METHUEN'S
MANUALS OF MODERN PSYCHOLOGY

(Founder Editor C. A. Mace 1946–68)
General Editor H. J. Butcher

Mental Deficiency
The changing outlook

Third edition

Mental Deficiency
The changing outlook

Third edition

Edited by

ANN M. CLARKE and A. D. B. CLARKE

 The Free Press
A Division of Macmillan Publishing Co., Inc.
NEW YORK

The Free Press
A Division of Macmillan Publishing Co., Inc.
866 Third Avenue, New York, N.Y. 10022

Reprinted by arrangement with Methuen and Company Limited

Library of Congress Catalog Card Number: 75-6314

First American publication of this Edition 1975

Printed in the United States of America

printing number

1   2   3   4   5   6   7   8   9   10

Contents

Figures

Contributors

J. M. Berg, M.Sc., M.B., B.Ch., M.R.C.Psych., Director of Research, Mental Retardation Centre; Staff Geneticist and Psychiatrist, Hospital for Sick Children, Toronto; and Associate Professor, University of Toronto. Formerly Clinical Research Consultant, Kennedy-Galton Centre, Harperbury Hospital, Hertfordshire.

R. M. Blunden, B.Sc., Research Officer, Wessex Research Project in Mental Handicap.

J. Carr, B.A., Ph.D., Lecturer, Department of Psychology, London University Institute of Psychiatry.

D. F. Clark, M.A., F.B.Ps.S., Consultant Clinical Psychologist, N.E. (Scotland) R.H.B. Services for the Handicapped, Ladysbridge Hospital, Banff, and Clinical Senior Lecturer, Department of Mental Health, University of Aberdeen.

A. D. B. Clarke, Ph.D., Professor of Psychology, University of Hull. Formerly Consultant Psychologist, The Manor Hospital, Epsom.

Ann M. Clarke, Ph.D., Honorary Research Fellow, Department of Psychology, and Lecturer, Department of Educational Studies, University of Hull. Formerly Principal Psychologist, The Manor Hospital, Epsom.

M. Fawcus, M.Sc., L.C.S.T., Senior Tutor, School for the Study of Disorders of Communication, London.

R. Fawcus, B.Sc., L.C.S.T., Lecturer in Human Communication Studies, Guy's Hospital Medical School, London.

H. C. Gunzburg, M.A., Ph.D., F.B.Ps.S., Consultant Psychologist, Director of Psychological Services, Hospitals for the Subnormal, Birmingham Area.

G. D. Hawks, M.Sc., A.B.Ps.S., Senior Psychologist, The Hospital for Sick Children, Great Ormond Street, London.

B. M. E. Hermelin, Ph.D., Research Psychologist, M.R.C. Developmental Psychology Research Unit, London.

C. C. Kiernan, B.A., Ph.D., Senior Lecturer in Child Development, Child Development Research Unit, University of London Institute of Education.

B. H. Kirman, M.D., F.R.C.Psych., Consultant Psychiatrist, Fountain and Carshalton Group and Honorary Associate Physician, St George's and Maudsley Hospitals, London.

A. Kushlick, M.B., B.Ch., M.R.C.P., D.P.H., R.C.P.S., M.R.C.Psych., F.F.C.M., Director of Research in Mental Handicap and Care of the Elderly, Wessex Regional Hospital Board. Member of M.R.C. External Scientific Staff.

P. J. Mittler, M.A., Ph.D., F.B.Ps.S., Director, Hester Adrian Research Centre for the Study of Learning Processes in the Mentally Handicapped and Professor of the Education of the Mentally Handicapped, University of Manchester.

N. O'Connor, M.A., Ph.D., Director, M.R.C. Developmental Psychology Research Unit, London.

E. Stephen, M.A., Dip.Ed., Principal Psychologist, Queen Mary's Hospital for Children, Carshalton.

J. Tizard, M.A., B.Litt., Ph.D., Research Professor of Child Development in the University of London Institute of Education. Formerly Professor of Child Development in the University of London Institute of Education.

Acknowledgements*

The contributors and editors have drawn heavily upon the publications of many workers in this field, to all of whom they wish to express their gratitude. They would like in particular to thank the following:

Dr J. M. Berg. The late Professor L. S. Penrose F.R.S. for providing Plate 5. The late Dr D. H. H. Thomas for permission to photograph the children who were in his care, shown in Plates 3, 6 and 7. Mr M. A. C. Ridler for his photography of all the patients shown in the plates.

Dr J. Carr. Dr H. Raech, Professor J. Tizard and Dr W. Wolfensberger for allowing quotations from their work. Dr L. Wing for access to data quoted in table 24.

Mr D. F. Clark. Dr H. C. Gunzburg for fig. 9, from his chapter in the previous edition of this volume. Professor Samuel A. Kirk, Dr Winifred D. Kirk and the University of Illinois Press for figs. 11 and 12, from *Psycholinguistic Learning Disabilities: Diagnosis and Remediation* (1971). Dr J. J. Parnicky, Dr H. Kahn, Dr A. Burdett and the editor of the journal for fig. 13, from the *American Journal of Mental Deficiency*, vol. 70 (1965) and vol. 75 (1971).

Professor A. D. B. Clarke and *Dr Ann M. Clarke.* Dr John Bowlby and the World Health Organization for allowing a quotation from *Maternal Care and Mental Health* (1951) on p. 215. Mrs M. W. G. Brandon for supplying data quoted on pp. 217–19. The late Dr H. M. Skeels for permission to quote much data from his studies.

Mrs M. Fawcus and *Mr R. Fawcus.* Shulamith Kastein for permission to quote material on p. 599. Mr James Paterson for data quoted on p. 611. Mr B. Schneider and Mr J. Vallon for permission to quote their writings on p. 598.

Dr H. C. Gunzburg. The late Dr C. J. C. Earl and Dr R. J. Stanley for their stimulating discussions which helped in the formulation of much of the material presented.

Dr C. C. Kiernan. The Department of Health and Social Security for support by means of Research Grants. J. F. Budde, F. J. Menolascino and the editor of the journal for fig. 17, from *Mental Retardation*, vol. 9 (1971). J. F. Budde for fig. 18, from *The Lattice Systems Approach: A Developmental Tool for Behavioral Research and Program Models* (Parsons Research Center, 1971). Dr H. F. Boozer for fig. 19.

* Some other acknowledgements will be found in the text.

Dr B. H. Kirman. Colleagues past and present in the Fountain and Carshalton Hospital Group for the privilege of sharing their collective understanding of the problem of intellectual limitation in its many aspects. Miss Phyllis Wolf for preparing the manuscript of Chapter 5.

Dr A. Kushlick and *Mr R. Blunden.* The Department of Health and Social Security, the Medical Research Council and the Wessex Regional Hospital Board for support and funding. Pergamon Press Ltd for permission to use material from *Foundations of Child Psychiatry,* edited by Emanuel Miller (1968).

Professor P. J. Mittler. Dr W. A. Bricker and Churchill Livingstone for fig. 14, from *Assessment for Learning in the Mentally Handicapped,* edited by P. J. Mittler (1973). Dr V. R. Hall and the American Speech and Hearing Association for fig. 16, from *A Functional Approach to Speech and Language,* edited by F. L. Girardeau and J. E. Spradlin (ASHA Monograph 14, 1970). Dr H. N. Sloane, Dr M. K. Johnston, Dr F. R. Harris and the Houghton Mifflin Company for fig. 15, from *Operant Procedures in Remedial Speech and Language Training,* edited by H. N. Sloane and B. D. Macaulay (1968).

Miss Elspeth Stephen and *Mrs Gail Hawks.* Dr H. V. Bice for permission to quote figures in table 15. Dr W. Cruickshank, Dr G. Raus and Syracuse University Press for permission to quote figures in tables 17 and 18, from *Cerebral Palsy: Its Individual and Community Problems* (1955). Dr M. I. Dunsdon and the National Foundation for Educational Research for permission to quote tables 14, 16, part of 18, 20 and 21, from *The Educability of Cerebral Palsied Children* (1952). Mrs F. E. Schonell for permission to quote figures in tables 15, 18, 19, 20 and 23, from *Educating Spastic Children* (Oliver & Boyd, 1956). Professor M. Rutter for permission to quote from the Isle of Wight Survey, *A Neuropsychiatric Study in Childhood* (1970). Dr Brian Kirman for help and advice.

Professor J. Tizard. Dr Henry V. Cobb for permission to quote from *The Prediction of Fulfilment* (Teachers' College Press, 1972). Dr Mervyn Susser for permission to quote from *Community Psychiatry* (Random House, 1968).

Foreword to the first edition

Traditionally mental deficiency has been a neglected field of study, with the exception of some aspects of neuropathology and genetics. Here some outstanding work has been done, although extremely rare conditions have often assumed relatively greater importance than their numbers might warrant, in comparison with much more common but less clear-cut manifestations of mental subnormality. The fact that there is no 'cure' for the vast majority of clinical conditions subsumed under the wide legal-administrative category of mental deficiency seems to have rendered this aspect of mental handicap the least attractive to therapists and research workers alike. The possibility of capitalizing on the defective's limited assets by the application of learning theories has not yet been sufficiently explored; too often textbooks have concentrated upon his deficits. Moreover, the relative complexity of subnormal personalities has all too often been overlooked. Fortunately, however, such pioneers as Binet, Burt and Wallin have laid firm foundations for subsequent work.

Early this century an extreme and oversimplified genetical theory raised profound fears that national degeneracy was imminent; it is nowadays realized, of course, that inheritance does not take place in the simple manner then postulated, and, as Burt has recently stated, it must be supposed that heredity produces differences as often as resemblances. Moreover, the pattern of differential fertility which originally gave rise to alarm is itself changing. Nevertheless, from this original and largely inaccurate premise, a logical belief arose that *custodial care* was the correct solution, on both humanist and scientific grounds, to the social and genetic problems of mental deficiency. This was further reinforced by unemployment between the two world wars, and the overall effect, among others, prevented any real evaluation of the certified defective's prospects in the community. Similarly, the equally extreme behaviourist view originating from the work of J. B. Watson also had its adherents in the field of mental deficiency research. Nowadays, however, better experimental controls and more sophisticated techniques are beginning to give us more accurate, if less sensational, information about environmental influences. Moreover, much of the earlier work concerned children only, and as this book will endeavour to indicate, the mentally deficient child may in some cases show a different picture in adult life, and certainly his problems will be different.

Mental deficiency is a social-administrative rather than a scientific concept, varying in different countries and within a given country at different times. With the major social and economic changes which have occurred during the last fifteen years, a re-evaluation of the problem has become possible. It is clear that advances have occurred in our understanding of the nature, causes, and treatment of the many conditions which we term mental deficiency, resulting in a steadily changing outlook. Much new research in this country, the United States and Scandinavia has been completed and there has also been increased public interest and understanding, culminating in Britain in the recent Royal Commission. It is being increasingly appreciated that this is a rewarding and often exciting field of study.

In the present volume we have three main aims; first, to summarize as comprehensively as possible the literature on psychological and social aspects of mental deficiency (particularly that of the last decade) against a background of genetics and neuropathology. Second, we have tried to show the intimate, reciprocal and enriching relationship between theory and practice, and the use of experimental method in both areas; and third, an attempt has been made to indicate in a practical manner how the learning difficulties and social problems posed by the subnormal may be ameliorated. We would like to express our gratitude to the contributors who have willingly fitted in with this general plan, and who have patiently tolerated editorial interference over a long period.

Dr Vernon Hamilton read the original manuscript and made many useful suggestions, and Mr Roy Brown provided valuable help at the proof stage; we are very much indebted to them. We are also glad to record our thanks to Dr J. F. MacMahon who has taught us so much and over many years provided facilities for, and encouraged us in, our endeavours to apply scientific method to the problems of mental deficiency; our debt to him is great. We are also grateful to Professor C. A. Mace, General Editor of the Methuen Manuals of Modern Psychology series, for his interest and assistance.

May 1958   A. M. C.
                                                             A. D. B. C.

Preface to the second edition

When the first edition of this book was published in 1958 it was necessary to include a short section on the neglect of mental deficiency. Even so, the trends initiated during that decade enabled us to justify our subtitle: 'The Changing Outlook'. Between 1958 and 1964, however, many developments have occurred, and the pace of change has been greatly accelerated. It may, therefore, be worth reviewing the immediate background in England and in the United States.

In England, the development of the Welfare State in the post-war years sensitized public awareness of deprived members of the population, and this led to particular concern for the conditions of those in mental and mental deficiency hospitals. In the early 1950s it became obvious that custodial care for mildly subnormal persons was no longer appropriate either on humane or economic grounds, and survey and other findings helped to identify the necessary bases for reform.

Public unease about the mental health services undoubtedly played a large part in bringing into being the Royal Commission on Mental Illness and Mental Deficiency, 1954–7, and ultimately the passing of the Mental Health Act, 1959. The main principles now were, firstly, an emphasis on voluntary rather than compulsory admission, and secondly, a shift from hospital care, often in remote isolated areas, to community provisions for the mentally subnormal. Local health authorities were empowered to build training centres for the severely subnormal, as well as hostels for these and for others of higher grade. A great expansion of community services is thus now in progress (Ministry of Health, *Health and Welfare: The Development of Community Care*, Cmnd 1973, London, HMSO, 1963).

In the United States, a similarly accelerated development has taken place during the last decade. This has been well reviewed by D. Gibson (Psychology in mental retardation: past and present, *Amer. Psychol.*, 1964, **19**, 339–41). Between 1946 and 1960, according to this writer, changing social conditions brought sharply increased community expectations for improved educational and other services. This renaissance in public and professional concern reached its peak in 1962 with the Report of the President's Panel on Mental Retardation. Indeed, it is clear that the Kennedy family's personal interest in these problems did much to focus attention on the whole field. And before his untimely death in November 1963, President Kennedy was able to sign two major pieces of legislation relating to mental retardation.

The trends outlined have, of course, not merely been confined to Britain and the United States; similar changes have occurred, or are in process of occurring, in many other countries. Indeed, this heightened interest was reflected in the 1960 London Conference on the Scientific Study of Mental Deficiency, attended by nearly 700 delegates coming from twenty-seven countries. During this, the first multidisciplinary international conference, a provisional committee was set up with the aim of fostering an international organization. This latter was inaugurated as a permanent body at The International Copenhagen Conference on the Scientific Study of Mental Retardation in August 1964, with national committees in many countries. Its aim is to encourage research and disseminate scientific information.

Mental deficiency poses two main problems; first, the task of primary prevention of these conditions, whether they be of biological or socio-cultural origin. The second problem is the amelioration of existing mental deficiency wherever possible, again whether by biological, social or educational means. There have been recent important theoretical advances in the first sphere, even though, as yet, little immediate practical outcome can be expected, and it is very unlikely that, in the immediate foreseeable future, mental deficiency will be substantially reduced in incidence. In the second, however, the increased awareness of mental deficiency as a special problem in learning has already borne practical fruit. Although not wishing to minimize our continuing ignorance, it is now obvious that much can be done to use, develop, and indeed sometimes to create, limited assets in a way thought impossible a mere ten or fifteen years ago. The ground has thereby been cleared and the way is now open for behavioural scientists to explore in depth the details of learning and other processes. Perhaps the most important recent development in the field of mental retardation is the increasing concern by experimental scientists with perception, attention, memory, speech, and concept attainment. Work of this nature takes time to yield applicable knowledge; it seems to us, however, that the foundations of adequate educational programmes for the future will be laid on the basis of research carried out under conditions sufficiently controlled to indicate causes of behavioural deficits and precise methods of overcoming them.

Mental deficiency is a meeting point of a very large number of disciplines; neurology, sociology, biochemistry, psychology, genetics, education and psychiatry all have some part to play. Work in this field is not only rewarding for its immediate theoretical interest, or practical implications for the handicapped person, but also for its bearing upon the wider study of mankind. As Penrose has put it, 'these unfortunate mentally handicapped individuals can reveal, unwittingly, information of the utmost value to the rest of the human community, and we may well be grateful to them for this service'.

In this, the second edition, we have been fortunate to retain the help of our original contributors. In addition, we welcome Dr J. M. Berg to our numbers, and are very grateful for his masterly overview of aetiological principles in pathological deficiency. We have found no reason to alter the general outline of the book, but all chapters have been revised, in some cases considerably.

Advances in various fields also made it necessary completely to rewrite and re-structure Chapters 1, 6 and 13. And with the greatly increased output of research, all contributors have been forced into a greater selectivity than was necessary in the first edition. Nevertheless, we hope that the student or research worker will find this book reasonably comprehensive, and that our 1,200 or so references will enable him to follow up his particular interests without major difficulty.

Mrs M. Phillips prepared the author and subject indexes and references with the assistance of Mr A. S. Henney; we are very grateful to them for undertaking this time-consuming task.

December 1964
A. M. C.
A. D. B. C.

Preface to the third edition

Advances in research on mental retardation in all disciplines have been immense during the last decade. The outlook since the second edition of this book was prepared in the mid-1960s has changed so considerably that a complete re-structuring and virtually complete rewriting of the volume has proved necessary, together with a great extension of coverage. The first and second editions comprised eighteen chapters each; the present one has been increased to twenty-five. Earlier editions were both made up of three sections; we have now found it more logical to delete the distinction between theoretical and applied work and divide the book into sections according to research area.

Although this book has altered almost beyond recognition, its general message remains the same: that careful empirical work in all disciplines pays off both in the short- and long-term. It has implications for prevention and amelioration of subnormality, as well as a more general understanding of man as a biosocial organism. We have not, however, changed the book's title. It is amusing now to recall that in 1958 we were criticized for using 'The Changing Outlook' as part of it. Our critic felt that this would date the book, particularly if there were to be future editions, for although the outlook had then changed, it could not continue to do so. Happily, such pessimism was unjustified. We prefer the term 'Mental Retardation' to its synonyms but have been urged to retain 'Mental Deficiency' in the title because of its familiarity.

In Chapter 1 we refer, among other things, to the recent pronouncement of the President's Committee on Mental Retardation (1972) that, using present techniques in the biomedical and behavioural sciences, it is possible to reduce the incidence of mental retardation by half by the end of the century. It is, of course, significant that the word 'possible' has been chosen. Whether a possibility will become a probability depends very largely upon the resources which society will allocate to the problems. So far as the culturally disadvantaged, a very large group, are concerned, it is not enough to intervene effectively to break the cycle of deprivation. Society must learn to understand and overcome its own pathology which currently allows the cycle ever to start. Similarly, so far as biological factors are concerned, now is the time to focus attention upon such problems as malnutrition and high maternal age in the aetiology of handicapping conditions.

In this, the third edition, we have been fortunate in retaining our 1958 and 1965 teams of contributors. We welcome to their numbers Mr R. Blunden, Dr Janet Carr, Messrs D. F. Clark and R. Fawcus, Mrs Gail Hawks, Drs Beate

Hermelin, C. C. Kiernan, B. H. Kirman, A. Kushlick and Professor P. J. Mittler. Their assistance has been invaluable.

Finally, we must again express gratitude to Mrs Moira Phillips who prepared the index and assisted with the compilation of references and the checking of proofs.

July 1973   A. M. C.

                                                                A. D. B. C.

PART ONE

Biosocial factors

1

A. D. B. Clarke and A. M. Clarke

The changing outlook

Introduction

The field of mental subnormality is a meeting point for all the biological and behavioural sciences, with implications both for our understanding of human development in general and retarded development in particular. In the first edition of this book (1958) we noted that 'traditionally mental deficiency has been a neglected field of study, with the exception of some aspects of neuropathology and genetics'. In the second edition (1965) we commented on this earlier statement, indicating that 'between 1958 and 1964, however, many developments have occurred, and the pace of change has been greatly accelerated'. By 1972, the President's Committee on Mental Retardation, in a booklet entitled *Entering the Era of Human Ecology*, stated that, '*using present techniques from the biomedical and behavioral sciences*, it is possible to reduce the occurrence of mental retardation by 50 per cent before the end of the century' (our italics), and this has, indeed, become a 'Major National Goal' in the United States. These are bold – or perhaps rash – words, but they at least indicate the extent of the change in outlook that has occurred in the last fifteen years.

In the past, as at present, different countries have employed different practices for, and concepts of, mental subnormality. Definitions, however, tend to use similar phrases, such as 'incomplete or insufficient general mental development', 'sub-average general intellectual functioning' or 'arrested or incomplete development of mind . . . which includes subnormality of intelligence'. Such descriptions are necessarily vague when upper borderlines between the milder conditions and dullness are arbitrary, and depend upon an interaction between social attitudes, the complexity of society, and the provision of services. These problems are considered in detail in Chapters 2, 3 and 25. In the meanwhile it may be helpful to show how British and international terminology relate to IQ level and to aetiology (see Fig. 1).

As implied above, the milder levels of subnormality cannot be regarded as a scientific category but rather comprise a theoretical, administrative group of well below average individuals some of whom, usually temporarily, are 'at risk' of needing special educational or social assistance. The natural history of the majority of such persons is vastly different from those below about IQ 50, and, as indicated in Chapter 2, only a minority is in receipt of any specialized services for any length of time.

The endeavours of biological and behavioural scientists can be subsumed under three headings. First, the description of the many conditions which comprise subnormality, whether at chromosomal, biochemical or behavioural levels. Second, much work – again biological and behavioural – is related to the task of primary prevention of handicapping conditions. Third, the two approaches include in their aims the amelioration of existing mental subnormality. This classification of research work is over-simple, but will serve its purpose for subsequent discussion. In particular, there is an overlap between prevention and

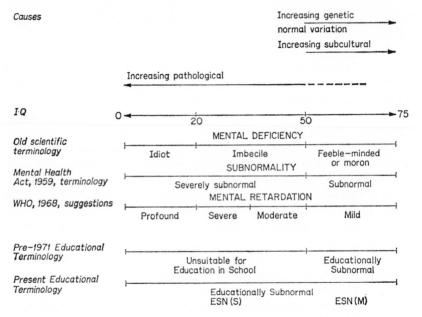

Fig. 1 Relation of IQ to aetiology and terminology, old and new.

amelioration, for really successful treatment becomes preventive of further retardation.

Belmont (1971), in an important paper, draws attention to the contents of symposia held on the occasion of the Joseph P. Kennedy Jr Foundation international awards for research, leadership and service in retardation. The vast majority of these papers were related to chromosomal aberrations and inborn errors of metabolism. These contributions which are very important nevertheless only apply to the aetiology of a minority of the subnormal. Belmont points out that retardation is a behavioural deficiency and the majority of these research workers have nothing to say about behaviour, other than that it is retarded. He calls for an increase in bio-behavioural research, an aim which we would endorse.

A World Health Organization (1968) document also stresses that no single profession has the key to the problems posed by mental subnormality, and calls for multi-disciplinary research. The primary aim of this book, however, is to offer and discuss the results of investigations into retarded behaviour, the main presenting feature of mental subnormality. In attempting this, however, we do not subscribe to a narrow professional viewpoint, and sufficient will be offered of the biological level of analysis to indicate its achievements, problems and limitations (see particularly Chapters 4 and 5).

Description of the mentally subnormal

Detailed studies of biological and behavioural deficits in the subnormal have been made on a very large scale in the last decade. A brilliantly succinct account of the biology of mental defect is given by Penrose (1972), indicating very considerable advances in the description and understanding of chromosomal aberrations and inborn errors of metabolism. The reader will find an account of some findings in this area discussed in Chapters 4 and 5.

Attempts to define the precise nature of behavioural deficits, undertaken by experimental psychologists, have resulted in the publication of numerous papers, which have led to some controversy concerning appropriate methodologies, and, in some cases, interesting and increasingly sophisticated theoretical reformulations. Reviews will be found in Chapters 10, 11 and 13.

The epidemiology and prevalence of various types of mental handicap are discussed in Chapters 2 and 3. Careful studies of this nature are essential as baselines for evaluating the effects of social changes, as well as for planning services (see Chapter 25).

Follow-up studies of defined groups may be variously concerned with, for example, longevity in mongols (Carter, 1959) or the adult social outcome for originally homogeneous groups of mildly retarded schoolchildren (Kennedy, 1966; Baller, Charles and Miller, 1967). Only by such precise descriptions can we learn about the natural history of handicapping conditions. Studies of this kind are likely to have a bearing upon our understanding both of aetiology and prognosis (see Chapters 3 and 9).

Careful evaluations have been made concerning the social contexts in which the mentally subnormal are reared, and in some cases the relation of these to aetiology (see Chapter 7). Important studies of institutions, their size, staffing structure and effects upon development have been undertaken by a number of research workers (see Chapters 3 and 25).

The prevention of mental subnormality

Since many factors are involved in the aetiology of subnormality, preventive measures must be similarly diverse. In this section an attempt will be made to indicate briefly some of the areas of work where research bears upon these problems. The most logical way of considering prevention is by means of a time scale for individual development from conception onwards, although this must be linked with some discussion of parental characteristics.

It has long been known that the age of the mother is correlated with the incidence of handicapping conditions, particularly in the case of Down's syndrome. Hence, earlier marriage and the earlier completion of families, which now takes place, is likely to have some effect. It has, for example, been calculated that if no children were born after maternal age 35, the incidence of Down's syndrome would be halved (Penrose, 1972).

Genetic counselling for families at risk is rapidly developing. Linked with this is the possibility of pre-natal diagnosis of chromosome anomalies by culturing foetal cells in a small amount of amniotic fluid, withdrawn in the fourteenth week of pregnancy. When the diagnosis is positive, termination of pregnancy may be offered (Steele and Breg, 1966; Penrose, 1972).

It has long been known that there are critical periods for the developing brain *in utero*. Rubella early in pregnancy, for example, carries with it a high risk of mental subnormality, blindness or deafness in the child. The development of a vaccine must be greatly welcomed. The whole field of nutrition in relation to brain growth, both pre- and post-natally, has also been the subject of intensive study during the last decade (e.g. Scrimshaw and Gordon, 1968; Kaplan, 1972). Research upon animals has yielded much information upon vulnerable periods for brain growth (e.g. Dobbing and Smart 1972; Dobbing, 1974). To delineate the effects of malnutrition upon both the brain and behaviour of man pose research problems of even greater complexity than in animals. As Dobbing and Smart (op. cit.) put it: 'The question whether early *malnutrition* causes *mental subnormality* ... is, in our view, wrongly posed. Rather it should be asked whether malnutrition or growth retardation, among the multitude of other important early environmental factors, can be identified as a contributor to the algebraic sum of those influences which determine adult "attainment".' From the work of Cravioto, DeLicardie and Birch (1966) it has, however, been inferred that protein-calorie deficiency in early life has an irreversible effect upon brain growth and behaviour. Such effects may be direct or indirect, via a lowered responsiveness of the child to his parents and to his environment. It has been established (Dobbing and Smart, 1972) that for full-term human babies, only about one-eighth of the vulnerable period for brain growth is foetal, the remaining seven-eighths of the growth spurt occurring in the first eighteen months postnatally. These authors summarize their excellent review of these complex problems by stating that there is a period of human development extending from the second trimester of gestation well into the second year, when the brain appears to have a once only opportunity to grow properly. A restriction of nutrition at these times 'may well have lasting behavioural consequences'. The elucidation of the role of malnutrition and, above all, the establishment of better conditions, will have a very important effect upon the inhabitants of developing countries.

Obstetric complications have long been known to be associated with handicapping conditions, although their effects may not be as often primary as has been supposed (Drillien, 1968). This investigator found that severe complications of labour and delivery appeared to be associated with additional neurological defects but not with the mental handicap itself. Over one-half of those below IQ 55 in this study showed congenital anomalies which must have arisen at an early stage of gestation. Obstetric factors remain of relevance, however, in the aetiology of some forms of subnormality, and here there is a social class correlation, apparently mediated by, among other things, the nutrition of the mother in her own childhood. Better nutrition will thus diminish these effects (Scrimshaw and Gordon, 1968; Kaplan, 1972).

The increased use of immunization techniques for the common childhood illnesses such as measles, mumps and whooping cough which can have neurological *sequelae* is also certain to have reduced cases of pathological subnormality. Clarke (1967) has recently developed a method of immunizing *rhesus*-negative mothers to prevent Rh sensitization by *rhesus*-positive foetuses, thus protecting subsequent pregnancies. Risk registers may also have been of value in alerting medical authorities to the possibility of handicapping conditions, and thus allowing remedial action.

Better ante-natal and obstetric care, among other factors, may be assumed to have had an impact on the incidence of subnormality, although probably counter-balanced as yet by the higher rates of survival of damaged infants (Tizard, 1964).

The individual qualities of the parents and the social class context into which the child is born set the stage for his own development. These in turn bear some relation to the parents' own upbringing. Social class differences emerge early in young children, and by the age of seven operate powerfully (Davie, Butler and Goldstein, 1972). For mild subnormality, membership of Social Class V has a particular relevance, although those whose condition is pathological in origin are to be found roughly equally in all social classes. Yet in slums mild subnormality is neither randomly distributed nor randomly caused. It appears to be particularly associated with a parent or parents of IQ below 80 (Heber, Dever and Conry, 1968), as well as with a complex of other adverse factors discussed in detail in Chapter 7. Heber is currently conducting a programme aimed at preventing the expected mental retardation in children from this background, and, although these are still too young for long-term predictions to be made with any confidence, has indicated a preliminary success well beyond expectations (see Chapter 7). His programme has operated both on the infants from birth onwards and upon their mothers.

These examples, which will be amplified later in this book, offer a brief indication of the biosocial principles underlying preventive measures. These are now developing so rapidly that some optimism must exist about prospects of primary prevention.

Amelioration

Unlike prevention, the field of amelioration implies an intervention of some kind aimed at modifying an existing or developing defect. Once again, however, a number of entirely different approaches are involved.

Biomedical treatment has had a part to play in ameliorating pathological conditions ever since the classic work on cretinism. If diagnosis is early, then replacement therapy with thyroxine is often partially effective in ameliorating the outcome. In general, however, these patients ultimately prove to be below average in intellectual status. More recently, considerable claims have been made for treatment of phenylketonuria by means of a phenylalanine-free diet. If therapy begins within the first two months of life, then the mean IQ attains a level of about 70, with a few cases reaching a normal level (Fuller, 1968). The picture is, however, complicated by the discovery that some infants who excrete phenylpyruvic acid develop normally anyway. Currently, therefore, the biochemical model of PKU is being re-evaluated (Bessman, Due Logue and Wapnir, 1968; Hsia *et al.*, 1968). Even more recent work, however, suggests a more hopeful outcome where treatment is started in the first month of life. Thus, in a series of 170 treated cases, R. Guthrie (personal communication) found only 3 who were mentally retarded at the age of 6.

Hydrocephalus has for many years been the subject of surgical attempts to relieve pressure upon the brain due to obstructed flow of cerebro-spinal fluid. In a large number of cases it has been treated successfully by means of a ventriculo-atrial shunt using the Spitz-Holter or Pudenz-Heyer valve which permits drainage of fluid from the ventricle through a tube via the internal jugular vein (Hilliard and Kirman, 1965).

As Penrose (1972) has indicated, 'the most direct forms of therapy are psychological, arduous procedures of training or teaching'. Here there have been considerable advances in research, as yet barely impinging upon practice. At least one conclusion emerges with absolute clarity from twenty years of experimental work; any human being, of whatever level, is capable of at least some learning. Sometimes this may be minimal and sometimes very considerable. Thus the question is now not so much whether a handicapped individual can with systematic tuition learn a basic skill which he would otherwise not spontaneously develop; the answer is usually affirmative. Rather the question has now become: 'What is the best way of teaching the particular skill, what circumstances of training and subsequent reinforcement favour its acquisition and retention, and what duration of tuition is necessary?' To take an extreme example, Sidman and Stoddard (1966) demonstrated perceptual discrimination learning in subjects devoid of language, including the severely and profoundly retarded, by means of careful programming and specially devised apparatus. Whether the gains demonstrated, or the investment of skilled manpower would be justified on a large scale, depends upon society's value judgements and the resources available.

These latter are ethical questions which must be considered separately from the scientific evidence.

In general, the balance of evidence suggests that while there are considerable differences between normals and subnormals in the rate of acquisition, the upper limits to attainment and to the amount and complexity of material learned, the learning processes themselves differ in degree rather than in kind. There is also some evidence for the view that a major deficiency is a relative inability to learn spontaneously from ordinary unstructured life experience. Experimental work on how far this relative inability might be diminished by training could be of the utmost importance.

The longer-term experimental studies yield results which suggest that the starting point in learning a task bears little or no relationship with potential responsiveness to training. These findings emerge from the 'backward learning curves' of Zeaman and House (1963) as well as from other studies of learning and social rehabilitation in the subnormal. It is probably because of this poor initial performance that the learning capabilities of the subnormal have been so commonly underestimated. Moreover, the psychometric approach, which employs solely a measure of initial performance, has reinforced this underestimation. Detailed discussion on these points is offered in Chapter 13 in which particular reference is made to the paper by Bortner and Birch (1970) who document the distinction between capacity and performance.

There is something of a lack of controlled studies of educational amelioration, although the work of Kirk (1958), Goldstein, Moss and Jordan (1965), Karnes, Teska and Hodgins (1970), and Weikart and Lambie (1970) are exceptions.

The whole question of 'compensatory education' for those already damaged by social adversity has been bedevilled by work which is naïve in its conception and methodology, usually of very short duration and limited in its application. This has enabled Jensen (1969) to write that 'compensatory education has been tried and it apparently has failed'. This view is factually correct in the vast majority of cases but these have mostly been not only short but scarcely educational at all. It needs substantial qualification where programmes are sharply focused, of long duration, and involve the families as well as their children (see Chapter 7). Yet compensatory education is a secondary approach to prevention. Ultimately society must learn to deal with its own morbid factors which lead to the conditions euphemistically termed 'cultural disadvantage'.

The rapid development of behaviour modification, discussed in Chapter 23, further indicates that much can be done for the 'untrainable', although the experimental methodology is often not beyond reproach (Gardner, 1969) and curiously little work on the less severely handicapped has been reported.

Finally, it should be recorded that improvement of some of the mildly subnormal appears to occur naturally and slowly as they enter adulthood. Sometimes this is no more than 'camouflage', or being 'propped up' but it sometimes occurs as a result of prolonged learning of social adaptation, and sometimes results from delayed maturation. It may well be that society begins to undo, or allows to be undone, some of its own effects which occurred earlier during individual development. In any event, both prevalence and follow-up studies indicate a tendency towards a better adult adjustment for the mildly handicapped than had been expected in the past (see Chapter 9).

Conclusions

This survey of the changing outlook has offered brief evidence from the research areas of description, prevention and amelioration. It is clear that the pace of change has accelerated dramatically during the last fifteen years in all disciplines. Not only are we learning more about subnormality, its prevention and treatment but, as Penrose once argued, more about man himself from studying man at his simplest.

References

BALLER, W. R., CHARLES, D. C. and MILLER, E. L. (1967) Mid-life attainment of the mentally retarded: a longitudinal study. *Genet. Psychol. Monogr.*, **75**, 235–329.

BELMONT, J. M. (1971) Medical-behavioral research in retardation. *Internat. Rev. Res. ment. Retard.*, **5**, 1–81.

BESSMAN, S. P., DUE LOGUE, D. and WAPNIR, R. A. (1968) Phenyl-ketonuria-certainty versus uncertainty. In RICHARDS, B. (ed.) *Proc. 1st Congr. Internat. Assoc. Scient. Stud. Ment. Defic.*, 182–93. Reigate: Michael Jackson.

BORTNER, M. and BIRCH, H. G. (1970) Cognitive capacity, and cognitive competence. *Amer. J. ment. Defic.*, **74**, 735–44.

CARTER, C. O. (1959) A life-table for mongols with causes of death. *J. ment. Defic. Res.*, **2**, 64–74.

CLARKE, C. A. (1967) Prevention of Rh-haemolytic disease. *Brit. med. J.*, **4**, 484–5.

CRAVIOTO, J., DELICARDIE, E. R. and BIRCH, H. G. (1966) Nutrition, growth and neurointegrative development: an experimental and ecologic study. *Pediatrics*, **38**, 319–72.

DAVIE, R., BUTLER, N. and GOLDSTEIN, H. (1972) *From Birth to Seven.* London: Longmans, in association with The National Children's Bureau.

DOBBING, J. (1974) The later development of the brain and its vulnerability. In DAVIS, J. A. and DOBBING, J. (eds.) *The Scientific Foundations of Paediatrics.* London: Heinemann.

DOBBING, J. and SMART, J. L. (1972) Early undernutrition, brain development and behaviour. In BARNETT, S. A. (ed.) *Ethology and Development.* Clinics in Developmental Medicine, No. 47. London: Heinemann.

DRILLIEN, C. M. (1968) Obstetric factors and mental handicap. In RICHARDS B. (ed.) *Proc. 1st Congr. Internat. Assoc. Scient. Stud. Ment. Defic.*, 113–24. Reigate: Michael Jackson.

FULLER, R. (1968) Treated phenylketonuria: analysis of psychological results. In RICHARDS, B. (ed.) *Proc. 1st Congr. Internat. Assoc. Scient. Stud. Ment. Defic.*, 305–13. Reigate: Michael Jackson.

GARDNER, J. M. (1969) Behavior modification research in mental retardation: search for an adequate paradigm. *Amer. J. ment. Defic.*, **73**, 844–51.

GOLDSTEIN, H., MOSS, J. W. and JORDAN, L. J. (1965) *The Efficacy of Special Class Training on the Development of Mentally Retarded Children.* Urbana, Ill.: Inst. for Research on Exceptional Children.

HEBER, R., DEVER, R. and CONRY, J. (1968) The influence of environmental and genetic variables on intellectual development. In PREHM, H. J., HAMERLYNCK, L. A. and CROSSON, J. E. (eds.) *Behavioural Research in Mental Retardation.* Eugene: School of Education, Univ. of Oregon.

HILLIARD, L. T. and KIRMAN, B. H. (1965) *Mental Deficiency* (2nd edn). London: Churchill.

HSIA, D. Y.-Y., BERLOW, S., O'FLYNN, M., BICKEL, H. and WAISMAN, H. A. (1968) Hyperphenylalaninemia without phenylketonuria. In RICHARDS, B. (ed.) *Proc. 1st Congr. Internat. Assoc. Scient. Stud. Ment. Defic.*, 441–54. Reigate: Michael Jackson.

JENSEN, A. R. (1969) How much can we boost IQ and scholastic achievement? *Harvard educ. Rev.*, **39**, 1–123.

KAPLAN, B. J. (1972) Malnutrition and mental deficiency. *Psychol. Bull.*, **78**, 321–34.

KARNES, M. B., TESKA, J. A. and HODGINS, A. S. (1970) The effects of four programs of classroom intervention on the intellectual and language development of four-year-old disadvantaged children. *Amer. J. Orthopsychiat.*, **40**, 58–76.

KENNEDY, R. J. (1966) *A Connecticut Community Revisited: A Study of the Social Adjustment of a Group of Mentally Deficient Adults in 1948 and 1960.* Hartford: Connecticut State Dept of Health, Office of Mental Retardation.

KIRK, S. A. (1958) *Early Education of the Mentally Retarded.* Urbana: Univ. of Illinois Press.

PENROSE, L. S. (1972) *The Biology of Mental Defect* (4th edn). London: Sidgwick & Jackson.

President's Committee on Mental Retardation (1972) *Entering the Era of Human Ecology.* Dept. of Health, Education and Welfare Publ. No. (OS) 72–7. Washington, DC.

SCRIMSHAW, N. S. and GORDON, J. E. (1968) *Malnutrition, Learning and Behaviour.* Cambridge, Mass.: MIT Press.

SIDMAN, M. and STODDARD, L. T. (1966) Programming perception and learning for retarded children. In ELLIS, N. R. (ed.) *International Review of Research in Mental Retardation*, Vol. 2. New York: Academic Press.

STEELE, M. W. and BREG, W. R. (1966) Chromosome analysis of human amniotic-fluid cells. *Lancet,* **i,** 383–5.

TIZARD, J. (1964) *Community Services for the Mentally Handicapped.* London: Oxford Univ. Press.

WEIKART, D. P. and LAMBIE, D. Z. (1970) Early enrichment in infants. In DENENBERG, V. H. (ed.) *Education of the Infant and Young Child.* London: Academic Press.

World Health Organization (1968) *Organization of Services for the Mentally Retarded.* Fifteenth Report of the WHO Expert Committee on Mental Health. WHO Tech. Rep. Ser. 392. Geneva.

ZEAMAN, D. and HOUSE, B. J. (1963) The role of attention in retardate discrimination learning. In ELLIS, N. R. (ed.) *Handbook of Mental Deficiency.* New York and London: McGraw-Hill.

2

A. M. Clarke and A. D. B. Clarke

Criteria and classification of subnormality

Some historical aspects of classification

The need to classify is deeply embedded in human beings, indeed it appears to be a fundamental basis of cognitive activities. As Bruner puts it, categorization allows the complexity of stimuli to be reduced by treating phenomena as equivalent when indeed they can be differentiated from each other in a variety of ways. It is thus important to recognize that the tendency to classify, either implicitly or explicitly, is part of the biological basis of man.

The categories which man will create are intimately related to the overall society in which he finds himself, and to his role in that society. For example, the 'man-in-the-street' and the architect will 'see' a given building in terms of very different selective categories. Moreover, the degree of selective categorization itself tends to change during individual development, as more and more knowledge is gained. Thus the young child's concept of a kangaroo will differ markedly from that of a zoologist, even though both have a clear and overlapping concept of this animal.

There is a close parallel between the use of classifications by the individual and those used by society. Different classifications of the same phenomenon serve different purposes and themselves change as the purposes change. This in turn is intimately related to prevailing social orientations at a given point in time. For example, the word 'crétin' is derived from the French 'chrétien' (Christian) and is testimony to the fact that in early times the severely handicapped were cared for by monastic communities.

Classification involves 'labelling' and there is a constant act of changing labels as new knowledge is acquired or as society's view of the concept changes. Langdon Down first described in 1866 the condition of mongolism, a label based upon the physical appearance of a particular clinical type, together with the aetiological notion of 'atavistic regression' which itself really implied that the 'Mongolian race' was inferior. In the mid-twentieth century, as world biological science expanded, it became necessary to reject this archaic label in the interest both of scientific precision, and to oppose the perpetuation of an offensive racist label. The 'Langdon Down syndrome' or 'Down's syndrome' was thus invented, and the word 'Syndrome' of course rightly underlines the constellation of possible symptoms in this condition. With even more recent genetic discoveries, sub-classifications of Down's syndrome such as 'Trisomy 21' or 'mosaicism' became necessary.

Labels for a given concept may also change in response to popular feeling. Thus in this country the terms 'mental deficiency', 'feeble-mindedness', 'imbecility' and 'idiocy' were dropped, in favour of 'subnormality' and 'severe subnormality', in the 1959 Mental Health Act, as being less pejorative. Similarly, the words 'mental retardation' are seen as less offensive than 'mental deficiency' in the United States. And now, 'mental handicap' shows every sign of being a more favoured label. Finally, it should be pointed out that a given label carries with it different connotations for different people, and may lead to great confusion in discussion if the number or quality of assumptions underlying the same label differs between two communicators (e.g. between a geneticist and a teacher, or a paediatrician and a relatively naïve parent).

Historical documents provide an insight into the varying social reasons why certain members of society have been classified as mentally subnormal. Early in history, the reasons for classification were clearly linked with administrative matters. In England, statutory mention of the mentally subnormal dates as far back as the reign of Edward I (1272–1307), when the distinction was made for the first time on record between the born fool and the lunatic. In the Statute of Prerogatives in the reign of Edward II, a similar division is recorded, between 'born fool' (*fatuus naturalis*) and the person of unsound mind who may yet have certain lucid intervals (*non compos mentis, sicut quidam sunt per lucida intervalla*). The purpose of this distinction in feudal times was to facilitate the disposal of property: thus, if a man were found by questioning to be a lunatic, the Crown took possession of his belongings only during the period of his illness; whereas, if a man were found to be an idiot, his property reverted permanently to the Crown, subject only to an obligation to provide for his person and estate.

Scientific views, however, began from the beginning of this century to make a larger impact upon administrative and social concepts. Thus over-simple and confused genetic theories, in the context of a type of social Darwinism, began to emerge with the work of Goddard (1912) and others. From then on one can perceive an interplay between social and scientific concepts.

Sarasen and Doris (1969) have given extended consideration to this interplay between the development of biological science and social attitudes towards mental subnormality. They trace the origin and consequences of the degeneration theory, the confusion between insanity and mental subnormality, the impact of social Darwinism, the development of the eugenics movement and the role of the intelligence testing movement, among other topics. Their book is essential reading for all those interested in the origins of different forms of provision and changing social attitudes. Here, however, space forbids little more than the briefest excursion into this area.

We propose to trace very briefly the changing use of the word 'idiot', a word derived from the Greek, and meaning 'a private person'. It has also been used to denote 'layman' (1660), and professional fool or jester, as in Shakespeare ('a tale told by an idiot'), or an ignorant, uneducated man. For a considerable period of time the word idiot appeared to denote anyone who was mentally subnormal, and it is of course impossible to know what level of impairment was then defined. John Locke (1623–1704) was fully aware of the distinction between insanity and subnormality: 'Madmen put wrong ideas together, and so make wrong propositions, but argue and reason right from them; but idiots make very few or no propositions, and reasons scarce at all'. In the late eighteenth century, Blackstone mentions that the 'idiot or natural fool is one that hath had no understanding from his nativity; and therefore is by law never likely to attain any'. At the beginning of the nineteenth century Pinel considered idiocy as being a variant of the general class of psychosis, involving a partial or total abolition of the intellectual powers. The idiots' natural indolence and stupidity might, however, be obviated by engaging them in manual occupations, suitable to their respective 'capacities'.

Esquirol (1772–1840) wrote that 'idiocy is not a disease, but a condition in which the intellectual faculties are never manifested; or have never been developed sufficiently to enable the idiot to acquire such an amount of knowledge, as persons of his own age, and placed in similar circumstances as himself, are capable of receiving'. In the United States, Howe in 1848 refers to the difficulty of distinguishing dementia from idiocy. He contrasts those whose understanding is undeveloped, or developed to a very feeble degree, with those who have lost their understanding, the demented: '... by far the greater part of the idiots are children of parents, one or both of whom were of scrofulous temperaments, and poor flabby organization'. Alcoholism was seen as a major aetiological factor; however, Howe began to distinguish between idiots, fools and simpletons.

The classic book by Séguin (1866) *Idiocy: its Treatment by the Physiological Method* perpetuated for a while the use of idiocy as a generic term. But increasing awareness of differences within the broad group, as well as differing prognosis, was fully recognized terminologically by the Idiots Act of 1886. Here lunacy, on the one hand, and idiocy and imbecility, on the other, are distinguished. Idiots and imbeciles from birth or from an early age would be placed in any registered hospital or institution for the care and training of such persons. In using the term imbecile, it indicated that a class of subnormals existed, less defective than the idiot. It also recognized that the idiot might be trained. Before long the Education Act of 1870 showed that there existed yet other groups, the 'educable imbecile and the feeble-minded'. In 1897 a Departmental Committee was set up, among other things, to 'report particularly upon the best practicable means for distinguishing on the one hand between the educable and non-educable children ...' In turn this led to the Elementary Education (Defective and Epileptic Children) Act of 1899 with its distinction between those who could, and those who could not, be sufficiently educated to become at least partially self-supporting in later life. Within a few years, Binet was to be faced with objectifying this same distinction (see Chapter 6).

The Royal Commission of 1904 reported in 1908, and as a result the Mental Deficiency Act of 1913 was passed. In this, idiots, imbeciles, feeble-minded persons and moral imbeciles were for the first time clearly defined: 'Idiots; that is to say, persons so deeply defective in mind from birth or from an early age as to be unable to guard themselves against common physical dangers . . .'

We need take this survey of 'idiocy' no further, for the 1913 definition, perpetuated in the amending Act of 1927, to all intents and purposes is synonymous with 'profound retardation' of the World Health Organization today. It has been clear that a specific meaning in Greek gave way to a number of alternatives in 'plain English'. It took on a pathological connotation in the seventeenth century, was seen in the nineteenth century variously as a form of psychosis, or the result of alcoholism and degeneration, or as the most severe degree of defect, as well as being used as a generic term for all grades of defect. Only at the end of the century was the more recent diagnostic synonym foreshadowed, while latterly the term has been omitted from the new vocabulary of scientists and administrators.

Society's changing outlook

What is subnormality? It is difficult to discuss this question without first examining the historical models of classification, and the assumptions made by those creating them.

Even in the simplest of societies from the beginning of history there have probably been those who perceived that some of their fellow men were socially incompetent and very stupid, and reasoned that these factors were causally connected. During the nineteenth century the 'disease model' became basic to a consideration of this population, for society placed those in need of care in the hands of the medical profession. At first, such persons seem to have been predominantly fairly severely retarded but by the end of the century, as legislation developed, a wider range of persons became designated as mentally deficient. As our brief considerations of the development of attitudes will show, the subnormal were regarded as a race apart in the early years of the present century. The social problems which some of them posed in a developing, complex, urban society, were 'explained' by reference to an over-simple genetic model, in the context of social Darwinism. This is well exemplified by Goddard's (1912) work on the Kallikak family which had very wide social and legislative repercussions both in the United States and this country. Both Goddard and Walter E. Fernald found themselves members of the same committee of the American Breeders' Association, and it is probably no accident therefore that through this connection Fernald (quoted by Sarason and Doris, 1969) was able to express such views in an alarming and succinct form to the Massachusetts Medical Society in 1912:

The social and economic burdens of uncomplicated feeble-mindedness are only too well known. The feeble-minded are a parasitic, predatory class, never capable of self-support or of managing their own affairs. The great majority ultimately become public charges in some form. They cause unutterable sorrow at home and are a menace and danger to the community. Feeble-minded women are almost invariably immoral, and if at large usually become carriers of venereal disease or give birth to children who are as defective as themselves. The feeble-minded woman who marries is twice as prolific as the normal woman.

We have only begun to understand the importance of feeble-mindedness as a factor in the causation of pauperism, crime and other social problems. Hereditary pauperism, or pauperism of two or more generations of the same family, generally means hereditary feeble-mindedness. In Massachusetts there are families who have been paupers for many generations. Some of the members were born or even conceived in the poor house.

Every feeble-minded person, especially the high-grade imbecile, is a potential criminal, needing only the proper environment and opportunity for the development and expression of his criminal tendencies. The unrecognized imbecile is a most dangerous element in the community.

Until fairly recently (the 1950s) such an analysis as that of Fernald, albeit in an attenuated form, underlay much thinking about subnormality. No doubt humane attitudes also played a part in legal provision, but basically legislation was conceived as protecting society. In this country, until 1959, the procedure was thus of 'certification as mentally deficient' provided the individual could be proved as 'subject to be dealt with'. Periodic reassessment or alleged reassessment took place, with visits of Justices of the Peace, followed in some cases by trial in daily employment, trial in residential employment and ultimately, if the 'patient' was fortunate, 'discharge from care'.

In any consideration of the classification of the mentally subnormal, two elementary but, none the less, important general points must be made. Classification always has a purpose. Its function has often been to allow some administrative action to be taken, sometimes investing it with a precision and scientific flavour it does not possess. Secondly, while no doubt boundaries do exist in nature, these are seldom as sharply defined or as rigid as we seek to make them. It is generally agreed that intellectual abilities, and also social competence, form graded continua, so that any dividing line must, in effect, be arbitrary.

Within the subnormal group, sub-classification equally has a purpose; sometimes the bias may be educational, sometimes aetiological or prognostic, and here again boundaries are often arbitrary, although those conditions in which the biological basis is fairly well understood (e.g. Down's syndrome) may be more precisely delineated than those in which it is not (e.g. autism).

During the latter half of the present century several factors have combined to alter considerably society's view of the mentally subnormal and therefore of appropriate provisions for them. These include (1) an awareness that genetic variation is a much more complex matter than was formerly realized; (2) evidence that the national degeneracy earlier predicted by certain prophets of doom was not taking place; (3) indications that nutritional and social factors may be implicated in some forms of subnormality; (4) the success of programmes of remediation undertaken in a few institutions which yielded hopeful results; and (5) a more humane and tolerant attitude towards at least mild forms of social deviation. It followed that the subnormal person should not be shut away in remote hospitals, but community care and integration became the watchwords, with plans for ultimately a very large number of hostel places. Moreover, in the 1970s the belief that half the present inmates of mental subnormality hospitals could and should find a place in the community is generally accepted. At the same time, voluntary admission as opposed to 'certification' caters for the vast majority, and legislation has shifted from primarily protecting society to primarily protecting the rights of handicapped individuals.

Purposes of classification

The different purposes of modern classification will now be briefly described.

(1) ADMINISTRATIVE

Some specific action may be needed on behalf of an individual, a group or for the sake of the home. The act of labelling a person as mentally subnormal enables the administrative machinery to take steps which, because of regulations or law, it otherwise could not do. They may be educational, institutional or protective. Nowadays a legally arranged deprivation of liberty, so common in the past, is unusual. The emphasis is upon voluntary admission to, for example, hospital or training centre.

(2) SCIENTIFIC

(a) *Diagnostic.* The social deviant (of whatever form) stands out as different from his peers. Natural curiosity suggests that the nature of this difference should be described – 'What is wrong with this person?' is the usual question in response to a grossly deviant appearance or grossly deviant behaviour. Then comes the question 'What is the cause or what are the causes of the condition?' and a diagnostic assessment may in itself suggest the approach to remediation, whether biochemical, educational or psychological (e.g. behaviour modification).

(b) *Prognostic.* Close on the heels of the question 'What is wrong?', comes the query 'What are his prospects?' Prognostic evaluation may often be linked with diagnosis, and can include an assessment of the likely contribution, and interaction, of biological and social factors in determining the handicap. It is appreciated, for example, that some children, drawn from very adverse social conditions, whose behaviour is indistinguishable from others in terms of their present personal characteristics, mature later, and during adolescence or early adult life show marked improvement in behavioural characteristics. Or again, some pathological conditions carry with them a prognosis of deterioration and early death. The complex question of prediction has recently been considered by Clarke and Clarke (1972 and 1973).

(c) *Research.* Classification, using well-defined criteria, allows scientists at different periods or from different areas to compare findings and communicate with each other. Is the survival rate for mongols increasing? Is the incidence of severe subnormality decreasing? Is encephalitis an equally grave cause of subnormality in Africa as in India? Do adults originally suffering from mild subnormality continue to improve after the age of 20, or indeed 40? These are but a few of the innumerable questions which can only be asked validly if the classification method and the constituent population are clearly defined.

Criteria of subnormality

Once the potential conceptual confusion of mental subnormality and mental illness has been clarified, three interlinked aspects of the behaviour of certain social deviants have been commonly considered: poor intelligence, lack of social skills, and poor academic achievements. The latter has never been advocated as a major or sole criterion, presumably since it has long been apparent to the most casual observer that many socially competent people are deficient in the skills of literacy or numeracy. Various authorities have, however, advocated intellectual or social incompetence, either separately or in combination, as being definitive of mental subnormality. These will, therefore, be examined for their validity and their adequacy.

(1) SOCIAL INCOMPETENCE AS A CRITERION

This concept is self-evidently so vague as nowadays rarely to be discussed seriously as a sufficient sole criterion of subnormality. Standards of what constitutes competence must be arbitrary, must differ not only between societies, but also within a society in different areas or social classes, as well as differing at various points in time. Social difficulties are clearly not confined to the subnormal but are symptomatic of a very wide range of causes, acting singly or in combination. Those who fail to conform to society's norms will include all criminals and *some* members of the following: the mentally ill, the mentally subnormal, the exceptionally brilliant, and the social or political innovator. In the latter case some countries appear to regard non-conformers as by definition socially incompetent and mentally ill.

Nevertheless, social incompetence as the major criterion of mental deficiency has been advocated by influential experts, with profound implications for legislation and the nature of the group thus classified. The 1913 British Mental Deficiency Act (amended in 1927) nowhere mentioned intelligence explicitly, but rather 'arrested or incomplete development of mind' was the central feature of the definition. The concept of mind was perceived as being wider than intelligence and included 'moral deficiency'. In discussing the then legal definition, Tredgold (1952) stated that although the Act made no reference to the permanency of the condition, there is no doubt that mental arrest, sufficient to cause the social incapacity envisaged by the Act, would be permanent and incurable. He further pointed out that when the Act referred to 'arrested development of mind', there was no legal justification for assuming that the only really important aspect of mind is the intellectual one: 'an arrested development of any process or department of mind, provided it resulted in social incapacity, constitutes mental deficiency'.

This latter interpretation has been advocated by several authorities and is typified by the British Medical Association and Magistrates' Association's memorandum of 1947 ('Interpretation of Definitions in the Mental Deficiency Act, 1927'), which states that 'the purpose of this memorandum is to point out that the concept of mind is wider than that of intellect, and that mental defect (i.e. deficiency of mind) is not the same thing as intellectual deficiency, though it includes it'. A similar point of view was later expressed by the Board of Control (1954) and the Royal Medico-Psychological Association (1954) in their memoranda to the Royal Commission on the Law relating to Mental Illness and Mental Deficiency. Thus, the Board of Control say: 'We regard the present definitions as enabling medical practitioners to certify mentally defective patients on the ground that they have characteristics from early youth which make them antisocial, although their intelligence might be quite normal.' The RMPA, in its discussion of the nature of mental deficiency, stated:

> This 'condition of arrested or incomplete development of mind' may, however, be manifested in very varied ways. A usual manifestation is failure to develop what is commonly known as intelligence-functions which can be measured by psychometric methods and assessed under such terms as 'mental age' or 'intelligence quotient'; but this is by no means invariable, and in other cases the undeveloped mind may be manifested chiefly by failure to attain normal control of the emotions or to achieve the qualities needed for normal social behaviour.

The practical outcome of this point of view was that in England a large number of individuals of dull-normal and normal intellect were certified as mentally defective and compulsorily detained. O'Connor and Tizard (1954) showed that in their 5 per cent sample of nearly 12,000 patients, over half were classified as 'feeble-minded'; they found, in conformity with their previous researches, and that of other psychologists working in institutions, that the *average* IQ of *young* adult feeble-minded defectives was a little above 70 points. Various tests have been used by different examiners with substantially similar results. Commenting on this state of affairs, the British Psychological Society (1955) wrote that 'During this century, the British concept of mental deficiency has widened until it is no longer closely related to biological, psychological, or genetic definitions of the condition'. It seems that something like one-quarter of all institutionalized mentally deficient patients had IQs of 70 or above at the time these reports were made, a fact never envisaged by Tredgold. As already implied, this position did not appear to have altered substantially during the mid-1960s (apart from a welcome and dramatic drop in the numbers compulsorily detained) after the passing of the 1959 Mental Health Act (Castell and Mittler, 1965). Since then, however, there has been a considerable reduction in numbers of mildly subnormal admitted to hospital (see Chapter 3).

(2) EDUCATIONAL RETARDATION AS A CRITERION

The MD Act of 1927 in its definition of those to be classed as feeble-minded says '. . . in the case of children, that they appear to be permanently incapable by reason of such defectiveness (already defined) of receiving proper benefit from the instruction in ordinary schools'. This definition was in effect amended by the 1944 Education Act, which makes provision for the teaching of educationally subnormal children of all sorts, including the cognitively defective (above IQ 50), without certification as mentally deficient. Persistent educational failure has never been regarded as a sole criterion of mental defect and, as Wallin (1949) pointed out, such a procedure would classify as subnormal, millions of children of backward and borderline levels of intelligence who could not be regarded as feeble-minded, socially considered. Nevertheless, it is commonly used as one of the facts supporting a diagnosis of mental subnormality, and deserves, therefore, a passing reference.

(3) THE IQ AS A CRITERION

The advantages and disadvantages of IQ measurements have been discussed by many writers and have been touched upon in Chapter 6 of this book. It is thus intended here to offer the briefest account of the problems, as follows: (1) the IQ is liable to some degree of measurement error, either because of imperfect standardization or because of individual cognitive or motivational fluctuations possessing no long-term significance; (2) the same IQ on different tests may not, for reasons of standardization, mean the same thing. In practice this may be overcome with the use of standard scores but this is seldom undertaken by clinicians or administrators; (3) intellectual growth over long periods of time (and particularly among some of the mildly subnormal) does not necessarily proceed in a constant fashion with reference to age peers. Like physical growth, intellectual growth may change, sometimes markedly, in its rate of increase.

This does not lead to error in the sense defined in (1) above; rather it indicates that IQ changes may reflect real growth changes.

The difficulty is expressed by Kushlick (1968) in his attempt to assess the prevalence and prognosis of mild subnormality. The IQ range 50 to 70, he writes, has not proved useful either clinically or administratively. Among the many examples he offers, the classification of children as educationally subnormal may be cited. The total number of children in ESN schools seldom exceeds half of the 2 per cent to be expected if all children of IQ 50–70 were to attend, but anyway a report indicates that almost 40 per cent of the ESN have IQs above 70. One cannot, therefore, escape the conclusion that a minority of the 50–70 IQ group actually find their way into ESN schools (see also Chapter 3).

From the foregoing it seems obvious that an upper borderline for subnormality is impossible to define with any degree of precision in IQ terms. Two considerations may, however, prove to be useful. First, to think of a proportion of the population as 'at risk' of needing special services at some time during their lives, while acknowledging that opinions will vary about what proportion this might represent (e.g. 2 per cent in England versus 3 per cent, as proposed by Heber, 1959). Second, an arbitrary upper limit should be imposed, if only to ensure that services designed as appropriate for an intellectually homogeneous section of the population are not misapplied by being extended to include a much wider range of the population, probably manifesting different needs. This appears in England to be occurring with an influx of ex-ESN children into some Adult Training Centres originally designed for the severely subnormal.

There does, however, appear to remain considerable agreement for the view expressed by Burt (1922) that for adults a mental age of 8 or IQ 50 is helpful in distinguishing between those who are almost invariably 'social parasites' and those who can, albeit at a low level, fend for themselves in the community. Despite the problems outlined above, some kind of classification system is necessary, (a) for administrative and (b) for scientific purposes. The major use here seems to be for research and for communication between scientists. We have suggested that mild mental subnormality is not a scientific category in itself. This does, of course, imply that scientific work on those so classified may not prove very useful.

In practice, behavioural criteria of subnormality are hard to define with precision. An extreme expression of this problem is given by Garfunkel (1964) and Brabner (1967) quoted by Sarason and Doris (1969). They argue that diagnostic categories or definitions confuse rather than clarify issues and that the concept of subnormality, like that of mental illness, is a useless one for understanding and modifying non-adaptive behaviour, primarily because the so-called 'condition' of subnormality is not an identifiable behavioural entity. Brabner goes on to state that medical men have initially lumped together in single categories several diseases of unknown aetiology. Later knowledge allows them to subdivide or re-classify these once vague categories.

The present writers have considerable sympathy with this view, and offer as an illustrative example the results of an attempt to account for those who might be presumed to be in need of assistance in a country offering well-established and extensive free services for the mentally subnormal. As already noted, it is generally estimated that about 2 per cent of the population may be regarded as intellectually subnormal and severely subnormal, in the porportion of three to one, respectively. With a population in England and Wales of about 48 million, therefore, one would expect to identify something like 960,000 subnormal persons of all grades. What do we know of the status of this large group? It is possible, in a rough-and-ready way, to account for a proportion by examining statistics for a given year, in this case 1966 (see Table 1).

TABLE 1. *Total identified subnormal population* (*subnormal and severely subnormal*)
in England and Wales, 1966

Population of England and Wales	approx.	48,000,000
2% of total population		960,000
In schools for the ESN	approx.	45,000
On ESN waiting lists	''	10,000
In mental subnormality hospitals	''	65,000
On mental subnormality hospital waiting lists	''	5,000
Under care of local health authorities	''	93,000
In Junior Training Centres	''	17,000
In Adult Training Centres	''	18,000
Total	''	253,000

Note: The total of 253,000 is considerably inflated because the Training Centre numbers are almost certainly also included in those under care of local health authorities. Moreover, in mental subnormality hospitals and training centres, the majority will be of severely subnormal grade.

It should be added that in 1966 there were a little over 4 million children under five; 2 per cent of this figure is 80,000. Of these, perhaps 60,000 are potentially ESN, but these will not have been identified until the school years. The balance, about 20,000, is severely subnormal and some of these pre-school children will be under the care of local health authorities or in special care units or in subnormality hospitals. All these considerations justify the conclusion that a relatively small percentage of the *mildly* subnormal (unlike the severely subnormal) are in receipt of special facilities at any one time. (Part of this information is taken from Table 7 in Worters, 1968.)

The table accounts for all those specifically designated subnormal (whether of mild or severe grade) and dealt with as such by various social agencies. It is certain that the table includes the vast majority of those who are severely subnormal. There remains the possibility, however, that other types of community provision include significant numbers of the mildly subnormal, of which the criminal population is the only one worth serious consideration. In an as yet unpublished recent study, Dr C. Banks (personal communication) gave individual Stanford-Binet tests to 900 randomly sampled men, aged 17–20, in detention, prison or borstal. She found that 2 per cent (i.e. roughly the expected representation from the total population) had IQs of 70 and below. Unfortunately, there is no study available of the intelligence of a randomly selected prison population, but according to Dr R. V. G. Clarke (personal communication) studies of selected samples of the prison population, while showing an over-representation of the dull normal, do not suggest any marked over-representation of the subnormal.

If one were to add, say, a further 25,000 (probably a considerable overestimate) to cover the mildly subnormal receiving care in prisons, borstals, approved schools, or charitable hostels, one would account only for less than a third of the estimated total subnormal and severely subnormal population. The conclusion seems inescapable that at any one point in time the majority of the *mildly subnormal* (who comprise three-quarters of the whole) function within the limits of community tolerance in a welfare state, receiving no special official provision. For these very reasons, little is known of the 'ordinary' mildly subnormal in the community, and precise data relate in the main to the most disadvantaged members of the group.

The rather crude analysis offered above is supported by the results of long-term social follow-up of mildly retarded persons (Charles, 1953; Miller, 1965). A large group identified as retarded and attending 'opportunity classes' was originally studied in the 1930s. Detailed analysis of the ways in which its members differed from the general population has been provided and the successively improving outcome carefully documented. A final monograph by Baller, Charles and Miller (1967) indicated that the majority were functioning adequately as low-average members of the population, working in unskilled or semi-skilled employment. Of average age 53 years, this group has 'continued to fare much better than could have been predicted or even hoped for'. See also Chapter 9.

If we perceive the mentally subnormal as a group of people 'at risk' of requiring special facilities provided by a welfare state (and this operational definition is at least as reasonable as any other), then it appears that *at any one point in time* only a third of those who may be presumed to represent the bottom 2 per cent of the distribution of intelligence are in fact using those facilities. The proportion *who at some period in their lives* require the special help of welfare agencies, will, of course, be greater. The above analysis is offered, not as evidence of some undisclosed qualities among the subnormal, nor as evidence of a necessarily perfect state of affairs. It does, however, imply (1) that a large proportion of the group at risk are not classified as subnormal for specific administrative purposes; and (2) where special help is required, it may be only temporarily.

In these terms, therefore, the mildly and severely subnormal are both 'at risk' of needing some form of community provision. The 'risk' is absolute so far as the lower group is concerned, and much less so in the higher group. In the former, the cause is primarily intellectual, and in the latter very often a compound of social, intellectual and environmental factors.

Decisions concerning the upper limit for the mildly subnormal will reflect an interaction of social provision, the threshold for social tolerance of deviant behaviour, the employment situation and, commonly, the existence of areas of social degradation, as well as the belief that it is wise in education or training not to deal with a group which is very heterogeneous in character.

It is concluded, therefore, that mild subnormality is primarily a social concept which may alter from time to time and which has some convenience so far as treatment is concerned. The label does not in practice constitute a scientific entity, which is not to say, of course, that the group so delineated may not be scientifically of very great interest, providing a very rewarding field of work.

THE AAMD COMMITTEE

In an endeavour to bring order into the chaotic status of terminology and classification in the field of mental retardation, the American Association on Mental Deficiency set up a broadly based committee of experts to inquire into the problem and make proposals. The recommended new system of classification was published (Heber, 1959), and represents an important advance in the field. Since the definitions and concepts proposed differ substantially from, for example, those embodied in the new British Mental Health Act, passed in the same year, it remains to be seen how effective the American Association on Mental Deficiency classification will be in producing a more uniform system of statistical reporting on an international basis.

The Manual starts with a section on definition, presenting a general concept of mental retardation which is interdisciplinary in character and which serves to distinguish mental retardation from other disorders of behaviour.

Definition: 'Mental retardation refers to subaverage general intellectual functioning which originates during the development period and is associated with impairment in one or more of the following: (1) maturation, (2) learning, and (3) social adjustment.'

'Subaverage' refers to performance more than one standard deviation below the population mean; 'general intellectual functioning' may be assessed by one or more of the various objective tests developed for the purpose; the upper age limit of the 'developmental period', although it cannot be precisely defined, is regarded as approximately 16 years; rate of 'maturation' refers to the rate of sequential development of self-help skills of infancy and early childhood and is regarded as of prime importance as a criterion during the pre-school years; 'learning ability' refers to the facility with which knowledge is acquired as a function of experience, and is particularly important as a qualifying condition during the school years. Social adjustment is particularly important as a qualifying condition of mental retardation at the adult level where it is assessed in terms of the degree to which the individual is able to maintain himself independently in the community and in gainful employment, as well as his ability to meet and conform to other personal and social responsibilities and standards set by the community. Since adequate population norms and highly objective measures of the various aspects of adaptive behaviour are not yet available, it is not possible to establish precise criteria of functioning in these areas.

The report stresses finally that within the framework of the present definition, mental retardation is a term descriptive of the *current* status of the individual.

The Manual outlines excellent classificatory schemes under medical and behavioural headings, and also includes a section on statistical reporting (Heber, 1959; see also footnote on p. 225 of this volume).

The reader is referred to an interesting polemic on some of the concepts used in the AAMD Manual between Garfield and Wittson (1960a, b) and Cantor (1960, 1961). In the last paper the author discusses at length the concept of 'incurability', and stresses the dangers inherent in the persistent tendency of clinicians to 'entitize' mental retardation.

WHO EXPERT COMMITTEE ON MENTAL HEALTH, 1968

The WHO Expert Committee (1968) takes account of most of the foregoing discussion of problems concerning criteria and classification. The report suggests IQ borderlines for the different grades of defect, assuming a population mean of 100 and a standard deviation of 15 points. Taken in conjunction with social factors, it is argued that the sub-classification of the mentally retarded should be associated with the following approximate IQ ranges: mild, −2·0 to −3·3 standard deviations from the mean (i.e. IQs 50–70); moderate, −3·3 to −4·3 standard deviations from the mean (i.e. IQs 35–50); severe, −4·3 to −5·3 standard deviations from the mean (i.e. IQs 20–35); and profound, more than −5·3 standard deviations from the mean. As the report indicates, 'It should again be stressed that these are not exact measurements, nor should they be considered the sole criteria; in practice, the categories will tend to overlap, but the IQ has some value within the range of mental retardation, both as a diagnostic and as a prognostic guide.' It might be added that the lower the IQ, the more profound are its implications both diagnostically and prognostically.

The Expert Committee's discussion on these points was related to the text of the eighth revision of the ICD (World Health Organization, 1967). The Committee thus accepted the sub-classification but made it more precise. It strongly opposed, however, the classification of those with an IQ in the range 68–85 as 'borderline mentally retarded' as shown in category 310. On this basis at least 16 per cent of the population would be labelled mentally retarded or borderline mentally retarded. The widening of the concept implied by this definition would greatly damage the quality of available services, which are geared to lower abilities, and would make mental retardation a repository for other deviant conditions. A similar viewpoint was advanced during a 1969 WHO Seminar held in Washington DC, where the following main recommendations were made for the ninth revision of the ICD: (1) A scheme of classification should be instituted requiring the recording of four types of information: (a) degree of mental handicap, (b) aetiological or associated biological or organic factors, (c) associated psychiatric disorder, and (d) psychosocial factors.

(2) The grades of mental retardation recommended in the 1968 report should be used, and the category 'borderline mental retardation' should be replaced by a category 'normal variations in intelligence'. Rather than being included in the ICD Manual, IQ ranges should be specified in an accompanying glossary which should draw attention to the limitations as well as to the usefulness of IQ data, and the need to take into account social and cultural background when evaluating grade of intellectual retardation (Moser, 1971, and personal communication).

The pathological / subcultural dichotomy

A most important classification, on the basis of aetiology, was proposed by E. O. Lewis (1933). Although subsequently modified, it remains fundamental, has influenced later classificatory systems and thus finds a penultimate place in this chapter.

Lewis stated that the term mental deficiency is an abstraction used to cover a heterogeneous and complex group of clinical conditions due to a variety of biological factors, and preferred, therefore, to speak of 'mental deficiencies'. On the basis of clinical studies in the field, he suggested that there are two forms of variation: (1) the *pathological* type, and (2) the *subcultural* type. Adopting Tredgold's classification of clinical varieties of secondary amentia, Lewis included in the pathological group all cases of mental deficiency attributable to trauma, inflammatory conditions, hydrocephalus, syphilis, epilepsy, cretinism, and nutritional and sensory defects. He also included several other conditions, such as mongolism, amaurotic family idiocy, hyperteliorism, naevoid amentiae, progressive degeneration, and many cases of sclerotic amentiae. In the causation of all these varieties of defect, one finds the intervention of some new or alien factors of a pathological character not found in the normal constitution. In Lewis's classification, such conditions as phenylketonuria and amaurotic idiocy, which are known to be due to recessive genes, were included in the pathological type.

On the other hand, the subcultural group included those cases of defect in which no alien factor was found, and where the deficiency was only an extreme variety of the normal variation of mental endowments. Thus, the higher grades of subcultural deficiency merged imperceptibly into the lower grades of dullness or temperamental instability in the normal population. Although Lewis inclined to the view that subcultural deficiency is inherited, he believed that unfavourable environmental factors may in some cases account for the condition.

As Penrose (1962) has indicated, an interesting change has occurred in our understanding of aetiological mechanisms. Whereas, in Lewis's day, most cases of pathological, mainly low-grade subnormality were thought to result from trauma, infection or toxicity, it is now increasingly recognized that rare (often recessive) genetic mechanisms are sometimes responsible for the damage (e.g. phenylketonuria). And whereas subnormals of about IQ 50 upward were at one time thought to owe their condition largely to unfavourable genetic mechanisms, evidence now suggests that early and prolonged social adversity is an important, though not the sole, feature. The pathological/subcultural dichotomy remains useful although there has been some reinterpretation of its aetiological mechanisms.

Clarke (1966, 1969) has suggested a tripartite system of aetiological classification, effectively splitting the Lewis subcultural category into subcultural versus normal genetic variation. Recognizing that parental-child intelligence correlations rarely exceed 0·5, he indicates that a proportion of the mildly subnormal groups must owe their status, not primarily to social factors, but to normal genetic variation. Fig. 1 in Chapter 1 indicated the relationship of these three aetiological headlines to terminology and to IQ.

Conclusions

Criteria and classification of subnormality possess a long history of development and change. At the root of all systems is the need of societies to take action of some kind. The nature of the procedures adopted is profoundly influenced by current perceptions of deviance on the one hand, and the type of responsibilities owed to their members on the other. From the thirteenth century consideration of problems concerning disposal of property, these concepts have changed to include, implicitly, biological and social theories of man. These ranged from the need for Christian brotherhood and charity for the oppressed, to post-Darwinian theories concerning the supposed evolutionary threat of 'feeble-mindedness' to civilized society. Currently, these have moved away from segregation to the notion of integration of the handicapped in the community and their maximal 'normalization'.

We have stressed throughout that subnormality is primarily an administrative concept, used for the purposes of social action. Our brief overview of the major criteria of subnormality, namely IQ below 70, social incompetence and educational retardation, has made clear that each is overinclusive of other conditions. It has been argued that (1) the IQ criterion includes many socially competent members at the above IQ 50 level; (2) that social incompetence is to be found in many other conditions than subnormality and is thus not specifically pathognomonic; and (3) that educationally, as Burt once put it, 'the dull are usually backward, but the backward are not necessarily dull'.

In combination, these criteria are highly intercorrelated in that small section of the population below about IQ 50. Above this level, in the individual case, an intercorrelation of all three will suggest the need for special help, which may be of a temporary or a longer-term nature. This combination provides the purest measure of administrative prevalence, that is, of society's need to take action.

References

BALLER, W. R., CHARLES, D. C. and MILLER, E. L. (1967) Mid-life attainment of the mentally retarded: a longitudinal study. *Genet. Psychol. Monogr.*, **75**, 235–329.

Board of Control (1954) *Memorandum of Evidence before the Royal Commission on the Law relating to Mental Illness and Mental Deficiency.* Day 1. London: HMSO.

BRABNER, G. (1967) The myth of mental retardation. *Training School Bull.*, **63**, 149–52.

British Medical Association and Magistrates' Association (1947) Interpretations of Definitions in the Mental Deficiency Act, 1927. London: BMA.

British Psychological Society (1955) Memorandum of Evidence before the Royal Commission on the Law relating to Mental Illness and Mental Deficiency. Day 17. London: HMSO.

BURT, C. (1922) *Mental and Scholastic Tests* (2nd edn, 1924). London: P. S. King.

CANTOR, G. N. (1960) A critique of Garfield and Wittson's reaction to the revised Manual on Terminology and Classification. *Amer. J. ment. Defic.*, **64**, 954–6.

CANTOR, G. N. (1961) Some issues involved in category VIII of the A.A.M.D. 'Terminology and Classification Manual'. *Amer. J. ment. Defic.*, **65**, 561–6.

CASTELL, J. H. F. and MITTLER, P. J. (1965) Intelligence of patients in subnormality hospitals: a survey of admissions in 1961. *Brit. J. Psychiat.*, **111**, 219–25.

CHARLES, D. C. (1953) Ability and accomplishment of persons earlier judged mentally deficient. *Genet. Psychol. Monogr.*, **47**, 3–71.

CLARKE, A. D. B. (1966) *Recent Advances in the Study of Subnormality.* London: National Association for Mental Health.

CLARKE, A. D. B. (1969) *Recent Advances in the Study of Subnormality.* (2nd edn). London: National Association for Mental Health.

CLARKE, A. D. B. and CLARKE, A. M. (1972) Consistency and variability in the growth of human characteristics. In WALL, W. D. and VARMA, V. (eds.) *Advances in Educational Psychology*, I. London: Univ. of London Press.

CLARKE, A. M. and CLARKE, A. D. B. (1973) Assessment and prediction in the severely subnormal. In MITTLER, P. J. (ed.) *Psychological Assessment of the Mentally Handicapped.* London: Churchill.

GARFIELD, S. L. and WITTSON, C. (1960a) Some reactions to the revised Manual on Terminology and Classification in Mental Retardation. *Amer. J. ment. Defic.*, **64**, 951–3.

GARFIELD, S. L. and WITTSON, C. (1960b) Comments on Dr Cantor's remarks. *Amer. J. ment. Defic.*, **64**, 957–9.

GARFUNKEL, F. (1964). Probabilities and possibilities for modifying behaviour of mentally retarded children: tactics for research. *Boston Univ. J. Educ.*, **147**, 45–52.

GODDARD, H. H. (1912) *The Kallikak Family*. New York: Macmillan.

HEBER, R. (1959) A manual on terminology and classification in mental retardation. *Amer. J. ment. Defic. Monogr. Suppl.*, **64.**

KUSHLICK, A. (1968) Social problems in mental subnormality. In MILLER, E. (ed.) *Foundations of Child Psychiatry*. Oxford: Pergamon.

LEWIS, E. O. (1933) Types of mental deficiency and their social significance. *J. ment. Sci.*, **79**, 298–304.

MILLER, E. L. (1965) Ability and social adjustment at midlife of persons earlier judged mentally deficient. *Genet. Psychol. Monogr.*, **72**, 139–98.

MOSER, J. (1971) World Health Organization activities concerning mental retardation. In PRIMROSE, D. A. (ed.) *Proc. 2nd Congr. Internat. Assoc. Scient. Stud. Ment. Defic.*, 546–7. Warsaw: Ars Polona; Amsterdam: Swets & Zeitlinger.

O'CONNOR, N. and TIZARD, J. (1954) A survey of patients in twelve mental deficiency institutions. *Brit. med. J.*, **i**, 16–18.

PENROSE, L. S. (1962) Biological aspects. *Proc. Lond. Conf. Scient. Stud. Ment Defic.*, **1**, 11–18.

Royal Medico-Psychological Association (1954) *Memorandum of Evidence before the Royal Commission on the Law relating to Mental Illness and Mental Deficiency*. Day 8. London: HMSO.

SARASON, S. B. and DORIS, J. (1969) *Psychological Problems in Mental Deficiency* (4th edn). New York: Harper & Row.

TREDGOLD, A. F. (1949) *A Text-book of Mental Deficiency* (7th edn reprinted; 8th edn 1952). London: Baillière, Tindall & Cox.

WALLIN, J. E. W. (1949) *Children with Mental and Physical Handicaps*. New York and London: Staples.

World Health Organization (1967) *Manual of the International Statistical Classification of Diseases, Injuries and Causes of Death, 1965 Revision*. Geneva.

World Health Organization (1968) *Organization of Services for the Mentally Retarded*. Fifteenth Report of the WHO Expert Committee on Mental Health. WHO Tech. Rep. Ser. 392. Geneva.

WORTERS, A. R. (1968) Subnormality – terminology and prevalence. In O'GORMAN, G. (ed.) *Modern Trends in Mental Health and Subnormality*. London: Butterworth.

3

A. Kushlick and R. Blunden

The epidemiology of
mental subnormality[1]

Introduction

In England and Wales at 31 December 1970 there were known to be 64,173 mentally handicapped people in NHS hospitals and contractual beds (DHSS, 1972a). There were also 104,140 such people receiving Local Authority mental health services (DHSS, 1971a). Table 1 shows the proportions of children and adults receiving provision together with details of some of the Local Authority services received.

TABLE 2. *Number of mentally handicapped people known to be in hospital or receiving Local Authority mental health services (England and Wales, 31 December 1970)*

Type of provision	Total number	Age Percentage aged	
		under 16	16 and over
NHS hospitals and contractual beds	64,173	10	90
Local Authority mental health services	104,140	29	71
Of these:			
Attending training centres	48,206	46	54
Resident in homes and hostels	6,685	26	74
Boarded out at LA expense	604	10	90

At the end of 1970 there were 1,792 children and 1,491 adults on the waiting list for admission to hospital (DHSS, 1970).

[1] Based upon a chapter by the first author in E. Miller (ed.) *Foundations of Child Psychiatry* (Oxford, Pergamon, 1968), by kind permission of the publishers.

Classification

These figures constitute the recognized or administrative prevalence of mental defect, that is the existing numbers at one time. However, mental defect is not a homogeneous entity; indeed it covers a wide range of abilities and incapacities. Table 3 shows the IQ range of the mentally handicapped and the terms which are used to describe the differing degrees. (See also Chapter 2.)

In this chapter we will use the classical terms idiot, imbecile and feeble-minded or severely and mildly subnormal to mean people in the IQ ranges shown in the table.

The official statistics reflect administrative practice rather than the 'true' prevalence of the condition. We are, however, able to make some generalizations about the 'true' prevalence of the condition in this country from the results of detailed studies conducted in smaller areas. These show that there are important differences between the severely subnormal (IQ under 50) and the mildly subnormal (IQ over 50). For this reason we will discuss these two major categories separately.

TABLE 3. *Different terms used to classify the degree of mental handicap with the approximate IQ ranges of the subjects in each grade (mean IQ of the population approximately 100)*

IQ range	Classification used in this chapter	Other terminology sometimes used	Mental Health Act (1959) classification	
0–20 or 25	Idiot ⎫ Severely ⎬subnormal Imbecile⎭ (SSN)	Low grade	⎫Severely ⎬subnormal⎭	S U
20 or 25–50 or 55		Medium grade		B
50 or 55–70 or 75	Feeble-minded Mildly subnormal (MSN)	High grade debile moron	Subnormal or subnormal and psychopathic	N O R M A L

The prevalence and prognosis of severe subnormality (IQ under 50)

In England and Wales about 3·7/1000 of the people who survive to the age of 15–19 are likely to be severely subnormal. Kushlick (1961) examined the records of all mental defectives known on 1 January 1961 to the Mental Health Department in Salford, a northern English industrial city of 153,000 people. Goodman and Tizard (1962) examined the records of all mental defectives known in 1961 to the Mental Health Department of Middlesex county, a major English conurbation with a population of 2,231,100. They also collected details of children of

IQ under 50 who were of school age but who were not known to the Mental Health Department because they were still attending schools within the ordinary educational system, private schools and private homes. Kushlick (1964) examined the records of all mental defectives known on 1 July 1963 in the area served by the Wessex Regional Hospital Board. The three county boroughs Southampton, Portsmouth and Bournemouth, and three counties Hampshire, Dorset and Isle of Wight, had a total population of 1,740,000 people. The records were obtained

TABLE 4. *Comparison of the prevalence rates of severe subnormality in age-groups where all subjects are likely to be known*

	Age-group	Total IQ under 50 per thousand	Mongol per thousand
England and Wales (Lewis) 1926–9:			
Urban	7–14	3·71	0·34
Rural		5·61	NK
Middlesex (Goodman and Tizard) 1960	7–14	3·45	1·14
	10–14	3·61	NK
Salford (Kushlick) 1961	15–19	3·62	0·90
Wessex (Kushlick) 1963:			
county boroughs	15–19	3·54	1·15*
counties	15–19	3·84	1·18*
Onondaga county 1953	5–17	3·6	NK
Baltimore (Lemkau *et al.*) 1936	10–14	3·3	NK
Rural Sweden (Åkesson) 1959	All ages	5·8	0·03
Edinburgh (Drillien *et al.*) 1962–4	7½–14½	5·0	1·8
Northern Ireland (Scally and MacKay) 1962	15–19	4·7	1·45
Camberwell (Wing) 1967	5–14	3·89	0·90
Aberdeen (Birch *et al.*) 1962	8–10	3·7	NK

* The Wessex Survey suggested that 10 per cent of mongols have IQ scores of more than 50.

from the Mental Health Departments of the Local Health Authorities, the psychiatric hospitals for the subnormal and the mentally ill, and from registered private homes serving the people in the region. The prevalence of severe subnormality found in these and other more recent UK surveys in comparable age-groups is shown in Table 4. The rates are very similar for both urban and rural areas.

Prevalence rates of severe subnormality in other Western countries are similar to those found here but differences in survey methods render comparisons with English results difficult. Lemkau *et al.* (1943) examined in 1936 the records of children known as imbecile or idiot in a part of Baltimore, USA, with a population of 55,000. He found a prevalence rate in the age-group 10–14 of 3·3/1000. A survey in the urban area of Onondaga County, New York, in 1955 found the prevalence rate of children of IQ under 50 in the age-group 5–17 to be 3·6/1000. The total population of children of 17 years and under in this urban area was 116,000. Åkesson (1961) tested all children and a sample of adults in 10 rural Swedish parishes with a total population of 11,500. He found the high rate of 5·8/1000 subjects of all ages with scores of IQ under 50.

The English studies suggest that distinct clinical entities are now contributing similar proportions to the condition of severe subnormality. Thus, Table 4 shows that the prevalence of mongolism at the age of 15–19 is very similar in all the surveys; most mongols are severely subnormal. Dunsdon *et al.* (1960) have estimated that 6–7 per cent of mongols scored IQs of over 45 while 1–2 per cent scored 55 and over. From this it can be seen that mongolism at present accounts for about a quarter of all cases of severe subnormality in this age-group.

The means of identifying severely subnormal subjects is similar in all industrialized countries. Some children are diagnosed as mentally handicapped in the first few days of their lives because of the presence of clinical signs like mongolism or microcephaly, which are often associated with future severe subnormality. Others are detected via family doctors, health visitors or paediatric services as a result of slow development in the early stages of childhood. These may then be referred to the appropriate social service agency if one is provided.

Where universal compulsory education is provided, severely subnormal children will be segregated, either by the provision of special education within the ordinary school system (as is done in Holland, Scotland, and now in England and Wales) or by excluding them altogether (as was done until 1971 in England and Wales).

It was found in the Salford survey that a third of the idiots (IQ under 20) had been notified to the Mental Health Department before the age of 5 and that 93 per cent had been notified by the age of 9. Among imbeciles (IQ 20–49) the corresponding percentages were 7 and 45 respectively. Most of the remaining severely subnormal children are excluded from the ordinary school system after a trial at school. However, Kushlick (1961) found that no less than a quarter of the severely subnormal children continued in the ordinary school system in special or ordinary schools and were notified to the Mental Health Department for supervision only on leaving school at 15 or 16.

Before April 1971, when services for the mentally handicapped in England and Wales were reorganized, nearly all severely subnormal people who had survived to the age group 15–19 had been notified to the existing Mental Health Departments of Local Authorities. Kushlick (1961) found that only a very small proportion of these people were notified for the first time after the age of 19. The reason for this appears to lie in the prognosis of people with severe subnormality. Only about 10 per cent of these subjects are able to hold employment in open industry. The remaining 90 per cent appear at the present time to remain permanently economically dependent and become, for this reason, known to the social agencies dealing with mental handicap.

Since April 1971 new Local Authority Social Services Departments have been set up and these include in their remit the responsibilities previously exercised by Mental Health Departments. It is not yet certain whether these new departments are being notified of people with severe subnormality to the same extent as were the Mental Health Departments.

Tizard (1958) reviewed the available follow-up studies of severe subnormality. He suggested that between 10 and 20 per cent may be capable of becoming economically independent. Ferguson and Kerr (1955) followed up 207 girls who had left Glasgow schools for the educationally subnormal six years previously. Only 2 out of 11 girls of IQ under 50 (range 40–49) had been employed since leaving school – one had worked for 2 years and one for 3 years. None of these girls had married. There is further indirect evidence that the severely subnormal are permanently economically dependent. Kushlick (1961) found that the prevalence rates of recognized severe subnormality in Salford remained constant from the age-group 15–19 until the age of 40, when it began to fall due to deaths among these subjects (see Table 5). In the same study the author was able to analyse all of the notifications to and deletions from the Salford register of mental defectives between 1948 and 1960. Subjects were deleted from the register when they died, emigrated to another area, when they could no longer be traced or when, because they made stable adjustments in the community and were no longer seen as being in need of supervision, they were discharged from care.

Stable employment and marriage were the main reasons for discharge. Only 7 per cent of the subjects discharged during 12 years were severely subnormal. The remainder had IQs of over 50.

Summary

Severely subnormal individuals are mainly identified in countries with compulsory universal education when they are found unsuitable for education within the ordinary school system.

Before April 1971 in England and Wales, the majority of these children were excluded from school and became the responsibility of the Mental Health Departments of the Local Authorities. About a quarter remained within the ordinary school system in special schools, and were notified to the Mental Health Departments after leaving school for supervision or when they failed to hold employment in open industry. In some countries, like Holland, a large proportion continued within the ordinary school system in schools for the severely subnormal. By the age of 15–19 nearly all severely subnormal subjects who had survived to this age were known to Mental Health Departments of Local Authorities in England and Wales. At this age the proportion of severely subnormal in the population is about 3·7/1000 in both urban and rural areas of England. Between a quarter and a third of these people have the clinical conditions of mongolism. An IQ of under 50 appears at present to be a severe incapacity leading to permanent dependence among about 90 per cent of affected individuals. Those subjects who did not die at an early age were eventually admitted to hospitals for the mentally handicapped. Once admitted they tended to remain there until they died.

Several changes in recent years could affect measures of administrative prevalence of severe subnormality, the form of residential provision for these people and their social prognosis. The administrative changes in April 1971 in this country involve both referrals to Education and Social Services Departments as well as the classifications used by these departments. The effects of these changes on administrative prevalence rates have yet to be examined.

Various forms of residential care other than traditionally organized hospital wards are being developed in this country and elsewhere. These include small locally based 'homes' and sheltered housing or group homes. It is also likely that new methods of teaching applied to the mentally handicapped may well reduce the proportions of those with severely disruptive behaviours and also increase the capacity of others for less dependent forms of existence.

The prevalence and prognosis of mild subnormality

The IQ range 50–70 has often been suggested as diagnostic of the grade of mild mental subnormality. This has not proved useful either clinically or administratively. There are many people in this IQ range who are never dealt with as subnormal and who do not appear to have problems arising from their low intelligence, and there are people of IQ well over 70 who are being dealt with by the services for the subnormal. In this country there has never been, nor is there now, an upper psychometric limit to this degree of subnormality. On a test standardized to give a mean of 100 and standard deviation of 15, the proportion of the population scoring between 50 and 70 would be nearly 20/1000. In the Salford survey the highest prevalence rate for mild subnormality was found among those aged 15–19; it was 8·7/1000 or under a half of the rate expected on the criterion of IQ alone. (See also Chapter 2.)

Although the Mental Health Act of 1959 included for the first time the criterion of low intellect in the diagnosis of subnormality, there is no sign that this has led to a lowering of the IQ level of people admitted to hospitals for the subnormal. A Working Party of the British Psychological Society (1963) examined the Wechsler IQ levels of 876 people admitted to these hospitals since the Act became operative. The average Wechsler IQ of those graded 'subnormal' was 71·4; that of admissions categorized 'severely subnormal' was 60·4. These levels are very similar to those reported by O'Connor and Tizard (1956) among patients in hospitals for the subnormal in 1954. The 1970 census of mentally handicapped hospital patients (DHSS, 1972a) showed that of 13,098 patients classed as mildly mentally handicapped and for whom an actual or estimated IQ or mental age was available, 21 per cent had an IQ of 70 or more, whilst 7 per cent had an IQ of 80 or more. These percentages were considerably higher for the 15–19 and 20–34 year age-groups.

Nor is the IQ level the sole determinant of who is to be classified as Educationally Subnormal (ESN) and given special education within the ordinary school system.[1] The total number of children in special schools seldom exceeds half of the 2 per cent to be expected if all children of IQ 50–70 were to attend, and the Report of the Chief Medical Officer (Ministry of Education, 1963) shows that nearly 40 per cent of children in the special schools scored over 70.

It is now clear that the classification of a person as subnormal is dependent on his presenting social and behavioural problems in addition to his poor performance in IQ tests. This was recognized by Heber (1961) in his definition of mental retardation as 'subaverage general intellectual functioning which originates during the developmental period and is associated with impairment in adaptive behaviour'. Adaptive behaviour in this context refers primarily to the effectiveness of an individual in meeting the natural and social demands and expectations of his environment.

Unlike the severely subnormal, most of whom are detected during or before their years at school, the majority of the mildly subnormal become so classified in this country when they are notified by the Education Authority to the Social Services Department as in need of supervision on leaving school. Thus, 90 per cent of the mildly subnormal people referred to Salford Mental Health Department between 1948 and 1960 were notified between the ages of 15–19 (Kushlick, 1961). This also explains why social services department registers have very few mildly subnormal people aged under 15 and why there is a sharp rise in their numbers in the age-group 15–19.

There is much evidence that, unlike severe subnormality, mild subnormality is a temporary incapacity related largely to educational difficulties experienced at school. After leaving school the majority of these people become socially and economically independent and are indistinguishable from the rest of the community (see Chapter 2).

Some of the evidence is indirect. Kushlick (1961) found that the prevalence rate of mild subnormality dropped precipitously after the age range 15–19. This finding was confirmed in the Wessex survey (Kushlick and Cox, 1967). The rapid fall in administrative prevalence was due to the discharge of subjects from the register, when they were judged by the service not to require supervision because they were in stable employment or because they had married. By adding to the 1961 Salford Register all of the subjects who had been discharged in the period 1948–60 it was found that at the time of the survey discharges had been achieved by two-thirds of the people who were in the age range 25–29, nearly 40 per cent aged 20–24 and over 10 per cent aged 15–19. Over 90 per cent

[1] In this country, before the Education Act of 1944, children who received special education had first to be 'certified' mentally defective of the feeble-minded grade. It is now possible for children to receive special education on the recommendation of the Education Authority without being classified as ESN.

of those discharged were mildly subnormal. It may be assumed that these people were making reasonable adjustments within the community, because those who subsequently became social failures were likely to have been discovered by the social agencies like the National Assistance Board and the Labour Exchange, and minatory agencies like the Police, the Courts and the National Society for the Prevention of Cruelty to Children, and to have been re-notified to the Mental Health Department. These agencies do refer people to the department.

The rapid decline in the prevalence of mild subnormality after the initial peak at school-leaving age was first observed by Penrose (1949). He calculated age-specific prevalence rates from Lewis's (1929) data obtained in the classical survey of mental defect in three rural and three urban areas in England and Wales. This phenomenon has since been observed in the many surveys of subnormality in England and in other countries. The results of some of these surveys are summarized in Table 5. The methods used and criteria of grading are summarized in the Appendix. In the Wessex and Salford surveys the highest prevalence rates of mild subnormality were found in the age group 15–19 because the subjects were referred to the Mental Health Department only when they had left school; as the remaining surveys included children still at school, their highest prevalence rates were found in the age group 10–14.

There is other indirect evidence of the favourable prognosis of the mildly subnormal. Unlike the severely subnormal subjects, only a minority of the mildly subnormal subjects are ever admitted to hospital. Kushlick (1961) found that the decline in numbers living at home with increasing age was not accompanied by a rise in hospital numbers.

There are no adequate follow-up studies in this country of complete samples of mildly subnormal subjects. However, the favourable prognosis among the majority of these subjects is confirmed in a number of longitudinal studies reviewed by Tizard (1958). One outstanding study is summarized by Tizard in this review. Baller (1936) began a follow-up study of 206 people (nearly every child) who had been in the 'opportunity rooms' of the Lincoln, Nebraska, public schools up to the time of the research for at least one year, had an IQ of not above 70 and were considered mentally deficient by the teachers and psychologists. Charles (1953) located 150 (three-quarters) of these people. Of this number 24 had died – 17 through illness and 7 from accidents or violence. (The death rate was above the average for the population as a whole.) Ten per cent of those still alive had been successfully discharged from institutions or were on parole. Nine subjects were in institutions. Eighty per cent of the sample had married – 21 per cent of these were divorced. (The divorce rate was lower than the average for the whole population.) Eighty per cent of those married had children – the average number of children per family was 2·62. (This was lower than the population average.) School records were available for 73 of the children. Two were in mental deficiency institutions; another was crippled. The IQs available for 46 of the children ranged from 50 to 138 (mean 95; SD 16). The majority of the homes were adequate and they ranged from 'filthy shacks' to costly new houses with

TABLE 5. *Prevalence rates of subnormality per 1,000 in each age-group**

| | Grade | | | | | | All grades | | | | | |
| | Severely S/N | | | Mildly S/N | | | | | | | | |
Age	Salford 1961	England 1926–9†	Wessex 1963	Salford 1961	England 1926–9†	Wessex 1963	Salford 1961	England 1926–9 (from Penrose)	Wessex 1963	Baltimore 1936	Onondaga 1955	Rural Sweden 1955
0–4	0·91	0·69	0·53	0·15	0·51	0·18	1·17	1·2	0·73	0·7	4·5	12·5
5–9	1·62	3·09	2·41	0·36	11·41	0·57	1·98	15·5	3·03	11·8	39·4	18·4
10–14	2·54	4·35	2·57	0·29	21·25	0·48	2·84	25·6	3·07	43·6	77·6	37·2
15–19	3·64	2·84	3·42	8·65	7·96	2·97	2·27	10·8	6·41	30·2	—	14·2
20–29	3·45	2·07	2·82	4·16	6·33	2·90	7·65	8·4	5·73	7·2‡	—	19·7
30–39	3·78	1·49	2·13	1·83	4·21	1·78	5·60	5·7	3·93	8·1‡	—	22·7
40–49	2·47	1·22	1·82	2·59	4·18	1·71	5·04	5·4	3·56	8·3‡	—	17·7
50–59	1·71	0·90	1·23	1·08	4·00	1·34	2·84	4·9	2·59	6·4‡	—	17·6
60+	0·37	0·48	0·51	0·43	2·42	0·56	0·84	2·9	1·09	2·6‡ 1·9‡	—	8·4
Totals	2·27	1·87	1·78	2·60	6·73	1·39	4·37	8·6	3·19	12·2	—	17·4

* See Appendix for methods used in the surveys.
† Calculated from Lewis (1929), Tables 17(A) and (C), and Penrose (1963), p. 23.
‡ Age-groups are 20–24; 25–34; 35–44; 45–54; 55–64; 65+.

landscaped gardens. All but 7 of the non-institutionalized people had at least
part-time jobs; most were regularly employed and 83 per cent (as in 1935) were
self-supporting. Half of those gainfully employed had been in the same type of
occupation for from 3 to 30 years. Their occupations ranged from managerial to
unskilled labour. The IQs of 24 retested subjects had increased from a mean of
58 (Stanford–Binet, 1915) to 81 (Wechsler–Bellevue). Forty per cent of subjects
still in Lincoln and 60 per cent of the men had violated the law since 1935, one-
quarter were traffic and three-quarters were civil offences (one-half of these were
for drunkenness and none was serious). Throughout the period 1935–50 20 per
cent had been admitted to institutions; under a half had required public assistance; over a third had been self-sufficient. The proportion requiring public
assistance decreased from one-quarter in the period 1936–40 to under 10 per
cent in the following years up to 1950. Similarly, the proportion who were self-
supporting increased from 40 per cent in the period 1936–40 to 65 from 1946–50.
In 1935, Baller had found only one-quarter self-sufficient and one-half were
receiving assistance.

A favourable prognosis has also been shown among ESN school-leavers in
Scotland. Ferguson and Kerr (1955) found that 6 years after leaving school, 55
out of 207 such girls were already married (26·6 per cent compared with the 1951
Census figure of 39·6 per cent for all 22-year-old women in Glasgow). There was
a tendency for them to marry men of a higher social class than that of their own
fathers; thus, 30 per cent married skilled tradesmen whereas only about 10 per
cent were the daughters of skilled tradesmen. Nor was the rate of illegitimacy
among these women much greater than that in the rest of the population for this
age-group; thus 7·9 per cent of survey women still single were known to have
borne children compared with 6 per cent of Glasgow women aged 22. Their
work histories since leaving school were also good; thus, of 145 women still unmarried, 7 had worked for less than 2 years; 4 for 2 to 3 years; 8 for 3 to 4 years;
17 for 4 to 5 years; and 89 for 5 years or more. Physical disability was partly
responsible for their poor work performance in 10 out of 19 cases where women
had worked for some period less than 4 years. Of 11 girls with IQs of less than 50
only 2 had done any work since leaving school. Only 10 of the girls were in
institutions at the time of the survey.

Brandon (1960) has described a follow-up study of 200 mildly subnormal
women who were discharged from a small unit of the Fountain Hospital. They
constituted 70 per cent of all such patients ever admitted. They had been admitted when they were in their early twenties and discharged some 15 years
later. The follow-up assessment took place between 1 and 36 years after their
discharge. The mean IQ of this sample was 84·1 on the Wechsler-Bellevue and
65·0 on the Terman-Merrill scales. Most of the subjects came from grossly
disrupted families and 75 per cent had personality disorders diagnosed at admission. 12·5 per cent were admitted through the courts. Out of 171 contacted,
'20 have returned to the hospital for short periods. Roughly a third each are
living independently or are living with relatives, only 10 per cent are not working

or housewives, 46 are married.' Seven unmarried women have had children since their discharge.

Edgerton's (1967) description of the strategies employed by adults classified as mildly subnormal to maintain an independent existence outside of hospital in the face of many difficulties has added an important dimension to the understanding of the epidemiological picture of mild subnormality. (See also Chapter 9.)

INCONSTANCY OF THE IQ

It has also been shown that people categorized mildly subnormal or educationally subnormal continue to make IQ increments for some years after it is believed that IQ growth is complete. This observation is important because it questions the concept of the constancy of IQ as an assessment of innate 'intelligence' among the mildly subnormal. Second, it complicates further any attempt to measure the prevalence of mild subnormality on the criterion of IQ. Third, this phenomenon appears to be characteristic of mild subnormality in the absence of brain damage and may partially explain the good prognosis of these subjects after they leave school. Fourth, it suggests that the ability of the mildly subnormal to profit from education may indeed improve from the time they leave school and emphasizes the need to provide them with adult education on leaving school.

Clarke and Clarke (1953, 1954) retested with the same test some 2 years later 59 hospitalized patients whose initial IQs had ranged from 35 to 98 with a mean of 66·2 (SD 14·0). The range at retesting was 40–97 and the mean had risen 6·5 points to 72·7 (SD 13·4). The 59 subjects were divided independently of their score into two groups, those from 'very bad homes'[1] and the remainder. The former showed a mean increment of 9·7 (SD 6·3) and the latter a mean of 4·1 (SD 4·9). Clarke *et al.* (1958) retested 6 years later 28 of the subjects who were still in hospital – the other 31 patients had already been discharged. Nine of the 28 came from the very bad homes; their mean IQ had risen to 75·8 (SD 10·3), a mean increment over the 6 years of 16·2 (SD 6·1). Among the 19 from less adverse homes the mean IQ had risen to 72·5 (SD 13·3), a mean increment over the period of 10·2 (SD 6·6). The average age at the final test was nearly 27.

Stein and Susser (1960a, b) examined a stratified sample of 50 of a total random sample of 106 subjects aged 20–24 years who had been 'ascertained' as educationally subnormal while at school in Lancashire County and Salford City. (Four cases were subsequently excluded – one because he was found to have been mis-diagnosed originally, and had an IQ of 114, and three others because they had severe hearing defects.) Comprehensive social and psychiatric histories were obtained, medical examinations were done and the subjects were given Wechsler

---

[1] The twelve criteria used were: 'NSPCC intervention, parental attitude antagonistic, no fixed abode, "Fit Person Order", home conditions bad, considerable neglect, irregular school attendance due to neglect, home dirty and neglected, gross poverty, crime in parents, rickets, child found begging'.

Adult Intelligence Tests. The results of these tests were compared wth those of their previous Terman–Merrill tests given at ages ranging from 7 to 16 (mean 11) years. Both the uncorrected and corrected (Roberts–Mellone corrections) Terman–Merrill scores were compared with the Wechsler scores. Sixteen subjects with definite or assumed signs of brain damage showed a mean IQ decrement of 1·2 (based on the uncorrected TM score) and of 5·25 (based on the corrected TM score); on the other hand, 30 subjects who were clinically normal (all of lower working class origin) had a mean increment of 8·3 (uncorrected) and of 4·3 (corrected).

These authors found no differences in the IQ increments of the clinically normal subjects among those who came from grossly disrupted families, intact multiple agency families or intact families with another backward child. The increments observed were smaller than those found by Clarke and Clarke (1954) and Clarke *et al.* (1958). Stein and Susser point out, however, that their subjects were younger at the retest than those of the Clarkes. They also suggest that the small size of their subgroups may have accounted for the absence of differences between the increments of the subgroups.

Finally, it has been shown that lack of motivation may cause working-class normal and mildly subnormal children to under-score in intelligence tests. Thus, Zigler and de Labry (1962) compared the test performances of a group of clinically normal retarded subjects, of normal working-class boys and of normal middle-class boys all matched for mental age. In response to the promise of a tangible reward the retarded and working-class boys performed better than the middle-class boys on a concept switching task. In response to an intangible reward the middle-class boys were superior.

Summary

Mildly subnormal persons are mainly identified in countries with universal compulsory education as a result of educational difficulties. In this country, and in many others, special education is provided for children specially selected within the ordinary school system. The prognosis after leaving school for the majority of these children is good as is the prognosis for those who in this country have in the past been classified as mentally subnormal when they were referred by the Education Authorities to the Mental Health Department after they had left school. There is some evidence for a good prognosis among mildly subnormal women discharged from hospitals for the subnormal.

Mild subnormality appears to be a temporary incapacity characterized mainly by educational difficulties experienced at school. Only a small proportion of subjects categorized as mildly subnormal in this country are ever admitted to hospitals for the subnormal.

There are no consistent prevalence rates of mild subnormality. This appears to reflect the somewhat arbitrary criteria employed in the diagnosis. Before the 1944 Education Act, children presently classified as ESN were certified as mentally defective. Since 1944 only those children notified to the Mental Health Departments for supervision on leaving school are classified as mentally subnormal.

While the data show that most of the severely subnormal subjects who do not die at an early age are eventually admitted to hospitals for the subnormal, this should not be taken to mean that this is the only or the best way to cater for their or their families' needs. It is merely demonstrated that they appear, at the present time, to have a type of incapacity requiring a form of special provision for the whole of their lives in contrast to the mildly subnormal whose incapacities and needs are largely temporary. Second, the respective prognoses illustrated for the two grades are valid only for large numbers of cases whereas the prognosis in an individual case requires the skilled consideration of many factors other than the IQ. Third, while it is clear that the people in the IQ over 50 category merge imperceptibly with the community at large, the medium grade IQ range 20–49 contains within it a wide variation of capacity which overlaps at the upper end with that of the category of IQ over 50.

Incapacities and abilities associated with mental handicap

The mentally handicapped population includes people with a wide range of both clinical conditions and physical and behavioural incapacities. The range of abilities and incapacities has been measured on a large scale in Wessex (Kushlick and Cox, 1968) and in the 1970 census of mentally handicapped hospital patients (DHSS, 1972a).

Table 6 shows the range of social and physical incapacities which occur within various clinical diagnostic categories. The data relate to severely subnormal people aged 15–19 who were identified in the 1963 Wessex survey.

Table 6 shows that by age 15–19, 71 per cent of severely subnormal people are continent, ambulant and with no severe behaviour disorders. In addition it is evident that the distribution of incapacities varies very little between clinical groups. Notable exceptions are the high proportion of those categorized as having cerebral palsy who are also non-ambulant, those who are epileptic and who have severe behaviour disorders and those with Down's syndrome who are not incapacitated or only mildly so.

Table 7 shows the distribution of social and physical incapacity found in all administratively identified mentally handicapped from a total population of 100,000.

It is clear that the majority of the severely incapacitated people are found among the severely subnormal, but it is striking that both grades contain a substantial number of people who are continent, ambulant and with no severe behaviour disorders. The majority of non-ambulant, severely behaviour disordered and severely incontinent people are in residential care. However, for every one of the very severely handicapped children in residential care there is very nearly one equally handicapped child at home, under the care of his or her

TABLE 6. *Distribution of social and physical incapacity within clinical diagnostic categories*

Clinical diagnosis*	SPI* { No or insufficient information	Non-ambulant	Incontinent and with behaviour disorder	Behaviour disorder only	Incontinent only	Mildly incapacitated	Not incapacitated	Total number = 100%
				Percentages across				
No or insufficient information	–	7	–	7	–	–	87	15
Down's syndrome	2	2	1	5	1	8	80	167
Conditions usually associated with sub-normality	–	28	9	–	9	19	34	32
Conditions not usually associated with subnormality	–	–	–	–	–	–	–	†
Cerebral palsy	–	38	3	3	10	15	31	61
Major congenital abnormalities	–	8	5	11	8	11	57	37
Epilepsy	1	3	11	22	15	15	34	74
Other brain damage	–	–	–	–	–	–	–	†
No brain damage	3	2	4	10	5	9	67	220
All diagnoses	2	8	4	9	6	10	61	608

* Each subject appears in only one category on each scale. On the social and physical incapacity scale each person enters the left most category for which he qualifies. On the clinical diagnosis scale each individual is entered in the highest applicable category.

† Two rows in the table contained only one individual and-so no breakdown is given.

mother. Whereas nearly 80 per cent[1] of SSN children live at home with their families, the majority of SSN adults are in hospitals for the mentally handicapped. However, the proportion of very severely handicapped SSN adults is much lower than among the children. The range of incapacities found among young SSN adults is very wide. However, by age 15–19 three-quarters of these people are continent, ambulant and have no severe behaviour disorders. This proportion increases with age because of the differentially high mortality rate among the most severely handicapped.

TABLE 7. *Social and physical incapacity for children and adults by grade and whether or not in residential care (Wessex survey, 1 July 1963)*
Rates per 100,000 total population (rounded to nearest whole number)

Age	Grade	Place of care	Social and physical incapacity			
			Non-ambulant	Ambulant but with severe behaviour disorder	Ambulant, no severe behaviour disorder, but severely incontinent	Continent, ambulant, no severe behaviour disorder
Under 16	SSN	Home care	3	4	2	20
		Residential care	5	5	3	5
	MSN	Home care	1	1	1	7
		Residential care	0	0	0	1
16 and over	SSN	Home care	2	2	1	45
		Residential care	6	14	6	53
	MSN	Home care	1	0	0	69
		Residential care	2	4	1	45

Of the SSN adults in residential care a large proportion are continent, ambulant and free of severe behaviour disorders. This is because some of the children with the most severe incapacities die, while others make progress. In addition, more of the very able SSN adults who have lived all their lives at home have later to be admitted to residential care when their parents become older, more infirm and ill or die.

Other aspects of incapacity and ability studied in Wessex include speech, self-help skills, literacy, and vision and hearing defects. Of the 81[2] SSN adults in residential care from a population of 100,000, no fewer than 39 are continent, ambulant, with no severe behaviour disorders and are *also* able to feed, wash

[1] This survey was not designed to detect SSN children aged less than 5 years or those aged 5–15 who were attending schools run by the Education Authorities. These made up 50 per 100,000 total population.
[2] These totals include a few people per 100,000 whose social and physical incapacity was not known and are therefore not included in Table 7.

and dress themselves without help. For MSN adults in residential care, the corresponding figure is 42 out of 55.[1] These findings have been confirmed in the national census of mentally handicapped hospital patients (DHSS, 1972a).

Thus the present hospital population contains a large number of relatively able people without any serious social or physical incapacity. This fact is recognized in the Government White Paper 'Better Services for the Mentally Handicapped' (DHSS, 1971b), which stipulates that hospital care will be required only for those with physical handicaps or behaviour problems that require special medical, nursing or other skills. Local Authorities in England and Wales have a statutory duty to provide residential care for all others and also for those who can leave hospital after a period of treatment there.

SOCIAL FACTORS AFFECTING THE DEGREE OF INCAPACITY OF THE SEVERELY SUBNORMAL

We have seen that most severely subnormal subjects will be to some extent socially and economically dependent for the whole of their lives and that most of them will, at some time, require admission for residential care. The degree of their incapacities may be determined by the extent and nature of the organic brain pathology, but social factors have been shown to be important in determining how far the limits set by the organic factors will be realized. The legal and clinical definitions of severe subnormality have implied a poor prognosis and have suggested that these children are 'ineducable' and we have seen that in this country and in other Western European countries they have been excluded from school. In the absence of well designed experiments which could assess the effect of highly qualified teaching on the prognosis of children suspected of being severely subnormal, our knowledge of their potential comes from epidemiological studies of existing cases of recognized subnormality as it has been dealt with in the past and from small experimental studies. They suggest that these children are actually being retarded by some of our present methods of care, either by being deprived of education by trained teachers or by institutionalization in hospitals which fail to provide the quality of care which has long been known to be necessary for the growth and development of normal children. However, the low standard of services may be maintained because designers of social policy feel that the inherent poor prognosis does not warrant the provision of better services.

The reason for the inadequacy of follow-up studies of children diagnosed as severely subnormal lies partially in the difficulty of making such a diagnosis at an early stage in the child's development. Doctors may also be reluctant to suggest such a diagnosis because of their fears as to the prognosis and because of the lack of adequate facilities to deal with the problem once a diagnosis has been made. Illingworth, who claims that a diagnosis of mental subnormality can be made in infants (1961), followed up 122 infants in whom he had made the diagnosis of mental inferiority in the first year of life (58 in the first 6 months and

[1] See footnote 2 on previous page.

64 in the second 6 months). Cases of mongolism, hydrocephalus and cretinism were excluded. Of the 122 cases, 30 died within 5 or 6 years of birth. All 10 cases who had post mortems showed gross abnormalities of the brain. Of the 92 survivors, 4 could not be traced and one was severely deaf. Of the remaining 87, 6 had an IQ of 100 or more on follow-up examinations; 3 had a score of 90–99; 9 had a score 80–89; 8 had a score of 70–79; 10 had a score of 50–69; and 51 had an IQ score of less than 50. It was known that 3 who died were idiots. Thus, apart from obvious conditions like mongolism, hydrocephalus and cretinism, Illingworth was able to identify 65 out of 87 (75 per cent) survivors scoring IQs of under 70. However, only 51 out of 87 (59 per cent) were severely subnormal (IQ below 50); 41 per cent proved not to be severely subnormal and 21 per cent were not intellectually subnormal by any standard.

There is a wide range of incapacities among those classified as severely subnormal (see, for example, Table 7). Kushlick (1961) found that 0·72/1000 (20 per cent) of 3·62/1000 severely subnormal subjects surviving to the age group 15–19 were idiots (IQ under 20). Tizard and Grad (1961) measured the Vineland Social Ages of a random sample of 250 idiots and imbeciles at home and in hospital. Of those aged 16, over 23 per cent had social ages of 0–2 years, 18 per cent of 3–5 years, 43 per cent of 6–9 years and 14 per cent had social ages of 10 years or more. Similar proportions were found among children aged 11–15 but among the younger children the proportion with low social ages was increased both as a result of their lower chronological ages and because they included a higher proportion of idiots. The authors point out that the scores obtained by subjects in hospital may underestimate their abilities because they had no opportunity to do the things assessed in the Vineland test. This lack of opportunity may also have actually retarded the subjects. Severe motor impairment, due largely to spasticity, was present in 15 per cent of children and about 10 per cent of adults. Behaviour problems rated as 'uncontrollable' and 'too low grade to rate' were present in a quarter of the children. However, among adults the main problem was 'underactivity'. This was present in nearly 30 per cent. The wide range of IQs obtainable by mongols who constitute almost a third of the severely subnormal subjects was shown by Dunsdon *et al.* (1960). They estimated that 6–7 per cent scored IQs of 45 while 1–2 per cent scored 55 and over. Rare mongols due to chromosomal mosaics may have normal IQs (Dent *et al.*, 1963).

Adult imbeciles previously believed unemployable have been taught fairly complex industrial skills (O'Connor and Tizard, 1956; Clarke and Clarke, 1958). Tizard (1962) has reviewed the subject of treatment of subnormality in its broadest sense. (See also Chapter 13.)

The retarding effect of traditional institutional placement on severely subnormal subjects has been demonstrated. Lyle (1959, 1960a, b) and Shotwell and Shipe (1964) have shown that admission of imbecile children to large hospitals for the mentally subnormal depresses their verbal IQ scores compared with those who live at home. Tizard (1960, 1964) has shown that this may be due to the social structure of the institution rather than to the institutional placement itself.

He removed a sample of imbecile children from a large institution where they had had daily formal education to a residential unit where the children lived in small family groups, learned informally through play and close contact with adults and had their own supply of clothes and toys. These children not only lost many anti-social features of behaviour and signs of psychoneurosis, but they also gained significantly in verbal IQ over a matched control sample who stayed in the institution where they received formal education. The increment in performance IQs of the control group was slightly greater than among the experimental group, but the difference was not statistically significant. Tizard (1964) has described the possible harmful effects on such children produced by the 'conveyor-belt' systems of feeding, dressing and toileting them in large institutions.

The importance of social contact to the development of the child and the retarding effect of isolation has also been shown. Clarke and Clarke (1960) have reviewed a number of cases of illegitimate children locked up in extreme isolation by their mothers until they were rescued at ages varying from 6–10 years. With the exception of one child, who continued to function at idiot level, their performance appears to have improved dramatically as did their ability to speak, and in one case, to read and write.

Even within their families severely subnormal children are likely to be at a disadvantage. The parental problems may lead to anxiety and conflict in their dealings with the child. Parents may also find it very difficult to tolerate behaviour appropriate to the child's mental age, and to adjust their own expectations accordingly. Thus, they may be intolerant of and discourage in a 7-year-old child with a mental age of 2, behaviour which is acceptable in a child of chronological age of 2, but embarrassing in one of 7. In this way, the child may be deprived of indulging in experimental behaviour which is important to its socialization (Hulme, 1964). On the other hand, infantile behaviour may also be encouraged either because parents underestimate the capacities of the child or because infantile behaviour is more easily manageable than that of a robust active child. Woodward (1963) has shown that adverse factors at home were associated with behaviour disorders of severely subnormal children admitted to hospital.

A major advance in the last ten years has been the development of highly specific educational techniques directed towards increasing skills and decreasing inappropriate behaviours of the severely mentally handicapped. Applications of the work of Skinner (1953) to the analysis of behaviour has encouraged the development of a technology of teaching of particular relevance to the educational needs of the mentally handicapped (Bijou, 1966, 1971). The literature on this subject is growing rapidly. The reader is referred to a useful comprehensive account of this work with respect to both children and adults in Gardner (1971) as well as in Chapter 23 of this book. The effect of this work is likely to alter radically the present static conceptualization of mental handicap and to provide a guide to future provision of services for the handicapped and their families. It is also likely to decrease the proportions of the non-ambulant, severely behaviour disordered and severely incontinent, and to increase the proportions of the more able among the people now categorized as mentally handicapped. Changes in the proportions of different degrees of handicap should be measurable by advances in monitoring techniques of the prevalence of mental handicap. Advances are also needed in methods of relating any such changes to the introduction of a range of components of service if their effectiveness is to be adequately assessed (Kushlick 1972a, b).

The causes of mental defect

We have seen that mental defect is not a distinct clinical entity. It is largely a social and administrative concept which enables complex industrial societies to deal with a form of abnormal or deviant behaviour. The extent to which biological factors on the one hand and social or cultural factors on the other are responsible for this deviant behaviour is different for the severely subnormal and the mildly subnormal. Table 8 compares, for subjects known to the 1963

TABLE 8. *Comparison of aetiological factors between SSN and MSN subjects aged 15–19 (Wessex region and Wiltshire, 1963)*

Aetiological factor	Grade	
	Severely S/N (%)	Mildly S/N (%)
INFECTIVE. Rubella, meningitis, encephalitis, etc.	3·6	5·8
TOXIC. Jaundice, rhesus incompatibility etc.	4·9	3·0
INJURY. Definite or suspected birth injury	13·8	10·4
METABOLIC. Muscular dystrophy, lipoidosis, hypothyroidism	0·7	0·8
NEW GROWTH. Cancer	0·2	0·0
PERINATAL MALFORMATIONS. Mongolism, hydrocephaly, etc.	34·7	8·1
NEUROLOGICAL. Epilepsy, motor disturbance	11·5	10·0
NON-NEUROLOGICAL. Cultural, familial, psychotic, severe personality disorder, other non-neurological factors, factor unknown	25·9	49·2
No information	4·9	12·9
TOTAL	100·0	100·0
	(N=608)	(N=539)

Note: The classification is such that each individual appears only once and is allocated to the highest category in the table for which he is eligible. For example, a subject diagnosed as epileptic and with birth injury would appear only in the INJURY category. Thus, nearly half of the mildly subnormal subjects are included in the non-neurological classification, including those with no definite or suspected aetiological factor, whilst the corresponding proportion of severely subnormal subjects is about one-quarter.

Wessex survey and aged 15–19, the distribution of definite or possible aetio-logical factors for severely subnormal and mildly subnormal subjects. The classi-fication follows that of the AAMD (Heber, 1961).

In a detailed clinical investigation among approximately 100 administratively defined mentally handicapped children aged 8–10 in Aberdeen, Birch *et al.* (1970) found that all children except one with IQ under 50 had clear evidence of central nervous system impairment, compared with one-third of children with IQ 50 or more.

Crome (1960) examined the brains of 272 hospitalized imbeciles and idiots. Definite abnormalities were found in 267. Our knowledge of the causes of brain pathology among these subjects is still very limited and a definite cause is identifiable in only a minority of cases. Berg and Kirman (1959) examined the records of 200 imbeciles and idiots, consecutive admissions to the Fountain Hospital. A 'definite' causal factor was found in only 9·5 per cent of cases, e.g. iso-immunization and prematurity kernicterus, tuberculous and influenzal meningitis, post-immunization encephalopathy and recessive genetic condi-tions such as phenylketonuria, galactosaemia and cerebral lipoidoses. 'Probable' factors were suggested in 4 per cent and 'possible' factors in 56 per cent. Twenty-three per cent of the subjects were mongols; these were included among the subjects with 'possible' factors. In 31 per cent no causal factor was identifiable.

Investigations among hospitalized subjects must be interpreted cautiously because of the possible bias of these samples. Furthermore, studies of the mildly subnormal, even in defined populations, face the problem of definition and, as we have seen, in mild subnormality unlike severe subnormality the criterion of IQ is not very helpful.

Lewis (1929) observed in his survey for the Wood Committee that most of the mildly subnormal people were clinically 'normal'. Penrose (1938) found that of 1,280 hospitalized mental defectives 627 (49 per cent) were mildly subnormal. Of these he found no organic pathology in 198 (32 per cent) but a further 148 (24 per cent) were classified as 'psychopaths'. Penrose uses the term to mean psychoneurosis and psychosis. Stein and Susser (1960c) found among 106 subjects born between 1933 and 1937, and selected at random from all subjects classified as ESN in Salford and Lancashire county, only 25 per cent had pre-sumptive or obvious signs of brain damage or severe sensory handicaps.

SOCIAL CLASS AND MENTAL SUBNORMALITY

The concept of social class can be a useful means for examining the complex interrelations between social and biological factors causing subnormality. It has long been known that in industrial societies parents of severely subnormal children are evenly distributed among all the social strata in the society, whilst those of mildly subnormal subjects are predominantly from the lower social classes. This has been shown in surveys of mental subnormality occurring within whole communities (Lewis, 1929; Lemkau, *et al.*, 1943; Birch *et al.*, 1970) as well as in surveys of hospital patients (Penrose, 1938; Sabagh *et al.*, 1959; Saenger, 1960).

There is now evidence which suggests that mild subnormality in the absence of abnormal neurological signs, epilepsy, electroencephalographic abnormalities, biochemical abnormalities, chromosomal abnormalities or sensory defects occurs mainly among the lower social classes. Indeed, there is evidence that almost no children of higher social class parents have IQ scores of less than 80 unless they have one of the pathological processes mentioned above.

Stein and Susser (1960c) classified the families of their 106 subjects into 'demotic' (of the people) – the parents were manual workers and neither parents nor siblings had attended grammar or technical schools – and 'aspirant' – the fathers were white collar workers or of higher social standing or, if manual workers, a member of the family had been to a grammar school or technical school. They examined all of the children from 'aspirant' families and 50 from 'demotic' families. All 7 of the children from 'aspirant' families showed clinical abnormalities – 1 had neurological signs, 1 had a severe hearing defect, 1 had an abnormal electroencephalograph and 4 were classified as imbeciles on the criterion of a Wechsler Adult Intelligence Quotient of under 55 and the clinical finding of an 'incomplete personality'. Of the 50 from 'demotic' families 30 were clinically normal.

Stein and Susser (1963), believing that they might have missed clinically normal subjects of 'aspirant' families because of a possible bias in the selection of ESN subjects, examined the medical and psychological records of all children referred as 'backward' to the Salford school health service from 1955–9. The social standing of the schools which had referred the children was rated independently as of High, Low and Intermediate Standing using 'such factors as occupation of parents, residential rating and educational levels in the areas surrounding the schools'. The rates of referral for backwardness were found to decrease from the schools of Low Standing (25/1000 children at risk) to those of High Standing (8·7/1000). Thus the schools of High Standing were indeed referring backward children although in smaller proportions. However, 85 per cent of children referred from schools of High Standing scored IQs of 90 or more, whereas 79 per cent of the referrals from schools of Low Standing scored less than 90 and 45 per cent scored less than 79.

In the IQ range 50–79 schools of Low Standing referred 10·7/1000 children at risk compared with 1·3/1000 from schools of High Standing. In this IQ range the referral rates of children without any clinical abnormalities fell from 9·4/1000 from schools of Low Standing to 1·3/1000 from schools of High Standing. They also looked for high social class backward children elsewhere in Salford. The private schools in the city failed to reveal any children more than one class behind the average child of the same age. The investigators also examined the results in Salford of the 11-plus group intelligence tests used in the selection of children for secondary education. Among 694 examinees from schools of High Standing only 0·9 per cent scored 50–79 compared with 10 per cent from schools of Low Standing. The clinically normal children in this IQ range represented only 0·4 per cent of the examinees from schools of High Standing.

The results of the Scottish Mental Survey of 1947 also confirm these findings. In this survey there were no children who scored less than the equivalent of an IQ of 86 whose fathers were in the professional class. Of children whose fathers were unskilled the proportion rose dramatically to 26 per cent (Scottish Council for Research in Education, 1953).

In the 1962 Aberdeen study, Birch and his colleagues found the overall administrative prevalence of subnormality among children in unskilled manual working-class homes to be nine times higher than in the non-manual segments of the population. This was accounted for mainly by the excessive number of cases of IQ 60 or more among the working-class children. For severe subnormality, there was no class gradient associated with evidence of central nervous system insult.

Summary

Severe subnormality (IQ under 50), a condition which occurs among all social strata of the community, is due largely to organic factors and abnormalities in the brain. The resulting social and intellectual capacity is severe and leads at present to the subject's permanent dependence.

Organic factors are found to cause a proportion of cases of mild subnormality (IQ over 50). The proportion varies according to the definition of mild subnormality used. Thus, if the IQ range 50–70 is taken as the criterion of mild subnormality, the proportion of subjects where organic factors are involved is likely to be very small. These cases, like those of severe subnormality, occur in all social strata of the community. Mildly subnormal subjects without neurological signs, epilepsy, electroencephalographic, biochemical or chromosomal abnormalities, or without sensory defects like blindness and deafness are almost entirely confined to the lower social classes.

GENETIC FACTORS IN MENTAL SUBNORMALITY

For a lucid account of the genetics of mental defect the reader is referred to Penrose's book *The Biology of Mental Defect* (1963). In this section we will discuss briefly the evidence for the genetic causes of mental defect.

There are some rare clinical entities which usually cause severe subnormality and in which the mechanism of inheritance is known to be a recessive gene. These include amaurotic idiocy and such metabolic disorders as phenylketonuria and galactosaemia. However, the genetic contribution to mild subnormality in the absence of clinical abnormalities is more difficult to estimate because of the complexity of the environmental variables known to be associated with mild subnormality.

The theory that this grade of subnormality is due to the additive effect of multiple genes is based on a number of types of evidence. First, Pearson and Jaederholm (1914) and Roberts *et al.* (1938) have shown that the intelligence scores above 50 of complete populations of children assume a Gaussian or Normal distribution. The Gaussian distribution is a random distribution assumed when the quality in question is the resultant of multiple factors, some of which may be genetic. As the IQs of 50–70 contribute to this distribution, it is reasoned that they are part of the normal distirbution. By the same reasoning the subjects of IQ under 50 are said to be pathological in origin because there are more than would be expected from a Gaussian distribution. This evidence has been questioned by O'Connor and Tizard (1956) who point out that many IQ tests have been specially constructed to assume such a distribution.

The second type of evidence is that while the mean IQ of the siblings, parents and other relatives of the severely subnormal have normal intelligence, the IQs of the relatives of mildly subnormal patients are below average (Penrose, 1938; Halperin, 1945). This might also be due to environmental factors associated with low social class. We have seen that the proportion of low social class children with low intelligence quotients is very much higher than in those from the higher social classes. As most of the mildly subnormal have low social class parents the low IQs of the subjects may be due to an environmental factor common to the lower social classes.

Third, Penrose (1963) has summarized the evidence that the degree of correspondence between the IQ levels of the relatives and those of mildly subnormal patients increases with their degree of relationship to the patient in the proportions predicted by the multiple gene theory. He points out, however, that these predictions assume that mating in the population is random. There is evidence, however, that people tend to marry within their own social class and to some extent within their IQ level. This assortative mating would be expected to produce even higher correspondences than those observed if the additive gene theory were correct.

The other evidence relates to the inheritance of measured intelligence rather than to subnormality. The IQs of fostered children have been shown to be more closely related to that of their biological parents than that of their adoptive parents. There is also evidence to the contrary. The latter observations may be the result of the administrative policy of placing children of high IQ with parents of high IQ and vice versa. The problems of assessing this evidence are discussed by Penrose (1963) and Clarke and Clarke (1958).

It has been shown that the concordance between the IQs of monozygotic twins is higher than that observed among dizygotic twins, and that the concordance of IQs of monozygotic twins separated from one another is greater than that among dizygotic twins reared together. This is also critically appraised by Clarke and Clarke (1958) and by Penrose (1963), who show that even these studies do not exclude environmental factors. A further difficulty in interpreting these results arises because the proportion of subnormal subjects among twins is higher than that among singletons (Berg and Kirman, 1960) and because the birth weight of twins is lower than that of singletons. The relationship of low birth weight to intelligence is discussed later in this chapter.

CULTURAL FACTORS AND MENTAL SUBNORMALITY

The evidence just summarized suggests the presence of a genetic factor which determines the social and intellectual capacities of individuals. However, the importance of non-genetic environmental factors has also emerged and it has become possible to investigate their contributions. One of these is the cultural factor. In this context the term culture means the social and material way of life. Characteristic ways of life of subsections of a community are called subcultures. Thus, if one uses the categories of social class within the community it is possible to speak of a working-class, middle-class or upper-class subculture.[1]

There is indirect evidence that mild subnormality of IQ 50–70 in the absence of clinical abnormalities is to a large extent the result of the working-class subculture. This theory suggests that given children of the same limited genetic potential from unskilled and semi-skilled working-class homes on the one hand, and from skilled working-class, white collar and professional families on the other, the children from the unskilled and semi-skilled working-class subculture will develop to an IQ level below that of their genetic equals from the higher social class subcultures. First, the virtual absence of clinically normal children of IQ 50–70 from higher social class homes is not easily explained on the basis of genetic factors alone (Susser and Watson, 1962). It has been shown that inter-marriage does indeed take place between the upper and lower social classes (Glass and Hall, 1954). Thus, if inheritance was largely responsible for this condition, it would be expected to occur among the higher social classes although to a lesser degree because of assortative mating.

Second, the effect of the subculture on intelligence appears also to account for the ethnic differences observed of mean intelligence as well as of prevalence of mental subnormality. Klineberg (1940) showed that among US army recruits the average Negro IQ in the whole country was lower than that of the whites, but that Negro units from the northern states scored higher than white recruits from the southern states.

The higher prevalence rates of subnormality among non-whites than among whites found by Lemkau *et al.* (1943) and the Onondaga survey (1955) were reduced when the factor of income or area of residence was considered. The lower the income and the poorer the area of residence, the higher the prevalence of subnormality among both whites and non-whites. Lemkau *et al.* also showed that it was much more difficult for Negroes than for whites to gain admission to special schools. (These surveys do not give separate rates for severe and mild subnormality. However, it is likely that the preponderance is mainly among the mildly subnormal.) Sabagh *et al.* (1959) have shown that the proportion of white and non-white first admissions of severely subnormal subjects

[1] Until recently the term subcultural has been used in the mental deficiency literature to imply inferiority. As there is no objective way of measuring the values implied by this use of the term and as it lacks precision the sociological usage outlined very briefly above will be used in this chapter. For a detailed review on this subject see Sarason (1959) and Susser and Watson (1962).

to the Pacific State Hospital was equal to their representation in the population among the highly educated but over-represented among non-whites who had been poorly educated. However, mildly subnormal subjects were under-represented among the high and medium-educated whites and non-whites but were over-represented among the poorly educated of both ethnic categories.

The importance of social class appears also to outweigh that of low birth weight as a cause of mild subnormality among clinically normal children. Only among children of birth weight under 3 lb is the mean IQ lowered (Douglas, 1960; McDonald, 1964). The proportion of these children who are mildly subnormal (IQ 50–69) appears to be increased among the boys from the expected 29/1000 (Scottish Council for Research in Education, 1953) to the observed 41/1000. Among the girls the rate observed is only 11/1000 (McDonald, 1964). However, among children born to fathers of social classes I and II, McDonald found no decline in the mean IQ even of children with birth weights of less than 3 lb. Both Douglas (1960) and McDonald (1964) demonstrated that within each social class, the mean IQ of children of birth weights under 4 lb and without gross physical abnormalities was not significantly lower than the mean IQ of mature children.

Drillien (1961) has found within all social classes that the mean IQ of children of 3·5 lb and less was lower than the mean IQ of mature children. However, she appears to have included the IQs of grossly abnormal children in her computation of the mean IQ, whereas McDonald and Douglas did not. Douglas, McDonald and Drillien all agree that at every level of birth weight under 4 lb (and Douglas shows that at any level of birth weight) the mean IQ of children without gross abnormality declines from high to low social class. The incidence of babies weighing less than 5·5 lb or 2,500 grams rises from higher to lower social classes (Baird, 1962; Registrar General, 1958).

For a full discussion on the relationships between prematurity and social class the reader is referred to the article by Baird and to Susser and Watson (1962). Some of these will be mentioned briefly here. Lower social class mothers who are tall tend to have higher IQs than those who are small, and are also more likely than the short women to marry husbands from a social class higher than that of their fathers. On the other hand, short mothers tend to be of lower IQ and to marry men of a lower social standing than their own (Illsley, 1955; Scott *et al.*, 1956). The incidence of the highest prematurity rate in Aberdeen was found among the low social class women who are also short (Baird, 1962). McKeown (1970) has reviewed the relationships of birth weight and period of gestation to social class and IQ score, and has provided useful data on large numbers of children born in Birmingham, England.

A mechanism exists by which the unskilled and semi-skilled working-class subculture could possibly result in the lowering of the Intelligence Quotient in the absence of brain pathology. Luria (1961) has suggested that language, besides enabling the child to reason in abstract terms, allows it to achieve a high degree of specificity in all of its actions. He has devised ingenious experiments which illustrate the importance of language to the total development of the child at different stages of its development. Bernstein (1960) has suggested that children of unskilled working-class parents have a distinct language structure which is lacking in certain components present in that of middle-class language structure. Moreover, he has suggested that this form of language might contribute to the social cohesion of its users and that it is therefore likely to persist. There are also other reasons why the lower working-class subculture and many of the social and material disadvantages associated with it are perpetuated in this country. More children of unskilled and semi-skilled than of skilled and professional fathers live in overcrowded homes without standard amenities, go to slum, overcrowded schools (Ministry of Education, 1963), and fail to gain a grammar school place for higher education in spite of their adequate scores at the eleven-plus selection examination (Douglas, 1963). They are also likely eventually to do semi- and unskilled work and to find a spouse from these social classes (Berent, 1954).

In their Aberdeen study Birch and his colleagues found evidence that mild subnormality in the working classes was associated with large families, poor housing and overcrowded conditions.

In any attempt to compare the social prognosis of mildly subnormal subjects with that of a control population it is important that the factor of social class is taken into account lest the subnormality is used to explain phenomena which are part of the subculture from which the mildly subnormal arise. Thus, in the United Kingdom lower social class girls marry earlier, their fertility is greater and they have larger families than their higher social class peers (Glass and Grebenik, 1954). More of the former are pregnant at the time of marriage or have children before they are married (Thompson, 1956). The boys from lower social status homes appear to have a higher chance of being convicted of a criminal offence and sent to borstals (Gibbens, 1963).

It is known that the mean IQ declines with increasing family size. The results of the Scottish Mental Survey showed that this phenomenon occurs within all social classes. This may also be explained by a cultural factor because the highest means were found among the youngest and the oldest children, that is those children who were likely to have had the greatest degree of contact with adults (Susser and Watson, 1962). Because lower social class families are, on average, larger than those of the higher social classes, this could also lead to a lowering of the mean IQ among working-class subjects.

SOCIAL CLASS AND MINIMAL BRAIN DAMAGE

Another environmental explanation for the association of mild subnormality and low mean IQ with low social class has been suggested by Lilienfeld and Pasamanick (1955). They presented evidence that the mildly subnormal, although showing no obvious signs of neurological impairment, may have 'minimal brain damage' due to perinatal complications. This subject is reviewed by

Masland (1958), Masland *et al.* (1958), MacMahon and Sawa (1961), Knobloch and Pasamanick (1962). In this country perinatal complications are known to occur far more commonly among wives of lower than among those of higher social class husbands, and there is no sign that these disadvantages are decreasing. The perinatal mortality survey of all births occurring in this country during a week of 1958 (Butler and Bonham, 1963) showed that unskilled and semi-skilled working-class wives were much less likely than were higher social class wives to have adequate ante-natal care or to be confined in hospital, even if this was indicated on clinical grounds. More of their children were of low birth weight and they lost more babies as stillbirths, neonatal and post-neonatal deaths. A study of 691, 640 single legitimate live and stillbirths that occurred in England and Wales in 1949 showed that the lower social classes experienced consistently higher mortality rates even after biological factors like maternal age and parity and social factors like area of residence had been taken into account (Scott *et al.*, 1956; Morris and Heady, 1955a, b; Daly *et al.*, 1955; Heady *et al.*, 1955 a, b). Morris (1959) has shown that the gap between the neonatal mortality rates of the high and low social classes appears to have widened since the last war. Thus, although the mortality rates among all classes have declined, the lower social classes appear to have benefited less than the higher classes from the gains that have been made.

These disadvantages appear to persist into childhood. Working-class children, because of the larger size of their families, are more likely than higher class children to acquire infections (Cruickshank, 1958). Douglas and Blomfield (1958) showed that among all single legitimate children born in a week of March 1946 in England, Wales and Scotland, the lower social class mother made less use of welfare clinics than her higher social class peer, and her child was more severely ill than the higher social class child before she consulted the general practitioner.

Summary

Although there is evidence that the social and intellectual capacity may to some extent be determined by additive effect of multiple genes, the cultural factors, i.e. the social and material way of life, appear to be crucial in determining the extent to which the child's genetic potential will be realized. The lower working-class subculture appears to be the main factor responsible for the occurrence of clinically normal individuals with IQs in the mildly subnormal range 50–70. The genetic theory cannot account adequately for the virtual absence of this condition outside the lower working class, although it is known that inter-marriage between the social classes does indeed take place.

The absence of certain components in the structure of lower working-class language might be a possible cultural mechanism by which children of IQ 50–70 could occur in the absence of brain damage. There are many factors tending to maintain the distinctive lower working-class way of life.

It is possible that some of the clinically normal subjects of IQ 50–70 may have 'minimal brain damage' as a result of perinatal complications which are known to affect lower working-class children more often than those from the higher social classes. These perinatal disadvantages among the lower social class mothers appear to be persisting in spite of advances in social and medical welfare. It must, however, be remembered that only a small proportion of children falling into the IQ range of mild subnormality (50–70) are ever identified as presenting educational problems of an order requiring special education, and decreasing proportions respectively are classified in this country as ESN and mildly subnormal. The social prognosis of the majority of even these categories is good. A still smaller proportion present social problems and are eventually admitted to institutions for the subnormal from which they may yet be discharged and take up their positions in society.

SOCIAL FACTORS INFLUENCING THE INCIDENCE OF SEVERE SUBNORMALITY

The incidence (that is the inception rate of new cases) of severe subnormality must be distinguished from its prevalence (that is the rate of existing cases). The prevalence is determined by the incidence as well as the duration of the condition and its mortality rates. It is likely that the incidence of severe subnormality is higher among the lower than among the upper social classes, although the difference is not as great as among the mildly subnormal. We have seen from prevalence studies of severe subnormality in whole populations that the condition is distributed throughout all social strata in the community, but all of these studies show that it is more prevalent among the lower social classes. However, the infant mortality rate is higher among the lower social classes. Thus the preponderance of severe subnormality observed in prevalence studies probably underestimate the excess that probably exists at birth. The reasons for this are likely to be the same as those given in the discussion of perinatal complications and social class. One of these is low birth weight.

LOW BIRTH WEIGHT AND THE INCIDENCE OF SEVERE SUBNORMALITY

We have seen that low birth weight itself does not appear to be associated with mild subnormality and that the association observed is due to the common factor of low social class. It appears, however, that low birth weight may cause severe subnormality although it is possible that the factor causing the low birth weight also causes the severe subnormality. McDonald (1964) showed that of single children of birth weight 4 lb or less, excluding those with cerebral palsy, blindness or deafness, the proportion of severely subnormal exceeded that expected in the normal population – 18/1000 instead of about 3·7/1000. At 3 lb or less the proportion rose to 36/1000. Among singleton children weighing 4 lb or less at birth with cerebral palsy, blindness or deafness, the proportion who were severely subnormal rose to 144/1000. Of all children (twins and singletons) under 4 lb (including blind, deaf and cerebral palsied) 26/1000 scored IQs of under 50. Because low birth weight is more common among lower social class births (Baird, 1962) this is one possible cause of the excess of severely subnormal subjects among children from low social class families. It is unlikely in this country to be a numerically important cause of severe subnormality because only 7/1000 of all live births weigh less than 3 lb 4 oz, and under half of these (43 per cent in 1971) survive for 28 days (DHSS, 1972a). It may, however, become more important because there is no sign that very low birth weight is decreasing but the survival rate of such children is increasing. In 1953 in England and Wales only 313/1000 live births of under 3 lb 4 oz survived 28 days (Ministry of Health, 1954). Baird (1962) has shown that in Aberdeen between 1948 and 1959 the survival rate in the first week of single births weighing under 3 lb 8 oz at birth increased from 346 to 553 per 1000 live births.

OTHER SOCIAL FACTORS AFFECTING THE INCIDENCE OF SEVERE
SUBNORMALITY

Both the age of the mother and the birth rank have been shown to influence the stillbirth rate, and the age of the mother at the birth has been shown to influence the incidence of a number of clinical entities associated with severe mental defect. Thus, Heady *et al.* (1955b) showed that primiparity was associated with higher rates of stillbirth at all maternal ages but that for all birth ranks the stillbirth rate increased with maternal age.

The most striking association of a rise in incidence with increasing maternal age is shown by the clinical condition of mongolism. The incidence is low, less than 1/1000 births, until the maternal age group 30–34. It then rises rapidly to reach proportions of 2 or 3 per cent in the age group 45–49. The crude incidence of mongolism at birth appears to have remained over a number of years at about 1·5/1000. The evidence is reviewed by Penrose (1963). The association of increasing maternal age with other chromosomal abnormalities and some forms of non-mongol severe subnormality is present but much less pronounced.

Important social consequences may arise from this association with the incidence of mongolism. First, half of all cases of mongolism are born to mothers aged over 36, an age by which most families will have been completed, and this is likely to mean that the most difficult stage of child rearing, the early years, will continue well into the parents' middle age. On the other hand, it means that mongol children will be more likely than other severely subnormal children to be born to experienced mothers who have raised other normal children. This may be a possible explanation for the suggestion that most mongol children have an easy and happy disposition. Rollin (1946) and Blacketer–Simmonds (1953) investigating hospitalized mongols and Tizard and Grad (1961) on home and hospitalized mongols have questioned this generalization, but none of these studies has examined the effect of maternal age and birth rank on behaviour. The results of the Wessex survey (see table 6) show that in a total community sample the highest proportion of very able SSN adults free of severe behaviour disorder occurs among the mongols. The incidence of mongolism is likely to fall with advances in, and widespread use of, contraception among women aiming to complete child bearing at an earlier age (Penrose and Smith, 1966).

Advances in therapy also affect the incidence and the prevalence of severe subnormality. The advent of penicillin as a cure for syphilis has contributed towards the decreasing in the incidence of severe subnormality due to this cause. However, the availability of streptomycin has resulted in an increase in the incidence of severe subnormality due to tuberculous meningitis, previously a fatal condition (Penrose, 1938; Berg and Kirman, 1959; McLaren Todd and Neville, 1964).

However, the increased survival rates of conditions, the incidence of which has remained constant, may also lead to an increase in the prevalence of subnormality. The increased survival rates at birth of children of very low birth weight has been discussed. The survival rate of mongolism has also increased. Carter (1958) showed that among 700 mongol children attending the Hospital for Sick Children between 1944 and 1955, 30 per cent of live born mongols lived less than 1 month, 53 per cent less than 1 year, and 60 per cent less than 10 years. These findings agree with those of Record and Smith (1955) who found that among 252 mongols born in Birmingham in the years 1942–52, nearly 40 per cent lived less than 1 month, over 50 per cent less than 1 year, and nearly 60 per cent less than 5 years. Carter showed that the mortality for children attending hospital from 1949 to 1955 was 40 per cent lower than those attending from 1944 to 1948. Assuming that the incidence of mongolism has remained constant at about 1·5/1000 live births, the increased survival rates are shown by the increase in prevalence of mongolism in this country. Lewis (1929) found the prevalence of mongolism in the age group 7–14 to be 0·34/1000. Comparable recent rates are given by Kushlick (1961) in Salford in the age group 15–19 (0·9/1000), Goodman and Tizard (1962) in Middlesex in the age group 7–14 (1·14/1000), Kushlick (1964) in the South of England in the age group 15–19 – counties (1·18/1000) and county boroughs (1·15/1000). Laurence (1964) has suggested that the survival rates of hydrocephalus may also be improved as a result of early treatment of the associated spinal defects like meningocoele.

IS THE PREVALENCE OF SEVERE SUBNORMALITY (IQ UNDER 50) INCREASING OR DECREASING?

It has been shown that the prevalence of this incapacity depends on trends in the incidence, the survival rates and the prognosis of children with this condition. Differences between current prevalence rates and those found by Lewis in 1929 must be cautiously interpreted because the expansion of services for the subnormal since then may have rendered the identification of such cases easier now than in 1926 to 1929, and the standardization of the IQ tests used then and now may differ. Such comparisons of current prevalence rates of severe subnormality at comparable ages in surveys in this country suggest that in spite of increased survival rates of mongolism the prevalence of severe subnormality has fallen since 1929. The apparent fall in prevalence may, however, be masking a real increase in the prevalence of severe subnormality as we now see it, i.e. characterized by permanent severe incapacity.

Thus, Goodman and Tizard (1962) showed that the prevalence of severe subnormality in the age group 7–14 had decreased from Lewis's figure of 3·71/1000 in the urban areas to 3·45/1000 in Middlesex in 1961; in the same period the prevalence of mongolism increased from 0·34 to 1·14/1000. They interpreted their findings cautiously as reflecting an apparent decrease in the prevalence of non-mongol severe subnormality. Similar apparent decreases have been found by Kushlick. The prevalence of severe subnormality in the age group 15–19 in Salford in 1961 was 3·62/1000 and in the Wessex county boroughs in 1963 it was 3·54/1000. Kushlick (1964) found the apparent decrease in the rural areas to be even higher. Lewis's 1926–9 rate in the rural area was 5·61/1000 in the age group 7–14 compared with the 1963 rate of 3·84/1000 in the Wessex counties in the age group 15–19, in spite of the increased prevalence in 1963 of mongolism.

On the other hand, there is also evidence of an increase in prevalence. The total prevalence rates of severe subnormality and the rates for those aged 15 and over were higher in Salford in 1961 than those found in Lewis's survey in 1926–9 (see table 9). Kushlick (1961) reconstructed the Salford register of severe subnormality for 1948 and showed that between 1948 and 1960 the total prevalence of idiots had increased by 83 per cent and that of imbeciles by 38 per cent.

A possible explanation of this paradox is that Lewis's severely subnormal subjects in the age group 7–14 might have included a large proportion of non-brain-damaged subjects with temporary incapacities similar to the subjects with mild subnormality, whereas most of the severely subnormal children in the recent surveys are brain damaged and permanently handicapped.

Table 9 shows that the prevalence of severe subnormality in Salford remains fairly constant between the ages of 15 and 40, suggesting that these subjects continue to require supervision in or out of hospital until they die. However, the 1926–9 rates drop immediately after school-leaving age like the rates for the subjects with mild subnormality. This suggests that some of Lewis's severely subnormal subjects in the age group 7–14 might have adjusted sufficiently well to the demands of society and that Lewis's rates in the subsequent quinquennium 15–19 are a truer reflection of the prevalence of severe subnormality characterized by permanent incapacity. It is, of course, possible, as Lewis himself suggests, that there were large numbers of severely subnormal people aged 15–19 unknown to the agencies used as sources by Lewis. Such agencies as the Labour Exchanges and the Public Assistance Committees might have been expected to know of the large numbers of unemployed imbeciles anticipated from the difference in rates between the age groups 7–14 and 15–19 – the unemployment rate was very high at the time of this survey.

Stein and Susser (1971) consider changes over time in both incidence and prevalence of mental retardation. For all forms of severe mental handicap, they conclude that incidence is decreasing although survival and life span have both increased. This has resulted in some increase in prevalence in recent years, principally caused by an increase in prevalence of Down's syndrome.

Information obtained from the Wessex register by Kushlick and Cox (1968) suggested that the overall prevalence of severe subnormality among adults was

TABLE 9. *Prevalence rates of severe subnormality per 1,000 in each age-group (Salford, 1961, and England and Wales, 1926–9)*

Age	Salford, 1961	England, 1926–9*
0–4	0·89	0·69
5–9	1·62	3·09
10–14	2·55	4·35
15–19	3·62	2·84
20–29	3·44	2·07
30–39	3·77	1·49
40–49	2·47	1·22
50–59	1·70	0·90
60 +	0·52	0·48
Total	2·24	1·87

* Calculated from Lewis, 1929, Tables 17(A) and (C), and Penrose, 1963, p. 23.

likely to increase, at least for the next few years. The effects of mortality on future prevalence of adult severe subnormality were calculated by examining mortality rates for a four-and-a-half-year period. These suggested that prevalence would increase particularly among the more able severely subnormal adults who are continent, ambulant and with no severe behaviour disorders. The prevalence of the more severely handicapped non-ambulant adults was expected to remain constant.

IS THE PREVALENCE OF MILD SUBNORMALITY (IQ OVER 50)
INCREASING OR DECREASING?

It is much more difficult to estimate the trends of mild subnormality because, unlike severe subnormality in which an IQ of under 50 appears to have considerable predictive value, the majority of people in the IQ range of mild mental subnormality (50–70) appear to adjust to the demands of society after leaving school and the criterion of the IQ in this range has little predictive value.

However, the social policy of most Western countries towards the mildly subnormal has been based on the prediction that only by their sterilization and/or segregation in colonies during the child-bearing period of their lives would an increase in the incidence and prevalence of mild subnormality be prevented. This prediction was based on the observations that these subjects came from families of above average size and the theory that the qualities which led to their social failure were both inherited and permanent. We have seen that the theoretical basis of these predictions has been questioned by later investigations. The prediction of a fall in national IQ level has also been shown to have been incorrect.

The results of the Scottish survey of the intelligence of 87,498 11-year-old children in 1932 and of 70,805 children in 1947 showed that the mean test score had, if anything, increased from 34·5 points (SD 15·5) to 36·7 (SD 16·1) due to the reduction in the proportion of low scorers (Scottish Council for Research in Education, 1949).

For other assessments of the trend of the problem of mild subnormality we must rely on numbers of people receiving the services for this category of person. This is an unsatisfactory method as there has always been a shortage of these provisions, and increasing provision is more likely to reflect improvements in the quality of the services than real increases in the extent of the conditions for which services are being provided. Thus in this country, provision for ESN children has increased. Whereas there were 11,000 in ESN schools in 1946, the number in 1962 was 40,000 and estimates suggest that 40 per cent of these children had IQs of over 70 (Ministry of Education, 1963).

In a study designed to measure the change in prevalence of mild subnormality known to a whole community, Kushlick (1961) found that between 1948 and 1961 there had been no change in the prevalence of mild subnormality known to the Mental Health Department in Salford. The changes envisaged in the Mental Health Act of 1959 will undoubtedly cause a decrease of the known mildly subnormal because it is no longer necessary for Local Education Authorities to refer cases for supervision after leaving school.

The proportion of mildly subnormal hospital patients is decreasing (52 per cent in 1954, 30 per cent in 1963, 28 per cent in 1970), and is also being accompanied by a decline in absolute numbers from 30,280 in 1954 to 17,395 in 1963 and 16,291 in 1970 (DHSS, 1970).

The fall in these numbers is probably due to a number of factors. The discharge rate of subnormal patients doubled in 1956 and has remained at a similar level since then. The proportion of patients in each age-group who are mildly subnormal is lower in 1970 than in 1954 and 1963 for all ages except the under-fives. This would suggest both an increase in discharge rates and a decrease in length of stay of those discharged – unless there is a high re-admission rate, the numbers of chronic mildly subnormal patients should continue to fall. The recent White Paper 'Better Services for the Mentally Handicapped' (DHSS, 1971b) places responsibility for the care of a large proportion of the present hospital population with Local Authorities and the implementation of this policy will lead to a substantial decline in the mildly subnormal hospital patients.

Many of the mildly subnormal were compulsorily hospitalized in the past because of the wide definitions of mental defect and the large number of conditions which rendered mental defectives 'subject to be dealt with' under the Mental Deficiency Act. When such problems arise today they are probably handled by social agencies not specifically concerned with mental defect.

The proportion of legally detained patients is now comparatively small. On 31 December 1970, 2,211 (11 per cent) of all mildly subnormal hospital patients were legally detained. Of these 664 were detained under the sixth schedule of the 1959 Mental Health Act which allowed patients who had been detained under previous legislation to remain so (DHSS, 1972a).

There has been very little systematic study of this problem. It is likely that if the recent liberalizing of custodial régimes in the hospitals for the mentally ill is adopted by the hospitals for the subnormal, the difficulty of meeting the requirements of a minority of the subjects may be passed on to the state security institutions. Systematic epidemiological studies into the reasons for, and the effects of, custodial care of subnormal subjects are urgently needed. The problems of providing 'security units' need close attention (Kings Fund Hospital Centre, 1972), as do the methods used for dealing with the different behaviours among their residents (Lehner *et al.*, 1971; Boren and Colman, 1970; Colman and Boren, 1969).

Another factor requiring systematic evaluation is the effect of unemployment levels on the numbers of mildly subnormal people who are unable to support themselves in the community.

SOCIAL FACTORS LEADING TO THE CLASSIFICATION OF PEOPLE AS MILDLY SUBNORMAL

We have seen that only a minority of subjects in the IQ range 50–70, and others of even higher IQ are classified and dealt with as mildly subnormal. This selection appears to depend largely on their having behaviour disorders which create disturbances outside the family. It also appears that these behaviour disorders are caused by the subjects' child-rearing experiences in profoundly broken homes and multiple placements in residential institutions or foster homes.

Burt (1937) observed that there was a much higher preponderance of boys to girls in the special classes and special schools than in the population from which the children were drawn. He also showed that there was an excess of such children from lower social classes and from broken homes.

Stein and Susser (1960a) found in their follow-up study of ESN school-leavers that those children who had lived in a family which provided them for the first 10 years of their lives with a set of enduring relationships had significantly better occupational histories than those who had spent their first 10 years of life in foster or children's homes. Even children from intact families known to one or more social agencies as problem families had favourable prognoses. Thus, 7 out of 10 male subjects reared for almost the whole of their first 10 years of life in children's homes or foster homes had legal charges against them compared to 17 out of 50 from normal intact families and 5 out of 8 from problem families. Six out of 22 subjects of both sexes who came from broken homes had been admitted to hospitals for the mentally subnormal. Only 1 of the remaining 84 was so admitted. Saenger (1960) found that only 23 per cent of mildly subnormal subjects in institutions had both parents compared with 56 per cent of subjects living in the community. The corresponding percentages among imbecile subjects (IQ 20–49) were respectively 56 per cent and 92 per cent. Saenger (1960) and Leeson (1962) have also shown that in contrast to imbecile subjects who were admitted to hospital on parental initiative because of problems within the home (either the subjects made heavy demands on an intact family, or the death or illness of a family member made it impossible to care for the subject at home), mildly subnormal subjects were admitted on the initiative of minatory agencies such as the police acting on their own initiative or with the support of parents because of disturbances caused by the subject outside the home. Leeson (1962) found that there were comparatively few mildly subnormal subjects on the Manchester Regional Hospital Boards' waiting list because most of these cases were admitted as emergencies directly from the courts.

These findings suggest that the social inadequacies of those subjects who fall into the hands of the social agencies and are classified as subnormal may arise from a lack of social skills normally acquired by children within their own families (Parsons and Bales, 1955). Their problems may also arise from the possession of social skills learned in and appropriate to large authoritarian institutions, but which prove dysfunctional when the subjects have to adjust to the complexities of social relationships outside institutions (Goffman, 1957; Coser, 1962).

The uses of epidemiology in developing and evaluating services for the mentally handicapped

The epidemiological approach lends itself to the development of a service which can both anticipate and deal with problems which are known to be present a long time before they come to the notice of the existing services, often worsened by delays (Morris, 1957). Many studies suggest strongly that much of the therapeutic and social pessimism which surrounds the subject of subnormality is the result on the one hand of ignorance and, on the other, of lack of adequate facilities. These problems are briefly considered here and in greater depth in Chapter 25.

Epidemiological methods have already contributed to the estimation of the overall size of the problem of mental handicap and of the nature of the problem in terms of the relative numbers of handicapped people with various levels of ability and incapacity. In addition, epidemiological studies provide data on the extent to which existing services are being provided and hence the shortfall between provision and need. The Government White Paper 'Better Services for the Mentally Handicapped' (DHSS, 1971b) incorporates the results of epidemiological studies carried out in the Wessex, Newcastle and Camberwell areas of England in order to estimate the numbers of places required in various forms of service provision and the extent to which these requirements are being met. On the basis of this type of information planners are assisted in the estimation of resource requirements and administrators in the setting of realistic goals for service developments.

In addition to providing national estimates, epidemiological data may be applied at the local level. From the overall prevalence rates the requirements of graphically comparable populations of any size can be roughly estimated. The rates can be used not only to plan new services but also to measure how far existing facilities in an area are meeting the community's needs.

There are also good reasons for actually developing such comprehensive services for local populations. First, in this country the medical, psychological, educational and recreational facilities used by the whole community, and needed also by the mentally handicapped, are being developed to serve catchment areas of between 50,000 and 250,000.

Obvious examples are the district general hospitals which supply the highly specialized diagnostic and therapeutic services, the educational and training facilities of the Local Authorities, the social work services and the child guidance clinics. Catchment areas of this size make these services readily accessible to the people who need them and to one another. Second, the residential units needed for the severely subnormal subjects of these catchment areas, if situated in these areas, would, in addition to being accessible to the people needing them and the other services, be very much smaller than those currently in use in this country and in most other highly industrialized countries.

We have seen that the main function of long-term residential care is to provide a substitute family for those people whose own intact families are unable to cope with the subject's excessive demands, or whose families because of illness or death are unable to manage even the 'reasonable' demands of the subjects. Smaller units may be better able to provide the care and socialization needed by them than the larger wards currently used in bigger institutions serving wider catchment areas. The advantages of small homes for normal children in need of such care has long been recognized in most advanced countries; the potential advantages of such units to the severely subnormal have also been demonstrated. Moreover, much is known of the disadvantages of the existing large institutions for the subnormal (Tizard, 1960, 1964).

Following the work of Goffman (1957) studies by King, Raynes and Tizard (1971) have clarified components of 'poor' or 'institution-oriented' care in residential facilities. These have questioned the other suspected factor of 'size' of institution as being a key variable determining the quality of care. The importance of lack of resources, particularly of residential-care staff, absence of defined organizational aims and therefore of staff tasks, and of inaccessibility of residential facilities to the families of the mentally handicapped as well as specialist facilities available outside the residential facilities, have also been highlighted as factors determining poor quality care (Kushlick, 1972a, b).

There are also a number of sociological studies of the problems inherent in the management of large bureaucratic organizations in general (Blau, 1963; Goffman, 1957) and psychiatric hospitals in particular (Caudill, 1958; Belknap, 1956; Jones, 1953; Stanton and Schwartz, 1954; Parsons, 1957). These show that many aspects of the complexity of the relationships in these organizations are often deflected by unrecognized but inherent problems of management. In addition, isolation of these 'total institutions' may lead them to develop a system of values different from that accepted as normal or humane in the society outside (Goffman, 1957).

Thus the estimates of the number of residential places needed by the severely subnormal arising from an area of 100,000 people provide not only the basis for developing small units as part of a comprehensive service but also for evaluating them and discovering the disadvantages associated with them (Tizard, 1965; Kushlick, 1965).

We have seen that the prevalence of severe subnormality in both rural and urban England is at present about 3·7/1000 in the age group 15–19. The prevalence at earlier ages must be at least as high because of the excess mortality rate among these children. In a community of 100,000 people with an annual birth-rate of 16/1000 (the average in England and Wales from 1948–62), 1,600 children would be born every year and there would be about 25,000 children aged under 16. We would expect to find in this community nearly 100 (25·6 × 3·7) severely subnormal children; 30 aged 0–4 and 66 aged 5–15. From these figures we can estimate roughly how many places would be required to serve the severely subnormal in a community of 100,000 people.

Crèche facilities are needed for the 3- and 4-year-olds: about 12 places. About 2 of these children were, in 1963, in institutions for the subnormal, a further 1 was awaiting admission and only 1 had training in day centres, leaving three-quarters without special services. (Such facilities are also needed for the slow developing children of lower social class origin, particularly those from broken homes. Kirk, 1958, has shown that these children benefit from a pre-school education programme.)

At present hospitals for the mentally handicapped typically serve populations of 500,000 or more, and patients from a particular geographical area will be distributed throughout one or more such hospitals. By developing services along the lines of the recent White Paper (DHSS, 1971b) hospitals will be 'aligned' (i.e. take only clients from a catchment area of about 250,000 population) and wards and community units will be 'sectorized' (i.e. take only clients from a sub-area of, say, 50,000 population). When this is achieved and Local Authority facilities are organized on a similar basis, a wide range of facilities and personnel will be available to the mentally handicapped from a given area.

Kushlick (1972c) has examined the possible improvement in the availability of services to the mentally handicapped, both at home and in residential care, which this arrangement might facilitate.

The available figures also reveal the existing lack of facilities. Table 10 shows the estimated need of the mentally handicapped from a population of 100,000 together with the estimated average level of provision in England and Wales in 1969 (adapted from DHSS, 1971b, p. 42).

TABLE 10. *Estimated need and average present provision of services per population of 100,000*

Type of service	Places for children (age 0–15)		Places for adults (age 16 +)	
	Required	Provided 1969	Required	Provided 1969
Day care or education for children under 5 years	8	1	–	–
Education for children of school age:				
In the community	62	48	–	–
In hospitals	13	10	–	–
Occupation and training for adults:				
In the community	–	–	150	50
In hospitals	–	–	45	62
Residential care in the community	12	4	75	10
Hospital treatment	19	16	65	108

It is evident that expansion of educational facilities is required both for children under 5 and for those of school age. An increase in occupation and training places for adults in the community is also needed. A need for an increase in Local Authority residential care facilities from 4 to 12 places for children and from 10 to 75 for adults reflects the recognition that many of the more able people at present in hospital could be provided for in Local Authority homes, foster homes or some form of lodging or sheltered flatlet. The provision of these places by Local Authorities would relieve the presently overcrowded hospitals for the mentally handicapped and allow them to develop the specialized skills needed for the care of the profoundly handicapped.

In addition to the resource requirements there are still major administrative problems involved in integrating the available professional skills into a single service able to provide continuous care to the subject and his family. However, the availability in sufficient numbers of the basic facilities required may go a long way to meeting some of these difficulties. Moreover, adequate evaluation of these services should provide answers to some of the existing questions. The most recent prevalence rates of subnormality in this country are, therefore, offered as the basis for developing and assessing the adequacy of some existing services in this country and, perhaps, in similar highly industrialized countries.

Having pointed to areas of need and provided data on which plans may be based, the epidemiologist is also able to contribute towards an evaluative assessment of the services being provided. By monitoring the extent to which individuals come into contact with various facilities, it is possible to examine the degree to which policy decisions are implemented and to point to areas of lack of progress where unforeseen difficulties may have occurred. An ongoing epidemiological study is also able to assess, in relatively crude terms, the effects of changing provision on clients and their families in terms of changes in incapacity and ability level and of changing patterns of contact with the services. This area offers an exciting challenge to the epidemiologist in the development of measures which are sufficiently sensitive and can be produced sufficiently quickly to be of use to administrators and planners. In some cases an epidemiological evaluation may point to areas where more detailed investigations on a smaller scale may be necessary or sociological studies of organizational difficulties may prove useful.

There are systematic studies which have investigated the extent to which, and the reasons why, our sophisticated diagnostic genetic counselling and social work services are failing to meet the needs (Holt, 1958; Tizard and Grad, 1961; Deisher *et al.* 1962; and Hudson, 1963) or failing to accept responsibility for long-term guidance (Rutter, 1964). Indeed, one of the most exciting fields for advance in modern medical care awaits the incorporation of the existing body of knowledge into the existing services for the chronically ill in general, and the mentally subnormal in particular.

Sociological studies of the changing structure and function of the 'normal' family in industrial societies (Parsons and Bales, 1955; Young and Wilmott, 1957) have revealed important mechanisms for the stress created by a chronically handicapped (deviant) member of the family (Susser and Watson, 1962). Moreover, other studies (Hollingshead and Redlich, 1958; Bernstein, 1964) have focused attention on unrecognized difficulties of communication which arise between the professionals and their clients because of their different social class origins. These findings have led to systematic studies of the problems of families of the subnormal (Holt, 1958; Leeson, 1960; Tizard and Grad, 1961; Susser and Watson, 1962; Jacobs, 1969) and these are now well understood. Katz (1961) has described the evolution and function of the voluntary organizations run by the parents of the mentally handicapped. It is now possible to deal with and relieve many of the family difficulties by the use of specialist services, whereas not long ago they were regarded as insoluble or remediable only by institutionalizing the subject.

COMPULSION AND SERVICES FOR THE SUBNORMAL

The services for the mentally disordered have evolved from a stage where legal and bureaucratic authority was used to care for and control patients and their families, to the present time when it is possible to use skilled professional authority and personal relationships to achieve these ends (Susser and Kushlick,

1961). The aspects of legal compulsion which remain, such as exclusion from school, removal of children from their families and detention of patients in hospital, need to be continuously evaluated with the object of maximizing the place of skilled professional authority which is accepted voluntarily by patients and their families because of their confidence in the service. The possibility that persons may be unnecessarily detained and deprived of their rights as a result of being classified subnormal or severely subnormal has led the Working Party of the BPS (1963) to recommend that among adults the upper level of subnormality should be fixed at a WAIS IQ of 70 points, and that of severe subnormality in which detention after the age of 25 years is easily effected, at 55 points. It is doubtful whether the implementation of this recommendation would do much to solve the problem. We have seen that the behaviour difficulties of the mildly subnormal (IQ 50–70) who are eventually admitted to hospitals for the subnormal arise largely from their lack of socialization within a family during the first 10 years of their lives, rather than from their low IQ level. Their needs, like those of children with higher IQs from similar backgrounds, would appear to require a combination of continuous, specialized social work, psychological, psychiatric, educational and recreational services within a substitute family until they have passed the critical stage of adolescence. In the absence of such a service the individuals of IQ over 70 now dealt with as subnormals would, because of the minor acts of delinquency committed by the men and the promiscuity of the women, merely be diverted to social agencies like the prisons and the welfare departments. At present, none of these agencies is staffed or equipped to meet these subjects' needs. Only the provision of alternative services relevant to the needs both of patients and their families is likely to prevent the inappropriate admission of such people to hospitals for the subnormal.

Thus, from our knowledge of the epidemiology of mild subnormality we can also see the limitations of the proposal in the early part of this century to lower the incidence of mild subnormality by a programme of compulsory sterilization. If every person in the IQ range 50–70 (about 2 per cent of the whole population) were sterilized, the resulting decrease in the incidence of mild subnormality might be of the order of less than 10 per cent. Thus, Penrose (1938) found that over 90 per cent of the mildly subnormal in his hospital survey had parents of normal or dull-average intelligence. The importance of family disruption as a cause of hospitalization of mildly subnormal subjects might even have led to an over-representation in his sample of subjects with mildly subnormal parents. No government other than that of the Nazis has ever suggested a hideous programme of this sort. However, some countries still practice compulsory sterilization of 'certified', 'ascertained' or hospitalized mildly subnormal people. Such a programme is unlikely to make any real impact on the incidence of the condition because of the very small proportion of people in this IQ range who are ever 'ascertained' or hospitalized. We have also seen that there has not been any decline in the national intelligence although social policy towards the mildly subnormal had been planned on the prediction of such a decline. Penrose (1963) has suggested that although environmentally induced increases in height and intelligence may be masking a genetic decrease, the risk of 'national degeneration' is both speculative because the evidence is to the contrary and academic because we cannot predict now the human qualities which will be needed by future generations. There is little doubt, however, that voluntary sterilization to limit family size may often relieve family problems and this should, of course, be made available to people who choose it.

Finally, it has been shown by Belknap and Steinle (1963) that the quality of medical care in comparably staffed and equipped hospitals is very much higher in those hospitals where the influential political and economic figures in the locality participate in the hospital administration, and where the attitudes of these people favour the provision of a high standard of service to the community as a whole. This finding is probably of great importance to the services for the subnormal. In the present atmosphere of community tolerance of the subnormal it is likely that radical improvements to the service might be possible if there were to be a move in this direction by skilled and well-informed professionals in the field.

Appendix (see Table 4)

Prevalence surveys of mental handicap: references, dates of surveys, populations sampled, methods of identification and criteria of grading used.

Author	Area investigated	Date	Population sampled
1. Lewis (1929)	England and Wales	1926–9	Six rural and six urban areas of 100,000 people each.
2. Lemkau *et al.* (1943)	Baltimore	1936	Urban area of population 55,000.
3. Onondaga county survey (1955)	Onondaga county	1953	Urban area. 116,000 population aged 0–18 yrs.
4. Åkesson (1961)	Rural Sweden	1959	Ten rural parishes of total population 11,500.
5. Kushlick (1961)	Salford	1961	Urban area of 153,000 total population.
6. Goodman and Tizard (1962)	Middlesex	1960	Urban area. 451,800 population aged 0–14 yrs.
7. Birch *et al.* (1970)	Aberdeen	1962	Urban area. 8,274 population aged 8–10 yrs.
8. Kushlick (1964)	Wessex county boroughs	1963	Urban areas. 46,000 population aged 15–19 yrs.
	Counties	1963	Urban and rural areas. 90,000 population aged 15–19 yrs.

Author	Area investigated	Date	Population sampled
9. Drillien *et al.* (1966)	Edinburgh	1962–4	Urban area. 39,500 population aged 7·5–14·5 yrs.
10. Scally and MacKay (1964)	Northern Ireland	1962	Urban and rural areas, total population 1,435,400.
11. Wing (1971)	Camberwell	1967	Urban area. 38,460 population aged 10–14 yrs.

How the subjects were identified:

Children	1, 2, 3, 4 and 7	All children both at school and known to social agencies.
	5, 11	Children known as mentally handicapped to Mental Health Department only.
	6	As in 5 plus hospitals, approved schools and private homes.
	8	As in 5 plus hospitals, private homes and hostels.
	9	As in 1 plus hospitals, private homes and hostels.
	10	All children known to the Special Care Services.
Adults	1	All adults known to all social agencies – score IQ under 65.
	2	All adults known to all social agencies diagnosed as mentally defective.
	4	All adults in population scoring IQ under 70.
	5	All adults known as mentally subnormal to Mental Health Department only.
	10	All adults known to the Special Care Services.

Criteria for grades:

Only in 1 and 5 are grades recorded by age for all age-groups.

1	Children – IQ under 45–50; IQ 45–50 to 70.
	Adults – IQ under 40–45; IQ 40–45 to 60–85.
5, 6 and 7	IQ under 50; IQ over 50.
10	IQ 0–19, IQ 20–49, IQ 50–69.

References

ÅKESSON, H. (1961) *Epidemiology and Genetics of Mental Deficiency in a Southern Swedish Population.* Univ. of Uppsala, Sweden.

BAIRD, SIR D. (1962) Environmental and obstetrical factors in prematurity, with special reference to experience in Aberdeen. *Bull. Wld Hlth Org,* **26,** 291–5.

BALLER, W. R. (1936) A study of the present social status of a group of adults who, when they were in elementary schools, were classified as mentally deficient. *Genet. Psychol.*, **18**, 165–244.

BELKNAP, I. (1956) *Human Problems of a State Mental Hospital.* New York: McGraw-Hill.

BELKNAP, I. and STEINLE, J. G. (1963) *The Community and its Hospitals: A Comparative Analysis.* Syracuse, NY: Syracuse Univ. Press.

BERENT, J. (1954) Social mobility and marriage: a study of trends in England and Wales. In GLASS, D. V. (ed.) *Social Mobility in Britain.* New York: Humanities Press.

BERG, J. M. and KIRMAN, B. H. (1959) Some aetiological problems in mental deficiency. *Brit. med. J.*, **2**, 848–52.

BERG, J. M. and KIRMAN, B. H. (1960) The mentally defective twin. *Brit. med. J.*, **1**, 1911–27.

BERNSTEIN, B. (1960) Language and social class. *Brit. J. Sociol.*, **11**, 271.

BERNSTEIN, B. (1964) Social class; speech systems and psycho-therapy. *Brit. J. Sociol.*, **15**, 54.

BIJOU, S. W. (1966) Application of experimental analysis of behavior principles in teaching academic tool subjects to retarded children. In HARING, N. N. and WHELAN, R. J. (eds.) *The Learning Environment: Relationship to Behavior Modification and Implications for Special Education.* Univ. of Kansas Publ., School of Education, No. 16.

BIJOU, S. W. (1971) *The technology of teaching young handicapped children.* Paper given to the First Symposium on Behavior Modification, Talapa, Mexico, January, 1971.

BIRCH, H. G., RICHARDSON, S. A., BAIRD, D., HOROBIN, G. and ILLSLEY, R. (1970) *Mental Subnormality in the Community. A Clinical and Epidemiologic Study.* Baltimore, Md.: Williams & Wilkins.

BLACKETER-SIMMONDS, L. D. A. (1953) An investigation into the supposed differences existing between mongols and other mentally defective subjects with regard to certain psychological traits. *J. ment. Sci.*, **99**, 702–19.

BLAU, P. M. (1963) *Bureaucracy in Modern Society.* New York: Random House.

BOREN, J. J. and COLMAN, A. D. (1970) Some experiments of reinforcement principles within a psychiatric ward for delinquent soldiers. *J. appl. Behav. Anal.*, **3**, 29–37.

BRANDON, M. W. G. (1960) A survey of 200 women discharged from a mental deficiency hospital. *J. ment. Sci.*, **106**, 355–70.

British Psychological Society (1963) Report of the working party on subnormality. *Bull. Brit. Psychol. Soc.*, **16**, 37–50.

BURT, C. (1937) *The Backward Child.* London: Univ. of London Press.

BUTLER, N. R. and BONHAM, D. G. (1963) *Perinatal Mortality.* London and Edinburgh: Livingstone.

CARTER, C. O. (1958) A life-table for mongols with the causes of death. *J. ment. Defic. Res.*, **2,** 64–74.

CAUDILL, W. A. (1958) *The Psychiatric Hospital as a Small Society.* Cambridge, Mass.: Harvard Univ. Press.

CHARLES, D. C. (1953) Ability and accomplishment of persons earlier judged mentally deficient. *Genet. Psychol. Monogr.*, **47,** 3–71.

CLARKE, A. D. B. and CLARKE, A. M. (1953) How constant is the I.Q.? *Lancet*, **ii,** 877–80.

CLARKE, A. D. B. and CLARKE, A. M. (1954) Cognitive changes in the feebleminded. *Brit. J. Psychol.*, **45,** 173–9.

CLARKE, A. D. B. and CLARKE, A. M. (1960) Some recent advances in the study of early deprivation. *Child Psychol. Psychiat.*, **1,** 26–36.

CLARKE, A. D. B., CLARKE, A. M. and REIMAN, S. (1958) Cognitive and social changes in the feebleminded – three further studies. *Brit. J. Psychol.*, **49,** 144–57.

CLARKE, A. M. and CLARKE, A. D. B. (1958) *Mental Deficiency: The Changing Outlook* (1st edn). London: Methuen.

COLMAN, A. D. and BOREN, J. J. (1969) An information system for measuring patient behaviour and its use by staff. *J. appl. Behav. Anal.*, **2,** 207–14.

COSER, R. L. (1962) *Life in the Ward.* East Lansing: Michigan State Univ. Press.

CROME, L. (1960) The brain and mental retardation. *Brit. med. J.*, **1,** 897–901.

CRUICKSHANK, R. (1958) A survey of respiratory illness in a sample of families in London. In PEMBERTON, J. and WILLARD, H. (eds.) *Recent Studies in Epidemiology.* London: Oxford Univ. Press.

DALY, C., HEADY, J. A. and MORRIS, J. N. (1955) Social and biological factors in infant mortality, Ill. The effect of mother's age and parity on social class differences in infant mortality. *Lancet*, **i,** 445–8.

DEISHER, R. W., BALKANY, A. F., PREWITT, C. D. and REDFIELD, W. J. (1962) Phenylketonuric families in Washington State. *Amer. J. Dis. Childh.*, **103,** 818–21.

DENT, T., EDWARDS, J. H. and DELHANTY, J. D. A. (1963) A partial mongol. *Lancet*, **ii,** 484–9.

Department of Health and Social Security (1970) *Mental Health Statistics for 1970: Number of Patients Awaiting Entry to Hospital, Admitted for Temporary Residential Care, or Admitted to Guardianship during 1970.* Statistics and Research Division, DHSS.

Department of Health and Social Security (1971a) *Digest of Health Statistics for England and Wales 1971.* London: HMSO.

Department of Health and Social Security (1971b) *Better Services for the Mentally Handicapped.* Cmnd 4683. London: HMSO.

Department of Health and Social Security (1972a) *Census of Mentally Handicapped Hospital Patients.* Statistical and Research Report Series, No. 3. London: HMSO.

Department of Health and Social Security (1972b) *On the State of the Public Health, The Annual Report of the Chief Medical Officer of the DHSS for the year 1971.* London: HMSO.

DOUGLAS, J. W. B. (1963) *The Home and the School.* London: Macgibbon & Kee.

DOUGLAS, J. W. B. (1960) 'Premature' children at primary schools. *Brit. med. J.*, **1**, 1008.

DOUGLAS, J. W. B. and BLOMFIELD, J. M. (1958) *Children under Five.* London: Allen & Unwin.

DRILLIEN, C. M. (1961) A longitudinal study of the growth of prematurely and maturely born children. Part VII. *Arch. dis. Childh.*, **36**, 233–40.

DRILLIEN, C. M., JAMESON, S. and WILKINSON, E. M. (1966) Studies in mental handicap. Part 1: Prevalence and distribution by clinical type and severity of defect. *Arch. dis. Childh.*, **41**, 528–38.

DUNSDON, M. I., CARTER, C. O. and HUNTLEY, R. M. C. (1960) Upper end of range of intelligence in mongolism. *Lancet*, **i**, 565–8.

EDGERTON, R. (1967) *The Cloak of Competence.* Berkeley: Univ. of California Press.

FERGUSON, T. and KERR, A. W. (1955) After-histories of girls educated in special schools for mentally-handicapped children. *Glasgow med. J.*, **36**, 50–6.

GARDNER, W. I. (1971) *Behaviour Modification in Mental Retardation.* London: Univ. of London Press.

GIBBENS, T. C. N. (1963) *Psychiatric Studies of Borstal Lads.* London: Oxford Univ. Press.

GLASS, D. V. and GREBENIK, E. (1954) The trend and pattern of fertility in Great Britain. A report on the family census of 1946. *Papers of the Royal Commission on Population*, Vol. VI, Parts I and II.

GLASS, D. V. and HALL, J. R. (1954) Social mobility in Britain: a study of inter-generation changes in status. In GLASS, D. V. (ed.) *Social Mobility in Britain.* New York: Humanities Press.

GOFFMAN, E. (1957) *The Characteristics of the Total Institution*, Walter Reed Symposium on Social Psychiatry. Washington, DC.

GOODMAN, N. and TIZARD, J. (1962) Prevalence of imbecility and idiocy among children. *Brit. med. J.*, **1**, 216–19.

HALPERIN, S. L. (1945) A clinico-genetical study of mental defect. *Amer. J. ment. Defic.*, **50**, 8.

HEADY, J. A., DALY, C. and MORRIS, J. N. (1955a) Social and biological factors in infant mortality, II: Variation of mortality with mother's age and parity. *Lancet*, **i**, 395–7.

HEADY, J. A., STEVENS, C. F., DALY, C. and MORRIS, J. N. (1955b) Social and biological factors in infant mortality, IV: The independent effects of social class, region, the mother's age and her parity. *Lancet*, **i**, 499–502.

HEBER, R. (1961) A manual on terminology and classification in mental retardation (2nd edn). *Amer. J. ment. Defic. Suppl.*, No. 64.

HOLLINGSHEAD, A. B. and REDLICH, F. C. (1958) *Social Class and Mental Illness*. New York: Wiley.

HOLT, K. S. (1958) The influence of a retarded child upon family limitation. *J. ment. Defic. Res.*, **2**, 28.

HUDSON, F. P. (1963) Phenylketonuria in the North of England. *The Medical Officer*, **110**, 69–71.

HULME, I. (1964) *A Comparative Study of the Play, Language and Reasoning of Severely Subnormal Children and Children of Similar Mental Age*. Unpubl. M. Ed. thesis, Manchester Univ.

ILLINGWORTH, R. S. (1961) The predictive value of developmental tests in the first year, with special reference to the diagnosis of mental subnormality. *J. Child. Psychol. Psychiat.*, **2**, 210–15.

ILLSLEY, R. (1955) Social class selection and class differences in relation to stillbirths and infant deaths. *Brit. med. J.*, **2**, 1520–4.

JACOBS, J. (1969) *The Search for Help: A Study of the Retarded in the Community*. New York: Brunner/Mazel Inc.

JONES, M. (1953) *The Therapeutic Community*. New York: Basic Books.

KATZ, A. H. (1961) *Parents of the Handicapped*. Springfield, Ill.: Charles C. Thomas.

KING, R. D., RAYNES, N. V. and TIZARD, J. (1971) *Patterns of Residential Care*. London: Routledge & Kegan Paul.

Kings Fund Hospital Centre (1972) Strategies for the mentally handicapped security patient. *Mental Handicap Papers*, No. 2. London.

KIRK, S. A. (1958) *Early Education of the Mentally Retarded*. Urbana: Univ. of Illinois Press.

KLINEBERG, O. (1940) *Negro Intelligence and Selective Migration*. New York: Columbia Univ. Press.

KNOBLOCH, H. and PASAMANICK, B. (1962) Medical progress: mental subnormality. *New Engl. J. Med.*, **266**, 1045–51, 1092–7, 1155–61.

KUSHLICK, A. (1961) Subnormality in Salford. In SUSSER, M. W. and KUSHLICK, A., *A Report on the Mental Health Services of the City of Salford for the Year 1960*. Salford Health Dept.

KUSHLICK, A. (1964) *The Prevalence of Recognised Mental Subnormality of I.Q. under 50 among Children in the South of England, with Reference to the Demand for Places for Residential Care*. Paper to the International Copenhagen Conference on the Scientific Study of Mental Retardation, Copenhagen.

KUSHLICK, A. (1965) Community care for the subnormal – a plan for evaluation. *Proc. Roy. Soc. Med.*, **58,** 374–80.

KUSHLICK, A. (1972a) *Evaluating Residential Services for the Mentally Handicapped.* Paper presented at the Second WPA Symposium on Psychiatric Epidemiology, Mannheim, July 1972.

KUSHLICK, A. (1972b) The need for residential care. In *Action for the Retarded.* London: National Society for Mentally Handicapped Children.

KUSHLICK, A. (1972c) *Some Implications of the White Paper Cmnd 4683, Better Services for the Mentally Handicapped.* Winchester: Wessex Regional Hospital Board.

KUSHLICK, A. and COX, G. (1967) Ascertained prevalence of mental subnormality in the Wessex Region. *Proc. Internat. Congr. Scient. Stud. Ment. Defic., Montpellier, 1967.*

KUSHLICK, A. and COX, G. (1968) Planning services for the subnormal in Wessex. In WING, J. K. and BRANSBY, B. R. (eds.) *Psychiatric Case Registers.* DHSS Statistical Report Series, No. 8. London: HMSO.

LAURENCE, K. M. (1964) The natural history of spina bifida. *Arch. dis. Childh.*, **39,** 41–57.

LEESON, J. (1960) A study of six mentally handicapped children and their families. *The Medical Officer*, **104,** 311.

LEESON, J. (1962) *Demand for Care in Hospitals for the Mentally Subnormal.* Manchester: Manchester Regional Hospital Board.

LEHNER, P., SCHIFF, L. and KRIS, A. (1971) Operant conditioning in a comprehensive treatment programme for adolescents. *Arch. gen. Psychiat.*, **25,** 515–21.

LEMKAU, P., TIETZE, C. and COOPER, M. (1942) Mental-hygiene problems in an urban district. Third paper. *Ment. Hyg.*, **26,** 275–88.

LEMKAU, P., TIETZE, C. and COOPER, M. (1943) Mental-hygiene problems in an urban district. Fourth paper. *Ment. Hyg.*, **27,** 279–95.

LEWIS, E. O. (1929) *The Report of the Mental Deficiency Committee being a Joint Committee of the Board of Education and Board of Control: Part IV – Report on an Investigation into the Incidence of Mental Deficiency in Six Areas, 1925–1927.* London: HMSO.

LILIENFELD, A. M. and PASAMANICK, B. (1955) Association of maternal and fetal factors with development of mental deficiency. Relationship to maternal age, birth order, previous reproductive loss and degree of mental deficiency. *Amer. J. ment. Defic.*, **60,** 557–69.

LURIA, A. R. (1961) The role of speech in the regulation of normal and abnormal behaviour. *Zeitschrift für ärztliche Fortbildung*, **51,** 503.

LYLE, J. G. (1959) The effect of an institution environment upon the verbal development of imbecile children: (1) Verbal intelligence. *J. ment. Defic. Res.*, **3,** 122–8.

LYLE, J. G. (1960a) The effect of an institution environment upon the verbal development of imbecile children: (2) Speech and language. *J. ment. Defic. Res.*, **4**, 1–13.

LYLE, J. G. (1960b) The effect of an institution environment upon the verbal development of imbecile children: (3) The Brooklands Residential Family Unit. *J. ment. Defic. Res.*, **4**, 14–23.

MCDONALD, A. D. (1964) Intelligence in children of very low birth weight. *Brit. J. prev. soc. Med.*, **18**, 59–73.

MCKEOWN, T. (1970) Prenatal and early postnatal influences on measured intelligence. *Brit. med. J.*, **3**, 63–7.

MCLAREN TODD, R. and NEVILLE, J. G. (1964) The sequelae of tuberculous meningitis. *Arch. dis. Childh.*, **39**, 213–25.

MACMAHON, B. and SAWA, J. M. (1961) Physical damage to the fetus. *Milbank Memorial Fund Quart.*, **39**, 14–73.

MASLAND, R. L. (1958) The prevention of mental retardation: a survey of research. *J. dis. Childh.*, **95**, 3–111.

MASLAND, R. L., SARASON, S. B. and GLADWIN, T. (1958) *Mental Subnormality: Biological, Psychological and Cultural Factors.* New York: Basic Books.

Ministry of Education (1962) *Report of the Chief Medical Officer of the Ministry of Education: The Health of the School Child, 1960 and 1961.* London: HMSO.

Ministry of Education (1963) *Half our Future. A Report of the Central Advisory Council for Education (England).* London: HMSO.

Ministry of Health (1954) *On the State of Public Health. The Annual Report of the Chief Medical Officer of the Ministry of Health for the Year 1953.* London: HMSO.

MORRIS, J. N. (1957) *Uses of Epidemiology.* Edinburgh and London: Livingstone.

MORRIS, J. N. (1959) Health and social class. *Lancet*, **i**, 303–5.

MORRIS, J. N. and HEADY, J. A. (1955a) Social and biological factors in infant mortality: I. Objects and methods. *Lancet*, **i**, 343–9.

MORRIS, J. N. and HEADY, J. A. (1955b) Social and biological factors in infant mortality: V. Mortality in relation to the father's occupation, 1911–1950. *Lancet*, **i**, 544–9.

O'CONNOR, N. and TIZARD, J. (1956) *The Social Problem of Mental Deficiency.* Oxford: Pergamon.

Onondaga County Survey (1955) A special census of suspected referred mental retardation. *Community ment. Hlth Res.* New York State Dept of Mental Hygiene Report.

PARSONS, T. (1957) The mental hospital as a type of organization. In GREENBLATT, M., LEVINSON, D. J. and WILLIAMS, R. H. (eds.) *The Patient and the Mental Hospital.* Glencoe, Ill.: The Free Press.

PARSONS, T. and BALES, R. F. (1955) *Family, Socialization and Interaction Process*. Glencoe, Ill.: The Free Press.

PASAMANICK, B. and LILIENFELD, A. M. (1955) Association of maternal and fetal factors with development of mental deficiency. I. Abnormalities in prenatal and paranatal periods. *J. Amer. med. Assoc.*, **159,** 155–60.

PEARSON, K. (1931) On the inheritance of mental disease. *Ann. Eugen., Lond.*, **4,** 362.

PEARSON, K. and JAEDERHOLM, G. A. (1914) *On the Continuity of Mental Defect*. London: Dulau.

PENROSE, L. S. (1938) A clinical and genetic study of 1280 cases of mental defect (Colchester Survey). *5p. Rep. Ser. Med. Res. Coun.*, No. 229. London: HMSO.

PENROSE, L. S. (1949) *The Biology of Mental Defect*. London: Sidgwick & Jackson.

PENROSE, L. S. (1963) *The Biology of Mental Defect* (3rd edn). London: Sidgwick & Jackson.

PENROSE, L. S. and SMITH, G. F. (1966) *Down's Anomaly*. London: Churchill.

RECORD, R. G. and SMITH, A. (1955) Incidence, mortality and sex distribution of mongoloid defectives. *Brit. J. prev. soc. Med.*, **9,** 10–15.

Registrar General (1958) *Decennial Supplement. England and Wales, 1951. Occupation Mortality, Part II; Civil.* London: HMSO.

ROBERTS, J. A. F., NORMAN, R. M. and GRIFFITHS, R. (1938) Studies on a child population: IV. The form of the lower end of the frequency distribution of Stanford Binet intelligence quotients and the fall of low intelligence quotients with advancing age. *Ann. Eugen. Lond.*, **8,** 319–36.

ROLLIN, H. R. (1946) Personality in mongolism with special reference to the incidence of catatonic psychosis. *Amer. J. ment. Defic.*, **51,** 219.

RUTTER, M. (1964) Intelligence and childhood psychiatric disorder. *Brit. J. soc. clin. Psychol.*, **3,** 120–9.

SABAGH, G., DINGMAN, H. F., TARJAN, G. and WRIGHT, S. W. (1959) Social class and ethnic status of patients admitted to a state hospital for the retarded. *Pacific Sociol. Rev.*, **2,** 76–80.

SAENGER, G. S. (1960) *Factors Influencing the Institutionalization of Mentally Retarded Individuals in New York City*. Report to the New York Inter-departmental Health Resources Board.

SARASON, S. B. (1959) *Psychological Problems in Mental Deficiency*. New York: Harper Bros.

SCALLY, B. G. and MACKAY, D. N. (1964) Mental subnormality and its prevalence in Northern Ireland. *Acta. psychiat. Skand.*, **40,** 203–11.

SCOTT, E. M., ILLSLEY, R. and THOMSON, A. M. (1956) A psychological investigation of primigravidae: II. Maternal social class, age, physique and intelligence. *J. Obstet. Gynaec. Brit. Emp.*, **63,** 340.

Scottish Council for Research in Education (1949) *The Trend of Scottish Intelligence*. London: Univ. of London Press.

Scottish Council for Research in Education (1953) *Social Implications of the 1947 Scottish Mental Survey, XXXV*. London: Univ. of London Press.

SHOTWELL, A. M. and SHIPE, D. (1964) Effect of out-of-home care on the intellectual and social development of mongoloid children. *Amer. J. ment. Defic.*, **68**, 693–9.

SKINNER, B. F. (1953) *Science and Human Behaviour*. New York: Macmillan.

STANTON, A. and SCHWARTZ, M. (1954) *The Mental Hospital*. New York: Basic Books.

STEIN, Z. and SUSSER, M. (1960a) The families of dull children: a classification for predicting careers. *Brit. J. prev. soc. Med.*, **14**, 83–8.

STEIN, Z. and SUSSER, M. (1960b) Families of dull children: Part II. Identifying family types and subcultures; Part III. Social selection by family type; Part IV. Increments in intelligence. *J. ment. Sci.*, **106**, 1296–1319.

STEIN, Z. and SUSSER, M. (1960c) Estimating hostel needs for backward children. *Lancet*, **ii**, 486–8.

STEIN, Z. and SUSSER, M. (1963) The social distribution of mental retardation. *Amer. J. ment. Defic.*, **67**, 811–21.

STEIN, Z. and SUSSER, M. (1971) Changes over time in the incidence and prevalence of mental retardation. In HELLMUTH, J. (ed.) *Exceptional Infants, Vol. 2: Studies in Abnormalities*. New York: Brunner/Mazel Inc.

SUSSER, M. W. and KUSHLICK, A. (1961) *A Report on the Mental Health Services of the City of Salford for the Year 1960*. Salford Health Dept.

SUSSER, M. W. and WATSON, W. (1962) *Sociology in Medicine*. London: Oxford Univ. Press.

THOMPSON, B. (1956) A social study of illegitimate pregnancies. *Brit. J. prev. soc. Med.*, **10**, 75.

TIZARD, J. (1958) Longitudinal and follow-up studies. In CLARKE, A. M. and CLARKE, A. D. B. (eds.) *Mental Deficiency: The Changing Outlook* (1st edn). London: Methuen.

TIZARD, J. (1960) Residential care of mentally handicapped children. *Brit. med. J.*, **1**, 1041–6.

TIZARD, J. (1962) Treatment of the mentally subnormal. In RICHTER, D., TANNER, J. M., LORD TAYLOR and ZANGWILL, O. I. (eds.) *Aspects of Psychiatric Research*. London: Oxford Univ. Press.

TIZARD, J. (1964) *Community Services for the Mentally Handicapped*. London: Oxford Univ. Press.

TIZARD, J. (1965) Community care for the subnormal. *Proc. roy. Soc. Med.*, **58**, 373–4.

TIZARD, J. and GRAD, J. C. (1961) *The Mentally Handicapped and Their Families*. London: Oxford Univ. Press.

WING, L. (1971) Severely retarded children in a London area: prevalence and provision of services. *Psychol. Med.*, **1**, 405–15.

WOODWARD, M. (1963) Early experience and behaviour disorders in severely subnormal children. *Brit. J. soc. clin. Psychol.*, **2**, 174–84.

YOUNG, M. and WILMOTT, P. (1957) *Family and Kinship in East London.* London: Routledge & Kegan Paul.

ZIGLER, E. and DE LABRY, J. (1962) Concept-switching in middle-class, lower-class and retarded children. *J. abn. soc. Psychol.*, **65**, 267–72.

4

J. M. Berg

Aetiological aspects of mental subnormality: pathological factors

Introduction

A wide variety of individuals with different clinical characteristics and different degrees of intellectual retardation are considered to be mentally defective or subnormal. Criteria of social competence and educational capability enter into such considerations, as well as the intellectual level *per se* as measured by tests of intelligence. Persons who can be classified as mentally subnormal on the basis of these criteria range from the helpless idiot to the dullard whose behaviour is regarded as disturbed or otherwise inappropriate. From the aetiological point of view, the term mental subnormality has no more meaning than, for example, a term such as diminished head size. Like smallness of the head, mental subnormality is not a disease entity but a symptom which can be determined by a large number of different causal agencies. These agencies operate, in given circumstances, to produce the symptom, in varying degrees of severity, together with other clinical manifestations. This chapter and Chapter 5 consider complementary aspects of these basic issues. (See also Chapter 2.)

General approach to the problem

Some subnormal persons, in particular those with severe mental defect, suffer from demonstrable organic disease or pathology which, however determined, can reasonably be regarded as being responsible for the subnormality. Aided by knowledge of the personal and family history, these pathological conditions may be detected, even pre-natally in certain particular circumstances,[1] by means of various diagnostic techniques including clinical, radiological, biochemical, cytological and neuropathological ones. In other cases of subnormality, no physical abnormality can be found which could account for the mental defect. A considerable clinical problem which arises in these cases is that of trying to decide whether the inability to demonstrate organic pathology is due to inadequacy of available methods of diagnosis or due to the absence of such pathology. Important diagnostic aids have been developed in recent years, notably in the fields of biochemistry and cytogenetics, which have led to the detection of

[1] Since this chapter was written, the scope of prenatal diagnosis has extended substantially. This trend will undoubtedly continue, with significant preventive implications in regard to some varieties of mental subnormality. Milunsky (1973) has published a comprehensive survey of developments in these spheres.

previously undifferentiated pathological types of mental subnormality. There is little doubt that more such types will be recognized in the future, though very many persons are likely to remain who function at a low intellectual level for reasons other than the operation of specific disease processes. Lewis (1933) called such cases 'subcultural', as opposed to 'pathological', and regarded them as representing the lower end of the normal variations in intelligence which occur in the general population. Most of these cases have relatively mild intellectual deficit and many are not obviously distinct from the normal population as a whole.

Lewis's (1933) subdivision of the mentally retarded into those who are organically diseased variants of the general population and those who are normal variants provides a helpful approach to the aetiology of mental subnormality. Two groups of causal agencies emerge for consideration:

1. Specific organic pathological processes directly responsible for, or closely associated with, mental defect. In the main, these lead to severe subnormality. However, a few (for example, the triple-X condition in females) are more usually associated with mild defect and many (for example, phenylketonuria) can result in intellectual states varying from gross idiocy to levels within the range of normality.
2. An interaction of genetical and environmental influences, of the same kind as those operating in the normal population, not responsible for specific physical disease but sufficient to produce some (usually mild) impairment of intellectual function. This will lead to a diagnosis of subnormality if the individual is considered also to be socially incompetent.

The influences mentioned in the second group are considered in Chapters 7 and 8 and will not be discussed further here. In this chapter an account is given of specific pathological causes of, and some distinct physical syndromes closely associated with, mental subnormality. The subject cannot be dealt with extensively within the confines of one chapter, so that the data are presented with emphasis on principles rather than details.

Heredity and environment in the causation of pathological types of mental subnormality

The pathological types of mental subnormality can be divided conveniently into those which are genetically and those which are environmentally determined. It should be borne in mind, however, that the two sets of causal factors are not mutually exclusive. The effects on the individual of abnormal events and diseases having their origin in the environment will be influenced by the inherited constitution of that individual; for example, the occurrence of an obviously environmental event, such as injury at birth, will be dependent to some extent on characteristics of the newborn infant, like his birth weight, which are partly genetically determined. Conversely, inherited defects can be determined by earlier environmental events as, for instance, when irradiation produces mutations in germ cells (ova and sperms) which are harmful to offspring derived from these cells. Further, even when mental subnormality is due to inherited disease, environmental influences, such as a stable and stimulating home, appropriate educational facilities, and specific medical treatments, can have a substantial effect on the actual level and quality of mental function achieved. Haemolytic disease of the newborn, due to *Rhesus* incompatibility between mother and foetus, provides a notable example of the interaction between hereditary and environmental factors in the production of mental effects. In this condition, an inherited antigenic difference between the mother and her foetus can result in the formation of maternal antibodies which constitute an environmental hazard to the foetus; its red cells may be haemolysed with consequent serious damage to foetal tissues, including those of the brain. Mental subnormality of variable degree can thus occur in survivors. Both mortality and morbidity rates have been reduced by the environmental alteration achieved by exchange transfusions undertaken soon after birth. This technique involves the removal of the infant's blood, containing harmful ingredients, and its replacement by normal donor blood. Even more important current developments, involving the use of prophylactic Rh immunoglobulin, could result in a decline of Rhesus haemolytic disease by as much as 95 per cent (Finn, 1970).

Without prejudice to the reservations made above, the conditions to be discussed in this chapter are subdivided into those of genetical and those of environmental origin. As Penrose (1963a) pointed out, the distinction between hereditary and environmental causes must be based upon temporal sequence; the former are determined prior to conception (in parental, or more remote ancestral, germ cells) and the latter subsequent to it (before, during or after birth). It is perhaps as well to add a reminder here that the terms hereditary and congenital are not synonymous. The latter term is more comprehensive in that it is applicable both to conditions which are inherited and to those which arise from events occurring during intra-uterine life. Thus, all hereditary conditions may be considered as congenital in origin, though some congenital ones are not hereditary. The point can be illustrated by reference to congenital cataract. One variety of this, described by Garland and Moorhouse (1953), occurs in association with subnormality and ataxia and is due to a recessively transmitted gene. Another variety is a well-known consequence, together with other abnormalities including mental defect, of foetal infection with the rubella virus during the early stages of pregnancy. A further point which emerges from this reference to congenital cataract is that genetical and environmental events can give rise to similar defects. Goitrous cretinism, discussed on page 90, provides another example of this.

I. MENTAL SUBNORMALITY OF SPECIFIC GENETICAL ORIGIN

Genetically determined conditions closely associated with pathological types of mental subnormality may be due to:

1. Harmful genes. Autosomal dominant, autosomal recessive and X-linked abnormalities are the main ones in this category. The genes resulting in pathological types of subnormality are rare specific ones, in contrast to commoner non-specific genes which may be supposed to be operating to produce what Lewis (1933) called 'subcultural' variation.
2. Aberrant chromosomes. These aberrations may involve the autosomes or the sex chromosomes and, sometimes, both.

Each of these will be considered in turn. An understanding of the mechanisms involved in the production of these abnormalities presupposes some knowledge of the characteristics of chromosomes and of the genetical units, or genes, which are regarded as an essential part of their nature. Some aspects of this subject are referred to in the context of the data presented below, though a comprehensive account of it is beyond the scope of the main theme of this chapter. Stimulating general introductions to the science of human genetics include those of Carter (1962) and of Penrose (1963b). Among valuable recent editions of more formal introductory textbooks, those of Roberts (1970) and Thompson and Thompson (1973) may be mentioned as examples.

(1) *Conditions due to harmful genes*

(a) *Autosomal dominant abnormalities.* Several conditions, in which mental subnormality is not uncommon, fulfil the criteria of dominant inheritance. Such conditions are due to a single gene transmitted by a parent (of either sex) to half the offspring, though actually, because human sibships are relatively small, frequently more or less than half the children are affected. The parent, say the father, is capable of transmitting the gene either because it has arisen by fresh mutation in his germ cells or because he himself inherited it. In the former case, the parent will not himself suffer from the disease and, in the latter, he must be sufficiently mildly afflicted to be capable of reproduction even though his affected offspring may be so grossly diseased as to be infertile. Fresh gene mutations and variability in the manifestations of disease therefore play an important role in dominant conditions associated with severe abnormalities. These considerations can make the demonstration of dominant inheritance of such abnormalities very difficult in practice.

Epiloia illustrates these points. Bourneville (1880) was the first to recognize the pathological features of the condition which he called *sclérose tubéreuse* (tuberous or tuberose sclerosis) in view of the tuber-like nodules which are found in the brain. Feeling the need for a name based on clinical rather than neuro-pathological considerations, Sherlock (1911) coined the term epiloia for the disease. Three of its main features are mental subnormality, epilepsy, and various skin anomalies of which the most important is adenoma sebaceum, consisting of multiple papules in a mainly butterfly-shaped distribution on both cheeks (see Plate 1). Mental subnormality is usually severe but can be absent. Though often noted in infancy, subnormality may not be apparent for a number, or even many, years, particularly when it is of a mild degree. Epilepsy commonly begins in the first year of life and may be the first sign of abnormality noted. There is wide variability in the frequency of fits, and remissions can occur, lasting for months or years, even without the use of anticonvulsants. Adenoma sebaceum, which is a most valuable diagnostic sign, does not usually appear till the child is a few years old, though it may possibly be present at birth (Walsh *et al.*, 1938) and has been observed also, for the first time, at the age of 26 years (Finlayson, 1955). In addition to these variable manifestations, many internal tissues, apart from those of the brain, can be involved (for example, the kidneys, heart and lungs) with the production of a wide range of clinical signs. Various combinations of pathological and clinical findings occur in individual cases, even in the same family, making it difficult to obtain accurate data concerning the familial and overall incidence of the disease. Incomplete forms, with some of the more obvious features absent, add to the difficulty. Nevertheless, many pedigrees show a dominant mode of inheritance. A considerable number of cases, perhaps about half, seem to occur sporadically and many of these are thought to be due to new gene mutations. Penrose (1963a) estimated the frequency of epiloia due to a dominant gene to be one in 30,000 in the general population of England. The condition is not unusual in populations of severely subnormal persons; there were 10 instances of it among 800 consecutive admissions of idiot and imbecile children to the Fountain Hospital, London (Berg, 1963).

Among other conditions which can reasonably be regarded as dominant, and which are not infrequently associated with mental subnormality, are neurofibromatosis, acrocephalosyndactyly and craniofacial dysostosis. As in epiloia, new gene mutations are thought to determine many instances of these conditions and they display considerable variation in symptomatology.

Neurofibromatosis (von Recklinghausen's disease), with an estimated incidence, in all its forms, of the order of 1 in 2,000 in the general population (Neel, 1954), is partially characterized by nerve tumour formation which may involve many parts of the body (see Plate 2). If there is cerebral involvement, mental subnormality can be one of the sequelae. Preiser and Davenport (1918) noted that 7·8 per cent of 243 reported cases of neurofibromatosis were feeble-minded, and, more recently, Canale *et al.* (1964) reported a 10 per cent incidence of retardation among 92 affected patients seen in a Detroit hospital. However, the disease is rare among the severely subnormal. In the Fountain Hospital series of 800 children referred to above, there were only 2 examples of it. Penrose (1963a) pointed out that many pedigrees are consistent with the hypothesis that an irregularly dominant gene is responsible for the disease.

Acrocephalosyndactyly (Apert's syndrome) is a condition in which, as the name indicates, a high, wide and short cranium is associated with malformation of the fingers and/or toes. A characteristic facial appearance, including widely set bulging eyes, underdeveloped maxillae, crowded teeth and a prominent lower jaw, facilitates correct diagnosis. According to Sirkin (1944), the intelligence of most reported cases is normal. However, Penrose (1963a) noted that mental defect, though not usually severe, is a common accompaniment. Blank (1960) distinguished two main clinical categories of acrocephalosyndactyly, 'typical' and 'atypical', interdigital osseous union being a conspicuous feature of the former and absent in the latter. He described the former as being commoner and estimated its incidence at birth to be about 1 in 160,000. Most cases are thought to be due to fresh gene mutations. Among additional varieties of acrocephalosyndactyly which have been recorded are two rare types in which there are extra, as well as fused, digits. One of these types (Noack's syndrome) is considered to be dominant, and the other (Carpenter's syndrome) recessive (McKusick, 1968).

Craniofacial dysostosis (Crouzon's disease) is another condition in which cranial deformity can be associated with mental subnormality. The physical characteristics of the condition include a thin, acrocephalic skull, prognathism, exophthalmos and optic atrophy. These characteristics are variable, and a considerable range of associated anomalies also are sometimes reported under the heading of Crouzon's disease. They may not all be instances of the same disease. The incidence of the condition in some families suggests a dominant mode of inheritance. In a well-illustrated example of such a family, recorded by Vulliamy and Normandale (1966), the authors were able to trace fourteen affected members over four generations. According to Dodge *et al.* (1959), about one-quarter of reported cases have no history of other relatives being affected.

(b) *Autosomal recessive abnormalities.* A larger number of recessive conditions are known to be closely associated with severe subnormality than is the case with dominant conditions. This is not surprising as the heterozygous carriers of genes responsible for recessive abnormalities are not themselves affected, in the sense of being diseased, and so are fertile despite the fact that the genes they transmit can produce, in the homozygous state, major defects resulting in infertility. It should be added that important advances have been made in recent years in the detection of heterozygous carriers of genes for recessive abnormalities by means of special examinations. Examples of such examinations are chemical loading or tolerance tests, in which the response to a standard oral dose of phenylalanine or galactose is measured, for purposes of detection of carriers of the gene for phenylketonuria and that for galactosaemia, respectively. Heterozygotes for each of these conditions usually show a higher rise and slower decline in the blood level of the relevant ingested chemical than do non-carrier controls. Another valuable method of carrier detection, with applications to some recessively determined biochemical types of subnormality, involves direct assays of body tissues for specific enzyme deficiencies.

Both parents must be carriers of the gene determining a recessive abnormality for that abnormality to occur in offspring. As this is more likely to happen if the parents are blood relations, there is a higher incidence of consanguinity among the parents of children with rare recessive defects than would be expected on the basis of chance alone. Parental consanguinity is thus a useful pointer to the presence of rare recessively inherited defects though, of course, many non-consanguineous parents have children with recessive abnormalities and many consanguineous parents have normal children only. The increased incidence of parental consanguinity in series of cases of severe subnormality indicates that rare recessive conditions are likely to be found in such series. Among 800 consecutive admissions of severely subnormal children to the Fountain Hospital, London, 10 (1·25 per cent) had parents who were first cousins (Berg, 1963, unpublished observations), compared with a figure of 0·4 per cent for children admitted to general hospitals in England (Bell, 1940).

When both parents are the carriers of a gene for any particular recessive abnormality, there is a one in four risk of any one child inheriting the gene in duplicate, one from each parent, and thus being affected. As with dominant conditions, however, small individual human sibships do not provide a statistically adequate sample for the precise Mendelian ratio of affected to unaffected children to occur often in practice, quite apart from the difficulty created by early death of some cases.

A brief account follows of some conditions, considered to be recessive, which are connected with mental subnormality. Each of these conditions is rare in the general population with frequencies usually less than 1 in 10,000.

Phenylketonuria, a metabolic disease discovered by Fölling (1934), is characterized chemically by an inability to convert phenylalanine to tyrosine, due to deficiency of a specific enzyme, phenylalanine 4-hydroxylase, in the liver. This leads to an accumulation of phenylalanine in blood serum and other tissues. One result is that phenylpyruvic acid is excreted in the urine from a few weeks after birth onwards, and this substance can be conveniently identified by the green colour reaction produced on the addition of ferric chloride solution to urine containing it. Mental subnormality, usually of a severe degree, is present in most cases though a number of persons with the disease have near normal, and even normal, intelligence. There may be substantial differences in intelligence between phenylketonurics even in the same sibship (Coutts and Fyfe, 1971). These considerations must be borne in mind in assessing the effect on mental level of a phenylalanine-low diet given as treatment. Though some controversy persists about the precise efficacy of such treatment, there is widespread agreement that an important prerequisite for its success is commencement in early infancy (before 3 months); less certain is the age at which dietary restrictions can be appropriately abandoned. A possible future therapeutic prospect, mentioned by Rosenberg and Scriver (1969), is that of liver transplants from normal donors as a source of missing enzyme.

The basic reason for mental subnormality in phenylketonuria is obscure, but post-mortem examinations of brains of affected cases show definite abnormalities including reduction in size and fibrous gliosis (Crome and Pare, 1960). In addition to intellectual deficit, behavioural peculiarities are fairly frequent (Pitt, 1971). Other clinical features include dilution of hair and eye colour in comparison with unaffected sibs, a tendency to dermatitis, broad, widely spaced incisors, brisk reflexes and, as in many other types of severe subnormality, reduced stature and head size and a liability to have fits. Gross physical deformities are relatively uncommon.

It has become apparent, in recent years, that the condition discussed above, now sometimes referred to as classical phenylketonuria, is not the only variety of disordered phenylalanine metabolism. Mild and transient variants have been described, as well as a benign persistent type, each with its own biochemical and clinical characteristics (Rosenberg and Scriver, 1969). An issue of particular relevance to mental subnormality is that concerned with hyperphenylalaninaemia in fertile women. High phenylalanine levels in such women have grave implications for foetal development. The seriousness of the problem is indicated in Yu and O'Halloran's (1970) review of sixty-eight offspring of phenylketonuric mothers. Sixty-five of these children were retarded, and some had such additional abnormalities as small heads, convulsions and heart defects. The authors emphasize the importance of careful dietary control prior to and during pregnancy in these circumstances.

Over the past two decades, a number of new diseases have been discovered which, like phenylketonuria, appear to be recessively inherited, are characterized by the excretion of specific amino-acids in the urine and are associated with mental subnormality. They include *maple syrup urine disease* (Menkes *et al.*, 1954), *argininosuccinicaciduria* (Allan *et al.*, 1958), *cystathioninuria* (Harris *et al.*, 1959), *homocystinuria* (Carson *et al.*, 1963), and *lysinuria* (Oyanagi *et al.*, 1970). Relatively few examples of these rare conditions are known as yet and available information about them is considerably more scanty than in the case of phenylketonuria. They illustrate, however, the progress being made in the differentiation of specific types of mental subnormality by the application of new techniques of investigation, in these instances mainly biochemical ones.

Galactosaemia is a disorder of carbohydrate metabolism in which the absence of a particular enzyme, known as galactose-1-phosphate uridyl transferase, prevents the normal transformation of galactose to certain glucose products. As galactose is an ingredient in milk, ordinary feeding of an affected baby exposes it to serious clinical consequences. These include failure to thrive, jaundice and liver enlargement in the early stages of the disease; subsequently, mental subnormality and cataract formation may be noted. The symptomatology can be attributed to undue concentrations of chemical substances both intracellularly and in body fluids (Harris, 1970). Many reports testify to the value of early treatment with a galactose-free diet in preventing or ameliorating these abnormalities. An instance has been recorded (Roe *et al.*, 1971) of an apparently healthy child born to a galactosaemic woman who had been maintained on a galactose-restricted diet since infancy.

Amaurotic idiocy is the term often used for conditions in which there are complex disturbances of lipid metabolism resulting in intracellular deposits of abnormal substances, mainly in the brain and retina. These disease states are associated clinically, as the name implies, with visual defects and mental subnormality. Manifestations appear at different ages, the two most documented varieties being the infantile type (Tay-Sachs disease) and the juvenile type (Batten's or Vogt-Spielmeyer disease). In the former, neurological and ophthalmological abnormalities develop within several months of birth and are distinctly progressive with gross mental defect, paralysis, epilepsy, a so-called 'cherry-red spot' in the macula, optic atrophy and blindness as common features, followed by death by the age of about 2 to 4 years (Frederickson and Trams, 1966). In the latter, symptoms are similar in some respects, but onset is usually delayed till the child is several years old and the disease advances more slowly until death occurs about five to ten years later (Sjögren, 1931). The two diseases appear to be separate entities in various regards.

Gargoylism (see Plate 3), like amaurotic idiocy, concerns disease in which abnormal substances accumulate within cells. Mucopolysaccharide metabolism is disordered, complex biochemical disturbances occur and many tissues are involved. The grotesque facies and deformed appearance, which produce a close resemblance between affected persons, led Ellis *et al.* (1936) to name the condition gargoylism, a term which has become widely accepted. Abnormalities can be observed in early infancy. The typical facies include coarse features, well-developed bony prominences, bushy eyebrows, corneal clouding, a broad nose and large mouth, lips and tongue. Among other clinical findings are hirsutes, a protuberant abdomen due to enlargement of the liver and spleen, dorso-lumbar kyphosis and limitation of extension of joints. Mental subnormality is usually of severe degree. An X-linked form of the disease, referred to by many as Hunter's syndrome, occurs. This differs clinically from the commoner autosomal recessive variety (frequently also called Hurler's syndrome), described above, in generally showing milder manifestations of later onset, including the absence of corneal involvement. Other, to some extent similar, conditions involving abnormal mucopolysaccharide metabolism also have been documented, often with eponymous designations (McKusick, 1969). These include the syndromes of Sanfilippo, Morquio, Scheie and Maroteaux-Lamy.

Cretinism can be conveniently discussed here as there is considerable evidence that some cases, in which various chemical defects in the synthesis and utilization of thyroid hormone occur, are recessively determined (Stanbury, 1966). Cretinism in these cases is associated with enlargement of the thyroid gland, a circumstance which also can be environmentally determined by insufficient iodine intake in the diet or by the ingestion of goitrogenic agents like thiouracil. Imperfect embryonic development of the thyroid gland, for whatever reason, can result in cretinism as well, in this instance without goitre. Recent data indicate that cretinism is less common than is often assumed. No more than 2 examples were noted among 800 (0·3 per cent) consecutive admissions of severely subnormal children to the Fountain Hospital, London (Berg, 1963). At the larger children's hospitals in Scandinavia, only one or two cases of congenital cretinism are diagnosed annually (Åkerren, 1955). The clinical features can include mental subnormality, general sluggishness, anaemia, small stature, coarse skin, large tongue, low temperature, slow pulse and chronic constipation. If treatment with thyroid extract is started early, the prognosis as regards physical development is generally considered to be good but the effect on mental development is more variable (Hubble, 1953; Lawson, 1955).

Microcephaly literally means smallness of the head and, as such, can be used as a descriptive term for a physical sign that is noted in various different types of mental subnormality. Among these are, for instance, many cases of phenyl-ketonuria and mongolism, and children born to mothers who were exposed to irradiation or to the rubella virus early in pregnancy. When used in this way the term is often restricted, rather arbitrarily, to persons with a head circumference below a certain size, for example less than 17 inches in adults or at least three standard deviations below the mean for age and sex in children. Microcephaly is considered in this section because there is convincing evidence that some mentally subnormal persons with small heads of a particular shape have re-cessively inherited their condition (Böök *et al.*, 1953; Komai *et al.*, 1955; van den Bosch, 1959). Penrose (1963a) pointed out that such individuals, sometimes referred to as 'true' microcephalics, have heads in which the height and width show relatively greater reduction than the length, and they tend to have a receding forehead and a face approaching the normal in size. Penrose regarded these features, combined with a well-developed, though dwarfed, body and a tendency to a stooping posture and quick, furtive movements, as highly characteristic; some observers (for example, Kirman, 1957), however, dispute this. Another type of microcephaly which appears to be recessively inherited, but is different from the condition discussed above in various respects, is known as Seckel's syndrome or bird-headed dwarfism. Affected persons have small heads with a 'bird-like' facies and show multiple congenital malformations. They are dwarfed in stature and retarded in intellect. McKusick *et al.* (1967) have de-scribed a sibship in which two sisters and a brother probably had the disorder.

(c) *X-linked abnormalities*. The abnormalities considered thus far are determined by genes located on the autosomes, consisting, in man, of twenty-two pairs of chromosomes. In addition to these abnormalities, there are a number, closely associated with mental subnormality, which are thought to be due to genes on the X chromosome. These abnormalities are referred to as X-linked. As there are two X chromosomes in females and only one in males (the other sex chromosome in males being a Y), a gene for recessive defects on the X chromosome has different effects in the two sexes. Males with one such harmful gene on the X chromosome would be affected whereas females with the one gene on an X chromosome would be heterozygous carriers of the abnormality; females would be affected if they were homozygous for the gene in question (i.e. if it were located on each of their X chromosomes).

In general, males are affected by X-linked recessive abnormalities and females are carriers, though it is possible for females to be affected also. An affected father, even if fertile, cannot transmit the abnormality to his sons though such a father's daughters would all be carriers despite the mother being normal. If the father is normal and the mother is a carrier, there is a one in two risk that a son will be affected and the same risk that a daughter will be a carrier. In the less likely circumstance of the father being affected and the mother being a carrier, sons will be normal or affected and daughters will be carriers or affected. If both parents were affected, and could have children, all of them would have the abnormality.

Because of its occurrence in royalty, one type of rare X-linked condition, the bleeding disease haemophilia, has become especially well known. The disease has no particular association with mental subnormality. An X-linked form of gargoylism, referred to on page 90, does have such an association and the following abnormalities are further examples.

Oculocerebrorenal syndrome is the name now most usually applied to a condition discovered by Lowe *et al.* (1952). Up to 1968, some seventy characteristic examples had been reported (Abbassi *et al.*, 1968). The disease is so called because of the association of eye abnormalities (such as cataract and glaucoma) with mental subnormality and kidney defects (manifested by excess amino-acids in the urine and other changes). The disease affects boys and is transmitted by females. Abnormalities, particularly cataracts, may be noted at birth or soon after. Life expectancy is substantially reduced, renal disturbances and secondary infections being common causes of death.

Lesch–Nyhan syndrome is the eponymous designation now often applied to a condition described by Lesch and Nyhan (1964) in two brothers, aged 5 and 8 years, in whom hyperuricaemia was associated with mental subnormality, choreoathetosis and an inclination to bite their lips and hands. Other reports of affected boys contributed to the further delineation of this syndrome of severe mental and physical handicaps. Among additional neurological features which may be noted are spasticity, convulsions, dysarthria and dysphagia. Also, increased levels of urinary uric acid can be connected with such manifestations as the passage of blood or calculi in the urine. Hoefnagel *et al.* (1965) raised the question of a possible X-linked recessive mode of inheritance, and subsequently-published pedigrees of afflicted families, for example by Shapiro *et al.* (1966), provided supportive evidence for this view.

Nephrogenic diabetes insipidus is a disease in which excessive excretion of dilute urine is associated with undue thirst. Manifestations appear in early infancy. Unlike other varieties of diabetes insipidus, the condition does not respond to treatment with antidiuretic hormone. Mental subnormality, of variable degree, occurs in some cases. In a study of eight children, aged from 5 to 11 years, with the disease, Ruess and Rosenthal (1963) reported IQ scores ranging from about 20 to 114. Unless adequate fluid intake is maintained, dehydration occurs and this can have an adverse effect on the mental level (Kirman *et al.*, 1956). The disease usually occurs in males, but females are sometimes affected (West and Kramer, 1955; Glaser, 1958). Heterozygous female carriers may be detected by a reduced ability to concentrate urine when fluids are withheld (Carter and Simpkiss, 1956).

Hydrocephaly (see Plate 7), like microcephaly (see p. 91), can be looked upon as a physical sign which may be due to a variety of causes, both genetical and environmental ones. Among the latter causes are, for instance, tuberculous meningitis which is discussed on page 104. Genetical types of hydrocephaly include a variety which is characterized by narrowing of the aqueduct of Sylvius and demonstrates an X-linked pattern of inheritance. Edwards *et al.* (1961) reported a family with a defect of this kind in which there were fifteen affected males and no affected females in three generations. Shannon and Nadler (1968) recently described another such family and briefly reviewed earlier reports. Whatever the cause of a particular case of hydrocephaly, cerebral pathology is present so that subnormality and neurological abnormalities, like spasticity and epilepsy, are common clinical consequences in survivors.

(2) *Conditions due to aberrant chromosomes*

(a) *Autosomal aberrations.* The nuclei of somatic cells in normal humans contain forty-six chromosomes, largely consisting of desoxyribonucleic acid (DNA), of which forty-four are known as autosomes and two as sex chromosomes. Twenty-two autosomes and one sex chromosome are derived from each of the two germ cells (ovum and sperm) which unite to begin the formation of the new individual. The relatively recent development of cytological techniques which enable each of the chromosomes to be clearly seen under the microscope, in suitable preparations of dividing human cells (see Plate 5), has led to the discovery of a substantial number of chromosomal aberrations which are closely connected with various abnormal clinical conditions. Standardization in identification and designation of each chromosome has been greatly facilitated as a result of international conferences held in Denver, London, Chicago and Paris in 1960, 1963, 1966 and 1971 respectively. Based on the proposals of these meetings (Chicago Conference, 1966; Paris Conference, 1971), individual chromosomes are distinguished by such criteria as their length, the position of a constriction called the centromere and characteristic banding patterns produced by certain special stains. They can thus be matched in pairs, numbered or lettered in a uniform manner, and abnormalities can be indicated by recommended notations or symbols. These abnormalities can occur both in the number and in the morphology of the chromosomes. It is possible also for the same person to have some cells in his body showing a chromosomal anomaly and other cells which are normal, or he may have more than one type of chromosomal aberration in different cells. This phenomenon is known as mosaicism.

The first reports of human chromosomal aberrations began to appear in 1959 and it was evident, from the outset, that the aberrations were often associated with mental subnormality. New discoveries have been comparatively frequent in this rapidly advancing field, and more than 100 different types of human chromosome disorders have now been described (Carr, 1969). It can be reasonably expected, in relation to these developments, that a good deal of additional data will be forthcoming on hitherto obscure forms of subnormality and other defects. The following are examples of types of mental subnormality now known to be connected with autosomal aberrations. Much still remains uncertain as to the aetiological factors which determine these aberrations and as to how the latter operate to produce abnormal clinical states.

Mongolism (Down's syndrome) is by far the commonest disease entity detected in subnormal populations. Among 800 consecutive admissions of severely subnormal children to the Fountain Hospital, London, there were 175 (21·9 per cent) cases of the syndrome (Berg, 1963). By contrast, the next most common entity was mental defect due to meningitis with an incidence of 2·8 per cent. The incidence of Down's syndrome in hospital populations of subnormal persons of all ages and grades of defect is often about 10 per cent. Despite the possible implications in the name 'mongolism', the disease is not especially characteristic of, and is not limited to, any particular race. For readers interested in a detailed comprehensive account of the condition, the textbook by Penrose and Smith (1966) is particularly valuable.

The frequency of Down's syndrome at birth was found by Carter and MacCarthy (1951) to be 1 in 666 in London and the Home Counties and this figure agrees closely with other European surveys as well as with a large Australian one (Collmann and Stoller, 1962a). The well-known and striking variation in incidence that occurs at different maternal ages is shown in a table by Penrose (1963a); at birth, the incidence is less than 0·1 per cent up to a maternal age of 34 years and then rises steeply to as much as 2·75 per cent in the maternal age-group of 45 years and over. Respiratory infections, heart defects and other causes result in a higher early mortality in cases of Down's syndrome than in the general population, so that the incidence of the condition falls in older age-groups. In 1958, the incidence was about 1 in 1,000, at the age of 10 years, in and around London (Carter, 1958). The mortality rate of cases of Down's syndrome has decreased markedly in the past few decades as it has also in children in general.

The clinical features of the syndrome have been recorded many times since Langdon Down's original description in 1866 and they will not be considered in detail here. Many, though by no means all (Zappella and Cowie, 1962), cases are recognized at birth; the diagnosis is usually made in the first year of life, and should, in general, be conveyed promptly to the parents (Berg *et al.*, 1969). A wide range of abnormalities occur though manifestations vary and many are found individually in persons not suffering from the disease. Stature is reduced and the limbs are hypotonic. The head tends to be small with greater reduction in length than in breadth. The characteristic facies includes slanting eyes, epicanthic folds, squint, Brushfield's spots (white specks) in the iris, and small nose and ears. The teeth often erupt late and some may be congenitally absent (Barkla, 1966a, b). There is a tendency for the little finger to be curved inwards and for a wide gap to occur between the first and second toes. A single transverse palmar crease is often present, and characteristic dermatoglyphic patterns occur on the hands and feet as they do also in some other conditions in which there are chromosomal aberrations (Penrose, 1963c). The incidence of leukaemia is increased in young children with Down's syndrome (Krivit and Good, 1957). Biochemical studies of the blood and urine have not revealed pathognomonic abnormalities.

Marked neurological handicaps, like epilepsy and cerebral palsy, are unusual and nearly all cases learn to walk. They are often cooperative and friendly. These aspects of their personalities, as well as the traditional views that they are especially fond of music and better mimics than other children, deserve further study. Many cases have IQs between 20 and 40; some, however, are gross idiots and others have IQs above 45 and can benefit from attendance in schools for the educationally subnormal (Dunsdon *et al.*, 1960).

Abnormalities in the pelvic bones (Caffey and Ross, 1956) and absence of a rib (Beber, 1965) have been reported, and many internal organs can be malformed. Heart malformations, of many kinds, are particularly frequent. Contrary to views expressed by some authors, Berg *et al.* (1960) have found no heart defect specific to Down's syndrome though some defects are particularly common. Malformation of the duodenum is also relatively frequent (Bodian *et al.*, 1952). The brain is reduced in weight and tends to be rounded with small frontal lobes, brain-stem and cerebellum, but it does not appear to show constant abnormalities on histological examination (Crome, 1957).

There is no known cure for Down's syndrome and claims for the efficacy of pituitary and thyroid preparations should be viewed with caution (Berg *et al.*, 1961). Advocacy of the value of siccacell treatment is also unconvincing (Bardon, 1964).

An outstanding advance in knowledge about Down's syndrome was made with the discovery that persons with the disease have forty-seven chromosomes in somatic cells instead of the normal forty-six (Lejeune *et al.*, 1959). In these cases there is an extra chromosome No. 21 and this circumstance is often referred to as trisomy 21. It is considered to arise as a result of non-disjunction whereby both, instead of one, members of the relevant pair of chromosomes enter the germ cell during the formation of the latter. The association in these cases of Down's syndrome with advancing maternal age implicates the ovum rather than the sperm. Propositions have been made that maternal exposure to various external agencies before or at about the time of conception, for example ionizing radiation (Sigler *et al.*, 1965) or the virus of infective hepatitis (Stoller and Collmann, 1965), could be aetiologically related to the syndrome. Opinions differ on these questions.

A number of variations in the chromosomal findings can occur in Down's syndrome. In a small minority of cases, forty-six chromosomes are found in somatic cells. The karyotype, however, is still unbalanced because, by a process known as translocation, a considerable portion of a No. 21 chromosome is fused with another autosome, which may be a No. 15 or a No. 22. These cases of the syndrome are not obviously different clinically from those with forty-seven chromosomes. However, in the 15 : 21 translocation type both maternal and paternal age is close to that in the general population, whereas in the 21:22 type advancing paternal (and not maternal) age may be aetiologically significant (Penrose, 1963d). Balanced translocations may be transmitted through several generations without producing clinical effects unless an extra amount of chromosome material is present. Another chromosomal variation in Down's syndrome is the occurrence of mosaicism, in which circumstance some cells can have a normal chromosome complement whereas others show trisomy 21. Such cases may have only limited signs of the disease. Down's syndrome can be associated also with the Klinefelter syndrome (see Plate 4). This occurs in males with forty-eight chromosomes in their cells, one of which is an extra No. 21 and the other an extra X (see Plate 5). Since the first case with this association was recorded (Ford *et al.*, 1959), a number of further instances have been reported. Down's syndrome with an extra No. 21 has been recorded occasionally also in persons with other additional chromosome abnormalities, such as XXX or XYY sex chromosome constitution and trisomy of a No. 13–15 or a No. 18 autosome (Laxova *et al.*, 1971).

Patau's syndrome occurs in persons who have a characteristic combination of congenital malformations including cerebral and heart defects, microphthalmos, malformed ears, harelip, cleft palate, polydactyly and capillary haemangiomata (Patau *et al.*, 1960; Taylor, 1967, 1968). In addition, diagnostically helpful dermatoglyphic deviations from the normal are often found on the hands and feet (Penrose, 1966). Affected children tend to be born before term, with a low birth weight, and most die soon after. However, even in early infancy, developmental retardation is noted and seizures are common. The condition is often referred to as trisomy 13–15 because there are usually seven chromosomes in this group instead of the normal six, and it has been uncertain to which of the three pairs (13, 14, or 15) the extra chromosome should be designated; it is now generally considered to be an additional No. 13. As with Down's syndrome, this trisomy is commoner among the offspring of older than of younger mothers.

Edwards's syndrome is another trisomic condition in which an extra autosome, either a No. 17 or a No. 18, is associated with multiple congenital abnormalities. These include an abnormally shaped head, peculiar facies, webbing of the neck, syndactyly, chest deformity and heart malformation (Edwards *et al.*, 1960; Taylor, 1967, 1968). Absence of true dermatoglyphic patterns on the finger tips (i.e. the presence of arch formations) is a strikingly frequent finding. Though birth often occurs at term, weight tends to be lower than in Patau's syndrome. In this condition also, delayed mental development is observed in infancy, a period which few survive, and, on the average, maternal age is increased. Taylor (1968) has estimated, from pooled data, that Edwards's and Patau's syndrome each have an incidence of the order of 1 in 7,000 live births. Because of the extremely high infantile mortality, examples of either syndrome are very rarely seen in mental subnormality practice.

The cri du chat syndrome is the name given to a condition, first described by Lejeune and his co-workers (1963, 1964), in which a peculiar cry resembling the mewing of a cat is a characteristic finding. Among other clinical features are gross retardation of mental development, a small head, low-set ears, oblique palpebral fissures and a broad nasal bridge. The initial reports concerned children, but the prospects of survival to adulthood became apparent with the documentation of older examples (Berg *et al.*, 1965; Breg *et al.*, 1970), including one aged 55 years. As the patients get older, the typical cry disappears, the face tends to lose its earlier rounded appearance and premature greying of the hair is quite often noted. The crucial chromosomal error in affected persons is deletion of part of the short arm of one of the No. 5 chromosomes. A like deletion can occur in the morphologically similar No. 4 chromosome, also resulting in mental subnormality, but no cat-like cry and a number of rather different physical consequences (Arias *et al.*, 1970; Miller *et al.*, 1970), such as a flat nose, cleft palate, a preauricular and/or sacral dimple or sinus, and hypospadias.

Partial deletion of No. 18 chromosome, involving either the long or the short arm of that chromosome, has been described in some forty instances and new examples are being documented from time to time. Reported features in persons having a deletion of the long arm (18q— in the Chicago Conference, 1966, notation), in addition to severe mental subnormality, include a small head, anomalies of the ears and eyes, hypotonia and an increased frequency of whorl patterns on the finger tips (de Grouchy *et al.*, 1964; Wertelecki *et al.*, 1966; Insley, 1967). The clinical characteristics of those showing short arm deletion (18p—) appear to have been less uniform, as indicated by Migeon's (1966) summary of twelve recorded cases. However, variable degrees of retardation in mental and physical development have been generally consistent findings in affected individuals surviving beyond infancy.

Other autosomal aberrations of diverse kinds have been found in humans and, particularly with increasing sophistication of techniques, including the important new banding procedures with fluorescent and Giesma dye stains (Hsu, 1973), it is virtually certain that more will be detected. The most frequently documented autosomal aberrations discovered to date include those described above. Trisomy may involve other autosomes also. For instance, Ellis *et al.* (1962) reported trisomy, probably of chromosome No. 22, in a subnormal person with epilepsy. It is also possible for cells to contain 69, 92, and even 184 chromosomes. Apart from abnormalities in the number of chromosomes, morphological aberrations can occur. Several examples of deletions are provided on this page, and translocation has been referred to on page 95. Other rare abnormalities of chromosome structure include duplications, inversions and ring chromosomes. Mental subnormality is commonly associated with many of these aberrations.

(b) *Sex chromosomal aberrations*. Of the two sex chromosomes normally present in humans, an X is derived from the mother and an X or Y from the father. Females have two X chromosomes in their cells and males have an X and a Y. As in the case of the autosomes, aberrations of the sex chromosomes can occur which are closely associated with various abnormal clinical states. Well-documented disorders in this category, particularly relevant to the field of mental subnormality, are the Klinefelter syndrome, the triple-X and double-Y conditions, and some variants of these situations.

The diagnosis of X chromosome anomalies is facilitated by the discovery made by Barr and Bertram (1949) that cell nuclei of normal females contain a sex chromatin structure, known as the Barr body, which is visible under the microscope. Examination of buccal smears shows that some cells contain one Barr body less than the number of X chromosomes in the sex chromosome constitution of that individual. Thus, a normal male (XY sex chromosome constitution), a normal female (XX), a Klinefelter male (XXY), and a triple-X female (XXX) have 0, 1, 1, 2 Barr bodies, respectively, in their cell nuclei. The examination of buccal smears for Barr bodies is a comparatively simple procedure so that a valuable screening test is available for investigations of X chromosome aberrations. Staining techniques, using quinacrine compounds, are currently being developed and refined to enable rapid recognition of the presence of one or more Y chromosomes. Characteristic fluorescent bodies, numerically equal to the number of Y chromosomes in a person's sex chromosome make-up, thus may be observed in appropriate preparations of some interphase nuclei, including those from buccal smears (Pearson *et al.*, 1970). These developments provide prospects for surveying populations for Y chromosome aberrations to complement the well-established X chromosome screening procedure referred to above.

Klinefelter syndrome is the name given to a combination of abnormalities described by Klinefelter *et al.* (1942). These abnormalities, which become apparent from puberty onwards, occur in males and include gynaecomastia, small testes, azoospermia, poor hair growth and an increased pituitary gonadotropin level. Many cases are mentally subnormal, often mildly so. Manifestations can be variable and not all individuals described as examples of the Klinefelter syndrome have the same features or necessarily suffer from the same disease. Some of these persons have a normal sex chromosome constitution, whereas others have an extra X chromosome and so are of the type XXY. The latter is the usual finding when the chromosome constitution is abnormal but, occasionally, cases with some degree of clinical similarity have 3 or 4 X chromosomes with one Y, or 2 Xs and 2 Ys, or even, though males, 2 Xs and apparently no Ys. Still others (mosaics) have an abnormal sex chromosome complement in only some of their cells. The association of Klinefelter syndrome and Down's syndrome in the same person has been referred to on page 96. Klinefelter syndrome is commoner among patients in hospitals for the mentally subnormal, and among those attending infertility clinics, than in the general population. A number of surveys of males in subnormality hospitals have revealed a frequency of chromatin-positive cases (i.e. those showing Barr bodies) of the order of 1 per cent, compared with, on average, only about one-sixth that frequency in live-born male babies (Court Brown, 1969).

The triple-X condition, which occurs in persons also referred to as 'super-females', is, like the Klinefelter syndrome, a condition in which an extra X chromosome is present. These persons, who are females, thus have an XXX sex chromosome constitution. The clinical features are not strikingly abnormal (Johnston *et al.*, 1961). Subnormality is present in some cases and most of these are mildly retarded. Menstruation can be absent or irregular but some have regular periods, are fertile and can have normal children. The condition is not usually found as frequently as the Klinefelter syndrome in hospitals for the mentally subnormal, and had an incidence of 0·4 per cent in one large series of retarded females studied (Maclean *et al.*, 1962). Chromosomal variants of the condition occur and these include females with 4 or 5 X chromosomes and others who are mosaics of the type XXX/XX or XXX/XO or even the combination XXX/XX/XO.

The double-Y condition, in which an X and two, instead of one, Y chromosomes are present, was first reported in a mentally normal man (Hauschka *et al.*, 1962), but subsequently shown to have an association with mental subnormality, aggressive behaviour and unusual tallness (Jacobs *et al.*, 1965). Later studies of males with these clinical features, in various psychiatric and penal settings, often also revealed an unduly high frequency of XYY sex chromosome complement in comparison with control groups (Court Brown, 1968; Marinello *et al.*, 1969). However, it is important to emphasize that by no means all persons with an extra Y chromosome show a characteristic stereotype of the kind referred to above. In fact, considerable physical differences are found in such persons, as well as a wide mental spectrum ranging from entirely laudable to grossly anti-social behaviour and from superior to severely deficient intellect (Berg and Smith, 1971). Marked deviations from normal intelligence, at either end of the scale, are unusual, most affected cases recorded to date being relatively mildly retarded. These considerations should be borne in mind in making prognostic judgments in a given instance, particularly when the additional Y chromosome is detected in infancy before any clinical peculiarities are apparent. As with other chromosomal disorders described in earlier sections, variants of the double-Y condition may be found, including, on rare occasions, two instead of one extra Y to produce an XYYY sex chromosome constitution, and mosaicism in which only some cells show the chromosome fault. The association of an extra Y with an extra No. 21 chromosome or with an extra X has been mentioned on pages 96 and 98 respectively.

Other sex chromosomal aberrations in humans are also now known and, as with autosomal aberrations, their number is likely to grow. One of these conditions, in which there is a total of forty-five chromosomes in somatic cells (with one X and no Y), is known as Turner's syndrome. Physical abnormalities involving the neck, ovaries, kidneys and heart occur but the condition does not appear to be associated particularly with mental subnormality. Still other rare aberrations consist of abnormalities in the form rather than in the number of X chromosomes. These chromosomes may be shortened, lengthened, or distorted in other ways.

The Y chromosome also may show various structural anomalies, as well as numerical aberrations of the kind already considered.

II. MENTAL SUBNORMALITY OF ENVIRONMENTAL ORIGIN

A large number of agents and events having their origin in the environment have been regarded as causes of pathological types of mental subnormality. Many of these circumstances have been convincingly established as being aetiologically significant whereas others have been postulated on more tenuous grounds. The occurrence of an abnormal environmental event or disease in a person subsequently noted to be subnormal is not, of itself, proof of a causal connection. The likelihood of such a connection is greatly increased if the particular abnormal event produces characteristic features which include signs of cerebral involvement, and if other causes of subnormality can be reasonably excluded.

Environmental events leading to pathological types of mental subnormality can occur before, during, or after birth and they are considered below in each of these categories.

(1) *Pre-natal causes*

The causes of mental subnormality discussed under this heading are those which operate during intra-uterine life. The causes themselves can originate from events occurring before or after conception. Examples in each of these categories are, respectively, maternal infection with the spirochaete producing syphilis and with the virus producing rubella. A brief account follows of these, as well as of some other, pre-natal agencies which can result in mental subnormality.

Congenital syphilis has long been recognized as a cause of mental subnormality in live-born offspring of infected mothers. The spirochaete responsible for syphilis can pass from the mother to the foetus and produce abortion, stillbirth, or mental and physical abnormalities in surviving children. Among the abnormalities which may be noted in childhood are mental defect, blindness, deafness, epilepsy, paralyses, and characteristic anomalies of the skull and teeth. In one variety, juvenile general paresis, manifestations often develop in late childhood or adolescence and include mental disturbance, as well as defect, and characteristic neurological signs. A general decline in the incidence of syphilis in many countries has resulted in a marked reduction of cases of subnormality due to this infection. Compared to a 4 per cent incidence of congenital syphilis found by Penrose (1938) in Colchester, and by Benda (1942) in Massachusetts, a more recent survey in London (Berg and Kirman, 1959) revealed a history of syphilis in only 0·6 per cent of 1,900 defectives.

Rubella in early pregnancy was first shown by Gregg (1941) to be a cause of congenital abnormalities in the offspring of infected mothers, and many reports on the subject have since been published. The most important structures involved are those of the brain, heart, eyes and ears with the production of a characteristic, though variable, symptomatology. Other tissues may be damaged also with, for instance, resultant skeletal and dental defects (Forrest and Menser, 1970). The proportions of affected children reported among those at risk have varied greatly in different studies, but have been of the order of 10 to 20 per cent in some of the more recent prospective surveys. An important fact which emerged from the earlier studies was that the incidence of affected live-born children falls markedly when the mother develops rubella after the first three months of pregnancy. The risk appears to be particularly great if rubella occurs in the first month of pregnancy (Pitt, 1961). Data from the Fountain Hospital, London, indicate that rather less than 1 per cent of cases of severe subnormality were due to maternal rubella (Kirman, 1955). The role of this infection in the production of minor degrees of subnormality is less clear. Developments of prophylactic measures against rubella by the use, in certain circumstances, of gammaglobulin and, more recently and significantly, of an appropriate rubella virus vaccine, though still fraught with unresolved problems (Robbins and Heggie, 1970), hold promise that the disease will become an increasingly rare cause of congenital defects and subnormality.

Irradiation, in the form of *excessive* exposure to x-rays, in the early stages of pregnancy is now well established as a cause of abortion and of mental subnormality, reduced head size, microphthalmia and other defects in surviving children. Early studies on the subject include those of Zappert (1926), Murphy (1928, 1929), and Goldstein (1930). Similar dangers to the foetus of radiation from other sources were demonstrated by Plummer (1952) and by Yamazaki *et al.* (1954) who investigated, respectively, effects of the Hiroshima and Nagasaki atomic explosions. Persisting defects in survivors who were thus exposed in utero were recorded in a twenty-year follow-up study by Wood *et al.* (1967).

Rhesus incompatibility between mother and foetus has been referred to on page 84. In these circumstances, the basal ganglia and other portions of the brain can become stained and damaged by bilirubin pigments, a pathological state to which the term kernicterus is frequently applied (Baar, 1959). Affected liveborn children are jaundiced soon after birth and survivors often suffer from mental subnormality, choreoathetosis, spasticity and deafness. The mental level varies from extreme idiocy to normality. Eleven out of 800 (1·4 per cent) severely subnormal children admitted to the Fountain Hospital, London, were considered to owe their defect to Rhesus incompatibility (Berg, 1963). Maternal-foetal incompatibility involving the ABO blood groups can produce similar effects and they are known to occur also in the absence of evidence of blood group incompatibility.

Other pre-natal causes of subnormality have been implicated or postulated on many occasions. Space does not permit a discussion of each of them in turn so that a brief general account is given in this section of some agencies not specifically considered above.

Many infections, apart from syphilis and rubella, can be transmitted to the foetus, but few of these have been convincingly shown to cause mental sub-normality. Interest in maternal virus infections, from this point of view, was stimulated with the discovery of the hazards of rubella. Cytomegalic inclusion-body disease, transmitted through the placenta, can produce microgyria, among other defects in the brain and elsewhere (Crome, 1961), and so result in subnormality. Maternal Asian influenza was noted by Coffey and Jessop (1959, 1963) to be associated with an increased incidence of central nervous system abnormalities in offspring, but Doll *et al.* (1960) did not find such an association. These and other viral infections, in relation to their possible deleterious effects on the foetus, have been considered in a useful review by Hardy (1965). Bacterial infection in pregnant women has not been proved to cause subnormality in their offspring but maternal toxoplasmosis, a protozoal infection, can do so. Other findings in congenital toxoplasmosis include abnormalities of head size, intra-cranial calcification and ocular defects (Couvreur and Desmonts, 1962). Malaria, another protozoal infection, can be transmitted to the foetus and was found by Archibald (1958) to be associated with a reduction in birth weight; follow-up studies of such children, compared with others, in regard to mental function would be interesting.

Teratogenic effects of various chemical agents have been demonstrated many times in experimental animals (Kalter, 1968). The possibility of grave hazards to the human foetus of particular chemical substances has received increased attention following the thalidomide tragedy which occurred about a decade ago. The commonest malformations resulting from thalidomide, taken during pregnancy, are those involving the limbs (Smithells, 1962; Leck and Millar, 1962) and there appeared to be no specific relationship of this drug with mental subnormality. Other drugs, however, may have such a relationship. Thiouracil (Elphinstone, 1953), for instance, and also large doses of insulin (Wickes, 1954) administered to pregnant women, have been occasionally associated with the birth of subnormal children. Treatment of mothers during pregnancy with radioactive iodine may result in the birth of children with cretinism, though the diagnosis might not be apparent initially (Green *et al.*, 1971). A retrospective survey by Gal *et al.* (1967) indicated that certain hormonal pregnancy tests might be connected significantly with the birth of some babies with meningomyelocele or hydrocephaly. Apart from the question of therapeutic or diagnostic chemical agents, extensive use of chemicals in agriculture and industry could, in certain circumstances, constitute a danger to the foetus. Reports have been published, for example, of serious neurological abnormalities in infants whose mothers inadvertently ingested, while pregnant, foodstuffs contaminated with mercury (Snyder, 1971). In addition, various deficiencies in the maternal diet may be harmful to the human foetus with the possibility of adverse effects on subsequent mental development (Hepner, 1958).

Deleterious effects on the foetus have been attributed also, from time to time, to various other events occurring during pregnancy. Few of these can be re-garded as established causes of mental subnormality. Among ancient explanations of the origin of foetal defects are supernatural intervention, either by gods or devils, intercourse during menstruation, and unpleasant sights and frights during pregnancy (Pitt, 1962). Claims also have been made that acute maternal anxiety and emotional stress can result in foetal malformation, but evidence for this view is unconvincing. Data bearing on this question have been discussed recently by James (1969). Physical trauma sometimes may cause damage to the foetal nervous system (Hinden, 1965). So may anoxia, and Courville (1959) has considered various circumstances where this could occur. Reduction in such variables as birth weight and head circumference has been noted among children of mothers who smoked during pregnancy (Kullander and Källén, 1971). Possibly harmful consequences of the unsuccessful use of chemical contraceptives and abortifacients deserve fuller study, as do a wide range of other factors.

(2) *Natal causes*

The two events at birth which are especially relevant to the question of causation of cerebral damage, and hence of mental subnormality, are mechanical injury and hypoxia or asphyxia. These events are closely associated, and it is often difficult, in clinical practice, to distinguish the role of each. A further difficulty is that of trying to decide whether evidence of birth trauma or hypoxia in a particular case represents the cause or the consequence of abnormality.

Birth injury is a term which is often used to cover the combined effects of mechanical trauma and of hypoxia or anoxia occurring in relation to the birth process. The types of central nervous system damage which can be a consequence of these occurrences have been reviewed by Towbin (1970). Birth injury has been blamed for anything from under 1 per cent to over 50 per cent of cases of subnormality. In general, the higher estimates have been based on retrospective evidence of obstetrical complications or of neonatal distress in subnormal persons, and in many of these cases a causal connection is not convincingly demonstrated. In a detailed study of 1,280 subnormal patients of all types, Penrose (1938) found only 11 cases (0·9 per cent) whose defect could be regarded, with reasonable certainty, as due to birth injury. He added, however, that trauma may have been an unrecognized aetiological factor in a number of other cases. Drillien (1963) concluded, on the evidence from an extensive longitudinal survey of Edinburgh children, that obstetrical hazard is not a major factor in the causation of gross defect.

The risk of birth injury is increased in premature births and this could be a factor in the poorer mental development that has been noted in prematurely born children, as a group, when compared to children in general. A greater liability for twins to be injured at birth may account also for some of the excess of twins found in subnormal populations (Berg and Kirman, 1960). Other circumstances, often interrelated, which have been considered to have a bearing on the problem of birth injury include maternal age, complications of pregnancy such as toxaemia, birth order, and various abnormalities of presentation and delivery.

(3) *Post-natal causes*

A large number of abnormal events and diseases having their origin in the post-natal environment can be responsible for mental subnormality. Though many of these events and diseases are themselves common, they often do not have an obvious effect on mental function. Variations between individuals in susceptibility to an illness, its severity, and the efficacy of treatment are among the factors which may influence the outcome. Mental retardation, when it does result, varies widely in degree from case to case.

The aetiological significance of post-natal agencies, particularly when they do not operate till a considerable time after birth, is frequently easier to assess than is the case with either pre-natal or natal events. This is because there is the opportunity of observing the child's development before, as well as after, the post-natal hazard occurs. However, the possibility must be considered that some diseases which are determined earlier, for instance certain types of amaurotic idiocy (see p. 89), may show clinical manifestations only some time after the child is born.

Several examples of post-natal causes of subnormality are described individually below and others are referred to in a general section.

Tuberculous meningitis, which was nearly always fatal before modern drugs for the treatment of tuberculosis became available, is now periodically seen as a cause of mental subnormality (see Plate 6). Many children with tuberculous meningitis are treated successfully, but some, who would probably otherwise have died during the acute illness, now survive and show mental and physical abnormalities of varying degrees of severity (Todd and Neville, 1964). Among 800 children with IQs below 50 admitted, from 1949 to 1960, to the Fountain Hospital, London, 11 (1·4 per cent) were considered to owe their subnormality to tuberculous meningitis (Berg, 1962a). Other handicaps in these children included, in order of frequency, spastic paralysis of the limbs, blindness, hydrocephaly, epilepsy and deafness.

Whooping cough encephalopathy is a term which may be used to designate the cerebral involvement which sometimes complicates this infectious fever. As a consequence of such involvement, mental subnormality, behaviour disturbances, epilepsy, paralysis, and impairment of vision and hearing can occur (Berg, 1962b). Definite, though variable, abnormalities are found in the brains of children with neurological complications who do not survive the acute illness. These include haemorrhagic, inflammatory and degenerative changes. Levy and Perry (1948) considered that subnormality seemed to be due to whooping cough in 2 per cent of 1,000 children with IQs of 70 or less in a Washington State institution. By contrast, this cause of subnormality has only very occasionally been established among severely subnormal children in the Fountain Hospital, London. Byers and Rizzo (1950), in a follow-up for several years of thirty-five Boston children who had whooping cough before the age of 2 years, found that six (17 per cent) suffered from intellectual or emotional difficulties of sufficient severity to 'compromise their competitive status'.

Lead poisoning in childhood is rarely reported in Great Britain but many cases have been recorded in some countries, notably the United States, Australia and Japan. Pica is a frequent precursor and painted woodwork is a particularly common source of the lead. The average toddler is said to take some three months to nibble away sufficient lead-containing paint to produce symptoms (Shrand, 1961). Apart from paint, other sources of the metal noted in affected children examined in London include red lead in putty, old battery casings and toys (Moncrieff *et al.*, 1964). Cerebral involvement is relatively common in children; clinical manifestations can include changes of temperament, tremors, convulsions, coma and papilloedema. Patchy, widespread lesions are found in the soft, oedematous brains of children who die during the acute illness (Blackman, 1937). Among persisting abnormalities in survivors are subnormality, behaviour disturbances, paralyses of the limbs, and blindness associated with optic atrophy. Intellectual, emotional and sensori-motor handicaps have been found in cases followed up after apparent complete recovery from the original illness (Byers and Lord, 1943). A useful review has been published by Gibb and MacMahon (1955).

Head injury is not infrequently blamed by parents for subnormality in their offspring. In fact, it is rarely established as the cause of gross mental defect in childhood (Berg, 1960). Less severe post-traumatic effects are commoner. Behaviour disturbances and personality changes leading to poor scholastic achievement were noted by Newell (1937) in five out of twenty persons who had had head injuries. A lasting adverse influence on their school careers was thought by Rowbotham *et al.* (1954) to be likely in eight out of eighty-two children with such injuries. A well-documented recent study of the frequency of acute head injuries and their psychiatric consequences in young schoolchildren has been presented by Rune (1970). It is often said that adults tolerate head injuries less well than children (Glaser and Shafer, 1932; Blau, 1936) so that harmful mental effects may be commoner following cerebral trauma in adulthood. In studies of subnormal patients of all grades and ages, post-natal cerebral trauma was thought to be aetiologically significant in 0·9 per cent of 1,280 cases in Colchester (Penrose, 1938) and in 1·5 per cent of 1,000 cases in New York State (Boldt, 1948).

Other post-natal causes also can be implicated, with a fair degree of certainty, in particular cases of pathological types of mental subnormality.

Various organisms can cause meningitis and lead to subnormality and physical defects similar to those due to the tubercle bacillus. Among these organisms are the pneumococcus, meningococcus, staphylococcus, and the influenza bacillus. Between them, they were responsible for the same percentage of cases of severe subnormality (1·4 per cent) as was due to tuberculous meningitis in the Fountain Hospital series referred to above.

Besides whooping cough, other acute infectious fevers (for instance, measles, chickenpox and scarlet fever) can sometimes be followed by mental deterioration. Careful follow-up of cases which appear to recover completely at the time of the acute illness may show a higher incidence of harmful mental effects than is often assumed to occur. Gibbs *et al.* (1956) did electroencephalographic studies on children with whooping cough, measles and mumps who showed no clinical evidence of neurological involvement during, or immediately after, the acute illness. On the basis of these studies, they thought that in some cases a 'state of disorder' is established which might take months or years to run its full course and which might sometimes manifest itself in clinical disorder long after the acute illness. Immunization against whooping cough very occasionally produces neurological complications, including subnormality, similar to those which can occur with whooping cough itself (Berg, 1958). Mental subnormality has also been noted, though rarely, following vaccination against smallpox.

Many other infections and infestations can result in cerebral damage and thus lead to subnormality. Among the various encephalitides, encephalitis lethargica attracted especial attention because of widespread epidemics of the disease in the earlier part of this century. Manifestations of the condition include antisocial behaviour, intellectual retardation, a mask-like expression, and muscular tremors and rigidity. Cerebral involvement also can complicate disease due to certain parasitic worms, protozoa and fungi, so that these are potential, though rarely implicated, causes of subnormality. Subnormality also has been observed as a sequel to gastro-enteritis accompanied by marked dehydration (Crome, 1952), and gross defect can follow sudden catastrophes, associated with anoxia, such as partial drowning or strangulation, carbon monoxide poisoning, and temporary cardiac arrest.

The effect of psychological and social influences on mental function has evoked a great deal of interest in recent years. Adverse influences in this category can play a role in the production of maladjustment and intellectual impairment and thus can be crucial in regard to a diagnosis of mental subnormality in certain cases. This subject falls outside the scope of the present chapter which is concerned with pathological types of subnormality due to organic disease processes. It is dealt with extensively in other sections of this book. (See Chapters 7 and 8.)

Conclusions

Organic disease or pathology is responsible for nearly all cases of gross mental defect and for some cases in which the defect is relatively mild. The pathological types of mental subnormality determined in this way have been considered in this chapter and shown to be due to the operation of a large number of harmful physical agencies of both genetical and environmental origin.

Clinical evidence of cerebral abnormality, such as paralyses of the limbs and epilepsy, is found in many persons with severe mental subnormality. Cerebral pathology, often widespread and of various kinds, is demonstrable also at post-mortem examination in the great majority of gross defectives (Crome, 1960). Nevertheless, the causes of such pathology, and hence of the subnormality, can be established in the present state of knowledge in only a minority of these cases.

In circumstances relatively favourable for diagnosis because of the availability of a great deal of relevant data, definite causes of, and distinct syndromes closely connected with, subnormality were found in only one-third of 800 children with IQs below 50 (Berg, 1963). If the 175 cases of Down's syndrome in this series of 800 children are excluded, only 100 of the remaining 625 children (16 per cent) are accounted for in terms of aetiology. These data give some impression of the great amount of knowledge that still needs to be accumulated before the causation of pathological types of mental subnormality can be regarded as being satisfactorily understood. It may be added that the causal basis of many clinically distinctive mental retardation syndromes, such as those of de Lange (Berg *et al.*, 1970) and of Rubinstein and Taybi (Rubinstein, 1969), is, thus far, entirely obscure. Even when clear-cut retardation syndromes, known to be closely connected with a specific biological fault, can be recognized, the exact aetiology and pathogenesis of the mental defect in these syndromes is not always altogether clear as yet. The precise reasons why subnormality occurs are still vague in, for instance, conditions associated with chromosomal aberrations and in phenylketonuria.

The problem of the elucidation of the many different causes of pathological types of mental subnormality is deservedly receiving increasing attention from the viewpoint of a variety of scientific disciplines. This problem is, indeed, a fundamental one because understanding of causation is an essential basis for rational preventive and curative measures.

References

ABBASSI, V., LOWE, C. U. and CALCAGNO, P. L. (1968) Oculo-cerebro-renal syndrome: a review. *Amer. J. Dis. Childh.*, **115**, 145–68.

ÅKERRÉN, Y. (1955) Early diagnosis and early therapy in congenital cretinism. *Arch. dis. Childh.*, **30**, 254–6.

ALLAN, J. D., CUSWORTH, D. C., DENT, C. E. and WILSON, V. K. (1958) A disease, probably hereditary, characterized by severe mental deficiency and a constant gross abnormality of amino acid metabolism. *Lancet*, **i**, 182–7.

ARCHIBALD, H. M. (1958) Influence of maternal malaria on newborn infants. *Brit. med. J.*, **2**, 1512–14.

ARIAS, D., PASSARGE, E., ENGLE, M. A. and GERMAN, J. (1970) Human chromosomal deletion: two patients with the 4p-syndrome. *J. Pediat.*, **76**, 82–8.

BAAR, H. S. (1959) Kernicterus. *J. Maine med. Ass.*, **50**, 111–17.

BARDON, L. M. E. (1964) Sicacell treatment of mongolism. *Lancet*, **ii**, 234–5.

BARKLA, D. H. (1966a) Ages of eruption of permanent teeth in mongols. *J. ment. Defic. Res.*, **10**, 190–7.

BARKLA, D. H. (1966b) Congenital absence of permanent teeth in mongols. *J. ment. Defic. Res.*, **10**, 198–203.

BARR, M. L. and BERTRAM, E. G. (1949) A morphological distinction between neurones of the male and female, and the behaviour of the nucleolar satellite during accelerated nucleoprotein synthesis. *Nature* (Lond.), **163**, 676–7.

BEBER, B. A. (1965) Absence of a rib in Down's syndrome. *Lancet*, **ii**, 289.

BELL, J. (1940) A determination of the consanguinity rate in the general hospital population of England and Wales. *Ann. Eugen.*, **10**, 370–91.

BENDA, C. E. (1942) Congenital syphilis in mental deficiency. *Amer. J. ment. Defic.*, **47**, 40–8.

BERG, J. M. (1958) Neurological complications of pertussis immunization. *Brit. med. J.*, **2**, 24–7.

BERG, J. M. (1960) Postnatal head injury as a cause of mental defect. *Arch. Pediat.*, **77**, 207–11.

BERG, J. M. (1962a) Meningitis as a cause of severe mental defect. *Proc. Lond. Conf. Scient. Stud. Ment. Defic.*, *1960*, **1**, 160–4. Dagenham: May & Baker.

BERG, J. M. (1962b) Whooping cough encephalopathy. *Indian Practitioner*, **15**, 559–61.

BERG, J. M. (1963) Causal factors in severe mental retardation. *Proc. 2nd Internat. Congr. Ment. Retard.*, *Vienna, 1961*, **1**, 170–3.

BERG, J. M. and KIRMAN, B. H. (1959) Syphilis as a cause of mental deficiency. *Brit. med. J.*, **2**, 400–4.

BERG, J. M. and KIRMAN, B. H. (1960) The mentally defective twin. *Brit. med. J.*, **1**, 1911–17.

BERG, J. M. and SMITH, G. F. (1971) Behaviour and intelligence in males with XYY sex chromosomes. In PRIMROSE, D. A. (ed.) *Proc. 2nd Congr. Internat. Assoc. Scient. Study Ment. Defic.* Warsaw: Ars Polona; Amsterdam: Swets & Zeitlinger.

BERG, J. M., CROME, L. and FRANCE, N. E. (1960) Congenital cardiac malformations in mongolism. *Brit. Heart J.*, **22**, 331–46.

BERG, J. M., GILDERDALE, S. and WAY, J. (1969) On telling parents of a diagnosis of mongolism. *Brit. J. Psychiat.*, **115**, 1195–6.

BERG, J. M., DELHANTY, J. D. A., FAUNCH, J. A. and RIDLER, M. A. C. (1965) Partial deletion of short arm of a chromosome of the 4–5 group (Denver) in an adult male. *J. ment. Defic. Res.*, **9**, 219–28.

BERG, J. M., KIRMAN, B. H., STERN, J. and MITTWOCH, U. (1961) Treatment of mongolism with pituitary extract. *J. ment. Sci.*, **107**, 475–80.

BERG, J. M., MCCREARY, B. D., RIDLER, M. A. C. and SMITH, G. F. (1970) *The de Lange Syndrome.* Oxford: Pergamon.

BLACKMAN, S. S. (1937) The lesions of lead encephalitis in children. *Bull. Johns Hopk. Hosp.*, **61**, 1–62.

BLANK, C. E. (1960) Apert's syndrome (a type of acrocephalosyndactyly) – observations on a British series of thirty-nine cases. *Ann. hum. Genet.*, **24**, 151–64.

BLAU, A. (1936) Mental changes following head trauma in children. *Arch. Neurol. Psychiat.* (Chicago), **35**, 723–69.

BODIAN, M., WHITE, L. L. R., CARTER, C. O. and LOUW, J. H. (1952) Congenital duodenal obstruction and mongolism. *Brit. med. J.*, **1**, 77–8.

BOLDT, W. H. (1948) Postnatal cerebral trauma as an etiological factor in mental deficiency. *Amer. J. ment. Defic.*, **53**, 247–67.

BÖÖK, J. A., SCHUT, J. W. and REED, S. C. (1953) A clinical and genetical study of microcephaly. *Amer. J. ment. Defic.*, **57**, 637–60.

BOURNEVILLE, D. M. (1880) Sclérose tubéreuse des circonvolutions cérébrales: idiotie et épilepsie hemiplégique. *Arch. Neurol.*, **1**, 81–9.

BREG, W. R., STEELE, M. W., MILLER, O. J., WARBURTON, D., DE CAPOA, A. and ALLDERDICE, P. W. (1970) The cri du chat syndrome in adolescents and adults: clinical findings in 13 older patients with partial deletion of the short arm of chromosome No. 5 (5p−). *J. Pediat.*, **77**, 782–91.

BYERS, R. K. and LORD, E. E. (1943) Late effects of lead poisoning on mental development. *Amer. J. Dis. Childh.*, **66**, 471–94.

BYERS, R. K. and RIZZO, N. D. (1950) A follow-up of pertussis in infancy. *New Engl. J. Med.*, **242**, 887–91.

CAFFEY, J. and ROSS, S. (1956) Mongolism (mongoloid deficiency) during early infancy. Some newly recognized diagnostic changes in the pelvic bones. *Pediatrics*, **17**, 642–51.

CANALE, D., BEBIN, J. and KNIGHTON, R. S. (1964) Neurologic manifestations of von Recklinghausen's disease of the nervous system. *Confin. neurol.* (Basel), **24**, 359–403.

CARR, D. H. (1969) Chromosomal abnormalities in clinical medicine. In STERNBERG, A. G. and BEARN, A. G. (eds.) *Progress in Medical Genetics*, Vol. 6. New York: Grune & Stratton.

CARSON, N. A. J., CUSWORTH, D. C., DENT, C. E., FIELD, C. M. B., NEILL, D. W. and WESTALL, R. G. (1963) Homocystinuria: a new inborn error of metabolism associated with mental deficiency. *Arch. dis. Childh.*, **38**, 425–36.

CARTER, C. O. (1958) A life-table for mongols with the causes of death. *J. ment. Defic. Res.*, **2**, 64–74.

CARTER, C. O. (1962) *Human Heredity*. Harmondsworth: Penguin.

CARTER, C. O. and MACCARTHY, D. (1951) Incidence of mongolism and its diagnosis in the newborn. *Brit. J. prev. soc. Med.*, **5**, 83–90.

CARTER, C. O. and SIMPKISS, M. (1956) The 'carrier' state in nephrogenic diabetes insipidus. *Lancet*, **ii**, 1069–73.

Chicago Conference on Standardization in Human Cytogenetics (1966) *Birth Defects: Original Article Series*, **II** (2). New York: National Foundation.

COFFEY, V. P. and JESSOP, W. J. E. (1959) Maternal influenza and congenital deformities: a prospective study. *Lancet*, **ii**, 935–8.

COFFEY, V. P. and JESSOP, W. J. E. (1963) Maternal influenza and congenital deformities: a follow-up study. *Lancet*, **i**, 748–51.

COLLMANN, R. D. and STOLLER, A. (1962a) Notes on the epidemiology of mongolism in Victoria, Australia, from 1942 to 1957. *Proc. Lond. Conf. Scient. Stud. Ment. Defic.*, *1960*, **2**, 517–26. Dagenham: May & Baker.

COLLMANN, R. D. and STOLLER, A. (1962b) A survey of mongoloid births in Victoria, Australia, 1942–1957. *Amer. J. Publ. Hlth*, **52**, 813–29.

COURT BROWN, W. M. (1968) Males with an XYY sex chromosome complement. *J. med. Genet.*, **5**, 341–59.

COURT BROWN, W. M. (1969) Sex chromosome aneuploidy in man and its frequency, with special reference to mental subnormality and criminal behavior. *Int. Rev. exp. Path.*, **7**, 31–97.

COURVILLE, C. B. (1959) Antenatal and paranatal circulatory disorders as a cause of cerebral damage in early life. *J. Neuropath.*, **18**, 115–40.

COUTTS, N. A. and FYFE, W. M. (1971) Classical and mild phenylketonuria in a family. *Arch. dis. Childh.*, **46**, 550–2.

COUVREUR, J. and DESMONTS, G. (1962) Congenital and maternal toxoplasmosis: a review of 300 congenital cases. *Developm. med. Child. Neurol.*, **4**, 519–30.

CROME, L. (1952) Encephalopathy following infantile gastro-enteritis. *Arch. dis. Childh.*, **27**, 468–72.

CROME, L. (1957) The pathology of certain syndromes. In HILLIARD, L. T. and KIRMAN, B. H. (eds.) *Mental Deficiency*. London: Churchill.

CROME, L. (1960) The brain and mental retardation. *Brit. med. J.*, **1**, 897–904.

CROME, L. (1961) Cytomegalic inclusion-body disease. *Wld Neurol.*, **2**, 447–58.

CROME, L. and PARE, C. M. R. (1960) Phenylketonuria, a review and a report of the pathological findings in four cases. *J. ment. Sci.*, **106**, 862–83.

DE GROUCHY, J., ROYER, P., SALMON, C. and LAMY, M. (1964) Délétion partielle des bras longs du chromosome 18. *Path. Biol.* (Paris), **12**, 579–82.

DODGE, H. W., WOOD, M. W. and KENNEDY, R. L. J. (1959) Craniofacial dysostosis: Crouzon's disease. *Pediatrics*, **23**, 98–106.

DOLL, R., HILL, A. B. and SAKULA, J. (1960) Asian influenza in pregnancy and congenital defects. *Brit. J. prev. soc. Med.*, **14**, 167–72.

DOWN, J. L. H. (1866) Observation on an ethnic classification of idiots. *Lond. Hosp. Rep.*, **3**, 259–62.

DRILLIEN, C. M. (1963) Obstetric hazard, mental retardation and behaviour disturbance in primary school. *Developm. med. Child. Neurol.*, **5**, 3–13.

DUNSDON, M. I., CARTER, C. O. and HUNTLEY, R. M. C. (1960) Upper end of range of intelligence in mongolism. *Lancet*, **i**, 565–8.

EDWARDS, J. H., NORMAN, R. M. and ROBERTS, J. M. (1961) Sex-linked hydrocephalus: report of a family with 15 affected members. *Arch. dis. Childh.*, **36**, 481–5.

EDWARDS, J. H., HARNDEN, D. G., CAMERON, A. H., CROSSE, V. M. and WOLFF, O. H. (1960) A new trisomic syndrome. *Lancet*, **i**, 787–90.

ELLIS, R. W. B., SHELDON, W. and CAPON, N. B. (1936) Gargoylism (chondro-osteo-dystrophy, corneal opacities, hepatosplenomegaly and mental deficiency). *Quart. J. Med.*, **5**, 119–35.

ELLIS, J. R., MARSHALL, R. and PENROSE, L. S. (1962) An aberrant small acrocentric chromosome. *Ann. hum. Genet.*, **26**, 77–83.

ELPHINSTONE, N. (1953) Thiouracil in pregnancy – its effect on the foetus. *Lancet*, **i**, 1281–3.

FINLAYSON, A. (1955) Tuberous sclerosis. *Amer. J. ment. Defic.*, **59**, 617–28.

FINN, R. (1970) The prevention of Rhesus haemolytic disease. In APLEY, J. (ed.) *Modern Trends in Paediatrics*, Vol. 3. London: Butterworth.

FÖLLING, A. (1934) Über Ausscheidung von Phenylbrenztraubensäure in den Harn als Stoffwechselanomalie in Verbindung mit Imbezillität. *Hoppe-Seyler's Z. physiol. Chem.*, **227**, 169–76.

FORD, C. E., JONES, K. W., MILLER, O. J., MITTWOCH, U., PENROSE, L. S., RIDLER, M. and SHAPIRO, A. (1959) The chromosomes in a patient showing both mongolism and the Klinefelter syndrome. *Lancet*, **i**, 709–10.

FORREST, J. M. and MENSER, M. A. (1970) Congenital rubella in schoolchildren and adolescents. *Arch. dis. Childh.*, **45**, 63–9.

FREDERICKSON, D. S. and TRAMS, E. G. (1966) Ganglioside lipidosis: Tay-Sachs disease. In STANBURY, J. B., WYNGAARDEN, J. B. and FREDERICKSON, D. S. (eds.) *The Metabolic Basis of Inherited Disease* (2nd edn). New York: McGraw-Hill.

GAL, I., KIRMAN, B. and STERN, J. (1967) Hormonal pregnancy tests and congenital malformation. *Nature* (Lond.), **216**, 83.

GARLAND, H. and MOORHOUSE, D. (1953) An extremely rare recessive hereditary syndrome including cerebellar ataxia, oligophrenia, cataract and other features. *J. Neurol. Psychiat.*, **16**, 110–16.

GIBB, J. W. G. and MACMAHON, J. F. (1955) Arrested mental development induced by lead poisoning. *Brit. med. J.*, **i**, 320–3.

GIBBS, E. L., GIBBS, F. A. and GROSSMAN, H. (1956) Electroencephalographic evidence of encephalitis in children with supposedly uncomplicated childhood diseases. *Trans. Amer. neurol. Ass.*, 81st Annual Meeting.

GLASER, L. H. (1958) A case of nephrogenic diabetes insipidus. *Brit. med. J.*, **2**, 780–1.

GLASER, M. A. and SHAFER, F. P. (1932) Skull and brain traumas; their sequelae. *J. Amer. med. Ass.*, **98**, 271–6.

GOLDSTEIN, L. (1930) Radiogenic microcephaly. *Arch. Neurol. Psychiat.*, **24**, 102–15.

GREEN, H. G., GAREIS, F. J., SHEPARD, T. H. and KELLEY, V. C.
(1971) Cretinism associated with maternal sodium iodide I 131 therapy
during pregnancy. *Amer. J. Dis. Childh.*, **122**, 247–9.

GREGG, N. M. (1941) Congenital cataract following German measles in the
mother. *Trans. ophthal. Soc. Aust.*, **3**, 35–46.

HARDY, J. B. (1965) Viral infection in pregnancy: a review. *Amer. J. Obstet.
Gynec.*, **93**, 1052–65.

HARRIS, H. (1970) *The Principles of Human Biochemical Genetics.*
Amsterdam: North-Holland Publishing Co.

HARRIS, H., PENROSE, L. S. and THOMAS, D. H. H. (1959) Cystathioninuria. *Ann. hum. Genet.*, **23**, 442–53.

HAUSCHKA, T. S., HASSON, J. E., GOLDSTEIN, M. N., KOEPF, G. F.
and SANDBERG, A. A. (1962) An XYY man with progeny indicating
familial tendency to non-disjunction. *Amer. J. hum. Genet.*, **14**,
22–30.

HEPNER, R. (1958) Maternal nutrition and the fetus. *J. Amer. Med. Assoc.*,
168, 1774–7.

HINDEN, E. (1965) External injury causing foetal deformity. *Arch. dis.
Childh.*, **40**, 80–1.

HOEFNAGEL, D., ANDREW, E. D., MIREAULT, N. G. and BERNDT,
W. O. (1965) Hereditary choreoathetosis, self-mutilation and hyperuricemia in young males. *New Engl. J. Med.*, **273**, 130–5.

HSU, T. C. (1973) Longitudinal differentiation of chromosomes. In ROMAN,
H. L., SANDLER, L. M. and CAMPBELL, A. (eds.) *Ann. Rev. Genet.*,
7, 153–76.

HUBBLE, D. V. (1953) Endocrine disorders. In MONCRIEFF, A. and EVANS,
P. (ed.) *Diseases of Children* (5th edn). London: Edward Arnold.

INSLEY, J. (1967) Syndrome associated with a deficiency of part of the long
arm of chromosome No. 18. *Arch. dis. Childh.*, **42**, 140–6.

JACOBS, P. A., BRUNTON, M., MELVILLE, M. M., BRITTAIN, R. P.
and MCCLEMONT, W. F. (1965) Aggressive behaviour, mental subnormality and the XYY male. *Nature* (Lond.), **208**, 1351–2.

JAMES, W. H. (1969) The effect of maternal psychological stress on the
foetus. *Brit. J. Psychiat.*, **115**, 811–25.

JOHNSTON, A. W., FERGUSON-SMITH, M. A., HANDMAKER, S. D.,
JONES, H. W. and JONES, G. S. (1961) The triple-X syndrome.
Clinical, pathological and chromosomal studies in three mentally
retarded cases. *Brit. med. J.*, **2**, 1046–52.

KALTER, H. (1968) *Teratology of the Central Nervous System.* Chicago:
Univ. of Chicago Press.

KIRMAN, B. H. (1955) Rubella as a cause of mental deficiency. *Lancet*, **ii**,
1113–15.

KIRMAN, B. H. (1957) In HILLIARD, L. T. and KIRMAN, B. H. (eds.)
Mental Deficiency. London: Churchill.

KIRMAN, B. H., BLACK, J. A., WILKINSON, R. H. and EVANS, P. R. (1956) Familial pitressin-resistant diabetes insipidus with mental defect. *Arch. dis. Childh.*, **31**, 59–66.

KLINEFELTER, H. F., REIFENSTEIN, E. C. and ALBRIGHT, F. (1942) Syndrome characterized by gynecomastia, aspermatogenesis without a-leydigism, and increased excretion of follicle-stimulating hormone. *J. clin. Endocr.*, **2**, 615–27.

KOMAI, T., KISHIMOTO, K. and OSAKI, Y. (1955) Genetic study of microcephaly based on Japanese material. *Amer. J. hum. Genet.*, **7**, 51–65.

KRIVIT, W. and GOOD, R. A. (1957) Simultaneous occurrence of mongolism and leukemia. *A.M.A.J. dis. Child.*, **94**, 289–93.

KULLANDER, S. and KÄLLÉN, B. (1971) A prospective study of smoking and pregnancy. *Acta obstet. gynec. scand.*, **50**, 83–94.

LAWSON, D. (1955) On the prognosis of cretinism. *Arch. dis. Childh.*, **30**, 75–82.

LAXOVA, R., MCKEOWN, J. A., SALDAÑA, P. and TIMOTHY, J. A. D. (1971) A case of XYY Down's syndrome confirmed by autoradiography. *J. med. Genet.*, **8**, 215–19.

LECK, I. M. and MILLAR, E. L. M. (1962) Incidence of malformations since the introduction of thalidomide. *Brit. med. J.*, **2**, 16–20.

LEJEUNE, J., GAUTIER, M. and TURPIN, R. (1959) Etudes des chromosomes somatiques de neuf enfants mongoliens. *C.R. Acad. Sci.* (Paris), **248**, 1721–2.

LEJEUNE, J., LAFOURCADE, J., BERGER, R., VIALATTE, J., BOESWILLWALD, M., SERINGE, P. and TURPIN, R. (1963) Trois cas de délétion partielle du bras court d'un chromosome 5. *C.R. Acad. Sci. Paris*, **257**, 3098–102.

LEJEUNE, J., LAFOURCADE, J., DE GROUCHY, J., BERGER, R., GAUTIER, M., SALMON, C. and TURPIN, R. (1964) Délétion partielle du bras court du chromosome 5. Individualisation d'un nouvel état morbide. *Sem. Hôp. Paris*, **40**, 1069–79.

LESCH, M. and NYHAN, W. L. (1964) A familial disorder of uric acid metabolism and central nervous system function. *Amer. J. Med.*, **36**, 561–70.

LEVY, S. and PERRY, H. A. (1948) Pertussis as a cause of mental deficiency. *Amer. J. ment. Defic.*, **52**, 217–26.

LEWIS, E. O. (1933) Types of mental deficiency and their social significance. *J. ment. Sci.*, **79**, 298–304.

LOWE, C. U., TERREY, M. and MACLACHLAN, E. A. (1952) Organic-aciduria, decreased renal ammonia production, hydrophthalmos, and mental retardation. *Amer. J. Dis. Childh.*, **83**, 164–84.

MCKUSICK, V. A. (1968) *Mendelian Inheritance in Man: Catalogs of Autosomal Dominant, Autosomal Recessive, and X-linked Phenotypes* (2nd edn). Baltimore: Johns Hopkins Press.

MCKUSICK, V. A. (1969) The nosology of the mucopolysaccharidoses. *Amer. J. Med.*, **47**, 730–47.

MCKUSICK, V. A., MAHLOUDJI, M., ABBOT, M. H., LINDENBERG, R. and KEPAS, D. (1967) Seckel's bird-headed dwarfism. *New Engl. J. Med.*, **277**, 279–86.

MACLEAN, N., MITCHELL, J. M., HARNDEN, D. G., WILLIAMS, J., JACOBS, P. A., BUCKTON, K. A., BAIKIE, A. G., COURT BROWN, W. M., MCBRIDE, J. A., STRONG, J. A., CLOSE, H. G. and JONES, D. C. (1962) A survey of sex-chromosome abnormalities among 4514 mental defectives. *Lancet*, **i**, 293–6.

MARINELLO, M. J., BERKSON, R. A., EDWARDS, J. A. and BANNERMAN, R. M. (1969) A study of the XYY syndrome in tall men and juvenile delinquents. *J. Amer. med. Assoc.*, **208**, 321–5.

MENKES, J. H., HURST, P. L. and CRAIG, J. M. (1954) A new syndrome: progressive familial infantile cerebral dysfunction associated with an unusual urinary substance. *Pediatrics*, **14**, 462–7.

MIGEON, B. R. (1966) Short arm deletions in group E and chromosomal 'deletion' syndromes. *J. Pediat.*, **69**, 432–8.

MILLER, O. J., BREG, W. R., WARBURTON, D., MILLER, D. A., DE CAPOA, A., ALLDERDICE, P. W., DAVIS, J., KLINGER, H. P., MCGILVRAY, E. and ALLEN, F. H. (1970) Partial deletion of the short arm of chromosome No. 4 (4p−): clinical studies in five unrelated patients. *J. Pediat.*, **77**, 792–9.

MONCRIEFF, A. A., KOUMIDES, O. P., CLAYTON, B. E., PATRICK, A. D., RENWICK, A. G. C. and ROBERTS, G. E. (1964) Lead poisoning in children. *Arch. dis. Childh.*, **39**, 1–13.

MILUNSKY, A. (1973) *The Prenatal Diagnosis of Hereditary Disorders.* Springfield, Ill.: Charles C. Thomas.

MURPHY, D. P. (1928) Ovarian irradiation; its effect on the health of subsequent children. *Surg. Gynec. Obstet.*, **47**, 201–15.

MURPHY, D. P. (1929) The outcome of 625 pregnancies in women subjected to pelvic radium or roentgen irradiation. *Amer. J. Obstet. Gynec.*, **18**, 179–87.

NEEL, J. V. (1954) Problems in the estimation of the frequency of uncommon inherited traits. *Amer. J. hum. Genet.*, **6**, 51–60.

NEWELL, H. W. (1937) The effect of head injury on the behavior and personality of children: a study of 20 cases. *Med. Clin. N. Amer.*, **21**, 1335–65.

OYANAGI, K., MIURA, R. and YAMANOUCHI, T. (1970) Congenital lysinuria: a new inherited transport disorder of dibasic amino acids *J. Pediat.*, **77**, 259–66.

Paris Conference on Standardization in Human Cytogenetics (1971) *Birth Defects: Original Article Series*, **viii** (7). New York: National Foundation.

PATAU, K., SMITH, D. W., THERMAN, E., INHORN, S. L. and
WAGNER, H. P. (1960) Multiple congenital anomaly caused by an extra
autosome. *Lancet,* **i,** 790–3.

PEARSON, P. L., BOBROW, M. and VOSA, C. G. (1970) Technique for
identifying Y chromosomes in human interphase nuclei. *Nature* (Lond.),
226, 78–80.

PENROSE, L. S. (1938) A clinical and genetic study of 1280 cases of mental
defect. *Sp. Rep. Ser., Med. Res. Coun.,* No. 229. London: HMSO.

PENROSE, L. S. (1963a) *The Biology of Mental Defect.* London: Sidgwick &
Jackson.

PENROSE, L. S. (1963b) *Outline of Human Genetics* (2nd edn). London:
Heinemann.

PENROSE, L. S. (1963c) Finger-prints, palms and chromosomes. *Nature,*
197, 933–8.

PENROSE, L. S. (1963d) Paternal age in mongolism. *Lancet,* **i,** 1101.

PENROSE, L. S. (1966) Dermatoglyphic patterns in large acrocentric trisomy.
J. ment. Defic. Res., **10,** 1–18.

PENROSE, L. S. and SMITH, G. F. (1966) *Down's Anomaly.* London:
Churchill.

PITT, D. B. (1961) Congenital malformations and maternal rubella: progress
report. *Med. J. Aust.,* **1,** 881–90.

PITT, D. B. (1962) Congenital malformations: a review. *Med. J. Aust.,* **1,**
82–7, 121–4.

PITT, D. B. (1971) The natural history of untreated phenylketonuria. *Med.
J. Aust.,* **1,** 378–83.

PLUMMER, G. (1952) Anomalies occurring in children exposed *in utero* to
the atomic bomb in Hiroshima. *Pediatrics,* **10,** 687–93.

PREISER, S. A. and DAVENPORT, C. B. (1918) Multiple neurofibromatosis
(von Recklinghausen's disease) and its inheritance: with description of a
case. *Amer. J. med. Sci.,* **156,** 507–40.

ROBBINS, F. C. and HEGGIE, A. D. (1970) The rubella problem. In
FRASER, F. C., MCKUSICK, V. A. and ROBINSON, R. (eds.)
*Congenital Malformations: Proceedings of Third International Conference,
The Hague, Netherlands, September 1969.* Amsterdam: Excerpta Medica.

ROBERTS, J. A. F. (1970) *An Introduction to Medical Genetics* (5th edn).
London: Oxford Univ. Press.

ROE, T. F., HALLATT, J. G., DONNELL, G. N. and NG, W. G. (1971)
Childbearing by a galactosemic woman. *J. Pediat.,* **78,** 1026–30.

ROSENBERG, L. E. and SCRIVER, C. R. (1969) Disorders of amino acid
metabolism. In BONDY, P. K. (ed.) *Duncan's Diseases of Metabolism*
(6th edn). Philadelphia: W. B. Saunders.

ROWBOTHAM, G. F., MACIVER, I. V., DICKSON, J. and BOUSFIELD,
M. E. (1954) Analysis of 1400 cases of acute injury to the head. *Brit.
med. J.,* **1,** 726–30.

RUBINSTEIN, J. H. (1969) The broad thumbs syndrome – progress report 1968. *Birth Defects: Original Article Series*, **5** (2), 25–41.

RUESS, A. L. and ROSENTHAL, I. M. (1963) Intelligence in nephrogenic diabetes insipidus. *Amer. J. Dis. Childh.*, **105**, 358–63.

RUNE, V. (1970) Acute head injuries in children: an epidemiologic, child psychiatric and electroencephalographic study of primary school children in Umeå. *Acta Paediat. scand.*, Suppl. 209, 1–122.

SHANNON, M. W. and NADLER, H. L. (1968) X-linked hydrocephalus. *J. med. Genet.*, **5**, 326–8.

SHAPIRO, S. L., SHEPPARD, G. L., DREIFUSS, F. E. and NEWCOMBE, D. S. (1966) X-linked recessive inheritance of a syndrome of mental retardation with hyperuricemia. *Proc. Soc. exp. Biol. Med.*, **122**, 609–11.

SHERLOCK, E. B. (1911) *The Feeble-Minded*. London: Macmillan.

SHRAND, H. (1961) Treatment of lead poisoning with intramuscular edathamil calcium-disodium. *Lancet*, **i**, 310–12.

SIGLER, A. T., LILIENFELD, A. M., COHEN, B. H. and WESTLAKE, J. E. (1965) Radiation exposure in parents of children with mongolism (Down's syndrome). *Bull. Johns Hopk. Hosp.*, **117**, 374–99.

SIRKIN, J. (1944) Acrocephalosyndactylia: report of a case. *Amer. J. ment. Defic.*, **48**, 335–8.

SJÖGREN, T. (1931) Die juvenile amaurotische Idiotie. *Hereditas*, **14**, 197–426.

SMITHELLS, R. W. (1962) Thalidomide and malformations in Liverpool. *Lancet*, **i**, 1270–3.

SNYDER, R. D. (1971) Congenital mercury poisoning. *New Engl. J. Med.*, **284**, 1014–16.

STANBURY, J. B. (1966) Familial goiter. In STANBURY, J. B., WYNGAARDEN, J. B. and FREDERICKSON, D. S. (eds.) *The Metabolic Basis of Inherited Disease* (2nd edn). New York: McGraw-Hill.

STOLLER, A. and COLLMANN, R. D. (1965) Incidence of infective hepatitis followed by Down's syndrome nine months later. *Lancet*, **ii**, 1221–3.

TAYLOR, A. I. (1967) Patau's, Edwards' and cri du chat syndromes: a tabulated summary of current findings. *Developm. med. Child Neurol.*, **9**, 78–86.

TAYLOR, A. I. (1968) Autosomal trisomy syndromes: a detailed study of 27 cases of Edwards' syndrome and 27 cases of Patau's syndrome. *J. med. Genet.*, **5**, 227–52.

THOMPSON, J. S. and THOMPSON, M. W. (1973) *Genetics in Medicine* (2nd edn). Philadelphia: W. B. Saunders.

TODD, R. MCL. and NEVILLE, J. G. (1964) The sequelae of tuberculous meningitis. *Arch. dis. Childh.*, **39**, 213–25.

TOWBIN, A. (1970) Central nervous system damage in the human fetus and newborn infant: mechanical and hypoxic injury, incurred in the fetal-neonatal period. *Amer. J. Dis. Childh.*, **119**, 529–42.

VAN DEN BOSCH, J. (1959) Microcephaly in the Netherlands: a clinical and genetical study. *Ann. hum. Genet.*, **23**, 91–116.

VULLIAMY, D. G. and NORMANDALE, P. A. (1966) Cranio-facial dysostosis in a Dorset family. *Arch. dis. Childh.*, **41**, 375–82.

WALSH, M. N., KOCH, F. L. P. and BRUNSTING, B. A. (1938) The syndrome of tuberous sclerosis, retinal tumors, and adenoma sebaceum: report of case. *Proc. Mayo Clin.*, **13**, 155–60.

WERTELECKI, W., SCHINDLER, A. M. and GERALD, P. S. (1966) Partial deletion of chromosome 18. *Lancet*, **ii**, 641.

WEST, J. R. and KRAMER, J. G. (1955) Nephrogenic diabetes insipidus. *Pediatrics*, **15**, 424–32.

WICKES, I. G. (1954) Foetal defects following insulin coma therapy in early pregnancy. *Brit. med. J.*, **2**, 1029–30.

WOOD, J. W., JOHNSON, K. G. and OMORI, Y. (1967) In utero exposure to the Hiroshima atomic bomb: an evaluation of head size and mental retardation twenty years later. *Pediatrics*, **39**, 385–92.

YAMAZAKI, J. N., WRIGHT, S. W. and WRIGHT, P. M. (1954) Outcome of pregnancy in women exposed to the atomic bomb in Nagasaki. *Amer. J. Dis. Childh.*, **87**, 448–63.

YU, J. S. and O'HALLORAN, M. T. (1970) Children of mothers with phenylketonuria. *Lancet*, **i**, 210–12.

ZAPPELLA, M. and COWIE, V. (1962) A note on time of diagnosis in mongolism. *J. ment. Defic. Res.*, **6**, 82–6.

ZAPPERT, J. (1926) Über rontgenogene fotale mikrozephalie. *Arch. Kinderheilk.*, **80**, 34–50.

5

B. H. Kirman

Individual differences
in the mentally subnormal

Introduction

It is a truism that all men are different. Of recent years there has been an enormous growth in the numbers of mankind. However, the genetic mechanism is so complex that no two people are identical in their genetic endowment (Dobzhansky, 1964).[1] The impact of the early environment may create considerable birth weight or other differences between identical twins (Penrose, 1963) who may later show appreciable differences in intelligence amounting, in extreme cases, to one being ranked mentally deficient and the other normal (Hobbs, 1941; Lewis, 1936; Penrose, 1937; Brandon *et al.*, 1959). The birth process itself places the second twin at a disadvantage and may predispose to mental handicap in twins (Berg and Kirman, 1961). At a later stage the structural differences between individuals are compounded by social differences; thus the Chronicles not only list the names of the descendants of Adam but identify some as belonging to the families of those 'that wrought fine linen' and others 'were the potters, and those that dwelt among plants and hedges'. From the beginning of human social development the interaction between structure and function must have been influenced by occupation, social status and artificial environment. A recent variation on the proverbial madness of the hatter has been the outbreak of Minamata disease (Miller, 1967). This term has been coined because a number of expectant mothers in Japan had eaten fish from a bay of that name, the fish having been contaminated with methyl mercury. They gave birth to children with brain abnormalities which were attributed to the effect of the mercury intake. This example shows that mercury in particular and pollution in general can have an untoward effect on the development of the unborn child. This warning is underlined by the recent publicity given to the dangerous levels of methyl mercury in tuna fish from the open ocean.

Clinical conditions

In considering mental handicap, the parent, teacher and psychiatrist are primarily concerned with behaviour and its variations. Abnormalities in structure, as

[1] With the exception of uniovular twins.

reflected in clinical diagnoses and classifications are of interest, but of limited practical importance as a guide to action. The interplay of factors mentioned above, the relationship between biological structure on the one hand and the social environment on the other, dictate normal variations in behaviour and intellectual attainment. This applies also to mental retardation, though with the grosser degrees of handicap there is more evidence of major single determinants and of qualitative alterations in structure. None the less a majority of cases of severe degrees of mental handicap remain undiagnosed at a clinical level or even at autopsy (Berg and Kirman, 1959a, b; Crome and Stern, 1967; Angeli and Kirman, 1970, 1971; Kirman, 1970, 1972; Angeli, 1971).

DOWN'S SYNDROME

Down (1866) noticed the structural similarity of a number of children some of whom had previously been described by Séguin (1843) as 'furfuraceous cretins'. His notion that they had some genetic similarity was confirmed in 1959 by the discovery in France of the 47th chromosome in affected infants (Lejeune *et al.*, 1959). The history of this syndrome illustrates the usual steps in scientific biology as applied to the study of the mentally retarded: first the collection of material, the attempts at classification, followed by a multitude of hypotheses to explain the dynamics of the phenomenon. Of these last, Penrose's (1933) suggestion that the condition was linked to maternal age held the key to aetiology. It is a cliché that the exception proves the rule, but it remains true. Investigation of children, born to young mothers, with the condition showed an undue proportion with 46 chromosomes including a translocated 21. The rule is that the condition occurs in association with high maternal age and is due to trisomy 21 whilst the exceptions are commonly in children of young mothers with translocation. Only the latter carry an increased risk of another child being affected (Berg and Kirman, 1961; Carter and Evans, 1961). These differences in genetic basis for the condition do not seem to be reflected in any psychological difference. Yet another exception is the case of mosaicism which permits every possible degree of dilution of the syndrome by normality.

The presence of an entity such as Down's syndrome only determines one element in the complex which forms the individual. Admittedly in this case the interference with normal development is gross and the effect of the additional acrocentric chromosome, small though it is, disrupts every aspect of normality. Stunting of physical growth is one of the most obvious consequences but shortening of life expectation is equally obvious. Despite the reduction in mortality (Carter, 1958) half the children with Down's syndrome are dead by age 5 years (Collmann and Stoller, 1963). However, it is in this respect that the tremendous individual variation in effect is best shown. At birth the incidence of Down's syndrome is about 1 in 600 live births, but the incidence at conception is probably of the order of 1 in 200 (Penrose and Smith, 1966). In a considerable number of cases the effect of the additional genetic material is such as to produce an early spontaneous abortion. In children who die in infancy with Down's syndrome there is often a heart lesion or other additional abnormality (Berg *et al.*, 1960). Even after infancy the expectation of life is far from normal. The majority of a cohort is dead by 50 but there are some individuals who reach the age of 70 or more.

There is considerable range in the expression of other physical features of the condition such as epicanthus (Donoghue, 1965): for example, a minority are not brachycephalic. But it has never been shown that there is any correlation between the extent of the expression of the physical abnormalities (mosaics excepted) and the psychological aspects of the condition. In regard to intelligence there is a very wide range of impact. In a recent study of the age of development of walking (Donoghue *et al.*, 1970), we found that the average age for children with Down's syndrome was 3·2 years, but two patients had not walked at 16 and 14 years respectively. This variation may be due in part to modification of the effect of the additional chromosome by the remainder of the genetic material inherited by the individual. In part it may be due to super-added problems. Children with Down's syndrome are not immune to perinatal damage, on the contrary they may be more prone to this. The brain sometimes sustains further damage, particularly in cases with a patent interventricular septum from an embolism (Crome, 1965). Epilepsy is not common in Down's syndrome but it does occur and may indicate such additional brain damage (Kirman, 1951). The frequent respiratory and other somatic illnesses which occur in conjunction with Down's syndrome may in some cases impair mental development. The writer has the impression that early hospitalized cases thrive less well and there is some evidence to connect an excessive mortality among the severely handicapped in general with admission to an overcrowded institution (Lind and Kirman, 1958).

Walking does not correlate very well with other attainments in the sense that some children who later prove to be profoundly retarded walk early whilst some of high intelligence walk late. There is, however, evidence that among ordinary children there is an impact on age of walking of socio-cultural conditions (Hindley *et al.*, 1966). In our study on walking mentioned above we found a suggestion that children with Down's syndrome committed to institutions at an early age walked later than those who began to walk at home. An element of selection may be involved. In regard to more socially conditioned activities such as talking the evidence is definite, showing that individual differences in this respect in children with Down's syndrome can be determined by the mode of upbringing, though as a group their speech is less well developed than that of other children with a comparable mental age (Lyle, 1959a, b, 1960). Some patients with Down's syndrome are profoundly retarded and are incapable of self care, a majority are trainable and become capable of sheltered work, a small minority achieve a level of measured intelligence in the mildly retarded range, perhaps 2 to 3 per cent (Evans and Carter, 1954). The ability to write more than a few relevant words is rarely developed, but a striking exception is Nigel Hunt whose book (1967) received much publicity.

An interesting phenomenon which may not be peculiar to children with Down's syndrome but is certainly well developed in them is an apparent sharp decline in intelligence in infancy. Assessments of babies often differ little from the norm, but at the age of 2 to 3 years a marked deficit may be obvious (Carr, 1970). If this represents genuine organic deterioration then it is possible that some of the difference between individual patients with Down's syndrome may be determined at this stage. It seems more likely, in the present state of our knowledge, that the deficit in Down's syndrome is made more obvious as assessment is applied at a later age to different functions which are more impaired than those which are used as a basis for assessment in the young infant, and which may be relatively undamaged. This may be connected with the relative specificity of cerebral changes in the syndrome, i.e. a greater reduction in the size of the brain stem and cerebellum than of the cerebral hemispheres (Davidoff, 1928) with impairment of phylogenetically recent structures in the cerebellum.

The literature is full of accounts which attribute special character traits to children with Down's syndrome, e.g. that they are fond of music, good at mimicry etc. It is difficult to validate these objectively. Apart from certain physiological differences from other trainable patients such as a skin resistance more like the normal, Hermelin and O'Connor (1963) found that eye movements were more frequent in children with Down's syndrome. They found also that they were worse in tactile discrimination and reproduction of designs (O'Connor and Hermelin, 1961; Hermelin and O'Connor, 1961). These authors suggest the possibility that low muscle tone may be related to the relative slowness in reaction time shown by these patients (Berkson, 1960). Certainly of all the neurological features of Down's syndrome in infancy this is the most regular and constant (Cowie, 1970). It should, therefore, be of interest to follow the results of the trial of administration of 5-hydroxytryptophane to infants with the condition (Bazelon *et al.*, 1967) if this is continued. This substance corrects the deficiency of 5-hydroxytrypamine in these subjects and can restore their muscle tone to normal.

As to differences in character and temperament between patients with this syndrome and others similarly retarded, a number of workers have failed to find convincing evidence (Rollin, 1946; Blacketter-Simmonds, 1953; Marrs, 1955). Attempts to define particular patterns of behaviour in relation to other syndromes rest on an even more slender foundation.

LESCH–NYHAN SYNDROME

This is a form of congenital hyperuricaemia which is sex-linked and therefore shows only in boys. It is due to a faulty enzyme and for some reason which is not understood it produces a tendency to self-mutilation in addition to severe mental retardation. Affected individuals may chew away whole areas of the lips (Lesch and Nyhan, 1964; Nyhan *et al.*, 1965). In this particular case there does seem to be a genuine association between a diagnosable disease entity and a particular type of behaviour, but this is exceptional and rare. Most of the other suggested associations must be regarded as not proven. Recently Professor Nyhan and the writer and their colleagues reported two cases of the Cornelia de Lange or Amsterdam type of dwarfism with self-destructive behaviour, but this is most likely coincidental (Shear *et al.*, 1971). Other cases reported have not shown this type of behaviour. Another condition associated with self-destruction is congenital insensitivity to pain (Kirman and Bicknell, 1968). This is not an entity but rather a miscellaneous group of conditions including some genetic anomalies. The self-destruction in these cases may be regarded as accidental rather than the result of a particular form of behaviour, and in this respect is like the damage to the joints and bones and other tissues which leads to the premature death of affected people.

MICROCEPHALY

Smallheadedness is not a diagnostic entity, though some authors like to distinguish 'true' microcephaly with a relatively long head and attributed to a recessive mode of inheritance. There are probably several different genetic forms of microcephaly as well as many environmental factors which interfere with brain growth, such as rubella (Gregg, 1941). Exposure to x-rays (Murphy, 1929), to atomic radiation (Hollingsworth, 1960), to toxoplasma and the cyto-megalic virus (Stern *et al.*, 1969) will produce this effect among other agents. The writer has not found genetically determined forms of microcephaly to be distinguishable anatomically from those which are caused by environmental factors (Brandon *et al.*, 1959). Penrose (1963), however, believes that recessive true microcephaly is a highly characteristic condition, patients being below average stature but active and physically fairly healthy, the body, apart from the cranium, being well developed with normal musculature. He mentions that 'some of these patients make quick, furtive movements which, together with their stooping posture, are reminiscent of some of the lower animals, and they were called "bird men" by Lombroso'. He adds that 'psychologically, true micro-cephalics found in hospitals for the mentally subnormal are usually of the low imbecile grade. Though reputed to be querulous and bad-tempered, if well treated they are among the happiest and most harmless of patients.'

As mentioned, genetic forms of microcephaly are many, one of the aspects of the sex-linked condition described by Dunn *et al.* (1963) being reduction in head size. In any one of these the variation in intelligence from one case to another is likely to be very considerable. In our study we found examples of retarded sibs, one of whom ranked as microcephalic by our standards while another fell just outside our criterion. This variation in physical expression is matched by variation in the effect on intelligence. The character traits attributed to the microcephalic in the description quoted above are very non-specific and would probably not stand up to objective analysis. Most patients are happy and friendly if well treated. Most undesirable and antisocial patterns such as self-destructiveness, aggression, smearing faeces, noisiness, and overactivity are considerably influenced by change of circumstances, particularly by relationships with people. In institutions the staffing ratio, the attitude of staff, the amount of physical restraint, the opportunities for exercise, activity and employment, and the extent of staff involvement are all critical. In particular cases behaviour can be modified by psychotherapy (O'Connor and Tizard, 1956) by re-designing the material and psychological environment (Tizard, 1965; Stephen and Robertson, 1972) or by behaviour shaping. These factors appear to the writer to be vastly more important as determinants of behaviour than either structural factors or drug therapy in this type of case.

Behaviour is, of course, profoundly influenced by the degree of motor disability, and in some cases of profound retardation there is remarkably good preservation of gross motor coordination so that the individual can climb in a monkey-like manner, apparently unafraid of danger. On the other hand in our survey we found that a majority of the cases of microcephaly which we provisionally classed as 'genetic' were associated with cerebral palsy and could be loosely described as 'Little's disease'.

PHENYLKETONURIA

This appears to be at first sight a very neat and self-contained biological category. Sufferers from the condition were discovered by Fölling (1934) on the basis of the ferric chloride test in the urine which produces a green colour in positive cases all of which appeared to be mentally retarded. The phenistix test later appeared more satisfactory but can also produce false positives and is not positive until a considerable number of days after birth. Therefore the Guthrie test which is dependent on the growth of bacillus subtilis in the presence of phenylalanine in the blood was introduced. But this test also needs confirmation by chemical measurement of the phenylalanine in the blood. But not all people with hyperphenylalaninaemia are mentally retarded and in those who are there is very wide variation in intelligence even if they are untreated (Cowie, 1951b; Cowie and Brandon, 1958). The writer has little doubt about the value of early treatment, though in some cases even if treatment is begun early the results are unsatisfactory. This may be due to excessive treatment, in some cases starving the organism of essential phenylalanine without which the brain cannot develop and function normally. In other cases due attention may not have been paid to a proper balance of the diet and to inclusion of the necessary vitamins, minerals and other ingredients. Reviews of treatment have not always been based on scientific principles and it is possible to criticize results destructively on this basis (Birch and Tizard, 1967; Tizard, 1967), but results accumulated by Hudson and his colleagues among others (Hudson, 1963; Hudson *et al.*, 1963, 1970; Partington, 1967; Baumeister, 1967; Pitt, 1968) seem to provide overwhelming evidence that patients treated before the age of 6 months do better than those untreated or treated too late.

Phenylketonuria provides another example of a condition to which a particular item of behaviour, namely digital mannerisms, has been linked (Cowie, 1951a). It now seems likely that this observation is based on coincidence and the relationship cannot be regarded as in any way specific or proven, such mannerisms being a very common feature of arrested development. They are, in simple form, equivalent to 'hand regard' in the young infant and represent an essential stage of normal development.

In considering individual variations in the effect of phenylketonuria a major place must be accorded to dietetic treatment which seems to have its chief impact at a time when growth and development of the brain including myelination is still taking place. Apart from this there is a wide range of variation in the effect on intelligence and other qualities. A large part of this is probably due to the total genetic composition of the individual, i.e. a pathogenic gene does not act in isolation but in the setting of all the other genes which make up the total genetic pattern. Some particular genes may be specially relevant to the pathogenic gene and may act as 'modifying genes'. This phenomenon is well known in the case of Rhesus incompatability. The production of antibodies to a Rhesus positive baby is modifiable by the ABO blood group system. If the mother and baby are also ABO incompatible then any of the baby's cells entering the maternal circulation are likely to be destroyed very quickly before the mother has had time to form any Rhesus antibodies.

The illustration of colour may also be used to understand the variable effect on mental function of phenylketonuria. It is known that the disease produces blonding (Berg and Stern, 1958) and texts often state that patients with phenylketonuria have blue eyes and fair hair. This is only partly true. The effect like all genetic effects is relative. Japanese children with the condition are not blond but they are fairer than ordinary children in that country. Thus the actual physical and psychological state of the individual is influenced by the total heredity, and those who inherit a major pathogenic fault are affected to a greater or lesser extent according to the remainder of their genetic make-up.

Another major consideration accounting for different effects of what at first appears to be the same biological condition, is that very often such an apparent entity dissolves on closer inspection. It is now clear (Woolf *et al.*, 1968) that there are several alleles involved in phenylketonuria which have a range of possible effects from severe retardation to normal intelligence with high blood phenylalanine. These effects stem not only from the difference between the alleles themselves but also from the possibility of interaction between them. A person who is homozygous for phenylketonuria may have two different abnormal alleles the effect of which may be intermediate between that of either of them in the homozygous state.

TUBEROUS SCLEROSIS

The discoveries of Mendel (1866, in Bateson, 1902) have played a fundamental part in the understanding of heredity but have from time to time been amplified as additional knowledge and new techniques have become available. Phenylketonuria is a classical Mendelian recessive trait whilst tuberous sclerosis is dominant. It is now recognized that these terms are relative and that recessive traits always have some effect on the phenotype of the heterozygote, and that the extent of the expression of dominant traits is very varied. Recessive traits, especially if they are very rare, may only be manifested after many generations during which the abnormal gene has been transmitted in the carrier. On the other hand, by definition dominant traits are manifest in each generation. Theoretically there may be exceptions to this rule in the sense that dominance is also relative. In practice there is no well-authenticated case of tuberous sclerosis 'skipping a generation'. It is a condition of the continuance of such conditions as tuberous sclerosis at the same level of frequency that there should be great variation in the severity of the condition. If all the patients were severely affected and if they were all of very low intelligence then none of them would have children and the condition would rapidly disappear from the population as an inherited trait. Cases would only occur sporadically as the result of new mutation. In fact it seems that at the present time a majority of recognized cases are due to this process and only a minority are the result of transmission by parents with a mild form of the condition (Zaremba, 1968; Bundey *et al.*, 1970; Bundey and Evans, 1969; Pampiglione *et al.*, 1968). It is not known how frequent the condition is in the general population and it is possible that many of the mild cases with little impairment of intelligence are missed.

Tuberous sclerosis is like several other conditions in which patients cluster clinically according to the severity of the disease. One group of affected children present with infantile convulsions and perhaps with white macules in the skin. Many of these are later recognized as being markedly retarded. Another group is mildly affected but members are recognized as parents of affected children. A third group attends the skin clinic with the persistent rash of adenoma sebaceum on the face, perhaps hoping for cosmetic improvement. Still others may be treated in epilepsy clinics. Mosaicism for Down's syndrome may have a similar effect in that one group present as children with Down's syndrome whilst another group are only recognized because they are mothers of affected children. A similar situation obtains for Klinefelter's syndrome. Some patients are sufficiently retarded to be in special schools or hospitals or training centres, whilst others of a better level of intelligence may attend a clinic for sterility or incomplete sexual development (Nielsen *et al.*, 1969).

Using a score sheet obtained from Dr Mildred Creak (Creak, 1961, 1964) the writer and his colleagues found that patients with tuberous sclerosis scored more points than other similarly retarded patients on the scale for childhood psychosis. It is, however, difficult to devise a sufficiently objective scale for this purpose and the numbers were small. There is certainly wide variation among patients with the condition and some have no psychotic features.

EPILEPSY

Fits are very common among the mentally retarded. More than one-third of the severely subnormal children at Queen Mary's Hospital for Children are currently epileptic. Epilepsy and other complications are somewhat commoner in hospitalized patients than in the mentally retarded living at home (Tizard and Grad, 1961). As a group among the severely subnormal, epileptics tend to have a lower intelligence than patients without this complication. In other words, epilepsy is commoner the severer the degree of mental defect. There are nearly as many myths about epilepsy as there are about mental retardation. The symptom is ill understood and much feared, despite many attempts at public education. In some units such as rehabilitation departments there is an automatic ban on patients with epilepsy, though this is illogical and unjustifiable. Two of the reasons for this attitude are that epileptics are thought to be subject to 'epileptic deterioration' and that they have a difficult temperament. Neither of these concepts has been proven (Chaudhry, 1959; Chaudhry and Pond, 1961; Pond, 1961).

Some epileptics do deteriorate. In some cases this is associated with progressive brain lesions such as chronic subacute encephalitis, which is now thought to be due in most cases to the measles virus (*British Medical Journal*, 1968, 1969a, b; Connolly *et al.*, 1971). Such cases are, however, a small minority and the overwhelming majority of epileptics owe their condition to a static brain lesion or malfunction. Occasionally *status epilepticus* occurs and this may lead to sudden, severe deterioration (Kirman, 1965) which may occasionally occur after a single episode (Bourne, 1956). These cases are also rare and the majority of epileptics do not deteriorate in any noticeable way. Similar considerations apply to personality deviations. There is a tendency to constellation of mental handicap, cerebral palsy, epilepsy and temperamental difficulty (Rutter *et al.*, 1970 a, b) in that all of these may be expressions of structural and functional abnormality of the brain. As suggested above, behaviour disturbances in the mentally retarded may be artefacts induced by the environment or they may be faculative and modifiable by an appropriate régime. On the other hand it must be accepted that limitations imposed in some cases by cerebral structure and function may be selective and qualitative, rendering the individual susceptible to fatigue, irritability and frustration in circumstances which might not be stressful to others. The analysis of perceptual and organizational difficulties in young, retarded and uncooperative children is difficult (Rutter, 1966), but there is much evidence to suggest that such special difficulties exist in children who have been labelled autistic, or more generally, psychotic (Hermelin and O'Connor, 1970). Some of this group are epileptic and some epileptic children share in these specific difficulties. In classical conditioning work Pavlov and his colleagues (Pavlov, 1931) were able to produce restlessness and neurotic features by imposition of tasks that were marginally too difficult, or where the time sequence between conditioned and unconditioned stimulus was too great, or where the volume of the stimulus was too great or too small for the particular individual. It seems likely that many situations which are acceptable to most children, including the retarded, are unacceptable or even noxious to particular individuals. If this hypothesis is accepted then it indicates an exploratory and experimental approach to remedial education and therapy for such difficult children, whether they be epileptic or not.

'BRAIN DAMAGE' AND 'MINIMAL BRAIN DAMAGE'

These two terms have been much abused. The former became, with Strauss and Lehtinen, synonymous with a particular pattern of behaviour (Strauss and Lehtinen, 1947; Strauss and Kephart, 1955). Similarly, Michel (1963) has defined a psychological syndrome related to minimal brain damage, but, as pointed out by Tizard (1965), there is no good evidence correlating the behavioural symptoms listed with structural lesions in the brain. Almost all severely subnormal children have severe brain damage, using this term in its widest sense (Crome, 1960) to include all structural abnormalities whether due to genetic or environmental factors. In our survey (Angeli and Kirman, 1971) we attributed a considerable number of cases of moderate, severe and profound retardation to perinatal brain damage, though this field is notoriously difficult for retrospective studies. So far as we know there is no particular critical level below which adverse perinatal factors cease to be operative. This consideration probably applies to a majority of noxious influences. This would lead to the logical conclusion that the effect of such adverse factors spreads throughout the whole range of human intelligence and is probably a major influence in causing normal variation as well as producing the milder forms of mental retardation. To the extent that such adverse factors produce structural lesions as opposed to more subtle effects such as may be determined by socio-cultural factors, there is a differential between the mildly retarded coming from favoured homes and those from poor homes. The former show a higher proportion of neurological features indicative of structural brain abnormality (Stein and Susser, 1960a, b; Susser, 1962). The British perinatal survey undertaken by Butler and his colleagues provides convincing evidence for the interplay and combination of adverse factors as well as permitting a tentative assessment of the role of individual adverse influences such as smoking during pregnancy. The same survey shows the very wide class discrepancies in this respect within the so-called 'Welfare State' (Butler and Bonham, 1963; Pringle *et al.*, 1966; Butler and Alberman, 1969). Pasamanick and colleagues (Knobloch and Pasamanick, 1958, 1962; Knobloch *et al.*, 1956) have used the term 'continuum of reproductive casualty'. The same notion is applicable to many adverse factors at any stage of development. Thus, a bad dental anaesthetic seldom produces catastrophic dementia but may well cause a small neuronal loss, and a cumulation of such incidents could produce significant intellectual deterioration. Similarly, dramatic loss of mental powers is not noticed very often in the participants in a particular boxing match but it is well known that chronic addicts to this sport are liable to the form of dementia known as punch drunkenness.

NEONATAL JAUNDICE

It is now well understood how and why jaundice of the newborn produces damage to the brain (Lathe *et al.*, 1958). The results are variable anatomically and clinically (Crome *et al.*, 1955). It is usually assumed for practical purposes that unless the bilirubin in the infant reaches a certain level, e.g. 18 mg per 100 ml, there is no need to intervene with exchange transfusion (Crosse, 1957; Crosse *et al.*, 1955). The dramatic results in the form of athetosis, deafness and mental retardation do not usually occur unless this level is reached (Dunn, 1963). However, it has been shown that neonatal jaundice is one of a series of adverse factors which, even in lesser degree, may contribute to or be associated with reduced intelligence (Feldman, 1961), but it requires surveys such as Butler's referred to above to separate the effects of prematurity, jaundice, neonatal hypoglycaemia, neonatal infection, illegitimacy, poor antenatal attention, difficult birth, anoxia and many other factors which may be positively correlated with each other.

LEAD ENCEPHALOPATHY

This may be chosen as another example of the operation of a noxious factor on the brain with, apparently, no critical level required to produce the effect. If the condition of lead encephalopathy is due to the deposition of the metal in the brain, it seems obvious that the continued effect of small doses over a long period may be similar to that of larger doses over a shorter period of time. It is not to be expected on this basis that there will be a close correspondence between the blood level at any particular point in time and the degree of mental impairment. It also seems likely that, especially in the past, when lead utensils were common and lead contamination of beverages such as beer was frequent, there must have been many minor incidents involving damage to the brain from lead which went undiagnosed. At the present time there are renewed dangers of mild brain damage from diffuse contamination of the environment by lead (Barltrop, 1969; Barltrop and Killala, 1969). The frequency of high blood lead levels in mental retardation has been shown by Clayton and her colleagues (Moncrieff *et al.*, 1964). It seems likely that in the majority of cases the mental retardation is not due to the lead but to the fact that mentally retarded children are specially liable to lead poisoning because they need longer to become discriminative in their feeding habits. On the other hand some cases of severe mental retardation are due to lead. A study by Bicknell considered different groups of patients: the cerebral palsied with no access to lead, ambulant retarded children with ordinary access to hospital precincts, and children with pica. The mentally retarded children with palsy had, as was expected, normal levels, the second group included some with high levels and the highest levels were found in the pica group (Bicknel *et al.*, 1968).

Lead poisoning shows a definite class distribution occurring predominantly among poor people and slum dwellers. In them it combines with a whole array of other adverse factors to lower intelligence. A similar situation applies among those who are already retarded. The brain of such children is likely to suffer additional damage as a result of the ingestion of lead.

Basis of individual differences

There are probably many as yet unknown mechanisms producing individual variation, amounting in some cases to mental retardation; but it may be useful to summarize at this point the main known ways in which variation is determined with particular reference to mental retardation.

Situations causing mental retardation

Point mutations with major pathogenesis, e.g. phenylketonuria or tuberous sclerosis.

Point mutations with minor effect, e.g. hyperphenylalaninaemia.

Multifactorial effect based on gene constellation.

Major chromosome error, addition or loss of genetic material.

Environmental effect with structural change, e.g. post meningitic state.

Environmental effect with functional change, e.g. social milieu producing illiteracy.

Complex multifactorial situation with genetic and environmental components, e.g. spina bifida.

Some examples have been given of the way in which these different types of factor or group factors may act. The above classification is tentative, fragmentary and incomplete. Knowledge in each of these areas is limited. It is, therefore, wise at all levels in considering the origin, classification and prognosis of mental handicap to avoid the dogmatic approach. Many notions which seemed to be well established have proved misleading or ill founded. No doubt further revision will be necessary. With increasing possibilities of controlling the material and social environment and of his own reproduction, Man may alter somewhat the factors which have hitherto determined the spread of variation of intelligence. Much attention has been paid to those who from Morel to Thomson foresaw imminent catastrophe in regard to national intelligence in rapidly changing conditions. Morel (1857) in his day was much concerned with the moral degeneration of the well-to-do and the corrupting effect that this might have on the artisan of Paris. He was concerned by the poor state of recruits for military service. Tredgold (1909) regarded Morel's doctrine as 'no myth but a serious reality'. This doctrine included the notion of the all-embracing 'neuropathic diathesis' which saw a causal relationship between insanity, idiocy, psychopathy, delinquency, alcoholism, poverty, tuberculosis and fecklessness. At present this unitary notion has been abandoned in favour of a factorial analysis approach to the determinants of intelligence, whether these be environmental or genetic. There are still, however, many contemporary echoes of the older approach, and the term which is often used, 'stigmata' of degeneration, is one of these. Another interesting fallacy is the apparent phenomenon of 'anticipation'. This was in line with Morel's general notion that the process of degeneration became worse from one generation to the next as a kind of mystic transmissible inner rot. Mott (1910) and Tredgold gave this a contemporary touch by equating the idea with 'damage to the germ plasm'.

Certain diseases do seem at first sight to support the notion of anticipation because of the extent of individual variation of their effects. If tuberous sclerosis and dystrophia myotonica are studied in this light it will be found that there are mild cases in the older generation and more serious cases beginning earlier in the younger generation. Thus, the older affected members of the family will have relatively slight effects on intelligence; they will have married and produced children, some of whom are affected gravely and are extremely retarded so that the 'evil' as Morel saw it would ultimately extinguish itself. This impression is, of course, due to sampling error. Severely affected members of older generations are dead and families that come under review are those with a young severely affected child who acts as the propositus and leads to the discovery of a mildly affected parent and perhaps of a grandparent too. The mildly affected members of the younger generation have as yet not developed obvious signs of the disease and therefore have not been diagnosed. This effect is possible in these conditions because they are transmissible in a dominant manner.

INDEFINITE SYNDROMES

The two conditions mentioned above can be seen each to constitute a biological entity in that they are both dominantly transmitted. Sporadic cases can be recognized by the highly characteristic lesions. The facial appearance of adenoma sebaceum is virtually unmistakable and other features such as the presence of white macules and, radiogically, the later calcification of the cerebral lesions are all helpful in establishing the diagnosis. In fatal cases the histology of the abnormal areas in the brain is like nothing else. Similarly the syndrome of dystrophia myotonica is very striking, with the particular features of difficulty in loosening the grip and characteristic electrophysiological changes associated with very slow muscle wasting and impairment of facial expression. Thus, although there are no laboratory tests which help to establish the diagnosis and although the severity of the syndromes varies greatly from one case to another there is little likelihood of a mistake by an expert.

Concepts of many syndromes which have been described must, however, be revised in the light of increasing knowledge. In an attempt to break down the total number of unclassified cases of mental defect earlier workers have used a great variety of classificatory systems. One method is to take a prominent symptom and to group together all cases presenting a particular feature. This has been done, for example, with retrolental fibroplasis in which condition the vision is impaired with disintegration of the structures in the posterior chamber of the eye. This occurs particularly in premature babies and is usually attributed to the effect of oxygen administration. This method of classification has, therefore, led to a very valuable effect in that oxygen is now used with moderation both in the proportion administered and the time during which the baby is exposed. Sjögren (1935) described forty defectives suffering from congenital bilateral cataracts in thirty sibships. In two cases the parents were first cousins. The condition was thought to be recessively transmitted, But Sjögren himself realized that his material was heterogeneous. Other workers have, however, accepted the concept of 'Staroligophrenie' as an entity. Whilst there may well be a core of homogeneous cases among those described by Sjögren, there are many conditions in which the association between mental handicap and cataract occurs. At the time when Sjögren wrote on this subject Gregg's classical discovery of the association between maternal rubella and congenital cataract had not been made, and it is possible that some of his series had this aetiology in those families where there was only one case. Some of Sjögren's cases had reduction in head size and it is well known that congenital cataract often accompanies microcephaly. Galactosaemia is a recessively transmitted defect which can cause both mental retardation and cataract. Although such a general basis for classification is inadequate the value of this approach can be seen in Gregg's discovery, since it was the occurrence of cataract in a number of infants which led him to connect the outbreak with rubella.

THE CORNELIA DE LANGE SYNDROME

Amsterdam dwarfism as a concept rests on the similarity between a number of dwarfs, in respect of facial appearance, hairiness, confluence of the eyebrows and imperfections of the limbs. There are no laboratory tests to support the diagnosis. Some of the published photographs show such a striking likeness that it seems very probable that they are examples of the same condition. The syndrome was first reported in Amsterdam (de Lange, 1933). The Dutch reports lay fallow for a number of years but they were then followed by the publication of accounts of a number of cases in the English literature (Ptacek *et al.*, 1963; Jervis and Stimson, 1963; Gans and Thurston, 1965; Falek *et al.*, 1966; Pearce *et al.*, 1967; Berg *et al.*, 1968). Although the condition is rare the evidence for the syndrome is similar to that used by Down and primarily rests on the fact that affected children look remarkably like each other. If this is, indeed, a syndrome or biological entity it has yet to be proven that there is any regular genetic pattern. If it should become established on the basis of additional criteria as a specific defect it will almost certainly be found that some cases have been misclassified under this head. On the other hand it will also be found in all probability that less typical cases have not been recognized.

MUCOPOLYSACCHARIDOSIS

This is a form of genetic error in which there is faulty metabolism of chemical substances which play an important part in the formation of cartilage, connective tissue, in the brain and in other organs. Several of the errors classifiable under this head were originally known as 'gargoylism' but it is now appreciated that there are a number of variants of this condition (McKusick, 1965). There is more than one form of inheritance. Whilst most cases are due to Mendelian recessive transmission, in some families the abnormality is sex-linked, being transmitted by females and only affecting males (Njå, 1945). There are also clinical differences between the different forms. Thus in the ordinary autosomal condition known as Hurler's syndrome clouding of the cornea with impairment of vision may occur, but this seems to be rare in the sex-linked variety. The opposite is true of deafness which is commoner in the sex-linked variety of the disease. In Morquio's syndrome the impact on the skeleton is more severe but the brain is less often severely involved. In all of these conditions excess of mucopolysaccharide is excreted in the urine, but in Morquio's syndrome the substance is keratosulphate which is chemically distinct from the chondroitin sulphate and heparitin found in the two forms of gargoylism. These diseases illustrate very well the principle that many examples of a syndrome do not conform to the textbook picture and may be mild or 'forma frustes'. The author saw two brothers a few years ago who were moderately retarded. He thought that one of them had some features suggestive of gargoylism. The other appeared anatomically normal. Both showed a positive urine test for gargoylism. A colleague elsewhere thought them examples of the sex-linked form on the basis of a study of the urine. It was realized that his criteria were in error when the sister of the two index patients also proved to have the condition; the patient whose appearance first suggested the diagnosis became more typical; he deteriorated physically and mentally and died. His brother has also gone downhill mentally but remains well grown, robust and still does not look a typical case of the condition. This example shows the great somatic differences within a sibship though the impact on intelligence was severe in all three cases. This family also illustrates the great difficulty which there may be in advising parents about prognosis for intelligence and life. Most children with the more severe degrees of mental handicap have a static brain lesion which does not become worse. As they grow, so a steady if slow increment in intelligence is to be expected, though in profound retardation this will be very limited. On the other hand a minority of conditions show progressive cerebral deterioration. It is, therefore, very desirable for counselling of parents to be able to distinguish this minority. Some progress has been made towards this by examination of white cells, rectal or appendicular biopsy, examination of the retina, and before long it should be possible to identify biochemical abnormality at enzyme level. The distinction is important for genetic counselling.

However, even when a clear diagnosis is established as in this case it is not possible to assess the rate of deterioration accurately. In the Tay–Sachs form of lipidosis there is usually rapid dementia with death at an early age. In gargoylism the deterioration proceeds much more slowly over many years, and the surviving brother in the case quoted has reached manhood in good physical health though there has been a decline from moderate to severe retardation. He may yet live many years. In counselling, therefore, the adviser should admit frankly that he is unable to predict accurately the course of the disease even when there is a definite diagnosis and the general trend can be forecast.

Practical application and implications for the services

Most of this chapter has been devoted to variations within recognized syndromes, to consideration of severe degrees of mental handicap with gross brain pathology, and to examination of the question of mild mental handicap in relation to the multitude of factors which produce diversity. The conclusion is that defects produced by a host of different factors can be very similar whilst defects produced by the same agency can be widely different. There are three major classes of defect: the first is the small minority which is progressive; the second is the bigger group of static structural defects; the third is the largest and this is the group of mild defect due to socio-economic deprivation, which is presumably in part remediable. The three categories are not sharply defined, they overlap, and this is particularly true of the second and third. The implications for the beneficial effect of improved conditions also cover, not only the third group but to some extent the second.

This brief survey has chosen only a few examples to indicate the scope of the problem and has not touched on, for instance, complex problems of human ecology accounting for the varying incidence and manifestation of such conditions as spina bifida, the different distribution of this and many other defects between the sexes, between the social classes and in different areas of such small countries as Wales (Laurence *et al.*, 1968).

The field is difficult enough to tackle at a theoretical, biological and social level. In practice it is even more complicated by the provisions which are made to deal with different aspects of mental handicap. There has been a rapid development in the provision of schools for the educationally subnormal. Few studies of the intellectual potential of children attending such schools have been done, but it would appear that they take children with a very wide range of intelligence. The population of such schools includes many who must be regarded as being within the normal range. If a separate category of 'borderline' or 'dull normal' is included in consideration of mental handicap this includes such a considerable proportion of the population that quite different orders of problem, more quantitative than qualitative, come up for consideration. The same applies to the hospital population in this country from the turn of the century, and increasingly after the first world war when the effect of the 1913 Act became obvious. The findings of the surveys by the British Psychological Society (Mittler, 1963, 1966) suggest that the proportion of patients within the normal range of intelligence in hospitals for the mentally handicapped may still be very considerable. The populations of Rampton and Moss Side also present a separate and qualitatively distinct problem.

There is a dearth of adequate studies of intelligence in hospital populations; this is even more true of the mentally handicapped in the community. Studies like those of Tizard and Kushlick (Goodman and Tizard, 1962; Susser and Kushlick, 1961; Kushlick, 1968, 1969) have deliberately concentrated on the profoundly, severely and moderately retarded. Figures about the mildly retarded are much less precise. In many areas little psychological expertise has been available to the training centre or for the assessment of those who for one reason or another are classed as subnormal. The overlap obviously operates to a greater extent in the other direction in that a high proportion of children within the mildly retarded range on intelligence testing remain within the ordinary educational framework and, when times are reasonably prosperous, enter open employment. (See also Chapter 25.)

Conclusions

All the evidence which is available would suggest that the existing differences between individuals, between classes and between societies in regard to mental ability may well reflect historical changes which have taken place in the relatively recent past. There seems to be some ground for cautious optimism in this respect in that there is no definite evidence of any general decline in intelligence and perhaps some indication of a general slight improvement and, at the same time, hope of elimination of some of the factors making for severe defect.

Attention has here been paid mainly to quantitative considerations in so far as loss of neurones or levels of intelligence are concerned. This is, of course, only one aspect of the picture. All the evidence shows that the criteria for successful employment above a certain basic level of intelligence, say a Wechsler IQ of 50, are much more concerned with steadiness, willingness, ability to get on with people, a capacity to engender a positive response in others, than with the level of intelligence. There is even a paradox in clinical practice that in a hostel population the most difficult patients to rehabilitate are the most intelligent. This is due to the fact that they are not in the general community through their emotional problems rather than limited intelligence. These difficulties range all the way from frank schizophrenia to bad temper.

In conclusion it may be salutary to remind ourselves that human society is probably built on individual differences in a way which we perhaps do not fully understand. These differences are essential to the human social group in providing a comprehensive understanding of the complex problems with which we are faced. They may also help to preserve the fluidity and adaptability of the social structure, to prevent it from fossilizing. The contradictions which they create may yet furnish the dialectic of survival of civilization.

References

ANGELI, E. (1971) *Genetic Prognosis in Mental Handicap.* Unpubl. M.D. thesis, Univ. of Athens.

ANGELI, E. and KIRMAN, B. H. (1970) Genetic counselling in relation to mental retardation. *Roy. Soc. Hlth J.*, **90**, 311–15.

ANGELI, E. and KIRMAN, B. H. (1971) Genetic counselling of the family of the mentally handicapped child. In PRIMROSE, D. A. (ed.) *Proc. 2nd Congr. Internat. Assoc. Scient. Stud. Ment. Defic.* Warsaw: Ars Polona; Amsterdam: Swets & Zeitlinger.

BARLTROP, D. (1969) Lead poisoning. *Brit. J. hosp. Med.*, **2**, 1567–73.

BARLTROP, D. and KILLALA, N. J. P. (1969) The factors influencing exposure of children to lead. *Arch. dis. Childh.*, **44**, 476–9.

BATESON, W. (1902) *Mendel's Principles of Heredity. A Defence. With a Translation of Mendel's Original Papers on Hybridisation.* Cambridge: Cambridge Univ. Press.

BAUMEISTER, A. A. (1967) The effects of dietary control on intelligence in phenylketonuria. *Amer. J. ment. Defic.*, **71**, 840–7.

BAZELON, M., PAINE, R. S., COWIE, V. A., HUNT, P., HOUCK, J. C. and MAHANAND, D. (1967) Reversal of hypotonia in infants with Down's syndrome by administration of 5-hydroxy-tryptophan. *Lancet*, **i**, 1130–3.

BERG, J. M. and KIRMAN, B. H. (1959a) Discussion on the aetiology of mental defect. *Proc. roy. Soc. Med.*, **52**, 789–91.

BERG, J. M. and KIRMAN, B. H. (1959b) Some aetiological problems of mental defect. *Brit. med. J.*, **2**, 848–52.

BERG, J. M. and KIRMAN, B. H. (1960) The mentally defective twin. *Brit. med. J.*, **1**, 1911–17.

BERG, J. and KIRMAN, B. H. (1961) Risk of dual occurrence of mongolism in sibships. *Arch. dis. Childh.*, **36**, 645–8.

BERG, J. M. and STERN, J. (1958) Iris colour in phenylketonuria. *Ann. hum. Genet. Lond.*, **22**, 370–2.

BERG, J. M., CROME, L. and FRANCE, N. E. (1960) Congenital cardiac malformations in mongolism. *Brit. Heart J.*, **22**, 331–46.

BERG, J. M., SMITH, G. F. and MCCREARY, B. D. (1968) The de Lange syndrome: diagnostic and aetiological considerations. In RICHARDS, B. (ed.) *Proc. 1st Congr. Internat. Assoc. Scient. Stud. Ment. Defic.* Reigate: Michael Jackson.

BERKSON, G. (1960) An analysis of reaction time in normal and mentally deficient young men. I. Duration threshold experiment. II. Variation of complexity in reaction time tasks. III. Variation of stimulus and of response complexity. *J. ment. Defic. Res.*, **4**, 51–77.

BICKNELL, J., CLAYTON, B. E. and DELVES, H. T. (1968) Lead in mentally retarded children. *J. ment. Defic. Res.*, **12**, 282–93.

BIRCH, H. G. and TIZARD, J. (1967) The dietary treatment of phenyl-ketonuria: not proven. *Developm. med. Child. Neurol.*, **9**, 9–12.

BLACKETTER-SIMMONDS, L. D. A. (1953) An investigation into the supposed differences existing between mongols and other mentally defective subjects with regard to certain psychological traits. *J. ment. Sci.*, **99**, 702–19.

BOURNE, H. (1956) Does virus encephalitis cause mental defect? *Amer. J. ment. Defic.*, **61**, 198–203.

BRANDON, M. W. G., KIRMAN, B. H. and WILLIAMS, C. E. (1959a) Microcephaly. *J. ment. Sci.*, **105**, 721–47.

BRANDON, M. W. G., KIRMAN, B. H. and WILLIAMS, C. E. (1959b) Microcephaly in one of monozygous twins. *Arch. dis. Childh.*, **34**, 56–9.

British Medical Journal (1968) Measles and panencephalitis. *Brit. med. J.*, **2**, 189 (editorial).

British Medical Journal (1969a) A measles vaccine withdrawn. *Brit. med. J.*, **1**, 194–5 (editorial).

British Medical Journal (1969b) Panencephalitis and measles. *Brit. med. J.*, **2**, 2 (editorial).

BUNDEY, S. and EVANS, P. R. (1969) Tuberous sclerosis: a genetic study. *J. Neurol. Neurosurg. Psychiat.*, **32**, 591–603.

BUNDEY, S., DUTTON, G. and WELLS, R. S. (1970) Tuberous sclerosis without adenoma sebaceum. *J. ment. Defic. Res.*, **14**, 243–9.

BUTLER, N. R. and ALBERMAN, E. A. (1969) *Perinatal Problems: The Second Report of the British Perinatal Morbidity Survey*. Edinburgh: Livingstone.

BUTLER, N. R. and BONHAM, D. G. (1963) *Perinatal Mortality*. Edinburgh: Livingstone.

CARR, J. (1970) Mental and motor development in young mongol children. *J. ment. Defic. Res.*, **14**, 205–20.

CARTER, C. O. (1958) A life-table for mongols with the causes of death. *J. ment. Defic. Res.*, **2**, 64–74.

CARTER, C. O. and EVANS, K. (1961) Risk of parents who have one child with Down's syndrome (mongolism) having another child similarly affected. *Lancet*, **ii**, 785–8.

CHAUDHRY, M. R. (1959) *Mental Deterioration in Epileptic Children*. Unpubl. M.D. thesis, Univ. of Punjab, Lahore.

CHAUDHRY, M. R. and POND, D. A. (1961) Mental deterioration in epileptic children. *J. Neurol. Neurosurg. Psychiat.*, **24**, 213–19.

COLLMANN, R. D. and STOLLER, A. (1963) A life table and data for mongols in Victoria, Australia. *J. ment. Defic. Res.*, **7**, 53–9, 60–8.

CONNOLLY, J. H., HAIRE, M. and HADDEN, D. S. M. (1971) Measles immunoglobulins in subacute sclerosing parencephalitis. *Brit. med. J.*, **1**, 23–5.

COWIE, V. A. (1951a) Phenylpyruvic oligophrenia. *J. ment. Sci.*, **97**, 505–31.

COWIE, V. A. (1951b) A typical case of phenylketonuria. *Lancet*, **i**, 272–3.

COWIE, V. A. (1970) *A Study of the Early Development of Mongols.* Oxford: Pergamon.

COWIE, V. A. and BRANDON, M. W. G. (1958) Follow-up note on an atypical case of phenylketonuria. *J. ment. Defic. Res.*, **2**, 55–8.

CREAK, M. (1961) Schizophrenic syndrome in childhood. *Cerebral Palsy Bull.*, **3**, 501–8.

CREAK, M. (1964) Schizophrenic syndrome in childhood. Further progress report of working party (April 1964). *Developm. med. Child Neurol.*, **6**, 530–5.

CROME, L. (1960) The brain and mental retardation. *Brit. med. J.*, **1**, 897–904.

CROME, L. (1965) The pathology of certain syndromes. In HILLIARD, L. T. and KIRMAN, B. H. (eds.) *Mental Deficiency.* London: Churchill.

CROME, L. and STERN, J. (1967) *Pathology of Mental Retardation.* London: Churchill.

CROME, L., KIRMAN, B. H. and MARRS, M. (1955) Rhesus incompatibility and mental deficiency. *Brain*, **78**, 514–36.

CROSSE, V. M. (1957) *The Premature Baby* (4th edn). London: Churchill.

CROSSE, V. M., MEYER, T. C. and GERRARD, J. W. (1955) Kernicterus and prematurity. *Arch. dis. Childh.*, **30**, 501–8.

DAVIDOFF, L. M. (1928) The brain in mongolion idiocy. A report of ten cases. *Arch. Neurol. Psychiat.*, **20**, 1229–57.

DE LANGE, C. (1933) Sur un type nouveau de dégénération (typus amstelodamensis). *Arch. Med. Enf.*, **36**, 713–19.

DOBZHANSKY, T. (1964) *Heredity and the Nature of Man.* London: Allen & Unwin.

DONOGHUE, E. C. (1965) Cited in KIRMAN, B. H., Down's disease (mongolism). In HILLIARD, L. T. and KIRMAN, B. H. (eds.) *Mental Deficiency* (2nd edn). London: Churchill.

DONOGHUE, E. C., KIRMAN, B. H., BULLMORE, G. H. L., LABAN, D. and ABBAS, K. A. (1970) Some factors affecting age of walking in a mentally retarded population. *Developm. med. Child. Neurol.*, **12**, 781–92.

DOWN, J. L. H. (1866) Observations on an ethnic classification of idiots. *Lond. Hosp. Rep.*, **3**, 259–62.

DUNN, H. G., REPENNINE, H., GERRARD, J. W., MILLER, J. R., TABATA, T. and FEDOROFF, S. (1963) Mental retardation as a sex-linked defect. *Amer. J. ment. Defic.*, **67**, 827–48.

DUNN, P. M. (1963) Obstructive jaundice and haemolytic disease of the newborn. *Arch. dis. Childh.*, **38**, 54–61.

EVANS, K. and CARTER, C. O. (1954) Care and disposal of mongolian defectives. *Lancet*, **ii**, 960–3.

FALEK, A., SCHMIDT, R. and JERVIS, G. A. (1966) Familial de Lange syndrome with chromosome abnormalities. *Pediatrics*, **37**, 92–101.

FELDMAN, A. M. (1961) *The Effect of Hyperbilirubinemia on Premature Infants. Progress Report.* Dept. of Psychiatry, New York Medical College.

FÖLLING, A. (1934) Uber Ausscheidung von Phenylbrenztraubensäure in den Harn abs Stoffwechselanomalie in Verbindung mit Imbezillitäb. *Hoppe-Seyler's Z. physiol. Chem.*, **227**, 169–76.

GANS, B. and THURSTON, J. G. B. (1965) De Lange's Amsterdam Dwarfs Syndrome. Report of four cases. *Developm. med. Child. Neurol.*, **7**, 42–5.

GOODMAN, N. and TIZARD, J. (1962) Prevalence of imbecility and idiocy among children. *Brit. med. J.*, **1**, 216–19.

GREGG, N. M. (1941) Congenital cataract following German measles in the mother. *Trans. ophthal. Soc. Aust.*, **3**, 35–46.

HERMELIN, B. and O'CONNOR, N. (1961) Shape perception and reproduction in normal children and mongol and non-mongol imbeciles. *J. ment. Defic. Res.*, **5**, 67–71.

HERMELIN, B. F. and O'CONNOR, N. (1963) *Speech and Thought in Severe Subnormality.* Oxford: Pergamon.

HERMELIN, B. and O'CONNOR, N. (1970) *Psychological Experiments with Autistic Children.* Oxford: Pergamon.

HINDLEY, C. B., FILLIOZAT, A. M., KLACKENBERG, G., NICOLET-MEISTER, D. and SAND, E. A. (1966) Differences in age of walking in five European longitudinal samples. *Hum. Biol.*, **38**, 364–79.

HOBBS, G. E. (1941) Mental disorder in one of a pair of identical twins. *Amer. J. Psychiat.*, **98**, 447–50.

HOLLINGSWORTH, J. W. (1960) Delayed radiation effects in survivors of the atomic bombings. A summary of the findings of the Atomic Bomb Casualty Commission, 1947–1959. *New Engl. J. Med.*, **263**, 481–7.

HUDSON, F. P. (1963) Phenylketonuria in the North of England. *Med. Off.*, **110**, 69–71.

HUDSON, F. P., DICKINSON, R. A. and IRELAND, J. T. (1963) Experiences in the detection and treatment of phenylketonuria. *Pediatrics*, **31**, 47–57.

HUDSON, F. P., MORDAUNT, V. L. and LEAHY, I. (1970) Evaluation of treatment begun in the first three months of life in 184 cases of phenylketonuria. *Arch. dis. Childh.*, **45**, 5–12.

HUNT, N. (1967) *The World of Nigel Hunt.* London: Darwen Finlayson.

JERVIS, G. A. and STIMSON, C. W. (1963) De Lange syndrome the 'Amsterdam type' of mental defect with congenital malformation. *J. Pediat.*, **63**, 634–45.

KIRMAN, B. H. (1951) Epilepsy in mongolism. *Arch. dis. Childh.*, **26**, 501–3.

KIRMAN, B. H. (1965) The backward baby. In HILLIARD, L. T. and KIRMAN, B. H. (eds.) *Mental Deficiency* (2nd edn). London: Churchill.

KIRMAN, B. H. (1970) Genetic counselling of parents of mentally retarded children. In BERG, J. M. (ed.) *Genetic Counselling in Relation to Mental Retardation.* Oxford: Pergamon.

KIRMAN, B. H. (1972) *The Mentally Handicapped Child*. London: Nelson.

KIRMAN, B. H. and BICKNELL, J. (1968) Congenital insensitivity to pain in an imbecile boy. *Developm. med. Child. Neurol.*, **10**, 57–63.

KNOBLOCH, H. and PASAMANICK, B. (1958) Seasonal variations in the births of the mentally deficient. *Amer. J. publ. Hlth*, **48**, 1201–8.

KNOBLOCH, H. and PASAMANICK, B. (1962) Medical progress: mental subnormality. *New Engl. J. Med.*, **266**, 1045–51, 1092–7, 1151–61.

KNOBLOCH, H., RIDER, R., HARPER, P. and PASAMANICK, B. (1956) Neuropsychiatric sequelae of prematurity. A longitudinal study. *J. Amer. med. Assoc.*, **161**, 581–5.

KUSHLICK, A. (1968) Social problems of mental subnormality. In MILLER, E. (ed.) *Foundations of Child Psychiatry*. Oxford: Pergamon.

KUSHLICK, A. (1969) Care of the mentally subnormal. *Lancet*, **iv**, 1196–7.

LATHE, G. H., CLAIREAUX, A. E. and NORMAN, A. P. (1958) In GAIRDNER, D. (ed.) *Recent Advances in Paediatrics*. London: Churchill.

LAURENCE, K. M., CARTER, C. O. and DAVID, P. A. (1968) Major central nervous system malformations in South Wales. *Brit. J. prev. soc. Med.*, **22**, 146–60.

LEJEUNE, J., TURPIN, R. and GAUTIER, M. (1959) Le mongolisme premier exemple d'aberration autosomique humaine. *Ann. de Génét.*, **1**, 41–9.

LESCH, M. and NYHAN, W. L. (1964) A familial disorder of uric acid metabolism and central nervous function. *Amer. J. Med.*, **36**, 561–70.

LEWIS, A. (1936) A case of apparent dissimilarity of monozygotic twins. *Ann. Eugen. Lond.*, **7**, 58–64.

LIND, E. B. and KIRMAN, B. H. (1958) Imbecile children. *Brit. med. J.*, **2**, 743, 1103.

LYLE, J. G. (1959a) The effect of institution environment upon verbal development of institutional children: I. Verbal intelligence. *J. ment. Defic. Res.*, **3**, 122–8.

LYLE, J. G. (1959b) *A Survey of the Verbal Ability of Imbeciles in Day Schools and in an Institution*. Unpubl. Ph.D. thesis, Univ. of London.

LYLE, J. G. (1960) The effect of an institution environment upon the verbal development of institutional children: (ii) speech and language, (iii) the Brooklands Residential Family Unit. *J. ment. Defic. Res.*, **4**, 1–13, 14–23.

MCKUSICK, V. A. (1965) The genetic mucopolysaccharides. *Circulation*, **31**, 1–4.

MARRS, M. (1955) *A Psychological Study of Institutionalised Defective Children*. Unpubl. M.A. thesis, Univ. of London.

MICHEL, G. (1963) Unpubl. paper cited in MACKEITH, R. and BAX, M. (eds.) Minimal cerebral dysfunction. *Little Club Clinics in Developm. Med.*, No. 10. London: Spastics Society and Heinemann.

MILLER, R. W. (1967) Prenatal origins of mental retardation. Epidemiological approach. *J. Pediat.*, **71**, 455–8.

MITTLER, P. (1963) Report of the working party on subnormality. *Bull. Brit. psychol. Soc.*, **16**, 37–50.

MITTLER, P. (1966) *Children in Hospitals for the Subnormal.* London: British Psychological Society.

MONCRIEFF, A. A., KOUMIDES, O. P., CLAYTON, B. E., PATRICK, A. D., RENWICK, A. G. C. and ROBERTS, G. E. (1964) Lead poisoning in children. *Arch. dis. Childh.*, **39**, 1–13.

MOREL, B. A. (1857) *Traité de dégénerescences physiques, intellectuelles et morales de l'espèce humaine.* Paris: Masson.

MOTT, F. W. (1910) Hereditary aspect of nervous and mental diseases. *Brit. med. J.*, **2**, 1013.

MURPHY, D. P. (1929) The outcome of 625 pregnancies in women subjected to pelvic radium or roentgen irradiation. *Amer. J. obstet. Gynec.*, **18**, 179–87.

NIELSEN, J., SØRENSEN, A., THEILGAARD, A., FRØLAND, H. and JOHNSEN, S. G. (1969) *A Psychiatric-Psychological Study of 50 Severely Hypogonadal Male Patients Including 34 with Klinefelter's Syndrome, 47, XXY.* Copenhagen: Universitetsforlaget.

NJÅ, A. (1945) A sex-linked type of gargoylism. *Acta Paediat.*, **33**, 267–86.

NYHAN, W. L., OLIVER, W. J. and LESCH, M. (1965) A familial disorder of uric acid metabolism and central nervous function. *J. Pediat.*, **67**, 257–63.

O'CONNOR, N. and HERMELIN, B. (1961) Visual and stereognostic shape recognition in normal children and mongol and non-mongol imbeciles. *J. ment. Defic. Res.*, **5**, 63–6.

O'CONNOR, N. and TIZARD, J. (1956) *The Social Problem of Mental Deficiency.* Oxford: Pergamon.

PAMPIGLIONE, G., EVANS, P. P., HARRIS, R. and MOYNHAN, E. J. (1968) Aspetti electroclinici della sclerosi tuberosa. *Conterenze di Aggiornamento Della Societa Italiana di Elettroencefalografia e Neurofisiologia*, 73–85.

PARTINGTON, M. W. (1967) Phenylketonuria and diet. *Canad. med. Assoc. J.*, **97**, 1033–4.

PAVLOV, I. P. (1931) Experimental neuroses. In *Conditioned Reflexes and Psychiatry.* New York: International Publishers.

PEARCE, P. M., PITT, D. B. and ROBOZ, P. (1967) Six cases of de Lange's syndrome: parental consanguinity in two. *Med. J. Aust.*, **1**, 502–6.

PENROSE, L. S. (1933) The relative effects of paternal and maternal age in mongolism. *J. Genet.*, **27**, 219–24.

PENROSE, L. S. (1937) Congenital syphilis in a monovular twin. *Lancet*, **i**, 322.

PENROSE, L. S. (1963) *The Biology of Mental Defect.* London: Sidgwick & Jackson.

PENROSE, L. S. and SMITH, G. F. (1966) *Down's Anomaly*. London: Churchill.

PITT, D. B. (1968) Phenylketonuria. *Proc. Aust. Assoc. Neurol.*, **5**, 149–53.

POND, D. A. (1961) Psychiatric aspects of epileptic and brain-damaged children. *Brit. med. J.*, **2**, 1377–82, 1454–9.

PRINGLE, M. L. K., BUTLER, N. and DAVIE, R. (1966) *11,000 Seven-year-olds*. London: Longman.

PTACEK, L. J., OPITZ, J. M., SMITH, D. W., GERRITSEN, T. and WAISMAN, H. A. (1963) The Cornelia de Lange syndrome. *Pediatrics*, **63**, 1000–20.

ROLLIN, H. R. (1946) Personality in mongolism with special reference to the incidence of catatonic psychosis. *Amer. J. ment. Defic.*, **51**, 219–37.

RUTTER, M. (1966) Behavioural and cognitive characteristics. In WING, J. K. (ed.) *Early Childhood Autism*. Oxford: Pergamon.

RUTTER, M., TIZARD, J. and WHITMORE, K. (1970a) *Education, Health and Behaviour*. London: Longman.

RUTTER, M., GRAHAM, P., YULE, W. and BIRCH, H. (1970b) *A Neuropsychiatric Study in Childhood*. London: Spastics International Medical Publications.

SÉGUIN, E. (1843) *Traitement Moral, Hygiène et Education des Idiots*. Paris and London: J. B. Baillère.

SHEAR, C. S., NYHAN, W. L., KIRMAN, B. H. and STERN, J. (1971) Self-mutilative behaviour as a feature of the de Lange syndrome. *J. Pediat.*, **78**, 506–9.

SJÖGREN, T. (1935) Klinische und vererbungs-medizinische Untersuchungen über Oligophrenie mit kongenitaler Katarakt. *Z. ges. Neurol. Psychiat.*, **152**, 263–92.

STEIN, Z. and SUSSER, M. (1960a) The families of dull children: a classification for predicting careers. *Brit. J. prev. soc. Med.*, **14**, 83–8.

STEIN, Z. and SUSSER, M. (1960b) Families of dull children: Part III. Social selection by family type; Part IV. Increments in intelligence. *J. ment. Sci.*, **106**, 1304–10; 1311–19.

STEPHEN, E. and ROBERTSON, J. (1972) Growing up in hospital. In *Mental Retardation*. Occasional Papers, Nos. 2, 3 and 4. London: Butterworth.

STERN, H., ELEK, S. D., BOOTH, J. and FLECK, D. G. (1969) Microbial causes of mental retardation: the role of prenatal infections with cytomegalovirus, rubella virus and toxoplasma. *Lancet*, **iii**, 443–8.

STRAUSS, A. A. and KEPHART, N. C. (1955) Progress in theory and clinic. Vol. II of STRAUSS, A. A. and LEHTINEN, L. E. (eds.) *Psychopathology and Education of the Brain-injured Child* (edn). New York: Grune & Stratton.

STRAUSS, A. A. and LEHTINEN, L. E. (1947) *Psychopathology and Education of the Brain-injured Child*. New York: Grune & Stratton.

SUSSER, M. W. (1962) Social medicine in Britain: a study of social class. In WELFORD, A. T., ARGYLE, M., GLASS, D. V. and MORRIS, J. N. (eds.) *Society: Problems and Methods of Study.* London: Routledge & Kegan Paul.

SUSSER, M. W. and KUSHLICK, A. (1961) *A Report on the Mental Health Services of the City of Salford for the Year 1960.* Salford Health Dept.

TIZARD, J. (1965) Psychological aspects. In HILLIARD, L. T. and KIRMAN, B. H. (eds.) *Mental Deficiency* (2nd edn). London: Churchill.

TIZARD, J. (1967) The dietary treatment of phenylketonuria: not proven? *Developm. med. Child Neurol.,* **9,** 511–13.

TIZARD, J. and GRAD, J. C. (1961) *The Mentally Handicapped and their Families.* Maudsley Monogrs., No. 7. London: Oxford Univ. Press.

TREDGOLD, A. F. (1909) The feebleminded: a social danger. *Eugen. Rev.,* **1,** 100–3.

WOOLF, L. I., GOODWIN, B. L., CRANSTON, W. I., WADE, D. N., WOOLF, E., HUDSON, F. P. and MCBEAN, M. S. (1968) A third allele at the phenylalanine hydroxylase locus in mild phenylketonuria (hyperphenylalaninaemia). *Lancet,* **i,** 114–17.

ZAREMBA, J. (1968) Tuberous sclerosis: a clinical and genetical investigation. *J. ment. Defic. Res.,* **12,** 63–80.

6

A. D. B. Clarke and A. M. Clarke

The changing concept of intelligence: a selective historical review

Introduction

Low or very low intelligence is about the only factor which the wide variety of those classified as subnormal have in common. Moreover, countless studies have shown that within this group, level of intelligence is relevant to type of care or training, and to prognosis. Hence, in this and the following chapter, an attempt will be made to review various theoretical positions on the nature of intelligence, to glance at the nature-nurture issue and to outline some of the more important studies of particular relevance to mental subnormality.

In considering the existing controversies, it will be important to begin by following the historical development of various ideas. Without some awareness of the underlying assumptions and presuppositions, the differing viewpoints of, for example, Jensen (1969) and Vernon (1970) are difficult to understand.

Modern interest in intelligence began in the 1890s, and the concept took on a new empirical precision in the first decade of this century. The invention of the IQ occurred in 1913, and with it the idea of IQ constancy. The latter represented the first real model for psychological development, and has had a profound influence. It advanced the view that, during development, individuals do not change their relative status and one can see in it some link with the predeterminism of psychoanalysis at about the same time. Unlike the ideas of Binet, the notion of constancy was a shot in the dark, totally lacking empirical support because longitudinal studies could not have been undertaken at that time. Particular attention will therefore be paid to Binet's later writings which are nowadays seldom studied.

History of the concept

Galton (1892) was well aware of 'the enormous difference between the intellectual capacity of men'. He goes on to say that he had 'not cared to occupy myself much with people whose gifts are below the average, but they would be an interesting study'. He quoted Séguin as stating that 50 per cent of idiots and imbeciles can be taught to work like 'the third of an average man'. More than

40 per cent can work 'like two-thirds of an average man' and 'from twenty-five to thirty per cent come nearer and nearer the standard of manhood, till some of them will defy the scrutiny of good judges, when compared with ordinary young men and women. In the order next above idiots and imbeciles are a large number of milder cases ... and so proceeding through successive grades, we gradually ascend to mediocrity.' Here Galton most clearly and explicitly stresses for the first time the gradation of human intelligence:

> ... there is a continuity of natural ability reaching from one knows not what height, and descending to one can hardly say what depth. I propose ... to range men according to their natural abilities, putting them into classes represented by equal degrees of merit, and to show the relative number of individuals included in the several classes ... The method I shall employ for discovering all this is an application of the very curious theoretical law of 'deviation from an average'.

Galton then refers to Quételet's work of 1849 and discusses in some detail the normal distribution curve for height. 'This is what I am driving at – that analogy clearly shows there must be a fairly constant average mental capacity in the inhabitants of the British Isles, and that the deviations from that average – upwards towards genius and downwards towards stupidity – must follow the law that governs deviation from all true averages.' In this connection his evidence rested upon stature, and probably also the circumference of the head, size of brain, weight of grey matter and number of brain fibres. 'The number of grades into which we may divide ability is purely a matter of option.' Galton maintains that the normal expectation would be of similar numbers in each class but argues that this would be 'egregiously mistaken'. He then calculates the numbers for each of sixteen classes and summarizes by stating that: 'Here we arrive at the undeniable but unexpected conclusion that eminently gifted men are raised as much above mediocrity as idiots are depressed below it; a fact that is calculated to considerably enlarge our ideas of the enormous differences of intellectual gifts between man and man.'

Another early writer on intelligence was Spearman (1904). He points out that in estimating intelligence the aim is to examine empirically all the various abilities having any prima facie claims to such title, ascertaining their relations to one another and to other functions. He then refers to four different kinds of intelligence. First, there is the classification according to school examination order, representing 'present efficiency'. Second, the age influences by taking the absolute difference between age and examination ranks. This is regarded as 'native capacity' after correction for a further number of factors. Third, another kind of intelligence is represented and measurable by the general impression produced on other people. Teachers' rankings are cited as an example. The fourth kind of intelligence is that known as 'common sense'.

It was by 'correlational psychology', then, that an understanding of intelligence would emerge. And there is no doubt that Spearman made an important contribution in drawing attention to the positive intercorrelations existing between all cognitive measures, almost however defined. In his 'two-factor theory' he postulated the existence of a general factor, common but in varying amounts, to all cognitive activities, and, secondly, specific factors. He was later to ascribe the success of the Binet method to the pooling of large numbers of test results and thus the maximizing of the general factor. Spearman's work stands squarely on the shoulders of Galton, and he proceeds by correlational argument to conclude that 'there really exists a something we may provisionally term "General Sensory Discrimination" and similarly a "General Intelligence", and further that the functional relationship between the two is not appreciably less than absolute'. This leads him on to state that whenever branches of intellectual activity are at all dissimilar, then their correlations with one another appear wholly due to their being all variously saturated with some common fundamental function.

Finally in his 1904 article, Spearman goes on to discuss the nature of this 'Function', as he terms it. He concludes that it appears to become fully developed in children by about their ninth year, and possibly even much earlier. 'From this moment, there normally occurs no further change even into extreme old age.' The Function almost entirely controls the relative position of children at school, 'and is nine parts out of ten responsible for success in such a simple act as Discrimination of Pitch'.

It is the present writers' guess that the final remarks stand as direct inspiration to the psychological model, constancy of the IQ, which served from 1913 almost unchallenged until the 1930s and 1940s. After all, one of the proponents was Cyril Burt, a pupil of Spearman who nevertheless by 1917 observed that in a group of subnormal children, tested over a five-year period, 'constancy of the mental ratio is but imperfectly realized'. Indeed, Burt was well aware that growth changes could take place and refers to 'an intrinsic irregularity of mental growth' in some children. On the whole, however, he believed that decline in IQ was much more common than increase in the mentally subnormal.

Before his death in 1911, Alfred Binet (quoted by Skeels and Dye, 1939) commented that

> Some recent philosophers appear to have given their moral support to the deplorable verdict that the intelligence of the individual is a fixed quantity, a quantity which cannot be augmented. We must protest and act against this brutal pessimism. We shall endeavour to show that it has no foundation whatsoever. . . . A child's mind is like a field for which an expert farmer has advised a change in the method of cultivating, with the result that in place of desert land we now have a harvest. It is in this particular sense, the only one that is significant, that we say that the intelligence of children may be increased . . . namely the capacity to learn, to improve with instruction.

Thus it is clear that the notion of intelligence as a fixed quantity was 'in the air' during the whole of this period: and it is probable that Binet was referring to Spearman.

Binet's and Simon's (1916) views on intelligence are particularly worthy of comment since this work and those of their followers bridge the gap between theoretical discussion and practical application. It is a tragedy that Binet should have died in 1911 in his mid-fifties. His writings suggest that, had he survived, the history of the intelligence testing movement might well have been very different.

In his 1905 paper, which forms Chapter 1 in the 1916 book, Binet refers to the Commission which was charged with the study of measures to be taken to ensure the benefits of instruction to defective children. No child should be admitted to a special class without first being subjected to a pedagogical and medical examination, from which it could be certified that because of the state of his intelligence he was unable to profit, in an average measure, from the instruction given in ordinary schools. But the Commission gave no guidance on how the child should be compared with normal children.

> It has seemed to us extremely useful to furnish a guide for future Commissions' examination. Such Commissions should understand from the beginning how to get their bearings. It must be made impossible for those who belong to the Commission to fall into the habit of making haphazard decisions according to impressions which are subjective. . . . Such a condition is quite unfortunate because the interests of the child demand a more careful method. To be a member of a special class can never be a mark of distinction and such as do not merit it, must be spared the record. . . . We are convinced, and we shall not cease to repeat, that the precision and exactness of science should be introduced into our practice, whenever possible, and in the great majority of cases it is possible.

The twin strands of humane concern and a search for scientific exactitude are outstanding features of all Binet's writings.

Binet and Simon point to the great confusion arising from subjective estimates of intelligence, to the low reliability between examiners and so on. Comparative statistics are worthless if the diagnoses upon which they are based are in doubt. Moreover,

> it is impossible to solve those essential questions concerning the afflicted, whose solution presents the greatest interest; for example, the real results gained by the treatment of inferior states of intelligence by doctor and educator; the educative value of one pedagogical method with another; the degree of curability of incomplete idiocy. . . . There is but one means of knowing if a child, who has passed six years in a hospital or a special class, has profited by that stay, and to what degree he has profited; and that is to compare his certificate of entrance with his certificate of dismissal, and by that means ascertain if he shows a special amelioration of his condition beyond that which might be credited simply to the considerations of growth.

This could be achieved only by standard methods. In summary, Binet and Simon found lacking in 1904 'a precise basis for differential diagnosis'.

The authors mention that psychological, as opposed to somatic, classification was quite recent, although it already existed in Séguin's book; 'in that singular work, so remarkable as a practitioner's, so weak as a theorist's, we find the extraordinary idea that idiocy depends on a weakness of will'. Binet and Simon criticize previous attempts at assessment and make the remark that in questioning the child 'it would be better to turn the question so as to oblige the child to somewhat develop his thought if he has one', a view which was to be developed in later work.

Binet's ultimate solutions are too familiar to need detailed exposition; his purpose

is to be able to measure the intellectual capacity of a child . . . in order to know whether he is normal or retarded. We should therefore study his condition at the time and that only. We have nothing to do with his past history or with his future; consequently we shall neglect his aetiology, and we shall make no distinction between acquired and congenital idiocy; for a stronger reason we shall set aside all considerations of pathological anatomy which might explain his intellectual deficiency. So much for his past. As to that which concerns his future, we shall exercise the same abstinence; we do not attempt to establish or prepare a prognosis and we leave aside the question of whether this retardation is curable or even improvable. We shall limit ourselves to ascertain the truth in regard to his present mental state.

Binet clearly believed that the study of particular assets and deficits in the abilities of the subnormal would be rewarding, but confined himself at this stage to the measurement of general intelligence, comparing the retarded with that of 'normal children of the same age or of an analogous level'. This was to be achieved by establishing a measuring scale composed of a series of tests of increasing difficulty, starting with the lowest level that could be observed and ending with that of average normal intelligence. Each group of tests in the series was designed to correspond with a different mental level. This scale, write the authors, does not permit the measure of intelligence 'because intellectual qualities are not superposable, and therefore cannot be measured as linear surfaces are measured, but are, on the contrary, a classification, a hierarchy among diverse intelligences; and for the necessities of practice this classification is equivalent to a measure'. By comparison with normals it would be possible to determine by how many years a child is advanced or retarded.

Binet and Simon then criticize those who create tests based on theoretical notions, and who have not patiently standardized them in schools. They stress that all their measures have been tried out repeatedly, and of course subsequent modifications and improvements took place in 1908 and 1911. A single sentence highlights their aims and their conception of the nature of intelligence: 'We have aimed to make all our tests simple, rapid, convenient, precise, heterogeneous, holding the subject in continual contact with the experimenter, and bearing principally upon the faculty of judgment.' They go on to write that it is the intelligence alone that they seek to measure. Here they separate 'natural intelligence and instruction'; they aim to disregard as far as possible the degree of instruction which the subject possesses. 'We believe that we have succeeded in completely disregarding the acquired information of the subject. We give him nothing to read and nothing to write, and submit him to no test in which he might succeed by means of rote learning. ... It is surely the level of natural intelligence that is taken into account.'

This is one of the few passages in the Binet and Simon (1916) book which in the 1970s seems naïve. It suggests in modern terms that these workers believed that they were measuring Intelligence 'A'. Yet in the section of 1911, the authors consider the findings of Decroly in Belgium which, using the Binet–Simon tests, were thought by some to have invalidated the scale. These findings were re-analysed. It was found that the majority of the Belgian children were advanced, and on average by a year-and-a-half. They suggested two possible reasons: (1) a greater indulgence in scoring, and (2) the children 'are not of the same social condition as ours'. Upon enquiry, it was found that the pupils 'belong to a social class in easy circumstances; they have parents who are particularly gifted and understand education in a broad sense; they are renowned physicians, university professors, well-known lawyers, etc.' Moreover, their education took place in classes of eight to ten at the most. So a superior social condition and an education which tended towards individualism were seen as responsible for Decroly's results. 'Is it a matter of education? Is it a matter of heredity? It would be difficult to establish a difference between the two factors which are here operating in conjunction.' But there remained an aspect of the findings which particularly intrigued Binet. There was a whole series of tests in which the Belgian children were even more advanced. These were associated with 'more training, attention, faculty of language, habit of looking at pictures, practical life, comprehension'. Language seemed the most important difference; 'the little children of the upper classes understand better and speak better. This verbal superiority must certainly come from the family life; the children of the rich are in a superior environment from the point of view of language and one that is more expressive.'

The recognition that socio-economic factors were associated with Binet's intelligence measures, and that this relationship might be directly influenced by the quality of the environment, would be seen by some as the flaw in his belief that he was measuring capacity unaffected by 'instruction'. In his penultimate chapter, he refers to the question of definition of intelligence as one of 'fearful complexity' and goes on to write that 'in our study we have sought to find the natural intelligence of the child, and not his degree of culture, his amount of instruction'. He goes on to state his belief that the intellectual faculty appears to be independent not only of instruction but of the scholastic faculty, the faculty of learning at school. To learn at school, other qualities such as attention, will, character, a certain docility, a continuity of effort are needed. Lack of attention or character, he believed, would scarcely be reflected in his tests. An intelligent pupil, for example, may be lazy. While there is a general parallelism between intelligence and the scholastic faculty, some striking discrepancies nevertheless occur. After detailed discussion Binet summarizes his findings: test results depend, first, upon intelligence pure and simple; second, on extra-scholastic acquisition capable of being gained precociously; third, on scholastic acquisitions made at a fixed date; and fourth, on acquisitions relative to language and vocabulary, which are at once scholastic and extra-scholastic, based partly on school and partly on home circumstances.

> Does our scale fail to do justice to a child of uncommon intelligence without culture, or with scholastic culture much inferior to his intelligence? We do not think so. Such a child will show his superiority in the repetition of figures, in the repetition of sentences, paper cutting, the arrangement of weights, the interpretation of pictures, etc. And it is a specially interesting feature of these tests that they permit us, when necessary, to free a beautiful native intelligence from the trammels of the school.

This was a brave hope that Binet would have had to modify if he had survived. School learning in those days was largely rote learning. Binet probably rightly concluded that he was measuring something other than knowledge acquired in this way, but did not closely examine the possibility of spontaneous learning from other situations. His principal conclusion to the 1908 work was that 'we actually possess an instrument which allows us to measure the intellectual development of young children whose age is included between three and twelve years'. Knowledge so gained would be of interest in itself, but in particular could influence the development of well-founded curricula by matching the content to the child's capabilities. Looking to the future Binet could perceive many possible applications, 'a future where the social sphere would be better organized than ours; where every one would work according to his known aptitudes in such a way that no particle of psychic force would be lost for society'. The more immediate practical ends were for parental knowledge and particularly for teachers who wish to know and understand their pupils but who are unsystematic in their observations. 'But we are of the opinion that the most valuable use of our scale will not be in its application to the normal pupils but rather to those of inferior grades of intelligence.' Differential diagnosis was at that time so subjective that Binet presents some detailed evidence that this was a real problem. But retardation, particularly at the higher levels, must be judged according to its context; a peasant, normal in his ordinary surroundings, may be considered a moron in the city. Moreover, to establish a diagnosis, account must be taken of two essential elements, the age and the intellectual level. The way in which these factors should be combined would not be known with certainty until extensive research had been performed. This would indicate the prognosis that can be made from certain retarded conditions. At that time, however, nothing was known of prognosis, the question was open; ' . . . one who is imbecile to-day may, by the progress of age, become a moron, or on the contrary remain an imbecile all his life. One knows nothing of that; the prognosis is reserved.' By the test of intelligence alone, one cannot know absolutely that a child is subnormal; situations are considered where there are doubts on the causes of scholastic backwardness; 'and in such a case, if to a serious retardation of scholarship is added a serious intellectual retardation, there is sufficient reason for sending a pupil to a special class'.

In his final chapter, Binet recognizes that short tests merely sample limited areas; thus a particular test, isolated from others, is of little value. One might almost say, he writes, that it matters very little what the tests are so long as they are numerous.

In summary, Binet's published works contain an astonishing wealth of insights into many of the problems surrounding intelligence testing and interpretation, which remain a burning issue to this day.

Burt's *Mental and Scholastic Tests* (1921, and finally 1962) passed through four editions and several impressions. In reviewing the development of the concept of intelligence he states that Binet, like Galton, was seeking to measure a capacity that is 'innate', 'inborn' or 'natural' as distinct from knowledge or skill that is acquired. Secondly, he was attempting to measure cognitive capacity, and thirdly, an all-round or general ability. Teachers, he points out, have no hesitation in assuming that some such general ability exists, and is definitely recognizable. Brushing aside the rival theories of Thorndike and Thomson, Burt believes that the universality of positive correlations is in itself sufficient to justify the assumption of a common factor entering into all the tests. He also believes that there exists a small set of group factors or special abilities. Moreover, differences in this general factor 'are largely the result of the individual's genetic constitution'. He goes on to say that since intelligence as thus defined is not an observable but merely a hypothetical quantity, we cannot measure it directly. 'But we can make fairly plausible estimates of its amount. . . .'

Burt notes that Spearman rejected the complex type of test used by Binet, the rough and ready tests of everyday activities, preferring the exact laboratory tests of elementary processes. Burt concluded, however, that one should select tests covering all types of cognitive activity from the lowest (like Spearman's tests) to the highest. A general factor still emerges but the tests yielding the highest correlations with this factor are those of the more complex processes. He thus concluded that intelligence must be essentially a synthesizing or organizing capacity. This is confirmed, he argued, in his own work on the most effective aspects of the Binet scale. He concludes that something corresponding to the definition ('innate, general, cognitive factor') really exists.

Burt considers in detail the nature of the well-known correlation between

Binet IQ and school attainment; is this a two-way causal process? By means of partial correlations, he concludes that

> with the Binet–Simon scale a child's mental age is a measure not only of the amount of intelligence with which he is congenitally endowed; not only of the plane of intelligence at which in the course of life and growth he has eventually arrived; it is also an index, largely though not perhaps mainly, of the mass of scholastic information and skill which, in virtue of attendance, more or less regular and by dint of instruction more or less effective, he has progressively accumulated. ... In determining the child's performance in the Binet–Simon scale, intelligence bestows only about two-thirds the share of school, and age but one-third the share of intelligence.

He summarizes by stating that numerous factors affect the measurement of IQ by Binet methods. Educational, and particularly linguistic, attainments influence it more profoundly than any other measurable factor. The IQ is thus by no means a pure measure of capacity as Spearman and Binet had expected. That being so, what of its validity? Here Burt believes that there is no standard of comparison which can surpass or supersede the considered estimate of an observant teacher, working daily with the individual children over a period of several months or years. In asking for estimates, emphasis was laid upon two facts: first, that practical out-of-school common sense should be weighed quite as attentively as scholastic ability; and second, that proper discount should be allowed for age. The correlations between the Binet–Simon scores and teachers' ratings averaged about ·50. For older children, one of Burt's reasoning tests correlated around ·70. Hence, in elementary schools, 'the Binet–Simon tests as tests of intelligence prove but moderately successful'. With the subnormal, however, the correlations average about ·62. In spite of the foregoing, and his view that 'the routine examiner ... remains generally unconscious of the frail foundation upon which his standards of comparison repose', Burt believed that

> while waiting for the slow and sure, we must make shift with the rough and ready ... a handy method which can be immediately applied by teachers, doctors and social workers; for a pocket rule, which will furnish diagnostic measurements in terms of some plain concept like the mental year, obvious, moderately exact and instantly intelligible. ... To satisfy such a demand, scientific exactitude may pardonably be postponed for the prompt delivery of a workable substitute. And such a substitute, provisional yet ready-made, is to be found in the Binet–Simon Scale. (Burt, 1962, pp. 260–2).

Terman (1919) found a similar relationship between teachers' ranking and IQs. He quotes a correlation of ·48 and states: 'That it is moderately high in so far corroborates the tests. That it is not higher means that either the teachers or the tests have made a good many mistakes.' Quoting Binet, he argues (1) that teachers do not have a very good idea of what constitutes intelligence; (2) they are too easily deceived 'by a sprightly attitude, a sympathetic expression ...';

and (3) 'the majority show rather undue confidence in the accuracy of their judgement'. Hence for Binet and Terman the 'fault was plainly on the part of the teachers'. Mistakes were most common with children who were either over age or under age for their grade, and mostly the former. It is the teacher's tendency, then, to estimate a child's intelligence according to the quality of his schoolwork in the grade where he happens to be located.

Dearborn (1928) tackles the problem of validity in much the same way. Success in school is determined by several other factors as well as by intelligence. The teacher's idea of what is normal or average is often faulty. Second, as noted earlier, he tends not to take account of the differences in the ages and lengths of previous training of pupils. Older, more retarded, pupils were thus often overestimated whereas younger, more advanced, pupils were underestimated. The Binet approach depends upon a full normative population, with CA taken into account. Dearborn goes on to outline some of the classic studies on the un-reliability of teachers' judgments and concludes that tests are much more reliable.

It is of interest that Dearborn was at this time a firm believer in constancy of the IQ 'in at least the majority of cases'. Indeed he refers to this 'discovery' as 'the most important contribution which has resulted from the use of intelligence tests' and quotes with approval a remark attributed to Spearman that 'it is born with one and can neither be improved by schooling nor dulled by neglect'. Some thirteen years later Dearborn (Dearborn and Rothney, 1941) was to offer a totally different interpretation: '. . . prediction of growth is hazardous'. It seems likely that some of these early workers were misled by studying group averages rather than individual growth curves.

Dearborn evaluates the Binet approach by stating that the best way of measuring intelligence would be to study the actual process of representative learning, but for practical reasons this is not possible:

> . . . a large majority of the tests in common use are not so much tests of the actual process of learning, of the actual operation of the intellect, but are tests of what has been learned; that is, they are tests of the products of intelligence. The assumption is made that tests of information or of knowledge show how well intelligence has worked in the past and will presumably work in the future. But this is not necessarily the case. Individuals differ greatly in the organization of their experiences. . . .

Dearborn goes on to discuss Burt's views, already noted, that the Binet IQ is not a pure measure of 'intelligence' and cites further the classic study of Gordon on canal boat children. 'Intelligence as tested depends as much upon the amount of schooling as does the educational attainment. Correlations between the IQ and the amount of school attendance is the same as between the educational ratios and school attendance.' The rank correlation between age and IQ was $-\cdot75$; the older the child the duller, a fact recently underlined by the findings of Heber and Garber (1971) also reporting upon a deprived population.

All this was written by Dearborn in the early years of the Harvard Growth

Study, but he was already at this time beginning to draw attention to the existence of some very large changes in relative growth rates. Pointing out that intelligence does not develop *in vacuo* he argues that 'nature is but a first habit'. And 'if we can modify the conditions under which an organism develops, we can determine its habits and hence its nature'. He hints then that there may be 'no fundamental distinction between what has been called innate and what has been called acquired'. He concludes in very modern terms that 'Nature sets certain general limits, but for each individual there is a "margin of safety" or a range of accomplishment which is a function of the environment, and the extent of which can only be ascertained by individual effort under the most favourable conditions.'

In this selective review of the history of the concept of intelligence we can now move forward two decades and consider briefly the views of more recent writers. Factor analytic techniques were greatly developed in the 1930s and later by L. L. Thurstone. By these methods, and from his realization that a general factor was insufficient to account for matrices of intercorrelations, he suggested the presence of group factors. He identified these as 'primary mental abilities' and lists them as perceptual speed, number, word fluency, verbal comprehension, space, associative memory and general reasoning (Thurstone, 1947). In his important book of 1950, Vernon draws upon the by now highly developed factorial studies and underlines the hierarchical nature of human abilities. The general factor was found to cover more than twice as much variance as all group factors combined. After the removal of *g*, tests fall into two main groups: the verbal–numerical–educational, and the practical–mechanical–spatial–physical.

Vernon draws attention to Thomson's 'anarchic' theory of intelligence, that a matrix of intercorrelations of cognitive items can be interpreted equally validly as either the expression of a *g* factor in the Spearman sense plus perhaps some group factors, or alternatively as expressing the number of shared neural bonds of which tasks make use.

> It may be seen from Thomson's theory that *g* is not a fixed, purely inherited quantity ... presumably [it] is largely dependent on some psycho-physiological and innate property of the higher nervous system, but there is no reason why its number [of bonds] should not be affected by the use made of the mind, and by its organic conditions such as brain injury and ageing. This fits in with modern research on the highly individual nature of mental growth, on the effects of schooling and the intellectual stimulus provided by people's jobs and on deterioration of mental efficiency in pathological conditions.

Factor analysis has been the main approach to intellect of J. P. Guilford (1959). He presents a three-dimensional model, involving operations (evaluation, convergent and divergent thinking, memory, cognition); products (units, classes, relations, systems, transformations, implications); and contents (figural, symbolic, semantic, behavioural). 'With about 50 intellectual factors already discovered, however,' he writes, 'we may say that there are at least 50 ways of being intelligent. ... The structure of intellect is a theoretical model that predicts as many as 120 distinct abilities. ... We do not know to what extent each factor is determined by heredity and to what extent by learning. The best position for educators to take is that possibly every intellectual factor can be developed in individuals at least to some extent by learning.'

Hebb (1949) drew attention to at least two valuable meanings for the word 'intelligence'. Intelligence (A) is

> an innate potential, the capacity for development, a fully innate property that amounts to the possession of a good brain and a good neural metabolism. The second is (B) the functioning of a brain in which development has gone on, determining an *average level of performance or comprehension* by a partly grown or mature person. Neither, of course, is observed directly; but *intelligence* B, a hypothetical level of development in brain function, is a much more direct inference from behaviour than *intelligence* A, the original potential.

Hebb emphasizes that these are not parallel forms of intelligence but two different meanings of 'intelligence'. For estimating B, a summation of observation of behaviour in different situations is required at different times. The relationship to A is less direct. Vernon (1955) added C, the intelligence test score. Some of the remainder of Hebb's (1949) arguments have been overtaken by events and will not be considered here. Suffice it to say that Hebb maintains that much of the confusion in the literature arose from the failure to make these distinctions. Commenting on racial differences he asks why the Negro's IQ does not have the same meaning as a white man's: 'Because Negro and white do not have the opportunity to learn to speak the language with equal range and accuracy, are not usually taught in equally good schools, and do not have equally good jobs or equal exposure to cultural influences that usually require a fairly good income.'

Finally, Hebb discusses the *completely necessary* innate potential interacting with a *completely necessary* environment, confesses ignorance of the precise role of the latter and believes that 'it should be a pressing concern for psychology to discover the conditions that will develop whatever potentialities a child may have'.

Ferguson (1954), in an important paper, presented a generalized theory which drew together in a single conceptual framework the study of human learning and the study of human ability. We can regard 'ability' as defined by an individual's performance, and two classes may be delineated. The first is more or less invariant with respect to repetition or its cessation; the second is not. In the first case some of the things the individual can do have a fairly high degree of permanence, others may exhibit great improvement with practice or show a decrement in the absence of repetition.

Ferguson's first hypothesis is that in adults in our culture those more or less stable attributes of behaviour which we ordinarily speak of as abilities, and which are defined in terms of performance in psychometric tests, refer to performance at a crude limit of learning. These abilities are thus overlearned acquisitions, and their stability is the result of overlearning. In our culture, children are exposed to an environment that demands rapid learning of many things. It is probable that children of a particular age are functioning fairly close to their upper learning limits.

Ferguson continues his argument by considering transfer, and noting the Hebb and McGeoch view that all learning is influenced by transfer, and that transfer may have a particularly important function early in life. He advances two hypotheses: first, that in many adult learning situations the most important variables exerting transfer effects on subsequent learning are the 'abilities' – those earlier acquisitions that have attained their limit of performance. Second, the overlearned acquisitions exert their effects differentially in any learning situation; different abilities exert different effects at different stages of 'new' learning, and abilities which have transfer effectiveness at one stage may be different from those that transfer at another stage.

In summarizing his paper, Ferguson underlines the complex interaction of biological propensities of the organism, prior learning and the age at which prior learning occurs. The role of ability in, for example, scholastic performance can be viewed as a problem of transfer. A two-factor theory of learning is proposed. The correlation among abilities is explained in terms of positive transfer, and the differentiation of abilities by their development with some specificity towards particular learning situations.

Recent writings have sharpened the nature-nurture issue. It seems obvious that this controversy, to which thousands of words have been devoted in the past, remains ill-understood, even by some of the main protagonists. As has been pointed out, the question of which is the more important, nature or nurture, is misconceived since both are involved and both are essential to the growth of psychological characteristics. This point can be illustrated by considering a non-emotive topic, the growth of physical stature. In a constant, nutritionally adequate environment, differing rates of growth and differing endpoints of stature must, by definition, result from unfolding genetic and constitutional programmes. Hence, differences between individuals are not in these circumstances environmental in origin. But the growth itself is obviously absolutely dependent upon the nutritional environment of the developing individual. It is thus a question of whether genetics or environment in a particular group are *seen* to be related to growth differences. As a further example, the ordinary person would not offer air pressure as of any importance in his life. It would be seen to be important only if he entered situations of very low or very high pressure. From such examples it is obvious that the perception of genetic or environmental factors as crucial will best be established in circumstances of change. Where environment is uniformly optimal, its importance in individual differences will not be obvious even though, like genetics, its operation is essential. Similarly, some of the rare recessively-determined conditions such as PKU mark their possessors as sharply different from their peers for obviously genetic reasons. And where drastic environmental change occurs in the development of the individual, if it is followed by corresponding growth changes, its importance will be obvious.

In the next section of this chapter we will consider very briefly the reliability and validity of the measurement of intelligence, and this discussion will not be anticipated here. As Uzgiris (1970) states: '. . . the evidence that intelligence tests measure nothing but achievement and that IQ scores vary systematically with a number of background conditions roughly correlated with opportunities for learning, such as socio-economic status, amount of schooling, etc., has been marshalled again and again. . . . Evidence that IQs of individuals change with change in their circumstances, especially during the childhood years, is also ample.' Vernon (1970) takes a rather similar view:

> To the theoretical psychologist, however, intelligence seems to have outgrown its usefulness, as have other faculties (e.g. attention and memory) or instincts and personality traits. It does not refer to any one thing but covers a multitude of cognitive skills, schemata or plans which mature or are built up in response to stimulation and exercise in increasingly complex forms – probably in the manner that Hebb, Piaget, Ferguson, G. A. Miller, Hunt, Bruner and others have described. Thus the measures of intelligence . . . are merely rather coarse indices of the general or average level of difficulty of the tasks which the individual can perform by means of these skills.

Later Vernon notes that 'the myth of measuring innate ability still persists' and that 'intelligence scores are achievement scores just as much as are reading or arithmetic scores. . . . The former does not "cause" the latter. At the same time, intelligence scores are useful predictors in so far as they sample the more general conceptual or reasoning skills which a child has built up largely outside school and which he should therefore be able to apply in the acquisition of more specialized skills in school.'

Hunt (1961) points out that a number of authorities have warned against seeking a general answer to the question of the relative contributions of genetics and environment to intelligence. However, 'the effort to find one never seems to die, and those answers available get implications attributed to them which they do not have.' He goes on to maintain that so long as samplings are based on any given set of existing conditions, the answer to the proportion question obtained from them says nothing about what answer might be obtained from another set of conditions. Hunt then argues powerfully that the analysis of variance model fits the data from the heredity-environment relationship too poorly to permit a meaningful answer. The model is based on the principle that the variances from heredity and environment are additive and without interaction. The evidence is certainly against this notion. As an alternative approach, Hunt suggests that specific questions should be asked which are significant either for programmes of education, child rearing and human welfare in general, or for specific issues in the theory of human development. How much can the intelligence of subnormal children be raised, he asks, and goes on to quote other specific examples.

Jensen's recent (1969) suggestions concerning Level I and Level II intelligence will be discussed in the next chapter.

Space precludes any detailed consideration of the explosion of research in the last decade inspired by the writings of Piaget. His theory of intellectual development (see Piaget, 1970, for a recent account) is clearly and explicitly interactionist. The child's intelligence develops through the gradual modification and structuring of his *schemata* as he adapts to the environment. This cognitive adaptation consists of an equilibrium between assimilation and accommodation. Assimilation implies changing the elements in a situation so that they can be incorporated into the structure of the organism, while accommodation refers to modification of the organism's structure so that it can adapt to the environment.

In commenting upon the relations between development and learning, Piaget insists again that knowledge results from interactions between the subject and the object, which are richer than what the objects can provide by themselves. In Piaget's view, learning theories such as those put forward by the behaviourists reduce knowledge to direct functional copies which do not enrich reality. 'The problem we must solve in order to explain cognitive development is that of *invention* and not of mere copying. And neither stimulus-response generalization nor the introduction of transformational responses can explain novelty or invention. By contrast the concepts of assimilation and accommodation and of operational structure (which are created, not merely discovered, as a result of the subject's activities), are oriented toward this inventive construction which characterizes all living thought.'

Unfortunately, as yet there have been few systematic experimental studies of how the cognitive *schemata* are acquired, and how these relate to biological and social factors. Furthermore, the seductive theory of stages is, as Tuddenham (1970) points out, implicit in standard intelligence tests such as the Stanford–Binet. Moreover, as Bovet (1970), one of Piaget's colleagues, indicates, 'We have to emphasize that we have hardly ever studied the reactions of subjects older than 12 years of age; therefore, the question of a possible acceleration or modification of cognitive processes in adults remains open.' Thus Piaget's theory of intellectual development is best seen as a useful model for stimulating systematic research rather than as an explanatory theory of the nature and development of intelligence.

Applications to mental subnormality

During the last twenty years, the laws concerning intellectual growth as measured by the IQ have increasingly been appreciated. In earlier editions of this book we have offered detailed evidence on test reliability. It is no longer necessary to repeat this and only a brief summary will be offered: longitudinal researches show consistently that (a) the predictive value of the IQ (as measured by test-retest correlations) decreases as the interval between the tests lengthens; and, as a corollary, (b) although the group or population average may not alter greatly, there will be considerable change of status of some individuals within that group (subsequent retests showing that to varying extents some subjects increase in IQ, some decrease, some fluctuate and some remain constant); and (c) mental tests given to children in the pre-school years usually have little if any predictive value in the long term. In particular, steadily decreasing correlations usually indicate genuine growth changes, not artefacts.

Test-retest correlations for very short intervals usually amount to ·90, or a little higher. The implications of such values have been discussed by Shapiro (1951) and Clarke and Clarke (1972). While they indicate great stability in the order of scores for the majority of the particular group, such correlations conceal, for the uninitiated, a minority for whom changes of relative position may be considerable. Since in longitudinal studies we are dealing with relationships usually much lower than ·9, it has been argued that variability of individual status over many years is more probable than great consistency (see Honzik *et al.*, 1948; Sontag *et al.*, 1958; Clarke and Clarke, 1972). Indeed, the latter authors have offered evidence that similar laws apply to personality development, the growth of scholastic skills and other human characteristics.

This being so, it is not surprising to find numerous studies of IQ changes in the midly subnormal, even under conditions where perhaps no obviously active attempts are made to promote such changes. Researches by Guertin (1949, 1950), Clarke and Clarke (1954), Mundy (1955), Marchand (1956), Clarke *et al.* (1958), Roswell Harris (1958), Rosen *et al.* (1968) and Brown (1972) have all been concerned with IQ increments, sometimes very substantial, over time. There seems to be some agreement that such improvements occur in adolescence and young adult life rather than earlier, in those drawn from subcultural surroundings. What happens when deliberate attempts at remediation are made, will be reserved for discussion in the next chapter.

In the meanwhile, we propose to outline in some detail the only recent study which challenges the interpretation given above.

Fisher and Zeaman (1970) have reported what in some ways is an impressive study on the growth and decline of retardate intelligence, using an institutional population and a semi-longitudinal method for data collection. Unlike longitutional research, this approach requires merely a few years. Each subject was tested at least twice, and many repeated measurements were not required; straight lines connect up adjacent results and these were averaged within each CA interval. In turn these averages are connected.

These authors list some of the studies on IQ stability or change in retardates. They point out that the results are often in apparent contradiction but maintain that retardates of different ages, levels and aetiologies have been examined, and that the growth of intelligence could conceivably change with these variables. One can account for the bulk of these studies by a quite simple rule; the younger the subject below age 16, the greater the likelihood of a spontaneous decrease in IQ with age. The older the subjects, the greater the likelihood of an increase in IQ.

Using Stanford–Binet IQs, MAs and IQs were plotted using the semi-longitudinal method for five levels of mental retardation. All levels fall precipitously from CA2 to 16 years. Then, because CA is fixed at about 16 in the MA/CA formula, the IQ starts to rise for the higher levels, because the MA is still growing. 'These data show that it is indeed possible to get either increases or decreases in IQ over time for retarded populations depending upon what ages and levels are chosen. Very few of the apparently discrepant published findings of IQ changes in the retardate are inconsistent with this general picture. . . .'

These authors go on to state that they do not attach any profound psychological significance to these changes in IQ. Indeed, they 'constitute a nuisance because of their inconsistency. Also, in a theoretical sense, if the test were aiming to measure a constant, genetically determined aspect of intelligence, it would be appropriate to try to find a transformation of the scale which would yield age invariant scores. In other words, it would be nice if we could find for each retardate a number, representing his intelligence, which would remain constant over a lifetime and would predictably describe the growth and decline of mental age' (Fisher and Zeaman, 1970, pp. 166–7).

These are indeed remarkable statements if one accepts the views of Vernon (1970) and many others on intelligence. They suggest that intelligence 'A' can be directly inferred from intelligence 'C' in an institutionalized population. The psychological significance or otherwise of large IQ increments will be discussed later. Suffice it to say that a ten-year study undertaken by the present writers on a young adult group of subnormals, who had earlier shown significant increases in IQ, failed completely because the vast majority of the group were no longer available for study, having achieved discharge from care. Or, to take an extreme example, the severely subnormal isolated and cruelly treated twins who were rescued at the age of 7 had IQs of 94 and 95 respectively by age 11 (Koluchova, 1972). No constant could be useful in this unusual situation (see Chapter 7).

Having earlier shown that mongoloid intelligence possesses a strong logarithmic component, the authors fitted a number of parameters by means of multiple regression analyses to the five levels of retardation. Fisher and Zeaman go on to produce a simplified equation as follows: $MA = 36K \ln CA + KCA + 44 \cdot 8K + 27 \cdot 1$. Each subject can be assigned a K value by substituting his MA and CA into the equation and solving for K. The authors provide a table for simplifying this procedure. 'The value of K should remain constant from early childhood to old age, interpretable much as the IQ is interpreted – a measure of relative intelligence (although in this case the result of both growth and decay processes).' It is finally argued that, unlike IQ, the K values show fairly stable test-retest correlations over time.

These notions, heroic in their aims, if perhaps old-fashioned in their conceptions, remain to be tested in longitudinal studies. In the meanwhile, the following points must be made:

1. The semi-longitudinal method may be a misleading approach to the whole growth curve of an individual.
2. There may well be sampling differences at the later ages, by which time, if the institution has any realistic scheme of rehabilitation, the more promising members of the group will have left and will therefore have been omitted from study. Assuming a constant intake to the institution, the data which indicate declining numbers with increasing CA may support this possibility.
3. The authors fail to discuss approaches to intelligence testing other than those of Binet, where artefactual changes at different ages are well known to occur. Their aim to compensate for such changes is of course laudable, and it is important for students of mental growth to be aware of such artefacts.
4. The techniques used were ultimately derived from averages over mostly rather short time intervals. It is well appreciated that averages are much more stable than individual curves.

In spite of these criticisms the study is of value in indicating the relation of growth to level and to age, but longitudinal work will indicate whether the doubts of the present writers are justified.

It seems clear that, in the mildly subnormal, growth changes are common. This being so, the reasons for such changes become of immediate interest. These will include the effects of test practice, errors of measurement or incorrect testing, as well as genuine variations in growth rates, sometimes genetic and sometimes environmental in origin. In this latter connection, experimental studies, as well as the results of natural occurrences which have been properly documented, have a bearing upon the limits to change and prospects for up-grading deprived members of the population. In some such studies the concept of regression to the mean is not infrequently invoked as a cause of substantial changes. It must, however, be appreciated that this concept is descriptive rather than explanatory, and is often used in a confused and illogical way (Clarke *et al.*, 1960).

Conclusions

1. All cognitive activities, however defined, intercorrelate positively. It is possible to sample cognitive processes by selecting tasks, the correlations between which are moderate to low (as in a wide-spreading intelligence test) or high, in which cases the processes are likely to be similar. The Spearman notion of a general factor plus specifics is insufficient to account for these relationships; group factors must at least be added. Nevertheless, an equally plausible theory merely suggests common neural bonds as underlying these correlations.
2. Intelligence, however defined, is multi-faceted.

3. Each facet of intelligence must have its own developmental history.
4. There is the plausible suggestion that the development of intelligence involves increasing differentiation, and that this is itself the result of frequent encounters with particular demands of the environment, building up particular facets by means of overlearning.
5. Once an ability has been created by genetic-environmental interaction it is not easily extinguished, except through gross disuse over long periods or through pathological changes in the brain.
6. So far as the basis of intelligence is concerned, one is dealing with absolutely necessary genetic factors interacting with absolutely necesssary environmental agencies. There is a suggestion that any analysis involving the pre-supposition of *additive* influences is based on a misconception of these interactive relationships. The more useful point is whether genetics or environment in a particular group are *seen* to be the more influential: thus in an optimum environment, observed differences between children must be genetic or constitutional in origin, but those same children raised in social isolation would be severely subnormal intellectually. Where children from vastly different environments are being compared, environmental differences will be *seen* as more relevant, but these will obviously be superimposed upon genetic influences. In any event, it is highly unlikely that any general statement about the relative influences of genetic/environmental interaction will cover all cases. This being so, a search of this type seems largely unprofitable (see Chapter 7).
7. During development there is a good deal more variability in individual growth than is commonly accepted (Clarke and Clarke, 1972). This leads then to a need to study the genetic and environmental factors involved in such changes.
8. In this whole field, in the writers' view, the most useful approach is to study the conditions facilitating the development of intellectual attainments, as well as those which retard them. The study of particular groups under properly defined and measured influences, durations and reinforcements is already beginning to lead to a better understanding of the growth of intellectual skills. Indeed, the study of intelligence in the context of research upon human skills is likely to prove far more rewarding than a search for an entity called intelligence.

References

BINET, A. and SIMON, T. (1916) *The Development of Intelligence in Children* (transl. E. S. Kite). Baltimore, Md.: Williams & Wilkins.

BOVET, M. (1970) Piaget's theory of cognitive development, sociocultural differences, and mental retardation. In HAYWOOD, H. C. (ed.) *Social-Cultural Aspects of Mental Retardation*. New York: Appleton-Century-Crofts.

BROWN, R. I. (1972) Cognitive changes in the adolescent slow learner. *J. Child Psychol. Psychiat.*, **13**, 183–93.

BURT, C. (1921) *Mental and Scholastic Tests*. LCC Rep. No. 2052. London: London County Council.

BURT, C. (1962) *Mental and Scholastic Tests* (4th edn). London: Staples Press.

CLARKE, A. D. B. and CLARKE, A. M. (1954) Cognitive changes in the feeble-minded. *Brit. J. Psychol.*, **45**, 173–9.

CLARKE, A. D. B. and CLARKE, A. M. (1972) Consistency and variability in the growth of human characteristics. In WALL, W. D. and VARMA, V. P. (eds.) *Advances in Educational Psychology: 1*. London: Univ. of London Press.

CLARKE, A. D. B., CLARKE, A. M. and BROWN, R. I. (1960) Regression to the mean: a confused concept. *Brit. J. Psychol.*, **51**, 105–17.

CLARKE, A. D. B., CLARKE, A. M. and REIMAN, S. (1958) Cognitive and social changes in the feebleminded – three further studies. *Brit. J. Psychol.*, **49**, 144–57.

DEARBORN, W. F. (1928) *Intelligence Tests: their Significance for School and Society*. Boston: Houghton Mifflin.

DEARBORN, W. F. and ROTHNEY, J. W. M. (1941) *Predicting the Child's Development*. Cambridge, Mass.: Sci.-Art Publ.

FERGUSON, G. A. (1954) On learning and human ability. *Canad. J. Psychol.*, **8**, 95–112.

FISHER, M. A. and ZEAMAN, D. (1970) Growth and decline of retardate intelligence. In ELLIS, N. R. (ed.) *International Review of Research in Mental Retardation*, **4**, 151–91. New York and London: Academic Press.

GALTON, F. (1892) *Hereditary Genius* (2nd edn). London: Macmillan.

GUERTIN, W. H. (1949) Mental growth in pseudo-feeblemindedness. *J. clin. Psychol.*, **5**, 414–18.

GUERTIN, W. H. (1950) Differential characteristics of the pseudo-feebleminded. *Amer. J. ment. Defic.*, **54**, 394–8.

GUILFORD, J. P. (1959) Three faces of intellect. *Amer. Psychol.*, **14**, 469–79.

HEBB, D. O. (1949) *The Organization of Behaviour*. London: Chapman & Hall.

HEBER, R. and GARBER, H. (1971) An experiment in prevention of cultural-familial mental retardation. In PRIMROSE, D. A. (ed.) *Proc. 2nd Congr. Internat. Assoc. Scient. Stud. Ment. Defic.*, 31–5. Warsaw: Polish Medical Publishers; Amsterdam: Swets & Zeitlinger.

HONZIK, M. P., MACFARLANE, J. W. and ALLEN, C. (1948) The stability of mental test performance between two and eighteen years. *J. exp. Educ.*, **17**, 309–24.

HUNT, J. MCV. (1961) *Intelligence and Experience*. New York: Ronald Press.

JENSEN, A. R. (1969) How much can we boost IQ and scholastic achievement? *Harvard educ. Rev.*, **39**, 1–123.

KOLUCHOVA, J. (1972) Severe deprivation in twins: a case study. *J. Child Psychol. Psychiat.*, **13**, 107–14.

MARCHAND, J. G. (1956) Changes of psychometric test results in mental defective employment care patients. *Amer. J. ment. Defic.*, **60**, 852–9.

MUNDY, L. (1955) *Environmental Influences in Intellectual Function as measured by Intelligence Tests.* Unpubl. M.Sc. thesis, Univ. of London.

PIAGET, J. (1970) Piaget's theory. In MUSSEN, P. H. (ed.) *Carmichael's Manual of Child Psychology* (3rd edn). New York: Wiley.

ROSEN, R., STALLINGS, L., FLOOR, L. and NOWAKISKA, M. (1968) Reliability and stability of Wechsler IQ scores for institutionalized mental subnormals. *Amer. J. ment. Defic.*, **73**, 218–25.

ROSWELL HARRIS, D. (1958) *Some Aspects of Cognitive and Personality Test Changes in a Group of 100 Feebleminded Young Men.* Unpubl. M.A. thesis, Univ. of Reading.

SHAPIRO, M. B. (1951) An experimental approach to diagnostic testing. *J. ment. Sci.*, **97**, 748–64.

SKEELS, H. M. and DYE, H. B. (1939) A study of the effects of differential stimulation on mentally retarded children. *Proc. Amer. Assoc. ment. Defic.*, **44**, 114–36.

SONTAG, L. W., BAKER, C. T. and NELSON, V. L. (1958) Mental growth and personality development: a longitudinal study. *Monogr. Soc. Res. Child Developm.*, **23** (68), 2.

SPEARMAN, C. (1904) 'General intelligence': objectively determined and measured. *Amer. J. Psychol.*, **115**, 201–92.

TERMAN, L. M. (1919) *The Measurement of Intelligence.* London: Harrap.

THURSTONE, L. L. (1947) *Multiple Factor Analysis.* Chicago: Univ. of Chicago Press.

TUDDENHAM, R. D. (1970) A 'Piagetian' test of cognitive development. In DOCKRELL, W. B. (ed.) *On Intelligence.* London: Methuen.

UZGIRIS, I. C. (1970) Sociocultural factors in cognitive development. In HAYWOOD, H. C. (ed.) *Social-Cultural Aspects of Mental Retardation.* New York: Grune & Stratton.

VERNON, P. E. (1950) *The Structure of Human Abilities.* London: Methuen.

VERNON, P. E. (1955) Presidential address: the psychology of intelligence and G. *Bull. Brit. Psychol. Soc.*, **26**, 1–14.

VERNON, P. E. (1970) Intelligence. In DOCKRELL, W. B. (ed.) *On Intelligence.* London: Methuen.

7

A. M. Clarke and A. D. B. Clarke

Genetic-environmental interactions
in cognitive development

Introduction

The topic implied by the title of this chapter is very complex, and space permits no more than a highly selective review. The nature-nurture issue was the subject of bitter debate in the 1930s, very much on an 'either-or' basis, with the hereditarians and environmentalists each taking an extreme stand. Superficially at least, the present debate is more sophisticated, with most research workers eager to indicate that they are interactionists. This term, however, permits a wide range of interpretations, with Jensen and Eysenck at one extreme (asserting that 80 per cent of the variance for intellectual differences is genetic in origin), and Skeels and Hunt at the other.

The problem of genetic and environmental interaction in the development of human characteristics is central to the behavioural sciences. For the field of mental subnormality, it is of particular relevance to the causation and treatment of mildly handicapped and disadvantaged children. Hence the topic will be treated quite generally in this chapter.

The first point to be considered is the argument by analogy that since important human characteristics like height are known to be strongly influenced by heredity, it is likely that others such as intelligence will also be. Furthermore, it has been shown that animals can, by judicious manipulation of genetic characteristics, be bred for certain behavioural traits. Two points arise in this connection. (1) It is known that various environmental factors affect the development of height, particularly nutrition; to quote an extreme example, a severely rachitic child will not develop to his potential stature. In another connection, a leading geneticist once pointed out that the best dairy cow will cease to give its abundant supply of milk if severely undernourished. (2) The evolutionary development in the highest primates of a complex and sophisticated system of communication, renders them capable of transmitting information from generation to generation, which raises the possibility that some intellectual strategies as well as elaborated verbal codes may be acquired rather than inherited, or, at the least, so modified on the basis of an unobservable hereditary potential as to alter substantially the position of intellectual development by comparison with purely physical characteristics.

We see then that an important conceptual distinction must be made between the operation of the physical environment on the development of elaborated behavioural characteristics and the potential operation of the social environment. In this connection a further distinction needs to be drawn between environmental factors which are likely to have a rapid effect, and those which are likely to operate slowly and cumulatively. In the former category we find certain events may rapidly and permanently damage the genotype, as demonstrated by abnormal mutations following exposure to an atomic bomb explosion; others may damage the developing foetus *in utero*; maternal rubella and placenta collapse being different examples of this. Yet others, such as acute cerebral infections or severe trauma, may render a normally intelligent child severely subnormal in a matter of days or weeks. In the second category, the effect of nutrition on height and other physical characteristics is a slow process, to be measured in years rather than weeks. There is no evidence, nor in our view is there ever likely to be any, that social factors operate rapidly; they must be seen as potentially long-term variables, if they operate at all.

Before considering the data, it may be helpful to outline the research models which are theoretically valid for elucidating the problem. These will include both those which for ethical reasons cannot be used, and those which can and have been used.

(1) EXPERIMENTAL MANIPULATION OF THE ENVIRONMENT

(a) If children born to *two* parents of known high IQ were to be experimentally placed at birth in conditions of poverty and deprivation, reared by foster parents *both* of known low IQ for, say fifteen years, and were found to be very bright, this would be powerful evidence for heredity being of overwhelming importance in determining intelligence.

(b) If children born to two parents of known low IQ were experimentally placed at birth with parents both known to be bright, and brought up in a stimulating and culturally rich environment, and resembled their true parents more than their foster parents, heredity would be presumed to be the powerful factor.

(c) If children born to two parents of known low IQ were experimentally manipulated in such a way that the potentially adverse effects of living with their parents were compensated for, yet developed low intelligence, once again heredity would emerge supreme.

(d) If a cohort of identical twins born to parents of known high (or low) IQ were separated at birth, one twin remaining with the natural parents and the other twin placed with parents varying from very unintelligent to highly intelligent; and if, after fifteen years, those whose environment differed substantially from the natural home resembled each other closely, heredity would be shown predominant.

In practice, of these experimental models (a) and (d) cannot be tried for ethical reasons; there is partial evidence on (b), and (c) is the subject of a recent ongoing experiment in which the results are suggestive, but the children are not as yet old enough for the results to be clearly evaluated.

(2) OBSERVED DATA FROM SITUATIONS WHICH HAVE ARISEN THROUGH NATURAL SOCIAL CAUSES

These form the vast bulk of available evidence on heredity and environment. The following are situations which have been used to elucidate the effects of either heredity or environment on intellectual performance. In all cases the tool used was a standardized intelligence test, usually with a verbal component. The following predictions may be made.

Genetics

1. Correlations between related individuals should show an increasing size according to the closeness of the familial relations.
2. Children separated from their natural mothers and reared in foster homes should resemble their mothers more closely than their foster mothers.
3. Much less certainly, some writers have predicted that there should be regression to the mean across generations. Galton noticed that children of very tall parents tended to be shorter, while children of short parents tended to be taller. It has been suggested that a similar effect will be found with respect to intelligence. One would expect to find studies with IQs of both parents and all their children available for the testing of this hypothesis.
4. Children resident in institutions where the range of environment is limited should show considerable individual differences.
5. Separated identical twins should show a higher intercorrelation of test scores than siblings, and, even if there are wide environmental differences for each member of the twin pair, their scores should be very similar, and the relationship should be much the same as for identical twins reared together.

Environment

1. Converse findings to those above should in general be available, except that correlations between related individuals should show an increasing size according to the closeness of the familial relationships for reasons of environmental similarities. This point is the same as (1) under Genetics.
2. Children whose environments change for a prolonged period should show changing growth rates in the direction predicted by the environmental change.
3. The amount of change noted under (2) above should relate to the degree and duration of environmental alteration.

As will be seen when data are examined, few studies are anywhere near to being crucial, but as Burt (1967) states: 'The logic of the argument should be carefully noted: as in all natural science, the mode of proof is indirect; hence the conclusions can never be "necessary" or "certain", but only probable. The critic . . . commonly misses this point and revels in demonstrating that some alternative can be conceived. But one can always think up alternatives; a hypothesis empirically shown to be probable can only be overthrown by proving that the proposed alternative *is still more probable.*'

The predictions mentioned above will now be compared with existing studies and, with one exception, poorer models not so far mentioned will be ignored. The exception relates to the correlates of social class; these variables appear so powerful and pervasive that, whatever the balance of forces that influences their origin, they are clearly of major general importance quite apart from their specific relevance to the problem of mild subnormality. In particular, the models described under Environment (2) and (3) will be closely examined because both natural and contrived experiments are now numerous, and because the methodological problems posed by these approaches are relatively straightforward.

Genetic factors

(1) Correlations between IQs of individuals and their relatives depend upon the closeness of the familial relationships. Erlenmeyer-Kimling and Jarvik (1963) have summarized 52 studies and present median correlations as well as their range. Thus, unrelated children reared together yield median IQ intercorrelations of ·23 (range: ·15 to ·32); foster-parent and child, ·20 (range: ·18 to ·40 – 3 studies); parent-child, ·50 (range: ·22 to ·80 – 12 studies); siblings reared apart, ·40 (range: ·33 to ·47 – 2 studies); siblings reared together, ·49 (range: ·30 to ·77 – 35 studies); dizygotic twins reared together, ·53 (range: ·38 to ·88 – 20 studies); monozygotic twins reared together, ·87 (range: ·76 to ·95 – 14 studies); monozygotic twins reared apart, ·75 (range: ·61 to ·87 – 4 studies). The ranges[1] around these median values are very considerable, and may reflect either (1) differences in design and execution of the studies, or (2) differences in populations studied with respect to genetic and environmental variables; or both.

The work of Erlenmeyer-Kimling and Jarvik is well known and quoted by all those writing upon the inheritance of intelligence (e.g. Jensen, 1969; Eysenck, 1971). It is also well appreciated that the majority of separated monozygotic twins are reared in similar environments (e.g. Shields, 1962). A problem in interpreting kinship data is that environments of relatives are likely themselves to be correlated, and with adequate measures might provide a hierarchy of correlations resembling the IQ correlation matrix. Thus, on an environmental hypothesis one would expect a low relationship between, say, cousins, and a very high correlation between identical twins reared together.

In favour of genetic factors, however, is the fact of very low correlations

---

[1] These ranges are approximate, having been estimated from a small graph.

between foster parents and children, and on an environmental hypothesis one would surely expect the usual correlation between parent and child IQ (when living together) to be higher than ·50, which is about the same as that for unrelated people who marry.

(2) The correlation between maternal and child IQ has been firmly established as averaging about ·50. Skodak and Skeels (1949) offered a final report on 100 children with inferior social histories adopted in infancy into superior homes. It was shown that these had a normal chance of superiority or inferiority (IQ range at 13 was 70 to 154, with a mean of 117) in spite of the fact that true mothers' IQs averaged well below 100. Nevertheless, by the age of 13 a correlation with true mothers' IQ of ·44 was established, even though there was a mean difference of over 20 points between the mothers and their children. This can only be interpreted as showing the influence of genetic factors on the differences between the children, as well as, of course, an environmental influence, even after allowing for regression to the mean (see below).

(3) Burt (1967) points out that people are apt to think of heredity as a tendency of like to beget like, whereas Mendelian theory is equally applicable to account for differences within families. One of the important areas of debate in this connection is regression to the mean, first noticed by Francis Galton in the context of height. For intelligence this would entail the paradox that if the parents are dull, their children will be brighter, and if the parents are bright, their children will be duller than they are, i.e. in each case the intelligence of the children will tend to be nearer to that of the population average than that of their parents. Of the several studies pertinent to the problem, the best known is one by Burt (1961), while Oden's (1968) report on the follow-up of Terman's gifted group and their children is also often quoted. Burt's evidence appears to provide perfect support for the usual genetic prediction of regression halfway to the mean. Thus with an average paternal IQ of 140, the mean IQ of the children was 121, and with an average paternal IQ of 85, the average of the children was 93.

There are a number of difficulties concerning this study: for example, perfect regression halfway to the mean would only be predicted genetically with random mating, whereas as mentioned above, there is substantial assortative mating for intelligence. The results appear suspiciously perfect, since this amount of regression would not be predicted in an assortatively mated population. The mothers' IQs thus constitute an unknown variable, and Burt's statements that his study 'is intended merely as a pilot enquiry', that 'the data are too crude and limited for a detailed examination by a full analysis of variance' and that 'For obvious reasons the assessments of adult intelligence were less thorough and less reliable' suggest that these findings are by no means as firm as some subsequent authors have interpreted them.

The whole issue of regression to the mean has been subject to misinterpretation and misunderstandings. Firstly, it is incorrectly thought, on the basis of the genetic model, that regression will be predicted *equally* from single parent and mid-parent intelligence. In fact, it only applies in the case of single parent-child correlations, and will, of course, be reduced by the extent to which assortative mating occurs. Secondly, and probably in part due to the first confusion, Burt's study has been treated as though it referred to mid-parent-child regression, whereas in fact the data are on fathers' and sons' intelligence levels only. Thirdly, it has been considered that parent-child regression is not predictable on any environmental hypothesis. In fact, in the case of single-parent-child regression, hypothetically it could be, but the same environmental argument loses plausibility if the fact of sibling differences is considered in conjunction with it. Thus the strength of the genetic explanation of regression does not hinge upon the parent-child relationship alone. However, in the case of mid-parent-child regression, as for example observed by Outhit (1933) and more recently by Reed and Reed (1965), this is not predicted by a simple additive polygenic model; regression here can only be explained on either environmental grounds, or on the basis of a radically different genetic model. In either case, test error would be implicated to some extent. It will thus be obvious that regression to the mean is the weakest and most confused of all the genetic arguments discussed here. The authors are greatly indebted to their colleague, Mr M. McAskie, for much of the section outlined under (3) above.

(4) Institutions usually offer a uniformity of environment, with poor adult-child ratios and relationships. Long residence under such conditions might be expected to produce a uniformity in intellectual functioning in ordinary children. While one or two studies indicate a decreasing IQ variability (e.g. Jones and Carr-Saunders, 1927) the majority show a wide range of individual differences surviving the impact of environmental uniformity (Burt, 1961; 1966).

(5) The universal finding that identical twin IQ correlations are very high, and much higher than sibling correlations, has been accepted as powerful evidence of the role of heredity. Even if one views this from an environmental view (i.e. that identical twins must have a closer environmental similarity than other members of the species, and that identical twins reared apart are commonly brought up in similar environments), there is no environmental reason why identical twins reared apart should correlate *more closely* than siblings reared together, except that in the former case there is identity in ages but not in the latter.

We will now consider twin studies in some detail, since these comprise the most widely quoted area of research in the genetics of intelligence. Various statistical methods have been evolved for estimating the proportion of the variance between individuals that can be ascribed to genetic factors, and Mittler (1971) provides a useful review. McClearn (1970) quotes some surprising results from the work of Vandenberg (1966) in which within-pair variances were calculated for MZ and DZ twins on the six Primary Mental Ability subtests. Significant hereditary determinants for verbal, space, number and fluency were suggested, but no evidence for hereditary determination of memory *or reasoning* was forthcoming.

Burt's (1966) study of identical twins reared apart is widely quoted as meeting the usual objection to such studies, namely that the separated individuals are commonly reared in similar environments. Admittedly there have been exceptions where a few cases, reared in markedly different circumstances, have shown considerable differences (Newman *et al.*, 1937). Apparently Burt had the opportunity over many years to build up a case study of some identical twins separated very early in life and reared in different social classes. His general findings indicated surprisingly high intercorrelations for IQ in spite of social class differences, but a social class effect on school attainments. Yet there are a number of puzzling features about this study which are seldom noticed. First, no raw data are presented, and in particular no indication of the mean IQs for each half of the twin pairs. It could be that the means would indicate social class correlates, yet the intercorrelations of IQ could still remain very high. Second, the class distribution of those remaining with their parents was as follows: social classes I − III = 19; social classes IV − VI = 34. The other twins were distributed in foster homes as follows: social classes I − III = 11; social classes IV − VI = 42. While it is clear that considerable differences in class distribution occurred, they are not overwhelmingly great in most cases. Only about half the sample had twins who experienced a shift of two or more social classes when fostered. Third, the method of assessment of IQ is not entirely clear. Thus Burt (1967), commenting on the views of some of his critics, stated that 'what I was discussing was not acquired knowledge or skill . . . but rather the psychologist's attempts to assess the individual's "innate general ability" – a purely "hypothetical factor". My object was to demonstrate that, when these assessments were reached, not by taking scores on some familiar "group test" just as they stand, but *by adopting the more elaborate procedures which my colleagues and I had used*, then the errors of assessment were comparatively slight' (our italics). Reference back to the 'elaborate procedures' in the 1966 paper shows that the tests used were: (1) a group test of non-verbal and verbal items; (2) an individual test, Burt's own revision of the Terman–Burt scale, 'used primarily for standardization, and for doubtful cases'; (3) a set of performance tests. The test results 'were submitted to the teachers for comment or criticism; and, wherever any question arose, the child was re-examined'. It is not stated how often such retests occurred, nor what their effect was. Did they, for example, involve a closer approximation of the IQs of twin pairs ? Table 2 in the 1966 paper includes the mysterious heading 'Final assessment' without indicating there or elsewhere how these were reached, but the effect on correlations was slightly to raise the relationship between IQs of identical twins reared apart.

It will be seen that Burt's paper raises a number of important questions which unfortunately can never be answered now. Knowing what we do about the 'experimenter effect' a much closer enquiry on the mode of assessment would have been desirable in order to exclude this as possessing any possible influence (e.g. knowledge of the hypothesis, knowledge of the other twin test scores). In particular the notion of establishing 'innate general ability', dated though it is, appears to beg the whole question. If those doing the assessments had been able to establish this, then by definition identical twins reared apart in different environments would possess identical innate general ability, which in fact approximates to Burt's reported findings.

Indices of heritability are usually based on the comparison of intra-class correlations between identical and fraternal twins. Using such formulae, whether Holzinger's H or Falconer's h^2, it is usually concluded that about 80 per cent of the variance is genetic in origin. Nevertheless, it is nearly always stated that such estimates are based upon North American or European populations and cannot necessarily be generalized, and that studies of minority populations are also needed.

It must be indicated, however, that there are still a number of problems in this type of approach. As Hunt (1961; already referred to in the last chapter) indicates, the analysis of variance model fits the data too poorly and assumes that genetic and environmental variances are additive and without interaction. A further point, in comparing fraternal twin intercorrelations with identical twin correlations, relates to twin studies in general. These are used because in non-separated twins, whether fraternal or identical, it is assumed that environment is held more or less constant for each member of the twin pair; if this is so, it is scarcely surprising that heredity should emerge as the more powerful variable. But the whole approach to estimating heritability in this fashion is also weakened by the range of findings in twin studies. Thus Erlenmeyer-Kimling and Jarvik (1963) quote the range of ·40 to ·65 for dizygotic twins of opposite sex reared together, ·63 to ·85 for monozygotic twins reared apart, and ·76 to ·95 for mono-zygotics reared together. Indeed, Jarvik and Erlenmeyer-Kimling (1967), who are among those most closely identified with arguments for the importance of genetic factors, protest that 'attempts to assess the relative contribution of genotypic differences to individual differences in psychological characters continue to appear in the literature', and that the 'heritability' estimate 'is usually regarded as an approximation to some true, fixed property of the characteristic under study. The foregoing assumption is incorrect'. They go on to indicate that heritability would receive its highest estimate for a genetically heterogeneous group which had undergone relatively homogeneous environmental circumstances, and would appear low when derived from comparatively homogeneous populations, experiencing a diversity of environmental conditions.

A further source of disagreement has recently been outlined by Jensen (1971). He argues that the established practice of squaring the correlation coefficient in order to obtain the percentage of variance due to genetic factors in kinship correlations is unjustified. Such correlations, unsquared, are themselves the genetic proportion.

McClearn (1970) discusses in some detail these problems and shows that the assumption that comparison of mono- with dizygotic twins will indicate the contribution of heredity is fraught with difficulties.

The straightforward application of twin study results to the population at large is prevented by two features of the twin situation. The magnitude of the genetic effect is assessed by comparing differences between genetically identical individuals to the differences between genetically diverse individuals; the genetic diversity, however, is only that which can exist among progeny of the same parents. This will involve much less variability than exists in the population as a whole. Similarly, the environmental forces whose impact is assessed by MZ pair differences are only those environmental differences that exist within a family. Again this must certainly underestimate the range of environmental forces at work in the population.

Moreover, Penrose (1972) has indicated that on the assumption of an 80 per cent hereditary contribution to intellectual differences, and with the fact of assortative mating, IQ correlations between parents and their children and between siblings should be much higher than they in fact are. He also suggests that psychologists should pay less attention to intra-familial differences in intelligence and more to special abilities.

In summary, in the present state of knowledge one can accept the existence of powerful genetic factors in the development of individual differences in intelligence, scholastic ability and other characteristics, without presuming, on the basis of less than adequate data, to ascribe a particular proportion of the variance to genetics or environment.

This section can be concluded by stating the obvious, that genetic factors exert a strong influence on intellectual development, and may be assumed to account for a large part of observed intellectual differences. Indeed with a genetic theory which is prepared to explain both similarities and differences within families, it is tempting to assume that inheritance accounts for virtually all of the variance in a population with respect to measured intelligence; in fact many serious students of this problem believe that it accounts for by far the major part. We have now to look at evidence on the effect of the environment to account for the fact that some have hesitation in adopting this position as firmly established.

Environmental factors

INTRODUCTION

The word environmental needs definition for the purposes of this section. It is perfectly correct to regard brain damage due to trauma, or resulting from the effects of maternal rubella in early pregnancy, or underdevelopment due to early malnutrition, as environmental in origin, and there is seldom any controversy over these or allied conditions. The present section, however, will be concerned only with the rather less obvious and much more controversial effects of social environments; thus in this section, environmental is used as a synonym for social-psychological.

It may be helpful to start with a logical argument. It does not seem possible, if evolutionary theory is accepted, to conceive of *any* behaviour which does not have a biological foundation – that is, in the final analysis of most cases a heredi-tary basis. No biological scientist is likely to accept the 'blank slate' hypothesis, and latterly the writings of Chomsky and Lenneberg have added powerfully to the logical argument in showing the biological basis of human language acquisi-tion. Those who work in the field of mental subnormality should have no difficulty in accepting the proposition that there are a few very rare cases of individuals born without a 'language acquisition device', whereas other members of the species appear to have a highly developed and sensitive ability to acquire language. In a beautifully succinct account of his theory, Lenneberg (1964) describes four criteria which may distinguish biologically from culturally determined behaviour, and illustrates these by contrasting walking (biologically determined) with *writing* (culturally determined, although with a biological basis).

Lenneberg does not argue that developed language is a genotypic phenomenon – he asserts that the culturally determined features in language are obvious, and his discussion focuses on the less obvious innate features.

It is self-evident that there is a large environmental component to language as used by any human being. It is an established fact that verbal intelligence tests correlate as well or better with school achievement as do any other behavioural measures. All the data in the previous section on genetic factors in intelligence were based on intelligence tests with a large verbal component. The question is to what extent does the language environment, in which a child develops, determine his efficiency on verbal reasoning tests; are there gross differences in language environment within one culture; are these differences reflected in intelligence tests and scholastic achievement? May some non-verbal strategies of reasoning be shaped by the environment?

THE CORRELATES OF SOCIAL CLASS

An attempt to describe differences within a culture will be mentioned. This is the report of Hess and Shipman (1965), based upon Bernstein's theories. They took a group of 163 Negro mothers of 4-year-old children representing four social classes: college-educated, professional and managerial; skilled, but not college educated; unskilled and semi-skilled, with mostly no high-school education; unskilled or semi-skilled level, but with fathers absent and mothers on public assistance. These mothers were interviewed twice in their homes, and brought to the university for testing and for an interaction session between mother and child in which the mother was taught three simple tasks by the staff member and then asked to teach these tasks to the child.

The results showed (a) a striking difference in verbal output differentiating middle-class mothers from those of the three other groups; (b) a difference in the use of abstract words, scores ranged from an average index of 5·6 for middle-class mothers to 1·8 for the recipient of public assistance; (c) a difference in the use of complex syntactic structures. There were differences in control systems: the middle-class mothers in response to questions concerning how they would deal with such situations as the child breaking school rules, failing to achieve, or having been wronged by someone, showed a marked tendency to offer person-oriented logical and elaborated explanations, while the lowest classes offered status-oriented orders. There were significant differences among the children on cognitive tasks which correlated with observed differences among the mothers in their mode of teaching their own child in an experimental session. On the other hand, the mothers of the four groups differed little in the affective elements of their interaction with their children.

The authors define cultural deprivation in terms of lack of cognitive meaning in the mother-child communication system. The 'meaning of deprivation is a deprivation of meaning, a cognitive environment in which behavior is controlled by status rules rather than by attention to the individual characteristics of a specific situation and one in which behaviour is not mediated by verbal cues or by teaching that relates events to one another and the present to the future.' The end result is the child responsive to authority rather than to rationale, non-reflective and without long-term goals.

Faced with pronounced differences betweeen social classes in their method of communicating with their children, it might be expected that there will be differences among children reflecting the language and cognitive environments in which they are reared. From the foregoing, it could be predicted that:

1. SES differences should be found not only in global IQ measures, but in the qualitative aspects of a child's preferred cognitive strategy. It is to be expected that children reared in circumstances favouring abstract strategies would perform well in tests demanding abstract thinking, and conversely those reared in cultures relatively devoid of cognitive meaning will encourage strategies relying on associative rote learning, at which such children might be expected to excel. (This is borne out by the data; see p. 176.)
2. Since successful achievement at school is increasingly dependent upon abstract cognitive strategies, one would expect a growing disparity between high and low social classes as age increases. (This is confirmed; see p. 177.)
3. One would expect a positive relation between ability to receive and profit from higher education and continued conceptual development. (Again this is confirmed; see p. 177.)

It is of interest that little difference may be found between social groups at around 15 to 18 months (Bayley, 1965; Hindley, 1965). Clear average IQ differences are present by 3 years (Hindley, 1965). Schaefer (1970) suggests that the appearance of differences is probably related to the shift in content from sensori-motor test items to a greater language content, and it is language differences which, as already noted, are obvious features in social class comparison. However, the consequences of a simplistic language, over and above the poor language itself, should not be ignored, nor the improverished surroundings in which such children are reared, nor the potential implications for the development of abstract non-verbal cognitive structures.

Lawton (1968) made a detailed study of language use by middle- and working-class boys, matched for verbal and non-verbal ability, at the ages of 12 and 15 years. Using three different language situations – essay writing, discussion and a structured interview – he obtained data which on the whole confirmed the social class differences postulated by Bernstein. The two major factors which differentiated the groups were, first, a more extensive use of the passive voice in middle-class children, and, second, their facility at switching from a restricted to a more elaborated code in appropriate circumstance.

If language impoverishment is indeed a main way in which low social class effects are mediated, then a remedial language programme for such children might overcome social class differences. There are problems in answering this clearly, because language programmes are seldom applied in isolation. However, Levenstein (1969), quoted by Schaefer (1970), claims to have promoted 17-point average IQ gains by stimulating mother-child verbal interaction over a seven-month period, involving the lending of books and toys (see later section on Head-Start Studies).

Jensen (1970a) has given detailed consideration to the basis of social class differences in intelligence. He believes that these cannot be comprehended without involving the existence of at least two relevant dimensions: (1) the cultural content of the test items; and (2) their complexity, degree of abstraction and problem solving. He cites the classic paper of Eells *et al.* (1951) which indicates that the largest social class differences did not appear in the most culturally loaded items, but rather on those that involved the highest degree of abstraction, conceptual thinking and problem solving ability. Moreover, these items possessed no great cultural content, in the sense of different degrees of exposure in different social classes. In addition, if all the social classes' IQ differences were due to differences in cultural experiences, it should be possible to devise intelligence tests that favour low groups over high. Jensen states that no one has succeeded in doing this, hence culture bias is only a trivial effect compared with intrinsic differences in abstractions and complexity. This seems to be an impressive argument but in reality may be circular if, as already noted in the work of Hess and Shipman (1965), abstractness and complexity may themselves be culturally biased. It is not being argued that Jensen's findings are either unimportant or invalid, but rather that we question the mechanisms by which Level I and Level II types of thinking evolve as the preferred strategies in individual cases.

At this point some discussion of Level I and Level II is necessary. Jensen has elaborated his theory of hierarchical cognitive abilities in various publications (1969), and most recently (1970b) in a chapter entitled 'A theory of primary and secondary familial mental retardation'. He excludes from his argument those mental retardates predominantly below IQ 50 whose condition is due to pathological agents, and goes on to examine the nature and cause of subcultural retardation. Jensen dismisses as unsound the notion that the common correlation between IQ and SES is to a large extent culturally determined, and gives the evidence for regarding genetic factors as the major cause of mild mental sub-normality.

Jensen argues that there is a great deal of evidence that mental abilities stand in some hierarchical relationship to one another. He acknowledges the controversial nature of factor analytic studies alone, but points to the considerable evidence from experimental studies of the training process such as Gagné's and those reviewed by White (1965) as showing that for many abilities there is a natural and invariable order of acquisition or emergence, such that when ability B is found A will always be present, but not conversely. He acknowledges that some basic abilities are learned, but suggests that there are other abilities which are practically impossible to account for except in terms of maturation. These latter abilities can also be seen as hierarchical, in the sense that normal maturation of a lower level of neural structure does not necessarily ensure later maturation of a higher level.

For Jensen the essential characteristic that most generally describes the levels of this hierarchy of mental maturation is the degree of correspondence between 'input' and 'output'. Lower levels in the hierarchy involve relatively little processing or transformation of input (whereas the higher levels do). A continuum is postulated, transcending task difficulty and stimulus complexity, in which tasks requiring little input transformation (e.g. conditioning, reaction-time, discrimination learning) are low in the hierarchy while complex concept learning and problem solving (as in verbal analogies and Raven's Progressive Matrices) are high. The theory states that although all tasks range along a single continuum, the latter is seen as the result of at least two types of ability: Level I or 'associative ability' and Level II or 'cognitive ability'.

Jensen asserts that, in every study performed by his research group, low SES and middle SES groups differ much less on Level I tests than on Level II (Jensen, 1970b).

One could predict Jensen's (1970b) experimental results from those of Hess and Shipman (1965) as well as from the theories of sociologists such as Bernstein. The interpretation of Jensen's findings would, however, be totally different from the one he advances, and consequently the educational implications would also differ. One might predict that the lower-class child would, over a period of many years, cumulatively come to depend upon Level I learning strategies, while the middle-class child would increasingly leave these behind and depend more and more upon Level II.

A series of experiments conducted by the authors on pre-school children of predominantly (but not exclusively) low social class indicated that in sorting tasks demanding, for their correct solution, the use of super-ordinate concepts, the children's initial strategy involved incorrect and often idiosyncratic associations. Training on different material, so organized as to force the child to use a conceptual strategy, resulted in substantially improved performance on transfer back to the initial task (Clarke et al., 1967; Clarke et al., 1969). It is suggested that the biologically normal child has potential for both Level I and II strategies but that his long-term interaction with cultural factors, favouring predominantly one or the other, may be crucial in determining which he employs in a given situation.

It seems, then, that Level II as an available mode of response is superior to, but depends upon, Level I. In suggesting this dichotomy Jensen seems to be doing little more than splitting cognitive processes into simple versus complex, and intelligence into basic, simple versus complex, abstract, symbolic. This may be a useful distinction to make (reminiscent of Bernstein's restricted versus elaborated linguistic codes) but unequivocal evidence on the origins of either is much more difficult to obtain than he suggests. Moreover, Stevenson (1972) indicates that the size of correlations (between ·38 and ·56) between the most extreme representatives of Level I and Level II tasks suggests that these levels are less independent than might be supposed.

It is not possible within the compass of this chapter to present all the evidence on the relationship between home background and intelligence as tested or as revealed in scholastic achievement. Goldberg (1970), in discussing psychosocial issues in the disadvantaged, confirms the second prediction made above (page 174): 'The findings cited throughout this section demonstrate not only a consistently negative relationship between disadvantaged status (economic and ethnic) and academic or intellective attainment; they demonstrate also that the retardation exhibited by such children is cumulative, growing greater and greater as they go up the grades. Whatever the explanation, the fact remains that as they grow older and stay in school longer, disadvantaged children fall further behind their more affluent age mates.'

There is substantial evidence from studies at those ages when educational opportunities are most diverse that higher education improves performance not only on attainment but also on intelligence tests. Vernon (1960) summarizes the position as follows:

... Many studies have shown that high school and college students continue to increase their scores from 15 up to 20 years and over. Indeed, Dearborn and Rothney (1941), on the basis of repeated testing of children in their 'teens, predict that the final maxim is not reached until 30. The only plausible way of reconciling these findings is to allow that growth continues so long as education or other stimulating conditions continue, though probably never beyond 25–30 years, and that when such stimulation ceases decline sets in.

A direct indication of the effects of advanced education is provided by Lorge's (1945) and Husén's (1951) investigations, where the same individuals were tested as children and as adults. Lorge reckoned that, at 34, adults who had received university education were 2 MA years superior to others who possessed the same intelligence at 14 but had had no further schooling. Husén tested 722 men entering the Army at 20 whose IQs at 10 years were known, and found that those who had matriculated had gained 12 IQ points relative to those who had had no secondary education.

That the quality rather than the length of schooling makes a difference is indicated by a research (Vernon, 1957) in which almost all the boys in the 14 secondary schools of an English city were tested at 14 years, and their results compared with their IQs at the time of secondary school selection 3 to 4 years earlier. Allowing for initial differences between boys entering different schools, and for regression effects, there were now differences of up to 12 points between boys in the 'best' and 'worst' schools. The combined grammar and technical school boys had apparently gained 7 points over the combined modern schools. Much of this difference might well be due to the grammar school boys coming from better homes, with more favourable attitudes to education; but this would none the less be an environmental effect.

In addition, Oden (1968), reporting on a follow-up of Terman's gifted group, reports a general increase in CMT score with increased educational level within this highly selective sample. However, she also reports that 146 subjects who did not go beyond high school earned exactly the same CMT score as that of a group of advanced graduate students at a leading university. Lerner (1968) summarizes from what he describes as 'a jungle of literature' the well-known relationship, demonstrated during the first world war in America, between adult intelligence and educational expenditure in the states from which the recruits were drawn.

Finally, in discussing the effects of social class, it must be pointed out that although average differences have long been appreciated, one is dealing with something more than the effects of social class membership. Within each class, there is the same range of ability; it is in their differing proportions of particular levels of ability that these differences reside (Maxwell, 1961). Thus the proportion with superior ability is very low in the children of social class IV and V parents, and very high in social class I. But because of the size of these lower socio-economic groups the absolute number of superior children is greater than for those of the small social group I.

It seems, therefore, that the context of social class influences provides a groundwork for the development of a particular average level of ability and attainment. But this average level for each class is surrounded by wide differences arising from genetic differences and constitutional differences (e.g. the effects of nutrition, the prevalence of illness, the effects of differing birth histories, etc.). Moreover, practices within each social class are far from being uniform and, as pointed out by Burt many years ago, the 'efficiency of the mother' has an enormous influence upon the child's development.

The correlates of social class have been well documented recently by Davie, Butler and Goldstein (1972), and some details of their study are offered later in this chapter. They note that 'One of the most striking features which emerges ... is the very marked differences between children from different circumstances which are already apparent by the age of seven ... the most potent factors were located in the home environment.' There are, of course, large actuarial differences between different classes in material prosperity, child-rearing practices and parental expectations, but in spite of these average differences, the situation within a single social class is obviously far from being uniform. Clearly in this field as in others, multiple genetic and environmental interactions are involved cumulatively and over the whole period of development.

STUDIES OF MAJOR ENVIRONMENTAL CHANGE

One of the most carefully documented studies of environmental change and its effect upon retarded children has been provided by Skeels and Dye (1939), Skeels (1966) and Skodak (1968). The initial observation was accidental. Two children under 18 months old, in residence at a state orphanage, gave unmistakable evidence of marked mental retardation. Kuhlmann–Binet intelligence tests were given to both, the results on one (at 13 months) being IQ 46, and on the second (aged 16 months) IQ 35. Qualitative and behavioural assessments supported these results. There was no indication of organic defects.

These two children were recommended for transfer to a state school for the mentally deficient but the prognosis was at the time regarded as poor. After transfer, they were placed in a ward of older girls whose ages ranged from 18 to 50 years and in mental age from 5 to 9 years. Six months later the psychologist visiting the wards of this institution was surprised to notice the apparently remarkable development of these children. They were accordingly re-examined on the same test as before, this time gaining IQs of 77 and 87 respectively. A year later their IQs had risen to 100 and 88. At the age of about $3\frac{1}{2}$ the two children's scores were 95 and 93.

The hypothesis to explain these results was that the ward attendants had taken a particular fancy to these two babies who were the only pre-school children in their care. They were given outings and special play materials. Similarly, the older and brighter inmates of the ward were particularly attached to the children and would play with them during most of their waking hours; for these two it was clearly a stimulating environment. It was considered that a further change would be desirable if the intellectual alteration was to be maintained, and accordingly they were placed in rather average adoptive homes at the age of $3\frac{1}{2}$. After about fifteen months in these homes re-examination, this time with the Stanford–Binet, resulted in IQs of 94 and 93 respectively. These unexpected findings raised a number of important questions. Observation suggested that similar children left in an orphanage nursery made no such gains in the rate of mental growth. Adult contacts were at a minimum and limited largely to physical care. Adoptive placement was clearly inappropriate, owing to the lack of certainty that progress would occur. The most reasonable solution would seem to lie in a repetition of the 'accidental experiment' but this time in a planned and controlled manner. Thus research was started involving an experimental group of thirteen children whose ages ranged from 7 to 30 months, and Kuhlmann–Binet IQs of 35 to 89. Mean age at the time of transfer to the state school was 19 months and mean IQ was 64. Once again, clinical observation supported the IQ classification; for example, a 7-month-old child in the group could scarcely hold his head up without support, while another at 30 months could not stand alone and required support while sitting in a chair. After the close of the experimental period it was decided to study a contrast group of children remaining in the orphanage. This group consisted of twelve children, whose ages ranged from 11 to 21 months, and IQs from 50 to 103. Mean age at the time of the first test was 16 months, with a mean IQ of 86. No marked differences in the birth histories of the two groups were observed, nor in their medical histories. Family histories indicated that the majority came from homes of low socio-economic levels with parents of low intellect, and there were no important differences between them.

The members of the experimental group in general repeated the experiences of the first two children and also attended the school kindergarten just as soon as they could walk. In the case of almost every child, some adult, either older girl or attendant, would become particularly attached to him or her and would figuratively 'adopt' him. This probably constituted an important aspect of the change. Members of the Contrast Group, however, had environments rather typical of the average orphanage. The outstanding feature was the profound lack of mental stimulation or experiences usually associated with the life of the young child in an ordinary home. Up to the age of 2 years, the children were in the nursery of the hospital. They had good physical care but little beyond this; few play materials were available and they were seldom out of the nursery room except for short walks or periods of exercise. At the age of 2, they graduated to cottages where over-crowding was characteristic. Thirty to thirty-six children of the same sex under 6 years of age were under the care of one matron and three or four untrained and reluctant teenage girls. The matron's duties were so arduous that a necessary regimentation of the children resulted. No child had any personal property. The contrast between these two environments is obvious (cf. Bowlby, 1951).

During the course of the experiment the average increase in IQ of the experimental group was 27·5 points, the final IQs at the conclusion having a mean of 91·8. Gains ranged from 7 to 58 points; three made increments of 45 points or more, and all but two increased by more than 15 points. The length of the experimental period depended in an individual case upon the child's progress, varying from 5·7 months to 52·1, with a mean of 18·9 months.

The development of the children in the contrast group was almost precisely the opposite from those in the experimental group. The average IQ at the beginning was 86·7 and at the end was 60·5, an average loss of 26·2 points. Apart from one child who gained 2 points, all showed losses varying from 8 to 45 points. Ten of the twelve children lost 15 or more points. The average length of the experimental period was 30·7 months.

In commenting upon these data, one notes (a) the initial superiority of the contrast group; (b) the reversal of the status of the two groups; and (c) the differing lengths of the evaluation periods for the groups.

As soon as the experimental group showed intellectual functioning approaching the normal range, with two exceptions they were placed in adoptive homes. The adoptive parents were, with one exception, lower middle class. The selection of relatively modest levels of adoptive homes was made because of the poor social background of the children and the fact that, at one time, they had all been mentally retarded. It was therefore felt advisable to select homes where aspirations for achievement might not be too high.

Contrast children, on the other hand, either remained in unstimulating and in some cases actively adverse orphanages or state schools for the mentally retarded.

Later, Skeels, with the assistance of Marie Skodak, carried out an impressive follow-up of both groups after being completely out of touch with their members for over twenty years (Skeels, 1966; Skodak, 1968). The aims of the follow-up were simple. What happened to the children as adults, how have the early childhood differences been reflected in adult achievement and adjustment, and have the divergent paths been maintained. A major problem was of course to locate the subjects, and the Skeels monograph describes in vivid detail the problems and frustrations in so doing.

Very marked differences between the two groups were found in educational and occupational status and general life style. The experimental group had completed an average of 11·68 grades of school (median 12); their spouses had virtually identical educational attainments. The contrast group, on the other hand, had completed an average of 3·95 grades of school (median 2·75).

In considering occupational levels, it should be noted that the experimental group contained only three males, while the contrast group contained eight.

There were marked differences in the occupational levels of the two groups. The three males in the experimental group were: a vocational counsellor, a sales manager for an estate agent, and a staff sergeant in the Air Force. Eight of the ten girls were married and of those who were employed, one taught elementary school grades, another was a registered nurse, another a licensed practical nurse, another had passed State Board examinations and practised as a beautician. Another girl was a clerk, another after graduating from high school passed the examinations and was accepted as a stewardess in an airline. Two were domestics in private homes.

In the contrast group, four were still residents in institutions, and unable to engage in employment. Seven were employed, one washing dishes in a nursing home, two were dishwashers in small restaurants, another worked in a cafeteria. One of the men had been in and out of institutions for years, and when out lived with his grandmother, doing odd jobs. Another man was a 'floater' travelling from coast to coast, engaging in casual and unskilled labour. Yet another was an employee in the state institution where he was originally a patient. Finally, the deviant of this group, to be referred to later, was a typesetter for a newspaper in a large city. It will be apparent that, of those who were employed, with the exception above (Case 19), all were in unskilled manual occupations. It might also be added that, unlike the experimental group which had shown considerable geographical mobility and whose members were very difficult to trace, there were only minor problems in locating by means of institutional records the members of the contrast group.

Space precludes a detailed consideration of all the evidence presented in the 1966 monograph. Although inevitably in a study of this kind there are some gaps in information available, sufficient data are presented on the status of the children as infants, the socio-economic and educational backgrounds of at least one parent, the status of the adoptive parents and the final outcome for the twenty-five children as adults, for certain conclusions to be drawn with considerable confidence.

Although the majority of the experimental group were adopted, two were not, for reasons which are not stated. The majority of the contrast group remained in poor institutions during their childhood, but there was one exception. What is clear is that the eventual outcome for all these children was closely related to the long-term environmental circumstances surrounding the major part of their later development. It is our belief, based on this and other evidence, that the relatively brief pre-school stimulation programme, which was initially a major focus of interest for Skeels and his colleague Skodak, is probably of little long-term relevance, except as initiating a differentiation between experimental and contrast groups, and thus providing the belief that the experimental children would not grow up to be mentally retarded.

This thesis will be illustrated with reference to the bare outlines of some specific case histories.

Case 10 (experimental group) at 23 months, before transfer to the 'stimulating conditions', had an IQ of 72. On retest at 45 months, his IQ was 79. His natural mother was educated to 8th grade, and had six months of high school education. His natural father was a theatre manager in a small town, and was presumably at least of reasonable intelligence. His adoptive father, educated to 9th grade, was a milkman and his adoptive mother had been educated to 8th grade. The subject himself graduated from high school, and attended college for two and a half years. At the time of follow-up he was sales manager in a real estate firm.

Case 11 (experimental group) at 26 months, before transfer, had an IQ of 75. On retest at 51 months, after the special programme, he had an IQ of 82. His natural mother had an IQ of 66 and was diagnosed as a psychotic mental defective. Nothing is known of his natural father. His adoptive father was a college graduate, the only one of the adoptive sample who occupied a professional post. The adoptive mother was a high school graduate, drawn from a somewhat affluent family. The subject himself was a university graduate, with a BA degree and some postgraduate work at the time of follow-up. His occupation was that of vocational counsellor in a state welfare programme.

By contrast, Case 2 (experimental group) had an IQ of 57 at 13 months. On retest, after the programme, at 37 months her IQ had risen to 77. Her natural mother had completed 8th grade at school and was said to be 'slow mentally'. The natural father, a farm labourer, was also said to be mentally slow; he, too, had completed 8th grade. The subject was never adopted, and completed only five grades at school. On follow-up, about 1942, she was in residence at the institution for the mentally retarded and 'in all probability will continue to show marked mental retardation to a degree necessitating continued institutionalization'. At final follow-up, she was a housewife married to a labourer and had been in domestic service.

Case 24 (contrast group) had an IQ of 50 at 22 months. On retest, at 52 months his IQ was 42. His natural mother went as far as 8th grade at school and then took a short evening class course in business studies. She worked as a telephone operator and did general office work. His natural father graduated from high school but was unemployed at the time of his birth. The subject was brought up in the institution for the mentally retarded where he did rather well. At the age of 20, his Wechsler IQ scores were: Verbal 76; Performance 106; Full Scale, 84. An attempt was made to place him in open employment but this proved unsatisfactory and he asked for return to the institution where, at the time of follow-up, he was assistant to the Head Gardener. He was reported to be an exceedingly good gardener but institutionalized.

Case 19 (contrast group) had an IQ of 87 at 15 months. On retest at 45 months this had decreased to 67. His natural mother graduated from high school and had an IQ of 84; his father was a farmer. Although he was never adopted, he was the only member of the contrast group not brought up in the institution for the mentally retarded. By chance he was included in an intensive stimulation programme as part of a doctoral research which emphasized language training and cognitive development. When he entered regular school he was discovered to have a moderate hearing loss following bilateral mastoidectomy in infancy. At about the time of retest, at the relatively late age of 6, he was accordingly transferred to a residential school for the deaf where the matron of his cottage took a special fancy to him as one of the youngest children, and one who had no family. He was a frequent guest in her home and in that of her daughter and son-in-law. He graduated from high school, had one semester of college and at the time of follow-up was employed as a compositor and typesetter. His marriage was stable, he had four intelligent children, owned his house in a comfortable middle-class district, and was earning as much as the rest of the contrast group put together.

In summary, the diverging early histories of both groups have been maintained in adult life. 'It seems obvious', writes Skeels (1966), 'that under present day conditions there are still countless numbers of infants born with sound biological constitutions and with potentialities for development well within the normal range, who will become mentally retarded and a burden to society unless appropriate intervention occurs ... we have sufficient knowledge to design programs of intervention which can counteract the devastating effects of poverty, sociocultural deprivation and maternal deprivation.'

This study was one of the spiritual fathers of Head-Start Programmes, and some general comments may be in order. As already stated in the previous chapter, infant IQs have virtually no predictive value. The early changing IQ of both Experimental and Contrast subjects are therefore difficult to interpret, and as Jensen (1969) notes, extreme caution must be exercised in evaluating IQ increments. The only university graduate had an IQ of 82 at the age of $4\frac{1}{4}$ years. Yet the long-term changes were congruent with the environmental opportunities the children were initially offered. What seems important is the vast differences among all twenty-five children, in their total histories and in their ultimate status. The intervention programme may be of no more long-term significance than in having inspired confidence in the investigators that the children were potentially adoptable.

The work of Kirk (1958), which was directly inspired by the early Skeels data, showed that although IQ increments can be engineered by careful pre-school programmes, contrast children who had not had such programmes began to catch up with those who had, during their first year in school. Furthermore, Kirk spells out the implications for children living in psycho-socially deprived homes, and writes, 'It should make us reconsider the belief that "a poor home or a poor mother is better than no home or no mother".' Until someone has been able to demonstrate the long-term effects of early intervention without subsequent environmental enrichment, the safest interpretation of Skeels' important data is that adult status is closely related to the whole environmental circumstances between the age of 5 and adulthood.

A few studies of individual children, socially isolated in an extreme and fortunately rare way, also illustrate the retarding effect of grossly adverse environments, as well as the remedial influences (from the age of 6 or 7) of enriched environments. The case described by Mason (1942) and independently by Davis (1947) is a classic but suffers from several omissions. Much more recently, Koluchova (1972) has described quite fully and carefully the rescue from isolation, neglect and cruelty, of twin boys aged 7.

Their mother died shortly after their birth. They were placed 'in care' for a year, after which they went to an aunt for six months. During this time they developed normally, and it is probably very important that their nutrition was normal. When they were 18 months old, their father married again, and their stepmother, an obviously unbalanced woman, took over the care of the twins. They had reached the age of 7 before it was discovered that for most of the intervening period the boys had been kept isolated in a cellar, had been cruelly treated, and were suffering from malnutrition.

Experts who examined them found that they were severely mentally handicapped, their IQs being in the forties. They could barely speak, they could hardly walk, they were terrified of ordinary household objects and were quite unable to recognize the meaning of pictures.

For some time the boys were given very active treatment – partly to repair the physical damage they had suffered and partly to bring their social behaviour and their abilities up to the level that might be expected of more 'normal' retarded children. When they were judged ready for it, they were placed in a school for the mentally handicapped. So good was their progress there that they were moved after a while to an ordinary school. Now they are doing well, though at 11 years of age they are still some years behind average in school attainment. But their IQs – in just four years – have more than doubled, are continuing to increase, and are now in the normal range (one is 94 and the other 95).

The twins have been adopted by dedicated people who are giving them a stable and happy home, and the improvement in their emotional maturity is very obvious. Of course, we do not know what will happen to them eventually, but it is interesting to hear that when they were first discovered a number of experts considered that their terrible condition and the extraordinary way they had been treated must mean that they were damaged beyond hope of recovery. (See also Clarke, 1972.)

On the contrary, it is clear now that the options remained open at the age of 7, even after almost unbelievable adversity. Our own work in the 1950s also illustrated the considerable long-term changes that could take place in adolescent and early adult life following removal from conditions of great adversity (Clarke and Clarke, 1954; Clarke *et al.*, 1958).

The Koluchova study is too recent to have received comment. The studies by Mason, Davis, Skeels and Skodak are, however, well known and the findings generally accepted. Referring to such research, Jensen (1969) offers the argument that environment only acts as a threshold variable. 'There can be no doubt', he writes, 'that moving children from an extremely deprived environment to good average environmental circumstances can boost the IQ some 20 to 30 points and in certain extreme rare cases as much as 60 or 70 points. On the other hand, children reared in rather average circumstances do not show an appreciable IQ gain as a result of being placed in a more culturally enriched environment.' (Here Jensen gives no references.) He goes on to say

While there are reports of groups of children going from below average up to average IQs as a result of environmental enrichment, I have found no report of a group of children being given permanently superior IQs by means of environmental manipulations (our italics).

In brief, it is doubtful that psychologists have found consistent evidence for any social environmental influences short of extreme environmental isolation which have a marked systematic effect on intelligence. This suggests that the influence of the quality of the environment on intellectual development is not a linear function. Below a certain threshold of environmental adequacy, deprivation can have a markedly depressing effect on intelligence. But above this threshold, environmental variations cause relatively small differences in intelligence. . . . When I speak of sub-threshold environmental deprivation, I do not refer to a mere lack of middle-class amenities. I refer to the extreme sensory and motor restrictions in environments such as those described by Skeels and Dye (1939) and Davis (1947) . . . culturally disadvantaged children are not reared in anything like the degree of sensory and motor deprivation that characterizes the children of the Skeels study.

This rather diffuse passage, then, suggests that social environment only possesses a marked effect on intelligence in extreme conditions Moreover, in the sentence which we have italicized it is quite unclear whether Jensen has (a) found no report or (b) has found reports but these had negative results. In either event, it is surprising that he fails to mention Husén's famous (1951) study (see p. 177). Suffice it to say, that having dismissed 'ordinary' environmental differences, Jensen has no need to weigh the evidence from many other studies.

A test of Jensen's threshold theory for the operation of environmental factors would be provided by a prospective and total intervention programme using the disadvantaged population living in their own homes and in their own community. As already noted, these in Jensen's view are above the threshold, since they do not suffer 'anything like the degree of sensory and motor deprivation that characterizes the children of the Skeels study'. The study which will be outlined fulfils these criteria and, although in its early stages, has results which are very suggestive.

Heber and his associates (Heber *et al.*, 1968; Heber and Garber, 1971; Heber, 1971) have been responsible for the most important and best-controlled prospective study designed to test the cultural deprivation hypothesis. It is indicated that over the past thirty years no more intense and bitter controversy has occurred than that concerning the aetiology of cultural-familial retardation, a group comprising perhaps 80 per cent of the total. The study was designed to have a bearing upon this question.

The first step was to institute a survey in an area of Milwaukee with the greatest population density, lowest median family income and the greatest rate of dilapidated housing. The major finding was that maternal intelligence proved to be the best single predictor of low intelligence in the offspring. Mothers with IQs less than 80, comprising less than half the total, accounted for almost four-fifths of children with IQs below 80. Moreover, the lower the maternal IQ, the greater the probability of her child scoring low. Paternal/maternal IQs were found to correspond fairly closely. A major early finding was that child IQs of the below 80 IQ mothers declined with increasing age, from an average of about 84 at age 5 to an average of about 78 at age 10 and considerably lower in adolescence. So far, the data could permit a number of differing explanations. It could be concluded, however, that in the slum, mental retardation was neither randomly distributed nor randomly caused. Thus the view that in a generic way the 'disadvantaged' environment affects cognitive development adversely is questioned. One cannot assume that conditions within a slum are uniform. Large families where maternal intelligence is low provide the context for mild retardation in depressed areas. Hence, whatever the mechanisms, there is a clear need to attempt the prevention of emergent retardation by a comprehensive family approach to rehabilitation.

Trained interviewers visited all mothers in the area with newborn children and used the PPVT as an initial screening device, also collecting extensive data on family history. Scores of 70 or less were checked by a full administration of the WAIS. Forty mothers, on the criterion of a WAIS Full Scale IQ of 75 or less, were randomly assigned to experimental or control conditions and were invited to participate in the study, the experimental part of which comprised (1) an infant stimulation programme, and (2) a maternal rehabilitation programme.

The teachers were paraprofessional, language facile, affectionate people who had had some experience with infants or young children and resided in the same general neighbourhood as the children. At 3 months of age the infant commenced attendance at the Centre. Each was then assigned a teacher who remained with the child until he reached 12 to 15 months of age. At that time he was gradually paired with other teachers and children. He was then grouped with two other children and came into contact with three different teachers. Each teacher was responsible for total care of the infant and had to follow and expand upon a prescribed set of activities. Each teacher of the 18 months and older group was responsible for ten children, seen in groups of two, three or four depending on age. She had to familiarize herself with one of three main academic areas (maths/ problem solving, language and reading). The teacher was expected to evaluate progress and to 'individualize instruction, as well as having a part to play in art, music, field trips and special holiday activities. She also had to establish as a major responsibility, contact and rapport with the child's mother.' The job was clearly a demanding one, and an ongoing training programme for teachers was established.

The philosophy of pre-school education was 'to prevent from occurring those language, problem solving and achievement motivation deficits which are known to be common attributes of mild mental retardation'. Intellectual functioning is regarded as the 'combination of abilities referred to as input, retention, interpretation, integration and utilization of symbols. The specific subject areas of our academic programme are simply vehicles through which we hoped to foster in our children these abilities which underlie normal intellectual development.' The curriculum had a cognitive-language orientation implemented through a structured environment by prescriptive teaching techniques on a daily basis (seven-hour day, five days per week).

Heber takes no particular theoretical stand other than that structured presentation of material is necessary. He considered that there were no ready-made programmes available so the project staff continually adapted existing methods and materials. The area chosen for particular emphasis was language and cognition, and the tasks to which the children were exposed were increased in complexity as they were mastered.

Language is emphasized for it is a tool for recording and processing information as well as for communication. Cognitive development is emphasized for it provides the child with a repertoire or responses enabling him to interpret and refine information. In addition, the child must have the desire to utilize these skills. . . . It is hoped that achievement motivation will be developed by introducing tasks designed to maximize interest, to provide success experiences, to provide supportive and corrective feedback from responsive adults, and to gradually increase the child's responsibility for task completion.

The author goes on to write that by utilizing a structured learning approach, the emphasis is on educating the teacher to plan and present relevant and organized learning situations. The content was presented in small logical steps, in which progress was evaluated and corresponding adjustments made to the programme. Heber's report gives details of the curriculum.

A two-phase programme for the mothers was instituted in parallel with the pre-school project. Attempts were made to give preparation for employment and to improve the home-making and child-rearing skills of the mothers in the experimental group.

Job training was undertaken in two large private nursing homes, both because permanent staff had an understanding of rehabilitation procedures and because employment opportunities existed. Reading, writing and arithmetic were emphasized to increase the mothers' self confidence before the on-the-job training commenced. In addition, they attended classes on home economics, interpersonal relations and child care.

The job training included five weeks on laundry work, three-and-a-half weeks housekeeping, nine weeks food service and nine weeks of simple nursing. During this period there was a remarkable development of group spirit and cohesion. Group counselling sessions on a daily basis were felt to be important. This whole programme was regarded as quite successful, but major problems with respect to adequacy of home-making skills and care and treatment of children remain to be resolved with a number of the families. Hence the maternal programme is now shifting to an increased emphasis on training in general care of family and home, budgeting, instruction and food preparation, family hygiene and the mother's role in child growth and development.

Heber presents the results of repeated measures on the experimental and control children. In the first two years of life these consisted largely of the application of general developmental scales. From then on, in addition, increased emphasis was given to direct measures of learning and performance. Tests are administered by someone not involved in either the maternal or child projects.

At the age of 60 months there was a 26-point difference in the mean IQs for the two groups (Stanford-Binet) and a 20-point difference on the WPPSI. The actual scores are difficult to interpret, due to repeated testing of all the children in both groups; however, the majority of the controls scored below 90. Similar differences were obtained on various measures of language use, including the ITPA.

Thus the data indicate a remarkable acceleration of development in the children of the experimental group. Moreover, their performance is quite homogeneous compared with the range exhibited by the control group, where a quarter function at or above test norms while the remainder show trends towards sub-average performance.

Heber exhibits proper caution in interpreting these data, and raises the question of whether the children in the experimental group have merely benefited from specific training relevant to the tests on which they have been assessed. If this were so, and it seems unlikely to the present writers, then one would expect transfer in a very non-specific manner to occur to other cognitive activities (Clarke *et al.*, 1967). Nevertheless Heber indicates that no comparable group of infants has ever been exposed to the intensive training experienced by the experimental group. But possibly they have merely reached certain developmental stages earlier than usual, asks Heber. Much will depend upon the context of their lives in primary school and later, but just as cumulative deficits can occur, so too a positively reinforcing situation is likely to maintain cumulative assets in the future. We consider that this will necessitate a continuing divergence in the life styles of experimental and control subjects. If this experiment were now to cease, and the experimental children were to revert to control conditions, remaining in these until adulthood, it would be our assumption that there would be little or no difference between these groups at the age of, say, 20. Further work will in fact test this hypothesis, but hopefully, this experiment may have implications for our understanding of human development and the genetic limits upon performance.

If, indeed, the divergence between experimental and control children is maintained or increased as they grow older, the question will ultimately be raised concerning the crucial ingredients of the two-way programme for mothers and their children. This will call for even more ambitious and costly research but it will have to be undertaken if there is to be any hope of general programmes for upgrading the vast section in the population. Experiments already planned with current groups will have some bearing on these problems.

Not only have Heber and his colleagues used standard psychometric procedures but, increasingly, experimental measures of, for example, colour-form matching, sorting, probability, discrimination, and an Ivanov-Smolensky discrimination procedure. These were chosen because they could be made increasingly complex as the child developed. More than half the very lengthy (1971) report is devoted to these experiments, all of which showed superiority of the experimental over the control group. Perhaps the most interesting were inspired by the work of Hess and Shipman (1965) in studying mother-child interaction in both groups.

The experimental techniques and the general plan of Heber's research are impressive. In our view, however, his theoretical position is less than adequately formulated. For example, he appears to accept uncritically the notion of critical periods, which even in the animal field are fast being modified, and the application of which to man is very debatable. This might well lead him to underestimate the need for later enriched experience during the 'critical period' of human development from 5 to 20! Moreover, the published material (as opposed to roneo'd progress reports) is very scanty and one awaits with the greatest interest (and impatience) a detailed and unified account of this work. In addition, the results must not be interpreted as showing equality of biological potential; as

Eysenck (1971) has indicated, Heber's results show the effect of an environment never previously encountered by children of this age. It remains to be seen what might be the effect of similar intervention on children of high IQ parents.

Since the above paragraphs were drafted, further reports by Heber *et al.* (1972) and by Heber and Garber (1974) have become available. As predicted by the present writers, for those members of the experimental group who have reached school age, and for whom the formal programme has ceased, there has been a relative decline, although they are still above average and the gap between them and the controls remains roughly constant. It is our guess that far longer intervention, perhaps 12 to 15 years, is necessary to establish any permanent development change.

SUBTLE ENVIRONMENTAL FACTORS: THE FIRST-BORN PHENOMENON

The most likely explanation of the known facts that children who are first-born in a family tend to be superior in a number of ways is, in the writers' opinion, the operation of subtle, intra-familial psychosocial factors. Jensen (1969), who recognizes that work in this field is a threat to his threshold theory, summarizes in seventeen lines some of the evidence showing that 'first-born children are superior in almost every way, mentally and physically' and goes on to write: 'Since the first-born effect is found throughout all social classes in many countries and has shown up in studies over the past 80 years . . . it is probably a biological rather than a social psychological phenomenon. It is almost certainly not a genetic effect.' If, however, this were a biological, not a genetic outcome, it would imply some uterine superiority for the first-born. There is no evidence for this, and indeed birth hazards, with consequent damage, are greater for first-born than later born children. Furthermore, although no systematic study has been conducted on the superiority of 'first reared' as opposed to first-born, observation suggests that these former also show superiority. Roe (1952) in her classic paper on sixty-four eminent scientists, notes that the majority (thirty-nine) were first-born, of the remainder five were eldest sons and two who were second-born were effectively 'first reared' because of the death of an elder child. For the remainder there was often a considerable difference in age between the subject and his next elder brother (averaging five years).

Without exception all studies of first-born children, as well as others which take this phenomenon into account, show a significant advantage over later born children in terms of achievement, a strong tendency first recognized by Galton in 1874. Schachter (1963) has reviewed earlier studies of relationships between birth order and eminence and birth order and intelligence, concluding that eminent people are far more likely to have been eldest or only children than to have been later born. No clear answer concerning the relationship with intelligence emerged. Bradley (1968), reviewing later evidence of first-born of both sexes in universities and colleges throughout the United States, showed that these and only children are consistently and massively over-represented. Detailed studies of the finalists in National Merit Scholarship competitions showed among the top half per cent of the population in successive large groups there was a 23 per cent over-representation of first-born and only children. The fact that first-born and only children are over-represented in American universities could be established because of the widespread policy of requiring birth order data for university admission. Comparable data for Britain are not available because ordinal birth position is not recorded on UCCA forms. Unpublished studies in the Psychology Departments of Sheffield and Hull Universities, however, confirm these findings. Altus (1966), after considerable research into the pre-eminence of first-born and only children in academic attainment, reported that he was unable to find a single study that showed a divergent trend. More recent writers have added to the picture (Chittenden *et al.*, 1968). Nevertheless, this area has been examined critically by Schooler (1972) who believes that almost no reliable evidence exists for birth order effects in men living in the United States in the mid-1960s. The nub of his argument is that (1) at different periods within a community there are variations in the numbers of families started and, consequently, in the proportion of first-born; and (2) that family size is negatively correlated with social class, that social class is correlated with academic achievement and hence that the chances of an academically achieving individual being first-born are greater than for the general population. It is perfectly correct that many studies have not taken into account the possibly confounding effects of social class, which could certainly be mainly responsible, but there are a number which have controlled for family size and hence probably for social class. For example, Nichols (quoted by Altus, 1966) reported that of the 568 representatives of two-child families who were finalists in the National Merit competition, 66 per cent were first-born (a 16 per cent over-representation); of the 414 from three-child families, 52 per cent were first-born (a 19 per cent over-representation); and of the 244 from four-child families, 59 per cent were first-born (a 34 per cent over-representation). Furthermore as Schooler himself recognizes, there is some evidence that first- and last-born children tend to be more achieving academically than those in an intermediate ordinal position (see also Altus, 1966).

Finally, studies are briefly reviewed which take into account social class effects in assessing first-born achievement.

Thus Douglas (1964) has indicated that first-born children stay at school longer, join more clubs, read better books and push themselves harder than other children. The first-born of two or three children, particularly from working-class families, won far more grammar school places than would be expected from their ability scores alone. Douglas, Ross and Simpson (1968) show that the virtually all-round superiority of elder over younger boys in the same family is established and maintained from about age 8 onwards. Douglas did not, however, find that only children were as a group superior. This leads him to a somewhat different interpretation than is offered in the American reviews, although both have in common the assumption that personality variables relating to need for achievement are involved (see also Sontag *et al.*, 1958). Since the numerous American studies show that the phenomenon includes only children, this interpretation emphasizes adult-child relations while Douglas stresses sibling relationships.

More recently yet another careful study (Davie *et al.*, 1972) shows the effect of birth order on a number of variables in a large random sample of children. Thus at age 7, the difference in reading attainment between first- and fourth- or later-born children was equivalent to 16 months of reading age; for height, first-born were 2·8 cm taller than fourth- or later-born children after allowing for other relevant factors such as social class. Moreover, for a given birth order, those children with no younger siblings were 1·1 cm taller than those with two or more younger siblings. It is also of interest that the number of younger children is associated with adjustment; those with two or more younger siblings are less well adjusted than those with none. The authors assume that findings such as these can best be attributed to the sharing of resources, including parental time and attention. The 'only child' phenomenon has even been observed in a group of young mongols; those reared in families without other children or other young children showed a slight acceleration of mental development over those in families with other young children (Carr, 1971).

Jensen's argument, although not disproved, seems to be a far less likely explanation for the achievements of the first-born.

HEAD-START STUDIES

Following the work of Kirk (1958), Skeels (1966) and many others, and the recognition that deliberate intervention could produce upward shifts in measures of child development, in some cases maintained into adult life, the stage was set in the 1960s for attempts to upgrade the culturally disadvantaged and deprived members of the population in the United States. Thus President Johnson's Anti-Poverty Bill encouraged the initiation of Head-Start Programmes of pre-school education. It was tragic that the wave of enthusiasm, which followed, led in most cases to work which was philosophically, psychologically, educationally and methodologically naïve. Three errors, obvious to any sophisticated observer at the time, were common.

(1) The use of a short duration programme of pre-school stimulation in the summer before school entry. It was hoped that this brief exposure to pre-school education would undo the effects of early deprivation and allow the child to benefit from ordinary schooling. In such studies, few, if any, attempts were made to consider the child in his total context, including the home. No literature on recovery from cultural deprivation (other than from rare and extreme social isolation) gave the slightest hint that developmental paths in childhood could be rapidly shifted in a permanent way, so the philosophy of such intervention was ignorant, even though paying lip-service to research findings.

(2) Coupled with the hope that intervention of short duration could undo the

effects of social deprivation was a failure to realize that early experience involving learning must be subsequently reinforced if there is to be any hope of building up a permanency of such effects (Clarke, 1968).

(3) Many of the pre-school educational programmes were scarcely educational at all, and few attempts were made to analyse the needs of deprived children. Too often they were offered what they already possessed – free activity.

There exist a number of reviews of these attempts, of which those by Bereiter and Engelmann (1966) and Jensen (1969) are perhaps the best known. The former authors begin their book by referring to the sort of evidence already covered in our section on social class. They indicate that in all cognitive measures, disadvantaged children are retarded, or at least below average. In practically every aspect of language development, young children of this type function at the average level of those a year or more younger. Similar findings apply to reasoning ability. Thus for school success, disadvantaged children are retarded in areas that count the most.

Bereiter and Engelmann consider that disadvantaged children lack learning, and not the fundamental capacity to learn. Deficits in the early years are amplified by the school situation and become cumulative; hence it is necessary to remedy this situation in the pre-school years. If they are to catch up, however, they must progress at a faster than normal rate.

The most widely endorsed approach to this problem is the strategy termed 'enrichment'. In the pre-school programme attempts are made to compress the maximum quantity of experiences believed to be associated with the advantaged child's superior performance. Such programmes, write the authors, are often watered down with a humanitarian content which the disadvantaged child is thought to deserve. The most obvious logical error in this 'catch-up' approach is that while the disadvantaged child is being exposed to the programme, the advantaged child is forging ahead. This, then, is a race which cannot be won if its success depends upon well above average rates of absorption of cultural experiences, for a limited period in the day and for a limited overall duration. Such a programme may comprise a mere 500 hours in comparison with the 20,000 hours in which cultural disadvantages have retarded learning. Hence there remain just two ways of approaching the problem: (1) by selecting experiences that produce more learning; and (2) by compressing more experience into the available time. In so doing one cannot replicate the slow, cumulative development of the normal child which builds up under conditions of minor daily increments. 'Normally the young child has a lot of time; but the disadvantaged child who enters a pre-school at the age of four-and-a-half has already used most of his up.'

The basic fallacy in the enrichment strategy is that disadvantaged children must have the same kinds of experience as the privileged. If this were true, there would be no hope of speeding up their learning. More potent experiences are needed if the gap is ever to be reduced. Thus, if a child is one year retarded, and if he is to catch up a further year, he must learn at twice the normal rate.

Hence a narrower than usual spectrum of learning must be offered if this hope is to be realized. Specifically, one must focus upon academic objectives and relegate all others to a secondary position. This logical solution is one that promotes revulsion among many, but as we shall see, is the only possible hope for the full realization of potential in these children. Bereiter and Engelmann go out of their way to answer such criticisms; 'the broad, unfocused educational program', they write, 'recognizes no priorities and tolerates no omissions'. The errors here are (1) that the child's future is not considered; (2) the notion that a well-rounded programme is required reveals an ignorance of the fact that a world exists outside the school, and it may well be that a narrow educational programme amplifies the child's possibilities of benefiting from ordinary non-school experience; (3) the skilful teacher can promote favourable attitudes and emotional adjustment through specific learning activities equally well as through 'broadening' experiences; (4) recent evidence suggests that the child is not just a passive receiver of environmental stimulation. Rather, education hands him the tools needed to pursue his own development actively. The school can offer the specific skills which enable him to develop properly; (5) the teacher who tries to meet all the child's needs is likely to extend herself and dilute herself beyond all effectiveness; (6) the pre-school programme must somehow compromise between the ideals of all-round development and dealing with the severity of the child's deficiencies. The 'whole child' approach amounts to dividing the time, offering a smattering of learning in many areas but leaving him with a lesser degree of all the deficiencies he had before. Bereiter and Engelmann single out language handicaps as the most crucial.

Almost all schools for the disadvantaged are modelled upon upper middle class nursery school methods. These have never been designed with scholastic objectives primarily in mind. Such schools produce small gains in wide behavioural areas. Nevertheless some authors have made much of these gains which are, however, extinguished in comparison with those of controls after some years in the ordinary school. The advantages of such pre-schools thus appear to be slight. Bereiter and Engelmann offer a simple rule that fits the results quite closely. On the average, disadvantaged children going through pre-school will progress half the way to the mean from their initial IQ. No group will ever reach 100 if it starts below this level. On the other hand, the few cases where groups have risen to an average level of 100 relate to programmes which have departed radically from the traditional approach. (But see Heber and Garber, 1970.)

The authors then offer a detailed discussion of the language handicaps which are part and parcel of cultural disadvantage and outline the two possible strategies for overcoming them. The first is to compress a vast amount of miscellaneous verbal material to the limited time available, and the second is to plan activities so as to focus as directly as possible on the objectives. Thus the preferred approach ensures that the child receives an amount of exposure, practice and correction sufficient to teach what is intended. The first has been termed 'verbal bombardment'; the second simply involves direct teaching or instruction. Both imply a radical departure from traditional methods, but the former is less satisfactory because it may miss certain objectives. The latter gives a greater opportunity of planning and control of the syllabus. This approach has been criticized on the grounds of feasibility and whether it is good for young children to be subjected to essentially classroom procedures. The fact that such an approach has long been effective with very young deaf children is quoted as a precedent.

Outlining fifteen educational objectives that a disadvantaged child should attain by the end of a pre-school programme, ranging from being able to distinguish words from pictures to being able to perform certain kinds of 'if-then' deductions, the authors outline their results on a group of severely deprived 4-year-old children. From being retarded in language abilities by one year, these children caught up with the average in language and IQ in nine months of instruction. In summarizing this study, the authors maintain that their approach does not minimize stress but tries to direct it into productive channels; it does not provide the children with 'mothering' but does promote close affectional ties with the teacher. It prepares the child, under the best conditions, for normal schooling. If creativity is equated with freedom, the disadvantaged child usually has too much of it already.

The remainder of Bereiter and Engelmann's book is taken up with a detailed and careful consideration of all aspects of the programme.

In contrast, we now turn to the famous review of Jensen (1969) which opens with the words 'Compensatory education has been tried and it apparently has failed'. He goes on to quote the 1967 evaluation of the US Commission on Civil Rights which concluded that 'none of the programs appear to have raised significantly the achievement of participating pupils, as a group, within the period evaluated by the Commission'. Thus Jensen proposed to examine the presuppositions which underlay this apparent failure, and particularly the social deprivation hypothesis. This suggests that, having lacked certain essential early experiences, the child is thereafter cumulatively handicapped.

Jensen devotes some space to examining the concept of intelligence and IQ, examining the stability of IQ measures, and, incidentally, criticizing the notion popularized by Bloom (1964) that the age at which half the variance in adult intelligence can be predicted (i.e. by a ·7 correlation) implies that half its development has taken place. Jensen concludes that although the IQ is certainly not constant, under normal environmental conditions it is at least as stable as developmental characteristics of a strictly physical nature (see Clarke and Clarke, 1972). He also notes that the question about the normality of distribution of intelligence is meaningless.

Jensen believes that in psychology the importance of heredity has been under-estimated, particularly in individual differences in intelligence. He suggests that this has led to a 'belief in the almost infinite plasticity of intellect, the ostrich-like denial of biological factors in individual differences . . .'. He goes on to consider in detail the results of animal studies and discusses the problems of estimating heritability. He argues that values of H do not represent what the heritability might be under any environmental conditions or in all populations, or even the same populations at different times. These estimates are specific to the population sampled, the point in time, how the measurements were made, and the particular test used to obtain the measurements. He considers evidence from twin studies (particularly Burt, 1966), foster parents versus natural parents and of direct measures of environment. From an examination of correlational studies Jensen concludes that heredity is the major factor in individual IQ differences.

In a section entitled 'How the Environment Works' he advances the notion of environment as a threshold variable, that is, environment only has a marked effect if extremely adverse. The argument here (as pointed out on p. 186) is most unclear, although later (1969, p. 90) Jensen claims that this point is established. Moreover, he refers to the work by Heber in which is demonstrated a declining IQ in children whose mothers (with IQs below 80) resided in a slum, and concludes that this is probably due to genetic factors. Referring to recent work on birth order and achievement, he suggests (without offering any evidence) that this is probably a biological rather than a social-psychological phenomenon (see Clarke and Clarke, 1972). Jensen then discusses social class differences in intelligence and rightly underlines this association as one of the most substantial and least disputed facts in psychology and education. He considers that IQ differences in different classes have hereditary, environmental and interaction components, but environmental factors associated with class status are not a major *independent* source of intelligence variance. After reviewing other areas of research, including race, Jensen tackles the problem of compensatory education in the last twenty pages of his article.

Jensen starts by pointing out that the magnitude of IQ gains arising from enrichment and cognitive stimulation programmes ranges from about 5 to 20 IQ points. Amount of gain is related to the intensity and specificity of the instructional aspects of the programme. Ordinary nursery school attendance – and here there is agreement with Bereiter and Engelmann – generally results in a gain of only 5 or 6 points. With the addition of special cognitive training, particularly in language, the average gain is about 10 points. When an intensive programme is extended into the child's home, with short but demanding daily sessions, about a third of the children have shown gains of as much as 20 points. But, writes Jensen, average gains of 10 or 15 points have not been obtained (1) 'on any sizeable groups' or (2) 'have not been shown to persist or to be replicable'. There have, however, been claims for average 20 point increments, 'achieved by removing certain cultural and attitudinal barriers to learning'.

Jensen states that he had 'found no evidence of comparable gains in non-disadvantaged children'. The exceedingly meagre gains arising from excellent pre-school programmes occurred because the children did not come from sufficiently deprived backgrounds; here Jensen foreshadows his threshold theory for environmental effects, to which attention has already been drawn. He then uses regression to the mean as an explanatory model for some studies. 'The group's mean will increase by an appreciable amount because of the imperfect correlation between test-retest scores over, say, a one-year interval. Since this correlation is known to be considerably lower in younger than older children, there will be considerably greater "gain" due to regression for younger groups of children.' This is a cart-before-horse argument of a type to which we have devoted some discussion in Chapter 6 and in Clarke *et al.* (1960).

Small but significant gains in the Stansford–Binet may also arise from improvement on only one or two items of the test for young children. Moreover, testing under optimal conditions – as opposed to first testing in unfamiliar surroundings – may boost the IQ. Here Jensen foreshadows the views of Labov (1969). Such gains are of the same magnitude as the effects of direct coaching upon the IQ.

Jensen asks 'what is really changed when we boost the IQ?' Is it a gain in 'g', or in something less central to our concept of intelligence? 'I have found no studies that demonstrated gains in relatively non-cultural or non-verbal tests . . .' By implication, therefore, the gains seem to represent acquisition of simple information. Moreover, such gains fade after the enrichment programme has ceased (but see Clarke, 1968). Pre-school programmes should, therefore, be evaluated according to long-term results. The present authors agree with Jensen, but would wish to add to this sentence 'and upon the reinforcement or non-reinforcement of the programme subsequently'.

There is little doubt that intellectual development can be stunted by a deprived environment, and that a shift to a good one can undo the damage very largely, writes Jensen. But can enrichment go beyond a mere amelioration of the stunting? Does it act as a hothouse, producing an earlier bloom, or as a fertilizer, producing better yields? As we have seen, the ongoing experiment by Heber and Garber has a bearing on this question.

Jensen concludes that the pay-off from compensatory programmes in terms of IQ gains is small except where methods are sharply focused, as in the Bereiter and Engelmann study where children receive twenty-minute periods of intensive instruction in language, reading and arithmetic. The largest gains were in scholastic performance, and this is the area which can most fruitfully be tackled. It is the present authors' view that Jensen is likely to be proved right in this assessment. We would add that if pre-school learning is regarded as foundational, and followed by a sequence of instruction based upon it (rather than putting the child in a class not geared to his needs) the widening gap in academic achievement characteristic of advantaged and disadvantaged children may well close. In view of the findings of Husén and others (summarized by Vernon, see p. 177) it is altogether possible that at, say, age 12 children progressively accelerated in this way would perform better on intelligence tests as well as in attainment. Some slight evidence for this view is provided by Halsey (1972).

In Volume I of a Report on Educational Priority, Halsey outlines the findings emerging from four English action-research projects. He indicates that, contrary to much American experience, gains induced by pre-school programmes can be maintained into the infant school. He attributes this to 'the high degree of pre-school cover, the continuity of approach from the pre-school groups (mostly attached to the infant schools) through into the schools, the exceptional stability of the area's population, and the considerable interest generated by the fact that the groups were the first to attend any form of pre-school'. We would, however, point out that with the passage of further time the effects could well be extinguished, although the involvement of the child's parents may combat this, depending upon the degree to which their attitudes and abilities have been affected by the programmes. Moreover, in one of the experiments reported, some of the children who had attended pre-school in the previous year were involved during their first school year in an individual instruction programme. Although these children had already made gains on the English Picture Vocabulary Test, they showed a further rise in vocabulary as a result of their further enrichment.

Halsey offers three conclusions from the experience of three years in four districts. First,

> pre-schooling is *par excellence* a point of entry into the development of the community school ... the point at which the networks of family and formal education can be linked. ... Second, [it] is the most effective instrument for applying the principle of positive discrimination, and this conviction rests partly on the theory that primary and secondary educational attainment has its social foundations in the child's experience in the pre-school years and partly on the evidence that positive discrimination at the pre-school level can have a multiplier effect on the overwhelmingly important educative influences of the family and peer group to which the child belongs. ... Third, there is no unique blueprint of either organization or content which could be applied mechanically as national policy.

Halsey goes on to state that 'The home is the most important "educational" influence on the child. Formal pre-schooling is marginal. It cannot in this sense be compensatory. It can, however, define its role as supportive to family influences where support is most needed.' It is necessary to encourage parents to join in the educational process, taking education into the home and bringing parents into the school.

One of the best-controlled minimal intervention studies has been reported by Gray and Klaus (1965, 1970). Two experimental groups started a ten-week per year pre-school programme at ages 3 and 4 respectively; local and distal control groups served for comparison purposes. The experimental programme, which was especially concerned with changing attitudes towards achievement as well as aptitudes relating to achievement, was supplemented by weekly meetings during the remainder of each year by a specially trained home visitor and the parents. Intervention caused a rise in intelligence which was quite sharp at first, then levelled off and finally began to show decline once intervention ceased. It is of interest that those who started the programme at age 4 were fairly consistently superior to those who commenced at age 3. Yet differences between experimentals and controls were still apparent three years after completion of the programme; we would expect these to have been extinguished if there is a later follow-up. Spill-over effects were apparent in the local control group, while the distal control group declined quite sharply. Gray and Klaus conclude that progressive retardation can be offset but such an approach cannot be expected to 'carry the entire burden of off-setting progressive retardation ... without massive changes in the life situation of the child, home circumstances will continue to have their adversive effect upon the child's performance'. These results are entirely consistent with those of Heber, the main variable being totality of intervention, and the authors are completely aware that, as they say, pre-school experience cannot be conceived of as a single-shot inoculation protecting the child for life against the effects of adverse conditions. Human performance is the result of continuous and complex interaction between the individual and his environment.

Conclusions

Throughout this chapter we have attempted to indicate that an 'either-or' discussion of genetics and environment is dated and in many ways ridiculous. Our general thesis, which should by now almost represent a truism but which nevertheless needs stating and restating, is that human development is mediated by slow, unfolding, cumulative and powerful biological and psychosocial interactions. Different processes may well emerge at a particular time by virtue of predominant influences of one or the other, but all testify to these essential interactions.

   In spite of the complexity of the field and of the data, we shall try to indicate certain consistencies and their implications.

1. Much has been outlined with respect to intelligence, but this has in the text sometimes been linked with attainment. We offer no apologies, and here we follow Vernon in accepting that an IQ test is just as much an attainment test as is a measure of reading. Unlike the latter, however, it taps a much wider range of cognitive skills. The view is also shared with Vernon that the IQ does not by itself 'cause' scholastic attainments, and indeed we consider there may well be two-way interactions between them. Test results may never be used as direct indications of biological potential. Here there is an open conflict with the views of the late Sir Cyril Burt (see pp. 150–6).
2. Some of the data for genetic influences determining cognitive development regardless of environment are less than satisfactory when examined closely, and some permit alternative explanations. The most compelling evidence, however, resides in the fact that long residence in the relatively uniform conditions of institutions is still associated with wide individual differences; that correlations between foster parents and foster children are normally lower than between parents and their children; and that no environmental reason exists for the higher correlation between separated identical twins reared apart than siblings reared together.

In commenting on some of the correlational data, Penrose (1972) argued that the assumption that intelligence has a real existence, although it can only be measured indirectly, still confuses discussions on social, racial and cultural mental differences. It would be more significant, both for educational and genetical purposes, if psychologists paid more attention to the intrafamilial correlations of special abilities.

3. The correlates of social class are well known, and appear quite powerful and pervasive in spite of the crudity of the criteria. While each social class contains within it the whole range of intelligence and scholastic attainments, it is in their proportions in each class that they differ. Membership of Social Class V carries with it, among other factors, a high probability of scholastic backwardness, and in subsections of it (see Heber and Garber, 1971) there is a very strong risk of mild mental retardation. Yet the data do not *of themselves* yield an unequivocal answer to the relative importance of hereditary and environmental influence. It is prudent to interpret them as showing complex and slowly cumulative interactions.

4. Much less equivocal evidence of environmental effects come from studies of children who have undergone a considerable change of circumstances. There are vast differences in long-term outcome for those reared in very poor institutions and those removed from them and adopted (Skeels and Dye, 1939; Skeels, 1966; Skodak, 1968). A similar picture emerges from a study of rare cases of children rescued from social isolation and neglect (Mason, 1942; Davis, 1947; Koluchova, 1972). Such findings are universally accepted and these prompted Jensen's (1969) threshold theory for environmental influences. In this view, only such grossly adverse conditions are likely to influence markedly the course of development, and Jensen specifically draws attention to the much less adverse situation of the culturally disadvantaged child. The threshold theory is thus held to explain why the vast bulk of Head-Start Programmes fail in the long term.

5. It is suggested that Heber and Garber's (1971) important study already provides evidence against the threshold theory for environmental action, although the long-term outcome has yet to be seen. Studies by Husén (1951) and Vernon (1957) have similar indications. We also suggest, contrary to Jensen, that the first-born effect is more likely to be a psychosocial than a biological phenomenon, and thereby has considerable implications for the existence of environmental differences within families.

6. Jensen's view that most Head-Start Programmes have failed is a statement of fact, as well as an indictment of the *naïveté* of those behavioural scientists who played a part in planning such programmes. Before accepting that genetic inferiority is the limiting factor, however, we offer as more plausible the likelihood that the main variables for long-term intervention effects are: (1) the quality of the original environment; (2) the degree to which it was changed; (3) the duration of change; (4) the type of change and the methods of intervention, including its totality or lack of it; (5) the quality and duration of

reinforcement; and (6) the length of follow-up. Unfortunately those organizing the majority of recent intervention studies appear to have believed that a few weeks' intervention would undo several years of under-stimulation, and that this single-shot approach would mark the child for life. A Head-Start Programme as a means of compensating for years of deprivation, followed by further deprivation, is like offering good nutrition to an under-nourished child for a short period before returning him to his original conditions. No Head-Start Programme on its own can ever have long-term effects, and a belief to the contrary testifies to the ubiquity and strength of the mythology surrounding the alleged long-term effects of early experience (Clarke, 1968; Clarke and Clarke, 1972). Early experience in general does not *by itself*, and if unreinforced, have long-term effects, and the notion of critical periods in psychological (as opposed to physical) development receives little if any support from the literature. Indeed, prediction of adult status from the best psychological methods does not become powerful until later childhood, and even then there is considerable intra-individual variability.

Development, whether of cognitive, physical, scholastic or personality processes, involves a slow and very long-term cumulative interaction between biological and psychosocial factors. Hence, if mild mental retardation is to be prevented in those at risk, very long-term programmes are needed. The bold claim of the President's Committee on Mental Retardation (1972) that, *using present techniques from the biomedical and behavioural sciences,* the incidence of mental retardation in general can be reduced by half by the end of this century, depends for its realization quite largely upon acceptance of these simple facts about human development, together with their implications.

References

ALTUS, W. D. (1966) Birth order and its sequelae. *Science,* **151,** 44–9.

BAYLEY, N. (1965) Comparisons of mental and motor test scores for ages 1–15 months by sex, birth order, race, geographical location, and education of parents. *Child Developm.,* **36,** 379–411.

BEREITER, C. and ENGELMANN, S. (1966) *Teaching Disadvantaged Children in the Pre-school.* Englewood Cliffs, NJ: Prentice-Hall.

BLOOM, B. S. (1964) *Stability and Change in Human Characteristics.* London: John Wiley.

BOWLBY, J. (1951) *Maternal Care and Mental Health.* Geneva: World Health Organization.

BRADLEY, R. W. (1968) Birth order and school related behaviour. *Psychol. Bull.,* **70,** 45–51.

BURT, C. (1961) The gifted child. *Brit. J. statist. Psychol.,* **14,** 123–39.

BURT, C. (1966) The genetic determination of differences in intelligence: a study of monozygotic twins reared together and apart. *Brit. J. Psychol.,* **57,** 137–53.

BURT, C. (1967) The genetic determination of intelligence: a reply. *Brit. J. Psychol.*, **58**, 153–62.

BURT, C. (1970) The genetics of intelligence. In DOCKRELL, W. B. (ed.) *On Intelligence*. London: Methuen.

CARR, J. (1971) *A Comparative Study of the Development of Mongol and Normal Children from 0–4 years*. Ph.D. thesis, Univ. of London.

CHITTENDEN, E. A., FOAN, M. W. and ZWEIL, D. M. (1968) School achievement of first and second born children. *Child Developm.*, **39**, 1223–8.

CLARKE, A. D. B. (1968) Learning and human development – the forty-second Maudsley Lecture. *Brit. J. Psychiat.*, **114**, 1061–77.

CLARKE, A. D. B. (1972) A commentary on Koluchova's 'Severe deprivation in twins: a case study'. *J. Child Psychol. Psychiat.*, **13**, 103–6.

CLARKE, A. D. B. and CLARKE, A. M. (1954) Cognitive changes in the feebleminded. *Brit. J. Psychol.*, **45**, 173–9.

CLARKE, A. D. B. and CLARKE, A. M. (1972) Consistency and variability in the growth of human characteristics. In WALL, W. D. and VARMA, V. P. (eds.) *Advances in Educational Psychology: 1*. London: Univ. of London Press.

CLARKE, A. D. B., CLARKE, A. M. and BROWN, R. I. (1960) Regression to the mean: a confused concept. *Brit. J. Psychol.*, **51**, 105–17.

CLARKE, A. D. B., CLARKE, A. M. and REIMAN, S. (1958) Cognitive and social changes in the feebleminded: three further studies. *Brit. J. Psychol.*, **49**, 144–57.

CLARKE, A. M., COOPER, G. M. and CLARKE, A. D. B. (1967) Task complexity and transfer in the development of cognitive structures. *J. exp. Child Psychol.*, **5**, 562–76.

CLARKE, A. M., COOPER, G. M. and LOUDON, E. H. (1969) A set to establish equivalence relations. *J. exp. Child Psychol.*, **8**, 180–9.

DAVIE, R., BUTLER, N. and GOLDSTEIN, H. (1972) *From Birth to Seven*. London: Longmans and The National Children's Bureau.

DAVIS, K. (1947) Final note on a case of extreme isolation. *Amer. J. Sociol.*, **52**, 432–7.

DEARBORN, W. F. and ROTHNEY, J. W. M. (1941) *Predicting the Child's Development*. Cambridge, Mass.: Sci.-Art Publ.

DOUGLAS, J. W. B. (1964) *The Home and the School*. London: MacGibbon & Kee.

DOUGLAS, J. W. B., ROSS, J. M. and SIMPSON, H. R. (1968) *All our Future*. London: Peter Davies.

EELLS, K., DAVIS, A., HAVIGHURST, R. J., HERRICK, V. E. and TYLER, R. (1951) *Intelligence and Cultural Differences*. Chicago: Univ. of Chicago Press.

ERLENMEYER-KIMLING, L. and JARVIK, L. F. (1963) Genetics and intelligence. *Science*, **142**, 1477–9.

EYSENCK, H. J. (1971) *Race, Intelligence and Education*. London: Temple Smith.

GOLDBERG, M. L. (1970) Sociopsychological issues in Education. In DAVITZ, J. R. and BALL, S. (eds.) *Psychology of the Educational Process*. New York: McGraw-Hill.

GRAY, S. W. and KLAUS, R. A. (1965) An experimental pre-school program for culturally deprived children. *Child Developm.*, **36,** 887–98.

GRAY, S. W. and KLAUS, R. A. (1970) The Early Training Project: a seventh year report. *Child Developm.*, **41,** 909–24.

HALSEY, A. H. (1972) *Educational Priority. Vol. I: E.P.A. Problems and Policies*. London: HMSO.

HEBER, R. (1971) *Rehabilitation of Families at Risk for Mental Retardation: a Progress Report*. Madison, Wis.: Rehab. Res. and Trg. Centre in Ment. Retard.

HEBER, R. and GARBER, H. (1971) An experiment in prevention of cultural-familial mental retardation. In PRIMROSE, D. A. (ed.) *Proc. 2nd Congr. Internat. Assoc. Scient. Stud. Ment. Defic.*, 31–5. Warsaw: Polish Medical Publishers; Amsterdam: Swets & Zeitlinger.

HEBER, R. and GARBER, H. (1974) Progress Report II: An experiment in the prevention of cultural-familial retardation. In PRIMROSE, D. A. (ed.) *Proc. 3rd Congr. Internat. Assoc. Scient. Stud. Ment. Defic.* Warsaw: Polish Medical Publishers (in press).

HEBER, R., GARBER, H., HARRINGTON, S., HOFFMAN, C. and FALENDER, C. (1972) *Rehabilitation of Families at Risk for Mental Retardation*. Madison: Rehabilitation Research and Training Center in Mental Retardation, Univ. of Wisconsin.

HEBER, R., DEVER, R. and CONRY, J. (1968) The influence of environmental and genetic variables on intellectual development. In PREHM, H. J., HAMERLYNCK, L. A. and CROSSON, J. E. (eds.) *Behavioural Research in Mental Retardation*. Eugene: School of Education, Univ. of Oregon.

HESS, R. D. and SHIPMAN, V. C. (1965) Early experience and the socialization of cognitive modes in children. *Child Developm.*, **36,** 869–86.

HINDLEY, C. B. (1965) Stability and change in abilities up to five years: group trends. *J. Child Psychol. Psychiat.*, **6,** 85–99.

HUNT, J. MCV. (1961) *Intelligence and Experience*. New York: Ronald Press.

HUSÉN, T. (1951) The influence of schooling upon IQ. *Theoria*, **17,** 61–88.

JARVIK, L. F. and ERLENMEYER-KIMLING, L. (1967) Survey of familial correlations in measured intellectual functions. In ZUBIN, J. and JERVIS, G. A. (eds.) *Psychopathology of Mental Development*. New York: Grune & Stratton.

JENSEN, A. R. (1969) How much can we boost IQ and scholastic achievement? *Harvard educ. Rev.*, **39,** 1–123.

JENSEN, A. R. (1970a) Hierarchical theories of mental ability. In DOCKRELL, W. B. (ed.) *On Intelligence*. London: Methuen.

JENSEN, A. R. (1970b) A theory of primary and secondary familial mental retardation. In ELLIS, N. (ed.) *International Review of Research in Mental Retardation,* **4,** 33–105. London: Academic Press.

JENSEN, A. R. (1971) Note on why genetic correlations are not squared. *Psychol. Bull.,* **75,** 223–4.

JONES, D. C. and CARR-SAUNDERS, A. M. (1927) The relation between intelligence and social status among orphan children. *Brit. J. Psychol.,* **17,** 343–64.

KIRK, S. A. (1958) *Early Education of the Mentally Retarded.* Urbana: Univ. of Illinois Press.

KOLUCHOVA, J. (1972) Severe deprivation in twins: a case study. *J. Child Psychol. Psychiat.,* **13,** 107–14.

LABOV, W. (1972) The logic of nonstandard English. In GIGLIOLI, P. P. (ed.) *Language and Social Context.* Harmondsworth: Penguin.

LAWTON, D. (1968) *Social Class, Language and Education.* London: Routledge & Kegan Paul.

LENNEBERG, E. H. (1964) The capacity for language acquisition. In FODOR, J. A. and KATZ, J. J. (eds.) *The Structure of Language: Readings in the Philosophy of Language.* Englewood Cliffs, NJ: Prentice-Hall.

LERNER, I. M. (1968) *Heredity, Evolution and Society.* San Francisco: W. H. Freeman.

LEVENSTEIN, P. (1969) *Cognitive Growth in Preschoolers through Stimulation of Verbal Interaction with Mothers.* Paper presented at the 46th Annual Meeting of the American Orthopsychiatric Association, New York.

LORGE, I. (1945) Schooling makes a difference. *Teach. Coll. Rec.,* **46,** 483–92.

MCCLEARN, G. E. (1970) Genetic influences on behavior and development. In MUSSEN, P. H. (ed.) *Carmichael's Manual of Child Psychology* (3rd edn), Vol. 1. New York: Wiley.

MASON, M. K. (1942) Learning to speak after years of silence. *J. speech hear. Dis.,* **7,** 245–304.

MAXWELL, J. (1961) *The Level and Trend of National Intelligence.* Scottish Council for Research in Education, No. 46. London: Univ. of London Press.

MITTLER, P. J. (1971) *The Study of Twins.* Harmondsworth: Penguin.

NEWMAN, H. H., FREEMAN, F. N. and HOLZINGER, K. J. (1937) *Twins: a Study of Heredity and Environment.* Chicago: Univ. of Chicago Press.

ODEN, M. H. (1968) The fulfilment of promise: 40-year follow-up of the Terman Gifted Group. *Genet. Psychol. Monogr.,* **77,** 3–93.

OUTHIT, M. C. (1933) A study of the resemblance of parents and children in general intelligence. *Arch. Psychol.* (N. York), No. 149, 60.

OWENS, W. A. (1953) Age and mental abilities: a longitudinal study. *Genet. Psychol. Monogr.,* **48,** 3–54.

PENROSE, L. S. (1972) *The Biology of Mental Defect* (4th ed.). London: Sidgwick & Jackson.

President's Committee on Mental Retardation (1972) *Entering the Era of Human Ecology.* Publ. No. (OS) 72–7. Washington, DC: Dept of Health, Education and Welfare.

REED, E. W. and REED, S. C. (1965) *Mental Retardation.* Philadelphia: W. B. Saunders.

ROE, A. (1952) A psychologist examines sixty-four eminent scientists. *Scient. Amer.,* **187,** 21–5.

SCHACHTER, S. (1963) Birth order, eminence and higher education. *Amer. sociol. Rev.,* **28,** 757–68.

SCHAEFER, E. S. (1970) Need for early and continuing education. In DENENBERG, V. H. (ed.) *Education of the Infant and Young Child.* London: Academic Press.

SCHOOLER, C. (1972) Birth order effects: not here, not now! *Psychol. Bull.,* **78,** 161–75.

SHIELDS, J. (1962) *Monozygotic Twins.* London: Oxford Univ. Press.

SKEELS, H. M. (1966) Adult status of children with contrasting early life experiences: a follow-up study. *Monogr. Soc. Res. Child. Developm.,* **31** (105), 3.

SKEELS, H. M. and DYE, H. B. (1939) A study of the effects of differential stimulation on mentally retarded children. *Proc. Amer. Assoc. ment. Defic.,* **44,** 114–36.

SKODAK, M. (1968) Adult status of individuals who experienced early intervention. In RICHARDS, B. W. (ed.) *Proc. 1st Congr. Assoc. Scient. Stud. Ment. Defic.,* 11–18. Reigate: Michael Jackson.

SKODAK, M. and SKEELS, H. M. (1949) A final follow-up study of one hundred adopted children. *J. genet. Psychol.,* **75,** 85–125.

SONTAG, L. W., BAKER, C. T. and NELSON, V. L. (1958) Mental growth and personality development: a longitudinal study. *Monogr. Soc. Res. Child Developm.,* **23** (68), 2.

STEVENSON, H. W. (1972) The taxonomy of tasks. In MÖNKS, F. J., HARTUP, W. H. and DE WIT, J. (eds.) *Determinants of Behavioural Development.* New York and London: Academic Press.

VANDENBERG, S. G. (1966) *The Nature and Nurture of Intelligence.* Paper presented at Conference on Biology and Behaviour, Rockefeller University, New York.

VERNON, P. E. (1957) Intelligence and intellectual stimulation during adolescence. *Indian Psychol. Bull.,* **2,** 1–6.

VERNON, P. E. (1960) *Intelligence and Attainment Tests.* London: Univ. of London Press.

WHITE, S. H. (1965) Evidence for a hierarchical arrangement of learning processes. In LIPSITT, L. P., and SPIKER, C. C. (eds.) *Advances in Child Development and Behaviour,* Vol. 2. New York: Academic Press.

8

A. M. Clarke and A. D. B. Clarke

Adoption and fostering of children of the mentally subnormal

Introduction

Children of the mentally deficient are often illegitimate, and their parents may be either incapable of, unwilling to, or are prevented from, rearing their own offspring. (For a discussion of characteristics ascribed to mentally deficient mothers, see pp. 216–17.) These, therefore, for a variety of reasons are separated from their parents and are thus *potentially* available for adoption or fostering, and doctors or psychologists are often asked to advise would-be adopters on their prospects. At the same time, although there are large numbers of children under public or private care, there is in fact a shortage of children considered suitable for adoption, and those who wish to take such children may have to wait years before achieving this. In the past, adoption agencies have shown an extremely cautious attitude towards recommending children of the mentally deficient for adoption, although at the present time, partly due to the general demand and partly due to changes in our knowledge, such attitudes are beginning to alter. Thus, a United Nations study (1953) indicates that:

> It was thought formerly that a child offered for adoption must be 'perfect' from every point of view. It has come to be realized that a great many adopters are quite willing to care for and love a child who has some defect, provided they are told about it. Many agencies report instances of children who were below par physically, slightly retarded mentally, or difficult to handle, who after a little while blossomed under the care of loving adoptive parents and became quite normal. (p. 55)

In the present chapter we shall consider under what circumstances the adoption of children of the mentally deficient is justified, and discuss the risks involved. So far as middle-class persons are concerned, adoption often takes place via private channels, and therefore much of our evidence concerns children from the lower socio-economic groups.

The main problem in any individual case is the problem of prediction of future development, for, commonly and rightly, adoption takes place at a very early age. The most elementary requirement of prospective adopters is that the child will not turn out to be mentally deficient, or, alternatively, they may per-haps desire an assurance that the child will be bright. But we have already seen that prediction of development is hazardous (Chapter 6) even in children of normal parents and that we can only deal in terms of probabilities.

The adoption agency has three main sources of information from which to make its prediction: the parental background and history, the examination of the infant, and the assessment of the prospective adopter. Each of these will be examined in turn with special reference to the problem of children of the mentally subnormal.[1] Before so doing, however, the main factor which has bedevilled scientific work on this subject must be mentioned; this is the selective placement commonly practised by adoption authorities. These, to varying extents, tend to place infants in foster or adoptive homes as near as possible in every way to the sort of homes they would have had if the need for adoption had never arisen. On account of this policy, therefore, if a child placed in a superior foster home develops into a person of superior ability, while one in an average home develops average ability, this might be due either to hereditary factors, noted by the adoption agency, or to the environmental factors of the new home, or indeed to a combination of both. Until we learn what happens to children randomly placed in different types of home it is exceedingly difficult to identify the various influences which are operative.

History of true parents

It has often been considered that children available for adoption have in some sense a 'tainted' history, particularly when, as in the majority of cases, they are illegitimate. Greenland (1957), however, has challenged this view. He demon-strated that illegitimate children have a much higher mortality rate (in 1953, the infant mortality rate was 30 per 1,000 live births, compared with 51 per 1,000 for illegitimate children) and indicated that many of the survivors face a host of new hazards – social, emotional, medical, moral, and legal. But he quoted evidence suggesting that premarital chastity is now the exception rather than the rule, and it is therefore no longer possible to regard the unmarried mother as necessarily less stable or less moral than her married sister when the only difference may be her very much higher fertility. His data

> do not appear to support the view that unmarried mothers as a whole, apart from having conceived out of marriage, differ in important respects from other women of the same age and social class. If there is a difference it is in their relatively higher reproductive capacity which has a physical as well as a psycho-logical basis. . . .

---

[1] The general problem of adoption is considered in detail in a United Nations study (1953) and, so far as mental health aspects are concerned, in a World Health Organization report (1953). It is also the subject of an important report by Seglow, Kellmer Pringle and Wedge (1972) who review the literature and outline findings of a national survey of adopted children and their non-adopted controls.

Nevertheless, an examination of the record of the true parents is the first and obvious step in considering whether a child is adoptable. Discussion in this chapter is of course confined to parents known to be mentally deficient; the following points are relevant.[1]

(1) The majority of subnormals are born to parents who cannot themselves be regarded as subnormal and so too the majority of the children of the mentally subnormal are not themselves subnormal, even when brought up by their own parents or in institutions, although on the average they test lower than the general population. This is one aspect of the phenomenon of biological regression; the children of parents at either extreme of the intelligence distribution on the average function at less extreme levels. While these generalizations are important, they are clearly of only limited help in an individual case. Perhaps the most important figures available are those given by the Departmental Committee on Sterilization (1934):

> These relate to 3,733 defective parents drawn from various parts of the country (3,247 females and 486 males). These defectives produced a total of 8,841 children; of this number 2,001 or 22·5 per cent had died, leaving 6,840 for investigation. Children under the age of 7 years were not included owing to the difficulty of ascertaining their mental status. Of those of the remainder who were over 13 years old, 32·4 per cent were *defective*, 13 per cent were *mentally retarded*, and 0·5 per cent were of *superior mentality*; in other words, 45·4 per cent of these children were suffering from either certifiable mental defect or dullness.

So far as the group between 7 and 13 years was concerned, 40·4 per cent were either defective or retarded.

Burt (1937) examined the children of 500 defectives, previously investigated by him, and found that 14 per cent were defective within the meaning of the Education Act, and another 32 per cent dull and backward. Eighty-seven per cent had an IQ of less than 100. He adds that among the children of the unmarried defectives the proportion was higher.

Penrose (1938) in his study of the antecedents and children of 1,280 patients in a Colchester institution found that 7·6 per cent of the parents available for assessment were mentally defective. Ninety-five of the total of 2,560 could not be traced, but if these were added, the percentage would probably rise to 11·9. The proportion of defective parents was largest (12·1 per cent) among the patients of simpleton (feeble-minded) grade, and the proportion was least (2·7 per cent) for idiots.

Of the 570 female patients studied, only 67 had offspring (there were also

[1] Throughout this chapter intelligence alone is considered in relation to fostering and adoption. We have not reviewed the evidence relating to the genetic basis of some forms of epilepsy and of schizophrenia, which might complicate the problem in those comparatively rare cases where these conditions coexist with mental deficiency. Nor have we discussed the controversial issues regarding the relative roles of heredity and environment in relation to temperamental differences.

2 males who were known to have had children). The children of the female patients numbered 124, of whom only 56 lived long enough to be included in this survey, and most of these were examined with standardized tests. Twenty-three of them were mentally normal, 16 were dull, 11 were simpletons, 3 were imbeciles, and 3 idiots, but the grade of the child appeared to be almost independent of the grade of the mother.

(2) During the period up to 1959, the interpretation of the British Mental Deficiency Act widened, and consequently relatively large numbers of persons presenting social problems, who were of normal or only mildly subnormal intelligence, were certified as feeble-minded. Recent English evidence suggests that even under the Mental Health Act 1959 the situation had not changed markedly up to the mid 1960s, although since then the numbers of mildly subnormal in hospitals has decreased. Thus, paradoxically, the label 'mentally deficient' applied to a mother of an illegitimate child does not necessarily connote a very low mental status. The first requirement is therefore an accurate assessment of the mother's IQ, and where anything is known of the father the best that can be hoped for is an inference of his ability from occupational level, and any other relevant details.

(3) The cause of the mother's or father's deficiency must if possible be established for it is highly relevant. If it can be shown that the condition was acquired through disease or injury then in general we can state that genetically that person is normal, so that his or her children have a normal chance in this respect. A good control in this sort of case is to find out as much as possible about the defective's siblings (i.e. the child's uncles and aunts) or about the parents (i.e. the child's grandparents). In a similar environment the child would be likely to resemble them rather than the affected mother. It should be noted, however, that although sometimes organic defect is easy to diagnose (e.g. history of normal development until severe meningitis in early childhood), at other times it may be extremely difficult.

If the mother or father suffered from a rare genetically-determined disorder (e.g. Huntington's chorea) or from some forms of epilepsy, then there would be an increased likelihood of the child being similarly affected, although occasionally the infant examination could rule this out. If, on the other hand, the defective parents had no history of organic involvement, nor of rare genetically determined conditions, then their IQ would be of some importance – the higher the better. Thus any certified person with an IQ of over about 80 must be regarded as genetically within the normal range of intelligence. This does not mean that children of parents below this figure can be automatically excluded from consideration for, as has been noted, the IQ must be related to the social background of the person. Thus if the mother comes from very adverse circumstances herself, her own IQ is likely anyway to increase until the age of 30, and even so, may well be depressed from her 'true potential' due to early experiences.

A further complicating feature is that it may well be that the ordinary principles of assortative mating (i.e. the mating of persons who tend in important ways to resemble each other) may not operate so strongly where illegitimate births by mentally deficient mothers are concerned. Sometimes the father, though of dubious morality, may be genetically well endowed intellectually, and this may counterbalance the mother's own mental subnormality.

Sometimes children have been excluded from adoption because of the parents' 'immoral way of life'; it is obvious that immorality is a learned form of behaviour which may have no relevance to genetical factors. The following case serves to illustrate the point.

William, aged 17, had a Wechsler verbal IQ of 89, performance IQ 96, and full scale IQ of 92. On the Progressive Matrices his equivalent IQ is 102. He had been in various homes and institutions all his life, being illegitimate, and as one might expect, he was a rather shy, withdrawn youngster with poor educational attainments. As a baby he had been placed in a home by a County Council but was later withdrawn when the owner was prosecuted for neglecting children in her care. At the age of 2 years William was reported to be 'quite suitable for adoption' but was later removed from the list because of the mother's immoral way of life; she was thought to be a prostitute. This lad demonstrated some of the features one would expect in a deprived child, yet was intellectually normal, and happened to be a devoutly religious person. There is no doubt that he was suitable for adoption and that he would have benefited from it inestimably, but he was denied this on the basis of what is in fact a hoary superstition. This took place as recently as 1942, and there must be many who have so suffered.

Finally, it should be stated that there is direct evidence (Skeels and Harms, 1948; Skodak and Skeels, 1949; Skeels, 1966; Skodak, 1968) that adopted children with inferior social histories and dull or mentally subnormal mothers usually develop to a higher level than might be expected from a knowledge of their true parents. In above average adoptive homes they have an average chance of normality, subnormality, or superiority. These studies need repetition and extension if there are to be advances in the understanding of the relevant factors. Some of the better intervention programmes (e.g., Heber, Garber and Conry 1971) are also relevant.

History and examination of the child

The history of the child needs careful scrutiny; prolonged labour, forceps delivery, asphyxia, or prematurity may all be of relevance if they depart markedly from the normal, as may be malnutrition, attempted abortion, and so forth. Most cases of severe mental or physical deficiency can be recognized at birth or within a few weeks, particularly where clinical stigmata are present. Thus the history and physical examination by the doctor are important first steps in excluding abnormality or serious subnormality. Illingworth (1955), in an excellent discussion of the whole problem of recognizing serious mental retardation at a somewhat later age in the infant and pre-school child, believes that such a diagnosis must be made in four essential stages:

(1) *Developmental history*, which must be exceedingly comprehensive, 'since the cardinal feature of mental retardation in an infant is that he is retarded in all fields of development, except occasionally in sphincter control'. Thus the dates of passing the milestones of muscular development, sensory development, and the growth of understanding, concentration, learning to take solid food, and the acquisition of passive and active vocabularies are all important.

(2) *Family and environmental history.* Illingworth points out that lateness in certain fields of development, especially walking, talking, and sphincter control, often 'runs in the family' and therefore a history of this must be sought. Detailed information is required on how the child is handled by the mother, including any superstitions she may hold which may have influenced her child-rearing practices. He points out that institutional infants are usually retarded and 'it is essential to take this into consideration in assessing such children for adoption'. Such children usually make good their loss if placed in an adequate foster home, and, it might be added, if such placement is early in life.

(3) *Physical examination*, as mentioned, involves exclusion of gross forms of mental deficiency. The optic fundi should be examined for choroido-retinitis, optic atrophy, or other abnormalities. Hearing should be tested where relevant. Assessment of the infant's developmental level should be done in the child's normal playtime under optimum conditions. Unfavourable signs are general apathy, lack of prolonged concentration, and the slowness with which acts are performed.

(4) *Interpretation of findings* must avoid positive or negative 'halo effects'; no diagnosis of mental retardation can be made on a few signs, mental or physical, unless these are crucial (e.g. phenylpyruvic acid in the urine).

Very often it is hoped that examination during the first few weeks or months of life will not only exclude gross defect but that it will be successful in predicting future development. Such a viewpoint has been most clearly expressed by Gesell (1940) who stated that:

> . . . in no instance did the course of growth prove whimsical or erratic. The behaviour biographies gave clear evidence of a high degree of latent predictability, even in infancy. . . . Such examinations indicate whether an infant or child is of 'normal' mentality, and therefore a good adoption candidate, or if he is so subnormal that he is not a fit candidate. They further can to some extent discriminate within the normal group children, among average, above-average, and below-average endowment – thus giving a good clue as to what kind of home each child would best fit. (p. 149)

There is no doubt that Gesell is correct in believing that many of the grosser forms of mental defect can be excluded by his standardized form of clinical examination, and there is little doubt, too, that one aspect of the validity of his technique, namely the assessment of *present* developmental status, can be accurately undertaken. There is considerable doubt, however, about the second aspect of validity, the power of the examination to predict the course of future development within a normal group. In a most able monograph Wittenborn and his colleagues (1956) specifically evaluate the predictive validity of the Yale Developmental Examination of Infant Behaviour. Earlier investigators had in fact suggested that the predictive validity of infant assessments was nil (e.g. Bayley, 1940; Honzik, 1938; Honzik *et al.*, 1948). Wittenborn stated that: '. . . we have sought exhaustively to disprove the hypothesis of no predictive validity of the infant examination . . .' Two samples were studied, one of 114 children mostly in their fifth or sixth year at the time of follow-up, and the other of 81 children mostly in their eighth or ninth year. Some of the children had been placed in homes before the infant examination, and others after it. The only reliable relationship between Gesell's General Maturity Quotient and Binet IQ was with the group placed *after* the infant examination and for whom at that time there had been a confident classification. The correlation was therefore likely to be an effect of selective placement.

Wittenborn stated in conclusion:

> . . . our exploration of the relationships between the numerous facets of the infant examination and the numerous criteria for development which we have employed has yielded a lengthy and monotonous series of correlations which were not only unreliable but which were too small to be of any practical interest had they been based on huge samples.

He goes on to say that the correlations between aspects of the infant examination and his criteria which were statistically significant and large enough to suggest some practical value were so infrequent that they might result from chance or from selective placement (see also Wittenborn, 1957).

Macfarlane (1953) has reviewed for the World Health Organization the uses and predictive limitations of intelligence tests for the appraisal of intelligence and intelligence potential in infants and young children, in order to answer the question whether such tests 'show enough predictive validity to be dependable criteria on which to base adoption policy'. She indicated that infant tests have little or no predictive validity of adult status, and believed that those adopting parents who could only give responsiveness to a child of very high ability should be discouraged from adopting infants and should wait until older children are available when more accurate predictions can be made (e.g. at the age of 8 or 9). If in the meanwhile, however, such children are retained in institutions, they are likely to suffer maladjustment as Bowlby (1951) has shown. Thus the prospective adopter might be sure of reasonably high intelligence in a child at the cost of poor mental health, to say nothing of the greater difficulty of integrating a child of this age into the family and of personal identification with it.

On the other hand, Illingworth (1966) has suggested that the infant examination has much more predictive power than is recognized, and offers seven main reasons for the widely-held view that developmental assessment in infancy has no predictive value. These are as follows: (1) reliance has been placed on purely objective tests with no attention being paid to physical findings, history, socio-economic status of the family and so forth; (2) there has been a failure to record the quality of the infant's performance, which is judged on an all-or-none basis; (3) there has been a total reliance on sensori-motor tests; (4) there has been little attempt to assess the rate of development; (5) there have been errors of interpretation; (6) there has been an absence of physical and neurological examination; finally (7) the exclusion of mentally retarded children from follow-up samples has removed some of the most powerful evidence for the predictive value of the infant examination. This book is essential reading for those interested in early development.

Commenting specifically on the problem of adoption (1966, pp. 345–51) Illingworth has eleven points of great importance: (1) it is impossible in early infancy to diagnose the mildest forms of cerebral palsy; (2) one cannot be sure whether certain early abnormal neurological signs will be permanent or not; (3) in the first two or three weeks the developmental potential of the new-born cannot be assessed; (4) in retrospect one cannot be certain whether a baby was premature or dysmature; (5) one cannot be sure that an apparently retarded baby is not a 'slow starter' with delayed maturation; (6) one cannot be sure that a baby will not undergo mental deterioration from, for example, a degenerative disease of the nervous system, head injury and so forth; (7) one cannot be certain on how far a child's status is due to emotional deprivation and how far this may be reversible; (8) one cannot promise that he will not exhibit personality disorders, whether inherited or acquired; (9) one cannot exclude the possibility of epilepsy; or (10) schizophrenia; finally (11) one may be able to say something about a baby's potential but one cannot say what he will do with it, for this depends upon stimulation, his social environment, the expectancies that surround his rearing and so on.

More recently Illingworth (1971) has discussed again the predictive value of examination around 6 months of age, and has offered data on 230 cases considered for adoption, none of whom were clinical cases. Some assessment could be made from social workers' reports of the true mother and putative father, as well as of the adopting parents, and the adopting father's employment. A full development and physical history of the baby was taken, together with the results of physical and developmental examination. The babies were graded as follows: Grade 1 – superior (1 case); Grade 2 – possibly above average (68 cases); Grade 3 – average (92 cases); Grade 4 – doubtful (54 cases); Grade 5 – inferior (15 cases). These grades were compared with the IQ results obtained at the age of 7–8 years by psychologists. The mean IQs were as follows: Grades 1 and 2 = 112; Grade 3 = 108; Grade 4 = 99; Grade 5 = 76. Among other important findings, Illingworth quotes the case of twenty-two babies from twenty-two certified mentally defective mothers. Their mean IQ was 100. 'It would have been a tragedy if one had rejected these babies because of the bad family history.' He goes on to say that he had tended to underestimate the potential of his group and that at least some of this may have been due to the deprivation the babies suffered while awaiting adoption for some months. Further, 'there can never be a high correlation between developmental assessment in infancy and subsequent IQ scores because of the numerous variables which will affect the child's later progress'. This is certainly borne out if one calculates the number misclassified by the results of the infant assessment in terms of their childhood IQ status. Using a cut-off point between IQ 104 and 105, close to the mean for the whole group, we find that of the 69 (infancy) Grades 1 and 2, 17 fall below IQ 105 at age 7–8. Of the 92 Grade 3 (average) babies, 38 lie below IQ 105; of these, however, only 5 have IQs of 84 or below. Of the 54 Grade 4 (doubtful) babies, 19 proved to have IQs of 105 and above. Finally, the 15 inferior babies were, with only 1 exception, below IQ 105.

The main problem in evaluating these fascinating results is the degree to which selective placement was employed. Illingworth points out that 'there was inevitably some selection of the adopting homes in that, before adoption was permitted, the homes were inspected and vetted by social workers'. What seems important, nevertheless, is the high risk of babies rated as inferior turning out as below average – for whatever reason.

It seems clear that Illingworth is correct in drawing attention to the possibility that the predictive power of infant examination has been under-estimated. And there can be little doubt that any such assessment should not merely be confined to the present behavioural status of the infant in question. But since it is clear that children's development shows at least a tendency to follow the general context of their lives, it seems still to be uncertain whether Illingworth has made a strong case for the predictive value of the infant examination *per se*. If his figures are taken as they stand, however, there is some degree of misclassification in Grades 1–4. It is our own belief that the success in prediction springs both from the infant assessment and from the intuitive assessment by Illingworth of the child's future home. Whatever may ultimately prove to be the more correct, these findings are important.

Assessment of prospective adopters

Some sort of assessment of prospective adoptive or foster parents is always made by adoption agencies. The main quality they look for is that these should be suitable to have care of a young child, and usually considerable effort is expended in ascertaining their respectability and standing.

Agencies believe that such time should be devoted to the home study as will permit a thorough knowledge to be gained of the motives of the adopting parents for wanting to adopt a child; of their ability to deal with the educational problems presented by a growing child; of their attitude to each other and to the proposed adoption; and of the attitude to the adoption of the other members of the family. . . . The essential aim of the home study is to determine whether the applicants possess the qualities that make for good parenthood, and secondly, to find out whether they are likely to be able to deal more successfully with a particular type of child. (United Nations, 1953)

Apart from these important questions however, attention is far more concentrated upon the child.

There is evidence suggesting that even more attention should be paid to the qualities of the home and the general attitudes of the couple to the bringing-up of children, because many important aspects of personality are thought to be linked with the cultural and emotional background in which the child is reared. This whole problem has been discussed in detail by Bowlby (1951, pp. 104–8). He points out that

> to dub a baby unfit for adoption is usually to condemn him to a deprived childhood and an unhappy life. Few are qualified to reach this decision and the grounds on which it is commonly reached today in Western countries are more often well meaning than well informed. For instance, many adoption agencies place an absolute bar on the children of incestuous relationships, however good the stock. Naïve theories of genetics may also lead to a child being blackballed for such reasons as having a sibling mentally defective or a parent suffering from mental illness. . . . In the days when it was the accepted psychiatric view that all mental illness was hereditary this may have been a reasonable policy. Now that this is no longer so it is unreasonable, except in those cases where the incidence of mental defect or illness in the family is clearly much above the average. . . .

Wittenborn's (1956) monograph once again reaches a new level in respect of care and experimental control. Using the same two samples of children he pointed out that a standard body of specific information concerning child-rearing practices had emerged from semi-structured interviews with adoptive mothers. This information was organized into clusters on psychological and statistical grounds (e.g. eagerness on the part of the mother, lack of sympathy, severity of toilet training, etc.). The interviews had also cast light upon the values in the home and its general atmosphere, in fact on the general conditions of child rearing.

Wittenborn obtained information about the child's personal and social development from the child's own statements about his behaviour, from the adoptive mother's description, and from the examiner's ratings. He pointed out that heredity may be suspected as a 'confounding third variable' in the correlations between developmental criteria and environmental measurements when the particular aspect was usually considered to have an hereditary component (e.g. intelligence). Such correlations would be a likely effect of selective placement.

Where, however, developmental aspects not considered to have an hereditary basis were shown to relate to conditions of child rearing, there would be some reason to believe that these were not due to selective placement but emerged as a response to these particular practices. It was, however, emphasized that the environmental measures were relatively crude and that confirmatory studies would be needed before their practical importance was completely established.

Wittenborn and his collaborators, for example, showed that in the younger sample there was a correlation of ·33 between phobic reactions and unsympathetic child-rearing practices (operationally defined). For the older sample, anxious reactions correlated to the extent of ·35 with unsympathetic child rearing.

The relationships described were not particularly strong, and if, as the authors suspected, many were an expression of the formative role of the environmental differences, they should not be taken as indications of the possible maximal importance of such differences; their importance may be much greater than indicated. It seems likely, the authors concluded, that inharmonious, incompatible, and rejective adoptive parents may tend to produce children who are aggressive and fearful. We might suspect that much of the effort commonly devoted to an exact evaluation of the children could more profitably be devoted to a study of the applicants who desire to be adoptive parents (see also Wittenborn, 1957).

Furthermore, some of the Iowa studies, already referred to in this chapter (see also Chapter 7), have a direct bearing on this problem. In general, the illegitimate children of mentally deficient mothers, when adopted early by families of above average socio-economic status, showed a normal distribution of intelligence quotients, when followed up later; as this statement implies, a proportion of them were below average in IQ with a small number of very subnormal persons. A corresponding number were of very superior intelligence, with IQs up to 150, and the rest were in the normal range (mean IQ for groups of this type was usually a little above 100). The reasons for this may have been a combination of biological regression, organic damage in a parent, non-assortative mating, and a superior environment from an early age. The main implication is, however, that most of these children developed normally and in a way quite different from what would have been predicted, on the assumption that each generation is a faithful copy of the previous one, by an analysis of the intellectual and social status of the true mothers.

Subnormal women as parents

In this connection Sarason (1953) states a number of hypotheses about child-rearing practices in mentally deficient families which he hopes will focus interest in this subject, although he fully expects that they will be modified by subsequent research. These can be summarized as follows:

1. The defective mother does not plan to have a child, probably its presence is an unnecessary annoyance, does not possess adequate knowledge of, or receive

guidance in, child care, and is probably more concerned with her own than the child's needs. In other words, the defective mother is not adequately aware of, or set to respond to, the child.

2. She will probably deny her child adequate fondling, caressing, and play.
3. She will probably lack reassuring responsiveness to the child when distressed, may be inconsistent and even punitive in her handling of it.
4. By virtue of her intellectual limitations, she is unlikely to understand the importance of correct feeding, or be able to make wise decisions in this connection.
5. Since the number of children may well be large, the infant may receive little maternal attention and may frequently be entrusted to siblings.
6. The defective mother is unlikely to stimulate the child's initial attempts at verbalization or locomotion, and in fact may restrict these if they interfere with her own activities.
7. The children of defective parents are unlikely to enjoy the stimulation of toys and educational material and may not be encouraged in the acquisition of correct discriminatory responses.

Burt (1951) has described vividly some of the material and psychological deprivations suffered by children reared in pre-war London slums, and focuses particular attention upon the 'efficiency of the mother' as being of major importance for the young child (p. 333). Obviously, in addition a higher incidence of disease, overcrowding, accidents, and the acquisition of subcultural moral standards combine to give the child reared in such surroundings the worst possible chance of developing to the full his innate potential, and may well determine a pattern of inadequate or irresponsible behaviour which may ultimately culminate in official intervention. Research work by Brandon (1957), however, has raised the issue of the desirability of mothers who have been classed as defective bringing up their own children. She examined the children of 73 certified mentally defective mothers from the Fountain Hospital, most of whom at the time of the study were working or living in the community. Those who were married were found on ratings to be 'at least average, for their broad social group, when rated as wives, housewives and mothers'. Of the 150 children, 41 had died, this figure including (personal communication) 8 miscarriages and 5 stillbirths. The average IQ of those who survived was found to be 91, but since 51 of the 109 children were below the age of 6, these results are more in the nature of an estimate without longterm implications in individual cases.

So far these results are in accord with those of previous investigations. Unfortunately, however, they do little to advance our knowledge, for much crucial evidence seems either to be lacking or not to have been presented. Thus, one general theme in Brandon's papers concerns genetic factors, and the considerable difference between mothers and children. In this connection the following difficulties arise:

(1) A near-zero correlation between parental and child IQs is quoted. Since,

however, most of her sample were very young, and since it is well known that the size of correlation is dependent on the age of the children (see Chapter 7 and also Jones, in Carmichael, 1954), we asked Mrs Brandon for the correlation for the group excluding those under 5 years of age. She found (personal communication) that the correlation between children's and averaged parental IQ became ·25, and when three severely defective children (probably 'organic') were excluded, this again rose to ·41, which is what would normally be expected. Her discussion of genetic factors was thus based on insufficient analysis.

(2) The probability that organic factors were of aetiological significance in at least some of the mothers is not mentioned. Such persons are likely to be genetically normal. The fact that maternal-child IQ correlation is much smaller than paternal-child correlation adds support to this possibility.

(3) Non-assortative mating and its genetical effects are not mentioned, but from further material, which Mrs Brandon kindly supplied, it seems likely that mating was non-assortative within the group.

(4) The number of children dealt with as mentally deficient or educationally subnormal was found to be 18, although not all these had very low IQs. Brandon calculates various percentages as proportions of her total group of 109 children, yet, since nearly half her sample is within the age range 0–5 years, it is clearly illegitimate to discuss educational subnormality, or indeed to assess mental deficiency accurately at such ages. In fact, if those who have at any time been dealt with as mentally deficient or ESN are calculated as a proportion of the 58 cases aged 6 and above, the percentage rises to 31.

(5) The exceptionally large proportion of the group which had died before 2 years of age (16 per cent), together with high miscarriage and stillbirth rates, needs explanation, as the author comments. Until such explanation is attempted, with full supporting evidence which is often very difficult to obtain, we can go little further than the Departmental Committee on Sterilization (1934) which drew attention to the striking death rate in children of such persons, and considered this to be due to the adverse circumstances in which many live, their inability to take proper care of their children, and to the possibility of some correlation between mental defect and poor physique. Brandon has informed us, however, that with six possible exceptions, the dead children were never in the care of their mothers.

(6) Several different intelligence tests seem to have been administered during the research, but taking the group of mothers who had been given the most appropriate test for their age, the Wechsler, a mean IQ of 83 was demonstrated. This placed them on the borderline of dull-normality, and an average of 10 points higher on this test than is representative of the certified feeble-minded in institutions. They may not therefore be completely typical cases. The estimated IQs of the fathers for some reason were not given, but Mrs Brandon (personal communication) states the average as 94. The children's mean IQ of 91 is thus entirely in accordance with expectation on the basis of a genetic theory.

More important than the IQs, however, is the problem of the success or otherwise of the mothers in rearing their children. While theoretically one would assume from the facts quoted that some of these women would be adequate as mothers, one would also assume, in the absence of crucial evidence to the contrary, that a large proportion of those certified as mentally deficient who are (a) really subnormal intellectually, and (b) have all too often themselves been reared in most adverse circumstances, would not make adequate mothers. In fact, there is little doubt that severely subnormal and unstable women often have a deplorable effect on their children (cf. Burt, 1937; Lewis, 1954, and others).

Mrs Brandon's belief that the mothers were average for their neighbourhood is not qualified by assessment of the neighbourhoods themselves; obviously it would mean very little for those living in slum conditions. Research from many viewpoints has stressed that deprived and institutionalized persons tend to hand on to their offspring their own environmentally-induced instabilities; moreover, Sarason's list of qualities one would expect in such persons (1953, Chapter 6) is also relevant. It would therefore be very surprising if many such mothers were able to adopt reasonable child-rearing practices and indeed examination of some illuminating but perhaps not typical case histories summarized in Brandon's Appendix 1 indicates the problems involved. The fact that inadequate or adverse mothering is not confined to the mentally deficient is, moreover, no great comfort to their children.

In summary, this is a very important investigation which must unfortunately be regarded as unsatisfactory because of a lack of detailed analysis of the data and gaps in the information available to its author. It seems that the whole problem of whether it is in the child's interests to be brought up by a truly subnormal mother is still very much an open question upon which planned, as opposed to retrospective, research is needed. Discussion with Mrs Brandon has, however, indicated that, due to a number of difficulties, it was impossible to collect some of the data which we considered essential.

Conclusions

Adoption, like ordinary parenthood, involves risks, and in a society in which a premium is placed upon intelligence it may be a grave misfortune for intelligent parents to have children below average or even of average ability. There is little doubt that for such persons the risks involved with children of the mentally deficient are much greater than the risks with their own children, although the difference is smaller than at one time was thought.

From all viewpoints – integration in the family, early security, emotional identifications, and so forth – early adoption or fostering is of great importance both to the child and to the adoptive parents. At such ages, however, prediction of future development from examination of the child (apart from excluding gross mental or physical handicap) is fraught with difficulties. Similarly, prediction of the child's future from a study of the true parents may also give a misleading picture, complicated in the case of mentally deficient parents by the possibility of organic defect in a genetically normal person, by biological regression, by non-assortative mating or by subcultural deficiency which may result, partly at least, from early adverse experiences which, though profoundly damaging to the person, will have no genetic effect. There is direct evidence of some value which shows the discrepancy between the status of mentally deficient parents and their children's development in above average adoptive homes.

It is a truism that mother-child relationships and cultural opportunity and stimulation are of the utmost importance. It may well be that closer study of variations in child-rearing practices will indicate more certainly those in the child's best interests and those which are not, and which are likely to lead to frustration, aggression, anxiety, and poor mental health. Preliminary work in this field is encouraging, and thus much more attention must be paid to the prospective adopters, their motivation and attitudes, than has commonly happened in the past.

When parents wish to adopt children of the mentally deficient they should be told the full facts about the child in so far as these are known, and they should seek advice from an expert competent to weigh the relevant factors; thus every case must be treated on its merits and wide generalizations are unwise, but it does seem worth re-stating one such rule, that the majority of the children of the mentally deficient, even though brought up by their own parents or in institutions, are not themselves mentally deficient, although under such conditions (as opposed to foster homes) they are generally dull, unless they are the offspring of subnormals with a clear 'organic' history.

Where some assurance of superior ability is desired by prospective adopters they should be discouraged from adopting children when these are very young. It should be explained that adoption of older children also has hazards in terms of emotional maladjustment, even though one can be more certain of prediction of intellectual abilities. Fostering a child followed by later adoption may be a possible compromise because the foster parents are not then fully committed, but this means having a child 'on approval' with all that this implies. Such an experiment with another human being can be damaging to all concerned. There is no doubt, however, that fostering is a minimal desirable requirement of every child who cannot be maintained by his own parents, and every child, unless grossly defective, should be given such a chance. At the present time this is increasingly being recognized, and there is in fact a change from the earlier belief that children of the mentally deficient should automatically be excluded from adoption; this is a welcome tendency and one in accord with our greater knowledge.

References

BAYLEY, N. (1940) Mental growth in young children. *Yearb. Nat. Soc. Stud. Educ.*, **39**, 11–47. Quoted by Jones in Carmichael, 1954.

BOWLBY, J. (1951) *Maternal Care and Mental Health*. Geneva: World Health Organization.

BRANDON, M. W. G. (1957) The intellectual and social status of children of mental defectives. *J. ment. Sci.*, **103**, Part I, 710–24; Part II, 725–38.

BURT, C. (1937) *The Backward Child*. London: Univ. of London Press.

BURT, C. (1951) *The Backward Child* (3rd edn). London: Univ. of London Press.

CARMICHAEL, L. (1954) *Manual of Child Psychology*. London: Chapman & Hall.

Departmental Committee on Sterilization (1934) *Report*. London: HMSO.

GESELL, A. (1940) The stability of mental growth careers. *Yearb. Nat. Soc. Stud. Educ.*, **23**, 149–60.

GREENLAND, C. (1957) Unmarried parenthood: ecological aspects. *Lancet*, **i**, 148–51.

HEBER, R., DEVER, R. and CONRY, J. (1968) The influence of environmental and genetic variables on intellectual development. In PREHM, H. J., HAMERLYNCK, L. A. and CROSSON, J. E. (eds.) *Behavioural Research in Mental Retardation*. Eugene: School of Education, Univ. of Oregon.

HONZIK, M. P. (1938) The constancy of mental test performance during the pre-school period. *J. genet. Psychol.*, **52**, 285–302.

HONZIK, M. P., MACFARLANE, J. W. and ALLEN, C. (1948) The stability of mental test performance between two and eighteen years. *J. exp. Educ.*, **17**, 309–24.

ILLINGWORTH, R. S. (1955) Mental retardation in the infant and pre-school child. *Brit. med. J.*, **2**, 1–7.

ILLINGWORTH, R. S. (1966) *Development of the Infant and Young Child: Normal and Abnormal* (3rd edn). Edinburgh and London: Livingstone.

ILLINGWORTH, R. S. (1971) The predictive value of developmental assessment in infancy. *Developm. med. Child Neurol.*, **13**, 721–5.

LEWIS, H. (1954) *Deprived Children*. London: Oxford Univ. Press.

MACFARLANE, J. W. (1953) The uses and predictive limitations of intelligence tests in infants and young children. *Bull. World Hlth Org.*, **9**, 409–16.

PENROSE, L. S. (1938) A clinical and genetic study of 1280 cases of mental defect. *Sp. Rep. Ser.*, Med. Res. Coun., No. 229. London: HMSO.

SARASON, S. B. (1953) *Psychological Problems in Mental Deficiency* (2nd edn). New York: Harper & Row.

SEGLOW, J., KELLMER PRINGLE, M. and WEDGE, P. (1972) *Growing Up Adopted*. Slough: National Foundation for Educational Research, for The National Children's Bureau.

SKEELS, H. M. (1966) Adult status of children with contrasting early life experiences: a follow-up study. *Monogr. Soc. Res. Child Developm.*, **31** (105), 3.

SKEELS, H. M. and HARMS, I. (1948) Children with inferior social histories: their mental development in adoptive homes. *J. genet. Psychol.*, **72**, 283–94.

SKODAK, M. (1968) Adult status of individuals who experienced early intervention. In RICHARDS, B. W. (ed.) *Proc. 1st Congr. Internat. Assoc. Scient. Stud. Ment. Defic.*, 11–18. Reigate: Michael Jackson.

SKODAK, M. and SKEELS, H. M. (1949) A final follow-up study of one hundred adopted children. *J. genet. Psychol.*, 75, 85–125.

United Nations (1953) *Study on Adoption of Children.* New York: United Nations Dept of Social Affairs.

WITTENBORN, J. R. (1956) A study of adoptive children. *Psychol. Monogr.*, 70, 1–115.

WITTENBORN, J. R. (1957) *The Placement of Adoptive Children.* Springfield, Ill.: Charles C. Thomas.

World Health Organization (1953) *Report on the Mental Health Aspects of Adoption.* Geneva: WHO.

9

J. Tizard

Longitudinal studies:
problems and findings

Introduction

Interest in longitudinal and follow-up studies of the retarded derives from several sources. Parents, physicians and administrators are interested in the expectation of life of persons suffering from particular diseases or handicaps, or from conditions which manifest themselves in mental handicap. Teachers want to know how many of the skills taught at school are retained, and what use is made of them. The effect on social competence of education and training is of obvious importance to those responsible for planning training programmes, and decisions about when to recommend institutional care, and under what circumstances to grant leave from institutions, must clearly be influenced by what has happened in the past to other mentally retarded persons. Concern has also been shown over the dysgenic implications of mental defect, and more recently, over the mentally subnormal as parents. In much of the literature these problems have not been treated separately so that the total picture is a confusing one.

Some of the sources of this confusion can be spelled out. Longitudinal studies of the mentally handicapped cannot be interpreted unless they take into account: (a) biological differences between so-called high-grade and low-grade defectives; (b) differences between 'pathological', 'clinical' or 'organic' mentally handicapped people on the one hand, and 'aclinical', 'endogenous' or 'subcultural' retardates on the other; (c) the distinction between low intelligence and mental retardation; (d) what is known of the epidemiology of mental handicap, and in particular of the systematic biases that result when generalizations from data relating to samples of diagnosed or 'ascertained' cases of mental retardation are applied to mentally retarded persons not so ascertained.

High-grade and low-grade retardates

The differences between those with handicaps associated with severe (or low-grade) mental defect on the one hand and mild or high-grade mental handicap on the other have been reviewed in Chapters 2 to 5. The severely retarded tend to be stunted physically as well as mentally; their handicaps are often recognizable at birth or during early infancy; they are much more backward in development throughout childhood, and usually remain dependent upon others throughout life; they have a greatly reduced expectation of life; they are rarely fertile; almost all of them suffer from gross structural damage to the brain. However, their relatives tend either to be normal in development or to suffer from severe mental and physical handicaps. Parents of the severely retarded are drawn from all classes of the population and not mainly from one depressed social group.

In all of these respects the mildly retarded differ from the severely retarded and there are indeed very strong reasons for the belief that the two classes of handicap are caused by different agents, and that they necessarily have very different outcomes.

For present purposes the importance of these distinctions lies in the different prognosis of persons diagnosed as either mildly or severely retarded.

In view of the importance of grade (i.e. severity) of mental handicap as a determinant of behaviour it would be valuable for clinical, as well as for statistical, purposes to specify the dividing lines which separate the two groups. There is however no single indicator, no sharp dividing line, and in 'borderline' cases the differential diagnosis is a matter of judgment. The best single indicator is IQ, but since the distribution of IQs in the population forms a continuum, to take any particular IQ as marking the boundary must be to some extent arbitrary (Tizard, 1972a; Chapter 2). In IQ terms earlier writers (e.g. Lewis, 1929) specified an IQ of 45–50 as marking the boundary of severe mental handicap in the case of children; for adults it was placed at about 40 points, though a small number of adults with mental ratios (IQs) in the border zone of 40 to 50 were diagnosed as imbeciles 'because they suffered from serious additional temperamental disabilities, for example, dangerous outbursts of temper'. More recently authorities have tended to use a definition expressed in terms of standard deviation units from the mean. Thus the AAMD Classification (Heber, 1961) has as its cut-off point a level more than 3 standard deviations below the mean (i.e. an IQ of 54 or less on Wechsler Scales or of 51 or less on the revised Stanford Binet Test of Intelligence). This boundary line is also adopted in the eighth revision of the *International Statistical Classification of Diseases, Injuries and Causes of Death* (WHO, 1968). On the other hand, the fifteenth WHO Expert Committee on Mental Health which considered the organization of services for the mentally retarded (WHO, 1968) recommended a cut-off point at IQ 50 (3·3 standard deviations from the mean on a Wechsler scale) and it seems likely that this will be adopted in the ninth revision of the ICD.

Inasmuch as diagnosis is based upon IQ alone, these differences in criteria will result in the same individual being differently classified by different authorities. The problems of classification are further complicated by sampling errors, the use of different tests and assessment procedures, and by the problems of IQ standardization and calibration, particularly as these affect scores which deviate markedly from the mean (see Chapter 2). Despite these uncertainties, there is none the less a substantial measure of agreement among clinicians as to the diagnosis of *severe* mental handicap. Moreover, prevalence rates show a remarkable degree of agreement from one survey to another. By far the most difficult problems arise in regard to the mildly handicapped.

The major reason why it is not meaningful to generalize about the prognosis of the mildly retarded is that the term mental retardation is an administrative one applied to persons who are both intellectually retarded and socially incompetent. This is explicitly recognized in the AAMD Classification of Mental Retardation (Heber, 1961). The Association has devised both behavioural and medical classifications. A critical factor in the AAMD concept of mental retardation is inclusion of the *dual* criteria of reduced intellectual functioning *and* impaired social adaptation. 'It is the impairment of *social* adaptation which calls attention to the individual and determines the need for social or legal action on his behalf as a mentally retarded person; it is the below-average *intellectual* function which distinguishes mental retardation from other disorders of human efficiency.'

As explained in Chapter 2 the phrase 'sub-average general intellectual functioning' is defined as performance more than 1 standard deviation below the mean of the standardization sample on the general test of intelligence. Approximately 16 per cent of the population will demonstrate sub-average general intellectual functioning as defined in these terms, 'a figure far exceeding our usual prevalence estimates'. However the Association points out that the majority of those near the cut-off score will not demonstrate significant impairment in adaptive behaviour; where this is found, the sub-average general intellectual functioning is considered to be at least a contributive factor in the adaptive impairment. For clinical purposes the use of dual criteria is entirely appropriate, whether or not one regards an IQ of less than 85 as a satisfactory cut-off point to define sub-average general intellectual functioning – see Chapter 2 (WHO, 1968; Tizard, 1972a). Since, however, only one of these criteria, namely intelligence, is as yet measurable – and that imperfectly – see Chapter 6 – it is only in cases of *severe* mental handicap, in which there is a high correlation between adaptive behaviour and measured intelligence, that reliable diagnosis becomes possible.[1]

Recognizing this, psychologists have made a number of attempts – none very successful – to measure social adjustment with the same precision as intelligence is measured. The AAMD classification postulates four levels of impaired adaptive behaviour and suggests that they be scored in standard deviation units; and a scale to permit this to be done is currently being developed – the AAMD Adaptive Behaviour Scale. To the writer, however, it seems extremely unlikely that psychologists will be any more successful in devising a *valid* 'adaptive behaviour scale' than they have been in devising valid personality measures of traits such as introversion or aggressiveness (see Mischel, 1968, for a critique of attempts to measure traits and states as personality constructs). The problems

---

[1] In the 1973 Revision of the AAMD *Manual on Terminology and Classification in Mental Retardation* (Grossman, 1973) 'borderline' retardation is no longer recognized; the upper limit of IQ is placed at 2 Standard Deviations below the mean or approximately IQ 70, not IQ 85. See also pp. 25–6.

of assessment of adaptive behaviour are compounded by the fact that the term implies a judgment by others of the character as well as the competencies of the person being judged, and these in the context of a changing social milieu. Barbara Wootton (1959) has discussed the issues that arise in such circumstances in very clear terms:

> . . . in a less sophisticated age we should all have said that one of the merits of full employment was that it made it easier for the mental defectives to obtain employment. Now apparently we have to say that it actually reduces the number of such defectives. To appreciate the full significance of this situation we may imagine what would happen if similar reasoning were applied to the analogous case of some incontestable physical disability, such as the loss of a limb. Full employment certainly makes it easier for legless persons to get jobs, but no one in his senses would take it to mean that under full employment there are fewer persons without legs.

She goes on to say:

> so long as defectives are subject as they are to legal and other disabilities, the significance of this difference (between criteria dependent and not dependent on social criteria) is more than semantic. If defectives are to be deprived of full civil rights and responsibilities, and even in some cases of their personal freedom, and if the number of defectives varies with the state of the employment market, it follows that some people are liable to lose their status of fully responsible citizens or to be deprived of their liberty merely because employment is bad.

The solution to this problem adopted in the AAMD Classification is that, in assessing mental retardation, *complete* emphasis is to be placed on the present level of functioning of the individual. 'A person may meet the criteria of mental retardation at one age level and not at another; he may change status as a result of "real" changes in level of intellectual functioning; or he may move from retarded to non-retarded as a result of a training programme which has increased his level of adaptive behaviour' (Heber, 1962). This does much to clarify the issues. However, it is important to bear in mind that the limitations inherent in the assessment of intelligence are greatly increased when assessments have to be made of social competence, particularly of persons who do not share, or who only partly share, the cultural background of the clinician. A wealth of experience shows that clinical judgments are usually much more subject to error than are psychometric tests. It follows, therefore, that longitudinal studies of mildly retarded persons are not likely to be very informative, because the initial diagnosis is so subject to error (Tarjan and Eisenberg, 1972).

The social class distribution of organic and subcultural mental handicap

Nearly all severely retarded persons are diagnosable on clinical neurological examination as having abnormalities of function which can reasonably be attributed to organic lesions in the central nervous system. About half of all mentally subnormal children, irrespective of grade of handicap, have definite signs of neurological damage, but this is most frequently found in children with the lowest IQs. Thus, in a major clinical and epidemiological study of mental subnormality in the community, Birch and others (1970) found that three times as many of the children with IQs below 60 had clear evidence of neurological disorder on examination as was the case for mentally subnormal children with IQs equal to or greater than 60. Of 101 mentally subnormal children aged 8 to 10 years in the city of Aberdeen, 50 had signs indicative of organic brain dysfunction. Of these, 36 had IQs below 60 and only 14 had IQs of 60 or more. Among those who did not exhibit central nervous system abnormality upon clinical examination 13 had IQs below 60 and 38 had IQs of 60 or more.

There is also evidence that even among the mildly retarded (those with IQs of 50 or more) children who have demonstrable evidence of central nervous system

TABLE 11. *Social class distribution of mentally subnormal children with IQ ⩾ 50 with and without clinical signs of central nervous system damage (taken from Birch et al., 1970, pp. 69–70)*

Social class of parents	No. of children in population	No. of MS children	
		Without cns damage	With cns damage
Non-manual	2,405	0	1
Skilled manual	3,552	15	10
Unskilled and semi-skilled	2,131	33	14
Total	8,088	48	25

damage do worse educationally than children matched for IQ who do not (Kirk, 1958; Susser, 1968). It is important, therefore, to look at other factors which differentiate between *mildly* handicapped children with and without demonstrable central nervous system damage. Birch *et al.* found, as others have done (Stein and Susser, 1960; Rutter *et al.*, 1970) that not only was there a significant excess of mildly subnormal children contributed by the lower social classes, and a marked under-representation in the upper social classes, but that the distribution of cases with and without clinical evidence of central nervous system damage differed markedly with social class. In Birch's study, *all* mildly retarded children from families in the non-manual social classes had clinical evidence of central nervous system damage. That is, no children with IQs less than 75 who did not also have 'organic' signs were found in the upper social classes. Children with IQs above 50 and with evidence of central nervous system damage were over-represented in the lower social classes; and in addition, there were three times as many subnormal children among the families of the unskilled and semi-skilled who had no neurological signs. The data are presented in Table 11.

Until recently the differences in the social class distribution of mild mental retardation were explained on a genetical hypothesis: people tend to marry spouses who resemble them in intelligence, and bear children whose intelligence resembles their own (but with some regression to the population mean, see Chapter 7). Stein and Susser (1960), on the basis of findings obtained in the city of Salford, England, which were essentially similar to those obtained later by Birch and his colleagues at Aberdeen, challenged this interpretation. They examined a number of hypotheses to account for their results: a simple genetic theory, a statistical model in terms of regression to the mean, and one based on assortative mating and social mobility. None of these satisfactorily accounted for the data. As Susser (1968) summarizes their argument:

> The social mechanisms of marriage and mobility which might segregate people according to their genes for intelligence, clearly do not have the force to separate the intellectual heritage of the social classes to the degree required to explain the existing distribution. While genetic models alone might conceivably account for much individual variation in intelligence, they cannot be made to account for the gross disparities between the social classes. On the basis of this analysis, one may remain firm in the conviction that most children with mild mental subnormality and with no detectable handicaps to learning suffer from the effects of the environment in which they were reared. The social class gradient of low intelligence is similar to the gradient for those other disorders and attributes that are closely related to social conditions, such as bronchitis, tuberculosis, heights and weights, infant deaths and fertility. A generally accepted interpretation of these social class differences, strongly supported by secular trends, is that they are chiefly the result of social conditions. The improvement in intelligence through time shown in the two Scottish National Education Surveys of 1932 and 1947 leads to the same interpretation (Scottish Council for Research in Education, 1953). These studies show the decline in the percentage of low scorers from 18·7 per cent to 15·4 per cent in a period of 15 years. A similar trend appears in the prevalence of mild mental subnormality in England at periods separated by 30 years. Estimates suggest that in the 1950s there were little more than half as many recognized cases as in the 1920s. Such rapid change must certainly have been the result of changing environment.

Susser believes that it is the non-material rather than the material aspects of culture which are chiefly responsible for this secular trend. The Scottish data indicated that the change was chiefly confined to verbal and scholastic ability and did not affect other abilities. However 'better nutrition, the decline in infectious diseases, and similar factors, cannot easily be dissociated from the non-material aspects of culture. Such factors also vary in accord with the secular changes in low scoring on intelligence tests and with the social class gradient on these tests. For example, children from large families score lower on IQ tests than do children from small families, and even in the 1960s in Britain children from large families eat less well. Nutrition may be connected directly with prematurity, and in turn prematurity has been connected with mental subnormality. Premature births are also associated with poor living conditions and services, so that high rates of prematurity and high prevalence of mild subnormality tend to co-exist. Malnutrition might thus be related to subnormality directly, through a connection with prematurity, or through a coincidental relationship with poverty.

Birch *et al.* (1970), in an elegant analysis of family characteristics of minimally and borderline subnormal children, looked at size of family, area of residence, degree of crowding, and mother's premarital occupation, singly and in combination, as well as at the sibs of the index cases in their study. They suggest that:

> a number of family characteristics distinguish the minimally and borderline subnormal children from other families in social classes IV and V. These characteristics are highly inter-related, and taken together, they identify those groups of the population with low status and aspirations, minimal education, poverty, family disorganisation, and unwillingness or inability to plan the major economic and marital aspects of their lives. Such characteristics serve to identify certain of the families of minimally subnormal children, but by no means all of them.

They postulate a 'micro-environmental setting associated with the highest prevalence of minimally and borderline subnormal children'. However they do not assume that low occupational class, large family size, overcrowding or slum living directly *cause* mental subnormality. Rather,

> children born to parents who have themselves been inadequately housed, nourished, and educated, are at risk to a variety of hazards – pre-natal, perinatal, and post-natal – and the combined weight of such hazards and interaction produces mental subnormality in a substantial proportion of those who survive. Improvements in the standards of medical care must be accompanied by improvement in education and social welfare if we are to reduce the numbers of minimally subnormal children.

These epidemiological studies of mental retardation carried out in Britain give rise to two broad sets of conclusions. First, demographically it is well established that (a) there is a social class gradient in mental retardation which is particularly marked in the case of mild mental retardation; (b) there is an almost complete absence of aclinical or endogenous mental retardation among children of non-manual parents, and a greatly reduced prevalence of organic retardation; (c) prevalence rates both of severe mental handicap (Goodman and Tizard, 1962; Tizard, 1964) and of mild mental handicap have fallen during the last thirty years. Second, case studies of individual retardates show that disproportionately more of them come from certain families and types of family among the unskilled working class (see above, also Heber and Dever, 1970).

There seems little doubt that the first set of findings can be accounted for in environmental terms. As standards of living rise, and as more attention is paid to the health and welfare of mothers and young children, so the proportion of handicapped children decreases. Where living conditions remain poor, and people are ignorant, the cycle of deprivation and handicap recurs. This is true both of handicaps associated with organic signs of central nervous system dysfunction, and of those which lead to a diagnosis of 'endogenous' mental handicap in childhood. There is evidence that the educational progress of children in the two groups differs – but we know much less about differences in adult adjustment.

The second set of problems, as to why it is that within what is in many respects a fairly homogeneous lower working class environment some families appear to be much more vulnerable than others, raises quite different questions. Do individuals select, so to speak, certain types of environment in which they 'find their own level' in society and reproduce their like in conditions which they themselves help to perpetuate? Why should some people and not others be affected in this way? Can anything be done to help them?

There is some evidence that lends support to the view that certain types of vulnerable personality do, in a sense, select particular types of environment. Thus, recent research in another field, namely that of the relations between social class and schizophrenia, has suggested that the high social class gradient (many more schizophrenics among the unskilled working-class population than among those in non-manual occupations) may have been brought about by occupational shifts: the fathers of schizophrenics are a cross-section of the working population, but the index cases 'drift' into unskilled occupations because their illness, or the personality factors which predispose them to their illness, prevent them from making use of available opportunities to improve or maintain their lot (see Birtchnell, 1971, for an excellent treatment of this complex problem). Similarly British studies (Birch *et al.*, 1970; Rutter *et al.*, 1970) which have examined the *grandparents* of educationally and intellectually backward children have shown them to be similar in social class distribution to grandparents of children in a control group. The social differences associated with intellectual retardation and with educational handicap had, in these studies, existed for only a single generation. In the Rutter *et al.* study it was noted that the over-representation of unskilled workers among the fathers of the intellectually and educationally backward was the result of different patterns of intergenerational mobility. There tended to be *downward* occupational mobility among the parents of the children with intellectual or educational retardation, but *upward* occupational mobility among the control group. It was thought possible that educational difficulties in the parents of the backward children might have been responsible for their downward mobility. Compared with the control group, over twice as many of the children with intellectual or reading retardation had parents who reported that they themselves had been backward in their schooling or had had great difficulty in learning to read. Unfortunately, in this study the numbers were too small to test, within groups, the association of parental difficulties and downward social mobility.

The significance of the Aberdeen and Isle of Wight studies lies in the demonstration that in societies in which geographical and occupational mobility is not sharply restricted, and in which social conditions are improving, it is not the case that the majority of the backward come from a 'submerged tenth' of the population which has remained in the lowest social strata for generations. On the other hand, short-term, intergenerational effects have been shown.

Detailed studies both of the biomedical and social characteristics of vulnerable groups of families and of the life histories of individuals who at one point in time were known to have been 'handicapped' also throw light on specific factors which influence the course of their development. In doing so they indicate possible areas for intervention. Birch and Gussow (1970) have for example reviewed the numerous studies on relations between low birth weight and subsequent development, and have shown convincingly that seemingly contradictory findings regarding outcome can be reconciled if one looks at characteristics of the low birth weight child's *subsequent* environment. Except in the case of children with very low birth weights who have suffered organic damage, where the subsequent environment is benign the children develop normally; where it is adverse they fall behind their sibs and other children growing up in similar circumstances. In broad terms there are complex interactions between adverse biomedical factors at one point in time and subsequent biomedical and social circumstances which affect development. (Work in progress indicates that the development of children hospitalized for severe malnutrition in Jamaica during the first two years of life is similarly influenced by the characteristics of the environment they return to: if this favours their physical growth – and is presumably also favourable in other ways – they are, during their years of primary schooling, similar in IQ and in their educational attainments to their sibs and to children of the same age in the same classes at school. If however the environment is such that they remain short in stature, they are also stunted intellectually and educationally.) We have here, then, one group of factors which can be shown to affect the development of vulnerable children.

Today psychologists are also examining factors in the *social* environment during infancy and early childhood which may be of crucial significance for later development. A widely publicized study by Heber and associates (Heber and Dever, 1970; Heber, 1971) which, however, has not as yet been written up in any detail in the scientific press, reports striking gains in IQ and in social competence among *all* of a group of twenty children, of Negro mothers having IQs of 75 or less, who were subjected to an infant stimulation programme which began at the age of 3 months. As part of this study an intensive habilitation programme for mothers was also undertaken. Preliminary data indicate a rapid acceleration of intellectual development on the part of experimental subjects whose performance is uniformly high, as contrasted with that of control groups where only about a fourth of the children test at or above test norms, the remainder trending towards sub-average performance. The difference between children in the experimental and control groups has increased with time, and it is a matter of the greatest interest to know how these children will fare in school, now that the oldest are reaching the age of school entry (see Chapter 7).

Essentially similar results have been reported, in preliminary form, by Robinson and Robinson (1971), on the basis of work done in an experimental nursery which provided for disadvantaged infants and pre-school children. They found differences between experimental and control groups at 18 months, and at ages 2–4 years Negro children attending the Centre attained a mean Stanford-Binet IQ of approximately 120 as opposed to a control Negro mean IQ of approximately 86. 'The crucial variables of day care, educational and health programmes cannot be identified in a pilot study, but that the "package" made a difference in the lives of the children is unmistakable.' The findings of these two studies are in agreement with Hindley's data (1968) on social class differences in the developing intelligence of young children in middle-class and working-class homes. They are in sharp contrast to those obtained in most Head-Start Programmes in which, however, instruction does not begin normally until the fourth year of life (see Chapter 7).

It is too early to say whether the preliminary findings of Heber and the Robinsons will hold up over time, and if they do, to what extent the improvement will be attributable to specific teaching, better nutrition and health care, or a more benign social environment in which kindly and consistent individual attention is given to children by the same maternal figure. Whatever the reason, if it is found that early intervention can cure or prevent most mild mental handicap, while later intervention is much less effective, the implications for mental retardation will indeed be profound, and the problems of prognosis will be seen in an entirely new light. So far the evidence in favour of this highly attractive hypothesis is by no means substantial; and until much more work has been done, and the findings have been replicated by others, most people will reserve judgment about their generality – without wishing to dismiss them or to deny their importance.

Mental handicap and low intelligence

Finally on this matter it should be added that one conclusion which has been drawn over and over again from longitudinal studies begun in early childhood is that 'intervention' at one point in time is unlikely to have long-term results unless there is 'follow-through' in the ameliorative effort. Eisenberg and Connors (1968), summarizing data on the beneficial effects of Project Head-Start Programmes upon the intellectual development of young children, have put the argument for this point of view succinctly. We are, they say, 'far from convinced that the gains (which they report) will endure, given the over-crowding, educational impoverishment, and generally negative attitudes towards the poor that characterize inner-city elementary schools. We would not, after all, anticipate that a good diet at age five would protect a child against malnutrition at age six. The mind, like the brain, requires alimentation – biochemical, physiological, and cognitive – at every stage of its development.' At present knowledge even about long-term effects of malnutrition and dietary deficiency upon the development of brain tissue is fairly sketchy; knowledge about mental alimentation scarcely exists at all. The real advance that has been made in the developmental sciences during the last decade or so has come from a realization that growth and development cannot be understood without detailed studies of the timing as well as the duration of a multitude of specific factors, interacting in highly complex ways to produce different outcomes. A very similar view is expressed in Chapter 7.

Until we know very much more about the specific determinants of growth and behaviour, firm conclusions about, for example, the relative contribution of hereditary and environmental influences is unwarranted. In short, as Birch and Gussow (1970) put it, 'the genetic inferiority theory which many have found insupportable can more properly be described as presently unsupportable, and non-intervention on the basis of such a theory is therefore clearly unjustified'.

Epidemiological considerations

As has already been indicated, longitudinal studies of children initially ascertained through administrative, educational referral to be 'mentally retarded' represent only a proportion of the numbers who would be so diagnosed if other criteria were uniformly applied to all persons in a population. Ascertained cases are, however, likely to include a higher proportion of the multiply handicapped, and of those with the most severe problems. Results cannot, therefore, be generalized unless it is established how typical such cases are.

The importance of taking these selective factors into account can be seen from the Wessex data (Chapter 3) and from any study of special school provision and its consequences. Thus Kushlick's study in Wessex showed that even if we consider only severely mentally retarded persons, something like a third of these were unknown to the authorities responsible for planning services. One simply cannot say from what is known about the numbers of ascertained cases what is happening to the others. When we move from severe to mild mental handicap the difficulties of working epidemiologically become insuperable, and usually the best that one can do is to review administratively collected data in the hope that they may provide rough guidelines for future practice, or give an inkling as to factors which might cause us to modify practice in the future. The issues raised here have been more fully discussed in other, specialized reviews: see, for example, Gruenberg (1964); Birch *et al.* (1970); Kushlick and Blunden (Chapter 3 of this book); Susser and Watson (1962); Susser (1968); Tizard (1972c). A lucid general discussion of methodological issues involved in longitudinal studies is contained in Wall and Williams (1970).

The longitudinal study of mildly retarded persons

Literally hundreds of studies have been published describing the life histories of persons who at one point in their lives have been regarded as mentally retarded. A valuable review has been written by Goldstein (1964) and an annotated bibliography of research up to 1966 has been prepared by Cobb and his associates; the same writers have undertaken an analysis of the literature up to 1969. Together these two reports assemble virtually all that has been published on this problem; they make a definitive statement of the issues which surround it. Because of Cobb's review and because many other, briefer summaries of the literature are readily available it is not proposed to assess the field once again. Instead, some conclusions, taken partly from Cobb but with additional comments, will be presented, together with an Appendix summarizing a few of the major studies, the findings and methods of which are fairly typical of those reported in other but less adequate studies.

Cobb ends his exhaustive review of the 'outcomes' of research with the statement that 'no neat and certain formulae for predicting adult success in the retardate have been achieved. To the contrary, if there is one clear conclusion to be drawn from this array of studies, it is that no simple formula for prediction is possible, that the relationship between predictors and criteria are enormously complex, and that outcome in terms of personal, social and vocational success are the product of manifold interactive determinants.' With this one can only agree. The 'problem' is essentially a practical one; to look for general solutions is misguided.

The main findings of research studies can conveniently be grouped under eight headings.

(1) DIAGNOSIS OF MILD RETARDATION

Identification (or 'ascertainment') of the mildly retarded almost always occurs during the years of compulsory schooling, most commonly with children at an age when the basic educational skills of reading and arithmetic are being mastered and made use of by ordinary children – that is, from the age of 8 or so. The identification of a child as mentally retarded generally follows from school failure. Not all school failures are of course diagnosed as mentally retarded. Moreover, formal ascertainment as retarded may not take place until the years of secondary schooling. In such cases however the child is likely to have been known to his teachers as educationally backward well before he is designated as mentally retarded. Some children are recognized (by parents, doctors, or others) to be developmentally backward, or intellectually slow. These, too, are likely to be later identified as mentally retarded (Illingworth, 1966).

Backward children most likely to be called mentally retarded are those of different ethnic origin, those of low socio-economic status, those living in poor environmental circumstances, and those in large families. Such children tend also to test low on IQ tests. In perhaps a majority of cases retarded children coming from adverse backgrounds suffer from more than one of the associated (from an educational point of view in contemporary Britain or the USA) disadvantages (see Birch *et al.*, 1970; Mercer, 1970; Heber and Dever, 1970; Rutter *et al.*, 1970).

(2) EDUCATIONAL BACKWARDNESS AND MENTAL RETARDATION

Some educationally retarded children, including a higher proportion of those who are most seriously handicapped educationally, are referred for special schooling in special classes or schools. One would expect the results of this special schooling to be unequivocably beneficial, in that the children are taught in smaller classes, and often by specially trained teachers. There is, however, little firm evidence to support the view that special schooling offers great advantages; instead, results of controlled studies are highly equivocal (Goldstein *et al.*, 1965; Blackman, 1967; Dunn, 1954; Goldstein, 1964, 1967; Goldstein *et al.*, 1969; Tizard, 1970). In a comment on this puzzling finding Goldstein *et al.* (1969) pointed out that the majority of investigations into the efficacy of special classes have concerned themselves mainly with actuarial and administrative variables related to special class composition and organization. Child variables are usually confined to traditional psychometric and socio-economic data. Teacher variables are rarely considered. Programme variables, where referred to at all, are stated in rather gross terms. It is assumed that the fact that teachers and children are together in a special classroom implies the presence of an educational programme *relevant* to the development of the children; also, that the presence of a teacher in a special class ensures the competence of the teacher to provide an effective educational programme; and thirdly, that a relevant educational programme and a competent teacher imply that the administration and management of the educational programme is systematic and methodologically appropriate for retarded children.

In practice none of these desiderata have been met. Even if they were, one could still add a fourth criticism of published experimental studies of the effects of special schooling. What is the value of showing – if indeed it can be shown – that specially trained teachers working with special programmes, smaller classes and in an appropriate educational milieu achieve better results than teachers who are not specially trained, who work with much larger classes of children, without special help, and in an educationally impoverished and inappropriate milieu? Demonstration projects can explore the value of new ideas or techniques, but for educational purposes the most useful comparisons are likely to be those which explore alternative ways of employing scarce resources – of specialist teachers, educational psychologists, technical aids and the like. One would like to see, therefore, studies in which equivalent resources were made available to teachers of children in ordinary schools and to teachers in special schools or classes. No such studies have as yet been carried out.

(3) MENTAL RETARDATION AND LOW INTELLIGENCE

A diagnosis of mild retardation implies that the person so diagnosed has a measured IQ which is substantially below the average. However, placement in a special class, as has been mentioned, is made on the basis of *educational* criteria rather than mental test performance. Hence as many as 40 per cent of 'educationally subnormal' children in special classes (in England) may have IQs which are greater than 70. These relatively bright children are however among those who are *educationally* the most backward: that is why they are placed in special classes. Similarly, in England and probably in most other countries, at least three times as many children with IQs less than 70 remain in ordinary classes. Such children are more likely to be girls than boys – in England there are three boys to every two girls in special schools for the educationally subnormal, though the number of girls with IQs below 70 is actually slightly higher than that of boys (Rutter *et al.*, 1970). The reason is clear. Boys give more trouble in school than girls.

This fact raises awkward problems for follow-up studies, since initial diagnosis is likely to be based on a hotchpotch of factors which differ from one place, and from one time, to another.

(4) CONSTANCY OF THE IQ

Low intelligence is a *sine qua non* of mental retardation but, as has been mentioned earlier, low intelligence is not synonymous with mental retardation. In general the IQ is a fairly stable measure over time, but in individual cases the prediction of IQ in adult life from scores obtained in childhood is subject to considerable error (see Chapters 6 and 7). Within the mildly subnormal range of IQ intelligence is a poor predictor of adult adjustment.

(5) CRITERIA OF ADULT ADJUSTMENT

Cobb states that the problem of defining and measuring the criteria of adult adjustment has been approached but by no means resolved. Older follow-up studies tended to use rather simple and readily tabulated biographical data: actual employment, marriage and divorce or separation, court convictions, institutional recidivism. Cobb himself is critical of this approach. He seems to regard factor scores based on factor analysis of correlational data as being more likely to provide answers to the 'problems of heterogeneity in the criterion variable'. If, however, we see the problem of prediction of adult adjustment as essentially a practical one, studies such as that by Stevens (1964) in which 'a factor analysis of 80 continuous point scales together with an additional 61 dichotomous variables' is carried out 'in an attempt to define systematically the full range of relevant criteria' look like using a computerized sledgehammer to crack a conceptual nut. In other words, all that can come out of sophisticated correlational analyses of 'criteria' is something we already know, namely that we cannot substitute one for another: people who are well adjusted in employment are not necessarily happily married, and those who are happily married are not necessarily law-abiding citizens. Hence, in sticking to simple and socially relevant criteria, the older studies were, if this view is accepted, working on the right lines. Analyses which substitute indirect measures for direct ones tend on the whole not to be useful.

(6) ACTUAL ADJUSTMENT IN ADULT LIFE

The conclusion to be drawn from studies such as that by Kennedy (1966) and by Baller *et al.* (1966) which are summarized in the Appendix is that:

> in terms of the criteria of employment, marriage and law abiding behaviour, studies over 50 years have shown that a high proportion of those identified as mildly retarded make satisfactory adjustments. Without any special service or treatment, they tend to disappear into the general lower class population from which they are hardly distinguishable as a social group . . . All of the major longitudinal studies report identifiable shifting from early instability to re-latively increased stability over time. Thus, as compared with a non-retarded control group, the retarded show a higher incidence of marital, civic and occupa-tional failure, especially in the early stages. The difference, however, tends to diminish over time. The group identified as retarded still tends to retain a difference in frequency of unsatisfactory adaptations from non-retarded controls, but these frequencies are relatively small and decreasing. (Cobb, 1969)

Cobb, like most writers, points out that this tendency is consistent with a hypo-thesis of cultural deprivation from which recovery is possible over time and with improvement in environmental conditions. What most psychologists do not also point out is that effects such as these are also consistent with a psycho-biological hypothesis of delayed maturation. There is no necessary contradiction between these two viewpoints – cultural and material poverty could conceivably delay psycho-biological maturation. (The situation is not dissimilar from that which obtains in regard to psychopathy and delinquency – both of these social disorders are most commonly found among young people, and show a decreasing prevalence with age.)

(7) PERSONALITY

The work which has been done on personality factors affecting adjustment is much more inconclusive than the studies of competencies and of intelligence. In general, tests and rating of personality 'factors' have proved of little value (Menolascino, 1970). Behaviour checklists, and factors such as those relating to employment, marriage and delinquency offer much more scope, and are in general more useful predictors of future behaviour.

(8) INSTITUTIONAL STUDIES

A special interest has attached to studies of mentally retarded persons who are or have been in institutional care, because, contrary to the expectations of institution staff, numerous investigations have shown that a high proportion of patients discharged to the community make a reasonably adequate social adjustment there. A painstaking review of published work has been undertaken by Windle (1962), and Cobb's reviews of this literature are as competent as his analysis of the rest of the field. No general interpretation of findings obtained from institutional studies can be given because in most of the early ones the only patients to be discharged were those carefully pre-selected for discharge – or those who escaped from legal detention. The latter group were, not unnaturally, difficult to trace – and if traced they were in any case usually classed as having 'failed' in the community because they were picked up and returned to the institution.

Conclusions

In the changing situation in which nearly all patients admitted to institutional care in Britain, as in some other countries, come in voluntarily and remain as voluntary 'patients', the problem of 'success' following discharge ceases to be of much importance. Readmissions to residential care are common – and why not? Today we see residential care in a different light. We see that whether or not a retardate ever goes into an institution in the first place depends upon a host of factors: the amount of provision available, the admission policy adopted, the alternative provision for care or education in the community, the community attitudes to mental retardates, the state of the labour market, the circumstances both material and social of the retardate's own family, the advice and help that the retardate and his family are given, the retardate's own handicaps both physical and mental. Similarly it has become obvious that how long a patient stays in hospital is also dependent upon a large number of factors, only a few of which relate to the personal qualities of the patient. The discharge or rehabilitation policy may be liberal or conservative; the community services may be generous or inadequate – in the way of opportunities for employment in the open market or in sheltered workshops in the case of adults, or in special classes or schools, or day hospitals, in the case of children or very severely handicapped adults; and the availability of services depends upon their proximity or on the transport which is provided. Furthermore the provision of hostels or alternative forms of residential care outside hospital greatly influences discharge policies, and the amount of social work which is provided profoundly affects the willingness of families to have a mentally retarded person at home on trial, and the extent to which they can cope with his problems. Such casework also assists in the finding of jobs for the retardate and in enabling families to deal with problems which are not related to his presence but which decrease their general efficiency and happiness and thus indirectly make it more difficult for them to cope with him at home.

Likewise, how long a patient stays outside an institution is today seen to be dependent upon constellations of factors which differ for different individuals living in differing environments. To regard the return to the community as 'success' and placement in a hospital or institution as 'failure' leads to the reactionary and absurd conclusions that the fewer beds there are available for the mentally disordered the better a country's health service. Judged by this Spain and Egypt are more advanced than England, and Mexico and Brazil more advanced than the United States.

Baller *et al.*'s study (1966) and that by Kennedy (1948) – see Appendix – and similar investigations carried out of the after careers of institutional defectives, make further purely descriptive studies of little general interest. It can indeed be said that half a century of investigations has done little more than correct the false ideas that have been put forward during the same period. The twentieth century discovered and gave labels to the high-grade retardate; perhaps his problems should now be seen in the wider context of providing adequate medical, social and educational services for all who are disadvantaged or handicapped. High level generalizations about prognosis have been, and are likely to remain, banal. Research can however make a contribution to the elucidation of *specific* problems. A valuable review of factors influencing employment has been prepared by Clarke and Clarke (1972), and similar, analytical studies of factors influencing other aspects of social adjustment are very much needed.

Appendix

LONGITUDINAL STUDIES OF INDIVIDUAL RETARDATES

Comprehensive reviews and summaries of longitudinal studies of persons who at one time or other during the course of their lives were classified as mentally retarded have been published by Goldstein (1964) and Cobb (1966, 1969). The following synopsis of some of the principal studies is intended merely for illustrative purposes: to give examples of some of the more influential studies (including older ones as well as more recent ones). Differences in methodological sophistication, the representativeness of the samples, the opportunities made available to the retardates and the economic situation at the time the investigations were carried out, as well as differences in the problems posed by the researchers, make quantitative comparisons between one inquiry and another unprofitable.

Goddard, H. H. (1910, 1912, 1914)

Goddard's famous studies purporting to show the overwhelming importance of heredity in mental retardation were based on three assumptions: (1) that mental defect could be diagnosed from reports about an individual's conduct;

(2) that the condition was determined wholly by heredity; (3) that it was incurable.

His first study, which was reported in a paper read to the American Breeders' Association in 1910, went into the family histories of a number of mental defectives at the Vineland Institution. Charts were produced showing the presence of mental defect in the families for generation after generation. No comment or conclusion was offered by Goddard, but the material itself strongly suggested to the audience the transmission of defect in a typical Mendelian way (Davies, 1930).

A year later this material was used by Davenport as the basis for formulating a clearly expressed statement about the transmission of mental defect. He says

> . . . there are laws on inheritance of general mental ability that can be sharply expressed. Low mentality is due to the *absence* of some factor, and if this factor that determines normal development is lacking in both parents, it will be lacking in all of their offspring. *Two mentally defective parents will produce only mentally defective offspring.* This is the first law of inheritance of mental ability. It has now been demonstrated by the study of scores of families at the Vineland Training School for defectives by Dr H. H. Goddard . . . The second law of heredity of mentality is that, aside from 'Mongolians', probably no imbecile is born except of parents who, if not mentally defective themselves, both carry mental defect in their germ plasm.

In 1912 Goddard published a study of the Kallikak family, purporting to show the transmission of mental defect in one family through five generations. (An earlier work on the Juke family published by Dugdale in 1910, which is also very well known, had been concerned with criminality and destitution rather than with mental defect, but about this time a further history of the family was written up, and the findings reinterpreted in terms of mental subnormality by Estabrook, 1915.)

Goddard published a second volume (1914) in which he presented 327 family histories of feeble-minded persons. This study can be regarded as the first major scientific attempt to discuss the hereditary aspects of mental deficiency in a systematic way. The data were collected by three field workers, and information was obtained about no fewer than 13,711 persons. Attempts were made to check the reliability of the data by having some families visited independently by more than one investigator; mental tests were used for the first time in a social inquiry, and alternative hypotheses to account for the facts were examined. In these respects the investigations were an advance not only over previous studies, but also over many which have followed them. Goddard traced his families back for several generations, deciding in each case whether an individual had been feeble-minded or not:

> Three generations back is easy, and six is not impossible. It is not difficult for one versed in the subject to tell whether or not a man was feeble-minded even though he lived 100 years ago, providing he made enough impression

upon his time for traditions of him to have come down . . . any person living or dead who was so abnormal that his neighbours or friends or descendants always spoke of him as 'not quite right' is certain to have been decidedly defective. (pp. 28–9)

Following Goddard's example, other investigators added to the list of families such as the Jukes and the Kallikaks (see Louttit, 1947, for reference to these studies). His work thus had a widespread influence on psychologists both in the United States and in this country. It formed a basis for the first article on mental defect to appear in the *Encyclopaedia Britannica* (1919). As late as 1933 Pintner cited the conclusions uncritically in his chapter on feeble-mindedness in Murchison's *A Handbook of Child Psychology*, summing up as follows: 'The chief cause of feeble-mindedness is heredity. Numerous family histories support this contention. A very small proportion of cases is due to disease or accident. There is at present no cure. The care and control of the feeble-minded consists of education, segregation, and sterilization' (p. 838).

As a comment it should perhaps be said that contemporary writing about mental handicap is highly critical of the work of Goddard and his followers: indeed nearly all that has been written since the first world war about the natural history of retarded persons has contradicted or qualified his basic postulates.

Fernald, W. E. (*1919*)

During the closing years of the nineteenth century and the first quarter of the present one, W. E. Fernald was the most influential medical superintendent of a mental deficiency institution in America. Throughout most of his life his attitude to the patients under his care was primitive and pessimistic. Wolfensberger (1969) has given an authoritative analysis of the mood of the period and an account of Fernald's part in shaping it (see also Davies, 1930; and Kanner, 1964). The following quotation accurately expresses Fernald's views reiterated on many occasions:

The social and economic burdens of uncomplicated feeble-mindedness are only too well known. The feeble-minded are a parasitic, predatory class, never capable of self-support or of managing their own affairs. The great majority ultimately become public charges in some form. They cause unutterable sorrow at home and are a menace and danger to the community. Feeble-minded women are almost invariably immoral and if at large usually become carriers of venereal disease or give birth to children who are as defective as themselves . . . Every feeble-minded person, especially the high-grade imbecile, is a potential criminal, needing only the proper environment and opportunity for the development and expression of his criminal tendencies. (Quoted in Davies, 1930)

In 1919, however, Fernald published the results of a survey he had undertaken of all patients who had left Waverly State School – which he ran – during the years 1890–1914. The findings were 'so much at variance with the then accepted theories dealing with mental deficiency' that he hesitated for two years to publish the results of this study. Fernald's work led others to carry out similar inquiries (reviewed in Goldstein, 1964) which had essentially similar results. The bleak, hostile stereotype of the incurable, irredeemable moron was shown to be false.

Subjects. These were 1,537 retardates who had left the institution between 1890–1914, of whom 612 had been transferred to other institutions and 279 could not be traced.

Method. Letters were sent to friends or relatives of the remaining 646 former patients (176 females, 470 males). A social worker then visited the community and questioned agency personnel, police, ministers of religion and others about the retardate. Findings were tabulated and analysed.

Results. Thirty-five per cent of females had been readmitted to institutional care, 14 per cent had died, and 51 per cent remained in the community. Of these 52 (58 per cent) were not presenting problems: 11 were married and keeping house, 8 were totally self-supporting and independent, 20 worked at home and 13 lived at home without working. There were 38 females (42 per cent) who presented problems: mainly sexual offences, alcoholism and theft. However, only 4 had been sent to prison.

Of the men 24 per cent had been readmitted and 12 per cent had died, while 64 per cent had remained in the community. Only 13 out of the 305 such men had married; wives were judged to be normal as were the 12 children born to them. Of the total group 28 were self-supporting and living independently; 86 were employed but living at home; 77 worked at home; and 55 lived at home but contributed little to the family. Only 32 had been sentenced to prison or detention centre, though during the twenty-five-year period another 23 had been arrested but not sent to prison.

Most of those employed were in unskilled jobs but some were doing skilled or semi-skilled work. In general those who were contributing nothing to their families were among the most retarded, while those in skilled work were among the least retarded.

Community adjustment both of men and women appeared to be related to the amount of guidance and support available either from the retardate's relatives or from others in the community.

Remarks. As Goldstein (1964), from whom the above summary is taken, noted, once this study was published administrators and workers in institutions were faced with a question: If some mentally retarded persons with serious records of misbehaviour, who had been discharged from the institution under protest of the administration, could make adequate adjustment in their communities despite minimal training, chance placement, and chance supervision, what might be expected of those who received relevant training, selective placement and supportive supervision?

The history of rehabilitation and habilitation services over the last fifty years can be viewed as a series of attempts to provide data to answer this question. The following eight studies are representative of the inquiries that have been published.

Bronner, A. F. (1933)

Subjects. Cases referred to Judge Baker Foundation.

Results. Three studies reported. In the first, 189 'defectives' with IQs between 75 and 103 were followed up over at least four years with these results: 53 per cent successful (i.e. regular work and no trouble caused); 21 per cent failures (irregular work, or court records, or placed in institution); 26 per cent doubtful (unstable work record, or caused concern through petty misdemeanour). Second study: 50 defectives, mean IQ 68, all with IQs under 75, matched for age and crime with 50 non-defectives, mean IQ 96, range 90–110. Defectives 20 per cent success; non-defectives 16 per cent success, defined as above. For a group of first offenders, 39 per cent success for defectives; 54 per cent success for non-defectives. Third study: 500 adolescents on probation, of whom 19 per cent were defectives. Five-year follow-up. Of 400 boys, non-defectives 44 per cent success; defectives 40 per cent success; of 100 girls, non-defectives 84 per cent success; defectives 68 per cent success.

General remarks

Summarizing the three independently conducted researches, it seems thoroughly justifiable to conclude that the defective, even the defective who in childhood or adolescence presents a problem serious enough to warrant referral to a guidance centre for study, may be so managed that he stands a fair chance of becoming no great burden to the community . . . equated for type and degree of offence there is little difference in outcome as related to intelligence.

Fairbank, R. F. (1933)

Subjects. These were 122 adults from a group of 166 who had been ascertained as mentally defective seventeen years before. Adjustment compared with that of 90 adults who had been regarded as normal children. Also 173 children of the 'defective' group, of whom 79 were at school and 64 given Stanford-Binet test.

Results. Totally self-supporting: 78 per cent as against 88 per cent for 'normal' group. Remainder: partially self-supporting 5 per cent, receiving family assistance 10 per cent, living with parents 4 per cent, state care or widow's pension 3 per cent. Owned or buying a home: 30 per cent as against 24 per cent for the 'normal' group; and 16 per cent as against 36 per cent were saving money.

More marriages and slightly more sex delinquency among subnormals; more dependence on charitable organizations; living conditions were not so good as those of the 'normals'; more juvenile court records but the police records were about the same; less migration to better parts of the city. Of their children only 3 were defective with a mean IQ of 66; 24 were dull, mean IQ 89; 7 were average, mean IQ 109; 4 were of superior intelligence, mean IQ 118.

General remarks. This study was carried out during the economic depression of the 1930s and ran counter to the predictions of Campbell who had considered that self-support was impossible for 22 of the original group, and a 'dubious probability for the remaining 144'.

Abel, T. M. and Kinder, E. F. (1942)

Subjects. Eighty-four mentally subnormal girls placed in industry over a three-year period, beginning work at age of 17. IQ range 50–90 on Otis Scale.

Method. Trained for from one to two years in adjustment classes in New York City, learning simpler processes of women's garment-making. Placed doing similar work; followed up by placement officer of their school; social worker visited their homes periodically. If not able to be placed on machine work, sent as factory workers doing packing or other unskilled work. Employers not told they were subnormal.

Results. During first year half the girls succeeded in one concern; 35 per cent unable to hold a job for more than two weeks. In third year, 55 per cent worked steadily in one concern, half total number doing work for which trade training was useful, and others doing light packing and factory work; 20 per cent failed. Remainder partially successful, working steadily for less than trade union rates. Factors contributing to success were IQ, other aspects of personality, employers' attitudes, work drive or ambition, home stability and luck.

General remarks. The book gives a useful, mainly qualitative account of the major problems of subnormal adolescent girls during the 1930s, and of the exacerbation of their problems through the economic depression. The authors comment that better placement could have been secured if more time had been given to training.

Ramer, T. (1946)

Subjects. These were 626 special school pupils and 589 control cases in Stockholm, born 1905–17. Purpose: to examine how many had failed in life, had to apply for public assistance, became invalids or were delinquents. S. between 26 and 38 years of age at the time of inquiry. IQs as children mainly 70–84.

Method. Examination of official records concerning outdoor relief, invalid pension, drunkenness, court records, etc. (It should be remembered that Swedish social records are extremely well kept.)

Results. More of the subnormal from broken families or from unstable homes; lower social status on the whole. Higher mortality, lower marriage rate, higher divorce rate, more in unskilled jobs. One in three of special class pupils and one in five of controls had been in receipt of poor relief or invalid pensions. More of subnormal group in institutions. No differences in criminal record or in types of crime. Twice as many of the *controls* in trouble for vagrancy. Little difference in alcholism.

General remarks. ' "Temperament" plays a greater part in criminality than intelligence.' Study very carefully carried out and appropriate statistical comparisons made. Data are not, however, analysed separately for the period of the economic depression and the later period of full employment. A valuable review of European literature given.

Hoyle, J. S. (1951)

Subjects. Mentally defective persons under supervision in the City of Leeds. Comparison made between situation in 1929 and 1949. (Both high-grade and low-grade cases are included.)

Method. Analysis of official returns.

Results. In 1929, of 772 defectives under supervision 12 per cent lived under good home conditions; 79 per cent under fair conditions; and 9 per cent under poor ones. In 1949, the corresponding figures were 66 per cent, 31 per cent, and 3 per cent. In 1929, 12 per cent over 16 years of age were self-supporting; 39 per cent partially self-supporting; 12 per cent useful at home; 29 per cent unemployable; and 8 per cent out of work. Corresponding figures for 1949 were 44 per cent, 20 per cent, 9 per cent, 26 per cent, and 1 per cent. An Industrial Centre employs 53 youths and 30 girls, included in the 'partially self-supporting group'. Full employment and better social services are responsible for the change

Hilliard, L. T. (1956)

Subjects. These were 250 feeble-minded women admitted to the Fountain Hospital between 1946–55, and placed in an eighty-bed hostel.

Method. Of all admissions 152, i.e. 60 per cent, have been discharged from the MD Act, and a further 40 employed in the community on licence – 12 in residential jobs, and 28 in daily employment. Six have been placed under Guardianship. 'Of 250 consecutive feeble-minded patients dealt with in this hospital under the MD Act, more than 75 per cent are living or working in the community.' Of the 152 discharged patients, 21 (14 per cent) subsequently married.

Ferguson, I. and Kerr, A. W. (1955, 1958)

Two studies describe the after-histories of girls and boys who left special schools for educable mentally handicapped (ESN) children in Glasgow.

Subjects. These were 207 women, 22 years of age, who were consecutive school-leavers from special schools for the educationally subnormal in Glasgow six years previously; 225 men aged about 25 who had left similar schools nine years previously.

Method. Study of records, and by interview.

Results.

The final impression left by the performance (of both boys and girls) is one of amazement that they have been so successful in holding jobs, even in their middle twenties, when the mad scramble for juvenile employment has largely passed. With meagre educational equipment, usually without the advantage of a pushing parent and often with all the handicaps of an indifferent home, the great majority have contrived to keep in steady work. Certainly many of the jobs they held were jobs that have to be done, even in this streamlined age. But if the picture from the employment point of view is reasonably satisfactory, the general social condition of many of these young people leaves much to be desired; for many have had little chance in life, little chance to make the most of what talents they have. The police records of these youths can only be viewed with grave concern; it is obvious that many of your young criminals are recruited from the ranks of high-grade mental defectives. Nor is this surprising; for too many are inhibited, dull and simple and find it easy, almost natural, to develop antisocial behaviour through suggestibility and lack of 'insight'. There is no lack of suggestion.

Remarks. This careful study shows the material and cultural poverty still to be found in a welfare state in the middle years of the century, and the distressing social consequences for handicapped young people and their families. The attention paid on the one hand to physical handicaps and on the other to material deprivation make it an unusually informative study.

Saenger, G. (*1957, 1960*)

Subjects. A carefully constructed representative sample of 520 severely retarded adults who had attended classes for the 'trainable retarded' in New York City between 1929 and 1955. Age range 17–40 years. IQs mainly between 40 and 50 points. Twenty per cent were mongols.

Method. Interviews by trained psychiatric social workers, using interview schedules and check lists. Careful attention paid to training of interviewer, piloting study and checking validity of conclusions.

Results. Most of retarded alert and lively, taking an interest in life around them. One-third markedly self-confident, only 13 per cent lacking in affect, and 7 per cent lifeless and inattentive. Neurotic trends suspected in 20 per cent and psychotic tendencies in 6 per cent.

Secondary physical handicaps in three-quarters; 20 per cent had motor disabilities; 40 per cent speech defects; but 83 per cent able to dress and feed themselves and take care of bodily functions. Two-thirds able to express themselves in complete sentences and one-third able to pick out a car fare and distinguish coins. But only one in nine able to read even simple passages.

Saenger gives a wealth of data on the factors affecting institutionalization, and on family adjustment. One-quarter were in institutions, and 14 per cent had spent some time in an institution. No relation was found between institutionalization and parental income, education, or family size. Nor did secondary handicaps influence placement to any marked degree. Behaviour problems and disturbed family relations were the most important factors.

The adjustment of the defectives in their own families was surprisingly good: 75 per cent of parents reported no major difficulties and only 5 per cent had serious problems. These in general were those commonly found in normal 5–6-year-old children, namely restlessness and tantrums, stubbornness, fears, and overdependence.

About half took responsibility for their own things, and rooms, 20 per cent assumed major housekeeping responsibilities, and an additional third did household chores; 80 per cent were left alone safely, and probably others could have been.

The great majority spent most of their leisure time in the home but went out occasionally. Only about one-half had friends and only half of these had friends of the opposite sex. Only 4 per cent appeared to have had sex relations and only twelve children had been born. Delinquency was extremely uncommon.

The employment data were remarkable: 27 per cent were working for pay, and an additional 9 per cent had worked in the past. Four times as many men as women worked and Saenger believes that the numbers could have been increased, perhaps even doubled.

General remarks. These two monumental studies by Saenger provide data of extraordinary interest and importance regarding the low-grade defectives and their families. They are, moreover, models of research design, and should be studied by anyone contemplating research in this field.

In conclusion three studies of exceptional interest are described. Two of them (by Kennedy, 1948 and 1966; and by Baller, 1936, continued by Charles, 1953, and Baller, Charles and Miller, 1966) are noteworthy in that they included an appropriately matched control group. In both studies the subjects were also followed up on more than one occasion, in order to survey their social adjustment over time, and in both a psychiatric study was made of the children of the retardates.

The other study summarized below (by Edgerton, 1967) looks qualitatively at factors influencing adjustment. In doing so it goes beyond the endlessly repetitive findings of traditional follow-up studies, and opens up new avenues of approach to understanding of the problems and way of life of retardates.

Kennedy, R. J. R. (1948)

Subjects. These were 256 'morons' living in the community (IQs 45–75), and diagnosed as mentally subnormal when at school. Mean age at the time of the inquiry was 24·5 years. Control group of 129 adults of normal IQ matched for age, sex, and socio-economic status.

Method. Careful and comprehensive social investigation. Adequate statistical treatment of results.

Results. Comparing the two groups, morons came from poor backgrounds, with more parental instability. No significant difference in number married or in number of children born to them. Morons with more step- and adopted children and with higher divorce rate. Some tendency for more morons to have an unsatisfactory work record. Little difference in economic adjustment. More morons in trouble with the police. Morons showed less tendency than controls to participate in recreational activities, including cinema, sport, and dancing. They read less and participated less in group activities.

General remarks

> In final summary, our study reveals that morons are socially adequate in that they are economically independent and self-supporting; and that they are not serious threateners of the safety of society, but are rather frequent breakers of conventional codes of behaviour . . . The morons we studied are, by and large, successful in their social adjustment within limitations . . . apparently imposed by their inferior mental capacities. Doll's remark . . . that 'they find some humble niche in society which they can fill without becoming such a social menace that society becomes gravely concerned about them', seems to fit the actual situation very well.

This account is remarkable for its detail and thoroughness, and for the inclusion of a control group, and the above summary does less than justice to the mass of detailed information given in it.

Kennedy, R. J. R. (1966)

In 1960 all available subjects (N = 179, 69·9 per cent of the original sample) and controls (102, 79·7 per cent of the original 129) were again followed up, and their children were studied and given intelligence tests.

Results. Marriages: 86 per cent of the retarded and 92 per cent of controls were married. Divorce rate not significantly different (<10 per cent). Mean number of children (2·1) the same; mean IQs 99·5 and 106·6. Children of control subjects were in general doing better at school, children of retarded *mothers* having most difficulties. The economic status of members of both groups had risen over the years and job stability was high. One-third of the retarded group were engaged in skilled work, apparently fairly successfully. There were few differences in regard to unemployment. Retarded persons however had a higher incidence of delinquency – though in 1960 this was only half as high as in 1948.

Remarks. '1. The overwhelming majority of both subjects and controls have made acceptable and remarkably similar adjustments in all three areas: personal, social and economic. The main differences are of degree rather than of kind.' 2. 'In the sphere of personal and familiar behavior, subjects show no striking divergencies from what is generally attained by the normal controls.' 3. Although controls exceeded retarded subjects in a number of criteria of social adaptation, both groups showed an upward mobility in economic functioning. While the retarded subjects showed more irregularity of behaviour than controls, they do not in any respect threaten the safety of society (Cobb, 1969).

Baller, W. R. (1936), Charles, D. C. (1953), Baller, W. R., Charles, D. C. and Miller, E. L. (1966)

The other major study is that begun by Baller in the 1930s and continued through the 1940s and 1950s by Charles, and into the 1960s by Baller, Charles and Miller.

Method. The original sample comprised 206 former pupils of 'opportunity rooms' in Lincoln, Nebraska, all of whom had been classified as mentally deficient because of educational failure, and scored IQs less than 70 on the Stanford–Binet Test of Intelligence. At the time of the study they were aged 21 or more. Each index case was matched by sex, age, race and ethnic origin with a control subject with an IQ on the Terman Group Test of Mental Ability ranging from 100–120. A second contrast group having IQs 75–85 was recruited by Baller (1939). This constituted the 'Middle Group' in the follow-up studies, the index cases making up the 'Low Group' and the normal controls the 'High Group'.

Full data were secured on just over half of each group in the follow-up studies, but the samples appeared to be representative of the groups as a whole. The subjects themselves were interviewed, as were relatives (spouses and children). Where possible intelligence tests were given. Information was obtained from social agencies, the courts and from bureaux of vital statistics.

Results. The Low Group was less geographically mobile than members of the other two groups, 65 per cent as against 45 per cent remaining in or near Lincoln. Only 9 out of 205 members of the Low and Middle Groups were in institutional care and most of these had severe physical handicaps and had been placed in institutions in childhood.

The Low Group had an excess mortality, about one-third having died between the ages of 5–56 years against an expected mortality of one-sixth. The mortality of the Middle Group resembled that of the High Group. Among the Low Group there was in adult life a raised incidence of accidental death, but between 1953 and 1964 (that is, after the subjects were aged 40 or so) only one accidental death occurred. The Low Group were less likely to have married, more had divorced, and in general their marital situation was less stable than was that of the Middle and High Groups. The proportion fully employed rose from 27 per cent in 1935 to 36 per cent in 1951 and 67 per cent in 1964, at which time 80 per cent of the men and 77 per cent of the women were reported to be 'usually employed', as compared with 93 per cent and 96 per cent of the other two groups fully employed. As would be expected, the Low and Middle Groups tended to be in unskilled jobs, though as many as 13 per cent of the Low Group had their own business or were engaged in non-manual commercial employment.

Baller reported in 1936 that breaches of the law were three to seven times as frequent among the retarded groups as among the control group (though the controls had more reported traffic offences). Charles (1953) reported that 40 per cent of the subjects still living in Lincoln, and nearly 60 per cent of the men, had been involved in violation of the law since 1935. One-quarter of the violations were traffic offences, and the rest civil, with drunkenness accounting for half of the civil cases. None of the offences had been serious. From 1951 onwards only two males and no females have been in civil conflict with the law, though fourteen males and two females have had a total of fifty-six traffic offences. A small number (15) tested and retested first on the Stanford–Binet, then on the Wechsler–Bellevue and finally on the WAIS showed IQ rises: the interpretation of this finding is uncertain because of changes of test and of standardization. However the results do demonstrate once again that low IQ in childhood is a poor predictor of adult adjustment, and an imperfect predictor of adult IQ:

> The great variation in the present abilities and achievements of the subjects should dispel any notion that persons who give evidence of low ability in childhood develop and perform according to a rigid stereotype . . . Psychologists, educators and parents may gain encouragement from the knowledge that many children whose test scores and academic performance suggest mental deficiency develop into self-sufficient and desirable citizens as adults. (Charles, 1953, p. 67)

Baller, Charles and Miller believe that the explanation for their findings lies in the cultural deprivation suffered by the retardates as children. Subsequent recovery was slow, but steady; and in the absence of special services to help them:

> . . . they had to learn from experience in society rather than in the home. This necessity forced a slow and fumbling start, and much experience of

failure. This 'slow start' was reflected in the records of many subjects whose adolescent and early adult years were marked by delinquency, dependency on relief, and generally poor adjustment, but whose later adult lives were reasonably satisfactory. (Baller *et al.*, 1966, p. 87)

Edgerton, R. B. (*1967*)

Edgerton's study is quite different from any of those summarized so far, in that he is concerned not about quantifiable characteristics of a sample of persons judged retarded at some earlier point in their lives but with 'a general description of the lives of mentally retarded persons in the community [proceeding] to a specific discussion of the problems they face, and the techniques they employ, in dealing with their stigma and their incompetence' (Edgerton, 1967, p. xiv). The method is 'anthropological': that is, the material was gathered through repeated non-structured interviews with the respondents. These consisted of fifty-three former patients of Pacific State Hospital who had settled within a fifty-mile radius of the hospital.

Edgerton's thesis is that the dominating feeling governing these persons' lives is 'a single-minded effort to "pass" or "deny" ': to pass as ordinary people with ordinary memories of families, current friends, an ordinary place in a literate, educated world, and to deny their institutional experience, their ignorance and their stupidity. In order to cope most of them are dependent upon 'benefactors' who help them to survive. It is the *stigma* of mental handicap which is their greatest burden, one which leads them to don a *cloak* of competence to try (unsuccessfully) to cover their incompetence. To cope with this problem is, Edgerton believes, an unsolved task for institutional services.

Remarks. Edgerton's study is the only full-length report on *institutionalism* (see Wing, 1962; Wing and Brown, 1970) in mental subnormality presented from the point of view of the patient. Though Edgerton leaves the impression that the feeling is perhaps an inherent part of mental handicap, it is more realistic to regard it as a consequence of a particular pattern of 'treatment'. This issue is discussed more fully in Wing (1962), Wing and Brown (1970), and by the present writer (Tizard, 1964, 1970; King *et al.*, 1971). See also Chapter 25.

References

ABEL, T. M. and KINDER, E. F. (1942) *The Subnormal Adolescent Girl.* New York: Columbia Univ. Press.

BALLER, W. R. (1936) A study of the present social status of a group of adults who, when they were in elementary schools, were classified as mentally deficient. *Genet. Psychol. Monogr.*, **18**, 165–244.

BALLER, W. R. (1939) A study of the behavior records of adults who, when they were in school, were judged to be dull in mental ability. *J. Genet. Psychol.*, **55**, 365–79.

BALLER, W. R., CHARLES, D. C. and MILLER, E. L. (1966) *Mid-Life Attainment of the Mentally Retarded, A Longitudinal Study.* Lincoln: Univ. of Nebraska.

BIRCH, H. G. and GUSSOW, J. D. (1970) *Disadvantaged Children: Health, Nutrition and School Failure.* New York: Harcourt, Brace, and Grune & Stratton.

BIRCH, H. G., RICHARDSON, S. A., BAIRD, D., HOROBIN, G. and ILLSLEY, R. (1970) *Mental Subnormality in the Community: A clinical and epidemiological Study.* Baltimore, Md.: Williams & Wilkins.

BIRTCHNELL, J. (1971) Social class, parental social class, and social mobility in psychiatric patients and general population controls. *Psychol. Med.*, **1**, 209–21.

BLACKMAN, L. S. (1967) Comments on Goldstein's 'The efficacy of special classes and regular classes in the education of educable mentally retarded children'. In ZUBIN, J. and JERVIS, G. A. (eds.) *Psychopathology of Mental Development.* New York: Grune & Stratton.

BRONNER, A. F. (1933) Follow-up studies of mental defectives. *Proc. Amer. Assoc. ment. Defic.*, **38**, 258–67.

CHARLES, D. C. (1953) Ability and accomplishment of persons earlier judged mentally deficient. *Genet. Psychol. Monogr.*, **47**, 3–71.

CLARKE, A. M. and CLARKE, A. D. B. (1972) Problems of employment and occupation of the mentally subnormal. In ADAMS, M. (ed.) *The Mentally Subnormal: The Social Casework Approach.* London: Heinemann.

COBB, H. V. (1966, 1969) *The Predictive Assessment of the Adult Retarded for Social and Vocational Adjustment: A Review of Research. Part I Annotated Bibliography; Part II Analysis of the Literature.* Dept of Psychology, Univ. of South Dakota.

DAVIES, S. P. (1930) *Social Control of the Mentally Deficient.* London: Constable.

DUGDALE, R. L. (1910) *The Jukes.* New York: Putnam.

DUNN, L. M. (1954) A comparison of the reading progresses of mentally retarded and normal boys of the same mental age. *Monogr. Soc. Res. Child Developm.*, **19**, 7–99.

EDGERTON, R. B. (1967) *The Cloak of Competence: Stigma in the Lives of the Mentally Retarded.* Berkeley: Univ. of California Press.

EISENBERG, L. and CONNORS, C. K. (1968) The effect of Head Start on developmental processes. In JERVIS, G. A. (ed.) *Expanding Concepts in Mental Retardation.* Springfield, Ill.: Charles C. Thomas.

ESTABROOK, A. H. (1915) *The Jukes in 1915.* Washington: Carnegie Institution.

FAIRBANK, R. F. (1933) The subnormal child – 17 years after. *Ment Hyg.*, **17**, 177–208.

FERGUSON, T. and KERR, A. W. (1955) After-histories of girls educated in special schools for mentally handicapped children. *Glasgow med. J.*, **36**, 50–6.

FERGUSON, T. and KERR, A. W. (1958) After-histories of boys educated in special schools for mentally handicapped children. *Scot. med. J.*, **3**, 31–8.

FERNALD, W. E. (1919) After-care study of the patients discharged from Waverley for a period of twenty-five years. *Ungraded*, **5**, 25–31. Cited by Goldstein, 1964.

GODDARD, H. H. (1910) Heredity of feeble-mindedness. *Amer. Breeders Mag.*, **1**, 165–78.

GODDARD, H. H. (1912) *The Kallikak Family*. New York: Macmillan.

GODDARD, H. H. (1914) *Feeblemindedness: Its Causes and Consequences*. New York: Macmillan.

GOLDSTEIN, H. (1964) Social and occupational adjustment. In STEVENS, H. A. and HEBER, R. (eds.) *Mental Retardation: A Review of Research*. Chicago: Univ. of Chicago Press.

GOLDSTEIN, H. (1967) The efficacy of special classes and regular classes in the education of educable mentally retarded children. In ZUBIN, J. and JERVIS, G. A. (eds.) *Psychopathology of Mental Retardation*. New York: Grune & Stratton.

GOLDSTEIN, H., MISCHIO, G. S. and MINSKOFF, E. (1969) *A Demonstration Research Project in Curriculum and Methods of Instruction for Elementary Level Mentally Retarded Children*. Yeshiva University Final Report to US Office of Education, Bureau of Education for the Handicapped.

GOLDSTEIN, H., MOSS, J. W. and JORDAN, L. J. (1965) *The Efficacy of Special Class Training on the development of Mentally Retarded Children*. Cooperative Research Project No. 619. Urbana, Ill.: Univ. of Illinois, Institute for Research on Exceptional Children.

GOODMAN, N. and TIZARD, J. (1962) Prevalence of imbecility and idiocy among children. *Brit. med. J.*, **1**, 216–19.

GROSSMAN, H. J. (1973) *Manual on Terminology and Classification in Mental Retardation: 1973 Revision*. American Association on Mental Deficiency Spec. Publ. Ser. No. 2. Baltimore, Md: Garamond Pridemark Press.

GRUENBERG, E. (1964) Epidemiology. In STEVENS, H. A. and HEBER, R. (eds.) *Mental Retardation: A Review of Research*. Chicago: Univ. of Chicago Press.

HEBER, R. (1961) *A Manual on Terminology and Classification in Mental Retardation in the United States of America* (2nd edn). Amer. J. ment. Defic. Monogr. Suppl.

HEBER, R. (1962) The concept of mental retardation; definition and classification. *Proc. Lond. Conf. Scient. Stud. Ment. Defic., 1960*, **1**, 236–42.

HEBER, R. (1971) *Rehabilitation of Families at Risk for Mental Retardation: A Progress Report.* Madison: Rehabilitation Research and Training Centre in Mental Retardation, Univ. of Wisconsin.

HEBER, R. and DEVER, R. B. (1970) Research on education and habilitation of the mentally retarded. In HAYWOOD, H. C. (ed.) *Social-Cultural Aspects of Mental Retardation: Proceedings of the Peabody – NIMH Conference.* New York: Appleton-Century-Crofts.

HILLIARD, L. T. (1956) Discussion on community care of the feebleminded. *Proc. Roy. Soc. Med.,* **49,** 837–41.

HINDLEY, C. B. (1968) Growing up in five countries: a comparison of data on weaning, elimination training, age of walking and IQ in relation to social class from European longitudinal studies. *Developm. med. Child Neurol.,* **10,** 715–24.

HOYLE, J. S. (1951) Home conditions and employment of mental defectives. *Amer. J. ment. Defic.,* **55,** 619–21.

ILLINGWORTH, R. S. (1966) *The Development of the Infant and the Young Child, Normal and Abnormal.* Edinburgh and London: Livingstone.

KANNER, L. (1964) *A History of the Care and Study of the Mentally Retarded.* Springfield, Ill.: Charles C. Thomas.

KENNEDY, R. J. R. (1948) *The Social Adjustment of Morons in a Connecticut City.* Hartford: Mansfield-Southbury Training Schools (Social Service Dept, State Office Building).

KENNEDY, R. J. R. (1966) *A Connecticut Community Revisited: A Study of the Social Adjustment of a Group of Mentally Deficient Adults in 1948 and 1960.* Hartford: Connecticut State Dept of Health, Office of Mental Retardation.

KING, R. D., RAYNES, N. V. and TIZARD, M. (1971) *Patterns of Residential Care: Sociological Studies in Institutions for the Handicapped.* London: Routledge & Kegan Paul.

KIRK, S. A. (1958) *Early Education of the Mentally Retarded.* Urbana: Univ. of Illinois Press.

LEWIS, E. O. (1929) *Report of the Mental Deficiency Committee,* Part IV. London: HMSO.

LOUTTIT, C. M. (1947) *Clinical Psychology of Children's Behaviour Problems.* New York: Harper & Row.

MENOLASCINO, F. J. (1970) *Psychiatric Approaches to Mental Retardation.* New York: Basic Books.

MERCER, J. R. (1970) Sociological perspectives in mild mental retardation. In HAYWOOD, H. C. (ed.) *Social-Cultural Aspects of Mental Retardation: Proceedings of the Peabody – NIMH Conference.* New York: Appleton-Century-Crofts.

MISCHEL, W. (1968) *Personality and Assessment.* New York: Wiley.

MURCHISON, C. (1933) *A Handbook of Child Psychology.* Worcester: Clark Univ. Press.

PINTNER, R. (1933) The feeble-minded child. In MURCHISON, C. (ed.) *A Handbook of Child Psychology*. Worcester, Mass.: Clark Univ. Press.

RAMER, T. (1946) The prognosis of mentally retarded children. *Acta Psychiat., Neurol. Suppl.*, **41,** 1–142.

ROBINSON, H. B. and ROBINSON, N. M. (1971) Longitudinal development of very young children in a comprehensive day care programme: the first two years. *Child Developm.*, **42,** 1673–84.

RUTTER, M., TIZARD, J. and WHITMORE, K. (1970) *Education Health and Behaviour*. London: Longmans.

SAENGER, G. (1957) *The Adjustment of Severely Retarded Adults in the Community*. Albany: New York State Interdepartmental Health Resources Board.

SAENGER, G. (1960) *Factors Influencing the Institutionalization of Mentally Retarded Individuals in New York City*. Albany: New York State Interdepartmental Health Resources Board.

Scottish Council for Research in Education (1953) *Social Implications of the Scottish Mental Survey*. London: Univ. of London Press.

STEIN, Z. and SUSSER, M. W. (1960) The families of dull children: classification for predicting careers. *Brit. J. prev. soc. Med.*, **14,** 83–8.

STEVENS, W. B. D. (1964) *Success of Young Adult Male Retardates*. Ann Arbor, Mich.: University Microfilms Inc. Cited by Cobb, 1969.

SUSSER, M. W. (1968) *Community Psychiatry*. New York: Random House.

SUSSER, M. W. and WATSON, W. (1962) *Sociology in Medicine*. London: Oxford Univ. Press.

TARJAN, G. and EISENBERG, L. (1972) Some thoughts on the classification of mental retardation in the United States of America. *Amer. J. Psychiat.*, **128,** 14–18.

TIZARD, J. (1964) *Community Services for the Mentally Handicapped*. London: Oxford Univ. Press.

TIZARD, J. (1970) The role of social institutions in the causation prevention and alleviation of mental retardation. In HAYWOOD, H. C. (ed.) *Social-Cultural Aspects of Mental Retardation: Proceedings of the Peabody – NIMH Conference*. New York: Appleton-Century-Crofts.

TIZARD, J. (1972a) A note on the international statistical classification of mental retardation. *Amer. J. Psychiat.*, **128,** 25–9.

TIZARD, J. (1972b) Planning and evaluation of special education. In *Proceedings of the European Association for Special Education International Conference 'Teaching the Handicapped Child'*, Norrkoping, Sweden.

TIZARD, J. (1972c) Research into services for the mentally handicapped: science and policy issues. *Brit. J. ment. Subn.*, **XVIII,** Part I, 34, 1–12.

WALL, W. D. and WILLIAMS, H. L. (1970) *Longitudinal Studies and the Social Sciences*. London: Heinemann, for the Social Science Research Council.

WINDLE, C. (1962) Prognosis of mental subnormals. *Monogr. Suppl. Amer. J. ment. Defic.*, **66**, 1–180.

WING, J. K. (1962) Institutionalism in mental hospitals. *Brit. J. Soc. Clin. Psychol.*, **1.**

WING, J. and BROWN, G. (1970) *Institutionalism and Schizophrenia.* London: Cambridge Univ. Press.

WOLFENSBERGER, W. (1969) The origin and nature of our institutional models. In KUGEL, R. B. and WOLFENSBERGER, W. (eds.) *Changing Patterns in Residential Services for the Mentally Retarded.* Washington, DC: President's Panel on Mental Retardation.

WOOTTON, B. (1959) *Social Science and Social Pathology.* London: Allen & Unwin.

World Health Organization (1968) *International Statistical Classification of Diseases, Injuries and Causes of Death, 8th revision.* Geneva: WHO.

World Health Organization (1968) *Organization of Services for the Mentally Retarded.* Tech. Rep. Ser. No. 392. Geneva: WHO.

PART TWO

The experimental analysis of subnormal behaviour

10

A. M. Clarke and A. D. B. Clarke

Experimental studies: an overview[1]

Introduction

During the last decade there has been a vast increase in experimental studies of subnormal behaviour. More often than not, these have been laboratory-based and short-term in nature. In this chapter, an overview of the main fields of work is offered together with a discussion of some of the methodological difficulties involved. Research on operant learning and behaviour modification is virtually excluded here because of its detailed treatment in Chapter 23. The literature review, for reasons of space, is necessarily selective and attempts to cover recent findings up to and including the year 1970. Discussion of experimental research is not, of course, confined to this chapter.

Theories of subnormal behaviour

In any new scientific field, after a period of large-scale data collection, some general hypotheses or general attitudes arise to which research workers, wittingly or unwittingly, adhere. Currently, three positions with respect to mental subnormality may be outlined. These are as yet embryonic and are perhaps less important in their own right as psychological theories than for the role they play in determining research projects and type of experimental design.

(1) THE DEFECT THEORY

Adherents to this view consider that the mentally subnormal differ from the normal not only quantitatively but qualitatively. The argument rests on the many studies comparing subnormal and normal subjects *matched for MA* which show inferior performance in the former group, and the special difficulties of most subnormals in the area of language development and verbal mediation.

[1] This chapter is based upon part of Chapter 6 in H. J. Eysenck (ed.) *Handbook of Abnormal Psychology* (London, Pitman's Medical Press, 1973), and is reproduced by permission of the editor and publishers. It was written while the authors were in receipt of a generous grant from the Association for the Aid of Crippled Children, New York.

Most defect theorists (Ellis, 1963; Spitz, 1963; Luria, 1961) have elaborated their own physiological models which serve as guidelines in formulating hypotheses for behavioural research. Although their views are sometimes ambiguous, a strong impression is gained that they see the mentally subnormal, regardless of aetiology or level of intellect, as neurologically different from the normal population. As Ellis (1969), one of the chief exponents of this theory, puts it, MA, IQ, or 'developmental level', however defined, are rejected as an *explanation* of behaviour. Given that there are behavioural differences between normals and retardates of equal CA, the primary task for a behavioural science is to describe these differences. In view of Ellis's position it is logical that he believes the term 'defectives' more accurately describes this population than 'retardates', the latter term holding connotations of a developmental lag, which might in time be made good.

(2) THE RETARDATION OR DEVELOPMENTAL LAG THEORY

This states that the cognitive development of the mentally retarded is characterized by a slower progression through the same sequence of cognitive stages as the normal, and by lower limits to full development. Thus, the difference between normal and subnormal is analogous with the difference between the very superior and normal. The developmental position generates the hypothesis that there are no differences in formal cognitive functioning between *familial* (biogenic) retardates and normals, matched on general level of cognition (typically measured by MA). Zigler (1969) has contributed an excellent statement of this position and critique of the defect theory. He (1967) believes that many of the reported differences in performance between normal and mentally retarded individuals of the same MA may be traced to such variables as motivation and experience, rather than to basic cognitive deficiencies.

Although the differences in theoretical position between adherents of these views of subnormality sometimes appear wide, in fact there is considerable overlap, and the most important point of contention probably resides in the question as to whether the broad aetiological classification (biogenic versus pathological) is so basic to a consideration of any problem in mental retardation that research workers are in error to include in one group subjects selected on intellectual level as the sole criterion. Zigler (1969) would have it that a developmental lag theory applies best to the familial/cultural subnormals, reserving the defect theory for the pathological. By contrast, Leland (1969) and others argue that it is not to the scientist's advantage to dichotomize mentally retarded groups on the basis of presumed aetiologies. Most of them are so labelled because of maladaptation and behavioural difficulties. The only serviceable classification system is one that groups individuals by their ability to cope with specific critical demands, and that provides a guide to the modification and reversal of these behaviours.

(3) THE SKINNERIAN POSITION

The latter position has something in common with Skinnerian theory, elaborated for retardation by Bijou (1963 and 1966), which is important not so much for its effectiveness in describing the nature of subnormality, as in focusing the research of its adherents on to the antecedent conditions, and future methods of shaping the behaviours of sometimes profoundly subnormal individuals who might not otherwise be seen as promising material for psychological research. (See section on Operant Learning, and Chapter 23).

Bijou eschews the use of hypothetical mental constructs such as defective intelligence and hypothetical biological abnormalities such as 'clinically inferred brain injury' in the classification of mental retardation. He maintains that, since it is the behaviour that is retarded, correlates must be sought for this retarded behaviour. These must be observable events that clearly limit or control behaviour; antecedent events are grouped in classes such as abnormal anatomical structure and physiological functioning, the consequences of severe punishment, or inadequate reinforcement history. Once the relationship is established the basis for behaviour control is reached.

In summary, the main point of contention in the recent experimental literature on mental subnormality has related to the first two hypotheses outlined above, and frequent references to this issue will be found in the following pages. The recent polemic between Milgram (1969), Zigler (1969), and Ellis (1969) suggests a considerable overlap between the 'defect' and the 'retardation' theories, as well as some misunderstanding by the main protagonists of the others' position. But Ellis now considers that a sharp distinction between developmental and defect approaches lacks substance. Be that as it may, it is clear that much research owes its parentage to one or other of these positions.

Problems of research design

A majority of the experimental studies reviewed in this chapter contrast a group or groups of mentally retarded subjects' performance on a task or tasks with that of normal subjects matched for MA or CA. In both cases, IQ differences between groups will be inevitable and sometimes considerable. With MA matches, up to 50-point IQ differences may be found and with CA matches, 30 points is usual and up to about 70 points has been reported, when retarded children are compared with groups of intellectually superior subjects. Although in many cases of MA-matched groups, psychologists have clearly stated that they were looking for qualitative differences between groups who on intelligence tests had performed similarly, the suspicion arises that, on occasion, inclusion of normal controls in a research design was due to a blind adherence to a fashionable trend. Only recently have scientists looked critically at research designs in common use and at the questions that may legitimately be answered in any particular case.

Zeaman (1965) points out that the psychologist may attack the problems of subnormality in at least two ways, either by finding the laws, principles, or regularities that govern the behaviour of retardates, or by finding the *unique* laws of their behaviour. If the latter is to be attempted, comparisons with normal children are essential, but control in such comparisons is fraught with difficulty. 'If you match for CA, then MA is out of control. It you match for MA, then CA is necessarily out of control. If you assume CA is not a relevant variable and match for MA, then other differences appear to be out of control. Length of institutionalization, home environments, previous schooling, tender-loving-care, and socio-economic status are factors likely to be different for retardates and normals.' To tackle such problems realistically would require heroic investigators matched by heroic budgets, hence, Zeaman and some others confine their interest to laws about subnormal behaviour rather than unique laws.

Baumeister (1967b) discusses in detail the difficulties encountered in comparing subnormals and normals. Obviously, the fundamental problem is one of ensuring that the task is an equivalent measure of the same psychological processes for both groups. If one is investigating some cognitive process, and differences emerge, it is necessary to be able to exclude sensory, motor, motivational, and other differences, but this can seldom be achieved. Obvious violations of this principle occur in studies of institutionalized subnormals and non-institutionalized normals. Zigler (1969) quotes the following example. Rohwer and Lynch (1968) compared the paired-associate learning efficiency of institutionalized retardates (having a mean CA of about 25) with groups of normal children of varying economic strata (having CAs ranging from about 5 to 12). The finding that the institutionalized retardate group did worse than MA-matched normals (and even normals having lower MAs than the retarded) was interpreted as convincing evidence of the erroneousness of the retardation theory. However, in another article in the same journal, Baumeister (1968a) reported a study of paired-associate learning of MA-matched groups of institutionalized retardates, non-institutionalized retardates, and children of normal intellect. There was no difference between the latter two groups, but the institutionalized retardates were inferior to both. Furthermore, there was a significant correlation between length of institutionalization and trials to criterion: the longer the child was institutionalized, the worse was his performance.

Another example of a questionable comparison of groups is provided by some early work on short-term memory in which innumerate severely subnormal children were contrasted with normal schoolchildren of digit repetition.

Transcending the developmental *v.* defect controversy, there is agreement that the essential problem of mentally retarded individuals is their intellectual or cognitive inadequacy. Zigler (1969) reasons that since cognitive functioning lies at the core of retardation phenomena, it is easy to see why, in this particular area, workers have concentrated on cognitive functioning, often totally ignoring the possibility that other factors such as temperament, educational opportunities, motivation, social class, and environmental background might contribute at all to the current status, and consequent task performance of the retardate. Indeed, this chapter is itself testimony to the imbalance of experimental research in mental deficiency since the interactions of these factors with cognitive development has' not been systematically explored. A notable exception is the work of Zigler and his colleagues (see section on Personality and Motivation).

A few investigators have argued against attempts to match experimentally on either an MA or CA basis, on the grounds that it is not always a valid assumption that either of these is the most relevant variable that could be used, and may lead to the introduction of systematic differences between groups on variables other than these. Furthermore, experimental matching normally results in biased selection of subjects due to the necessity for discarding those who cannot be paired with others, or who alter means of variance on the matching variable. Stanley and Beeman (quoted by Prehm, 1966b) advocated statistical matching: subjects should be drawn at random from a specified population, and assigned at random to the various treatment conditions, a procedure that should result in subjects varying at random on any antecedent variable. Matching of subjects could then be accomplished through analysis of covariance. Prehm (1966b) discussed this suggestion, and adopted it in a study of paired-associate learning (Prehm, 1966a); however, experimental matching remains the preferred method by a majority of investigators.

Baumeister argues that comparison of subnormals and normals is most appropriate where their behaviour is observed as a function of systematic variations in task or environmental variables; this calls for a multiple factor design in which subject characteristics are co-manipulated with experimental factors. The question then posed is not whether the subnormal is inferior but whether experimental manipulation will produce the same behavioural adjustment in both groups. One is thus no longer concerned with showing that there are deficits in the subnormal (this is taken for granted) but with determining the conditions that produce variability in group differences. This procedure does not assume that the task is exactly the same for the two groups, but that task and subject characteristics are constant for all values of the experimental variables. This latter is normally a far safer assumption.

Where after an MA match, performance differences emerge, the researcher has identified a difference not residing in the MA scores themselves. 'That this difference is any more fundamental and theoretically meaningful than one which happens to correlate with test performance is dubious. One might say that such a result shows that intelligence tests do not measure all adaptive behaviours . . . we may have done nothing more than to discover another way of diagnosing mental retardation' (Baumeister, 1968a). Moreover, the MA is itself compounded of many factors, equal MAs may be reached by several routes, and are a reflection of an interaction between the content of the test, the experience of the subject and his 'true' ability. As such, the MA has little explanatory value. Baumeister notes that far more attention has been devoted to MA than to other variables such as reinforcement history, comprehension of instructions, and so on. In effect, like Zeaman, he concludes that to understand the behaviour of subnormals one must study the behaviour of subnormals, and the study of normal behaviour 'is quite irrelevant to this purpose'. He does not entirely dismiss the usefulness of comparative studies, but considers that observations of normals will not, of themselves, tell us about the behaviour of subnormals. At best it may raise hypotheses.

'Floor' and 'ceiling' effects are a further source of difficulty in group comparisons, particularly in learning studies. Clarke and Blakemore (1961), for example, compared adults, adolescent and child imbeciles from the same institution on their learning and transfer on various pairs of perceptual-motor tasks. They found that there was greater transfer in the children than in the adolescents and adults. This resulted from a 'ceiling effect' which prevented the adolescents and adults from improving their performance on tasks not especially difficult for them. When Clarke and Cooper (1966) repeated some of this work but adjusted task difficulty to achieve equal starting points for older and younger subnormals, no transfer differences were found.

Ellis (1969) makes a masterly contribution to this whole problem. The apparent rationale of an equal MA match is that this equalizes 'development'. Rarely, however, is the meaning of 'development' scrutinized. There is the additional and already noted problem of whether equal MA scores are based on equal subtest performance, and there is also the possibility that MA may reflect past and present motivational status as well as cognitive factors.

Ellis believes that the equal CA matching procedure is directed to the primary characteristic of subnormality. There are, however, serious problems with this design. Behavioural differences (except for the mildly retarded) are often so great that measurement on the same scale is impossible. 'Floor' and 'ceiling' effects (noted above) are inevitable hazards (Ellis and Anders, 1968). Nevertheless, Ellis argues that for certain purposes CA matches appear to carry more theoretical significance than a comparison of adult mental retardates with normal children on the basis of an MA match.

Finally, Baumeister (1968b), who makes a habit of tackling difficult methodological problems which are easily swept under the carpet, has pointed to the problem of greater performance variability of defective than normal subjects, a matter that must surely have been observed by all research workers who have studied both groups. He reviews the literature, which is not extensive, and concludes that it is almost certain that the two intelligence groups do differ on this characteristic to a significant extent; he suggests, tentatively, that variables related to arousal, attentional, or motivational processes may be implicated in normal-retardate efficiency differences.

These problems have been outlined at some length because, although they permit no easy solution, it seems essential that research workers should be aware of them, since the conclusions derived from much of the early experimental work on mental retardation must be regarded as equivocal, due to a failure on the part of investigators fully to understand the many pitfalls. Furthermore, the fact that in most areas included in this review both results and interpretations by different authors conflict, is acknowledged to be largely due to differing methodological preferences.

Bortner and Birch (1970) review a large number of studies of subnormal and normal children and experimental animals which demonstrate that performance levels under particular conditions are but fragmentary indicators of capacity (or potential). Glaring differences occur in the estimates of potential when significant alterations are made in the conditions for performance. This distinction between capacity and performance, more often implicit in the literature than explicit, has led some workers to start investigating systematically the appropriate conditions, both cognitive and motivational, for maximizing performance.

In considering the following text, which reviews a selection of studies published up to 1970, readers should bear firmly in mind the problems discussed above and, also, that the subjects used in the various experiments range from helpless idiots (see Operant Learning), through imbeciles (often malformed, malcoordinated with severe speech defects) to the mildly subnormal, many of whom in later life are barely distinguishable from members of the normal working population, but who, while young, by virtue of learning difficulties, find their way into special classes, schools, or institutions for the retarded.

Perceptual processes

Although sensory perception may be considered basic to cognitive functioning, psychologists have concerned themselves much less with the operation of sensory and perceptual processes in the mentally subnormal than with problems of learning and memory. Spivack (1963) reviewing this field concluded that the paucity of research data on perceptual processes is striking, and the results are too fragmentary to permit of meaningful integration. 'Too often the "single-shot" study raises more questions than are answered and is rarely followed up by others.' The situation has not changed substantially to date and, with certain important exceptions, there is as yet little theoretical debate of the sort likely to give rise to hypothetico-deductive studies. Moreover, the problem is complicated by the fact that some influential clinical theorists, notably Goldstein and Scheerer (1941), Werner (see Diller and Birch, 1964), Strauss and Lehtinen (1947), and Strauss and Kephart (1955) suggested that cortical lesions interfere with perception and in consequence special training and educational methods have been devised to take account of the effects of brain injury (either demonstrable or assumed). A vast literature exists on the psychological diagnosis of brain damage, and the differentiation of exogenous from endogenous mental defectives. This will not be reviewed here, but the reader is referred to a summary by Diller and Birch (1964), who raise a number of methodological problems that affect interpretation of the data. Haywood (1966), in a discussion of training programmes for the perceptually handicapped, concludes that no definite criteria reliably differentiate the perceptually handicapped (or minimally brain damaged) child from the emotionally disturbed or generally mentally retarded. No systematic research has been conducted to demonstrate the validity of these programmes, and it is suggested that 'perceptual handicap' may be 'an artifact of our ignorance and lack of solid descriptive research' (see also Sternlicht *et al.*, 1968).

The difficulty some brain-damaged children experience with visuo-motor tasks, such as copying a diamond or reproducing a block design, by comparison with controls matched for mental and chronological age, has given rise to a debate as to whether the basic problem is visuo-perceptual or visuo-motor. Bortner and Birch (1960), working with adult hemiplegics and cerebral-palsied children, found that these subjects made many more errors than did control subjects in copying block designs. However, in the vast majority of cases the brain-damaged subjects were able to select the correct design (over their own reproductions and a standard incorrect copy) when the task was presented in multiple-choice version. The investigators concluded that the difficulty of the brain-damaged lies not in the perceptual system but in the perceptual-action system.

Support for this view is provided by Ball and Wilsoncroft (1967) who used the phi-phenomenon to investigate perceptual-motor deficits. The technique used was based on Orlansky's (1940) demonstration that type of form used as stimuli influences phi-thresholds. If two squares are used, a certain threshold is obtained; if a square is paired with a diamond, the threshold changes signifinificantly. It is assumed that if a subject obtains thresholds that differ for homogeneous (two squares) and heterogeneous (square and diamond) forms, it is due to his perceptual ability to discriminate these forms. Three groups, normals, institutionalized retardates, and cerebral-palsied were studied; the latter two groups were tested on the Stanford–Binet task of copying a diamond (MA 7) as well as reproduction of a straight line and a diamond on a peg-board. Since all subjects had MAs over 8, the inability by some to copy or construct a diamond represented a specific perceptual-motor deficit. There were no differences in ability to discriminate form as measured by phi-thresholds among the groups and subgroups studied, although there was a significant difference in overall reactivity to phi motion in favour of the normals. The authors conclude that the results substantiate the position advocated by Bortner and Birch (1960) and are at variance with Kephart's theory which emphasizes the role of perception in accounting for perceptual-motor deficits.

On the other hand, Deich (1968) challenged this conclusion by demonstrating that retardates at two MA levels, matched on the variable with normal children, aged 6 and 8·9 years, were significantly inferior in both reproduction *and* recognition of block designs, although all groups performed better on the latter than the former. Deich believes her results support the view that retardates are perceptually impaired, at least for complex visual stimuli. In this connection, Gaudreau (1968) points to the great difficulty of discriminating between the roles played by perception and those by intelligence when complex problems are used. Krop and Smith (1969) showed that performance by retardates on the Bender–Gestalt test improves with participation in an educational programme, and further improvement resulted from specific instruction in drawing geometric patterns.

A marked contrast to the single-shot studies of perception, deplored by Spivack, is provided by the systematic work on illusions conducted recently over several years by Herman Spitz and his colleagues. Spitz (1963) offers a cogent defence of Gestalt theories in the study of mental retardation; more specifically, the application of Köhler and Wallach's (1944) theory of cortical satiation to the results of experiments on figural after-effects (Spitz and Blackman, 1959), kinesthetic after-effects (Spitz and Lipman, 1961), and perspective reversal (Necker cube) led him to postulate (1964) that cortical changes take place more slowly in retardates than in normals. Therefore retardates should be *less* susceptible to 'physiological' illusions than normal subjects, but *equally* susceptible to 'experiential' illusions, a classification applied to those illusions induced primarily by distorting the stimulus and/or reducing the viewer's observing power, apparently causing the viewer to resort to faulty assumptions and inferences based on past experience (Spitz, 1967).

Mental retardates were found to be less capable than equal CA controls of perceiving visual after-effects, and had a lower reversal rate on the Necker cube. Winters (1965) and Winters and Gerjuoy (1965, 1967) compared college students with high-grade retardates on sensitivity to gamma-movement (the apparent expansion and contraction of a briefly exposed figure) and concluded that, unlike normals, retardates do not perceive gamma at ·2 sec, but that it was possible to induce gamma in retardates by lengthening the exposure time. The authors believe that slower electro-chemical processes in the cortex rather than an attention deficit account for the differences observed between their groups (see section on EEG Studies).

Of the experimental illusions, Spitz (1964) found retardates equally susceptible as normals on the rotating trapezoidal window illusion, and on the distorted room illusion (Spitz, 1967). In the latter study, adolescent retardates were compared with college students on a table model of the Ames distorted room – a trapezoidal room which simulated rectangularity – and a control room that was truly rectangular. Loss of size constancy in judging two unequal circles was the illusion indicator. No significant differences between groups was found on either room. Even under visual restraint retardates maintained as much size constancy as equal CA normals.

Spitz (1965) has also reported *greater* susceptibility on the part of retardates than of normals to a physiological illusion that can be countered by an awareness of the depth cue of interposition (the rotating cube illusion). The results of all these experiments lend support to Spitz's contention that retardates differ from normals in their sensitivity to 'physiological' and 'experiential' illusions.

Winters (1969) took the argument further by postulating that if the only prerequisite for demonstrating physiological visual illusions is that a subject possesses a healthy central nervous system, then young normals (of equal MA to retardates) should demonstrate physiological illusions to the same degree as older normals (matched for CA to retardates), but should differ from older retardates; furthermore, that on a presumably experiential illusion different age-groups will be differentially affected. Winters contrasted perception of gamma-movement (physiological illusion) with two-dimensional size constancy (experiential illusion) using institutionalized male retardates (CA 16·4; IQ 63·7), normal adolescent males (CA 16·7; IQ 103·8) and normal male children (CA 10·8, no IQs available). The retardates did not demonstrate the physiological illusion, whereas both normal groups did, though not differing from each other. All three groups exhibited size constancy, with greater constancy of retardates over equal MA normals reaching only marginal significance. Winters interprets the results as confirming the defect theory of mental deficiency and offering evidence against the retardation theory.

The important question of the interdependence of perceptual and intellectual development was considered by Doyle (1967). Starting with the observation of an adult retardate whose perceptual skills appeared so well developed that by capitalizing on them she was able to perform tasks beyond her intellectual capacity, Doyle advanced the hypothesis that perceptual skill development might proceed independently of intellectual development. One hundred and eight children from special classes for the mentally retarded were allocated to CA groups (at 7, 9, and 11) and MA groups (at 7, 9, and 11) so that each MA level was represented at each CA level, and vice versa. The children's susceptibility to the horizontal-vertical illusion for hearing, sight, and touch was determined by the method of constant stimuli. Susceptibility to the illusion was associated with independently varied MA and CA; (e.g. retarded children in the highest CA group were less susceptible to the illusion than their younger MA counterparts) and the findings were interpreted as supporting the hypothesis. Although this conclusion should probably be accepted with caution until more studies have been conducted, the experimental design might be used to good effect to investigate other aspects of perception.

EEG studies

There is some, but by no means conclusive, evidence that EEG tracings are related to IQ (Ellingson, 1966; Vogel and Broverman, 1964, 1966).

The literature up to and including 1961 has been well reviewed by Berkson (1963), and Clevenger (1966) has provided an annotated bibliography of over 100 references. The former author distinguishes five main parameters of the alpha rhythm that have been studied. These are: (1) the frequency of alpha rhythm; average frequencies for normals and subnormals are closely similar, although there is a suggestion that the range for subnormals is greater; (2) the average amplitude of alpha rhythm; and (3) the proportion of time during a resting period for the subjects, when the rhythm is exhibited. Some studies show a relationship with MA while others do not; (4) and (5) are measures of response to short duration stimuli. If the subject is resting quietly in a darkened room, the alpha rhythm is most pronounced. With the presentation of a short-duration stimulus (e.g. light flash) the alpha rhythm is blocked, and the length of the block has been termed perseveration time. Berkson offers no information on speed of alpha blocking except from an unpublished study where no differences were found between normals and subnormals. The perseveration time of normals was, however, rather longer. Later work by Wolfensberger and O'Connor (1965) failed to confirm this finding. This later study also yielded information that subnormals were slower to block than normals.

Baumeister and Hawkins (1967) note the above discrepancies in the published findings and believe that difficulties may arise when widely disparate intelligence groups are compared. They aimed, therefore, to study the relationship between alpha phenomena and intelligence within subnormal groups, using twenty-one male adult cultural-familial subnormals. One-second duration light stimuli were used during the presence of alpha rhythm for twenty trials. IQ and alpha block duration were not correlated within this group, but the correlation between IQ and number of blocks was significant ($\cdot$05 level), the more intelligent blocking more frequently. Brighter subjects were also slower to block, and a significant habituation effect was noted, the block duration decreasing over trials. This appeared to be unrelated to other measures. These findings are interpreted as indicating that decreasing intelligence seems to be associated with a reduction in responsiveness to external stimulation, a view that corresponds closely to clinical impressions, which should be considered in conjunction with the conclusions of Butler and Conrad (1964). These authors interpret the EEG findings as indicating an impaired speed of integration of complex sensory information.

Vogel and co-workers (1969) noted the lack of studies of behavioural correlates of abnormal EEG phenomena among the mentally subnormal, and attributed this to a consensual assumption that a group of people with abnormal EEGs will, on average, evidence more cortical pathology and therefore more maladaptive behaviour than those with normal EEGs. They investigated forty-five retardates with abnormal EEGs and an equal number with normal EEGs, matched for age and diagnosis. The groups were compared for test intelligence, school, and occupational performance, personal skills, social behaviours, and psychiatric status for three separate periods: year of admission, year of EEG examination, and current year. EEG abnormality was associated with deficits on intelligence test performance, but not with deficits in broader categories of adjustment. However, mean alpha frequency of EEG was associated with behavioural adjustment as reflected in personal skills (e.g. dressing) and social behaviours (e.g. cooperation with ward staff), as well as test intelligence and classroom performance. The authors suggest that quantitatively derived EEG indices, such as alpha frequency, which are thought to reflect particular underlying neurological processes, relate more effectively to retardates' behaviour than do clinically derived categories such as EEG 'normality' or 'abnormality'.

Reaction time

Studies of reaction time (RT) using mentally subnormal subjects have been carried out by several investigators, particularly Baumeister and Berkson and their associates.

Baumeister and Kellas (1968c), reviewing the literature, concluded that:

1. Intelligence is functionally related to RT, not only when normal and subnormal subjects are compared (Scott, 1940), but also within the retarded population (Pascal, 1953; Ellis and Sloan, 1957; Berkson, 1960b). Although there has been some dispute on the nature of the function, it is suggested that it can best be described as linear.

2. Intensity of the stimulus influences retardates' response speed more than that of normals (Baumeister *et al.*, 1964; Baumeister *et al.*, 1965a, b). As the intensity of the signal to respond increases, RT correspondingly decreases. However, at stimulus values near threshold, normals and retardates are similarly affected.

3. Compound reaction stimuli appear to decrease RT in a manner similar to intensity. Holden (1965) showed that trimodal stimulation (auditory, visual, cutaneous) yielded faster reactions than any of these stimuli presented singly, possibly implying increased arousal. However, compound warning stimuli did not influence RT (Baumeister *et al.*, 1965c).

4. In conditions of stimulus complexity requiring choice, response speed of normals and defectives are equally affected (Berkson, 1960a, b). Berkson also found that when both stimulus and response complexity were varied, IQ interacted with the latter but not the former. Berkson concluded that IQ is not relevant to making a choice or planning a movement, but is related to the performance of that movement. Hawkins *et al.* (1965) compared college students and retardates on simple and choice RT tasks, using a verbal rather than motor response. Normals were faster than defectives and both groups showed slower choice RTs, but there was no interaction between type of task and intelligence level.

5. Temporal factors are related to the performance of mental defectives; these include the uncertainty, length of warning interval, psychological refractory period, and warning signal duration.

6. Attempts have been made to relate parameters of the alpha rythm to RT of retardates. Since it has been shown that alpha blocks are shorter in defectives than normals (Baumeister *et al.*, 1963; Berkson *et al.*, 1961), it seems possible that EEG responsivity is related to slow RT. Furthermore, reaction signals presented during the period of alpha block are associated in normal subjects with faster RT than stimuli presented during a no block period (Fedio *et al.*, 1961; Lansing *et al.*, 1959). Thus, Baumeister and Hawkins (1967) suggested that retarded subjects whose alpha waves are particularly responsive to visual stimulation might be rapid responders. Their findings failed to support the hypothesis. Hermelin and Venables (1964) used visual warning stimuli of different

duration and a wide range of warning interval. Reaction times to a sound stimulus were equally fast during periods of alpha and during alpha blocks.

7. Incentive conditions have been found to influence speed of RT (Baumeister and Ward, 1967).

8. Within-subject variability of RT is greater in defectives than normal subjects. Berkson and Baumeister (1967), examining variability in RTs of bright and dull subjects, found substantial correlations between medians and standard deviations (see also Baumeister and Kellas, 1968a, b; Baumeister, 1968b). Baumeister believes that greater variability of response generally characterizes the defective individual, and suggests that to determine the source of this variability offers an important subject for future research.

Baumeister, Wilcox and Greeson (1969) used a reaction-time experiment to test the hypothesis that mental retardates are at a particular disadvantage in situations that require rapid adjustment to a complex and uncertain environment. Two experiments were conducted to compare the reaction times of normals and retardates as a function of the relative frequency of reaction signal occurrence, using a buzzer and a light as signals. The results indicated that both groups displayed increased reaction times as the probability of a particular stimulus decreased. Only when the frequencies of stimulus occurrence were markedly different did the interaction between intelligence group and event probability reach significance.

Hyperactivity and distractibility

Clinicians have noted that among the retarded, and particularly severely retarded brain-injured children, many are hyperkinetic and distractible to a point where these characteristics actively interfere with attempts to educate or train them. Strauss and Lehtinen (1947) vividly describe the difficulties presented by such children; recently, research workers have attempted to explore factors affecting activity level and distractibility in the mentally retarded. Cromwell and co-workers (1963) summarize findings and theories concerning activity level, and rightly question whether it can be considered a unitary topic of review. The same point can justifiably be made concerning distractibility, and in consequence only a few very recent studies from these areas are included here.

Tizard (1968a) notes that, although hyperkinesis is a very real phenomenon to parents and teachers, it has proved strangely elusive to laboratory investigation. Neither McConnel *et al.* (1964) nor Schulman *et al.* (1965) were able to establish a relation between observers' ratings of overactivity and objective measures (by ballistograph or actometers). On the other hand, Hutt and Hutt (1964), who measured locomotion, found higher movement scores in hyperkinetic than normal children, and suggested that their activity was comparatively unmodifiable by any environmental influence, whether social or otherwise. In a preliminary study, Tizard observed two groups of severely subnormal children, rated very overactive and not overactive, during free play. The overactive children moved about significantly more often than the control children but were not rebuked more often nor did they receive more attention from their teachers. They were not more aggressive than the non-overactive group, but they made significantly fewer friendly contacts. The classical hyperkinetic syndrome was not seen; instead, the overactive children showed a wide range of personality characteristics. There was some evidence that they had suffered brain damage of a different kind from that found in the control group.

Since theories to account for overactivity postulate an inhibitory defect, as a result of which the child is unable to stop attending to, or responding to, irrelevant stimuli, or is slow to habituate, Tizard (1968b) conducted an experiment to determine (a) the effect of stimulus variation on the amount of locomotion, and (b) the effect of increasing familiarity with the environment on the amount of locomotion. Overactive and non-overactive severely subnormal children were tested four times, with and without toys, in an experimental room. There was no significant difference in the movement scores of the two groups and no significant habituation in the amount of movement recorded over four sessions for either group. Stimulus variation did not affect overall movement score, although it did affect the nature of the children's activity. Tizard concludes from the two studies that overactivity is a real characteristic of children designated overactive and one that is difficult to modify, and that delayed maturation or general retardation are inadequate concepts to account for the behaviour studied.

In an attempt to investigate the 'inhibitory defect' theory, Tizard (1968c) tested the responsiveness of overactive imbeciles to auditory stimuli using EEG and skin potential changes as measures of response, and the habituation of these responses while awake and while asleep. Control groups of non-overactive imbeciles and normal children were used. Only the normal children showed habituation of skin potential while awake; while asleep no habituation occurred in any group. There was no difference in the frequency of EEG and skin potential changes in response to sound in the three groups; a difference in alertness while awake was a confounding variable. Tizard (1968d) analysed the all-night EEGs, electro-oculograms, and movement records for the three groups. Apart from clinical EEG abnormalities, few group differences were found. The overactive group tended to have more but briefer periods of deep sleep, while the normal children tended to have longer waking periods. Over half the imbeciles, and a quarter of the normal children had periods resembling Stage I Rapid Eye Movement sleep without REMs. All groups spent longer in deep sleep, and less time in Stage I REM sleep than adults. Tizard notes with interest that children whose daytime behaviour is very abnormal and severely retarded, and in whom electro-physiological habituation is disturbed, have sleep patterns barely distinguishable from those of normal children.

Turning now to studies of distractibility, the experimental literature suggests that comparisons of the intellectually normal with the mentally retarded (and particularly brain-injured) do not always support the view that the latter are more distractible. Schulman and co-workers (1965) suggest that in view of the wide range of types of brain damage, the failure to differentiate between hetero-geneous groups of brain-injured and non-brain-injured is not surprising. It is also clear that 'distractibility' cannot be viewed as a unitary characteristic, but one that must be seen both in terms of individual differences and situational variables. Ellis and colleagues (1963) compared 'familial', 'subcultural', 'brain-injured', and defectives of unknown aetiology and normal children of equivalent MA on an oddity problem under two kinds of distraction: attention value of stimulus objects and the presence of a large mirror. The main hypothesis, that defective subjects would be more distractible than normal, was not confirmed, and the mirror actually facilitated the normal group's performance. Similarly, Baumeister and Ellis (1963) found that a potential distractor resulted in improved performance in a group of retardates. Girardeau and Ellis (1964) found no effect of various background noises (train noise, buzzer, playground noise, music, conversation, automobile horn, dog barking) on serial and paired-associate learning by normal and mentally retarded children. Sen and Clarke (1968) conducted a series of experiments, using subnormal subjects of two IQ levels, which showed that: (1) subjects' susceptibility to extraneous stimuli designed to act as distractors is clearly related to the level of task difficulty, and (2) not all external stimuli operate as distractors for a given task. In addition it was sug-gested that the following variables are important: (a) nature of the task; (b) its duration; (c) intensity of the distracting stimuli; (d) relevance of the distractors to the task; and (e) in case of conversation or stories, their attention value. The findings of these studies are consistent with the view that retardates, as a group, are more likely to show distractible behaviour than normal subjects (since more tasks will be at a level of difficulty producing distractible behaviour), but also suggest that a blanket description of retardates as distractible serves only to cloud the issue of why and in what circumstances they manifest this behaviour, and how it may be overcome.

Rather similar conclusions were reached by Belmont and Ellis (1968), who studied the effects of extraneous stimulation on discrimination learning in normals and retardates. Bright lights produced a decrement in 2-choice discrim-ination learning of normal subjects, but *facilitated* retardate learning. In two further experiments, retardates learned a series of six 2-choice problems, on which post-response extraneous stimulation (meaningful pictures) was at first found to facilitate learning. The same stimuli distracted the subjects later in the series. It was concluded that current notions regarding distractibility in retarda-tion require serious qualification.

Operant learning

The application of operant conditioning techniques to the mentally subnormal has aroused considerable interest within the last few years, and it is clear that further developments are to be expected. (See Chapter 23 for full details.)

This area is, however, different from the others reviewed, in that no comparative studies have been undertaken, and there has, until recently, been little controversy over method and interpretation of findings. The question raised by the Skinnerians is rarely 'Can a subnormal person learn by operant methods task X as well as a normal person matched on MA or CA?' The orientation is much more that since operant methods have been shown to be useful in shaping behaviour in animals and normal human beings, the same principles should result in efficient shaping in the subnormal at all levels. The evidence suggests that this faith has been justified.

As Dent (1968) indicates in an admirably succinct review, man's interaction with his environment results in the development of both simple and complex forms of behaviour. According to behaviour theory, these behaviours are acquired, altered, or maintained by the reinforcement received from the environment; the frequency of a response is subject to the consequences of that response. Broadly speaking, reinforcement may be positive (pleasant, rewarding) or negative (noxious, punishing). The former is assumed to increase, and the latter to decrease, the frequency of a particular response. There are four simple schedules of reinforcement: fixed ratio; variable ratio; fixed interval; and variable interval. Dent stresses that since society skilfully dispenses its reinforcement on a variable interval schedule, the ultimate goal in training the subnormal is to achieve control of the particular behaviour in such a way that it will eventually be maintained by society. This, in turn, suggests that the desired response should be established by means of a fixed ratio reinforcement schedule (i.e. rewards given in a fixed ratio to the subject's response rate) which is then gradually shifted to variable interval reinforcement; at the same time there should be a shift from primary reinforcers (e.g. edibles) to secondary (e.g. social approval).

Operant techniques are important, since they have often been applied to subnormals with IQs below 35, and in particular to those of idiot grade who are normally regarded as unresponsive to the more usual modes of training. Positive reinforcement is used to create desirable forms of behaviour and negative (e.g. aversive) reinforcement to eliminate undesirable traits such as aggressive, destructive, or self-destructive behaviour. Various studies have concerned the development, by means of operant conditioning, of personal self-care skills and social and verbal skills. Useful and comprehensive reviews have been produced by Watson and Lawson (1966); Spradlin and Girardeau (1966); Watson (1967); and Baumeister (1967a). An Orwellian twist has been provided by Henker, according to Dent (1968). She contends that the mentally subnormal can be trained to apply operant procedures in the training of other subnormals. This will create 'therapeutic pyramids' whereby a small number of professionals train a larger number of subnormals who, in turn, train a still larger number of their peers.

Of the general reviews, the most detailed appears to be that of Watson (1967) to whose work the writers are indebted. He discusses four types of positive reinforcement: edible, manipulatable, social, and token or generalized. In considering a number of studies in which comparisons between different reinforcers were made, he concludes that token reinforcement possesses two major advantages: first, it is possible that a summation effect may occur because of numerous associations with each of the edible, manipulatable, or social reinforcement with which it has been related; and second, it is relatively independent of specific deprivation states. A very useful annotated bibliography with over 100 references has been provided by Gardner and Watson (1969).

Positive reinforcement is not always a sufficient condition for developing certain behaviours while eliminating others, and the use of negative reinforcement at the same time has been found appropriate (Giles and Wolf, 1966; Watson, 1967). Time-out procedures have been used effectively to eliminate head banging, window-breaking, and other aggressive behaviour (Watson, 1967).

Studies have been mainly carried out in the following areas and some examples are given below:

1. Toilet training (Baumeister and Klosowski, 1965; Bensberg *et al.*, 1965; Hundziak *et al.*, 1965; Giles and Wolf, 1966; Watson, 1967).
2. Self-feeding (Gorton and Hollis, 1965; Henriksen and Doughty, 1967).
3. Self-dressing (Bensberg *et al.*, 1965; Gorton and Hollis, 1965; Roos, 1965; Watson, 1967).
4. Self-grooming (Girardeau and Spradlin, 1964; Bensberg *et al.*, 1965; Gorton and Hollis, 1965).
5. Social play behaviour (Girardeau and Spradlin, 1964; Bensberg *et al.*, 1965; Watson, 1967).
6. Undesirable behaviour (Girardeau and Spradlin, 1964; Giles and Wolf, 1966; Hamilton *et al.*, 1967; Watson, 1967; Wiesen and Watson, 1967).
7. Speech (Kerr *et al.*, 1965; Doubros, 1966; Hamilton and Stephens, 1967; Sloane and MacAulay, 1968). See also section on Language.
8. Work skills (Girardeau and Spradlin, 1964; Bensberg *et al.*, 1965).

In controlling undesirable behaviour, Gorton and Hollis (1965) and Bensberg *et al.* (1965) found that, with few exceptions, operant procedures were effective in maintaining desirable behaviour without the aid of tranquillizers, energizers, or sleeping medication. As Watson and Lawson (1966) put it, 'instrumental learning research is providing the basis for a new, effective technology of educating and training mental retardates, with both academic and social implications. ... Of significance is the fact that ... (these conditioning techniques) ... have succeeded with the severely and profoundly retarded, where other training methods have failed.'

Despite the large number of studies reported, Watson (1967) concluded that, although they indicate that severely and profoundly retarded children can develop skills when systematic training procedures are used, it is not clear what variables are responsible for the success of these programmes and which are either irrelevant or possibly even interfering. Gardner (1969) examined the methodology and results of operant conditioning techniques, and concluded that

to some extent all the studies have violated one or more of the following requirements of good experimental design: (1) exact specification of *all* relevant independent variables; (2) proper sampling techniques; (3) use of adequate controls;
(4) proper assessment of the dependent variable; and (5) evaluation of long-term
gains. Gardner recommends: (1) direct and indirect measures of both specific
and general changes in behaviour; (2) individual as well as group presentation
of results; (3) pre- and post-treatment evaluations, including periodic assessment
to measure long-term gain; and (4) multivariate manipulation of the independent
variables, particularly specific techniques. Progress in elucidating these problems
can confidently be expected.

Learning sets and transfer of learning

As Deese (1958) puts it, 'There is no more important topic in the whole of the
psychology of learning than transfer of training. Nearly everyone knows that
transfer of training is basic to educational theory. Practically all educational and
training programs are built upon the fundamental premise that human beings
have the ability to transfer what they have learned from one situation to another.'
The question at once arises whether the subnormal in addition to his deficiencies
in acquisition is also defective in the extent to which previously learned responses
may be generalized to new situations.

The first part of this section is concerned with learning set formation in the
mentally subnormal; studies of transfer of training among problems of disparate
classes, and the effects of special programmes of instruction upon test performance are reviewed later.

LEARNING SET ACQUISITION

A learning set (Harlow, 1949) is acquired through practice on problems that have
a common basis for solution. Once the solution is apparent, performance on
subsequent problems of the same type changes from a trial-and-error response
pattern to one approximating single-trial learning. Learning set acquisition is
based on a history of discrimination experience and represents a particular kind
of transfer of training, transfer among many problems of a single class. The main
variable of interest is, thus, interproblem learning as opposed to intraproblem
learning.

Watson and Lawson (1966) provide a detailed review of the vast number of
experiments using mentally retarded subjects on the Wisconsin General Test
Apparatus, most of which have been concerned with object-quality discriminations, reversal learning and oddity learning. Only a highly compressed summary
of some of the findings will be included here.

The relation between mental age and speed of acquisition of an object-quality
learning set was one of the first problems to be investigated. Ellis (1958) investigated object-quality discrimination at 'low' (5·05) and high (8·02) MA levels.

Ten successive problems were given and on each the subject had to reach a criterion of twenty successive correct responses ('finding the marble'). While both MA groups developed discrimination learning sets, the higher made fewer errors per problem and acquired learning sets more rapidly. Efficiency in learning set formation thus appeared to be a function of MA but, as Watson and Lawson point out, the possible effect of IQ was not partialled out. Stevenson and Swartz (1958) carried out a somewhat similar study but comparing two not greatly different MA groups. The lower of these (MA 4·1) failed to develop a set. Ellis and colleagues (1962), however, were able to show that even those with lower MAs were in some circumstances able to form object-quality discrimination sets. It seems probable that discrepancies between the findings of different studies can be accounted for by such factors as the nature of the discriminanda, number of problems, length of training, learning criterion, background experience, and type of reinforcement offered, as well as to such factors as MA (see also Wischner *et al.*, 1962). Kaufman (1963) and Girardeau (1959) also point to the influence on discrimination of factors other than MA. Hayes and co-workers (1953) believed that learning set acquisition is a joint function of trials-per-problem and level of performance.

Studies of reversal discrimination learning show that, in general, the subnormal learn a position discrimination reversal most easily, followed in order of difficulty by intradimensional reversal shift and extradimensional reversal shift (Watson and Lawson, 1966). Subnormals with MAs as low as two years were able to master reversal position problems (House and Zeaman, 1959). Some studies have found no difference between the reversal performance of retardates and equal MA normals (Plenderleith, 1956; Stevenson and Zigler, 1957). There appears to be little relationship between MA and position reversal performance, but there may be a relationship between MA and stimulus reversal, particularly where an extradimensional shift is required.

Oddity discrimination learning has been shown to be related to MA. The general finding is that subnormals with MAs below five years do not form oddity learning sets, but above this level, speed of learning set acquisition is related to MA (Ellis and Sloan, 1959; Ellis *et al.*, 1963; House, 1964).

Watson and Lawson point out that all conclusions concerning the relationship between MA and discrimination learning are open to the alternative interpretation of an IQ relationship, since both MA and IQ control procedures were not used. Furthermore, it is possible that institutionalized retardates, who were the subjects of these studies, may by virtue of the restricted environment be specifically deficient with respect to learning visual discriminations. These authors also conclude that the learning set acquisition is a function of the particular method employed. For maximizing the possibility of a low MA subnormal acquiring, for example, an object-quality set it is necessary to: (1) use many trials per problem or a high learning criterion; (2) employ a non-correction stimulus presentation technique; and (3) present the negative stimulus only on the first trial of each new problem.

Zeaman and House (1963) have provided an important theory of retardate discrimination learning that distinguishes two responses: (1) attending to the relevant stimulus dimension, and (2) approaching the correct cue of that dimension. From a large amount of data on visual discrimination learning in severely retarded subjects, they plotted the forward learning curves of sub-groups of subject homogeneous with respect to the number of trials taken to reach criterion of learning. From this it emerged that slow learners stayed close to chance performance for varying numbers of trials, but once performance started to improve, it moved relatively fast. Plotting the same data as backward learning curves (Hayes, 1953) showed that the final rates of all groups, fast or slow, were similar. It was concluded that the difference between fast and slow learning was not so much the rate at which improvement takes place *once it starts*, but rather the number of trials taken for learning to start. It was concluded that the difficulty retardates have in discrimination learning is related to the attention phase of the dual process, rather than to approaching the correct cue of the relevant stimulus dimension. Those who are familiar with studies of animal discrimination learning will note the similarity of this theoretical formulation with that of Sutherland (1964) and Mackintosh (1965). Zeaman and House present a number of stochastic models organized by the dual process theory and demonstrate the application of these to discrimination experiments with lower-level retardates, including original learning, reversals, effects of intelligence, stimulus factors, schedules of reinforcement, and transfer operations.

The discrimination reversal problem has been used to test verbal mediation deficiency hypotheses in mental retardates; these studies are reviewed in the section on Verbal Mediation.

Shepp and Turrisi (1966) have provided an important review (forty-six references) of work on learning and transfer of mediating responses in discrimination learning. In addition to discussing individual papers as well as methodological problems, these authors offer some general process laws. As already noted, intra-dimensional shifts are learned faster than extra-dimensional and this is held to support the proposition that the mediating process is dimensional in nature. Subjects learn to respond to a discriminative cue common to a class of stimuli, and they can transfer these responses to subsequent discriminations. Secondly, intra-dimensional shift performance improves with increasing amounts of overtraining, this being directly implied in the theories of Sutherland and Zeaman and House. These state that the strength of a relevant mediator approaches its asymptote slower than does the strength of an instrumental response. 'Consequently, with a weak criterion or just a few overtraining trials, the relevant mediator may be weak, and any intradimensional and extra-dimensional shift difference may be attenuated. With increasing amounts of overtraining, the strength of the relevant mediator increases, and the probability of this response approaches unity. There is also some evidence that extra-dimensional shifts become progressively more difficult with increases in amount of overtraining. This finding also supports the notion that the relevant mediator becomes stronger as a function of overtraining' (Shepp and Turrisi, 1966).

A third and much less certain 'law' is related to the type of irrelevant dimension presented during original learning (Shepp and Turrisi, 1966). In most experiments that have shown dimensional mediating-response transfer, the irrelevant dimension during training was presented with a variable-within arrangement. In one study, however, the irrelevant dimension was constant and there was subsequently no intra- or extra-dimensional shift difference and no evidence for mediating response transfer. Now mediating-response theories have not specified the variable-within irrelevant condition as a prerequisite for the acquisition of a mediating response. This poses an important theoretical question, and the authors suggest that the two types of shift should be compared with constant irrelevant and variable irrelevant dimensions to settle the question of whether the acquisition of a mediating response requires a variable irrelevant dimension during training.

RETENTION OF LEARNING SETS

Wischner and colleagues (1962) used a large number of problems (12 a day for 10 days) with mildly subnormal subjects, to study the formation of object-quality learning sets. The authors studied retention 6 months later, using an additional 2 days of practice on 12 3-trial problems a day. For those who had reached criterion in the earlier learning, the additional practice was sufficient to restore performance to its final level. For those who had earlier learned less well, however, performance was only a little above chance at the end of the 2 days of practice.

Clarke (1962) reported that a group of adult imbeciles, retested on the learning of the 4 Minnesota formboards 7 years after initial learning (32 trials), showed greatly enhanced performance, particularly on the first board. This could not be attributed to maturation but may, however, have resulted from the reinforcement provided by perceptual-motor experience in industrial workshops. However, Clarke and Cookson (1962) showed impressive retention of perceptual-motor learning by child and adult imbeciles over 6 months and 1 year, respectively, of non-reinforcement. In both these studies learning had been taken to asymptote, and motivation was apparently very high indeed.

Kaufman (Kaufman and Prehm, 1966), however, carried out a study on retention by mongols of three-trial object-quality problems. This experiment was marred by an institutional epidemic but limited findings failed to indicate retention by this group.

Much more information is needed on the degree to which learning sets may be retained. Apart from the nature of the tasks, at least two powerful factors seem to be involved. Firstly, the amount of learning and overlearning undertaken is clearly relevant, and secondly, the degree to which the ordinary life experience of these subjects possesses relevant reinforcers or makes direct use of the induced sets. (See also the section on Memory.)

TRANSFER OF TRAINING

Despite the acknowledged importance of transfer effects on all human activities, surprisingly little systematic research has been conducted in this area using mentally retarded subjects. In their comprehensive review, Kaufman and Prehm (1966) point to the diversity of work in this area and to the difficulty of coming to any precise conclusion concerning the conditions under which retardates will show positive (or negative) transfer.

An illustration of the importance of method to experimental outcome and thus to conclusions, is given in a later section on the Role of Input Organization in Memory. Gerjuoy and Alvarez (1969) failed to find any effect on amount recalled or amount of clustering one week after a single training session of five trials in which material to be recalled was presented clustered. By contrast, the present authors, using a different design, a long-term training procedure, and only one day between the end of training and initial transfer tests, did find significant effects. Both types of experiment are clearly necessary if the precise conditions in which transfer will occur are ever to be specified.

In the absence of data on which to base an analysis of transfer effects in the subnormal, this section will be confined to a summary of the only two long-term programmes of research on transfer reported in the literature, apart from the already discussed and monumental work by Zeaman and House on learning sets. This will be followed by discussion of three attempts to alter test behaviour on the basis of widely based programmes of instruction.

Using pairs of perceptual-motor learning tasks of equal difficulty, each of which made similar demands but had a different content from the other, Clarke and Blakemore (1961) showed that transfer, using a time score for twenty trials, was easily demonstrated, particularly among the younger imbeciles. Subsequent work suggested that this latter result was due to a ceiling effect for the adults. Clarke and Cookson (1962), using similar tasks and the same subjects, showed that earlier easier learning transferred six months later to more difficult learning, without intervening practice. Clarke and Cooper (1966) evolved a method for directly comparing adult and child imbeciles on the same tasks. Either the difficulty of the task pairs could be increased for the adults so that the time taken for initial performance was equal to that of the children, or difficulty could be decreased for the children so that their starting point was the same as for adults. Both methods gave similar results, showing that adults and children in these tasks exhibited similar learning and transfer curves. More importantly, it seemed that task complexity might, within limits, facilitate transfer. This notion was now tested by Clarke *et al.* (1966) who evolved a new experimental design, and, holding age constant, gave matched groups of imbeciles training on conceptual sorting tasks of different complexity. It was found that: (1) transfer was related to training task complexity; (2) it occurred across tasks that possessed no identical elements other than that they were conceptual problems; (3) differential effects of differing degrees of complex training were subsequently persistent over ten trials of the transfer task; and (4) the amount of overlearning of the complex training task was also relevant. This work was replicated, with rather more striking results on normal pre-school children (for review of these studies see Clarke *et al.*, 1967a).

The question of the nature of transfer between different conceptual tasks using normal pre-school children was then studied by Clarke *et al.* (1967b). Among other findings, it seemed that improved performance did not result from an increased arousal arising from exposure to a difficult problem, but rather from the practice of relatively unpractised processes – in this case the reduction of stimulus variability by categorization. The authors interpreted these and some later findings in terms of the subject's increased sensitivity to the categorical properties of the stimuli (Clarke *et al.*, 1970) a process not normally high in the hierarchy of preferred responses for these populations.

Bryant (1964) used apparently simple discrimination tasks and tested the ability of his severely subnormal subjects to abstract. Half were given verbal instruction on the first task, while the others were not. Against Bryant's expectancies, it emerged that verbal instruction heavily impeded transfer. A later experiment (Bryant, 1965a) showed that verbalization had interfered with the component on which imbeciles tend to base their transfer in discrimination learning, namely, learning to avoid the irrelevant dimension. Nevertheless, verbal instruction improved learning at the time when the instruction was given.

Subsequent work by Bryant (1967a) was aimed at elucidating the effect of verbal instruction: first, on the response about which instruction was being given, and second, on the response about which no instruction was given. Subjects were required to sort cards of two different colours into different boxes. Without verbal instructions, errors were equal for both. With instruction, errors were reduced but equal; and with instruction about one colour, errors were reduced for that colour, but for the other, errors remained equal to the earlier situation where no instruction was given. A transfer post-test showed many more errors with unfamiliar than the familiar colours. It seems, writes Bryant (1968) that learning strategies adopted by subnormals might be maladaptive to the introduction of language.

The author raises the question whether verbal instruction improves learning by direct attention or by affecting memory processes. His preliminary investigations (1965b, 1967b) suggested that memory is improved only when verbal labelling relates to a verbal problem, and that attentional processes are affected only when the stimulus array is a complex one.

The effects of specific, fairly long-term programmes of instruction, as measured by standard tests, have been explored in three recent studies.

Rouse (1965) found significant changes in educable retarded children after exposure to a special curriculum aimed at enhancing productive thinking. The training programme for the 47 experimental subjects comprised 30 half-hour lessons over a period of 6 weeks, and included a wide range of carefully specified activities; members of a control group meanwhile attended their regular classes.

Budoff and colleagues (1968) repeated the experiment, but their subjects failed to show gains on the Minnesota Tests of Creative Thinking commensurate with those previously reported; the authors were unable to offer precise reasons why the outcome of the two experiments differed.

Corter and McKinney (1968) conducted an experiment on flexibility training with educable retarded and bright normal children. Although much work on the alleged rigidity of the subnormal can be found in the literature, the authors were unable to identify any previous attempts to improve flexibility.

The major purpose of the study was to develop a process-oriented programme of training designed to provide subjects with reinforced practice in making cognitive shifts. The effectiveness of this training was then evaluated on 'flexibility tasks', the Binet scale, and five tests developed by the authors selected from a larger number by factor analytic techniques.

Training employed a large number of different exercises involving a variety of materials. Three general areas, perceptual, conceptual, and spontaneous flexibility, were sub-divided into two kinds of exercises for each. The perceptual area, for example, involved figure-ground reversal and embedded figures. The conceptual exercises used similarities-differences and concept shifting. For spontaneous flexibility, exercises included tasks in both structured and constructured fluency such as class naming, rhymes, and cancellation. Efforts were also made to teach appropriate verbal concepts such as 'figure', 'ground', 'part', 'whole', 'alike', and 'different'.

The subjects were 32 mildly subnormal children attending special education classes and 32 normal children in kindergarten, matched for MA and sex, and allocated randomly to teaching or control conditions. The experimental groups received cognitive flexibility training for 20 days in sessions that lasted between 30 and 45 minutes. Control groups participated in their usual classroom activities. At the conclusion, experimental and control groups were retested on the Stanford–Binet and with the Cognitive Flexibility test battery. The Stanford-Binet retests were carried out by 3 experienced examiners, who had not pre-tested the same children and had not taken part in the training programme.

Results indicated that for the experimental groups the mean change in flexibility score between pre- and post-test was highly significant ($p < \cdot 001$). The mean change for the retarded controls was not significantly different from zero, although the normal controls had achieved significantly higher scores ($p < \cdot 001$). Mean IQ increases for experimental groups were as follows: for retarded, 6·25 and for normals 10·19, these both being significant. For the controls, however, non-significant gains were reported.

The authors consider that their results support earlier findings of greater difficulty in concept shifting in retardates as compared with normals, but, as they indicate, their normals were 'bright' and the two groups were not matched for social class so that such results are somewhat equivocal. However, the training programme was effective in producing significant increases in flexibility, and it is of interest that a hypothesis that retardates and normals would respond differentially was unsupported. The IQ increases were significantly greater for the trained than the controls, and this appeared to indicate generalization from training to other areas of cognitive functioning. However, the authors properly list the limitations of their study and are cautious in their interpretations. An important point emerging from this study is that, although retardates may gain significantly from a training programme, it is likely that normal children, subjected to the same programme, will gain more, particularly if, as in this case, they are above average in intelligence.

The present authors conclude with Kaufman and Prehm (1966) that there is a need for greatly increased research activity on transfer of training. It is difficult to see how efficient programmes for use in schools and rehabilitation centres can be evolved without a great deal more knowledge of factors underlying the generalization of learning in the subnormal.

Memory

Studies of memory in the mentally retarded have focused attention on the problem of identifying deficits in short-term memory, long-term memory, and the role of input organization, usually by contrast with normal control groups, matched for MA or CA. Most of the studies on short- and long-term memory have used rote memory or rote learning techniques and either digits, letters of the alphabet, or conceptually unrelated words or pictures. Those interested in input organization have used word lists or picture displays in which the stimulus material can be grouped into common conceptual categories.

SHORT-TERM MEMORY (STM)

The importance of short-term memory is emphasized in a number of psychological theories (e.g. Broadbent, 1958; Miller *et al.*, 1960) which assume that if information cannot pass from STM into permanent storage, learning will not occur. It should follow that where the major distinguishing feature of a group is their inability to learn as efficiently as others of similar age, the key to their deficiency might well be found in the process underlying STM.

Ellis (1963) elaborated a theory embodying two constructs, stimulus trace and central nervous system integrity, to account for the behavioural inadequacies of the mentally retarded. The stimulus trace is a hypothetical neural event or response which varies with the intensity, duration, and meaning of the stimulus situation. CNS integrity is defined by indices of adaptability such as intelligence test score, and serves as a limiting function for the stimulus trace. The central hypothesis is that the duration and amplitude of a trace are diminished in the subnormal organism. Ellis further hypothesized that the apparent learning deficit in the subnormal organism is due to noncontinuity of events as a result of an impoverished stimulus trace. He presents an account of his physiological model and cites evidence in support of it from a wide range of behavioural research with mental defectives. These included the areas of serial verbal learning, paired associate learning, reaction time, EEG studies, and factor analytic studies of intelligence test profiles.

Further support for this theory is provided by Hermelin and O'Connor (1964; O'Connor and Hermelin, 1965), whose evidence suggested that recall deficits in STM might be due to both memory decay and input restriction, and Madsen (1966) who reported a series of five experiments involving the assessment of the recall performance of normal and retarded subjects for a single paired associate, under different conditions. Performance of the retarded subjects was consistently inferior to that of the normal controls. On the other hand, Butterfield (1968a) investigated several predictions from the stimulus trace theory concerning serial learning in normal and retarded subjects, and concluded from a review of the research literature that these predictions had not been supported. In order to determine whether the central organismic variable of stimulus trace theory (i.e. neural integrity) was more closely related to MA or IQ, Butterfield (1968b) compared digit span performance of groups who were matched on either MA or CA but who differed in IQ. Differences were found between normal, borderline, and retarded IQ groups matched on CA, but not between those matched on MA. It was concluded that stimulus trace theory may best be regarded as a developmental rather than a defect approach to mental retardation. Further experimental studies on STM are reported by Ellis and Munger (1966), Ellis and Anders (1968), and Baumeister *et al.* (1967).

Neufeldt (1966) conducted a series of experiments to investigate STM in mental retardates using the dichotic listening technique initiated by Broadbent (1954). The experiments were devised to discover whether STM *capacity* and/or *strategy of encoding information* would account for some of the differences between retardates and normals. Four groups of subjects were compared: two groups of retardates (IQ range 53 to 79), one Organic and one Cultural-Familial in aetiology; a normal group matched for MA, and a second normal control group matched for CA. The evidence indicated that STM capacity was indeed an important difference between retardates and CA controls, but not between retardates and MA controls. The most important differences lay in the superior strategies manifested by both normal control groups, who, by comparison with the retardates, demonstrated a marked degree of flexibility in their adaptation of different recall strategies to various rates of informational input, and an ability to use more ambiguous strategies; familial defectives were somewhat better in this respect than organic retardates. The differences between the two normal control groups (of different ages) were indicative of the degree to which both memoric capacity and ability to apply useful strategies develops in normal individuals over time. The discussion and interpretation of these findings is consistent with the 'developmental lag' theory of familial retardation.

Kouw (1968) investigated the stimulus trace construct as an explanatory mechanism in retardate STM. He argued that (a) the capacity of retarded subjects to perform a delayed response task will vary as a function of CNS integrity; and (b) their delayed response capacity will vary as a function of both the intensity and duration of the pre-delay stimulus as well as the interaction of these variables. Using the Knox Cubes Test to classify 181 retardates as high or low on STM adequacy, he found that stimulus intensity affected delayed response as predicted, but that stimulus duration had no effect on performance. The author does not accept the latter results as necessarily conclusive, suggesting refinements in the technique for further investigation. He concludes that the limitations imposed on behavioural adequacy in STM functioning in organisms with subnormal CNS integrity were shown to change in the direction of greater adequacy, and this change was greatest for those with the lowest degree of CNS integrity. He concurs with Ellis's (1963) suggestion that the investigation of learning difference between retardates and normals must focus attention on the acquisition aspects, rather than long-term retention.

Gordon (1968) showed how stimulus presentation rate may both enhance and hinder recall of stimuli, depending on the interacting effects of stimulus complexity and the level of intellectual competency of the subjects. Using mildly subnormal and normal adults, three levels of stimulus complexity and three rates of presentation (40, 60, or 120 units per minute) he showed that: (a) subnormal subjects were inferior to normals in all conditions; (b) while normal subjects recalled simple concepts at a high level under all rate conditions, subnormal performance was adversely affected by high-speed presentation; (c) the normal group curve of performance was positively decelerated with increasing stimulus complexity, while the retarded group curve was negatively decelerated; (d) the variance in normal performance decreased with increase in presentation rate, while the opposite occurred for the retarded; and (e) that the error pattern for the two groups differed, suggesting differences in both accuracy of perception and in the ability to organize, encode, or associate what has been perceived.

Scott and Scott (1968) in reviewing a vast literature on STM, comment on the importance of Ellis's theory in providing a focal point for investigation in this area, and suggest, further, that two relatively new experimental techniques show promise of major theoretical importance. These are Broadbent's dichotic listening technique used by Neufeldt (1966) and the miniature experiment technique elaborated by House and Zeaman (1963), which are seen as providing an essential bridge between research on attention and memory and the relations between these two processes.

Latterly, Ellis and his colleagues, E. A. Holden and K. G. Scott, have reported important methodological advances, experimental results and theoretical models (Ellis, 1970; Holden, 1971; Scott, 1971), which give promise of a comprehensive account of retardate memory processes within the context of a general theoretical model of memory. Although there are differences in approach, the major conclusion of these writers is the complexity of human memory processes and the potential importance of rehearsal strategies. Since the projects and the thinking underlying the three statements are ambitious and as yet in tentative form, no attempt will be made to summarize them as a whole. Ellis's own position (1970) may, however, be briefly stated. Two processes are involved in the short-term storage of supraspan messages; one is Primary Memory, a limited capacity system, capable of retaining transiently only a few items. Rehearsal strategy is seen as the mechanism whereby information is passed to the Secondary Memory and Tertiary Memory (equivalent to LTM, see pp. 287–8). It is assumed that the latter is normal in retardates. Active rehearsal strategies are essential for one of the short-term storage processes but not the other. When the Primary Memory system is maximally loaded, the Secondary Memory serves to store the 'overload'. It is this which is weaker in retardates while Primary Memory is assumed to be normal. But the main reason for this weakness is seen as a probable failure of rehearsal mechanisms. As Ellis indicates, this model suggests the need to investigate the role of language in rehearsal strategies, and studies are planned to attempt to teach retardates how to rehearse.

SERIAL ANTICIPATION AND THE MCCRARY–HUNTER HYPOTHESIS

If a list of items is learned to perfection and the number of errors made in the course of learning is plotted for each item in the series, according to its position, a bow-shaped curve is obtained. The degree of bowing may be influenced by several conditions such as distribution of practice, rate of presentation, familiarity of material, and individual differences in learning ability. McCrary and Hunter (1953) showed that, if the curve is plotted in terms of *percentage* of total errors occurring at each position, the effect of differing conditions and subject differences disappears and the distribution of errors remains invariant.

Lipman (1963) reviews many of the studies of this hypothesis using contrasted groups of subnormals and normals. Subsequent work by Girardeau and Ellis (1964), McManis (1965), and Sen and Sen (1968) has confirmed the invariance hypothesis, using subjects of different intellectual levels under various conditions of learning. Butterfield (1968a) reviewing studies of serial learning in mental retardates, points out that the McCrary–Hunter procedure does not take account of learning efficiency, and suggests that a correction be made to subject's percentage error scores prior to evaluating the relation between learning rate and the shape of the serial curve. He re-analysed data and found a significant interaction between rate of learning and serial position, reflecting the fact that slow learners made relatively more errors in the middle positions of the list. Butterfield points to the growing body of evidence showing the inadequacy of trace-interference explanations of the serial position curve, and suggests that strategy analysis might provide a testable framework within which to study individual differences in rate of learning and relative position errors.

The von Restorff effect has been investigated in mental retardates by McManis (1966), Sternlicht and Deutsch (1966), and Sen *et al.* (1968), with results that are consistent with the view that while serial learning performance in the subnormal is inferior to the normal, the effects of varying experimental conditions operate in a similar way in both groups. McManis (1969a), however, obtained results that supported a stimulus and response generalization explanation of the isolation effect for normals but not for retardates.

In summary, the findings in the area of short-term memory and serial learning generally support the thesis that comparisons of mental retardates with normally intelligent subjects, whether matched for CA or, in some cases, MA, is likely to result in a demonstration of inferior performance on the part of the mentally subnormal, but that the effects of varying conditions operate in a similar way for both groups. Any precise theoretical interpretation of these findings must await the resolution of some of the methodological problems that bedevil this area, and that were discussed earlier in this chapter.

LONG-TERM RETENTION

Although learning ability in the subnormal is typically impaired, their retention of learned material is usually found to be as good as that of normal subjects. Haywood and Heal (1968) provide the following succinct review of the literature:

> Experimenters have typically failed to find differences in long term retention between retardates and non-retardates of comparable mental age (MA) (Cantor and Ryan, 1962, relearning of picture paired associates; Johnson, 1958, recognition, recall, and relearning with nonsense syllables learned serially; O'Connor and Hermelin, 1963a, recall of word paired associates; Plenderleith, 1956, reversal learning with picture paired associates). Furthermore, experimenters have failed to find differences in retention between retardates and non-retardates of comparable chronological age (CA), provided adjustments were made for differences in learning level (Klausmeier, Feldhusen, and Check, 1959, savings in reworking simple arithmetic problems; Lance, 1965, savings scores with nonsense syllable paired associates; Pryer, 1960, savings scores with words in a serial anticipation task; Vergason, 1964, 30-day savings scores with picture paired associates). Only Heber, Prehm, Nardi and Simpson (1962, relearning with nonsense syllable paired associates adjusted for original learning by co-variance) and Vergason (1964, 1-day savings scores with picture paired associates) have reported poorer retention by retardates than by non-retardates of comparable CA when adjustments were made for original learning level.

Nevertheless, interpretation of these data must take account of a number of methodological problems, discussed in detail by Belmont (1966), who considers the literature in the light of critical analyses made by Underwood (1954, 1964) and Keppel (1965). Belmont abstracts certain principles considered essential to the construction of a viable experiment:

(a) level of learning, defined as probability of performance, must be equalized for all subjects, especially where subject variables are studied independently;

(b) the optimum level of learning must be less than maximal at the beginning of the retention interval; and

(c) there must be a criterion against which retention test performance will be judged. This criterion should take the form of a reliable evaluation of what subjects would have done had there been no retention interval, thus permitting an evaluation of the retention interval *per se*.

Implicit in this analysis are two further principles: the original learning phase must be regulated to yield sufficient acquisition data for all subjects, while avoiding asymptotic performance, and the retention test conditions must be identical to the conditions prevailing at the time of immediate memory assessment. Belmont reviewed twelve studies of retention in the mentally retarded and found that most suffered in varying degree from one or more methodological weakness, principally failure to demonstrate equal original learning and problems of floor versus ceiling effects. The single study (by Klausmeier *et al.*, 1959) which seemed to overcome these problems found that normals and retardates were equal in long-term memory.

Haywood and Heal (1968) conducted a retention experiment in the light of the foregoing analysis, taking account of the important methodological principles arising from it.

Experimentally naïve institutionalised retardates at four IQ levels were trained in a group procedure by the study-test technique over 15 presentations of a visual code task. Each IQ level was divided into the top, middle, and bottom thirds according to the number of codes correctly recalled during the 15 acquisition trials. Retention tests were given all Ss at post-training intervals of one hour, 24 hours, one week, two weeks, and four weeks. There were no differences among IQ levels in either training or retention performance. Those in any IQ group who made more correct responses during acquisition retained the learned associations best and appeared to forget them at a slower rate.

THE ROLE OF INPUT ORGANIZATION

Miller's (1956) paper on memory and the storage of information is too familiar to need summarizing. Suffice it to say that considerable research investment in the general area of input and storage organization has subsequently been made.

A further stimulus had been provided by Bousfield (1953) who studied associative clustering in free recall. Words from the same category tend to be recalled consecutively even though they may have been presented randomly. Recall of word lists is improved where categorizable words are included. Tulving (1962, 1964, 1966) took matters further by demonstrating the presence of organizing activities even with apparently unrelated words. It seems clear that this organizational process takes place at or during memory storage.

Turning to the field of subnormality, Osborn (1960) carefully selected two groups of 'organic' and 'familial' mildly subnormal institutionalized patients, together with normal MA-matched school controls. Using pictures, rather than words, as experimental material, no significant differences were found between 'organics' and 'familials', both groups recalling and organizing them in recall as efficiently as the controls. Osborn draws attention, however, to some qualitative differences that might be the result of inappropriate learning habits.

Rossi (1963) compared the clustering of normal and subnormal children using a list of 20 stimulus words, 5 from each of 4 categories, randomized in 5 different ways. Each subject was given 5 trials with the same words arranged in different order to minimize serial learning order effects. The words were almost identical with those employed by Osborn (1960). Using 3 PPVT MA levels for normal children (4–6; 7–3; and 10–0), he matched 3 subnormal groups, finding that there was no significant difference between normals and subnormals in amount of recall. The normals showed a superior clustering performance only when a special clustering measure which eliminated categorical intrusions was employed. Practice effects as well as MA were associated with clustering within each diagnostic group.

Evans (1964) used Rossi's methods with adult subnormals, which he divided into two intelligence groups with mean WAIS IQs of 69 and 47, respectively. Each was subdivided into subgroups with or without material incentives. This latter had a negligible effect, but the brighter subjects tended to recall more words than the duller. Neither main group differed on clustering. Evans also discusses the problem of intrusions in relation to indices of clustering.

Gerjuoy and Spitz (1966) review the literature and in the findings point to inconsistencies that may result from the use of two different measures of clustering. Moreover, neither measure takes into account the number of words recalled by the subject. The investigation summarized here had as its aims the study of the growth of clustering and free recall as a function of age, intelligence, and practice, as well as an elucidation of the relationship between clustering and free recall. Five populations were used: 20 middle-grade subnormals (mean IQ 53), 20 high-grades (mean IQ 72), 19 matched normal MA subjects (mean IQ 107), 14 matched CA subjects (mean IQ 117) and finally, a group of 20 college students.

The experimental material consisted of 20 nouns, 5 from each of 4 categories (animals, body parts, clothing, and food). Using an identical procedure to that of Rossi (1963), 5 separate randomizations of this test were used.

Two measures of clustering were used; the first was the amount of clustering above chance. Chance clustering, or expected repetitions was defined as follows:

$$E(R) = \frac{m_1^2 + m_2^2 + m_3^2 + m_4^2 - l}{n}$$

where m_1, m_2, m_3, and m_4 are the number of items recalled from the categories, and n the total number of items recalled. Observed repetitions, $O(R)$, were defined as the number of times a stimulus word was followed by one or more stimulus words from the same category. Categorical or irrelevant intrusions, and perseverations were not counted. The amount of clustering of each subject was defined as the difference between expected and observed repetitions.

The authors developed a second measure of clustering: the observed/maximum ratio, which again takes into account the number of stimulus words recalled. Maximum possible clustering, Max (R), was defined as $(m_1 - 1) + (m_2 - 1) + (m_3 - 1) + (m_4 - 1)$. The observed/maximum ratio formula is:

$$\frac{O(R) - E(R)}{\text{Max } (R) - E(R)}$$

which indicates the amount of above chance clustering achieved in relation to the maximum possible clustering based on the number of stimulus words recalled.

Data for middle- and high-grade subnormals were pooled since there were no significant differences between them on recall or amount of clustering. Comparison of the subnormals with the other populations was made by means of a Lindquist Type I analysis of variance. Significant Population and Trial effects (both with $p < \cdot 001$) with nonsignificant interactions were demonstrated. There were no significant differences between the two lower MA groups, nor between the two higher MA groups. The latter, however, both recalled more words than the former.

Subnormals and their MA matched controls clustered very little, and only on Trial 5 for the subnormals were the scores significantly above chance. Equal CA normals clustered significantly on Trials 4 and 5 ($p < \cdot 02$), and college students on Trials 3, 4 and 5 ($p < \cdot 001$). Significant correlations between clustering and recall were found only for equal CA normals on Trial 5 ($r = \cdot 55, p < \cdot 05$) and for college students on Trials 4 ($r = \cdot 81, p < \cdot 01$) and 5 ($r = \cdot 85, p < \cdot 01$).

A second experiment was planned to determine whether conditions designed to increase clustering would aid the recall of the retarded. Two different methods were used: the Presented Clustered (PC) method where the stimulus words were presented in categories, and the Requested Clustered (RC) method where the experimenter requested the words by category name. Fifteen institutionalized subnormals were randomly assigned to each condition, and the same stimulus material was used as earlier. For the first group (PC), however, 5 new orders of the 20 stimulus words were produced with the 5 words of each category placed consecutively but with the order of categories, and the order of words within categories, randomized.

The recall data were compared with those from the subnormals in the first experiment. There were significant effects of Treatment ($p < \cdot 005$), Trials ($p < \cdot 001$), and Treatment $\times$ Trials ($p < \cdot 005$). Results from the two induced clustering groups did not differ significantly but induced clustering significantly increased the recall of both of these groups and produced steeper learning curves.

The clustering data were equally interesting. The PC group on Trial 1 clustered almost twice as much as the subnormals in the first experiment, and significantly above chance. On Trial 4 the correlation between clustering and recall ($r = \cdot 63, p < \cdot 05$) was significant, decreasing to a non-significant $\cdot 39$ on

Trial 5. The observed/maximum clustering scores on the PC group were ·72, ·35, ·19, ·24, and ·26 for the five trials, respectively.

Irrelevant intrusions were few in all three conditions, but categorical intrusions were somewhat higher. The RC group gave significantly more categorical intrusions that the first experiment or PC subjects.

Spitz (1966) offers an important review of the literature and concludes that subnormals are primarily deficient in the categorization and chunking of incoming information rather than in simple memory. In a sense this notion is supported by much work on long-term memory which indicates that this process may be specifically less defective than some others.

Madsen and Connor (1968) investigated the extent to which high-grade subnormals categorize verbal material during the storage process in comparison with college students. Small groups were selected and given pre-training in the coding of 18 categories of 4 words each. They were then tested for the free recall of lists of 12 words which differed in the amount and type of categorization. With increased degrees of categorization in the lists, an increased recall score by both groups was apparent. When an uncorrected categorization score was used, the students showed a significantly higher rate than the subnormals. When, however, the score was based on the number of words recalled, there were no significant differences. These results are in marked contrast with those of Gerjuoy and Spitz (1966) and may result from the pre-training procedure used by Madsen and Connor, which ensured that the categories and words were available to the subjects. It is clear that the mildly subnormal can use clustering processes and information reduction under the above-stated conditions.

Gerjuoy and Alvarez (1969) failed to produce a set to cluster in educable retarded adolescents (CA 15·2 years, IQ 59·4) and normal children matched for MA, using 1 training session of 5 trials and a transfer session one week later. Two lists of 20 familiar words were used, 5 words from each of 4 categories. Half the subjects in each population received List 1 during training and List 2 for transfer, and the other half had the converse. Half the subjects were trained with randomized word lists, while the other half were given clustered presentation; all subjects had randomized lists in the second (transfer session). Both populations exhibited increased clustering and recall when the list was presented in a clustered, rather than a randomized order, thus confirming previous findings. Neither practice and familiarity with the task, nor experience with a clustered list aided performance at the second session.

By contrast, Clarke and co-workers (1970) found significant effects of a learned set on the free recall of retarded adults (mean PPVT IQ 60). Two groups of subjects matched for score on a pictorial similarities test and ability to recall unrelated words, were trained as follows: the Blocks Group was required to recall a list of 16 words, 4 in each of 4 categories, presented in clusters (i.e. 'blocks'), twice every day until a criterion of 4 consecutive scores of 15 or 16 out of 16 words was reached, *or* they had completed 24 trials. The orders of words within clusters, and position of clusters within the list, were systematically changed from trial to trial. The Random Group was required to recall a list of 16 unrelated high-frequency words (Thorndike-Lorge) to the same criterion, the order of presentation of words varying from trial to trial. Both groups were subsequently presented with the same new list of 16 words, 4 words in each of 4 categories in which no 2 conceptually related words were ever juxtaposed, and neither words nor categories were common to either of the 2 training lists. There was a significant difference in *amount* recalled ($p < ·025$) on the first 2 trials of transfer, favouring the Blocks Group, but neither group showed much tendency to cluster; on Trials 3 and 4 the differences between the groups in terms of amount recalled was reduced to non-significance, but there was a significant difference ($p < ·05$) in cluster index (taking account of score) in favour of the Blocks Group. A further study by the authors, using memory for pictures as the transfer task, and groups of subjects, including an equal number of educable and trainable (imbecile) adolescents, showed a significant difference in score only between Blocks and Random Groups on Trials 1 and 2 of transfer, and no difference whatever in clustering, educable subjects in both groups clustering above chance, and the imbeciles showing little tendency to cluster. It was concluded that if categorical relations among words are repeatedly demonstrated by clustered presentation, a set to perceive inter-item associations develops. This is available for use with new categorizable material so that the categorical relations are perceived at the input-coding stage with consequent augmentation of total output (recall score). Clustering at any significant level is a reflection of organization of input material in store, and is an activity that occurs after at least two repetitions of a list, predominantly among subjects of higher intelligence. The results point to the importance of total recall score as a measure of categorization, in addition to clustering, which latter may well depend on different psychological processes.

Language, verbal mediation, and conceptual behaviour

LANGUAGE

The proposition that language development in the mentally subnormal tends to fall below the general level of their abilities has commanded almost universal support for many years. Recently, Alper (1967), analysing the WISC test results of 713 institutionalized children aged 5 to 16, found performance IQs were significantly higher than verbal IQs; within the verbal scale the Comprehension and Similarities subtests were consistently higher than Arithmetic and Vocabulary, while within the performance scale Picture Completion and Object Assembly tended to be high and Picture Arrangement and Coding lower. Belmont and colleagues (1967) compared WISC performance of a total population sample of home-based educable mental retardates aged 8 to 10, in Aberdeen, with the performance of normal children. The subtest profile for the subnormal group differed from that of the normal, the outstanding feature being their lack of verbal facility, with Vocabulary the lowest subtest score. The factorial organization of intellectual patterning also differentiated the groups and led to the suggestion that the limited level of functioning in the retarded children may be directly related to their less-developed verbal skills and to the non-availability of such skills in the service of perceptual-motor performance.

As in other areas of research, however, two divergent positions, the 'developmental lag' and the 'defect' theories, have been used to account for such findings; Luria (1961) and Luria and Vinogradova (1959) have been the chief exponents, along with other Pavlovian 'defectologists', of the latter view. Thus, Luria has contended not only that speech and thinking are intimately related, and that speech plays a vital part in the regulation and integration of normal behaviour, but that in the retarded there is a pathological inertia of the nervous processes. Unlike the normal child, the subnormal also suffers a dissociation between speech and motor signalling systems. These facts are said to account for 'the extreme difficulties with which their training is connected'.

Luria's approach has involved ingenious experimentation but there remains some doubt about his methodology. In the famous Luria and Vinogradova (1959) experiment, for example, it was shown that imbeciles generalized to homonyms, while normal children generalized to synonyms. It is, however, unclear whether the words used were equally familiar to the subnormals as to the normals. If the words were not understood very well by the former, the results are entirely to be expected.

Work on language has been well reviewed by O'Connor and Hermelin (1963b) who also outline their own experiments. While these authors find some merit in the approach of Luria they believe the prediction that the dissociation between speech and motor behaviour cannot be overcome to be too pessimistic. Part of the subnormal's incapacity to handle symbols comes from a reluctance to use them. Thus, 'a verbal disinclination as well as a verbal disability seems to be present' (1963b).

Lenneberg (1967), unlike Luria, espouses a developmental view of language. Recognizing that each disease giving rise to retardation has its typical manifestations, he nevertheless states that: 'the development of language, insofar as it occurs at all in these patients, follows some general laws of evolvement which may be traced among all of these conditions, and which, indeed, are not different in nature from the unfolding of language in healthy children. Among the retarded the entire developmental process is merely slowed down or stretched out during childhood and is regularly arrested during the early teens.' Support for this view is provided by Lenneberg et al. (1964) who studied over a three-year period sixty-one mongoloid children reared in their own homes. The children were visited periodically, and data consisted of psychological test results, tape recordings of spontaneous utterances during play, performance on an articulation test and a sentence-repetition test, assessments of vocabulary, understanding of commands, and nature of vocalization. Lenneberg points out that the IQ threshold for language development is quite low, and that above it, chronological age is the better predictor for language development. In this sample, the sequence of learning phases and the synchrony of emergence of different aspects of language was normal; progress in one field of language learning was well correlated with progress in all fields other than articulation. Poor articulation seemed to be to some extent a motivational factor and not primarily due to structural abnormalities.

Two important review papers on language functions in mental retardation have been published by Spreen (1965a, b). In the first, evidence is presented on the relationship between intellectual and language development and consideration is given to specific types of retardation and to factors identified as contributing to the severity of language handicaps. The second concentrates on the role of language in higher intellectual functions such as abstraction, concept formation, learning, and verbal mediation.

Spreen indicates that language dysfunction occurs in 100 per cent of those below IQ 20, in 90 per cent of those between IQ 21 and 50, and in around 45 per cent for the mildly subnormal. It is also argued that the abstract-concrete dimension in vocabulary definitions is of some value in differentiating subnormals matched for mental age with younger normals, and there is some indication that the brain damaged are more handicapped in abstraction ability than familial subnormals.

In Spreen's second paper, attention is again directed to the work of Luria, and to the broad question of verbal mediation. He reviews the Dissociation Hypothesis as put forward by Luria, where, in the final stage (about the age of 6 in the normal child) spoken language becomes more and more replaced with inner language which 'constitutes the essential component of thought and volitional action'. If this is so, the fact that subnormals are on the average markedly deficient in language in comparison with their other deficiencies, may be particularly significant. That this view is at least oversimple has been shown in the work of Furth and Youniss (1964) and Furth and Milgram (1965). All that can be repeated with certainty is that there tends to be a particular language deficit in the subnormal, and this may have a bearing on the rest of their cognitive development. Spreen concludes his review of this complicated problem by suggesting that although some of the evidence points to a specific innate verbal deficit in the retarded, the effects of environment and interpersonal communication, and the effects of general anxiety and motivation are probably important additional factors in determining the retardate's poor performance in this area.

Blount (1969) has reviewed studies of language in the more severely retarded, below IQ 50. He points to the dearth of research in this area and draws attention to the important work of Lyle (1959, 1960a). Lyle (1960b), in collaboration with Tizard, studied the experimental manipulation of environment and its effect on verbal development in a sample of imbecile children. In this, the Brooklands experiment, a control group was left in impoverished institutional surroundings while the experimental group was moved to a small 'child centred' family unit. Over a two-year period very significant verbal gains (e.g. on the Minnesota

Pre-School Scale) were demonstrated in the experimental group. Later work (Lyle, 1961) also supported the findings of Karlin and Strazzulla (1952). The more severely retarded are delayed in language development but follow the same sequence as normals. Poor home environments as well as the restricting effects of institutionalization are among the relevant factors. Other important descriptive studies have been provided by Mein and O'Connor (1960), Mein (1961) and Wolfensberger *et al.* (1963).

Beier and co-workers (1969) studied vocabulary usage in 30 institutionalized mentally retarded male subjects aged 11 to 24, IQ range 23 to 75, who were known to talk and whose articulation was good. Data on normal children, aged 12 and 16, IQ range 90 to 110, were available from a previous study. The subnormal group spoke more slowly than normals; used more positive words such as 'yes' and 'okay', and used more self-reference words. There was very little difference between the samples in extent of vocabulary: both had a vocabulary of about 40 words which comprised 50 per cent of their language; the same high agreement was true for the 10 most frequently used words. The authors conclude that the deficit in mental retardation is not so much in vocabulary as in conceptualization, organization, language structure, grammar, and syntax usage.

It would be surprising if some degree of language remediation were not possible with the mentally retarded. Indeed, Lyle's (1960b) experiment showed that considerable gains could be induced in a deprived imbecile group. A much shorter five months' programme by Kolstoe (1958) with a mongol group was, however, largely unsuccessful. On the other hand, a two-year study by Harvey *et al.* (1966) showed highly significant improvements. In the present writers' view, a major research attack on the question of remediation of verbal deficiencies is now overdue; these need to be explored in much the same way as did earlier experimental work on manual skills. In particular, the question of length of training as well as the most appropriate methods need to be evaluated. It seems probable that if significant effects are to be obtained, training programmes will have to be carried out over long periods of time.

VERBAL MEDIATION

Since there is general agreement that the mentally subnormal tend to be particularly handicapped in the area of language development, a number of experimental studies have been undertaken to determine whether they can use verbal mediators to facilitate learning, and whether, as suggested by Jensen and Rohwer (1963) and Jensen (1965), retardates have a specific deficit in this ability. The methods used have commonly been reversal and non-reversal shift learning and paired-associate learning.

O'Connor and Hermelin (1959) found that 11-year-old imbeciles were greatly superior to 5-year-old normal subjects (matched for MA) on a reversal shift, although the groups had not differed on the original discrimination. However, the normal children would verbalize the principle, while the imbeciles would not.

A second group of imbeciles, required to verbalize their choices on the initial discrimination, showed no facilitation on reversal, resembling the normal controls in that discrimination and reversal scores were equal. A possible interpretation is that the original learning was not under verbal control in the retarded subjects and, consequently, they did not have to inhibit a strong pre-experimental verbal set in the reversal situation, as did the normal children.

Balla and Zigler (1964) replicated this experiment, and found no difference in discrimination or reversal learning between retardates and normals at MA levels 5 and 6. They challenged the view that the cognitive functioning of retarded subjects is inherently different from normal children of equivalent MA.

Milgram and Furth (1964) compared normal and educable retarded children at two MA levels on a variety of reversal, non-reversal, and control shift conditions. They found evidence for the mediational deficiency hypothesis in significant age and IQ differences on dimension reversal, the greater difficulty of non-reversal over reversal shift, and in the relation of retrospective verbalization about relevant cues with age and task variables.

The finding reported by Kendler and Kendler (1959, 1960) and others that reversal shifts are easier than non-reversal shifts for normal elementary school-children was confirmed by Sanders *et al.* (1965). Retarded children of similar MA, however, performed equally well on each problem, thus presenting ambiguous data for a theory that proposes presence or absence of verbal mediation as the basis for the difference in ease of learning the two types of problem.

Heal and colleagues (1966) compared retarded children (MA 6·4, CA 14–8) with normal children (MA 6·5, CA 5–4) on three reversal problems. While the groups did not differ on original learning, the retardates were inferior to the normals in overall reversal, results discrepant with those of O'Connor and Hermelin (1959). The authors suggested two deficits in retardates: inability to inhibit a previously acquired habit, and susceptibility to disruption by novel stimuli, and speculated that increasing mental age may be associated with increasing retardate inferiority on a discrimination reversal.

The data on reversal shifts are thus to some extent inconsistent, and it seems unlikely that this method will yield crucial evidence on possible mediational deficiencies in retardates (see also section on Learning Sets).

Evidence on mediation in retardates from studies of paired-associate learning is more extensive, and excellent summaries are provided by Prehm (1966a, b), Goulet (1968), Mordock (1968), and Baumeister and Kellas (1971).

Of those early workers who matched subjects for CA, Eisman (1958), Akutagawa and Benoit (1959), and Vergason (1964) failed to find significant differences between their retardates and normals. Berkson and Cantor (1960) compared normal and retarded children matched for CA in a three-stage mediation paradigm, where the mediator was based on laboratory acquired associations. They found no difference between the groups for mediated facilitation, but the normal subjects learned the test stage faster than the retardates. Blue (1963), Carrier *et al.* (1961), Madsen (1963), and Ring and Palermo (1961) also found differences between groups on rate of initial learning. Of those workers who matched on MA, Cantor and Ryan (1962), Girardeau and Ellis (1964), and Vergason (1964) found no differences between normal and subnormal groups, while Blake (1960) and Heber *et al.* (1962) did find retardates significantly inferior.

Lipman (1963) suggested that the meaningfulness of the stimulus material was a major variable in determining outcome of experiments such as these; the less meaningful the material, the greater would be the performance deficit in retardates. Evidence in support of this notion comes from Noble and McKeely (1957), Cieutat *et al.* (1958), Lance (1965), and Prehm (1966a). Mordock (1968), commenting on these findings, points out that although there is empirical support for Lipman's contention, the relationship between decreasing meaningfulness and deficit in retardates is not linear, since both Lance and Prehm imply that at certain levels decreases in meaningfulness do not further handicap the subnormal.

The effect of different exposure times and anticipation intervals is considered to be another possible source of variation among reported results (see section on Reaction Time). Recently, Penney and colleagues (1968a) used a similar experimental design to that of Berkson and Cantor (1960), but matched their subjects on MA. They found that the retardates were mediationally deficient relative to normal children when a relatively short anticipation interval was used during the mediation test. Lengthening the interval facilitated mediation in the former group but was detrimental to the latter.

The nature of the stimulus and response items and their relative similarity or dissimilarity is also relevant to the outcome of comparative studies of paired-associate learning. It is suggested by Mordock that since subnormal subjects have weaker associative strengths to the same words than have average subjects (Evans, 1964; Silverstein and McLain, 1966), it is possible that stimulus differentiation will be more difficult for them. Furthermore, if subnormal and average subjects are differentially affected by stimulus similarity, then they should differ in R–S recall. Rieber (1964) found that subnormal subjects do not differ from average in learning simple verbal responses to stimuli but they do differ considerably in their ability to use these responses; this suggests a relative inability in the retardate to acquire mediating responses, and a greater rigidity once these have been established.

Milgram has investigated the mediational deficiency hypothesis in a series of studies. A comparison of educable and trainable retardates of comparable MA with young normal children at two age levels on paired associate learning with response competition, showed a relationship between susceptibility to interference and a combination of MA and IQ variables (Milgram and Furth, 1966). Retardates were found to be inferior in long-term retention of a mediational set (Milgram, 1967), although they had benefited significantly from verbal mediation instructions. Milgram draws attention to Maccoby's (1964) distinction between *production deficiency* (failure to employ verbal statements that are potentially available and useful) and a genuine *mediation deficiency* (actually producing these verbalizations without using them to elicit effective covert mediating responses) and suggests that his data support a production deficiency in retardates (see also section on Concept Learning). This line of argument is further elaborated by Milgram (1968) in a study of verbal mediation in paired-associate learning in severely retarded subjects compared with 4-year-old children. Mediational facilitation was of borderline significance for the retardates, but was effective in the young normals. However, Milgram, drawing on a great deal of evidence, suggests that as yet the question of production versus mediational deficiency has not been resolved.

Prehm (1968) gives the following summary of a series of experiments by Martin and his associates (Martin *et al.*, 1968; Berch, 1967; Bulgarella, 1967; Hohn, 1967; Van der Veen, 1967):

Martin, Boersma and Bulgarella studied the use of associative strategies (mediators) by retarded and normal adolescents. Using a seven-level schema for classifying subjects' verbal reports about how they learned pairs of dissyllables developed in a previous study (Martin, Boersma, and Cox, 1965), they found that significantly more normal than retarded subjects used high-level, and fewer normal than retarded subjects used low-level, strategies. Both groups used intermediate-level strategies to a comparable degree. Hohn provided groups of retarded and normal subjects with associative strategy aids and found that, although the provision of aids facilitated the performance of the retarded subjects, their acquisition performance was still below that of unaided normal subjects. Berch found that the performance of retarded subjects who were made familiar with stimulus elements was superior to the performance of subjects who were familiar with the entire stimulus. Bulgarella found that retarded subjects could be conditioned to use high-level strategies and that acquisition performance of subjects so conditioned was superior to control subjects.

Baumeister and Kellas (1971) present a model of acquisition strategies in paired-associate learning based on studies of normal and retarded subjects. There are four main features: (1) *strategy selector* – the one chosen probably depends on (a) meaningfulness level of task items, (b) the amount to be learned, (c) response required, (d) rate of presentation, (e) subject's pre-experimental history, and (f) ongoing self-evaluation of own performance; (2) *coding*, including visual imagery and mediational techniques (e.g. clustering, chunking, rhyming); (3) *rote repetition*, the coding product is itself subject to rote repetition; and (4) *feedback loop*, involving hypothesis testing and possible change of strategy by the subject.

Evidence that mental retardates can be persuaded to use mediators, granted the appropriate learning opportunities, is provided by two recent papers. Borkowski and Johnson (1968) replicated the Berkson and Cantor (1960) experiment, but used an MA control group as well as a CA control. Furthermore, the control paradigm in the three-stage chaining experimental model differed from the mediational paradigm in stage II rather than in stage I to prevent the occurrence of differential stimulus familiarity in stage III learning. The paired-associate learning of retardates was inferior to that of MA and CA controls when mediators were not available. However, when mediating links were provided, retardates used these associations in learning as well as the MA control group though not as efficiently as the CA controls. Furthermore, comparison of higher IQ levels with lower, within the retarded group, showed that the beneficial effects of mediation were not restricted to the former.

In a further carefully controlled study, again using a three-list paired-associate task, Penney *et al.* (1968b) explored the possibility of creating a set to mediate, by giving half their mentally retarded subjects a learning set task, while the other half were given an operant task. Both groups were then again given the three-list paired-associate task as a post-test of their mediational ability. The results showed that learning-set training enhanced mediation, while operant conditioning retarded mediation; the former result is consistent with the emerging notion that mentally retarded subjects can learn to organize behaviour verbally and to use mediators. The latter result, which was unexpected, is, however, difficult to explain.

The important question of the retention of mediational sets in retardates has not as yet been adequately explored; thus, this remains a crucial area for investigation, with the probability of major theoretical and practical implications.

Gallagher (1969) used a variant of the three-stage chaining paradigm to investigate with normal and retarded subjects (MA 8·76, CA 15–16) the influence of free association strength (FAS) as an *inferred* mediator between word pairs that are non-associated according to normative data (e.g. table-chair: A–B stage chair–sit: B–C stage; both normal associations, should lead to table-sit: A–C faster than a control condition, A–D, where no associative links are available). Each subject received a list of six pairs. Two pairs had high FAS between both the A–B and B–C links; two pairs had low FAS between these links, and two pairs were non-associated. As predicted on the basis of previous work with normal subjects, paired-associate learning was a function on the multiplicative value of the FAS values from stages A–B and B–C for both normal and retarded subjects. Normals learned faster than retardates for both types of A–C pairs (high and low multiplicative FAS values), and for the A–D control pairs. The findings are further evidence that retardates use verbal associations to facilitate learning, although dependence on their natural repertoire may result in less efficient learning than laboratory controlled associations (Berkson and Cantor, 1960; Borkowski and Johnson, 1968).

STUDIES OF CONCEPTUAL BEHAVIOUR

The material to be reviewed in this section overlaps to a considerable extent with much of the foregoing research data on verbal mediation, and organization of input for memory storage. The chief difference lies in the type of problem studied, being less dependent on rote learning or memory components (as in paired-associate learning) and more dependent on spontaneous processes of abstraction. Useful summaries of some of the evidence are provided by Rosenberg (1963) and Blount (1968).

An important study by Miller and associates (1968) sought to determine a hierarchy of problems that might differentiate the mentally retarded from normal controls. The investigation is unique in that it employed a repeated measures design and used films in presenting 9 different tasks to 96 retarded adolescents, 100 normal adolescents of similar CA, and 109 normal children of similar MA to the retarded. The tasks included: paired-associate learning, discrimination learning, probability learning, incidental learning, concept of probability, conservation of volume, age estimation, verbal memory, and ability to construct anagrams. All subjects were non-institutionalized and testing took place in school classrooms.

The results offer clear evidence of less effective performance in learning and problem solving tasks by retarded subjects than by normal people of either similar CA or MA. The only task in which retarded subjects performed at a higher level than normals was probability learning (confirming previous findings by Stevenson and Zigler, 1958); on paired-associate and discrimination learning the differences failed to reach the ·05 level of significance; on all other tasks, significant inferiority of performance by the retarded, as compared with CA or MA matched peers, was demonstrated. The authors conclude that the ability of the retarded to organize verbal material, and to apply conceptual schemes to its analysis, is more drastically impaired than is their ability to modify their responses in a learning task as a consequence of the information they receive. A very important subsidiary finding lay in the difference between normals and retardates in their pattern of relations between IQ and performance on the 9 tasks. The correlations for the 2 groups of normal subjects were consistently positive and significant for the majority of tasks. By contrast, few significant correlations between IQ and performance were found for the retarded subjects. The authors suggest that variables other than intelligence, possibly motivation and attention (see Zigler, 1967), play a greater part in retardate than normal performance.

The results of Miller et al. (1968) lead to the proposition, which many assume tacitly, that if out of a number of tasks (given in the same circumstances to groups of normal and retarded subjects) some differentiate between the groups better than others, those that differentiate will be: (a) more difficult, and (b) have a larger verbal/conceptual component than those that do not. A study by Milgram and Furth (1963) is important in showing that these two factors are not always correlated. They compared retarded schoolchildren in the IQ range 50–75 with normal children matched by CA to subgroups of MA 6, 7, 8, and 10 (approximately) on 3 tasks previously used by Furth (1961) in a study of deaf children. The Sameness task involved discrimination between 2 identical geometrical figures and 2 different shapes; the Symmetry task required discrimination between symmetrical and asymmetrical figures (both these tasks were assumed to be predominantly perceptual); the Opposition task, which was assumed to involve language-mediation, required choosing the opposite to 1 exemplar among a series of objects varying (on any one occasion) in size, volume, length, member brightness, position, and texture. Size opposition was used as the standard, subjects being required to reach a criterion of 6 consecutive correct choices; the others (1 trial each) were used as transfer tasks. Trials to a given criterion were used as the measure to compare groups, which did not differ on the Sameness discrimination task, differed in favour of the retarded on Symmetry ($p < \cdot05$), and differed very significantly in favour of normal subjects ($p < \cdot001$) on Opposition. Further analysis of the data, however, revealed that this latter task was much the *easiest* of the 3 for both retarded and normal subjects. The authors interpret their findings as showing that the retarded are not adept at the discovery and application of a language-relevant concept within their realm of comprehension, but do as well as normals in (more difficult) problems where perceptual rather than verbal modes of solution might be more appropriate.

An important theoretical point arises from the work of Furth on concept learning in the deaf, elaborated by Furth and Milgram in studies using mentally retarded subjects of different levels of ability. Furth and Milgram (1965) challenge the commonly held assumption that thought and language are so inextricably related as to be to all intents and purposes identical. While not disregarding the presumed interaction of language and cognitive behaviour, they believe that many views about the relationship of the two are oversimplified and potentially confusing, and point out the dangers inherent in procedures adopted by Piaget, Vigotsky, and Kendler which rely on verbal operations as mechanisms for advanced stages of conceptual ability. It might be added that the hazards involved in demanding a verbal response as evidence even of verbal comprehension (let alone potential non-verbal concepts) are underlined by Lenneberg (1962) who described a case which he claims is typical of a larger category of patients, where an organic defect prevented the acquisition of the motor skill necessary for *speaking* a language but the patient showed evidence of a complete *understanding* of language.

In an attempt to explore non-verbal and verbal classificatory behaviour, Furth and Milgram (1965) constructed a pictorial similarities task. Eighteen sets of 7 pictures were presented, and from each set the subject was required to select 3 (out of 7) which belonged together (*picture sorting*). The subjects were presented with the 18 sets of 3 conceptually related pictures and asked to explain why they belonged together (*picture verbalization*); the material was presented verbally, i.e. 18 sets of 7 words (*word sorting*); and subjects were given 3 related words and asked to verbalize the basis for the relation (*word verbalization*). In the first of a series of experiments, 38 non-institutionalized retardates (CA 12 years, IQ 70, MA 9 years) were compared with 38 normal schoolchildren (CA 9·1). Half the children in each group were used for the first 2 tasks, and half for the latter. For both groups the 2 word tasks were more difficult than the picture tasks;

there was no difference between the groups on picture sorting; retardates were, however, significantly inferior to the normals on the remaining 3 verbal tasks.

In a further experiment the authors used lower CA–MA groups: 16 retardates (CA 9·2; IQ 66·9; MA 6) and 16 normal children (CA 6·1). As before, the groups were equal on picture sorting; they were also similar on picture verbalization, a fact interpreted as showing with normal children that, developmentally, verbal formulation lags behind cognitive behaviour at the 6-year level. A statistical analysis of the data from both experiments showed a significant IQ × CA × Modality (pictures/words) interaction, suggesting that retardates improve (from MA 6 to 9) significantly less than do normals on the verbalization task by contrast to the sorting task.

Milgram (1966), using the same procedure, compared severely retarded (trainable, institutionalized), mildly retarded (educable, non-institutionalized) and normal groups of similar MA (6) but with an IQ difference of 30 points between adjacent groups. No difference was found among the three groups on picture sorting, but the severely retarded were significantly inferior to the other two groups with respect to verbalization. As before, at this MA level, the mild retardates and normals did not differ on verbalization. Milgram concludes that the greater the severity of mental defect, the greater the deficiency in verbal formulation of adequate conceptual performance.

Somewhat different results are reported by Stephens, who conducted a series of investigations into the presence and use of categories by mentally retarded schoolchildren. He (1964) compared 30 mildly subnormal (mean IQ 60) boys with 30 normals (mean IQ 101) using a CA match. Cards, each containing 7 pictures, 4 of which represented a particular category, were presented to the subjects. The experimenter named the category and the boy was required to point out the 4 exemplars. The normals gave significantly more correct responses than the subnormals and could identify all exemplars of more categories.

Stephens (1966a) repeated the earlier study, using CA matched groups. The subnormals were selected in three CA ranges: 90 to 101 months; 102 to 113 months; and 114 to 126 months. On this occasion, the cards were demonstrated twice. First, the subject was asked to point out which 4 pictures went together and why; and second, with the same instructions as in the earlier experiment. The normals were able to indicate more of the exemplars of categories, and could also label more of the correctly identified categories under both experimental conditions. It appeared that the concepts were present but were poorly delineated in the subnormals, with, for example, not all exemplars being correctly identified.

In a further study (Stephens, 1966b) subnormals did not differ from MA controls, both these groups being significantly less efficient than CA controls. All subjects were more effective when the category was named by the experimenter than when they had to discover the category for themselves.

Stephens (1968) studied the linguistic deficiencies of mentally subnormal children by investigating the types of errors they exhibited when required to provide verbal labels for concepts they had used successfully. Seven types of error were discovered, ranging from over- or undergeneralization to inability to state a category by name. Further support is thus provided for the view that it is possible successfully to use categories for problem solving without being able to provide an appropriate verbal label (see Furth and Milgram, 1965). The author suggests two possible conclusions. 'On the one hand, there may exist a developmental sequence in concept learning and utilization which begins with no knowledge of a concept, proceeds to a functional ability to use the concept, and is concluded by the higher level development of the ability to label the concept appropriately, as well as to employ it correctly.' The second possibility is that it may be 'easier, and less threatening, to respond to a labelling task by citing a series of low level descriptive features of the stimuli than by risking failure'. This reference to a possible problem of motivation is reminiscent of O'Connor and Hermelin's (1963b) conclusion that there is a disinclination on the part of the subnormal to use speech. Allen and Wallach (1969) found that educable retardates (IQ range, 41 to 77) were considerably less efficient at word definition than recognition on the PPVT (with the recognition score corrected for guessing) and conclude that the major functional weakness of this population is verbal encoding.

The relative importance of the alternative explanations will be determined only after a great deal more experimental work has been undertaken contrasting retarded groups with normal (IQ 90 to 110) and normal with superior (IQ 130 and above), at all ages, including adults.

A series of experiments on conceptual behaviour has been reported by Griffith and his colleagues. Griffith and Spitz (1958) presented 8 groups of 3 nouns each, requiring institutionalized retarded subjects (IQ 66, CA 17 years) to state the relationship of the words in the triad, i.e. to abstract. An additional vocabulary test included 18 of the 24 words already used, and the subject was asked to define these. The definitions of each word in the triad were checked for the presence of identical characteristics having been stated which might serve as a common abstraction. The data were then compared with results from the other test (order of presentation having been controlled). Subjects who defined at least 2 of the triad words by mentioning a common characteristic were 10 times more likely to offer the abstraction common to the triad. Conversely, if they defined less than 2 words with a mention of common characteristics, they were unlikely to offer the abstraction common to the words in the triad. Had the subnormals been 'testing hypotheses', only one abstraction suitable to relate the constituents of the triad would need to appear in the definitions; hence, the authors concluded that they were not testing hypotheses. Moreover, the subnormals, while offering adequate definitions, found it difficult to produce adequate abstractions.

Griffith and colleagues (1959) used a similar procedure with institutionalized retardates but added normal MA matched controls. Their purpose was to cast light on the relationship between concept formation and the availability of mediators. Retardates and normal 7-year-old children were not very successful in concept attainment unless they defined at least two words in terms of an acceptable abstraction. Normal 9-year-olds, however, were relatively successful even when they defined only one word in terms of an abstraction. The authors consider that conceptual tasks are sensitive indicators of retardation.

Further work by Griffith (1960) aimed to establish whether retarded subjects' performance in reporting similarities depended on their defining a threshold number or some constant proportion of the presented stimulus words in terms of an appropriate similarity for the entire set of presented words. Subjects were required to respond to 3- and 6-word sets of stimulus words. Those with IQs below 65 showed little success unless they could define, in terms of a possible abstraction, approximately two-thirds of the words. The results for those of IQ 65 and above did not clearly support either hypothesis.

Miller and Griffith (1961) studied the effect of a brief period of training (three sessions) upon abstraction. Social reinforcement appeared to exercise little influence on abstraction performance, but training produced significant conceptual effects on materials used in training. This did not transfer to new material. The conclusion that any improvement in the conceptual behaviour of retardates, effected through training, may be limited to the materials used, must, however, be viewed in the context of the short duration of these experiments.

Concept attainment by induction and deduction was investigated by Blake and Williams (1968) using retarded, normal, and superior subjects, all from state schools. Two sets of subjects were used, one equated for MA (approximately 11), and the other for CA (approximately 14), with the same group of retardates in each set. The task was concept-identification with object-level words from 4 categories used as specific instances to be associated with 2-digit numerals, which served as category labels. Subjects were allocated to the following conditions: induction-discovery, induction-demonstration, or deduction. No significant groups effect was shown in the equal MA comparison; it was, however, significant in the equal CA comparison (where analysis of covariance was used to adjust for a superior group younger than the retarded group). In this comparison the superior group exceeded the normal and the retarded, while the normal exceeded the retarded. Furthermore, the difference between the superior and the normal was larger and more significant than that between the normal and retarded. Although the authors do not comment on it (perhaps because the groups were statistically rather than experimentally matched for age), this finding raises the question of whether differences between superior and average 'normal' children may be as great as differences between mildly retarded and normal (see Osler and Fivel, 1961; Osler and Trautman, 1961), an important point in considering the 'defect' versus 'retardation' view of mental subnormality. The methods of concept attainment did not differentially affect the relationships among the groups. Deduction was the most effective method for all three types of subject; induction was less effective, and no difference was found between the discovery and demonstration methods. The authors rightly suggest, in view of findings with normal populations, that the lack of qualitative difference should be interpreted with caution, and may not hold with different tasks and different material.

Gozali (1969) investigated cognitive style in mental retardates, using a method devised by Kagan (1966) for normal children. A circular version of Kagan's Matching Familiar Figures test was administered to eighty educable retardates and measures of response latency, number of errors and order of errors were obtained. The findings were similar to those reported for normal children: subjects with long time response latencies and few errors (reflective children) made consistent efforts to solve test items; subjects with short latencies and high error scores (impulsive) tended to employ a position response set. The findings are important in showing the lack of homogeneity in behaviour among a retarded group which was representative of a limited age range (8 to 10·5 years), IQ range (55 to 78) and drawn from special classes within one city.

The question of some variables affecting the development of relative thinking by retardates has been explored by McManis (1968), using a technique designed by Piaget (1928) and investigated with normal children by Elkind (1961, 1962). The 'right-left' test and 'mother-sister' test both assess a subject's ability to handle certain abstract relations without a necessary reference to himself. Thus, questions in the former test range from concrete, 'Show me your left hand, show me your right hand', to the abstract connotation of spatial relations between three objects *opposite* to the subject; in the latter test, questions range between 'How many brothers have you, how many sisters?' to 'Ernest has three brothers: Paul, Henry, and Charles. How many brothers has Paul? Henry? Charles?'

The subjects were 140 institutionalized subnormals with an IQ range of 30 to 60, CA 7 to 8 to 21 to 11, and MA from 5–0 to 8–11. The normal controls were provided from Elkind's data. A succinct description of the results has been provided by McManis. 'Retardate MA and normal CA correspondence was good for concrete understanding of both concepts. Abstract right-left understanding was CA related (low IQ retardates > high IQ retardates > normals). Abstract understanding of kinship, however, was not a simple function of either MA or CA (high IQ retardates > normals > low IQ retardates). Understanding of the class concept of brother-sister was a function of IQ (normals > high IQ retardates > low IQ retardates).

Commenting on these results, McManis points out that his data support the view that relative thinking development is hierarchically ordered. Success at the abstract-relative level was invariably associated with success with the concrete problems but the reverse relationship was not found.

In a study of mass, weight, and volume conservation, McManis (1969b) found conservation to be MA rather than CA related, and more or less in the expected order of difficulty, although there were several reversals. Conservation of volume was poor for both groups, and both failed to show MA related improvement on this task. In a further study, McManis (1969c) showed that retardates attained transitivity of weight and length considerably later than normals. Conservation developed prior to transitivity, with more retardates between MA 7 and 10 being in a transitional stage of the sequence.

In view of the recent plethora of Piagetian studies on normal children, one must expect this fashionable trend to extend to the field of subnormality. It is to be hoped that experimenters will not be content with describing Piagetian stages in relation to MA, CA, and IQ, but will also conduct rigorous, long-term learning experiments to establish the conditions in which conservation, transitivity, and other processes may be acquired.

Evidence already exists to suggest that neither the hierarchical sequences nor the developmental ages at which these types of thinking occur can be regarded as anything like as clear and predictable as has been claimed by Piagetian enthusiasts.

Personality and motivation

The emphasis of this chapter is on research connected with aspects of cognitive functioning, and important problems such as the general motivation, need achievement, or anxiety level of subjects taking part in the many experiments have largely been ignored. Writing on personality disorders and characteristics of the mentally retarded, Heber (1964) stated:

> Despite the generally acknowledged importance of personality factors in problem solving there has been relatively little experimental work relative to personality development and characteristics of the retarded. Not one of such commonly purported attributes of the retarded as passivity, anxiety, impulsivity, rigidity, suggestibility, a lack of persistence, immaturity, withdrawal, low frustration tolerance, unrealistic self-concept or level of aspiration can be either substantiated or refuted on the basis of available research data.

It is beyond the scope of this chapter to summarize research findings in the area of personality assessment; we will confine ourselves to a brief outline of two related theories of personality and motivation which in each case have served as a focus for systematic investigation. Both Cromwell and Zigler have been concerned to analyse the motivational effects of failure experiences and failure expectancies; Zigler has concentrated on the outcome of general deprivation suffered by most retardates in institutions.

Cromwell (1963) summarizes his social learning theory, emphasizing the critical role of failure experience and generalized expectancies for failure which typically characterize the retardate. Based on careful studies over many years he concluded that retardates: (1) enter a novel situation with a performance level which is depressed below their level of constitutional ability, (2) have fewer tendencies to be 'moved' by failure experience than normals, and (3) have fewer tendencies than normals to increase effort following a mild failure experience. Evidence was also obtained which gave partial support to the notion of separate approach and avoidance motivational systems. Stronger avoidance tendency was sometimes, but not always, shown by retardates. From this research there gradually developed a theoretical formulation that posited a success-approach and failure-avoidance motivational system which was separate from the hedonistic system typically described in terms of primary and secondary drives.

Zigler and his colleagues believe that many of the reported differences between the retarded and their normal MA matched controls may arise from a variety of differences in their motivational systems, associated with their impoverished experience and social deprivation. Zigler's interest arose in connection with a careful testing of the 'rigidity' hypothesis first advanced by Lewin and Kounin, a typical 'defect' theory of subnormality. This hypothesis was rejected, and in its place a social deprivation motivational hypothesis proposed (Zigler, 1966). Differences in 'rigidity' between the subnormal and their MA matched controls may be related to motivational differences for obtaining adult contact and approval. Those in institutions are likely to suffer a degree of deprivation and be more highly motivated to seek contact and approval. This view was supported by experimental evidence and led to an extension of the hypothesis that 'the greater the amount of pre-institutional social deprivation experienced by the feeble-minded child, the greater will be his motivation to interact with an adult, making such interaction and any adult approval or support that accompany it more reinforcing for his responses than for the responses of a feeble-minded child who has experienced a less amount of social deprivation' (1966, p. 85). For example, 60 retarded children were divided into 2 groups, high and low socially deprived, but matched on all other relevant variables. The study employed a 2-part satiation game and 3 out of 4 predictions were confirmed. The more socially deprived children: (1) spent a greater amount of time on the game; (2) more frequently made the maximum number of responses allowed; and (3) showed a greater increase in time spent on part 2 over that on part 1 of the game. The predictions that the more socially deprived would make fewer errors, however, reached only borderline significance.

Zigler pursued the point by demonstrating significant differences in performance of institutionalized retardates by comparison with home-based retardates and normal children matched for MA, the latter two groups showing no difference in performance; further, he found similar differences between institutionalized children of normal intelligence, by comparison with non-institutionalized controls (summarized in Zigler, 1966).

Butterfield and Zigler (1965) studied two institutions in the same state, having identical admission policies, but very different social climates in terms of staff attitudes to rehabilitation of their charges. In one institution, all except the most severely retarded were regarded as potentially capable of returning to the community, granted adequate preparation; in the other, a custodial attitude predominated. Butterfield and Zigler found that retardates in the latter institution had a greater need for social reinforcement than had those in the former (see also, Butterfield, 1967).

Additional research yielded data supporting the following hypotheses:

(1) Institutionalized retarded children tend to have been relatively deprived of adult contact and approval, and hence have a higher motivation to secure such contact and approval than do normal children.

(2) While retarded children have a higher positive-reaction tendency than normal children, due to a higher motivation to interact with an approving adult, they also have a higher negative-reaction tendency. This higher negative-reaction tendency is the result of a wariness which stems from retarded children's more frequent negative encounters with adults.

(3) The motive structure of the institutionalized retardate is influenced by an interaction between pre-institutional social history and the effects of institutionalization. This effect is complicated by the fact that institutionalization does not constitute a homogeneous psychological variable. Instead, institutions differ, and underlying psychological features of the particular institutions must be considered before predictions can be made concerning the effects of institutionalization on any particular child.

(4) The positions of various reinforcers in a reinforcer hierarchy differ as a function of environmental events. Due to the environmental differences experienced by institutionalized retarded children, the positions of reinforcers in their reinforcer hierarchy will differ from the positions of the same reinforcers in the reinforcer hierarchy of normal children.

(5) Institutionalized retarded children have learned to expect and settle for lower degrees of success than have normal children.

(6) An inner- versus outer-directed cognitive dimension may be employed to describe differences in the characteristic mode of attacking environmentally presented problems. The inner-directed person is one who employs his own thought processes and the solutions they provide in dealing with problems. The outer-directed person is one who focuses on external cues provided either by the stimuli of the problem or other persons in the belief that such attention will provide him with a guide to action. The style which characterises the individual's approach may be viewed as a result of his past history. Individuals whose internal solutions meet with a high proportion of failures will become distrustful of their own efforts and adopt an outer-directed style in their problem-solving. Since retardates unquestionably experience a disproportionate amount of failure, they are characterized by this outer-directedness. Many behaviours that are thought to inhere in mental retardation, e.g. distractibility, may be a product of this cognitive style. (Zigler, 1966)

Zigler's position must not be misconstrued as denying cognitive deficiencies of varying degree and quality in the mentally subnormal. He is, however, persistent in his assertion that factors other than 'pure' cognition determine performance in most behavioural situations, and that research workers should attempt some control of these factors in selecting groups for comparison (Zigler, 1969). He has shown that the institutionalized retarded, when confronted with an experimental task, tend to look for cues and solutions provided by others, rather than relying on their own judgment, as the intellectually normal tend to do (Turnure and Zigler, 1964; Sanders *et al.*, 1968).

The emphasis by both Cromwell and Zigler on failure experiences as an important motivational factor find support in Zeaman's (1965) summary of his research on discrimination learning sets. 'We have, on the other hand, observed *failure sets*. Prolonged failure on difficult problems leads to an inability to solve even the easiest problems, ordinarily solved in a trial or two' (p. 112).

Gardner (1968), in a careful review of research on personality characteristics, notes the paucity of systematic studies (other than those by Cromwell and Zigler), and that the results reported in the areas of self concept and anxiety level are conflicting and inconclusive. He can see no reason why personality character-istics in the subnormal should not be studied in an objective and meaningful fashion provided that the special problems of measurements in a population characterized by language deficits can be overcome.

Overview

If the reader of this chapter expected to gain clear knowledge from experimental studies of the precise nature and extent of the retardate's deficiencies and the methods by which these can be ameliorated, he will have been disappointed. In almost every area in which the methods of experimental psychology have been applied, apparently conflicting results have been reported. The wide range of subject and situational characteristics (including age, intellectual ability, and social background), experimental techniques, stimulus material, and criterion measures that have been employed, makes a critical evaluation of the literature exceedingly difficult, and it would at present be unwise to attempt to draw many firm conclusions. There is, however, an increasing awareness of methodological problems, and an increasing sophistication in the planning of experiments, which, combined with the differing attitudes of experimenters towards the problem of subnormality should, it is to be hoped, bring about a deeper under-standing of this branch of psychology during the next decade.

The evidence summarized leads the authors to the following selective evaluation:

1. The question of whether the mentally subnormal is qualitatively deficient, due to general CNS impairment, or a retarded normal, remains to be resolved, if indeed it is susceptible of resolution. The fact that a large section of institu-tionalized populations are known to be the victims of chromosomal or metabolic defects, or conditions involving brain injury, makes the defect position tempting. There are, however, two problems: first, the fact that there is by no means clear evidence that the behaviour of diagnosed organically impaired retardates differs from matched groups in whom no impairment can be demonstrated (Haywood, 1966; Sternlicht *et al.*, 1968; Zeaman, 1965); second, that the few comparisons

made of normal with super-normal children tend to show similar differences to those between normals and the mildly subnormal (Osler and Fivel, 1961; Blake and Williams, 1968; discussed on p. 304). If the hundreds of studies comparing retarded with normal subjects were repeated, but comparing normal children (preferably from orphanages or other institutions) with superior children, it might be concluded that on the whole people with IQs above 130 are qualitatively superior to those with IQs of 100, and that the latter were inferior in CNS functioning to the former. Such a (hypothetical) conclusion might be entirely valid, but would invalidate suggestions that the majority of the mentally subnormal are to be regarded as a race apart.

Despite the persuasive evidence presented by Spitz (1967) and Winters (1969) suggesting that normal and subnormal subjects differ with respect to their perception of 'physiological' but not to 'experiential' illusions (pp. 267–8), the present authors conclude with Zeaman (1965) that the emphasis of psychological research is best directed to an examination of the laws governing the retardate's behaviour, rather than a search for unique laws (p. 262). In this connection, there is no systematic evidence suggesting that the laws governing learning, including language acquisition, or retention, are essentially different from those underlying these processes in normal human beings, or, in some cases, other animals. Zeaman and House's analysis of discrimination learning in the subnormal bears a striking similarity to that of Sutherland (1964) and Mackintosh (1965) in the field of animal behaviour. The principles of operant learning, successfully applied in many cases to the subnormal, all originated in the animal laboratory.

Baumeister and others found that, although RT is functionally related to intelligence, alteration of experimental conditions similarly affected reaction times of normals and subnormals (pp. 270–1); Sen and Clarke showed within a defective population that susceptibility to external distractors was related to task difficulty, as previously demonstrated with normal subjects (p. 273); factors affecting verbal mediation, such as meaningfulness, exposure time and free-association strength (pp. 297–8) appear on balance to apply similarly to retardate behaviour and to the normal population. Blake and Williams (p. 304) showed that methods of concept attainment did not differentiate superior, normal, and mildly retarded subjects, although there was a clear difference in levels of performance. Baumeister and Kellas (1971) have concluded that differences in verbal learning behaviour across IQ levels seem to be quantitative rather than qualitative and are best understood in terms of a developmental rather than a pathological conceptualization. Other examples could be cited from the text.

2. Altogether too much of the evidence concerning different aspects of behaviour in the subnormal is based on institutionalized samples. Since a majority of the subnormal never go to an institution, and those who do must be regarded as an unrepresentative sample (see Introduction) there is a danger that inaccurate generalizations may be made.

There is sufficient evidence suggesting that institutionalized retardates differ from non-institutionalized retardates of similar level (Kaufman, 1963, learning sets; Baumeister, 1968a, paired-associate learning; Lyle, 1959, 1960a, language; Zigler, 1966, personality and motivation) to render suspect any conclusions relating to cognitive difference based on differences between institutionalized retardates and normal subjects. Fortunately, this point seems at last to have been taken, and recent studies have tended to compare normal and subnormal children in the same schools, or retardates of different levels in the same institution or workshop.

3. Zeaman and House's (1963; Zeaman, 1965) careful analysis of retardate discrimination learning have led them to conclude that this process is mediated, not by verbal behaviour, but by attention. Discrimination learning involves a chain of at least two responses, the first being that of attending to the relevant dimension, the second being to approach the positive cue of that dimension; it is in the former aspect that retardates are deficient (this behaviour being MA-related) rather than in the latter. Learning and extinction, once the process starts, do not appear to be related to intelligence (p. 278).

4. Although studies of short-term memory greatly outnumber those on long-term retention, and there is no consensus as to whether retardates generally are inferior to MA-matched controls, as they clearly are to CA-matched on short-term memory (pp. 283–4), there do seem to be reasonable grounds for tentatively concluding that the acquisition of new material is the chief area of deficit in the subnormal, while retention of well-learned material is good (pp. 287–8).

5. The fact that subnormals often show variability of performance (Baumeister, 1968b), low degree of intercorrelation among tasks, and low correlation with intelligence test performance (Miller *et al.*, 1968) suggests either a lack of a firmly based, well-ordered repertoire of response tendencies enabling the subject to select an appropriate strategy when first confronted with a task, or fluctuating motivation to succeed, or both in combination.

Work on verbal mediation (Borkowski and Johnson, 1968; Penney *et al.*, 1968b; Gallagher, 1969) suggests that mental retardates can be shaped in the laboratory to use mediators, but the strong possibility exists that without long-term over-learning they would quickly lapse back into their lower-order response habits. Milgram (1967) found that retardates, although benefiting significantly from verbal mediation instructions, were inferior to normal controls in their long-term retention of a mediational set.

6. There is impressive evidence that retardates are particularly handicapped with respect to verbal and higher-order conceptual abilities (Alper, 1967; Belmont *et al.*, 1967; Miller *et al.*, 1968). This is to be expected, almost by definition, and may reasonably be accepted as evidence of constitutional deficits. It should, however, be immediately apparent that differences between the sub-normal and normal in these respects find a direct parallel in differences between the average and intellectually gifted, and the entire nature-nurture controversy (which will not be elaborated here) can be applied to the findings (see Introduction). It has been suggested that, even among the severely retarded,

environmental factors significantly influence the level attained (Lyle, 1959, 1960a, b).

It is equally clear from the work of many investigators, and particularly Furth and Milgram (pp. 301–2) that even fairly low-grade subnormals are not wholly devoid of conceptual categories, but that the greater the severity of defect, the greater the deficiency in *verbal formulation* of conceptual activity.

Bortner and Birch (1970) make the important point that the performance of a subnormal or normal child in a particular experimental situation does not necessarily give an accurate indication of his capacity, or of his potential for learning. These authors assert that 'it is clear that we have but begun to explore the universe of conditions for learning and performance which will facilitate most effectively the expression of the potentialities for adaptation which exist in mentally subnormal children'.

Granted that the subnormal are impaired in their ability to learn, verbalize, and abstract, the question remains open concerning the extent to which they can be made more competent in these respects. Such evidence as is available suggests that they might. On the other hand, the criticisms voiced by Watson (1967) and Gardner (1969) of studies of operant learning would with profit be borne in mind by any potential researcher in this area. Neither short-term periods of specific instruction nor blunderbuss educational programmes are likely to lead to the detailed understanding of how verbal and conceptual training of the retarded should most effectively proceed. Obvious, but frequently overlooked problems, are 'Hawthorne' effects and the personal qualities of the instructor. Both of these should be controlled in the experimental design, in addition to other variables. Research on higher cognitive processes, to be of any value, will probably need considerable financial support, and the services of a team of scientists; it seems to the present writers that it offers a most challenging and potentially interesting area for endeavour – whatever the outcome.

References

AKUTAGAWA, D. and BENOIT, E. P. (1959) The effect of age and relative brightness on associative learning in children. *Child Developm.*, **30**, 229–38.

ALLEN, M. R. and WALLACH, E. S. (1969) Word recognition and definition by educable retardates. *Amer. J. ment. Defic.*, **73**, 883–5.

ALPER, A. E. (1967) An analysis of the Wechsler Intelligence Scale for Children with institutionalized mental retardates. *Amer. J. ment. Defic.*, **71**, 624–30.

BALL, T. S. and WILSONCROFT, W. E. (1967) Perceptual-motor deficits and the phi-phenomenon. *Amer. J. ment. Defic.*, **71**, 797–800.

BALLA, D. and ZIGLER, E. (1964) Discrimination and switching learning in normal, familial retarded, and organic retarded children. *J. abn. soc. Psychol.*, **69**, 664–9.

BAUMEISTER, A. A. (1967a) Learning abilities of the mentally retarded. In BAUMEISTER, A. A. (ed.) *Mental Retardation: Appraisal, Education and Rehabilitation.* London: Univ. of London Press.

BAUMEISTER, A. A. (1967b) Problems in comparative studies of mental retardates and normals. *Amer. J. ment. Defic.*, **71**, 869–75.

BAUMEISTER, A. A. (1968a) Paired-associate learning by institutionalized and non-institutionalized retardates and normal children. *Amer. J. ment. Defic.*, **73**, 102–4.

BAUMEISTER, A. A. (1968b) Behavioral inadequacy and variability of performance. *Amer. J. ment. Defic.*, **73**, 477–83.

BAUMEISTER, A. A. and ELLIS, N. R. (1963) Delayed response performance of retardates. *Amer. J. ment. Defic.*, **67**, 714–22.

BAUMEISTER, A. A. and HAWKINS, W. F. (1967) Alpha responsiveness to photic stimulation in mental defectives. *Amer. J. ment. Defic.*, **71**, 783–6.

BAUMEISTER, A. A. and KELLAS, G. (1968a) Distributions of reaction times of retardates and normals. *Amer. J. ment. Defic.*, **72**, 715–18.

BAUMEISTER, A. A. and KELLAS, G. (1968b) Intrasubject response variability in relation to intelligence. *J. abn. Psychol.*, **73**, 421–3.

BAUMEISTER, A. A. and KELLAS, G. (1968c) Reaction time and mental retardation. In ELLIS, N. R. (ed.) *International Review of Research in Mental Retardation*, Vol. 3. New York: Academic Press.

BAUMEISTER, A. A. and KELLAS, G. (1971) Process variables in the paired-associate learning of retardates. In ELLIS, N. R. (ed.) *International Review of Research in Mental Retardation*. New York: Academic Press.

BAUMEISTER, A. A. and KLOSOWSKI, R. (1965) An attempt to group toilet train severely retarded patients. *Ment. Retard.*, **3**, 24–6.

BAUMEISTER, A. A. and WARD, L. C. (1967) Effects of rewards upon the reaction time of mental defectives. *Amer. J. ment. Defic.*, **71**, 801–5.

BAUMEISTER, A. A., HAWKINS, W. F. and HOLLAND, J. M. (1967) Retroactive inhibition in short-term recall in normals and retardates. *Amer. J. ment. Defic.*, **72**, 253–6.

BAUMEISTER, A. A., HAWKINS, W. F. and KELLAS, G. (1965a) The inter-active effects of stimulus intensity and intelligence upon reaction time. *Amer. J. ment. Defic.*, **69**, 526–30.

BAUMEISTER, A. A., HAWKINS, W. F. and KELLAS, G. (1965b) Reaction speed as a function of stimulus intensity in normals and retardates. *Percept. mot. Skills*, **20**, 649–52.

BAUMEISTER, A. A., HAWKINS, W. F. and KOENINGSKNECHT, R. (1965c) Effects of variation in complexity of the warning signal upon reaction time. *Amer. J. ment. Defic.*, **69**, 860–4.

BAUMEISTER, A. A., SPAIN, C. J. and ELLIS, N. R. (1963) A note on alpha block duration in normals and retardates. *Amer. J. ment. Defic.*, **67**, 723–5.

BAUMEISTER, A. A., WILCOX, S. and GREESON, J. (1969) Reaction times of retardates and normals as a function of relative stimulus frequency. *Amer. J. ment. Defic.*, **73**, 935–41.

BAUMEISTER, A. A., URQUHART, D., BEEDLE, R. and SMITH, T. E. (1964) Reaction time of normals and retardates under different stimulus intensity changes. *Amer. J. ment. Defic.*, **69**, 126–30.

BEIER, E. G., STARKWEATHER, J. A. and LAMBERT, M. J. (1969) Vocabulary usage of mentally retarded children. *Amer. J. ment. Defic.*, **73**, 927–34.

BELMONT, I., BIRCH, H. G. and BELMONT, L. (1967) The organization of intelligence test performance in educable mentally subnormal children. *Amer. J. ment. Defic.*, **71**, 969–76.

BELMONT, J. M. (1966) Long term memory in mental retardation. In ELLIS, N. R. (ed.) *International Review of Research in Mental Retardation*, Vol. I. New York: Academic Press.

BELMONT, J. M. and ELLIS, N. R. (1968) Effects of extraneous stimulation upon discrimination learning in normals and retardates. *Amer. J. ment. Defic.*, **72**, 525–32.

BENSBERG, G. J., COLWELL, C. N. and CASSEL, R. H. (1965) Teaching the profoundly retarded self-help activities by behavior shaping techniques. *Amer. J. ment. Defic.*, **69**, 674–9.

BERCH, D. (1967) *Comparison of Training Methods in Effective Utilization of High-Level Associative Strategies.* Unpubl. paper presented at the 91st Annual Convention, Amer. Assoc. on Ment. Defic., Denver, Colorado.

BERKSON, G. (1960a) An analysis of reaction time in normal and mentally deficient young men. II. Variation of complexity in reaction time tasks. *J. ment. Defic. Res.*, **4**, 59–67.

BERKSON, G. (1960b) An analysis of reaction time in normal and mentally deficient young men. III. Variation of stimulus and of response complexity. *J. ment. Defic. Res.*, **4**, 69–77.

BERKSON, G. (1963) Psychophysiological studies in mental deficiency. In ELLIS, N. R. (ed.) *Handbook of Mental Deficiency.* New York: McGraw-Hill.

BERKSON, G. and BAUMEISTER, A. A. (1967) Reaction time variability of mental defectives and normals. *Amer. J. ment. Defic.*, **72**, 262–6.

BERKSON, G. and CANTOR, G. N. (1960) A study of mediation in mentally retarded and normal school children. *J. educ. Psychol.*, **51**, 82–6.

BERKSON, G., HERMELIN, B. and O'CONNOR, N. (1961) Physiological responses of normals and institutionalized mental defectives to repeated stimuli. *J. ment. Defic. Res.*, **5**, 30–9.

BIJOU, S. W. (1963) Theory and research in mental (developmental) retardation. *Psychol. Rec.*, **13**, 95–110.

BIJOU, S. W. (1966) A functional analysis of retarded development. In

ELLIS, N. R. (ed.) *International Review of Research in Mental Retardation*, Vol. 1. New York: Academic Press.

BLAKE, K. A. (1960) Direct learning and transfer. In JOHNSON, G. O. and BLAKE, K. A. (eds.) *Learning Performance of Retarded and Normal Children*. New York: Syracuse Univ. Press.

BLAKE, K. A. and WILLIAMS, C. L. (1968) Induction and deduction and retarded, normal and superior subjects' concept attainment. *Amer. J. ment. Defic.*, **73**, 226–31.

BLOUNT, W. R. (1968) Concept usage research with the mentally retarded. *Psychol. Bull.*, **69**, 281–94.

BLOUNT, W. R. (1969) Language and the more severely retarded: a review. *Amer. J. ment. Defic.*, **73**, 21–9.

BLUE, C. M. (1963) Performance of normal and retarded subjects on a modified paired-associate task. *Amer. J. ment. Defic.*, **68**, 228–34.

BORKOWSKI, J. G. and JOHNSON, L. O. (1968) Mediation and the paired-associate learning of normals and retardates. *Amer. J. ment. Defic.*, **72**, 610–13.

BORTNER, M. and BIRCH, H. G. (1960) Perception and perceptual-motor dissociation in cerebral palsied children. *J. nerv. ment. Dis.*, **130**, 49–53.

BORTNER, M. and BIRCH, H. G. (1970) Cognitive capacity and cognitive competence. *Amer. J. ment. Defic.*, **74**, 735–44.

BOUSFIELD, W. A. (1953) The occurrence of clustering in the recall of randomly arranged associates. *J. gen. Psychol.*, **49**, 229–40.

BROADBENT, D. E. (1954) The role of auditory localization in attention and memory span. *J. exp. Psychol.*, **47**, 191–6.

BROADBENT, D. E. (1958) *Perception and Communication*. Oxford: Pergamon.

BRYANT, P. E. (1964) The effect of a verbal instruction on transfer in normal and severely subnormal children. *J. ment. Defic. Res.*, **8**, 35–43.

BRYANT, P. E. (1965a) The transfer of positive and negative learning by normal and severely subnormal children. *Brit. J. Psychol.*, **56**, 81–6.

BRYANT, P. E. (1965b) The effects of verbal labelling on recall and recognition in severely subnormal and normal children. *J. ment. Defic. Res.*, **9**, 229–36.

BRYANT, P. E. (1967a) Verbal labelling and learning strategies in normal and severely subnormal children. *Quart. J. exp. Psychol.*, **19**, 155–61.

BRYANT, P. E. (1967b) Verbalisation and immediate memory of complex stimuli in normal and severely subnormal children. *Brit. J. soc. clin. Psychol.*, **6**, 212–19.

BRYANT, P. E. (1968) Practical implications of studies of transfer. In RICHARDS, B. (ed.) *Proc. 1st Congr. Internat. Assoc. Scient. Stud. ment. Defic.*, 865–8. Reigate: Michael Jackson.

BUDOFF, M., MESKIN, J. D. and KEMLER, D. J. (1968) Training productive thinking of E.M.R.'s: a failure to replicate. *Amer. J. ment. Defic.*, **73**, 195–9.

BULGARELLA, R. (1967) *Conditionability of Associative Strategies among Educable Retardates.* Unpubl. paper presented at the 91st Annual Convention Amer. Assoc. on Ment. Defic., Denver, Colorado.

BUTLER, A. J. and CONRAD, W. G. (1964) Psychological correlates of abnormal electroencephalographic patterns in familial retardates. *J. clin. Psychol.*, **20**, 338–43.

BUTTERFIELD, E. C. (1967) The role of environmental factors in the treatment of institutionalized mental retardates. In BAUMEISTER, A. A. (ed.) *Mental Retardation: Appraisal, Education and Rehabilitation.* London: Univ. of London Press.

BUTTERFIELD, E. C. (1968a) Serial learning and the stimulus trace theory of mental retardation. *Amer. J. ment. Defic.*, **72**, 778–87.

BUTTERFIELD, E. C. (1968b) Stimulus trace in the mentally retarded: defect or developmental lag? *J. abn. Psychol.*, **73**, 358–62.

BUTTERFIELD, E. C. and ZIGLER, E. (1965) The influence of differing institutional social climates on the effectiveness of social reinforcement in the mentally retarded. *Amer. J. ment. Defic.*, **70**, 48–56.

CANTOR, G. N. and RYAN, T. J. (1962) Retention of verbal paired-associates in normals and retardates. *Amer. J. ment. Defic.*, **66**, 861–5.

CARRIER, N. A., MALPASS, L. F. and ORTON, K. D. (1961) *Responses of Bright, Normal, and Retarded Children to Learning Tasks.* Office of Education Co-operative Project No. 578. Carbondale: Southern Illinois Univ.

CIEUTAT, V., STOCKWELL, F. and NOBLE, C. (1958) The interaction of ability and amount of practice with stimulus and response meaningfulness (m, m') in paired-associate learning. *J. exp. Psychol.*, **56**, 193–202.

CLARKE, A. D. B. (1962) Laboratory and workshop studies of imbecile learning processes. *Proc. Lond. Conf. Scient. Stud. Ment. Defic.*, **1**, 89–96.

CLARKE, A. D. B. and BLAKEMORE, C. B. (1961) Age and perceptual-motor transfer in imbeciles. *Brit. J. Psychol.*, **52**, 125–31.

CLARKE, A. D. B. and COOKSON, M. (1962) Perceptual-motor transfer in imbeciles: a second series of experiments. *Brit. J. Psychol.*, **53**, 321–30.

CLARKE, A. D. B. and COOPER, G. M. (1966) Age and perceptual-motor transfer in imbeciles: task complexity as a variable. *Brit. J. Psychol.*, **57**, 113–19.

CLARKE, A. M., CLARKE, A. D. B. and COOPER, G. M. (1967a) Learning transfer and cognitive development. In ZUBIN, J. and JERVIS, G. (eds.) *Psychopathology of Mental Development.* New York: Grune & Stratton.

CLARKE, A. M., CLARKE, A. D. B. and COOPER, G. M. (1970) The development of a set to perceive categorical relations. In HAYWOOD, H. C. (ed.) *Social-Cultural Aspects of Mental Retardation.* New York: Appleton-Century-Crofts.

CLARKE, A. M., COOPER, G. M. and CLARKE, A. D. B. (1967b) Task complexity and transfer in the development of cognitive structures. *J. exp. Child Psychol.*, **5**, 562–76.

CLARKE, A. M., COOPER, G. M. and HENNEY, A. S. (1966) Width of transfer and task complexity in the conceptual learning of imbeciles. *Brit. J. Psychol.*, **57**, 121–8.

CLEVENGER, L. J. (1966) Electroencephalographic studies relating to mental retardation. *Ment. Retard. Abstrs.*, **3**, 170–8.

CORTER, H. M. and MCKINNEY, J. D. (1968) Flexibility training with educable retarded and bright normal children. *Amer. J. ment. Defic.*, **72**, 603–9.

CROMWELL, R. L. (1963) A social learning approach to mental retardation. In ELLIS, N. R. (ed.) *Handbook of Mental Deficiency*. New York: McGraw-Hill.

CROMWELL, R. L., BAUMEISTER, A. A. and HAWKINS, W. F. (1963) Research in activity level. In ELLIS, N. R. (ed.) *Handbook of Mental Deficiency*. New York: McGraw-Hill.

DEESE, J. (1958) *The Psychology of Learning*. New York: McGraw-Hill.

DEICH, R. (1968) Reproduction and recognition as indices of perceptual impairment. *Amer. J. ment. Defic.*, **73**, 9–12.

DENT, H. E. (1968) Operant conditioning as a tool in the habilitation of the mentally retarded. In RICHARDS, B. (ed.) *Proc. 1st Congr. Internat. Assoc. Scient. Stud. Ment. Defic.*, 873–6. Reigate: Michael Jackson.

DILLER, L. and BIRCH, H. G. (1964) Psychological evaluation of children with cerebral damage. In BIRCH, H. G. (ed.) *Brain Damage in Children*. New York: Williams & Wilkins.

DOUBROS, S. G. (1966) Behavior therapy with high level, institutionalized retarded adolescents. *Except. Child.*, **33**, 229–33.

DOYLE, M. (1967) Perceptual skill development – a possible resource for the intellectually handicapped. *Amer. J. ment. Defic.*, **71**, 776–82.

EISMAN, B. (1958) Paired associate learning, generalization, and retention as a function of intelligence. *Amer. J. ment. Defic.*, **63**, 481–9.

ELKIND, D. (1961) Children's conception of right and left: Piaget replication study IV. *J. genet. Psychol.*, **99**, 269–76.

ELKIND, D. (1962) Children's conception of brother and sister: Piaget replication study V. *J. genet. Psychol.*, **100**, 129–36.

ELLINGSON, R. J. (1966) Relationship between E.E.G. and test intelligence: a commentary. *Psychol. Bull.*, **65**, 91–8.

ELLIS, N. R. (1958) Object-quality discrimination learning sets in mental defectives. *J. comp. physiol. Psychol.*, **51**, 79–81.

ELLIS, N. R. (1963) The stimulus trace and behavioral inadequacy. In ELLIS, N. R. (ed.) *Handbook of Mental Deficiency*. New York: McGraw-Hill.

ELLIS, N. R. (1969) A behavioral research strategy in mental retardation: defense and critique. *Amer. J. ment. Defic.*, **73**, 557–66.

ELLIS, N. R. (1971) Memory processes in retardates and normals. In ELLIS, N. R. (ed.) *International Review of Research in Mental Retardation,* Vol. 4. New York: Academic Press.

ELLIS, N. R. and ANDERS, T. R. (1968) Short-term memory in the mental retardate. *Amer. J. ment. Defic.,* **72,** 931–6.

ELLIS, N. R. and MUNGER, M. (1966) Short-term memory in normal children and mental retardates. *Psychon. Sci.,* **6,** 381–2.

ELLIS, N. R. and SLOAN, W. (1957) Relationship between intelligence and simple reaction time in mental defectives. *Percept. mot. Skills,* **7,** 65–7.

ELLIS, N. R. and SLOAN, W. (1959) Oddity learning as a function of mental age. *J. comp. physiol. Psychol.,* **52,** 228–30.

ELLIS, N. R., GIRARDEAU, F. L. and PRYER, M. W. (1962) Analysis of learning sets in normal and severely defective humans. *J. comp. physiol. Psychol.,* **55,** 860–5.

ELLIS, N. R., HAWKINS, W. F., PRYER, M. W. and JONES, R. W. (1963) Distraction effects in oddity learning by normal and mentally defective humans. *Amer. J. ment. Defic.,* **67,** 576–83.

EVANS, R. A. (1964) Word recall and associative clustering in mental retardates. *Amer. J. ment. Defic.,* **69,** 413–18.

FEDIO, P. M., MIRSKY, A. F., SMITH, W. J. and PARRY, D. (1961) Reaction time and E.E.G. activation in normal and schizophrenic subjects. *Electroencephalog. Clin. Neurophysiol.,* **13,** 923–6.

FURTH, H. G. (1961) The influence of language on the development of concept formation in deaf children. *J. abn. soc. Psychol.,* **63,** 386–9.

FURTH, H. G. and MILGRAM, N. A. (1965) The influence of language on classification: a theoretical model applied to normal, retarded and deaf children. *Genet. Psychol. Monogr.,* **72,** 317–51.

FURTH, H. G. and YOUNISS, J. (1964) Colour-object paired-associates in deaf and hearing children with and without response competition. *J. consult. Psychol.,* **28,** 224–7.

GALLAGHER, J. W. (1969) Mediation as a function of associative chains in normal and retarded children. *Amer. J. ment. Defic.,* **73,** 886–9.

GARDNER, J. M. (1969) Behavior modification research in mental retardation: search for an adequate paradigm. *Amer. J. ment. Defic.,* **73,** 844–51.

GARDNER, J. M. and WATSON, L. S. (1969) Behavior modification of the mentally retarded: an annotated bibliography. *Ment. Retard. Abstrs.,* **6,** 181–93.

GARDNER, W. I. (1968) Personality characteristics of the mentally retarded: review and critique. In PREHM, H. J., HAMERLYNCK, L. A. and CROSSON, J. E. (eds.) *Behavioral Research in Mental Retardation.* Corvallis: Oregon State Univ.

GAUDREAU, J. (1968) Interrelations among perception, learning ability and intelligence in mentally deficient school children. *J. learning Dis.,***1,** 301–6.

GERJUOY, I. R. and ALVAREZ, J. M. (1969) Transfer of learning in associative clustering of retardates and normals. *Amer. J. ment. Defic.*, **73**, 733–8.

GERJUOY, I. R. and SPITZ, H. H. (1966) Associative clustering in free recall: intellectual and developmental variables. *Amer. J. ment. Defic.*, **70**, 918–27.

GILES, I. K. and WOLF, M. M. (1966) Toilet training institutionalized, severe retardates: an application of operant behavior modification techniques. *Amer. J. ment. Defic.*, **70**, 766–80.

GIRARDEAU, F. L. (1959) The formation of discrimination learning sets in mongoloid and normal children. *J. comp. physiol. Psychol.*, **52**, 566–70.

GIRARDEAU, F. L. and ELLIS, N. R. (1964) Rote verbal learning by normal and mentally retarded children. *Amer. J. ment. Defic.*, **68**, 525–32.

GIRARDEAU, F. L. and SPRADLIN, J. E. (1964) Token rewards in a cottage program. *Ment. Retard.*, **2**, 345–51.

GOLDSTEIN, H. (1964) Social and occupational adjustment. In STEVENS, H. A. and HEBER, R. (eds.) *Mental Retardation*. Chicago: Univ. of Chicago Press.

GOLDSTEIN, K. and SCHEERER, M. (1941) Abstract and concrete behavior: an experimental study with special tests. *Psychol. Monogr.*, **53**, 25–42.

GORDON, M. C. (1968) Some effects of stimulus presentation rate and complexity on perception and retention. *Amer. J. ment. Defic.*, **73**, 437–45.

GORTON, C. E. and HOLLIS, J. H. (1965) Redesigning a cottage unit for better programming and research for the severely retarded. *Ment. Retard.*, **3**, 16–21.

GOULET, L. R. (1968) Verbal learning and memory research with retardates: an attempt to assess developmental trends. In ELLIS, N. R. (ed.) *International Review of Research in Mental Retardation*, Vol. 3. New York: Academic Press.

GOZALI, J. (1969) Impulsivity-reflectivity as problem solving styles among educable mentally retarded children. *Amer. J. ment. Defic.*, **73**, 864–7.

GRIFFITH, B. C. (1960) The use of verbal mediators in concept formation by retarded subjects at different intelligence levels. *Child Developm.*, **31**, 633–41.

GRIFFITH, B. C. and SPITZ, H. H. (1958) Some relationships between abstraction and word meaning in retarded adolescents. *Amer. J. ment. Defic.*, **63**, 247–51.

GRIFFITH, B. C., SPITZ, H. H. and LIPMAN, R. S. (1959) Verbal mediation and concept formation in retarded and normal subjects. *J. exp. Psychol.*, **58**. 247–51.

HAMILTON, J. W. and STEPHENS, L. Y. (1967) Reinstating speech in an emotionally disturbed, mentally retarded young woman. *J. speech hear. Dis.*, **32**, 383–9.

HAMILTON, J., STEPHENS, L. and ALLEN, P. (1967) Controlling aggressive and destructive behavior in severely retarded institutionalized residents. *Amer. J. ment. Defic.*, **71**, 852–6.

HARLOW, H. F. (1949) The formation of learning sets. *Psychol. Rev.*, **56**, 51–65.

HARVEY, A., YEP, B. and SELLIN, D. (1966) Developmental achievement of trainable mentally retarded children. *Training School Bull.*, **63**, 100–8.

HAWKINS, W. F., BAUMEISTER, A. A., KOENINGSKNECHT, R. A. and KELLAS, G. (1965) Simple and disjunctive reaction times of normals and retardates. *Amer. J. ment. Defic.*, **69**, 536–40.

HAYES, K. J. (1953) The backward curve: a method for the study of learning. *Psychol. Rev.*, **60**, 269–75.

HAYES, K. J., THOMPSON, R. and HAYES, C. (1953) Discrimination learning sets in chimpanzees. *J. comp. physiol. Psychol.*, **46**, 99–104.

HAYWOOD, H. C. (1966) Perceptual handicap: fact or artifact? *Ment. Retard.* (Canada), **16**, 9–16.

HAYWOOD, H. C. and HEAL, L. W. (1968) Retention of learned visual associations as a function of I.Q. and learning levels. *Amer. J. ment. Defic.*, **72**, 828–38.

HEAL, L. W., ROSS, L. E. and SANDERS, B. (1966) Reversal and partial reversal in mental defectives and normal children of a comparable mental age. *Amer. J. ment. Defic.*, **71**, 411–16.

HEBER, R. (1964) Personality. In STEVENS, H. A. and HEBER, R. (eds.) *Mental Retardation.* Chicago: Univ. of Chicago Press.

HEBER, R., PREHM, H., NARDI, G. and SIMPSON, N. (1962) *Learning and Retention of Retarded and Normal Children on a Paired-Associate Task.* Paper read at the Annual Meeting, Amer. Assoc. on Ment. Defic., New York.

HENRIKSEN, K. and DOUGHTY, R. (1967) Decelerating undesired meal time behavior in a group of profoundly retarded boys. *Amer. J. ment. Defic.*, **72**, 40–4.

HERMELIN, B. F. and O'CONNOR, N. (1964) Short-term memory in normal and subnormal children. *Amer. J. ment. Defic.*, **69**, 121–5.

HERMELIN, B. F. and VENABLES, P. H. (1964) Reaction time and alpha blocking in normal and severely subnormal subjects. *J. exp. Psychol.*, **67**, 365–72.

HOHN, R. (1967) *Facilitation in Associative Learning Ability among Educable Retardates.* Unpubl. paper presented at the 91st Annual Convention, Amer. Assoc. on Ment. Defic., Denver, Colorado.

HOLDEN, E. A. Jr. (1965) Reaction time during unimodal and trimodal stimulation in educable retardates. *J. ment. Defic. Res.*, **9**, 183–90.

HOLDEN, E. A. Jr. (1971) Sequential dot presentation measures of stimulus trace in retardates and normals. In ELLIS, N. R. (ed.) *International*

Review of Research in Mental Retardation, Vol. 5. New York: Academic Press.

HOUSE, B. J. (1964) The effect of distinctive responses on discrimination reversals in retardates. *Amer. J. ment. Defic.*, **69**, 79–85.

HOUSE, B. J. and ZEAMAN, D. (1959) Position discrimination and reversals in low-grade retardates. *J. comp. physiol. Psychol.*, **52**, 564–5.

HOUSE, B. J. and ZEAMAN, D. (1962) Reversal and non-reversal shifts in discrimination learning in retardates. *J. exp. Psychol.*, **63**, 444–51.

HOUSE, B. J. and ZEAMAN, D. (1963) Miniature experiments in the discrimination learning of retardates. In LIPSITT, L. P. and SPIKER, C. C. (eds.) *Advances in Child Development and Behavior*. New York: Academic Press.

HUNDZIAK, M., MAURER, R. A. and WATSON, L. S. (1965) Operant conditioning in toilet training of severely mentally retarded boys. *Amer. J. ment. Defic.*, **70**, 120–4.

HUTT, S. J. and HUTT, C. (1964) Hyperactivity in a group of epileptic (and some non-epileptic) brain damaged children. *Epilepsia J.*, **5**, 334–51.

JENSEN, A. R. (1965) Rote learning in retarded adults and normal children. *Amer. J. ment. Defic.*, **69**, 828–34.

JENSEN, A. R. and ROHWER, W. D. (1963) The effect of verbal mediation on the learning and retention of paired-associates by retarded adults. *Amer. J. ment. Defic.*, **68**, 80–4.

JOHNSON, G. O. (1958) *Comparative Studies of Some Learning Characteristics in Mentally Retarded and Normal Children of the Same Mental Age*. Syracuse, NY: Syracuse Univ. Press.

KAGAN, J. (1966) A developmental approach to conceptual growth. In KLAUSMEIER, H. J. and HARRIS, C. W. (eds.) *Analysis of Concept Learning*. New York: Academic Press.

KARLIN, I. W. and STRAZZULLA, M. (1952) Speech and language problems of mentally deficient children. *J. speech hear. Dis.*, **17**, 286–94.

KAUFMAN, M. E. (1963) The formation of a learning set in institutionalized and non-institutionalized mental defectives. *Amer. J. ment. Defic.*, **67**, 601–5.

KAUFMAN, M. E. and PREHM, H. J. (1966) A review of research on learning sets and transfer of training in mental defectives. In ELLIS, N. R. (ed.) *International Review of Research in Mental Retardation*, Vol. 2. New York: Academic Press.

KENDLER, T. S. and KENDLER, H. H. (1959) Reversal and non-reversal shifts in kindergarten children. *J. exp. Psychol.*, **58**, 56–60.

KENDLER, T. S., KENDLER, H. H. and WELLS, D. (1960) Reversal and non-reversal shifts in nursery school children. *J. comp. physiol. Psychol.*, **53**, 83–8.

KEPPEL, G. (1965) Problems of method in the study of short-term memory. *Psychol. Bull.*, **63**, 1–13.

KERR, N., MEYERSON, L. and MICHAEL, J. (1965) A procedure for shaping vocalizations in a mute child. In ULLMAN, L. P. and KRASNER, L. (eds.) *Case Studies in Behavior Modification*. New York: Holt, Rinehart & Winston.

KLAUSMEIER, H. J., FELDHUSEN, J. and CHECK, J. (1959) *An Analysis of Learning Efficiency in Arithmetic of Mentally Retarded Children in Comparison with Children of Average and High Intelligence*. Madison: Univ. of Wisconsin Press.

KÖHLER, W. and WALLACH, H. (1944) Figural aftereffects: an investigation of visual processes. *Proc. Amer. Phil. Soc.*, 88, 269–357.

KOLSTOE, O. P. (1958) Language training of low grade mongoloid children. *Amer. J. ment. Defic.*, 63, 17–30.

KOUW, W. A. (1968) Effects of stimulus intensity and duration upon retardates' short-term memory. *Amer. J. ment. Defic.*, 72, 734–9.

KROP, H. D. and SMITH, C. R. (1969) Effects of special education on Bender-Gestalt performance of the mentally retarded. *Amer. J. ment. Defic.*, 73, 693–9.

LANCE, W. D. (1965) Effects of meaningfulness and overlearning on retention in normal and retarded adolescents. *Amer. J. ment. Defic.*, 70, 270–5.

LANSING, R. W., SCHWARTZ, E. and LINDSLEY, D. B. (1959) Reaction time and E.E.G. activation under alerted and non-alerted conditions. *J. exp. Psychol.*, 58, 1–7.

LELAND, H. (1969) The relationship between 'intelligence' and mental retardation. *Amer. J. ment. Defic.*, 73, 533–5.

LENNEBERG, E. H. (1962) Understanding language without ability to speak. *J. abn. soc. Psychol.*, 65, 419–25.

LENNEBERG, E. H. (1967) *Biological Foundation of Language*. New York: Wiley.

LENNEBERG, E. H., NICHOLS, I. A. and ROSENBERGER, E. F. (1964) Primitive stages of language development in mongolism. In *Disorders of Communication*, Vol. XLII. Res. Publ. Assoc. Res. Nerv. Ment. D.B.

LIPMAN, R. S. (1963) Learning: verbal, perceptual-motor, and classical conditioning. In ELLIS, N. R. (ed.) *Handbook of Mental Deficiency*. New York: McGraw-Hill.

LURIA, A. R. (1961) *The Role of Speech in the Regulation of Normal and Abnormal Behaviour*. Oxford: Pergamon.

LURIA, A. R. and VINOGRADOVA, O. S. (1959) An objective investigation of the dynamics of semantic systems. *Brit. J. Psychol.*, 50, 89–105.

LYLE, J. G. (1959) The effect of an institution environment upon the verbal development of imbecile children: I. Verbal intelligence. *J. ment. Defic. Res.*, 3, 122–8.

LYLE, J. G. (1960a) The effect of an institution environment upon the verbal development of imbecile children: II. Speech and language. *J. ment. Defic. Res.*, **4**, 1–13.

LYLE, J. G. (1960b) The effect of an institution environment upon the verbal development of imbecile children: III. The Brooklands residential family unit. *J. ment. Defic. Res.*, **4**, 14–23.

LYLE, J. G. (1961) A comparison of the verbal intelligence of normal and imbecile children. *J. genet. Psychol.*, **99**, 227–34.

MCCONNEL, T. R., CROMWELL, R. L., BIALER, I. and SON, C. D. (1964) Studies in activity level VII. *Amer. J. ment. Defic.*, **68**, 647–51.

MCCRARY, J. W. and HUNTER, W. S. (1953) Serial position curves in verbal learning. *Science*, **117**, 131–4.

MACKINTOSH, N. J. (1965) Selective attention in animal discrimination learning. *Psychol. Bull.*, **64**, 124–50.

MCMANIS, D. L. (1965) Relative errors with serial lists of different lengths. *Amer. J. ment. Defic.*, **70**, 125–8.

MCMANIS, D. L. (1966) The von Restorff effect in serial learning by normal and retarded subjects. *Amer. J. ment. Defic.*, **70**, 569–75.

MCMANIS, D. L. (1968) Relative thinking by retardates. *Amer. J. ment. Defic.*, **73**, 484–92.

MCMANIS, D. L. (1969a) Intralist differentiation and the isolation effect in serial learning by normals and retardates. *Amer. J. ment. Defic.*, **73**, 819–25.

MCMANIS, D. L. (1969b) Conservation of mass, weight, and volume by normal and retarded children. *Amer. J. ment. Defic.*, **73**, 762–7.

MCMANIS, D. L. (1969c) Conservation and transitivity of weight and length by normals and retardates. *Developm. Psychol.*, **1**, 373–82.

MACCOBY, E. E. (1964) Developmental psychology. *Ann. Rev. Psychol.*, **15**, 203–50.

MADSEN, M. C. (1963) Distribution of practice and level of intelligence. *Psychol. Rep.*, **13**, 39–42.

MADSEN, M. C. (1966) Individual differences and temporal factors in memory consolidation. *Amer. J. ment. Defic.*, **71**, 501–7.

MADSEN, M. C. and CONNOR, K. J. (1968) Categorization and information reduction in short-term memory at two levels of intelligence. *Amer. J. ment. Defic.*, **73**, 232–8.

MARTIN, C. J., BOERSMA, F. J. and BULGARELLA, R. (1968) Verbalization of associative strategies by normal and retarded children. *J. gen. Psychol.*, **78**, 209–18.

MARTIN, C. J., BOERSMA, F. J. and COX, D. L. (1965) A classification of associative strategies in paired associate learning. *Psychon. Sci.*, **3**, 455–6.

MEIN, R. (1961) A study of the oral vocabularies of severely subnormal patients: II. Grammatical analysis of speech samples. *J. ment. Defic. Res.*, **5**, 52–9.

MEIN, R. and O'CONNOR, N. (1960) A study of the oral vocabularies of severely subnormal patients. *J. ment. Defic. Res.*, **4**, 130–43.

MILGRAM, N. A. (1966) Verbalization and conceptual classification in trainable mentally retarded children. *Amer. J. ment. Defic.*, **70**, 763–5.

MILGRAM, N. A. (1967) Retention of mediation set in paired-associate learning of normal children and retardates. *J. exp. Child Psychol.*, **5**, 341–9.

MILGRAM, N. A. (1968) The effect of verbal mediation in paired-associate learning in trainable retardates. *Amer. J. ment. Defic.*, **72**, 518–24.

MILGRAM, N. A. (1969) The rational and irrational in Zigler's motivational approach to mental retardation. *Amer. J. ment. Defic.*, **73**, 527–31.

MILGRAM, N. A. and FURTH, H. G. (1963) The influence of language on concept attainment in educable retarded children. *Amer. J. ment. Defic.*, **67**, 733–9.

MILGRAM, N. A. and FURTH, H. G. (1964) Position reversal versus dimension reversal in normal and retarded children. *Child Developm.*, **35**, 701–8.

MILGRAM, N. A. and FURTH, H. G. (1966) Response competition in paired associate learning by educable and trainable retarded children. *Amer. J. ment. Defic.*, **70**, 849–54.

MILLER, G. A. (1956) The magical number seven, plus or minus two: some limits on our capacity for processing information. *Psychol. Rev.*, **63**, 81–97.

MILLER, G. A., GALANTER, E. and PRIBRAM, K. (1960) *Plans and the Structure of Behavior*. New York: Holt, Rinehart & Winston.

MILLER, L. K., HALE, G. A. and STEVENSON, H. W. (1968) Learning and problem solving by retarded and normal Ss. *Amer. J. ment. Defic.*, **72**, 681–90.

MILLER, M. B. and GRIFFITH, B. C. (1961) The effects of training verbal associates on the performance of a conceptual task. *Amer. J. ment. Defic.*, **66**, 270–6.

MORDOCK, J. B. (1968) Paired associate learning in mental retardation: a review. *Amer. J. ment. Defic.*, **72**, 857–65.

NEUFELDT, A. H. (1966) Short-term memory in the mentally retarded: an application of the dichotic listening technique. *Psychol. Monogr.*, **80**, 1–31.

NOBLE, C. E. and MCKEELY, D. A. (1957) The rôle of meaningfulness (m') in paired-associate verbal learning. *J. exp. Psychol.*, **53**, 16–22.

O'CONNOR, N. and HERMELIN, B. F. (1959) Discrimination and reversal learning in imbeciles. *J. abn. soc. Psychol.*, **59**, 409–13.

O'CONNOR, N. and HERMELIN, B. F. (1963a) Recall in normals and subnormals of like mental age. *J. abn. soc. Psychol.*, **66**, 81–4.

O'CONNOR, N. and HERMELIN, B. F. (1963b) *Speech and Thought in Severe Subnormality*. Oxford: Pergamon.

O'CONNOR, N. and HERMELIN, B. F. (1965) Input restriction and immediate memory decay in normal and subnormal children. *Quart. J. exp. Psychol.*, **17**, 323–8.

ORLANSKY, J. (1940) The effect of similarity and difference in form on apparent visual movement. *Arch. Psychol.*, **246**, 85.

OSBORN, W. J. (1960) Associative clustering in organic and familial retardates. *Amer. J. ment. Defic.*, **65**, 351–7.

OSLER, S. F. and FIVEL, M. W. (1961) Concept attainment: I. The rôle of age and intelligence in concept attainment by induction. *J. exp. Psychol.*, **62**, 1–8.

OSLER, S. F. and TRAUTMAN, G. E. (1961) Concept attainment: II. Effect of stimulus complexity upon concept attainment at two levels of intelligence. *J. exp. Psychol.*, **62**, 9–13.

PASCAL, G. R. (1953) The effect of a disturbing noise on the reaction time of mental defectives. *Amer. J. ment. Defic.*, **57**, 691–9.

PENNEY, R. K., SEIM, R. and PETERS, R. de V. (1968a) The mediational deficiency of mentally retarded children: I. The establishment of retardates' mediational deficiency. *Amer. J. ment. Defic.*, **72**, 626–30.

PENNEY, R. K., PETERS, R. de V. and WILLOWS, D. M. (1968b) The mediational deficiency of mentally retarded children: II. Learning set's effect on mediational deficiency. *Amer. J. ment. Defic.*, **73**, 262–6.

PIAGET, J. (1928) *Judgement and Reasoning in the Child*. London: Routledge & Kegan Paul.

PLENDERLEITH, M. (1956) Discrimination learning and discrimination reversal learning in normal and feeble minded children. *J. genet. Psychol.*, **88**, 107–12.

PREHM, H. J. (1966a) Associative learning in retarded and normal children as a function of task difficulty and meaningfulness. *Amer. J. ment. Defic.*, **70**, 860–5.

PREHM, H. J. (1966b) Verbal learning research in mental retardation. *Amer. J. ment. Defic.*, **71**, 42–7.

PREHM, H. J. (1968) Rote verbal learning and memory in the retarded. In PREHM, H. J., HAMERLYNCK, L. A. and CROSSON, J. E. (eds.) *Behavioral Research in Mental Retardation*. Corvallis: Oregon State Univ.

PRYER, R. S. (1960) Retroactive inhibition in normals and defectives as a function of temporal position of the interpolated task. *Amer. J. ment. Defic.*, **64**, 1004–11.

RIEBER, M. (1964) Verbal mediation in normal and retarded children. *Amer. J. ment. Defic.*, **68**, 634–41.

RING, E. M. and PALERMO, D. S. (1961) Paired associate learning of retarded and normal children. *Amer. J. ment. Defic.*, **66**, 100–7.

ROHWER, W. D. and LYNCH, S. (1968) Retardation, school strata, and learning proficiency. *Amer. J. ment. Defic.*, **73**, 91–6.

ROOS, P. (1965) Development of an intensive habit training unit at Austin State School. *Ment. Retard.*, **3**, 12–15.

ROSENBERG, S. (1963) Problem-solving and conceptual behavior. In ELLIS, N. R. (ed.) *Handbook of Mental Deficiency*. New York: McGraw-Hill.

ROSSI, E. L. (1963) Associative clustering in normal and retarded children. *Amer. J. ment. Defic.*, **67**, 691–9.

ROUSE, S. T. (1965) Effects of a training program on the productive thinking of educable mental retardates. *Amer. J. ment. Defic.*, **69**, 666–73.

SANDERS, B., ROSS, L. E. and HEAL, L. W. (1965) Reversal and non-reversal shift learning in normal children and retardates of comparable mental age. *J. exp. Psychol.*, **69**, 84–8.

SANDERS, B., ZIGLER, E. and BUTTERFIELD, E. C. (1968) Outer-directedness in the discrimination learning of normal and mentally retarded children. *J. abn. Psychol.*, **73**, 368–75.

SCHULMAN, J. L., KASPAR, J. CHARLES and THRONE, F. M. (1965) *Brain Damage and Behavior. A Clinical-Experiment Study.* Springfield, Ill.: C. C. Thomas.

SCOTT, K. G. (1971) Recognition memory: a research strategy and a summary of initial findings. In ELLIS, N. R. (ed.) *International Review of Research in Mental Retardation*, Vol. 5. New York: Academic Press.

SCOTT, K. G. and SCOTT, M. S. (1968) Research and theory in short-term memory. In ELLIS, N. R. (ed.) *International Review of Research in Mental Retardation*, Vol. 3. New York: Academic Press.

SCOTT, W. S. (1940) Reaction time in young intellectual deviates. *Arch. Psychol.*, **36**, 1–64.

SEN, A. K. and CLARKE, A. M. (1968) Some factors affecting distractibility in the mental retardate. *Amer. J. ment. Defic.*, **73**, 50–60.

SEN, A. K. and SEN, A. (1968) A test of the McCrary-Hunter hypothesis in mentally retarded subjects. *J. ment. Defic. Res.*, **12**, 36–46.

SEN, A. K., CLARKE, A. M. and COOPER, G. M. (1968) The effect of isolating items in serial learning in severely retarded subjects. *Amer. J. ment. Defic.*, **72**, 851–6.

SHEPP, B. E. and TURRISI, F. D. (1966) Learning and transfer of mediating responses in discriminative learning. In ELLIS, N. R. (ed.) *International Review of Research in Mental Retardation*, Vol. 2. New York: Academic Press.

SILVERSTEIN, A. B. and MCLAIN, R. E. (1966) Associative process of the mentally retarded: III. A developmental study. *Amer. J. ment. Defic.*, **70**, 722–5.

SLOANE, H. and MACAULAY, B. (1968) *Operant Procedures in Remedial Speech and Language Training.* Boston: Houghton-Mifflin.

SPITZ, H. H. (1963) Field theory in mental deficiency. In ELLIS, N. R. (ed.) *Handbook of Mental Deficiency*. New York: McGraw-Hill.

SPITZ, H. H. (1964) A comparison of mental retardates and normals on the rotating trapezoidal window illusion. *J. abn. soc. Psychol.*, **68**, 574–8.

SPITZ, H. H. (1965) The effect of a single monocular depth cue deficit on retardates' perception of the rotating cube illusion. *Amer. J. ment. Defic.*, **69**, 703–11.

SPITZ, H. H. (1966) The rôle of input organization in the learning and memory of mental retardates. In ELLIS, N. R. (ed.) *International Review of Research in Mental Retardation*, Vol. 2. New York: Academic Press.

SPITZ, H. H. (1967) A comparison of mental retardates and normals on the distorted room illusion. *Amer. J. ment. Defic.*, **72**, 34–49.

SPITZ, H. H. and BLACKMAN, L. S. (1959) A comparison of mental retardates and normals on visual figural aftereffects and reversible figures. *J. abn. soc. Psychol.*, **58**, 105–10.

SPITZ, H. H. and LIPMAN, R. S. (1961) A comparison of mental retardates and normals on kinesthetic figural aftereffects. *J. abn. soc. Psychol.*, **62**, 686–7.

SPIVACK, G. (1963) Perceptual processes. In ELLIS, N. R. (ed.) *Handbook of Mental Deficiency*. New York: McGraw-Hill.

SPRADLIN, J. E. and GIRARDEAU, F. L. (1966) The behavior of moderately and severely retarded persons. In ELLIS, N. R. (ed.) *International Review of Research in Mental Retardation*, Vol. 1. New York: Academic Press.

SPREEN, O. (1965a) Language functions in mental retardation: a review I. Language development, types of retardation, and intelligence level. *Amer. J. ment. Defic.*, **69**, 482–94.

SPREEN, O. (1965b) Language functions in mental retardation: a review II. Language in higher level performance. *Amer. J. ment. Defic.*, **70**, 351–62.

STEPHENS, W. E. (1964) A comparison of the performance of normal and subnormal boys on structured categorization tasks. *Except. Child.*, **30**, 311–15.

STEPHENS, W. E. (1966a) Category usage by normal and mentally retarded boys. *Child Developm.*, **37**, 355–61.

STEPHENS, W. E. (1966b) Category usage of normal and subnormal children on three types of categories. *Amer. J. ment. Defic.*, **71**, 266–73.

STEPHENS, W. E. (1968) Labelling errors of mentally subnormal children in a concept attainment task. *Amer. J. ment. Defic.*, **73**, 273–8.

STERNLICHT, M. and DEUTSCH, M. R. (1966) Cognition in the mentally retarded: the von Restorff effect. *J. ment. Defic. Res.*, **10**, 63–8.

STERNLICHT, M., PUSTEL, G. and SIEGEL, L. (1968) Comparison of organic and cultural-familial retardates on two visual-motor tasks. *Amer. J. ment. Defic.*, **72**, 887–9.

STEVENSON, H. W. and SWARTZ, J. D. (1958) Learning set in children as a function of intellectual level. *J. comp. physiol. Psychol.*, **51**, 755–7.

STEVENSON, H. W. and ZIGLER, E. F. (1957) Discrimination learning and rigidity in normal and feeble minded individuals. *J. Personal.*, **25**, 699–711.

STEVENSON, H. W. and ZIGLER, E. F. (1958) Probability learning in children. *J. exp. Psychol.*, **56**, 185–92.

STRAUSS, A. A. and KEPHART, N. C. (1955) *Psychopathology and Education of the Brain Injured Child. Vol. II, Progress in Theory and Clinic.* New York: Grune & Stratton.

STRAUSS, A. A. and LEHTINEN, L. E. (1947) *Psychopathology and Education of the Brain Injured Child.* New York: Grune & Stratton.

SUTHERLAND, N. S. (1964) The learning of discriminations by animals. *Endeavour*, **23**, 148–52.

TIZARD, B. (1968a) Observations of over-active imbecile children in controlled and uncontrolled environments: I. Classroom studies. *Amer. J. ment. Defic.*, **72**, 540–7.

TIZARD, B. (1968b) Observations of over-active imbecile children in controlled and uncontrolled environments: II. Experimental studies. *Amer. J. ment. Defic.*, **72**, 548–53.

TIZARD, B. (1968c) Habituation of E.E.G. and skin potential changes in normal and severely subnormal children. *Amer. J. ment. Defic.*, **73**, 34–40.

TIZARD, B. (1968d) A controlled study of all-night sleep in over-active imbecile children. *Amer. J. ment. Defic.*, **73**, 209–13.

TULVING, E. (1962) Subjective organization in free recall of 'unrelated' words. *Psychol. Rev.*, **69**, 344–54.

TULVING, E. (1964) Intratrial and intertrial retention: notes towards a theory of free-recall verbal learning. *Psychol. Rev.*, **71**, 219–37.

TULVING, E. (1966) Subjective organization and effects of repetition in multi-trial free-recall learning. *J. Verb. Learn. Verb. Behav.*, **5**, 193–7.

TURNURE, J. and ZIGLER, E. (1964) Outer-directedness in the problem solving of normal and retarded children. *J. abn. soc. Psychol.*, **69**, 427–36.

UNDERWOOD, B. J. (1954) Speed of learning and amount retained: a consideration of methodology. *Psychol. Bull.*, **51**, 276–82.

UNDERWOOD, B. J. (1964) Degree of learning and the measurement of forgetting. *J. Verb. Learn. Verb. Behav.*, **3**, 112–29.

VAN DER VEEN, C. (1967) *Verbalization of Associative Learning Strategies among Educable Retardates and Normal Children.* Unpubl. paper presented at the 91st Annual Convention, Amer. Assoc. on Ment. Defic., Denver, Colorado.

VERGASON, G. A. (1964) Retention in retarded and normal subjects as a function of amount of original learning. *Amer. J. ment. Defic.*, **68**, 623–9.

VOGEL, W. and BROVERMAN, D. M. (1964) Relationship between E.E.G. and test intelligence: a critical review. *Psychol. Bull.*, **62**, 132–44.

VOGEL, W. and BROVERMAN, D. M. (1966) A reply to 'Relationship between E.E.G. and test intelligence: a commentary'. *Psychol. Bull.*, **65**, 99–109.

VOGEL, W., KUN, K. J., MESHORER, E., BROVERMAN, D. M. and KLAIBER, E. L. (1969) The behavioral significance of E.E.G. abnormality in mental defectives. *Amer. J. ment. Defic.*, **74**, 62–8.

WATSON, L. S. (1967) Application of operant conditioning techniques to institutionalized severely and profoundly retarded children. *Ment. Retard. Abstrs.*, **4**, 1–18.

WATSON, L. S. and LAWSON, R. (1966) Instrumental learning in mental retardates. *Ment. Retard. Abstrs.*, **3**, 1–20.

WIESEN, A. E. and WATSON, E. (1967) Elimination of attention seeking behavior in a retarded child. *Amer. J. ment. Defic.*, **72**, 50–2.

WINTERS, J. J. (1965) Gamma movement: a comparison of normals and retardates. *Amer. J. ment. Defic.*, **69**, 697–702.

WINTERS, J. J. (1969) A comparison of normals and retardates on physiological and experiential visual illusions. *Amer. J. ment. Defic.*, **73**, 956–62.

WINTERS, J. J. and GERJUOY, I. R. (1965) Gamma movement: field brightness, series, and side of the standard. *Psychon. Sci.*, **2**, 273–4.

WINTERS, J. J. and GERJUOY, I. R. (1967) Gamma movement: a comparison of normals and retardates under several temporal conditions. *Amer. J. ment. Defic.*, **71**, 542–5.

WISCHNER, G. J., BRAUN, H. W. and PATTON, R. A. (1962) Acquisition and long-term retention of an object quality learning set by retarded children. *J. Comp. Physiol. Psychol.*, **55**, 518–23.

WOLFENSBERGER, W. and O'CONNOR, N. (1965) Stimulus intensity and duration effects on E.E.G. and G.S.R. responses of normals and retardates. *Amer. J. ment. Defic.*, **70**, 21–37.

WOLFENSBERGER, W., MEIN, R. and O'CONNOR, N. (1963) A study of the oral vocabularies of severely subnormal patients. *J. ment. Defic. Res.*, **7**, 38–45.

ZEAMAN, D. (1965) Learning processes of the mentally retarded. In OSLER, S. F. and COOKE, R. E. (eds.) *The Biosocial Basis of Mental Retardation*. Baltimore, Md.: Johns Hopkins Press.

ZEAMAN, D. and HOUSE, B. J. (1963) The rôle of attention in retardate discrimination learning. In ELLIS, N. R. (ed.) *Handbook of Mental Deficiency*. New York: McGraw-Hill.

ZIGLER, E. (1966) Research on personality structure in the retardate. In ELLIS, N. R. (ed.) *International Review of Research in Mental Retardation*, Vol. 1. New York: Academic Press.

ZIGLER, E. (1967) Familial mental retardation: a continuing dilemma. *Science*, **155**, 292–8.

ZIGLER, E. (1969) Developmental versus difference theories of mental retardation and the problem of motivation. *Amer. J. ment. Defic.*, **73**, 536–56.

11

N. O'Connor and B. Hermelin

Specific deficits and coding strategies

Introduction

Failure to learn is the basic psychological characteristic of subnormality and Binet and Simon (1909) first drew attention to this problem in his classical studies of Parisian schoolchildren. His development of the concept of capacity, as distinct from acquisition, set the tone for subsequent work on intelligence and intelligence testing. Binet was, of course, reflecting a viewpoint that had already gained support in the nineteenth century. Galton (1892) held that individuals differed from each other in their physical and mental abilities and he maintained that the effects of training had strict limits. He was easily able to confirm both hypotheses, and indeed such opinions might be regarded now as commonplace. By drawing on statistical records, Galton was able to show that many characteristics were distributed in a relatively static population in a fairly constant way. Spearman (1904) was already correlating mental and physical characteristics and discussed the concept of intelligence in terms of proficiency and native capacity rather as Binet was to do. He estimated intelligence in terms of the relationship between achievement and chronological age. However, he also pointed out that many tests correlated together when individual scores on different kinds of performance were compared. (See also Chapters 6 and 13.)

Perhaps the most important observation made by Spearman which relates to our present subject is that which he made concerning the part played by general ability in different activities. At one point he suggests that a 'central function, whatever it may be, is hardly anywhere more prominent than in the simple act of discriminating two nearly identical tones'; in other words, even in such an apparently simple function as discrimination, central ability was thought to be playing a vital part. The extent to which 'g' (General Ability) contributed to specific functions varied in Spearman's view from dominant to subsidiary. The same idea has been expressed in a similar way by Vernon (1950), but other opinions also referred to by Vernon such as that of G. H. Thomson (1939) have a rather different character. Thomson suggested that the fact that many test scores correlate positively and may be represented by a single factor does not prove that this factor corresponds to any unitary faculty in the mind. His theory of multiple bonds, reflexes and associations allows that any one task or test might call into play a number of such bonds. These might appear to have the character of factors, but should not be thought of as faculties or organs.

All these authors, therefore, and others such as Burt (1937) and Thurstone (1935) have propounded views of intelligence of a more or less hierarchical character mostly distinguishing performance at any one time from native ability and mostly attributing some degree of acquisition in specific functions to a central general ability probably inherited. Hebb (1949) discussed the question of intelligence in terms of inherited potential, the state of the nervous system (Intelligence A) and the actual functional performance or comprehension of the person (Intelligence B). He points out that 'An innate potential for development is not logically a guarantee that the development will occur.' He argues on the basis of deprivation experiments that experience is essential to development. In Chapter 6 there is a selective historical review of the changing concept of intelligence where these points are discussed in detail. Both this kind of argument and questions concerning damage to the central nervous system, therefore, become of some importance when we try to account for the subnormals' cognitive incapacity. Duncan (1942) and others have remarked on brain injury as shown in patterns of performance on IQ tests. The verbal versus performance differences shown by subnormals could be of significance in examining specific deficits and their relationship to more general defects.

Specific disabilities and neuropsychology

The continued finding of different verbal and performance levels in the subnormal has led to such investigations as those of Sylvester (1966) and Blundell (1966), which point to the existence of localized lesions in addition to generalized damage in severe subnormality. Workers like Kirk and McCarthy (1961) have drawn attention to patterns of psychological response and their presumed neurological basis, and Strauss and Lehtinen (1947) noted the possible consequences of specific or more general lesions when found in the subnormal. However, despite attempts made by Reitan (1966) and his colleagues, a developed neuropsychology of subnormality does not exist. The problems of neuropsychology, as seen by Teuber (1959) and Teuber and Liebert (1958), deal with phenomena which are characteristic of lesions occurring at particular stages of development, and in this sense might be relevant to studies of subnormality. As has been shown, notably by Crome (1954) but also in much of the clinical literature, brain damage in the severely subnormal is diffuse and has general consequences which make the detection of specific effects more difficult.

Clearly, therefore, the detection of behavioural patterns in subnormality has to be set against the presence of widespread neurophysiological maldevelopment. Patterns of behaviour are not clearly associable with neurological lesions as they sometimes can be shown to be in adults suffering from dysphasias, short-term memory loss or disturbance of spatial perception.

The dilemma presented by Binet has been dealt with in part by the concept of islets of intelligence in autism as suggested by Creak (1961). It has also been considered by Binet and Simon (1909) himself and by subsequent workers such as Scheerer, Rothman and Goldstein (1945) in the concept of the *idiot savant*. However, despite clear evidence for unusual memories, and some evidence for *grands calculateurs*, e.g. Binet (1894) and Hunter (1962), examples are infrequent. They are clearly insufficient in number to provide a convincing case in favour of patterns of cognitive behaviour in subnormality as examples of specific abilities or deficits.

Specific theories of learning deficit

None the less, in recent years a number of attempts have been made to explain the subnormals' failure to learn, in terms of the weakness of a specific cognitive process. Such attempts have ignored the problem of neurophysiology or accepted a general theory of a molecular kind, in other words, a model with a presumptive neuroanatomy. Amongst these theories which, in a sense, oppose wholistic 'intelligence' type explanations, and which try to explain the learning problems of the subnormal in terms of specific deficits, are those of Ellis (1963, 1970) and Zeaman and House (1963) and Luria (1961). Ellis and his colleagues have suggested that a state of low cortical arousal which might be characteristic of subnormals results in a poor or weak trace in short-term memory (STM) and a consequent failure to establish events in long-term memory (LTM) in a more categorized form. This early form of a 'trace decay' hypothesis has been criticized by O'Connor and Hermelin (1965) and by Belmont and Butterfield (1969). Belmont and Butterfield have summarized material which shows that most results would accord with our own views of the importance of processes occurring at the input phase of learning. More recently, Ellis (1970) has examined STM in a theoretical framework which concedes the normality of LTM and discusses STM in terms of primary and secondary systems. Adopting different stimulus presentation rates, Ellis notes that subnormals differ from normals in material requiring rehearsal, e.g. the earlier items in a series of digits. Failure to rehearse is therefore advanced as an explanation of normal, subnormal differences in STM. Whatever the theoretical and practical variations of this short-term memory deficit as an explanation of failure to learn in the subnormal, it is given here as an example of a specific deficit hypothesis. It tends to advance failure to rehearse and hence failure of the secondary part of short-term memory as the reason for learning failure in the subnormal subject.

Another example of the specific type of hypothesis is that advanced by Zeaman and House (1963). This two-stage learning model assumes deficits in an attentional rather than in an S–R process, and in this respect resembles the dimensional theories advanced by Estes (1959) and Sutherland (1959). It is basic to such attentional theories that connection forming or the formation of stimulus response relations is rapid once the subject understands what is the nature of the stimuli. However, he must first have the capacity to orient his attention in the direction of the appropriate dimension within any one modality, for example, shape rather than size, within the visual modality. Some support for this view is contained in the studies of subnormal transfer carried out by Bryant (1965). (See also Chapter 10.)

Some criticisms of specific hypotheses

However, although this theory appears to be a specific hypothesis, it may prove to be more closely allied with a more general developmental view of the sub-normals' failure to learn. For example, Zeaman and House (1963) have them-selves suggested that dimensional orientation varies with development and may follow a definite emergent order. The evidence for the emergent nature of orientation to dimensions with development is questionable in view of evidence summarized by Pick and Pick (1970) concerning the primacy of modalities and the results of Bower's (1967) studies concerning infants' perception of form. However, more damaging to the specific character of the Zeaman and House hypothesis may be an observation made by Folkard (1971) as a result of vigilance studies carried out with normal and subnormal adolescents on a signal detection basis. He suggests that in their analysis of subnormal learning, they assume that the low probability of observing one dimension entails the high probability of observing another. This view is based on the assumption that probabilities must sum to unity, which in turn requires that only factors within the learning situa-tion are being attended to and that subnormals, like normals, can restrict their attention to one dimension. If subnormals are distractible, Folkard argues, they might be unable to focus attention at all, rather than failing to attend to the correct dimension. This would substitute an arousal hypothesis for one concern-ing lack of attention to specific dimensions. Such an arousal hypothesis would be a neurologically general one, rather than a specific theory.

Even if Folkard's objection did not apply, it could be argued that the emergence or orientation towards particular perceptual dimensions is a developmental hypothesis, and that developmental arrest as an explanation of failure to learn is like Woodward's (1963) adaptation of Piaget's (1953) and Piaget and Inhelder's (1969) theories, a general account of learning failure, applying to all types of performance, rather than to just one function such as dimensional orienta-tion.

Luria's (1961) very well known and brilliant exposition of verbal difficulties in the subnormal is based on the work of Vygotsky (1962) and also draws on Luria's (1961) extensive knowledge of neurology. The claim of his theory of verbal deficit in subnormals to account for their failure to learn is based on the important assumption that language, or in Pavlovian terms, the second signal system, is a more efficient medium for the acquisition of knowledge and in some situations the only one. As the theory of language as the initiator of thinking is one which may underlie some of Luria's arguments concerning subnormality, and as this view has been disputed, notably by Binet and Simon (1909) and Piaget

(1970), it is of interest to determine whether or not this relatively specific theory can be accepted as an explanation of learning failure. To some extent our own previous investigations in this field noted the failure of subnormals to use words effectively in learning procedures, and Bryant's studies of transfer showed that words had not the significance for subnormals in aiding transfer as they had for normals. However, as Bryant's studies also showed, the same was true of the use of signs by severely subnormal children. To express this differently, not only words but all symbols lacked generality when used by the subnormal.

The question of the primacy of thought or language is a subject on which Binet, Piaget and Vygotsky have each expressed views. Piaget's ideas are perhaps too well known to need emphasis, but Binet's (1909) are seldom quoted. He gives examples of single word answers to questions such as 'Have you read this book?' A negative word such as 'No' is a general negative and in no way indicates a particular answer to such a particular question, Binet argues. Even if we suppose that the answer is a series of words such as 'No, I have not read the book about which you speak', it could be shown by reference to imbeciles who lack more than a few words of speech that equally meaningful one-word answers can be evoked by questioning. In a similar fashion, Binet argues that an image such as one we might have in thinking about a planned expedition is inadequate fully to express the thought, just as words are. We think neither of the future, nor of the expedition, but often just of one aspect of the proposed journey. Binet concludes his discussion as follows: 'All this comes back to the conclusion that the thought is distinct both from the image and from the word, that it is quite another thing, that it constitutes a different element.'

Vygotsky (1962) expresses remarkably similar views concerning the way in which thought and language come to be related: '1. In their autogenetic development, thought and speech have different roots. 2. In the speech development of the child, we can with certainty establish a pre-intellectual stage, and in his thought development, a prelinguistic stage.' Vygotsky believes, however, that at a certain stage the two streams become one, whereas Binet obviously does not.

From the point of view of the subnormal person his failure to learn cannot always be explained in terms of a specific verbal deficit as many of Binet's examples suggest. Our own suggestions concerning language and thinking in the subnormal were that cross-modal coding was inadequate because subnormals often do not verbally describe the operations which they can none the less perform correctly, and hence are not able to carry out similar operations in a different context without further instruction. This original observation is subject to the findings made by Bryant subsequently, that failure to transfer is a product of failure to observe the general character of any signal whatsoever.

A number of explanations for learning deficiency have been listed and described above, and in each case we have attempted to offer reasons why such accounts are inadequate. If our arguments are valid, the general nature of the learning deficit in subnormal and severely subnormal people would have received some confirmation because of the failure to establish a strong case for a specific cause for failure to learn. Even had the theories reviewed made a very strong case, they would still face the logical objection that the presence of a particular deficit does not exclude the possibility of a general deficit in addition. Thus, for example, Down's syndrome children are known to have poorly-developed cerebella, but in addition to the poor stereognosis to which this gives rise, they suffer from widespread CNS damage and maldevelopment which impairs their general ability in other respects.

What, then, is undifferentiated subnormality?

The problem presented by Binet, therefore, and examined by his factorist successors, remains with us. What is the nature of the deficit which appears to affect a variety of measures of performance in the subnormal? What is the effect of retarded development which most characterizes subnormality and distinguishes it from the syndromes which show obvious specific deficits?

Our previous attempts to answer similar questions have led us to favour two main hypotheses, one arising from experiments concerned with subnormal and one arising from experiments with autistic children. The first offered an explanation in terms of a failure of coding at the input phase (O'Connor and Hermelin, 1965), and the second favoured an explanation in terms of a central logical deficit (Hermelin and O'Connor, 1970). In both series of experiments, the basic cognitive problem of these two groups was seen as a failure of categorizing or coding following immediate perception or short-term storage.

From such a standpoint we could criticize such views as those advanced by Ellis (1963) and Zeaman and House (1963) because they make use of concepts of formal descriptive faculties such as perception, learning and memory, without at the same time analysing the process common to these operations. Previous work of our own could also be criticized for an incompletely clear appreciation of the underlying unity of these processes.

Being led to analyse perceptual, associative and retrieval processes in this way, investigators have also concentrated on specifying deficits in such operations as if they were operations isolated in themselves and differing one from another. As a result there has been a tendency to look for diagnostically based and specific deficits. Diagnostic groups have been examined because of the presumed specificity of localized defects, as for example, in Down's syndrome (motor defects) or autism (language deficiency).

However, although such an approach is not without merit and effectiveness, it does fail to analyse the organizing process which underlies each such specific operation. Our own attempts to analyse cross-modal coding brought us towards such an appreciation of a common element in all learning operations, but did not, at that time, lead us to a definitive statement of its nature. Though we examined cross-modal coding in a variety of studies with subnormals, we did not propose that coding was an element basic to all processes connected with the acquisition of knowledge. Cognate problems have been discussed elsewhere by O'Connor and Hermelin (1971b).

A new attitude to cognitive deficits

Coding might be defined as the translation of an item from one sign system to another. Each sign stands for a class or category of items or an individual member of such a class. It appears to us that the process of learning includes in any operations such as perception, recall and recognition in each of which coding, either on input or at a later stage, plays an important part. It is possible to go further and suggest that the classification of any particular input, and its appropriate tagging for reference, constitutes the basic operation in perception, learning or recall and that this operation is coding. Therefore coding plays a central part in learning, and if subnormals fail to learn, the factors possibly affecting coding need careful examination.

Another reason for examining factors affecting coding is to test what might seem to be a possible example of Hebb's (1949) phase structure theory of learning. This theory posits that learning cannot occur in the absence of one of its basic stages. If a step in the process is missed out, normal development is arrested. The experiments of many of Hebb's colleagues such as Bexton, Heron and Scott (1954), and others whom he quotes such as Riesen (1947) and von Senden (1932), were directed towards showing that lack of experience led to developmental arrest. Many other workers tried to extend the theory to higher mammalian and to human behaviour, for example, Harlow (1958) and Spitz (1945). In general, so far as humans are concerned such experiments have not been too successful. However, Hebb's theory, in providing an explanation of learning failure, may also offer a behavioural theory of intellectual deficit and to some degree an account of the nature of (low) intelligence.

In examining coding, therefore, we might be considering a function which is basic to learning. In considering specific deficits which might affect coding, we would be examining the relationship between specific and general impairments. Therefore we began to consider cross-modal coding and the effect of specific sensory impairments on this process. It could be the case that some aspects of coding are supra-modal and dependent on a kind of operation which is either independent of, or common to, all modalities. Other coding functions may be modality specific. Questions of this kind concerned us when we began recent studies which are now described.

CODING OF TEMPORAL AND SPATIAL SEQUENCES

Many authors have drawn attention to the significance of coding as an operation which might be affected by cognitive handicap. Our own studies with subnormals, reported in O'Connor and Hermelin (1963) and with autistic children (Hermelin and O'Connor 1970) yield examples of such findings of coding deficits.

Whether the deficit in coding operations is confined to cross-modal coding, or to problems of feature extraction, or of sequential ordering, remains undecided at this stage. It is possible that different deficits involved in the process could be associated with different diagnostic conditions.

We attempted to examine the effects of blindness and deafness on coding operations. Our concern with coding was to determine whether it was affected by restriction of input modality. We also wished to determine whether it was a supra-modal operation or one which was specific to each modality. In general, we could examine the effect of restriction of input modality, i.e. a specific restriction on a presumedly more general function.

This aim determined our selection of subject groups: blind and deaf groups in whom input was presumably restricted, normal hearing and sighted controls whom we sometimes temporarily deprived of sight or hearing, subnormals in whom deficit was supposedly general rather than specific. The experiments reported below are concerned with the discrimination of temporal interval and with temporal or spatial-sequential coding. The former topic serves merely as an introduction to the latter.

DISCRIMINATION OF DURATION

In the first of these experiments, we tested cross-modal coding and temporal discrimination (O'Connor and Hermelin, 1971c).

Evidence on cross-modal transfer with children is inconclusive. Smith and Tunick (1969) carried out an experiment with retarded children where discrimination had to be transferred from touch to vision and vision to touch. When the same cues or stimulus objects were used, transfer was achieved across modalities. Blank and Bridger (1966) reported positive transfer of discrimination between sounds and lights provided that there was adequate verbalization during training. Blank, Altman and Bridger (1968) subsequently demonstrated positive transfer between touch and vision even in children unable to name the stimuli. While Birch and Belmont (1965) have reported deficits in matching auditory with visual patterns in cerebral palsied children, Rudel and Teuber (1968) found brain damaged and retarded children not to be different from controls in visual-tactile and tactile-visual shape recognition. In view of the contradictory evidence, it seemed appropriate to consider cross-modal transfer in terms of developmental deficits, associated with diffuse brain damage, and also in relation to such lasting impairment as might arise as a result of blindness or deafness. We therefore selected deaf, blind, subnormal and normal children matched for mental age.

Blind, normal, subnormal and deaf children were taught to discriminate between touch stimuli lasting either 6 seconds or 2 seconds. Appropriate motor responses to the long and the short stimulus were taught to each subject. The learning task involved discriminating between a rotary probe in the palm of the hand which lasted for 6 seconds and another which lasted for 2 seconds.

When the basic touch task had been learned, the subjects were asked to do a transfer task. The transfer stimuli were two touch signals of a different kind from that in the learning task, air puffs, and sounds or lights for the blind and deaf and their control groups respectively. Stimuli were of 2 seconds or of 6 seconds.

The results showed that the initial touch discrimination transferred to another kind of touch stimulus, but not to light or to sound. Absence of speech was no special handicap as the deaf did at least as well as other groups. Analysis of variance of transfer error scores showed that transfer was greatest within the modality and least across modalities. Differences between groups were not significant. Thus cross-modal transfer of a learned discrimination was not affected by restriction of sensory input. In the experiment reported above we had used successively presented stimuli in a temporal discrimination task. The relative failure of the subjects to judge two durations as being either the same or different may have been specifically related to the stimulus modality used, or to the successiveness of the exposures. Thus stimuli in another sense modality, or a simultaneous rather than a successive stimulus exposure, might yield different results.

It has been argued that hearing is a process which integrates successive stimuli. Although Savin (1967) suggests that the results of many experiments tend to confirm such a view, simultaneous sounds are also obviously integrated by the auditory system, as, for example, in the appreciation of harmony or the recognition of different speech accents. Conversely, though the eye deals with a wide visual field which presents information simultaneously, successive focusing on different points also occurs. The experiment reported below was designed to investigate the effect of simultaneous and successive presentation of stimuli on temporal and non-temporal discriminations when stimuli were presented in either the visual or auditory modality. Eighty 5-year-old children were asked to examine visual and auditory displays. The visual displays consisted of lines of different lengths (5, 10 or 15 cm) which could remain on for durations of 2, 4 or 6 seconds. The auditory display consisted of high,- medium- and low-pitched tones (1,200, 500 and 400 Hz) which could vary in duration from 2 to 4 or 6 seconds.

The procedure was designed to compare the effect of stimuli presented either simultaneously or successively, in either the visual or auditory modalities, and in terms of the dimensions of space or pitch, as compared with time. In all conditions 24 pairs of stimuli were presented to the subjects who had to judge whether these stimuli were the same or different. Each correct response was reinforced by the experimenter saying 'good' and each incorrect one was followed by the experimenter saying 'no'. The pairs of stimuli were either visual or auditory and varied in one of two ways. Either they varied in duration or alternatively they varied in another dimension, e.g. length in the case of visual and pitch in the case of auditory stimuli. When duration was invariant, this second dimension varied, and when the alternative dimension was invariant, duration was varied from trial to trial. When duration was invariant, exposure time was always 4 seconds, but when it was variable, stimuli were either both exposed for 2 seconds or both for 6 seconds, or one for 2 seconds and one for 6 seconds. A similar rule applied to the constancy or variation of length and pitch. When duration was varied, an intermediate length (10 cm) or pitch (800 Hz) was used. When the non-temporal dimensions were variable, combinations of the extremes (5 and 15 cm; 400 and 1200 Hz) were used, while duration was held constant at 4 seconds.

Instructions were always similar, e.g. 'Two lights (tones) will come up here and there. Watch (listen to) them carefully and when they have gone, tell me whether they were the same or different.' Successive displays were separated by a 5 second gap. Simultaneous displays always commenced at the same time, and the visual stimuli appeared one above the other, with a 5 cm gap between them.

Results showed that durational judgments were more difficult than the non-durational ones, though this difference was more marked when lights rather than when sounds were the stimuli.

Durational judgments were more efficient when the stimuli were exposed together than when one followed the other, and this was true with lights as well as with sounds. The patterns of responses for durational judgments were very similar for both stimulus modalities, indicating similar response strategies. In contrast to one of the previously advanced hypotheses, simultaneous presentation of stimuli varying in duration resulted in better performance with auditory as well as with visual signals.

These results also showed clearly that the relationship between modality of stimulus, manner of presentation and tendency for temporal or non-temporal coding needed further investigation. The results had shown that, particularly with visual stimuli, orientation towards the temporal dimension was not readily obtained. On the other hand, they had failed to provide evidence that successive stimulus presentation facilitated temporal orientation. The next series of studies further tested temporal and non-temporal coding when the material was either visually or auditorily presented.

INPUT MODALITY AND TEMPORAL AND SPATIAL CODING

For the following study we adopted a technique originally used by Attneave and Benson (1969) who tested the coding of tactile information. This consists of stimulating the finger ends of both hands and associating each separate tactile stimulus with a spoken word. After learning to associate a word with a stimulated finger, hand positions are reversed for the second part of the experiment. With sighted subjects, association between a word and a particular location in space were stronger than those between words and fingers. McKinney (1964), in a study of hand schema in blind children, concluded that these children relied on tactual cues as a guide to a spatial schema. We were interested to know whether the blind or children temporarily deprived of sensory input would use spatial schemes which differed from those of sighted children.

Blind and autistic children were matched on chronological age with sighted children, one group of whom were blindfolded for the experiment. Another group of blindfold adults was added to obtain further information. The autistic children had been diagnosed by a psychiatrist and had an onset before 18 months of age. Their mean IQ was 85. The blind were either totally blind from birth or had only light, without pattern vision. Their IQs had a mean of 118 and a range from 100 to 142 on the Williams (1950) test.

Ss were tested individually. They were first told that they had to learn four words. These were: 'run', 'sit', 'walk', 'stand'. The index and middle fingers of each hand were then placed on a 6 × 16·5 inch board in the position illustrated in Fig. 2.

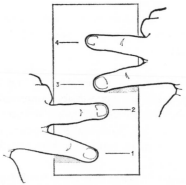

Fig. 2 A test of the coding of tactile information: association of tactile stimulus with the spoken word.

Half the children began with the right hand extended in front of the left, and for the other half these positions were reversed. The top of a finger was then lightly brushed with a toothbrush while E said, 'This is "run" ', or while touching another finger, 'This is "sit" ', etc. Care was taken not to indicate whether 'this' referred to the stimulation of a particular finger or its particular position.

After this demonstration the subject had to learn to respond to stimulation with the brush by uttering the correct word. Stimulation was administered in a predetermined random order. After the association had been learned to a criterion of 19 out of 20 trials the position of the hands was reversed, and E said, 'We will just go on.'

Results show that location or absolute spatial responses were predominant in those who carried out the task using touch and vision, and that finger responses were more common in those who carried out the task using touch alone. For example, 10 blind children gave 276 finger responses out of 400, whereas sighted children gave only 158. Oddly enough, blindfold adults gave no location responses and autistic children behaved as did the sighted normal. Neither chronological age nor psychiatric diagnosis affected this clear finding that space schema vary according to input restriction. If an input-independent concept of visually represented space were built up only gradually by experience, one might expect adults to respond more frequently than children in accordance with such an internal visual schema. This did not occur in the present experiment, where blindfolded adults gave more rather than fewer consistently finger-determined responses than did blindfolded children. The results showed that the absence of sensory input might have an effect on coding. Also, modality restriction appeared to be more important than handicap and for both these reasons we decided to use an input restriction paradigm in further experiments.

The method of the experiment to be reported next was developed from a study of short-term memory by Murdock (1969). In our study, subjects who

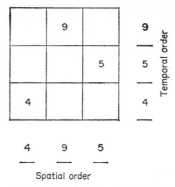

Fig. 3 A test of spatial *v.* temporal coding.

were either blind, deaf or normal were presented with 3 digits, either visually on a display panel or auditorily through three loudspeakers arranged in a semi-circle to the left, in front and to their right. The 3 digits were presented successively in such a way that their temporal sequential order differed from their left to right spatial order. An example might be presented as in Fig. 3 where the temporal sequential order is shown vertically and the left-right order is shown horizontally.

After each presentation the subject was asked to name or write down 'the middle number'. The question is ambiguous and the answer depends on whether the subject processes the digits in temporal sequence or left-right sequence. If a subject coded temporally his answer to the above example would be '5', and if spatially his answer would be '9'.

The hypothesis to be tested was that modality of presentation was the critical factor which would determine the choice of strategy. It was predicted, therefore, that blind children would respond temporally because receiving auditory input, and deaf children spatially, because their input would be visual. Normal children with auditory presentation were expected to respond temporally and normals with visual input were expected to code spatially, as would the deaf.

Eighty children took part in the experiments. In the first 10 deaf children and 2 groups of 10 normal children matched for digit span and chronological age were tested with visual material. One group of normal children wore earmuffs which restricted hearing. Ten blind children of a similar chronological age, and 2 groups of 10 normal children, one of them blindfolded and matched for chronological age, were tested with auditory material. The children were all chosen from average groups in their school classes, so that their mental ages would be approximately equal to their chronological ages. No tests of intelligence were made. The chronological ages of the groups were between 13 and 14 years and simple analysis of variance showed the groups to be statistically equal in age. The digit spans for each group exceeded the total length of the presentations by at least 2 digits.

The 3 digits were presented over a 2 second period, and the average pause between any 3 digits was 8 seconds, range 6 to 12 seconds. The results were that in the deaf and in both the 2 normal control groups, organization of visual items was predominantly spatial, as the spatially central digit was chosen as the middle one in an overwhelming number of instances. In the blind and the two control groups, with auditorally presented digits, the chosen central or 'middle' digit was predominantly a temporal one.

Results from this experiment are so clear that conclusions can be stated very simply. In an ambiguous situation, modality of presentation determines whether stimuli will be organized spatially or temporally. Thus an auditory presentation determines that subjects will regard the temporally central digit as the 'middle one' rather than the spatially central. A visual presentation determines that subjects will select the spatially central digit and ignore the temporal one. The fact that blind children always choose the temporal middle and deaf children the spatial is a result of the fact that their input is confined to auditory and visual modalities respectively. This is demonstrated by the response of the control groups. In nearly all cases they showed results characteristic for modality of presentation. The blind and deaf children responded in a manner like that of the hearing and sighted in their functioning modality.

Essentially our results indicate that modality of input induces either a temporal or spatial set: that is, the nature of the intuition, to use the terminology of Kant (1781), influences the selection of one or other category or concept. The term 'dimensions' as used by Sutherland (1959) and Zeaman and House (1963) might be mentioned. One could say that the input modality was the trigger which switched on the appropriate dimension for coding the stimuli. Thus the nature of the input to a great degree determines the code used to organize it.

The selection of one 'middle' digit was a task which could be accomplished without drawing on memory, and was in itself a decision and not a recall function. If instead of a decision process recall was required, it might be possible to emphasize and increase the frequency of sequential responses. We therefore modified the task of the previous experiment to ask for the recall of all 3 digits instead of the selection of the 'middle one'.

The experiment was carried out with normal children aged about 9 years who either spoke or wrote down the 3 digits presented. Results as predicted were entirely sequential even with visual presentation. However, when the same technique was used with normal IQ deaf children of the same CA, recall was not temporal-sequential but, in the case of most children, spatial. This result would appear to accord with theoretical expectations and would be explicable in terms of the failure of the deaf to rehearse or recall presented digits verbally. We were interested also in the behaviour of subnormal subjects and believed that their recall of 3 digits would be sequential because of their relatively normal verbal development at least to a limited mental age. We therefore tested severely subnormal adults of IQ 50 to 60, and with mental ages of 8 or 9 years. Responses, unexpectedly, were spatially ordered. This result cannot be easily explained in terms of a simple verbal deficit, unless this were such a deficit as that mentioned by Ellis, namely a rehearsal incapacity in the presence of a reasonable vocabulary.

Recognition scores confirmed the recall findings. For recognition the digits were presented in the same manner as for recall. Then the subjects were shown on some trial series the temporal sequence along with the same digits arranged randomly. On another trial series they were shown the spatial or left-right sequence along with an alternative random arrangement of the same digits. Both 3 digit numbers were presented together on a card and the subject was asked to point to the one he had just seen on the display panel.

Deaf children chose the spatial rather than the random series in 130 out of 160 trials, but gave responses on a chance level when asked to recognize temporal sequence. Normals on the other hand chose the temporal rather than the random sequence 114 times out of 160, but failed to recognize spatial order. Scores for the autistic children were closely similar to those for the deaf, and subnormal children behaved similarly but their bias was less marked.

Thus both in recall and in recognition a differential pattern of input processing occurred in which group differences were marked. Normal children, given a visual input, noted the temporal sequential order of the items, and recalled or recognized this order, whereas deaf, autistic and many subnormal children noted and recalled or recognized the spatially ordered sequence. These results differ from those found in the experiment concerned with the choice of the middle digit. In that case, modality of presentation appeared to determine the elective strategy, whereas in this case the results would appear to be divided according to groups. As the most obvious difference between normals and the other three groups is verbal competence, an explanation should perhaps be sought in these terms.

Specific deficits and general functions

The experimental findings described in the preceding section fall into several distinct patterns of results. In the first two studies, i.e. those concerned with cross-modal coding (O'Connor and Hermelin, 1971c), and with the judgment of duration (Hermelin and O'Connor, 1971a), neither different modalities of stimulus presentation, nor different groups of subjects used, gave differential result patterns. Thus the processes investigated by these studies, i.e. cross-modal coding and durational judgments, seem to be independent of both modality and diagnostic factors.

In the second set of experiments concerned with spatial and spatial-temporal coding (Hermelin and O'Connor, 1971b; O'Connor and Hermelin, 1971a), the crucial variable which affected response patterns was that of presentation modality. Auditory stimuli gave rise to temporal and visual signals to spatial organization of the stimuli. These experiments used single item selection tasks, in which a particular strategy, once adopted, would determine the set of sub-sequent responses. Thus, while response strategies may be elective in single item selection tasks, there are suggestions in the literature that short-term memory for verbal material is temporally organized, regardless of the mode of its pre-sentation. Thus Tulving and Madigan (1970) state that 'information about the temporal data of the occurrence of an item is an absolutely necessary condition for the recall or recognition of this item'. Similarly, Murdock (1969) also supports this view.

We thus predicted that, with normals at any rate, visually presented digits which had to be recalled or recognized would be temporally rather than spatially coded. This, in fact, was what occurred, and though normal children had selected a spatially central digit as the middle one in the previous experiment, they ordered the same digits temporally when they had to recall them. Deaf, autistic and some subnormal subjects, on the other hand, recalled and recognized the digits in a spatial left-to-right order, ignoring temporal sequence. However, the level of recall and recognition obtained did not differ between the groups, demonstrating that memory could be effectively organized in a non-temporal manner.

An explanation of the difference between the decision or 'middle' experiment and the 3-digit recall and recognition studies requires us to assume that in the case of normal subjects recalling 3 digits after their visual display, some verbal coding occurred either at input, during storage or at retrieval. If the input stage is favoured as an explanation, evidence could be adduced in support of the likeli-hood of some subnormals failing to use verbalization at this stage, including studies by Luria (1956), O'Connor and Hermelin (1959), and Bryant (1967). Subnormals notoriously do not verbalize or describe in words the input which they may be receiving. This is obviously true of the deaf and may be true of autistic children. As not all subnormals coded spatially in the 3-digit recall task, it must be assumed that only some fail to code verbally. If an explanation in terms of spontaneous verbal coding is acceptable as an account of the difference between the two sets of results, the 'middle' results should be reversible in the case of normal subjects if they vocalized the 3 digits before deciding which was the middle one. This hypothesis remains to be tested. Thus whether because of the modality of input, or because of failure to code verbally, coding strategy is affected. While, therefore, we cannot say that a specific impairment has led to a general deficit, it has led in some cases to a higher level coding strategy effect. In the case of each of the last three sets of experiments, some aspect of the nature of specific input has affected the subject's conceptual schema, whether spatial in the 'run, sit, walk, stand' experiment, the concept of 'middle' in the auditory and visual presentation experiment, or the choice of spatial or temporal sequential coding in the last experiment. These effects on coding must be considered as general effects although, of course, they are not in any sense deficits. The conclusion must be therefore that in certain instances specific impairments result in conceptual schemas which differ from the schemas characteristic of normals.

Conclusions

Such results, therefore, while not confirming a theory of phase sequence in the sense advanced by Hebb (1949), would be an example of limitation of sensory input affecting the operation of a process which, because supra-modal, must be seen as general. The theories of the mode of operation of specific deficits given at the beginning of the chapter were judged to be unsatisfactory in some respects as accounts of failure to learn. The examples we have given may also be inadequate in so far as they show not so much how children fail to learn, but how they tend to observe or record one event or series of events rather than another. However, these experiments may suggest ways in which learning patterns could diverge and lead to different conceptual frameworks in case of specific input handicap. They also show that subnormals, perhaps because they notoriously do not verbalize input, may provide examples of temporal coding deficit. Our results show that not all, but only some, subnormals behave as do deaf and autistic children. The reason for their failure to code temporally requires further study.

In a previous paragraph we referred to earlier attempts on our part to explain learning failure in handicapped groups in terms of a failure of coding at input. The results reported above tend to confirm this conclusion and show further the mechanisms by which characteristics of coding may be affected.

References

ATTNEAVE, F. and BENSON, L. (1969) Spatial coding of tactual stimulation. *J. exp. Psychol.*, **81**, 216–22.

BELMONT, J. M. and BUTTERFIELD, E. C. (1969) The relations of short-term memory to development and intelligence. In LIPSITT, L. P. and REESE, H. W. (eds.) *Advances in Child Development and Behaviour*, Vol. 4. New York: Academic Press.

BEXTON, W. H., HERON, W. and SCOTT, I. H. (1954) Effects of decreased variation in the sensory environment. *Canad. J. Psychol.*, **8**, 70–6.

BINET, A. (1894) *Psychologie des Grands Calculateurs*. Paris: Hachette.

BINET, A. and SIMON, T. H. (1909) A scheme of thought. In *The Intelligence of the Feeble-minded. L'Année Psychologique*, 1–147. Reprinted 1966, Baltimore, Md.: Williams & Wilkins.

BIRCH, H. G. and BELMONT, L. (1965) Auditory-visual integration in brain damaged and normal children. *Developm. med. Child. Neurol.*, **7**, 135–44.

BLANK, M. and BRIDGER, W. H. (1966) Conceptual cross-modal transfer in deaf and hearing children. *Child Developm.*, **37**, 29–38.

BLANK, M., ALTMAN, L. D. and BRIDGER, W. H. (1968) Cross-modal transfer of form discrimination in pre-School children. *Psychon. Sci.*, **10**, 51–2.

BLUNDELL, E. (1966) Parietal lobe dysfunction in subnormal patients. *J. ment. Defic. Res.*, **10**, 141–52.

BOWER, T. G. R. (1967) Phenomenal identity and form perception in an infant. *Perception and Psychophysics*, **2**, 74–6.

BRYANT, P. E. (1965) The transfer of positive and negative learning by normal and severely subnormal children. *Brit. J. Psychol.*, **56**, 81–6.

BRYANT, P. E. (1967) Verbalisation and immediate memory of complex stimuli in normal and severely subnormal children. *Brit. J. soc. clin. Psychol.*, **6**, 212–19.

BURT, C. (1937) *The Backward Child*. London: Univ. of London Press.

CREAK, M. (1961) Schizophrenic syndrome in childhood: progress report of a working party, April 1961. *Cerebral Palsy Bull.*, **3**, 501–4.

CROME, L. (1954) Some morbid-anatomical aspects of mental deficiency. *J. ment. Sci.*, **100**, 894–912.

DUNCAN, J. (1942) *The Education of the Ordinary Child*. London: Nelson.

ELLIS, N. R. (1963) The stimulus trace and behavioural inadequacy. In ELLIS, N. R. (ed.) *Handbook of Mental Deficiency*. New York: McGraw-Hill.

ELLIS, N. R. (1970) Memory processes in retardates and normals. In ELLIS, N. R. (ed.) *International Review of Research in Mental Retardation*, Vol. 4. New York: Academic Press.

ESTES, W. K. (1959) The statistical approach to learning theory. In KOCH, S. (ed.) *Psychology: A Study of a Science*, Vol. 2. New York: McGraw-Hill.

FOLKARD, S. (1971) *Attentional Deficits in ESN Children*. Unpubl. Ph.D. thesis, Univ. of London.

GALTON, F. (1892) *Hereditary Genius*. London: Macmillan.

HARLOW, H. F. (1958) The nature of love. *Amer. Psychol.*, **13**, 673–85.

HEBB, D. O. (1949) *The Organisation of Behaviour*. London: Chapman & Hall.

HERMELIN, B. and O'CONNOR, N. (1970) *Psychological Experiments with Autistic Children*. Oxford: Pergamon.

HERMELIN, B. and O'CONNOR, N. (1971a) Children's judgements of duration. *Brit. J. Psychol.*, **62**, 13–20.

HERMELIN, B. and O'CONNOR, N. (1971b) Spatial coding in normal, autistic and blind children. *Percept. mot. Skills*, **33**, 127–32.

HUNTER, I. (1962) An exceptional talent for calculative thinking. *Brit. J. Psychol.*, **53**, 243–58.

KANT, I. (1781) *Kritik der reinen Vernunft*. Riga. J. F. Hartknoch. 1933 edn, transl. N. Kemp Smith, London: Macmillan.

KIRK, S. A. and MCCARTHY, J. J. (1961) The Illinois test of psycho-linguistic abilities – an approach to differential diagnosis. *Amer. J. Ment. Defic.*, **66**, 399–412.

LURIA, A. R. (1956) Problems of the higher nervous activity of normal and abnormal children. *Acad. Pedagog. Sci.* Moscow: RSF SR.

LURIA, A. R. (1961) *The Rôle of Speech in the Regulation of Normal and Abnormal Behaviour*. Oxford: Pergamon.

MCKINNEY, J. P. (1964) Hand schema in children. *Psychon. Sci.*, **1**, 99–100.

MURDOCK, B. B. (1969) Where or when: modality effects as a function of temporal and spatial distribution of information. *J. Verb. Learn. Verb. Behav.*, **8**, 378–83.

O'CONNOR, N. and HERMELIN, B. (1959) Discrimination and reversal learning in imbeciles. *J. abn. soc. Psychol.*, **59**, 409–13.

O'CONNOR, N. and HERMELIN, B. (1963) *Speech and Thought in Severe Subnormality*. Oxford: Pergamon.

O'CONNOR, N. and HERMELIN, B. (1965) Input restriction and immediate memory decay in normal and subnormal children. *Quart. J. exp. Psychol.*, **XVII**, 323–8.

O'CONNOR, N. and HERMELIN, B. (1971a) Seeing and hearing and space and time. *Perception and Psychophysics* (in press).

O'CONNOR, N. and HERMELIN, B. (1971b) Cognitive deficits in children. *Brit. med. Bull.*, **27**, 227–31.

O'CONNOR, N. and HERMELIN, B. (1971c) Inter and Intra-modal transfer in children with modality specific and general handicaps. *Brit. J. soc. clin. Psychol.*, **10**, 346–54.

PIAGET, J. (1953) *The Origins of Intelligence in the Child* (transl. M. Cook). London: Routledge & Kegan Paul.

PIAGET, J. (1970) *Genetic Epistemology* (trans. E. Duckworth). New York: Columbia Univ. Press.

PIAGET, J. and INHELDER, B. (1969) *The Psychology of the Child* (transl. H. Weaver). London: Routledge & Kegan Paul.

PICK, H. L. and PICK, A. D. (1970) Sensory and perceptual development. In MUSSEN, P. (ed.) *Carmichael's Manual of Child Psychology*. New York: Wiley.

REITAN, R. M. (1966) A research programme on the psychological effects of brain lesions in human beings. In ELLIS, N. R. (ed.) *International Review of Research in Retardation*, Vol. I. New York: Academic Press.

RIESEN, A. H. (1947) The development of visual perception in man and chimpanzee. *Science,* **106,** 107–8.

RUDEL, R. and TEUBER, H. L. (1968) Pattern recognition within and across sensory modalities in normal and brain-injured children. *Annual Report, MIT Dept of Psychology.*

SAVIN, H. B. (1967) On the successive perception of simultaneous stimuli. *Perception and Psychophysics,* **2,** 479–82.

SCHEERER, M., ROTHMAN, E. and GOLDSTEIN, K. (1945) A case of 'idiot savant': an experimental study of personality organization. *Psychol. Monogr.,* **58.**

SMITH, J. and TUNICK, J. (1969) Transfer of discrimination by retarded children. *J. exp. Child Psychol.,* **7,** 274–84.

SPEARMAN, C. (1904) 'General intelligence': objectively determined and measured. *Amer. J. Psychol.,* **115,** 201–92.

SPITZ, R. A. (1945) Hospitalism: the inquiry into the genesis of psychiatric conditions in early childhood. In EISSLER, R. S., FREUD, A., HARTMANN, H. and KRIS, E. (eds.) *The Psychoanalytic Study of the Child,* Vol. I. New York: Internat. Univ. Press.

STRAUSS, A. A. and LEHTINEN, L. E. (1947) *Psychopathology and Education of the Brain-injured Child.* New York: Grune & Stratton.

SUTHERLAND, N. S. (1959) Stimulus analysing mechanisms. In *Proceedings of Symposium on the Mechanisation of Thought Processes,* Vol. 2, 575–609. London: HMSO.

SYLVESTER, P. E. (1966) Parietal lobe deficit in the mentally retarded. *J. Neurol. Neurosurg. Psychiat.,* **29,** 176–80.

TEUBER, H. L. (1959) Some alterations in behaviour after cerebral lesions in man. In *Evolution of Nervous Control.* Washington, DC: Amer. Assoc. Adv. Sci.

TEUBER, H. L. and LEIBERT, R. S. (1958) Specific and general effects of brain injury in man. *Arch. Neurol. Psychiat.,* **80,** 403–7.

THOMSON, G. H. (1939) *The Factorial Analysis of Human Ability.* London: Univ. of London Press.

THURSTONE, L. L. (1935) *The Vectors of the Mind.* Chicago: Univ. of Chicago Press.

TULVING, E. and MADIGAN, S. A. (1970) Memory and verbal learning. *Ann. Rev. Psychol.,* **21.** Palo Alto: Annual Review Inc.

VERNON, P. E. (1950) *The Structure of Human Abilities.* London: Methuen.

VON SENDEN, M. (1932) *Raum und Gestaltauffassung bei operierten Blind-geborenen vor und nach der Operation.* Leipzig: Barth.

VYGOTSKY, L. S. (1962) *Thought and language.* New York: MIT and Wiley.

WILLIAMS, M. (1950) *Williams' Intelligence Test for Children with Defective Vision.* Birmingham: Univ. of Birmingham Institute of Education.

WOODWARD, M. (1963) The application of Piaget's theory to research in mental deficiency. In ELLIS, N. R. (ed.) *Handbook of Mental Deficiency.* New York: McGraw-Hill.

ZEAMAN, D. and HOUSE, B. J. (1963) The role of attention in retardate discrimination learning. In ELLIS, N. R. (ed.) *Handbook of Mental Deficiency.* New York: McGraw-Hill.

12

B. Hermelin and N. O'Connor

Rules and structures: some studies with autistic children

Introduction

AUTISM AND MENTAL SUBNORMALITY

Though Wing (1966) remarks that early childhood autism can occur at any intelligence level, most surveys show that there is a strong bias towards the lower levels of intellectual functioning, i.e. below IQ 60. Lotter (1966) found that about 70 per cent of children in his sample had IQs below 55 (22 out of 32) and of the remaining 10, 6 were below IQ 80 as measured on the Seguin Form Board. Three were within normal limits on this test, and 1 was above normal expectation. Rutter (1966) tested 63 'psychotic' children. Of those, 26 had IQ scores of 50 or below, or no reliable score was obtainable; 19 had IQs between 50 and 69; and a further 11 between 70–89. Only 7 children had an IQ of 90 or above. When compared with a control group matched for IQ, the 'psychotic' children showed a greater variability on subtests. They were at their worst on those demanding abstract thought or symbolic or sequential logic, and at their best on those problems which required manipulative, or visual-spatial ability, or immediate verbal rote memory. Thus Bartak (personal communication) found that about 50 per cent of autistic children obtained scores in the average or superior range on Coloured Matrices. Gillies (1965) found that 13 out of 28 autistic children scored below 50 on non-verbal tests; 13 had IQs between 50 and 80; and 2 between 80 and 90. On a vocabulary test, 4 were untestable, a further 22 scored below IQ 50, and the remaining 2 below 70. No child achieved an all round normal score, though some children approached or reached a normal level on some test items.

In view of these and similar findings, one of the first questions to be asked must be whether there are any qualitative differences in psychological and cognitive functioning between those children diagnosed as autistic, and the rest of the mentally subnormal child population.

WHAT ARE AUTISTIC CHILDREN LIKE?

The first comprehensive description of the syndrome of Early Infantile Autism was made by Kanner (1943). He described a group of children encountered over the years who essentially showed what he described as 'autistic aloneness', as well as a tendency to ritualistic and stereotyped forms of behaviour, language impairment or complete absence of speech, motor mannerisms, and inappropriate responses to sensory stimuli. Kanner also stressed the children's 'insistence on sameness', i.e. an insistence on a fixed routine and resistance to change. Though his definition specifically excluded neurological damage, in fact symptoms of autism are accompanied by some indication of CNS damage in perhaps one-third of cases. In the more severely affected children, there is a high incidence rate of subsequent occurrence of epileptic seizures (Rutter *et al.*, 1970). Age of onset at birth or in the first two years has been determined largely by definition, and by differentiation from childhood schizophrenia.

Rutter (1967) has given a comprehensive assessment of criteria of differential diagnosis, taking account of the view of Kanner (1943), Despert (1955), Anthony (1962), Van Krevelen (1952), Bender (1956), Eisenberg (1966), Creak (1963) and others. Creak *et al.* (1961) have provided a description involving nine behavioural criteria. Creak's criteria included gross and sustained impairment of emotional relationships and a background of serious retardation with islets of normal or exceptional intellectual function. These two symptoms were regarded as key points. The other seven were: apparent unawareness of personal identity, pathological preoccupation with particular objects, sustained resistance to change, abnormal response to perceptual stimuli, acute and illogical anxiety, complete absence or abnormality of language, and distorted motility patterns. Of all the symptoms, Rutter (1968) found that only the language disorder was present in all the children and at all stages. Moreover, it is often the first symptom to be observed and it appears to be the most important prognostic factor. On the other hand, the symptom of autistic withdrawal has no significant association with outcome and it may show improvement or remission with no accompanying improvement in other symptoms.

The clinical features subsumed under the label of language abnormalities are manifold and differ from child to child. However, all autistic children show delayed development of speech, and many are suspected of deafness at some stage due to a lack of response to sounds. The majority of children who do learn to speak show echolalia, which in turn may give rise to the frequently observed tendency to reverse the pronouns 'you' and 'I'. Other features comprise symptoms reminiscent of developmental aphasia, lack of apparent interest in communication by either speech or gestures, failure to comprehend meaning, and marked 'concreteness' of the language used.

The other apparently most persistent symptom of early childhood autism refers to the ritualistic and stereotyped component present in many aspects of behaviour of autistic children in all stages of their development. Like every single feature described, it is also found in other psychiatric disorders. Manifestations of this phenomenon in autistic children appear to be mannerisms of hand and body movements, or stereotyped behaviour sequences found in spontaneous 'play', as well as in tasks requiring the solution of a problem or the execution of demands.

More complex examples of the same phenomenon are the 'insistence on same-ness', resistance to change, morbid attachments to objects and preoccupation with single thoughts. It has been suggested (Wing, 1966; Rutter, 1968) that the com-pulsive-ritualistic phenomena arise as a secondary means of the autistic child's dealing with his handicaps. If the autistic child, as a result of his inability to per-ceive meaning, is surrounded by a chaotic and unpredictable world, it seems plausible that this may evoke strong structuring tendencies in order to provide some rigid pattern in the environment. However, it is also possible that spon-taneously generated rigid patterning may impede the recognition of lawfulness in the environment. In the present chapter, we will describe a series of experiments which were carried out by us (Hermelin and O'Connor, 1970) and by Uta Frith (1969, 1970a, b), and which are concerned with two main features of autistic behaviour, the language abnormalities and the tendency to stereotopy. The question we asked was whether both these behaviour abnormalities could be associated with a generally impaired ability to perceive, remember and use structures, order, and pattern in a wide range of environmental features.

The autistic children taking part in the series of experiments to be reported here came from a sample of thirty children, all attending special schools and con-forming to the diagnostic criteria described by Rutter (1968). All children showed language abnormalities with associated cognitive disorders, some degree of autistic withdrawal and obsessional-ritualistic behaviour. Descriptive psycho-logical data on this sample have been obtained by Bartak (personal communica-tion). The average chronological age of the sample was 10 : 4 years (6 : 10 to 15 : 6), the social age as measured by the Vineland Social Maturity Scale was 6 : 4 years (3 : 4 to 10 : 6), the WISC Verbal Score IQ was 58 (45 to 89), the WISC Performance Scale IQ was 65 (44 to 115), the verbal IQ as assessed by the Peabody Picture Vocabulary Test (PPVT) was 66 (40 to 91).

Two control groups were used, one of normal children with chronological and mental ages between 3 and 6 years, and one of subnormal children who were matched for mental as well as chronological age with the autistic group. The non-autistic subnormal children came from schools for the educationally subnormal or from junior training centres.

Noise, voice, loudness and meaning

In the first study we want to report, autistic and subnormal children were pre-sented simultaneously with a visual and an auditory stimulus (O'Connor and Hermelin, 1965a). On each presentation of two such stimuli, the children could elect to approach one or the other of the stimulus sources, where they found a reward. There were thus no incorrect responses. In the experimental session, the children were tested individually in a room which was empty, except for loud-speakers and lights placed in the left-hand and right-hand corners of the room. The room was dimly lit, and three display combinations were presented. They were either a light from one side, and simultaneously a sound, or the words 'come here', from the other side. Visual and auditory stimuli were either of an equal and medium level of intensity, or the light was bright and presented together with the noise or the words at a low intensity, or lastly, the auditory stimuli were presented loudly, together with a low intensity light. With equal intensity, all children tended to approach the light rather than the sound stimulus, but an increase in the intensity of the sound increased the relative number of responses to it. However, when a word instead of a sound was simultaneously presented with light, subnormal children went towards the loudspeaker which had emitted the words, even when the relative intensity was lower than that of the visual signal.

This was not so for autistic children. They treated the words as equivalent to the noise, and only shifted their responses away from the light source when it was of very low relative intensity. It thus seemed that the autistic children were governed by the physical characteristics of the auditory stimulus, i.e. its intensity, rather than by its qualitative characteristic. They responded to words in the same way as to noises. Another study (Frith, 1969) investigated this further. It was based on observations that children learning to speak show consistent structural peculiarities of language (Brown and Fraser, 1963). They reduce English sentences in a systematic way, as in 'telegraphic English'. In this abbreviation 'keywords' (or content words) are retained and 'connecting words' (or function words) are omitted. Since keywords carry most of the information in a sentence and connecting words are largely predictable from the context, the former might be retained as a result of a communication analysis. On the other hand, keywords might be retained because they usually receive more emphasis, in terms such as higher intensity or longer duration. In normal speech, the two conditions cannot be disentangled; they could, however, be studied separately by putting emphasis on function words and leaving content words unstressed.

Thirty-two children acted as subjects in the study described. The mean chronological age of sixteen normal children, drawn from a nursery school, was 4 years 3 months. The autistic children had a mean chronological age of 11 years 6 months. All these children had been diagnosed as autistic by psychiatrists, all had early onset (before 3 years) of the psychosis, marked speech abnormalities and reported social and emotional abnormalities. Many showed obsessional features and bizarre motor movements. None appeared to be impaired in sight or hearing. Creak's (1961) nine criteria were applied to all these children, and at least four diagnostic features were shown by each of the subjects.

The groups were matched according to their Digit Span, since the method used in the experiment required that the subjects were comparable in their capacity for immediate recall of auditory material. In the Digit Span test recall was required of all presented digits in the same order as in the presentation. The criterion of success was at least one correct answer out of four trials.

In addition, the subjects' verbal ability was assessed in terms of mental age on the Peabody Picture Vocabulary Test (Dunn, 1959). The mean mental ages of the groups were not significantly different from each other and in relatively good accordance with the Digit Span scores. The mean verbal mental age for the normals was 3 years 11 months (ranging from 2 years 5 months to 5 years 7 months). For autistic children it was 4 years 9 months (ranging from 2 years 1 month to 10 years 5 months).

Word lists of 4, 6, 8, 10, 12, 14 words were constructed using words from Mein and O'Connor's (1960) list of words used by subnormals, in order to control the frequency of occurrence. Each list had on average word frequency of *c.* 50 per cent.

Half the words in each list were keywords, i.e. nouns, verbs, adjectives, adverbs; half were connecting words, i.e. pronouns, articles, auxiliary verbs and conjunctions. With each list first and second half were balanced in so far as they contained an equal number of keywords and connecting words.

Each word message was read aloud, using two different patterns of 'stress'. In one presentation keywords were stressed, and in the other connecting words were stressed. 'Stress' was defined as a relatively higher intensity level. Stressed words were spoken at a loudness of 78–83 db, unstressed words at a loudness of 60–68 db. The rate of presentation was 2 words per second; this approximates the rate of normal speech.

As the messages contained more words than the children could remember, the question asked was: Which words would be recalled? Keywords, which carried most of the information, regardless of the level of intensity with which they were presented, or stressed words, regardless of whether or not they were keywords? The results showed that those autistic children with a short digit span relied more on the intensity level of the words than on the amount of information they contained. They were more responsive to stress than to information content.

Thus the results of this study are in agreement with those from the previous experiment, that autistic children seem to extract the physical rather than the meaningful characteristics of speech. Indeed, the clinically observed echolalia in autism, where the children often repeat words with a similar accent and intonation to that heard, confirms these findings. It thus seems possible that the relative unresponsiveness to language stimuli, which can be observed in autistic children, may be less a function of lack of orientation towards auditory stimuli, but rather a consequence of their inability to extract meaning from language.

A SERIES OF SQUARES

While there are, of course, many aspects and definitions of 'meaning', it may depend, at least to some extent, on the appreciation of ordered structures. In relation to language, we call this structure 'grammar'. But grammar in this sense is not exclusive to language. There is also a 'grammar of perception', which enables us to compare, order, and classify the things we see. In the next series of experiments, we asked whether the impairment in the understanding of meaning was perhaps associated with a more general inability to extract order from a wide range of environmental stimuli.

In the next study we would like to report (O'Connor and Hermelin, 1965b), two groups of autistic children, one who did have some speech and one who had not, and groups of young normal and subnormal children were compared on a simple ordering task. The material consisted of five cardboard squares of decreasing size. The experimenter set these out in a row, starting with the largest and finishing with the smallest. The squares were then taken up and given to the child for the reproduction of this arrangement.

We found that though the task was relatively easy for the normals and subnormals, speaking as well as non-speaking autistic children did find it a very difficult one. They needed many repeated demonstrations and corrections before they could reproduce the series, and many of them did not achieve this at all. The autistic children tended to persist in setting out the squares in a random order, and did seem to have difficulties in appreciating that they should form an orderly sequence of decreasing size. Their appreciation of the principle of seriation involved was obviously impaired.

COLOUR PATTERNS

Seriation, according to Inhelder and Piaget (1964), does imply more than the simple ordering of elements. Piaget argues that seriation is only possible when the child has reached a level of mental development at which he is able to carry out reversible operations. In this context this means that any element in a series can be classified in two ways, i.e. in a series of items of graded sizes each item, except the two extremes, is smaller than some and larger than other items in the series. Thus the construction of a true series requires bi-directional comparisons to be made.

It might thus be argued that the previous seriation test involved more than the simple appreciation of order. The next study to be reported (Frith, 1970a) therefore uses simple binary sequences, where two items, in this instance red and green counters, were arranged in a pattern which the child had to reproduce. The simplest patterns which can be formed with such material appear to be repetitions, such as 'red, red, red, red', where one element is followed by the same one, or alternations, such as 'red, green, red, green', where one colour is followed by another. If a child is presented with either kind of series in a length which exceeds his immediate visual memory span, he has to extract the dominant rule governing the pattern in order to reproduce it correctly.

In the case of a regular alternation or repetition series, this is relatively easy. In the case of more complex structures, such as 'red, green, green, red', it is more difficult, and the more irregular the pattern becomes, the more difficult it will be to extract a dominant feature. The patterns used in the present experiment contained either predominantly repetitions or alternations. Also, in some patterns a change from one colour to another occurred only once, while two such changes occurred in others. Thus the dominant feature of a pattern could be clearly identified in terms of 'Alternation' or 'Repetition' rules as could the degree of regularity or irregularity it contained.

The children had to learn to make up four such patterns with green and red counters of 3·6 cm diameter, which they placed in a row inside a groove on a board just wide enough to hold a counter. The patterns were never shown beforehand, so that they had to be learned gradually, aided by corrections.

Each session, which lasted about half an hour, started with a sorting task to make sure that there was no difficulty in colour discrimination. The Ss had to sort green and red counters into two boxes. There were 36 counters of each colour.

The instructions for the experimental task relied mainly on a demonstration and a practice trial. The task was readily understood even by completely mute children.

The task was to place the counters from the two boxes one by one in a row so as to make a certain pattern. If the wrong colour were chosen, this was at once corrected by the E. As soon as one pattern was completed, the counters were immediately covered by a lid. The Ss had to repeat each pattern nine times, but each time the just-completed pattern was covered, so that direct copying was impossible. The order of the four patterns was balanced and so was the order of the colours within a pattern.

The overall performance level for both normal and autistic children was 75 per cent correct choices. The scores used for the analysis of differential performance and of learning indicated how often a S had used the incorrect colour in any position in a given pattern. There was a significant learning effect and a significant interaction of Group × Pattern. This interaction indicated that the level of errors of the normal children was clearly different for the four patterns, while the level of errors of the autistic children was similar in all patterns. For normal children, the patterns fell into two groups with significantly different error scores. The two easier patterns contained only one change from one colour to the other, i.e. consisted of two 'chunks', while the two more difficult patterns contained two such changes, i.e. had three 'chunks'.

Other analyses were carried out in order to investigate whether the errors were random or whether they were systematically related to the dominant feature of a given pattern. Since the given patterns were such that the dominant feature could be defined in terms of Alternation or Repetition rules, types of errors in accordance with those features would be expected to occur more frequently. Thus errors in 'Repetition dominant' patterns should be due to excessive application of the Repetition rule and errors in 'Alternation dominant' patterns should be due to excessive application of the Alternation rule.

It was thus possible to determine which errors were in accordance with the dominant feature. For example, an error due to alternation in an Alternation-dominated pattern was considered a positive instance of feature extraction, while an error due to perseveration in such a pattern would be considered a negative instance. An analysis of variance showed that normal children made more errors which were in accord with the dominant feature of the pattern; errors not complying with the dominant feature were significantly less frequent. In autistic children all errors were equally frequent, whether or not in accordance with the dominant feature of the pattern.

Thus the performance of normal children indicated that the four patterns were not equally easy to learn. Autistic children did not perform differently in the different types of patterns, in spite of their differing complexity. This finding is consistent with the hypothesis that autistic children are less sensitive to input characteristics than normal children. Even more support for this hypothesis is provided by the error analysis. Most errors made by normal children were consistent with the predominant rule of the given pattern. This would appear to indicate that feature extraction did occur. In autistic children little evidence of feature extraction could be found. Most of their errors were not consistent with the predominant rule of the pattern as given.

WORD PATTERNS

Both these last two studies could be regarded as being concerned with some aspects of the 'grammar of perception', though 'grammar' is simply defined in this context as a set of rules, and not necessarily the same rules as those of language. The next study by Frith (1970b) investigated the ability to appreciate similar rules, and use them for recall when the material presented were sets of words. As there were more words in a message than the children could remember, an efficient strategy would be to extract the dominant rule which governed the pattern, and use it for the reconstruction of the series. If, for instance, a series of such items would contain mostly repetitions of one word, with only an occasional switch to alternating two words, the rule to be extracted may be that of repetition, and the alternation element may be dropped or diminished in subsequent recall. Of course this process, like that of adopting other cognitive strategies, need not occur on a conscious level. For instance, in experiments on probability matching, where the subject recalls or predicts the probability of occurrence of one of a series of possible items, it has been found that the response frequencies after a while approach the actual proportions of the occurrence of these items in the series. However, the subject is often unable to state the principle which governs his responses.

In the following experiment the autistic children were compared with control groups matched in terms of their immediate digit span. There were Low and High Span groups. The Low Span groups consisted of 10 normal, 10 subnormal and 10 autistic children with a digit span of either 3 or 4. The normal children were between 4 and 5 years old and in their last year at nursery school. The subnormal children were between 10 and 16 years old, the autistic children between 7 and 13 years. Despite this discrepancy in chronological age, all children had a similar mental age of $4\frac{1}{2}$ years on the PPVT. It was found later that within groups age did not correlate significantly with performance on the experimental task itself. In addition, the subjects of the present experiment comprised 2 more groups of 10 normal and 10 autistic children with a digit span between 5 and 7.

Not enough subnormal children with such a high digit span could be found. The High Span groups had a PPVT mental age of approximately 6 years, which was also the chronological age of the normal children. The autistic children were between 8 and 15 years old. All children heard strings of 2 words arranged in different orders. The task of the child was to repeat what he had heard, as precisely as possible.

The Low Span subjects recalled 8 different patterns each 6 items long; the High Span subjects recalled 11 different patterns, each 12 items long. Examples of patterns presented for immediate recall are shown below, substituting the symbols '*a*' and '*b*' for any two different words actually presented in each list.

Examples of patterns

a b a b a b   a b b a b b   a b a a b a

In the trials, words were substituted for the symbols 'a' and 'b', for instance 'spoon mouse mouse mouse spoon spoon'.

Analysis of the results showed that autistic children were as good as the control groups in recalling the 'quasi-random' patterns, but were significantly

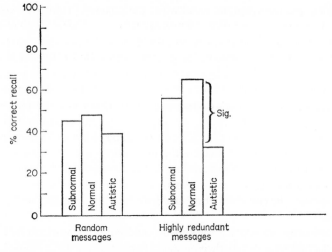

Fig. 4 Amount of correct recall for redundant and non-redundant patterns.

poorer than the control groups in recalling the other, more redundant patterns which showed a more consistent rule. This is illustrated in Fig. 4. The number of correctly recalled items of the quasi-random sequences for all children was the same or less than their digit span. However, in the more redundant, regular sequences, the control groups could recall significantly more items correctly. This implies that these children were processing the input efficiently. The features they extracted and stored increased recall above the limit of the immediate memory capacity. Autistic children, on the other hand, were not able to increase their recall significantly by the provision of greater redundancy in some of the patterns. Recall of autistic children suggested a strong recency effect as the only organizing principle, while recall of the control groups suggested feature extraction as an efficient processing strategy.

'Feature extraction' may be a similar process to that of finding an implicit rule contained in the input sequence. For example, the sequence *ababaa* is largely, if not completely, governed by the Alternation rule. If a child can extract and use this rule he can recall the sequence partially correctly by, for instance, producing *ababab*. The errors in this response can be assumed to be due to the exclusive and exaggerated application of the Alternation rule. Indeed, errors of this type can be used as evidence that a particular rule has actually been inferred. If there was no exaggeration, for instance, if the child would have recalled *aba*, then it could be that part of the input sequence was echoed and that processing was not involved. If recall was perfect, then again the conclusion that processing took place would be uncertain, since the child might have recalled the sequence by rote. Thus the following analyses are based only on incorrectly recalled lists.

If the incorrectly recalled sequences contained strings of either Alternations or Perseverations which were at least one item longer than the corresponding strings in the presented sequence, then this was considered a 'feature exaggeration'. For example, the presented sequence *ababaa* was recalled by one child as *ababab*, by another child as *aaaa*. The response of the first child would be scored as exaggeration of the Alternation rule, the response of the second child would be scored as exaggeration of the Repetition rule. While the first child applied the dominant rule, the second child used another, non-dominant rule. The number of children showing one type of exaggeration more often than the other in a given type of pattern is shown in Figs. 5 and 6.

The figures show that the control groups, regardless of developmental level, tended to exaggerate the predominant rule if exaggerations occurred at all, i.e. in approximately a third of all incorrect responses. Chi^2 tests indicated that Low Span normal children ($\chi^2 = 9 \cdot 14$, $p < \cdot 001$), Low Span subnormal children ($\chi^2 = 3 \cdot 14$, $p < \cdot 05$) and High Span normal children ($\chi^2 = 8 \cdot 64$, $p < \cdot 01$) extracted the dominant rule successfully. In contrast, more autistic children, both in Low Span and High Span groups, showed only exaggerations of repetitions and not exaggerations of alternating features, regardless of the dominant rule of the presented sequence.

It follows from these results that the type of errors of autistic and control children in the reproduction of very simple Repetition dominated patterns are similar. The specific processing deficit in autistic children becomes apparent only if more complex types of structures are introduced. In this case, the responses of autistic children do not reflect the dominant features of the different structures, and instead they show a response bias towards perseveration. Thus the results are consistent with the hypothesis that autistic children were little influenced by the crucial characteristics of the input.

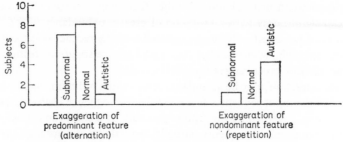

Fig. 5 Exaggerations in given Alternation Patterns.

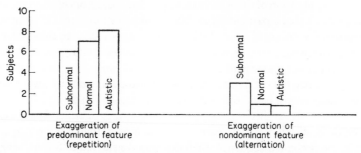

Fig. 6 Exaggerations in given Repetition Patterns.

SENSE AND NON-SENSE

After having established that autistic children are impaired in their ability to extract simple structural rules from visually or verbally presented material, the next question was whether this deficit extended to grammatical structures.

Grammar, as Chomsky (1961) points out, is not explicable in terms of learned sequential contingencies, and the understanding and production of sentences cannot therefore be explained through probability learning. Sentences with an equally low probability of contiguity between the words contained in it can nevertheless be appreciated as being either more or less grammatically correct. Contiguity of parts of speech instead of single words is an equally inadequate set of axioms for language structure. Indeed, what is necessary for understanding and producing language is a set of rules concerning the relationships of different grammatical patterns, i.e. active, passive, declarative, interrogative, negative, etc. These relationships are the rules of transformation and they are applied to the analysis of input data as well as for the planning and organizing of the output. Thus, knowing the language depends on the acquisition of a set of organizing principles.

With normals, immediate memory for verbal material is better for grammatically structured than unstructured messages (Epstein *et al.*, 1963; Marks and Miller, 1964). However, the improved scores to be found for patterned or structured messages may not be due to any improvement in the memory storage system, but may be attributable to successful guessing and predicting on the basis of one's knowledge of the characteristics of the language. The following experiment (Hermelin and O'Connor, 1967), therefore, investigated the relationship between immediate verbal recall and grammatical structure in 12 normal, 12 subnormal and 12 speaking autistic children. The normals were aged between 4 and 6 years. The other subjects were aged between 8 years and 14 years 5 months, with a mean age of 10 years 8 months. They were matched on the Peabody Vocabulary Test, which requires the visual recognition of spoken words. Mental ages on this test ranged from 2 years 6 months to 10 years 8 months, mean 4 years 3 months. The subjects were also matched individually on their immediate auditory-vocal memory span for digits, which ranged from 2 to 7, with a mean span of 4·5 digits. The material we used were one-syllable words, selected from a vocabulary list for subnormals (Mein, 1961). This list contains 1,720 words and their frequency of occurrence in the speech of a sample of 80 cases.

The selected words were presented in messages which consisted either of a simple English sentence, or of words of the same frequency, but occurring in random order. For each child, the length of the messages to be recalled exceeded his immediate memory span by 2 words. The comparison made was between recall scores for sentences, as compared to an unconnected string of words. Examples of the material are:

Sentences	*Random words*
We went to town	Light what leaf the
Today the weather has been fine	Some no dog for rain a

The messages were presented vocally at the rate of 2 words per second. The order in which sentences and random words were presented to each subject was determined by a balanced design. Recall after each message was immediate, but the rate of recall itself had to be unpaced. Though all children could be persuaded to try and repeat as many words as they remembered, it was not possible for them to do this at a fixed rate. Every effort was made consistent with a cooperative and optimal performance by the child, to ensure that his rate of recall was similar to that of other subjects and relatively constant.

The results of this recall experiment were scored in terms of number of messages correct, and are illustrated in Fig. 7. A correct message was one in which all words were repeated in the correct order. These scores were then treated by analysis of variance.

A comparison was made between scores obtained for the recall of sentences, and words of the same frequency presented in a random order. The result was a highly significant Groups by Conditions interaction. This showed that the subnormal children did much better with sentences than with unconnected words. This difference between the two kinds of material affected the recall of the autistic children far less. In fact, for them the difference between their recall scores for sentences and random word arrangements was not statistically significant.

Thus this experiment provided us with two results. The first was a confirmation of previous observations that autistic children have auditory-verbal immediate memories, which are at least as good as those of normals or subnormals of similar mental development. The second one was that when words were presented in the form of sentences, they were easier to recall for subnormal children than when they were presented in random order. This, however, did not apply to the same extent to the autistic children. If the greater ease with which organized material is remembered is due to the subject's ability to predict the items on the basis of the order in which they are organized, then it follows that the autistic child fails to make use of such an order, possibly because he may not recognize it

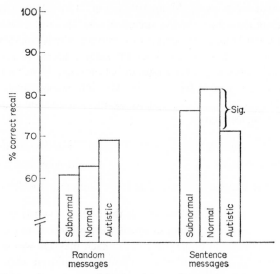

Fig. 7 Correct recall for random and sentence sequences.

as familiar. It is thus possible that autistic children, though they might understand single words, nevertheless do not understand sentence structure adequately.

As we argued earlier, the improved recall found in normals for semantically or sequentially connected material could be due to the subject's ability to retrieve verbal items through associating or guessing on the basis of familiarity with the properties of the language. Reliance on an 'echobox' type store (Craik, 1966) in conditions of auditory-vocal recall would result in favouring the most recent or last item in a series to be recalled. If, on the other hand, a classified storage system were used, structure would determine recall more than recency. The following experiment (O'Connor and Hermelin, 1967) tested these assumptions. Thirty-six children acted as subjects. There were 24 normals, 12 of them aged 4 years 11 months to 5 years, and 12 aged 3 years 6 months to 4 years 8 months. Twelve speaking autistic children were aged between 7 years 4 months and 15 years 8 months, mean 11 years 9 months. All subjects were individually matched for memory span for digits across groups, and the verbal sequences used for the experimental procedure were twice the subject's individual memory span in all cases.

The words in the passages to be presented for recall were selected from Mein and O'Connor's (1960) vocabulary, which gives frequency of occurrence of words in the speech of severely subnormal subjects. The words had frequencies between 30 per cent and 90 per cent and all messages were matched for an average frequency of 50 per cent. Each child was presented with 4 examples for each of the 4 types of message set out in the table. Order of presentation of conditions was balanced and randomized between subjects. Presentation rate was at the speed of 2 words per second, and recall was immediate and unpaced.

It can be seen from the material illustrated below that in one condition randomly arranged words have to be recalled, while in another it is 2 short sentences of equal length. In the remaining condition, a random arrangement of words is followed by a sentence of equal length, or, conversely, randomly arranged words follow a sentence. The question was: Which words would be recalled? Would it be the sentences, independent of whether they occurred at the beginning or the end of a message, or the last few words most recently heard, irrespective of whether they were in sentence or random form?

Examples of eight-word messages

Random-Random
| day | she | farm | when-cat | fall | back | rake |

Random-Sentence
| wall | long | cake | sand-where | is | the | ship? |

Sentence-Random
| read | them | your | book-way | spoon | here | like |

Sentence-Sentence
| ride | home | by | car-write | to | us | now |

The results were scored separately for the first and second half of each message, so that the number of words correctly recalled for first or second half, and from sentences and random arrangements, could be compared. The results of these comparisons are illustrated in Fig. 8.

An analysis of variance of the recall scores resulted in two highly significant interaction terms, viz. Groups by Positions and Groups by Conditions. The first of these confirmed that though all groups showed the effect of recency on recall, this was far more marked in the autistic children than in the other group. The second interaction illustrated that though sentences were recalled better than random arrangements by all subjects, this effect was much more marked in the normal than in the autistic children. Recall scores for randomly arranged words were the same for all groups, while sentences were significantly better recalled by the normal than by the autistic children. Thus the control group recalled sentences better than non-sentences, independently of their relative position in the message. The autistic children, on the other hand, recalled the last part of a message better than the first part, irrespective of whether this was a sentence or not.

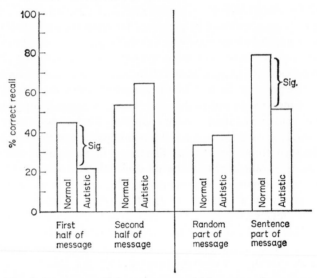

Fig. 8 Correct recall for sentences and last part of messages.

Conclusions: storage of programming deficits

The experiments summarized in this chapter seem to indicate to us a clearly definable cognitive pathology in autistic children. Whereas young normal as well as subnormal children on the whole made use of structures and extracted rules according to their mental ages, the autistic children behaved in a qualitatively different way. This means that even the subnormal draw on the linguistic associations available to them, whereas autistic children cannot do this. They therefore draw on the contents of their (superior) immediate memory, which, of course, favours recent material. One could propose a model for cognitive deficit which posited deficiency either in the appropriate programme or in size of the memory store of the system. If we were to use this model as the basis for explaining our findings, we might suggest that the subnormal have a very limited storage capacity, while the coding and ordering operations by the autistic seem incorrectly programmed.

References

ANTHONY, J. (1962) Low grade psychosis in childhood. In RICHARDS, B. W. (ed.) *Proc. Lond. Conf. Scient. Stud. Ment. Defic.*, **2**. Dagenham: May & Baker.

BENDER, L. (1956) Schizophrenia in childhood: its recognition, description and treatment. *Amer. J. Orthopsychiat.*, **26**, 499–506.

BROWN, R. and FRASER, C. (1963) The acquisition of syntax. In COFER, C. N. and MUSGRAVE, B. S. (eds.) *Verbal Behaviour and Learning.* New York: McGraw-Hill.

CHOMSKY, N. (1961) An elementary linguistic theory. In SAPORTA, S. (ed.) *Psycholinguistics.* New York: Holt, Rinehart & Winston.

CRAIK, F. I. M. (1966) Short-term memory: echo box plus search process. *London Conference of the British Psychological Society.*

CREAK, M. and others (1961) Schizophrenic syndrome in childhood: progress report of a working party. *Cerebral Palsy Bull.,* **3,** 501–4.

CREAK, M. (1963) Childhood psychosis: a review of 100 cases. *Brit. J. Psychiat.,* **109,** 84.

DESPERT, J. L. (1955) Differential diagnosis between obsessive-compulsive neurosis and schizophrenia in children. *Psychopathic Child,* **30,** 240–53.

DUNN, L. M. (1959) *Manual for the Peabody Picture Vocabulary Test.* Minneapolis: Amer. Guidance Service Inc.

EISENBERG, L. (1966) Psychotic disorders in childhood. In COOKE, R. E. (ed.) *Biological Basis of Pediatric Practice.* New York: McGraw-Hill.

EPSTEIN, W., MILLER, G. A. and ISARD, S. (1963) Some perceptual consequences of linguistic rules. *J. Verb. Learn. Verb. Behav.,* **2,** 217–28.

FRITH, U. (1969) Emphasis and meaning in recall in normal and autistic children. *Language and Speech,* **12,** 29–38.

FRITH, U. (1970a) Studies in pattern detection in normal and autistic children. Reproduction and production of colour sequences. *J. exp. Child Psychol.,* **10,** 120–35.

FRITH, U. (1970b) Studies in pattern perception in normal and autistic children. Immediate recall of auditory sequences. *J. abn. Psychol.,* **76,** 413–20.

GILLIES, S. M. (1965) Some abilities of psychotic children and subnormal controls. *J. ment. Defic. Res.,* **9,** 89–101.

HERMELIN, B. and O'CONNOR, N. (1967) Remembering of words by psychotic and subnormal children. *Brit. J. Psychol.,* **58,** 213–18.

HERMELIN, B. and O'CONNOR, N. (1970) *Psychological Experiments with Autistic Children.* Oxford: Pergamon.

INHELDER, B. and PIAGET, J. (1964) *The Early Growth of Logic in the Child: Classification and Seriation.* London: Routledge & Kegan Paul.

KANNER, L. (1943) Autistic disturbances of affective contact. *Nerv. Child,* **2,** 217–50.

LOTTER, V. (1966) Epidemiology of autistic conditions in young children. I: Prevalence. *Soc. Psychiat.,* **1,** 124–37.

MARKS, L. and MILLER, G. (1964) The role of semantic and syntactic constraints in the memorisation of English sentences. *J. Verb. Learn. Verb. Behav.,* **3,** 1–5.

MEIN, R. (1961) *A List of Words used in Conversation of Severely Subnormal Patients.* Cell Barnes and Harperbury Group Hospital Management Committee.

MEIN, R. and O'CONNOR, N. (1960) A study of the oral vocabularies of severely subnormal patients. *J. ment. Defic. Res.,* 4, 130–43.

O'CONNOR, N. and HERMELIN, B. (1965a) Sensory dominance in autistic imbecile children and controls. *Archiv. gen. Psychiat.,* 12, 99–103.

O'CONNOR, N. and HERMELIN, B. (1965b) Visual analogies of verbal operations. *Language and Speech,* 8, 197–207.

O'CONNOR, N. and HERMELIN, B. (1967) Auditory and visual memory in autistic and normal children. *J. ment. Defic. Res.,* 11, 126–31.

RUTTER, M. (1966) Behavioural and cognitive characteristics. In WING, J. (ed.) *Early Childhood Autism: Clinical Educational and Social Aspects.* Oxford: Pergamon.

RUTTER, M. (1967) Psychotic disorders in early childhood. In COPPER, A. J. (ed.) *Brit. J. Psychiat.,* Spec. Publ.

RUTTER, M. (1968) Concepts of autism. A review of research. *J. Child Psychol. Psychiat.,* 9, 1–25.

RUTTER, M., BARTAK, L. and NEWMAN, S. (1970) *Autism, A Central Disorder of Cognition and Language?* Paper to the Study Group of Infantile Autism at the Ciba Foundation.

VAN KREVELEN, D. A. (1952) Early infantile autism. *Acta Paedopsychiat.,* 30, 303–23.

WING, J. K. (1966) Diagnosis, epidemiology, aetiology. In WING, J. K. (ed.) *Childhood Autism: Clinical, Educational and Social Aspects.* Oxford: Pergamon.

PART THREE

Assessment

13

A. M. Clarke and A. D. B. Clarke

Severe subnormality: capacity and performance[1]

Introduction

This group of people are those most easily recognized as mentally handicapped in any community. The vast majority owe their condition to one or other of a variety of unusual genetic or environmental events which render them permanently damaged organisms, who will never be capable of leading a properly independent existence in the community. In societies with a high rate of child mortality, relatively few survive to adulthood; in advanced societies providing good medical care their survival may present a considerable problem to their families. Probably about a third live permanently in hospitals or other institutions, and about two-thirds are reared by their parents, but will by virtue of their handicaps require some form of supervised residential provision all their lives.

The recognition that many severely retarded children and adults are susceptible to training, and in later life can contribute to varying extents to their own support in sheltered conditions, has been one of the major advances in the study of the mentally subnormal.

With the greater understanding of the potential adverse effects of the large institution on the subnormal (Lyle, 1959, 1960a, b; Tizard, 1960; Morris, 1969), there is an increasing tendency to keep the severely retarded in the community. This implies a requirement to provide skilled teaching from a very early age and at least into late adolescence in order to normalize the child (Grunewald, 1969). Considerable advances have taken place in the educational technology required to develop social, language and vocational skills in the severely retarded, and it is no longer considered desirable for a majority either to 'put them away' from society or to keep them occupied with leisurely activities such as painting and dancing.

Until the early 1950s there had been little interest in the psychology of moderately and severely retarded persons. Clinical descriptions in textbooks

[1] Partly based upon a paper presented to the Ciba Foundation and Institute for Research into Mental Retardation, Study Group No. 5, London, December 1971. Published in P. J. Mittler (ed.) *Psychological Assessment of the Mentally Handicapped* (London, Churchill, 1973). Reproduced in part by kind permission of the editor and publishers.

concentrated upon what they *cannot* do rather than what they might achieve with training. The view of various authors can be summarized as follows:

1. At best they find it extremely difficult to concentrate and, more typically, seem capable only of involuntary and momentary attention.
2. They are incapable of comparing and discriminating even on the simplest plane, and of appreciating the relationship between cause and effect.
3. They are quite incapable of adapting themselves to anything out of the ordinary.
4. They are only able to perform the simplest routine tasks under constant supervision.
5. All this makes them unable to contribute appreciably towards their own support.

The traditional concepts referred to above were sanctified by repetition as recently as 1956 in the ninth edition of Tredgold's well-known text (Tredgold and Soddy, 1956), as the following excerpt indicates:

Imbeciles, as a class, stand above the idiots in that they can be taught to understand and protect themselves against many common physical dangers. For instance, they will not deliberately walk into a pond or put their hands into the fire, and they will attempt to get out of the way of a motor-car. They stand below the feeble-minded in that, whilst many of them can be trained to perform simple routine tasks under supervision, they are incapable of earning their living or of contributing materially towards their support. Most of them can wash, dress, and feed themselves under supervision. They are markedly defective in educational capacity, and as a class they cannot be taught to read beyond words of one syllable, to spell more than a few two- and three-letter words, or to do simple mental addition and subtraction beyond the smallest units. They can tell their name, say whether it is morning or afternoon, winter or summer. They can recognize and name common objects, and can say for what they are used, but they cannot give a description of them.

It is increasingly recognized that these negatives have much validity for the institutionalized severe subnormal who has not enjoyed an active training programme, but that they seriously underestimate, in their general tone, the possibilities of remediation. Indeed a review of only fifteen studies in the first edition of this book forced us in 1958 to conclude that:

... in this neglected field of imbecile learning, it is clear that much more research is needed and that the investigations reported have merely laid a basis for later work. Even so, there is little doubt that already some traditional concepts of imbecile abilities and trainability are in need of qualification or revision; consequently this must also apply to our methods of helping and training the low-grade patient.

This view was further documented in the second edition written in 1964. During the intervening years there had been something of an explosion of interest in this field and our review had become necessarily selective. In rewriting this chapter in 1972 it was obvious that even greater selectivity would be required, for a detailed coverage of the literature would demand a book in its own right. Thus we propose to organize the discussion around two broad topics, first, the psychometric, and second, the experimental approach to severe subnormality. In so doing we shall merely sample the considerable literature. It should, however, be stated at the outset that we believe that modern research gives guidance on some broad general principles of remediation. It seems to us that the most important general deficits in the severely subnormal are, firstly, a *severe inability to learn spontaneously from ordinary life experience* which includes social contacts with parents, peers and the community at large; secondly, there is almost always a severe language impairment; and thirdly, there is a considerable slowness in learning. Thus, if they are merely exposed to normal social and educational situations they will, on the whole, fail to profit from them. If, however, a situation or task is analysed for them and their attention directed to the relevant aspects by means of *structured training*, a very different picture will emerge, granted a sufficiently lengthy period (Clarke and Clarke, 1973). Thus the older generalizations noted above are true of those who have not been exposed to programmes of directed training with adequate rewards; they tend initially to be very bad at any task. However, the starting level (unlike that of normal people) bears little or no relationship to the final level after training, and, furthermore, on *simple* tasks they are usually able to achieve the same speed and quality as normals, but the time taken to reach this standard is very much longer.

Limitations of the psychometric approach

Psychometric assessment has four main functions:

1. to describe the individual as he is at a particular point in time, upon intellectual, social, emotional, educational or other variables with reference to a normative or contrast population;
2. to predict the individual's probable status at later points in time;
3. to provide a behavioural profile of assets and deficits as a starting point for remedial programmes;
4. to provide an objective means of checking progress of an individual or a group.

These categories of assessment in mental subnormality are intimately related to the services society provides, and thus to the demands for different types of information made upon the psychologist. If, for one reason or another, only custodial care is offered and no attempts at remediation, then assessment will only be concerned with the establishment of a clear borderline, related to the amount of provision, the estimated demands and the degree of handicap. In such a situation an individual intelligence test and an assessment of social competence will be essential. If, on the other hand, an adequate remedial service becomes available, then assessment becomes a starting point for action and a means for evaluating its results.

Most assessment procedures aim as far as possible to give an indication of native ability or capacity. It is nowadays recognized that it is impossible to measure 'pure' ability, unaffected by life experience, which must be largely unknown to the psychologist. On the whole, however, the vast literature on psychological assessment in the normal population is generally interpreted as indicating that properly standardized measures of ability or aptitude are at least useful in helping to predict achievement granted 'normal' life experience and 'normal' educational experience without any special remedial element. Two *caveats* are, however, increasingly accepted: that prediction is strongly affected by (1) the age at which it is undertaken, the earlier the measure the lower its predictive power; and (2) the length of time over which predictions are made, the longer the period, the less the accuracy. It has recently been argued that these generalizations apply not only to intelligence but also to personality measurements and attainment tests. Moreover, examination of data suggests that in the mildly subnormal, average and supernormal populations there is much more variability in growth than has been accepted. The contrary view results from a misunderstanding of the implications of correlation coefficients between repeated measurements over time. Even a ·9 correlation describes a situation in which a minority may make considerable changes of status, and in longitudinal studies one is normally dealing with much lower relationships and thus considerably greater proportions of significant individual change. Such an analysis is borne out by all really long-term studies (e.g. Baller *et al.*, 1967; Oden, 1968). In brief, predictive assessment is in general less accurate over the long term than is generally assumed (Clarke and Clarke, 1972). There is, however, a lack of long-term data on the severely subnormal but a consensus that, under conditions of minimal remediation, there will be little achievement. Global predictions are thus possible and probably fairly accurate.

The main argument of this chapter is that assessment, as outlined in the first three headings (and particularly in the first two), is of limited value in the field of subnormality. In Britain it has been classically regarded as the main contribution of psychologists. As currently employed it appears more often as an epiphenomenon keeping them busy, stimulating often unprofitable research and leading to a perpetual quest for the philosopher's stone (better and better tests) which will ensure more and more accurate predictions. It will be argued that, for a number of reasons, such hopes are misguided and that more profitable alternatives already exist.

THE BACKGROUND – AN OVERVIEW

Post-war research on severe subnormality began with the work of Tizard and his colleagues Gordon and Loos. This showed that, granted individual attention and training in simple and not-so-simple laboratory tasks, the traditional picture of the behaviour of the severely subnormal needed substantial revision. For example, good motor dexterity and good spatial judgment could be achieved within a reasonable period of training, the skills gained were retained, and learning transfer could be demonstrated as a powerful function on some tasks. Within a few years Clarke and Hermelin showed that the results of these laboratory studies could be replicated in sheltered 'real life' industrial working conditions. Later still it was concluded that the combination of typically poor starting points yet subsequently good learning, both on laboratory and industrial tasks, could only be explained by postulating a relative inability in these subjects to learn spontaneously from ordinary life experience (Clarke and Cookson, 1962).[1] It was thus easy to understand the traditional view of the lack of capacity in the severely subnormal; Tredgold and others had taken initial performance as a sample of potential learning ability, and therefore that the SSN were incapable of learning, full stop.

There are two sources of learning which may interact with the biologically determined potential of any developing human organism: (1) unstructured situations, the majority, and (2) structured learning situations, the minority. As we see it, the highly intelligent 'spontaneous' learner will profit greatly from the former, as well as from the latter, the less gifted will rely increasingly on the latter, and the severely subnormal will profit rather little from unstructured situations. The notion that the best learning is self-generated has for years been the basis of 'progressive' education, associated in this country with the names of A. S. Neill and Bertrand Russell among others. It has become a major article of faith in Colleges of Education, and has become logically attached to the developmental theory of Piaget. Teachers in training are encouraged to use informal assessment of Piagetian stages to discover whether their pupils are 'ready' to learn certain concepts, or, indeed, certain skills like reading. Since what they are assessing is the spontaneous acquisition of certain elaborate behaviours based upon innate abilities interacting with the environment in an unknown way over an unknown period, by the time the child shows 'readiness' he requires little formal teaching. If one assesses the severely subnormal in Piagetian terms (as in any other terms) one will be likely to conclude that he is not ready to learn.

It appears that the severely subnormal child may lose out under both headings mentioned above. First, there is an obvious constitutional deficit which imposes severe limits upon his development, and includes, if we are correct, a relative inability spontaneously to structure ordinary experience. Moreover, as a mainly passive baby and child, his role in the dyad with his parents will tend to evoke

---

[1] It is difficult to define spontaneous learning ability without embarking on a discussion of the nature of intelligence. However, it includes the ability to organize or code incoming stimuli in a variety of ways and to build up schemata appropriately which enable the individual both to respond selectively and to embark upon the next stages of learning. It includes the ability to perceive relationships and make deductions without the intervention of another human agent. We are not arguing that the SSN have no spontaneous learning ability, merely that it is very greatly impaired.

less responsiveness and thus less stimulation. Second, the current move away from structured situations, already referred to, avoids the conditions which for him are almost the sole possibility of learning.

The early background work can be summarized by stating in more modern terms that in the severely subnormal there is a profound gap between psychological capacity and initial performance, a gap which has its origin in constitutional factors on the one hand, and mode of handling on the other.

SOME DETAILED EVIDENCE

Assessment usually involves a one-trial measure on a particular variable, and hence indicates initial performance. Brief evidence has already been offered on the inadequacy of initial performance as a predictor, and hence on the inadequacy of normal assessment methods for prediction in this population. It may, however, help to put some flesh on the bare bones of the argument, to select for purposes of illustration a stream of work which illustrates the theme and with which Tizard and ourselves have been concerned. For this we take the Minnesota Spatial Relations Test, normally an industrial selection test, but used as a learning task on several occasions in the last twenty years. This consists of 4 very large form-boards each containing 58 holes into which the corresponding 58 pieces have to be fitted, these being first set out in a pre-determined order. The boards comprise 2 pairs, A and B, and C and D. For each pair, a single set of pieces is common although the corresponding holes are in very different places in each board. For efficient performance on this difficult task, not only is it necessary accurately to perceive form, but clustering behaviour, involving the selection of sets of 3 or 4 identical shapes (differing in size), aids the speed and efficiency of solution, these being the test criteria.

The classic assessment approach might raise the following problems:

1. How good or bad is the individual on a spatial relations task (i.e. *on 1 trial of 1 board*)?
2. On the basis of the test (i.e. single trial), can we predict the subject's suitability for, e.g., industrial training?
3. From his performance can we predict his future status on this task?

The inadequacy of these questions will be obvious from what follows. With hindsight, it can be assumed that the individual's spatial ability is to varying extents damaged, that prediction of future status on the basis of initial test score is very limited, that however poor his initial performance, he will respond to training, that the degree of his disability will only affect the speed of responsiveness and that therefore a specific individual programme is hardly necessary. Let us see how learning experiments built up this somewhat different picture.

Tizard and Loos (1954) showed that a group of SSNs selected as being thought virtually unemployable in an institution workshop with average IQs of about 35 exhibited exceedingly poor performance (averaging about 20 minutes) on Trial 1 of the first board (the normal average being about 4 minutes). Their learning curves were impressive and over the succeeding 3 boards they showed considerable transfer. Time scores for correct solutions were used, and by Trial 32 had reduced to 3 or 4 minutes, the average Trial 1 score for normals. This work was confirmed and amplified by Clarke (1962), Clarke and Cooper (1966) and Radon and Clarke (1971).

In an oversimplified way some of these findings may be summarized: (1) initial (i.e. assessment) score bears no relationship to final score; (2) while initial scores are very poor and vary widely between individuals, final scores after 32 trials are very homogeneous and good (i.e. the 'funnel effect'); (3) learning transfer takes place between boards and is an impressive function; (4) over very long periods of time without direct practice, a retest indicates that initial scores are greatly improved probably because of exposure to other industrial tasks involving spatial relationships; (5) clustering behaviour, which ordinarily occurs poorly but spontaneously can be differentially increased by a particular type of training.

These facts being established for this type of perceptual-motor activity, single trial assessment of spatial ability together with individual predictions, or selection on this basis, are misconceived. Rather, the more economical assumption with the SSN subject is that he will show initial inadequacy and thus a programme to overcome it needs to be prescribed.

Of course it may well be that the work on the Minnesota Test, which has been summarized, by chance capitalized upon particular potential assets and the findings might not, for example, apply to a complicated language programme. All one can say, however, is that on initial performance (i.e. test assessment) one scarcely gained the impression that these gravely damaged subjects had any spatial assets at all. But certainly in this area at least, the total inadequacy of assessing 'spatial ability' or 'clustering ability' by exposure to a single trial or even a few trials is obvious. Indeed, had Tizard and Loos (1954) merely used this task for its usual purpose, a 1-trial assessment test, and had we then accepted this as a predictor, the course of subsequent work might have been very different. It was this difference between Trial 1 prediction and outcome that stimulated Clarke and Hermelin (1955) to undertake experiments on industrial work. Using *the same subjects* as Tizard and Loos in a recently created industrial unit, these authors sought to establish whether the laboratory findings would be confirmed, and whether more complex skills might be taught. They employed 3 tasks: (1) the use of a guillotine to cut insulated wire to exact lengths; (2) the soldering of 4 different coloured wires to the correct terminals of an 8-pin television plug; and (3) the assembly of a bicycle pump, involving 9 operations which had to be performed in the correct order.

The table overleaf summarizes some of the findings.

The Guillotine data, based on only 2 hours of training, separated by a week of non-practice, show very considerable improvement which no doubt would have continued had the minimal training been prolonged. The relation of initial to final scores for 6 subjects was: 35–46; 23–33; 40–52; 36–56; 16–48; 15–57.

The Television Plug results show widely different starting points and great improvement, leading to very similar endpoints (the 'funnel effect').

The Bicycle Pump Assembly data indicate precisely similar results to the above.

In all cases, Trial 1 performance (the typical assessment device) is very poor, nor is it any guide to ultimate level of improvement, nor is it correlated with ultimate level. The authors concluded that the main difference on simple tasks between the ability of these subjects and normals was not so much the endpoint as the time taken to achieve it. Had Trial 1 been used for assessment purposes, it would have been concluded that these subjects were below all norms, and that they were therefore unsuitable for any sort of industrial work, which would also have been predicted from Trial 1 of the Minnesota Test. Data from these two

TABLE 12. *Some basic data*

	Initial range	Final range	Duration of training
Guillotine	15–40 wires cut per 5 min.	33–57 wires cut per 5 min.	2 × 1-hour periods
Television plug	4 min.–19 min. per plug	1 min. 42 sec.– 3 min. 30 sec. per plug	34 trials
Bicycle pump	4 min. 20 sec.– 10 min. 45 sec. per assembly	54 sec.– 1 min. 50 sec. per assembly	30 trials

experiments have been presented in some detail because they appear to offer the key to understanding the inadequacy of most assessment methods in this population.

Let us also consider another example, namely some very recent work which, on the face of it, appears to contradict the argument advanced so far but which, in reality, probably supports it. This is some very careful work by Grant (1971) whose concern includes the problem of prediction of workshop industrial ability. Some 13 industrial assessment tests were given to a sample of trainees in an Adult Training Centre, and from these 17 predictor variables were identified. These scores were correlated with performance on 8 industrial tasks on the average of the first 3 successful trials. The findings indicated that a far greater proportion of the tests produced significant correlations with job performance for males than females. 'A tentative explanation for this', writes Grant, 'would be that the previous work experience of males and females has been so different over the years that attributes such as those measured have developed differentially between the sexes.' This notion, which seems entirely reasonable, implicitly supports the view of Ferguson (1954) that specific abilities arise from, among other things, overlearning of typical sequences. The second main finding of Grant was that, on the whole, the correlations were of moderate to high value. Thus, for the males 56 out of 136 correlations were ·70 or above, and for the females, 37 out of 136.

These data appear to yield quite impressive relationships and suggest the possibility of developing a more refined test battery for the accurate prediction of industrial performance. However, as the author seems implicitly aware, the outlook may well be less rosy, because what he has in effect done is to correlate initial performance on assessment tasks, themselves designed to sample the basic perceptual-motor processes involved in industrial work, with initial performance (on the average, the first five trials) on industrial tasks. That initial industrial-type performance correlates quite well with initial industrial performance, while interesting, does not necessarily imply that these devices would in any sense predict final achievement levels after training.

As a further example, the work of Cobb (1969) can be cited. He has provided in two volumes a summary of the research literature on the predictive assessment of the adult retarded for social and vocational adjustment. He reaches thirteen conclusions, of which three will be alluded to here. His views in this particular field bear striking similarity with some of the more general points we have made.

1. The most consistent and outstanding finding of all follow-up studies is the high proportion of the adult retarded who achieve satisfactory adjustments, by whatever criteria are employed. This is, of course, especially true of those at mild level, on whom most of the studies have been done; but it also holds for the retarded at moderate and even severe levels. This should guide the counselor to the adoption of more generally optimistic expectation than has generally prevailed in the past. Indeed, the evidence suggests that it is more appropriate to make an assumption of positive adaptation on some meaningful criteria of employability and social integration until negative evidence appears rather than to assume a poor prognosis until positive evidence appears. The latter attitude, which has been highly prevalent in the past, has the general effect of creating its own proof by failing to provide available means for facilitating successful adaptation. Every follow-up validation of predicted successes and failures has shown a higher rate of false negatives than of false positives. . . .

3. Evidence from the major follow-up studies indicates that adult adaptation of the retarded may take considerable time, especially when retardation is related to social and cultural deprivation. The movement from instability to stability may take years but it may be greatly facilitated by flexible, open-ended programs of social-vocational training. Failure at any point should never be taken as conclusive. The general principle, supported throughout the research literature, is that predictions of adaptive success are generally more reliable than predictions of failure. This might lead a counsellor who is interested only in building a good record of successful closures to concentrate

all his attention on the clearly positive cases and exclude all the 'risk' cases. But it will lead the counsellor who is really client-centered to be very cautious in accepting negative prognosis as final evidence of unfeasibility. . . .

6. Of particular significance to case workers is the finding from Parnicky's research that predictive validity decreases rapidly over time and over the stages of training. This finding suggests that we are on much firmer ground in using predictive measures more as estimates of preparation for the *next step* in training or placement than as determiners of the longer-range future.[1]

In this section some brief attention has been devoted to spatial ability, industrial performance and to social and vocational adjustment. To round off this survey, a short account will be given of a different area, namely 'clustering', a higher-order cognitive ability in which it might reasonably be expected that subnormals would be clearly deficient. Gerjuoy and Spitz (1966) studied clustering and free recall as a function of age, intelligence, and practice. Five populations were used: 20 middle-grade subnormals (mean IQ 53), 20 high-grades (mean IQ 72), 19 matched normal MA subjects (mean IQ 107), 14 matched CA subjects (mean IQ 117) and finally, a group of 20 college students.

The experimental material consisted of 20 nouns, 5 from each of 4 categories (animals, body parts, clothing, and food). Using an identical procedure to that of Rossi (1963), 5 separate randomizations of this test were used, together with 2 different measures of clustering. Data for middle- and high-grade subnormals were pooled since there were no significant differences between them on recall or amount of clustering. Comparison of the subnormals with the other populations showed significant Population and Trial effects (both with $p < \cdot001$) with nonsignificant interactions. There were no significant differences between the 2 lower MA groups, nor between the 2 higher MA groups. The latter, however, both recalled more words than the former.

Subnormals and their MA matched controls clustered very little, and only on Trial 5 for the subnormals were the scores significantly above chance. Equal CA normals clustered significantly on Trials 4 and 5 ($p < \cdot02$), and college students on Trials 3, 4 and 5 ($p < \cdot001$). Significant correlations between clustering and recall were found only for equal CA normals on Trial 5 ($r = \cdot55$, $p < \cdot05$) and for college students on Trials 4 ($r = \cdot81, p < \cdot01$) and 5 ($r = \cdot85$, $p < \cdot01$). The implications are clear; no clustering above chance levels for the subnormals on the first 4 trials. Traditional assessment using Trial 1 would thus confirm a total deficiency in this area. However, a second experiment was planned to determine whether conditions designed to increase clustering would aid the recall of the retarded. Two different methods were used: the Present Clustered (PC) method where the stimulus words were presented in categories, and the Requested (RC) method where the experimenter requested the words by category name. Fifteen institutionalized subnormals were randomly assigned to

[1] Here Cobb is really stating that initial performance at any stage correlates with initial performance at the next step.

each condition, and the same stimulus material was used as earlier. For the first group (PC), however, 5 new orders of the 20 stimulus words were produced with the 5 words of each category placed consecutively but with the order of categories, and the order of words within categories, randomized.

The recall data were compared with those from the subnormals in the first experiment. There were significant effects of Treatment ($p < .005$), Trials ($p < .001$) and Treatment $+$ Trials ($p < .005$). Results from the 2 induced clustering groups did not differ significantly, but induced clustering significantly increased the recall of both of these groups and produced steeper learning curves.

The clustering data were equally interesting. The PC group on Trial 1 clustered almost twice as much as the subnormals in the first experiment, and significantly above chance. On Trial 4 the correlation between clustering and recall ($r = .63$, $p < .05$) was significant, decreasing to a non-significant $.39$ on Trial 5. The observed/maximum clustering scores on the PC group were $.72$, $.35$, $.19$, $.24$, and $.26$ for the 5 trials, respectively.

Irrelevant intrusions were few in all three conditions, but categorical intrusions were somewhat higher. The RC group gave significantly more categorical intrusions than the first experiment or PC subjects. This second experiment therefore indicates that under certain conditions clustering can be induced.

Yet another experiment underlines what has been said about duration of training. Thus Gerjuoy and Alvarez (1969) failed to produce a set to cluster in educable retarded adolescents (CA 15·2 years, IQ 59·4) and normal children matched for MA, using 1 training session of 5 trials and a transfer session 1 week later. Two lists of 20 familiar words were used, 5 words from each of 4 categories. Half the subjects in each population received List 1 during training and List 2 for transfer and the other half had the converse. Half the subjects were trained with randomized word lists, while the other half were given clustered presentation; all subjects had randomized lists in the second (transfer session). Both populations exhibited increased clustering and recall when the list was presented in a clustered, rather than a randomized order, thus confirming previous findings. Neither practice and familiarity with the task, nor experience with a clustered list aided performance at the second session.

By contrast, Clarke and co-workers (1970) found significant effects of a learned set on the free recall of retarded adults (mean PPVT IQ 60), all members of an Adult Training Centre. Two groups of subjects, matched for score on a pictorial similarities test and ability to recall unrelated words, were trained as follows: the Blocks Group was required to recall a list of 16 words, 4 in each of 4 categories, presented in clusters (i.e. 'blocks'), twice every day until a criterion of 4 consecutive scores of 15 or 16 words was reached, *or* they had completed 24 trials. The orders of words within clusters, and position of clusters within the list were systematically changed from trial to trial. The Random Group was required to recall a list of 16 unrelated high-frequency words (Thorndike-Lorge) to the same criterion, the order of presentation of words varying from trial to trial. Both groups were subsequently presented with the same new list of 16 words, 4 words in each of 4 categories in which no 2 conceptually related words were ever juxtaposed, and neither words nor categories were common to either of the 2 training lists. There was a significant difference in *amount* recalled ($p < \cdot 025$) on the first 2 trials of transfer, favouring the Blocks Group, but neither group showed much tendency to cluster; on Trials 3 and 4 the differences between the groups in terms of amount recalled was reduced to non-significance, but there was a significant difference ($p < \cdot 05$) in cluster index (taking account of score) in favour of the Blocks Group. A further study by the authors, using memory for pictures as the transfer task, and groups of subjects, including an equal number of ex-ESN and ex-JTC adolescents in an Adult Training Centre, showed a significant difference in score only between Blocks and Random Groups on Trials 1 and 2 of transfer, and no difference whatever in clustering, the ESN subjects in both groups clustering above chance, and the JTC Ss showing little tendency to cluster. It was concluded that if categorical relations among words are repeatedly demonstrated by clustered presentation, a set to perceive inter-item associations develops. This is available for use with new categorizable material so that the categorical relations are perceived at the input-coding stage with consequent augmentation of total output (recall score). Clustering at any significant level is a reflection of organization of input material in store, and is an activity that occurs after at least two repetitions of a list, predominantly among subjects of higher intelligence. The results point to the importance of total recall score as a measure of categorization, in addition to clustering, which latter may well depend on different psychological processes.

It is clear that both types of experiment, that by Gerjuoy and Alvarez (1969) and Clarke *et al.* (1970) with their negative and positive results, respectively, are important in delineating the conditions which favour or inhibit the development of a higher order activity. In the latter investigation, those of very low intelligence failed to profit by this type of training, while those of higher ability did. It may be that the use of conceptual categories in the organization of randomly presented verbal material, in contrast with the growth of clustering on the Minnesota Form boards, cannot be achieved by those with severe verbal impairment but this for us remains an open question.

Alternatives to the psychometric approach

We have perhaps laboured the point that initial performance on any task is an inadequate predictive device. It should also be stressed that in our experience structured training diminishes individual differences, so that from rather heterogeneous initial performance a group will tend to reach a more homogeneous final performance. It will be apparent below how this limits prediction by the more usual psychometric methods, although not by the third method we outline. The 'funnel effect' to which we have already referred (i.e. decreasing variability as learning improves) is also implicitly supported by the work of House and

Zeaman on 'backward learning curves' first suggested by Hayes (1953). These workers show that in discrimination learning there are apparently wide differences in performance. The plotting of backward learning curves shows, however, that once learning has commenced, the curves are very similar for different individuals.

For useful predictive assessment there are three normative possibilities, the first two of which are essentially psychometric: (1) a considerable dispersion of initial scores; (2) a considerable dispersion of final scores after, e.g. training or a mere lapse of time. If these two criteria are met, then a correlation coefficient is a short-hand way of expressing the predictive ability of the assessment, although, as already noted psychologists seldom understand the implication of such coefficients and are easily led up the garden path by them. It has already been indicated, however, that the second possibility is seldom fulfilled, and this is a roundabout way of restating the main argument. There must in the vast majority of cases be low correlations between initial performance and final attainment after training. We now come to point (3), however. The learning experiment, of which we have given a few examples earlier, can examine any aspect of any function both *ab initio* and also its modification by particular forms of structured training. It is then possible to specify the endpoint, together with its rather limited dispersion of scores, and hence the training objective. Subsequently the effect of different forms of training, different durations and reinforcements will provide a technology of remediation, a process which has barely begun. Rather similar conclusions have been reached by Bortner and Birch (1970) who have surveyed the scattered literature from mainly cognitive fields in their important paper on cognitive capacity and cognitive competence. In summarizing their survey, they state that:

Our consideration of the relation between cognitive capacity and cognitive performance in mentally subnormal children, as well as in normal children and experimental animals, permits a general conclusion. It is clear from all these data that performance levels under particular conditions are but fragmentary indicators of capacity. Possessed concepts and skills, and particular conceptual abilities, as well as levels of learning when manifested in performance, all reflect the interaction between possessed potentialities and the particular conditions of training and task demand. Glaring differences occur in the estimates of potential when meaningful alterations are made in the conditions for performance. It is clear that we have but begun to explore the universe of conditions for learning and performance which will facilitate most effectively the expression of the potentialities for adaptation which exist in mentally subnormal children. Clearly, the most effective facilitation of development will be dependent on the ingenuity with which such conditions are elaborated. It is hoped that placing this question in the broader context of psychology will contribute to the invention of more effective strategies for training and for the maximization of competence.

It appears that the severely subnormal person is initially to some extent a *tabula rasa*; his limited achievements are directly and almost solely related to the structured and directed training, whether social or vocational, he has undergone, together with its subsequent reinforcement, and to the demands made upon him and to their motivational consequences. These rather simple ideas have as yet made virtually no impact upon practice, as Grant (1971) has clearly indicated. In his experiment, for example, he demonstrated eight industrial tasks to each supervisor, who was himself encouraged to try the assembly. He was then asked to estimate (1) whether each trainee could learn each of the tasks, and (2) how many trials would be required for the successful trainee to reach the criterion standard. As the author indicates, supervisory predictions were emphatic, but when compared with the actual mimimal training outcome, large numbers turned out to be successful job performers who appeared to have been written off as failures by their supervisors. Further, the abilities of the females were underestimated to a far greater extent by their supervisors. Failure sets apparently do not only apply to the mentally handicapped: '. . . many supervisors must be unaware of much latent ability, and this attitude is probably in part accountable by the simplicity of work normally undertaken in centres' (Grant, 1971). And, one might add, lack of awareness of the points to which this chapter is devoted.

Discussion

So far the inadequacy of predictive assessment of potential achievement has been presented in the context of attempts at remediation. To give an overall picture, however, it must be noted that predictive assessment will be highly accurate on any task if one knows that the individual is not subsequently to be exposed to structured learning opportunities and good incentive conditions. This is perhaps stating the obvious but this is justified when varying claims for prediction are made without reference to their context. This point was well recognized even in the mid-1950s when the British Psychological Society gave evidence before the Royal Commission on the Law relating to Mental Illness and Mental Deficiency, 1954–7. Responsiveness to training was then suggested as a main predictive device. It is possible that some measure might be developed to predict the time period necessary for the subject to achieve a given level of proficiency.

Across the Atlantic the Skinnerians have got into gear, and the impetus in research on developing socially adaptive skills in the severely subnormal has shifted from Britain to America. Mittler (1973) expresses concern that psychologists in this country are not being involved in the establishment and day-to-day running of new diagnostic units in hospitals, clinics and schools. Since virtually all recent knowledge on perceptual and cognitive processes in the subnormal has been developed by psychologists, as well as all the major programmes of educational remediation in the last half century, it is indeed curious and sad that this should be so.

We would like to suggest that one reason is that British psychologists, both theoretical and applied, have concerned themselves too much with assessment and too little with learning processes. Possibly the success of the Skinnerians with the subnormal has been due in large measure to their (otherwise unfortunate) disinclination to make assumptions about internal processes, but instead to manipulate observed behaviour in a systematic way.

Kirk and McCarthy's (1961) construction of the ITPA was aimed not primarily at producing a better diagnostic test for predictive purposes, but rather as an attempt to provide a more detailed guide for the design of remedial education programmes. Marianne Frostig advocates the use of a battery of tests for a similar purpose. On the other hand Tyson (1970) points out that in connection with the design of remedial programmes for people above the level of severe subnormality:

> Having stated that an essential pre-requisite . . . is first of all a clear diagnosis of the child's difficulties, it is necessary now to qualify this statement in that, given the crudity of some of the psychological tools available at present, it may not be possible initially to pin-point the exact area of disability. In this case, to an even more important degree than in more clear-cut diagnosis, *the teaching itself carries the burden of diagnosis*, in that the pay-off from different approaches gives some indication as to where difficulties lie; but some general idea at least of the area of difficulty must be available in order to establish the initial teaching techniques that are to be employed. (our italics)

Neither Heber (1971), Bereiter and Engelmann (1966) nor Gray and Klaus (1970) (all of whom work with the socially deprived mildly subnormal) have shown much interest in assessment procedures, except as an essential tool for evaluating changes in their experimental subjects. They are all involved in the much more interesting task of modifying behaviour.

We fail to see what purpose can be served by applied psychologists carrying out detailed and elaborate assessment procedures in new diagnostic units, unless they can offer some prescription for remediation. Furthermore, we are strongly inclined to the view that developmental and cognitive psychology will be entirely rewritten on the basis of the research, as yet to be carried out, of psychologists who become involved in the systematic modification of behaviour at different intelligence levels over a long period of time.

Few psychologists would consider that Skinner has elaborated a satisfactory theory of human behaviour. Perhaps this is because he and his colleagues have ignored a detailed description of the constitutional differences that exist among animals. On the other hand, Piaget, who essentially describes elaborated behaviour, and psychologists such as Hermelin and O'Connor (1970) who conduct brilliantly creative experiments, shedding light on important constitutional differences, seem to pay little attention to the fact that the behaviour they observe has, by the time they observe it, been shaped to an unknown extent by several years of interaction with the physical and social environment, and might (or might not) be modifiable.

Surely the time has come for more psychologists to address themselves to bridging this gap. It seems obvious to us that children with different constitutionally determined assets and deficits interact (probably from birth) differently with their environment, and no adequate theory of behaviour can be developed until these interactions are (a) observed and (b) controlled.

Conclusions

Both for reasons of constitutional deficits and, to an as yet unknown extent, inappropriate handling, the severely subnormal exhibit an initial performance which often appears well below their capacity. While a careful description of the individual on a particular variable may be found helpful, if that individual is then to be exposed to structured learning opportunities, its main function will be merely to mark the start, at a particular point in time, of a remedial process. As a check upon progress, this initial assessment will be essential, and this takes us back to the fourth function of assessment, described at the outset, and indeed the only one about which no reservations have been expressed in this paper.

In the past, and to an extent still at the present time, the function of assessment has all too frequently been solely administrative, and the direct benefit to the individual has more often than not been dubious resulting all too often in deprivation of liberty or of learning experiences. The assessment movement, from Galton and Binet onwards, has depended upon single-shot sampling of an area of behaviour, and from this an estimate of capacity inferred. From all that has been said it is clear that in the severely subnormal this approach can offer little useful long-term guidance, nor indeed can very short-term experimental approaches do so. The alternative is the long-term carefully-conceived prospective experimental study which can outline the 'artificial' development of processes which otherwise will lie dormant, either because ordinary experience fails to stimulate their emergence, or because of failure sets or other factors. It is clear that we are coming to the end of the period of sterile psychometrics and are at the threshold of something of greater interest both theoretically and practically. In summary, there are at least three major variables which must be taken into account in the prediction of achievement: (1) the constitution of the subject, (2) the nature of the task, and (3) the nature, demands and duration of the learning experience, with its motivational consequences. At the present time prediction should be based upon knowledge of the development of a process following remediation rather than upon test results related to initial performance. Capacity can only be inferred when the limits to performance have been reached by systematic, prolonged and structural training.

References

BALLER, W. R., CHARLES, D. C. and MILLER, E. L. (1967) Mid-life attainment of the mentally retarded: a longitudinal study. *Genet. Psychol. Monogr.*, **75**, 235–329.

BEREITER, C. and ENGELMANN, S. (1966) *Teaching Disadvantaged Children in the Preschool.* Englewood Cliffs, NJ: Prentice-Hall.

BORTNER, M. A. and BIRCH, H. G. (1970) Cognitive capacity and cognitive competence. *Amer. J. ment. Defic.*, **74**, 735–44.

CLARKE, A. D. B. (1962) Laboratory and workshop studies of imbecile learning processes. In RICHARDS, B. W. (ed.) *Proc. Lond. Conf. Scient. Stud. Ment. Defic.*, **1**, 89–9. Dagenham: May and Baker.

CLARKE, A. D. B. and CLARKE, A. M. (1972) Consistency and variability in the growth of human characteristics. In WALL, W. D. and VARMA, V. (eds.) *Advances in Educational Psychology.* London: Univ. of London Press.

CLARKE, A. D. B. and COOKSON, M. (1962) Perceptual-motor transfer in imbeciles: a second series of experiments. *Brit. J. Psychol.*, **53**, 321–30.

CLARKE, A. D. B. and COOPER, G. M. (1966) Age and perceptual-motor transfer in imbeciles: task complexity as a variable. *Brit. J. Psychol.*, **57**, 113–19.

CLARKE, A. D. B. and HERMELIN, B. F. (1955) Adult imbeciles: their abilities and trainability. *Lancet*, **ii**, 337–9.

CLARKE, A. M. and CLARKE, A. D. B. (1973) What are the problems? An evaluation of recent research relating to theory and practice. In CLARKE, A. D. B. and CLARKE, A. M. (eds.) *Mental Retardation and Behavioural Research.* Edinburgh: Churchill Livingstone.

CLARKE, A. M., CLARKE, A. D. B. and COOPER, G. M. (1970) The development of a set to perceive categorical relations. In HAYWOOD, H. C. (ed.) *Social-Cultural Aspects of Mental Retardation.* New York: Appleton-Century-Crofts.

COBB, H. V. (1969) *The Predictive Assessment of the Adult Retarded for Social and Vocational Adjustment*, Parts I and II. Vermillion: Psychology Dept, Univ. of Dakota.

FERGUSON, G. A. (1954) On learning and human ability. *Canad. J. Psychol.*, **8**, 95–112.

GERJUOY, I. R. and ALVAREZ, J. M. (1969) Transfer of learning in associative clustering of retardates and normals. *Amer. J. ment. Defic.*, **73**, 733–8.

GERJUOY, I. R. and SPITZ, H. H. (1966) Associative clustering in free recall: intellectual and developmental variables. *Amer. J. ment. Defic.*, **70**, 918–27.

GRANT, G. W. B. (1971) *Some Management Problems of Providing Work for the Mentally Disordered with Particular Reference to the Mentally Handicapped.* Unpubl. M.Sc. thesis, Univ. of Manchester Institute of Science and Technology.

GRAY, S. and KLAUS, R. A. (1970) The Early Training Project: a seventh year report. *Child Developm.*, **41**, 909–24.

GRUNEWALD, K. (1969) *The Mentally Retarded in Sweden.* Stockholm: National Board of Health and Welfare.

HAYES, K. J. (1953) The backward curve: a method for the study of learning. *Psychol. Rev.*, **60**, 269–75.

HEBER, R. (1971) An experiment in prevention of 'cultural-familial' mental retardation. In PRIMROSE, D. A. (ed.) *Proc. 2nd Congr. Internat. Assoc. Scient. Stud. Ment. Defic.* Warsaw: Polish Medical Publishers; Amsterdam: Swets & Zeitlinger.

HERMELIN, B. F. and O'CONNOR, N. (1970) *Psychological Experiments with Autistic Children.* Oxford: Pergamon.

KIRK, S. A. and MCCARTHY, J. J. (1961) The Illinois test of psycho-linguistic abilities – an approach to differential diagnosis. *Amer. J. ment. Defic.*, **66**, 399–412.

LYLE, J. G. (1959) The effect of institution environment upon verbal development of imbecile children: I. Verbal intelligence. *J. ment. defic. Res.*, **3**, 122–8.

LYLE, J. G. (1960a) The effect of an institution environment upon the verbal development of imbecile children: II. Speech and language. *J. ment. defic. Res.*, **4**, 1–13.

LYLE, J. G. (1960b) The effect of an institution environment upon the verbal development of imbecile children: III. The Brooklands residential unit. *J. ment. defic. Res.*, **4**, 14–22.

MITTLER, P. (1973) *Psychological Assessment of the Mentally Handicapped.* London: Churchill.

MORRIS, P. (1969) *Put Away: a Sociological Study of Institutions for the Mentally Retarded.* London: Routledge & Kegan Paul.

ODEN, M. H. (1968) The fulfilment of promise: 40-year follow-up of the Terman Gifted Group. *Genet. Psychol. Monogr.*, **77**, 3–93.

RADON, M. and CLARKE, A. D. B. (1971) The effects and persistence of different training methods on transfer using the Minnesota formboards. In PRIMROSE, D. A. (ed.) *Proc. 2nd Congr. Internat. Assoc. Scient. Stud. Ment. Defic.* Warsaw: Polish Medical Publishers; Amsterdam: Swets & Zeitlinger.

ROSSI, E. L. (1963) Associative clustering in normal and retarded children. *Amer. J. ment. Defic.*, **67**, 691–9.

TIZARD, J. (1960) Residential care of mentally handicapped children. *Brit. med. J.*, **i**, 1041–6.

TIZARD, J. and LOOS, F. M. (1954) The learning of a spatial relations test by adult imbeciles. *Amer. J. ment. Defic.*, **59**, 85–90.

TREDGOLD, R. F. and SODDY, K. (1956) *A Textbook of Mental Deficiency* (9th edn). London: Baillière, Tindall & Cox.

TYSON, M. (1970) The design of remedial programmes. In MITTLER, P. (ed.) *The Psychological Assessment of Mental and Physical Handicaps.* London: Methuen.

14

D. F. Clark

Psychological assessment in mental subnormality – 1 General considerations, intelligence and perceptual-motor tests

Introduction

At about the time when this volume was first published, psychologists investigating the problems of subnormals by the use of tests were often set to their task by psychiatric colleagues who asked for help with diagnosis or for a guide to classifying subnormals in terms of cognitive variables such as IQ or Social Age. This help is still available, but changes in the climate both of psychology and psychiatry have inexorably led to less preoccupation with diagnosis and its bedfellow, prognosis, and more with the *process* of assessment as a constructive, more flexible, continuous activity leading not to a fixed prescription of 'treatment' till 'cure' is achieved but to an on-going programme which may be frequently modified in the interests of the subnormal's life situation and of a reduction in his current specific difficulties. This change of attitude has not wholly eliminated the need for the psychologist to concern himself with diagnosis or to attempt prediction where he is equipped to do so, but it has weakened the concept of prognosis. The latter presupposed a kind of 'destiny' for the client which all remedial measures, treatment or behaviour modification emerging from assessment are trying to subvert. One is compelled to ask therefore whether making a prognosis, in its original sense, is a meaningful task (see also Chapter 13).

The move away from a medical disease model of mental deficiency to a psychological developmental model has been endorsed by recent publications (Stevens and Heber, 1964; Mittler, 1970) which have made it patent that, especially in the field of mental subnormality, assessment should not be confused with diagnosis. It is true that both involve the eliciting of information, signs and symptoms from the client. It will be apparent, however, that whereas diagnosis is a descriptive process defining a relatively clearly delineated present condition in terms of aetiology, family history, signs and symptoms, etc., assessment is an altogether more comprehensive activity, sometimes encompassing diagnosis but also relating the client and his behaviour to present and future events and circumstances. It owes nothing to the medical model of illness and cure. Like diagnosis, it may be a kind of consummation of intervening decisions resulting in the prescription of subsequent activity but, unlike diagnosis, it continues in time, it shows varying emphases over quite brief periods, and seldom is communicated through relatively simple coherent concepts like those of 'measles', 'fracture of femur' or 'pyelonephritis'. Not that psychologists and others have always been aware of the importance of longitudinal assessment; time was when a Stanford–Binet IQ of less than 70 spelt doom for many a 5 year old! Another way of expressing the current change of emphasis would be to suggest that diagnosis is a decision made *about* the subject whereas assessment is more commonly decision making *for* or on *behalf of* the subject.

In drawing a distinction between diagnosis and assessment it is appropriate to stress that the theoretical standpoint of the psychologist is likely to bias the nature of the assessment he is likely to carry out just as a psychiatrist in 'diagnosing' a high grade subcultural subnormal will proceed as he would in diagnosing a case of phenylketonuria or mongolism. He will describe a disease entity rather than a person. Illnesses are diagnosed. Persons are assessed. One difficulty with the diagnostic approach is that there tends to be an assumption of organic or structural defect underlying many manifestations of subnormality. These physical defects are often real enough, but since they frequently cannot be directly tackled, there is a tacit assumption that therapeutic endeavour, once such a diagnosis has been made, will be unavailing. Indeed, there is a school of thought headed by Tredgold (1952) which would postulate that even the 'familial' or subcultural defective suffers from microscopic imperfections of nervous tissue which, while not so far discerned by neuropathological techniques, will nevertheless be laid bare in the fullness of time by improved technology. This is a perfectly tenable assumption. Unfortunately, it is not a necessary assumption and the more eclectic view that purely functional or psychological disturbance may underlie much neurotic, psychotic and defective behaviour is better reflected by a process of assessment which is ongoing, which traces the natural history of the deficiency in time and place and which is conceptually more diverse and complex than is the process of diagnosis rooted in symptoms and aetiology.

Organic factors, of course, cannot in many instances be denied. In the words of Benton (1964):

> The concept of mental retardation held by most clinicians in the field at the present time is that it is a form of behavioural maladaptation determined by structural cerebral deficit and that clinically similar behavioural pictures which are not ascribable to such defect do not represent instances of 'true' mental retardation. However . . . an increasing number of workers are prepared to admit the possibility of forms of mental retardation which are not primarily determined by structural cerebral alterations of the 'classic' type. In any event, whether the latter type of case is viewed as belonging within the conceptual framework of mental retardation or not, an important goal of the psychological

examination is to ascertain whether there are behavioural criteria which permit differentiation between the two types.

This is an entirely legitimate task with important implications for mental sub-normality theory. The subcultural/pathological, primary/secondary, brain-damaged/non-brain-damaged dichotomies are still the subject of considerable debate, but the issue is often an academic one. The psychologist in mental retardation practice, as distinct from the pure researcher, will frequently be applying his skill in testing with a view to describing his patient accurately so that remedial efforts can be both directed to improving the patient's understanding of the world and his skills in social adjustment, and be measured as effective. The underlying pathology, organic or functional, may often, though not always, be irrelevant as Clark (1958, 1966) has illustrated in a variety of ways in other contexts.

Placing tests in their setting

Sundberg and Tyler (1962) define assessment as 'The systematic collection, organization, and interpretation of information about a person and his situation.' In line with traditions generated early in the United Kingdom, Gwynne Jones (1970) has added to this, 'the prediction of his behaviour in new situations'. The latter goes on to illustrate the general thesis that, in essence, assessment is a developed sequence of decision-making which passes through a variety of stages ranging from specification of the problem, collection of data in a routine way, specification of further problems which emerge from the routine collection of data, often via a case conference procedure, then specific investigations, some-times including experimental methods on the single case (Shapiro, 1970) and specialized testing. Subsequent to this there is a revaluation of the data and action decisions by the psychologist, by his colleagues and, not uncommonly, by the client.

There is little to be questioned in such a clear application of hypothetic-deductive method to the task of assessment, and most clinical psychologists will wish not only to choose and administer appropriate tests correctly but will also consider a key element of their task to be the setting of the test results in their context, a context which takes account not only of the standardization data but also of the circumstances of testing and of the individual characteristics of the person tested. For this reason, therefore, the research-like situation of having to rationalize test data 'blind' must be contrasted with psychological assessment in clinical work in that the latter almost invariably demands that the psychologist: (a) has an opportunity to observe the patient, whether he actually does the testing or not; (b) talks with the patient; and (c) responds to the patient like a human being who understands him, has some feeling for his cultural and personal back-ground and problems, but who has cultivated sufficient professional expertise to be a detached observer of what is occurring in the patient and in himself during the course of this transaction. 'Accurate empathy, non-possessive warmth and genuineness' are appropriate not only in psychotherapy.

THE CLINICAL INTERVIEW

The clinical interview provides such opportunities and while it may be true, as Riesman and Benney (1956) put it, that 'interviewing itself is a middle-class profession, in pursuit of middle-class concerns', this is not in itself an indictment. Much more serious is the comment of many researchers epitomized by the statement of Kahn and Cannell (1957) that 'the interview must be considered to be a measurement device which is fallible and which is subject to substantial errors and biases'. There is the now classical study of Rice (1929) which showed that interviewers with personal or political social biases would very easily interpret data (already elicited from the subjects by them with the same biases operating) in terms of these biases and that, moreover, these biases would be generated in the subjects interviewed by the interviewer. For example, in studying New York destitutes one social worker who was a keen prohibitionist reported that the main cause of 62 per cent of his group being destitute was strong drink, whereas another interviewer of left-wing political views considered that the vast majority of his group of destitutes had become such because of distressed industrial conditions, unemployment and poor labour relations. What was especially noteworthy in Rice's study was not simply that this was interviewer's interview-based opinion of comparable groups but also that members of these groups, having been interviewed by these interviewers, themselves began to attribute the causes of their situation and difficulties to drink and hard industrial conditions, respectively.

A similar type of bias calling in question the validity of the interview was demonstrated by Raines and Rohrer (1955, 1960) who, in two careful studies concerned with idiosyncratic patterns of diagnosis by psychiatrists, showed that two psychiatrists interviewing the same man would both observe different traits in this man and also report different characteristic defence mechanisms to be used by this man. Secondly, psychiatrists were found to have a preferred personality classification or diagnosis which they were under some unconscious pressure to utilize because of aspects of their own early life experience making them more sensitive to certain aspects of the patient's attitudes and behaviour. In their second paper, Raines and Rohrer (1960) confirmed this 'projection' hypothesis by relating the kinds of diagnosis made by psychiatrists to the personality characteristics of the assessing psychiatrist.

A further factor complicating the assessment of the value of the interview is that examined by Pope and Siegman (1968) who were able to demonstrate that the relative 'warmth' and the specificity of the interviewer might have an effect on the productivity of the interviewee. Not unexpectedly, the authors found that respondents would be significantly more productive when the interviewer was 'warm' and accepting in manner and when he was less rather than more specific in questioning. It is important to note, however, that this was only true when the 'warm' rather than the 'cold' interview was first in the series of two. Secondly, while increased productivity may be prima facie desirable in the interview the psychologist still has the task of selecting what is relevant, of differentiating, as it were, 'signal' from 'noise'.

From the studies of Ash (1949), Kelly and Fiske (1951), Meehl (1954) and others reviewed by Matarazzo (1965), it is clear that often the predictive validity of the interview is low. Much of the difficulty arises, however, either when too much is attempted with the interview or when the predictions made utilize concepts of questionable value, e.g. when one interview is used to develop rapport, to collect case history information and to assess personality traits, or when psychiatric diagnosis is made following interview, and patients are allocated to categories such as 'schizophrenic' and 'depressive' which themselves are of indeterminate value (Eysenck, 1960) or relate only vaguely to treatment procedures (Bannister *et al.*, 1964).

Interestingly, the classical study of the unreliability of the interview provided by the work of Hollingworth (1922) in which 12 experienced executives each interviewed and rank ordered 57 salesmen applicants and in which, for example, Applicant C was ranked 1 by one executive and 57 by another, has been the stimulus for later re-scrutiny of such phenomena, and Matarazzo (1965) quotes a similar study from Bingham *et al.* (1959) where results apparently as discouraging as those of Hollingworth's were found. Nevertheless, when the rank order of candidates by any one evaluator is matched against the consensus or average rank assigned to any candidate by all evaluators, quite high indices of agreement are calculated. The authors consider that the data 'reveal not merely a wide range of opinion regarding almost every applicant; they show that in spite of these variations there was a fairly definite agreement among a majority of the interviewers on many of the applicants'. For example, Interviewer A's rankings on each of the 24 applicants correlated ·77 and Interviewer B's ·69 with the consensus of all the judges.

Many of the difficulties in achieving higher reliabilities in interview data arise, in the words of Vernon (1953), 'because the influences of selectivity or homogeneity in the experimental population are not allowed for'. When interviews are standardized, more limited in their goals, utilize clearly defined cues and strict recording techniques, then reliabilities climb to the ·8 or ·9 level (Wing, 1966; Wing *et al.*, 1967). It may seem platitudinous but worthy of repetition that in a recent review by Ulrich and Trumbo (1965) it is suggested that the interview can be more useful if it is recognized as being better suited to some tasks than others! In any event, it should be borne in mind that the strictures of Kahn and Cannell (1957) quoted earlier were directed to the interview 'as a measurement device'. With the mentally defective it is not proposed that it be used in this way, however, but that it have a more limited value in establishing rapport and collecting information which enables test procedures to be carried out validly and reliably and finally to be interpreted in a manner which is responsive to the individual characteristics of the patient and his background.

No excuse is made therefore for the above digression on the interview in psychological assessment. In spite of the tendency for the academic psychologist to recoil from it as a method of psychological inquiry because of the many critical studies, it is now apparent that used shrewdly and with simple rather than multiple, complex goals it can be both reliable and clinically defensible. It is a 'face to face verbal interchange, in which one person, the interviewer, attempts to elicit information or expressions of opinion or belief from another person' (Maccoby and Maccoby, 1954). What seems to have bedevilled many of the studies of reliability and validity is the fact that often the interviewer has not distinguished between different levels of information received (e.g. hearsay as distinct from behavioural evidence) and has not differentiated expressions of opinion and belief from information. Moreover, he has often simultaneously attempted to combine the foregoing tasks with attempts to create and maintain rapport, to test hypotheses about the patient's behaviour and to administer formal tests. Little wonder that the resulting amalgam of impression, hard data, speculations and interpersonal feelings has dubious scientific value! The baby must not, however, be thrown out with the bath water. Patients, even subnormals, have long been impressed by the significance of speech even if their own use of it is limited. They expect to be interviewed. They also expect to ask questions of the interviewer, and unless their speech behaviour is reinforced at this stage by attentiveness and social smiling on the part of the examiner, testing and test analysis may be severely limited. Apart from that, the examiner is given practice in listening to what may be a strong dialect or poorly articulated speech.

The subnormal patient will, like others, wish the psychologist to note his individuality, and he will see himself as having more scope for the expression of this in the interview rather than in the test situation. It is, after all, the differences between rather than the similarities which make people interesting to each other. Indeed this is one reason why libraries are filled with books written by novelists rather than by statisticians. The psychometric approach, however valuable to the researcher with his nomothetic interest in the size and distribution of variables in groups of persons, will frequently require to be complemented by a more ideographic analysis of the individual patient where descriptions and predictions are made about the distribution and interaction of many variables in one person – a much trickier task. Again, the interview may play a large part in enabling the psychologist to ascertain the subject's conformity with a group for whom norms are available, or what is the variability of the patient's responsiveness in the test situation.

Although he rightly points out that they may well overlap at times, Hetherington (1970) has divided interviewing into the fact-finding, the diagnostic and personality assessment, and the therapeutic interview. It is odd that, in spite of the fact that almost every cognitive and personality test manual will have, as a preamble to the detailed instructions for administration of the test, some adjuration to the examiner to ensure that rapport has been achieved and that the subject is both attending and motivated favourably, the interview as a rapport-creating situation is not included in this classification. It is, after all, in the first face-to-face encounters with a patient that the psychologist will attempt to form, and subsequently modify, his theoretical model of what questions need to be asked at the assessment or diagnostic level, of what kind of answers are required and what can be done if such answers are achieved. He has scant chance of employing any of his other professional skills if he cannot persuade or make it obvious to the patient that the latter may be at ease, may be tolerated though dirty, smelly, inarticulate or bizarre, and may show without fear of condemnation or retribution the full range of his usual behaviours and attitudes. Unless he feels secure and unthreatened he will simply flee the room or have recourse to negativism, aggression, withdrawal and/or mutism, together with the whole range of avoidance techniques open to any other sick or inadequate individual. Indeed, in many institutions perhaps 25 per cent of patients (Castell and Mittler, 1965; BPS, 1966) may prove to be untestable for a variety of reasons – hyperactivity, sensory handicap, psychotic withdrawal and so on – but it is equally likely from the same evidence that, of that 25 per cent, some 22 per cent may be assessed, if not tested in the traditional sense. Individual experimentation and systematic observation of developmental level may well lead to worthwhile assessment. It may be over-severe to claim that the statement that a mentally subnormal patient is 'untestable' is as much an indictment of the psychologist as it is of the patient; but to equate the administration of standardized tests with the process of assessment is at best misleading and at worst therapeutic nihilism.

Test selection and programming of the assessment

Seeing and talking to the patient, collecting background information from case notes and other sources, will often direct the psychologist's attention to one or more psychological test procedures which may go some way towards completing a descriptive picture or leading to the prescription of training or treatment. Gwynne Jones (1970) has, however, pointed out how there is a constant interaction in decision-making of this sort between the utility and the probability of relative events or outcomes. It may be possible to use tests which are highly reliable and highly valid even within a limited field, but which contribute relatively little to estimating the patient's future life style, disposal, or planning his activities. Assessment procedures must therefore pay heed to the utility of outcomes, and it may often be better to use tests which predict accurately the behaviour with which the psychologist is concerned even if the procedure is in some other ways crude and limited in, for example, its theoretical coherence, rather than to use apparently exotic techniques of considerable statistical sophistication. For example, studies of subnormals who were found later to show significant gains in IQ (Clarke *et al.*, 1958; Craft, 1962) illustrate that scrutiny of the patients' social history contributed more to the accuracy of prognosis than did a survey of specific aspects of detailed psychological test findings. Windle (1962) in a comprehensive monograph, further illustrates the considerable diversity of factors contributing to prognosis in mental deficiency. Sometimes the highly sophisticated test techniques which one might be tempted to use may simply increase the complexity of the decision-making process forced on the psychologist. As Gwynne Jones (1970) has stressed, in complex decision-making human beings

> appear to find it difficult to combine conflicting attributes of alternatives even in rather simple choice situations, and as soon as the choice becomes at all complicated, the natural decisions deviate markedly but systematically from the optima. Despite the claims made for the human brain as a computer (based largely on its operation in perceptual situations) interactions between factors tend to be ignored and complex multi-dimensional problems tend to be simplified by collapsing them along a single simple evaluative dimension.

There is importance too in the sequence of decision-making in assessment. Goals may change over quite brief spells of time and there may well be better or poorer strategies which may be adopted in both clarifying what these goals are and which should be achieved first. While this has general relevance in clinical psychology it is of even greater relevance to the process of assessment in mental subnormality, where developmental processes may be inhibited both by failures of maturation and failures of learning and where, by dint of long institutionalization, there may be changes both in the subject and in his erstwhile background which warrant total review of the situation at periodic intervals. Such a procedure does carry certain risks. In establishing both subgoals and strategies the psychologist may build up his model of the client and the client's problems in terms of his own methodological problems. He may find himself telling colleagues that this is a difficult problem to conceptualize at the same time as the patient is telling his friends that all he wants is a suitable job but the psychologist keeps giving him more and more tests. The opposite problem of oversimplifying the patient's difficulties is, however, perhaps the one of which the psychologist is more frequently guilty.

Assessment must be both descriptive and prescriptive. One needs to know the appropriate terms to use for a clear description of the patient at different points in time which will allow fair comparison and worthwhile longitudinal study – an activity relatively easily indulged in by psychologists in mental subnormality but surprisingly seldom carried out. Equally, one needs to predict particular behaviours in particular situations and to specify clearly the strength and weaknesses of individual patients so that remedial action can be planned and executed. Finally, the effects of the measures taken must be assessed reliably, not only to ascertain whether they have wrought more for the patient than no measures would have done but also whether they have been positively deleterious to him.

Hand in hand with the process of formulating a theoretical schema about the patient will go the process of selecting the appropriate tests on which the assessment will be based. Watson (1951) has suggested that such a selection will be adequate only if the following criteria are met. He maintains that any tests used must be:

1. relevant to the problem;
2. appropriate to the patient;
3. familiar to the clinician;
4. adaptable to the time available;
5. must meet established standards of reliability, validity and normative breadth.

In looking more closely at requirement 1, it can be seen that the above discussion of general issues in assessment has come full circle to Gwynne Jones's strictures on utility. Relevance to the problem will certainly include consideration of the actual or potential utility of that problem's being solved. For example, a high-grade patient may have been admitted to hospital because of disruptive and disinhibited behaviour at home. It may be relevant to test the effects of drugs and/or training régime by repeated administration of, e.g., the Eysenck–Withers Personality Inventory to assess whether the patient's N and E scores have been significantly reduced. A letter from the patient's home saying that his parents have died and his brother refuses to have him, however, signally reduces the utility of the test information to the patient if not to the psychologist. Such an example illustrates too how the goals of assessment may change even as it proceeds.

It is probable that only a case conference method can effectively mediate such changing assessment needs. The bringing together round the conference table of psychologist, psychiatrist, social worker, nurse, occupational supervisor and so on may enable decision-making about the relevance and pay-off value of testing to be evaluated better in the light of changing conditions in the patient's social background, personal moods and adaptations. In a previous edition of this volume, Gunzburg (1965) aptly describes the situation of the psychologist bringing his data to the case conference.

The test situation is assumed to provide a sample of behaviour which is representative of a person's habitual mode of acting, his intellectual grasp, and his mode of tackling new situations. The test can, of course, give only tentative leads to a full estimate of the interaction of individual and environment since many variables, such as motivational factors of interest, zeal, financial reward, or even the effect of mere chance, cannot be directly assessed in the test procedure. The ensuing comparative scantiness of observational data, and the difficulty of evaluating their relevance, makes it imperative to proceed with great caution when interpreting a person's test scores. Determination of the aetiology, the assessment of personality and the prediction of behaviour are based on inference and deduction, and, though the observational clues obtained in the test may be reliable and valid, it will depend on the skill, knowledge, and experience of the clinician to give the tests the weight and proportion appropriate to the individual under consideration'. (p. 284)

The issue of selecting tests which are appropriate to the patient is one which is usually covered by a comment to the effect that normative data congruent with a patient's age-group and subpopulation are available; that subtests must not depend on the existence of motor or sensory capacities that the patient patently does not possess; and that the content of the test is fitted to the age and experience of the testee. These criteria may all be met, and still the mentally subnormal subject may be troubled and his performance made less reliable because he cannot see the relevance of the test – as he will say, 'What is it for?' Explanation beyond the minimum instructions therefore may well be called for when one attempts, for example, tests of eye-blink or GSR conditionability, the Bene Anthony Family Relations Test, or the pursuit rotor task.

The questions of familiarity to the clinician and of the time available also raise the issue of whether it is better for the psychologist to develop high expertise in a fixed battery of tests as against a fair acquaintanceship with many. In the subnormality field not many decades ago the tendency to favour a routine battery of tests was reinforced by the paucity of tests available with adequate normative data and suitable content. Moreover, the preoccupation with classification rather than remediation limited the battery to perhaps a few tests giving reliable IQs or differentiating verbal from performance skills. This is no longer the case, and indeed clinicians may well feel that the repetitious use of a battery of tests might be stultifying to the psychologist, in that he will no longer explore experimentally or therapeutically the specific individuality of the patient and may risk fitting the patient to the tests rather than vice versa. The argument for an established battery of tests was perhaps first put by Rapaport (1945) who writes, 'The advantages of . . . a battery of tests are that indicators, which for some reason are absent in one or several of the tests, are likely to be present in others; that indicators in the different tests are likely to support and supplement each other; and that the presence of indicators in some of the tests may call attention to more subtle indicators in others which might otherwise have been overlooked.' It appears, however, that he was arguing there for the use of several tests rather than one test only as a basis for assessment, and most psychologists would concur with that. There is a danger of rigidity of 'psychological outlook' arising from the use of a fixed battery of tests (even if this were feasible over the entire age range from infancy to old age) and the current position is rather that psychologists will use several instruments with the single patient for the reasons Rapaport gives, but that they will wish to vary within the range of their developed expertise the content of the battery from one patient to another.

This is the more defensible approach since it meets many of the arguments in favour of developing a battery with which one is familiar while avoiding the pitfalls. For example, the use of a subset of tests from a well overlearned total set allows comparable data on frequently used tests to become available for research, as well as allowing the individual psychologist to develop 'norms in his head' – a sense of how the test is commonly performed by different types or grades of patient. The routine battery can be selected to check on features of cognition and personality already considered and shown to be important for specific or global predictions of status or performance. Finally, it lets the psychologist gain familiarity with the common interactions between both test results and qualitative test performance which is the essence of clinical acumen. Against that, the preoccupation with a battery of tests may lead the psychologist to waste both his and the patient's time by over-testing, to a mechanical approach which disregards the need to reassess and to take a longitudinal as well as a cross-sectional view of the patient, and to a dulling of sensitivity to particular problems of a patient whose needs might best be served by experimental testing or intensive probing of a given area by specialized techniques. Watson (1951) concludes, without saying in so many words, that pay-off determines practices. There is the ring of truth in his statement that 'As a matter of fact many (clinicians) who would insist that they select a new battery for each patient will be found using the same instrument time after time nearly as often as those who hold the opposed positions.'

The earlier comment that tests must be selected in relation to the time available is more likely to be applicable to the psychologist seeing patients in an out-patient setting, especially where they may have come a considerable distance and time is limited because of public transport difficulties and the pressure on the clinician to see a number of patients. The crucial issue becomes not what test should be used, but what is the primary issue to be resolved, and does it require the use of a test at all, bearing in mind that whatever test is used there will be vast areas of behaviour which remain unexplored and all of which contribute to the difficulty of interpreting the test data. It is probably at this point that the psychologist who has built up expertise in several tests, which he knows well, will profit most, and where his interpretation of the tests eventually applied will be most useful to the patient. The possibility of using abbreviated tests will be discussed later.

Finally, the tests used must be given strictly in accordance with standardization instructions. The reliability, validity and already established norms mean nothing if the wording or manner of presentation of the test is varied. The skilled examiner will retain flexibility and opportunism in his testing of difficult patients and still present the test according to the Manual. Pauses and interruptions may occur but even so, he will not, for example, slip into the habit of inserting definite or indefinite articles in the PPVT nor will he fail to reverse the Porteus Maze Test forms when appropriate. It is an excellent idea, in fact, for even experienced psychologists to record on tape (video or sound) their own behaviour while testing, since it is all too easy to allow small defects of test practice to grow into one's technique over the years – especially with the tests with which one is most familiar. Furthermore, if this accuracy is maintained both in administration and in the recording of test responses, preferably verbatim where appropriate (as in vocabulary tests or Wechsler verbal subtests), then the psychologist has some chance of contributing both to the general store of norms and to his personal bank of test experience. It is cautionary to remember that statistics *measure* but do not *produce* reliability, and the psychologist must therefore take care that the conditions under which he tests produce the reliability for which he strives.

MD—O

Gunzburg (1965) originally outlined an assessment programme for subnormals which was planned to 'gauge different and relevant aspects of the subject', and he rightly indicated that the proposed tests could primarily refer to the subject's status at the time of testing, but that they might be seen in the light of his past performance as measured in other ways (as, for example, when assessing deterioration), or, thirdly, for presaging evidence of personality disturbance which is latent and soon to emerge in behaviour. As he puts it, the use of this first selection

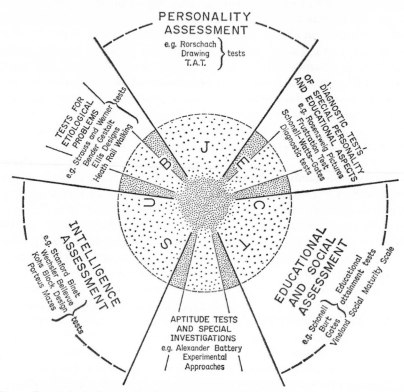

Fig. 9 Psychological investigation in mental deficiency. Primary and secondary assessment (from Gunzburg, 1965).

of tests will indicate whether a second selection should be used, to clarify certain points emerging from the first examination.

Gunzburg, however, does not outline any strategy for the sequential deployment of these tests, and his inclusion of 'special investigations' along with 'aptitude tests' suggests an incomplete grasp of how Bartlet and Shapiro (1956) or Gwynne Jones (1970) envisaged their proposals being applied in practice. They consider that specific hypotheses be set up which will be tested by specially designed tests. Pay-off in decision-making about the patient and his behaviour in terms of utility both to the patient and psychologist and probability of significant results being achieved needs to be high, and careful step-by-step elimination of variables, the use of control groups, and the operational definition of goals and effects will ensure that what may appear to be an *ad hoc* procedure in fact has validity for the patient in his present circumstances and will be reliable enough to allow similar procedures to be repeated for similar patients by other psychologists. In this way theory is likely to emerge from practice and process to become as important as status. In the general psychiatric field Beech and Parboosingh (1962) and in retardation Ravenette and Hersov (1963) have illustrated these principles, but on the whole the considerable amount of painstaking work which Shapiro (1970) has shown to be involved has deterred many psychologists from pursuing this approach. This is a pity, and one looks forward to the emergence of much more research along those lines with subnormal and abnormal populations alike.

In the light of these comments, therefore, a more defensible schema for the assessment of the subnormal might be suggested which uses the well-known flow chart format of the computer era.

It should be noted that in the flow chart (overleaf) the term 'test' is used in a wider sense than usual and should be taken to include any formal controlled experimental procedure or any systematic observations which can be adequately validated, e.g. Piaget-type 'situation experiments'. The modules and steps illustrated are, of course, simplified as compared with many systems analyses in practice, but are intended to indicate a plan of attack which, unlike the programme in Fig. 10 does not so much spell out which tests should be used as reveal the strategy and sequence of decisions which underlie the selection and usage of tests. While reliability and normative width and applicability have found a place in the schema, validity has not. One wishes to distinguish between measuring validity on the one hand and arranging conditions so that a valid test behaviour sample is secured. As Watson (1951) puts it, 'all procedures which make for accurate diagnosis contribute validity. Validity is a function of the use to which the results are put; test results in themselves are not valid or invalid. They possess validity only when they are used for some purpose and their degree of validity must be evaluated in terms of their use.' He stresses that a test may therefore have not one but a number of validities. The Porteus Maze Test, for example, gives a test quotient which is a valid test of foresight and planning (Porteus, 1959), but the 'Q' score derived from it may also be used as a valid test of delinquent tendencies or impulsivity (Foulds, 1951; Porteus, 1959). Too often validity is expressed simply as a correlation coefficient with a criterion measure which itself may be arbitrarily chosen, and members of the club of 'intelligence' test constructors will seek high correlations between their new test and the SB, LM or WAIS with the unquestioning assiduousness of novices in a monastery.

Finally, the procedure outlined in the flow chart allows of frequent recycling of part or whole of the programme, at different points of time in the assessment process or in the subnormal's life, thus giving opportunity for longitudinal as well as cross-sectional study of the patient. It is less wasteful in that evidence which is not useful for decision making need not be collected but it still permits

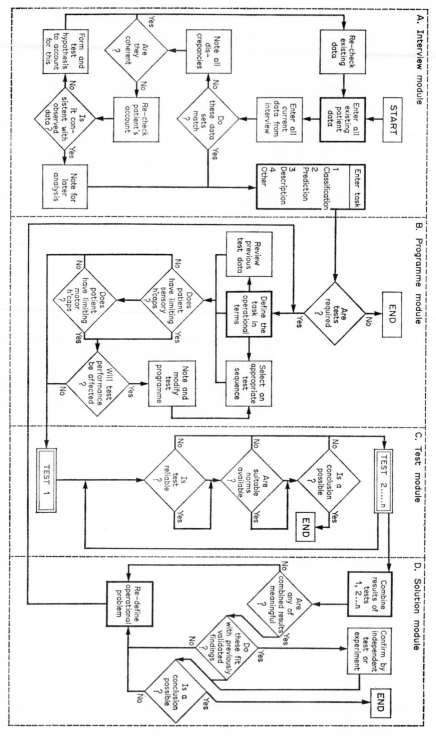

Fig. 10 Flow chart of the decision-making process underlying the use of tests in assessment.

exhaustive investigation to be carried out, if need be, in certain areas. Not only may the test/experiment module be re-run with different tests to the *n*th time but the programme module can be entered for different tasks, many of which may be more specific than the broad aims of classification, prediction or description suggested here.

The essential professional skill of the psychologist in assessment, however, lies in knowing the right question to ask and in translating it into sound operational terms. This is one of the reasons for considering sight of and discussion with the patient in the interview so important a preamble to later testing. Secondly, he will take account in his analysis of results of the various factors which are known to contribute to the variance of test scores, such as inherent differences within the subject, chance and errors of measurement, the reliability of the tests, the patient's current situation, practice effects of previous testing, long- and short-term motivation in the patient, and not least, the examiner himself who is subject to errors in (a) administering the test, (b) recording the subject's responses, (c) scoring these responses and (d) interpreting the results.

The remainder of this and the subsequent chapter will therefore be concerned with looking at some of the commonly used intelligence and perceptual-motor tests in the field of mental subnormality, and second, at procedures for the assessment of social competence, rehabilitation indications and personality. These will be scrutinized in the light of usage within the frame of reference set out above, their reliability, normative background and predictive value.

Intelligence tests

In practice, the three intelligence tests which are most frequently used with the mentally retarded have been found by Silverstein (1963) to be the Stanford–Binet Intelligence Scale, the Wechsler Intelligence Scale for Children and the Wechsler Adult Intelligence Scale. In more recent days a survey by Stevens and Heber (1964) indicated that these same three tests were in fact widely used with retardates throughout the world. There are of course several other less comprehensive tests which play a large part in the armamentarium of many psychologists working with retardates, but the three mentioned above have characteristics which are fairly common to tests attempting to measure intelligence by sampling several kinds of problem-solving behaviour in a variety of media.

Most intelligence tests can be subdivided into (a) verbal and (b) non-verbal types of test, a verbal test relying on material which has been learned and is conceptualized and expressed in terms of words and numbers. Individuals who have had their environments restricted, having been brought up in hospitals, institutions or deprived families, or whose cultural habits do not conduce much to the use of speech or to discovery of the intricacies of language, are likely to perform poorly on a verbal intelligence test because it tends to compare these people with others who have had normal cultural opportunities. The ravages of age also seem to work themselves out less on verbal skills than they do on performance skills, particularly where the latter are adversely affected by tremor or perceptual motor incapacities of a more severe type. In a society where verbal skills are, however, the evidence of our cultural achievement and where they are so necessary for social interaction it is nevertheless important that this aspect of behaviour be adequately measured.

A non-verbal or performance test, by contrast, avoids as far as possible the use of words and requires motor activity in the form of manipulation of test materials such as blocks and pieces of wood or the matching of figural designs or of pictures. In short, instead of saying something, in response very often to spoken instructions, the subject is asked to carry out some task involving reasoning but also the handling of materials or the mental or actual manipulation of shapes. The difference between these two types of test is often thought to be more clear-cut than it is in practice since even in carrying out performance tests there is the suggestion (Sarason, 1949) that these tests involve mediation by speech or a process of 'talking over to oneself' what is going on. Not only that, but very often the instructions for the manipulation of the materials are in purely verbal terms and do not allow, as in some cases, adequate demonstration by mime alone. It is not unlikely that when subjects are carrying out performance tests they may be 'verbalizing' about the task in a way which uses words idiosyncratically or in a less accurate and coherent manner than would be demanded of them in overtly verbalizing a response to an examiner on a verbal subtest.

Subjects who have the deprived background commented on above are often thought to perform more reliably on performance tests because they will not then be handicapped in relation to the standardization population to the same degree as they were because of their lack of verbal capacity, but the research evidence concerning this is rather mixed. The relationship between a performance dominance and cultural background may be more complex than has been thought before, as will be brought out in later discussion of separate tests.

THE STANFORD–BINET INTELLIGENCE SCALE, THIRD REVISION, FORM L-M (TERMAN AND MERRILL, 1960)

This scale plays such a large part in the historical development of psychometric testing that it cannot but be commented on again. The second and third revisions of the test (Terman and Merrill, 1937, 1960) show the same features that marked not only the first revision but also Binet and Simon's original scale, including, for example, the use of age standards of performance, the inclusion of a wide range of items involving the more complex mental processes including perceptual accuracy, memory, verbalization, grammatical syntax and numerical reasoning. There is reliance on a concept of general intelligence that includes a large component of 'mental adaptability to new problems' and on all revisions intellectual level is expressed in terms of mental age. All forms of the test, including the recent revision, contain a number of pictorial and manipulative items but are rather heavily weighted with verbal items and, unlike the Wechsler tests, no attempt is made separately to measure different aspects of ability. The items on the 1960 revision remain arranged in order of difficulty by age level but the test has only one form, L-M, which contains the best 122 items from forms L and M plus an alternate item at each level.

The standardization sample for the second revision consisted of 3,184 white American subjects equally divided by sex ranging in age from $1\frac{1}{2}$ years to 18 years. In spite of care being taken, it was found that the sample proved to be slightly higher in socio-economic status than the general population according to census returns at the time, and also included a rather larger number of urban subjects than was desired. The present third revision did not involve a re-standardization but instead a check of existing standards against current census data. The records of 4,498 subjects tested in four years during the 1950s were compared with the subjects of the standardization sample and items were either retained, eliminated, replaced or rescored on the basis of this comparison.

One of the most important differences of the third revision from the first and second is that whereas IQ was formerly defined in terms of the ratio of mental age to chronological age and IQ tables were provided up to age 16, IQ is re-defined as a standard score with a mean of 100 and a SD of 16 and IQ tables now extend upwards to age 18. The test still remains relatively unsuitable for use with adults, and especially with mentally defective adults, the content being quite clearly related to a child population and indeed a child population which has attended school. Perhaps the occasion when the test is most appropriately used with subnormals is when the latter are so defective that other scales do not extend their norms low enough, or at later stages of life when the person is so defective that he is likely to fall below norms on any other tests available.

Some of the strictures directed to earlier revisions of the Stanford–Binet Test have been met in the new revision, for example, the criticism that the standard deviation of test scores varied at different age levels, but a number of serious criticisms remain and some of these have been dealt with at length by Berger (1970). In particular he is concerned that the test has not been restandardized and that many of the procedures introduced as a substitute have methodological limitations which make them an unacceptable alternative. For example, they do not ensure that the subtest difficulties are unbiased estimates of their population values, and he adds that it must therefore follow that the selection of subtests and their organization into mental age tests has produced a scale of unknown diffi-culty for the contemporary population. Berger makes the further point, a less critical one but quite important for clinical psychologists, that although revision of the test allowed subtests to be constructed by drawing from both the L and M forms of the Stanford–Binet, this has had the effect of eliminating the possibility of a parallel test when it is common knowledge that practising psychologists are likely to be in greater need of parallel forms than of alternative subtests for one form.

In his general conclusions, Berger (1970) makes the point that the inter-pretation of intelligence test scores is dependent in the first instance on the way in which the test is constructed. The nature of test construction is such that each operation determines the adequacy of the procedures which follow it, and as with any sequence of interdependent operations deficiencies in the early stages undermine the structure. Sampling and the determination of the item difficulty are two of the most basic operations in the construction of intelligence tests and they predetermine the meaning of scores derived from these scales.

In spite of Berger's rather stringent criticisms, however, a recent review of the use of the Stanford–Binet with retardates by Himelstein (1968) produces general evidence that the test is still relatively valuable for the population for which early standardization work was carried out. He points out that the new scale was developed by heavy reliance on internal consistency, which assumes that the test as a whole is valid, rather than on the use of external criteria. Dingman and Meyers (1966) point out that this method of 'validating' a test tends to increase test reliability but leaves unanswered the problem of the validity of form L-M. Indeed, since a similar comment could be made about earlier revisions of the SB it would have to be assumed that users of these scales are willing to accept them as valid almost entirely on the basis of an internal consistency factor. Silverstein (1969) studied the internal consistency of the SB and found a reliability co-efficient of ·95. He points out that this value corresponds to the mean split-half correlation that would result from dividing the test in all possible ways, taking into account the fact that the items are arranged in order difficulty by age level. Silverstein concluded that the internal consistency of the test is high enough and of a magnitude comparable to that of the test-retest and alternate form reliabilities reported by other investigators such as Rushton and Stockwin (1963), Barclay and Goulet (1965).

So far as alternate form reliability is concerned, Budoff and Purseglove (1963) compared performance on the second and third revisions of the Stanford–Binet given in counterbalanced order with one month between tests. Correlation between the two forms was ·90 and neither the means nor standard deviations differed significantly. The investigators concluded that the two forms were comparable and interchangeable in spite of the fact that new IQ tables were applicable to form L-M and that the latter used a deviation IQ as distinct from a mental age ratio IQ. Hiskey and Sadnavitch (1958), however, compared changes in IQ defined as a ratio with those in IQ defined as a standard score, using a test-retest interval of three years. Both the means and standard deviations of the ratio IQs differed significantly but those of the standard score IQs did not. The balance of evidence is probably in favour of the latter form. Test-retest reliability studies have mostly been carried out on the old forms L and M, one of the most comprehensive being that of Collmann and Newlyn (1958) where a test-retest coefficient of ·93 was achieved.

It is true that there are substantial correlations between the SB and other intelligence tests, but this of course assumes that the other scales are valid and unfortunately many of these scales have claimed validity only on the grounds of their high correlation with the SB. Terman and Merrill (1960) consider that validity is ensured first by the fact that their choice of items for form L-M assures that it is measuring the same thing as is measured by the previous forms; secondly, that there are regular increases in mental age from one chronological age to the next; and thirdly, that each item is correlated with the test as a whole even more highly on the third revision than on the second. Silverstein (1970) restates the view that it is quite reasonable to expect performance on test to relate significantly to various other test and non-test behaviours that are themselves presumed to reflect intelligence, such as measures of adaptive behaviour, school achievement and learning ability. So far as the SB L-M is concerned this is generally confirmed although the magnitude of the relationships is somewhat variable. The limitation of these measures as criteria, however, is well known and it is quite likely that the test is better standardized than the criteria against which it is measured. Rohs and Haworth (1962) compared performance on the Binet with the WISC and report a correlation of ·69 between WISC full-scale IQ and SB IQ for their forty-six familial and organic subjects, and correlations of ·72 and ·50 for form L-M and WISC verbal and performance scales respectively. Fisher, Kilman and Shotwell (1961) compared institutionalized adult subnormals on the SB form L-M and WAIS in spite of the fact that existing normative data on the L-M do not supply norms for mental age derived from patients of the chronological ages that these authors were interested in. They reported correlations ranging from ·777 at the 55 to 73 year level to ·736 at the 18 to 34 year level. They found that the mean WAIS IQ was significantly larger than the SB IQs at each of four age-groupings ranging from a mean difference score of 22·56 IQ points in the older age bracket to 13·60 IQ points in mid-adulthood. Not surprisingly, their analysis of the different scores indicated that age but not IQ level was significant in determining the discrepancy. Another study by Krosk, Fretwell and Cupp (1965) similarly reports WAIS IQs to be higher than form L-M IQs for subnormals who are hospitalized. There was a difference in their study of approximately 11 IQ points. McKerracher and Scott (1966) reported results in the same direction with a British sample.

The study by Rohs and Haworth (1962) in which they compared mean scores of children on the WISC with the SB L-M showed a significantly lower mean score on the WISC full scale than on the SB L-M. Himelstein (1968) points out that previous research with the 1937 SB had demonstrated that mental subnormals obtained lower mean IQs on that test than on the WISC. Rohs and Haworth explained this finding in terms of the use of deviation IQs on the 1960 revision, but as Himelstein points out it would be difficult to apply this explanation to the findings by Fisher, Kilman and Shotwell (1961) and by Krosk, Fretwell and Cupp (1965) in which they were comparing WAIS with SB IQs. It seems likely nevertheless that the fact that the SB was standardized on young people rather than adults may offer a clue towards the interpretation of this difference, together with the fact that there is likely to be heightened variability on the Binet with its SD of 16 as against the WISC with its SD of 15. Even if the tests were perfectly correlated the Binet mean would be somewhat lower than the

WISC and WAIS means, the magnitude of the difference depending on the degree of retardation. In the same way one might expect the Binet SD to be somewhat larger than the WISC and WAIS SDs.

One of the occasions when the Stanford–Binet L-M is especially valuable is in attempting to test extremely retarded subnormals. Quite often in these circumstances it is impossible to achieve a basal level at age 2 and the problem arises whether or not one is justified in assuming a basal level of $1\frac{6}{12}$ if the subject succeeds on any subtest at age 2. Sternlicht (1965) attempted to study this specific issue. He correlated the IQ obtained in this manner with scores on the Kuhlmann Test of Mental Development and concluded that it was safe to assume such a basal if at least one subtest on the scale at age 2 were answered correctly. The correlation he found between the Kuhlmann Test and the Binet was ·90 and neither the means nor the SDs differed significantly.

Some attempts have been made to assess the possibility of brain injury from scatter on the form L-M, and Hartlage (1966) has suggested that configural patterning on the SB can be of little value in assessing brain damage because there is a lack of uniform spacing at different levels of difficulty as Berger (1970) has pointed out. There have been studies attempting to explore SB differences between the two groups and, although not directly concerned with this problem, that of Rohs and Haworth (1962) did obtain some differences between familial and organic retarded children. Their groups had been equated for age and performance on an earlier Binet and the authors found that organic retardates showed significantly more scatter on the test. However, when they looked at individual items and compared performance of the two groups on these they found a significant difference on only one of them. This seems much too tenuous a finding for basing decisions about any individual case on it.

It is not unlikely that the age of subjects and their length of institutionalization might wreak some effect on SB scores. Sternlicht and Siegel (1968) investigated the Binet performance of subjects between the ages of 5 and 11 who were tested initially soon after admission to an institution and subsequently at three-yearly intervals. The results showed a general decline of 10 IQ points over this period confirming the investigators' hypothesis that institutionalization might result in a lowering of the level of intellectual functioning as measured by test performance. This is an important finding based of one of the few longitudinal studies that have been made in this area. More commonly, cross-sectional studies are carried out in which each subject is tested just once and with perhaps different groups of subjects being tested at different dates. As Silverstein has pointed out more than once, the problem with the cross-sectional approach is that changes found from test to test may be due to differences among the groups in factors other than age and length of institutionalization. He illustrates this by a study of Bensberg and Sloan (1950) who investigated SB results of subjects aged 30 to 55 and found what appeared to be a progressive decline in the means with age, a decline represented by an average decrement over 20 years of something like 13 IQ points. However, comparable differences were found in the means on the first revision of the Binet given when the subjects were between ages 15 and 24. In their interpretation of this, the investigators suggested that the brighter subjects failed to be retained by an institution and therefore were not likely to be included in groups measured in the older age bracket.

Because of these criticisms Silverstein (1969) tackled the subject using both a semi-longitudinal and cross-sectional approach. He looked at the SB performance of patients ranging in length of institutionalization from 0 to 30 years and the results of the two methods agreed in demonstrating a progressive decline, but whereas the average decrement over a period of 25 years was 15 IQ points when assessed cross-sectionally, it was reduced to 8 points when assessed longitudinally. The results therefore confirmed the hypothesis mentioned above that the subjects who are likely to be tested 30 years after admission are likely to be duller subjects than those who were probably released well before that time.

So far as adapting the test to physically handicapped subjects is concerned (and this is not an uncommon problem in assessing the retardate) many clinicians will themselves devise a method of selecting items from the SB which are relevant for patients with motor defect, cerebral palsy or perceptual defect. Both Katz (1956) and Allen and Jefferson (1962) have presented tables for the items on form L-M which will illustrate whether vision, hearing, speech or hand/arm coordination are required and whether the item concerned can be suitably adapted.

While most psychologists agree that the short form of any test is to be used only when pressure of time is extreme, there has nevertheless been a great deal of time spent in devising short forms of tests which might better have been spent in administering the whole test. So far as the Stanford–Binet L-M is concerned the manual provides one method that will eliminate nearly one-quarter of the usual time, viz. using only four subtests at any age level. Wright (1942) suggested a modification of this whereby basal and ceiling levels were obtained on the basis of the full six tests and only the four selected tests were used to complete the intervening age levels. Silverstein and Fisher (1961) and Silverstein (1963a) compared the two short forms of the form L-M with the full scale for retarded adults and children respectively. For the adults the Terman–Merrill short form correlated ·98 with the full RSB IQ while the Wright method correlated ·99 with the full scale. For children, the corresponding correlations were ·95 and ·98 respectively. Silverstein (1966) later analysed the results from short forms in terms of agreement with the full RSB on subnormals classified by degree of retardation. So far as the adult groups were concerned the Wright short form IQ agreed on classification of 91 per cent of the cases and so far as the children were concerned agreed on 93 per cent of the cases, with the Terman–Merrill short form only a few percentage points behind in both instances. Silverstein was confident that this procedure would therefore misclassify only one of 10 cases at the most.

In a recent study by Achenback (1970), the L-M revision of the Stanford–Binet was administered by one examiner to 79 non-retarded subjects and 62 familially retarded subjects. As a result 54 pairs were formed in which non-retarded and retarded subjects were closely matched for mental age ranging from 4 to 11 years and sex. Comparison of the proportion of non-retarded and retarded subjects passing each item revealed few significant differences. Generally speaking, the items in which retarded subjects did well tended to be concrete and practical whereas those in which the non-retarded excelled involved more abstract intelligence. Individuals differing in IQ and CA, therefore, but matched for MA differ little in their performance on this test. Similarly Achenback found an absence of significant differences between black and white retarded subjects, and the occurrence of a significant difference between black retarded and white non-retarded subjects on only one item VI (4) which did not differentiate the racially matched pairs of non-retarded and retarded subjects indicate that Binet performance by individuals obtaining the same MA scores may be generally similar even if they are of different races.

THE WECHSLER ADULT INTELLIGENCE SCALE (WAIS) (WECHSLER, 1955) THE WECHSLER INTELLIGENCE SCALE FOR CHILDREN (WISC) (WECHSLER, 1949)

While the SB L-M may be the choice of test for young retardates because of its lower 'floor' most psychologists testing mental defectives will prefer to use the WAIS, WB 2, or WISC tests with their outstanding characteristic of a breakdown of test response into its verbal and performance aspects. More important still, all of these tests define IQs as a standard score with a mean of 100 and standard SD of 15 and rely on Wechsler's concept of intelligence as 'the global capacity to act purposefully, think rationally and deal effectively with one's environment' (Wechsler, 1955). With the exception of an older group chosen without reference to census specifications for the standardization of the WAIS for ages 65 to 75, both the WAIS and WISC tests were standardized on large (c. 2,000) samples which took account of variables such as sex, geographical distribution, socio-economic level, urban/rural residence, and most importantly, included a subsample of defectives drawn from institutions and special schools.

Not being geared to the concept of mental age the Wechsler tests attempt to measure this 'global capacity' for intelligent behaviour by using 11 subtests – 6 verbal and 5 non-verbal – which include measures of aspects of functioning such as information level, comprehension, arithmetic reasoning, verbal abstraction and vocabulary level, on the verbal scale; and on the performance scale, measures designed to reflect synthetic and analytic ability, perceptual accuracy and motor/perceptual skill. This approach does not presume that two different kinds of intelligence exist, only that intelligence may be demonstrated in different ways. Nevertheless, both with normals (Maxwell, 1960; Sprague and Quay, 1966) and with subnormals (Baumeister and Bartlett, 1962a, b) factor analytic studies of the various Wechsler tests have confirmed general, verbal and performance factors together with a fourth factor originally reported, but unexplained, by Satter (1955) but interpreted by Ellis (1963) following the work of Baumeister *et al.* as a stimulus trace or immediate memory factor. Ellis's theory takes the view that the stimulus trace in retardates is reduced in duration and amplitude as compared with non-retarded subjects. Thus it follows that defectives should perform at lower levels than normal subjects on tasks which require short-term memory. Such tasks as delay of response, delay of reinforcement and serial learning are situations in which short-term memory is vitally necessary for an adequate performance, and elements of these tasks can be found in subtests of the Wechsler scales.

Not unexpectedly a wealth of studies have been carried out on one or another of the Wechsler tests. Guertin, Frank, Ladd and Rabin (1966) have, for example, reviewed 179 relatively recent papers on the WAIS alone, and Baumeister (1964) has reviewed the use of the WISC with retardates. Silverstein (1970) has reviewed much of his own and other work with both of these tests and compared them with SB L-M in a number of respects. He has also (Silverstein, 1963a) submitted a downward extrapolation of scaled scores of the WISC and the WAIS for use with the mentally retarded.

Wechsler (1958) has presented split-half, test-retest and correlational data showing the WAIS verbal, performance and full-scale IQs to have higher reliability than the Wechsler Bellevue and higher full-scale IQ than performance IQ reliability. This has later been confirmed (Cook and Hirt, 1961; Prado and Schnadt, 1965) and similar findings have been reported of the WISC and the WAIS (Fisher, 1962a; Webb, 1963). On the whole, reliability coefficients for FS IQ are in the range ·90 to ·97 with verbal IQ and performance IQ between ·84 and ·96. Clinicians will, however, wish to take account of the varying reliabilities of the subtests, since some of these demonstrate lower reliability than the overall IQ reliabilities. Field (1960) has presented valuable tables which not only comment on the reliability of scores but also on their abnormality, a distinction which is important when subtest differences and verbal performance discrepancies are analysed.

It is often difficult to separate problems of validity and reliability and some fairly serious criticisms of the validity of the WAIS as a measure of intelligence in the retarded have been made by Fisher (1962a, b). His work stems from that of Fisher, Kilman and Shotwell (1961) who compared Binet and WAIS performance of subjects between the ages of 18 and 73 and found that the WAIS mean was significantly higher than the Binet mean at all ages. Importantly, the difference was significantly greater for the older subjects than for the younger ones. These writers commented that since the WAIS norms make an allowance for normal deterioration with age it would be logical to assume that the WAIS is the more accurate measure of intelligence than the Binet. However, they also noted the possibility that this allowance might not be applicable to defectives and suggested that longitudinal studies might go some way to resolving this issue. As a result Fisher conducted two studies, first comparing performance on Binet and WAIS with that on the Binet given twenty to twenty-six years earlier. The

Binet means were quite comparable but the WAIS mean differed markedly from that on the first Binet. Moreover there was a correlation of ·37 between age and the difference between the WAIS and the second Binet. Fisher concluded that the Binet was a reliable measure of intelligence for defectives over a long period of time whereas the WAIS overestimated their intelligence increasingly with advancing age and was therefore of questionable validity. Fisher's (1962b) second follow-up study compared performance on the WAIS with that on the WISC given six years earlier, and he predicted that roughly the same degree of discrepancy would obtain between early WISC and later WAIS means as between early Binet and later WAIS means. This prediction was confirmed, the differences between the WAIS and WISC means being within 1 IQ point of that between the WAIS and the Binet means for the same age-group in the first follow-up study. Fisher took this to be additional evidence that the WAIS was not entirely valid as an intelligence measure for retardates. Silverstein (1970) has commented that Fisher provided 'a convincing demonstration that the WAIS is not functionally equivalent to the Binet and the WISC, and he has correctly pointed out the need for systematic exploration of the possibility that the rate of normal deterioration with age may vary as a function of intellectual level. However, functional equivalence is not synonymous with validity, and it is difficult to accept his conclusion that the WAIS is not valid without other sorts of evidence than that provided by comparisons among the tests.' In any event comparisons among the tests on the whole show very high correlations ranging in the case of correlations between SB L-M and WAIS from ·74 to ·78 for defectives of differing age and IQ levels (Fisher *et al.*, 1961) and between the SB and WAIS V IQ and P IQ of ·79 and ·78 (Brengelmann and Kenney, 1961). One study has been carried out (Davis, 1966) on the internal consistency of the WISC. The writer determined the odd-even reliability of all the subtests except Digit Span Coding and Mazes to which this procedure is not applicable, and also the verbal, performance and full scales including these three subtests. The reliabilities averaged ·92, ·83 and ·93 for the verbal, performance and full scales and showed a tendency to increase as a function of intellectual level. There seems little doubt that the internal consistency of the test therefore is satisfactory.

The reliability and stability of Wechsler IQ scores for institutionalized subnormals has been looked at in detail by Rosen, Stallings, Floor and Nowakiska (1968). As might be expected, the reliabilities of the Wechsler were somewhat lower when calculated by retest than by split-half techniques. For the WAIS, the reliability coefficients for FS IQ are ·97 and ·88 for split-half (Wechsler's data) and test-retest (present data) methods respectively. For the WISC, the comparable coefficients are ·94 and ·81 respectively. In the same study, WAIS test-retest reliability of the P IQ V IQ differences score was ·86 which is roughly comparable with the reliabilities of the three IQ scores, whereas for the WISC this value drops to ·60 which is somewhat lower than the reliability of the WISC IQs. The difference score was most frequently in a positive direction (i.e. P IQ greater than V IQ) but this tendency was most noticeable on the

WISC. The authors suggest, in keeping with some other studies, that there would be some limitation on the use of different scores of this sort diagnostically, especially with adults of indigent status who have been long-term residents in institutions. In these cases differential changes in P IQ relative to V IQ over time may detract from the stability of this score. This would be consistent with the work of Clarke and Clarke (1959) who have demonstrated that subjects from very bad homes are likely to show IQ increments when removed to a better environment. In the Rosen *et al.* (1968) research this was confirmed and they also noted the fact that children below the age of 15 did not show this effect, thus demonstrating that the later effects in older subjects was due to what the Clarkes have explained as the fading of 'intellectual scars' induced by bad home conditions. Butterfield and Zigler (1970) have very recently produced evidence using the Stanford–Binet test which is closely related to the finding of the Clarkes. The Butterfield and Zigler study secured ratings of pre-institutional social deprivation for all the subjects, some of whom were familial and some were non-familial subnormals, who were given the SB L-M prior to institutionalization and each year thereafter for five years. The non-familials were characterized by less severe pre-institutional deprivation and through the course of institutionalization increasingly greater losses in IQ. The extent of the IQ decrease was clearly related to the degree of pre-institutional deprivation among both familials and non-familials, and their findings were interpreted as being consistent with the hypothesis that IQ changes reflect changes in debilitating motivational factors rather than changes in cognitive functioning. This being so, differences between the findings of this and earlier studies seem to suggest that different institutions have different effects on their residents.

So far as the WAIS is concerned a number of short forms have been developed which have proved clinically valuable when time is limited (Clayton and Payne, 1959; Fisher and Shotwell, 1959; Ross, 1963; McKerracher *et al.*, 1968). Doppelt (1956) suggested a short form WAIS of four subtests based on analysis of the standardization data in terms of regression equations, but Himelstein (1957) found that simple pro-rating of the subtest scores was virtually as effective as the regression equation method in calculating scores. It has been commented by more than one writer that psychologists have probably spent more time devising short forms of the Wechsler tests than they have saved in using them, but nevertheless there seems to be a large demand for such short forms and they continue to proliferate. So far as Doppelt's (1956) short form is concerned, the subtests used are arithmetic, vocabulary, picture arrangement and block design and the validity coefficient of ·96 is reported for these. With defectives Fisher and Shotwell (1959) used this short form and the validity coefficient dropped only to ·93.

Finally, the prognostic significance of Jastak's AQ was evaluated in subnormals by Silverstein, Fisher and Owens (1963). In three analyses, the AQ was a less valid predictor than IQ of subsequent IQs three to six years later, of release from the hospital and of diagnosis as retardate versus pseudo-retardate. Several studies in the past have reported high correlations between AQ and IQ – about ·85 to about ·90 – which suggest that it has little to add in any prediction beyond IQ.

Factors affecting performance

There are a number of elements in the contemporary forms of WISC and WAIS which require to be modified for United Kingdom subjects, wording and quantities in the verbal subtests in particular. While certain work has been done on this, recent changes to decimal currency necessitate a reversion to a form of the arithmetic test which is perhaps nearer to the original form. It has also been noted that there are significant differences in the difficulty level particularly on the picture completion and vocabulary subtests.

Many subnormals, are, of course, physically or perceptually handicapped and this poses a variety of problems in the use of tests which are designed essentially for normal subjects. Most psychologists using the Wechsler tests settle for the use of one or other of the verbal or performance batteries depending on the type of defect which the subject presents, or by selecting appropriate subtests and pro-rating scores. Recent studies have, however, focused on some of the special problems of left-handed people in performing, for example, the digit symbol or coding subtest. McCarthy (1961) noted that such people were frequently penalized because they tend to cover the key with their hand and slow down their performance. McCarthy's solution was that left-handed individuals be provided with a separate set of key items which may be placed in a position where it might be viewed more conveniently by them, but Bonier and Hanley (1961) noted that this kind of interference was likely to be more significant for those who used 'crabbed' hand position in writing than for those who used a more conventional left-hand position. Some suggestion has been made that the digit symbol subtest be commenced at the right rather than left side of the rows but of course this interferes with the relative repetitions of similar symbols and may make the subtest slightly more difficult.

Measures of brain damage

Wechsler (1958) developed a deterioration quotient following the principle that age curves of his subtests on the WAIS declined at different rates for different subtests, and by assessing the disparities he noted those greater than might be expected for a given age level. Much inconclusive work has resulted from the use of this index and in general it is not considered to be a particularly appropriate measure especially in view of the other complicating factors in assessing the scores of subnormal patients (Sloan, 1947; Bensberg and Sloan, 1950). Hewson (1949) approached the problem by investigating 13 ratios based on the Wechsler subscales, and although this development was criticized (Rabin and Guertin, 1951) the Hewson ratios have attracted a good deal of interest and there is growing evidence that they have some validity in differential diagnosis in organic disorders and senile dementia. Even so, Bolton *et al.* (1966) suggest that the deterioration measures derived from the WAIS should be used in conjunction with normal data to make sound statements about intellectual impairment rather than as psychiatric indices, and this would certainly be more in keeping with current trends in assessment technique.

There have, of course, been many studies exploring verbal-performance discrepancy and relating the direction of this to different syndromes or categories. Fisher (1960) classified 508 low IQ subjects into 8 primarily aetiological categories. The groups 'infection' or 'other' CNS pathology actually had V IQ greater than P IQ but 'undifferentiated', 'familial', 'functional', 'epilepsy' and 'suspected but not confirmed' groups did not have significant V IQ/P IQ differences. However, there has been some suggestion that the level of IQ measured has also an effect on the V IQ/P IQ discrepancy (Brengelmann and Kenney, 1961; Warren and Kraus, 1961). On the whole, the research literature continues to validate the finding that the 'garden variety type of neuro-pathology' is manifest most apparently in the poor performance of relatively non-verbal tasks in the Wechsler tests, and Guertin et al. (1966) quote many authorities to support this. Nevertheless, it is not always easy to define in psychophysiological or neuro-logical terms what is meant by the description 'cerebral pathology', 'brain damage' or 'organic damage' and quite often the hemisphere of the brain that is involved will promote differential performance on the Wechsler tasks. In the same way, the chronicity of the disorder has been found to be another factor influencing performance. Generally, individuals with cerebral pathology limited to the right hemisphere reveal good capacity on verbal tasks, in respect to their own performance on the performance task as well as the performance on the verbal tasks of those with cerebral pathology limited to the left hemisphere. However, the longer one is afflicted with the disorder, right or left hemisphere specific, the less differentiation between these kinds of people can be made. As Guertin et al. point out, 'For the present, it is relatively safe to assume that a V IQ greater than P IQ pattern is not just characteristic of cerebral pathology, *sui generis*, but may be indicative of pathology in the right hemisphere or of a more diffuse kind; the reverse pattern (P IQ greater than V IQ) though typical of most cerebral disorders differentially characterizes the left hemisphere disturbance.' They go on to add,

Probably no single combination of scores has had the heuristic value of the V IQ/P IQ discrepancy. Unfortunately, this extensive work has yielded limited and as yet tentative results, namely, the V IQ is probably less than the P IQ whenever education (especially reading) has been poor, there is long term social maladjustment, the environmental emphasis has been on 'doing' and not 'thinking' (e.g., sociopaths and 60 to 80 IQ mental retardates), and/or the dominant hemisphere has been damaged. On the other hand, ego involvement with verbal ability, little interest (e.g. psychosis and depressives), and impaired abstract reasoning, visual motor co-ordination, or spatial analysis (e.g. generalized or right hemisphere brain damage or psychosis), may produce

V IQ greater than P IQ. These results have not always been replicated and, furthermore, except possibly within the brain damaged subjects, the V IQ/ P IQ discrepancy has been of little value in individual diagnosis. Perhaps most neglected in this area is the comparison of obtained V IQ and P IQ with expected IQ based upon education, work history, or premorbid academic achievement test scores.

THE PEABODY PICTURE VOCABULARY TEST (DUNN, 1959, 1965), FORMS A AND B

The Peabody Picture Vocabulary Test was designed in the USA to provide an estimate of 'verbal intelligence' through measuring the subject's recognized vocabulary. It was originally designed for use with the mentally handicapped and to this extent is unlike the tests previously discussed. However, it can be used more generally with subjects between the ages of $2\frac{1}{2}$ and 18 years, the norms for the 18 years age-group being used for adult subjects. As a consequence the test has wide validity clinically, and is specially applicable to subjects who are non-readers, who are speech impaired because of aphasia or stuttering, and can be used with autistic, withdrawn children or subjects who have motor defects or even limited vision.

The test consists of 150 numbered plates each containing 4 drawings printed in clean bold lines on a plastic surface. The subject is asked to indicate by speech, pointing or even eye pointing which of the pictures represents best a word spoken by the examiner. There are 3 example plates and it is a test where rapport is easily established; where the administration time is limited to about 15 minutes; where the test is untimed and free from the stress of having to make hasty decisions; and alternate forms are available for repeated measures. Scoring is, of course, completely objective, and raw scores can be converted to mental age scores, to percentiles or verbal IQs. The IQs are deviation IQs in the form of standard scores with a mean of 100 and SD of 15.

The PPVT was standardized on 4,012 cases fairly evenly divided between age levels at year intervals from $2\frac{1}{2}$ to 18. All subjects were white Central American children from the state of Tennessee. The overall sample was known to demonstrate a normal distribution curve of intelligence on the basis of other validated tests. One study of the use of the PPVT with adolescents and young adults above available normative ages (Kahn, 1966) shows good reliability coefficients ranging from ·80 to ·85 up to a three-year interval, and acceptable distributions of scores were achieved.

Alternate form reliability coefficients for the PPVT correlating the raw scores range from ·67 at the 6-year level to ·84 at the 18-year level with a median correlation of ·77 (Dunn, 1965). Blue (1969) has studied the temporal stability of the test over a 1-year period together with alternate form reliability in a population restricted in IQ range but heterogeneous in CA. Alternate form correlation coefficients range from a low of ·77 for IQ scores at the youngest age level ($6\frac{1}{2}$)

to a high of ·92 for raw and mental age scores for the total group. Temporal stability coefficients range from a low of ·75 for raw scores at the youngest level to a high of ·93 for mental age scores for the total group. Blue concluded therefore that the PPVT demonstrated high alternate form reliability at a one-year interval in test-retest regardless of the form of scores employed or the age groupings. Gardner and Birnbrauer (1968) suggest that form B tends to be easier for institutionalized children under 16 although there was some tendency for form A to be easier for older children. This was a finding which was not confirmed in children of normal intelligence but was held to be true only of subnormals. No explanation is offered for this finding.

Pool and Brown (1970) have evaluated the PPVT as an intelligence test for an adult hospital patient population and have compared it with the Doppelt short form of the WAIS. The tests correlated ·81, but additional analyses demonstrated that the PPVT underestimated the D-WAIS scores in the lower ranges and grossly overestimated them in the upper ranges. Mein (1962) had already found that the PPVT tended to underestimate MAs below the vocabulary quotient of 55. Indeed Mein's study also demonstrated what has since become apparent to many United Kingdom testers, that a number of the plates are misplaced in order of difficulty and that minor variations in wording might improve the test's usefulness with English-speaking subjects in this country.

The fairly consistent finding that the PPVT overestimates the corresponding Stanford–Binet score in subnormals is commented on by Himelstein (1968). Probably the main reasons for differences of results on the discrepancy between PPVT and, for example, SB IQs may be the finding by Koh and Madow (1965) that the relationship between the two scales is curvilinear and that the PPVT MA overestimates SB MA at the higher levels in subnormals and underestimates at lower MA levels. Most authorities (Hammill and Irwin, 1965; Koh and Madow, 1965; Kicklighter, 1964) agree that the PPVT is a valid instrument although there are various suggestions that it may include a specific sensitivity to language deficits (Shaw *et al.*, 1966). The curvilinear relationship between PPVT and SB L-M commented on above has been substantiated by Budoff and Purseglove (1963) who report a high degree of relationship with low-grade defective subjects and a low relationship with high-grade subjects. Recent work by Hammill and Irwin (1965) focuses upon the apparently higher equivalency of the two instruments for trainable subjects than for the educable. With trainable subjects MA differences between PPVT and form L-M were no more than ·4 years apart at any CA level. With educable subjects the discrepancy was slight until age 10 and the difference of 1·3 MA years (with the PPVT higher) was obtained at CA 14 to 15 years. However, when the educable groups were divided by aetiology it was found that the organic group was the critical factor in the MA discrepancy. Trainable subjects are more than likely to be brain involved, and educable subjects are likely to be the result of a variety of aetiological factors. Hammill and Irwin see the type of response (focal versus non-focal) as a possible explanation for their findings. As Himelstein comments, their study would seem to be additional evidence that research with the mentally retarded should not group subjects into broad classifications such as retarded or educable as though the members within the group are homogeneous.

Kaufmann and Ivanoff (1968) also investigated the practicality of using the PPVT with mentally retarded adult subjects. The findings of their investigation were consistent with studies that reported higher correlations of the PPVT IQ with the WAIS verbal scale and full-scale IQ than with the WAIS performance scale IQ (Burnett, 1965). Of special significance in the study of Kaufmann and Ivanoff (1968) was the fact that their obtained correlations between the PPVT and the variables they used (WAIS and WRAT) were found to be considerably higher when the PPVT Mental Age equivalents were substituted for the reported standard score equivalents or IQs. It seems therefore that the given PPVT MA equivalents might, for retarded subjects of adult years, be more usable than the PPVT IQ scores in prognosticating intellectual functioning.

There can be relatively little need of short forms in the case of the PPVT since it already adopts a scanning technique in its administration. It is, for example, not necessary to start with the first pictures for subjects who are over $7\frac{1}{2}$ when it is acceptable to start with picture number 50 and work back to a basal level if need be and then work up until the criterion level of 6 failures in any 8 items is achieved.

Although the PPVT is more commonly used in a subnormal population because of its wide range, Brimer and Dunn (1962) have produced English revisions of the test using substantially the same drawings and words for children of age ranges 5 to $8\frac{11}{12}$ and 7 to $11\frac{11}{12}$. A standardization was carried out on 5,000 Wiltshire schoolchildren adequately sampled by age, sex and school background, and reliabilities are quoted ranging between ·87 and ·92 for Test 1 and from ·88 to ·96 for Test 2 (Brimer and Dunn, 1962). To assess the validity of the EPVT against other tests may be somewhat less than fair since it nominally seeks to assess the construct 'listening vocabulary' rather than verbal intelligence, but it is interesting to note that Phillips and Bannon (1968) found a correlation coefficient of EPVT with the SB L-M of ·80, thus making it 'one of the most useful short measures of verbal ability available in this country'.

The question has arisen from time to time of performance on a picture vocabulary test being a function in part of visual perceptual acuity, since it is possible that the difficulty of the items might rest on visual perceptual subtleties in analysing the pictures rather than on a knowledge of the words which are uttered by the examiner. Brimer and Dunn (1962) comment that the visual perceptual element has been reduced in construction and in picture selection by the following precautions:

(a) the picture is focused on the essential attribute to which the word refers;
(b) distractors were avoided which depended for their operation upon differences in degree of representational accuracy;
(c) the pictures are clear line drawings of high quality;

(d) shadow images are reduced by using paper of high opacity for Test 1 and by using black masking paper for Test 2;
(e) the distraction of facing pages is avoided by the examiner presenting only one page at a time for Test 1 and by using the black masking paper for Test 2.

The question of validity of both the EPVT and the PPVT is discussed at length in the relevant manuals and in many of the papers quoted above. It seems that it cannot be concluded, in spite of relatively high correlations with other test criteria such as WAIS and WISC verbal IQs and Stanford–Binet IQs, that the PPVT and the EPVT are measures of general intelligence or even of language comprehension as distinct from recognition of words. However, it seems apparent that there is a sufficiently close relationship with all of these constructs to make the test of value, primarily as a screening device and secondarily to augment 'performance' types of test in a battery designed to clarify, for example, reading difficulties and vocabulary development in a subnormal population. It appears to be highly acceptable and unthreatening to subnormals of a wide range of age and intelligence and is simply administered and scored.

STANDARD PROGRESSIVE MATRICES (RAVEN, 1938 TO 1956)
COLOURED PROGRESSIVE MATRICES (RAVEN, 1947)

Raven produced his well-known Matrices Test at a time when the hunt for Spearman's 'g' factor was at its height. He evolved the tests in an attempt to clarify a concept of intelligence largely concerned with the discernment of relevant relationships and the education of relevant correlates. There is little doubt that following its very wide use in HM Forces during the last war Vernon and Parry (1949) considered it as 'an almost pure test of "g" ', and Spearman himself (Spearman and Jones, 1950) regarded the Progressive Matrices in the same light. More recent work (Vernon, 1947, 1950; Emmet, 1949) have demonstrated that 'g' accounts for rather over 62 per cent of the variance with a small spatial factor playing a subsidiary part. Tizard and O'Connor (1950) did not identify their single factor finding with Spearman's 'g' but as a more complex non-verbal practical factor probably more related to performance than to verbal intelligence.

In spite of this the test has been used very extensively by many agencies in Great Britain and been found to be well worthwhile especially when combined with an appropriate vocabulary test, commonly the Mill Hill Vocabulary Scale (Raven, 1943, 1958).

The test consists of a booklet containing 5 sets of design in the case of the Standard Matrices and 3 sets, including 2 of those in the Standard set, in the Coloured Matrices. One section of each matrix design is missing and the subject is asked to complete the design by choosing from either 6 or 8 alternative parts of the matrix printed below the main design. If need be, the test can be administered entirely by mime and the colour element in the simpler form is merely a device to secure more definitely the attention of duller subjects. Indeed this may be one of the great difficulties in using the test with subnormals, in that many such patients are liable to become bored with the repetitiveness of the task and to settle for a position response making quick idiosyncratic decisions through a sheer lack of content novelty in successive problem pages. Nevertheless, the Matrices continue to have great value as a screening device where estimates of general visual/perceptual reasoning level are concerned and the test is, to the subnormal, refreshingly free of verbal or 'educational' content. In its Coloured form it has a low 'floor' and the slight negative skew is not a disadvantage at sub-average intelligence levels. There is some anxiety, mainly expressed by Bortner (1965) that the validity and reliability of the Matrices is equivocal. The information in the manuals is limited and the inability of the test to measure a variety of aspects of cognitive functioning is a deficit, especially in the clinical sphere. On the whole, Matrices results correlate quite well with other tests. Clarke, Clarke and Reiman (1958) quote an r of ·81 with the Wechsler Full Scale IQ in high-grade defectives, although the Matrices results tended to be fractionally lower than the Wechsler results. A lower correlation of $r = ·68$ with the Wechsler Full Scale IQ was found by Stacey and Gill (1954) but the same writers quote a correlation of ·86 with the Stanford–Binet for the same patients. Orme (1961) quotes an r of ·93 between the WISC and the Coloured Matrices; and although the latter, because they have fewer items, may hold the attention of defectives rather longer, they suffer the defect that the scatter of scores is rather less and that there is something wanting in the normative background from the point of view of interpreting the raw scores of different kinds of defective patients. Although the data was originally interpreted in percentile form, Gwynne Jones (1956) and Orme (1961) have supplied data for conversions of raw scores into IQs of other tests.

The original manual quotes a retest reliability varying with ages from ·83 to ·93. Since 1956, the problems constituting the 1938 series have been rearranged to give a more uniform probate distribution since the difficulty value of these items was clearly mistaken in the first editions. Similarly, the alternatives between which choice had to be made were also rearranged to give a more uniform distribution of common and uncommon errors of judgment. One of the major objections to the test was the fact that it gave hardly more than a quantitative percentile score and did not reveal qualitative information that might be clinically valuable. Miller and Raven (1939), Bromley (1953), Crawford (1955) and Maher (1960) all investigated the errors connected with 'position preference' since it had been suggested that answers tended to be selected because of their position in the top row of alternatives or at the right-hand of the page. Maher (1960), in particular, compared subnormal children with college students and found no support for the hypothesis that differences in intelligence lead to differential position preferences nor even for the existence of position preferences.

As well as norms in the more usual sense being supplied, norms are also available which allow the reliability of results to be established by checking the scatter of success against these 'subtest' patterns. In the case of testing retardates it is almost certain that the individual test will be administered and percentile points in the normative tables were calculated from the raw scores of 735 Colchester children. The self-administered or group test for adults depends on a larger standardization population of some 5,700 individuals, more than half of whom were military. In the case of the Coloured Matrices a standardization sample of 608 Dumfries schoolchildren between the ages of 5 and 11½ years of age were used, and further percentile points for a group of 51 old people aged approximately 70, plus or minus 7 years, are available. Orme (1961, 1966) has provided normative information for subnormal and other older groups.

Perhaps the greatest advantage of the Progressive Matrices Test is its value for a variety of cultural and subcultural groups and especially for subgroups of, for example, deaf pupils (Gaskill, 1957), and for patients who may be spastic or have other difficulties of motor control or who have expressive aphasias or articulation defects. As in the case of the PPVT the response of the subject may be verbal or motor or may be limited only to eye-pointing or nodding in response to alternatives being indicated by the examiner. Most examiners will tend to prefer the Coloured Matrices with defectives since Philips and Bannon (1968) have indicated that this abbreviated version of the Matrices differentiates very well in the lower ranges of ability in a way which it does not do among children of better than average ability around 11 years of age. These authors also quote a correlation coefficient of ·68 with the SB L-M which compares favourably with the co-efficient of ·66 with the SB form L quoted in the manual for a sample of children at age 9 years.

In view of the very wide usage given to both forms of the Matrices in this country it is surprising that more work has not been published on the relation-ship of test scores to work or social behaviour. Whether or not familiarity has bred contempt or whether users have been deterred by the alleged tendency for defectives to perserverate on a particular position response in answering (e.g. always choosing the extreme right-hand possible answer) is not clear, but the fact that such a perserverative response does not usually set in until the subject has reached extreme difficulty threshold might well be itself a subject for further exploration. Clark (1958) examined a sample of Industrial Rehabilitation Unit clients with a mean Standard Matrices score of 14·21 (SD 3·57) and subdivided his total group of 175 into subgroups of 127 who were not diagnosed as neurotic or unstable and 48 who were. There were no significant differences between the mean test scores of neurotic and stable cases but the former group were found to be very much less likely to be actively resettled in industry than the latter. In that study, however, no detailed analysis was made of patterns of failure in particular Matrices performances.

THE MAZE TEST (PORTEUS, 1959)

Porteus (1959) maintained that the major weakness of commonly used intelligence tests was their failure to measure 'planfulness' or 'prehearsal'. He considered that this capacity was essential for adaptation to most practical life situations and the failure of tests to provide a measure of it resulted in faulty diagnoses and incomplete assessments of the individual. In his own words, 'A necessary component of . . . a basic intelligence index is a measure of planfulness'; and 'no diagnostic examination should be considered complete without some measure of planfulness as an essential factor in intelligence'. He offered, consequently, his standardized series of Mazes not as a substitute for general intelligence, but rather as 'a test of a very important segment or area of general intelligence inadequately covered by another series of tests . . .'.

The test provides two scores, a test quotient (TQ) presumed to measure non-verbal foresight and planning ability, and a qualitative (Q) score based upon the style and quality of test performance. The latter score is a measure of impulse control and has been demonstrated to differentiate between various groups differing in impulsiveness (Docter and Winder, 1954; Fooks and Thomas, 1957; Porteus, 1945). More recently, the Q score has been shown to differentiate between delinquents who behave well in a training school situation and those who do not (Erikson and Roberts, 1966).

Repeated studies since his test was first published have clearly established the validity of the test as a rather sensitive instrument in measuring differences which are not clearly observed by more commonly used tests. In a review of published reports on its effectiveness Tizard (1951) summarized his findings by saying 'because planning activity enters all adaptive behaviour and because the Maze is a very good test of planning capacity, the Maze tends to correlate with other tests to the extent to which they themselves are measures of "planfulness".' Tizard found 28 correlations recorded between the Stanford–Binet and the Porteus Mazes ranging from ·54 to ·69. These correlations are reasonably high for a test which, as Porteus has always argued, is not a substitute for the SB, but is a supplementary test measuring at least partly different functions. Tobias and Gorelick (1962), using a population of retarded adults, quote correlations of ·69 for the Porteus Maze Test with the full WAIS, ·41 for the test with the verbal and ·67 with the performance IQs. A large number of reports indicate that well-adjusted individuals tend to make significantly higher scores on the Maze Test than on the Binet while the maladjusted group, including thieves, truants, sex offenders and subjects with other behaviour disorders, tend to obtain relatively low Maze TQs compared with the Binet IQ (Poull and Montgomery, 1929; Karpeles, 1932).

The institutional adjustment ratings (Porteus, 1950) of feeble-minded patients correlated higher with the Maze than with the Binet or other intelligence tests. Tobias and Gorelick (1962) showed that a cut-off score of 8·5 on the Maze was more accurate in identifying successfully employed ex-trainees of a workshop than was the performance IQ of the WAIS. More recently, Roberts and Erikson (1968) explored the relationship between a behavioural and verbal measure of delay of gratification, Porteus Maze Test measures of planning ability and foresight (TQ) and impulse control (Q), and ratings of adjustment in a school for delinquent adolescent males. Both measures of delay of gratification were significantly related to the Porteus measures and the adjustment ratings. Delay of gratification was also found to be related in part to age and ethnic group membership, but not IQ.

Low scores on the test may be due to low intelligence or to maladjustment, but maladjustment does not exclude high scores and differential diagnosis calls for a qualitative analysis of the performance. It was in response to this need that Porteus developed his Q score because it quickly becomes apparent on the observation of patients doing this test that it is close to being a projective test as well as a cognitive task. Attention must be paid to the subject's response to frustration and failure, whether he becomes rigid and unable to shift or whether he becomes impulsive, 'rattled', or confused and inclined to take quick short cuts without reference to the conditions imposed on him. It becomes an easy task to consider whether his performance is due to intellectual inability or to failure of temperament in the face of stress. A series of studies (Porteus, 1950; Wright, 1944; Grajales, 1948; Docter and Winder, 1954; Tobias and Gorelick, 1962; Roberts and Erikson, 1968) show that analysis of the Q score enables remarkably accurate classifications between delinquents and non-delinquents to be made. However, only the penultimate paper by Tobias and Gorelick suggests that the critical Q score is equally valid in the feeble-minded population.

The test appears to be particularly sensitive to temperamental factors and indeed Foulds (1951, 1952) has outlined characteristic kinds of test performance presented by normal intelligent subjects with different psychiatric diatheses. It is clear from the nature of the test that with duller subjects quite wide differences in score may be achieved on retest, possibly because of differences in attention level or the circumstances surrounding the test occasion. More importantly, the fact that the calculation of test quotients is rather a gross procedure based on a mental age concept tends to lead to wide variations in final score, which may depend on one little slip of the pen or one moment of distraction on the part of the examinee. As Gunzburg (1965) has said,

> there is no doubt that this test has far more in common with the techniques of personality assessment which have been clinically accepted despite their weak scientific grounding, than with well standardized, validated, and reliable intelligence tests. Being a measure of a single mental task, the test can obviously not do justice by itself to such a complex problem as social adaptation which requires many capacities and abilities.

However, the most recent papers quoted show some evidence that the test has certain prognostic value, particularly when both the TQ and Q scores are used as predictors of adjustment and resettlement following rehabilitation in dull or delinquent subjects. Further follow-up studies are necessary to confirm this and until these emerge it will be difficult to judge the value of the Maze as a measure of 'social intelligence' or trainability.

BLOCK DESIGN TEST (KOHS, 1923)

This test consists of sixteen multi-coloured cubes and a series of designs, the subject being asked to manipulate the cubes in such a way as to reproduce with great accuracy enlarged copies of designs which increase in complexity from very simple to quite difficult patterns. The solution of these problems requires only the capacity to analyse the design into its component square units and to re-synthesize the pattern in the form of blocks after this analysis has been completed. In this way the subject's ability to learn to use logical procedures and to construct planfully are measured. It is therefore one of the most popular single measures of intelligence measured in a 'performance type' task and a good deal of stress has been laid by some writers on the importance of auto-critical faculty for the effective performance of the task. Nevertheless, attention and adaptability are also called for and many subnormals find the more difficult items troublesome in that they fail to attend long enough to recapitulate, thus accumulating moves.

Subnormal subjects are found to do better on the Block Design than on the Stanford–Binet on a number of occasions, and it has been said by Kohs (1923) that the test appears to be 'a fairer index of their functional efficiency in various occupations than the Binet'. Sarason and Potter (1947), Wile and Davis (1930) and Gunzburg (1956) have all demonstrated that the good performer on the Kohs Block Test tends to be personally stable and have good social adjustment, whilst poor performance on this test can be due to maladjustment, brain injury, confusion of visual organization and so forth. The test has, of course, been used in various combinations, including in the Wechsler as a smaller subtest with reliability coefficients of ·82 to ·86 quoted when used in this context. The use of the test in the assessment of brain damage has been illustrated mostly by Goldstein and Scheerer (1941) and by Shapiro (1951, 1954).

Gunzburg (1965) has suggested that large and striking discrepancies between the Kohs performance and the efficiency in other tests might be indicative of disordered cerebral functioning, whilst a less dramatic lowering of this perfor-mance may suggest only emotional disturbance. The qualitative features of the performance are worthy of observation and have been commented on by a number of authorities (Wile and Davis, 1930; Earl, 1937, 1940).

DRAW A PERSON TEST (GOODENOUGH, 1926; HARRIS, 1963)

It seems not unlikely that the Draw a Person Test in one form or another is amongst the most popular of projective and/or cognitive tests used in the English-speaking psychological world. However, reviews of the figure-drawing literature (Roback, 1968; Swensen, 1968) and the more recent work of Adler (1970) tend to be rather pessimistic about the validity of the instrument as it is commonly used. Gunzburg (1965) has quoted a number of studies producing significantly good correlations with intelligence tests, in the region of ·7 with the Stanford–Binet, but is inclined to agree that the DAP test becomes less valid as a measure of intelligence the more the subject deviates from normality. However, it is clearer from the contemporary literature that so far as mentally subnormal subjects are concerned, the drawing test as a cognitive measure can have substantial value (Gunzburg, 1955a; Murphy, 1956; Harris, 1963). Levy (1971) has recently produced evidence that using the educable and adolescent mentally retarded as subjects, test-retest reliability for the Harris revision (the most commonly used scoring system) of the Goodenough Draw a Man Test reaches ·81 on the full scale with an intra-scorer reliability of ·99. However, in his study, correlation between the Goodenough Draw a Man Test and the 1960 revision of the Stanford–Binet was only ·27, a fact that throws in question the validity of the test. Up till that time it had been thought to correlate sufficiently with more generally used intelligence tests to be measuring largely some general quality which was congruent with intelligence. Indeed the work of Nichols and Strumpfer (1962) had demonstrated that a single factor, 'the overall quality of the drawing', accounted for almost all of the variance common to thirty figure drawing scales. The same study indicated three lesser factors – one a size factor, one associated by the authors with defence and constriction, and one tapping sexual differentiation. It may well be, therefore, that some of these other factors were playing a larger part in the variance of scores from a sample such as that described by Levy (1971). The debate about the test goes on and even in the limited population of the mentally retarded Silverstein (1966) was able to demonstrate that in children anxiety played a part in depressing the quality scale of the test, and Maloney and Payne (1969) have indicated that it is not, as currently scored, a very clear measure of body image.

Adler, in a study similar to that of Nichols and Strumpfer, also elicited four factors which accounted together for 44·7 per cent of the total variance. The nature of their first and clearly most powerful factor was similar in that it reflected the formal accuracy of the drawn figure and the degree to which the figure is differentiated with regard to detail and individuality. However, unlike Maloney and Payne (1969), Adler considers that the overall estimate of body concept sophistication on a five-point scale as described by Witkin loads ·91 on this first factor, which suggests that it is an acceptable quick estimate of that dimension. What is important in his view is that a high score reflects an accurate realistic reproduction of a person involving some degree of technical ability but essentially requiring less aesthetic talent and more a developed cognitive skill in body image representation.

The second factor of size and placement seems to be a stable factor confirming Nichols and Strumpfer's work and a clearly independent factor which may be of some predictive usefulness but which has had little further work done on it. Adler remarks that this factor may reflect the drawing variables associated in the literature with the personality dimension of expansiveness/constriction and therefore it seems worthwhile to pursue this further. It may also be related to constancy defects in certain patients. The third factor in Adler's study appeared to be promising and the items which loaded highest on it were an overly large head, bizarre or mixed profile, disintegration of the body structure reflecting a disturbed relationship between the discrete parts of the figure and other internal inconsistencies. This factor was associated by clinicians with the presence of cerebral dysfunction, and there seems to be a case for further scrutiny of it. There is, however, a clear disparity in the descriptions attributed to the fourth factor between Nichols and Strumpfer and the Adler studies, the latter taking it to represent simply a failure of behavioural control or lack of concern about control in the execution of the drawing rather than representing failure of sexual differentiation.

These two main studies make it clear that analysis of figure drawings will be most productively pursued along factor-analytic lines, but unfortunately neither of them deal with drawings of subnormals as an experimental population. Reproductions of the Adler and Nichols and Strumpfer work with the subnormal population is therefore clearly to be desired.

Some of the general methodological problems facing the psychologist who has a persistent interest in the 'draw a person' type of test have been presented by Wanderer (1969) and Hammer (1969) who make it clear that in the general psychiatric setting at least the debate continues with unabated vigour. Gunzburg (1955a) has enumerated criteria in drawings which make it possible to differentiate between the normal productions of uncomplicated subnormals and the abnormal drawings of pathological subnormals. The absence of these signs suggests that the drawing has not been interfered with and can be assumed reasonably to correspond with the intellectual level established by an intelligence test. There are many difficulties with this type of exploration and serious misclassifications can occur if the test is used outside a battery. For example, even if one can demonstrate that a particular sign will be found only in the drawings of schizophrenic subjects but not in all schizophrenic subjects, then all subjects showing this sign will be correctly classified, but many who should be so classified will escape because the sign is not showing; that is, unless other tests which will isolate these cases are being concurrently administered. This indeed is a further example of the need to use a series of 'meshes' in classifying patients and also in using a temporal strategy for the selection of tests depending on the information to be derived from them. Perhaps one of the greatest risks in the Draw a Person Test is that of the wide qualitative range of the drawings. The sometimes rather florid abnormalities which one finds can lead to the danger of indiscriminate over-interpretation. Certainly expressive material of this sort which can be controlled and matched to other cognitive and emotional performances makes the test a field for further research both into cognitive development and personality investigation. The fact that it is usually acceptable to subnormals, even into middle age, makes it particularly useful in this field, but at the moment it is perhaps best used as a measure of general intellectual development with a component of social and interpersonal observation rather than as a projective or personality test.

THE ILLINOIS TEST OF PSYCHOLINGUISTIC ABILITIES (MCCARTHY AND KIRK, 1961)

It is not too much to say that this test, which has recently emerged in a revised edition (Kirk, *et al.*, 1968), marks a milestone in the development of the psychological assessment of handicap. It concerns itself essentially with the assessment of linguistic maturity in children from the age of 2 years 4 months to the age of 10 years 3 months, but evidence is beginning to emerge (Gunzburg, 1964) that it may have applicability to mental defectives of greater age. The importance of language disorders in an assessment of handicap has been recently stressed by Mittler (1970) and in a variety of papers reviewed by him in preceding years.

The authors of the test have based their work on Osgood's (1957, 1963) theoretical communication model which owes something to models of communication developed by cyberneticists and engineers. In particular, Osgood attempts to distinguish between levels of organization, psycholinguistic processes, and channels of communication. The first is mainly concerned with the subject's ability to deal with meaningful symbols at the representational level, and at the automatic sequential level is concerned with 'non-meaningful use of symbols, principally their long-term retention and a short-term memory of symbol sequences' (McCarthy and Olson, 1964). Psycholinguistic processes are more concerned with the development of habits which become part of normal language functioning. A distinction is made between the techniques of 'decoding' used to obtain meaning either from visual or auditory linguistic inputs, and 'encoding' which make possible the expression of meaning in words or gestures. Thirdly, a process of association is posited which is an intermediate stage involving the inner manipulation of linguistic symbols. The channels of communication are taken to be the sensori-motor paths for the transmission or reception of linguistic symbols. Transmission may result in either a motor or a verbal output.

It cannot be stressed too much, as the authors comment in their introduction to the new manual, that the revised edition (Kirk *et al.*, 1968) as well as the original ITPA was conceived as a diagnostic rather than a classificatory tool. Its object is to delineate specific abilities and disabilities in children in order that remediation may be initiated when needed. Its aim is to provide both the framework within which can be conceptualized and tested discrete and educationally significant abilities and also a base for the construction of remedial programmes for children who show disparate development of these separate abilities. Fig. 11 indicates the three-dimensional model of the ITPA. (See also Chapter 17.)

In the words of the authors,

the psycholinguistic model on which the ITPA is based attempts to relate those functions whereby the intentions of one individual are transmitted (verbally or non-verbally) to another individual, and, reciprocally, functions whereby the environment or the intentions of another individual are received and interpreted. It attempts to inter-relate the processes which take place, for example, when one person receives a message, interprets it, or becomes a source of a new signal to be transmitted. It deals with the psychological functions of the individual which operate in communication activities.

The adoption of this theoretical model for the battery served two purposes: (a) it was a parsimonious device by which the essential features of communication

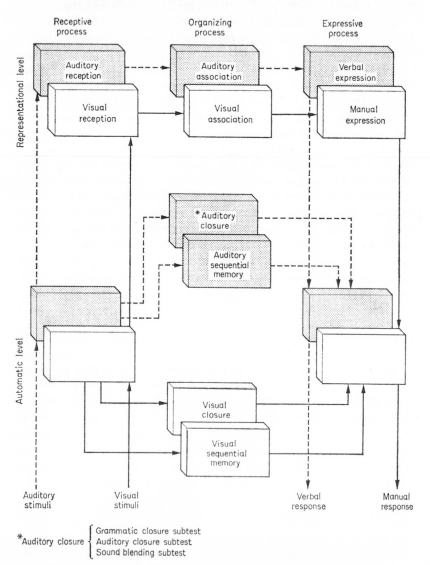

Fig. 11 Clinical model of the ITPA (from Kirk and Kirk, 1971).

were delineated so that their relationships were specified; (b) it provided a framework in which to observe and evaluate a child, making it possible to verify and elaborate on test results and to suggest remedial measures.

By using the above model the authors have generated ten separate tests and two supplementary tests for the purpose of assessing specific abilities and disabilities in children. Their intention is that analysis of the pattern of these abilities and disabilities would lead quite clearly to a programme whereby concentration on the individual's particular strengths might ensure confidence and practice, and remedial programmes might also be developed to boost the subject's weaknesses where they were not essentially mediated by a remediable physical or other defect.

The twelve subtests of the ITPA are recommended as being given in the order presented on the record form:

1. Auditory Reception
2. Visual Reception
3. Visual Sequential Memory
4. Auditory Association
5. Auditory Sequential Memory
6. Visual Association
7. Visual Closure
8. Verbal Expression
9. Grammatic Closure
10. Manual Expression
11. Auditory Closure
12. Sound Blending

The tests can eventually be expressed in terms of a raw score, a language age or a standard score together with an overall total score for the test. Profile analysis for the individual subjects may be made as indicated in Fig. 12. The work of Tubbs (1966) made a comparison between groups of normal, subnormal and psychotic children roughly matched on non-verbal tests and resulted in profiles approximately equivalent to those indicated in Fig. 12 being achieved. Tubbs's work indicated that psychotic children tended to do worse than younger matched normals on auditory decoding, auditory vocal association, motor encoding, auditory vocal automatic, visual motor sequential and vocal encoding. As Mittler points out (1970) it will be apparent that there was no difference on the auditory sequential task, confirming the clinical and experimental evidence that psychotic children are unimpaired at reading back from an immediate memory store. Similar group differences were compared by Olson (1961) who reported a study of deaf, receptive and expressive aphasic children with the ITPA. It was clear that his three groups could be differentiated on all except one of the subtests, and that children diagnosed as expressive aphasic were far from being homogeneous from a psycholinguistic point of view, so confirming clinical evidence relating to the variety of handicaps often found in such patients.

A survey by Bateman (1965) reports a number of studies where the ITPA has been used in the way which will probably become more common, not in studying groups but in reporting individual cases where the diagnostic use of the tests has resulted in significant improvements in the psycholinguistic areas which were noted as being significantly depressed. It is an interesting general comment about the type of test epitomized by the ITPA that it relates much more closely to the individual experimental analysis of cases suggested by the work of Bartlet and Shapiro (1956), who investigated reading difficulties in a 9-year-old of apparently low IQ who had failed to benefit from special coaching. In brief the experimental analysis demonstrated that the subject's difficulties stemmed from inability to

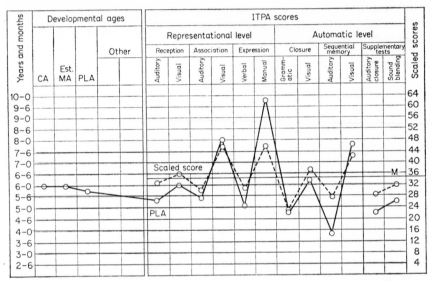

Fig. 12 ITPA profile analysis in terms of psycholinguistic ages and of scaled scores (from Kirk and Kirk, 1971).

form associations between sensory modalities, and went on to suggest lines along which remedial teaching could take place. This is exactly the procedure which the use of ITPA adumbrates, and there is clearly a sense in which each administration of the test is in fact a series of experiments with individual subjects rather than the aim being to classify a subject by locating his position on one main variable. (See also Chapter 17.)

Reliability coefficients are not quoted by the authors in the manual, but earlier work indicated test-retest coefficients of ·82 (Smith, 1962), ·94 over 9 months (Mueller and Smith, 1964) and ·83 over a 4-month interval with adult defectives (Gunzburg, 1964). These figures indicate that the battery is reliable enough diagnostically but it seems likely that the authors would not be over-apprehensive about lower coefficients since there is the essential paradox that the more intensively one strives for higher reliability the more one is tending to stamp out of the test characteristics which make it susceptible to measuring intra-individual differences from week to week. Since it is measuring a dynamically interrelated series of skills and processes which are likely to be interfered with, or modified favourably by, remediation programmes, it would not be surprising if reliability coefficients showed a measure of variability greater than in most traditional intelligence or other cognitive tests. In any event, the main advantage of the instrument for assessment is that it allows the various processes involved in language to be broken down into their components.

The original standardization of the ITPA was on 700 children between 2½ and 9 but there are some suggestions that the use of the test below 4 years is likely to prove difficult for practical reasons. The raw scores can in each case be converted to scaled scores for each of the subtests, and an overall psycholinguistic age which is relatively comparable to a traditional IQ can be used to assess overall performance. Gunzburg's (1964) study analysed the performance of 50 young male subnormals on the ITPA, and he supplies a table for the calculation of language ages based on a shortened battery of subtests. The subtests which were eliminated on the grounds of relatively low reliability coefficients were the auditory decoding, auditory-vocal automatic and visual motor association tests. This, of course, is a problem with all subtests in batteries and was originally commented on by Wechsler. Standard errors of measurement calculated by Gunzburg for the separate subtests was slightly larger than those given by Kirk and McCarthy (1961), so that their advice that a 'raw score difference of less than 4 points between test and retest should not be regarded as reliable' is applicable to adult subnormals. In the same way, the standard error of measurement for the total ITPA psycholinguistic age is approximately 6 raw score points for the child sample and 9 points for Gunzburg's adult sample. Consequently the rule of thumb suggested by the authors that 'no difference of less than 10 raw score points should be regarded as reliable' would still apply.

The development of understanding, conceptualization and reasoning appears to be related so closely to the development of speech and language, especially in subnormals, that the latter constitute the main channels by which we attempt to assess the state of mental functioning in humans. The use of the ITPA, therefore, is likely to uncover knowledge relevant to the functioning or malfunctioning of various aspects of language and its growth which is bound to reflect some light on the whole area of mental development. The drawing together of many experimental threads is imminent and is beginning to appear in some of the literature (Mueller and Weaver, 1964; Lucas, 1970). It has been demonstrated by Zeaman and House (1963), as a result of their investigations of discrimination learning in retardates, that attention deficit or failure to attend to relevant stimulus cues may be the reason for the defective's difficulty in learning discrimination tasks. Luria (1963) has postulated that the bond between the verbal or 'secondary signalling system' and motor behaviour is poorly developed in retardates and leads to inadequate regulation of motor behaviour by verbal signals. Thirdly, a series of investigations reported by O'Connor and Hermelin (1963) were designed to explore in institutionalized moderately retarded subjects coding behaviour which can be thought of as a translation of stimuli from one modality to another without changing the meaning. Their results indicated that defectives tended to give more stereotyped responses if the stimulus and response items were presented in the same sensory modality. Cross-modal conditions, according to these authors, appear to necessitate translation from one type of sensory image to another resulting in a more specific association between words and images and improving accuracy of responses on recognition tasks. However, Hinshaw and Heel (1968) replicated O'Connor and Hermelin's (1961) investigation using American subjects and failed to find significant differences between like and cross-modal conditions. A tendency was found for like-modality presentation to be superior to cross-modal conditions in subjects with MA of 4 to 6 years. These investigations appear to indicate a need for further exploration of the relationship of modality preferences or strength to performance on specific learning tasks across modalities. Conflicting results of different investigations regarding unimodal versus cross-modal efficiency suggest that other variables than coding or even mental age may be related to the results found. Lucas (1970) has looked into this problem using six subtests of the ITPA to divide her population into high auditory and high visual modality groups. Each group was given a recognition task under unimodal (visual/visual or auditory/auditory) or cross-modal (visual/auditory or auditory/visual) conditions of presentation and recognition. She found no relationship between assessed modality strength on the ITPA and performance on the recognition task. The visual presentation/visual recognition task condition resulted in significantly higher scores than the cross-modality or auditory/auditory task conditions. The efficacy of cross-modal coding and facilitating recognition in moderately retarded subjects was not supported by results. The data therefore fail to support O'Connor and Hermelin's (1961, 1963) finding of a clear beneficial effect of cross-modal conditions on stimulus recognition with defectives and tend to support the results of Hinshaw and Heel (1968). Visual presentations therefore appear to be more effective and this needs to be borne in mind when the education and training of the moderately retarded are at stake, visual cues and materials being used on all possible occasions. However, the apparent conflict between the results quoted above may be resolved since it is possible that task difficulty may interact with cross-modality conditions and that as task difficulty increases cross-modality conditions may facilitate recognition. Only further experimentation will confirm this possibility. On the whole the work of Mueller and Weaver (1964) and of Bilovsky and Share (1965) with Down's syndrome subjects all using the ITPA makes it clear that there are certain general patterns of response likely to be observed in a retardate population.

Defectives at the trainable level have significantly greater difficulty in coding language compared to their overall language age, and have greater difficulty in the utilization of the auditory vocal channel than of the visual motor channel. Language age scores tend to be approximately nineteen months lower than mental age scores in this type of population although significant correlations are found between LA and speech ratings. So far as the Down's syndrome group are concerned, their primary deficits are also in the auditory vocal channel on the automatic sequential level, whereas their main strength lies in motor encoding and visual decoding channels at the representation level.

The ITPA subtests generally are of sufficiently wide range to allow them to be applied to fairly wide populations of retardates up to mental age 10, but it is clear that a good deal of further work by way of accumulation of norms and characteristic response patterns needs to be done before the results can be interpreted with sufficient confidence when the test is applied to subjects of increased chronological age. The great strength of the test lies in its representing a move away from the attribution of a number like an IQ to a person and towards the analysis of strengths and weaknesses which may be positively tackled in the workshop, classroom and ward and the effects of this effort monitored from time to time.

DEVELOPMENTAL TEST OF VISUAL PERCEPTION (FROSTIG, MASLOW, LEFEVER AND WHITTLESEY, 1964; FROSTIG, LEFEVER AND WHITTLESEY, 1966)

The changing interests of psychologists in their testing of subnormal patients is reflected not only in the ITPA but also in the development of this new test of development of visual-perceptual processes. Marianne Frostig and her co-workers have been impressed by the frequency with which limitation or impairment of ability to perform different visual perceptual tasks was observed in children with learning difficulties. Sometimes this appeared to be related to brain damage, sometimes to emotional disturbances, and sometimes simply to slow development. Furthermore, it seemed to these writers that what was normally referred to as visual perception consisted of several subskills each of which may be relatively independent of one another. It was not felt that existing visual-perceptual tests were completely adequate to explore this so they developed the following five subtests measuring operationally defined perceptual skills:

Test 1. Eye-motor coordination, which is a test of eye-hand coordination involving the drawing of continuous straight, curved or angled lines between boundaries of various width or from point to point without guide lines.

Test 2. Figure ground perception, which involves shifts in the perception of figures against increasingly complex backgrounds in which intersecting and 'hidden' geometric shapes are used.

Test 3. Shape constancy, which is a test involving the recognition of certain geometric figures presented in a variety of sizes, shadings, textures and positions in space and their discrimination from similar figures.

Test 4. Position in space, which involves the discrimination of reversals and rotations of figures presented in series. Schematic drawings representing common objects are used.

Test 5. Spatial relationships, which is a test involving the analysis of simple forms and patterns consisting of lines of various lengths and angles which the child is required to copy using dots as guidepoints. This test is reminiscent of the marble board test (Strauss and Lehtinen, 1947).

While the authors consider that in the future the test may become a useful tool in the diagnosis of brain damage, no immediate assumptions were made that it measures this although the latter has been shown seriously to affect perceptual ability. This test, as well as the ITPA, is an interesting tool for use in analysing reading and other defects of symbol usage. The author's research together with that of others indicates that the test correlates between ·40 and ·50 with reading achievement in the normal early school years. However, the test is not predictive of reading disability in the higher grades. The test consists of a thirty-five page expendable booklet, the back cover of which can be used as a scoring sheet, and the book also provides space for personal data and comments. There are a number of demonstration cards and three transparent scoring tissues for some of the subtests. Subjects require four well-sharpened coloured pencils in contrasting colours together with an ordinary pencil. The examiner may use a blackboard, slate or spare white paper for demonstrations at administration.

Normative data for the test, which may be administered to a group, is available for normal children between the ages of 4 and 8 years and is reported in quarter-year intervals. The 1963 standardization is based on the responses of over 2,100 children who were tested with the 1961 (third) edition, and the norms currently in use are based on nursery school and public school children who lived in southern California and were between the ages of 3 and 9 years. Normative curves drawn from the standardization sample indicate that maximum perceptual development in the areas measured occurs between the ages of 4 and 7, with less growth after the age of approximately $7\frac{1}{2}$ when cognitive functions begin to predominate. The test therefore is designed mainly for use with young children, and early exploratory ventures with adult subnormals have had very limited publication. Norms were developed using the concept of perceptual age level whereby the latter for each subtest was defined in terms of the performance of the average child in the corresponding age-group. Means are available, however, in the present standardization for such measures to be converted by conversion tables to scale scores, and from these to perceptual quotients.

Early reliability studies carried out by the authors in 1961 give a test-retest correlation coefficient of ·98 when the test was administered individually some weeks apart, and a coefficient of ·80 when the test was administered to small groups two weeks apart. Separate subtest coefficients range from ·42 (Subtest 2) to ·80 (Subtest 3). It is interesting to note that the lowest reliability coefficients are on Subtests 1 and 2 which assess visual motor functioning, and these subtests would be expected to be much more affected than others by the physical condition and emotional state of the child as well as by wider environmental influences. The authors expect test-retest correlation coefficients to be low, especially after longer intervals or if training is interpolated between tests, because of the rapid development of visual perception which seems to be more strongly influenced by experience than is thought to be the case with general intelligence. Split-half reliabilities for total score range from ·78 at age 8 to 9 to ·89 at age 5 to 6.

So far as validity of the test is concerned, correlations have been found between scores on the Frostig Test and teacher ratings of classroom adjustment of ·441, with motor coordination ·502, and with intellectual functioning of ·497. In passing, it is perhaps worth commenting in this context that the authors felt that the Goodenough DAP Test might be used as an indicator of intellectual functioning, perceptual development (particularly of body image) and as a projective technique. The authors obtained product moment correlation coefficients between the perceptual quotient and the Goodenough IQ. These range from ·46 at the kindergarten level to ·37 at second grade school level. The authors took it that the relatively low coefficients indicated that the two tests were measuring factors relatively distinct from each other but that there was some degree of overlap most evident at the lower age level. However, they comment that the coefficients may also reflect the relatively low reliability of the Goodenough IQ which is reported by Goodenough (1955) as ·77 computed by the split-half method for the ages in question.

The test has the advantage that it can be administered with minimum use of language and consequently can be given to deaf, hard of hearing or even non-English-speaking children by gesture and the use of additional examples. Spastic children or other children with severe motor handicaps may be given the subtests with the possible exception of Subtest 1, allowing them to outline the required items with the finger or hand rather than with pencils. With defective children the authors suggest that scale scores and perceptual quotients be computed using both the chronological age and the mental age of the children, since the current evidence seems to indicate that scale scores and perceptual quotients computed on the basis of the mental age may be more helpful to the teacher in pinpointing subtest areas which need to be dealt with by educational measures.

Neurologically handicapped samples of children have been studied by Frostig, Lefever and Whittlesey (1963), who pointed out that in attempting to help a child with disabilities of visual perception, knowledge of aetiology matters less than knowledge of the extent and nature of the symptoms. However, most research studies in this area have reported an impressive correlation between perceptual disabilities and neurological handicaps, and as a result it has been suggested that a test of visual perception might become a useful tool within a battery of tests for the diagnosis of brain damage. The work reported above indicated that in 71 children with known learning difficulties, a high percentage of whom had been medically referred with a diagnosis of 'neurologically handicapped', a much greater scatter of age equivalent subtest scores was found than in the responses of normal children and the total scores were lower. More recently Abercrombie *et al.* (1964) reported a study comparing the incidence of some aspects of perceptual and visual motor disorders within the main categories of cerebral palsy, and investigated their relationships with motor handicap, strabismus and somatic sensory disorders. In this study, the two parts of subtest 2 (intersecting figures and hidden figures) were scored separately and the authors tentatively concluded that, for example, strabismus increases the difficulty of perceiving hidden figures. These authors found that disturbances of visual motor performance as measured by one or more of the tests in their battery were associated with spasticity and not with aethetosis; the incidence of such disturbance in spastics was very high.

Although the DTVP was standardized on a sample of children with an age range from 3 to 9 years, Silverstein, Ulfeldt and Price (1970) carried out a study in which they applied the test individually to 148 schoolchildren at Pacific State Hospital between the ages of 10 and 17 years with a mean age of 14, SD = 2·20, and a mean IQ (WISC) of 47, SD 9·93. They were able to demonstrate that the average scores were at about the same level as those of the average 5-year-old child in the standardization sample. Although the authors of the DTVP feel that scale scores on the PQ should not be used for children above the age of 9, in this study the subjects' mean PQ (48·5) was very close to their mean IQ (47·8), and there is a suggestion therefore that the test may be relatively usable with older subjects. The correlations of the subtest with both age and IQ were positive and mostly significant. Both the intercorrelations among the subtests and their internal consistency reliabilities were appreciably higher than those reported for the standardization sample, and moreover their common variance was also higher and their specific variance lower. The components of variance differed markedly from those reported by Silverstein (1968) for the standardization sample, in which the average common, specific and error variance was ·21, ·51 and ·28 respectively. It had been assumed by the authors of the DTVP that the subtests tapped five different and essentially independent abilities, but the results of the Silverstein *et al.* (1970) study are not consistent with this assumption and suggest that the differential screening of perceptual dysfunctions may not be so easily carried out as the authors of the DTVP assume. Similarly, Ward (1970) has shown that factor analysis of the test results in the emergence of only one main perceptual motor factor.

The test, however, has much to offer and it is clear that further experimental work with more extended samples is called for. Previous studies of the test with normal children have shown that results on this test are positively related to classroom adjustment, motor coordination and intellectual functioning, to scores on the Goodenough Test, and to reading achievement. They are negatively related to learning difficulties and neurological handicaps. That it has considerable relevance to the field of retardation will already be apparent.

Just as the ITPA allows the planning of remedial programmes so also the use of the Frostig Test has led to the development of a programme of visual perceptual training. Frostig and Horne (1964), for example, in evaluating large numbers of youngsters with learning difficulties found that the most frequent accompanying symptom was disturbance in visual perception. They further demonstrated that the period during which the greatest amount of perceptual development normally takes place is between the ages of $3\frac{1}{2}$ and $7\frac{1}{2}$ years of age, so that attention to deficiencies should be paid during the preschool rather than early school years or at an equivalent mental age level. The authors have therefore developed a training programme following the use of the Frostig Test which sets out classroom or remedial techniques to be routinely administered to children with visual perceptual difficulties diagnosed by the test. Walsh and D'Angelo (1971) have recently demonstrated the value of this with children attending a Head-Start Centre and have shown that visual training did produce significant gains in visual performance. Jacobs (1967) had previously noted that little perceptual development appears to occur for the age-group concerned as a result of maturation alone.

It is a moot point, however, whether the perceptual training provided by the Frostig programme will effectively transfer to activities required in school. Bosworth (1968) found that the application of a training programme in visual motor skills for kindergarten children did produce significant gains in a test of word discrimination and in visual motor ability, but Rosen (1966) by contrast found that a brief programme of visual training produced gains in visual perception but not in reading scores for first-grade subjects. It is clear therefore that considerably more work needs to be done to confirm transfer effects from the programme to a wider range of communication and perceptual skills. By the same token, many psychologists in mental retardation are utilizing programmes of sensory training, motor and perceptual skill training, but have not often reported on the detailed effects of these in a systematic fashion. Perhaps the groundwork triggered off by the Kirks and by Marianne Frostig will supply an adequate stimulus for this work to go forward with the vigour that deserves to be applied to it. Psychologists with an interest in remediation and assessment will find Myers and Hammill (1969) and Kirk and Kirk (1971) very useful in practice.

Perceptual-motor tests

The Bender Gestalt Test (Bender, 1938) has proved popular with many psychologists interested in perceptual-motor functioning, often more on the grounds that it is an easily administered design-copying task for the subject than on the grounds that there is clear-cut evidence for its usefulness in a number of fields. Billingslea (1963) reviewed this test and concluded that despite its many weaknesses it has continued to be of value in the clinician's repertory. The scoring methods of Pascal and Suttell (1951) for adults and of Koppitz (1964) for children seem to be those which have gained most use. Attempts to differentiate between organic and non-organic mental subnormals on performance in the Bender (Baroff, 1957; Feldman, 1953; Silverstein and Mohan, 1962) have examined both qualitative and quantitative differences, but Feldman (1953), for example, reported a diagnostic classification accuracy of 67 per cent which, though useful for screening purposes, is hardly adequate for individual diagnosis. Pacella

(1965), however, produced evidence that organic and non-organic hospitalized subnormals could be distinguished at the ·01 level of confidence if they were given three successive trials on the Bender Gestalt with the instructions that they should do it again and see how well they could do it this time. On all occasions scoring was by the Pascal and Suttell method. In general, the organics failed to show learning and significant improvement whereas the non-organics did.

A recent and promising development using the Bender Gestalt Test both with psychiatric and with subnormal populations has been devised by Canter (1966, 1968) and pursued by Adams (1970). This is known as the Background Inter-ference Procedure (BIP), which requires the subject first to copy the Bender figures on standard blank paper followed by his repeating the task on specially prepared paper which has the appearance of an assembled jigsaw pattern. In Canter's (1966) study it was shown that increased decrement of performance on the BIP mode relative to the standard mode was characteristic of organic brain disorder when the Pascal and Suttell method of scoring the Bender Test results had been used for both modes. In his second study, Canter (1968) examined two samples of psychiatric patients having from 36 to 38 per cent base rates of organic brain disorder. Two scorers were used and a good degree of correspondence between BIP Bender classification of organic disorder and independent medico-neurological classification was shown by either of the two scorers. In general, the sensitivity of the BIP Bender as a diagnostic screen may be evaluated by the inverse probability given by the Bayes's formula (Meehl and Rosen, 1955) viz.

$$P_0 = \frac{Pp_1}{Pp_1 + Qp_2}$$ where P_0 equals the probability that an individual has an

organic brain disorder, given that his BIP Bender is Class C, i.e. 'organic'; P = the base rate of actual organic brain disorder in the population examined; $P + Q = 1$; p_1 equals the proportion of 'valid positives' on the BIP Bender; and p_2 equals the proportion of 'false positives' on the BIP Bender. If one assumes the base rate of organic brain disorder amongst referrals to the psychologists in the medical psychiatric setting to be ·35 (Satz, 1966), the valid positive rate to be ·81 and the false positive rate to be ·05 (from the averages of Canter's 1968 study), then $P_0 = ·92$. It is interesting to note therefore that the BIP Bender seems to have a high degree of accuracy in screening out the non-organic patients. The 'valid negative' rate, i.e. proportion of non-organics correctly identified as such, is ·95. This represents a considerable improvement over the simple base rate of ·65 for non-organics in the population examined.

Broadhurst and Phillips (1969) have recently looked at the Koppitz system of scoring children's Benders and give full information on the reliability and the validity of the test when applied to a large and representative sample of British schoolchildren. These authors demonstrated inter-scorer reliabilities of from ·79 to ·84 (Koppitz scoring), that the part played in performance by 'g' is very small but that the test must be used with caution. They go on, however, to make the important point that 'Copying the Bender designs without errors is a complex task involving functions which probably differ at different age levels. Maturation and integration of these functions by the age of eleven make the task a relatively easy one for most children, and therefore by that age or somewhat earlier it should be possible to demonstrate a clear association between failure in the test and those clinical states in which perceptual motor disability is part of the syndrome. But if a child suffers a functional deficiency in some component skill it is not necessarily revealed by an analysis of the protocols for certain kinds of error. The more mature subject can employ strategies to surmount difficulties which others do not experience. Some children use language to monitor performance in copying; others approach the task with greater care and deliberate planning than the majority of their peers find necessary. Clinical use of the Bender Test is most productive when such features of performance are observed and evaluated.' The remote scoring of the completed drawings may therefore lose some of these qualitative characteristics of test performance and make establishment of validity indices rather harder.

A similar type of test, the Graham–Kendall Memory for Designs Test (MFD) (1946, 1960) involves the presentation of simple geometric designs and reproduction of these from memory. Difficulty in performance of this task has been assumed to be associated with organic impairment. Unfortunately, the original tables supplied by the authors reveal the 50 per cent misclassification of organics; but more recently the test has been further standardized to provide age and intelligence standardization, and although significant differences between brain damage and control groups can now be found using a cut-off point scoring system there remains considerable overlap with other diagnostic groups. Broadly, however, investigations of Brilliant and Gynther (1963) and Korman and Blumberg (1963) suggest that this is one of the most consistently successful motor-perceptual measures for identifying brain damage. Richie and Butler (1964) quote a test-retest reliability coefficient of ·77 for this test in a population of retardates, and inter-judge correlations by different judges scoring the tests reach as high as ·96.

In the same field, the Benton Visual Retention Test (VRT) (Benton, 1963) can yield interesting and useful results with retarded subjects (Alley, 1969; Brown and Rice, 1967). In fact Alley's work originated from the finding of Sternlicht, Pustel and Siegel (1968) that other constructional praxis tasks, which had been previously used to differentiate organically impaired from cultural-familial mentally retarded groups, had yielded such conflicting results. The latter authors found in their own studies of the scoring systems of the Bender Gestalt and the MFD that only the mentally retarded children's adaptation of the Pascal and Suttell scoring system of the Bender Gestalt significantly differentiated organic impairment in two institutionalized groups of retardates. The Koppitz (1964) scoring of the Bender Gestalt and the MFD administered either as a memory or copying task yielded non-significant differential results. The authors were able to differentiate the organic from the non-organic groups on three variables at the 5 per cent level, with the cultural familials obtaining significantly higher mean absolute scores on 'distortion' score, 'card 2' error score and 'card 10' error score. Additionally, the absolute mean scores favouring the cultural/familial group on the number correct score, total error score, size score, 'card 3' error score, 'card 5' error score, 'card 7' error score and 'card 9' error score all obtained statistical significance at the ·01 level. These authors gave no information about base rates, but it appeared to them that the practical level for a cut-off score to differentiate organically impaired mentally retarded children would be to use two standard deviations below the normative group's mean 'number correct' score and/or two SDs above the normative group's mean 'total error' score for each of the respective chronological age levels.

However, there is in subnormality a growing tendency for psychologists to feel less impressed by the organic/familial dichotomy as a practical distinction as distinct from an academic one, and the continuing use of the ITPA and the Frostig Tests tends to endorse this. What is of critical importance for the patient and directly for the psychologist is whether or not remedial measures can effect change in performance. The distinction between organic and non-organic therefore becomes significant only if it can be clearly demonstrated that changes can not be wrought in one or another of these two groups. Probably because psychologists have in the past been more concerned to classify than to remedy or treat, relatively little work has been done to establish how much behavioural or cognitive change can be effected in different groups of subnormal subjects. If the effect of such change can be fully demonstrated then the extent of the change will be quantifiable and the pay-off to be derived from concentrating on familial as distinct from organic perhaps will become more apparent. At that stage we may expect a resumed interest in the use of tests to make the organic/familial distinction once more.

Note: General conclusions, together with a consolidated list of references, will be found at the end of the next chapter.

15

D. F. Clark

Psychological assessment in mental subnormality – 2
Social competence, vocational and rehabilitative prospects, personality measures

Introduction

Although the bulk of psychometric research effort in mental subnormality has been in the field of testing intelligence or other cognitive skills, authorities have generally insisted that subnormality cannot be defined only in terms of IQ and that additional criteria of defect must be sought. Dangerous as it can be (see Chapter 2), some estimate of social adaptation, competence and personality is often made in the attempt to describe effectively current characteristics of subnormals and to predict the response to training and treatment in such persons.

This chapter will consider some attempts to quantify and test social competence, vocational prospects and indications for successful rehabilitation derived from test data together with some of the approaches to personality assessment in subnormals.

Measures of social competence

VINELAND SOCIAL MATURITY SCALE (DOLL, 1936)

Legislators and clinicians alike have for long been convinced that some assessment of social competence over and above intellectual capacity is of critical importance in making predictions about the subnormal. For many years the standard instrument in the area has been the Vineland Scale of Social Maturity, which consists of 117 items arranged in order of difficulty and covering categories of behaviour such as general self-help, self-help in eating and dressing, occupation, communication, locomotion and socialization. It assumes that such social development will continue from birth to approximately age 25 and attempts to represent the stage of development by a social age or social quotient derived from the total score and based on norms from 620 subjects, 10 of each sex for each year from birth to 30 years. The scale, however, is not a test in its traditional sense, depending on the eliciting of information from some informed person who knows the subject to be rated relatively well, such as parent, nurse or teacher. As a consequence, the reliability of a score from such a scale may be affected by the examiner, by the informant or by certain characteristics of the scale. Nevertheless, Doll himself reported an overall reliability coefficient of ·92 and another study (Hurst, 1962) has suggested that it is unlikely to drop below ·80.

The Vineland has many items which could be taken to reflect aspects of intelligent behaviour built into it, especially at the lower age levels, and it is not surprising therefore that correlation coefficients between IQ and SQ range from ·41 to ·82 and between mental age and social age from ·66 to ·96 (Shakespeare, 1970). Himelstein (1968) has already pointed out that in the view of Terman and Merrill general intelligence can be thought of as 'mental adaptability to new problems' and that the area of social competency would seem to be at least as involved in the validity of a test of intelligence as, say, achievement in school. It is not surprising therefore that correlations of the order quoted should be achieved. Indeed according to Heber (1962) the Vineland SMS is 'probably the best single measure of adaptive behaviour currently available'.

Lockyer and Rutter (1970), in a study of infantile psychosis, have found that, taking into account the scores on both the Wechsler Verbal Scale and the Peabody Picture Vocabulary Test as measures of verbal ability, there is evidence that more psychotic children than control children have verbal abilities which are inferior to their abilities on performance tasks. Also, among the psychotic children there was little difference between the IQ and SQ as measured by the VSMS when the former measure was based on either the Wechsler full or verbal scales. However, the SQ was appreciably below the Wechsler performance IQ, the difference not quite reaching significance. This may be contrasted with the situation in the control group where the mean SQ was higher than the mean IQ in all three comparisons, although the difference was only significant in the case of the full scale and performance IQs. This finding of the inferior social maturity of children with infantile psychosis (compared with non-psychotic children of the same age and IQ) agrees with the results of Gillies (1965).

One of the main problems with the VSMS is that there is an insufficient number of items critical to the narrower range of retarded subjects which makes it difficult to discriminate finer degrees of social competency or incompetency, either when one is comparing two children or comparing one child with himself at a later date. The test is quite useful for relating an individual's social performance to that of his age and cultural peers, but there can be little doubt that further more specific definitions of social competence are required to amplify the VSMS test results in subjects at the lower age levels, regardless of their intelligence, largely because of the relatively few items by which progress can be noted at, for example, early adolescent and early adulthood age levels.

In more recent years a variety of other assessment procedures concerned with the social competence of retardates have emerged (Cain et al., 1963; Matthew, 1964), and of these probably the best appears to be the Cain–Levine scale which has test-retest reliabilities of ·98 and ·94. Congdon (1969) has in fact suggested that this scale and the VSMS may well be substituted for one another if only a raw scores comparison of one child with another were important, since they correlate very highly (·77).

The need to design specific programmes for specific patients, however, rather than simply to relate the standing of one patient in relation to his normal peer group, has led Gunzburg (1960, 1963) to develop his Progressive Assessment Chart method. This is basically an inventory of particular social skills divided by areas, including those of self-help, communication, socialization and occupation. These describe how much better or worse a retarded individual is in relation to other retardates or in relation to himself at a previous period. The chart is in essence an inventory of some 120 skills, graded according to difficulty, the items being simple pass/fail scores attributed by a nurse, supervisor or other person who is in a position to observe the subject for a substantial period in different situations. The passing or failing of an item is recorded by shading in the item on a chart consisting of concentric circles divided into quadrants. The easiest items appear at the centre of the circle and as they become harder move to outer positions, each quadrant representing one of the areas of social competence indicated above. Elliot and Mackay (1971) have produced correlational evidence showing PAC scores (calculated in terms of the average percentage of items passed per group) to be closely related to VSMS social age – ·86 overall and separate subscale correlations of from ·72 (occupation) to ·82 (communication). Although general norms are not available and in fact may not be appropriate in this setting, this rating of behavioural competence does allow the examiner to establish with reasonable objectivity whether the subject's achievements are at a standard appropriate to his intellectual level or better or worse for the group in which he is living. Moreover, the specificity of the individual items allows a clear-cut programme of remedial measures to be instituted in sensory training or nursing situations. Periodical assessments of the individual therefore can ensure that the commonly reported deterioration in social competence resulting from institutionalization does not occur. Since each patient is used as his own control the question of general norms can be set aside and individual regimes for patients set up on essentially an experimental basis.

One of the greatest difficulties in the interpretation of any measure of social competence is assessing how far the present state represented will be predictive of the competence of the subject in a different environment. For example it may be that a subject scores positively on the item 'is reasonably careful with tools, machines, broken glass etc. to prevent injuries' when in the relatively low pressure atmosphere of the hospital workshops, but may be somewhat more flustered when he goes out to work in the local sawmill and has just had a row with the foreman. At the moment these assessment procedures are likely to be of more value in ascertaining the progress of a subnormal patient in hospital or hostel rather than predicting his behaviour in the wider environment.

ASSESSMENT OF EDUCATIONAL LEVEL

Closely associated with the level of social maturity is the level of attainment in more specific educational areas which the retardate may have or have not achieved. Burt (1922), Schonell (1942) and Watts (1944) have already supplied a number of suitable scales for the assessment of reading, arithmetic and other levels. These demonstrate the subject's position in relation to a normal school population and, where some literacy or numeracy prevails in the subject, can show up a disparity in his level of attainment relative to his potential as assessed from other tests. Most subnormal patients are, however, not at a level of cognitive development to make these tests applicable and, indeed, so closely associated with school activities are they that indiscreet application in unsuitable cases may be traumatic or anxiety-provoking at least. With the development of the ITPA and the careful scrutiny of subtest scores in the Wechslers, very often only a brief scrutiny of the reading level need be carried out. The Burt/Vernon Reading Scale (1938) is a simple word reading test whereas the Holborn Reading Scale (Watts, 1944) has the advantage of a comprehension assessment over and above a simply scored word recognition task.

It is important to recognize, however, as Gunzburg remarks, that

A most important aspect of such investigation is to ascertain the degree to which the person is capable of using his attainments. Obtaining a certain fluency in 'barking at print' does not in itself imply adequate comprehension and use of the printed word. Even mastery of the 'four rules' does not guarantee that the defective is able to check his change at Woolworths. More profitable from the point of view of assessing capacity for social functioning is an investigation of how far an individual is able to make use of meagre school knowledge and how far, and in what way, he has been able to overcome his educational shortcomings. The examination should, therefore, include both a standard test of reading comprehension and practical arithmetic, and expand into a prolonged systematic interview which should explore the use made of these skills as well as the command of 'civic knowledge'. It will be valuable to know whether he reads the newspapers, whether he has some inkling of what is going on in the world, whether he looks up advertisments and whether he can account for a day's shopping, or write a letter home. The use of the telephone, his realization of statutory deductions, his ability to obtain information, the manner of spending wages, and planning leisure time activities, will give a fuller picture of his educational standing than a mere reading or arithmetic attainments test.

Literature pertaining to this aspect of educational testing is sparse and suggests that rehabilitation programmes have not considered the effect of meagre educational knowledge. An exact mapping out of the vast blank spaces in a defective's educational knowledge will help to pinpoint many sources of insecurity, escape mechanisms and evasion tactics, and provide the basis for a wider educational approach than simply arranging for instruction in the '3 Rs'. The educational assessment results will then contribute to the therapeutic and rehabilitation aims in the same way as psychometric and personality testing.

Test data as rehabilitation predictors

Windle's (1962) major monograph on the whole topic of prognosis in mental subnormals extensively reviewed the literature on this topic up till that time and in his summary of conclusions suggested that patients with general familial or undifferentiated diagnoses were more likely to be released from institutions than were patients with specific clinical disorders. He adds that there had been many interesting suggestions about the prognostic importance of the difference between organic and psychological aetiologies of subnormality, but up till that time convincing demonstrations of the prognostic usefulness of the distinction had not made themselves apparent. Secondly, intelligence had been found to be highly related to a likelihood of release from hospitals but had not been found to be prognostic for adjustment after release. It was suggested that the absence of this relationship, which would be expected on the basis of common sense, indicates a selective bias in the nomination of patients for release whereby the brighter hospital patients must have more severe complicating handicaps than less bright patients to fall in the same population. Thirdly, there was a general consensus on the view that superior performance to verbal scores on intelligence tests had a more favourable outcome. Again, however, this pattern score, just as in the case of IQ, is prognostic for likelihood of release but not for success after release. Fourthly, little work has been done on personality assessment and its relationship to follow-up, but what has been done shows little relationship for failures to be worse in subjects who have adverse personality traits although there did seem to be some slight evidence that having a 'better' personality led to a greater likelihood of release from hospital. Finally, there appears to be a significant relation between some types of psycho-motor ability and likelihood of release from an institution.

In his monograph, Windle has much to say on the difficulty of assessing the literature imposed by the widely varying criteria selected by authors in studies relating intelligence and other test scores to post-hospital settlement or behaviour. Many of these studies report criteria of community adjustment which have been described dichotomously, e.g. return versus non-return to hospital or success versus failure in one or more occupations following hospital (Jackson and Butler, 1963; Madison, 1964; Shafter, 1957; Warren, 1961). As is pointed out by Song and Song (1969), when the criterion is described in such broad terms some of the factors which cause individuals to be placed in one or another of these are usually masked, and yet these factors which are masked are often personal and social factors rather than job efficiency factors which determine success or failure. Because of this great difficulty with criteria it has been difficult to identify clearly vocational efficiency predictors (Kolstoe and Shafter, 1961).

Even when dichotomous criteria are not used there is a strong tendency to use rating scale measures from one or more raters who may be clinically sophisticated or not. These are generally considered to be closer approximations to some significant hypothetical construct than are straightforward administrative classifications (Reynolds and MacEachern, 1956) but much work remains to be done to establish reasonably meaningful criteria. Something along the lines of factorially established set of criterion variables suggested by Rosen, Kivitz, Clark and Floor (1970) appears the most likely approach.

In any event there are certain strictures which must obtain in such predictive studies and which though fairly fundamental to scientific method in psychology seem to be strangely lacking in many of the reported papers. The experimenter must, for example, choose experimental conditions which will test his hypothesis with the greatest sensitivity. In order to do this he requires a reasonably homogeneous sample of sufficient size which is randomly selected from the population about which he is aiming to generalize. Secondly, he requires predictive indices relevant to his hypothesis which can be obtained before placement takes place. Windle (1962) would also agree that the decision should be made at this point as to how contingency factors should be treated either as predictive indices or as outcomes to be predicted. When criterion measures are obtained, even should these be ratings by individuals dealing with the experimental subjects, the characteristics of the criterion rated need close description and the reliability of the rating should be ascertained and any relations between the different dimensions rated established. Needless to say, both the statistical significance of differences and measures of the degree of relationships of variables should be determined.

Subsequent to Windle's (1962) work the relatively contentious nature of the general topic of prediction of behaviour from IQ was emphasized by a series of papers by MacAndrew and Edgerton (1964, 1965) and Baumeister (1965). The former writers take as a starting point the comment of Sarason (1959) that while intelligence tests may be adequate or even excellent predictors of academic achievement they may be poor indicators of non-test or non-academic intellectual activity. Sarason considers that IQ testing is 'at best non-productive' and Buddenhagen (1967) in another context has suggested that IQ may be one of the most trivial items of information to be ascertained, particularly about a severely retarded individual. MacAndrew and Edgerton subsequently employed 6 non-professional employees to rate a sample of 74 patients from a hospital ward who were of very low IQ and relatively wide range of age from 15 to 52. The raters rated the patients on 35 different dimensions and the 6 raters' individual rankings were averaged for each patient. Full rankings of the 74 patients were later correlated with their most recent IQ scores and the appropriate correction for attenuation using the reliability of the pooled rankings and the test-retest reliability of the IQ was made. Tests and ratings were separated by an average period of 3·1 years. Sixteen of the rated dimensions were found to correlate at a highly significant level ranging from about ·60 to ·76 with the IQ, and the authors concluded that IQ scores of patients at this level of retardation were not only remarkably stable over time but were significantly related in a non-artifactual manner to 16 non-test dimensions. Examples of the rated dimensions would include 'ability to think about the future', 'knows what is going on around him', 'has different definite preferences in food or dress' and so forth. The dimension 'has a calm even disposition' was one example of a dimension which was entirely unrelated to IQ ($r = \cdot 04$).

In his reply to the previous paper Baumeister (1965) points out that the authors were not demonstrating that the IQ was related to 16 independent dimensions of behaviour and that it was valid only for predicting attendant's ratings of 16 items of behaviour in severely retarded patients. Baumeister criticized a number of the dimensions since they seemed to contain characteristics that might well be measured by a good intelligence test. Furthermore, Baumeister very properly points out that the MacAndrew and Edgerton finding may be reflecting little more than the raters' biases concerning what they felt should be related to intelligence. In essence his criticism is that of Windle and others who make unfavourable comments on criterion measures. Furthermore, the IQ was here measuring the level of performance in a ward situation rather than predicting future performance in a working situation.

The work of Wagner and Hawver (1965) pursued the notion that cognitive tests might be useful predictors of at least sheltered workshop performance in very severely retarded adults. This they took to be the group inclusive of sub-groups commonly labelled 'imbecile' or 'idiot' with IQ well below 50 and to that extent they were comparable with the groups discussed by MacAndrew and Edgerton. It has been shown by Gunzburg (1957) and Gage and Wolfson (1963) that although some defectives at this level can be capable of regular employment, generally subjects of very low IQ are considered suited only for sheltered workshop activities. Wagner and Hawver attempted to predict success in a sheltered workshop by means of tests, and along with a number of dexterity and manipulative tests they also included the Goodenough Harris DAP, the Bender Visual Motor Gestalt Test and the Stanford–Binet L-M. Yet again, their criterion measure was an overall ranking by the chief instructor in the workshop which took account of the subject's responses to authority and instruction, together with his quality of work co-operativeness and development of skills. For each test, scores were ranked as were the subjects on the basis of the rating scale, and Spearman rho's were worked out. The authors themselves admit that the sample size was small (27) and they do not quote the reliability coefficient of the criterion ranking. Further, they admit that no cross validation had occurred since no new subjects had as yet been accepted into the workshop on the basis of test scores. However, the extent of the correlations of the tests used with the criterion (ranging from $\cdot 50$ to $\cdot 89$) was such as to encourage the belief in some single factor of a rather complex nature compounded both of basic psychological and psycho-motor efficiency might be responsible for the workshop success of these subjects. Tizard and O'Connor (1950) had already adumbrated this and other studies have since confirmed it. Perhaps one of the most intriguing findings of all in this study was that the highest correlation with the criterion was achieved by the Bender Gestalt Test which yielded a ·89 correlation with the criterion, rendering, in the view of the authors, the use of the other tests redundant.

More recently, a paper by Elkin (1968) has pursued the same 'holy grail' of an adequate predictor variable for the workshop performance in the retarded. Her sample was larger than the previous one but also more intelligent. For this reason it seems likely that her criterion variable, which was assessed in a rather more sophisticated manner using rating scales and an already standardized social knowledge scale, was more worthwhile and she found that psycho-motor and intellectual abilities were highly inter-correlated and significantly related to performance on the job. On the whole, correlations were lower than in the previously quoted study and it was noteworthy that the PPVT failed to demonstrate any significance for predicting success in the job, whereas the WAIS performance IQ consistently yielded coefficients around ·60 with the criterion. This study, however, again encountered difficulties both in assessing objectively performance on the work and assessing subjects who work in dissimilar work situations. There were, for example, many differences in correlations between tests and criteria between the sexes which may have been in a large part due to the different kinds of work that these subjects were carrying out. Elkin properly makes the case that outside the experimental setting job performance in subnormals is probably very complexly related to total adjustment both in the community and in the institution. (See also Chapter 13.)

On quite another tack, Johnson (1970) obtained census data on as many as 23,211 individuals from 19 American institutions for the retarded. There were available for very large numbers of these subjects the latest IQ and SQ scores together with the types of test from which these were obtained, ratings of the patients' capacities for self-help and also information about the frequency with which the subject had behaved in a variety of antisocial ways. The reliability of these data was reported on by Abelson and Payne (1969). Johnson then submitted his data to a series of correlational analyses by which the effectiveness of psycho-metric scores and the relative effectiveness of IQ versus SQ scores in predicting behaviour could be established. Much of the value of this paper derives from the fact that very large samples were dealt with and that the sample contained a wide range of age and intelligence. In this study again, there is the problem that the criterion measures tend to be somewhat arbitrary and describe behaviours such as 'requires help in dressing', 'is on a work project', 'is aggressive', 'does not understand speech of others' and so forth. Nevertheless, the correlational data produced by the author enabled him to make a statement that IQ or SQ test data

> . . . allow one to predict, at a level of success far greater than chance, the probability of the subject emitting certain behaviours involving independent functioning, self-help, and helping others, and of being exposed to or judged capable of learning from certain varieties of training experience. Test scores

tell far less about the probability that certain 'problem' behaviours, generally involving disturbed relations with peers or with authority figures, will occur, but still in a number of instances allow prediction at a probability of success better than chance.

An interesting by-product of this study was that the writer had thought that a pool of subjects who were tested, and on whom both IQ and SQ was available, would show increased correlations between test score and behaviour than either IQ or SQ subjects alone. This was due to his belief that IQ tests might be used generally with the brighter subjects and SQ with the more seriously backward. However, this was not so and correlations were of the same magnitude whether for IQ or SQ. The major criticism of the work is that while his test data adequately predict these behaviours, there remains the problem of assessing the validity of such a prediction for the emergence of these behaviours in a non-institutional setting, or for the relevance of these behaviours to resettlement in an occupation or social resettlement in the outside world.

The most important papers in this area in recent years are probably those where an attempt has been made to predict job efficiency of retardates after they have emerged from the institution into the community (Jackson and Butler, 1963; Madison, 1964; Song and Song, 1969; Rosen *et al.*, 1970). These writers have between them identified a number of predictive variables including Wechsler IQ, school achievement, age, personality ratings and early home conditions which discriminate between those defectives who are successful in the community and those who are not. In some of these investigations the relationship of each of the predictor variables with the criterion was evaluated separately without regard to the simultaneous influence of the other variables. The Song and Song (1969) study did not use, as so many studies before it, a dichotomous criterion variable, but selected a more defensible Vocational Adjustment Rating Scale of work ability and work habits with a mean criterion rating for their 45 subjects of 56·18 and SD 14·41. Their subjects were all working as unskilled or semi-skilled in industrial jobs. The Vocational Adjustment Rating Scale has a test-retest reliability of ·92 (Bae, 1968). The importance of Song and Song's work was that they carried out a multiple regression analysis using a combination of 18 zero order correlation coefficients to produce an R of ·77 with a standard error of ·07 which was significant at P ·05. The multiple regression analysis showed a different group of patient variables as predictors to the criterion from those which were identified by zero order correlation. The predictors in rank order of their respective contributions to the criterion were information, similarities, performance IQ, comprehension, full scale IQ (all of the Wechsler) and ratings of work habits. School achievement, behaviour ratings and demographic data did not contribute significantly to the prediction. The authors take the view therefore that their results confirm other studies which have found IQ and work history as being important discriminators of vocational adjustment after hospitalization, but the results demonstrate clearly that in order to obtain a high level prediction one should not consider one patient variable at a time but should consider several variables simultaneously. This is exactly the process that so many psychologists pay lip-service to as an exercise of clinical judgment, and one is reminded of Gwynne Jones's (1970) comments at the beginning of Chapter 14 that psychologists are all too ready to collapse complex predictor variables into one simple, easily handled dimension when the data become difficult to handle in combination. It could be suggested that using a multiple regression analysis of this sort may give scope for further studies in which other predictor variables not used in the Song and Song study may be inserted, such as family and social background of the patient, employment conditions in the district and the patient's relationship with family members and previous work colleagues.

Subtlety in the combination of predictor variables has been extended to subtlety in the assessment of the criterion variables by the work of Rosen, Kivitz, Clark and Floor (1970). It was perhaps the unsubtlety of both predictor and criterion variables that led Windle (1962) to conclude that in spite of the numerous predictive studies in the literature the findings had limited reliability and the conclusions were of a highly restricted generalizability, and Masland, Sarason and Gladwin (1958) to note that 'Criteria customarily used to define mental retardation are not adequate to predict social and occupational adjustment at the extremes' and that 'our conventional tests leave much to be desired both as evaluators and predictors'. Rosen, Kivitz, Clark and Floor (1970) therefore evaluated 29 demographic, psychometric and behavioural rating variables as predictors of 22 criteria of adjustment for a group of mentally retarded subjects who had been discharged to independent life in the community. In summary, tests of perceptual-motor abilities and behavioural ratings of employment potential showed the highest number of predictive relationships with criteria; tests of verbal abilities and ratings of social adjustment being poor predictors. The results suggested that accurate decisions regarding selection for discharge may ultimately be made from psychometric scores and assessment of work performance within the institution. Their technique was, broadly speaking, a factor-analytic one in which they isolated 5 main factors amongst the predictive variables, whereas variance in the correlation matrix of the criterion variables could be accounted for by 6 factors.

Predictor factor 1: Verbal and symbolic intellectual skills
Predictor factor 2: Perceptual-motor skills
Predictor factor 3: Age
Predictor factor 4: Employability rating
Predictor factor 5: Sex
Criterion factor 1: Coping behaviour
Criterion factor 2: Job satisfaction (A)
Criterion factor 3: Job stability
Criterion factor 4: Job satisfaction (B)

Criterion factor 5: Unlabelled
Criterion factor 6: General adjustment

A significant feature, in view of the data quoted on the Bender Gestalt earlier in this section, was that the tests contributing most of the verbal skills factor (WAIS Verbal IQ and the Metropolitan Achievement Test) were relatively less important as correlates of post-institutional adjustment than were those tests loading most strongly on the perceptual-motor skills factor and including especially the Porteus Maze Test and Bender Gestalt Test. This particular finding, that non-verbal abilities tend to be better predictors of community functioning than verbal skills endorses the practice of assessing concrete-practical and perceptual-motor skills in evaluating the rehabilitation potential of the subnormal, and is consistent with other investigations reporting performance IQ bias on the WAIS as a predictor of favourable outcome (Fitzpatrick, 1956; Ferguson, 1958).

Contrasts between the performance of retardates on verbal and performance tests are frequently drawn and are thought to have considerable diagnostic or prognostic significance in spite of the findings of Tizard and O'Connor (1950), who considered that 'the pattern hypothesis' of performance dominance had not been satisfactorily established. A year later, Seashore (1951) analysed VIQ–PIQ differences for retardate subjects from the standardization sample of the WISC and found that the average difference was two IQ points in favour of the performance scale. He concluded from this that it would not be safe to accept the generalization that retardates are less retarded on performance tasks. These early studies did not lend much credence to the view that there was profit to be had from studying verbal-performance discrepancy, but nevertheless there have been studies of this with retardates, in particular those of Sloan and Schneider (1951), Stacey and Levine (1951), Vanderhost, Sloan and Bensberg (1953) and Alper (1967) all of whom found significant differences in favour of the performance scale of the WISC, while Baroff (1959) found a non-significant difference in the same direction. In studies using the WAIS, Warren and Kraus (1961) found a significant difference in favour of the performance scale while Brengelmann and Kenney (1961) found a non-significant difference in the same direction. There is therefore a general consistency of results with the commonly expressed belief that performance subtests are completed more effectively by subnormals although on the whole the differences are rather small for prognostic comfort.

Several other early studies not using the WAIS (Earl, 1940; Roberts, 1945; Gunzburg, 1959) report that superiority on perceptual-motor tasks over verbal or language tests is associated with favourable community adjustment.

The likelihood of release predicted by such discrepancies may, of course, simply be an artifact of the weeding out of persons where the reverse condition obtains (i.e. higher verbal than performance ability) a condition which may often be more associated with 'organic' diagnosis. Rosen, Stallings, Floor and Nowakiska (1968) have shown that favourable prognoses as measured by IQ increment are closely associated with familial rather than organic diagnoses and almost always involve increases in performance IQs rather than in verbal IQs. The Ferguson and Fitzpatrick studies quoted above also support the Rosen, Kivitz, Clark and Floor work in demonstrating that the WAIs full-scale IQ correlates significantly with outcome criteria suggesting that performance IQ alone rather than the verbal performance discrepancy is the crucial variable.

Rosen *et al.* make an important point that if their results are upheld in a cross-validation study they might well lead one to question whether there is substance in the accepted practice of using the quality of interpersonal relationships and social adaptation of the patient within the institution to judge his later coping behaviour outside. Ratings of social behaviour in their study were often widely discrepant from judgments about employment potential, even though the employment measures also encompassed social skills which might play a part in their job functioning. They add,

> . . . it may be that social and inter-personal behaviours of retarded persons within institutions are not representative of the types of social behaviours required once the individual returns to the community. This would suggest that social conformity and adherence to institutional regulations should not be necessarily interpreted as a favourable prognostic for discharge to the community. Similarly, an institutional history of management problems and poor inter-personal relationships need not necessarily be considered indicative of unfavourable post-institutional prognosis.

Vocational assessment of the subnormal

It must be clear to psychologists who have used these tests that the Strong Vocational Interest Blank (1943) or the Kuder Preference Record (1951) which are commonly used with other populations require a reading skill and level of comprehension considerably beyond that achieved by even the mildly retarded. In any case, these tests are concerned with job areas and levels which it would not be realistic to expect the subnormal to aim for. There are, of course, one or two picture tests of vocational interest available and while it is true that such tests make it unnecessary for the subject to read they remain inappropriate for use with defectives for the reasons already quoted.

It is apparent from a number of studies elsewhere in this chapter that while certain intelligence tests have a measure of predictive value with regard to the post-hospital settlement of patients it is equally true that work interests, habits, motivations and understanding of job requirements are as critical variables as the patient's specific job skills. For many of the subnormal the unskilled or semi-skilled work that they are likely to cope with will be work where it is less important to develop specific skills or generate knowledge and more to appreciate an employer's point of view, his expectations of his worker and the capacity to get along with others together with some awareness of the characteristics of the job in general. Parnicky, Kahn and Burdett (1965, 1971) appear to be the only workers who have made a determined effort to assess vocational interests systematically in subnormals and to have set themselves the goal of devising an objective test which (a) would be reading free; (b) would have appropriate content for subnormals; (c) would differentiate subjects' vocational interests; and (d) would permit evaluation of a subnormal's knowledge of job conditions. They developed two versions of their test, one to cover a range of specific occupations considered feasible for retarded individuals and another to include such general variables as working alone or in a group, being supervised or unsupervised, working outdoors or indoors, doing heavy or light work, and working with the same sex or with the opposite sex. This they describe in their recent paper as the Vocational Interest and Sophistication Assessment technique (VISA). The test consists of 75 pictures for males and 53 for females which have to be sorted by the subject. Examples are illustrated in Fig. 13(a). The job clusters, factorially established, for males are farm and grounds, food service, garage, laundry, light industrial, light maintenance and materials handling; and for females, business/clerical, food service, housekeeping and laundry. The 3,000 standardization subjects drawn from institutions, workshops and schools in 7 north-eastern USA States had a mean IQ of 66 with a range of 45 to 84. The authors made no special effort to stratify the sample with respect to either urban/rural residence or socio-economic status but feel that the diversity of locations and programmes in the agencies concerned would suggest acceptable representation across these dimensions.

For the administration of VISA the picture items are bound in a numerical sequence into a booklet in which they are preceded by additional items, 1 for each of the job areas and 3 which are used for explanation of the task to the subject. The sequence of administration is (a) sophistication enquiry, (b) explanation of task and (c) interest enquiry. The first of these consists of obtaining responses to 7 questions for each of the job areas. The questions cover the subject's knowledge of what the worker depicted was doing, his title, range of duties, working conditions and pay. Explanation of the task involves establishing for each subject identification of the figures used in the subsequent interest items. In the interest enquiry the subject indicates whether he would or would not like to do this job depicted in each picture. Based on previous work, responses to each of the sophistication items were assigned scores of 0 to 2 points. 'Dislike' responses on interest items were assigned the score of 1, 'like a little' responses received a score of 2, and 'like a lot' responses were given a score of 3. Earlier experience with the technique established that degree of preference responses could be elicited from subnormals but degree of aversion responses could not. The factor-analyses were computed on initial and retest data to yield interest clusters. These were compared with each other and with the clusters obtained in the early pilot investigation.

The findings supported the procedure of one set of norms for males and one for females, and a high degree of construct validity was established for both male

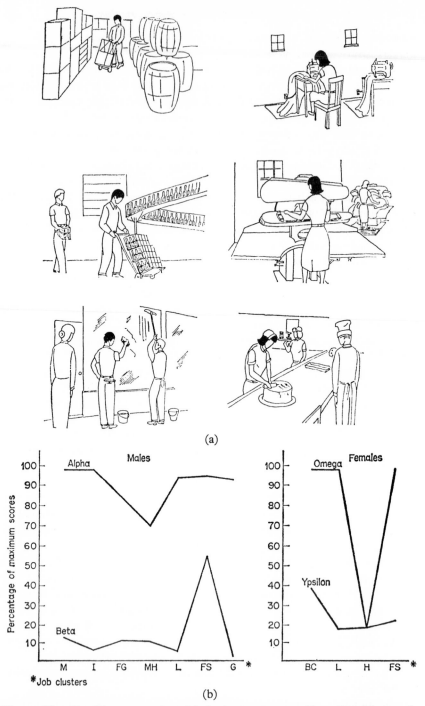

(a)

(b)

Fig. 13 Vocational interest and sophistication assessment (from **Parnicky** *et al.*, 1965, 1971) (a) Sample pictures from the VISA. (b) Illustrative interest profiles.

and female forms of the interest scales. Data obtained from subjects' trainers and supervisors tended to corroborate the VISA scores. The reliability and stability of interest factors was found to be high with reliability coefficients, in short run retest ranging between ·70 and ·78 and in the long run ranging from ·81 to ·99. The one exception to these coefficients was that for materials handling where it dropped to ·46. Interest scores were found to be relatively independent of variables such as CA, IQ and job knowledge, and sophistication scores were of sufficient reliability to warrant practical application of the test.

In general, this appears to be a technique which may have considerable application to populations outside the original standardization population since the content of jobs and the characteristics of the test appear to have good face value for a Western European culture. It seems possible in view of the discussion of IQs and other scores as predictors in the case of the severely subnormal, and in view of the standardization sample used by Parnicky, Kahn and Burdett, that this test will be applicable only to moderately retarded subjects, but in view of the paucity of other available test techniques in this area it seems likely to be the subject of further research and validation.

Personality and other tests

PROJECTIVE AND QUESTIONNAIRE TYPE TESTS

The field of personality testing of the subnormal is a neglected one mainly because the vast majority of tests devised for psychiatric patients in this area have depended on verbal skills not shared by the subnormal. Furthermore, since theories of personality tend to determine the tests which emerge and since there has been very little theorizing about the personality-determined responses of subnormals rather than their cognitive development the field has not been much tapped by psychologists. It is true that Klopfer and Kelley (1942) state quite categorically that the Rorschach test is 'of particular value in its application to problems of the mentally deficient', but on the whole the literature shows relatively little in the way of positive results. Most Rorschach studies tend to suffer from the usual handicaps of being carried out with small groups showing inadequate control of variables and dubious criteria. The general dissatisfaction of many psychologists with the psychometric characteristics of the Rorschach can be understood on perusal of the very extensive literature, and the rather stereotyped responses of most subnormals to the test do not encourage one to continue to use it as it stands.

It seems more likely that responses of greater value might be achieved from rather more structured material of, for example, the Thematic Apperception Test or the Symonds Picture Story Test. The latter is particularly useful in the case of the adolescent subnormal who finds the identification with the depicted figures rather easier than in the TAT. Nevertheless, the literature reveals very few studies in which these tests have been used as predictors of specific behaviour patterns in the subnormal, and while they may help in the task of describing the subnormal's present psychological situation and attitudes the relevance of such tests would be greater in, for example, a psycho-therapeutic rather than a retraining situation.

The same difficulty of low level of verbal skill has prevented the extensive use of questionnaires with subnormals until development of the Eysenck/Withers Personality Inventory (Eysenck, 1965). This scale is designed particularly for subjects with IQs between 50 and 80 and derives directly from the work of Eysenck on the EPI, being congruent with his general theory of personality, and measuring the orthogonally related factors of Extraversion and Neuroticism together with a Lie Scale. The standardization group consisted of 426 subnormal subjects, rather more men than women, who had been hospitalized in various institutions for the subnormal. Split-half reliability for the three scales is $E = \cdot 70$, $N = \cdot 88$ and $L = \cdot 70$, and test-retest reliabilities for the same scales are $\cdot 71$, $\cdot 83$ and $\cdot 92$. The standardization population had a mean age of $35 \cdot 633$, SD $14 \cdot 925$, and although there were no sex differences with regard to E, women had rather higher scores on N as is found with normal adults and children. Men showed a slightly greater tendency to get higher scores on the L scale. Consequently, the sexes must be kept apart for statistical and experimental analysis.

Although the supposition that subjects scoring high on N may well find it harder to make adjustments in work outside the hospital or even to cope with certain hospital situations, and that subjects who are particularly extraverted may rehabilitate better in face-to-face personal interaction situations than more introverted subjects, to date there is little evidence of confirmatory work in this area. Thorpe, Bardecki and Balaguer (1967) have looked at that hypothesis with seventy-two SN subjects. They conclude that retest reliability is higher when the subject's responses are recorded by the examiner, that there is an examiner effect on Lie scores and that the instrument in its present form will not be of appreciable value from a predictive point of view regarding the individual case. The constructors admit that the inventory is more a research instrument than a clinically applicable device, and until further normative information is forthcoming it appears best to use the test on an intra-individual basis or with large groups to measure trends at the moment.

A second approach to personality development that has recently emerged has been to use the semantic differential as a technique already shown to have potential usefulness with the retarded (Rybolt, 1969). Its particular value is in allowing some freedom in the selection of scales and concepts which would suit the area to be investigated, and previous work with the test on intellectually average subjects (Masters and Tong, 1968; Kear-Colwell and McAllister, 1970; Bhagat and Fraser, 1970) have emphasized its value. The study by Bhagat and Fraser has confirmed the observation by Osgood *et al.* (1957) that retarded subjects would polarize their choices, and Rybolt (1969) has lately confirmed that the three major factors (evaluative, potency and activity) would be found in retardates' responses just as in those of normals. The Bhagat and Fraser study made it clear that presenting the test in booklet form would be useless for subjects of under IQ 45, but above that retarded offenders' responses to concepts relevant to delinquency were similar to those of an intellectually average group of young offenders. There were some significant differences, but the authors conclude that 'the semantic differential . . . appear to reflect the common-sense distinctions one might expect in heterogeneous groups of retardates. The socially crippled institutionalized subject, the socially competent discharged subject, and the sociopathic individual are, to some extent, distinguishable by the responses on this instrument.' They feel that the test is usable primarily as an adjunct to the interview and they show that it is a practical instrument with retardates even over a wide range of low intelligence. A few simple comprehensible adjectives allow the retardate to express intrinsic attitudes which he would otherwise find difficult to encode, and the selection of areas for analysis allows the continuing use of clinical acumen and adaptation to the particular circumstances of the patient.

PSYCHO-PHYSIOLOGICAL TESTS

One may look in the future to further developments in the application of psycho-physiology to problems in retardation. This was adumbrated by the work of Tong (1959, 1960) but has been pursued more vigorously by Karrer (1966) and Karrer and Clausen (1964) with lower grade subjects. All of these writers, together with Berkson (1963) and Claridge (1970), make it clear that the application of psycho-physiological methods to clinical psychological topics generally is fraught with many difficulties posed by resting levels, signal/noise ratio and specificity of response, and it is perhaps an awareness of these and difficulties with the associated complex equipment that has prevented psychologists from making more use of the technological advances that have occurred in the last five to ten years. Most of the work in this area on conditioning, habituation, and arousal levels is concerned with the classification of subjects rather than remediation, and this would appear likely to continue (Tong and Murphy, 1960; Wolfensberger and O'Connor, 1965). However, a more direct connection with treatment procedures can be seen where the psychologist is concerned to monitor the effects of drugs and changes of drugs on the learning processes of subnormal subjects. This is something which may be particularly important where high levels of sedation, tranquilization, or anti-convulsant drug therapy are being maintained, and where at the same time some programme of sensory training or intellectual training is being proposed. Ten years ago Franks and Franks (1962) attempted to use classical conditioning procedures as an index of vocational adjustment among MDs' and confirmed their prediction that those subjects whose vocational adjustments were poor were also those who were relatively poor at forming conditioned eyeblink responses in the laboratory. The three groups of females who differed in work adjustment did not differ significantly with respect to age, IQ, indices of physical health or proportion of subjects with

CNS damage. This positive result, however, should not lead psychologists to a simplistic view and much more work needs to be reported before such techniques replace other predictive instruments.

TESTS OF MOTOR SKILLS

'It is a truism in psychology that the mechanism of the mind stands on a sensori-motor basis. The world outside can stimulate the mind only through one of the senses; and, in return, all that the greatest intellects can do is to contract a set of muscles and move a set of bony levers. The end product of every mental process is simply a muscular reaction' (Burt, 1937). In view of this it is remarkable that relatively little work has been pursued in the relationship of both motor proficiency and motor development to more generalized aspects of human functioning in the defective. The most important original work was, of course, concerned very much to relate motor proficiency to intelligence (Sloan, 1951; Rabin, 1957; Distefano *et al.*, 1958), Sloan in particular using the Oseretzky Test of motor proficiency. Doll (1946) found mental defectives to be significantly inferior to children of average intelligence in motor proficiency, and he concluded that there was a positive relationship between intelligence and motor skill but that motor proficiency was not 'a distinct aspect of functioning which can be isolated from general behaviour but is rather another aspect of the total functioning of the organism'.

Perhaps the most commonly used measures of motor skill are measures of balance and locomotion such as the Rail Walking Test (Heath, 1942) which consists of three wooden rails, 6 to 9 feet long, varying in width from 1 to 4 inches. The subject is asked to traverse the rails, heel to toe, unsupported. Heath (1953) reports correlations of ·57 to ·62 between rail walking and MA for familial defectives, but low correlations of ·15 to ·23 between these variables in brain injured subjects. The nature of the result, however, does not suggest that the test is appropriate for differentiating between these types of defective although differences are reported between the groups. Early work by O'Connor and Tizard (1951) and by Tizard, O'Connor and Crawford (1950) showed that Rail Walking performance in particular and tests of motor performance in general could contribute much to the prediction of occupational success, and discriminated too between retardates and normals and between 'endogenous' and 'exogenous' subnormals.

Rotary pursuit performance has also been shown to have value with a SN population (Baumeister *et al.*, 1966; Dingman and Silverstein, 1964; Bilodeau and Rosequist, 1964), and the by now extensive work on reaction time measurement on retardates has been fully and recently reviewed by Baumeister and Kellas (1968) and by Weaver and Ravaris (1970).

Malpass (1963) has thoroughly reviewed the field with particular reference to tests of motor development such as the Lincoln Oseretzky. One of the difficulties currently experienced by many psychologists interested in this area is, however, that norms are available only for children and relatively little work with adults other than specific experiments using very specific test situations has emerged.

Stott (1966) has developed a test of motor impairment in children which Whiting, Clarke and Morris (1969) have tried to validate. The latter authors point out that:

> The term motor impaired has been used to indicate the subnormal performances of certain children in everyday activities. Many attempts have been made to attribute the cause to neural disfunction arising from minimal brain damage that is the result of malformation, infection or injury. Such impairment may reflect a general disfunction or a specific inability to perform certain related tasks. The absence of severe disabilities, the difficulty of detecting the cause and evaluating the consequences of the mild cases of motor impairment present an acute problem for the educationalist. One may observe a certain lack of control or apparent awkwardness, but there exists no valid means whereby one can identify the specific area of motor impairment and so help the child with his difficulties. When he is not seen to be organically impaired, it's often assumed that there is no justifiable reason why the child's performance should be below that of any other.

The number of children impaired in this way has never been so far established, but some guidance was available from a study of the incidence of visual motor impairment amongst schoolchildren which was carried out in 1967 by Brenner *et al.* The battery they used included items of dexterity, perceptual analytic capacity and constructional skill, and it identified 6·7 per cent of the sample of supposedly normal children with an IQ of above 90 whose performance suggested a specific developmental disability. These children were significantly poorer than the controls on tests involving manual skill and special judgment, and teachers tended to classify them as being clumsy in movement or in fine control so that they had to contend with their variety of difficulties in learning tasks in the classroom. Children who have this kind of difficulty are often likely to be rebuked or punished for their apparent carelessness and untidiness, and as a result of this experience of repeated failure the child may well be emotionally damaged or inhibited. As Whiting, Clarke and Morris (1969) point out, the child who experiences difficulties of this sort may well tend to withdraw from as well as to dislike activity which brings these difficulties to light, and the child may also seek forms of achievement and recognition that may be socially undesirable as a compensation for his other difficulties. It is of the greatest importance, therefore, that such a child's difficulties be correctly and appropriately identified by a suitable test as early as possible. This was the aim which Stott (1966) had in mind in developing his test of motor impairment.

The work of Whiting, Clarke and Morris (1969) showed that, while the Stott Test was designed in the first instance to detect cases of minor impairment which might be missed by routine medical inspection, it was comforting to note that there was some overlap between the screening of the test and that of the medical diagnosis. It was noted, nevertheless, that the test tended to fail in some instances to define a particular area of impairment that was expected. This might suggest a failure in the diagnoses, the factor structure of the test or both. Some support for suggesting a weakness in the factor structure of the test comes from noting that test items for the component of balance include tests of static balance, dynamic balance and balancing objects. Fleishman (1954) has in fact shown these areas of balance to be independent of one another. In addition, Whiting *et al.* (1968) were able to show that a test score based on three items only of the test was as efficient a screening device as a score based on all five items. The commonly related relation between birth injury and abnormalities in motor impairment was not supported by the clinical investigation of Whiting, Clarke and Morris.

The possibilities of using mirror-writing, the pursuit rotor, steadiness tests of various types, pegboards and so forth with adults have been sporadically reviewed, but perhaps the greatest impetus to a new interest in this area has been given by the recent development of remedial systems and appropriate tests which will, like the ITPA and the Frostig, explore areas of perceptual and perceptual-motor development. Perhaps the work of Roach and Kephart (1966) has also contributed to an interest in motor skills, and these authors have presented a well-established treatment programme for learning disorders which emphasizes the sequential development of motor generalizations. The training programme focuses simultaneously on visual, receptive, assimilative and motor expressive behaviour at the lower level, gradually moving on to an improvement of more symbolic behaviour (Bateman, 1967). As a result there is a new interest not only in the relationship between intelligence, simple and complex motor deficiency (Groden, 1969; Hofmeister, 1969), but also in the relationship of sensori-motor training programme to the development of skill in this area (Maloney *et al.*, 1970; Maloney and Payne, 1970).

It is clear in spite of this work, however, that psychologists interested in the development of motor skills especially in an adult SN population will have to devise appropriate tests with appropriate norms before this can be other than a limited procedure from which generalizations will not be immediately possible. The technology of this, however, is not complicated, and with the groundwork already completed in the work of the above-mentioned authors there is every incentive for experimentally minded clinical psychologists in mental deficiency further to explore this interesting and productive field, especially since it has direct pay-off in terms of patient rehabilitation.

DEVELOPMENTAL ANALYSIS

Finally, the tenuous line that can be drawn between assessment and remediation is emphasized by the work adumbrated earlier by Woodward (1963) and subsequently restated by the same author (in Mittler, 1970). She makes it clear that her techniques and analyses of development derive directly from the difficulties of carrying out assessments on children who were lower than —3 SD from the mean on conventional test scores. Techniques of assessment based on Piaget's studies of sensori-motor development in the first eighteen months of life were particularly devised to solve this problem. In the same way techniques used to assess the development of the child's concept of number and space could be developed for older subnormals, and in all of these cases the intention of the author was to obtain information from the behaviour of subjects in different experimental situations that could be used to place the child in an appropriate learning situation with a view to making a further assessment when the child had been given a chance to learn something in that situation. There is insufficient space here to recapitulate the work of either Woodward or Piaget, but perhaps a brief resumé analysing the process of development during the period of sensory operations (0 to 2 years) with the likely behaviours to be demonstrated would be helpful.

For example, the child will exercise its reflexes during the first month and the presence or absence of these spontaneously operating can be noted. Secondly, coordination of reflexes and responses can be expected to occur in the next three months so that the examiner need simply observe whether the child is reaching, grasping, sucking and so forth. Thirdly, a child will intentionally repeat responses during the fourth to eighth months and it can be observed whether he will kick at a toy to swing it or move it or begin to search for lost objects or misplaced objects. Fourthly, he will begin to differentiate means from ends, to use responses to obtain results from about 8 months to 11 months, and consequently can be observed to remove an obstacle to get at a hidden toy or other such task. Fifthly, active experimentation, exploration, variation and modification of behaviour would be looked for from the eleventh to the twelfth month and beyond, so that it can be noted whether a child presented with toys will pull strings to move them or likes to make things happen, especially new things, by, for example, banging on different surfaces to make different kinds of noise or pushing objects over in a semi-random manner. Sixthly, there comes, towards the end of the second year, the emergence of the capacity to respond to and think about objects not directly observable and to invent new means of accomplishing results through 'mental combinations'. This is a stage when one is rapidly approaching the type of test response elicited at the early stages of the Minnesota pre-school scale or the Stanford–Binet LM.

These general principles can of course be adapted by the ingenious experimenter for clarificatory purposes and are probably best used on the longitudinal study of the individual patient rather than in an attempt to confirm general norms for patients of a given chronological or other age level.

It is in the analysis of the problem of the individual where already standardized tests are not going to prove helpful, either because appropriate norms are not available or because total cooperation of the subject cannot be achieved, that the experimental method is of greatest value. The techniques involved in the individual experiment with patients will be determined by the expertise, confidence and experience of the individual psychologist but the general principles involved are already clearly outlined by Shapiro (1961, 1966, 1970). It is when remediation is the end result of assessment that one is forced to consider ideographic much more than nomothetic analyses of the present position and of the subject. The specification of training by workbooks and practices such as those in the Frostig Remedial Program forces the clinical psychologist to make fairly specific predictions about what changes will occur in his subject if his teachers, trainer or nurses behave in this or that way towards the subject or carry out this or that programme of treatment or training. Kirk (1966) and Kirk and Kirk (1971) quote several examples of very specific changes in ITPA profiles, following equally specific remediation programmes devised on the basis of pre-testing with these techniques. The scene is clearly set for a considerable leap forward both in techniques of testing and assessment and in techniques of treatment – a leap forward which has gained impetus from the new interest in the patient rather than in the test, and in processes rather than properties.

Conclusions

The use of psychological tests in the assessment of psychiatric and subnormal patients has a long history and one of which it can properly be proud in terms of academic ingenuity and of attempts to combine rigour with usefulness. That some of these tests will be more useful and more rigorous than others, thus isolating them from the plethora of available materials, will already be evident and a few of the more commonly used have been discussed. None of these tests will, however, be more use to the patient or to the psychologist than the acumen of the latter and the cooperation of the former will allow, and there may be occasions when the psychologist might be better advised to discard the use of the routine battery and to supplant it with informed insight, careful history-taking and detailed analysis of the patient's past circumstances, present condition and future hopes and possibilities. One must always ask oneself whether it is better to use instruments, the quality of which one may know to be relatively low, rather than to utilize techniques which are as yet unproven but where the probability is that they might be of high value. The conflict between 'band width' and 'fidelity' will keep cropping up in new guises and can only be resolved by detailed and accurate analysis of the presenting problem.

It is probably indefensible to utilize a number of tests which are patently measuring the same variable and where one's predictions gain little from more than one test being used. It is equally indefensible to use a test which will not improve one's predictions at all, unless it provides useful descriptive characteristics not achieved in other ways.

If any trend is to be detected in the use of tests in assessment over the last decade it is probably towards a renewal of interest in ideographic as distinct from nomothetic methods, an interest which is not a denial of the scientific but a reassertion of a new application of science to specific problems of individuals. The newfound readiness of psychologists to involve themselves in treatment, training and rehabilitation and to take responsibility for specifying the details of such programme for individuals and for groups has led to a trend in testing in which the emphasis is towards a clear description of the *status quo* of the patient in respect of a number of discernible variables, with the clear-cut implication that active steps can be taken to produce change, hopefully for the better, in these variables. Just as counsellors are moving into schools to concern themselves with the clinical as well as the educational, so also clinical psychologists are concerning themselves with the remedial and educational aspects of their patients' problems, especially in the field of mental subnormality. This is not to say that there is to be any less preoccupation with the adequacy of tests as methods of describing population samples or defining the distributions of variables across large populations. This need remains and will no doubt be catered for by the emergence of new and better tests as time passes. What appears to have happened is that clinical psychology in subnormality has become more pragmatic and, although it has had to work without a background of unified cognitive or personality theory, its healthy empiricism has produced a trend which will serve both to help the individual patient and to produce a climate and a series of practices from which it seems more likely that sound, general theory can emerge.

No test can be used unthinkingly nor will it ever be better than the psychologist who uses it. It can never be a substitute for clear thinking, nor for the exercise of common sense, perceptiveness, and humanity on the part of the clinician carrying out the assessment. The ultimate responsibility for posing his problem in operational terms, for using his tests and experimental techniques advisedly, and for drawing his conclusions or making his predictions rests on the psychologist himself.

References

ABELSON, R. B. and PAYNE, D. (1969) Regional data collection on state institutions for the retarded: reliability of attendant ratings. *Amer. J. ment. Defic.*, **73**, 739–44.

ABERCROMBIE, M. L. J., GARDINER, P. A., HANSEN, E., JONCKHEERE, J., LINDON, R. L., SOLOMON, G. and TYSON, M. C. (1964) Visual perceptual and visual motor impairment in physically handicapped children. *Percept. mot. Skills*, **18**, 561–625 (Monogr. Suppl. 3-VI8).

ACHENBACK, T. M. (1970) Comparison of Stanford-Binet performance of non-retarded and retarded persons matched for M.A. and sex. *Amer. J. ment. Defic.*, **74**, 488–94.

ADAMS, J. (1970) Canter background interference procedure applied to the diagnosis of brain damage in mentally retarded children. *Amer. J. ment. Defic.*, **75**, 57–64.

ADLER, P. T. (1970) Evaluation of the figure drawing technique: reliability factorial structure, and the diagnostic usefulness. *J. consult. clin. Psychol.*, **35**, 52–7.

ALLEN, R. M. and JEFFERSON, T. W. (1962) *Psychological Evaluation in the Cerebral Palsied Person: Intellectual, Personality, and Vocational Applications.* Springfield, Ill.: Charles C. Thomas.

ALLEY, G. R. (1969) Comparative constructional praxis performance of organically impaired and cultural familial mental retardates. *Amer. J. ment. Defic.*, **74**, 279–82.

ALPER, A. E. (1967) An analysis of the Wechsler Intelligence Scale for Children with institutionalized mental retardates. *Amer. J. ment. Defic.*, **71**, 624–30.

ASH, P. (1949) The reliability of psychiatric diagnosis. *J. abn. soc. Psychol.*, **44**, 272–7.

BAE, A. (1968) Factors influencing vocational efficiency of institutionalized retardates in different training programmes. *Amer. J. ment. Defic.*, **72**, 871–4.

BANNISTER, D., SALMON, P. and LEIBERMAN, D. M. (1964) Diagnosis – treatment relationships in psychiatry: a statistical analysis. *Brit. J. Psychiat.*, **110**, 726–32.

BARCLAY, A. and GOULET, L. R. (1965) Short term changes in intellectual and social maturity of young non-institutionalized retardates. *Amer. J. ment. Defic.*, **70**, 257–61.

BAROFF, G. S. (1957) Bender-Gestalt visuo-motor function in mental deficiency. *Amer. J. ment. Defic.*, **61**, 753–60.

BAROFF, G. S. (1959) W.I.S.C. patterning in endogenous mental deficiency. *Amer. J. ment. Defic.*, **64**, 482–5.

BARTLET, D. and SHAPIRO, M. B. (1956) Investigation and treatment of a reading disability in a dull child with severe psychiatric disturbances. *Brit. J. educ. Psychol.*, **26**, 180–90.

BATEMAN, B. (1965) *The I.T.P.A. in Current Research: Summaries of Studies.* Urbana: Univ. of Illinois Press.

BATEMAN, B. (1967) Learning disabilities – yesterday, today and tomorrow. In FRIERSON, E. C. and BARB, W. B. (eds.) *Educating Children with Learning Disabilities.* New York: Appleton-Century-Crofts.

BAUMEISTER, A. A. (1964) Use of the W.I.S.C. with mental retardates: a review. *Amer. J. ment. Defic.*, **69**, 183–94.

BAUMEISTER, A. A. (1965) The usefulness of the I.Q. with severely retarded individuals: a reply to MacAndrew and Edgerton. *Amer. J. ment. Defic.*, **69**, 881–2.

BAUMEISTER, A. A. and BARTLETT, C. J. (1962a) A comparison of the factor structure of normals and retardates on the W.I.S.C. *Amer. J. ment. Defic.*, **66**, 641–6.

BAUMEISTER, A. A. and BARTLETT, C. J. (1962b) Further factorial investigations of W.I.S.C. performance of mental defectives. *Amer. J. ment. Defic.*, **67**, 257–61.

BAUMEISTER, A. A. and KELLAS, G. (1968) Reaction time and mental retardation. In ELLIS, N. R. (ed.) *International Review of Research in Mental Retardation*. New York and London: Academic Press.

BAUMEISTER, A. A., HAWKINS, W. F. and HOLLAND, J. (1966) Motor learning and knowledge of results. *Amer. J. ment. Defic.*, **70**, 590–4.

BEECH, H. R. and PARBOOSINGH, R.-C. (1962) An experimental investigation of disordered mental expression in a catatonic schizophrenic patient. *Brit. J. soc. clin. Psychol.*, **1**, 222–7.

BENDER, L. (1938) *A Visual-Motor Gestalt Test and its Clinical Use*. Amer. Orthopsychiat. Assoc. Res. Monogr., No. 3.

BENSBERG, G. J. and SLOAN, W. (1950) A study of Wechsler's concept of 'Normal Deterioration' in older mental defectives. *J. clin. Psychol.*, **6**, 359–62.

BENTON, A. L. (1955) *Benton Visual Retention Test* (rev. edn). New York: Psychological Corporation.

BENTON, A. L. (1963) *The Revised Visual Retention Test: Clinical and Experimental Applications*. New York: Psychological Corporation.

BENTON, A. L. (1964) Psychological evaluation and differential diagnosis. In STEVENS, H. A. and HEBER, R. *Mental Retardation: A Review of Research*. Chicago and London: Univ. of Chicago Press.

BERGER, M. (1970) The third revision of the Stanford-Binet (L.M.): some methodological limitations and their practical implications. *Bull. Brit. Psychol. Soc.*, **23**, 17–26.

BERKSON, G. (1963) Psychophysiological studies in mental deficiency. In ELLIS, N. R. (ed.) *Handbook of Mental Deficiency*. New York: McGraw-Hill.

BHAGAT, M. and FRASER, W. I. (1970a) The meaning of concepts to the retarded offender. *Amer. J. ment. Defic.*, **75**, 260–7.

BHAGAT, M. and FRASER, W. I. (1970b) Young offenders' images of self and surroundings: a semantic enquiry. *Brit. J. Psychiat.*, **117**, 381–8.

BILLINGSLEA, F. Y. (1963) The Bender Gestalt; a review and perspective. *Psychol. Bull.*, **60**, 223–51.

BILODEAU, I. M. and ROSEQUIST, H. S. (1964) Supplementary feedback in the rotary pursuit tracking. *J. exp. Psychol.*, **68**, 53–7.

BILOVSKY, D. and SHARE, J. (1965) The I.T.P.A. and Down's Syndrome: an exploratory study. *Amer. J. ment. Defic.*, **70**, 78–82.

BINGHAM, W. V. D., MOORE, B. V. and GUSTARD, J. W. (1959) *How to Interview*. New York: Harper & Row.

BLUE, C. M. (1969) P.P.V.T. temporal stability and alternate form reliability with the trainable mentally retarded. *Amer. J. ment. Defic.*, **73**, 745–8.

BOLTON, N., BRITTON, O. G. and SAVAGE, R. D. (1966) Some normative data on the W.A.I.S. and its indices in an aged population. *J. clin. Psychol.*, **22**, 184–8.

BONIER, R. J. and HANLEY, C. (1961) Handedness and D.S. performance. *J. clin. Psychol.*, **17**, 286–9.

BORTNER, J. (1965) A review of Progressive Matrices. In BUROS, O. K. (ed.) *Sixth Mental Measurements Year Book.* New Jersey: The Gryphon Press.

BOSWORTH, M. (1968) Pre-reading: improvement of visual motor skills. *Dissertation Abstr.*, **28**, 35–45.

BRENGELMANN, J. C. and KENNEY, J. T. (1961) Comparison of Leiter, W.A.I.S., and S.B. I.Q. in retardates. *J. clin. Psychol.*, **17**, 235–8.

BRENNER, N. W., GILLMAN, S., ZANGWILL, O. L. and FARRELL, M. (1967) Visual motor disability in school children. *Brit. med. J.*, **4**, 259–62.

BRILLIANT, P. J. and GYNTHER, M. B. (1963) Relationships between performance on three tests for organicity and selected patient variables. *J. Consult. Psychol.*, **27**, 474–9.

BRIMER, M. A. and DUNN, L. M. (1962) *Manual for the English Picture Vocabulary Test.* Bristol: Educational Evaluation Enterprises.

British Psychological Society (1966) *Children in Hospitals for the Subnormal.* London: British Psychological Society.

BROADHURST, A. and PHILLIPS, C. J. (1969) The reliability and validity of the Bender Gestalt Test in a sample of British schoolchildren. *Brit. J. soc. clin. Psychol.*, **8**, 253–62.

BROMLEY, D. B. (1953) Primitive forms of response to the Matrices Test. *J. ment. Sci.*, **99**, 374–93.

BROWN, L. G. and RICE, J. A. (1967) Form equivalence of the Benton V.R.T. in children of low IQ. *Percept. mot. Skills*, **24**, 737–8.

BUDDENHAGEN, R. G. (1967) Toward a better understanding. *Ment. Retard.*, **5**, 40–1.

BUDOFF, M. and PURSEGLOVE, E. M. (1963a) Forms L and M of the Stanford-Binet compared for an institutionalized adolescent mentally retarded population. *J. clin. Psychol.*, **19**, 214.

BUDOFF, M. and PURSEGLOVE, E. M. (1963b) Peabody Picture Vocabulary Test: performance of institutionalized mentally retarded adolescents. *Amer. J. ment. Defic.*, **67**, 756–60.

BURNETT, A. (1965) Comparison of the P.P.V.T., Wechsler-Bellevue and Stanford-Binet on educable retardates. *Amer. J. ment. Defic.*, **69**, 712–15.

BURT, C. (1922) *Mental and Scholastic Tests* (2nd edn, 1924). London: P. S. King.

BURT, C. (1937) *The Backward Child.* London: Univ. of London Press.

BUTTERFIELD, E. C. and ZIGLER, E. (1970) Pre-institutional social deprivation and IQ changes among institutionalized retarded children. *J. abn. Psychol.*, **75**, 83–9.

CAIN, L. F., LEVINE, S. and ELZEY, F. F. (1963) *Manual for the Cain–Levine Social Competency Scale.* Palo Alto, Calif.: Consulting Psychologists Press.

CANTER, A. A. (1966) A background interference procedure to increase sensitivity of the Bender Gestalt Test to organic brain disorder. *J. consult. Psychol.*, **30**, 91–7.

CANTER, A. A. (1968) B.I.P. Bender Test for the detection of organic brain disorder: modified scoring method and replication. *J. consult. clin. Psychol.*, **32**, 522–6.

CASTELL, J. H. F. and MITTLER, P. (1965) Intelligence of patients in subnormality hospitals: a survey of admissions in 1961. *Brit. J. Psychiat.*, **111**, 219–25.

CLARIDGE, G. S. (1970) Psycho-physiological techniques. In MITTLER, P. (ed.) *The Psychological Assessment of Mental and Physical Handicaps.* London: Methuen.

CLARK, D. F. (1958) The industrial rehabilitation of the mentally subnormal. *Occ. Psychol.*, **32**, 89–101.

CLARK, D. F. (1966) Behaviour therapy of Gilles de la Tourette's Syndrome. *Brit. J. Psychiat.*, **112**, 771–8.

CLARKE, A. D. B. and CLARKE, A. M. (1959) Recovery from the effects of deprivation. *Acta Psychologica*, **16**, 137–44.

CLARKE, A. D. B., CLARKE, A. M. and REIMAN, S. (1958) Cognitive and social changes in the feebleminded – three further studies. *Brit. J. Psychol.*, **49**, 144–57.

CLAYTON, H. and PAYNE, D. (1959) Validation of Doppelt's W.A.I.S. short form with a clinical population. *J. consult. Psychol.*, **23**, 467.

COLLMANN, R. D. and NEWLYN, D. (1958) Changes in Terman Merrill I.Qs. in mentally retarded children. *Amer. J. ment. Defic.*, **63**, 307–11.

CONGDON, D. M. (1969) The Vineland and Cain–Levine; a correlation study and program evaluation. *Amer. J. ment. Defic.*, **74**, 231–4.

COOK, R. A. and HIRT, M. L. (1961) V.I.Q. and P.I.Q. discrepancies on the W.A.I.S. and W.B. Form 1. *J. clin. Psychol.*, **17**, 382–3.

CRAFT, M. (1962) The rehabilitation of the imbecile: a follow-up report. *J. ment. Subnorm.*, **70**, 714–16.

CRAWFORD, A. (1955) An analysis of children's wrong answers on Raven's Progressive Matrices Test 1938. *Bull. Brit. Psychol. Soc.*, **26**, 2, 31–33 (inset).

DAVIS, L. J. (1966) The internal consistency of the W.I.S.C. with the mentally retarded. *Amer. J. ment. Defic.*, **70**, 714–16.

DINGMAN, H. F. and MEYERS, C. E. (1966) The structure of intellect in the mental retardate. In ELLIS, N. R. (ed.) *International Review of Research in Mental Retardation*, Vol. 1. New York: Academic Press.

DINGMAN, H. F. and SILVERSTEIN, A. B. (1964) Intelligence, motor disabilities and reaction time in the mentally retarded. *Percept. mot. Skills*, **19**, 791–4.

DISTEFANO, M. K., ELLIS, N. R. and SLOAN, W. (1958) Motor proficiency in mental defectives. *Percept. mot. Skills*, **8**, 231–4.

DOCTER, R. F. and WINDER, D. L. (1954) Delinquent vs. non-delinquent performance on the Porteus Qualitative Maze Test. *J. consult. Psychol.*, **18**, 71–3.

DOLL, E. A. (1936) *Vineland Social Maturity Scale.* Minneapolis: Amer. Guidance Service Inc.

DOLL, E. A. (1946) *The Oseretzky Tests of Motor Proficiency: A Translation from the Portuguese Adaptation.* Minneapolis: Educ. Test Bureau.

DOPPELT, J. E. (1956) Estimating the full scale score on the W.A.I.S. from scores on four subtests. *J. consult. Psychol.*, **20**, 63–6.

DUNN, L. M. (1959) *The Peabody Picture Vocabulary Test Manual.* Minneapolis: Amer. Guidance Service Inc.

DUNN, L. M. (1965) *Expanded Manual for the P.P.V.T.* Minneapolis: Amer. Guidance Service, Inc.

EARL, C. J. C. (1937) The performance test behaviour of adult morons. *Brit. J. med. Psychol.*, **17**, 78–92.

EARL, C. J. C. (1940) A psychograph for morons. *J. abn. soc. Psychol.*, **35**, 428–48.

ELKIN, L. (1968) Predicting performance of the mentally retarded on sheltered workshop and non-institutional jobs. *Amer. J. ment. Defic.*, **72**, 533–9.

ELLIOT, R. and MACKAY, D. M. (1971) Social competence of subnormal and normal children living under different types of residential care. *J. ment. Subn.*, **17**, 48–53.

ELLIS, N. R. (1963) The stimulus trace and behavioural inadequacy. In ELLIS, N. R. (ed.) *Handbook of Mental Deficiency.* New York: McGraw-Hill.

EMMET, W. G. (1949) Evidence of a space factor at 11 plus and earlier. *Brit. J. Psychol.* (Stat. Sect.), **2**, 3–16.

ERIKSON, R. V. and ROBERTS, A. H. (1966) A comparison of two groups of institutionalized delinquents on Porteus Maze Test performance. *J. consult. Psychol.*, **30**, 567.

EYSENCK, H. J. (1960) Classification and the problem of diagnosis. In EYSENCK, H. J. (ed.) *Handbook of Abnormal Psychology.* London: Pitman.

EYSENCK, S. B. G. (1965) *Manual of the Eysenck–Withers Personality Inventory for subnormal subjects.* London: Univ. of London Press.

FELDMAN, I. S. (1953) Psychological differences among moron and border-line mental defectives as a function of aetiology. *Amer. J. ment. Defic.*, **57**, 484–94.

FERGUSON, R. G. (1958) *Evaluation of the Potential for Vocational Rehabilitation of M.R. Youths with Muscular, Orthopaedic and Emotional Impairment.* Second Annual Report, Sheltered Workshop of the MacDonald Training Centre, Tampa, Florida.

FIELD, J. G. (1960) Two types of tables for use with Wechsler's intelligence scales. *J. clin. Psychol.*, **16**, 3–7.

FISHER, G. M. (1960) Difference in WAIS verbal and performance IQ's in various diagnostic groups of mental retardates. *Amer. J. ment. Defic.*, **65**, 256–60.

FISHER, G. M. (1962) A note on the validity of the W.A.I.S. for mental retardates. *J. consult. Psychol.*, **26**, 391.

FISHER, G. M. (1962b) Further evidence of the invalidity of the W.A.I.S. for the assessment of intelligence of mental retardates. *J. ment. Defic. Res.*, **6**, 41–3.

FISHER, G. M. and SHOTWELL, A. M. (1959) An evaluation of Doppelt's abbreviated form of the W.A.I.S. for the mentally retarded. *Amer. J. ment. Defic.*, **64**, 476–81.

FISHER, G. M., KILMAN, B. A. and SHOTWELL, A. M. (1961) Comparability of intelligence quotients of mental defectives on the W.A.I.S. and the 1960 revision of the S.B. *J. consult. Psychol.*, **25**, 192–5.

FITZPATRICK, F. K. (1956) Training outside the walls. *Amer. J. ment. Defic.*, **60**, 827–37.

FLEISHMAN, E. A. (1954) Dimensional analysis of psychomotor abilities. *J. exp. Psychol.*, **48**, 437–54.

FLEISHMAN, E. A. (1964) *Structure and Measurement of Physical Fitness.* Englewood Cliffs, NJ: Prentice-Hall.

FOOKS, G. and THOMAS, R. R. (1957) Differential qualitative performance of delinquents on the Porteus Maze. *J. consult. Psychol.*, **21**, 351–3.

FOULDS, G. A. (1951) Temperamental differences in Maze performance. Pt. I. *Brit. J. Psychol.*, **42**, 209–17.

FOULDS, G. A. (1952) Temperamental differences in Maze performance II: the effect of distraction and E.C.T. on psycho-motor retardation. *Brit. J. Psychol.*, **43**, 33–41.

FRANKS, C. and FRANKS, V. (1962) Conditionability in defectives and in normals as related to intelligence and organic deficit: the application of a learning theory model to a study of the learning process in mental defectives. In RICHARDS, B. W. (ed.) *Proc. Lond. Conf. Scient. Stud. Ment. Defic.*, **2**, 577–83. Dagenham: May & Baker.

FRANKS, V. and FRANKS, C. M. (1962) Classical conditioning procedures as an index of vocational adjustment among M.Ds. *Percept. mot. Skills*, **14**, 241–2.

FROSTIG, M. (1964) *The Marianne Frostig Development Test of Visual Perception* (3rd edn). Palo Alto, Calif.: Consulting Psychologists Press.

FROSTIG, M. and HORNE, D. (1964) *The Frostig Program for the Development of Visual Perception.* Chicago: Follett.

FROSTIG, M., LEFEVER, D. W. and WHITTLESEY, J. R. B. (1963) Visual perception in the brain injured child. *Amer. J. Orthopsychiat.*, **33**, 665–71.

FROSTIG, M., LEFEVER, D. W. and WHITTLESEY, J. R. B. (1966) *Manual for the Developmental Test of Visual Perception.* Palo Alto, Calif.: Consulting Psychologists Press.

FROSTIG, M., MASLOW, P., LEFEVER, D. W. and WHITTLESEY, J. R. B. (1964) The Marianne Frostig Developmental Test of Visual Perception, 1963 standardization. *Percept. mot. Skills*, **19**, 463–99 (Monogr. suppl. 2-V19).

GAGE, R. M. and WOLFSON, I. N. (1963) Four years of experience with day work programme at Letchworth village. *Amer. J. ment. Defic.*, **67**, 563–8.

GARDNER, A. M. and BIRNBRAUER, J. S. (1968) A note on possible form differences in the P.P.V.T. *Amer. J. ment. Defic.*, **73**, 86–7.

GASKILL, P. (1957) In EWING, A. W. G. (ed.) *Educational Guidance and the Deaf Child*. Manchester: Manchester Univ. Press.

GIBSON, D. and FIELDS, T. L. (1970) Habilitation forecast in mental retardation: the configural search strategy. *Amer. J. ment. Defic.*, **74**, 558–62.

GILLIES, S. (1965) Some abilities of psychotic children and subnormal controls. *J. ment. Defic. Res.*, **9**, 89–101.

GOLDSTEIN, D. and SCHEERER, M. (1941) Abstract and concrete behavior: an experimental study with special tests. *Psychol. Monogr.*, **53.**

GOODENOUGH, F. L. (1926) *Measurement of Intelligence by Drawings*. New York: World Book Co.

GOODENOUGH, F. L. (1955) *Measurement of Intelligence by Drawings*. New York: Harcourt, Brace.

GOULET, L. R. and BARCLAY, A. (1962) The Vineland Social Maturity Scale: utility in assessment of Binet M.A. *Amer. J. ment. Defic.*, **67**, 916–21.

GRAHAM, F. K. and KENDALL, B. S. (1946) Performance of brain-damaged cases on a memory-for-designs test. *J. abn. soc. Psychol.*, **41**, 303–14.

GRAHAM, F. K. and KENDALL, B. S. (1960) *Memory for Designs Test*. Missoula: Psychological Test Specialists.

GRAJALES, M. L. (1948) *Porteus Qualitative Maze Test as a Measure of Delinquency*. Unpubl. thesis, Fordham Univ., New York. Quoted by Porteus, 1950.

GRODEN, G. (1969) Relationships between intelligence, simple, and complex motor proficiency. *Amer. J. ment. Defic.*, **74**, 373–5.

GUERTIN, W. H., FRANK, G. H., LADD, C. E. and RABIN, A. I. (1966) Research with the Wechsler Intelligence Scales for Adults: 1960–1965. *Psychol. Bull.*, **66**, 385–409.

GUNZBURG, H. C. (1955a) Scope and limitations of the Goodenough drawing test method in clinical work with mental defectives. *J. clin. Psychol.*, **11**, 8–15.

GUNZBURG, H. C. (1955b) Projection in drawings: a case study. *Brit. J. med. Psychol.*, **28**, 72–81.

GUNZBURG, H. C. (1956) A short version of the Kohs Block Design Test. *J. Midl. ment. Defic. Soc.*, **2**, 20–6.

GUNZBURG, H. C. (1957) Therapy and social training for the feebleminded youth. *Brit. J. med. Psychol.*, **30**, 42–8.

GUNZBURG, H. C. (1959) Earl's moron battery and social adjustment. *Amer. J. ment. Defic.*, **63**, 92–103.

GUNZBURG, H. C. (1960) *Social Rehabilitation of the Subnormal.* London: Baillière, Tindall & Cox.

GUNZBURG, H. C. (1963) *Progress Assessment Chart (P.A.C.) (Form I, Form II).* London: National Association for Mental Health.

GUNZBURG, H. C. (1964) The reliability of a test of psycholinguistic abilities (I.T.P.A.) in a population of young male subnormals. *J. ment. Subn.*, **10**, 101–12.

GUNZBURG, H. C. (1965) Psychological assessment in mental deficiency. In CLARKE, A. M. and CLARKE, A. D. B. (eds.) *Mental Deficiency: The Changing Outlook.* London: Methuen.

GWYNNE JONES, H. (1956a) Comments on 'The validity and interchangeability of Terman–Merrill and Matrices Test data'. *Brit. J. educ. Psychol.*, **26**, 141–3.

GWYNNE JONES, H. (1956b) The evaluation of the significance between scaled scores on the W.A.I.S.: the perpetuation of a fallacy. *J. consult. Psychol.*, **20**, 319–20.

GWYNNE JONES, H. (1970) *Principles of psychological assessment.* In MITTLER, P. (ed.) *The Psychological Assessment of Mental and Physical Handicaps.* London: Methuen.

HAMMER, E. F. (1969) D.A.P.: Back against the wall? *J. consult. clin. Psychol.*, **33**, 151–6.

HAMMILL, D. and IRWIN, O. C. (1965) P.P.V.T. as a measure of intelligence for mentally subnormal children. *Training School Bull.*, **62**, 126–31.

HARRIS, D. B. (1963) *Children's Drawings as Measures of Intellectual Maturity.* New York: Harcourt, Brace.

HARTLAGE, L. (1966) Common psychological tests applied to the assessment of brain damage. *J. Proj. Tech. pers. Asses.*, **30**, 319–38.

HEATH, S. R. (1942) Railwalking performance as related to mental age and aetiological type among the mentally retarded. *Amer. J. Psychol.*, **55**, 240–7.

HEATH, S. R. (1953) The relations of rail walking and other motor performances of M.Ds. to mental age and aetiological types. *Training School Bull.*, **50**, 110–27.

HEBER, R. (1962) The concept of mental retardation; definition and classification. In RICHARDS, B. W. (ed.) *Proc. Lond. Conf. Scient. Stud. Ment. Defic.* 1960, **1**, 236–42. Dagenham: May & Baker.

HETHERINGTON, R. R. (1970) The clinical interview. In MITTLER, P. (ed.) *The Psychological Assessment of Mental and Physical Handicaps.* London: Methuen.

HEWSON, L. R. (1949) The Wechsler Bellevue Scale and Substitution Test as aids in neuro-psychiatric diagnosis. *J. nerv. ment. Dis.*, **109**, 158–83.

HIMELSTEIN, P. (1957) Evaluation of an abbreviated W. A.I.S. in a psychiatric population. *J. clin. Psychol.*, **13**, 68–9.

HIMELSTEIN, P. (1968) Use of the Stanford-Binet, LM, with retardates: a review of recent research. *Amer. J. ment. Defic.*, **72**, 691–9.

HINSHAW, E. M. and HEAL, L. W. (1968) Like and cross modality recognition in retardates. *Amer. J. ment. Defic.*, **72**, 798–802.

HISKEY, M. S. and SADNAVITCH, J. M. (1958) Minimising exaggerated changes in Binet rating of retarded children. *Except. Child.*, **25**, 16–20.

HOFMEISTER, A. (1969) Motor proficiency and other variables in educable mentally retarded children. *Amer. J. ment. Defic.*, **74**, 264–8.

HOLLINGWORTH, H. L. (1922) *Judging Human Character*. New York: Appleton-Century-Crofts.

HUBSCHMAN, E., POLIZZOTTO, E. A. and KALISKI, M. F. (1970) Performance of institutionalized retardates on the P.P.V.T. and two editions of the I.T.P.A. *Amer. J. ment. Defic.*, **74**, 579–80.

HURST, J. G. (1962) The meaning and use of difference scores obtained between performance on the S.B. Intelligence Scale and the Vineland Social Maturity Scale. *J. clin. Psychol.*, **18**, 153–60.

JACKSON, S. and BUTLER, A. (1963) Prediction of successful community placement of institutionalized retardates. *Amer. J. ment. Defic.*, **68**, 211–17.

JACOBS, J. (1967) An evaluation of the Frostig Visual Perception Training Program. *Educational Leadership*, **25**, 332–40.

JOHNSON, R. C. (1970) Prediction of independent functioning and of problem behaviour from measures of I.Q. and S.Q. *Amer. J. ment. Defic.*, **74**, 591–3.

KAHN, H. (1966) Evidence for long term reliability of the P.P.V.T. with adolescent and young adult retardates. *Amer. J. ment. Defic.*, **70**, 895–8.

KAHN, R. L. and CANNELL, C. F. (1957) *The Dynamics of Interviewing: Theory, Technique and Cases*. New York: Wiley.

KARPELES, L. M. (1932) A further investigation of the Porteus Maze Test as a discriminative measure in delinquency. *J. appl. Psychol.*, **16**, 427–37.

KARRER, R. (1966) Autonomic nervous system functions and behaviour: a review of experimental studies with mental defectives. In ELLIS, N. R. (ed.) *International Review of Research in Mental Retardation*, Vol. 2. London and New York: Academic Press.

KARRER, R. and CLAUSEN, J. (1964) A comparison of M.D. and normal individuals upon four dimensions of autonomic activity. *J. ment. Defic. Res.*, **8**, 149–63.

KATZ, E. A. (1956) A method of selecting S.B. Intelligence Scale test items for evaluating the mental abilities of children severely handicapped by cerebral palsy. *Cerebral Palsy Rev.*, **17**, 13–17.

KAUFMAN, H. I. (1970) Diagnostic indices of employment with the mentally retarded. *Amer. J. ment. Defic.*, **74,** 777–9.

KAUFMAN, H. I. and IVANOFF, J. M. (1968) Evaluating the mentally retarded with the P.P.V.T. *Amer. J. ment. Defic.*, **73,** 396–8.

KEAR-COLWELL, J. J. and MCALLISTER, J. A. (1970) A new method for the analysis of individual meaning systems. *Brit. J. med. Psychol.*, **43,** 49–56.

KELLY, E. L. and FISKE, D. W. (1951) *The Prediction of Performance in Clinical Psychology.* Ann Arbor: Univ. of Michigan Press.

KICKLIGHTER, R. (1964) *Comparison of P.P.V.T. and R.S.B. Test Scores of Educable Mentally Retarded Children.* Atlanta, Ga.: State Dept of Education.

KIRK, S. A. (1966) *The Diagnosis and Remediation of Psycholinguistic Disabilities.* Urbana: Univ. of Illinois Press.

KIRK, S. A. and KIRK, W. D. (1971) *Psycholinguistic Learning Disabilities: Diagnosis and Remediation.* London, Chicago and Urbana: Univ. of Illinois Press.

KIRK, S. A. and MCCARTHY, J. J. (1961) The Illinois test of psycholinguistic abilities – an approach to differential diagnosis. *Amer. J. ment. Defic.*, **66,** 399–412.

KIRK, S. A., MCCARTHY, J. J. and KIRK, W. D. (1968) *The Illinois Test of Psycholinguistic Abilities* (rev. edn). Urbana: Univ. of Illinois Press.

KLOPFER, B. and KELLEY, D. (1942) *The Rorschach Technique.* New York: World Book Co.

KOH, T. H. and MADOW, A. A. (1965) Relationship between P.P.V.T. and S.B. Intelligence Scale in institutionalized mentally retarded. *Amer. Psychol.*, **20,** 466.

KOHS, S. C. (1923) *Intelligence Measurement.* New York: Macmillan.

KOLSTOE, O. P. and SHAFTER, A. J. (1961) Employability prediction for mentally retarded adults: a methodological note. *Amer. J. ment. Defic.*, **66,** 287–9.

KOPPITZ, E. M. (1964) *The Bender Gestalt Test for Young Children.* New York: Grune & Stratton.

KORMAN, M. and BLUMBERG, S. (1963) Comparative efficiency of some tests of cerebral damage. *J. consult. Psychol.*, **27,** 303–9.

KROSK, W. H., FRETWELL, L. M. and CUPP, E. (1965) Comparison of the Kahn intelligence tests: experimental form, Stanford-Binet, and the W.A.I.S. for familial retardates. *Percept. mot. Skills*, **21,** 428.

KUDER, G. F. (1951) *Kuder Preference Record Administrators Manual.* Chicago: Science Research Associates Inc.

LEVY, I. S. (1971) The Harris Goodenough Drawing Test and educably mentally retarded adolescents. *Amer. J. ment. Defic.*, **75,** 760–1.

LOCKYER, L. and RUTTER, M. (1970) A five to fifteen year follow-up study of infantile psychosis: IV. Patterns of cognitive ability. *Brit. J. soc. clin. Psychol.*, **9**, 152–63.

LUCAS, M. S. (1970) Assessment of coding behaviour of trainable retardates. *Amer. J. ment. Defic.*, **75**, 309–15.

LURIA, A. R. (1963) Psychological studies of mental deficiency in the Soviet Union. In ELLIS, N. R. (ed.) *Handbook of Mental Deficiency.* New York: McGraw-Hill.

MACANDREW, C. and EDGERTON, R. (1964) I.Q. and the social competence of the profoundly retarded. *Amer. J. ment. Defic.*, **69**, 385–90.

MACANDREW, C. and EDGERTON, R. (1965) A reply to Baumeister. *Amer. J. ment. Defic.*, **69**, 883.

MCCARTHY, D. (1961) Administration of D.S. and coding subtests of the W.A.I.S. and W.I.S.C. to left-handed subjects. *Psychol. Rep.*, **8**, 407–8.

MCCARTHY, J. J. and KIRK, S. A. (1961) *Illinois Test of Psycholinguistic Abilities: Experimental Edition.* Urbana: Institute for Research on Exceptional Children, Univ. of Illinois.

MCCARTHY, J. J. and OLSON, J. L. (1964) *Validity Studies on the Illinois Test of Psycholinguistic Abilities.* Milwaukee: Univ. of Wisconsin.

MACCOBY, E. E. and MACCOBY, N. (1954) The interview: a tool of social science. In LINDZEY, G. (ed.) *Handbook of Social Psychology*, Vol. I. Reading, Mass.: Addison-Wesley.

MCKERRACHER, D. W. and SCOTT, J. (1966) I.Q. scores and the problem classification. *Brit. J. Psychiat.*, **112**, 537–41.

MCKERRACHER, D. W., WATSON, R. A., LITTLE, A. J. and WINTER, K. S. (1968) Validation of a short form estimation of W.A.I.S. in subnormal and psychopathic patients. *J. ment. Subn.*, **14**, 96–7.

MADISON, H. L. (1964) Work placement success for the mentally retarded. *Amer. J. ment. Defic.*, **69**, 50–3.

MAHER, B. A. (1960) Position errors and primitive thinking in the Progressive Matrices Test. *Amer. J. ment. Defic.*, **64**, 1016–20.

MALONEY, M. P. and PAYNE, L. E. (1969) Validity of the Draw a Person Test as a measure of body image. *Percept. mot. Skills*, **29**, 119–22.

MALONEY, M. P. and PAYNE, L. E. (1970) Note on the stability of changes in body image due to sensory-motor training. *Amer. J. ment. Defic.*, **74**, 708.

MALONEY, M. P., BALL, T. S. and EDGAR, C. L. (1970) Analysis of the generalizability of sensory-motor training. *Amer. J. ment. Defic.*, **74**, 458–68.

MALPASS, L. F. (1963) Motor skills in mental deficiency. In ELLIS, N. R. (ed.) *Handbook of Mental Deficiency.* New York: McGraw-Hill.

MASLAND, R. L., SARASON, S. B. and GLADWIN, T. (1958) *Mental Subnormality: Biological, Psychological and Cultural Factors.* New York: Basic Books.

MASTERS, F. G. and TONG, J. E. (1968) The Semantic Differential Test with Borstal subjects. *Brit. J. Crimin.*, **8**, 20–31.

MATARAZZO, J. D. (1965) The interview. In WOLMAN, B. B. (ed.) *Handbook of Clinical Psychology*. London: McGraw-Hill.

MATTHEWS, C. G. (1964) The social competence of the subnormal school leaver. *J. ment. Subn.*, **10**, 83–8.

MAXWELL, A. E. (1960) Obtaining factor scores on the W.A.I.S. *J. ment. Sci.*, **106**, 1060–2.

MEEHL, P. E. (1954) *Clinical Versus Statistical Prediction*. Minneapolis: Univ. of Minnesota Press.

MEEHL, P. E. and ROSEN, A. (1955) Antecedent probability and the efficiency of psychometric signs, patterns, or cutting scores. *Psychol. Bull*, **52**, 194–216.

MEIN, R. (1962) Use of the Peabody Picture Vocabulary Test with severely subnormal patients. *Amer. J. ment. Defic.*, **67**, 269–73.

MILLER, F. M. and RAVEN, J. C. (1939) The influence of positional factors on the choice of answers to perceptual intelligence tests. *Brit. J. med. Psychol.*, **18**, 35–9.

MITTLER, P. (1970) *The Psychological Assessment of Mental and Physical Handicaps*. London: Methuen.

MUELLER, M. W. and SMITH, J. O. (1964) The stability of language age modifications over time. *Amer. J. ment. Defic.*, **68**, 537–9.

MUELLER, M. W. and WEAVER, S. J. (1964) Psycholinguistic Abilities of institutionalized and non-institutionalized trainable mental retardates. *Amer. J. ment. Defic.*, **68**, 775–83.

MURPHY, M. M. (1956) A Goodenough Scale evaluation of human figure drawings of three non-psychotic groups of adults. *J. clin. Psychol.*, **12**, 397–9.

MYERS, P. I. and HAMMILL, D. B. (1969) *Methods for Learning Disorders*. London: Wiley.

NICHOLS, R. C. and STRUMPFER, D. J. (1962) A factor analysis of Draw a Person Test scores. *J. consult. Psychol.*, **26**, 156–61.

O'CONNOR, N. and HERMELIN, B. (1961) Like and cross modality recognition in subnormal children. *Quart. J. exp. Psychol.*, **13**, 48–52.

O'CONNOR, N. and HERMELIN, B. (1963) *Speech and Thought in Severe Subnormality*. Oxford: Pergamon.

O'CONNOR, N. and TIZARD, J. (1951) Predicting the occupational adequacy of certified mental defectives. *Occup. Psychol.*, **25**, 205–11.

OLSON, J. L. (1961) Deaf and sensory aphasic children. *Except Child.*, **27**, 422–4.

ORME, J. E. (1961) The Coloured Progressive Matrices as a measure of intellectual subnormality. *Brit. J. med. Psychol.*, **34**, 291–2.

ORME, J. E. (1966) Hypothetically true norms for the Progressive Matrices Test. *Human Developm.*, **9**, 222–30.

OSGOOD, C. E. (1963) Psycholinguistics. In KOCH, S. (ed.) *Psychology: A Study of a Science*. New York: McGraw-Hill.

OSGOOD, C. E., SUCI, G. J. and TANNENBAUM, P. H. (1957) *The Measurement of Meaning*. Urbana: Univ. of Illinois Press.

PACELLA, M. J. (1965) The performance of brain damaged mental retardates on successive trials of the Bender Gestalt. *Amer. J. ment. Defic.*, **69**, 723–8.

PARNICKY, J. J., KAHN, H. and BURDETT, A. (1965) Preliminary efforts at determining the significance of retardates' vocational interests. *Amer. J. ment. Defic.*, **70**, 393–8.

PARNICKY, J. J., KAHN, H. and BURDETT, A. (1971) Standardization of the (VISA) Vocational Interest and Sophistication Assessment Technique. *Amer. J. ment. Defic.*, **75**, 442–8.

PASCAL, G. R. and SUTTELL, B. J. (1951) *The Bender Gestalt Test*. New York: Grune & Stratton.

PHILLIPS, C. J. and BANNON, W. J. (1968) The Stanford–Binet, Form L.M., Third Revision: a local English study of norms, concurrent validity and social differences. *Brit. J. educ. Psychol.*, **38**, 148–61.

POOL, D. A. and BROWN, R. (1970) The P.P.V.T. as a measure of general adult intelligence. *J. consult. clin. Psychol.*, **34**, 8–11.

POPE, B. and SIEGMAN, A. (1968) Interviewer warmth in relation to interviewee verbal behaviour. *J. consult. clin. Psychol.*, **32**, 588–95.

PORTEUS, S. D. (1945) Q-Scores temperament and delinquency. *J. soc. Psychol.*, **21**, 81–103.

PORTEUS, S. D. (1950) *The Porteus Maze Test and Intelligence*. Palo Alto, Calif.: Pacific Books.

PORTEUS, S. D. (1959) *The Maze Test and Clinical Psychology*. Palo Alto, Calif.: Pacific Books.

POULL, L. E. and MONTGOMERY, R. P. (1929) The Porteus Maze test as a discriminative measure in delinquency. *J. appl. Psychol.*, **13**, 145–51.

PRADO, W. M. and SCHNADT, F. (1965) Differences in W.A.I.S.-W.B. functioning in three psychiatric groups. *J. clin. Psychol.*, **21**, 184–6.

RABIN, A. I. and GUERTIN, W. H. (1951) Research with the W.T. Test: 1945–1950. *Psychol. Bull.*, **48**, 211–48.

RABIN, H. M. (1957) The relationship of age, intelligence and sex to motor proficiency in mental defectives. *Amer. J. ment. Defic.*, **62**, 507–16.

RAINES, G. N. and ROHRER, J. H. (1955) The operational matrix of psychiatric practice. I: Consistency and variability in interview impressions of different psychiatrists. *Amer. J. Psychiat.*, **111**, 721–33.

RAINES, G. N. and ROHRER, J. H. (1960) The operational matrix of psychiatric practice. II: Variability in psychiatric impressions and the projection hypothesis. *Amer. J. Psychiat.*, **117**, 133–9.

RAPAPORT, D. (1945) *Diagnostic Psychological Testing*, Vol. I. Chicago: Year Book Medical Publishers.

RAVEN, J. C. (1938) *Progressive Matrices*. London: H. K. Lewis.

RAVEN, J. C. (1943) *Mill Hill Vocabulary Scales*. London: H. K. Lewis.

RAVEN, J. C. (1947) *Progressive Matrices (Coloured) Sets A, Ab, B*. London: H. K. Lewis.

RAVEN, J. C. (1956) *Standard Progressive Matrices 1938*. London: H. K. Lewis.

RAVEN, J. C. (1958) *Mill Hill Vocabulary Scales–Manual* (2nd edn). London: H. K. Lewis.

RAVENETTE, A. T. and HERSOV, L. A. (1963) Speed of function and educational retardation: the psychological and psychiatric investigation of the individual case. *J. Child Psychol. Psychiat.*, **4**, 17–28.

REYNOLDS, M. C. and MACEACHERN, D. G. (1956) The prediction of the adult status of high grade mental defectives. In WRIGHT, M. E. and CROLEY, H. T. (eds.) *Research in the Management of the Mentally Retarded Child*. Winfield, Ka.: Winfield St. Training School.

RICE, S. (1929) Contagious bias in the interview: methodological note. *Amer. J. Sociol.*, **35**, 420–3.

RICHIE, J. and BUTLER, A. J. (1964) Performance of retardates on the M.F.D. Test. *J. clin. Psychol.*, **20**, 108–10.

RIESMAN, D. and BENNEY, M. (1956) The sociology of the interview. *Mid-West Sociologist*, **18**, 3–15.

ROACH, E. G. and KEPHART, N. C. (1966) *The Purdue Perceptual-Motor Survey*. Colombus, Ohio: C. E. Merrill Books.

ROBACK, H. (1968) Human figure drawings: their utility in the clinical psychologists' armamentarium for personality assessment. *Psychol. Bull.*, **70**, 1–19.

ROBERTS, A. D. (1945) Intelligence and performance test patterns among older mental defectives. *Amer. J. ment. Defic.*, **49**, 300–3.

ROBERTS, A. H. and ERIKSON, R. V. (1968) Delay of gratification, Porteus Maze Test performance, and behavioural adjustment in a delinquent group. *J. abn. Psychol.*, **73**, 449–53.

ROHS, F. W. and HAWORTH, M. R. (1962) The 1960 S.B., W.I.S.C. and Goodenough Test with M.R. children. *Amer. J. ment. Defic.*, **66**, 853–9.

ROSEN, C. (1966) An experimental study of visual perceptual training and reading achievement in first grade. *Percept. mot. Skills*, **22**, 979–86.

ROSEN, M., KIVITZ, M. S., CLARK, G. R. and FLOOR, L. (1970) Prediction of post-institutional adjustment of mentally retarded adults. *Amer. J. ment. Defic.*, **74**, 726–34.

ROSEN, M., STALLINGS, L., FLOOR, L. and NOWAKISKA, M. (1968) The reliability and stability of Wechsler I.Q. scores for institutionalized mental subnormals. *Amer. J. ment. Defic.*, **73**, 218–25.

ROSS, D. (1963) A short form of the WAIS for use in mental subnormality. *J. ment. Subnorm.*, **9**, 9–94.

RUSHTON, C. S. and STOCKWIN, A. E. (1963) Changes in Terman Merrill I.Qs. of educationally subnormal boys. *Brit. J. educ. Psychol.*, **33,** 132–42.

RYBOLT, G. A. (1969) Stability characteristics of the semantic differential responses of the mentally retarded. *Psychol. Rep.*, **24,** 103–8.

SARASON, S. B. (1949) *Psychological Problems in Mental Deficiency* (2nd edn, 1953). New York: Harper Bros.

SARASON, S. B. (1959) *Psychological Problems in Mental Deficiency* (3rd edn). New York: Harper Bros.

SARASON, S. B. and POTTER, E. H. (1947) Color in the Rorschach and Kohs Block Designs. *J. consult. Psychol.*, **11,** 202–6.

SARASON, S. B. and SARASON, E. K. (1946) The discriminatory value of a test pattern in the high grade familial defective. *J. clin. Psychol.*, **2,** 38–49.

SATTER, G. (1955) Retarded adults who have developed beyond expectation. Part III: Further analysis and summary. *Training School Bull.*, **51,** 237–43.

SATZ, P. (1966) A Block Rotation Task: the application of multi-variate and decision theory analysis for the prediction of organic brain disorders. *Psychol. Monogr.*, **80,** No. 629.

SCHONELL, F. J. (1942) *Backwardness in the Basic Subjects*. Edinburgh: Oliver & Boyd.

SEASHORE, R. H. (1951) Work and motor performance. In STEVENS, S. S. (ed.) *Handbook of Experimental Psychology*. New York: Wiley.

SHAFTER, A. J. (1957) Criteria for selecting institutionalized mental defectives for vocational placement. *Amer. J. ment. Defic.*, **61,** 599–616.

SHAKESPEARE, R. (1970) Severely subnormal children. In MITTLER, P. (ed.) *The Psychological Assessment of Mental and Physical Handicaps*. London: Methuen.

SHAPIRO, M. B. (1951) Experimental studies of a perceptual anomaly. I: Initial experiments. *J. ment. Sci.*, **97,** 90–110.

SHAPIRO, M. B. (1954) An experimental investigation of the Block Design rotation effect. *Brit. J. med. Psychol.*, **27,** 84–8.

SHAPIRO, M. B. (1961) A method of measuring psychological changes specific to the psychiatric patient. *Brit. J. med. Psychol.*, **34,** 151–5.

SHAPIRO, M. B. (1966) The single case in clinical-psychological research. *J. gen. Psychol.*, **74,** 3–23.

SHAPIRO, M. B. (1970) Intensive assessment of the single case: an inductive-deductive approach. In MITTLER, P. (ed.) *The Psychological Assessment of Mental and Physical Handicaps*. London: Methuen.

SHAW, D. J., MATTHEWS, C. G. and KLOVE, H. (1966) The equivalence of W.I.S.C. and P.P.V.T. I.Qs. *Amer. J. ment. Defic.*, **70,** 601–4.

SHOTWELL, A. M., O'CONNOR, G., GABET, Y. and DINGMAN, H. F. (1969) The relation of the Peabody Picture Vocabulary Test I.Q. to the Stanford–Binet I.Q. *Amer. J. ment. Defic.*, **74,** 39–42.

SILVERSTEIN, A. B. (1963a) An evaluation of two short forms of the S.B. LM for use with mentally retarded children. *Amer. J. ment. Defic.*, **67**, 922–3.

SILVERSTEIN, A. B. (1963b) Psychological testing practices in state institutions for the mentally retarded. *Amer. J. ment. Defic.*, **68**, 440–5.

SILVERSTEIN, A. B. (1966a) Anxiety and the quality of human figure drawings. *Amer. J. ment. Defic.*, **70**, 607–8.

SILVERSTEIN, A. B. (1966b) A further evaluation of two short forms of the Stanford Binet. *Amer. J. ment. Defic.*, **70**, 928–9.

SILVERSTEIN, A. B. (1968) Variance components in five psychological tests. *Psychol. Rep.*, **23**, 141–2.

SILVERSTEIN, A. B. (1969) The internal consistency of the Stanford-Binet. *Amer. J. ment. Defic.*, **73**, 753–4.

SILVERSTEIN, A. B. (1970) The measurement of intelligence. In ELLIS, N. R. (ed.) *International Review of Research in Mental Retardation.* New York and London: Academic Press.

SILVERSTEIN, A. B. and FISHER, G. M. (1961) An evaluation of two short forms of the Stanford-Binet (LM), for use with mentally retarded adults. *Amer. J. ment. Defic.*, **65**, 486–8.

SILVERSTEIN, A. B. and MOHAN, P. J. (1962) Bender Gestalt figure rotations in the mentally retarded. *J. consult. Psychol.*, **26**, 386–8.

SILVERSTEIN, A. B., FISHER, G. M. and OWENS, E. P. (1963) The altitude quotient as an index of intellectual potential: III. Three studies of predictive validity. *Amer. J. ment. Defic.*, **67**, 611–16.

SILVERSTEIN, A. B., ULFELDT, V. and PRICE, E. (1970) Clinical assessment of visual perceptual abilities in the mentally retarded. *Amer. J. ment. Defic.*, **74**, 524–6.

SLOAN, W. (1947) Validity of Wechsler's deterioration quotient in high grade mental defectives. *J. clin. Psychol.*, **3**, 287–8.

SLOAN, W. (1951) Motor proficiency and intelligence. *Amer. J. ment. Defic.*, **55**, 394–406.

SLOAN, W. (1955) The Lincoln–Oseretsky motor development scale. *Genet. Psychol. Monogr.*, **51**, 183–252.

SLOAN, W. and SCHNEIDER, B. (1951) A study of the Wechsler Intelligence Scale for Children with mental defectives. *Amer. J. ment. Defic.*, **55**, 573–5.

SMITH, J. O. (1962) Group language development for educable mental retardates. *Except Child.*, **29**, 95–101.

SONG, A. Y. and SONG, R. H. (1969) Prediction of job efficiency of institutionalized retardates in the community. *Amer. J. ment. Defic.*, **73**, 567–71.

SPEARMAN, C. and JONES, L. L. W. (1950) *Human Ability.* London: Macmillan.

SPRAGUE, R. L. and QUAY, H. C. (1966) A factor-analytic study of the responses of retardates on the W.A.I.S. *Amer. J. ment. Defic.*, **70,** 595–600.

STACEY, C. L. and GILL, M. R. (1954) The relationship between Raven's Coloured Matrices and two tests of general intelligence for 172 subnormal adult subjects on the Stanford–Binet and W.I.S.C. *Amer. J. ment. Defic.*, **55,** 590–7.

STACEY, C. L. and LEVINE, J. (1951) Correlational analysis of scores of subnormal subjects on the Stanford–Binet and W.I.S.C. *Amer. J. ment. Defic.*, **55,** 590–7.

STERNLICHT, M. A. (1965) A downward application of the 1960 Revision S.B. with retardates. *J. clin. Psychol.*, **21,** 79.

STERNLICHT, M. A. and SIEGEL, L. (1968) Institutional residents and intellectual functioning. *J. ment. Defic. Res.*, **12,** 119–27.

STERNLICHT, M. A., PUSTEL, G. and SIEGEL, L. (1968) Comparison of organic and cultural familial retardates on two visual motor tasks. *Amer. J. ment. Defic.*, **72,** 887–9.

STEVENS, H. A. and HEBER, R. (1964) *Mental Retardation: A Review of Research.* Chicago and London: Univ. of Chicago Press.

STOTT, D. H. (1966) A general test of motor impairment for children. *Developm. Med. Child. Neurol.*, **8,** 523–31.

STRAUSS, A. A. and LEHTINEN, L. E. (1947) *Psychopathology and Education of the Brain-injured Child.* New York: Grune & Stratton.

STRONG, E. K. (1943) *Vocational Interests of Men and Women.* Stanford, Calif.: Stanford Univ. Press.

SUNDBERG, N. D. and TYLER, L. E. (1962) *Clinical Psychology.* New York: Appleton-Century-Crofts.

SWENSEN, C. H. (1968) Empirical evaluations of human figure drawings. *Psychol. Bull.*, **70,** 20–44.

TERMAN, L. M. and MERRILL, M. A. (1937) *Measuring Intelligence.* London: Harrap.

TERMAN, L. M. and MERRILL, M. A. (1960) *Stanford–Binet Intelligence Scale Manual for the Third Revision Form L-M.* Boston: Houghton Mifflin.

THORPE, J. G., BARDECKI, A. and BALAGUER, A. B. (1967) The reliability of the Eysenck Withers Personality Inventory for subnormal subjects. *J. ment. Defic. Res.*, **11,** 108–15.

TIZARD, J. (1951) The Porteus Maze test and intelligence. A critical survey. *Brit. J. educ. Psychol.*, **21,** 172–85.

TIZARD, J. and O'CONNOR, N. (1950) The employability of high-grade mental defectives. *Amer. J. ment. Defic.*, **54,** 563–76; **55,** 144–57.

TIZARD, J., O'CONNOR, N. and CRAWFORD, J. M. (1950) The abilities of adolescent and adult high grade defectives. *J. ment. Sci.*, **96,** 889–907.

TOBIAS, J. and GORELICK, J. (1962) The Porteus Maze Test and the appraisal of retarded adults. *Amer. J. ment. Defic.*, **66,** 601–6.

TONG, J. E. (1959) Stress reactivity in relation to delinquent and psychopathic behaviour. *J. ment. Sci.*, **105,** 935–56.

TONG, J. E. (1960) G.S.R. studies of sex responsiveness in sex offenders and others. *J. ment. Sci.*, **106,** 1475–85.

TONG, J. E. and MURPHY, I. C. (1960) A review of stress reactivity research in relation to psychopathology and psychopathic behaviour disorders. *J. ment. Sci.*, **106,** 1273–95.

TREDGOLD, A. F. (1952) *A Textbook of Mental Deficiency* (8th edn). London: Baillière, Tindall & Cox.

TUBBS, V. K. (1966) Types of linguistic disability in psychotic children. *J. ment. Defic. Res.*, **10,** 23–4.

ULRICH, L. and TRUMBO, D. (1965) The selection interview since 1949. *Psychol. Bull.*, **63,** 100–16.

VANDERHOST, L., SLOAN, W. and BENSBERG, G. J. (1953) Performance of mental defectives on the Wechsler-Bellevue and W.I.S.C. *Amer. J. ment. Defic.*, **57,** 481–3.

VERNON, P. E. (1938) *The Standardization of a Graded Word Reading Test.* Scottish Council for Research in Education, No. 12. London: Univ. of London Press.

VERNON, P. E. (1947) The variations of intelligence with occupation, age and locality. *Brit. J. Psychol.*, **1,** 52–63 (Stat. Sect.).

VERNON, P. E. (1950) An application of factorial analysis to the study of test items. *Brit. J. Psychol.*, **3,** 1–13 (Stat. Sect.).

VERNON, P. E. (1953) *Personality Tests and Assessments.* London: Methuen.

VERNON, P. E. (1966) *Personality Assessment: A Critical Survey.* London: Methuen.

VERNON, P. E. and PARRY, J. B. (1949) *Personnel Selection in the British Forces.* London: Univ. of London Press.

WAGNER, E. E. and HAWVER, A. H. (1965) Correlations between psychological tests and sheltered workshop performance for severely retarded adults. *Amer. J. ment. Defic.*, **69,** 685–91.

WALSH, J. F. and D'ANGELO, R. (1971) Effectiveness of the Frostig Program for Visual Perceptual Training with head-start children. *Percept. mot. Skills*, **32,** 944–6.

WANDERER, Z. W. (1969) Validity of clinical judgments based on human figure drawings. *J. consult. clin. Psychol.*, **33,** 143–50.

WARD, J. (1970) The factor structure of the Frostig D.T.V.P. *Brit. J. educ. Psychol.*, **40,** 65–7.

WARREN, F. (1961) Ratings of employed and unemployed mentally handicapped males on personality and work factors. *Amer. J. ment. Defic.*, **65,** 629–33.

WARREN, S. A. and KRAUS, M. J. (1961) W.A.I.S. verbal minus performance I.Q. comparisons in mental retardates. *J. clin. Psychol.*, **17**, 57–9.

WATSON, R. I. (1951) *The Clinical Method in Psychology*. New York: Harper Bros.

WATTS, A. F. (1944) *The Language and Mental Development of Children*. London: Harrap.

WEAVER, L. A. and RAVARIS, P. (1970) The distribution of reaction times in mental retardates. *J. ment. Defic. Res.*, **14**, 295–304.

WEBB, A. P. (1963) A longitudinal comparison of the W.I.S.C. and W.A.I.S. with educable mentally retarded negroes. *J. clin. Psychol.*, **19**, 101–2.

WECHSLER, D. (1949) *Wechsler Intelligence Scale for Children: Manual*. New York: Psychological Corporation.

WECHSLER, D. (1955) *Wechsler Adult Intelligence Scale*. New York: Psychological Corporation.

WECHSLER, D. (1958) *The Measurement and Appraisal of Adult Intelligence* (4th edn). Baltimore, Md.: Williams & Wilkins.

WHITING, H. T. A., CLARKE, T. A. and MORRIS, D. R. (1969) A clinical validation of the Stott Test of Motor Impairment. *Brit. J. soc. clin. Psychol.*, **8**, 270–4.

WHITING, H. T. A., JOHNSON, G. F. and PAGE, M. (1968) *A Factor Analytic Study of Motor Impairment at the Ten Year Old Level*. Unpubl. paper, Leeds Univ.

WILE, I. S. and DAVIS, R. (1930) A comparative study of the Kohs block design tests. *Amer. J. Orthopsychiat.*, **1**, 89–103.

WINDLE, C. (1962) Prognosis of mental subnormals. *Amer. J. ment. Defic. Monogr. Suppl.*, **66**, 1–180.

WING, J. K. (1966) The measurement of psychiatric diagnosis. *Proc. Roy. Soc. Med.*, **59**, 1030–2.

WING, J. K., BIRLEY, J. L. T., COOPER, J. E., GRAHAM, P. and ISAACS, A. D. (1967) Reliability of a procedure for measuring and classifying present psychiatric state. *Brit. J. Psychiat.*, **113**, 499–515.

WOLFENSBERGER, W. (1962) The correlation between P.P.V.T. and achievement scores among retardates: a further study. *Amer. J. ment. Defic.*, **67**, 450–4.

WOLFENSBERGER, W. and O'CONNOR, N. (1965) Stimulus intensity and duration effects on E.E.G. and G.S.R. responses of normals and retardates. *Amer. J. ment. Defic.*, **70**, 21–37.

WOODWARD, M. (1963) The application of Piaget's theory to research in mental deficiency. In ELLIS, N. R. (ed.) *Handbook of Mental Deficiency*. New York: McGraw-Hill.

WRIGHT, C. A. (1942) A modified procedure for the abbreviated revised S.B. in determining the intelligence of mental defectives. *Amer. J. ment. Defic.*, **47**, 178–84.

WRIGHT, C. A. (1944) The qualitative performance of delinquent boys on the Porteus Maze Tests. *J. consult. Psychol.*, 8, 24–6.

ZEAMAN, D. and HOUSE, B. J. (1963) The role of attention in retardate discrimination learning. In ELLIS, N. R. (ed.) *Handbook of Mental Deficiency*. New York: McGraw-Hill.

16

E. Stephen and G. Hawks

Cerebral palsy and
mental subnormality

Introduction

Of recent years increasing interest has been shown in cerebral palsy both in this
country and in America. Although Little first described a case of spastic paralysis
(or Little's disease) in 1862, it is probably true that the intensive work in this
field dates from the 1930s. Since then, there have been a large number of articles
written on all aspects of the subject and a corresponding development of services
for the cerebral palsied.

At first, the interest in cerebral palsy was mainly medical. In 1930, however,
Lord published an account of her pioneer work and since then psychologists
have given increased attention to the subject. It is, however, worth noting that
in her original study, Lord asked some of the important questions which still
remain largely unanswered. She was, for example, interested in discovering a
psychological method of evaluating mental status in spite of motor handicap;
this is still a main problem for the psychologist.

This chapter is an attempt to discuss psychological and educational aspects
of cerebral palsy with particular reference to mental subnormality. Experiments
in which cerebral palsied patients have been studied in order to investigate
psychological dysfunction associated with brain injury, or maldevelopment in
general, are not included here. No attempt has been made to cover the strictly
medical aspects of cerebral palsy, or to consider the literature on the ancillary
medical services, such as physiotherapy, occupational therapy and speech
therapy (see Chapter 18). It is true that co-operation between the different
services exists in practice, possibly in varying degrees. However, although the
need for teamwork involving a galaxy of talent drawn from many disciplines is
repeatedly mentioned in the literature, studies of the results of such teamwork
are slow to appear in the journals.

DEFINITION AND PREVALENCE

Yannet (1944) defines cerebral palsy as a 'motor defect present or appearing
soon after birth and dependent on pathologic abnormalities in the brain'. This

definition excludes motor defects due to lesions of the spinal cord or peripheral nerves, or progressive neuromuscular disease. It appears that all writers on the subject would subscribe to this wide definition.

Considering the definition of cerebral palsy, Rutter, Graham and Yule (1970) write that this widely used diagnosis is an artificially derived category, not a disease entity. Nevertheless, it has some administrative usefulness and facilitates comparison between different studies; for these reasons it was retained in their investigation and defined as 'an unequivocally pathological motor disorder in which there was evidence of a non-progressive lesion above the brain stem. As the study was confined to children under the age of 15 years, it was implicit that the lesion occurred in an immature brain.'

According to Walshe (1952) there are four main categories of motor disorder:

1. Where the pyramidal system is acting defensively or not at all.
2. That resulting from loss or impairment of the extra-pyramidal mechanisms.
3. From cerebellar lesions.
4. Where the lower motor neurone is involved.

Studies of the prevalence of cerebral palsy in children of school age have varied between rates of 3·4 and 4·8 per 1000, as reported in the New Jersey survey of 1938, to rates of 1 to 2 per 1,000 reported by Asher and Schonell (1950), Dunsdon (1952), Hansen (1960) in Denmark and Henderson (1961) in Eastern Scotland. Rutter, Graham and Yule (1970) discuss the whole question of prevalence. They attribute differences in rates reported in different studies:

1. to differences of definition and methodology;
2. in clinic and administrative studies, to inadequacies in case-finding methods, and they emphasize the need for multiple screening methods (Ingram, 1955); and
3. to chance variation.

They conclude that the true rate of cerebral palsy, at least in Great Britain, is probably somewhere between 2 and 3 per 1,000. They suggest that as ongoing studies, for example in the Isle of Wight, report rates at least as high as those reported by Ingram (1955) and Henderson (1961), it seems unlikely that there has been any decline in the incidence of cerebral palsy over the last decade (cf. Woods, 1963).

Classification of cerebral palsy

The classification of the cerebral palsies seems still to be in considerable confusion. Clear descriptions of the present systems of classification are given by Illingworth (1958, Chapter 1) and Mitchell (Henderson, 1961, Chapter IV). More recently Rutter, Graham and Yule point out the difficulties which arise in attempting to classify cerebral palsy, and attribute them to the 'wide variety of manifestations of cerebral palsy, from the lack of clear differentiation between them and from the fact that in any individual child the manifestations tend to change as he grows older'.

The following section gives a comparative outline of the forms of classification.

I. CLASSIFICATION ACCORDING TO TYPE

In this chapter the four main types are considered to be the spastic, the athetoid, the ataxic and a mixed type.

1. In spasticity the pyramidal system is involved. Spasticity is characterized by a 'clasp-knife' rigidity of the muscles and exaggerated reflexes.

2. In athetosis the lesion involves the extra pyramidal system and basal ganglia (Wyllie, 1951). Athetosis is characterized by slow wormlike writhing movements.

3. Ataxia is characterized by disturbance of balance.

In their Isle of Wight study, Rutter, Graham and Yule used a classificatory system based on that of Ingram (1964). They had thirty-five cases which only allowed them a fairly broad classification into three categories: first, those with paresis, which they further subdivided according to the number of limbs involved; second, those with dyskinesia, cases where involuntary movements of the limbs produced the major disability, there being little or no paresis; and, lastly, those with ataxia, where incoordination and impaired balance were the main manifestations, and where there was little paresis.

TABLE 13. *The distribution of cerebral palsy by type* (%)[1]

	Athetoid	Spastic	Mixed	Other
Dunsdon (1952) England and Wales				
(a) Diagnostic selection	13·0		81·0	6·0
(b) Special inquiry areas	7·8		82·7	9·5
Asher and Schonell (1950)				
349 cases of congenital CP in children	10·0	83·0	5·0	1·9
Hopkins, Bice and Colton (1951) New Jersey				
1,406 cases	23·6	45·1	3·4	26·9
Hansen (1960) Denmark				
2,621 cases	9·3	78·5	4·6	7·6
Henderson (1961) Eastern Scotland				
240 cases	11·7	77·1	9·6	1·6
				Extra-pyramidal
Crothers and Paine (1959)				
406 cases		64·6	13·1	22·0

[1] In a number of the quoted tables it will be noted that the percentages given by the various authors do not always total 100.

Some form of spasticity is the most frequently found type of cerebral palsy in all surveys, but apart from this common finding there seems to be considerable variation between the incidences of the main types as noted by the different workers. It seems possible that this is due to differences in diagnostic criteria. Sarason and Doris (1969) write: 'However, in many cases both pyramidal and extrapyramidal tracts are involved and there are relatively few cases showing pure spasticity or pure athetosis.' This is also Wallin's (1949) point of view. At present there seems no other explanation of the fact that there are apparently more athetoids in America than in Great Britain. The relative number of spastics and athetoids is important for psychologists and educationists if, as some writers seem to assume, they form separate groups with regard to certain psychological or educational characteristics.

II. CLASSIFICATION ACCORDING TO NUMBER OF LIMBS INVOLVED

Some authorities apply this principle of classification mainly to spastics; others, for example Wyllie, Dunsdon, Bice and Hopkins, apply it to all types of cerebral palsy. Wyllie (1951) suggests the following classification:

1. Congenital symmetrical diplegia (bilateral symmetrical paralysis, most common in lower limbs).
2. Congenital paraplegia; this is a mild form of the above in which the legs only are involved.
3. Quadriplegia, bilateral hemiplegia, or tetraplegia; paresis of all four limbs, most marked in upper limb or of equal severity in all four limbs.
4. Triplegia, three limbs involved; a very rare condition.
5. Hemiplegia, both limbs on one side involved.
6. Monoplegia, one limb affected; very rare,

'With additional qualifications of (a) spasticity, (b) flaccidity, (c) mixed types, (d) athetosis, (e) ataxy.'

TABLE 14. *Three recent surveys* (%)

	Spastic mono-plegia	Para-plegia	Hemi-plegia	Di-plegia	Tetra-plegia
Hansen (1960) 2,057 spastic patients (78·5% of 2,621 CP patients)	4·3	14·5	41·9	21·0	18·3
				Tri-plegia	
Henderson (1961) 240 CP patients	5·0	12·1	37·0	3·8	19·2
Crothers and Paine (1959) 406 patients	0·4	2·8	40·5	1·9	19·0

TABLE 15. *Incidence by subtypes in the New Jersey Study (1951)*

Subtype	Spastic						Athetoid						Rigidity					
	Boys	*%*	*Girls*	*%*	*Total*	*%*	*Boys*	*%*	*Girls*	*%*	*Total*	*%*	*Boys*	*%*	*Girls*	*%*	*Total*	*%*
Quadriplegia	99	26·4	61	22·5	160	24·8	172	89·5	120	85·1	292	87·6	51	53·1	37	45·6	88	49·7
Triplegia	32	8·8	23	8·1	55	8·5	1	0·5	1	0·7	2	0·6	2	2·0	5	6·1	7	3·9
R. hemiplegia	94	25·1	63	23·2	157	24·3	8	4·1	12	8·5	20	6·0	26	27·0	17	20·9	43	24·2
L. hemiplegia	82	21·9	60	22·1	142	21·8	8	4·1	7	4·9	15	4·5	15	15·6	15	18·5	30	16·9
Paraplegia	63	16·8	61	22·1	124	19·2	2	1·0	1	0·7	3	0·9	2	2·0	7	8·6	9	5·0
Monoplegia	4	0·1	3	1·1	7	0·5	1	0·5			1	0·4						
Totals	374		271		645		192		141		333		96		81		177	

TABLE 16

Neurological syndrome	Isle of Wight Survey (%)	Dundee Survey (%)	Edinburgh Survey (%)
Hemiplegia	37·1	37·5	36·1
Diplegia	34·3	41·2	43·7
Bilateral hemiplegia	22·9	1·3	3·9
Dyskinesia	2·9	8·4	8·2
Ataxia	2·9	1·7	7·2
Other	0·0	10·0	1·0

It seems to the writers that this implies a continuum of motor disturbance, rather than clearly defined types. The concept of a continuum does offer a partial explanation for the apparent discrepancies between the incidence of each class quoted by different workers in the tables, and the different subclasses used.

There is general agreement in the major studies that hemiplegias comprise one-third of all cerebral palsies (Perlstein, 1957). Rutter, Graham and Yule (1970) add that half are either diplegic or quadriplegic and that dyskinesia and ataxia are relatively rare. Reynell (Mittler, 1970) writes that athetosis is usually estimated at not more than 10 per cent of the total cerebral palsied population.

III. CLASSIFICATION ACCORDING TO TIME OF ONSET (ANTE-NATAL, NATAL OR POST-NATAL)

One would expect this to be an important area of study. Several workers, including Wallin (1949) and Wyllie (1951), have suggested that ante-natally acquired cerebral palsy is more likely to be associated with general mental defect than natally or post-natally acquired cerebral palsy. There seems to be little work reported on this subject, possibly because of the difficulty of distinguishing between ante-natal, natal, or early post-natal cerebral palsy. Perlstein (1957) states that only 10 per cent of cerebral palsy is post-natally acquired, while nearly one-third of spastic hemiplegia is postnatal in origin. Wyllie (1951) gives a clear account of this problem. Rutter, Graham and Yule found only four cases of post-natally acquired hemiplegia in their small sample.

IV. CLASSIFICATION ACCORDING TO DEGREE OF INVOLVEMENT

Schonell (1956) classifies her sample of 340 cerebral palsied children as slightly handicapped, 87 (25 per cent); moderately handicapped, 148 (44 per cent); severely handicapped, 85 (25 per cent); very severely handicapped, 20 (6 per cent). Her descriptions of each category appear to involve subjective judgments of the severity of the total handicap for each child, involving sensory as well as motor dysfunction. Mitchell (Henderson, 1961) classified his sample of 227 patients under the age of 21 as: mildly handicapped, 97 (42·7 per cent); moderately handicapped, 79 (34·8 per cent); and severely handicapped, 51 (22·5 per cent). Mitchell makes the point that the large number of mildly handicapped cases in his series is mainly due to the fact that the majority of cases of hemiplegia, the commonest form of cerebral palsy, fall into this category. Hansen (1960) classifies his patients in terms of six grades relating to motor disability, but these grades are also defined in terms of self-help – approximately 64 per cent of his sample were able to look after themselves with regard to daily living functions. What seems to emerge from these classifications is the need to assess total handicap in relation to placement.

Rutter, Graham and Yule assessed degree of handicap in terms of the extent to which the child's disability interfered with his daily life. They write that attention was accordingly confined to the actual restriction of activities, regardless of whether this seemed to be due to mental, physical or motivational factors. Significantly for the mentally handicapped they found that motivational factors seemed to play only a very minor part in the handicap, but intellectual factors were more important, and that in most cases where there was a severe mental defect there was also a severe physical defect. They describe their scale in detail; in their emphasis on daily living their scale resembles that of Hansen. Some of their findings were, firstly, that all the children excluded from school by reason of mental subnormality (in their small samples) were severely physically handicapped, whereas only one in eight (12 per cent) of those attending schools were severely physically handicapped. Secondly, they found that the proportion of severely handicapped children in their series (37 per cent) was similar to that reported by Ingram, but higher than that found by Mitchell. By severe physical handicap they meant that substantial help was needed with daily activities such as dressing, undressing, washing, bathing and feeding. The rating was also applicable where the child required special transport or was unable to go out unaccompanied. They do not relate severity of physical handicap to mild subnormality or placement in school for the educationally subnormal.

The impression left by this attempt to consider methods of classifying the cerebral palsied is one of some confusion, but the situation is becoming clearer as more information is added by further surveys of total populations by Hansen, Henderson and Ingram, studies of specific aspects by Wedell and Abercrombie, and follow-up studies by Crothers and Paine and Gardner (1970).

Aetiology

Wyllie (1951) writes: 'Infantile cerebral palsy covers a wide variety of clinical forms and underlying them a far greater number of aetiological factors. There is no uniformity of gross anatomy of the brain or in histology for the different clinical types. The infantile brain in its response to abnormal growth has a limited range of expression.'

He adds that a survey of causes contributing to infantile cerebral palsy must include pre-natal, natal and post-natal factors. He also makes the point that it is difficult, in some cases, to distinguish between natal and post-natal causation in early infancy. 'Most activities of the new born infant depend on reflex pathways in the brain-stem and spinal cord and signs of pyramidal involvement of a higher level take a variable time to appear' (1951, p. 151).

In this short chapter it is only possible to mention the views and findings mainly of the psychologists on this subject. Hansen (1960) and Mitchell (Henderson, 1961) give full and interesting analyses of the aetiological factors found in their samples.

Sarason (1949) commented on the tendency to discount factors of birth as primary in the causation of cerebral palsy, 'one reason being the increasing caution with which birth histories are evaluated'. He goes on to say that in many cases of cerebral palsy, where the motor defect is very severe, there have been no indications of a difficult or complicated birth, also 'the anatomical defects and malformations found in many cases of cerebral palsy are not of the type that one would expect as a result of birth injuries. Difficult labour may be the result of malformation rather than vice versa.' Sarason stated that studies of cerebral palsy among the mentally deficient had shown that:

1. the average age of the mother at birth of the cerebral palsied child was significantly greater than that found in the general population;
2. there was no significant difference between the percentage of affected children who were first-born and the percentage expected on the basis of chance selection;
3. in families of cerebral palsied children where there was more than one child, there was a slight tendency for another sibling to have a similar condition;
4. the incidence of mental subnormality among the non-affected siblings seemed to be greater than in the general population;
5. cerebral palsy cases in which a definite history compatible with the diagnosis of birth trauma was present comprised approximately 10 per cent of institutionalized cerebral palsy cases.

It is important to note that these findings apply to mentally defective cerebral palsies and might not be found in a study of cerebral palsy amongst the non-defective.

Dunsdon (1952) found that 66 per cent of 327 cerebral palsied children were first-born. She gives the birth order of the cerebral palsied types as follows:

	First pregnancy
Athetoid	75%
Spastic	64%
Others	64%

It has been argued that first pregnancies tend to be associated more often than succeeding ones with difficult labour and therefore possible birth injury. It seems interesting that although 66 per cent of Dunsdon's group were first-born, in only 14 per cent was there a history of birth injury. A possible difficulty in estimating the incidence of birth injuries may be that we have no reliable or valid measures, and slight cases may be missed. A continuum theory of brain damage implies that all brains are more or less damaged.

Other abnormal features associated with the birth of 190 cerebral palsied children and noted by Dunsdon are:

Prematurity	39%
Instrumental delivery	30%
Birth injury	14%
Jaundice	19%
Asphyxia	40%
Convulsions	20%

Sarason sums up the present position:

> ... it has been recognized that no single aetiological factor accounts for all cases of cerebral palsy. ... If one were to consider only those cases which all workers consider not to be due to birth injury, he would have to conclude, on the basis of the available evidence, that the aetiological factors are unknown.

On the aetiology of athetosis Asher and Schonell (1950) found that in their series of 400 cases of cerebral palsy among children the evidence suggested that athetosis is usually the result of birth injury, asphyxia or neonatal jaundice. Wyllie (1951) also believes that the commonest type of athetosis is due to a venous vascular lesion, caused by asphyxia or anoxia at birth and affecting the basal ganglia. 'Uncomplicated cases of athetosis with extra pyramidal rigidity occasionally occur among cerebral palsies and may be due to rhesus incompatibility, rare survivors of kernicterus.' Cruickshank and Raus (1955) after discussing the 1951 New Jersey Survey, say 'the genetic component appears to be another variable in the galaxy of problems related to cerebral palsy'.

INTELLIGENCE AND CEREBRAL PALSY

Sarason (1949) summarizes the earlier American studies as follows:

> In a study of 50 cases, Smith (1926) found 22 per cent normal, 16 per cent morons, 40 per cent imbeciles and 22 per cent idiots. Schroeder (1929) reported that 66 per cent of 146 children classified as cerebral palsied were mentally retarded. ... McIntire (1938) reported that 26 per cent of his series of 143 cases were mentally defective.

There is considerable variation in the incidence of mental deficiency reported in these studies. Greater reliance can perhaps be placed on the following figures from more comprehensive and recent surveys. It should be noted that in the 1951 New Jersey Survey (Table 17) 15 per cent of the total group were found to be untestable; also that Hansen (1960) based his classification of intelligence on 'a general evaluation, in which intelligence measurements have been of assistance in only a minor number of cases'.

These studies agree in indicating that approximately 48 per cent of cerebral palsied children, who are testable, have IQs below 70. This finding is in line with the conclusions of Bice and Cruickshank (1955) in their detailed comparison of the major American and English surveys.

The two facts that emerge are: (1) that amongst cerebral palsied children and adults, an unduly high proportion are mentally defective on intelligence tests,

TABLE 17. *IQ distribution of children with cerebral palsy* (%)

IQ	Rutter, Graham and Yule (1970)	Ingram (1955)	Cock-burn (1961)	Dunsdon (1952)	Floyer (1955)	Asher and Schonell (1950)	Holeran (1955)	Herlitz and Redin (1955)
100 or more	24	18 ⎫	26	9	10 ⎫	25 ⎫	25 ⎫	
85–99	9	14 ⎭		15	14 ⎭			43
70–84	12	24	25	17	29	28	36 ⎭	
50/55–69	18	22	21	24	17	24	21	19
Below 50/55	36	22	27	35	29	23	18	38

New Jersey (Cruickshank and Raus, 1955): 1,000 cases tested in 1951.

IQ	0–49	50–69	70–89	90–109	110–129	130 and above
%	28·4	20·4	22·7	21·6	5·3	1·6

Denmark (Hansen, 1960): classification of 2,621 patients according to intelligence

Estimated normally intelligent	47·7%
Presumably retarded (observation for mental retardation)	9·4%
Retarded, hardly mentally defective	11·0%
Feeble-minded	9·8%
Imbecile	10·3%
Idiots	7·0%
Classification as to intelligence uncertain	4·8%

usually the Binet in the case of children; and (2) that about 40–50 per cent of cerebral palsy patients are not mentally defective. This could suggest that in relation to general intelligence the cerebral palsied are a fairly heterogeneous group. Mental deficiency may occur more frequently among the cerebral palsied than among the normal population because cerebral palsy tends to be associated with damage to, or maldevelopment of, other parts of the brain than the motor cortex.

Hansen's is the only comprehensive survey in which the severely subnormal patients are classified as idiots or imbeciles.

INCIDENCE OF MENTAL SUBNORMALITY AND TYPES OF CEREBRAL PALSY

It has been stated by several authors that, in athetosis, intelligence is relatively unaffected because the damage is to the basal ganglia and is therefore subcortical. This seems to have been a fairly widely held view in America. However, in England, Schonell (1956) and in America, Hopkins, Bice and Colton (1954) in their 1951 New Jersey Survey found there was no difference between the mean IQs of athetoids and spastics. Dunsdon supports this finding. Among 104 athetoid children, she found that 49·9 per cent had IQs below 70. The more recent surveys in Denmark and Eastern Scotland are in line with this.

Schonell (1956) gives the following useful table (18) of the means and standard deviations of the estimated IQs of 340 children grouped according to the form of cerebral palsy.

TABLE 18. *IQs according to type of cerebral palsy*

Type	Spastic	Athetoid	Ataxic	Mixed
Mean IQ	67·9	67·6	62·3	62·4
SD	27·7	25·5	19·3	21·5
N	277	41	4	18
Not yet assessable	9	4	–	1

Cockburn (*1961*) Eastern Scotland	All spastics	Spastic tetra-plegias	Spastic except tetra-plegias	Athetoids
Number	177	51	126	19
Average IQ	66·7	35·4	78·9	77·4

Schonell's table suggests that in terms of general intelligence as measured by the Binet, there is no significant difference between the two main forms of cerebral palsy. The mean IQ for all types seems to be significantly lower than for the normal population. Cockburn's table is of interest because it illustrates a point, emphasized by the tables which follow. She writes 'the most clear cut finding is that the spastic tetraplegics who were the most extensively handicapped among the spastics, tended to be of lower intelligence than any other subgroup of the cerebral palsied'.

Tables 19 and 20 also indicate a correlation between the extent of handicap and mental subnormality. The average IQ of all spastics may be the same as the average IQ of all athetoids in recent surveys because, as Hansen points out, the hemiplegics comprise one-third of the spastic group. In his sample 60·8 per cent

TABLE 19. *Intelligence and extent of handicap (number of limbs involved) (from Schonell, 1956)**

	L. Hemi-plegia	R. Hemi-plegia	Para-plegia	Quadri-plegia
Mean IQ	77·9	76·8	74·3	50·2
SD	20·1	26·0	23·6	27·6
N	41	57	85	80
Not yet assessable	1	2	2	4

* This table is confined to pure spastics.

TABLE 20. *Per cent incidence (these are likely to be severely handicapped) (from Dunsdon, 1952, Special School applicants)*

	IQ under 55	IQ 55–69	IQ 70–84	IQ 85–99	IQ 100–114	IQ 115–129	IQ 130 plus
Quadriplegia	30·3	10·7	9·7	5·6	1·5	1·3	0·6
						Total 59·6	
Hemiplegia	3·9	4·1	3·4	1·5	0·6	0·2	0·0
						Total 13·7	
Paraplegia	10·0	6·2	4·1	4·3	1·5	0·4	0·2
						Total 26·7	
All	44·2	21·0	17·1	11·4	3·6	1·9	0·8
						Total 100	

of the hemiplegics were normally intelligent. In their Isle of Wight sample, Rutter, Graham and Yule found that all those children with bilateral hemiplegia had IQs of less than 55.

CEREBRAL DOMINANCE AND IQ

Assuming that the left hemisphere is the dominant one for most people, it has been hypothesized by several workers that right (R) hemiplegics and quadriplegics would tend to be less intelligent than left (L) hemiplegics. McIntire's (1947) findings in the New Jersey Survey, 1938, tend to support this hypothesis. From 800 cases he selected 287 who fulfilled the following conditions: (1) spastic hemiplegics or quadriplegics, (2) the result of cerebral lesion, (3) mental diagnosis being available. This resulted in a group of 97 (R) hemiplegics and

77 (L) hemiplegics. Of the former, 70 per cent, and of the latter 29 per cent, were mentally defective. The difference between the (L) and (R) types seems significant but they may have been very severely handicapped spastics, thus not truly representative of the spastic population. In the 1951 New Jersey Survey, the mean IQ of the (R) hemiplegics was significantly lower than that of the (L) hemiplegics. However, numbers were small. Cruickshank and Raus (1955) and Crothers and Paine (1959) found that patients with (L) hemiplegia were slightly more intelligent than patients with (R) hemiplegia.

Conflicting evidence comes from Perlstein (1957), Woods (1963) and Schonell (1956). Perlstein from his study of 334 infantile spastic hemiplegics found that the laterality of involvement did not seem of much significance in relation to intelligence. He says himself that his sample was not representative of all spastics. Schonell's figures (see Table 19) support Perlstein's findings. Woods comments that from her figures the (L) hemiplegics tend to show a lower IQ rating than the (R) hemiplegics.

It does not seem possible to draw any firm conclusions from these studies, and this is an area in which further work is needed.

INCIDENCE OF CEREBRAL PALSY AMONGST MENTAL DEFECTIVES

Although there appears to be a widespread belief that many of the cerebral palsied are wrongfully detained in mental deficiency institutions, there seems little, if any, published evidence to support this. Remarkably little research seems to have been undertaken on the incidence of cerebral palsy among defectives. Kirman (1960) writes:

> The proportion of cerebral palsied cases in mental deficiency institutions will be less than 9·5 per cent of the whole, or some 6,000 in England and Wales – even less information is available about mental defectives under supervision and/or in hospital. It may be that there are some 7,000 further cases of cerebral palsy among mental defectives in the community, making a total of 13,000. Further elucidation is very necessary as this estimate is little better than guesswork.

In their chapter on the physically handicapped child, Chapter 10 in *Mental Deficiency*, Hilliard and Kirman (1957) emphasize the frequent association between mental and physical handicap. They write 'the same anatomical abnormality of the brain which gives rise to mental defect may also produce cerebral palsy or epilepsy, two conditions which frequently complicate mental deficiency'. They stress the need to diagnose physical handicap in cases of mental defect only on the evidence of clearcut physical handicap, because of the 'special educational and occupational problems which it implies'. It is now recognized that patients with mental and physical handicap represent a long-term hard-core problem on the borderland between several branches of medicine, education and social welfare. Hilliard and Kirman define the problem in relation to children and mental deficiency by describing three main groups of children:

1. Children in whom the physical defect is the main problem.
2. Trainable imbeciles with double defect.
3. Idiocy associated with other defects.

The first group they describe is wrongly diagnosed as mentally deficient. From the point of view of cerebral palsy it would include: (a) children in whom the physical defect exaggerates the apparent mental defect; (b) children with an undetected sensory defect, such as deafness in athetosis, masking an average intelligence; and (c) cases where the physical handicapping is so widespread that it makes education and training impossible even if intelligence is within the normal range, as in some spastic quadriplegics and athetoids with gross impairment of speech and manual ability. Fortunately modern technological advances are providing new methods of training and communication so that within the past few years the position of the most severely handicapped has become a little brighter.

The second group, the trainable imbeciles, they say is fairly large, and although the presence of a double defect makes training difficult, 'it is sometimes possible to get gratifying results' (cf. Quibell *et al.*, 1961).

In the third group, the idiots, the mental defect is the main problem and the physical defect may merely complicate the nursing problem.

Hilliard and Kirman also make the important point that the larger group of educationally subnormal children tend to have more physical defects than normal children, and in relation to cerebral palsy this is confirmed by all the major surveys of intelligence. This is of great importance because it does seem that it is now being increasingly recognized that all methods of treatment have a useful part to play in the habilitation of educationally subnormal and imbecile children with cerebral palsy.

Of the cerebral palsied patients in a mental deficiency hospital for children, Crome (Chapter 5 in Hilliard and Kirman, 1957) writes:

experience at the Fountain Hospital suggests that in the majority of patients with cerebral palsy and mental deficiency, birth injury can be excluded by scrutiny of the history and the morphological findings.

It is sometimes possible to relate the type of palsy to the distribution of lesions. Thus hemiplegia may be associated with hemiatrophy, lobar atrophy, porencephaly or microgyria in the contralateral cerebral hemisphere. But the second hemisphere is seldom entirely spared in mental defectives. Usually it is also affected by similar, albeit slighter changes.

This is in line with the general finding in the surveys that quadriplegics tend to be the most severely mentally handicapped group amongst the cerebral palsied.

Hilliard and Kirman (1957, Chapter 10) give the following useful table showing the incidence of ˙cerebral palsy at the Fountain Hospital recorded over a five-year period.

Form of palsy	Total No.	%	With epilepsy No.	%
Spastic diplegia	103	45	51	50
Hemiplegia	35	15	18	17
Athetosis	19	8	4	4
Ataxia	5	2	0	0
Unclassified	66	29	30	29
Total	228		103	

From this table it appears again that spastic diplegia is the commonest form of cerebral palsy amongst mental defectives.

Doll (1933) considered that 6 to 10 per cent of the mentally defective patients at Vineland had motor handicaps due to birth lesions. Kirman's (1956) figures for the Fountain Hospital in 1955 were 23 per cent cerebral palsied. The apparent difference between these percentages may be due to differences in the intelligence level of patients, and in the implied diagnosis of cerebral palsy. Henderson (1961) points out the difficulties which may arise in connection with cerebral palsy and mental deficiency. He writes:

no fewer than 61 of the 301 children (20 per cent) regarded as cases of cerebral palsy who were examined by the paediatrician were found not to have the condition. Most of these children had uncomplicated mental deficiency, their characteristic clumsiness being mistaken for cerebral palsy. No doubt the knowledge that the mentally normal child with cerebral palsy is often wrongly considered to be mentally defective and that mental deficiency is often associated with cerebral palsy had added to the confusion.

The Vineland training school probably contained a larger proportion of high-grade defectives than the Fountain, which was mainly a hospital for ineducable severely subnormal children. Kirman writes 'in most cases the cerebral lesion is probably more gross and widespread than in those children with cerebral palsy who attend school'. Perhaps as one goes down the scale of intelligence, brain damage becomes more diffuse and widespread and tends to be associated with general developmental anomalies, not relatively clear-cut lesions. This would seem to be supported by the general finding that spastic tetraplegics, where the lesion is presumably widespread, tend on the average to be of lower intelligence than other cerebral palsied patients.

Sarason (1953) quoted McIntire's (1938) figures of the incidence of the different types. McIntire's findings for defectives with cerebral palsy were: 29 per cent borderline, 27 per cent moron, 22 per cent imbecile, and 21 per cent idiot (to the nearest per cent). There is a need for an up-to-date detailed study of mentally defective patients with cerebral palsy. Cockburn found of 59 mentally handicapped children of school age 21 were uneducable, 11 were trainable, and 27 were educable.

Associated defects

Speech defects and cerebral palsy

Dunsdon (1952) gives the following table (21) of the frequency of articulatory defects amongst 500 cerebral palsied children aged $4\frac{1}{2}$ to 14 years.

TABLE 21. *Articulatory defects in cerebral palsied children*

Type	No.	Speech defects (%)	No speech (%)	Development delay (%)
Athetoid	83	71	14	48
Ataxic	35	86	20	60
Quadriplegic	185	71	22	42
L. Hemiplegic	30	37	3	30
R. Hemiplegic	34	91	29	56
Paraplegic	133	39	6	26

From these figures there appear to be significantly more speech anomalies amongst the (R) than the (L) hemiplegics. On the question of delayed speech Perlstein's findings (1957) appear to be different. Perlstein found that in his sample the (L) hemiplegics walked and talked slightly earlier than the (R) hemiplegics but the difference was not statistically reliable. Dunsdon attributes the greater frequency of speech anomalies amongst (R) hemiplegics to the localization of the speech areas mainly in the (L) hemisphere, the one damaged in (R) hemiplegia. It is relevant that Goodglass and Quadfasel (1954), in a review of the literature on language laterality, suggest that cerebral dominance for speech is not fully established in children up to the age of 9 years. Before this age a shift in laterality can take place, according to their evidence. Woods (1957) gives an interesting table of hearing and speech defects in her sample, but she was not concerned with this problem; like Dunsdon she found that athetoids and quadriplegics showed a high frequency of speech defects. In this table Woods also gives the frequency of hearing defects, and this shows that while 30 out of 33 athetoids had speech defects, 12 had hearing defects.

The speech defects shown by the cerebral palsied obviously vary in severity, type and aetiology. Some may be due to the motor dysfunction itself, some may be central in origin associated with damage involving the speech areas, some may be associated with hearing loss. It should be noted that of 42 patients without speech in Cockburn's sample of 223, 33 had IQs below 50. This relationship is confirmed by Ingram's (1964) findings.

The practical implications of the findings are that a large proportion of the cerebral palsied may require speech therapy and, probably, specially adapted teaching methods. This is especially true for the severely subnormal.

VISUAL DEFECTS

Dunsdon found that of 575 children nearly one-third had peripheral visual defects such as of refraction and of muscle control. In the 1951 New Jersey Survey 21·4 per cent of 1,300 cases had visual defects. Douglas (Henderson, 1961, Chapter 12) gives a full account of the ophthalmological aspects of the Dundee Survey. In relation to mental deficiency and cerebral palsy it is significant that he writes 'severe visual, physical and mental handicaps are frequently found in association'. Abercrombie (1960) has studied eye movements in relation to perception in a group of cerebral palsied children. These more detailed studies, by describing particular concomitant disabilities, should lead to more effective treatment. (See also section on visuo-spatial and visuo-motor defects.)

HEARING DISABILITIES

Mowat (Henderson, 1961, Chapter 13) reviews the literature on hearing disabilities and cerebral palsy, and gives a detailed analysis of hearing in the Dundee (Eastern Scotland) sample. He also writes 'the results suggest that the incidence of deafness, but not necessarily the severity, varies directly with the degree of physical and mental handicap'. He believes the true incidence of deafness is probably between 20 per cent and 25 per cent.

EPILEPSY

Dunsdon found that 14 per cent of 796 children with cerebral palsy had a history of convulsions or seizures, the greatest incidence being amongst children of low IQ. Kirman (1956), in his study of certified defective children, reports a tendency for cases of cerebral palsy with epilepsy to be less intelligent than those without epilepsy. He found that in 265 cases of epilepsy 37 per cent had cerebral palsy. Floyer (1955), in her Liverpool Survey, found that 29 per cent of children with cerebral palsy had a history of one or more seizures. In the 1951 New Jersey Survey 29·2 per cent had a history of seizures. Woods (1957, Chapter XVI) gives an interesting table showing the incidence of fits in the different types of cerebral palsy in her Bristol sample of children. The percentage incidence of fits in her whole sample was 38 per cent.

MANUAL DEFECTS

Manual ability is of prime importance in relation to all aspects of life, but it appears to have been somewhat neglected in the major surveys. There may be two reasons for this: (a) it is too obvious; (b) up to now the main interest has been in children of school age rather than in adult patients: the vast majority of cerebral palsied patients have at least one hand which is normal enough to make them socially and educationally adequate as children. However, in adult life, particularly in employment, it may be that normal hand ability is more necessary, and that even a slight disability is an obstacle to full adult independence. Cockburn has studied this aspect and her findings are of considerable interest.

1. In her sample of 223 patients, manual defects were more common than speech defects and only 32 were rated as having normal hands.
2. Of the patients 179, or 80 per cent, had one hand at least that was normal or only slightly affected (they could use a pencil).
3. When severe speech and manual defects occurred together, gross mental deficiency was frequently present too.

VISUO-SPATIAL AND VISUO-MOTOR DEFECTS

It has been widely recognized that cerebral palsied children tend to suffer from a variety of defects of visual perception apart from the peripheral sensory ones already mentioned. This is to be expected since the brain pathology giving rise to the motor defect will not necessarily be confined to these areas, and other functions may be affected. Further visuo-perceptual difficulties could arise either as a result of damaged central mechanisms or of the interaction between central and peripheral factors. The defects observed may vary, therefore, in different individuals and appear on different types of task. Holt and Reynell (1966) have outlined some of the situations in which deficits occur and distinguished between disorders of visual perception, visuo-spatial perception, visuo-motor action and body image disturbances which may be linked with the other types. They point out that where there are visuo-perceptual difficulties, deficits will usually be observed on visuo-motor tasks, but the reverse is not necessarily true as Ball and Wilsoncroft (1967) were able to show, using specially selected tests.

There have been various studies in recent years designed to investigate these disorders. Abercrombie (1964) provided a useful review and also provided summaries of work done up to that time. Tasks frequently used in these investigations involve the matching of shapes and figures or copying them in such a way as to minimize the purely motor aspect of the task (e.g. Wedell, 1960). Constructional tasks such as formboards and block designs have also been used as well as standard tests involving aspects of visual perception (e.g. Neilsen, 1966). There is not always a close relationship between performance on different types of task confirming that the defects are not unitary.

Taylor (1959) compared children with different types of brain lesions on various perceptual motor tasks and showed that those with extrapyramidal lesions tended not to have difficulty with them unlike the other groups, particularly those with spastic cerebral palsy. Most workers have found that spastics tend to have more difficulty than athetoids, for example Dunsdon (1952), Cruickshank, Bice and Wallen (1957) and Wedell (1960), and this is probably a function of the part of the brain affected in the two groups. Spastic children with left-sided motor handicap are often found to have more of these visuo-perceptual defects than those with right-sided handicaps, in line with the general finding that adults with non-dominant brain lesions have more difficulty with a number of perceptual tasks. In Wedell's 1960 study, for example, he compared four groups of cerebral palsied children and one of normal controls matched for age and IQ and showed that spastics with bilateral or left-sided motor handicaps did worse on his tasks than those with right hemiplegia. Visuo-motor defects are generally found to be more frequent in subjects of lower intelligence but are not always related to severity of handicap (Neilsen, 1966). This last finding may depend on the limbs involved to some extent (cf. Luszki, 1966).

The possibility of sex differences in this area is an interesting question which has largely been ignored. In normal subjects sex differences in favour of males have been widely demonstrated on a number of tasks involving spatial ability (Sherman, 1967). There is a suggestion from the work of Floyer that this may be an important variable in cerebral palsied groups as well. She matched her subjects on sex as well as age and IQ and found that the girls made significantly worse performances than controls while in the boys the difference was less marked.

Other factors which may have an influence on the occurrence of visuo-motor disorders have been discussed by Abercrombie (1968). She stresses the possibility that the motor disorder in cerebral palsy may interfere with the development of visuo-spatial perception and also that a conflict of attention to stimuli in different sensory modalities, i.e. visual and somaesthetic, may be an important factor.

Emotional factors can also have an important influence as Williams (1960) found in a study of the effect of parental attitudes on children's performance. Neilsen (1966) found no relation between disorders of visuo-motor functioning and of personality in her sample, however.

The nature of the disorders observed is another question which has been considered, specifically whether the behaviour is the result of a delay in normal development or is different from that observed at any stage in normal children. Wedell's (1961) follow-up study of thirty-six children showed that they all improved in their performance on perceptuo-motor tasks after $2\frac{1}{2}$ years, providing some support for the developmental delay viewpoint. Further work by Wedell (1964) and a study by Nelson (1962) indicated that developmental aspects may be more important on some tasks than others, suggesting that this is not a sufficient explanation. Schalling and Cronholm's (1968) data on adults indicates that on their tasks at least the deficit is still present, and the work of Ounsted, Annett and Lee (1961), providing evidence that in general hemiplegic children acquired visuo-spatial ability in preference to other abilities, also seems to cast doubt on a purely developmental theory. See Abercrombie (1964) for further discussion of this question.

The occurrence of visuo-motor defects in cerebral palsied children is an important area for study because of its practical relevance to education. These children frequently have problems in learning to read and write, for example, and information which gives rise to appropriate teaching methods is of obvious value. The question of interference with treatment has also been stressed in the past but Reynell (1963) holds that the importance of this has been exaggerated.

OTHER SENSORY DEFECTS

Some disabilities result from injury to the sensory cortex. Some hemiplegics, for example, show disturbance of sensation. Tizard *et al.* (1954) studied impairment of sensation and visual defects in 106 children with hemiplegia. Impairment of sensation was found in 50 per cent of the cases, both those with hemiplegia, presumably acquired at birth, and among those with brain injury, usually acquired later in childhood. The incidence of hemianopia was slightly less than 25 per cent and hemianopia without sensory deficit was found to be very rare. The types of sensation most frequently affected were the cortically localized discriminatory faculties. The usual types of sensation tested were touch, pain, temperature, position sense, passive motion, vibration, location sense, sharp-dull discrimination, two-point discrimination, and stereognosis. In his summary, Tizard says that sensory impairment is in some instances the major reason for disuse of the arm affected with hemiplegia; if present, it is important in constituting a limiting factor for the results that may be expected from physical therapy, apparatus or orthopaedic surgery. Woods (1963) studied sensory defects in all the cases in her series of 301 children with cerebral palsy, except those who were too young or too backward to cooperate in testing. Sensory loss was detected in 47 cases and she writes that there was also evidence of a loss of body image and a finger agnosia. She considers that the sensory defects were cortical in nature.

To sum up this section, undoubtedly there is a tendency for children with cerebral palsy to have more, and a wider variety of concomitant defects than one would expect to find in the general population. Although the cerebral palsied are not a homogeneous group we are beginning to see how they can usefully be grouped for educational purposes. For example, present evidence suggests that the mentally retarded will be the most severely physically handicapped. Cockburn (1961) sums up the present position; with regard to children with cerebral palsy, she writes: 'within the group (the Dundee sample) the wide range of intelligence and of disability means that provision must be diverse and that the cerebral palsied form not one but several educational groups. On the basis of their educational needs, many can be classified with other broad categories recognized for educational purposes'. She gives the following table showing the educational classification of 133 children of school age in her sample.

Rutter, Graham and Yule (1970) found in their sample that half the

TABLE 22. *Educational classification (from Cockburn, 1961)*

1	2	3	4	5	6	7	8
	Mentally handicapped			Blind	Deaf	Remainder	Total
	Imbecile	Trainable	Educable				
Number	21	11	27	3	1	70	133

hemiplegic children attended ordinary school and none of them came under the mental subnormality services – no child with bilateral hemiplegia was at ordinary school, one was at a school for spastics and seven came under the care of the subnormality services. They point out that, although their total sample of cerebral palsied children was small, their findings are in close agreement with the other major English surveys.

From the point of view of mental deficiency, cerebral palsied patients will tend to be severely handicapped in other ways as well.

The assessment of intellectual functioning

There are two main points to be considered in discussing the assessment of general intelligence in the cerebral palsied. The first involves the usefulness of the assessment. Sarason (1953) quoted Strother (1945):

> The parent, the doctor or the teacher is interested in knowing the child's intelligence, not to satisfy idle curiosity, but to help them determine what to do for the child. The specific questions they have in mind are questions such as: Is the child able to profit from surgery or physiotherapy? Can he be taught to talk? Can he profit from education? Is he ready to enter school? . . . What special materials or methods of instruction does he need?

In cases of severe and multiple handicap particularly, follow-up studies of different educational and treatment methods are required to provide information on which to base predictions. Some results are already available. Quibell, Stephen and Whatley (1961), for example, have shown that some severely handicapped cerebral palsied children with IQs 45–69 respond to surgery and/ or physiotherapy. Pollock and Stark (1969) found that intelligence was one of the most important factors predicting the employability of a group of school leavers, none of those with IQs below 70 being in employment. Bowley (1967) has reported preliminary findings on the school placements and progress of a group of children who attended a nursery centre. With regard to the educability of the most severely physically handicapped children, however, Gardner and Johnson (1964) have stressed the need for long-term assessment before a final decision is made.

The second point at issue is the extent to which the cerebral palsied can be validly assessed using formal tests of intelligence standardized on children and adults without cerebral palsy. This involves the reliability of the tests under these circumstances and the extent to which the motor and in many cases sensory handicaps interfere with the assessment of the individual's 'intelligence' as far as this is a distinct phenomenon unaffected by his limited or distorted experience. Studies of the reliability on retesting of IQ results for cerebral palsied children have been reviewed by Neilsen (1966, 1968). She concluded that in 65 to 75 per cent of cases there was fairly good agreement, less than 10 points difference in IQ, which compares well with findings for normal children. This indicates that in a majority of cases assessments can be made using standard tests which are reliable enough to allow predictions to be made. Larger discrepancies are reported to occur more often, as would be expected, with younger children and among those with associated sensory handicaps and speech disorders, and also for those in the low normal range of intelligence (IQs 70–90). This last finding has received further confirmation in a fourteen-year follow-up study by Klapper and Birch (1967) who discuss possible reasons and emphasize the educational implications.

Beyond the reliability of the tests, their validity for the assessment of the intelligence of the cerebral palsied has not received very much attention. Studies which have used a battery of tests for assessment have chosen these to cover a wide range of abilities rather than to determine the agreement between tests purporting to measure general intelligence. The same tests have frequently not been used for the whole sample but one or more chosen as being the most appropriate for each subject. In the absence of data on the correlations between results on different tests, information on validity must be sought from other sources such as the concurrent agreement with ratings by teachers and others (cf. Pearson, 1969) or accuracy of prediction of certain eventualities on follow-up. The examples of follow-up studies already mentioned are a beginning in the right direction, but much more needs to be done. An alternative approach would be in identifying the factors that interfere with the validity of a particular test for these children, e.g. in cases with visuo-spatial deficits or lack of manual dexterity. These particular factors should be relatively easy to assess but others such as lack of experience would be less so, whether this is in the broad sense of restriction of environment or more specifically as a lack of sensori-motor experience resulting from manual handicaps. Reynell (1970) has pointed out that the comparison of children with physical handicaps with and without involvement of the central nervous system (Abercrombie *et al.*, 1964) implies that this is not such an important factor as has sometimes been supposed. Further studies could provide more detailed information on this question.

The practical difficulties which may be encountered when using formal intelligence tests with the cerebral palsied, especially in cases of more severe or multiple handicap, have received attention from various authors including Dunsdon (1952), Cockburn (1961), Holt and Reynell (1966) and Francis-Williams (1971). The most obvious problem is frequently in the selection of response mode since an individual with motor incoordination or a severe speech defect will be physically incapable of complying with the requirements of many tests. Even where the person appears capable of responding appropriately he may still be handicapped to an unknown extent, particularly on timed tests. There may also be a defect associating hand and eye movements so making finger pointing unreliable, and this may be exacerbated by difficulty in maintaining sitting posture and head position. Cerebral palsied children, especially, tend to tire easily and to have a shorter span of attention than normal so the session may have to be tailored accordingly. Visual and hearing disorders or epilepsy obviously require appropriate modifications of approach.

In the face of these difficulties the temptation to depart from standardized procedure or to make allowances in scoring may be very great but, as Sarason (1953) has pointed out, 'the unfeasibility of adhering to procedures standardized on normal individuals is not obviated by relying on impressions and unsystematic observations as a basis for evaluation'.

PRESENT TESTING PRACTICE

Versions of the Stanford–Binet have frequently been used in assessing the general intelligence of children with cerebral palsy. Many of the major surveys have used this method including Cockburn (1961) and Neilsen (1966) although in some cases certain modifications of varying degrees of formality were found necessary or other tests used in addition. Most of the authors considered that the test was applicable to the majority of their cases, Dunsdon (1952) and Schonell (1956) reporting particularly low incidences of untestable children. One reason for the use of the Stanford–Binet has been that until the advent of the Wechsler scales it was a generally better test than the others available for the assessment of normal children, and in cases of cerebral palsy it could often be administered where hand function was impaired since it is a predominantly verbal test. The most severely physically handicapped individuals, however, tend to have sensory handicaps and to lack certain experiences which limit their performance. Since the content of the test is not homogeneous there is no way of estimating the extent of this.

More recently, for example in the Isle of Wight study, there has been a tendency to use the WISC rather than the Stanford–Binet mainly because of the possibility of separating verbal and non-verbal functioning using scale scores or purer factor scores. Some of the items require motor manipulation, however, and many have time limits, so for children with multiple handicaps similar problems arise.

Various alternative approaches are potentially available especially in the assessment of the individual case where procedures can be selected with that person's handicaps in mind rather than those most applicable to a whole group with many and varied handicaps. It seems likely that no one method will ever be the most suitable for all cases of cerebral palsy. For example, where a child is deaf or blind he will probably need to be assessed using tests appropriate for these groups. Gibbs (1968) considers that it will probably never be possible to produce effective standardizations on a group with such heterogeneous handicaps as the cerebral palsied. Of the tests standardized on normal subjects, untimed performance tests can sometimes be used, and those requiring a minimal response such as pointing or eye pointing (Holt and Reynell, 1966). For example, Raven's Progressive Matrices, the Columbia Mental Maturity Scale or the various picture vocabulary tests offer a high degree of flexibility, although they may tap rather a limited area of function or may be sensitive to visuo-spatial disorders.

Anastasi (1961) considered that a more satisfactory approach than that frequently adopted, of making informal modifications to standard tests, lies in developing procedures which can be applied to individuals with all degrees of handicap. This could either be adaptations of existing tests such as those for the Stanford–Binet by Katz (1958) and Allen and Jefferson (1962), or in the development of new approaches, for example the assessment of Luria's 'verbal regulation of behaviour' in cerebral palsied children (Schubert, 1969; Burland, 1969) or of the formation of object discrimination learning sets (Pearson, 1969). Preliminary findings suggest that some cerebral palsied children who are assessed as mentally retarded using standard tests do better than expected on these tasks and that this bears a relation to their response to education or to their rated intelligence. If these approaches can be adequately validated they appear to hold promise of being useful indices for prediction.

There is a particular lack of test procedures suitable for the assessment of the young pre-school child with physical handicaps. Developmental scales used for normal children have a large motor component and so are not suitable. The Columbia scale already mentioned can be used, but this task is repetitive and tiring for young children and only taps a fairly specific area of functioning. Reynell has developed a useful measure of verbal comprehension and work in other areas of functioning would be valuable.

Related to the lack of methods of assessment of young children there is also little for use with the physically handicapped of subnormal intelligence especially those of very low mental age, although Woodward's (1959) work provides one means of approach. Now that all children are deemed educable this has become a more urgent problem.

Apart from the test procedures used, workers in the field differ in the type of results they prefer to obtain from testing, in the use of qualitative as opposed to general measures which may either be in the form of IQs or of allocation to broader categories, for example Crothers and Paine (1959). This seems to depend largely on the purpose of the assessment. If an index of intelligence is required for predictive purposes or in research to assess the general relationship between intelligence and other factors in the cerebral palsied, a general measure seems most useful. The use of IQs in this connection has the advantage that they are internationally understood and a measure of intelligence alone, whereas categories may vary between different workers and if based on a general rating rather than on the result of a particular test may be affected by educational level and social competence. On the other hand, it may not be possible to obtain a valid IQ in cases of severe handicap and this method may give a misleading impression of the reliability of the assessment. Where a more broadly based assessment of a child's abilities and handicaps is required in order to make specific recommendations for education and treatment more information may be required from the assessment. Reynell (1970) advocates the use of a qualitative assessment of different aspects of functioning while some other workers prefer a more quantitative approach using a variety of suitable procedures. Whatever end-point is preferred most workers emphasize the need for reassessment both to provide confirmation of previous results and to determine progress and new objectives. (See also Chapter 13.)

Where it is not possible to make a precise evaluation of the level of intelligence of a child or adult with very severe handicaps or additional defects using methods available at present, a minimum estimate of this can often be established. This could be useful although interpretations should be made with caution since, as Neilsen (1966, 1968) has pointed out, it may be more dangerous to over-evaluate than to under-evaluate the intelligence of the child because of the possible emotional effects of frequent experience of failure. Furthermore it may for some purposes be useful to have an assessment of what the child is capable of achieving on a test in comparison with normal children even if this does not represent his optimal level of functioning. For example when children cannot respond to standard tests because of communication difficulties they are unlikely to respond to standard educational methods either. The majority of cerebral palsied adults will have to live in and make an adjustment to normal society. Latent intellectual abilities will be of no use in practice if education has not allowed them to be realized. In all cases the assessor needs to be fully aware of all the factors which may be contributing to the child's performance and, while being concerned to avoid placing limits on his opportunities on insufficient grounds, to make use of all information which will provide a reasonable basis for planning the most valuable approaches to teaching and remediation.

Personality and cerebral palsy

Many workers stress the importance of personality factors in the study of cerebral palsy, and research has been directed mainly towards two aspects of this subject, the emotional adjustment of cerebral palsied children and the emotional adjustment of their parents. This last reflects an increased concern with parents' difficulties in the whole field of work with handicapped children. The need to study the relations between parental attitude and children's adjustment is commented on by Sarason (1953) when he points out the need for a large-scale follow-up study and says that in such a study it would be necessary for the psychologist to study the parent-child relationship. The findings of Shere (1954) in a twin study and of Schonell (1956) emphasize this need. Shere's work is an unpublished doctoral dissertation, reviewed by Cruickshank and Raus (1955, p. 118). The pilot study by Williams, referred to earlier, is concerned with one effect of parental attitudes on one group of cerebral palsied children, i.e. that adverse parental attitudes may impede the perceptual development of children with a weakness in this area.

EMOTIONAL ADJUSTMENT AMONG CEREBRAL PALSIED CHILDREN

Dunsdon (1952) assessed the prevalence of instability among children with cerebral palsy, using school reports as a basis. One of the difficulties for psychologists is the lack of standardized objective measures of personality traits; the use of teacher's judgments seems one of the most useful procedures at present. In a special school for cerebral palsied children, Dunsdon found that of sixteen with IQs below 70, only two seemed reasonably stable; of fifty children with IQs over 70 instability was noted in 38 per cent.

Floyer (1955) also considered the frequency of instability. The characteristics of instability which she describes resemble those defined by Straus and Lehtinen (1947) as typical of the 'brain-injured' child. The criticisms made of this concept are also applicable when it is related to cerebral palsy. Floyer found that 42 per cent of a group of 100 cerebral palsied children showed excessive emotionality; excessive emotionality being defined in terms of distractibility, lack of drive, tension, disinhibition, fluctuation in performance, history of fits, and perseveration. However, her procedure is not very clear. She notes that 58 per cent did not show excessive emotionality and had apparently equal environmental strain and additional handicaps. This, she says, suggests innate factors predetermining emotionality, an interesting suggestion which requires further investigation.

In contrast to Floyer, Schonell (1956) quotes Gesell and Amatruda (1947): 'In general temperamental characteristics are the least affected by cerebral injury. The child has an underlying individuality which makes itself manifest.' One would expect, from studies of brain-damaged adults, that the latter part of this statement at least is likely to be true. It does however require to be made more precise. Schonell believed that her research findings tended to confirm Gesell's point of view. Her study of the pupils at a special school for cerebral palsied children revealed that they had no innate limitations on the temperamental side, but 'it was on the acquired side of personality that there was need for help'. This is an important suggestion of the need for research on personality changes in cerebral palsied children. It may be that we are not yet ready to investigate innate and acquired characteristics, it might be more fruitful to carry out a prospective long-term study of adjustment changes in a group of cerebral palsied children. In a small unpublished study, Quibell and Stephen's findings suggest that some dull cerebral palsied boys become more maladjusted at adolescence. In their small series, adjustment did not appear to be related to response to treatment or to family background – but this requires further study; it is merely suggestive of the need for more precise research in this area. Crothers and Paine

(1959) in an interesting chapter on 'Emotional Status in Adolescence and Early Adult Life' describe some cases illustrative of the reactions of cerebral palsied patients and their parents to the changing demands of their environment. Crothers and Paine distinguish two groups of patients, in terms of their manner of dealing with emotional problems. The first group consisted of all the patients who developed difficulties comparable to the 'catastrophic reaction' of Goldstein. They were thought to have lesions in the cerebral hemispheres. The second group, those with extrapyramidal lesions, 'never, as far as we know, had disorders which resembled the catastrophic reaction. They were frequently very much disturbed, often resentful, but they never retreated into helplessness.' Schonell, like Phelps (1948), says that she found the following characteristics were shown by spastics: fearfulness, timidity, dislike of loud noises, fear of falling or being left alone. Athetoids tended to be extroverted, friendly and affectionate. However, these findings appear to be based on impression, rather than systematic enquiry.

Cruickshank and Bice (1955) describe a study in which the Bender Visual Gestalt test (1938) was administered to 216 children with cerebral palsy, to determine whether the use of tests involving different types of perceptual or conceptual abilities could contribute to an understanding of their personality or adjustment problems. This is a promising and interesting line of inquiry, but so far they appear to be still concerned with the exploration of differences in perception between the various diagnostic groups.

EMOTIONAL ADJUSTMENT AMONGST PARENTS OF CHILDREN WITH CEREBRAL PALSY

Boles (1959) and Thurston (1960) have investigated the attitudes and emotional reactions of parents of cerebral palsied children. Boles in New York City compared the parental attitudes of sixty mothers of cerebral palsied children with a control group of sixty mothers of normal unhandicapped children. The two groups were carefully matched and were given a questionnaire to elicit their attitudes in relation to anxiety, guilt, protection, rejection, lack of realism towards their children, marital conflict and social withdrawal. The results were broken down in terms of the age of the child and the religious affiliation of the mother. The only significant differences between the two groups, irrespective of religion or age of child, were that the mothers of the cerebral palsied children were more over-protective and had more marital conflict than the mothers of the normal children. An interesting finding was that the scores for anxiety, measured by the Taylor Manifest Anxiety Scale, were equally high for both groups. Their results also showed that personal, social and cultural factors influenced maternal attitudes and that these changed with the age of the child. This is a careful, well-planned study. Thurston's study is directly relevant to this chapter because he was concerned with the attitudes and emotional reactions of parents of institutionalized cerebral palsied retarded patients. He studied the effects of long-term institutionalization of these children on the parents by sending the Thurston Sentence Completion form to 610 parents and relatives. The Thurston Sentence Completion form explores such areas as:

  (i) personal reactions and concerns;
 (ii) attitudes about comfort and discomfort of patient in the institution;
(iii) reactions of brothers and sisters;
 (iv) reactions of community, friends and neighbours;
  (v) attitudes to institution and its staff;
 (vi) hopes and expectations for the handicapped child;
(vii) general attitudes.

Two hundred and fifty-five, or 41·4 per cent, returned the Sentence Completion form. The results are given in order of frequency for each area and are interesting and suggestive. One of the important findings was that on average considerable emotional upset remained for parents even ten years after birth of child and placement in an institution. This was a retrospective study but it has implications suggesting the need for long-term social work supporting the parents of institutionalized mentally retarded cerebral palsied patients.

Cockburn (1961) studied the homes in her sample of cerebral palsied patients. She writes:

about one quarter of the cases studied came from homes deemed unsatisfactory or unsuitable, though in most cases these homes would have been unsuitable for any child. . . . The handicap of cerebral palsy was better understood in homes of good intellectual status, and in cases where the handicapped person was older, and the handicap more severe, but acceptance of the handicap bore little relation to the intellectual status of the home, or to the age or the degree of handicap, of the cerebral palsied person. . . . One home in five was considered to provide an unstimulating background. . . . Only 48, 31 per cent, of the cerebral palsied over 7 years of age were considered to be persons with interests.

Tizard and Grad (1961), in a sample of sixty adult defectives living at home, found that eight had slight motor impairment and six severe motor impairment. They present an illustrative case of severe motor impairment in an adult defective with spastic diplegia: 'he was heavy and had to be carried to bed, washed, dressed and kept in napkins like a baby.' He could not speak but understood speech. This indicates the total problem which the parents of severely handicapped cerebral palsied defective patients have to deal with.

Hewett (1970) and Rutter, Graham and Yule (1970) have explained the social problems of the families of cerebral palsied children. Hewett studied the problems of a Midlands sample of 180 cerebral palsied children aged 1 to 9 years using the Newsom's normal 4-year-old Nottingham sample as a control group. This is a fascinating study. Rutter *et al.* looked at the impact of the child's disorder on the family in their Isle of Wight study of children with neuro-psychiatric disorders. Both studies made use of parental interviews. One of the most important findings relevant to this chapter, found in both studies, is that families of children with cerebral palsy combined with severe mental handicaps suffered most. Rutter *et al.* noted most disorganization in families of SSN. children and in them 'disorganisation often stemmed from behaviour difficulties'. Surprisingly they found that parents often referred to the need for services which already existed. It seems a sad, but true, comment on the present state of our knowledge of the emotional problems of the cerebral palsied, that Rutter, Graham and Tizard can write: 'In spite of a considerable literature on various aspects of the association between brain dysfunction and child psychiatric disorder, it remains a largely uncharted territory with most of the basic questions still unanswered.' They found in their sample that over a third of the children with neuro-epileptic disorders including cerebral palsy showed psychiatric disorder, a rate five times that found in the general population.

The authors' personal impression after reading the reports on the problems of families of handicapped children is that although the present services available to them may be inadequate, they do exist and could be improved and extended by the application of existing knowledge of their needs and difficulties (see Chapter 24).

Educational attainments of cerebral palsied children

The findings in general indicate that cerebral palsied children tend to be educationally retarded. Dunsdon found that her group of thirty-five special school children were retarded in either one or both of the basic subjects, usually in both. Floyer (1955) studied educational attainment in half her sample. She

TABLE 23. *Reading level and different types of cerebral palsy* $(N = 213)$

Readers	Spastic		Athetoid		Ataxic		Mixed	
Mean reading quotient	88·7		94·5		78·0		89·5	
Standard deviation	15·7		20·46		–		15·0	
	No.	%	No.	%	No.	%	No.	%
Readers	98	56	12	43	1	50	2	25
Non-readers	77	44	16	57	1	50	6	75

found that in 38 per cent reading attainment and mental ages were nearly equivalent, and 62 per cent showed an average retardation of nearly two years. In arithmetic 88 per cent showed retardation relative to mental age of three years on the average. Schonell gives an interesting table of the reading level of 213 children, over 7 years of age, with different forms of cerebral palsy.

In a study of the attainments of left hemiplegics, right hemiplegics, para-plegics and quadriplegics, Schonell found no statistical differences between the means of the reading ages. She also found that in her severely handicapped group 75 per cent were non-readers.

Cockburn (1961) considered the educational attainments of her series in relation to their mental ability. She found that of 153 cases, aged 7 years and over, 41 had no measurable educational attainments but all of these had IQs of 70 and under; the remaining 112, 73 per cent, made some score on reading attainment tests but almost two-thirds, 71, scored below the level expected in relation to their ability. Cockburn says that a very small percentage of the cere-bral palsied children in her series had educational attainments which would have been considered good for the average child, and that better attainment tended to be associated with higher intelligence and milder handicap. More recently Rutter, Graham and Yule (1970) found that 41 per cent of their Isle of Wight sample of cerebral palsied children were at least two years retarded in reading even allowing for their general intelligence.

What emerges is the wide range of attainment in the cerebral palsied group and the high incidence of educational retardation. Like Cockburn, in Schonell's group the highest incidence of non-readers came in the severely handicapped group.

RECOMMENDATIONS ON THE EDUCATION AND TRAINING OF CHILDREN WITH CEREBRAL PALSY

Dunsdon's recommendations are based on her study of the children in a dual-purpose school for the cerebral palsied, and an estimated population of 5,300 school-age children with cerebral palsy in England and Wales. As this estimate was based on a prevalence rate of 1 per 1,000 and the school-age population in 1948, it underestimates the size of the present problem.

Cockburn's findings are based on a recent survey of one region of Scotland but she agrees on several important points with Dunsdon.

Both suggest that the majority of cerebral palsied children can be adequately catered for within the present system, without the provision of separate units for the cerebral palsied, which will only be needed for a relatively small number of children.

Dunsdon estimated that of the 5,300 children of school age, 50 per cent would be able to attend ordinary schools because they were lightly handicapped. A further 20 per cent could be absorbed in special schools either for the physically handicapped, or the educationally subnormal. This would leave 30 per cent, but many of these would be severely subnormal mentally, possibly 20 per cent of the whole group.

Dunsdon's recommendations are worth careful study. She was concerned with the educability of cerebral palsied children, therefore she was not primarily interested in the trainability of ineducable children with cerebral palsy. In her study of the highly selected children in a dual-purpose school for the cerebral palsied, she found that the children who made a 50 per cent rate of progress educationally were almost without exception children with IQs over 85. Interestingly, although her main concern was with educable children, Dunsdon points out that it is the group of children who are not formally educable, because of their combination of mental and physical handicap, but whose needs may not be met in training schools for the severely subnormal, who require special attention. The needs of this group of children are again emphasized by Cockburn (1961). She found that of 26 children with cerebral palsy unsatisfactorily placed (out of a total of 133), 16 were mentally handicapped. She writes 'the greatest need encountered amongst those unsatisfactorily placed in this group was for education suitable for mentally handicapped children'.

Dunsdon based her recommendation that an IQ of 85 was the baseline for formal education on the reasonable assumption that cerebral palsied children tend to have so many handicaps that they require a relatively high IQ and chronological age in order to make worthwhile educational progress, and on the evidence of the group of children in a special school, quoted above.

Schonell envisaged schools as dual-purpose centres for all ages; unlike Dunsdon, who considered that the main emphasis should be on a social and motor training up to 9–10 years and then on education from 10–16 years. Schonell's recommendations appear to stem from one study of the reading attainments of children attending the Carlson House Special School for cerebral palsied children. The experimental group consisted of seventeen special school-children; the control group comprised seventeen children with cerebral palsy from special schools for the physically handicapped, ordinary schools and no schools at all. The two groups were paired for mental age, chronological age, physical, sensory and speech handicaps. The age range was 7–10 years. Schonell found that the mean reading age of the experimental group was significantly higher than that of the control group. She also gives a useful table of the educational placement of the cerebral palsied children in her survey, as does Cockburn. Rutter *et al.* (1970), in their Isle of Wight survey, found that only a third of their children with cerebral palsy attended ordinary schools. They write:

> The major difference in school placement between the children with cerebral palsy and those with lesions below the brain stem is the more striking because the physical handicaps of both groups were fairly similar. However, the cerebral palsied children had a much higher rate of associated handicaps (such as intellectual retardation, and psychiatric disorder). A special school placement is rarely necessary purely on account of a physical disability, even severe. Usually the presence of multiple handicaps gives rise to the need for special provision.

There seems general agreement that the majority of educable cerebral palsied children can attend existing ordinary and special schools, but most workers would also agree that some would benefit from special schooling as cerebral palsied children. The size and identity of this group is a matter for further research.

The great need of the mentally handicapped child with cerebral palsy for special consideration is mentioned by most workers.

SPECIAL METHODS OF EDUCATION

Up to the present there has been little detailed description or scientific evaluation of specific methods of education to be used with children with cerebral palsy. There are statements in the literature that special training is necessary for teachers of spastic children; although this is probably true, there is a lack of published evidence on the efficacy and nature of special methods of teaching which may be due to the fact that the special schools in England have not been in existence for very long.

In considering the literature on the education of the cerebral palsied, the following points emerge. Commonsense techniques to obviate physical handicaps are widely used. Some authorities, Schonell (1956) and Johnson (1955) among them advocate the use of modern teaching methods such as centres of interest and reading readiness programmes. Orville Johnson, in discussing the education of mentally retarded cerebral palsied children, suggests that they require ordinary methods of teaching but that each stage will take much longer than with normal children. There seems to be a fairly widely held belief that cerebral palsied children learn slowly, even if they are of at least average intelligence, and that therefore they require at least three or four years of extra schooling. This seems to be a hypothesis which could be usefully tested.

In America, teaching techniques based on the work of Strauss and Lehtinen (1947) and their concept of the 'brain injured child' have been used in the teaching of the cerebral palsied. Their method consists of the avoidance of all irrelevant stimuli and the clear simple presentation of the material to be learned. An empirical criticism is that Strauss and Lehtinen have not shown that this method is more effective than others. They describe various devices to aid in the teaching of reading, writing and arithmetic; these are related to their concept of brain injury and are, therefore, intended to overcome the dysfunctions which they ascribe to brain injury.

Other remedial programmes for brain injured children which have been outlined include those by Cruickshank, which is especially oriented towards hyperactive children, and Frostig, which concentrates largely on visuo-perceptual training (see Loring, 1968). The usefulness of these programmes has not so far been thoroughly evaluated. A more carefully designed approach, such as that used by Gallagher (1960) to study the methods of tutoring effective with brain injured mentally retarded children, might be more productive. Short periods of individual tuition were found to be more effective than longer periods in a group in this study, and work is needed to see if this finding also pertains to the more specific group of cerebral palsied and over the normal intelligence range. Frostig also stresses the individual approach and the need for basing the plan for teaching on the pattern of assets and deficits of each child, and modifying these where necessary as the pattern changes.

More radical approaches to the education of the cerebral palsied child which at present have received only limited application are the use of operant conditioning techniques (for example Connolly, 1968) and the development of technological devices for use especially by the severely physically handicapped, for example the Touch Tutor (Thompson and Johnson, 1971) and the Possum typewriter (Jenkin, 1967). These techniques are receiving particular attention in the special schools run by the Spastics Society. This society has also established a school for severely subnormal cerebral palsied children which is developing methods of education appropriate to that group.

The evidence on the education of cerebral palsied children is not satisfactory. It may be that there are some cerebral palsied children who are best educated separately, but even this has not yet been clearly shown. It may be that the main advantage of a special school, or centre, for the cerebral palsied is the availability on the premises of physiotherapy and speech therapy. A consideration of some of the current assumptions about the education of cerebral palsied children suggests that there may be many untested theories underlying the educational provisions made for other categories of children.

At present cerebral palsied children are educated and receive physical treatment in a wide range of hospitals, schools and institutions. It would seem an excellent time to carry out prospective research into the efficacy of different methods of education and treatment for comparable groups of children. This should be carried out in conjunction with research work in the assessment centres which are developing for young and/or multiply and severely handicapped children. One sometimes gets the impression that the medical and educational placement of the cerebral palsied tends to be dealt with separately in the published studies, although this may not be so in practice. Rutter, Graham and Yule (1970) stress the need for close links between paediatricians and the school health service.

FOLLOW-UP STUDIES OF PATIENTS WITH CEREBRAL PALSY

Although there has been little long-term study of educational methods with cerebral palsied children, there are follow-up studies of patients with cerebral palsy. Crothers and Paine (1959) in their classic study were concerned with the natural history of cerebral palsy, and not with assessing the results of any specific treatments; however, they do provide much useful information on the adult status of the patients in their sample.

Quibell, Stephen and Whatley (1961) carried out a retrospective study of the progress in daily living functions of 40 physically handicapped children, IQ 48–70, age 2 to 16 years, 30 of whom were cerebral palsied. All these children had been treated in a long stay children's hospital and school for at least one year, and improvement was assessed on a scale of activities essential for daily living. Thirty-one of the children made demonstrable gains in functional independence, including 2 children of imbecile level. They comment: 'It appears that the minimum IQ, or mental age, necessary in order to make useful progress in daily living functions is much lower than may sometimes have been assumed. Our survey suggests that the children who did not show improvement, could not, because of the severity of the physical handicap, rather than because of mental dullness.' From these studies it appears that some mental defectives with cerebral palsy show marked improvement after treatment.

In a follow-up study of children assessed for school placement Gardner (1970) found: (1) that of 57 children recommended for schools for cerebral palsied children of normal intelligence, 10 were placed elsewhere 5 years later – 8 of the 10 were in ESN schools and 2 were in SSN schools – a $17\frac{1}{2}$ per cent disagreement; (2) of 39 children recommended for ESN/CP schools, on follow-up 3 had moved up and 2 had moved down – that is, a 13 per cent disagreement 5 years later.

Gardner recommends improved assessment procedures and more educational provision for the 42 per cent of his sample with multiple handicaps and for those with 'minimal' cerebral palsy.

ADULT PATIENTS WITH CEREBRAL PALSY

Most surveys of patients with cerebral palsy have been concerned with children, therefore there are no firm figures on the prevalence rate of adults with cerebral palsy.

Crothers and Paine (1959) found a death rate of 14 per cent among their sample of 847 patients born in 1915–55 and concluded that 'the majority of cerebral palsied patients have a considerable life expectancy'. Ingram (1964) found in his follow-up 10 years later of 144 cerebral palsied patients, 7 had died between the ages of 10 and 20 years: 'All had been classified as having severe physical handicaps, all had severe associated disabilities and a prediction of institutional life had been made in all cases.' The remainder Ingram classified as follows:

1. Patients leading a normal social life for their age, sex and social class (over 21 per cent).
2. Patients leading a restricted social life (over 25 per cent).
3. Patients who attended clubs for the disabled, and whose friends were disabled (over 13 per cent).
4. Patients who attended clubs for the disabled and whose social life was otherwise confined to their immediate family circle (approximately 6 per cent).
5. Patients whose social life was confined to their immediate family circle (16 per cent).
6. Patients who never left the house for social activities (approximately 6 per cent).
7. Patients in institutions for the mentally handicapped (just over 10 per cent).

Degree of physical handicap seemed to be the determining factor in categories 1, 2, 3 and 4, but in 5, 6 and 7 degree of mental handicap was the determining factor.

Henderson (1961) in his sample found a prevalence rate of 1·54 for ages 15–18. Tizard & Grad (1961) in their London sample of 150 mentally defective children and 100 mentally defective adults found that:

> cerebral palsy and various types of paralysis were the most common of the special disabilities. These conditions, or unsteadiness of gait or muscular weakness, were seen in nearly one-third of the children and more than one-fifth of the adults. Of the children, 15 per cent were rated as suffering from slight motor impairment and 15 per cent from severe motor impairment. Among the adults, 14 per cent showed slight motor impairment and 8 per cent, severe motor impairments.

Six per cent of the adults with severe motor impairment were living at home.

There is some information on the frequency of mental deficiency amongst adults with cerebral palsy. Holeran (1955) in a survey of young adult cerebral palsied patients in Leeds found that out of a total of 78, 15 had been notified to the Mental Deficiency Authority before the age of 15 and 2 were in occupation centres, i.e. 22 per cent were mentally deficient. Hansen (1960) reports that 27 per cent of 1,127 adult patients with cerebral palsy 'were fit to be dealt with as mentally defective'. In both these surveys the mentally deficient adult patients were among the unemployed. In discussing the placement of young adults in her sample, Cockburn (1961) writes 'almost half of those over school age were unemployable and in the majority of cases this was due to serious mental handicap'.

Pollock and Stark (1969) followed up a group who had attended a special school for educable children with severe physical handicaps. Sixty per cent of their sample were in employment or still in training and those who were not tended to be the less intelligent and to have more severe physical disabilities.

There is little published evidence so far on the results of vocational guidance and training in this country. The American and Danish surveys indicate a large wastage in training (at least 50 per cent). This may now be unavoidable but suggests that new methods should be inquired into.

Ingram (1964) has followed up the patients surveyed by himself (1955, 1964) and Henderson (1961). This is a fascinating study of all aspects of the lives of adult patients with cerebral palsy in two areas of Scotland. One of his interesting recommendations is that 'because of the low prevalence rate of cerebral palsy, services for cerebral palsied patients must be planned at a national level'.

RESIDENTIAL CARE

The majority of cerebral palsied children of normal intelligence live at home and attend day schools, but for some a residential placement will be necessary particularly in cases of more severe handicap in conjunction with mental retardation or where social factors require it. As their life expectancy becomes increasingly normal a larger number of adults previously living with their families are coming to need alternative care for part of their lives. Hewett (1970) has shown that handicapped children are less likely than their siblings to be looked after by a relative in an emergency but go to an institution. There is therefore some need for short- and long-term facilities for children and adults especially those with the most severe handicaps.

Until recently hospital care was the only possibility available. It is now widely recognized that except where constant medical attention is required the advantages of this are debatable, for example physiotherapy can be provided in other settings. Hospitals impose severe limitations on the independence and experience of their patients. Oswin (1971) has compared some aspects of the lives of handicapped children in different types of institutions. The merits of smaller less structured institutions have been stressed by the voluntary societies who have gone some way towards providing suitable alternative accommodation.

Summary and conclusions

In recent years studies have confirmed the earlier findings on the prevalence of cerebral palsy and on the range of intelligence amongst school age children with the disorder, for example Henderson (1961). More detailed information is now available on the overlap between cerebral palsy and mental subnormality from which it is now clear that there is a tendency for severity of physical handicap and frequency of sensory handicaps to be associated with severity of mental retardation (Hilliard and Kirman, 1957; Henderson, 1961; Rutter *et al.*, 1970).

New areas have been explored including the attitudes and problems of parents of children with cerebral palsy (Hewett, 1970), and follow-up studies have provided information on educational placement of children and employability of adults (e.g. Crothers and Paine, 1959; Pollock and Stark, 1969; Gardner, 1970).

Increasing interest is being shown in the area of minimal brain damage and thus of minimal cerebral palsy, i.e. cases of very mild handicap frequently not diagnosed as such but regarded as normal children who show clumsiness, awkwardness or mild behaviour disorder, the organic basis of which is not recognized. This may be related to learning difficulties at school as well as being manifest in general behaviour.

Regarding the education of cerebral palsied children there has been a swing of opinion away from the provision of special education for the less severely handicapped cases. While there would appear to be sound commonsense grounds for this in that it should facilitate the child's integration with non-handicapped people there does not appear to have been any research into the effects of alternative methods of education on children with various degrees of handicap.

There is still much to be learned about cerebral palsy: about the motor deficit itself, the other defects that tend to be associated with it and about appropriate methods of assessment, treatment and education. Pre-school children in particular have been little studied although Francis-Williams (1970) has looked at a group of these of normal intelligence. The feasibility of early diagnosis is an important question here. More studies with adults are also needed and there is a useful body of experimental work on other types of brain lesions for comparison.

References

ABERCROMBIE, M. L. J. (1960) Perception and eye movements. Some speculations on disorders in cerebral palsy. *Cerebral Palsy Bull.*, **2**, 142–7.

ABERCROMBIE, M. L. J. (1964) Perceptual and visuo-motor disorders in cerebral palsy. A Survey of the Literature. *Little Club Clinics in Developm. Med.*, No. 11. London: Spastics Society and Heinemann.

ABERCROMBIE, M. L. J. (1968) Some notes on spatial disability: movement, intelligence quotient and attentiveness. *Developm. med. Child Neurol.*, **10**, 206–13.

ABERCROMBIE, M. L. J., GARDINER, P., HANSEN, E., JONCKHEERE, J., LINDON, R., SOLOMON, G. and TYSON, M. (1964) Visual perceptual and visual motor impairments in physically handicapped children. *Percept. mot. Skills Monogr. Suppl.*, **V**, 561–625.

ALLEN, R. M. and JEFFERSON, T. W. (1962) *Psychological Evaluation of the Cerebral Palsied Person: Intellectual, Personality and Vocational Applications.* Springfield, Ill.: Charles C. Thomas.

ANASTASI, A. (1961) *Psychological Testing* (2nd edn). New York: Macmillan.

ASHER, P. and SCHONELL, F. E. (1950) A survey of 400 cases of cerebral palsy in childhood. *Arch. dis. Child.*, **25**, 360–79.

BALL, T. S. and WILSONCROFT, W. E. (1967) Perceptual motor deficits and the phi phenomenon. *Amer. J. ment. Defic.*, **71**, 797–800.

BICE, H. V. and CRUICKSHANK, W. M. (1955) The evaluation of intelligence. In CRUICKSHANK, W. M. and RAUS, S. (ed.) *Cerebral Palsy: Its Individual and Community Problems.* Syracuse, NY: Syracuse Univ. Press.

BOLES, G. (1959) Personality factors in mothers of cerebral palsied children. *Gen. Psychol. Monogr.*, **59**, 159–218.

BOWLEY, A. (1967) A follow-up study of 64 children with cerebral palsy. *Developm. med. Child Neurol.*, **9**, 172–82.

BURLAND, R. (1969) The development of verbal regulation of behaviour in cerebrally palsied (multiply handicapped) children. *J. ment. Subn.*, **XV**, 2, 85–9.

COCKBURN, J. M. (1961) in HENDERSON, J. L. (ed.) *Cerebral Palsy in Childhood and Adolescence*, 281–324. Edinburgh and London: Livingstone.

CONNOLLY, K. (1968) The application of operant conditioning to the measurement and development of motor skills in children. *Developm. med. Child Neurol.*, **10**, 697–705.

CROTHERS, B. and PAINE, R. (1959) *The Natural History of Cerebral Palsy.* London: Oxford Univ. Press.

CRUICKSHANK, W. M. and BICE, H. V. (1955) Personality characteristics. In CRUICKSHANK, W. M. and RAUS, S. (ed.) *Cerebral Palsy: Its Individual and Community Problems.* Syracuse, NY: Syracuse Univ. Press.

CRUICKSHANK, W. M. and RAUS, S. (ed.) *Cerebral Palsy: Its Individual and Community Problems.* Syracuse, NY: Syracuse Univ. Press.

CRUICKSHANK, W. M., BICE, H. and WALLEN, N. (1957) *Perception and Cerebral Palsy.* Syracuse, NY: Syracuse Univ. Press.

DOLL, E. A. (1933) The psychological significance of cerebral birth lesions. *Amer. J. Psychol.*, **45**, 444–52.

DUNSDON, M. I. (1952) *The Educability of Cerebral Palsied Children.* London: Newnes, for National Foundation for Educational Research.

FLOYER, E. B. (1955) *A Psychological Study of a City's Cerebral Palsied Children.* Manchester: British Council for the Welfare of Spastics.

FRANCIS-WILLIAMS, J. (1970) *Children with Specific Learning Difficulties.* Oxford: Pergamon.

FRANCIS-WILLIAMS, J. (1971) *Psychological Investigation of Handicapped Children.* London: National Association for Mental Health.

GALLAGHER, J. J. (1960) *The Tutoring of Brain Injured Mentally Retarded Children: An Experimental Study.* Springfield, Ill.: Charles C. Thomas.

GARDNER, L. (1970) Assessment and outcome. *Spec. Educ.*, **59**, 11–14.

GARDNER, L. and JOHNSON, J. (1964) The long-term assessment and experimental education of retarded cerebral palsied children. *Developm. med. Child Neurol.*, **6**, 250–60.

GESELL, A. and AMATRUDA, C. S. (1947) *Developmental Diagnosis, Normal and Abnormal Child Development* (2nd edn). New York: Harper Bros. and Paul Hoeber Inc.

GIBBS, N. (1968) The psychological assessment of preschool spastic children. In LORING, J. (ed.) *Assessment of the Cerebral Palsied Child for Education.* London: Spastics Society and Heinemann.

GOODGLASS, F. A. and QUADFASEL, F. (1954) Language laterality in left-handed aphasics. *Brain*, **77**, 521–48.

HANSEN, E. (1960) *Cerebral Palsy in Denmark.* Copenhagen: Munksgaard.

HENDERSON, J. L. (1961) *Cerebral Palsy in Childhood and Adolescence: A Medical, Psychological and Social Study.* Edinburgh: Livingstone.

HERLITZ, G. and REDIN, B. (1955) The prevalence of cerebral palsy. *Acta Paediat. Scand.*, **44**, 146.

HEWETT, S. (1970) *The Family and the Handicapped Child.* London: Allen & Unwin.

HILLIARD, L. T. and KIRMAN, B. H. (1957) *Mental Deficiency.* London: Churchill.

HOLERAN, I. (1955) The employability of cerebral palsied young people. *Med. Off.*, **94**, 337–9.

HOLT, K. S. and REYNELL, J. K. (1966) *Assessment of Cerebral Palsy II.* London: Lloyd Luke.

HOPKINS, T., BICE, H. V. and COLTON, K. (1954) *Evaluation and Education of the Cerebral Palsied Child.* Washington, DC: Internat. Counc. Except. Child.

ILLINGWORTH, R. S. (1958) *Recent Advances in Cerebral Palsy.* London: Churchill.

INGRAM, T. T. S. (1955) A study of cerebral palsy in the childhood population of Edinburgh. *Arch. dis. Childh.*, **30**, 85–98.

INGRAM, T. T. S. (1964) *Paediatric Aspects of Cerebral Palsy.* London: Livingstone.

JENKIN, R. (1967) Possum: a new communication aid. *Spec. Ed.*, **56**, 1.

JOHNSON, G. O. (1955) Mental retardation and cerebral palsy. In CRUICKSHANK, W. M. and RAUS, S. (eds.) *Cerebral Palsy: Its Individual and Community Problems.* Syracuse, NY: Syracuse Univ. Press.

KATZ, E. (1958) The 'Pointing Modification' of the Revised Stanford–Binet Intelligence Scales Forms L and M, Years II through VI. *Amer. J. ment. Defic.*, **62**, 698–707.

KIRMAN, B. H. (1956) Epilepsy and cerebral palsy. *Arch. dis. Childh.*, **31**, 1–7.

KIRMAN, B. H. (1960) Cerebral palsy and mental handicap research aspects. *Spastics Quart.*, **19**.

KLAPPER, Z. S. and BIRCH, H. G. (1967) A 14-year follow up study of cerebral palsy: intellectual change and stability. *Amer. J. Orthopsychiat.*, **37**, 540–7.

LORING, J. (1968) *Assessment of the Cerebral Palsied Child for Education.* London: Spastics Society and Heinemann.

LUSZKI, W. A. (1966) Intellectual functioning of spastic cerebral palsied. *Cerebral Palsy J.*, **27**, 7–9.

MCINTIRE, J. T. A. (1938) The incidence of feeblemindedness in the cerebral palsied. *Proc. Amer. Assoc. ment. Defic.*, **43**, 44–50.

MCINTIRE, J. T. A. (1947) A study of the distribution of physical handicap and mental diagnosis in cerebral palsied children. *Amer. J. ment. Defic.*, **51**, 624–6.

MITTLER, P. (1970) *The Psychological Assessment of Mental and Physical Handicaps.* London: Methuen.

MOWAT, J. (1961) In HENDERSON, J. L. (ed.) *Cerebral Palsy in Childhood and Adolescence*, 242–53. Edinburgh and London: Livingstone.

NEILSEN, H. H. (1966) *A Psychological Study of Cerebral Palsied Children.* Copenhagen: Munksgaard.

NEILSEN, H. H. (1968) Assessment of intellectual potential. In LORING, J.

(ed.) *Assessment of the Cerebral Palsied Child for Education*, 26–32. London: Spastics Society and Heinemann.

NELSON, T. M. (1962) A study comparing visual and visual-motor percep-tions of unimpaired, defective and spastic cerebral palsied children. *J. genet. Psychol.*, **101**, 299–332.

OSWIN, M. (1971) *The Empty Hours*. London: Allen Lane.

OUNSTED, C., ANNETT, M. and LEE, D. (1961) Intellectual disabilities in relation to lateralised features in the E.E.G. *Little Club Clinics in Developm. Med.*, **4**, 86–112.

PEARSON, D. (1969) Object discrimination learning set acquisition in young cerebral palsied children in relation to tested and rated intelligence. *J. cons. clin. Psychol.*, **33**, 478–84.

PERLSTEIN, J. A. and HOOD, P. N. (1957) Infantile spastic hemiplegia, intelligence and age of walking and talking. *Amer. J. ment. Defic.*, **61**, 534–43.

PHELPS, W. M. (1948) Characteristic psychological variations in cerebral palsy. *Nerv. Child*, **7**, 10–12.

POLLOCK, G. A. and STARK, G. (1969) Long term results in the manage-ment of 67 children with cerebral palsy. *Developm. med. Child Neurol.*, **11**, 17–34.

QUIBELL, E. P., STEPHEN, E. and WHATLEY, E. (1961) A survey of a group of children with mental and physical handicap treated in an orthopaedic hospital. *Arch. dis. Childh.*, **36**, 58–64.

REYNELL, J. K. (1963) *Factors affecting Response to Treatment in Cerebral Palsy*. Unpubl. Ph.D. thesis, Univ. of Sheffield.

REYNELL, J. K. (1970) Children with physical handicaps. In MITTLER, P. (ed.) *The Psychological Assessment of Mental and Physical Handicaps*, 443–69. London: Methuen.

RUTTER, M., GRAHAM, P. and YULE, W. (1970) A neuropsychiatric study in childhood. *Clinics in Developmental Medicine*, 35/36. Spastics International Medical Publications.

RUTTER, M., TIZARD, J. and WHITMORE, K. (1970) *Education, Health and Behaviour*. London: Longmans.

SARASON, S. B. (1949) *Psychological Problems in Mental Deficiency*. New York: Harper & Row.

SARASON, S. B. and DORIS, J. (1969) *Psychological Problems in Mental Deficiency* (4th edn). New York: Harper & Row.

SCHALLING, J. and CRONHOLM, B. (1968) Effects of early brain injury on perceptual-constructive performance in adults. *J. nerv. ment. Dis.*, **147**, 547–52.

SCHONELL, F. E. (1956) *Educating Spastic Children*. Edinburgh: Oliver & Boyd.

SCHROEDER, P. L. (1929) Behavior difficulties in children associated with the results of birth trauma. *J. Amer. med. Assoc.*, **92**, 100–4.

SCHUBERT, J. (1969) The VRB apparatus: an experimental procedure for the investigation of the development of verbal regulation of behaviour. *J. genet. Psychol.*, **114**, 237–52.

SHERE, M. O. (1954) *An Evaluation of the Social and Emotional Development of the Cerebral Palsied Twin.* Unpubl. doctoral dissertation, Univ. of Illinois College of Education. Quoted by Cruickshank and Raus (1955).

SHERMAN, J. (1967) Problem of sex differences in space perception and aspects of intellectual functioning. *Psychol. Rev.*, **74**, 290–9.

SMITH, S. B. (1926) Cerebral accidents of childhood and their relationships to mental deficiency. *Welf. Mag.*, **17**, 18–33.

STRAUSS, A. A. and LEHTINEN, L. E. (1947) *Psychopathology and Education of the Brain-injured Child.* New York: Grune & Stratton.

STROTHER, C. R. (1945) Evaluating intelligence. *Crippled Child*, **23**, 82–3.

TAYLOR, E. M. (1959) *Psychological Appraisal of Children with Cerebral Defects.* Cambridge, Mass.: Harvard Univ. Press.

THOMPSON, D. A. and JOHNSON, J. D. (1971) Touch Tutor at Hawksworth Hall. *Spec. Educ.*, **60**, 1.

THURSTON, J. R. (1960) Attitudes and emotional reactions of parents of institutionalized cerebral palsied retarded patients. *Amer. J. ment. Defic.*, **65**, 227–35.

TIZARD, J. and GRAD, J. C. (1961) *The Mentally Handicapped and their Families.* Maudsley Monogr., No. 7. London: Oxford Univ. Press.

TIZARD, J. P. M., PAINE, R. S. and CROTHERS, B. (1954) Disturbance of sensation in children with hemiplegia. *J. Amer. med. Assoc.*, **155**, 628–32.

WALLIN, J. E. W. (1949) *Children with Mental and Physical Handicaps.* New York and London: Staples Press.

WALSHE, F. M. R. (1952) *Diseases of the Nervous System.* Edinburgh and London: Livingstone.

WEDELL, K. (1960) Variations in perceptual ability among types of cerebral palsy. *Cerebral Palsy Bull.*, **2**, 149–57.

WEDELL, K. (1961) Follow-up study of perceptual ability in children with hemiplegia. *Little Club Clinics in Developm. Med.*, **4**, 76–85.

WEDELL, K. (1964) Some aspects of perceptual-motor development in young children. In LORING, J. (ed.) *Learning Problems of the Cerebral Palsied*, 146–9. London: Spastics Society.

WILLIAMS, J. R. (1960) The effect of emotional factors on perception and concept formation in cerebral palsied children. *Little Club Clinics in Developm. Med.*, **2**, 123–32.

WOODS, G. (1957) *Cerebral Palsy in Childhood.* Bristol: Wright.

WOODS, G. E. (1963) A lowered incidence of infantile cerebral palsy. *Developm. med. Child Neurol.*, **5**, 449.

WOODWARD, M. (1959) The behaviour of idiots interpreted by Piaget's theory of sensori-motor development. *Brit. J. educ. Psychol.*, **29**, 60–71.

WYLLIE, W. S. (1951) Cerebral palsies. In FEILING, A. (ed.) *Modern Trends in Neurology*. London: Butterworth.

YANNET, H. (1944) The etiology of congenital cerebral palsy. *J. Pediat.*, **24,** 38–45.

PART IV

Amelioration of mental subnormality

17

P. J. Mittler

Language and communication[1]

Introduction

The ability to use language is obviously closely bound up wtih the development
of intelligence, but the relationship between them is far from simple. The fact
that a child is mentally subnormal should not be regarded as providing a satisfactory explanation for his inability to speak, nor should failure to learn to speak
at the appropriate time be regarded as evidence of mental subnormality.

Many studies have demonstrated the severe language difficulties of the
mentally subnormal and suggested that they are underfunctioning in relation to
their level of skills in other areas of development. It is therefore important to
consider the nature of the difficulties in some detail, since some of these might
under certain circumstances be preventable and others might lend themselves
to remediation (see Chapter 18).

This chapter will therefore begin with a discussion of some of the skills
necessary for normal language functioning and consider implications for delayed or deviant development. This will be followed by an account of some of the
more important features of recent work in linguistics and psycholinguistics
concerning the structure of language, with special reference to the distinction
between competence and performance, and the rule-governed aspects of language,
again stressing the implications of such work for subnormality. A separate
section is devoted to comprehension, as opposed to production of language,
since this has important cognitive and educational implications. This is followed
by a review of biological and environmental influences on language development,
which stresses their complex interactions in the subnormal. Another section
reviews knowledge on the nature and frequency of language difficulties in
subnormals, and discusses questions concerned with the relative importance of
developmental delay as opposed to specific deficits, and with the role of verbal
mediation in thinking and problem solving. Developments in assessment
techniques are next considered in some detail, reflecting the shift of emphasis

[1] The preparation of this chapter was supported by a grant from the Social Science
Research Council.

from standardized tests towards criterion-referenced observational and developmentally orientated measures, and from a preoccupation with spoken language towards an interest in receptive skills. The final section is devoted to a full discussion of the principles and techniques which have been applied in the teaching of language skills to subnormal individuals, with special reference to the use of systematic teaching methods derived from behaviour modification.

Communication skills

In order to be able to use and understand language, an individual needs to develop a number of skills which can be separately identified and which may be differentially sensitive to subnormal intellectual functioning. One well-known attempt to isolate some of these skills is found in the Illinois Test of Psycholinguistic Abilities (Kirk *et al.*, 1968), which has been discussed above (see section on 'Assessment'). But assessment is by no means limited to psychometric approaches and tests alone cannot sample more than a small part of the communication system of which language is only one part. The processes involved can usefully be considered in terms of information processing strategies which are not unlike those required for perceptual stimuli. Thus, for language functioning to be effective, according to Eisenson (1966), the subject has to:

(a) be able to receive stimuli produced in sequential order;
(b) maintain a sequential impression of the message so that its components can be integrated into a pattern;
(c) scan the pattern from within to categorize the data and compare it with an existing store;
(d) respond differentially to perceptual impression.

Some of these are the very abilities that have been shown to be severely impaired in the mentally subnormal. Experimental studies have consistently indicated that they have particular difficulties in dealing with incoming sensory information, and that many of their learning difficulties can be regarded as stemming from a disorder of attention. Information processing of auditory material is particularly difficult but is also seen in dealing with visual material (O'Connor and Hermelin, 1963; Denny, 1964; Baumeister, 1968). It is therefore important to try to differentiate between a large number of deficits, all of which could result in apparent language impairment, but some of which might be due to basic perceptual and attention disorders. It is not easy to make such a differentiation with the crude assessment techniques currently available, but an experimental analysis can often be suggestive. Needless to say, a programme of language therapy often needs to begin by teaching the child to attend, listen, discriminate and respond selectively to auditory and other material (Bricker and Bricker, 1970a).

Language skills may concern phonology, morphology, syntax and semantics and are defined as follows by Carroll (1967).

(a) Phonology: the specification of the units of sounds (phonemes) which go to compose words and other forms in the language.
(b) Morphology: the listing of the words and other basic meaningful forms (morphemes) of the language and the specification of the ways in which these forms may be modified when placed in various contexts.
(c) Syntax: the specification of the patterns in which linguistic forms may be arranged and of the ways in which these patterns may be modified or transformed in varying contexts.
(d) Semantics: the specification of the meanings of linguistic forms and syntactical patterns in relation to objects, events, processes, attributes and relationships in human experience.

Research and theory are currently emphasizing possible forms of interaction between these different components, particularly the relationship between syntax and semantics, but principles of skills analysis can be fruitfully applied to the study of language.

In an extensive discussion of this topic Herriot (1970) stresses the parallels between motor and language skills by drawing attention to certain common elements. In the first place, language is probably hierarchically organized within as well as between skills; some skills are essential prerequisites for the development and use of others; thus certain minimal articulatory skills are normally prerequisites of syntactical or grammatical skills. Some qualification is necessary in the case of subnormals, however, because the developmental sequence of language acquisition may occasionally be different. Thus, as we shall see, although comprehension normally precedes production, the order may be reversed on occasion; as a corollary, a child may have an advanced level of language comprehension, but have relatively undeveloped productive skills, due to damage to the peripheral speech mechanisms or even because of a primary expressive aphasic disturbance (Lenneberg, 1962).

The second aspect of skills analysis discussed by Herriot is that of feedback. The speaker needs to be able to monitor his own performance in relation to his 'plan' or intention in each instance, and to modify his utterance accordingly. But this process may be faulty in subnormals. For example, a subnormal person may be aware that what he is trying to communicate is being severely disrupted by inadequate articulation or inappropriate syntax or semantics. In other words, the speaker is to a greater or lesser degree aware that his language performance does not match his thought or communicative intent. A second aspect concerns the subnormal person's ability to assimilate feedback information from others. In the two-person communication situation, he may not be as aware as a normal person of feedback information such as lack of comprehension, boredom, embarrassment, etc. Furthermore, the normal listener may in fact suppress such signals and pretend a polite interest for the sake of encouragement and courtesy to the subnormal speaker, thus depriving him of essential cues which might otherwise help him to accommodate to the requirements of the listener.

A third aspect of language skill is automatization, which concerns the skill of emitting chains or sequences of behaviour without the need for fully conscious control. Spoken language is organized in sequences of this type, both at a phonological and also at a grammatical level. Thus, a child rapidly learns that certain sequences are 'permissible' while others are not; for example, that words can begin with g + l and k + l, but not d + l; similarly, syntactic sequencing normally requires the adjective to precede the noun ('big boy', not 'boy big' etc.). The extent to which automatization occurs must depend to a large extent on the size of the units which can be stored in short-term memory; subnormals may therefore be at a disadvantage in acquiring such skills because of shortcomings both in short-term memory and in ability to chunk or cluster both input and output. Furthermore, studies using the ITPA suggest that subnormals have specific deficits in both auditory and visual sequencing tests (see below).

Fourthly, Herriot draws attention to anticipation as a feature of language skill. The listener needs to be able to anticipate what the speaker is going to say, and in doing so uses a variety of linguistic as well as non-linguistic cues. Some of these derive from the context in which the utterance is made, others are related to the syntactic and semantic organizations of the utterance. Anticipation is also an essential element in planning one's own utterances. It is apparent, however, that subnormals are likely to be at a disadvantage in planning and anticipation, since these skills depend heavily on general intelligence.

Hierarchical organization, feedback, automatization and anticipation may be regarded as essential aspects of language skill which lend themselves to analysis in much the same way as comparable motor skills. Notable advances have been made in the fine grain analysis of motor skills both for normals and subnormals which have led directly or indirectly to remedial programmes designed to overcome specific deficits in one or other aspect of motor skill (Annett, 1971; Whelan, 1973). One task that awaits the research worker is the application to the field of language, of principles of skills analysis as detailed as those which have characterized studies of motor function. This may in time lead not merely to an increase in our understanding of specific language impairments in subnormal individuals, but to the formulation of soundly based remedial strategies.

LANGUAGE AND SPEECH

Carroll (1953), writing as a linguist, defines language as a 'structured system of arbitrary vocal sounds and sequences of sounds which is used, or can be used, in interpersonal communication by an aggregation of human beings, and which rather exhaustively catalogues the things, events and processes in the human environment'. In a later discussion, he stresses the distinction between language and speech in relation to mental handicap: 'when we talk therefore about the *language* of mental retardates, we are talking . . . about the *system* that they have learned. When we refer to the *speech*, of mental retardates we are referring . . . to the actual behaviour of these individuals in using language' (Carroll, 1967).

The distinction between speech and language is not accepted by all authorities in this field but is generally adopted as a matter of convenience. It is a useful distinction in the study of deviant or delayed development, because speech and language may be differentially affected in such cases. To take an extreme example, an articulate and intelligent adult may receive a cerebral injury, such as a gunshot wound, which destroys or impairs speech but leaves his ability to understand language and to write books relatively unaffected. Similarly, a severely retarded child may be able to speak without difficulty, but his language may be primitive and undifferentiated in so far as he has only a minimal grasp of the system of language (in Carroll's sense). In other words, speech and language represent different aspects of verbal behaviour which sometimes get out of step with one another. Hydrocephalus is often quoted as an example of a condition in which the sufferer appears to be able to keep up a continuous chatter despite gross brain damage and physical handicap but whose use of language as a system of rules reflecting ideas and concepts is rudimentary (see Parsons, 1971, for a comprehensive review).

A survey of the literature suggests that more studies have been concerned with speech than with language abilities of the mentally handicapped, and have typically described the nature and incidence of disorders of voice, respiratory coordination (hesitation, stammer etc.), or speech sound production due to demonstrable dysfunction or structural abnormalities of the tongue, lips, teeth or palate. Such disorders are frequent and severe, though precise estimates are not available on account of the difficulty of defining criteria (but see Webb and Kinde, 1968; Fawcus, 1965 and this volume; and Schiefelbusch *et al.*, 1967, for useful accounts of earlier work).

Language structure

The last twenty years have witnessed a complete reorientation in the field of language research. While these changes have been productive of much theory and of further research, their impact on people concerned with handicap and remediation has so far been slight. Nevertheless, it is hardly possible to consider actual or potential developments in language studies in mental subnormality without at least a brief examination of some of the main issues that have been raised by psycholinguistics. Only the bravest or the most fool-hardy research worker would now design a study concerned with language which took no account of this work.

It would not be appropriate to characterize, let alone summarize, the nature of the revolution that has taken place in language studies, since the publication of Miller's (1951) *Language and Communication*, if only because it has now been ably done by many others (e.g. Brown, 1965; Hayes, 1970; Herriot, 1970; Olson, 1970; McNeill, 1970a). But it may be useful to single out a few distinctive features, which have influenced psychologists and educators both positively and negatively, and which will need to be taken into consideration in the planning of future work.

COMPETENCE AND PERFORMANCE

The distinction between competence and performance is fundamental to much recent research and theory in the area of language development, though its implications for grossly delayed or deviant development have not been adequately explored.

Competence relates to a child's knowledge of a language which will enable him to understand and generate an infinite number of grammatical sentences, and no non-sentences of that language. Performance refers to the actual use made of that knowledge. It is widely agreed that competence is influenced and distorted by performance factors, but cannot itself be directly measured. In this respect it is similar to Hebb's concept of Intelligence A, i.e. physiological and genetic aspects of intelligence which are not directly measurable but which form the basis of Intelligence B, intelligence as used in everyday life, and Intelligence C, which is what is measured by the appropriate tests. Although linguists treat the competence-performance distinction as fundamental to an understanding of language, more empirically orientated psychologists tend to regard it as an interesting theoretical construct which does not of itself lead to many testable hypotheses (e.g. Herriot, 1970). Chomsky (1957, 1965) and his followers postulate the existence of an '*ideal* speaker-listener', but it is clear that such an abstraction is of doubtful relevance in the field of mental handicap. One can only hope that a study of language pathology in the broadest sense may eventually lend a wider perspective to psycholinguistics.

Chomsky's original concept of competence has been considerably developed and refined by later writers, some of whom have drawn distinctions between different aspects of competence and performance, which have some bearing on applications to language pathology. Recent writings by Campbell and Wales (1970) may be taken as a convenient example. They tend to dismiss as 'non-essential' the kind of limitations to the expression of language competence which might be imposed by short-term memory or the 'various low-level sensori-motor capacities involved in the perception and production of speech' (p. 246). This aspect of competence, characterized for their purposes as 'weak', might well be considered as more significant for the student of language pathology, since it is often at this level that impairment is found. A significant degree of hearing impairment or structural abnormalities of the speech organs are cases in point. The second aspect of competence is characterized as communicative competence, the area with which psycholinguistics has so far been largely concerned and which has been discussed above. It includes such traditional areas of enquiry as linguistic and psychological aspects of the relationships between speaker and listener, and ways in which these are modified in different contexts and situations. Recent work has also placed more emphasis on interactions between syntactic and semantic aspects of language. Campbell and Wales criticize many studies of syntactic development for failing to take account of situational variables, and stress the importance of studying the context within which speech occurs with the same thoroughness as the speech samples themselves. This is particularly important in studying the language of subnormal populations or individuals, since many of their utterances are so primitive that a knowledge of context is necessary to clarify meaning. It is also necessary to create particular contexts for eliciting specific types of utterance – e.g. objects varying in size are essential for eliciting comparative forms.

RULES OF LANGUAGE

It has been said that the task of the linguist is to discover the system of rules which a speaker appears to be using; similarly, the task of the speech pathologist or student of language disorders is to try to assess the extent to which these rules operate in the child's understanding and use of language. It is also important to try to determine at what point the child's use of rules is faulty, and to try to help him to master them.

One of the rule systems that has been studied concerns morphology, in particular the ability to provide appropriate inflectional endings to signal plurals, tenses, comparatives and superlatives etc. The most influential study is that of Berko (1958) who presented children with drawings purporting to illustrate nonsense words and then asked questions designed to elicit specific inflections. For example, a drawing named as a 'wug' was shown to fifty-six children at each age between 4 and 7 years; two further examples of the same picture were then shown to elicit the plural, which was always given as 'wug/z.' Similarly, the past tense was elicited from nonsense syllables such as 'spow', 'rick', 'gling', etc. In general, there were rather few age differences in the range which she studied, suggesting that regular rule systems were fairly well established at the age of 4. That this does not apply to irregular constructions is suggested by her own and a number of later studies, and is also a matter of common observation. The child who says 'digged', 'gooses', 'mans' etc. is presumably misapplying a rule for forming the past tense and for pluralization; he is unlikely to be imitating.

These rules continue to be misapplied for quite some time after children have acquired considerable linguistic proficiency. They are not merely misapplied to nonsense words but also appear to be implicit in their production of phrases and constructions which they are unlikely to have heard – phrases which represent a new construction involving grammatical rules wrongly applied to exceptional instances – 'wented', 'breaked', 'betterdn't we?' etc.

The Auditory Vocal Automatic subtest of the Illinois Test of Psycholinguistic Abilities is designed to sample morphological skills in children between the ages of 3 and 10. Instead of nonsense words, the test employs lexical items and appropriate pictures, and the child is required to complete a statement with an inflected word ('Here is a man: here are two –'; 'The thief is stealing the jewels; here are the jewels he – '). In a study of 100 normal 4-year-olds, only 19 per cent could correctly pluralize 'man' and fewer still could provide irregular past inflections, such as 'wrote', 'hung' or 'stole'. Irregular comparatives and superlatives were also found difficult (Mittler, 1970a). This test appears to be particularly sensitive to social class differences; children from social classes I and II differed by the equivalent of thirteen months of language development from those in classes IV and V. (See also Giebink *et al.*, 1970; George, 1970; Howard *et al.*, 1970.)

Subnormal children seem to show marked difficulty or at least a delay in acquiring morphological rules. In a study comparing the performance of three groups of normal, ESN and SSN children on the revised ITPA, this subtest (now renamed Grammatic Closure) discriminated strongly between normal and both subnormal groups, even though all groups were equated for EPVT vocabulary age (Marinosson, 1970). Similar studies using adaptations of the original Berko material indicate that subnormal children perform at a consistently inferior level compared to both CA and MA matched controls (Lovell and Bradbury, 1967; Blake and Williams, 1968; Dever and Gardner, 1970).

These studies suggest that an analysis both by tests and by structured observations of a child's ability to use morphological rules may provide valuable insight about competence as well as performance. But we can do little more at this stage than speculate about possible reasons for the relative inferiority of subnormal children in these tasks.

Even normal children, however, strongly resist attempts made by adults to modify their own idiosyncratic version of the rules of the language. Ervin (1964) reports one unsuccessful attempt to replace a child's '*Nobody don't like me*' with '*Nobody likes me*'. The correct version was presented to the child eight times. At the ninth attempt, the child brightened and said, 'Oh, I see: *nobody don't likes me.*' Children also tend to preserve the word order of their own telegraphic utterances, even though the mother regularly expands them, and do not seem to be able to expand the length of their utterances beyond a specific number of morphemes, even under considerable adult pressure. Thus the child's imitations do not increase as a function of the length of the adult's sentence, but a pattern of regularity is maintained in which nouns, main verbs and adjectives appear to be retained, while articles, prepositions, auxiliaries and the final '-ing' form tend to be omitted.

The fact that children's utterances cannot easily be expanded or made grammatically more advanced should not necessarily be taken as evidence for a biological or maturational view of language development. Even if such a model satisfactorily accounted for most of what we now know about language development, we would not be justified in withholding educational or language therapy programmes designed to accelerate development. Examples of such teaching programmes are discussed later in this chapter ('Language Teaching').

Comprehension

Most parents and teachers seem to identify language with what a child says rather than with what he understands. This is a curious placing of the developmental cart before the horse, since it is generally thought that comprehension precedes production of language and is an essential foundation for further development. The implications for remediation are obvious; it may be important to begin a language facilitation programme by assessing and then furthering the child's comprehension of spoken language rather than concentrating exclusively on expressive aspects. The factors that prevent a child from speaking are not necessarily the same as those which prevent him from understanding. There may be biological and neurological obstacles to the development of speech, including abnormalities or disorders of the tongue, lips or palate (see Fawcus and Fawcus, Chapter 18). The processes involved in language comprehension are probably more directly cognitive in nature, and include listening, auditory discrimination, reference to store and interpretation.

In an important discussion of this topic, Friedlander (1970) stresses other important psychological differences between listening and speaking, chiefly those relating to control and also to divergence and convergence. The speaker has

> total freedom to control the formulations of his message, while the listener must accommodate his information processing tactics to the requirements of the message . . . speech is generative, egocentric, essentially unconstrained in the possibilities over which it may range, unlimited in its options, and subject to continual branching off in new directions. Listening is fundamentally reconstructive, constrained to processing the speech of others, operates towards the progressively more limited options of interpreting inputs, often must select among inputs from two or more message sources at the same time, and is directed towards the attainment of specifiable objectives. Speech is open-ended in its possibilities while listening is closed-ended in its constraints. (p. 22)

These considerations appear to be of particular relevance to the mentally subnormal, since they frequently lack the social and behavioural skills which would allow them to indicate to the speaker that he was not being understood, thus depriving the speaker of the kind of cues which would enable him to modify his utterance accordingly. A normal child learns as he gets older to send out signals of non-comprehension: he frowns or looks puzzled, or asks for something to be repeated, just as a person in a foreign country may ask the speaker to speak more slowly or more distinctly. These are essential social skills in a communication situation, which the normal child may acquire without conscious effort, but which may have to be systematically taught to the subnormal child.

If comprehension is to a large extent a matter of guesswork, then the less intelligent child will be at a disadvantage; not only does he lack a sufficiently wide range of experience against which to match new utterances, but he may be less receptive to the minimal and sometimes quite subtle cues which form part of the communication situation, and which facilitate the discriminations on which adequate comprehension depends.

A normal child between the age of 18 and 24 months knows from frequent examples the context within which a large number of single words is normally spoken, but this is not to say that he is equal to the task of decoding a long and syntactically complex sentence, even though he may know each individual word in the sentence. The child who goes to sit at the dinner table in response to the mother saying 'get ready for your dinner' is not really proving that he has understood the mother's statement. He needs to understand no more than the word 'dinner', and might have reacted similarly (though perhaps with some surprise) if she had said 'dinner your for ready get', or produced some other low order approximation to English. A parallel may be drawn here with a child with a partial hearing loss who hears only vowels and very few consonants but can follow what is being said by using the minimal cues that are available.

It is important to remember that cues are not only verbal but also non-verbal. Mothers and teachers are not always aware of the extent to which they use gestures, or hand and eye pointing; it is instructive to observe the effect on the child of complete elimination of all gestural and situational cues, leaving him with nothing but the verbal component of the instruction. By doing this on one or two occasions, the mother can make a more realistic appraisal of her child's comprehension. It is one thing to understand language when it is supported by numerous other cues, and another thing to react appropriately to language without situational context. A teaching programme based on such a simple experiment might begin by providing the child with a large number of non-verbal cues, including gesture, pointing, eye contact and other redundant information; these prompts would then be faded one by one, leaving him at the end of the programme responding to the verbal message alone, divorced as far as possible from pragmatic expectation or visual or personal cues.

When a subnormal child fails to carry out a 'simple request' it is often assumed that he has not 'understood'; by this we imply that he is unable to cope with the demands which are being made on his limited intelligence, whereas it is possible that a careful rephrasing of the same request may reveal that it is syntactic or semantic rather than the cognitive aspects of the instruction that are responsible for his difficulty. In either case, it would be useful to equip the child with a non-verbal signal to indicate that the message has not been understood. Such signs exist in the Paget system which has been widely used with the deaf; modifications have been developed by Levitt (1970) with SSN spastic children. Needless to say, it is not enough to teach the system; the child has also to learn the social conventions governing its use. It is not only normal children but also highly intelligent adults who may be reluctant to admit that they are having comprehension difficulties.

The use of gesture need not be dismissed as a recourse to 'primitive' methods of communication, but should be seen as an important step in a graded teaching programme, to be discarded as soon as the child can dispense with it. It is important for teachers of the subnormal to avoid the controversies between 'oral' and 'manual' methods which have divided teachers of the deaf for so many years (Lewis, 1968), and to try to relate teaching techniques to the particular developmental needs of the child rather than to the requirements of fashion or theory.

Processes underlying comprehension of language are difficult to isolate, but appear to have a strong cognitive component. The child needs to be able to attend, listen, discriminate between sounds, and later to adapt to the sequential aspects of incoming language, and to appreciate the significance of different word orders. Linguists and psychologists have very recently begun to construct provisional models of the processes involved in language comprehension, but it is still too early to work out the educational implications of these theories (Herriot and Lunzer, 1971; Olson, 1972; Trabasso, 1972). We might suggest, however, that the cognitive processes that have been implicated are precisely those in which subnormal children have been shown to have specific difficulties and deficits. We know from the experimental literature that they have particular difficulties in information processing generally, not merely in language, but also in tasks where they have to discover and attend to the relevant as opposed to the irrelevant features of a visual stimulus display (Zeaman and House, 1963). It has also been suggested that one of their characteristic difficulties lies in their inability to profit from 'incidental learning' (Denny, 1964). A difficulty in learning spontaneously and without specific guidance would be likely to handicap a child in a situation where he has to attend to a wide spectrum of cues, both of a verbal and a non-verbal nature.

The fact that psychologists have isolated a number of specific cognitive deficits which appear to be critical to comprehension of language does not mean that they are unamenable to remediation. We might try to help a child to improve basic skills, such as attention, discrimination between sounds, words and sentences of gradually increasing length and complexity. For example, the child might need to be taught to listen to loud, simple and meaningful sounds which would first be paired with significant events (the rattle of a spoon on a cup to precede food), and then as part of a series of increasingly complex discriminations between different sounds. Such techniques are not uncommonly used by teachers, but they are rarely part of a graded programme and often begin at too advanced a level. At one point it might be possible to teach a child that reward always follows the quieter of two sounds, or the highest of two notes. It is important not to keep the child as a passive listener, but to try wherever possible to allow him to produce the sounds himself.

Particular emphasis has been placed on language comprehension and on possible means of developing receptive skills in children, since these seem to be of a more cognitive nature, and may lend themselves to the design of an appropriately designed remedial programme based on research findings. In fact, recent work in psycholinguistics has been closely concerned with language comprehension and has largely proceeded on the assumption that comprehension might provide a fruitful means of studying 'competence'. But the assessment of language comprehension is no easy matter, either for the research worker or the applied psychologist, and presents particular difficulties with subnormal children, to be further discussed later (p. 554).

Biological and environmental influences

The work of Chomsky and his associates has richly influenced students of language and psychology, but has made less impact in educational circles, partly perhaps because teachers have understandably reacted against the notion of an innately determined Language Acquisition Device (LAD), and also against a biologically orientated and strictly maturational model of language development. It is sometimes objected that by the time Chomsky and (*a fortiori*) Lenneberg (1967) have finished, there is precious little left for the teacher (or parent) in providing environmental variables, such as appropriate teaching or a 'stimulating language environment'. In the same way, Piaget is sometimes criticized for providing the intellectual foundations of over-rigid 'readiness' notions in teaching number, scientific or moral concepts etc. It is true that both groups emphasize the unfolding of maturationally determined potentialities, and tend to characterize development by reference to distinct stages; it has been left to others to devise means of facilitating progress from one stage to the next, and to investigate the contribution of experiential and learning factors to development.

But to describe the stages of growth is not necessarily to describe the process. Thus, the existence of well defined and frequently validated stages of development need not inhibit the teacher from trying to accelerate the child's progress from one stage to the next. Such attempts need not necessarily be unacceptable to theorists and model-builders, most of whom might be prepared to adopt some kind of interactionist position rather than placing exclusive emphasis either on a biological-maturational or an environmental-learning view. We should surely have learned enough from the nature-nurture controversies of the 1930s to know that heredity cannot operate outside an appropriate environmental context, or vice versa. But although we pay lip service to interactional processes, we have not made much progress in understanding them. Biological and genetic factors may set the limits to development, but environmental factors may also retard growth (Mittler, 1971).

Although biological factors obviously play a crucial role in both speech and language disorders, they must be seen as interacting with environmental variables. A child with severe articulation difficulties is likely to suffer secondary language disorders in addition to his primary speech disorders; his efforts at communication are often unsuccessful, he will be misunderstood or even ignored, and may come to regard his attempts at communication as inefficient and not worthwhile. In this situation he may resort to non-verbal means of communication, such as gestures and mime, and hope that his needs will be understood without the use of language.

It is important not to polarize biological and environmental accounts of language development, and to avoid the danger of treating as irreconcilable two theories which to some extent are concerned with different stages as well as different processes of language development. Skinner's (1957) theory is an attempt to explain the development of speech on a selective reinforcement basis; a baby exposed to and also initially producing a wide range of human speech sounds learns to associate certain regularly occurring patterns with specific perceptual or personal situations (such as feeding). Thus a conditioned stimulus (the word 'dog') comes to be associated with the unconditioned stimulus (a dog, or picture of a dog) and eventually comes to evoke the appropriate conditioned response in the child. This has been likened to a classical conditioning paradigm, whereas the child's own speech is explained in terms of operant conditioning, the strength of the operant response being regarded as a function of the strength of the positive reinforcement.

In his celebrated review Chomsky (1959) accused Skinner of 'complete naïveté with respect to grammatical mechanisms', of ignoring the whole problem of 'meaning', and of circularities in defining stimulus, response and reinforcement. From a psychological point of view, Osgood (1963) concluded that Skinner was 'not false but insufficient'. He agrees with linguistic criticisms that there is nothing in Skinner's model about the meaning of signs or about semantic generalization and adds that decoding processes are also not adequately catered for.

These two points of view are not as irreconcilable as they seem. In the first place, each theory concentrates on a different stage of language development. Learning theories seem to concentrate on the earliest stages of *speech* development, whereas generative grammarians and most psycholinguists concentrate on the acquisition of early *grammars*, beginning with two-word utterances, and have relatively little to say about pre-grammatical language such as babbling or the origins of single-word responses. This is obviously an over-simplification, especially since neo-behaviourists such as Staats (1968) have begun to work with child grammars. The dispute is moreover a real one in so far as it concerns possible models or processes which might affect language growth.

Secondly, language skills almost certainly comprise both innate and learned components; only the most extreme theorists would now claim that the two were mutually exclusive.

Finally, it is worth emphasizing that a language skill can be facilitated or taught even if it can be shown to be a 'linguistic universal'.

One difficulty arises from the use of the term 'environment' as a global term, denoting a set of amorphous and ill-defined forces. No one could possibly deny a general statement along the lines that 'environment' affects 'language'; the problem is to break down these global terms and to study the exceedingly complex interactions between them. For example, we know far too little about the nature of the language used by mothers to their normal children in everyday situations, or in guided play situations, though we do have some preliminary evidence of social class differences in conversational and maternal teaching strategies (Hess and Shipman, 1965; Robinson, 1971). It is far from easy and perhaps not altogether desirable to specify what kind of language stimulation is most conducive to language development in the child. Even if we could do this with some confidence for normal children, would the same conclusions necessarily apply to mentally handicapped children?

INSTITUTIONALIZATION

A further example can be taken from studies comparing institutionalized children with those living at home. Almost without exception, such studies document the inferiority of the institutionalized group (Schlanger, 1954; Lyle, 1960; Muller and Weaver, 1964). The consistency of the findings does not easily allow the data to be dismissed as a mere selection artefact. The adverse effects of institutionalization are neither irreversible nor inevitable, as Tizard's (1964) Brooklands experiment demonstrated. Substantial increments in verbal and social development took place when children were removed from hospital and cared for in family groups along modern 'child-centred' lines. No improvements were apparent in non-verbal tests – confirming other evidence which suggests that performance on non-verbal tasks might be more genetically determined than on verbal or social tests (Vandenberg, 1968). Nor was improvement maintained when the children were eventually returned to the original hospital conditions (Tizard, personal communication).

The example of institutionalization is well known, but illustrates the difficulty of penetrating beyond a 'global' conception of environment. We know at a general level that 'environment' or even 'institutionalization' adversely affects language, but we need to identify the critical characteristics in any given situation, and proceed from there to conduct experiments in which these independent variables are systematically manipulated so that the effects of such manipulations on language can be examined. Few such studies are available, though recent work by Barbara Tizard (1971) carries some interesting implications. She found that merely increasing the staff/child ratio did not by itself lead to better language performance, since adults were likely to spend more time talking to each other, and did not necessarily spend more time with the children in their care. Her study also stresses that it is not institutionalization as such which affects language development, but the type of child care practices to which the child is exposed.

In the absence of experimental data, we can do no more than formulate the problem in terms of more or less plausible models. Spradlin (1968), for example, invokes a learning theory approach by emphasizing (no doubt rightly) that the hospital environment tends to reinforce non-verbal rather than verbal behaviour. 'If the retarded child lines up and follows the other children, he may end up in the dining-room or the picture show. If he imitates the verbal responses of a peer, it is unlikely that anything very dramatic will occur.' Put in cognitive terms, we might say that he has little opportunity to differentiate relevant foreground from irrelevant background. The constant background of radio or piped music during the day and the tranquillizing use of television from late afternoon till bedtime present him with a problem of differentiating 'signal' from 'noise'. Adults rarely talk to him from close quarters, and he tends to hear language addressed to others rather than to him individually. The existence of a set routine reduces the need for communication, and the best way to gain adult attention is often non-verbal. It is extremely difficult to set up an institutional environment that reinforces rather than discourages language.

We should also note that some aspects of language are more likely to be affected by some aspects of environment than others. It is possible, for example, that an institutional environment may be more deterimental to language production than to language comprehension, or, as a corollary, that children brought up at home might be less competent at understanding than at speaking. Even if this were so, we should still need to try to isolate which aspects of a particular environment were critical.

SOCIAL CLASS AND FAMILY INFLUENCES

Many studies have examined socio-economic status or social class as a crude index of environment. Although massive social class differences have been found in children's language development (McCarthy, 1954; Lawton, 1968), it is not clear whether these represent real differences in language abilities or merely social class differences in general intelligence. Few studies have attempted to partial out or control for IQ (see also Chapter 7).

Although social class differences have been consistently reported for normal populations, it is possible that these are more marked for some language abilities than for others. This possibility was examined in a recent study in which the ITPA was administered to a sample of 100 normal children who were all within four weeks of their fourth birthdays (Mittler and Ward, 1970). Social class differences were highly significant, but were stronger on the auditory-vocal than on the visual-motor channel. This finding can be compared with a parallel study in which the ITPA was administered to 100 twin pairs of the same age. Twins showed an average retardation of 6 months of language development at 48 months; their performance on non-verbal tests was within the average range, so that the language retardation could not be attributed to general intellectual retardation alone (Mittler, 1970b). Comparisons between identical and fraternal pairs in the context of a classical twin study design suggested that genetic factors (expressed in terms of heritability) accounted for a greater proportion of the variance on visual-motor than on auditory-vocal tests (Mittler, 1969). Thus, the findings of the twin study provide the corollary of those on the normal controls, and suggest that tests on the auditory-vocal channel are heavily influenced by environmental variables (expressed in terms of social class), whereas tests on the visual-motor channel appear to carry a stronger genetic loading. These findings are broadly consistent with findings from behaviour genetics and twin studies in suggesting that some cognitive skills are more environmentally determined than others (Mittler, 1971).

There have been surprisingly few studies which have concerned themselves with social class influences on the severely mentally retarded, though the critical role of socio-economic variables on the mildly subnormal (ESN) pupil is better documented (e.g. Tizard, 1970). The few studies that have examined this question have not found any consistent social class differences. In a study of over 2,000 admissions to mental retardation treatment centres in Ontario, Singer and Osborn (1970) could not find any clear-cut or consistent social class differentials in respect of IQ scores. A detailed longitudinal study of forty-seven mongol babies in the London area (Carr, 1970) using the Bayley mental scales showed no difference between working-class and middle-class children at any age between 6 weeks and 2 years. In fact, the middle-class children were somewhat worse, though this was largely accounted for by two very low scorers. Normal controls, however, showed clearcut social class differences at all ages. Results on the motor tests of the Bayley scale showed that middle-class mongols were slightly better than working-class mongols at 6, 10 and 15 months, but this was reversed at the age of 2 years. In the case of the normal controls, working-class children remained consistently above middle-class children on the motor scale.

We can do no more than speculate on possible reasons why the social class differentials which in normal children operate strongly in favour of middle-class children do not appear to produce the same effects in the case of the severely subnormal. The lack of clear-cut differences in language development between middle- and working-class subnormal children has still to be properly established, but a number of possibilities suggest themselves. In the first place, the finding may be no more than an artefact of the association between language and general intelligence. We would not necessarily expect middle-class SSN children to score higher on intelligence tests, partly because the impairment of general intelligence is largely a result of biological factors. Since language and general intelligence are closely associated, both developmentally and psychometrically, the absence of social class differential on language tests is hardly surprising. But we are still justified in asking what aspects of 'environmental stimulation' are critical to the development of language skills in the mentally handicapped, and whether these differ in any essential sense from those which apply in the case of normal children.

Unfortunately, we have few guidelines from research to help us towards the answers to these questions. We know very little about how parents or teachers actually talk to subnormal children. A number of studies have demonstrated how adults typically restrict the range and diversity of their utterances when talking to retarded children (Spradlin and Rosenberg, 1964) and that the more retarded a child is perceived to be, the less people talk to him (Rosenberg *et al.*, 1961). The effect of this is to remove language stimulation from the child who needs it most. Moreover, since many subnormal people are underfunctioning in respect of language skills, their lack of language may give others the impression that they are more subnormal than they really are, thus further reducing the language stimulation from the environment.

It would be useful to have more information about ways in which mothers and teachers actually talk to and interact verbally with subnormal children in everyday situations, and to study adult utterances in terms of their communicative efficiency and their relevance to the language skills of the retarded person. Jeffree and Cashdan (1971) reported a tendency for mothers of subnormal children to fire a constant barrage of questions at them in order to get them to talk, and that most of these questions were of the 'what's this called?' type – i.e. calling for one word answers, usually nouns. This behaviour occurred in a situation in which mothers were asked to take their child round a model zoo, and talk to them about the various animals and situations in the same way as if they were visiting a real zoo. A previous study of mothers of normal nursery school children had shown substantial social class differences (Adkins, 1969); however, mothers of subnormal children of comparable levels of development differed significantly in their behaviour from mothers of normal children. 'They failed to set the scene or to explain what was happening, or to feed in information or fantasy.' Instead, they tended to fire simple questions at the child. Further work is needed to establish whether they would use similar language at home, and the extent to which findings such as these might be due to a special artefact of the testing situation.

However, even if parents are intent on providing a rich and complex language environment, this is not necessarily appropriate for a language retarded child. To a child with a severe comprehension difficulty the use of long sentences or of an elaborated type code may be meaningless and confusing, and may succeed only in teaching him that adult language is best ignored. A programme of language therapy, whether formally planned or informally administered, needs to take note of the child's ability to benefit from the kind of adult language stimulation which is generally considered appropriate for normal children (Rutter and Sussenwein, 1971). Similarly, it is of little use exposing a child to a stimulating verbal environment such as a normal nursery school on the assumption that he will learn from other children. The consensus of research evidence indicates that language is best learned from individual interaction with adults rather than from mere exposure to other children. On the other hand, one should be cautious about advising parents to 'keep talking to him', since they might then maintain a continuous chatter which is largely unintelligible to the child and which will lead him to regard adult language as unrewarding, and eventually to stop listening (Rutter and Mittler, 1972).

Language disorders in subnormals

Our knowledge of language development in the mentally handicapped is lamentably limited; in fact, there is little that we can assert with confidence, beyond the much-documented truisms that language develops late and that it remains primitive and undifferentiated. We lack detailed longitudinal studies of language development in subnormal populations; even the numerous cross-sectional and survey type studies have tended to concentrate on global estimates of language development and have so far made little use of the kind of detailed and fine-grain measures which would clarify whether some aspects of language considered as a group of skills were more impaired than others.

INCIDENCE

We shall confine ourselves in this section to a brief consideration of surveys of language as distinct from speech disorders. The distinction is obviously not a hard and fast one, but will follow the lines proposed at the beginning of this chapter. Even so, many of the surveys express their findings in global fashion ('difficulties of communication'), and do not differentiate at a detailed level between different aspects of language functioning.

In a review of earlier studies, Spreen (1965a) documents the expected relationship between IQ and both speech and language disorders. The frequency of language disorders is 100 per cent below IQ 20, around 90 per cent in the IQ range 21–50, and about 45 per cent in mildly retarded groups. These figures are based on a large number of reports, but definition criteria and survey methods obviously vary widely. Problems also arise on account of overlap in item content between intelligence tests and language measures; many IQ test items are verbal, and many items in language tests are similar to those found in intelligence tests. That some measure of independence does exist, however, is suggested by factorial studies and by studies which correlate items of low redundancy. Although it would be unrealistic and meaningless to demand 'pure' measures of either language or intelligence, some attempt to differentiate between them is necessary, partly because of the possibility which exists both for individual subjects and for populations that language functions are specifically depressed in relation to other aspects of development. If this is the case, there is justification in designing remedial compensatory measures.

It seems probable that some aspects of language are more affected than others. For subnormals who have developed some degree of language ability, there appears to be little difference in size of vocabulary between normals and subnormals matched on MA; in fact, a study of Thompson and Magaret (1947) suggested that subnormals were better. On the other hand, they were substantially inferior on higher level language skills. Lyle (1961) reported that subnormals scored lower than matched normals on naming of familiar objects, word definitions, grammatical accuracy and complexity of utterances, and also used much more jargon, sign language and irrelevant remarks. Mein (1961), on the basis of interviews and semi-structured picture descriptions of institutionalized subnormal adults, suggested that they tended to rely unduly on nouns, and that this was particularly marked in mongols, who were not otherwise impaired in word production or fluency. Other studies have noted discrepancies based on measures of sentence length, relative to normative data reported by Templin (1957). However, O'Connor and Hermelin (1963), on the basis of experiments on noun, verb and adjective usage, could not find differences between normal and subnormals in respect of language structure.

In general, the evidence suggests that subnormals are likely to show specific difficulties or protracted delay in the structural aspects of language, particularly in respect of sentence length, and syntax and sentence complexity (for other reviews see Jordan, 1967; Webb and Kinde, 1968; Schiefelbusch, 1963, 1972; and Schiefelbusch *et al.*, 1967. Relevant recent studies include those by Saunders and Miller, 1968, and Beier *et al.*, 1969).

LANGUAGE AND DOWN'S SYNDROME

Mongols appear to show a pattern of inferiority on some aspects of language, and also to be particularly vulnerable to the effects of institutionalization (Lyle, 1960; Schlanger and Gottsleben, 1957). In Lyle's study, there was a difference corresponding to nine months of verbal MA between mongols and non-mongols, but this discrepancy was not significant in comparable samples living at home and attending training centres. But he also showed that much depended on the level of language development attained by the child prior to hsopitalization. Children who had acquired some language skills adjusted better to hospital than those who had failed to do so. In a recent longitudinal study of mongol children living at home, Carr (1970) showed that 'motor' development was consistently ahead of 'mental' development, as measured by the Bayley scales.

A number of ITPA studies have suggested a specific mongol profile on this test, characterized by outstandingly high scores on motor encoding (use of gesture), poor performance on the auditory-vocal channel (particularly the auditory-vocal automatic subtest concerned with morphology) and relatively high scores on the visual-motor channel (Bilovsky and Share, 1965; McCarthy, 1964). Their language development is also markedly slow compared to other aspects of development. In Thompson's (1963) sample no child showed language skills commensurate with mental age.

We cannot in the present state of knowledge easily relate deficits of the kind described to specific physiological or biological deficits. Even if it were possible to demonstrate a link between a specific clinical syndrome and a characteristic pattern of language function, we still need to examine the extent to which environmental variables constitute contributory factors. This is a relevant question for research using groups, but is even more pertinent when we are considering an individual child. Although the relative contribution of biological and environmental factors to language development cannot be precisely assessed even in the individual case, the educator will clearly be concerned with environmental influences which may have unduly prevented or further retarded language development, and will also try to mobilize environmental resources as effectively as possible in order to facilitate further development, whatever the cause of the previous failure. (See Evans and Hampson, 1968, for a review.)

DELAYED OR DEVIANT?

It is sometimes asked whether subnormal children are merely very slow developers, or whether they show specific deficits in one or other aspect of language skill over and above what might be expected on the basis of their mental subnormality. This sounds a reasonable question, but we have no proper basis on which to answer it, and what evidence we have suggests that both developmental delay and specific deficit can be held responsible. On a developmental view, the mentally handicapped person is held to pass through the same stages of development as a normal person, but at a slower rate and with a reduced likelihood of reaching the stages attained by normal children at the age of about 8. A defect position is supported if it can be shown that subnormals are inferior on a learning task or language skill compared with normal children matched for mental age. It will be apparent that the issue revolves largely around mental age matching procedures. But the assumptions behind MA matching have now been questioned for a variety of reasons (e.g. Baumeister, 1967) and the contrast between developmental and deficit positions may be more apparent than real. (See also Chapter 10.)

A number of studies have provided preliminary if not conclusive evidence. The study by Lenneberg *et al.* (1964) is usually quoted in support of a developmental position, but it is open to more than one interpretation. They examined the language development of sixty-one mongol children living at home, between 3 and 22 years of age, and with IQs ranging between the 20s and 70s. A strong relationship was found between language and motor development – especially age of walking, dressing and feeding independently. In general, language development was more strongly related to chronological age than to IQ. Moreover, mongols seemed to go through the same stages of development as normal children in respect of babbling and early one-word utterances, though articulation disorders were frequent. However, language development stopped far short of that reached by normal children; the rate of progress was slowed down as the children became older, so that they seemed to lag further behind the older they became. Thus, what begins as a developmental disorder in childhood finishes as a deficit at maturity.

It is also relevant to ask not merely whether language is developmentally delayed, but the extent to which it is delayed. Evidence on this question is hard to find, partly because it is difficult to estimate the level of language development that should be expected in a subnormal person or population with given characteristics. But it is reasonable to assume that many mentally handicapped persons are underfunctioning in so far as their language development is well below what might be expected from a knowledge of their level of development in other areas of development. For example, it is not at all uncommon to encounter patients in hospitals for the subnormal with a mental age around 5 years whose language development is well below a 3-year level. The normal 2-year-old has a vocabulary of several hundred words and is rapidly mastering the rules of syntax and morphology, but few subnormal children can expect to reach the level of linguistic competence reached by the normal child of 5 or 6. In a study of an institutionalized population, Blanchard (1964) found few patients whose level of language development went beyond a 4-year level. An unpublished study by Webb (cited in Webb and Kinde, 1968) showed that 70 per cent of a sample of adults in a sheltered workshop scored 2 years below MA on ITPA total Language Age scores.

Unfortunately, we do not precisely know the level of language development that can be expected at any particular stage of intellectual development. Clearly, there is cause for concern about a child whose mental and social development corresponds to a 4- or 5- year level but whose language development is well below a 2- year level. But what about a child with a mental age of 5 and a 'language age' of 4 years? Discrepancies as small as this may be of little real significance, and may be no more than measurement artefacts. Moreover, we have no basis for assuming that there should be a one-to-one relationship between intellectual development on the one hand and language development on the other. Even if the test results were reliable and accurate, we could not assume that a child with a mental age of 5 and a language age of only 4 was necessarily 'under-functioning'. Similar problems occur at a later stage in considering the equally complex relationship between mental age and reading age (cf. Graham, 1967; Burt, 1967).

Although it seems likely on the whole that a considerable degree of under-functioning is to be found in the mentally subnormal, the precise amount is difficult to determine and will, in any case, vary considerably depending on individual circumstances. Thus, developmental delay can be seen not only in relation to normal populations, but also by comparison with other aspects of the subnormal person's own development. The existence of both developmental disorders and specific deficits is suggested in the comparative study by Marinosson (1970) in which the revised edition of the ITPA was administered to 30 normal, 30 educationally subnormal (ESN) and 30 severely subnormal (SSN) children, carefully matched for vocabulary age on the English Picture Vocabulary Test. Although all the groups had a VA between 5–0 and 6–0, the normal children were consistently superior on all the ten subtests, the SSNs lowest, while the ESN children showed intermediate scores. The profiles of the three groups were on the whole parallel, suggesting that the pattern of linguistic organization was similar. Both groups of subnormal children showed substantial underfunctioning in relation to the normal controls. However, the subnormal children showed specific impairments on the two sequential memory tests; both ESN and SSN children produced very low scores on the visual sequential memory test, whereas the impairment on auditory sequential memory was less marked for the ESN subjects.

Some groups of children also seem to have particular difficulty in structuring incoming auditory material. Autistic children, for example, are in some respects at least quite different from SSN children. Although they show exceptionally good immediate rote memory, and do not show the characteristic deficits of sequencing found in the SSN, they seem to be extraordinarily unselective in what they remember, and perform equally well if they are asked to recall unstructured nonsense strings as they do when presented with structured and meaningful sentences (Hermelin and O'Connor, 1970; Hermelin, 1971; Frith, 1971). This suggests specific deficiencies in coding and categorizing processes which are relatively more marked in autistic than in matched subnormal or normal controls (see also Chapter 12).

It is worth recalling in this connection that factorial studies on the Wechsler scales tend to suggest the presence of a short-term memory factor which is present in subnormals but not in normals (Baumeister and Bartlett, 1962a, b).

LANGUAGE AND PROBLEM SOLVING

A further example of a possible specific deficit arises from work on the verbal regulation of behaviour. A subnormal person may show deficiencies in language functions when these are analysed in terms of communication or skills analysis, but may be relatively proficient in the use of language in problem solving situations. At these times he may be making use of what has been described as 'inner' or 'covert' language. That such a language system exists is suggested by a substantial body of research with intelligent but profoundly deaf subjects (Furth, 1966).

The nature of the relationship between language and thinking has preoccupied philosophers and psychologists for a long time. Luria (1961, 1963) and other Soviet psychologists have developed Pavlov's later distinction between first and second signalling systems. Luria has described four stages in which behaviour comes under increasing control of the second signalling system. His experimental situation required the child to press (or not to press) a button on the appearance of a particular signal, usually a light or buzzer, though this basic paradigm has been extensively varied.

In the first stage, any utterance by the experimenter (E) causes the subject (S) to press, regardless of whether E says 'Press' or 'Don't press'. This is essentially the *orienting* phase, the words primarily serving to attract the child's attention. In the second stage, the child can inhibit pressing in response to E's 'Don't press'. This is described by Luria as the *releasing* or *impulsive* function of language which seems to cue the child to do what he was already going to do. Thirdly, the child tells himself aloud what to do, and can be heard quietly rehearsing 'Press', 'Don't press', or 'Yes', 'No'. At this stage, language has acquired a *selective* function. The final stage consists primarily of covert self-instruction (pre-selection) in which the child can respond appropriately to an instruction in the form 'Press if the red light comes on, but don't press if the green light comes on'. This stage is not normally reached until around 5 years. Even at this stage, the child may repeat the instructions to himself more or less verbatim, but later comes to condense them to telegraphic form. Luria particularly stresses the role of language in *inhibiting* behaviour, and argues that subnormals have a particular deficit in this respect. A small number of normative and experimental studies have been reported in recent years which suggest that Luria's model is potentially of diagnostic as well as theoretical significance (Burland, 1969; Schubert, 1969; Hogg, 1973) though a study by Miller *et al.* (1970) failed to confirm the increasing use of verbal mediation with age.

The effects of language on thinking and problem solving are usually demonstrated by studying the effects of labelling or other verbal cues on a discrimination learning task. A study by Barnett *et al.* (1959) demonstrated that subnormal subjects who learned names of objects on a delayed recall task performed significantly better than those who did not, and that this effect was equally marked for both higher and lower MA levels. This subject was also extensively investigated by O'Connor and Hermelin (1963), in a series of studies in which the contribution of verbal mediation was systematically varied in tasks involving generalization, transfer and cross-modal coding. A brief summary of this and later research is contained in a recent review (O'Connor and Hermelin, 1971). It appears that subnormal children could perform certain visual discriminations without verbal labelling, but they were not retained. They tend not to use verbal labels spontaneously, as normal children do, but can be helped to acquire and use them under certain conditions. Thus, the original formulation of Soviet psychologists in terms of a dissociation between first and second signalling systems was not supported, and one cannot any longer confidently assert that subnormals suffer from a 'specific verbal mediation deficiency', over and above what would be expected for the MA level.

Different results were obtained in tasks calling for cross-modal coding. The necessity for verbal coding in translating a stimulus from one modality to another seemed to facilitate learning, though this was less effective in conditions in which the verbal coding was difficult.

Later work by Bryant (1967) has indicated that verbal labelling at the initial learning phase does not necessarily make for transfer. He also showed that while verbal labelling facilitates recall, there are no clear effects on recognition, though matched normal subjects demonstrated effects on both recall and recognition. Similar lack of transfer in subnormals is shown as a result of providing specific verbal instructions about the relevant dimension in a discrimination learning task.

Absence or deficiency in verbal mediation may be a positive advantage in those cases where self-imposed verbal mediation strategy may provide misleading information. This has also been suggested in some studies of highly intelligent children in concept attainment tasks (e.g. Osler and Trautman, 1961). An example of such a situation occurs in a non-reversal learning shift situation: in a study reported by Sanders *et al.* (1965) subnormals were actually found to be superior to MA matched normals (see Reese and Lipsitt, 1970, for a fuller discussion of this question). It has also been suggested that verbal mediation may not be the most parsimonious explanation, and that the problem may take the form of a production deficiency in which children have the necessary cognitive skills but can neither make use of them nor produce verbal formulations of the reasons for their solutions (Flavell *et al.*, 1966).

From a practical point of view, it is important to stress that the degree of meaningfulness of the material is a particularly critical variable for subnormals. Weir and Stevenson (1959) showed that learning was facilitated if the subject had to name the stimulus before responding, while Jensen and Rohwer (1963) showed that mediators provided in the form of a sentence were superior to mere labelling, though long-term retention did not seem to show any benefit.

Spreen (1965b) summarizes the conditions that must be fulfilled if learning is to be furthered by verbal mediation: (i) the discrimination stimuli must be similar enough to allow generalization to occur initially; (ii) the responses to be learned must be discrete; (iii) the names learned during pre-training must be distinctive; (iv) the names must all be learned to a high criterion. Even Kendler and Kendler (1967), the most dedicated proponents of verbal mediation theory, have now conceded that a mediator need not necessarily be verbal. In fact, any response, whether implicit or a motor act, may have the effect of adding distinctiveness or signalling properties to cues, and thus enhance learning. The systematic use of non-verbal cues both by teachers and by subnormals themselves seem to be an important development in compensatory education for this population, but has not yet been tried on any scale. The most promising work has in fact been done on chimpanzees (Gardner and Gardner, 1969; Premack, 1970).

Assessment

Although adequate assessment procedures are essential both for the subnormal individual and for research, priorities have recently shifted from assessment to teaching. This is partly due to dissatisfaction with currently available assessment tests, and partly to a greater appreciation of what can be achieved by teaching. But the Skinnerian precept, 'Don't test, teach,' might be rephrased as 'Don't teach without testing', since it is difficult to evaluate the effects of teaching without previously assessing the child's language skills. But there is considerable uncertainty at the present time both about the strategy and the tactics of testing, not only in language but in relation to other aspects of cognitive development. Doubts are being expressed about the rationale of using normative instruments which compare the subnormal with the normal population on which the test has been standardized, about the reliance on such measures for the planning of remedial programmes (Mittler, 1970a, 1973a) and about the assumption that a test adequately samples 'real' skills and abilities as reflected in ordinary situations. Moreover, existing tests are often unsuitable for subnormal individuals with only limited language development; the ITPA, for example, although standardized on a normal population ranging in age from $2\frac{1}{2}$ to 10, suffers from 'floor' effects and is difficult to use below a 4-year level of language development. Finally, a formal test involving language skills may be inappropriate for motivational reasons in a subnormal population.

Increased emphasis is therefore being placed on assessment techniques which rely on observational methods. Samples of language can be collected in various real-life situations – in school, on the ward and at home, as well as in free play situations in an assessment class or clinic. The degree of sophistication which is then applied to the analysis of the data depends on the specific interests of the investigator. Greater use is also being made of developmental scales completed by someone who is familiar with the child. This includes parents as well as professionals.

OBSERVATIONAL METHODS

Reliable sampling of a child's language in everyday situations presents fewer problems with retarded children who say relatively little during the course of a single observational session than in the case of a larger class of normal pre-school children. A teacher in an assessment class would not be able to listen to more than one child during a session but it should not be impossible for her to record everything the child says during a given period of time. Observation and recording of language in 'real life' situations has advantages over the artificial sampling of language skills in a formal test situation, but the interpretation of the data collected presents more problems. Analysis of utterances can obviously range in sophistication from a simple count of the number of words spoken (assuming we can agree on the definition of 'word') to a complex analysis of the generative transformational complexity of the child's grammar. Whatever the level of analysis used, it is essential that the data be systematically collected, otherwise the observations and the time spent on them will be wasted. The data can be kept in cumulative record form merely for the teacher's own information, so that a regular check on the nature or complexity of the child's utterances is available. At the simplest level it need be little more than a slightly more systematic version of the kind of language diary which many mothers keep on their own children at the earliest stages of language development. If a full record is kept of everything that the child says in a fifteen-minute session over one or more days, together with comments on the general context in which the utterances took place, it should be possible to note changes in length or complexity of utterances over a period of time.

The way in which language data is analysed clearly depends on the purposes to which the analysis is put. Although it is useful to keep the analysis to a simple level for ordinary purposes, it is also important to be aware of somewhat more complex though time-consuming methods. One of the earliest but most useful indices of language maturity is based on the mean length of utterance over a given period. This method was used by earlier investigators such as McCarthy (1954), Davis (1937) and Templin (1957) who collected a great deal of data on utterance length as a function of age, sex, social class, etc. Rules for the use of this method are clearly described by Templin (1957). Mean length of response appears to be a sensitive index of language development; Shriner and Sherman (1967) reported that this was the most useful of several other measures, including mean of five longest responses, number of one-word responses, the number of different words and a structural complexity score. A more complex system has been developed by Miner (1969).

Length of utterance is by itself a fairly limited criterion of language development, and needs to be supplemented by an analysis of level of linguistic complexity. Such measures are influenced by recent work in developmental psycholinguistics. Lee and Canter (1971) have recently reported a procedure for estimating the complexity of the sentence structure used by children between 3 and 7 years. Although percentile norms are provided for this particular age range, the method is not a standardized test and still depends on collecting the language samples in natural play situations. Developmental Sentence Scoring (DSS) provides a method of estimating the extent to which a child has learned grammatical 'rules' concerned with the use of indefinite and personal pronouns, verbs, negatives, conjunctions, interrogative reversals and 'wh-' questions. Suggestions are given for ways in which the teacher or speech pathologist can plan a series of teaching situations which introduce such structures in an appropriate sequence.

Teachers of very young or severely handicapped children may feel that these methods assume a more advanced level of language development than that shown by children in their class. It is therefore necessary to devise assessment techniques, whether based on formal tests or systematic observation, which are relevant to much earlier stages of development. To cater for this need, Lee (1966) devised a Developmental Sentence Type Chart to estimate the child's ability to use two-word utterances, simple phrase structure rules and transformations of kernel sentences. Going back further still, it is possible to carry out a straightforward classification of single-word utterances by dividing them into different 'parts of speech' – e.g. nouns, verbs, adjectives, interjections, etc. Note should also be taken of whether the utterance is in response to another person, whether it is a repetition of what someone has just said, and whether it is spoken to someone else or to no one in particular.

DEVELOPMENTAL SCALES

Most of the examples already considered refer to children whose language development has reached the point where they have a vocabulary of at least single words or where they have already started to combine two words meaningfully. Many mentally handicapped children have not yet reached either of these stages, particularly the younger ones who are increasingly being admitted to special schools or observation units. It is often a case of assessing the 'language' abilities of a child who does not yet have any meaningful speech. This is not a contradication in terms, since language comprises many skills, only some of which concern expressive language. These skills can be tentatively assessed by comparing the child's performance with approximate sequences of normal development.

The value of normative data should not be underestimated. Although there are still many gaps in our knowledge, a great deal of research has been done on the development of language in the normal child with the result that we know a good deal about the stages or sequences of development. It seems reasonable to assume, at least as a preliminary basis for study of an individual or group, that the stages will be similar for normal and subnormal children, provided we bear in mind that individual discontinuities and distortions will occur in many cases. For example, a stage or step may be omitted; this is not uncommon in physical development, when we find that a child progresses to the walking stage with little or no time spent crawling. Similarly, one occasionally hears anecdotal evidence about a child who suddenly begins to speak in long sentences, having previously been heard to speak only in single-word utterances. Such cases are rare, and few have been adequately documented, but it is worth bearing in mind that they may exist. Unevenness of development may also occur horizontally as well as vertically; Down's syndrome children are commonly relatively more advanced in physical than in language development, and in one aspect of language compared with another (Evans and Hampson, 1968).

But the normative approach has certain limitations. These can best be illustrated by an examination of published scales of language development. In the first place, many of the items on such a scale are difficult to interpret and score ('Quieted by voice', 'Searches for sound with eyes', 'Shouts for attention', etc.). Secondly, the scales assume agreement on the meaning of 'the word' as a stage of development. Darley and Winitz (1961) after an exhaustive review of the numerous studies investigating 'age at first word' concluded that 'children begin to speak when their parents think they do'. In the case of subnormal children, it is particularly difficult to know whether a certain sound is consistently used in the context of a particular situation or object; it is all too easy to attribute meaning or consistency to a sound, when it may exist in the ear of the listener rather than in the mind of the child. Furthermore, the scales are lacking in detail after the age of about 12 months and tend to be confined to a few items only (e.g. one clear word at 12 months, three at 13 months etc.).

In addition to the normative approach, it is useful to attempt an assessment which, while still being roughly developmental in character, is based on an attempt to describe the development of specific language skills from a criterion point of view. Such an attempt was made in the context of a workshop for parents of young mentally handicapped children, which had as one of its objectives the training of parents in a form of developmental assessment of their own child, based on observation and the use of specially prepared developmental schedules (Cunningham and Jeffree, 1971). The chart was designed to help parents and others to structure their observations, and to consider different aspects of language, including the growth of vocabulary, the use of language for communication, sentence structure, comprehension and imitation. It was also hoped that the chart would highlight specific needs and hence lead to a programme of structured play and language stimulation. Parents appeared to welcome the opportunity to carry out an assessment of their own child's development, and generally succeeded in filling in the charts, once ambiguities and difficulties had been clarified in small tutorial-type discussion groups. The profile approach enabled them to understand the unevenness of development both between and within areas of development. Thus, a young mongol child may be relatively advanced in imitation, but may be poor at understanding instructions or in vocalization. Parental assessment was not compared with that carried out by 'experienced testers', but the aim was not so much accuracy of normative placement as the sharpening of observational skills.

A number of published scales are now available which consist of a more or less detailed check list of skills and abilities reached by normal children at different ages. Some are rapid screening devices containing only a few items, others are longer and more comprehensive schedules with many items at each period. Among the shorter American scales are the Denver Developmental Screening Test (Frankenburg and Dobbs, 1967), the Utah Test of Language Development (Mecham *et al.*, 1967), the Houston Test for Language Development (Crabtree, 1958). Relevant British scales that include but are not exclusively concerned with language have been prepared by Sheridan (1973) and Gunzburg (1966).

A final limitation of developmental charts is that many aspects of behaviour may be critical to the development of a skill but are difficult to place on a scale. One example of this concerns the importance of play as a precursor to language. The child whose play is representational or symbolic, who shows, for example, that he is able to make one thing stand for another, is laying essential foundations for language development.

LANGUAGE COMPREHENSION

The importance of comprehension in language acquisition has already been discussed, but it may be useful to refer to methods of assessing comprehension, since this is clearly essential in the case of people whose expressive language skills are limited or non-existent. It is frequently claimed that a child 'understands everything you say', but such statements should be treated with caution, since he is likely to be using a wide variety of non-verbal, contextual and situational cues, and it is difficult to distinguish these from the processes involved in understanding language itself.

How then can we assess comprehension? It is not difficult to test for comprehension of single words, and standardized tests are available for this purpose. Perhaps the best known is the Peabody Picture Vocabulary Test (Dunn, 1959). This test merely requires the child to point to one of four pictures in response to a stimulus word spoken by the experimenter. The number of words correctly identified can be compared against available norms, and expressed in terms of a vocabulary age, percentile equivalent or IQ. The test begins at a 21-month level, and usually presents few difficulties of administration, since the child merely has to be able to select one of four pictures by pointing. It is a useful test to administer at the beginning of an assessment session, though results must be interpreted with caution. Although the test shows acceptable levels of reliability, it does not always correlate well with other language tests such as the Illinois scales (Carr *et al.*, 1967) or with a test of general intelligence such as the Wechsler (Shaw *et al.*, 1966). To use it as an intelligence test may therefore be misleading; it is, however, of interest as a simple measure of vocabulary recognition, yielding a vocabulary age. Shortened English versions are also available, though only from a 3-year level upwards (Brimer and Dunn, 1965).

One of the difficulties of tests of the Peabody type is finding visual referents which provide an equal amount of information to the child. The very young or the very handicapped child may point to the most interesting picture of the four, or the one that provides the most novelty. It is almost impossible to hold visual variables constant, so that one picture does not prove to be more salient or prominent to the child than any other. If the child is correct, then we can safely assume that he knows the word being tested: if he points to the wrong picture, or appears to be pointing quite randomly, then we do not really know whether this is because he does not know the word, or because he cannot carry out the visual search operations necessary to enable him to look at each picture successively; furthermore, he might be unable to integrate the visual scanning task with the verbal signal from the examiner: in other words, he might have difficulties in cross-modal coding, or in short-term memory. Most commonly, however, the very young child tends to point to the picture that first captures his attention, and sometimes does so even before the examiner has had a chance to say the stimulus word.

The Peabody test is merely the most obvious instance of our ignorance of the psychological processes underlying what appears at first sight to be a commonplace task. In fact, we have not begun to study all the relevant variables involved in tests of this kind, and there is reason to be dissatisfied with most tests that purport to measure comprehension of language but which depend heavily on the need to scan visual material, and then to make fairly complex discriminations in which the relative prominence of auditory and visual cues is difficult to control.

Similar problems arise when we ask a child to carry out comprehension tasks using small toys and other three-dimensional material. Here again, such items as 'put the spoon in the cup' or 'Give me the car' are highly predictable, and are just the kind of actions which the child might carry out even if no instructions had been given. Toys have the additional disadvantage of being too interesting, so that a child might become so absorbed in playing with them that he is not really listening to the examiner asking him to carry out certain actions. He might therefore be correct because most of the commands might be guessed by chance, or he might be wrong for any of the reasons discussed earlier but also because the test has become too much of a play situation for him.

These sources of error or bias must not be exaggerated, but it is also important not to assume that a child's failure is due to lack of comprehension when other variables may be involved which have not been adequately controlled in the test, and which generally remain uninvestigated. For this reason, it is necessary to ask the child to carry out fairly unexpected actions with the test material, though this too may have the disadvantage of violating too many pragmatic expectations. If, for example, one is investigating the child's comprehension of prepositions, he may not expect you to say 'Put the spoon *under* the cup', and conclude that you must obviously be asking him to 'Put the spoon *in* the cup'.

It is apparent therefore that the listener trying to understand a message is dealing not only with the language used by the speaker but also with a very large number of communication cues. If we want to assess the extent to which a child understands language, we should try as far as possible to exclude as many non-linguistic cues as possible. To some extent this is bound to be an artificial exercise, since the child normally has so many non-linguistic cues available to help him. But these cues will obviously vary considerably from one situation to another, so that it seems important to try to differentiate between linguistic and non-linguistic information, and in particular to vary the nature of the linguistic input in a systematic manner.

Work is now in progress in the Hester Adrian Research Centre to develop a sentence comprehension test. This test was originally devised with Angela Hobsbaum at Birkbeck College, London, and has now undergone various modifications (Hobsbaum and Mittler, 1971). The child is presented with 4 examples of 15 types of sentence of varying complexity and grammatical structure. His task is to identify which of 3 or 4 pictures corresponds to the sentence spoken by the examiner. Each picture illustrates an alternative grammatical interpretation. Thus, in response to the sentence '*The cat is sleeping*', the child is shown pictures of a *dog* sleeping, and also of a cat *playing* with a ball of string, i.e. the noun and the verb have been systematically varied. Similarly, in response to the sentence '*The girl is cutting the cake*', the child is shown the following pictures:

The girl is cutting the cake (stimulus)
The *boy* is cutting the cake (subject varied)
The girl is *eating* the cake (verb varied)
The girl is cutting the *loaf* (object varied)

Other sentence types tested include comparatives and superlatives, past and future tenses, passives, negatives, plurals, prepositions and embedded clauses.

Data are now available on 150 normal nursery school children between 34 and 54 months; the test has also been administered to 200 SSN children matched for mental age with the normal controls (mean MA 3–7). Order of difficulty was very similar for normal and subnormal children (rho = ·78), suggesting that the test is measuring comparable processes in the two groups. It also shows acceptable levels of test reliability (Mittler and Wheldall, 1971; Mittler *et al.*, 1974).

Other attempts to assess sentence comprehension have also been reported in recent years. Carrow (1968) presents a useful table (reproduced in Berry, 1969) showing the approximate ages at which 60 per cent of normal children understand specific grammatical structures, such as nouns, verbs, adjectives, adverbs, prepositions, tenses and genders. The North West Syntax Screening Test (Lee, 1969, 1970) consists of 20 sentence pairs to be identified respectively by picture selection, and 20 comparable pairs to be produced in response to stimulus pictures. Norms for both receptive and expressive skills are presented in percentile graphs, but as the name implies, the test provides only a rapid screening measure yielding a global total score, and is not intended as a detailed grammatical analysis of receptive language.

These tests are still at the research stage, and are mentioned mainly in order to illustrate the difficulty in differentiating between comprehension of language and the child's response to the total communication situation of which language forms only one element. It is important to bear in mind that failure on a test is no proof of inability to perform a cognitive task; it is possible that the child has not adequately understood what is required of him, that he has been distracted by an irrelevant feature of the test situation or that he is in a general sense inattentive to the task. When dealing with mentally handicapped children, we cannot assume, as we usually do for normal children, that they are attending to or understanding our instructions, or that they are interested in carrying them out. In this sense, we need to pay special attention to the complexity of the language which we use in testing or talking to children with intellectual or linguistic handicaps.

STANDARDIZED TESTS

Perhaps the best known and certainly the most ambitious test of language abilities is the Illinois Test of Psycholinguistic Abilities (ITPA). An experimental edition of the test was published in 1961 (McCarthy and Kirk, 1961) and a revised edition is now available in Britain (Kirk *et al.*, 1968; Paraskevopoulos and Kirk, 1969). The test is based on a model of communication processes first proposed by Osgood (1957). Basically, the model distinguishes between channels of communication, levels of organization and psycholinguistic processes. The model aims to provide a specification for all the processes and all the levels that appear to be involved in both understanding and speaking a language, but the test itself only samples ten features of the model. Each test purports to assess a different aspect of language functioning, and can be scored in terms of raw score, language age and standard scores. A total language score can also be derived.

A substantial literature has now grown up around the experimental edition (Bateman, 1965, 1968; Kirk, 1968; Kirk and Kirk, 1971; see also Clark, this volume, Chapter 14). The test was initially enthusiastically received in North America, but its reception in Britain has been more conservative.

The need for a multifactorial test of language should be seen in the context of a reaction against the traditional monopoly enjoyed by intelligence tests such as the Binet and Wechsler scales, and a growing interest in attempts to identify and isolate specific cognitive skills, not only in respect of language abilities, but also in the area of perception, memory, learning and intelligence itself. It was hoped that a 'profile' approach would yield an analysis of specific strengths and weaknesses which could then be used as the basis of a remedial programme tailor-made to the needs of the individual child. In other words, the test was designed to be diagnostic, but did not confine itself to mere classification.

Nevertheless, the test has latterly come under increasing criticism, partly on technical grounds, and partly as a result of a growing disenchantment with formal tests in general. Technical criticisms throw doubt on the claim to have identified specific language abilities; factorial studies suggest that a substantial proportion of the variance is accounted for by general linguistic ability (Mittler and Ward, 1970; Smith and Marx, 1971). In a review of eighteen factorial studies, Ryckman and Wiegernink (1969) found little consistency of factor structure between age-groups, but showed an increase in the number of factors as age increased. At younger ages the test appears to function in a more global manner, presumably because language abilities have not been or cannot be differentiated at these early stages of development. Technical and psychometric criticisms have also been made by Weener *et al.* (1967).

The ITPA represented a useful development when it was first developed in the 1950s, but now suffers from having been overtaken by events. The model of language on which it was based now seems outmoded in the light of the developments that have taken place in psycholinguistics. Apart from a brief reference to the work of Berko (1958), the test owes little or nothing to models of language structure developed by Chomsky or to theories of the language acquisition process proposed by some of his followers (e.g. McNeill, 1966, 1970a; Menyuk, 1969; Slobin, 1971a). Osgood himself has modified the original (1957) model on which the ITPA was based towards one more influenced by transformational generative grammar (Osgood, 1968), but these developments are not reflected in the test.

Nevertheless, the ITPA represents an important advance and deserves some (if not all) the popularity which special educators and psychologists have bestowed on it. It has helped us to take a more multifactorial view of language, with the result that we are now more cautious in using global shorthand in describing handicapped children. But it should not be thought that the ITPA provides a comprehensive or relevant analysis of language skills. It is too far removed from 'real life' language behaviour, and is not based on any attempt to analyse minimum language requirements for a child in a given community. Such a requirement is particularly relevant for the older mentally handicapped child whether he is living in the community or being considered for discharge from residential care. The very success of the ITPA may, in fact, have hindered the development of more functionally orientated assessment techniques (Rosenberg, 1970). It may also have prevented psychologists and educators from subjecting recent language research to critical scrutiny of its possible practical significance.

OTHER LANGUAGE SCALES

Mention should also be made of a number of other scales which have become available in recent years.

(1) *The Reynell Developmental Language Scales (Reynell, 1969)*

The Reynell Scales have normative data based on children between the ages of 6 months and 6 years, but were designed from the outset with the needs of handicapped children in mind. They distinguish between receptive and expressive aspects of language. The Verbal Comprehension scale (A) requires mainly a simple pointing response or the manipulation of appropriate play materials. The child is required to point to objects or pictures which have to be identified or manipulated according to instructions of gradually increasing complexity. There is an alternative form of the Comprehension Test (B) for use with physically handicapped children who cannot pick up or even point to toys. The expressive tests aim to elicit samples of the child's spoken language in free conversation and in response to standard materials, and to score these in terms of structure, content and vocabulary. The RLDS is of particular value in the assessment of children whose language development is immature or uneven, and for whom more precise information is needed than that provided in general tests of language development. The distinction between receptive and expressive skills is a particularly important contribution towards assessment. It has not been available long enough for validation or subpopulation studies to be carried out on a large scale, but a dissertation by Rogers (1971) suggests that mongol children produce substantially lower receptive than expressive scores.

(2) *Renfrew Language Attainment Scales (Renfrew, 1971)*

The Renfrew Scales are primarily designed to help speech therapists and other experienced examiners to assess relevant aspects of language and speech in children between 3 and 7 years.
They consist of the following tests:

(i) *Articulation Attainment Test.* This test is designed to 'provide a standardized estimate of the extent to which use is made of all the English consonants'. The test makes use of 38 words containing 100 consonants, and is phonetically balanced in so far as each consonant is represented with the same frequency as in everyday speech. Spontaneous naming of the objects in pictures is required, as well as serial counting and imitation of phrases.
(ii) *Word Finding Vocabulary.* This scale assesses the ability of children to find

words, as distinct from recognizing them in association with pictures (as in the Peabody tests). The items are modified from those originally used by Watts (1944), and call for the identification of parts of the body, the naming of objects and shapes, the use of common and proper nouns, verbs, prepositions and other parts of speech.

(iii) *Action Pictures*. This test is designed to stimulate the child to give short samples of spoken language for purposes of a simple grammatical analysis. The child is shown nine pictures illustrating common activities, and asked questions designed to elicit the use of present, past and future tenses in regular and irregular forms, singular and plural nouns and simple and complex sentence constructions. The test is separately scored in terms of information and grammar.

(iv) *A Test of Continuous Speech*. A sample of continuous speech is elicited by first telling the child an interesting story, illustrated by suitable pictures (e.g., 'The Bus Story'), and then asking him to tell the story to the examiner. Scoring criteria are in terms of information and sentence length.

Some of the Renfrew tests have been under constant development and modification for a period of years, and data are available on a large number of children tested in various parts of Britain. Although problems of scoring and interpretation remain, the tests promise to be a useful addition to the better known and more ambitious scales already described.

(3) *Michigan Picture Language Inventory (Lerea, 1958; Wolski, 1962)*

The Michigan Inventory represents an early ingenious technique for the separate assessment of receptive and expressive skills, using identical linguistic content. Lerea, who originally devised the test, used the 'missing word' technique which is also found in the Grammatic Closure Test of the ITPA, and is intended to elicit specific grammatical constructions from the child, including regular and irregular nouns and verbs, different tenses, demonstratives, articles, pronouns, etc. The limitations of this method have been criticized elsewhere (Mittler, 1970a), but it is now widely agreed that knowledge of morphological rules may provide a sensitive reflection of linguistic competence. Berko's (1958) original study of morphological skills has given rise to a number of psychometric instruments (e.g. Blake and Williams, 1968; Berry and Talbot, 1966; Berry, 1969).

(4) *Sentence Repetition Tasks*

Elicited imitation has until quite recently been neglected as an assessment device, partly because imitation was thought to be a purely mechanical or perceptual-motor skill, and partly because such tasks were conventionally associated with memory testing. It is now becoming apparent that imitation involves the structuring and at least partial comprehension of the material, and that a detailed analysis of the imitation strategies and the exact type of errors made can provide a means of assessing linguistic maturity. The advantage of imitation as an assessment technique lies in the element of control which can be exercised over input, so that the complexity of the utterance can be made progressively more difficult, while keeping length and memory load constant as far as possible. It also has the advantage of being reasonably interesting to the child, as long as the test is not too long and is played almost as a game. Unfortunately, the use of imitation tasks is still in its infancy. Work is now in progress in Manchester on the construction of an imitation test for subnormal children (Berry, 1971; Mittler *et al.*, 1974).

Conclusions

In considering the status of language assessment techniques, we need to strike a sensible balance between clinging to tests merely because they provide scientific respectability or because we happen to be familiar with them, and abandoning them in favour of an enthusiastically but perhaps indiscriminately planned and applied teaching programme. According to one view, assessment for assessment's sake is educationally sterile and there is neither psychological nor indeed ethical justification for subjecting an individual to tests unless it can be shown that the procedures are designed to help him. In the case of a handicapped child, this would limit the use of tests largely to situations in which a remedial programme was to be designed on the basis of test findings.

It is also questionable whether the monopoly of testing traditionally enjoyed by psychologists is not now something of an anachronism. It has been argued elsewhere (Mittler, 1970c, 1973a) that intensive courses of training should be established for special educators in the principles and practice of psychological assessment, with the objective of having in each special school at least one teacher (not necessarily the head teacher) who is trained not merely in testing but in the use of assessment procedures to plan remedial programmes. School psychologists should by this means be freed from much of what is now called 'routine testing' in order to act as specialists and consultants in problem cases. There will always be complex or experimental tests which should be restricted to psychologists – perhaps ITPA was (or still is) in this category – but many other tests are comparatively simple and straightforward to administer, score and interpret.

Language teaching

STIMULATION AND STRUCTURE

In view of the evidence of serious underfunctioning, delay or deficit in language abilities, the question of teaching assumes added importance. Until quite recently, however, the fashion has been to rely on 'exposure' methods to a rich and linguistically stimulating environment, in the hope that the subnormal child will acquire language partly by 'learning from others', partly by listening to stories, and partly by needing to communicate his needs and thoughts in a social situation. This is presumably the rationale underlying the use of normal nursery schools for speechless or language disordered children. We have argued elsewhere that this may be more an act of faith than judgment unless specific efforts are directed to obtaining the desired verbal interaction (Rutter and

Mittler, 1972; Mittler, 1973b). A lively and stimulating environment is no doubt valuable, but it may not be enough. Some children have to be helped or even taught to adapt to such an environment, and may need to begin at an earlier developmental level by learning language at 'mother-distance' (Sheridan, 1964). Schiefelbusch *et al.* (1967) draw attention to certain prerequisites of language development which may have to be taught or recapitulated in the case of subnormal or severely language disordered children. These essentially concern stages in social development, and include sensory stimulation and smiling, attachment, word acquisition and social exploration, and lastly language acquisition and experience.

A further disadvantage in relying exclusively on exposure and stimulation is that such methods do not take account of the difficulties which subnormals appear to experience in spontaneous or incidental learning (Denny, 1964; Clarke and Clarke, 1973a) or in discriminating the relevant from the irrelevant in a learning situation. If these are 'real' deficits which are likely to occur with high frequency in a subnormal population, then the design of an appropriate learning environment both for the individual and for the group will need more careful thought than has so far been forthcoming. A wide variety of methods is in use, but very little research has been devoted to their effectiveness or to long-term results. Bereiter and Engelman (1966) advocate highly structured formal language lessons, designed to teach children to exploit the grammatical and syntactical possibilities of language to the full. Other workers have described less formal approaches, which place less reliance on drills and try to help the child to develop language skills in the context of enjoyable and relevant play and learning experiences (e.g. Klaus and Gray, 1968; Gahagan and Gahagan, 1970).

At this stage the problem appears to be one of finding a balance between stimulation and structure, and of realizing that they do not represent incompatible educational objectives or philosophies. But stimulation by itself is probably not enough for the majority of subnormal children, though it provides an essential background against which more structured approaches may be developed. It may be useful to think in terms of designing a series of graded environments which would provide for the needs of the individual child at various stages of his development. This might involve initially teaching him in fairly quiet conditions, in short sessions by himself or with only one or two others, and then gradually introducing him to progressively more stimulating and demanding situations. In other words, the relative prominence of stimulating or structured methods should be determined by the stage of development and the needs of the child, and this in turn can only be discovered as a result of systematic assessment.

What, then, do we mean by a rich and lively language environment, and what is it that constitutes stimulation?

THE LANGUAGE ENVIRONMENT

The child is in some form of language environment the moment he enters the classroom. The modern 'child-centred' approach to education is one of activity and movement, and encourages conversation between children, and between children and teachers. Inevitably and appropriately, it is likely to be noisy. But some children cannot tolerate what to them may be excessive stimulation, just as others react adversely to individual contact with an adult, even for a brief period. In the first group are children who can be seen to put their hands over their ears in conditions that would not strike an outsider as particularly noisy, or who retreat into a corner to pursue their own interests or to do their work. In the second group are children who are reasonably active and busy until an adult makes an individual approach or begins to make demands, when they avert their eyes or move away. Individual differences such as these exist in most classrooms and may be based on 'real' differences of personality or biological constitution. But this does not mean that they are necessarily resistant to modification. Some children may need to be taught or helped to function intellectually as well as socially in a group, while others may need help to allow them to cope with the demands of a one to one relationship.

It is also relevant to consider the function of adult utterances to children. Some of our utterances are in the form of commands ('Come here', 'Sit down', etc.) and some are merely offered as a running commentary or as a general encouragement ('That's a nice picture'). The running commentary is a powerful means of focusing the child's interest and helping to create a link between his own activity and the teacher's verbal formulation ('Oh, I see, you're making a train with your bricks, here's the engine, and here's the guard's van', etc.). Similarly, the teacher can try to extend the range of a child's representational play. If a pile of bricks is being used to make a train, she can ask (or ask the child to show) what else they can be used for – e.g. to make a station, a signal etc. The use of language in such circumstances comes as second nature to many teachers, and it is hardly necessary to provide a psychological rationale. Other teachers and many parents, however, tend to get discouraged if the child does not answer them, and may reduce the amount of verbal interaction with such a child without being fully aware of it. This is understandable, since we are conditioned by years of contact with normal children and adults to expect a reply and an interchange sooner or later, and some mothers in particular feel embarrassed by talking to a child who does not reply and who may not even show that he is understanding her.

Once a child does begin to say a few words, the teacher will obviously consider ways in which she can not only encourage him to extend his present level of language functioning, but also talk to him in ways that will help him to attain the next stage. For example, a child's spoken language may be confined to a small number of single words, all of which happen to be nouns. The teacher may want to introduce more nouns, in order to reinforce the principle that 'things' have 'names' – a breakthrough which may be as dramatic and as significant as it was in the case of Helen Keller and Miss Sullivan. At the same time, she may be considering how to introduce him to verbs, by using and perhaps encouraging him to use verb forms to describe his own activities ('eating', 'painting', 'running' etc.). Chalfant (1968) has reported a kind of 'do and say' programme for young mongol children, who are encouraged to use a single verb or verb phrase in the form of a pacing commentary on their own activities. (See also Mittler *et al.*, 1974.)

It is also instructive to listen to a tape recording of an adult with a group of retarded children, and then to carry out a simple analysis of the kinds of questions which children are asked. Many questions are phrased in such a way as to make it almost impossible to answer in anything other than single words, most of which are likely to be nouns. It is natural for adults to encourage children to talk by asking questions, but these need not be exclusively of the 'What's this called?' or 'What colour is it?' variety. In fact, a good deal of what is said to retarded children seems to take this form. At the very least, it should be possible to phrase questions so that the child has to make a choice ('Would you like milk or juice?' 'Shall we go for a walk now or later?'). More open-ended questions follow at a slightly later stage ('What shall we buy at the shops?' 'What are you going to do now?'). The skilled teacher knows how to talk to the child at his own level and in the natural context of his play or other activities without appearing to turn the conversation into a formal language lesson, so that the child learns that language is not only a natural accompaniment to play but can help to extend and develop it. If language experiences are relevant and enjoyable, the child may adopt a more positive attitude to more formal or structured approaches which may be introduced at a later stage.

There are, of course, some practical limitations to the introduction of more structured language programmes, the chief of these being shortage of staff, since most of the methods that have been reported involve a one to one working relationship between teacher and child. This need not present insuperable obstacles to the teacher wishing to experiment with these methods. In the first place, a structured approach calls for a carefully considered definition of short-term and long-term objectives for each child, and for detailed planning of how these aims can be met. Secondly, it may only be appropriate to carry out such a programme for a relatively short period. Few would advocate that structured teaching should take place all day and every day, though critics of these methods sometimes talk as though this was all that happened in such a classroom. The important principle is to know what one's objectives are, and to exploit every possible teaching opportunity to achieve them. This calls for an alert sensitivity to the child's language needs, and to his particular developmental pattern. Children develop in ways and at a speed that we do not necessarily expect; a systematically planned teaching programme should be flexible enough to be modified or abandoned in the light of cues provided by the child.

It is also worth emphasizing that teachers and even administrators in special education are working towards the principle of the two-teacher class. Once we achieve this objective, or even approach it by having at least a second adult such as a nursery nurse in each special school classroom, one teacher will be free to devote parts of the day to individual teaching, while the other is concerned with the rest of the group. Ideally, this principle involves an architectural innovation in special schools: the addition of a small room for individual teaching alongside each main classroom. This is hardly ever found.

EVALUATING RESULTS

Although a number of attempts at language improvement have been reported, the studies are often poorly controlled and of short duration. Earlier studies were well reviewed by Spradlin (1963) in the context of a critical discussion of the methodological problems which arise in designing and evaluating language teaching programmes. More recent studies have been brought together in two publications by Schiefelbusch (Schiefelbusch *et al.*, 1967; Schiefelbusch, 1972). Characteristic of the more recent work is a broadly behavioural approach to both assessment and teaching, with an emphasis on functional as opposed to psychometric analysis of language behaviour, followed by the systematic use of principles of programming and reinforcement (Sloane and Macaulay, 1968). Most of these studies deal with small samples and use the individual as his own control, whereas earlier workers tended to use pre- and post-test measures, often with a control or contrast group. Summarizing group studies of this type, Spradlin (1963) indicated that seven out of twelve reported some improvement in language skills, and an eighth was inconclusive. The four studies that reported insignificant or negative findings all used a form of control, though these were not regarded as satisfactory either. Only four of the seven studies among those reporting successful treatment included an element of control in the experimental design. One is reminded of an earlier parallel in the field of drug trials in psychiatric populations; Foulds (1958) showed that most of the studies reporting positive effects were poorly designed or statistically inadequate, whereas those characterized by proper control tended to report negative findings.

The difficulty of evaluating change is partly one of constructing appropriate control groups, and partly one of choosing relevant measures of language behaviour. The former difficulties are now more widely recognized, and investigators appreciate the problems of matching groups for comparison purposes, whether the match is based on a test score or on a specific criterion, such as being on a waiting list (Baumeister, 1967; Clarke and Clarke, 1973b). The second group of problems derives from the uncertain status of currently available measures of language functioning (see section on 'Assessment'). The fact that scores on a test such as ITPA change in an upward direction following a programme of language teaching cannot necessarily be ascribed to the teaching programme. At the lowest level of explanation, it may be due to the unreliability of the tests for the particular group under investigation. In other cases, the nature of the teaching is so closely based on a test-based diagnosis of the language difficulties that it is sometimes questionable whether the programme has done more than teach the children to do the tests more effectively. However, the reliability of standardized language tests is at least known with some measure of confidence. This is not usually the case with observations by skilled or unskilled observers of the child's language in everyday situations, though proper attention to time sampling and to observer reliability should make it possible to objectify such observations, and to reduce unreliability to the minimum. At least naturalistic observation eliminates the artificiality of a formal test, usually carried out by a stranger who is often required by the conventions of research to be not only unfamiliar with the child but ignorant of the 'treatment' he has received.

Methodological problems of evaluation of the effects of language teaching can be illustrated by reference to a study by Kolstoe (1958) which is frequently cited as an example of a successful programme. An experimental group of fifteen institutionalized mongol children receiving speech therapy was individually matched on Kuhlmann MA with a no-treatment control group. The treatment, which was based on principles of verbal and social reinforcement, was given in forty-five minutes sessions five days a week over a period of over five months, and used a variety of methods, including pictures, mechanical toys, films and records. The results indicated a loss on the Kuhlmann for both groups, though the experimental group lost fewer points than the controls, and children with higher IQs stood to gain more from the programme than those with lower IQs. It is possible that the largely negative findings of this study were due to the fact that the IQ of both groups was in the low 20s. Other measures also failed to reflect any significant benefit, but the experimental group did show higher scores after treatment on the Differential Language Facility Test – an early version of the experimental edition of the ITPA. Spradlin considers that this is one of the few studies with an adequate design; but it is a pity that the control group did not receive an equal amount of adult attention.

A study involving a more elaborate design and using children of greater ability was reported by Lassers and Low (1960), whose subjects were between 7 and 15 and had IQs ranging between 40 and 79. Two experimental groups were created, one receiving traditional speech therapy with an emphasis on sound discrimination and production in a 'clinic' setting, the other being encouraged by means of simulated 'real life' situations to increase their language skills. A control group was also used. After fifteen weeks of therapy, differences between the three groups were shown only on an articulation test, and not on a sound discrimination test or on the San Francisco Inventory of Communicative Effectiveness. Spradlin points out that even on the articulation test there was a confounding between examiners and treatments which might have resulted in bias. Treatment studies are also reported by Schlanger (1953), Strazzula (1953), Mecham (1955), and Johnson *et al.* (1960).

One feature of most of the studies reviewed by Spradlin and also characterizing a number of later reports lies in the absence of detail concerning the aims and objectives of therapy, and the exact techniques used by the therapists. A considerable variety of aims and methods seem to have been involved, so that it is difficult to know whether improvements should be related to one part of the programme rather than another. Similarly, more success might have been achieved if the therapy had been restricted to specific aspects of language ability.

BEHAVIOUR MODIFICATION: PRINCIPLES

Since the mid-1960s an increasing number of workers in this field have been using a variety of techniques and models which are based to some degree on principles of behaviour modification. Some are undoubtedly strictly operant and neo-Skinnerian in character, while others make use of one or other principle or technique based on operant theory. For example, a number of workers employ systematic reinforcement, but without necessarily subscribing to a consistent theoretical framework, or basing their treatment on a preliminary functional analysis of behaviour.

Work in this area owes much of its impetus to advances made over a wide front in abnormal psychology in treating individuals with disorders of behaviour, both in building up new behaviours and in removing undesirable or un-adaptive behaviours. In the field of language, it derives from the premise that language is in principle no different from other aspects of behaviour in being subject to modification as a consequence of the applications of systematic reinforcement. Different workers might disagree, however, about the limits of what can be achieved by such methods.

It would not be appropriate here to embark on a full exposition of the principles of behaviour modification. These can be found in chapter 23 of this volume, and also in Gardner (1971), Kiernan (1973), Weisberg (1971), and many others. A useful volume summarizing operant work in relation to speech and language disorders has been brought together by Sloane and Macaulay (1968). Bricker's work represents perhaps the most consistent theoretical as well as practical approach to the teaching of language skills to the mentally retarded, and is also notable for the attempt to relate behaviour modification to cognitive and develop-mental psychology in general and to psycholinguistics in particular (Bricker and Bricker, 1970a, b, 1973; Bricker, 1972).

Operant theory regards a retarded person as characterized by a limited repertoire of behaviour, and as being in a sense a product of his reinforcement history (Bijou and Baer, 1967). The practical question confronting the therapist concerns the principles and techniques which should underlie a systematic attempt to increase the retarded person's repertoire. In order to do this, it is necessary to begin with a functional analysis and assessment. This, according to Kiernan (1973), involves (i) a clear definition and description of the behaviour, (ii) an attempt to specify the precise stimulus conditions which appear to be related to the occurrence or non-occurrence of the behaviour under study (i.e.

stimulus and setting conditions), and (iii) specification of the events which are acting as reinforcers. This analysis is the foundation of the treatment programme, in so far as the treatment provides for a manipulation of the stimulus and setting conditions in relation to specific target behaviours. Indeed, as Kiernan points out, it is only through the attempt to modify behaviour which arises out of functional analysis that the appropriateness of the analysis can be examined.

It is worth pointing out, however, that functional analysis is more appropriate for some language skills than for others. In many cases, the therapist is confronted by a total absence of language or even vocalization, so that it is hardly possible to specify the conditions under which the child vocalizes or not. It may be necessary in such cases to implement a form of 'diagnostic therapy' by embarking directly on a course of treatment, by means, for example, of shaping techniques, with the object of finding out whether the individual's vocalizations can in any specifiable sense be brought under operant control. On the other hand, a view of language which was not simply confined to expressive aspects allows a programme of treatment to consider what kind of skills are necessary to the development of speech, to apply a functional assessment to these skills and to plan an appropriate regime of treatment to compensate for deficiencies in areas which are deemed critical to development. We have already discussed the importance of receptive skills, and suggested that it may be important at certain states of development to assess and if necessary further listening and receptive language. It has also been suggested that imaginative and representational play forms an important foundation to language development, since the ability to play in such a way as to make one object or activity stand for another is the precursor of learning not only that things have names, but that language can be used creatively and generatively.

It is in this connection that a hierarchical model of language development becomes relevant, in the sense that it may be necessary to assess and develop looking, listening, sound discrimination, word recognition and finally sentence discrimination before embarking on a speech and language programme.

The importance of planning a language training curriculum in the context of a consistent theoretical and procedural framework is repeatedly stressed in Bricker's writings. He uses the device of a procedural lattice to specify the terminal states which he wishes to reach in specific and individual areas of language skill, and the training sequences which will be necessary to achieve these aims. Fig. 14 provides a convenient illustration of his approach (Bricker and Bricker, 1973).

The lattice specifies a number of programme steps in a language training curriculum and also shows how they are related in time and in order. Boxes above the diagonal represent various terminal behaviour states, those below the diagonal specify the subprogrammes that are likely to be needed to achieve these goals. The lattice begins on the left with initial behaviour control and attention training achieved through reinforcement procedures, and proceeds through stages such as discrimination, memory, vocabulary, imitation, articulation, syntax and morphology. Furthermore, more detailed procedural lattices

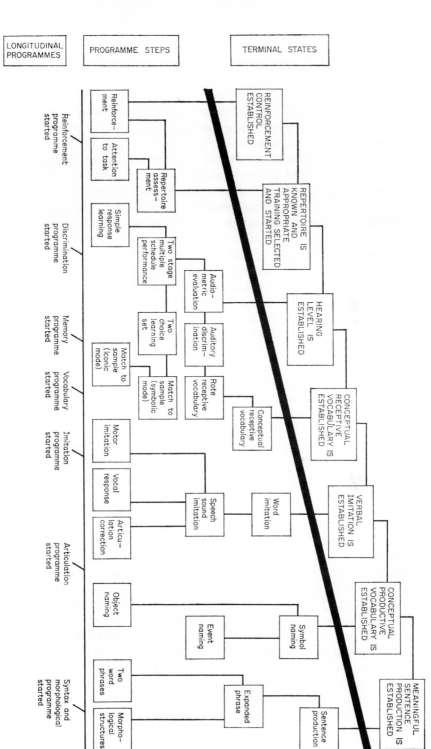

Fig. 14 Language Training Lattice (from Bricker and Bricker, 1973).

have been worked out for specific parts of the language training programme; examples are given for steps and methods that might be used to teach the comprehension and production of two-word utterances, such as 'want milk'. Bricker emphasizes that the key feature of this model is that as the training progresses, each subsequent step involves a change in the antecedent stimulus, the reinforced response, or both.

A disadvantage of the lattice system is that it can only be used by professionals who are already trained behaviour modifiers, since it assumes a knowledge of operant terminology and techniques. The Brickers also describe the use of flow charts which can be used with relatively untrained personnel, since it specifies in detail both the antecedent and the subsequent stimulus events that are regarded as necessary to move behaviour from one point to another.

It will be apparent from the discussion of the principles of behaviour modification that some of the techniques to which these principles have given rise offer certain advantages both in the design and implementation of treatment programmes, and also in relation to the problem of evaluating results. In the first place, this approach largely dispenses with the need for standardized tests and for comparison of an individual with a hypothetical population average. It largely replaces the traditional normative test with a criterion-referenced evaluation which is focused on the question of whether or not the individual is capable of a particular skill. Secondly, it forges a direct link between assessment and treatment, so that the response to treatment partly determines the validity of the assessment. Thirdly, it allows the individual's response to treatment to be described in relation to the level of his own prior performance. In other words, progress is evaluated in relation to an objectively established baseline. Using the individual as his own control also provides a partial solution to the problem of designing matched control groups when comparing the effects of different treatments.

In principle there is no reason why these methods cannot be combined with a more traditional form of evaluation, including analysis of variance and 'repeated measures' designs. In an important paper, Gardner (1969) criticizes many behaviour modification studies in subnormality for failing to specify or take account of important independent variables such as age, duration of institutionalization, physical condition, diagnosis, psychometric test scores, as well as the nature, type and schedule of reinforcement used. He also criticizes the absence of control groups, biased samples, imprecise measures even of the dependent variable, and absence of long-term follow-up. A similar article evaluating behaviour therapy with children includes a table showing the very small number of studies which have adopted at least some of the more stringent evaluation criteria available (Pawlicki, 1970). It seems likely that future studies will increasingly combine individual and group designs.

BEHAVIOUR MODIFICATION: PRACTICE

After the foregoing discussion of principles, a few examples of application will now be considered, though these are intended merely as illustrations of a rapidly growing area of work. The most comprehensive recent summary of operant studies has been compiled by Sloane and MacAulay (1968); an unannotated bibliography up to 1968 has been prepared by Peins (1969), and a section of speech and language is regularly included in *Mental Retardation Abstracts*.

The importance of imitation as the foundation for a language teaching programme has already been emphasized. Before a child can begin to imitate or produce speech, he must clearly be able to interact with the teacher and be sufficiently responsive to commands and cues to enter a language programme. But many children need first to be taught to imitate, and a number of workers have reported in detail on methods that have been employed to this end. Peterson (1968) summarizes a series of studies originally carried out at the University of Washington (e.g. Baer and Sherman, 1964; Sherman, 1965; Risley, 1966). Later work on generalized imitation and specific setting events is reported by Peterson and Whitehurst (1971) and Peterson *et al.* (1971).

The technique frequently adopted in these studies is to begin by trying to establish a simple imitative behaviour which can be physically prompted. For example, the teacher taps the table, takes the child's hand and taps the table and provides immediate reinforcement. The physical prompt of holding the child's hand is then gradually faded, while continuous reinforcement is provided for responding. At this stage, some workers introduce the discriminative stimulus 'Do this', following this by the behaviour to be imitated. In order to establish a hierarchy and to avoid entering the programme at too advanced or complex a level, it is common to begin with gross movements such as standing, sitting, jumping, clapping, and then to begin to localize imitation to the head (head shaking and nodding), and finally to the mouth, tongue, lips and throat. Here again, it is useful to introduce a verbal discriminative stimulus by saying 'Do this: stand up', etc., in order to maintain control at later stages. A number of relevant movements of the mouth and tongue can be imitated by this means: opening and shutting the mouth, tongue in and out, tongue in various placements (on lower lip, behind teeth, tongue click), blowing, hissing, an aspirated 'h', 'ppph' and 'fff', etc. It may be necessary to produce prompts in the form of guidance of the child's lips, tongue and mouth, or to put the child's hand on the teacher's throat to feel the vibrations produced by vocalizations and to provide a discriminative stimulus to the child that a voiced response is required. Similarly, a hand placed in front of the mouth will enable the child to feel voiceless plosive or fricative sounds. Phonetic placement procedures are discussed by MacAulay (1968) following Van Riper (1954).

At this point the most difficult stage of imitating voiced sounds has been reached, and failure is frequently encountered. Sherman (1965) suggests a backdown and chaining procedure to try to overcome this. It involves pairing a verbal response (e.g. 'ah') with a previously learned motor response. Thus, standing up might be paired with 'ah'; the child is more likely to produce the verbal imitation if it is chained to a previously learned motor response, which can then in turn be faded (see also Nelson and Evans, 1968, for a useful account of a collaborative project between a psychologist and a speech therapist).

MacAulay (1968) describes her teaching procedures in detail, and reports results in a series of individual case studies. The teaching programme incorporates a number of stages: individual sounds, blending sounds into words, a naming vocabulary and, where possible, word phrases. She makes systematic use of colour cues, employing black alphabet cues for consonants and a different colour for each of ten vowel sounds. The colour cues consisted originally of rectangles, but these were later 'shaped' to the appropriate letters of the alphabet.

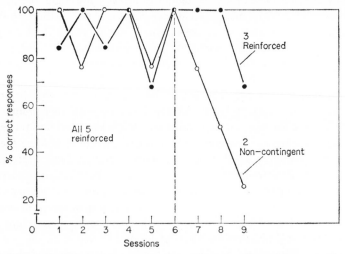

Fig. 15 Effect of reinforcement on accuracy of tacting (from Sloane *et al.*, 1968).

A particular feature of her method lies in her use of similar principles to teach both speech and basic reading skills. Her subjects ranged in IQ from 27 to 92, but most of the detailed case studies in her report are in the severely subnormal range. Five of her eleven subjects were originally mute and had previously not responded to speech therapy. All of these children learned to produce sounds and in some cases words. Improvements in articulation were also reported, and the graphs show a substantial rise in the percentage of sounds which came under discriminative control. She reports that most children acquired a full repertoire of speech sounds within four to six months while being seen only twice a week. One wonders whether results could have been achieved more quickly if daily sessions had been used.

MacAulay's study did not include formal control procedures, either through control groups, by using the individual as his own control, or by experimentally removing contingent reinforcement. A more controlled design was used by

Sloane *et al.* (1968), who measured the effects of non-contingent reinforcements. An example is provided in Fig. 15.

The child was required to name five pictures and was reinforced with ice cream for each correct response. After the sixth session, reinforcement was provided for only three of the pictures, and ice cream was given on a non-contingent basis for the remaining two. Accuracy of naming for the two pictures fell from 85 to 25 per cent, but remained at 85 per cent for the other three. Unfortunately, no data are given for a return to the experimental condition for

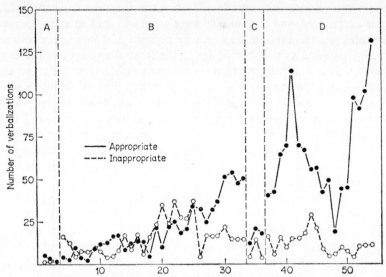

Fig. 16 A record of appropriate and inappropriate verbalization (from Hall, 1970). A = Baseline period prior to contingent reinforcement. B = Reinforcement period, verbalizations reinforced by food, play materials and the E's attention. C = Reversal period, return to baseline conditions of non-contingent reinforcement. D = Second reinforcement period, return to procedures of contingent reinforcement.

the two pictures, though it is likely on the basis of other studies that near 85 per cent accuracy would have been restored. Use was also made of 'time out' from reinforcement immediately after inappropriate behaviour or incorrect responding, though this was rarely needed after the initial sessions. A notable feature of this report is the involvement of mothers as co-therapists. The mothers were initially trained in the laboratory by being cued over an intercom when to start, reinforce, correct errors, etc. These prompts were gradually removed, and the training continued in the home, with frequent reports to staff, first in person, and then by telephone.

The importance of experimentally reversing and reinstating reinforcement contingencies is also illustrated in a single case study reported by Hall (1970), illustrated in Fig. 16.

The subject of Hall's study was a 6-year-old boy who had been diagnosed as brain damaged and autistic, and suffering from moderately severe mental retardation. Although he could produce a few words of appropriate speech, most of his utterances consisted of jargon and nonsense syllables, and he barely responded to verbal direction. Following three baseline sessions in which a mean of 3·3 appropriate verbalizations were recorded, reinforcement was provided only for appropriate verbalization, though this did not produce a marked improvement for about sixteen sessions. Nevertheless, the mean rate of responding rose 20·0 per session during the reinforcement periods. At this point three reversal sessions were introduced during which appropriate verbalizations were not reinforced, and bites of food were given non-contingently. Compared to the three preceding sessions in which the percentage of appropriate responses were 48·3, 44·8 and 53·7, responses during the reversal sessions dropped to 9·6, 6·7 and 1·6. Reinforcement was then reintroduced with the result that responses immediately returned to a rate of 43·7. This was maintained despite a change from continuous to a variable ratio of reinforcement, and despite the introduction of a new training regime which required him to imitate and produce 'I want'. The overall increase in the percentage of appropriate verbalizations reached 78·5, and recordings taken at home indicated that the language training programme had partially generalized to the home situation, and was mantained three months after the end of the experiment.

Hall's study is included in a useful monograph (Girardeau and Spradlin, 1970) which contains other highly relevant examples of training and evaluation procedures which are reported in sufficient detail to allow others to repeat and modify similar methods (see particularly Yoder and Reynolds, and important methodological and review chapters by Girardeau and Spradlin and Spradlin and Girardeau). Significant contributions to this field have also been made by Hewett (1966), Kerr *et al.* (1965), Lovaas (1966), Risley and Wolf (1967), Johnston (1968) and many others. One of the most exhaustive accounts of a language training programme has recently been reported by Buddenhagen (1971) who incorporated recent developments in phonetics into his teaching of four profoundly language-retarded mongols. His monograph is also notable for its highly critical discussion of the implications (or lack of them) of psycholinguistics in general and of the work of Chomsky in particular for language teaching of the mentally subnormal. Reference should also be made to a growing tendency to combine behaviour modification principles and teaching techniques with formal methods of evaluation of the results, including pre-and-post testing of experimental and control groups on standardized tests (even including Binet IQ) and observational studies of language behaviour in both free and structured situations (e.g. Talkington and Hall, 1970; MacCubrey, 1971).

A number of recent studies have incorporated, but also modified, models and theories derived from developmental psycholinguistics. The work of Bricker and his associates is the most notable example of an attempt to use both operant techniques and a systems analysis approach in order to try to teach young subnormal children to reach the stage of using two-word utterances of the 'pivot-open type' (Bricker and Bricker, 1973). 'Pivots' are words which occur with high frequency on which a larger number of 'open' class words are hung. Thus 'allgone' might be a pivot preceding open class words such as 'dinner', 'potty', 'Daddy', etc. According to linguists (e.g. Slobin, 1971b; McNeill, 1970a) the pivot-open structure is an innately determined linguistic universal, and part of the 'Language Acquisition Device' common to all known languages. But this does not necessarily debar the educator from trying to teach children to acquire it; indeed, as Bricker (1972) points out, this constitutes a powerful challenge to the educator. There are also important implications for cognitive development in the acquisition of two-word structures, since the child equipped with even a small number of two-word utterances can begin to express increasingly complex intentions and meanings (e.g. no dinner, my car, more dinner, etc.). He has progressed from the stage of labelling, using mainly nouns, to his first statements about situations and relationships.

A small study designed to teach pivot-open structures has recently been completed in Manchester (Jeffree *et al.*, 1973). Two 4-year-old mongol boys who were developmentally equated and who were both using only single-word utterances were used in a design involving both within subject and between subject control procedures. Both boys were initially taught the appropriate use of ten nouns, as well as the participle 'gone'. Play for the experimental child was then structured with the help of appropriate apparatus and teaching with a view to eliciting pivot-open utterances, using five of the ten nouns, together with 'gone'. The control child had identical conditions but no pivot-open models were given. When criterion level was reached for the first child, he was exposed to the second five nouns, suggesting that some generalization had occurred. At this point, the control child who had not previously produced two-word utterances was switched to the experimental condition, and quickly learned both to imitate and generalize the appropriate pivot-open construction.

A study by Fygetakis and Gray (1970) is of considerable interest for its close attention to programming variables and its systematic attempt to teach linguistic constructs. The subjects were three children with severe language disorders which mainly took the form of distorted and inadequate syntactic constructions reflecting inability to differentiate between singular and plural subject or between present and past tense. They did not demonstrate usage of many of the transformation rules for reordering and changing the underlying deep structure into the appropriate surface structure. Consequently they did not make the word order changes necessary in forming questions. The paper then describes a form of 'programmed conditioning' designed to develop the base structure rules involved in using *is* in sentences with a singular noun phrase and a verb phrase containing either an adjective or prepositional phrase. The subjects not only learned the task, but were able to use it in free play and conversation outside the experimental situation. In addition, considerable success was obtained in a second programme designed to teach transformational rules involved in the reordering of words in question form.

Although the authors of this study argue that they have directly taught competence, this issue will be regarded as theoretical by many; even those who subscribe to a theory of linguistic universals would not necessarily object on principle to remedial measures which are designed to develop linguistic skills, whether these are related to competence or performance. But the question is not as theoretical as it might seem, since some skills may lend themselves more easily to remediation than others. Educators and behaviourists have been applying themselves to a wide range of language behaviours, including simple noun-labelling responses, two-word utterances and more complex and elaborate syntactic skills. Major advances have also been made in the technology of establishing communication systems with chimpanzees. By careful use of programmed techniques, chimpanzees have been taught both to understand and to produce three-dimensional representations of fairly complex syntactic constructions – including statements of the form 'Sarah, put the banana into the pail and the apple into the dish' (Premack, 1970). In addition, components of the American Sign Language for the Deaf have been taught to chimpanzees who learned to use and maintain a form of conversational behaviour (Gardner and Gardner, 1969).

Without in any way adopting an extremist behaviourist position that anything is teachable if properly taught, it is rarely justifiable to conclude that the failure of a teaching programme is necessarily due to the fact that the child is not 'maturationally ready' or that he is 'too dull to benefit', or to withhold treatment on the grounds that a specific deficit is 'constitutional'. Nor is it enough for psychologists merely to demonstrate that subnormals have specific deficits in this or that cognitive or linguistic skill; they could usefully continue their studies by considering whether the deficits that they have demonstrated yield in any measure to specific programmes of remediation designed with the same detail as the experiment which demonstrated the deficit in the first place. Such remedial programmes can be short term or long term; in other words, they can be begun in the 'laboratory', as one of the experimental conditions, and developed by gradual stages into a classroom teaching programme. The important point here is that we should not conclude that initial performance on a learning task is necessarily predictive of how the individual will respond to a programme of teaching, or that failure to learn is necessarily due to 'innately low intelligence', 'laziness', 'psychosis' or any other quality in the individual (Clarke and Clarke, 1973). Such variables may impose limits on the amount that can be learned, and the time that will be taken to learn, but much can also be achieved by careful attention to teaching methods.

A survey of the work now proceeding on the teaching of language skills to the mentally subnormal gives good ground for optimism. In particular, the principles and practice of behaviour modification appear to be productive, not only in the hands of psychologists but also when systematically taught and applied by nurses, teachers and, most significantly of all, by parents. However, both principles and the practice are not without their limitations, and many of the studies reported are still inadequate in conception, badly carried out and unsystematically reported. Behaviour modifiers have on occasion not taken account of knowledge in related fields, including linguistics, phonetics and even developmental psychology, in selecting target behaviours which they wished to teach. Should one, for example, begin by shaping and developing sounds that are already in the child's repertoire, or start with sounds which we know from studies of normal speech development are the earliest or the easiest in the developmental sequence? How far should the therapist be guided by the child's interests and how far by the demands of the teaching regime in, for example, determining the criteria for 'time out' or the length of the sessions? In reporting the results of language training programmes, is it necessary to concentrate largely on single case-studies, or can we in future incorporate stricter methods of design and statistical evaluation?

Systematic attempts to improve language skills in the mentally subnormal have hardly begun, but seem to offer reasonably promising prospects. It may therefore be premature to come to any firm conclusions about the ultimate level of language skill that a mentally subnormal child may be expected to reach at adulthood. It would be equally unrealistic to exaggerate what could be achieved even if the best teaching methods were more widely available.

Conclusions

Both parents and professionals agree on the central importance of language in the development of the child, but we know more about the language deficiencies of the mentally handicapped than about ways of tackling them. Much of the recent psycholinguistic research has taken the form of theorizing and model building, and has on the whole discounted the role of environmental factors in language development. Educational practice has in its turn tended to be influenced by a maturational orientation which has resulted in a somewhat uncritical reliance on techniques that have been developed with younger normal children. It might have been hoped that psychology would play a mediating role between psycholinguistic research and educational practice; instead, many psychologists have tended to concentrate on the development of assessment techniques, and on perfecting techniques of demonstrating deficits.

Nevertheless, there are encouraging signs of a more positive approach. Research and practice are coming closer together, though the gap between them is still uncomfortably wide. Research into the structure of language and a growing interest in normal language acquisition have resulted in an interest in the underlying processes of development, and in the variables associated with growth from one stage to another, rather than in descriptions of the stages themselves. This process-orientated approach has in its turn led to attempts to isolate specific skills and abilities. Global concepts identifying language exclusively with the spoken word are being replaced by a growing appreciation that some aspects of language may be less affected than others both in the individual and in groups.

Experimental techniques have been applied to clinical populations to describe characteristic strategies of dealing with language input, and useful parallels have been drawn both with motor skills and with models of information processing. The emphasis of recent psycholinguistic research on the structure of language has led to a greater awareness of the complexity of language input both at a semantic and a syntactic level. Techniques which have so far been used mainly in the laboratory seem likely to be adapted for the classroom and for assessment purposes in order to assess the degree to which an individual is able to impose order and structure and to extract relevant features from incoming information. More emphasis is also being placed on the extent to which spoken language is understood, and on the interaction between non-verbal and verbal cues both in speaking and in listening.

It is becoming apparent that the emphasis which has recently been placed on maturational components of development do not necessarily deny the contribution of environmental factors. Biological and environmental variables are now seen as interacting in a complex relationship which is only partly understood and certainly under-investigated. Most of the research studies have been concerned with one or other group of variables, but the interaction between them does not easily lend itself to systematic study, though its existence seems theoretically plausible.

Perhaps the most positive development in recent years can be found in a more positive approach to teaching and remediation. With a growing awareness of the central importance of language skills in the total development of the child, a number of teachers and research workers have been adopting an increasingly systematic approach to teaching, and have been less inclined than in the past to wait for language to develop spontaneously or to limit themselves to providing an appropriately stimulating environment. Some teaching programmes have been based on theories and models of language structure and language processes derived from cognitive psychology and psycholinguistics, and have therefore concentrated on attempts to help the child to acquire basic skills connected with morphology, syntax and appropriate language use. But the most substantial body of work has depended heavily on learning theory and on principles of behaviour modification, including functional analysis, and the use of a graded programme involving shaping, successive approximation and consistently applied schedules of reinforcement.

There can now be little doubt that behaviour modification techniques constitute a powerful therapeutic weapon in the teaching of language and other cognitive skills. While it would be dangerous to exaggerate what might be achieved, it would be even more shortsighted to neglect the potential contribution which systematic teaching can make in this field. Many reports have now been published which testify to the effectiveness of these methods, and it is likely that they will be increasingly applied in educational programmes in the future. An immediate problem arises from the shortage of staff who are trained in the use of behaviour modification techniques, and who can in their turn train not merely psychologists, but other professional and paraprofessional groups, including teachers, nurses and nursing assistants, and above all parents. Results obtained so far certainly justify some degree of optimism in experimenting with new approaches to the teaching of language skills.

References

ADKINS, S. (1969) *The Language Addressed by Mothers to their Three and Four Year Old Children*. Unpubl. dissertation, Univ. of Manchester.

ANNETT, J. (1971) Acquisition of skill. *Brit. med. Bull.*, **27**, 266–71.

BAER, D. and SHERMAN, J. A. (1964) Reinforcement control of generalised imitation in children. *J. exp. child Psychol.*, **1**, 37–49.

BARNETT, C. D., ELLIS, N. R. and PRYER, M. W. (1959) Stimulus pre-training and the delayed reaction in defectives. *Amer. J. ment. Defic.*, **64**, 104–11.

BATEMAN, B. (1965) *The Illinois Test of Psycholinguistic Abilities in Current Research: Summaries of Studies*. Urbana: Univ. of Illinois Press.

BATEMAN, B. (1968) *Interpretation of the 1961 Illinois Test of Psycholinguistic Abilities*. Seattle: Special Child Publications.

BAUMEISTER, A. A. (1967) Problems in comparative studies of mental retardates and normals. *Amer. J. ment. Defic.*, **71**, 869–75.

BAUMEISTER, A. A. (1968) Learning abilities. In BAUMEISTER, A. A. (ed.) *Mental Retardation: Appraisal, Education, Rehabilitation*. London: Univ. of London Press.

BAUMEISTER, A. A. and BARTLETT, C. J. (1962a) A comparison of the factor structure of normals and retardates on the WISC. *Amer. J. ment. Defic.*, **66**, 641–6.

BAUMEISTER, A. A. and BARTLETT, C. J. (1962b) Further factorial investigations of WISC performance of mental defectives. *Amer. J. ment. Defic.*, **67**, 257–61.

BEIER, E. G., STARKWEATHER, J. A. and LAMBERT, M. J. (1969) Vocabulary usage of mentally retarded children. *Amer. J. ment. Defic.*, **73**, 927–34.

BEREITER, C. and ENGELMANN, S. (1966) *Teaching Disadvantaged Children in the Pre-School*. Englewood Cliffs, NJ: Prentice-Hall.

BERKO, J. (1958) The child's learning of English morphology. *Word*, **14**, 150–77.

BERRY, M. F. (1969) *Language Disorders of Children*. New York: Appleton-Century-Crofts.

BERRY, M. F. and TALBOTT, R. (1966) *Exploratory Test of Grammar*. Cited in Berry, 1969.

BERRY, P. (1971) *Imitation of Language in Subnormal Children*. Unpubl. M.Ed. thesis, Univ. of Manchester.

BIJOU, S. W. and BAER, D. M. (1967) Operant methods in child behaviour and development. In BIJOU, S. W. and BAER, D. M. (eds.) *Child Development: Readings in Experimental Analysis*. New York: Appleton-Century-Crofts.

BILOVSKY, D. and SHARE, J. (1965) The ITPA and Down's Syndrome: an exploratory study. *Amer. J. ment. Defic.*, **70**, 78–82.

BLAKE, K. A. and WILLIAMS, C. L. (1968) *Use of English Morphemes by Retarded, Normal and Superior Children Equated for CA*. Athens: Univ. of Georgia.

BLANCHARD, L. (1964) Speech pattern and etiology in mental retardation. *Amer. J. ment. Defic.*, **68**, 612–27.

BRICKER, W. A. (1972) A systematic approach to language training. In SCHIEFELBUSCH, R. L. (ed.) *The Language of the Mentally Retarded*. Baltimore, Md: Univ. Park Press.

BRICKER, W. A. and BRICKER, D. D. (1970a) A program of language training for the severely language handicapped child. *Except. Child.*, **37**, 101–11.

BRICKER, W. A. and BRICKER, D. D. (1970b) Development of receptive vocabulary in severely retarded children. *Amer. J. ment. Defic.*, **74**, 599–606.

BRICKER, W. A. and BRICKER, D. D. (1973) Behaviour modification programmes. In MITTLER, P. (ed.) *Assessment for Learning in the Mentally Handicapped*. London: Churchill Livingstone; Baltimore, Md: Williams & Wilkins.

BRIMER, M. A. and DUNN, L. M. (1965) *English Picture Vocabulary Test*. Bristol: Educational Evaluation Enterprises.

BROWN, R. (1965) *Social Psychology*. New York: The Free Press.

BRYANT, P. E. (1967) Verbal labelling and learning strategies in normal and severely subnormal children. *Quart. J. exp. Psychol.*, **19**, 155–61.

BUDDENHAGEN, R. G. (1971) *Establishing Vocal Verbalizations in Mute Mongoloid Children*. Champaign, Ill.: Research Press.

BURLAND, R. (1969) The development of the verbal regulation of behaviour in cerebrally palsied (multiply handicapped) children. *J. ment. Subn.*, **15**, 85–9.

BURT, C. (1967) Capacity and achievement. *Education*, 198–201.

CAMPBELL, R. and WALES, R. (1970) The study of language acquisition. In LYONS, J. (ed.) *New Horizons in Linguistics*. Harmondsworth: Penguin.

CARR, D. L., BROWN, L. F. and RICE, V. A. (1967) The PPVT in the assessment of language deficit. *Amer. J. ment. Defic.*, **71**, 937–40.

CARR, J. (1970) Mental and motor development in young mongol children. *J. ment. Defic. Res.*, **14**, 205–20.

CARROLL, J. B. (1953) *The Study of Language: A Survey of Linguistics and Related Disciplines in America*. Cambridge, Mass.: Harvard Univ. Press.

CARROLL, J. B. (1967) Psycholinguistics in the study of mental retardation. In SCHIEFELBUSCH, R. L., COPELAND, R. H. and SMITH, J. O. (eds.)

Language and Mental Retardation. New York: Holt, Rinehart & Winston.

CARROW, M. A. (1968) The development of auditory comprehension of language structure in children. *J. speech hear. Dis.*, **33**, 99–111.

CHALFANT, J. (1968) Systematic language instruction: an approach for teaching receptive language to young trainable children. *Teaching except. Child.*, **1**, 1–13.

CHOMSKY, N. (1957) *Syntactic Structures.* The Hague: Mouton.

CHOMSKY, N. (1959) Review of Skinner's *Verbal Behavior. Language*, **35**, 26–58.

CHOMSKY, N. (1965) *Aspects of the Theory of Syntax.* Cambridge, Mass.: MIT Press.

CLARKE, A. D. B. and CLARKE, A. M. (1973a) Assessment and prediction in the severely subnormal. In MITTLER, P. (ed.) *Assessment for Learning in the Mentally Handicapped.* London: Churchill Livingstone; Baltimore, Md: Williams & Wilkins.

CLARKE, A. M. and CLARKE, A. D. B. (1973b) What are the problems? In CLARKE, A. D. B. and CLARKE, A. M. (eds.) *Mental Retardation and Behavioural Research.* London: Churchill Livingstone; Baltimore, Md: Williams & Wilkins.

CUNNINGHAM, C. and JEFFREE, D. (1971) *Working with Parents: Developing a Workshop Course for Parents of Young Mentally Handicapped Children.* Manchester: National Society for Mentally Handicapped Children, North-West Region.

CRABTREE, M. (1958) *The Houston Test for Language Development.* Houston Test Co.

DARLEY, F. L. and WINITZ, H. (1961) Age of first word: review of research. *J. speech hear. Dis.*, **26**, 272–90.

DAVIS, E. A. (1937) *The Development of Linguistic Skill in Twins, Singletons and Sibs and Only Children from 5–10.* Inst. Child Welf., Monogr. No. 14. Minneapolis: Univ. of Minnesota.

DENNY, M. R. (1964) Research in Learning and Performance. In STEVENS, H. A. and HEBER, R. (eds.) *Mental Retardation: A Review of Research.* Chicago: Univ. of Chicago Press.

DEVER, R. B. and GARDNER, W. I. (1970) Performance of normal and retarded boys on Berko's test of morphology. *Language and Speech*, **13**, 162–81.

DUNN, L. (1959) *The Peabody Picture Vocabulary Test.* Minneapolis: Amer. Guidance Service Inc.

EISENSON, J. (1966) Perceptual disturbances in children with central nervous system dysfunctions and implications for language development. *Brit. J. dis. Comm.*, **1**, 21–32.

ERVIN, S. M. (1964) Imitation and structural change in children's language. In LENNEBERG, E. H. (ed.) *New Directions in the Study of Language.* Cambridge, Mass.: MIT Press.

EVANS, D. and HAMPSON, M. (1968) The language of mongols. *Brit. J. dis. Comm.*, **3**, 171–81.

FAWCUS, M. (1965) Speech disorders and therapy in mental subnormality. In CLARKE, A. M. and CLARKE, A. D. B. (eds.) *Mental Deficiency: the Changing Outlook* (2nd edn). London: Methuen.

FLAVELL, J. H., BEACH, D. R. and CHINSKY, J. M. (1966) Spontaneous verbal rehearsal in a memory task as a function of age. *Child Developm.*, **37**, 283–300.

FOULDS, G. A. (1958) Clinical research in psychiatry. *J. ment. Sci.*, **104**, 259–65.

FRANKENBURG, W. K. and DOBBS, J. B. (1967) *Denver Developmental Screening Scale*. Denver: Univ. of Colorado Medical Center.

FRIEDLANDER, B. Z. (1970) Receptive language development in infancy: issues and problems. *Merrill-Palmer Quart. Behavior Developm.*, **16**, 7–51.

FRITH, U. (1971) Spontaneous patterns produced by autistic, normal and subnormal children. In RUTTER, M. (ed.) *Infantile Autism: Concepts, Characteristics and Treatment*. London: Churchill Livingstone.

FURTH, H. (1966) *Thinking without Language: Psychological Implications of Deafness*. New York: The Free Press.

FYGETAKIS, L. and GRAY, B. B. (1970) Programmed conditioning of linguistic competence. *Behavior Res. Therapy*, **8**, 153–63.

GAHAGAN, D. M. and GAHAGAN, G. A. (1970) *Talk Reform: Explorations in Language for Infant School Children*. London: Routledge & Kegan Paul.

GARDNER, J. M. (1969) Behavior modification research in mental retardation: search for an adequate paradigm. *Amer. J. ment. Defic.*, **73**, 844–51.

GARDNER, R. A. and GARDNER, B. T. (1969) Teaching sign language to a chimpanzee. *Science*, **165**, 664–72.

GARDNER, W. I. (1971) *Behavior Modification in Mental Retardation*. Chicago: Aldine Atherton.

GEORGE, R. ST. (1970) The psycholinguistic abilities of children from different ethnic backgrounds. *Austral. J. Psychol.*, **22**, 85–9.

GIEBINK, J. W., NEVILLE, A. R. and DAVIDSON, R. E. (1970) Acquisition of morphological rules and usage as a function of social experience. *Psychology in the Schools*, **7**, 217–22.

GIRARDEAU, F. L. and SPRADLIN, J. E. (1970) *A Functional Analysis Approach to Speech and Language*. ASHA Monogr. No. 14. Washington, DC: American Speech and Hearing Association.

GRAHAM, C. (1967) Ability and attainment tests. *Education*, 902–3, 948–9, 1000–2.

GUNZBURG, H. C. (1966) *Progress Assessment Charts*. London: Nat. Assoc. Ment. Health.

HALL, V. R. (1970) Reinforcement procedures and the increase of functional speech by a brain-injured child. In GIRARDEAU, F. L. and SPRADLIN, J. E. (eds.) *A Functional Approach to Speech and Language*. ASHA

Monogr. No. 14. Washington: American Speech and Hearing Association.

HAYE, J. R. (1970) *Cognition and the Development of Language.* New York and London: Wiley.

HERMELIN, B. (1971) Rules and language. In RUTTER, M. (ed.) *Infantile Autism, Concepts, Characteristics and Treatment.* London: Churchill Livingstone.

HERMELIN, B. and O'CONNOR, N. (1970) *Psychological Experiments with Autistic Children.* London: Pergamon.

HERRIOT, P. (1970) *An Introduction to the Psychology of Language.* London: Methuen.

HERRIOT, P. and LUNZER, E. (1971) *Comprehension and Cognitive Development.* Paper delivered to Research Workshop on 'Language Comprehension and the Acquisition of Knowledge', Durham, North Carolina, April 1971.

HESS, R. D. and SHIPMAN, V. (1965) Early experience and socialisation of cognitive modes in children. *Child Developm.,* **36,** 869–86.

HEWETT, F. M. (1966) Teaching speech to an autistic child through operant conditioning. *Amer. J. Orthopsychiat.,* **35,** 927–36.

HOBSBAUM, A. and MITTLER, P. (1971) *Sentence Comprehension Test. Experimental Edition.* Hester Adrian Research Centre, Univ. of Manchester.

HOGG, J. H. (1973) Personality assessment of the subnormal as the study of learning processes. In MITTLER, P. (ed.) *Assessment for Learning in the Mentally Handicapped.* London: Churchill Livingstone; Baltimore, Md: Williams & Wilkins.

HOWARD, M. J., HOOPS, H. R. and MCKINNON, A. J. (1970) Language abilities of children with differing socio-economic backgrounds. *J. learning Dis.,* **3,** 32–9.

JEFFREE, D. and CASHDAN, A. (1971) Severely subnormal children and their parents: an experiment in language improvement. *Brit. J. educ. Psychol.,* **41,** 184–94.

JEFFREE, D., WHELDALL, K. and MITTLER, P. (1973) The facilitation of two word utterances in two Down's syndrome boys. *Amer. J. ment. Defic.,* **78,** 117–22.

JENSEN, A. R. and ROHWER, W. D. (1963) The effect of verbal mediation on the learning and retention of paired associates by retarded adults. *Amer. J. ment. Defic.,* **68,** 80–4.

JOHNSON, G. O., CAPOBIANCO, R. J. and MILLER, P. Y. (1960) Speech and language development of a group of mentally deficient children enrolled in a training program. *Except. Child,* **27,** 72–7.

JOHNSTON, M. (1968) Echolalia and automatism in speech. In SLOANE, H. N. and MACAULAY, B. D. (eds.) *Operant Procedures in Remedial Speech and Language Training.* New York: Houghton Mifflin.

JORDAN, J. E. (1967) Language and mental retardation. In SCHIEFELBUSCH, R. L., COPELAND, R. H. and SMITH, J. O. (eds.) *Language and Mental Retardation.* New York: Holt, Rinehart & Winston.

KENDLER, T. S. and KENDLER, H. H. (1967) Experimental analysis of inferential behavior in children. In LIPSITT, L. P. and SPIKER, C. S. (eds.) *Advances in Child Development and Behavior.* New York: Academic Press.

KERR, N., MEYERSON, L. and MICHAEL, J. (1965) A procedure for shaping vocalisation in a mute child. In ULLMAN, L. P. and KRASNER, L. (eds.) *Case Studies in Behavior Modification.* New York: Holt, Rinehart & Winston.

KIERNAN, C. K. (1973) Functional analysis. In MITTLER, P. (ed.) *Assessment for Learning in the Mentally Handicapped.* London: Churchill Livingstone; Baltimore, Md: Williams & Wilkins.

KIRK, S. A. (1968) The Illinois Test of Psycholinguistic Abilities: its origins and implications. In HELLMUTH, J. (ed.) *Learning Disorders,* Vol. 3. Seattle: Special Child Publications.

KIRK, S. A. and KIRK, W. (1971) *Psycholinguistic Learning Disabilities: Diagnosis and Remediation.* Urbana: Univ. of Illinois Press.

KIRK, S. A., MCCARTHY, J. J. and KIRK, W. (1968) *Illinois Test of Psycholinguistic Abilities. Revised Edition.* Urbana: Institute for Research in Exceptional Children.

KLAUS, R. A. and GRAY, S. W. (1968) The early training program for disadvantaged children. *Monographs of the Society for Research in Child Development,* **33,** 120.

KOLSTOE, O. P. (1958) Language training of low grade mongoloid children. *Amer. J. ment. Defic.,* **63,** 17–30.

LASSERS, I. and LOW, G. (1960) *A Study of the Relative Effectiveness of Different Approaches of Speech Therapy for Mentally Retarded Children.* Report to Office of Education on Contract 6904. (Cited in Spradlin, 1963.)

LAWTON, D. (1968) *Social Class, Language and Education.* London: Routledge & Kegan Paul.

LEE, L. (1966) Developmental sentence types: a method for comparing normal and deviant syntactic development. *J. speech hear. Dis.,* **31,** 311–30.

LEE, L. L. (1969) *The Northwestern Syntax Screening Test.* Evanston, Ill.: Northwestern Univ. Press.

LEE, L. L. (1970) A screening test for syntax development. *J. speech hear. Dis.,* **35,** 104–12.

LEE, L. and CANTER, S. (1971) Developmental sentence scoring: a clinical procedure for estimating syntactic development in children's spontaneous speech. *J. speech hear. Dis.,* **36,** 315–40.

LENNEBERG, E. H. (1962) Understanding language without ability to speak: a case report. *J. abn. soc. Psychol.,* **65,** 419–25.

LENNEBERG, E. H. (1967) *Biological Foundations of Language*. New York: Wiley.

LENNEBERG, E. H., NICHOLS, I. E. and ROSENBERGER, E. F. (1964) Primitive stages of language development in mongolism. In *Disorders of Communication*, XLII. New York: Assoc. Res. nerv. ment. Dis.

LEREA, L. (1958) Assessing language development. *J. speech hear. Res.*, **1**, 75–85.

LEVITT, L. M. (1970) *A Method of Communication for Non-speaking Severely Subnormal Children*. London: Spastics Society.

LEWIS, M. M. (1968) *The Education of Deaf Children: the Possible Place of Finger Spelling and Signing*. London: HMSO.

LOVAAS, I. (1966) A program for the establishment of speech in psychotic children. In WING, J. K. (ed.) *Early Childhood Autism: Clinical, Social, and Educational Aspects*. London: Pergamon.

LOVELL, K. and BRADBURY, B. (1967) The learning of English morphology in educationally subnormal special school children. *Amer. J. ment. Defic.*, **71**, 609–15.

LURIA, A. R. (1961) *The Role of Speech in the Regulation of Normal and Abnormal Behaviour*. London: Pergamon.

LURIA, A. R. (1963) *The Mentally Retarded Child*. London: Pergamon.

LYLE, J. G. (1960) The effect of an institution environment upon the verbal development of institutionalised children. *J. ment. Defic. Res.*, **4**, 1–23.

LYLE, J. G. (1961) Comparison of the language of normal and imbecile children. *J. ment. Defic. Res.*, **5**, 40–50.

MACAULAY, B. D. (1968) A program for teaching speech and beginning reading to nonverbal retardates. In SLOANE, H. N. and MACAULAY, B. D. (eds.) *Operant Procedures in Remedial Speech and Language Training*. New York: Houghton Mifflin.

MCCARTHY, D. (1954) Language development. In CARMICHAEL, L. (ed.) *Manual of Child Psychology*. New York: Wiley.

MCCARTHY, J. J. (1964) Research on the linguistic problems of the mentally retarded. *Ment. Retard. Abstrs.*, **2**, 90–6.

MCCARTHY, J. J. and KIRK, S. A. (1961) *Illinois Test of Psycholinguistic Abilities. Experimental Edition*. Urbana: Inst. for Research in Exceptional Children.

MACCUBREY, J. (1971) Verbal operant conditioning with young institutionalised Down's Syndrome children. *Amer. J. ment. Defic.*, **75**, 696–701.

MCNEILL, D. (1966) Developmental psycholinguistics. In SMITH, F. and MILLER, G. A. (eds.) *The Genesis of Language*. Cambridge, Mass.: MIT Press.

MCNEILL, D. (1970a) *The Acquisition of Language: The Study of Developmental Psycholinguistics*. New York and London: Harper & Row.

MCNEILL, D. (1970b) The development of language. In MUSSEN, P. H. (ed.) *Carmichael's Manual of Child Psychology* (3rd edn). New York and London: Wiley.

MARINOSSON, G. (1970) Language abilities of normal, ESN and SSN children: a comparative study. In MITTLER, P. (ed.) *The Work of the Hester Adrian Research Centre: A Report for Teachers*. Monogr. suppl., *Teaching and Training*, 8, 17–21.

MECHAM, M. J. (1955) The development and application of procedures for measuring speech improvement in mentally defective children. *Amer. J. ment. Defic.*, 60, 301–6.

MECHAM, M. J. and JEX, J. L. (1962) *Picture Speech Discrimination Test*. Provo, Utah: Brigham Young Univ. Press.

MECHAM, M. J., JEX, J. L. and JONES, J. (1967) *Utah Test of Language Development*. Salt Lake City: Communication Research Associates.

MEIN, R. (1961) A study of the oral vocabularies of severely subnormal patients. II. Grammatical analysis of speech samples. *J. ment. Defic. Res.*, 5, 52–9.

MENYUK, P. (1969) *Sentences Children Use*. Cambridge, Mass.: MIT Press.

MILLER, G. A. (1951) *Language and Communication*. New York: McGraw-Hill.

MILLER, S. A., SHELTON, J. and FLAVELL, J. H. (1970) A test of Luria's hypotheses concerning the development of verbal self-regulation. *Child Developm.*, 41, 651–65.

MINER, L. E. (1969) Scoring procedures for the length-complexity index: a preliminary report. *J. Comm. Dis.*, 2, 224–40.

MITTLER, P. (1969) Genetic aspects of psycholinguistic abilities. *J. Child Psychol. Psychiat.*, 10, 165–76.

MITTLER, P. (1970a) The use of morphological rules by four year old children; an item analysis of the Auditory-Vocal Automatic Test of the ITPA. *Brit. J. dis. Comm.*, 5, 99–109.

MITTLER, P. (1970b) Biological and social aspects of language development in twins. *Developm. med. Child Neurol.*, 12, 741–57.

MITTLER, P. (1970c) *Psychological Assessment of Mental and Physical Handicaps*. London: Methuen.

MITTLER, P. (1971) *The Study of Twins*. Harmondsworth: Penguin.

MITTLER, P. (1973a) *Assessment for Learning in the Mentally Handicapped*. London: Churchill Livingstone; Baltimore, Md: Williams & Wilkins.

MITTLER, P. (1973b) The teaching of language. In CLARKE, A. D. B. and CLARKE, A. M. (eds.) *Mental Retardation and Behavioural Research*. London: Churchill Livingstone; Baltimore, Md: Williams & Wilkins.

MITTLER, P. and WARD, J. (1970) The use of the Illinois Test of Psycholinguistic Abilities with English four year old children: a normative and factorial study. *Brit. J. educ. Psychol.*, 40, 43–53.

MITTLER, P. and WHELDALL, K. (1971) Language comprehension in the severely subnormal. *Bull. Brit. Psychol. Soc.*, 24, 227A (abstr.).

MITTLER, P., JEFFREE, D., WHELDALL, K. and BERRY, P. (1974) *Assessment and Remediation of Language Comprehension and Production in Severely Subnormal Children*. Final Report to Social Science Research Council (unpubl.). Hester Adrian Research Centre, Univ. of Manchester.

MULLER, M. W. and WEAVER, S. J. (1964) Psycholinguistic abilities of institutionalised and non-institutionalised trainable mental retardates. *Amer. J. ment. Defic.*, **68**, 775–83.

NELSON, R. O. and EVANS, I. (1968) The combination of learning principles and speech therapy techniques in the treatment of non-communicating children. *J. child Psychol. and Psychiat.*, **9**, 111–24.

O'CONNOR, N. and HERMELIN, B. (1963) *Speech and Thought in Severe Subnormality*. London: Pergamon.

O'CONNOR, N. and HERMELIN, B. (1971) Cognitive deficits in children. *Brit. med. Bull.*, **27**, 227–31.

OLSON, D. R. (1970) Language acquisition and cognitive development. In HAYWOOD, H. C. (ed.) *Social-Cultural Aspects of Mental Retardation*. New York: Appleton-Century-Crofts.

OLSON, D. R. (1972) Language use for communication, instruction and thinking. In CARROLL, J. B. and FREEDLE, R. (eds.) *Language Comprehension and the Acquisition of Knowledge*. Washington, DC: Winston.

OSGOOD, C. E. (1957) A behaviouristic analysis. In OSGOOD, C. E. (ed.) *Contemporary Approaches to Cognition*. Cambridge, Mass.: Harvard Univ. Press.

OSGOOD, C. E. (1963) Psycholinguistics. In KOCH, S. (ed.) *Psychology: Study of a Science*, Vol. 6. New York: McGraw-Hill.

OSGOOD, C. E. (1968) Towards a wedding of insufficiencies. In DIXON, T. R. and HORTON, D. L. (eds.) *Verbal Behavior and General Behavior Theory*. Englewood Cliffs, NJ: Prentice-Hall.

OSLER, S. F. and TRAUTMAN, G. E. (1961) Concept attainment. II. Effect of stimulus complexity upon concept attainment at two levels of intelligence. *J. exp. Psychol.*, **62**, 9–13.

PARASKEVOPOULOS, J. N. and KIRK, S. A. (1969) *The Development and Psychometric Characteristics of the Revised Illinois Test of Psycholinguistic Abilities*. Urbana: Univ. of Illinois Press.

PARSONS, J. G. (1971) *Aspects of Verbal Behaviour in Hydrocephalic Children*. Unpubl. Ph.D. thesis, Univ. of Sheffield.

PAWLICKI, R. (1970) Behavior therapy research with children: a critical review. *Canad. J. behav. Sci.*, **2**, 163–73.

PEINS, M. (1969) *Bibliography on Speech, Hearing and Language in Relation to Mental Retardation 1900–1968*. Washington, DC: US Dept of Health, Education and Welfare.

PETERSON, R. F. (1968) Imitation: a basic behavioral mechanism. In SLOANE, H. N. and MACAULAY, B. D. (eds.) *Operant Procedures in Remedial Speech and Language Training*. New York: Houghton Mifflin.

PETERSON, R. F. and WHITEHURST, G. J. (1971) A variable influencing the performance of generalised imitative behaviors. *J. appl. Behav. Anal.*, 4, 1–9.

PETERSON, R. F., MERWIN, M. R. and MOYER, T. J. (1971) Generalised imitation: the effects of experimenter absence, differential reinforcement and stimulus complexity. *J. exp. child Psychol.*, 12, 114–28.

PREMACK, D. (1970) A functional analysis of language. *J. exp. Anal. Behav.*, 14, 107–25.

REESE, H. W. and LIPSITT, L. P. (1970) *Experimental Child Psychology.* New York: Academic Press.

RENFREW, C. E. (1971) *Renfrew Language Attainment Scales.* Oxford: Churchill Hospital.

REYNELL, J. K. (1969) *The Reynell Developmental Language Scales.* London: NFER.

REYNOLDS, L. J. (1970) Reinforcement procedures for establishing and maintaining echoic speech by a nonverbal child. In GIRARDEAU, F. L. and SPRADLIN, J. E. (eds.) *A Functional Approach to Speech and Language.* ASHA Monogr. No. 14. Washington, DC: American Speech and Hearing Association.

RISLEY, T. (1966) *Establishment of Verbal Behavior in Deviant Children.* Unpubl. Ph.D. thesis, Univ. of Washington. (Cited by Peterson, 1968.)

RISLEY, T. and WOLF, M. (1967) Establishing functional speech in echolalic children. *Behav. Res. Therapy*, 5, 73–88.

ROBINSON, W. P. (1971) Social factors and language development in primary school children. In HUXLEY, R. and INGRAM, E. (eds.) *Language Acquisition: Models and Methods.* London and New York: Academic Press.

ROGERS, M. G. H. (1971) *A Study of Language Development in Severe Subnormality.* Unpubl. dissertation, Institute of Child Health, Univ. of London.

ROSENBERG, S. (1970) Problems of language development in the retarded. In HAYWOOD, H. C. (ed.) *Social-Cultural Aspects of Mental Retardation.* New York: Appleton-Century-Crofts.

ROSENBERG, S., SPRADLIN, J. and MABEL, S. (1961) Interaction among retarded children as a function of their relative language skills. *J. abn. soc. Psychol.*, 63, 402–10.

RUTTER, M. and MITTLER, P. (1972) Environmental influences on language development. In RUTTER, M. and MARTIN, A. (eds.) *The Child with Delayed Speech.* London: Spastics Society and Heinemann.

RUTTER, M. and SUSSENWEIN, I. (1971) A developmental and behavioral approach to the treatment of preschool autistic children. *J. Autism and Childhood Schizophrenia*, 1, 376–97.

RYCKMAN, D. B. and WIEGERNINK, R. (1969) The factors of the Illinois Test of Psycholinguistic Abilities: a comparison of 18 factor analyses. *Except. Child.*, 36, 107–13.

SANDERS, B., ROSS, L. E. and HEAL, L. (1965) Reversal and non-reversal shift learning in normal children and retardates of comparable mental age. *J. exp. Psychol.*, **69**, 84–8.

SAUNDERS, E. and MILLER, C. J. (1968) A study of verbal communication in mentally subnormal patients. *Brit. J. dis. Comm.*, **3**, 99–110.

SCHIEFELBUSCH, R. L. (1963) Language studies of mentally retarded children. Monogr. Suppl., *J. speech hear. Dis.*, **10**, 1–108.

SCHIEFELBUSCH, R. L. (1972) *Language of the Mentally Retarded.* Baltimore, Md.: Univ. Park Press.

SCHIEFELBUSCH, R. L., COPELAND, R. H. and SMITH, J. O. (1967) *Language in Mental Retardation.* New York: Holt, Rinehart & Winston.

SCHLANGER, B. B. (1953) Speech therapy results with mentally retarded children in special classes. *Training School Bull.*, **50**, 179–86.

SCHLANGER, B. B. (1954) Environmental influences on the verbal output of mentally retarded children. *J. speech hear. Dis.*, **19**, 339–43.

SCHLANGER, B. B. and GOTTSLEBEN, R. H. (1957) Analysis of speech defects among the institutionalised mentally retarded. *J. speech hear. Dis.*, **22**, 98–103.

SCHUBERT, J. (1969) The V.R.B. Apparatus: an experimental procedure for the investigation of the verbal regulation of behavior. *J. genet. Psychol.*, **114**, 237–52.

SHAW, H. J., MATTHEWS, C. G. and KLOVE, H. (1966) The equivalence of WISC and PPVT IQs. *Amer. J. ment. Defic.*, **70**, 601–4.

SHERIDAN, M. D. (1973) *Developmental Progress of Infants and Young Children.* London: NFER.

SHERIDAN, V. (1964) Development of auditory attention and the use of language symbols. In RENFREW, C. and MURPHY, K. (eds.) *The Child Who Does Not Talk.* London: Spastics Society and Heinemann.

SHERMAN, J. A. (1965) Use of reinforcement and imitation to reinstate verbal behavior in mute psychotics. *J. abn. soc. Psychol.*, **70**, 155–64.

SHRINER, T. H. and SHERMAN, D. (1967) An equation for assessing language development. *J. speech hear. Res.*, **10**, 41–8.

SINGER, B. D. and OSBORN, R. W. (1970) Social class and sex differences in admission patterns of the mentally retarded. *Amer. J. ment. Defic.*, **75**, 160–2.

SKINNER, B. (1957) *Verbal Behaviour.* London: Methuen.

SLOANE, H. N. and MACAULAY, B. D. (1968) *Operant Procedures in Remedial Speech and Language Training.* New York: Houghton Mifflin.

SLOANE, H. N., JOHNSTON, M. K. and HARRIS, F. R. (1968) Remedial procedures for teaching verbal behavior to speech deficient or defective young children. In SLOANE, H. N. and MACAULAY, B. D. (eds.) *Operant Procedures in Remedial Speech and Language Training.* New York: Houghton Mifflin.

SLOBIN, D. I. (1971a) *Psycholinguistics.* London: Scott Foresman.

SLOBIN, D. I. (1971b) Universals of grammatical development in children. In FLORES D'ARCAIS and LEVELT, W. (eds.) *Advances in Psycholinguistics*. Amsterdam: North Holland.

SMITH, P. A. and MARX, R. W. (1971) The factor structure of the revised edition of the Illinois Test of Psycholinguistic Abilities. *Psychology in the Schools*, **8**, 349–56.

SPRADLIN, J. E. (1963) Language and communication in mental defectives. In ELLIS, N. R. (ed.) *Handbook of Mental Deficiency*. New York: McGraw-Hill.

SPRADLIN, J. E. (1968) Environmental factors and the language development of retarded children. In ROSENBERG, S. and KOPLIN, J. H. (eds.) *Developments in Applied Psycholinguistics Research*. New York: Macmillan.

SPRADLIN, J. E. and ROSENBERG, S. (1964) Complexity of adult verbal behavior in a dyadic situation with retarded children. *J. abn. soc. Psychol.*, **68**, 694–8.

SPRADLIN, J. E. and GIRARDEAU, F. L. (1970) The implications of a functional approach to speech and hearing and therapy. In GIRARDEAU, F. L. and SPRADLIN, J. E. (eds.) *A Functional Approach to Speech and Language*. ASHA Monogr. No. 14. Washington, DC: American Speech and Hearing Association.

SPREEN, O. (1965a) Language functions in mental retardation: a review. I. Language development, types of retardation and intelligence level. *Amer. J. ment. Defic.*, **69**, 482–94.

SPREEN, O. (1965b) Language functions in mental retardation: a review. II. Language in higher level performance. *Amer. J. ment. Defic.*, **70**, 351–62.

STAATS, A. W. (1968) *Language, Learning and Cognition*. New York: Holt, Rinehart & Winston.

STRAZZULA, M. (1953) Speech problems of the mongoloid child. *Pediatrics*, **8**, 268–73.

TALKINGTON, L. W. and HALL, S. M. (1970) Matrix language program with mongoloids. *Amer. J. ment. Defic.*, **75**, 88–91.

TEMPLIN, M. C. (1957) *Certain Language Skills in Children*. Minneapolis: Univ. of Minnesota Press.

THOMPSON, M. M. (1963) Psychological characteristics relevant to the education of the preschool mongoloid child. *Ment. Retard.*, **1**, 148–51.

THOMPSON, C. W. and MAGARET, A. (1947) Differential test responses of normals and mental defectives. *J. abn. soc. Psychol.*, **42**, 285–93.

TIZARD, B. (1971) Environmental effects on language development: a study of residential nurseries (paper delivered to Annual Conference of The British Psychological Society, Exeter, April 1971). *Bull. Brit. Psychol. Soc.*, **24**, 232.

TIZARD, J. (1964) *Community Services for the Mentally Handicapped*. London: Oxford Univ. Press.

TIZARD, J. (1970) The role of social institutions in the causation, prevention and alleviation of retarded performance. In HAYWOOD, H. C. (ed.) *Social-Cultural Aspects of Mental Retardation.* New York: Appleton-Century-Crofts.

TRABASSO, T. (1972) Mental operations in language comprehension. In CARROLL, J. B. and FREEDLE, R. (eds.) *Language Comprehension and the Acquisition of Knowledge.* Washington, DC: Winston.

VANDENBERG, S. G. (1968) *Progress in Human Behavior Genetics.* Baltimore: Johns Hopkins Univ. Press.

VAN RIPER, J. (1954) *Speech Correction: Principles and Methods.* Englewood Cliffs, NJ: Prentice-Hall.

WATTS, A. F. (1944) *Language and Mental Development of Children.* London: Harrap.

WEBB, C. E. and KINDE, S. (1968) Speech, language and hearing of the mentally retarded. In BAUMEISTER, A. A. (ed.) *Mental Retardation.* London: Univ. of London Press.

WEENER, P., BARRIT, L. S. and SEMMEL, M. I. (1967) A critical evaluation of the Illinois Test of Psycholinguistic Abilities. *Except. Child.,* **33,** 373–84.

WEIR, M. and STEVENSON, H. W. (1959) The effects of vocalisation in children's learning as a function of chronological age. *Child Developm.,* **30,** 143–9.

WEISBERG, P. (1971) Operant procedures with the retardate: an overview of laboratory research. In ELLIS, N. R. (ed.) *International Review of Research in Mental Retardation,* Vol. 5. New York and London: Academic Press.

WHELAN, E. (1973) Developing work skills: a systematic approach. In MITTLER, P. (ed.) *Assessment for Learning in the Mentally Handicapped.* London: Churchill Livingstone; Baltimore, Md: Williams & Wilkins.

WOLSKI, W. (1962) *The Michigan Picture Language Inventory.* Ann Arbor: Univ. of Michigan Press.

YODER, D. (1970) The reinforcing properties of a television presented listener. In GIRARDEAU, F. L. and SPRADLIN, J. E. (eds.) *A Functional Approach to Speech and Language.* ASHA Monogr. No. 14. Washington, DC: American Speech and Hearing Association.

ZEAMAN, D. and HOUSE, B. J. (1963) The role of attention in retardate discrimination learning. In ELLIS, N. R. (ed.) *Handbook of Mental Deficiency.* New York: McGraw-Hill.

18

M. Fawcus and R. Fawcus

Disorders of communication

Introduction

A disorder of communication may be described as any chronic limitation of an individual's ability to engage in social behaviour involving verbal and sometimes non-verbal processes.

Breakdown in communication may occur at any point in the complex sensori-motor cycle and in some cases will occur at several stages. A retarded child, for example, frequently has any deviant articulatory pattern blamed upon his low intelligence. Whilst this may possibly be responsible for the slow development of language, the suggestion ignores the likelihood of sensori-motor dysfunction, hearing loss and unfavourable environmental factors.

Intellectual abilities have a bearing on many features of both learning and performance of communication skills. The normal infant may be expected to achieve considerable control of the necessary perceptual, semantic and syntactic phonological skills over a remarkably short period. Within the group of children of normal and superior intelligence there is, as might be anticipated, considerable variation in the rate of development of the integral skills. The principal feature of the linguistic development of the subnormal child is a delay in semantic and syntactic processing which may or may not be accompanied by a delay in phonological skills.

The acquisition and performance of linguistic skills involves a high level of information processing and represents the most complex universally observable area of skilled behaviour. Vowels, diphthongs and continuant consonants (*w, m, n, ng, l, r, y*) consist of complex patterns of harmonics achieved by momentary postures of the upper respiratory tract. The variable resonance chambers modulate the laryngeal tone to produce such diverse information as dialectal differences, intonation patterns and affective states.

Plosive, fricative and affricative consonants play a major part in providing a phonological skeleton in most languages. Voiceless consonants (*p, t, k, f, v, th, s, sh, ch*) generally consist of characteristic high frequency patterns differentiated by duration, mode and place of production. The frequency range of this group is from 1,000 Hz to the upper limits of the audio frequency range.

The voiced counterparts of this group are formed by combining the high frequency elements with the low frequency larynx output (*b, d, g, v, th, z, j*). Complex perceptual processing is obviously vital to the development of communication. The auditory channel is of primary importance in all except children with a severe hearing loss. At higher levels of cerebral function, the neural analogues of acoustic information are correlated with stored previous inputs to achieve semantic matching.

The output stage of language demands the selection of specific neural information with as much, if not greater, precision than the input process. Generation of a speech sound, a syllable or a chain of syllables requires the organization of a series of major and minor feedback loops. Although hearing is of singular importance during the development of language, it is the kinaesthetic feedback channel which is pre-eminent in the performance. A child with little or no useful hearing may go on to learn reasonably fluent intelligible speech whilst a mature speaker may lose his hearing completely and yet retain a fluency and accuracy only a little below his previous performance.

Incidence and prevalence

Two facts emerge very clearly from studying the literature on the prevalence of speech disorders in the mentally subnormal: firstly, that there is a very much higher incidence of communication problems than amongst the normal population, and secondly that, not surprisingly, the incidence increases as the IQ decreases. Surveys have also shown (Schlanger and Gottsleben, 1957; Blanchard, 1964) that there is a particularly strong link between mongolism and communication disorders. This is perhaps not surprising when one considers some of the physical abnormalities associated with Down's syndrome. These will be discussed later under articulation and voice. Only one area of conflicting findings seems to exist, and this is in the prevalence of stuttering.

One of the problems in any 'head-counting' survey is the fact that criteria will obviously differ in deciding whether or not there is a communication problem. For example, dialectal variants with which one is not familiar may render speech unintelligible. Within the subject's own 'speech environment', however, no such problem exists. In such circumstances it is very easy to label speech as 'poor' or 'deviant' when it is the listener's ear which should really be considered at fault. Taking these factors into account, however, there seems little doubt that a great many subnormal subjects have handicapping communication problems which probably prevent them functioning at their highest potential level.

A statistical survey carried out in London by Burt in the 1920s (Burt, 1951) showed that 'severe defects of speech' occurred in just over 1 per cent of normal children (the control group); in over 5 per cent of backward children; and in nearly 11 per cent of those children considered to be mentally deficient. Burt also mentions the results of a survey carried out by Lloyd in Birmingham at the same time, in which severe speech defects were found in ·5 per cent of the (normal) control group, in just over 5 per cent of the backward, and in nearly 15 per cent of the mentally deficient. In the London survey, and taking mild defects into account, Burt estimated that nearly one-quarter of mentally deficient children surveyed showed some defect of speech. It is interesting to compare these figures with those of Wallin (1949) who states that in St Louis over 26 per cent of pupils in special schools had defective speech, compared with 2·8 per cent in 'the regular elementary and high school grades'. Wallin also showed that there are a higher number of articulatory disorders among the mentally deficient children examined than among the normal group – just over 81 per cent of all defects in the former and 57 per cent in the latter.

A more recent survey carried out by Schlanger and Gottsleben (1957) among 516 residents at The Training School, Vineland, New Jersey, showed that no less than 79 per cent had 'varying types and levels of speech defectiveness'. They comment, 'It is interesting to note that practically all the subjects with voice and stuttering defects had, in addition, some degree of articulatory impairment.' The authors attempted to discover the incidence of defective speech amongst the different aetiological groups which come under the broad heading mental retardation. They found that the greatest incidence occurred in the mongol group (of whom 95 per cent had defects of articulation, 72 per cent had voice disorders, and 45 per cent stammered). In the organic group, defective articulation occurred in 84 per cent, 56 per cent had a voice disorder, and 18 per cent stammered. They discovered that the lowest incidence of defective speech was in the familial group, where 66 per cent had some defect of articulation, 22 per cent had voice disorders, and 10 per cent stammered. The lower incidence amongst the familial group 'is to be expected because of a lesser degree of pathology underlying their retardation'. Schlanger and Gottsleben themselves suggest that the very high incidence of defective speech at The Training School is in part due to the fact that only 12 per cent of the school population come in the familial group. In addition, both authors have training and considerable experience in speech pathology and therapy, and their criteria are therefore probably more strict in deciding what constitutes defective speech.

Although there have been several studies of the incidence of speech defects amongst the mentally retarded, not all of these have shown the relative incidence in what were recognized as the three main grades. Kennedy (1930) attempted such a survey, and found that 42 per cent of 249 feeble-minded patients had speech disorders ranging from slight to severe; 71 per cent of 27 imbeciles had speech defects; and none of the 32 idiots examined showed meaningful speech. The age range of the group studied was 5 to 38 years.

In a study of 2,522 institutionalized patients, Sirkin and Lyons (1941) found that 31 per cent of patients with IQs over 69 had speech defects; 47 per cent of the feeble-minded group showed defective speech; and 74 per cent of the imbecile group. Sachs (1951) in a study of 210 feeble-minded and imbecile patients (aged 10–20 years) reported that 57 per cent had defective speech. An analysis of the patients with speech defects showed that 18 per cent of the 'borderline' group had speech defects, 44 per cent of the feeble-minded group, and 79 per cent of the imbecile group.

Three more recent studies have all confirmed earlier findings on the prevalence of communication problems amongst the institutionalized retarded. Saunders and Miller (1968) assessed 1,005 patients at the Manor Hospital, Surrey: 482 males between the ages of 5 and 82 years, and 523 females between 7 and 80 years. They looked at comprehension and use of spoken language, intelligibility of speech, fluency and voice quality. The patients' verbal communication was assessed, and the results examined according to sex, chronological age and intelligence. They concluded that 'normal speech did not occur in more than 42 per cent of any of the groups and a large number of patients were considered to have inadequate verbal communication'.

Of 216 patients examined at Porterville State Hospital (Sheehan *et al.*, 1968) 50 per cent had no speech at all or else severely delayed language development. They found that dental abnormalities and articulation disorders were common, and only 12 per cent of the patients seen had normal speech. This was followed up by a further study (Martyn *et al.*, 1969) at Camarillo State Hospital, California. 'Individual diagnostic speech evaluations' were made on a total of 346 patients. In this study, more than a third of the patients had articulation disorders and almost a third showed lack of or delayed language development.

Two further studies amongst the educable mentally retarded show widely differing results: Donovan (1957) found that 8 per cent of 2,000 educable children had severe defects of articulation, whilst Steinman, Grossman and Reece (1963) considered that 53 per cent of 1,000 children examined had defective speech. As Matthews (1957) points out, 'Variations in the incidence figures are probably due to differences in criteria of what constitutes a speech defect, and to differences in the composition of the retarded group studied.' This high incidence of speech defects would seem to suggest that mental deficiency is the *cause* of many of these disorders of speech and language. As Kastein (1956) has pointed out, however, 'The child's label of gross (mental) impairment does not necessarily indicate the cause for his language and speech deficiency.'

Matthews (1957) has said, 'In view of the high incidence of speech and hearing problems among mentally retarded children, it is not surprising that communication disorders are often thought to result from mental deficiency.' He goes on to say, 'The well-trained speech and hearing therapist should recognize that there may be many explanations of delayed or defective speech which have no relation to intellectual retardation.'

Becky (1942), in a study of fifty children with delayed speech, found that there were a number of constitutional, environmental, and psychological factors, other than mental retardation, to explain the retardation of speech. Matthews (1957) lists brain injury, glandular dysfunction, emotional disturbance, and hearing loss as aetiological factors of speech disorders in mental deficiency.

Berry and Eisenson (1956) are in agreement with these findings and point of view. They say,

Despite the very high incidence of speech defects among the feeble-minded, low intelligence is probably not a direct cause of defective speech production, though it is undoubtedly directly associated with poor linguistic ability. There are many organic conditions, such as cretinism, mongolism and brain damage, which are responsible at once for both the lowered intelligence and the defective speech of the individual. The amount of intelligence needed for the correct production and control of speech sounds is not great.

These writers emphasize the point that there may be a common aetiological factor (or even factors) underlying both the mental deficiency and the speech or language problem. Furthermore, it will be shown that the speech disorder itself may be largely or in part responsible for the retarded intellectual development.

The efficacy of remedial measures

Because of the generally pessimistic view of achieving any lasting improvement, the field of subnormality was not a popular area with many speech therapists. As some of the early therapists came from the field of speech training, the emphasis tended to be on improving articulation. For a number of reasons, such procedures generally proved to be unproductive: treatment periods were too widely spaced, the children were frequently too immature and therapists lacked the necessary knowledge of learning theory and training procedures. Over the past two decades, however, attitudes have changed and many therapists are now working with both the mildly and severely subnormal. Too many of these appointments are still on a very limited sessional basis, but in the United Kingdom there are now a number of full-time appointments in institutions for the more severely handicapped. A number of influences have been responsible for this change – including work by Clarke and Clarke (1953) and others, showing that the IQ was not so constant a factor as had been imagined, and the increasing awareness of the adverse effects of poor environment on intellectual development. In addition it has been increasingly realized that many retarded children and adults are not functioning at their highest potential level because of communication problems.

There is still a continuing shortage of speech therapists, and often a lack of funds to provide an adequate establishment in centres for the subnormal. The question of training aides has been discussed and Aronson (1968) has reported on their successful use with severely subnormal children at North Jersey Training School. She found a marked improvement in both language development and IQ (from 10–20) at the conclusion of a two-year training programme. Guess, Smith and Ensminger (1971) have also reported favourably on the use of former psychiatric aides as 'language developmentalists'.

The use of speech therapy aides is naturally a controversial one, but speech therapists are realizing the need to cooperate more closely with parents, teachers and others in developing language and improving every aspect of communication. Where a speech therapist has only one or two sessions in training schools for the subnormal, then it would seem to be a more realistic goal to work in an advisory capacity with parents and teachers, rather than try to see a handful of the children needing speech therapy for a single half-hour session each week.

Without speech as an adequate means of self-expression and communication, the child's intellectual and emotional development will suffer, and the resulting anxiety and frustration may produce behaviour problems. Regarding the effect of defective speech on education, Burt (1951) has this to say: 'The handicaps imposed by defective articulation are most easily seen in oral and linguistic subjects. More particularly it is liable to hinder the child's early efforts at phonic analysis, and so prevent him from learning to read as quickly as the rest.' Defective speech may, in fact, be a considerable factor in producing backwardness and, further still, in preventing the child from benefiting from special educational or training programmes available.

Nisbet (1953) has made an interesting contribution on the relationship between environment, verbal ability, and intellectual development. He says,

> Previous studies have shown from the testing of children from institutions, of only children, and of twins, that lack of contact with adults results in retardation of verbal development; and there is substantial evidence to suggest that ability with words is of importance not only in verbal tests but in all abstract thinking.

He quotes Terman and Merrill (1937), who say, 'Language, essentially, is the shorthand of the higher thought processes, and the level at which this shorthand functions is one of the most important determinants of the level of the processes themselves.'

While it is generally recognized that there is an intimate connection between thought and language, what is not always appreciated is the effect of language deprivation on the thought processes of a child, for example, the deaf mute. It is obvious that thought must use symbols of some sort, or what Pavlov (1941) termed 'the signals of signals'. Clearly the deaf mute builds up some sort of process of symbolization, but words are the most obvious, the most flexible, discriminative, and the widest in range of all possible symbols. Nisbet (1953) quotes Ballard's (1934) conclusion: 'Admitting frankly that thought can function without language, we must also point out that it cannot function well without it, and that though it can do without it, it very rarely does.' Thus speech deprivation may not only restrict communication and experience, but depending upon its degree, may even limit the development of the thought processes, and hence intelligence.

The now famous study of twins of normal intelligence by Luria and Yudovich (1959) is relevant in this context. A pair of twins were studied who, at the age of 5 years, communicated only with one another, possessing a very limited vocabulary. Their comprehension was also limited, and they showed no interest in listening to stories. 'While our twins understood perfectly speech that was directly related to an object or action which preoccupied them, they were not in a position to understand speech when it was not directly connected with a concrete situation and took a developed narrative form.' Their play was primitive and monotonous. There was no constructional play, and any meaningful or creative activities were rare. They were unable to draw or model in clay. Speech which consisted mainly of exclamations was, as Luria described it, 'locked in activity', and was not used in any way to organize or direct activity. After an initial period of observation, the two children were removed from the twin situation, and were each placed in a separate kindergarten group. This separation rapidly resulted in an improvement in play activity and the development of constructional activity, with the ability to formulate a project. Instead of scribbles, the children's drawings became, to use Luria's words, 'Goal driven, differentiated and objective'. 'Even more significant', he said, 'was the fact that the whole structure of the mental life of the twins was simultaneously and sharply changed. Once they acquired an objective language system, the children were able to formulate the aims of their activity verbally, and after only three months we observed the beginnings of meaningful play.'

Furthermore, language training in one twin resulted in increased perception of speech and certain intellectual operations, such as the ability to classify. Hermelin and O'Connor have commented, 'The role of language may be decisive for the degree of efficiency with which imbeciles may be able to master problems as distinct from acquiring skills' (1963).

Schneider and Vallon (1955) have published the results of their work with mentally retarded children at the Westchester School for Retarded Children, and have concluded that

There is definitely a place for speech therapy in the educational or training programmes for the moderately and severely retarded child, and that not only can speech therapy be successfully integrated into almost any training programme for such children but that inherent in such a programme are potential values that challenge the imagination.

Supporting their contention that speech therapy has a place in the rehabilitation of the defective child, they say,

Those children who proceeded to develop the ability to communicate verbally have gained considerably more than can be measured by the number of words they have learned. The mere ability to express one's wants or needs in a socially acceptable manner, let alone the facility of fulfilling one's wants or needs through verbal communication, is indeed an invaluable asset to the child on an intellectual, an emotional, and a social level. . . . With greater facility in verbal expression seemed to come a reduction in anxiety-producing situations, which in turn led to a reduction in a-social behaviour, and has, in many instances, made for a happier and better adjusted individual.

Rittmanic (1958) reported a noticeable improvement as a result of a three-month oral language programme, in which a group of institutionalized but educable mentally retarded children were seen five times a week for a period of fifteen to twenty minutes. Kolstoe (1958) found that language training with low-grade mongoloid children resulted not only in an increase in language abilities, but also in a statistically significant increase in IQ. Of 169 institutionalized patients selected for a three and a half year therapy programme (mean length of treatment five months), Sirkin and Lyons (1941) reported that 52 per cent of the total benefited. Divided into categories, improvement was shown in 79 per cent of the borderline, 59 per cent of the educationally subnormal, and 26 per cent of the moderately subnormal group.

Encouraging reports on the results of speech and language therapy with mentally retarded children have also been published by Schlanger (1953a, b) and Strazzulla (1953).

A successful response to speech therapy may be predicted, provided that:

1. the patient has sufficient ability to cooperate with the therapist in carrying out simple instructions;
2. the patient's attention can be gained and then maintained for a reasonable period of time;
3. rapport between patient and therapist has been established, so that the patient has confidence in the therapist and will cooperate with her;
4. anxiety has been eliminated from the learning situation, enabling the patient to function at his highest intellectual level;
5. all distracting stimuli have been removed, such as noise and unwanted equipment;
6. the patient is adequately motivated;
7. the material used is meaningful, and so presented that the patient's interest is stimulated;
8. stages in treatment are so graded that the patient may always succeed at one stage before the next is attempted;
9. speech correction can be carried out at frequent intervals (at least two or three times a week), or else followed up by regular and wisely supervised practice periods;
10. the cooperation of parents, teachers, and all those responsible for the patient's welfare has been gained;
11. the physical handicaps are such that they may to some extent be overcome.

Where the prognosis is in any doubt when the patient is first assessed, a trial period of speech therapy may provide the answer to the question, 'Can this child benefit from treatment?' As Kastein (1956) says, 'The child's response to integrative language and speech therapy should be taken into consideration before his mental potential can be assessed with any degree of accuracy. His response to such therapy is, in fact, an index of his potential.' The same may be said to be true of the adult patient. As Berry and Eisenson (1956) comment, 'Low intelligence undoubtedly is responsible for many cases of delay in speech, but speech delay also is the cause for much apparent low intelligence.' Furthermore,

There is some evidence to the effect that when children are taught to speak there is a concomitant increase in their IQs. Whether this increase results directly from the ability of the child to use language in a conventional manner, or whether the child who speaks generally makes a more adequate adjustment to his environment, and to the taking of intelligence tests, is not certain.

Hubschman (1967) used behavioural shaping techniques and reinforcement procedures in a daily programme of language stimulation for nine institutionalized mongols, matched for age, sex, IQ and mental age with a control group. No improvement was reported after a period of six months, but by eighteen months there were significant increases in mental age, intelligence quotient and social quotient.

With the improvement in language assessment techniques, the measurement of response to therapy is becoming a more reliable procedure. Guess, Smith and Ensminger (1971) describe the use of the Illinois Test of Psycholinguistic Abilities (McCarthy and Kirk, 1961) and the Mecham Verbal Language Development Scales (Mecham, 1958) in assessing the results of an eighteen-month language programme. Small groups of moderately and severely retarded children responded encouragingly to 'systematic and intense language training'. Discussing the results, the authors comment, 'the type of low functioning, fairly old and in some cases, multiply handicapped children included in the programme have traditionally been considered a difficult group with whom to work effectively'.

Let Matthews (1957) have the final word: 'In making a decision it would be well to remember that in a high-grade defective adequate speech may make the difference between self-sufficiency and dependency – between a lifetime in an institution at tax-payers' expense and vocational adjustment in society.'

With increasing awareness of the importance of differential diagnosis in all communication problems, and with improvement in assessment techniques, there is far less chance of a child being labelled 'mentally deficient' and other causative factors being overlooked. What we must always be on the alert for are discrepancies in test results which may indicate that the child's verbal ability is not in line with his mental age. It is still all too easy, in a child who obviously 'hears', to overlook quite handicapping degrees of high frequency hearing loss. Having labelled a child as mentally defective, then all communication failures may be blamed on his lack of intelligence when, in fact, his overall performance may be depressed by his verbal limitations. There seems little doubt that, if programmes are of sufficient intensity and duration and are planned on appropriate lines, then significant improvement in language and social skills does take place. It also seems clear that the progress made cannot be measured in terms of language achievement alone, but also in terms of increased confidence and social adjustment.

Disorders of language

(a) DEVELOPMENTAL DELAY

Speech therapists are frequently asked to advise the parents of pre-school children who exhibit no evidence of neuromuscular or perceptual dysfunction, are of normal intelligence with no serious behavioural problems who may be delayed up to two years in either understanding or production of language (Greene, 1967).

The introduction of more sensitive assessments of language has resulted in a substantial improvement in the service which speech therapists can offer to teachers, psychologists, paediatricians and parents. The ITPA is at present employed by a few therapists working in close conjunction with psychologists. The RDLS (Reynell, 1969) is more commonly employed. It is faster to administer and consists of items which are interesting and attractive to the vast majority of children for whom it was designed. The age range is from 18 months to 6 years, and an alternative form of receptive language assessment is specially provided for children with severe physical handicaps.

(b) THE EFFECTS OF LOW INTELLIGENCE

A useful distinction may be drawn between the different conditions which prevail in the familial and pathological groups of subnormal children. The child in the familial group is usually required to learn linguistic skills with a relatively normal but slowly developing sensori-motor mechanism, below average intellectual capacity and an environment in which neither the necessary interest nor skill in teaching language is likely to be present. The child with a history of pathology may have to develop in a similar milieu with the added problems of a damaged sensori-motor system and even less intellectual capacity. Many of the latter group, however, are born into families where both interest and some skill in language teaching are clearly in evidence.

Vocabulary acquisition may be impeded by environmental factors, retarded conceptual development or disordered processing at either peripheral or central stages.

Brook (1966) and Mein and O'Connor (1960) give details of the vocabulary of different populations of institutionalized severely subnormal individuals. Brook comments that:

The usual tests of vocabulary, the general approach and strategy employed by the speech therapist in schools and general hospitals and so forth, are not valid in such an institution. To illustrate, a 'sister' is no longer a relative, but is the female nurse in charge of a ward. Words in everyday use outside such as 'bus', 'grocer' and 'Father' are found to have few practical associations for these patients. On the other hand words such as 'Charge Nurse', 'stocktaking' and 'injection' are familiar words full of real meaning.

In cases of gross intellectual deficiency the patient is unlikely ever to develop meaningful speech. He may acquire a vocabulary of a few familiar words, and even understand simple commands, but he will not use speech as a means of communication in any real sense. In some low-grade defectives 'there may be an excessive flow of words, but the thought content is elementary, frequently irrelevant, and the vocabulary is limited' (Morley, 1957). Of 32 profound subnormals examined, Kennedy (1930) found that 20 were mute, 10 'jabbered' with an occasional intelligent word, 1 showed echolalia, and 1 had irrelevant speech.

Various investigators have shown that the age at which children first begin to use words and sentences is directly related to intelligence, and general mental retardation is probably the most common single factor in speech retardation. However, only in cases of gross intellectual deficiency would it be true to say that mental retardation is responsible for failure to develop speech at all.

The moderately subnormal vary considerably in their language ability, and much will depend on the stimulation provided by their environmental background. They show a very marked delay in the acquisition of speech: Wallin (1949) found that they used their first words at 2 years 3 months, and their first sentences at 3 years 7 months on the average. They will be unable to comprehend complex commands, and will experience difficulty in formulating sentences for narrative purposes – in describing a picture for example. Attempts may be telegrammatic in form, but they can communicate, and may 'converse' on a simple, concrete level. Vocabulary is limited to words within their more immediate physical environment.

Educationally subnormal children (mild) may use normal sentence construction, but may always prove to be linguistically inadequate in giving complex explanations. Onset of first words and sentences may be retarded, but much of their later verbal limitations may be the result of a restricted language background. This is particularly true where the familial group is concerned.

(c) HEARING LOSS

If hearing loss is sufficiently profound, and is either congenital or acquired before the development of speech, then speech and language will fail to develop once the babbling stage has passed. The child may learn to lip-read and understand simple and familiar speech without special training, but will be able to communicate himself solely through gesture and sublinguistic utterances. Should speech fail to develop, then the possibility of hearing loss should be investigated as early as possible. Unfortunately, deafness may not be detected, so that the most critical period for listening to and learning speech may be lost (Fry and Whetnall, 1964). Once again, the importance of early investigation and careful differential diagnosis cannot be over-stressed – not only because of the importance of early auditory training, but also because of the danger of incorrectly labelling the child as mentally defective. This is particularly true of the child with high-frequency deafness (Foale and Paterson, 1954).

Ives (1967) has outlined the specific tests available for the assessment of conceptual and linguistic development in children with disorders of hearing.

(d) APHASIA

Developmental aphasia is a rare disorder of language or symbolization in which the child fails to comprehend the spoken or written word (receptive or sensory aphasia), or is unable to express himself through language (expressive or motor aphasia). Few cases show an isolated receptive or expressive disturbance, and most patients show some impairment of other language faculties, such as reading (dyslexia) or writing (dysgraphia). Aphasia is a not uncommon condition in the middle-aged and elderly, associated with cerebral vascular lesions, but it is symptomatic of any infective or traumatic lesion involving appropriate areas of the cerebral cortex. Associated with these disturbances of language is a condition known as apraxia. Russell Brain (1952) defines apraxia as 'an inability to carry out a purposive movement, the nature of which the patient understands, in the absence of severe motor paralysis, sensory loss, and ataxia'.

In mental deficiency, and in considering delay or failure in speech development, we are naturally much more interested in developmental aphasia. Mykelbust (1957) mentions anoxia, Rh incompatibility, rubella, cerebral haemorrhage due to birth injury, and encephalopathic diseases such as meningitis and encephalitis, as the most common aetiological factors in aphasia in children. Aphasia may or may not be associated with mental retardation. Receptive aphasia is believed to be an uncommon condition in children, but varying degrees of expressive aphasia may be more common than is realized. The possibility of aphasia should be considered where a child shows an atypical or patchy performance on intelligence tests, performing well on performance tests, but showing a markedly lower score on verbal tests. West (1957) has said, 'The striking thing about the aphasic is the disparity between his language associations and the rest of his mental processes; his power to associate experiences is relatively normal, except for those which have only arbitrary and symbolic meanings.' He continues, 'He thinks in terms of real objects. Words are abstractions; they constitute a type of association with which he cannot deal.'

(e) LACK OF STIMULATION AND MOTIVATION

Cases are sometimes referred for treatment where speech has failed to develop in the absence of any apparent mental retardation, organic cause, or emotional disturbance. Such cases may occur when the young child is left alone a great deal, and generally deprived of human contact. On the other hand, the need for speech may never be created if parents are over-solicitous and anticipate the child's every need. As Van Riper (1952) says, 'The law of least effort is a rather fundamental determinant of human effort, and when children can get their wishes fulfilled without employing speech, they never acquire this all-important tool.'

Deprivation of affection and maternal care (such as may result in the case of children from institutions and large families) may be a very potent factor in the delayed acquisition of speech. The deprived child has little stimulation or motivation to acquire speech, and may therefore be very backward in learning to talk. Nisbet (1953) has already been quoted in this chapter on the relation of family size to verbal ability, and he also mentions the verbal retardation of institutionalized children.

Ainsworth (1962) has said: 'The specific aspects more seriously affected by continuing deprivation have been found repeatedly to be in language and social development.' The whole question of deprivation and its effect on language, and in turn the possible effects on intellectual growth, suggests the importance of a comprehensive and systematic programme of language training. (See Chapter 7.)

Remedial measures

Treatment will obviously depend on the aetiological factors involved in each case. The importance of making a careful differential diagnosis has already been stressed, not only because it is all too easy to blame mental retardation for delayed or inadequate language development, but also because a failure to recognize the real cause may deprive the child of the appropriate treatment or training he needs.

The speech therapist, working in the ESN School or Training School, will usually spend far more time on language stimulation and development than on speech correction of articulatory defects. Indeed, it is in encouraging the development and use of language that there is most possibility of achievement. Irwin (1959) stated that, 'For the mentally defective child the improvement of language is a much more realistic goal than the correction of specific sound defects', and she recommends a programme in which 'improvement in language should take precedence over the correction of specific sounds'.

In the Hospital Service similar emphasis has been placed on the educational nature of the 'therapy' and the importance of language. The speech therapist, whether working in the hospital or in the community, will typically be engaged in:

(a) *An advisory role* in relation to parents of very young retarded children. Medical advice is rarely explicit and frequently terse and pessimistic. Advice could also be given by psychologists, but their knowledge of language development and language stimulation techniques is usually more rudimentary than a speech therapist's.

(b) *Demonstration and training* for parents or surrogates. Demonstration is far more useful than even a series of talks. The vast majority of parents and surrogates tend to know what to do but are anxious about 'doing the wrong thing' when attempting to help with language stimulation. Sociolinguists have underlined class differences in language teaching practices. Normally, it is found that unless domestic and possibly psychiatric factors are extremely burdensome, parents will usually cooperate (Cashdan, 1969). Observation of differences in parental cooperation would suggest that the affective state of the mother will have a profound effect on the enthusiasm with which she engages in language training. Precise delineation of goals and careful encouragement will greatly assist parents or ward staff in their efforts to help the child.

(c) *Intensive training*. Some speech therapists consider that it is important to augment advice and demonstration by brief intensive periods of language stimulation. These are particularly valuable if:

(i) the child has apparently reached a plateau (e.g. six months with no obser-vable change in language or intelligibility) – the most cooperative and capable of parents will often become discouraged if no improvement is evident;

(ii) no parental or substitute assistance is forthcoming. So far only very limited domiciliary facilities are available, but with many families this would provide the only answer to overwhelming domestic difficulties. Peripatetic teachers visit pre-school children diagnosed as suffering from hearing loss and there would appear to be no reason why parents of children with other communi-cation handicaps should not receive this type of assistance.

(d) *Behaviour modification*. The achievement of such basic steps as encouraging the child to listen or to concentrate for any period is of primary importance. Traditional methods whether employed by parents, teachers or therapists have consisted of establishing a relationship with the child and gradually attempting to increase both the duration and depth of concentration. Spradlin (1968) and Yule and Berger (1971) describe behavioural modification techniques designed to remove the 'hit or miss' element from language teaching techniques with the sub-normal. Although the reinforcing stimuli may be identical with those employed by parent or therapist, the basic difference lies in the systematic mode of pre-sentation and the careful recording of the subject's responses. Wing (1966) sug-gests that individuals in the environment of the subnormal or autistic child should be given specific training in behaviour modification techniques in order to facilitate language development. This approach is described in great detail in Chapter 23.

(e) *Language stimulation*. In the case of the physically neglected and emotionally deprived child, every effort should be made so to adjust the environment that his physical and emotional needs are satisfied. The therapist can do much to help parents provide home conditions which will facilitate the optimum development of language within the framework of the child's mental ability and his level of physical maturation. Parents need an acceptance and understanding of the child's limitations, and an awareness of his need for additional stimulation and en-couragement. He must be treated as a 'belonging' member of the family unit, in which he may feel loved and secure. He needs an environmental background in which he is exposed to (but not bombarded by) rich and varied sensory experi-ence. He needs, far more than the normal child, to be played with and talked to and must experience success at his own level of attainment. His speech attempts, however poor and late these may be, must be received with pleasure and approval if further attempts are to be made. The therapist must help the critical and demanding parents to accept their child's limitations, and to realize how much their attitude is responsible for the child's lack of speech attempt.

Goda (1960) has given an interesting account of very early sound and language stimulation in non-speaking children, and says, 'Speech stimulation methods for each of these children should be consistent with his or her level of development.'

The therapist may work with these children individually, or in small groups matched for chronological and mental age, and for the type of language difficulty presented. A group has the advantage of simulating a more natural social situation; it creates a greater need for speech; and the therapist may make good use of the competitive element inherent in it.

Where the environment provides little stimulus for speech (e.g. in an institution) the therapist must endeavour to create a need for speech; help build the vocabulary and language to meet this need; and give adequate praise and encouragement when speech is attempted, however inadequate that attempt may be. Within the confines of the institution she must be responsible for increasing the child's experience as far as possible (by taking him shopping, or for a bus ride).

Where the child has been subjected to too much pressure to acquire speech, she must be undemanding in her approach. Once he recognizes that no demands are being made on him, and that his speech attempts, however poor, are accepted without adverse comment (or even with enthusiasm), then he will begin to explore the possibilities of using speech as a means of communication.

The possibility of deafness should of course always be investigated. The responsibility for the development of language and the teaching of speech in the deaf child is normally in the hands of the teacher of the deaf, and there are special schools for the child who is both deaf and mentally deficient. Children may be excluded from these schools, however, having failed to make progress or because of behaviour problems, and sent to residential institutions for the mentally deficient, where they then become a problem for the speech therapist. The therapist working with the born deaf will be primarily concerned with the acquisition of language, and only secondarily with the teaching of speech.

The speech therapist will need to make the greatest possible use of visual aids, and lip-reading will be taught concurrently with language work. As with aphasics, work begins with the association of words with concrete objects and easily demonstrated activities. A great deal of repetition will be necessary in the initial stages, and the associations must be as vivid as possible. New and more abstract words must be explained within the framework of the language the child already knows. As language increases, so the child becomes more accessible, and behaviour problems tend to decrease. Intellectual development is stimulated as language concepts are acquired and the child becomes more capable of abstract thought.

Any residual hearing present should be developed as far as possible, not only by the issue of a hearing aid but also by a thorough and systematic programme of auditory training. Where hearing loss is profound, the teaching of articulate speech will depend on the use of visual and tactile methods of approach. The intelligibility of the speech obtained will be affected by several variable factors, including the degree of hearing loss, the intelligence of the child, and the age at which speech training commences.

In the treatment of developmental aphasia, whether predominantly expressive or with some associated receptive difficulties, progress will inevitably be very slow, and therapy will necessarily extend over a period of several years. It is impossible here to do more than outline treatment. In view of the complexity of the problem, the rehabilitation programme will need to be very carefully planned to cover all aspects of language function. Basically, the therapist aims to build strong and vivid associations between concrete objects or activities, and the verbal symbols or words which we use for them. Rather than bewilder the child with a wealth of auditory stimuli, the therapist aims to establish a small vocabulary of familiar words. The whole speech situation is built up round the new word: for example, 'Give me the ball. Throw the ball. Catch the ball.' Abstractions are avoided, and the initial stages of therapy are based upon the most concrete material. Nouns and verbs are taught first, and only as language begins to develop are more abstract language concepts taught. Lea (1968) describes a comprehensive programme for matching auditory with visual stimuli devised in the course of his work with intelligent developmental dysphasic children.

Emotional conflict or trauma may be responsible for a child's failure to communicate. There are many possible causes of such conflict, which cannot be enumerated here, which careful investigation of the child's background may reveal. A negative attitude towards speech, with a complete refusal to make any speech attempt, may result when a mentally retarded child is over-stimulated by demanding or ambitious parents.

Failure to develop speech, or failure to use speech meaningfully (or to make any attempt at communication), may be symptomatic of autism in children. They may exhibit echolalia, in which the whole or last part of speech addressed to them is echoed without apparent understanding or meaning.

There are many practical problems in making a differential diagnosis between autism and mental deficiency. The subnormal child who has been rejected, or who, through institutionalization, has been emotionally deprived in the early years, may also present a picture of emotional disturbance. If sufficiently severe, this may lead to the problem of non-communication. The autistic child tends to perform at infantile levels of behaviour, which may make accurate assessment of aetiology even more difficult.

O'Connor and Hermelin (1971) describe a range of experiments designed to investigate the basic differences in perception and other capacities between autistic children, normals and the severely subnormal.

Any delay in speech development, or failure to develop adequate language as the child grows older, may be due to a complex aetiology in which two or more physical, intellectual, or emotional factors may be involved. Any of the conditions outlined above may be associated with varying degrees of mental retardation. The label 'mentally defective' may well obscure the child's need for special help with specific language difficulties or emotional problems.

Disorders of articulation

(a) FUNCTIONAL

A disorder of communication may be due to purely social or emotional causes with no direct association with learning problems, anatomical or physiological disorder. It is widely recognized that the majority of stutterers, for example, do not differ significantly from the majority of the normal population in anything but their specifically learned patterns of behaviour.

The effect of any communication disorder, however, is normally to give rise to stress which may exacerbate the original problem. A deviant pattern of articulation in a young mentally handicapped child will often be of more concern to even intelligent parents than the far more serious limitation in language development. This tends to occur because the language problem may be concealed if a child is able to engage in appropriate social responses.

Communication disorders in the subnormal may be the same in essence as those which affect the intelligent or may be derived from the specific condition and environment of individuals with low intelligence. Articulatory skills may be subject to delay in accordance with a total pattern of retarded sensori-motor development. In institutions and some families it may be found that a child conforms to the norms of his peers and is unintelligible to outsiders.

Most of the disorders of articulation prevalent among the subnormal tend to be associated with features of learning. In some cases the deviations are similar to patterns of immature articulation. A statement such as:

[mɪ mʌ̃ ˈtaʊ mɪ ʔɪ wɛ̃ ˈkʌ̃ʔɪ aˈmɒwə]

('My Mum told me she wasn't coming tomorrow')

bears a close resemblance to the dialectal forms in use in both the child's ward and the home in which he was brought up. The number of 'errors' or 'defects' to be counted depends completely upon qualitative judgments by the observer.

There is a vast difference between 'careful, polished, precise' articulation and the common patterns of even so-called 'educated speakers'. There is a tendency for all speakers to 'cut corners' physiologically, particularly in natural conversation. Most of the simplifications occur outside the conscious awareness of both speaker and listener and are only obvious to the phonetician or other trained listener. Many dialects abound with assimilations and elisions and successful communication is only achieved by the processes of continual exposure, a limitation of contexts and the general level of linguistic redundancy. Riello (1958) reports on the articulatory performance of a group of boys (N = 55) and girls (N = 45) with mean MA 7 years 9 months and CA 11 years 6 months.

41 per cent had defective articulation.

50 per cent of the deviant patterns were described as substitutions.

28 per cent of the deviant patterns were described as omissions.

19 per cent of the deviant patterns were described as distortions.

Beresford and Grady (1966) insist that this type of analysis ignores the influence of an individual's idiolect and that these phonological deviations must be regarded as features of a total language structure.

(b) ANATOMICAL MALFORMATION

Minor anatomical anomalies of the tongue, soft palate or lips will frequently be compensated for and overcome by children of normal and above average intelligence. The suggestion that this appears to occur less frequently in the subnormal has not been verified but is generally accepted.

Within the normal population there appears to be less successful adaptation to excessively deviant skeletal and muscular structures. The phonetic effects of such obvious features as irregular or missing dentition, disproportion of the mandible, maxilla, or tongue tie are more likely to be an indication of relative tongue mobility and the patency of the sensori-motor pathways (Tulley, 1964; Fawcus, 1969). In the United States intensive research is being directed upon problems of oral sensation and related motor behaviour. Preliminary results suggest that this will continue to be an increasingly important study (Bosma, 1970).

Tredgold and Soddy (1956) state that 'anomalies of teeth are very common' in the mentally deficient, and they go on to say, 'A good set of teeth is rare in mental defectives. Often late to appear, malformed and unhealthy when present, and prone to early decay and disappearance.' Whilst this statement suggests a higher incidence than may be found in actual fact, poor dentition is frequently found amongst the mentally deficient patients referred for therapy. Rather than being a 'stigma of degeneracy', however, these anomalies are more probably due to such factors as poor nutrition, neglect of dental care, and lack of orthodontic treatment, and may also be associated with disease, such as congenital syphilis.

In cases of mongolism, the tongue may appear dystonic and abnormally large in relation to the oral cavity, giving rise to clumsy and indistinct articulation. Macroglossia is not, however, an inevitable concomitant of this condition, and many mongols have surprisingly good speech. Tongue-tie, popularly regarded as the cause of many speech defects, is a relatively uncommon condition, and seldom found in the cases referred for speech correction.

(c) CLEFT PALATE

Figures quoted by Tredgold and Soddy (1956) show that the incidence of cleft palate and lip in mental deficiency is no higher than the incidence among the normal population, and they thus assume that these conditions cannot be regarded as 'stigmata of degeneracy'. (Figures quoted by Morley, 1945, show that cleft palate occurs once in approximately every 1,000 births.) On the other hand, Tredgold and Soddy (1956) show that there is a higher incidence of high, narrow, arched palates amongst mentally deficient patients.

Whilst the chief problem of an unrepaired (or unsuccessfully repaired) cleft of the hard and/or soft palates is excessive nasal resonance, the presence of an incompetent palato-pharyngeal sphincter may also give rise to defective articulation, characterized by nasal escape on consonant sounds, and in some cases sound distortions, omissions, and substitutions. Many of the latter represent the child's attempt to compensate, however inadequately, for the physiologically inefficient mechanism with which he was born. For example, being unable to build up sufficient oral air pressure for plosive consonants such as *p* and *t*, he will produce the sound at a level where air pressure can be built up and then released – that is, below the level of the closed glottis, producing the glottal stop sound which is such a characteristic feature of the speech of some cleft palate patients. Fricatives such as (*s*) and (*sh*) may also be produced in the larynx.

Other children articulate consonants in the correct position, but due to nasal escape of air and inadequate oral pressure, plosive, fricative, and affricate sounds are weak and even inaudible. Nasal escape may be gross, so that speech is virtually unintelligible. Where nasal escape is less severe, speech will be intelligible, but with marked nasal resonance and characteristic nasal grimace on speaking.

Dental irregularities may also be present, associated with a unilateral or bilateral cleft of alveolus and lip. These will all contribute to the child's difficulties in producing normal patterns of articulation.

(d) NEUROPHYSIOLOGICAL DYSFUNCTION

Dysarthria is a disorder of articulation due to a breakdown in the control and coordination of the muscular movements of tongue, lips, jaw, and palate required for speech. There may be a gross disturbance of articulation in cases of ataxic, athetoid, or spastic forms of cerebral palsy. On the other hand, there may be a dysarthria associated with minimal motor disability, or even in the absence of other neurological signs. Morley (1957) has given a comprehensive account of developmental dysarthria, and other disorders of articulation. Dyspraxic dysarthria (Morley, 1957) is a disorder of articulation in which the patient has difficulty in initiating and organizing the complex movements required for speech, in the absence of any muscular paralysis. The degree of difficulty experienced may vary greatly, and may show itself in a tendency for articulation to deteriorate to a marked extent in connected speech, whilst isolated sounds and words may be produced correctly. Ingram (1964) has contested the validity of the diagnosis of dyspraxia for all children who exhibit difficulties in imitation, but considerably more evidence is required before the situation becomes even remotely clear.

(e) HEARING LOSS

Hearing loss must be considered in terms of its effect on language development, the articulatory pattern, and on the pitch, volume, and quality of voice.

The effects of impaired hearing on speech will depend on the type of hearing loss, the severity of that loss, and the age of onset. A congenital high-frequency deafness, for example, will mean that certain sounds (e.g. *s*, *sh*, and *t*) will not be perceived, and will therefore not be incorporated into the speech pattern. The child born with a very profound hearing loss will, in the absence of special training, fail to develop speech at all.

Research undertaken by Foale and Paterson (1954) at Lennox Castle Institution showed that 13 per cent of 100 feeble-minded boys given audiometric tests showed hearing loss sufficient to 'handicap them in ordinary life activities'. They compare these findings with the figure of 6 per cent in Scottish (normal) schools, and from 5·17 per cent to 8·35 per cent as the incidence of all grades of deafness in schools in England and Wales. The same authors quote the investigation of Birch and Matthews (with rather lower grade boys) at Polk State School in the United States. They found an even higher incidence of deafness (32·7 per cent). Foale and Paterson conclude that, 'Impaired hearing may be a contributory factor in low scoring in intelligence tests and a person carrying out psychometric tests should be alert for signs of such impairment, particularly when the subject being tested has an articulatory speech defect.' Of the child with high-frequency deafness, they remark that he is

> most handicapped by his inability to appreciate fully the finer shades of meaning in spoken language. He has to rely more on context and is handicapped in anything which relies on spoken explanation and he, therefore, can become educationally retarded, show inadequate responses to social situations, and have only a limited vocabulary. Handicapped as he is, he may well become emotionally unstable because he is less able to cope with his environment. The clinical picture is thus similar to that found in feeble-mindedness.

Kodman (1958) in a survey of data on hearing loss amongst the mentally retarded says, 'The results agree in one direction; namely, that the incidence of hearing loss amongst mentally retarded children is significantly greater than the incidence of loss among our public school children.' He goes on to predict that 'improved testing techniques and uniformity in reporting the results will find the incidence of 30 *db* or greater losses among the mentally retarded to be three or four times that found in our public school children'. The findings of Lloyd and Reid (1967) would tend to support this suggestion. Pure tone audiometry carried out on 428 institutionalized subjects (age range 6–22 years) indicated a hearing loss present in 138.

Perceptive hearing loss may occur in association with cerebral palsy, mongolism and as a sequala of meningitis. Conductive hearing loss may result from neglect of middle ear infections. As with dental problems, the child with communication difficulties may be unable to indicate the source of his discomfort and can thereby be deprived of available treatment.

Remedial measures

Mental deficiency presents its own special problems in speech therapy which will inevitably affect the prognosis to some extent. Lack of motivation is one of the most important problems to be encountered, and this is particularly true where the patient is institutionalized, or the member of a large family of low social and intellectual status. Conversely, the question of over-stimulation arises where the mentally retarded child has intellectually superior and demanding parents, rendering the child thoroughly negative and unresponsive to all attempts at speech correction.

Far from the mental and physical lethargy popularly associated with mental deficiency, the therapist is often faced with the treatment of an over-active and highly distractible child. In such cases, it may prove extremely difficult to gain and then keep the patient's attention, and it is essential that distracting stimuli should be reduced to the minimum and that optimum conditions for learning should be obtained before therapy is attempted.

Emotional factors, including a tendency to defeatism in many high-grade patients, may make the initial stages of speech correction difficult, but these will tend to become progressively less of a problem as good rapport between therapist and patient is established. Resentment and anxiety may result in a refusal to speak and to cooperate in treatment, or in an exhibition of aggressive behaviour. Whether such problems of behaviour arise will depend to a great extent on the patient's awareness of, and attitudes towards, his mental retardation and/ or speech defect. The adjustment of negative attitudes, with consequent reduction of feelings of inferiority, anxiety, and embarrassment, are very much the therapist's concern, and should, wherever the problem occurs, constitute an essential and major part of therapy.

Finally, the patient's mental and/or physical limitations must be considered. Successful therapy can only be carried out where these limitations are properly understood. Otherwise, the resultant failures in reaching unrealistic goals will produce a state of anxiety and frustration which will adversely affect the patient's performance still further.

Where physical anomalies exist, and are thought to be a contributing factor, patients should be referred for corrective treatment (e.g. orthodontics) wherever possible. Routine hearing tests are always advisable to eliminate the possibility of hearing loss. Where hearing loss is found to be substantial, and felt to be responsible for either the speech disorder or educational retardation, the child should be issued with a hearing aid and, furthermore, be taught how to use it. A thorough programme of auditory training should be carried out, in order that the fullest possible use is made of the child's residual hearing.

The services of a qualified teacher of the deaf are rarely available for the sub-

normal child. There has been an unfortunate tendency in education to concentrate scarce resources upon the intelligent handicapped child to the detriment of
the subnormal child with hearing loss, visual handicap or cerebral palsy.

The challenge of the not uncommon subnormal child with all three handicaps
has only begun to be met.

Exercises for muscular control and coordination are only required where there
is an obvious impairment of tongue, lip, or jaw movement. Where there is evidence of an articulatory dyspraxia, then visual stimulation through the medium
of mirror work will be an essential adjunct to auditory stimulation. Where the
patient is able to read, then reading practice may help to establish the correct
patterns of movement required for speech (Morley, 1957).

A phonetic assessment of the patient's speech should be made before correction is attempted. The aim of such a speech analysis is to discover which of the
speech sounds are omitted, distorted, or have incorrect substitutions – and
whether these deviations occur both in isolated words or only in connected
speech. With the mentally retarded patient it is advisable to commence correction of a sound which can be both seen and heard, and is therefore comparatively
easy to imitate. These patients are easily discouraged, and everything must be
done to reward their efforts with success. A patient who experiences constant
failure, because speech correction work is too difficult, and beyond the scope of
his abilities, will soon become discouraged from making any effort at all. Each
step must be so carefully graded that the physical and mental effort required in its
attainment are kept to a minimum – failure to do so will result in the rapid onset
of fatigue, confusion, and anxiety.

The next important stage in treatment is to make the patient aware of his
articulation errors. Providing he is sufficiently intelligent to respond to simple
instructions, a fairly intensive programme of auditory training should be undertaken. The aim of such training may be at first to help the patient recognize and
discriminate between gross sounds (e.g. money clinking, matches being rattled in
a box); secondly, to discriminate between phonically dissimilar speech sounds;
thirdly, to hear the difference between acoustically related sounds; and finally, to
recognize the difference between errors and the correct pronunciation. Such a
training should be fundamental to all speech correction work in disorders of this
kind. Providing the patient's attention can be gained, and his interest held, simple
hearing training techniques can be very effective. Speech correction, following
such auditory training, will tend to proceed far more smoothly and rapidly, and
sounds may come spontaneously during this period, even before any direct
attempt has been made to elicit them.

Either following on or overlapping with hearing training techniques, the
defective or omitted speech sounds must be elicited in isolation. With younger
pupils, most of these sounds are obtained through play activities, and it has been
found extremely useful to associate speech sounds with some concrete activity or
object (thus, *sh* becomes associated with running water for the bath, and *p* is the
sound made when blowing out a candle). Such associations help to make the

sounds more vivid in the child's mind, and also make the whole business of speech correction more pleasurable and interesting for him. The use of a mirror may prove invaluable in maintaining the mentally deficient child's interest, and so may the provision of his own 'speech book', in which pictures can be drawn and credit stars stuck.

More sophisticated feedback devices including storage oscilloscopes, modified DAF systems and videotape recording are beginning to come into use in a few clinical centres.

The next step, in which the correct sound is integrated into words, obviously cannot proceed until the sound can be produced easily and at will in isolation. It must be stressed that in carrying out speech correction work with the mentally deficient, each step must be firmly consolidated before the next step is attempted, otherwise there is a tendency for any achievements to break down under the pressure of new demands made upon it. This is not to say that patient and therapist should persevere with a new sound until it is absolutely correct, whatever the amount of time and difficulty involved – rather should the therapist move to a different and easier sound, and when this has been achieved or improved, return to the original sound. Correction should proceed as Greene (1955) suggests, 'by horizontal strata rather than by vertical sections. This means that the ground covered must be traversed again and again, each time aiming at a higher level of attainment, but this gives the patient a sense of achievement and raises the whole standard of speech in a very short time.' The aim is achievement, however modest that achievement may be, and it is the therapist's task so to plan treatment, and modify her methods and approach, that the speech defective has the satisfaction of making some progress each time he comes for treatment.

Whilst Sommers *et al.* (1970) describe encouraging effects of intensive articulatory training in the subnormal, they emphasize the difficulties of 'carry-over' in treatment generally and in the course of a relatively short experiment.

Perseveration presents a particular problem in the treatment of articulatory defects. It will be found that once a new sound has been elicited and fairly well established, the patient will tend to perseverate in using it when another consonant is being corrected. For this reason, the correction of two phonically similar sounds should never be attempted simultaneously or consecutively.

The use of a tape-recorder is an invaluable asset in the treatment of articulation disorders, since the playback of the recording enables the patient to hear and analyse his defects more objectively. It also provides a useful source of motivation. Van Riper and Irwin (1958) give many valuable suggestions for hearing training procedures and other remedial techniques for articulation disorders.

Everything possible should be done to make the learning process as vivid as possible, and to develop the fullest possible use of auditory, visual and kinaesthetic senses in speech correction.

CEREBRAL PALSY

The aetiological background of this condition has already been fully discussed in Chapter 16 and so will not be mentioned here. It has been estimated that from 60 to 70 per cent of the cerebral palsied have some type of speech defect. Where there are difficulties in sucking, chewing, and swallowing, and there is incoordination of the movements of respiration, we may well expect phonation to be uncontrolled and speech to be dysarthric. Whilst dysarthria is generally the most obvious and severe speech problem, the speech therapist may find associated language difficulties, and sensory defects affecting speech.

There is a fairly high incidence of deafness associated with cerebral palsy, particularly of the perceptive type, which will obviously have an adverse effect on the acquisition of both language and normal articulation. In some cases, there may be evidence to suggest a developmental aphasia. Language will also tend to be retarded where severe physical handicaps have resulted in a limited environment and consequently limited experience.

Any attempt at speech may precipitate athetoid movements, or the patient may go into spasm, even when passive movements are attempted. Incoordination and phonation will affect the voice. West, Kennedy, and Carr (1947), describing phonation, say, 'The voice lacks flexibility, resonance and control; instead of a well-modulated, even flow of voice, erratic intensity and sudden pitch changes occur irregularly.'

The first aim in treatment is to establish correct feeding habits as fast as possible, since little can be done to improve speech until this has been done. It is also important to correct head and neck posture, and movements of respiration in the early stages of treatment.

Bobath and Bobath (1952) have described the reflex inhibiting postures in which the cerebral palsied child may experience normal muscle tone, and in which movement, active or passive, may be carried out with a minimum of interference by abnormal spasm or involuntary movement. Accounts of the application of this approach in the field of speech therapy have been given by Marland (1953) and Parker (1957). Phelps (1958) has described the Bobath technique as well as other methods of physical therapy in the treatment of cerebral palsy.

General relaxation is also widely used, and the therapist normally works from facilitated or assisted movements of vocalized babbling, so that the child may experience some of the sensations of normal effortless speech.

Cerebral palsy is an extremely specialized field, and speech therapy is always part of a total programme of physical treatment. Many therapists have evolved their own approach to the problems encountered, through clinical practice and their associations with other workers (e.g. physiotherapists and occupational therapists).

Severely subnormal children with physical handicaps have been successfully taught to employ a gestural means of communication where spoken language was not possible (Levett, 1969).

Disorders of voice

Attempts have been made to classify voice disorders by the aspect of voice affected; that is, problems of pitch, volume or quality. In practice, however, it is seldom that one of these facets of voice production is affected without the other two. To give a typical example: in cases of laryngitis, the quality is husky or hoarse, the volume is markedly diminished and the pitch range, particularly for the higher frequencies, is reduced.

It is useful to classify disorders of voice under the broad headings of organic and functional, but even here some overlap may exist. In addition, 'functional' may refer to a problem which reflects psychogenic disturbance or results from a period of habitual misuse of the vocal mechanism.

The only voice disorder which we may regard as 'characteristic' of mental retardation is the hoarse voice sometimes associated with mongolism. Blanchard (1964) found 'a low-pitched harsh monotone' in 29 of 50 mongoloid subjects examined. Schlanger and Gottsleben (1957) found that 72 per cent of the mongols in their study had voice problems. Zisk and Bialer (1967) have listed factors which have been claimed as responsible for the particular voice quality found in a number of mongols, including a higher placement of the larynx, a thicker and fibrotic laryngeal mucosa, lack of proper mutation, incorrect breathing patterns and hypotonia of abdominal muscles. Luchsinger and Arnold (1965), however, say that the 'rough coarse loud voice' is caused by 'the pronounced congestion and chronic swelling of the vocal cords'. Due to a hormonal imbalance, there is a chronic oedema of the mucous membranes of the larynx. They claim that vocal nodules (a benign thickening on the free edge of the vocal cords, occurring bilaterally) may result from continued overuse of the voice in a forced and strained manner.

Vocal misuse and abuse is probably one of the most common causes of functional voice disorder – the resulting dysphonia may be transient (for example, following voice use at high intensity levels in enthusiastic support of a football team), or it may be chronic as a result of habitual misuse. Here the dysphonia is typically associated with the professional voice user; but may result in any case where the voice is used for considerable periods in an inappropriate way (i.e. with excessive laryngeal tension and at improper pitch or volume levels). Furthermore, there may be adverse environmental conditions, such as background noise or chemical irritants. In addition, there may be emotional problems associated with the onset or the continuation of the voice problem.

A profound hearing loss for the lower frequencies of voice (approximately 100–250 Hz) will have an indirect effect on both the volume pitch and intonation of voice, although the larynx itself is normal. The voice of the patient with a severe impairment of hearing is characteristically monotonous, and may show little variation in volume, which is frequently too loud.

Where articulation is affected due to lesions of the central or peripheral nervous system (as in cerebral palsy, or conditions associated with the adult patient such as Parkinsonism and disseminated sclerosis), then we may also find phonation involved giving rise to the condition known as dysarthrophonia. Voice problems may result from endocrine disorders – in fact, dysphonia may be an early diagnostic sign in cases of myxoedema. Cretinism may be associated with dysphonia, varying from slight vocal dysfunction in the subclinical form to a marked dysphonia in more severe degrees of cretinism. The voice has been described as dull and husky and there is a very limited vocal range, from a few semitones to a single octave.

REMEDIAL MEASURES

Voice therapy will be largely determined by the cause of the voice disorder, and in some cases medical and/or surgical treatment is more appropriate than speech therapy. A careful assessment of the individual and his mode of voice use must be made before an appropriate treatment plan is made. Some of the indications may be:

use of voice at appropriate pitch and intensity levels;
improvement of breath control;
correction of poor postural habits;
reduction of laryngeal tension;
optimum use of resonating cavities.

The aim is to achieve optimum voice use with the minimum of effort. Where the voice disorder is associated with dysarthria, and is organically based, treatment is part of a total programme to improve respiration, phonation and articulation.

Voice disorders generally represent a relatively small proportion of the speech therapist's caseload in most settings and it is therefore considered beyond the scope of this chapter to include conditions which are less common and are not particularly associated with mental retardation.

Voice loss of sudden onset, or which is associated with certain communicative situations, indicates a psychogenic voice disorder (sometimes quite inappropriately called hysterical dysphonia). These cases are frequently very amenable to appropriate treatment. One of the most effective approaches is non-directive counselling as described by Rogers (1942). Very quiet use of the voice, which may lead to communication problems where there is background noise, may indicate nothing more than lack of confidence and feelings of inadequacy on the part of the speaker and may be regarded as personality-tied.

On the whole, unless volume is severely affected, voice disorders do not often have a serious effect on communication, and speech therapy is probably seldom indicated where presented by the mentally retarded subject. An exception would be made where faulty voice use is leading to vocal fatigue, strain and discomfort which, if continued, would ultimately lead to organic changes in the larynx, such as chronic laryngitis or vocal nodules. Whether treatment is given or not would further be determined by the degree of subnormality and the amount of cooperation one might reasonably expect in carrying out a remedial programme.

The successful treatment of voice disorders arising from habitual misuse demands a high degree of motivation and cooperation on the part of the patient. Therefore, unless the mentally retarded child or adult is seriously handicapped by problems of phonation, treatment would not be contemplated.

Disorders of resonance

(a) INSUFFICIENT NASAL RESONANCE

This may occur where some form of nasal obstruction (e.g. adenoids, chronic catarrh) results in an inadequate airway. This may lead to mouth breathing and characteristic 'cold in the nose' speech. Not only will the production of the nasal consonants (*m*, *n*, and *ng*) be difficult, but vowel quality will also be affected.

(b) EXCESSIVE NASAL RESONANCE

This condition has already been discussed at some length under Cleft Palate, but there are several other causes of the same speech condition: sub-mucous cleft; a short soft palate associated with a congenitally large pharynx; paresis of the soft palate associated with a developmental dysarthria (this often occurs in cerebral palsy); paralysis of the palate following an infective lesion such as bulbar poliomyelitis.

Excessive nasal resonance may be a temporary, or in a few cases a more permanent, sequel to adenoidectomy. Occasionally, the presence of a large adenoid pad makes normal speech possible where the child would otherwise be unable to make adequate closure between the soft palate and the posterior wall of the pharynx. Removal of the adenoids in these cases results in a sudden deterioration in speech, with gross nasal escape. Where the adenoid pad has *prevented* full movement of the palate, and the sphincter mechanism is otherwise adequate, the nasal escape results from a purely functional condition, and speech should improve rapidly and spontaneously. Caution should be exercised, however, in carrying out routine removal of adenoids in association with tonsillectomy, particularly in cases of successfully repaired cleft palate, or where there is any evidence of a sub-mucous cleft.

REMEDIAL MEASURES

In cases of insufficient nasal resonance due to enlarged adenoids, surgical treatment will be necessary. In some cases, speech therapy may still be necessary after the obstruction has been removed, due to the persistence of poor speech habits, and the continued tendency to mouth breathing.

In the treatment of cases of excessive nasal resonance auditory training is essential if the patient is to discriminate between his faulty voice production and that which is required of him. As Morley (1945) says, 'Not only is the ear of the child becoming accustomed to the sound he hears himself producing, but these abnormal auditory images are being inevitably correlated in his mind with the normal sounds he hears around him, and which he is trying to imitate.'

In cases of cleft palate, the speech therapist's work normally begins where the surgeon's ends. When an unrepaired cleft is encountered, the possibilities of surgical repair should be explored. Should operative treatment not be recommended, the patient may be referred for prosthetic treatment. Following an anatomically and functionally successful repair before the onset of speech, normal speech may develop, and therapy prove unnecessary. The speech therapist is therefore concerned with those cases where surgery has failed to provide a competent palato-pharyngeal sphincter, or where a successful repair was carried out after poor speech habits had been established, and which therefore persist post-operatively. Such cases, in addition to audible nasal escape of air during speech, frequently present deviant articulation. The patient, because of nasal escape which he cannot prevent, is unable to obtain sufficient air pressure to produce plosive and fricative consonants correctly. The problem of speech correction in cleft palate cases may be further complicated by the presence of gross dental irregularities and a short and/or immobile upper lip.

The speech prognosis in cases of an incompetent palato-pharyngeal sphincter has, in the past, been considered poor, but Greene (1955) indicates that good results, and even normal speech, may be obtained in such cases, and she outlines an excellent programme of speech rehabilitation. In considering the factors influencing prognosis in these cases, she rates cooperation in treatment higher than intelligence. This observation is of particular significance in connection with the possibilities of achieving results with high-grade defectives.

In cases of excessive nasal resonance, due to an incompetent palato-pharyngeal sphincter, speech therapy aims to: stimulate movement of the soft palate as far as possible; encourage oral breath direction, with the minimum of physical effort, and the consequent elimination of the characteristic nasal grimace; correct excessive resonance on vowel sounds, principally through ear-training, and by encouraging more 'open' production of vowel sounds; and finally, correct articulation of consonants, both by reducing nasal escape of air, and by correcting placement of speech sounds (e.g. where glottal stops and pharyngeal fricatives have been substituted for normal consonant sounds).

Stuttering

Whilst the cause of stuttering is still a subject of considerable controversy, it is now fairly generally held, both in the UK and the USA, that it arises from the normal non-fluencies that occur to a greater or lesser extent in the speech of most young children. Wendell Johnson's very extensive research (1959) indicated that non-fluencies (in the form of effortless prolongations and repetitions) were a feature of the speech of children between the ages of 3 and 4 years. Qualitatively and quantitatively he considered these non-fluencies to be the same whether manifested by an experimental group of children 'diagnosed' as stutterers by their parents, or as the 'normal' non-fluencies shown by a matched group of normal children. From these findings he formulated his semantogenic or diagnosogenic theory of stuttering, which suggested that these non-fluencies become a problem only when they are evaluated as stuttering by the anxious parent.

Bloodstein (1969) extended Johnson's ideas and suggested that expectations of 'speech failure' of various kinds (e.g. articulation errors) might also lead to the 'anticipatory struggle behaviour' which marks the onset of true stuttering. He states: 'An important source of the stutterer's belief in the difficulty of speech are the anxieties and demands focused by parents with ranging degrees of subtlety on the communicative process.' Such a child, Bloodstein feels, is particularly vulnerable to environmental pressures and he may be 'quick to accept a concept of himself as a failure'.

With this point of view in mind the findings of Andrews and Harris (1964) are of particular interest. In a careful survey carried out in Newcastle-upon-Tyne they found that the speech of a group of 86 stutterers was characterized by a history of late and poor talking, and that they showed poor attainment on tests of intellectual ability. IQ tests on 86 stutterers matched with 86 non-stutterers showed small but statistically significant differences: the experimental group had an average IQ of 95, whilst the control group had an average IQ of 100. Taking the positive family history into account, and the poor and late speech development, they suggested that stuttering may be a question of multifactoral inheritance – 'genetic loading' plus unfavourable environment 'exceeding a certain threshold'. In other words, 'certain adverse environmental factors acting upon a genetic matrix'. Weuffen (1961) reported lower scores for stutterers in a test of word-finding ability. 'This is of interest, among other reasons, because of its possible relationship to speech fluency', comments Bloodstein (1969).

Wendell Johnson's observations that non-fluencies reach their peak between 3 and 4 years suggests that the breakdown in fluency occurs at a stage in speech development when the child is particularly vulnerable to speech stress or disruption. In the subnormal child, whose acquisition of stable speech skills proceeds at a much slower rate, there is obviously a much longer period of vulnerability. We may therefore anticipate a higher incidence of stuttering amongst the mentally retarded. There is conflicting evidence, however, about the prevalence of stuttering in the subnormal population. Sheehan, Martyn and Kilburn (1968) at Porterville State Hospital, California, examined 216 patients, and found only 1 stutterer and 1 clutterer amongst them.

Sheehan, Martyn and Slutz (1969) followed this up by a further study at Camarillo State Hospital, California. Among 346 institutionalized, retarded patients, they found 3 stutterers. 'Thus,' comments Sheehan (1970), 'assertions that stuttering appears more frequently among the retarded, or related to either end of the distribution of intelligence, appear totally unfounded.'

Schlanger and Gottsleben (1957) in their survey of speech defects at Vineland Training School found that 17 per cent of the 517 residents examined exhibited stuttering. In the aetiological groups considered, the highest incidence was amongst the mongoloid subjects (45 per cent). There were only 10 per cent of stammerers in the familial group, and 18 per cent in the remainder of the organic group. Their findings are supported by those of Schubert (1966) who found 15 per cent of a group of 80 institutionalized mongols stuttered and 8·8 per cent of a group of institutionalized non-mongols, matched for functioning level, chronological age and sex.

Beech and Fransella (1968), surveying the conflicting literature, came to the following conclusion: '. . . while the difficulties of assessment must play some part in determining the different figures for incidence among subnormals, the consistency of the findings strongly suggests that, at lower levels of intelligence, the occurrence of stammer plus intelligence are in some way associated.'

It is not within the scope of this chapter to do more than mention theories which are still current but which are no longer so widely held in the UK and the USA. The two main theories hold that stuttering is (a) symptomatic of an underlying emotional disturbance or conflict, for which symptomatic therapy will be neither appropriate nor effective; or (b) caused by an underlying neurological diathesis, the value of which is not yet fully known or understood.

The 'secondary symptoms' of stuttering develop as the child becomes increasingly aware of his non-fluencies as an embarrassing and sometimes socially penalized piece of behaviour. In place of the effortless repetitions and prolongations we find tense and often voiceless blocks as the stutterer tries to inhibit the non-fluencies. Finding that he has interfered only too successfully with the forward flow of speech, he must now devise a method of forcing his way out of the block he has unintentionally created. One of the most famous quotations in the literature is Wendell Johnson's observation that 'stuttering is what the stutterer does to stop stuttering'.

As the stutterer begins to 'predict' and anticipate feared situations and words, he starts to approach words in an abnormal fashion incompatible with normal speech, so that his prediction is fulfilled and he blocks just as he had anticipated he would. The initial arousal response may be viewed as a type of classical conditioning and the subsequent struggle behaviour as an operant response. He may also develop very effective strategies of word and situation avoidance. Whilst helping to create a superficial fluency, they none the less do little to remove the anxiety of stammering and may severely limit his verbal output and affect his mode of expression.

We may expect that the development of such approaches will depend on the level of intelligence of the subnormal patient and on the amount of adverse environmental reaction he has encountered. Certainly word avoidance, by the substitution of a word similar or identical in meaning, demands a fairly good level of intelligence. Lerman, Powers and Rigrodsky (1965) looked at the stuttering behaviour of subnormal children and found it comparable to that of children of normal intelligence in its early stages. They observed, however, that fears, avoidances and secondary symptoms can and do occur.

Cabanas (1954) regards the hesitances of the mongol as cluttering, since he found no evidence of anticipations, substitutions or other avoidance devices, or even a memory of past blocking. Lack of awareness of non-fluencies is regarded by many as one of the most crucial signs of cluttering as opposed to stuttering.

The approach to therapy will be determined by a number of factors, including the pattern of stuttering presented, the age and intelligence of the stutterer and, most important, his awareness of stuttering. If speech is characterized by non-fluencies not associated with either tension or anxiety, then the aim is to prevent the development of stuttering. This is normally done through careful parent counselling and management of the child's environment. Factors which precipitate or aggravate non-fluencies (such as interruptions or lack of attention on the part of the listener) need to be modified or eliminated. In order to 'canalize' the parents' natural anxiety into useful channels, they can be shown how to develop the child's language ability so that he is better able to meet the demands on his speech skills. This is particularly important in the case of the mentally retarded child who is linguistically at a disadvantage. Finally, social penalties of any kind – which may make the child aware that his non-fluencies are a problem – must be removed.

Where awareness and tension have occurred, then a symptomatic approach may be used to modify any abnormal speech behaviour which has developed. Verbal communication in all speech situations must be encouraged and word and situation avoidance discouraged. Syllable-timed speech (Andrews and Harris, 1964; Brandon and Harris, 1967) has proved to be one of the simplest and most effective techniques in the treatment of stuttering. Clinical observation suggests that this approach will be particularly appropriate with the mentally retarded stutterer.

Conclusions

It is recognized that speech and language are essential to the individual's intellectual and emotional development. Therefore, any impairment of speech and language functions which prevents communication and the satisfaction of his emotional and physical needs will tend to produce maladjustment and behaviour deviations. Furthermore, the absence of linguistic concepts will hinder abstract thought, and prevent the individual from functioning at his highest potential mental level.

The speech therapist's gradual change in emphasis from 'speech and language' to 'communication' has opened a wider range of possibilities within the field of subnormality. Within a generation there has been a growing trend from virtually no provision to a realization that most ESN and SSN children should be assessed by a speech therapist and many should receive specialized help. This may lie in the form of parental advice, collaboration with teachers or direct intervention according to specific circumstances.

Research into linguistic development has begun to influence practical measures designed to overcome communication problems, but can only evolve through close collaboration between psychologists and specialists in linguistics and communication disorders.

References

AINSWORTH, M. D. (1962) *Deprivation of Maternal Care: A Reassessment of its Effects*. Geneva: WHO.

ANDREWS, G. and HARRIS, M. (1964) *The Syndrome of Stuttering*. London: Heinemann.

ARONSON, H. V. (1968) Development of a training and supervisory programme for speech aides at a state institution for the mentally retarded. *Welfare Reporter*, **19**, 25–8.

BALLARD, P. B. (1934) *Thought and Language*. London: Univ. of London Press.

BECKY, R. E. (1942) A study of certain factors related to retardation of speech. *J. Speech Dis.*, **7**, 232–49.

BEECH, H. R. and FRANSELLA, F. (1968) *Research and Experiment in Stuttering*. Oxford: Pergamon.

BERESFORD, R. and GRADY, P. A. E. (1966) An investigation into the apparently unintelligible speech of a ten year old boy. In *Speech Pathology: Diagnosis, Theory and Practice. Brit. J. Dis. Communication Suppl.* Edinburgh: Livingstone.

BERRY, M. F. and EISENSON, J. (1956) *Speech Disorders*. New York: Appleton-Century-Crofts.

BLANCHARD, I. (1964) Speech pattern and aetiology in mental retardation. *Amer. J. ment. Defic.*, **68**, 612–17.

BLANCHARD, I. (1968) Diagnostic patterns of articulation. In WALDON, E. F. (ed.) *Differential Diagnosis of Speech and Hearing of Mental Retardates*. Washington, DC: Catholic Univ. of America Press.

BLOODSTEIN, O. (1969) *A Handbook on Stuttering*. Chicago: National Easter Seal Society for Children and Adults.

BOBATH, K. and BOBATH, B. (1952) A treatment of cerebral palsy. *Brit. J. phys. Med.*, **15**, 107–17.

BOSMA, J. F. (1970) *Oral Sensation and Perception*. Springfield, Ill.: Charles C. Thomas.

BRAIN, W. R. (1952) *Diseases of the Nervous System*. London: Oxford Univ. Press.

BRANDON, S. and HARRIS, M. (1967) Stammering: an experimental treatment programme using syllable-timed speech. *Brit. J. dis. Comm.*, **2**, 64–8.

BROOK, J. R. (1966) The spontaneous spoken vocabulary of a group of severely, mentally subnormal children. *Brit. J. dis. Comm.*, **1**, 131–5.

BURT, C. (1951) *The Backward Child* (3rd edn). London: Univ. of London Press.

CABANAS, P. (1954) Some findings in speech and voice therapy among mentally deficient children. *Folia Phoniat.*, **6**, 34–9.

CASHDAN, A. (1969) The role of movement in language learning. In WOLFF, P. H. and MACKEITH, R. (eds.) *Planning for Better Learning*. London: Heinemann.

CLARKE, A. D. B. and CLARKE, A. M. (1953) How constant is the IQ? *Lancet*, **ii**, 877–80.

DONOVAN, H. (1957) Speech programme for the mentally retarded children in the New York City public schools. *Amer. J. ment. Defic.*, **62**, 455–9.

FAWCUS, R. (1969) Oropharyngeal function in relation to speech. *Developm. med. Child Neurol.*, **11**, 556–60.

FOALE, M. and PATERSON, J. W. (1954) The hearing of mental defectives. *Amer. J. ment. Defic.*, **59**, 254–8.

FRY, D. B. and WHETNALL, E. (1964) The auditory approach in the training of deaf children. *Lancet*, **i**, 583.

GODA, S. (1960) Vocal utterances of young moderately and severely retarded non-speaking children. *Amer. J. ment. Defic.*, **65**, 269–73.

GREENE, M. C. L. (1955) The cleft palate patient with incompetent palato-pharyngeal closure. *Folia Phoniat*, **7**, 172–82.

GREENE, M. C. L. (1967) Speechless and backward at three. *Brit. J. dis. Comm.*, **2**, 134–45.

GUESS, D., SMITH, J. O. and ENSMINGER, E. E. (1971) The role of non-professional persons in teaching language skills to mentally retarded children. *Except. Child.*, **37**, 447–53.

HERMELIN, B. F. and O'CONNOR, N. (1963) *Speech and Thought in Severe Subnormality*. Oxford: Pergamon.

HUBSCHMAN, E. (1967) *Experimental Language Programme at the Nursery*. Chicago: American Association on Mental Deficiency.

INGRAM, T. T. S. (1964) Late and poor talkers. In RENFREW, C. and MURPHY, K. (eds.) *The Child Who Does Not Talk*. London: Heinemann.

IRWIN, R. B. (1959) Oral language for slow learning children. *Amer. J. ment. Defic.*, **64**, 32–9.

IVES, L. A. (1967) Deafness and the development of intelligence. *Brit. J. dis. Comm.*, **2**, 96–111.

JOHNSON, W. (1959) *The Onset of Stuttering*. Minneapolis: Univ. of Minnesota Press.

KASTEIN, S. (1956) Responsibility of the speech pathologist to the retarded child. *Amer. J. ment. Defic.*, **60**, 750–4.

KENNEDY, L. (1930) *Studies in the Speech of the Feeble-minded.* Unpubl. Ph.D. dissertation, Univ. of Wisconsin.

KODMAN, F. (1958) The incidence of hearing loss in mentally retarded children. *Amer. J. ment. Defic.*, **62**, 675–8.

KOLSTOE, O. P. (1958) Language training of low grade mongoloid children. *Amer. J. ment. Defic.*, **63**, 17–30.

LEA, J. (1968) Language and receptive aphasia. *Spec. Educ.*, **57**, 2.

LERMAN, J. W., POWERS, G. R. and RIGRODSKY, S. (1965) Stuttering patterns observed in a sample of mentally retarded individuals. *Training School Bull.*, **62**, 27–32.

LEVETT, L. M. (1969) A method of communication for non-speaking severely subnormal children. *Brit. J. dis. Comm.*, **4**, 64–6.

LLOYD, L. L. and REID, M. J. (1967) The incidence of hearing impairment in an institutionalised mentally retarded population. *Amer. J. ment. Defic.*, **71**, 746–63.

LUCHSINGER, R. and ARNOLD, G. E. (1965) *Voice-Speech-Language: Clinical Communicology, its Physiology and Pathology.* London: Constable.

LURIA, A. R. and YUDOVICH, F. I. (1959) *Speech and the Development of Mental Processes in the Child.* London: Staples Press.

MCCARTHY, J. J. and KIRK, S. A. (1961) *Illinois Test of Psycholinguistic Abilities – Examiner's Manual.* Urbana, Ill.: Institute for Research on Exceptional Children.

MARLAND, P. M. (1953) Speech therapy for cerebral palsy based on reflex inhibition. *Speech*, **17**, 65–8.

MARTYN, M. M., SHEEHAN, J. and SLUTZ, K. (1969) Incidence of stammering and other speech disorders among the retarded. *Amer. J. ment. Defic.*, **74**, 206–11.

MATTHEWS, J. (1957) Speech problems of the mentally retarded. In TRAVIS, L. E. (ed.) *Handbook of Speech Pathology.* New York: Appleton-Century-Crofts.

MECHAM, M. J. (1958) *Verbal Language Development Scale: Manual of Item Definitions.* Minneapolis: Amer. Guidance Service Inc.

MEIN, R. and O'CONNOR, N. J. (1960) A study of the oral vocabularies of severely subnormal patients. *J. ment. Defic. Res.*, **4**, 130–4.

MORLEY, M. E. (1945) *Cleft Palate and Speech.* Edinburgh: Livingstone.

MORLEY, M. E. (1957) *The Development and Disorders of Speech in Childhood.* Edinburgh and London: Livingstone.

MYKLEBUST, H. R. (1957) Aphasia in children – diagnosis and training. In TRAVIS, L. E. (ed.) *Handbook of Speech Pathology.* New York: Appleton-Century-Crofts.

NISBET, J. D. (1953) *Family Environment: A Direct Effect of Family Size on Intelligence.* Occasional Papers on Eugenics, No. 8. London: Cassell.

O'CONNOR, N. and HERMELIN, B. (1971) *Psychological Experiments with Autistic Children*. Oxford: Pergamon.

PARKER, L. P. (1957) The preparation for speech in the very young cerebral palsied child. *Folia Phoniat.*, **9**, 54–7.

PAVLOV, I. P. (1941) *Conditioned Reflexes and Psychiatry* (transl. W. Horsley Gantt). New York: International Publishers.

PHELPS, W. M. (1958) The role of physical therapy in cerebral palsy. In ILLINGWORTH, R. S. (ed.) *Recent Advances in Cerebral Palsy*. London: Churchill.

REYNELL, J. (1969) A developmental approach to language disorders. *Brit. J. dis. Comm.*, **4**, 33–40.

RIELLO, A. (1958) *Articulatory Proficiency of the Mentally Retarded Child*. Unpubl. Ph.D. dissertation, New York Univ.

RITTMANIC, P. A. (1958) An oral language program for institutionalized educable mentally retarded children. *Amer. J. ment. Defic.*, **63**, 403–7.

ROGERS, C. W. (1942) *Counselling and Psychotherapy*. Boston: Houghton Mifflin.

SACHS, M. H. (1951) *A Survey and Evaluation of the Existing Interrelationships between Speech and Mental Deficiency*. Unpubl. M.A. thesis, Univ. of Virginia.

SAUNDERS, E. A. and MILLER, C. J. (1968) A study of verbal communication in mentally subnormal patients. *Brit. J. dis. Comm.*, **3**, 99–110.

SCHLANGER, B. B. (1953a) Speech therapy results with mentally retarded children in special classes. *Training School Bull.*, **50**, 179–86.

SCHLANGER, B. B. (1953b) Speech examination of a group of institutionalized mentally retarded children. *J. speech hear. Dis.*, **18**, 339–49.

SCHLANGER, B. B. and GOTTSLEBEN, R. H. (1957) Analysis of speech defects among the institutionalized mentally retarded. *J. speech Dis.*, **22**, 98–103.

SCHNEIDER, B. and VALLON, J. (1955) The results of a speech therapy program for mentally retarded children. *Amer. J. ment. Defic.*, **59**, 417–24.

SCHUBERT, O. W. (1966) *The Incidence Rate of Stuttering in a Matched Group of Institutionalised Mental Retardates*. Paper presented at 90th Annual Meeting of the American Association on Mental Deficiency, Chicago, Ill.

SHEEHAN, J. G. (1970) *Stuttering: Research and Therapy*. New York: Harper & Row.

SHEEHAN, J. G., MARTYN, M. M. and KILBURN, K. (1968) Speech disorders in retardation. *Amer. J. ment. Defic.*, **73**, 251–6.

SIRKIN, J. and LYONS, W. F. (1941) A study of speech defects in mental deficiency. *Amer. J. ment. Defic.*, **46**, 74–80.

SOMMERS, R. K., LEISS, R. H., FUNDRELLA, D., MANNING, W., JOHNSON, R., OERTHER, P., SHOLLY, R. and SIEGEL, M. (1970)

Factors in the effectiveness of articulation therapy with educable retarded children. *J. speech hear. Res.*, **13**, 304–16.

SPRADLIN, J. E. (1968) Environmental factors and the language. In ROSENBERG, S. and KOPLIN, J. H. (eds.) *Developments in Applied Psycholinguistic Research*. New York: Macmillan.

STEINMAN, J., GROSSMAN, C. and REECE, R. E. (1963) An analysis of the articulation of the educable retarded child. *Amer. speech hear. Assoc.*, **5**, 791.

STRAZZULLA, M. (1953) Speech problems of the mongoloid child. *Quart. Rev. Pediat.*, **8**, 268–73.

TERMAN, L. M. and MERRILL, M. A. (1937) *Measuring Intelligence*. London: Harrap.

TREDGOLD, R. F. and SODDY, K. (1956) *A Textbook of Mental Deficiency* (9th edn). London: Baillière, Tindall & Cox.

TULLEY, W. J. (1964) The tongue: that unruly member? *Dent. Practit.*, **15**, 27.

VAN RIPER, C. (1952) *Speech Correction*. New York: Prentice-Hall.

VAN RIPER, C. and IRWIN, R. W. (1958) *Voice and Articulation*. London: Pitman.

WALLIN, J. E. W. (1949) *Children with Mental and Physical Handicaps*. New York and London: Staples Press.

WEST, R. (1947) The neuropathologies of speech. In WEST, R., KENNEDY, L. and CARR, A. (eds.) *The Rehabilitation of Speech*. New York: Harper & Row.

WEST, R., KENNEDY, L. and CARR, A. (1947) *The Rehabilitation of Speech*. New York: Harper & Row.

WEUFFEN, M. (1961) Untersuching der Worfindung bei normal sprechenden und stotternden Kindern und Jugendlichen in Alter von 8 bis 16 Jahren. *Folia Phoniat.*, **13**, 255–68.

WING, J. K. (1966) *Early Childhood Autism*. Oxford: Pergamon.

YULE, W. and BERGER, M. (1971) Applications of behaviour modification principles to speech and language disorders. In RUTTER, M. and MARTIN, J. A. M. (eds.) *Young Children with Delayed Speech*. Clinics in Developm. Med. London: Heinemann.

ZISK, P. K. and BIALER, I. (1967) Speech and language problems in mongolism: a review of the literature. *J. speech hear. Dis.*, **32**, 228–41.

19

H. C. Gunzburg

Educational planning
for the mentally handicapped

Introduction: The purpose of education for the mentally subnormal

It is essential for educational planning that primary objectives should be stated clearly in relation to the different capabilities and to a realistic assessment of the role of the mentally subnormal adult. Educational targets, which refer to the 'development of the mentally handicapped child's potential', avoid the crucial issue of stating clearly which potential is to be developed. After all, the mentally handicapped child has a potential, even though limited, in many areas of education and, given ample time and dedicated teaching, might be able to develop a reasonable degree of competence in many different aspects. Yet, not all of these educational skills will be of equal value to the mentally handicapped adult. Instead of developing the 'potential' into any conceivable direction, determined by the particular interests of teachers and other interested people, the designers of an educational syllabus will have to consider how far particular attainments and skills acquired at school will help the subnormal in his adulthood.

Subnormal children have disabilities associated with some loss of skills or functions. These impairments result in handicaps, the size and severity of which may not be directly related to the basic impairment itself, because they are affected by environmental factors, by personality, by the development of compensatory skills, or by reorganizing one's style of living. Thus, it might be possible to achieve a reasonable degree of competence by decreasing the handicap even though the impairment itself remains. Special education in particular attempts to deal systematically with this task (Younghusband et al., 1970; Gulliford, 1971.) In the case of the mentally handicapped child the primary educational goal should be modest, but realistic: to assist in the maximum development of his social potential and to enable him to function later on in his particular adult community as unobtrusively and as competently as possible. This means that he must become socially acceptable and able to contribute, if he can, to his own support, so that he is, at least, less dependent on his immediate environment.

This is an aim which is implied in 'normal' education, but is not specifically mentioned because it is more or less a natural result of development. In the case of the mentally handicapped child it is a conscious effort of striving for a level of social functioning through a formal teaching operation. Education of this kind must aim primarily at making the subnormal less of a liability to society, which will often assist him in attaining a satisfactory level of contentedness and cannot, as a rule, reasonably hope to make the mentally handicapped child into an asset for society as in the case of the education of the normal child. Systematic teaching of social competence is a legitimate task of education and appreciable achievements in that area are more vital to the mentally subnormal person's happiness and emotional adjustment than proficiency in the conventional areas of education. Yet it must be clearly understood that aiming at 'social competence' must not be interpreted as only attempting to teach how to catch a bus, how to pay for food, how to eat decently, or how to converse. In addition to these technical and essential skills, 'learning to live' means also encouraging the interests and desires of the child and helping him to develop as a person, and not simply as an efficient social automaton. 'Social education' cannot be over-emphasized too much, but it can certainly be taught in too unimaginative and narrow terms (Gunzburg and Gunzburg, 1973).

From this point of view, serious doubts have been expressed regarding the use of teaching programmes, derived from normal teaching practice, even though adjusted to the mentally handicapped child's limited abilities. It is pointed out that the severely subnormal child will never be able to apply meaningfully and flexibly academic knowledge, even though he may be able to acquire reasonable competence in the mechanical execution of processes. Thus, competence in reading mechanically without understanding would be less useful to a mentally handicapped adult than the ability to 'fit in' with others and to be a useful member of his particular community. It is argued that the mentally defective child is (a) a slow learner who is handicapped in interpreting the meaning and significance of social situations around him and, therefore, unlikely to benefit as much as the normal child by informal learning; (b) over-protected by anxious parents and not encouraged to learn in situations which are thought to be potentially harmful or dangerous; and (c) often deprived of normal and natural learning opportunities by being in institutional, custodial facilities. In consequence, it is suggested that in view of the overwhelming importance for the adult of a relative degree of social competence, it is essential that education ensures, first of all, that *he is adequately prepared for his role in the community* – modest as it is – and that the design of an educational syllabus should serve this particular aim. Conventional school subjects will play a part in this, but how big a part will be determined by practical considerations, as for example:

(a) time available for teaching;
(b) relative importance;
(c) capabilities of pupils.

Factors of this kind, and the nature of the target to be aimed at, make it imperative to accept that education for the mentally defective must extend far outside the classroom boundaries and must be directed even to those aspects which are usually left to the informal and haphazard teaching by life itself. This would apply particularly to mentally defective children who are institutionalized and thereby not only deprived of normal life experience but also subjected to abnormal conditions (Skeels and Harms, 1948; Skodak and Skeels, 1949).

Special education

It is a curious aspect of educational work in mental subnormality that few educationists seem to have paid attention to the fact that *all* definitions of mental deficiency contain an explicit statement regarding the social incompetence of the defective (see Chapter 2). This is the first criterion to be considered in the diagnosis of mental deficiency, but next to no systematic effort has been evolved to deal constructively with this conspicuous shortcoming. Indeed, though there is considerable concern regarding the mentally subnormal person's social inadequacy, which makes him a social liability, nearly all educational work concentrates on how to overcome his academic weaknesses, even though these weaknesses can be tolerated by the community quite well and have comparatively little impact on the main problem.

Much time and effort has been, and is still being, devoted to studying in some detail the nature of the intellectual deficiencies which are responsible for the academic shortcomings in an effort to find educational ways and means by which to teach successfully a minimum of 'normal educational knowledge'. This approach is usually modified as far as the amount of school knowledge is concerned when dealing with different levels of intellectual ability, but is seldom adjusted by considering what will be *needed* in later adult life by different levels of ability. There is a widespread belief underlying much educational action that though the lowered IQ score necessitates a decrease of educational work and expectations, this means simply less in quantity but unchanged in quality. There is also a slight hope that a magical educational touch might lead to academic success of a much higher order than one would ordinarily dare to expect (Schmidt, 1946; Kolburne, 1965.)

It is surely a disservice to the subnormal adult if his childhood education represents a prolonged imitation of an academic, even if 'normal' school life, whilst the preparations for his adult life are disregarded. The further down the IQ ladder a child has to be placed, the less justification there is for giving 'normal' education, even though less of it, and the greater necessity for providing 'special' education which prepares him for *his* way of living at a later stage.

'Special education' is, therefore, not to be regarded as providing only 'special means', but also as having 'special contents' for teaching. It could well be that the mentally handicapped child should receive a special-different education and not that ordinary education be taught by special means. This different education must aim at making the mentally handicapped socially competent, because this is the very area which is mainly responsible in adult life for a large multitude of failures and perpetual requests for assistance. Hungerford (1948) pointed out that in normal education the order of emphasis is: academic proficiency, occupational competency and competency in social adjustment; whilst in the case of the mentally retarded the sequence of priority should be 'social competency, occupational or vocational competency and academic proficiency', and Johnson (1958) states three objectives: 'personal and emotional adjustment, social adjustment and economic adjustment'.

A syllabus of education does, of course, not exclude the traditional and well-tried basic academic education, but it will apportion carefully the available time in relation to the possible future usefulness to the mentally handicapped adult. It is reasonable, for example, to give less attention to reading in the case of the severely retarded compared with the mildly handicapped, because even a relatively high degree of technical competence will not enable the severely retarded to read with understanding.

(a) SOCIAL EDUCATION – DEFINITION

It must be appreciated that 'social education' is a term which indicates not only the direction and contents of the educational work but is also far more comprehensive in its application than is the traditional interpretation of 'education'. 'Social education' is not limited to activities which relate directly to a widely recognized mode of living, e.g. how to use public transport, how to fill in forms, how to budget one's earnings and so forth, but relates to any form of activity which purposefully aims at making the mentally retarded child participate in some way in the world around him. This means that social education is applicable even to those profoundly mentally handicapped children whose responsiveness is minimal and on a very primitive level. In their case, attention has to be paid to needs which are ordinarily seen to by parents and nursery life, but which will have to be met by professional educational assistance if it is not available or inadequate. In practical terms this means that stimulation, the arousing of interest in the surroundings and the encouragement of responses, are legitimate tasks of social education which demand highly skilled techniques – which have by no means been adequately developed as yet – and which cannot be left to chance or well meaning 'minding' efforts, and that education in the form of systematic stimulation has to start as early as possible (Lorenzo, 1968).

Such considerations must not in any way revive the dichotomous practice which differentiated sharply between the trainable and educable, the child 'unsuitable for education at school' and the slow learner at school. These terms refer to non-essential aspects of education – the educable child being a child who can be taught to use reading, writing and arithmetic meaningfully, and the less able child who would be unable to apply these skills flexibly to various situations even though he can be taught the mechanics to some extent. The dividing line is usually assumed to be around IQ 50 (Williams and Wallin, 1959; Rychlak and Wade, 1963), but should really only be used as a rough guide, whether academic education would be beneficial or not considering the intellectual abilities. Irrespective of this, all children must receive generous and intensive social education, but the proportions of various aspects must be adjusted to their capabilities and the use they are likely to make of their skills. An educational programme which is firmly directed towards the educational objective of social competence will, therefore, attempt to give different proportions of time and attention to different aspects of education according to future needs. Those children whose disabilities result in only a mild handicap may be best served by a 'normal' school curriculum, though modified by scope and method. Others, more handicapped, will need less academic and more social 'know-how' to make it possible for them to fit in with the demands of their communities; whilst the more severely handicapped needs most of all enough social skills to make him function better in the 'planned dependence' (Gardner, 1969) which the community will have to arrange.

(b) MULTIPLY HANDICAPPED CHILDREN

Increasing awareness of the existence of additional physical and sensory handicaps has resulted in demands for special schools for mildly handicapped and/or physically handicapped blind children, for hearing-impaired and maladjusted children, for deaf and subnormal physically handicapped children. There is in fact a bewildering variety of possible permutations of categories of handicap. Moreover, major physical handicaps are often associated with intellectual and social handicaps and very soon it becomes clear that the educational requirements for the mentally handicapped are very similar, even identical with other children with different handicaps.

A recent investigation (Younghusband et al., 1970) pointed out that 'whereas earlier legislation specified children who required special schooling on account of defects (deafness, blindness, physical defects, intellectual defects and epilepsy), the 1945 "Handicapped Pupils and School Health Service Regulations" introduced the concept of need for special educational treatment. This shift from a criterion of defect to one of educational need was particularly clear in the broad definitions of educational subnormality and maladjustment.' The compilers point out 'that this trend should be taken further and categorization be viewed not so much as a categorization of handicaps nor categorization of children, but as a categorization of special needs and moreover the concept of special needs should include personal and social needs as well as more strictly educational ones'. Indeed, the report concludes that these considerations may 'release us from too close an adherence to notions inherent in the words, "school" and "education". A somewhat different concept of education is developing, not limited to the acquisition of attainments and skills nor to the work of the teacher and the classroom.'

The preoccupation, one might even say the obsession, with intellectual disabilities has detracted attention from the fact that a significant proportion of mentally handicapped children are also multiply handicapped and require special education which utilizes special means and methods. It is not always appreciated that in such cases their learning abilities are not only less but also different. Bland's survey (1968) of 31 schools in hospitals for the subnormal indicated that 9·4 per cent of the children had defects of hearing and/or vision, 16·5 per cent had physical handicaps and 48·3 per cent displayed speech defects. Tizard and Grad (1961) found in their sample of non-institutional severely subnormal children 16 per cent with mild cerebral palsy, 16 per cent with fits and 29 per cent with other disabilities besides subnormality. Marshall (1967) obtained similar results from her sample of severely mentally defective children living at home – 9 per cent with mild cerebral palsy, 15 per cent with fits and 25 per cent with additional disabilities (see also McCoull, 1971).

Morris (1969) found in her survey of hospitalized subnormal children that only 41·7 per cent did not apparently have additional handicaps. The percentage of paralysed children was high (22·6 per cent),

and 11·3% showed autism, 6·1% a severe speech defect and 2·2% were blind. Only 0·8% had been diagnosed as having severe deafness but since very few hospitals carry out routinely audiometric investigations, this figure could be very misleading and underestimate seriously the handicapping effect of high tone frequency on educational progress. Epilepsy was found in 32·3% of the children.

Specific groups of children whose special handicap had not always been correctly diagnosed are beginning to attract attention. Psychotic-autistic features were shown to be present in 4·6 per 10,000 schoolchildren aged 8 to 10 (Lotter *et al.*, 1966) and it is estimated that of some 13,000 cerebral palsied schoolchildren in England some 2,500 are probably severely subnormal. There are no reliable national figures regarding visual defects (Kellmer Pringle, 1964; Williams, 1966) nor hearing defects among subnormals, but a survey of 403 children resident in 17 hospitals gives some indication of the size of the problem (British Psychological Society, 1966). The investigation found that 23 per cent of the sample were reported to have a visual, auditory or motor handicap, cerebral palsy being the most frequent of the motor handicaps. A minimal estimate of 'Behaviour Disorder' indicated that about one-quarter of the sample displayed pronounced deviant traits. Generally, the presence of the multi-handicap in most, if not all, severely retarded children, such as visual – hearing – motor, language handicaps, requires such different teaching techniques that these problems can usually only be tackled by a multi-disciplinary team which includes at least the medical (Burns and Simon, 1968) and psychiatric specialist (O'Gorman, 1970), the psychologist, (Woodward 1962a; Mein 1968), speech therapist (Sampson 1962, 1964, 1966) and physiotherapist (e.g. Bobath, 1966; Cotton and Parnwell, 1973). Compared with the moderately and mildly retarded child, this severely mentally handicapped child represents a considerably more complex challenge at various fronts, many of which have so far eluded diagnosis. Nevertheless, it appears that in practice educational treatment and training towards a degree of social adaptation can be successfully carried out even without defining definitely the aetiology of the handicap, though it has often to deal with basic elements such as attention span, memory, verbal concepts, or transfer (Brown, 1966; Bryant, 1967).

To leave the difficult child unstimulated will not only result in intellectual deterioration as has been shown so often, but also cause a significant increase of behaviour disturbance (Pitt, 1968).

Some educationists, acceding perhaps to pressure by parents, attempt to deal with the severely mentally handicapped child as if he were simply a more reluctant, dimmer and slower learner, who could eventually be led along the path taken by the mildly subnormal child by showing more kindness, patience and by developing new techniques. There are indeed isolated instances of unexpected achievements (Williams, 1966), but these have not been attained with the majority of this pathological group where the central nervous system itself has been damaged, and where success seems to be more likely by exploring aspects which are less directly involved and which will benefit the child in later life (see also Hunt, 1967; de Vries-Kruyt, 1971).

Assessment – educational diagnosis – planned learning

The educationist dealing with the mentally handicapped child is no longer content with the information conveyed by an intelligence measurement, indeed it is considered to be scarcely a starting point. Though a careful analysis of a test record can suggest certain lines of further enquiry, it is nowadays felt that the assessment of specific functions with a view to initial remedial action is more relevant for the educational task than the measurement of global intelligence.

Thus, those instruments which gauge aspects involved in the learning processes, such as language (e.g. Kirk Illinois Test of Psycholinguistic Abilities; Reynell Developmental Language Scale), or perceptual processes (e.g. Frostig Developmental Test of Visual Perception, Bender Visual Motor Gestalt) attract particular attention because they provide a direct guidance in curriculum planning.

Very often these fairly sensitive diagnostic asssessment instruments are used for checking the effectiveness of educational action.

A. ASSESSMENT OF THE MENTALLY HANDICAPPED CHILD/ADULT

Whilst no one will deny the superiority of a trained and experienced teacher's sensitive observations (Stevens, 1968), it will be advantageous for her, and essential for the not so well qualified teacher to augment this knowledge by consistently and regularly applied objective assessments of aspects which are relevant to the teaching targets.

Considering the very concrete objectives of education for different degrees of mental handicaps the most important assessment procedures used in educational work with mental defectives can be conveniently discussed under three headings:

(a) assessment of social functioning;
(b) assessment of academic functioning;
(c) assessment of specific aspects.

(a) *Assessment of social functioning*

It would obviously be most important to become aware of a child's disabilities as early as possible. Thus, an early assessment should not be regarded as attempting a prediction of very doubtful reliability, but as drawing attention to a child at risk (Younghusband *et al.*, 1970) for whom the timely start of remedial action could mean a lessening of his handicap in later life. Assessments at that stage are therefore primarily a screening procedure, because workers are fully aware of the unreliability of predictions at a very early age. Practically all scales are based on the Gesell research (Gesell, 1954) indicating the 'milestones' of normal child development at key ages – 4, 16, 28, 48 weeks – 12, 18, 24, 36 months. Gesell and other workers (Cattell, 1947; Griffiths, 1954; Sheridan, 1960; Illingworth, 1966; Gunzburg's Primary P-A-C and P-P-E-I- see p. 637) sample various aspects of development such as motor behaviour, adaptive behaviour, language behaviour and personal-social behaviour and arrive at developmental stages, ages and quotients, indicating an individual child's standing in relation to the performance of a large number of children of similar age.

The Griffiths Scale (1954) is the only infant scale standardized on English children and assesses five aspects: locomotion, personal-social, hearing and speech, eye and hand, and performance. However, though this type of assessment will give a reasonably valid indication of the child's functioning at the time of testing, great care is required if used for predictive purposes (Hindley, 1960).

There is some doubt about the reliability of these developmental scales for predictive purposes, probably because the subject himself – the young child – is 'unreliable' in that he varies widely in his rate of growth in different areas of development. There is almost no evidence about the reliability of the scale when applied to mentally handicapped children.

Uncertainty regarding the reliability affects, of course, the validity of the screening procedure. Unless the severely subnormal child has pronounced physical characteristics (e.g. gargoylism, mongolism, etc.,) even a careful developmental assessment will misclassify some young children. Using a very full developmental assessment procedure, Illingworth and Birch (1959) followed up their own early diagnoses of mental retardation when the children were of school age. They found that their predictions of severe mental retardation were confirmed later in 82 per cent of the cases when the child was found to be ineducable, whilst in the cases of their early diagnosis of moderate or slight retardation 28 per cent and 10 per cent respectively were subsequently considered ineducable. Illingworth (1961) also reported another follow-up where his early diagnoses of mental defect was correct in 75 per cent of the cases.

Whilst it is quite obvious that a high number of children 'at risk' can be traced by using developmental assessments at an early stage, some children could be seriously handicapped unless subsequent, frequent assessments are made to correct initial misplacements. In Illingworth and Birch's study (1959) sixteen children developed better than had been expected and four children did worse. In Illingworth's (1961) study, 25 per cent of his children had IQs above 70 despite the early diagnosis of mental defect. It is certainly important to consider not only the child by himself but also the many environmental factors which may contribute decisively to retarded mental and social development (Clarke and Clarke, 1954; Mundy, 1957; Craib and Woodward, 1958; Stott, 1962a, b; Williams, 1966).

An interesting departure from the conventional landmarks of childhood development is offered by the investigations of Piaget and Inhelder relating to exploration of cognitive processes and concepts. Their work indicated four major phases of development (sensori-motor, pre-operational, concrete operational and formal operational) which occur during the period from birth to approximately 12 years of age and are each characterized by certain types of behaviour patterns.

Using this approach in the field of mental subnormality, Woodward (1959) found that this procedure was particularly suited to such difficult assessment problems as are offered by the child with multiple handicap (Woodward and Stern, 1963) or behaviour disturbances (Woodward, 1963a). A comprehensive summary of this approach with particular reference to subnormality is found in several recent writings by Mary Woodward (1963b, 1970).

In childhood and adolescence the Vineland Social Maturity Scale is still considered the best instrument for the assessment of social functioning, and it was, until a few years ago, unique in that respect.

Doll set out to develop a serviceable instrument for appraising an individual's social competence which is defined 'as the sum total purposive effect of correlated aptitudes and integrated experiences'. He emphasizes that 'the person as a social unit stands above the mere quantitative synthesis of his distinctive characteristics' and postulates 'a relation between constitutional aptitude and environmental activity'. Thus 'deviation or variation from the normal in these respects, whether arising from physical, mental, or social causes, is ultimately mirrored in some measurable increase, decrease, or other modification of social competence' (Doll, 1953).

The scale, which measures and describes in operational terms a subject's competence in defined spheres of behaviour, is in fact a standardized interview of people who are in close contact with the subject. It thus does not require the subject's collaboration and is not affected by temporary emotional disturbances. The scale records observed habitual behaviour in areas like self-help, locomotion, occupation, self-direction, communication, and socialization. The inventory of performance is based on a statistical evaluation of their frequency for successive age periods. 'The items are conceived as integrative composites of such specific "trait" qualities as personality, habit, motivation, memory, judgment, emotion, special skills.' The scale is not 'a direct measure of intelligence, skill, personality, or the like, but only of their conative capitalization for social effectiveness' (Doll, 1953).

There have been so many studies of the use of this particular scale among the mentally subnormal that a short reference would be wholly inadequate and the interested reader is referred to the full review in Doll's manual (1953).

In conclusion it must be pointed out that many items of the scale are typically American and refer to that culture. It would require a new standardization in England to make the scale a basis for adequate comparison, though it has been used here occasionally for research work (Bodman, 1946; Rudolf, 1949; Kellmer Pringle, 1951, 1960, 1966). The scale purports to evaluate 'social maturity' and this is not necessarily equivalent to social competence and adequacy. The latter term, though related to, and mostly dependent on, 'maturity', is also a consequence of environment which may have prevented expression and mastery. Social maturity is also relatively independent of social adjustment and the Vineland Scale does not seem, for example, to differentiate between favourable licence and unfavourable licence prospects (Whitcomb, 1945). From the prognostic point of view this latter study illustrates the limitation of a scale which neglects the important factors of personality make-up and emotional maturity, and overemphasizes a person's ability to exist independently rather than his ability to live together with others.

The scale attempts to assign a social standing to a person, just as an intelligence test assigns an intellectual standing to him. But, it should be noted, this rank is again only describing a facet, an acquired reaction pattern, and in itself gives little understanding of why he functions as he does.

Recently a few additions have been made to the lower end of the scale to make it more sensitive in work with young children (Mecham, 1958; Doll, 1966).

In recent years a number of new scales have been developed in the USA and the UK.

The Social Competency Scale by Cain, Levine and Elzey (1963) was the result of a major investigation of the efficiency of training efforts (Cain and Levine, 1963). At the Wisconsin Institution the Scalar Techniques have been worked out (Balthazar and English, 1969; Balthazar, 1972, 1973), and at the Parsons State Hospital the Scale of Adaptive Behaviour (Leland *et al.*, 1968) was developed. Subsequently, the American Association on Mental Deficiency published the Adaptive Behavior Scales in 1969 (Nihira *et al.*, 1969). Lunzer published the Manchester Scales of Social Adaptation (1966) for children up to 15 years.

An assessment instrument which has been designed specifically for the use of teachers of mentally retarded children and adolescents is the Progress Assessment Chart of Social Development (P-A-C) in its various versions. The P-A-C is basically an inventory of skills which contribute to social competence. The skills are distributed among the four areas of self-help, communication, socialization and occupation and are arranged either according to degree of difficulty (Primary P-A-C, P-A-C 1) or in accordance with their usefulness in situations of varying social complexity (P-A-C 2). It is noteworthy that the 'shading in' of the circular diagrams of the P-A-C does not result in an overall score but attempts to give a visual plotting of the assets and deficits in social ability. The author maintains (H. C. Gunzburg, 1968, 1974b) that it is more important for the teacher to have available a qualitative picture of functioning than an overall score which fails to give adequate information about its composition. As Jastak (1949, 1952) had pointed out many years ago, an identical IQ score could be the result of very different performances in the various aspects contributing to the total score. The variations in the composition of the global score could provide evidence for interpretation and action. This is, of course, also the approach underlying the use of the psychogram.

The inventory of skills in the P-A-C selected for their relevance to social functioning, represents a kind of basic syllabus of social education, and the assessment provides the opportunity for designing a tailor-made programme of remedial action for the individual pupil (H. C. Gunzburg, 1968).

A further development of this assessment technique is the Progress Evaluation Index (P-E-I) which is available in four versions, corresponding to the four P-A-C forms. The P-E-I gives an opportunity for comparing the individual qualitative P-A-C records with 'average attainment levels'. Unlike most similar instruments the reference point for comparison is, however, not the average score of a sample of the general population, but the average level of social attainments of mentally handicapped children and adults. It is suggested that it is unimportant for the teacher to know how far below the normal average is the performance of a particular mentally retarded child, but that it is very essential for her to realize whether a particular mentally retarded child is functioning below the average attainment level of other mentally retarded children of the same age-group. In other words, this procedure enables the teacher to identify the 'backward' mentally handicapped child with reference to the 'average' and 'above average' functioning mentally handicapped child. The vital educational issue is to make a teacher aware that *more* could reasonably be expected from a retarded child and that in consequence a more demanding approach would be justified. The average attainment levels of the P-E-I can, therefore, be regarded as 'expectancy levels' – educational targets of a temporary nature, which will have to be redefined from time to time when more effective educational action results in higher efficiency levels.

The combination of the P-A-C and P-E-I instruments provides the education-ist, in the classroom and as a researcher, with the necessary initial data to pose in each case the vital question: 'Why can this child not do as well as others of comparable age and handicap? In many cases the answer may be very obvious, e.g. because the child suffers from an additional handicap, but in many other instances the teacher will become aware that it is a matter of lack of opportunity and experience, which can be remedied by redesigning the educational programme (Matthew, 1964; Marshall, 1967; H. C. Gunzburg, 1968; Schiphorst, 1968; Elliott and MacKay, 1971; Bland, 1974; Morley and Appell, 1974).

(b) *Assessment of academic functioning*

There is a large variety of attainment tests relating to the conventional school subjects such as reading, writing and arithmetic, the usefulness of which in the field of subnormality is strictly limited. All of them show the discrepancies between the individual performance by the mentally handicapped child and the rather hypothetical 'norm' of a national average performance of different age-groups. These norms reflect ordinary school curricula methods and standards throughout the country and become far less of a guide when 'ordinary' conditions do not apply. Even their value for research purposes, to provide a measuring device, is limited because they tend to be fairly insensitive to small differences at the lower end of the scale, which is practically the only useful assessment area in mental retardation.

Though the attainment age is still retained in most educational assessment procedures, there is nowadays a feeling that it is more helpful to relate attainments to levels which a severely subnormal child could be expected to reach, rather than comparing him with a normal child. From this point of view an educational attainment test is a diagnostic test to initiate action rather than to define the size of the gap between the subnormal and normal achievement.

(1) *Number work.* Comparatively little useful work is available relating to the assessment of number comprehension as distinct from mechanical number skills. It is necessary to make this distinction because teachers and parents are too often misled by being given the assessment results referring to the ability to add up mechanically on paper, whilst the practical application of this skill to everyday situations lags much behind.

A useful approach to this problem is given by the Piaget research as applied to the number concepts of mentally handicapped children (Woodward, 1961, 1962b) and adults (Locking, 1966).

(2) *Reading.* The assessment of reading ability should not only pay attention to the figure which expresses what has been called disrespectfully 'barking at print' – namely the ability to read mechanically – but should also give some idea of reading comprehension. Though intelligence level will determine the maximum extent of comprehension, there are aspects of reading skill, such as short-term recall, ability to separate essentials from inessentials, complexity of vocabulary, etc., which can be improved by remedial action and which in their turn will help the development of better reading comprehension.

There are a few diagnostic tests of reading which give some essential information; the Neale Analysis of Reading Ability (Neale, 1966a) is applicable to ages 6 to 13 years and provides a comprehensive tool for a 'reading diagnosis'.

The Standard Test of Reading Skill (Daniels and Diack, 1958) also attempts to provide more qualitative information than is found in conventional reading assessment. The authors avoid the measuring approach related to the average attainments of a normative population and provide a scale of reading growth by analysing reading development into stages. This appears to be a promising approach because it is independent of 'average – normal' performances, and helps to direct attention to the essential task of furthering growth.

(3) *Assessment of language ability*. The assessment of the command of and understanding for the spoken word is not traditionally included in the 'academic' attainment tests, though vocabulary tests have been used extensively in mental subnormality during the last few years.

Whilst traditional vocabulary tests require oral definitions by the child or adult and are therefore particularly difficult to apply with mentally handicapped children, the picture vocabulary tests require simply an identification of a picture among several, which associates with the one word spoken by the examiner. The Peabody Picture Vocabulary Test (Dunn, 1959) was designed for mentally retarded children and an English version was produced by Brimer and Dunn (1966).

A good deal of literature on this test has been published, relating to mentally handicapped children (e.g. Shaw *et al.*, 1966; Carr *et al.*, 1967); however, most interest centred in recent years on diagnostic tests of communication abilities which provide educationists with a lead to remedial work.

The Illinois Test of Psycholinguistic Abilities (McCarthy and Kirk, 1961) was developed from a theory of communication put forward by Osgood (1957). The model from which the test was derived postulates two channels of communication: (a) auditory and visual input and (b) vocal and motor output. It involves two levels of organization; representational or meaning level and automatic-sequential level. Three processes are needed: decoding, which refers to those abilities required to obtain meaning from visual and auditory linguistic stimuli; association, which refers to the ability to manipulate linguistic symbols internally; encoding, which is the sum of all abilities required to express ideas in words or gestures. A battery of nine tests permits the exploration of each level or process through one of the channels of communication, thus pinpointing the location of weakness in communication.

The test does not attempt to serve as a classification instrument and avoids a global diagnosis. It does not make any assumptions with respect to neurological and neurophysiological correlates of behaviour. Its emphasis is on assessing behaviour manifestations in the psycholinguistic field, in relating the assets and deficits to a behavioural (not a neurological) model, and in extending this type of behaviour diagnosis to a remedial teaching situation (Kirk and McCarthy, 1961).

The test in its present form and in an earlier version known as a Differential Language Facility test (Sievers, 1959; Sievers and Rosenberg, 1960; Sievers and Essa, 1961) has produced some interesting work. The reliability correlation coefficients on test-retest reported so far, ·82 for over 3 months (Smith, 1962),

·94 over 9 months (Mueller and Smith, 1964) and ·83 over an average interval of 4 months with adult mental defectives (Gunzburg, 1964a), suggest that the battery is reliable as a diagnostic instrument. The last-named investigator also reports test-retest coefficients relating to the 9 subtests which range from ·38 to ·79, but points out that the test was used for adults though it was standardized on young children.

Recently a revised version of this test has been published (Kirk *et al.*, 1968) which taps essentially the same abilities as the original ITPA but incorporates several additions (Visual and Auditory Closure Tests, a Sound Blending Test) as well as new norms (from 2 years 4 months to 10 years 3 months).

There is a good deal of literature on this assessment instrument (so far nearly entirely based on the original edition) which has been collected and summarized by Bateman (1965). Recent studies using the ITPA in mental deficiency work indicate its usefulness for increasing awareness of problem areas (Olson, 1961; Tubbs, 1966).

Another diagnostic assessment procedure of communication abilities particularly suitable for mentally handicapped children is the Parsons Language Sample (Spradlin, 1963a, b).

Reynell's Developmental Language Scales (1969) were designed for assessing verbal comprehension and expressive language of young children, aged 1 to 5 years.

(c) *Assessment of specific aspects*

This is the area where much specialist help is required in view of the many complicating factors which could account for difficulties in the learning process.

In recent years deficiencies in perceptual skills have been in the foreground of interest. Following the early work by Strauss and his co-workers (Strauss and Lehtinen, 1947; Strauss and Kephart, 1955), a few systematic assessment procedures have been developed in the form of batteries of subtests (Frostig *et al.*, 1961) leading to a form of perceptual training (Frostig and Horne, 1964). Practically none of the assessment procedures of perceptual development (Bender, 1938; Benton, 1955) pay sufficient attention to the difficulties of differentiating between low ability and brain injury and it needs much expertise to avoid misuse of these instruments (Feldman, 1953; Birch, 1964; Abercrombie, 1964; Horne and Justiss, 1967; Birch *et al.*, 1967).

With the realization that many of the subnormal children are multiply handicapped, assessment procedures have to be considered which will compensate for faulty and inadequate evidence obtained by conventional techniques. As far as educational assessments are concerned, the importance of augmenting the information by specialized assessments cannot be over-emphasized too much, considering that a misclassification at school age can deprive a child permanently of his place in the open community for which he has adequate ability.

In recent years this problem has been discussed particularly in relation to autistic children in the school situation, who, it is claimed, are permanently misclassified as severely subnormal (Mittler *et al.*, 1966; Mittler, 1968). The differential diagnosis is extremely difficult and must be left to the psychiatric experts. To some extent the degree of responsiveness to an intensive educational programme appears to indicate the diagnosis (Eisenberg and Kanner, 1956; Scanlan *et al.*, 1963).

Even more attention has been focused on the child who has an unsuspected auditory handicap such as high tone frequency and is thereby unable to participate fully. His behaviour often resembles that of a mentally defective child and a careful specialist assessment is vital. The problem is often to become aware in the course of a conventional assessment procedure that additional assessments should be made, in order to avoid a diagnostic misclassification. Inconsistencies within the test, such as marked discrepancies between the verbal and non-verbal parts of the Wechsler test (or the profile of a developmental scale such as the Ruth Griffith Scale), are very often the first signs of a hitherto unsuspected auditory impairment. There is much information on this aspect available (Webb and Kinde, 1967; Reed, 1970), though in practice it is often difficult to obtain adequate specialist assistance.

One of the most disappointing fields of educational assessments is represented by the efforts to discover special vocational interests. Aptitude testing has been carried out with older children and adolescents but has not been widely accepted in the training and education of the mentally handicapped.

Tizard (1950) applied a battery of tests aiming to measure spatial aptitude, form perception, eye-hand coordination, motor speed, finger dexterity, and manual dexterity. Though he found that apparently 'motor coordination and precision of movement are more difficult for defectives than are tasks demanding form and space perception', he was hesitant about the reliability and validity of his findings on statistical grounds. He also pointed out that a good deal more research needs to be done before such tests can be used for vocational purposes.

Summing up their researches on the use of batteries of various selected tests for the prediction of occupational success, O'Connor and Tizard (1956) concluded that so far 'ratings have been more successful predictors than were objective tests'.

B. THE 'ADEQUACY' OF TEACHING EFFORT

In the last resort any theory and programme of teaching will depend entirely on the enthusiasm and ability of the teacher involved. Cain and Levine in their study (1963) made an attempt to judge the quality of teaching. The criteria for 'high adequacy' of an instructional time period were:

> materials easily accessible and sufficient for conducting the activity; a high degree of teacher supervision during the activity with individualized attention in evidence; most or all students engaged in the activity with additional tasks provided for children finishing early; differentiation among the children's ability levels relative to the activity; opportunities for assuming responsi-

bilities provided for by the teacher; general and/or specific evaluation statements of the children's work made by the teacher or by the teacher eliciting evaluation statements from the children; deviant or distracting behaviour handled by the teacher with minimal interference with the ongoing activity.

Based on these criteria the assessors came to the disturbing conclusions that of the 25 per cent of classroom time judged to be concerned with 'instructional-social competence' (which was part of only 44 per cent of time categorized as instructional), only half was considered of 'high adequacy' in the community-based schools. As far as the institutional classroom time was concerned, all instructional time devoted to social competence was judged to be of 'low adequacy'.

There are many aspects of social behaviour which require attention outside the classroom and the institutional ward could provide a useful extension for socialization work. Yet, for various reasons – not necessarily overcrowding and understaffing – the staff on the wards are not adequately involved in such work. Thormalen's study (1965) investigated the work on children's wards. The findings are perhaps not atypical for the situation:

1. The technicians (psychiatric nurses) interacted with the children in a manner that promoted independent behaviour in the children on the wards for 12 per cent of the total time observed. Formal training was included in this category.
2. The ward personnel formally trained children for 1·9 per cent of the total time observed.
3. Interaction with the children in a manner that promoted neither independent or dependent behaviour accounted for 51 per cent of all technician time.
4. Technicians interacted with the children in a manner that promoted dependent behaviour 37 per cent of the total time observed.

A few other investigations corroborate the impression of misdirected effort and minimal and irrelevant results. Marshall (1967), in her studies of training centres in England, came to the conclusion that children leave at CA 16 with educational intellectual and social attainments which, on average, correspond to those of children between 5 and 6 years, although their emotional and physical needs and their work capacity are likely to be far above this level.

It is probable that the unsatisfactory results of educational efforts are not only due to an inadequate appreciation of the specific goals of the special education for the mentally retarded, but also to the low expectation teachers generally have about the possible attainments of their low ability pupils (Cain and Levine, 1963). This attitude is of course directly related to the knowledge of low MAs which seem to explain the unsatisfactory school results, and provide a ready-made excuse for diminished educational pressure.

It is alarming to find how little educational assessment work is actually being carried out in the teaching situation. Regular assessments are essential procedures for evaluating a particular situation and for judging the effectiveness of steps taken to improve such a situation. On the other hand, assessments are also used for selection purposes and in this role they can become a potentially dangerous procedure if they defer specific educational steps rather than initiate a particular form of educational approach. This inappropriate interpretation of assessment results can cause permanent damage in the case of the profoundly handicapped child whose education might be abandoned on account of his unresponsiveness to an assessment procedure. It is well recognized that there are stages of long duration where apparently no development is taking place and where no effective responses can be elicited and it is then likely that an assessor may draw the conclusion that the child is not yet 'ready' to benefit from education. The reassessment some time later, which is meant to provide a safeguard against the danger of permanently losing sight of the child, will regretfully have to repeat the previous verdict – because the child was unable to progress without receiving the assistance of which the initial assessment had deprived him. An educational assessment in such cases must not only be carried out by a multi-disciplinary team, which is able to investigate many aspects which may have bearing on functioning, but must also be based on a reasonably long period of observation combined with an educational programme appropriate for the severity of the handicap (Mittler, 1968). A reassessment of the situation is only justified after some action has been taken which has to be the more determined, the more severe the disability has been pronounced.

Manipulating the educational environment

Three problem complexes are being consistently discussed in the professional literature on education for the subnormal: the difficulties concerning appropriate staff training, the decision relating to where special education should be carried out, and the importance of providing an 'extra' in educational stimulation to compensate for deprivation and decreased responsiveness. It is being accepted more widely than ever before that teaching must not only be systematic and to the point, but must be reinforced outside the school situation. This leads, in its turn, to reappraisal of the general provisions for the mentally handicapped.

(a) STAFF TRAINING

Much of the unsatisfactory situation regarding the results obtained through educational efforts could be ascribed to inadequate teaching which does not take into account the results of educational and psychological research. Qualified teachers with specialist training are nowadays the rule rather than the exception as far as children in the mildly (educable) handicapped category are concerned. However, qualifications were not always considered essential when dealing with the most difficult educational problem, the severely retarded child – who has in fact until recently been regarded as 'unsuitable for education at school'.

In England, the 'trainable' child was not the responsibility of the Education Authorities before 1971. For a considerable time a majority of people to whom the education and training of these children was entrusted possessed no teaching qualifications at all and only a small number held a one-year diploma in teaching the mentally handicapped. A survey carried out by the Government in 1959 (Scott Report, 1962) revealed that only 18 per cent of teachers in the training centres and hospital schools had obtained this relevant diploma. Much effort was made to improve the situation in the following year and a survey by the British Psychological Society in 1962 (British Psychological Society, 1966) established that 22 per cent of the teachers in hospitals were now qualified compared with 3 per cent in 1959. Ministry of Health figures for 1964 indicate that 33 per cent of staff were holding the diploma. Smaller and limited surveys gave similar figures, e.g. Marshall (1967) found 29 per cent in training centres, Norris (1968) 20 per cent, but Bland (1968) found that only 13·7 per cent of assistant teachers in hospital schools and 38·2 per cent of the head teachers held the diploma. This was confirmed by the result of the survey by Morris (1969) who found that 13·7 per cent of the 307 teaching staff in hospital schools held the relevant qualification.

The presumably 'better' qualification of generally qualified teachers was held by only 3 per cent of teachers at the time of the Scott Report, 13 per cent of teachers at hospital schools in 1962, and by 4 per cent assistant teachers and 38 per cent head teachers of hospital schools in 1968 (Bland, 1968). Morris's report (1969) showed that 9·3 per cent of the teachers in her sample (N 307) held a teaching certificate.

Generally the educational situation is more inadequate in hospital schools than in the community, though the children total about 12 per cent of the hospital population (Morris, 1969) and should, even on that account alone, receive much attention.

It is recognized that adequate specialized training of the teachers of the retarded is essential but there is lack of agreement what particular forms it should take. There is much support for 'normal' teacher training followed by a specialist qualification, but the argument is also put forward that relevant specialized training from the beginning will produce a better teacher for the subnormal. Qualified teachers themselves feel frequently that their training did not adequately prepare them for their work (Mackie *et al.*, 1960). In Cain and Levine's investigation (1963) two-thirds of the teachers felt that they had been inadequately prepared for teaching the mentally retarded, partly because college instructors had no experience with the trainable child, partly because the focus of teacher education programmes is on the educable child.

The conditions under which teaching has to be carried out in the hospital environment are usually very unsupportive and result in increasing isolation and deterioration of teaching efficiency (Bland, 1968; Morris, 1969).

Since April 1971 the education of all mentally handicapped children in England has become the responsibility of the Education Authorities and new arrangements for teacher training will no doubt be worked out in due course. To some extent the description of the teaching scene, as outlined in the preceding paragraphs, may therefore be relatively irrelevant past history in the near future, but it is important to see the comparatively poor results so far obtained against the background of conditions which are less than helpful. The limited progress made by mentally handicapped children must not entirely, or even mainly, be ascribed to their innate defects as long as the influence of appropriate teaching programmes and stimulating environments is consistently neglected.

These new provisions, however, will not affect the many other staff who care for and supervise the mentally handicapped child's life outside school hours, in hostels, homes or institutions. It would be quite wrong to look at education only as taking place between set hours in a particular place and given by a particular person. In the case of the mentally handicapped child/adult it is particularly important that the education initiated in one place should be consolidated in other ways and that there should be a consistency of teaching approach to overcome by its unified impact the mentally handicapped's slow responsiveness.

It has therefore been acknowledged that other staff too have an educative role and should be involved on all levels within an educational framework. This applies particularly to institutional facilities where nurses should not assist in education on account of expediency because there are not enough teachers, but because they can continue and reinforce educational efforts (O'Hara, 1968).

This merging of disciplines becomes particularly pronounced in certain aspects of social competence, such as self-help skills (eating, dressing, etc.), which are within the professional competence of many people who wish to help the child. The new psychological techniques of behaviour therapy and conditioning are used by either discipline and can even be passed on to the mentally handicapped himself (Whalen and Henker, 1969, 1971). Whilst there is obviously a special expertise acquired by appropriate training, the educational task is so monumental that no educationist can afford to neglect the assistance which can be given by delegating to other people particular aspects of work which can be carried out by them under guidance.

(b) SPECIAL CLASS *v.* REGULAR CLASS FOR THE MILDLY HANDICAPPED

Much attention has been paid to the most advantageous placement for the mildly retarded – would he benefit more by being with other children of similar level of intelligence in a special class where instruction could be adjusted generally to his ability, or would he be encouraged to work harder if placed with normal children? Particular concern is naturally felt about the possibility of increasing emotional reactions to experiences of failure and inferiority when having to compete with other children endowed with better ability.

Various researches have made use of matched samples but the presence of many variables has usually made it impossible to come to definite conclusions.

Mullen and Itkin (1961) came to the conclusion that placement in special classes was helpful for the lower ability range of children with IQs 50–74, for the emotionally disturbed and for those coming from lower socio-economic background.

Thurstone (1960) found that mentally retarded children in regular classes were rejected and isolated, whilst the special class children were better adjusted and had more friends. The special class children seemed to gain more in academic work than the regular class children.

Stanton and Cassidy (1964) pointed out that children in special classes showed better social adjustment, but significant academic gains were achieved by mentally handicapped children in the regular classes. Peck and Sexton (1960) however, found, no significant differences in the achievements of mentally retarded children in ordinary classes, a special class and a class in an institution. Goldstein, Moss and Jordan (1964) carried out a careful study of 129 children with IQs between 56 and 85 over 4 years. They came to the conclusion that (a) children in special classes did not show more rapid intellectual development than children in regular classes; (b) there was some suggestive evidence that children in special classes achieved more success in academic subjects; and (c) children in special classes achieved a greater degree of personal adjustment.

There is no scarcity of investigations into these particular aspects (Ainsworth, 1959) but the results are not always consistent. There is, however, some general agreement on the better social adjustment, the lesser degree of resentment and hostility among mentally retarded children who are not exposed to the competition and expectancy of the regular classroom situation (Blatt, 1958; Cassidy and Stanton, 1959; Kern and Pfaeffle, 1962; Francey, 1966).

However, it has been pointed out that it becomes increasingly more difficult to provide separate special educational facilities for the increasing variety and complexity of needs. In consequence,

we have moved forward from the position of identifying defects of mind and body as a basis for education in special schools to the recognition of special needs for education and personal care resulting from a complex of personal and environmental factors and that these needs may be met in a special school, in special classes or units in ordinary schools or be the subject of some extra attention and care within the ordinary work of schools. The concept of special need is broader than previous ideas associated with handicapped children and special schooling. Recognition of a relatively large number of children showing some degree of emotional unsettlement, educational retardation and social disadvantage, means that measures for providing special help in ordinary schools must receive more attention in terms of organization, methods of teaching and the training of teachers. It is no longer possible to make a sharp division between special and ordinary schools; this is another line of demarcation which is disappearing (Gulliford, 1971).

(c) THE EDUCATIONAL MANIPULATION OF THE ENVIRONMENT

Though many investigations have drawn attention to the detrimental effects of adverse environmental conditions on the educational development of the retarded child, very little work has been done about the implication of such findings (Butterfield, 1968). The President's Panel (1962) asserted that perhaps half or more of all new cases of mental retardation could be prevented with a broad attack on the fundamental adverse conditions, and stated specifically that educational opportunities could prevent 'mental retardation from setting in'. This section, however, is not concerned with preventative measures, but with ameliorating a condition which requires an educational attack which is not limited to classroom activities.

This refers not so much to educable children whose educational responsiveness and needs have much in common with normal children, and who also tend to grow up in 'normal circumstances', but is particularly important to severely mentally handicapped children who have to be institutionalized for one or the other reason.

Comparisons of the educational achievements of institutionalized and non-institutionalized children are plentiful, and there is much consensus among the investigators that the attainments of the child living at home or in a homelike environment are superior. This applies particularly to language (Lyle, 1960) and social competence (Mitchell, 1955; Schiphorst, 1968; Elliott and McKay, 1971), and these findings provide much ammunition for those who would abolish institutional care altogether. The real difference, however, may be between the individual care given to a few at home and the pernicious management practices which develop when a few staff have to administer far too many, often highly dependent children (Tizard, 1962; MacAndrew and Edgerton, 1964; Blatt and Kaplan, 1966; White and Wolfensberger, 1969). There is evidence that children in small community houses might not be better off than in larger institutions (Raynes and King, 1968; King and Raynes, 1968) because there are considerable differences in institutional climates which have significant influence on the social competence of the children (Butterfield and Zigler, 1965; Klaber *et al.*, 1969; Barrett, 1971). It has also been shown that adults may recover in the institution from the effects of adverse conditions outside (Clarke and Clarke, 1954; Clarke *et al.*, 1958) or may not be significantly affected by institutional living (Sternlicht and Siegel, 1968). The popular generalization that institutions *per se* are 'bad' and provisions of any other kind are preferable should be qualified in the light of recent work suggesting that the decisive factor is the type of behavioural management practised rather than the administrative framework itself (Wolfensberger *et al.*, 1963; Raynes and King, 1968; King and Raynes, 1968; Klaber, 1969; Balla *et al.*, 1974; Mackay, 1974).

Nevertheless, there are scarcely any educational programmes which stress sufficiently that the social education of the so-called trainable requires not only a different emphasis but demands the involvement of the whole environment rather than only a single department. The education of this child must not simply be regarded as an easier version of the syllabus designed for the more able educable mentally retarded child, but must, because of its different nature, be carried on outside the immediate school environment, so that the child can benefit by practice and experience. Thus, the institution itself has to be reshaped to become an educational environment where the school as such forms only one important aspect in an educational programme. As it is at present, practically all institutions represent storage communities which provide education in a department, but no educational experience *in toto* (Bland, 1968; Gunzburg, 1970; Gunzburg and Gunzburg, 1973).

Some pointers to the importance of environmental settings in mental and social development are given by a few investigations which study the institutionalized child's progress when removed from an unstimulating environment to normal stimulating conditions. Lyle (1959, 1960) found that such children gained appreciably in verbal skills after having been exposed to such influence for a period of twelve to eighteen months. Kirk's extremely well designed study (1958) compared two community-placed groups of young children with two groups of institutionalized young children. One group in the community and one in the institution were given a regular nursery school programme and individual tutoring. The results on the Stanford–Binet, the Kuhlman and the Vineland Tests showed clearly that the extra attention given to one group of community-placed children did not give them much advantage over the control group which had not received extra tuition. On the other hand, the institutional group which was given enriched teaching showed significant positive changes compared with the institutional control group which deteriorated and was never able to catch up on the experimental group at a later stage. It was concluded that the school programme prevented deterioration and overcame the lack of stimulation in the institution. Heber and Dever (1970) summarized twenty-one major studies in which a comparison of the detrimental effect of an adverse environment and the incremental effect of removal from an adverse environment was made, and concluded that stimulation led to slight rises in IQ. (See Chapter 7, however, for a review of intervention studies.)

Even though it has been shown that the introduction of intensive educational programmes can counteract the effects of institutionalization to some extent (Kirk, 1958; Gallagher, 1960, 1962), it could be argued that this addition of educational stimuli to the unstimulating institutional setting could have even more impact if the whole environment could be made to support these efforts.

The necessity for enriching the environment by offering a variety of stimuli could, it might be thought, cause confusion in the mentally retarded child, who is unable to bring order into the complexity of an 'enriched' environment. Some theoretical and experimental support for this view is drawn from the work of Strauss and Lehtinen (1947) who pointed out the brain-injured child's distractibility, and perceptual disturbances. In their view, the environment, such as a classroom, should be as non-stimulating as possible, without pictures, flowers and other distractions. The results of approaches based on these theories (Gallagher, 1960, 1962; Cruickshank *et al.*, 1961) have not been very convincing but nevertheless suggest that enrichment of the environment might lead to bewilderment unless accompanied by guidance and educational support. In other words, the enriched environment should be used actively by the educator as a life-sized classroom providing realistic learning situations. Considering the mentally retarded child's difficulties in sorting out the life around him, the stimuli should relate to meaningful 'normal' experiences.

Particular difficulties are encountered in 'normalizing' an institutional setting, and it has been argued that this is a contradiction in terms. A compromise solution is to provide in institutions smaller domestic type units for only seventeen to fifteen 'residents' which have some autonomy and where more individual attention can be given. Whilst such units are directly to be modelled on the 'normal' practices, the continued use of purpose-built hospital or institutional facilities is advocated for the profoundly retarded who requires more intensive care (Department of Health and Social Security, 1971). The needs are not regarded so much as educational, but as requiring the most efficient method for dealing with them, e.g. toileting, observation, etc. (Watson, 1968). If, however, the educational needs of the subnormal require that he must be encouraged to learn, dealing with such simple techniques, then the environment must be shaped to provide learning opportunities. Advocates of conditioning will suggest that the environment should be designed to facilitate the acquisition of relevant techniques (Gorton and Hollis, 1965; Bensberg *et al.*, 1969; Roos, 1970; Grunewald, 1971) even though it would thereby deviate considerably from a 'normal' environment, whilst some proponents of the normalization principle feel that a carefully designed 'normal' environment with built-in learning opportunities will be more suitable (Dybwad, 1967, 1970; A.L. Gunzburg, 1967, 1974; Bayes and Francklin, 1971; Gunzburg and Gunzburg, 1973), particularly because it will also encourage the staff to act 'normally'.

Normalization

In recent years there has been much pressure from parent organizations and professional circles to create conditions for the mentally handicapped which are as 'normal' as possible, to give him opportunities to absorb and adapt to them at his own slow speed. The essence of this particular creed is that 'normal' behaviour cannot be encouraged in abnormal conditions, such as a hospital or segregated educational facilities. Much of the theory and the probably most far advanced practical application of the 'normalization' principle comes from the Scandinavian countries (Bank Mikkelsen, 1969; Nirje, 1969, 1970), and the implications of this approach have been discussed in the USA (Wolfensberger, 1972) and the UK (Gunzburg, 1970). 'Normalization' represents a large scale and intensive manipulation of the environment for educational purposes and is the logical outcome of our knowledge that learning is by doing and that social competence is by far the most important aim of educational effort. Bengt Nirje

(1970) lists a number of aspects which are experienced by the child in an 'abnormal' way if he is brought up in an environment which cannot emulate the home conditions. They are:

(a) Rhythm of the day – institutions, hospitals, etc., adopt a routine which deviates sharply from normal practices, e.g. getting-up time, going to bed, eating, etc.
(b) Rhythm of the week – the different activities experienced by the mentally handicapped, such as training, special therapies, recreation, take place in the same setting, whilst ordinary people usually live in one place, work, or at least shop, in another, and find their leisure activities in a variety of places.
(c) Rhythm of the year – seasonal changes which bring with them a variation of work, food, cultural events, sports, general leisure time and outdoor activities are not experienced in the institution in the same full way as in the normal society surrounding it.
(d) Development of experiences of the life cycle – children require to be fed with positive stimuli, and small children live in a world especially structured for them and are guided and taught by a few significant adults – for children of school age wide social experiences outside the classroom have important impact – but growing up in a deviant institutional society offers only a limited range of experience.
(e) Respect for choices, wishes and desires – mentally subnormal children are seldom encouraged to participate actively in decisions and arrangements concerning them though normal people claim the right of having a say in issues relating to them.
(f) Recognition of the bisexual world – until a short time ago, sex segregation was insisted on and even today some institutions still continue to separate the sexes among patients and the staff – quite contrary to normal life practice.
(g) Recognition of normal economic standards – the subnormal too should be given those basic financial privileges which are available to ordinary people.
(h) Physical facilities for the subnormal should be modelled on those provided for ordinary people. Indeed, not only should they be 'normal looking' of a domestic size but also contain specially arranged learning opportunities to encourage 'learning by doing'.

The most effective way of avoiding the pernicious influence of such factors as outlined by Nirje appears to many workers the placing of the child into a normal environment in the community and to let him experience life in as normal conditions as possible (Kushlick, 1966; Tizard, 1968; Morris, 1969). The proposal for small hostels and foster homes is not new and indeed the available evidence suggests strongly that it has measurable favourable consequences (Skeels and Dye, 1939; Skeels and Harms, 1948; Lyle, 1959, 1960). Scandinavia, which is not burdened with a vast and traditional hospital and institution heritage, quite deliberately pursues a policy of education in the community which will avoid the educational segregation still taking place in the UK and USA.

On the other hand, these countries will have to find a way for utilizing the many institutional facilities whilst at the same time overcoming the detrimental influences which seem to be inherent in the concept of the institution, the asylum (Goffman, 1961; Barton, 1961; Vail, 1967). If this environment is to be made into an educational tool it will be necessary to break away from the traditional medical-nursing tradition (Gunzburg, 1970; Tizard, 1970; Gunzburg, 1973), and indeed to reshape the overall organization completely in order to replace the medical by an educational structure, where it is necessitated by the needs of the mentally handicapped child (Zarfas, 1970).

Conclusions

'Normalization' appears to be as much a principle underlying management practices as a final target to be aimed at; i.e. absorbing the individual into the 'normal' community. As a guide for avoiding the dangers of the 'abnormal situation' it cannot be bettered. It has still to be shown that it also provides an equally useful guide for determining the most effective practices and approaches in meeting the mentally handicapped's needs.

Note: Chapters 19, 20 and 21 are closely linked, both in subject matter and in authors cited. Thus a consolidated list of references will be found at the end of Chapter 21.

20

H. C. Gunzburg

The education of the mentally handicapped child

Introduction

For a long time there has been an indefensible dividing line between children with IQs above the 50 mark who were given 'education' and those below IQ 50 who were given 'training'. This artificial division served not only administrative convenience but determined the quality of attention given, the qualification of staff and the provisions made. Only quite recently – with the Education (Handicapped Children) Act, 1970 – has it been abolished in England, and all children, irrespective of the degree of their mental disability, are now the responsibility of the Education Authorities. No child will be excluded from the education system, even though its responsiveness to educational stimulation may be regarded as minimal. The dividing line has not simply been placed at a lower level of ability, but has disappeared altogether.

Whilst it must be regarded as an historical advance in English legislation that no child is excluded from educational attention on account of his mental disability, it is necessary to point out that the abolition of an administrative dividing line must not suggest that there are not differences in handicaps, which necessitate different types of programmes and divisions, depending on realistic educational targets for different needs. It would be a retrograde step if education for all were interpreted as meaning the 'same education' to different degrees.

Neale and Campbell (1963) phrased this consideration very neatly when they stated: 'The guiding principle here is, "To each according to his needs", and this is being placed ahead of desert ("To each according to his merit") and capacity ("To each according to his ability").' And they quote Warner et al. (1946) as stating that to treat all pupils alike is like putting little chicks, ducklings, baby swans, kittens and bear cubs all in a pond together and waiting to see how they respond to this 'equal opportunity'. On the other hand, Kolburne (1965) argues that 'academic education is probably the most important phase of a child's life'. Since we live in a democratic society 'a complete educational programme for the trainable mentally retarded should include academic instruction'.

It is, therefore, proposed to discuss the programming for three major levels of educational work, which should be regarded as having no definite borders and which should be applied flexibly as circumstances require. On each of these levels educational and psychological research have made useful inroads.

The first level is characterized by the dominance of 'care problems' and the need for nearly full-time attention to the self-help items, such as toileting, washing, eating, dressing. Most, but not all, children on this level of functioning are profoundly retarded and have IQs below 20. Though their physical care requires the most direct attention, they have emotional problems, they are in need of stimulation and activation to prevent deterioration and can achieve a reasonable level of functioning despite their disability. They will, however, always be high dependency people.

The second level is characterized by the fact that the lowish IQ range (extending up to approximately IQ 55) gives not much indication of the level of social competence that can finally be achieved. 'Academic' achievements, which can be used meaningfully in ordinary life situations, are very meagre or non-existent, but with appropriate education and training a degree of social functioning can finally be achieved which enables many mentally handicapped persons to live comparatively independently and with little assistance by others.

The third level of education has been very widely explored and is most similar to 'normal' education. A large number of children who would benefit by this type of education have been deprived of cultural stimulation or have been emotionally disturbed. Education means, therefore, for them a suitable presentation of normal stimuli, which are well within their mental grasp, and 'academic' work is purposeful on this level. In later adult life a majority of these children merge inconspicuously with the normal population.

The contents of educational work are determined to a large extent by the social future of the mentally handicapped child and the fact that a lower IQ indicates not only a slower rate of learning but also the likely presence of a multitude of additional handicapping factors.

Level 1: The profoundly handicapped child

These children require generally nursing attention, though this can be given by untrained but reasonably careful persons. A number of them, however, e.g. hemiplegia, quadriplegia, are in need of a degree of physical nursing which can in the long run only be met adequately by trained nursing staff. Most of these children are without the ability to look after themselves in the simple skills of toileting, washing, dressing and they are also very unresponsive to stimulation.

The educational objectives are, therefore, primarily concerned with reducing the amount of assistance required in the self-help area and to encourage the child to respond to the environment (Kolburne, 1965).

For quite some time these children were left in the 'back wards' of institutions and Special Care Units, being nursed physically and only by the personal interest of nurses did they ever achieve higher levels of functioning. Recent developments in conditioning methods has resulted in much advance in this area (see Chapter 23).

Operant conditioning in the ward to achieve a higher degree of self-help skills has been described by Colwell and Cassell (1955), Orlando and Bijou (1960), Linde (1962), Hundziak *et al.* (1965), Bensberg *et al.* (1965), Whelan and Haring (1966), Hamilton and Allen (1967), Hollis and Gorton (1967), Minge and Ball (1967), Roos and Oliver (1969), and Treffry *et al.* (1970).

The same approach has also been used for tackling behavioural disturbance in the severely handicapped child (Ellis *et al.*, 1960; Girardeau, 1962; Headrick, 1963; Girardeau and Spradlin, 1964).

These investigations and training schemes are of direct relevance to the child's well-being and are thus of great interest to those who have to evaluate efficient management practices for children with severe handicaps. The nursing press reflects to some extent the successful adoption of similar training programmes by the nurses, often without direct guidance by scientific workers.

Other studies of a more academic nature indicate that there is a capacity of responsiveness even in the severely handicapped child which could be utilized if the right approach can be found and consistently pursued.

Skinner (1965) describes the case of a 40-year-old microcephalic idiot with a mental age of about 18 months, who was partly toilet trained and only able to dress himself with help. This man was taught by carefully programmed instruction to make subtle form discriminations and to use a pencil.

There are now several bibliographical articles on behaviour shaping in mental subnormality (Gardner and Watson, 1969; Nawas and Braun, 1970).

It might be argued that much of the success of the behaviour shaping techniques is due to the attention by staff and consistency of approach rather than the technique itself. Some of the evidence presented is not very convincing on account of methodological inadequacies (Gardner, 1969). However, from the practical point of view, the mere fact that successful guidance in the management of intractable problems has been provided makes it certainly worthwhile to pursue this approach. Little is known yet about the long range effects of such programmes in maintaining the level of behaviour after conclusion of training. Lawrence and Kartye (1971) investigated this aspect in a group of 21 children, aged 8 years to 14 years with IQs ranging from 23 to 36 and SQ (Vineland) from 8 to 42. After a year's training the 14 incontinent children in the sample had been toilet trained and all children were able to feed themselves with a spoon, though none of them had been able to do so at the beginning of the programme. Seventeen children had learned to dress and undress themselves though none of them had originally been able to do this. Training extended to other areas, such as ability to use gestures and to verbalize needs (communication), the ability to perform activities without direction and to carry out peer group activities. After conclusion of the programme there was a four months' period without any formal training, after which a new assessment was made. It was found that the children had regressed significantly in initiative, communication and social skills but not in self-help skills. The authors suggested that the main reason for maintaining the level of competence in this area was due to the daily routine of the ward, which 'provided the residents with opportunities for additional practice and reinforcement in maintaining skills in the area of Self-Help. Dressing, undressing and eating are activities which must be carried out, even in the absence of a formal training program.' This comment reflects the great weakness of the educational approach on this level, when systematic education is only carried out within the framework of a formal training programme, but is not considered as a necessity at all times. The achievements in communication, social skills and initiative could probably have been maintained if staff had provided as many opportunities for these skills as for the self-help items. This is a criticism which applies to this type of exploratory work as well as to much other educational research, which seems to be primarily and solely interested in establishing that a particular method can achieve significant results, rather than in ensuring that it is of a kind which can be applied in practice. There is still a tremendous gap between the laboratory conditions of the research worker and the adoption of his findings in ordinary conditions (Keith and Lange, 1974; Kiernan, 1974).

Many references in modern literature on the very severely disabled child indicate the growing concern for the educational deprivation suffered by these children. Whilst it is clearly recognized that education on that level must be of a fundamentally different character, one feels also that behaviour shaping techniques by themselves will only assist in making the child, and later the adult, more acceptable to others and less dependent on them, but will not be sufficient in encouraging more responsiveness to people and the world around. The two frequently-used key words in this context are stimulation and activation, which are interpreted as ranging from providing coloured balls on a string above the cot of the severely handicapped child to nursery play. Educational efforts for children on that level are mostly seen as providing systematically sensory stimulation in the form of more or less formal exercises, such as following moving objects with eyes, tactile stimulation by presenting various pieces of textures, listening to auditory cues etc.

The child's prolonged unresponsiveness weakens the parents' determination for eliciting responses and the decreased effort in its turn decreases chances for success. It becomes, therefore, important that a stimulation programme is initiated as early as possible to avoid a premature 'setting' due to weak or absent stimulation. Though Heber's investigation (1968, 1971) aims at preventing mild subnormality in children, the methods used may well have relevance to the profoundly handicapped child. Heber reports that babies in this group attended daily special nursery groups with a daily programme of sensory and language stimulation and aiming particularly at problems solving skills and language development. Though the children were not removed from home the mothers were given special training in homemaking and child care skills in order to reinforce the teaching in the nursery. When reassessed at age $3\frac{1}{2}$ the differences in intelligence scores, compared with a control group, were striking. As Heber suggests, 'the trend of our present data engenders the hope that it might prove to be possible to prevent the kind of mental retardation associated with both poverty and parent of limited ability'. Lorenzo (1967) describes a programme in Uruguay designed 'to diagnose and treat at a very early age high risk babies'. This leads to providing 'enriched multi-sensorial stimulation and rich environmental stimulation' to promote a better development of so-called 'high risk babies'. The same author stresses also (1970) that the stimulation required must come from the whole environment and not be limited to set times and places, such as a classroom. This is an important reminder – not only relevant to work with the highly mentally disabled child – that educational work must be extended to all situations, the home, the ward, the nursing staff and the parents, to become really effective. And if sensory stimulation is considered essential in triggering off interest in the surroundings, then it is highly doubtful that either the anaemic, hygienic conditions of a good ward or the barren and dilapidated conditions of a poor ward are conducive to stimulation. One may well think that there could be more enrichment of the severely subnormal child's environment by providing a variety of environmental sensory stimulation for smelling, sensing, hearing and feeling.

Level 2: The moderately handicapped child

Contrary to traditional assessments of the moderately retarded adult's role in the open community, it is now widely accepted that a far larger number of people with intellectual limitations can function outside a protected environment than has been assumed in the past (see Chapter 2). To prepare for the adult role, the education programme will have to be directed primarily towards achieving finally a measure of self-sufficiency and occupational competence.

A careful consideration of the role of education in the social rehabilitation of the subnormal child indicates that objectives have to be formulated not as 'subjects', e.g. reading, writing, arithmetic, but rather as areas of competence. Most modern workers have come to broadly similar conclusions, even though individual preferences often add a quaint note. Generally they have stressed that the subnormal should be taught among other skills:

(a) how to get on with other people;
(b) how to accept the work situation and give reasonable satisfaction;
(c) how to manage money;
(d) how to get about and make use of public services;
(e) how to manage leisure time.

Whilst teaching objectives of the kind mentioned above are realistic and feasible because they are essential for tackling life situations and can be taught within the limits imposed by time and school structure, other educational aims mentioned in the literature appear to be so ambitious as to be unrealistic. 'Acquiring knowledge of, practice in, and zeal for democratic processes; becoming sensitive to the importance of group action in the attainment of social goals;

developing meaning for life' (Nickell, 1951) are statements of aims which seem rather out of place when dealing with mentally subnormal children (Kirk and Johnson, 1951; Ingram, 1953; Kirk *et al.*, 1955; Wallin, 1955; Stevens, 1958; Williams and Wallin, 1959; Gardner and Nisonger, 1962; Kirk, 1962; Gunzburg, 1963a).

The fact that the subnormal person's limitations prevent him from achieving normal standards must not prevent the educationalist from striving towards a relative competence within each individual's capability. Only relative degrees of social, personal and economic adequacy can be expected, yet even these limited skills will help the defective to live in the world – in many cases limited to his immediate surroundings – with some confidence and feeling of security (Hudson, 1955; Rosenzweig, 1959).

Educational programmes provide guidance to the many varying and confusing experiences of shopping, of the use of public transport or the telephone, queuing up for buses or at shops, buying little refreshments, etc. Even though teachers realize that knowledge of community demeanour requires experience in the community, the educational classroom situation provides rehearsal and preparation opportunities (Neale and Campbell, 1963; Gunzburg, 1963a; Stevens, 1971). It is also recognized that the acquisition of the technical skills of social competence eases the mentally handicapped person's adjustment difficulties. The mentally handicapped child tends for various reasons to live a withdrawn and sheltered existence which affects his ability to establish and maintain human relationships. One of the foremost tasks of the educational programme is, therefore, the development of those social skills which encourage cooperation, the give and take of living together, the recognition of authority, the willingness to be directed, the acceptance of rules and property of others – all of which will contribute substantially to a reduction of friction when living in 'normal' society.

Level 3: The mildly handicapped child

The educational literature on the mildly handicapped or educationally subnormal child – ESN(M) – has increased to such an extent that it would be quite unjustified to deal with it in only a few paragraphs. It will therefore be more helpful to discuss in the space available the relative weight of various 'subjects' in the school curricula of the three levels of ability.

Special subjects

Training programmes and their effect on the intellectual and social functioning of severely subnormal children have been described by Francey (1966), Bland (1968), Mitchell and Smeriglio (1970), and Stevens (1971).

Whilst it is nowadays widely accepted that social education must be the prime objective in curriculum planning, there are considerable differences in actual practices regarding how much time should be devoted to that aspect in comparison with the conventional school subjects, such as reading, writing and arithmetic, to which nowadays a new 'subject' tends to be added, namely language development. Some guidance in drawing up curricula and timetables is offered by considering carefully the use a mentally handicapped adult can make of a particular skill, such as reading, and also by assessing its place in the list of needs required for a reasonable adjustment to a particular level of the community.

Reading

(a) THE SEVERELY RETARDED CHILD

It is nowadays generally accepted that the teaching of reading skills should be guided by the practical use to which such an attainment can be put. Though it has been demonstrated by educators, parents and researchers that a reasonable degree of mechanical reading skill, disrespectfully referred to as 'barking at print', can be attained, it becomes a meaningless skill if the reader cannot comprehend what he is reading. There may be, of course, an emotional benefit for the child and the parent, who derive satisfaction from the organization of a technique which is basic to normal school education (Kolburne, 1965); but, it could be argued, a similar feeling of achievement can be obtained by concentrating on competence in number and money skills, which are of immediate practical usefulness.

There seems to be some justification to define the reading targets in accordance with the understanding a child could be expected to have (Kirk, 1940), though it might be dangerous practice to make teaching targets correspond too closely to MA and IQ, which themselves might be affected by reading difficulties (Quay, 1963).

As far as the profoundly and severely mentally retarded is concerned, a prevailing practice is to teach him by sight a vocabulary of cautionary and admonitory words which would help him in daily living (reading for protection).

A list of socially useful words, a social sight vocabulary (Gunzburg, 1968; Bell, 1970), includes, for example: Ladies, Gentlemen, Wet Paint, Danger, No Smoking, No Exit, Entry, etc.

The conventional method of teaching a social sight vocabulary is by exposing flashcards showing the 'word picture' in different sizes and types of print. An interesting variation on this technique is the 'symbol accentuation', developed by Miller (1968). This method refers to 'a motion picture animation technique of integrating spoken and printed language with objects and events in a way that enables those with limited capacity meaningfully to relate words to objects and letters to sounds'.

It is comparatively simple to extend the size of such a sight vocabulary, and Hermelin and O'Connor (1960) found the number of words read by the severely handicapped, with IQs between 35 and 50, ranged from 0–200, with a mean of 45 words read. They also found that there was no significant correlation between the number of words read and the child's IQ, but that mental age and chronological age were significantly correlated with the reading score.

There is, however, a definite danger that a teacher might sacrifice energy and valuable teaching time to the pursuance of a goal which is not necessarily first on the list of priorities for this level of functioning, though it figures as such in 'normal education'.

(b) THE MODERATELY RETARDED CHILD

With the moderately retarded child, reading targets can be set more ambitiously than with the profoundly retarded, but the teacher must still keep in mind that technical mastery of reading will give an illusion of competence which can never exist because the limited mental abilities set a ceiling to the comprehension of the written word. At the same time, it is necessary to remember that within the group will be found many socially deprived children whose academic and intellectual achievements are well below their abilities and require careful encouragement (Dunn, 1968; Tansley and Gulliford, 1960; Bell, 1970; Gulliford, 1971).

On this level, many of the research findings on different methods are of importance. There is now a decided preponderance of work suggesting that mixed linguistic and phonic methods are of greater value than the sight recognition approaches employed with the more disabled child.

As far as the proponents of the sight recognition methods are concerned, they emphasize arguments based on considerations concerning the child's or adolescent's reactions rather than on the efficiency of the learning method itself. Thus, it is suggested that a slow and so far unsuccessful learner – a reading failure – will gain an immediate feeling of success by learning words which he recognizes as being important and useful. Since contents and meaning can be adjusted to individual interests and specific targets, the method is flexible and carries a large factor of inbuilt motivation. It provides a good start, which can gradually merge with the phonics and analytical methods which are required for further development of reading competence. Such a method for mentally retarded non-readers has been described and developed by H. C. Gunzburg (1968).

On the other hand, a phonic system represents a systematic step by step approach in which the child is taught a method which can be developed and transferred and is, from this point, far more flexible than an approach based largely on memorizing visual pictures (Daniels and Diack, 1960; Keating, 1962; Chall, 1967).

Within this framework of phonic methods, as used with mentally retarded children, two approaches are of special interest. A linear programme using simultaneous presentation of visual and auditory stimuli was developed by Brown and Bookbinder (Brown, 1967; Brown and Bookbinder, 1966, 1968). Teaching machines and programmed instruction were used by Bijou (1965), Stolurow (1963), though the efficacy of this method has been challenged (Blackman and Capobianco, 1965).

Great interest has been shown in investigating using the phonetic Initial Teaching Alphabet (ITA). This is based on forty-four symbols of sounds and is said to provide an easy introduction to the complexities of conventional English spelling and phonetics. Smith (1966) used this system with eight children (age range 10–12, IQ 53–65), who had reading ages well below their chronological ages. Results after fifteen months indicated significant increases and little difficulty when transferring to ordinary spelling and reading. Similar favourable results were reported by Dunn and Mueller (1966), particularly when combined with a language development programme (Dunn *et al*, 1967), but doubts have been expressed by Labon (1967).

The main purpose of reading on this level is obtaining information and instruction which will help the mentally handicapped child in orientating himself in a world which relies on short written instruction, advice etc.

For this reason classrooms should contain items like telephone directories, railway and bus timetables, newspapers and television programmes. Children should be encouraged to study these and some assignment cards will both give them practice in seeking information and opportunities to follow instructions. Any attempt to link reading with real life situations brings into play the Utility Motive, for children are more likely to see the purpose and relevance of the activity. Opportunities for this type of activity often arise naturally in other subjects of the curriculum. (Bell, 1970)

(c) THE MILDLY RETARDED CHILD

Children whose intellectual abilities and awareness for life around them are near normal are likely to make better and more frequent use of their technical reading facility. In their cases, reading need not only be a laboriously acquired technical tool applied clumsily with little confidence to everyday situations, but can be used with pleasure and advantage in a multitude of situations. Competence in reading on this high 'normal' level will depend not only on technical fluency but on other factors, such as familiarity with the vocabulary, with idioms used, conventions in literary style, ability to discriminate between essentials and inessentials, etc.

There is very little evidence available regarding the actual difficulties in comprehension experienced by children with a mild intellectual handicap when faced with literature apparently suitable for their level.

Gunzburg (1948) investigated the comments on their reading matter made by 14–16-year-old boys in the IQ range 50–75. He found that these children's reading tastes and preferences are very similar to those of normal children. They are attracted by descriptions of fighting, shooting and other dramatic events, descriptions of escapes, last-minute rescues and happy family reunions. However, difficulties are caused by the complexity and unfamiliarity of vocabulary. References to well-known events and persons are not understood, and historical stories using old-fashioned phraseology and vocabulary lead to much confusion. He came to the conclusion that the mentally handicapped does not use his reading skill adequately because of 'disillusionment with his reading matter. He is quite incapable of selecting reading matter which is within his grasp and which is not confusing. Not being of a very persistent nature, he will soon give up the struggle, and a reading skill which has taken years to acquire is left to deteriorate for lack of practice' (H. C. Gunzburg, 1968).

These comments suggest that it is essential that teaching should devote systematic attention to the development of aspects which contribute to comprehension of reading matter, and must not take it for granted that fluency in reading itself will encourage adequate use of that skill.

Only a few assessment tools have been developed which will assist in drawing attention to difficulties in reading comprehension. The Neale Test has already been mentioned (see p. 639). Gates (1935) published a diagnostic battery to measure four different aspects of comprehension: (A) to appreciate general significance; (B) to predict the outcome of given events; (C) to understand precise directions; (D) to note details. Other authors (Sangren, 1927; Watts, 1944) followed similar lines, and exercises based on the analysis of the poorly developed aspects of an individual's reading comprehension have been shown to be of considerable help (Duncan, 1942).

Generally speaking, a systematic and well-programmed reading course which attends to reading comprehension appears to be particularly important at this mental level. Reading competence is socially a very approved and appreciated skill, which is taken for granted in normal life, and inadequate competence will make the retarded feel isolated and inferior. Encouraging him in learning to use his reading skill flexibly is, therefore, as much a therapeutic action of gaining his confidence as a purely utilitarian move to make it easier for him to adjust to a literate community.

Gann (1945), who made a careful analysis of the personality of backward, good and average readers on the basis of projective tests, came to the conclusion that the poor readers are 'emotionally less well adjusted and less stable. They are insecure and fearful in relation to emotionally challenging situations and they are socially less adaptable to the group.' She suggested that 'the building of reading adequacy in those who have experienced difficulty with the process would involve, therefore, the resolutions of inhibiting personality forces and negative attitudes, as well as increased interest and skill in reading itself'. It may also happen in some cases, as Burt (1922) has suggested, that the reading matter may be associated with emotionally disturbing memories and thus create a blank leading to miscomprehension and inability to follow the thread of the story. Burt compared these blanks 'to those lapses of speech and memory, the slips of the pen and the trippings of the tongue, which in adults have been shown by psychoanalysis to be so richly symptomatic of the profounder secrets of the individual's mental attitude'.

Though the relationship between emotional maladjustment and reading disability is by now widely accepted, opinions differ whether therapy should precede reading instruction (Axline, 1947; Ewerhardt, 1938), or whether the improvement in reading in itself will lead to better adjustment (Kirk, 1934).

It is often difficult to decide whether emotional disturbance leads to reading failure or the lack of progress in reading causes emotional difficulties. Kirk (1934), investigating the effects of remedial reading on the institutionalized mentally retarded children, noted that progress in reading was associated with better adjustment in the classroom and decreased signs of personality maladjustment. On the other hand, Ewerhardt (1938) concluded from his work that the treatment of the emotional problems of retarded children led to better results in reading.

There are now several detailed reviews of work in this field available, which should be consulted (McCarthy and Scheerenberger, 1966; Kirk, 1964; Pope and Haklay, 1970) particularly regarding specific reading disabilities such as 'word blindness', developmental dyslexia, etc.

Number work

It could be argued with much success that it is nearly impossible for a mentally subnormal child or adult to 'get on' in life without some understanding for numbers, even though he might become very successful in the general community without being able to read. Many of the motivational schemes for the very retarded depend to a large extent on the appreciation of comparative sizes of rewards and the wide use of monetary incentives. The attempt to introduce realistic situations into institutions and schools, the aim of training the subnormal to become a wage earner who can make sensible use of his wage packet, all these require that the subnormal should have a reasonably useful level of competence in this area. Despite its great usefulness fairly little systematic educational work has been published relating to teaching the severely subnormal.

Kirk (1964) summarized the results of research into the relation of arithmetical achievement to mental age as follows: 'Basically, retarded children appear to achieve in harmony with their mental age expectance in arithmetic fundamentals, but are below their expectancy in arithmetic reasoning problems requiring reading.'

(a) THE SEVERELY MENTALLY HANDICAPPED CHILD

There is nowadays much awareness of a need for establishing basic number concepts (Finley, 1962; Thresher, 1962) following a developmental sequence. The work of Piaget has provided guidelines for structuring educational work on a low level, which might have more impact on the subnormal than the more conventional approaches. Many of the devices used in number work may become real obstacles in the development of logical number thinking if the child becomes impressed with spatial, visual relations and carries those misleading, concrete examples into a later stage, relying on 'visual' rather than logical evidence. Piaget's experiments in 'conservation of quantity', 'ordination' and 'cardination' point to the need to lay far more systematically the foundation for an understanding of numbers before beginning the more formal tasks of teaching number work (Woodward, 1961, 1962a, b).

Woodward (1962a) discusses the use of the usual type of classroom apparatus in relation to Piaget's sequence in development and suggests the correct order of presentation. Richards and Stone (1970) reported significant gains on conservation through a training programme with transfer to related behaviour in a group of 7–12–year–old children with IQs between 44 and 77.

Laying the initial foundations for an adequate understanding of number concepts requires also attention to a number vocabulary (Cruickshank, 1946; Silverstein *et al.*, 1964). Kirk and Johnson (1951) point to the necessity of acquiring a working vocabulary of arithmetical terms encountered in everyday life. It is quite surprising, and a cause of needless misunderstanding, how vague many subnormals are with regard to the meaning of terms concerned with length and distance (inch, foot, yard, etc.), to measurements (quarter, half, dozen, etc.), to amounts (pair, twice, increase, decrease, etc.), to time (day, week, month, etc.), and others. Though they know how to count, the meaning of ordinal figures (first, second, third, etc.) is often unknown.

The limitations imposed by the mental abilities of the pupil, time and educational organization make it imperative to develop a curriculum which deals primarily and perhaps solely with those skills which are of direct use to the defective. As Burns (1961) points out, the introduction of each new arithmetical skill and operation should depend on questions like: 'Is it important enough to teach? If it is to be taught, how can it be introduced in a concrete way? How can the abilities connected with the topic be practised enough to assure real learning?' Nicholls (1963) gives a list of some 200 number words, which is reduced to a more manageable extent by Bell (1970).

(b) THE MODERATELY HANDICAPPED CHILD

This is the child who, when an adult, might have to handle small money transactions in everyday situations. Most of the emphasis of teaching is, therefore, usually placed on encouraging competence in money operations and there is much agreement that 'paper and pencil sums' should give way to actual handling of money, first in mock-up situations and later in practical situations outside the schoolroom.

Brown and Dyer (1963) studied the results of two teaching methods. One group was given coaching in a work situation, where arithmetic problems could be directly related to work in hand. The other group was given conventional teaching in the classroom. The authors showed that there were significant increases in the arithmetical competence of the pupils when taught in a realistic setting.

In the same way as it is necessary to differentiate between the mechanical reading skill (barking at print) and the flexible use made of the skill (comprehension), it will be utterly important in number work to assess the achievements in mere rote memory (e.g. counting of objects) and in number concepts where the child has to apply his knowledge to many different situations (e.g. handing over three objects, counting in threes, reporting that there are three chairs, fetching three books, three children on command etc.). This requires many different types of learning situations for practising (Burns, 1961; Locking, 1966; Ross, 1970).

(c) THE MILDLY RETARDED CHILD

Once the elementary money operations have been satisfactorily mastered, educational targets can be set higher for those who have the innate ability to understand more complex financial operations. With a view to future adult status, more demanding financial situations can be tackled, such as budgeting of a wage packet and the implications of hire purchase arrangements. Programmes suitable for this level of ability are found without difficulty in the literature relating to the teaching of the educationally subnormal child (Duncan, 1942; Tansley and Gulliford, 1960).

Language

Not only do the results of verbal and non-verbal intelligence tests suggest poor verbal functioning, but specific investigation points to the mentally subnormal person's difficulties in verbal expression and understanding. Earl (1961) discussed at great length the language development of mildly and moderately handicapped children. He points out that certain personality aspects typical for the mentally handicapped, such as weakness of drive, simplicity and viscosity affect their ability to express themselves, resulting in a language of their own make, the 'sub-speak'. This is a primitive language with a small vocabulary, little syntax and less grammar, which helps in reinforcing their feelings of being at home in their own world and excluding the adult, normal world, which is beyond the subnormal's grasp.

Various investigations have confirmed the mental defective's difficulties in thinking abstractedly and in manipulating concepts, and it has been pointed out that institutionalization (Papania, 1954; Badt, 1958; Mein and O'Connor, 1960) was in many ways responsible for the low level of abstractness when compared with children of the same ability but receiving home training (Schlanger, 1954; Lyle, 1959): it is usually ascribed to the lack of environmental stimulation in the hospital. Whilst this explanation is generally correct, it must also be remembered that institutions deal probably with the more difficult children because only these tend to be admitted from urgent waiting lists. Mein and O'Connor (1960) studied the oral vocabulary of severely subnormal hospital patients and compared it with that of normal children of approximately the same mental level. The patients used about 1,000 fewer words than did the normal children. Sampson (1964) studied carefully the conversation of severely subnormal children living at home, following up her earlier work (1962) on language development of this type of child. The problems of language and communication have been ably summarized by Spradlin (1963a) in the case of the mentally handicapped and by Renfrew and Murphy (1964) for handicapped children in general. Brook (1966) studied the spontaneous speech of severely subnormal institutionalized children, and Beier *et al.* (1969) analysed their vocabulary usage and concluded that 'there is no particular deficit in the type of memory function needed to retain a vocabulary, but that the mentally retarded deficit is likely to be found in conceptualization, organization, language structure, grammar and syntax'.

Major studies in this area are found in Luria (1963), O'Connor and Hermelin (1963), Adler (1964), McCarthy (1964), Mecham *et al.* (1966), Schiefelbusch *et al.* (1967), and Spradlin (1968). They and many others are reviewed in Chapter 17.

Some systematic work in encouraging language competence has been reported (Richardson, 1967), usually as the result of diagnostic assessments of specific language weaknesses, though many educationalists prefer to 'integrate' language activities in a general programme rather than treating them as a subject (Harrison, 1959; Irwin, 1959; Mecham, 1963; Olson *et al.*, 1965; Jeffree and Cashdan, 1971). Generally, the difficulties in communication are tackled in two different ways. Many teachers advocate the need for expanding environmental stimulation by play, activities and discussions. Using informal but natural situations they still attempt to induce a desire for communication in everyday life (Lyle, 1960). There is obviously the danger that the not so expert teacher will miss many teaching opportunities, will be unable to encourage progress and will not remedy in time weaknesses and deficits in language competence. To avoid these possible disadvantages, systematic language training has been advocated to promote the the use of language for thinking, for forming concepts and abstractions. These programmes, usually based on the results of the analysis of language use and understanding, treat language as a subject, following a syllabus step by step (Bereiter and Engelmann, 1966).

(a) THE SEVERELY SUBNORMAL CHILD

Several studies of the language competence of severely subnormal children have been published which have implications on language programmes (Blount, 1968). The language disorders of mongols have attracted particular attention Lenneberg *et al.*, 1964; Bilovsky and Share, 1965; Evans and Sampson, 1968; Weinberg and Zlatin, 1970) and Jeffree (1971) describes a language teaching programme designed for a particular 8-year-old mongol child. This was an unusually carefully designed programme, which took into account her assets and interests (such as writing, interest in drawing and in humorous pictures), and her immaturities in expressive language (such as short phrases, preponderance of nouns over verbs, preference for gestures, etc.). Five different teaching approaches were developed and the effect of each on both quantity and quality of language was systematically examined. The interaction of language and behaviour in the cerebrally palsied child was described by Burland (1969).

(b) THE MODERATELY RETARDED CHILD

The Illinois Test of Psycholinguistic Abilities (McCarthy and Kirk, 1961) encouraged much systematic classroom work (Kirk and Bateman, 1962; Wiseman, 1965). Smith (1962) reported significant increases in ITPA scores after only thirty-three lessons but also instability of achievement over time (Mueller and Smith, 1964). Kirk (1962) and Kirk and Bateman (1962) give several examples of the use of this test, not only for diagnosis but for suggesting in each individual case a remedial programme to correct the linguistic disability. Language programmes have been described by various educationalists (Dawe, 1942; Harrison, 1959; Irwin, 1959; Mecham, 1963; Olson *et al.*, 1965; Sampson, 1966).

(c) THE MILDLY RETARDED CHILD

Using the Peabody Language Development Kit (Dunn and Smith, 1964), Dunn and his collaborators (Dunn and Mueller, 1966; Dunn *et al.*, 1967) found considerable gains in language ages with socially mildly disadvantaged children, depending on the length of language education. They stress particularly overlearning to facilitate retention, but the approach has been severely criticized by Rosenberg (1970). An example of the classroom use is provided by Carter (1966) who obtained significant gains as the result of an intensive forty-hour programme over ten weeks.

Whilst the dullness of the usual systematic language programme makes it difficult to assess its permanent effect on communication abilities, there is little doubt that this aspect of mental functioning cannot be left to informal and haphazard teaching approaches, which will most likely fail to apply educational pressure on those fronts where it is needed most. It will be essential to stress the language aspect throughout an educational programme, to provide for a variety of experience in other than language lessons, but at the same time adhere closely to a defined programme of language use which is related to the subnormals' interests and life.

Other teaching areas

Compared with the importance of those aspects already discussed, other 'school subjects' assume subordinate and often very minor roles. However, it is very clear that they too, if properly integrated into a programme with clearly defined objectives, can contribute substantially towards its realization. The aim would then be to reinforce learning in the main areas by approaching these objectives in different ways and contexts and presenting the teaching contents in a variety of different situations.

Ross (1970), for example, reports the efficacy of a general programme for teaching basic number concepts and social skills, utilizing table search games, card games, guessing games, board games and active racing. The progress of a group of children was compared with that of a control group in the classroom. It was found that the experimental group obtained higher scores on all measures – rote and rational counting, specific quantitative terms, time, money, shape and colour.

Significant increases in language ability, productivity and good classroom behaviour were the results of an art and movement programme, which aimed to achieve higher competence in self care, language and motor skills as a 'by product' of carefully planned play lessons (Neale, 1966b).

Nature study can provide realistic opportunities for training perception and encouraging sensory discrimination, and Barham (1971) describes such a programme in relation to aspects as measured by the Illinois Test of Psycholinguistic Abilities.

Conclusions

Though some of the educational research has given valuable suggestions and has demonstrated that results can be achieved, the transfer from the laboratory situation to classroom teaching has on the whole been pretty unsuccessful. This is primarily due to a reluctance on the teachers' part to exchange familiar methods and syllabi, hallowed by their long use in 'normal' education, for new, unproven and demanding procedures. It is even more due to the fact that no one has yet 'proved' that the direct teaching of various aspects of social education has substantially increased the mentally handicappeds' prospects of social adjustment, whilst, on the other hand, no one would seriously challenge the value of the basic acquisition of reading, writing and arithmetic. As it is, shifting of emphasis from academic to social education is more an act of faith than the result of demonstrated relevance to the overall aim.

There is also a feeling that thinking of 'adult aims' will violate the right of the severely subnormal child to be treated as a child, who wants to play and to explore. There is really no reason why thinking in terms of a systematic programme of preparation for adulthood should interfere with the need of the child for a stimulating education adjusted to his level. For many, however, the main difficulty is to accept that different final aims may well require different teaching approaches and different teaching contents at comparatively early stages.

Note: Chapters 19, 20 and 21 are closely linked, both in subject matter and in authors cited. Thus a consolidated list of references will be found at the end of Chapter 21.

21

H. C. Gunzburg

Further education
for the mentally handicapped

Introduction

It is the rule rather than the exception that the mentally handicapped child is regarded an adult by the time he reaches age 16 or thereabouts. Educational provisions are then no longer available to him as a right, but he may continue at school if it is considered to be beneficial, and if resources permit. More often than not, pressures on staff and accommodation necessitate a transfer to other facilities, such as Adult Training Centres and the adult section of hospitals if he can not be placed in the 'open community'. This decision is greatly encouraged by the fact that many of these children have 'outgrown' the junior level of schooling. By that time, the discrepancies between physical, emotional and mental growth have become more marked and there is a necessity for providing facilities and programmes which take into account the needs of young adults, who have the emotional make-up and the inadequate attainments of much younger children.

Many educationists regard the transfer of a mentally handicapped child to an adult environment with considerable disquiet because, in practice, this move tends to deprive the adolescent of opportunities for further learning. There are several reasons for further systematic education after the age of 16.

First of all, it is argued that the usual practice of having severely subnormal children attending 'school' because they are of 'normal' school age is, to some extent, less effective than is expected. Though it is quite clear that the children must receive stimulation and activation, perhaps best given in a nursery type environment (Tizard, 1964), at that stage of their development the mental ability of severely subnormal children (as expressed in MA terms) is too low to profit much by more formal education. Wolfensberger *et al.* (1963) pointed out that 'a child of chronological age 10, intelligence quotient 30, and mental age of 3·0 may not be able to profit much from quasi-academic learning tasks, while an adolescent of chronological age 18, intelligence quotient 30 and mental age of about 5·0 or slightly higher, may.'

There are a few studies suggesting that there is intellectual development after the age of 16 in mentally handicapped people, but the data of standardized tests indicate that this is true for the general population. The norms of the WAIS indicate that the average peak of intellectual efficiency is reached between the ages of 20 and 34 years, and this would apply to the subnormal provided he is given stimulation in the same way as a normal person in normal conditions. O'Connor and Hermelin's (1961) findings suggested that the ability of imbeciles to deal with cognitive problems improved significantly after age 16, and Hermelin and O'Connor (1960) showed a significant correlation (·62) between chronological age and reading score with mental age held constant. Clarke and Clarke's work on IQ changes of hospitalized adults (1954; Clarke *et al.*, 1958) put forward the view that the intellectual assessment of a number of mentally handicapped people does not reflect their potential because disturbing factors make them under-achievers. A removal from these adverse environmental factors – even without special training and education – might result in better mental functioning because they are now able to apply themselves to the task in hand. Thus, IQ changes are in fact indicating restoration of mental ability which has been dormant, rather than the maturation of mental ability after the age of 16. Whatever interpretation is attached to changes of IQ in adulthood (Walton and Begg, 1957; Roswell-Harris, 1958; and see Chapter 7) it appears that many handicapped people might become more receptive to stimulation and educational effort at this adolescent stage than in their childhood, and discontinuing systematic efforts at this time may well put an artificial ceiling on further development.

There is a strong case for continuing with some suitable form of education after the age of 16, which could be considered to be a kind of induction course to adulthood. Though it is accepted that work, and preparation and training for it, are legitimate concerns of an educational programme for adults, it is also thought that few mentally handicapped children will have received sufficient grounding in their schooldays to make it unnecessary to continue with a form of 'academic education' past age 16. There is, therefore, a growing body of opinion for arranging further education for the adolescents and tailing it off gradually into full-time work training (Gunzburg, 1963b).

Many of the pupils at this age may not have been transferred directly from special schools but may have experienced a short and unsuccessful period at work and in the community. To some extent, this may help towards increasing their awareness of and desire for social competence and education. Provided that teaching and instruction at that stage are to the point and are appreciably related to reality, such unsuccessful experiences could give additional motivation for learning.

Social learning ability in adolescence

The adolescent slow learner has the capacity to learn, to retain and to apply his learning, academic and social; the evidence for this is increasing and supports strongly the demand for continuing systematic education after the usual school-leaving age.

Though there is obviously a relationship between intelligence and social competence the available information indicates also that there is nearly always at least one year's difference between the higher social ability level and the lower mental level. Goulet and Barclay (1962) reported that 78 per cent of their 164 cases had SA scores greater than their MA scores. Baranyay's study (1971) of 12 severely subnormal young men and women aged 16 to 20 with IQs ranging from 21 to 50 indicated discrepancies between social and mental ability at admission, ranging from 1 year to 11 years 5 months and averaging 3 years 3 months. Gunzburg (1964b) presented the assessments of 31 young adults between the ages 16 and 25 living in the community with an average discrepancy of over $1\frac{1}{2}$ years between MA and SA in favour of the latter. In 9 cases the discrepancy exceeded 3 years.

The mere fact that the adolescent mentally handicapped has lived longer, has had more opportunities to learn by experience, and is being taught persistently a limited number of elementary practical skills, makes it not further surprising that his social age could be well above the level suggested by an intelligence assessment (Goulet and Barclay, 1962; Barclay *et al.*, 1964). There is at present no clear indication in the literature of the maximal level of competence in various aspects of social functioning that could be attained by people with varying degrees of intellectual handicap, provided they are given good training and have ample adult experience.

Gunzburg's Progress Evaluation Index 2 (1969) gives average attainment levels in self-help, communication, socialization and occupation, for moderately, mildly and borderline mentally handicapped adolescents, but no indication of maximal achievements within their abilities. However, several investigations have indicated that appreciable improvements can take place as a result of directed training under favourable conditions.

An analysis of the results of a systematic teaching of social skills to adults (IQ 41 to 83, age 16 to 30) over 9–15 months' institutional residence, was undertaken by Gunzburg (1974a). It was clearly shown that considerable progress could be achieved by systematic education and training, by following a training programme and providing the relevant learning opportunities. The achievements were most marked in the area of self-help and socialization which are less dependent on cognitive abilities, but even in the area of communication, which contains the skills of reading, writing and arithmetic, substantial progress was noted.

H. C. Gunzburg (1968, pp. 188–97) described in detail the results of an educational programme for young men and women, aged 16 to 25 with IQs below 55 (mean MA 5 years 11 months). Their social competence as assessed on the Vineland Scale was generally on the level of 7- and 8-year-old children at the beginning of the training period. After two years of training, it was shown that the mean SA had increased to 10·3 years from 7·6 whilst the mean social age of the comparable control group (receiving no training) had only increased from 7·4 to 7·9 years.

It is particularly important to note that the significant and important changes in efficiency were due to a systematic training programme whilst those adolescents who had only opportunities for incidental learning 'at home' did not generally improve very markedly.

Baranyay (1971), reporting further results of the same educational demonstration as Gunzburg, and having available the records of forty-four adolescent trainees showed that the mean increase in social age for this group was 1·5 years indicating 'remarkable results in developing the social aspects of the trainees' personalities'. She reports that the 'highest increases by an individual trainee were from 7·7 to 14·1, a rise of 6·4 years in social age. The two next highest results were from 10·8 to 14·4 and from 7·7 to 11·3 an increase of 3·6 years in social age in each case.'

It must be stressed that these increases would probably not have taken place in 'normal' circumstances, and Doll (1953) in fact suggests that 'the amount of SA increase over MA during this period (14–24 years) is relatively slight, reaching on the average a maximum of 2·0 years at LA 23'.

On the assumption that further education aims to make the mentally handicapped as competent as possible to fit into his particular community (which need not necessarily be the normal community without protection) various aspects of educational work will be discussed under three headings: formal education, social education, and activity training.

A. Formal education

Generally speaking, educational work with the adolescent mentally subnormal as reported in literature seems to be a direct continuation of the syllabus carried out at the junior level, though sometimes efforts are made to give the elementary work a more adult content.

(a) FINANCE

The continued emphasis on a financial education cannot be stressed too much because many social breakdowns of mentally handicapped adults are connected with their inadequate competence in this area. Thompson (1962) investigated the arithmetic problems of school leavers who had been classified as educationally subnormal. Eighty-eight per cent of the problems met were connected with the use of money in shopping and paying, and there were problems associated with budgeting, simple measuring, timetables, rents, rates, insurance and hire purchase. Matthews (1964) in his study of educationally subnormal school leavers found that only 39 per cent of his sample were able to do the calculations necessary for the purchase of larger items involving sums over £1, and only a small proportion (12–30 per cent) were knowledgeable about income tax and

National Insurance contributions. The author stresses how much these inadequacies proved to be 'a source of anxiety, frustration and conflict with authority'.

Brown and Dyer (1963) studied the effects of two methods of teaching arithmetic to twenty-two young adults with common age of approximately 20 years and mean IQ 65. In one method the young men 'were given two 45 minute periods of coaching each week in the industrial unit, while the other group received a similar amount of education in the school'. They came to the conclusion that the 'practical education appeared the more efficient method' in a good work environment which was defined as one which approximated to work conditions in the community and also had a training aspect.

(b) READING

Though much of the formal work in this area is similar to the syllabus for younger, normal children, there is an awareness, at least at the research front, of the need to tackle certain aspects which relate to an increase in social competence. An interesting example for this is the effort to train visual social cue interpretations (Edmonson *et al.*, 1965, 1967) because it is argued that some of the behaviour difficulties are due to the mentally handicapped person's 'failure to match his behaviour to the situational norm' on account of 'the slowness and inaccuracy with which he detects and reads the customary social signals or cues'.

A reading scheme designed for the illiterate adolescent subnormal and incorporating 'social situations' has been developed by H. C. Gunzburg (1968). The programme is based on the initial acquisition of a specific number of social sight vocabulary words such as 'Ladies', 'Gentlemen', 'Wet Paint', 'Exit', etc., which provide a useful first aid skill in orientating oneself in a world relying much on notices, signboards, warnings, etc. This vocabulary represents the first step in reading competence aiming to support social adequacy and is acquired with the help of flash cards and specially designed reading books. The second step aims at learning to read in the conventional way by using the words of the social sight vocabulary in the sentences and stories of a series of books dealing with socially important situations (post office, supermarket, doctor, café, etc.). Lastly, in a third step of the programme the level of reading skill (approximately RA $9\frac{1}{2}$) is consolidated by reading of social problem situations, such as encounters with landladies, foremen, shop assistants, etc., and thereby becoming acquainted with certain difficulties with which young people might be faced. In this way, an attempt is made to provide at any stage of the programme a useful reading competence and to utilize the process of teaching reading to support the aims of social education.

(c) LANGUAGE

It is most disappointing to note the scarcity of useful work on the language competence of the adolescent retarded. The language abilities of severely subnormal hospitalized children and adult patients were studied by Mein and O'Connor (1960) and compared with the achievements of normal children of approximately the same mental level. The patients used abcut 1,000 fewer words than did the normal children. Gunzburg (1964a) applied the Illinois Test of Psycholinguistic Abilities to fifty men aged 16 to 31 with a mean IQ of 70. The results indicated that this group had a limited primitive vocabulary (average language age: 8 years), that there was difficulty in deciphering visual symbols which provide guidance and help in finding one's way about in life (average language age: 7 years 6 months). The group was functioning on an average language age of 8 years when relating auditory impressions, but was less capable when dealing with visual impressions (average language age: 7 years), and the group was poorest in encoding processes (average language age: 6 years 8 months) because of their limited 'subcultural' vocabulary, and their efficiency was further lowered by a reluctance to support the spoken word by appropriate gestures (average language age: 6 years 5 months). An analysis of the sample according to mental ability indicated that this pattern of relative successes and failure applied to various groups irrespective of intelligence level.

Wolfensberger *et al.* (1963) studied the oral vocabularies of severely subnormal patients and suggested that at least within the mental age range of their investigations (2–9 to 7–4) 'word training should result in greater expressiveness and perhaps mediation' and that 'word training may be more warranted in lower intellectual groups than had been considered feasible'.

B. Social education

This area of education is, of course, a further development of an approach which has been initiated in the junior stage. Owing to increased maturity, changed interests and more mobility, a number of new aspects can be added to the programme which are of adult interest and importance.

The main aim will now be to make the mentally subnormal person familiar with those arrangements of community life which are so self-evident to the ordinary person that one hardly realizes that they may often present sizeable obstacles to the handicapped. The fact that houses are numbered odd and even on the opposite sides of the street, that a return ticket may be cheaper than two single tickets, that a post office offers facilities for saving, that one has to register with a doctor, are only a few instances where a mental defective, particularly one who has been institutionalized for a long period, might find himself in as embarrassing a situation as a foreigner in a country with an unfamiliar culture. The defective, who may be too shy to request information and vaguely conscious of making a fool of himself, attempts to hide his ignorance and shortcomings by various subterfuges.

Neither institutional life, whether in a residential school or hospital, nor the culturally impoverished upbringing in the defective's home is able to offer opportunities for an unconscious absorption of these useful, but unconnected, pieces of social knowledge and information, and it thus occurs that a systematic effort has to be made to teach them at this late stage.

It will be helpful, and ease the subnormal's adjustment, to stage for him interview situations which make him familiar with the usual questions and to let him practise filling in forms of application with the usual headings: surname, christian name, address, age, sex, nationality, signature.

Similarly, to learn to find one's way about an unknown district, to select appropriate public transport, to locate a given address and to follow verbal directions ('Take first turn to the left, till you come to the church, then turn right'), is an acquisition of great importance, quite literally widening the defective's horizon and creating in him a feeling of confidence in his abilities.

Social activities, such as buying clothes, putting money into the savings bank, obtaining tickets for a variety theatre performance, etc., have, of course, to be practised in the community itself and should not merely be discussed in the classroom (Baranyay, 1971). Similarly, insistence on the acquisition of the 'social graces', which will assist in making the defective less conspicuous in small groups (youth clubs, cycling clubs, etc.), as well as instruction in attending to personal needs (preparing a simple meal, or attending to personal clothing), will contribute in many cases to a smoother adjustment to society (Gunzburg, 1960, 1963b; Baranyay, 1971). Only in this way may we hope to build up familiarity and knowledge with social practices which may assist the patient later on in independent life.

(a) SEX EDUCATION

Social education work tends nowadays to comprise not only the practical techniques of shopping and moving about on public transport, but also assistance in certain aspects of living (e.g. motivation), some of which had been quite neglected in the past. The relationship of the sexes had been considered formerly only in terms of devising the most efficient techniques for avoiding any problems, but progressive workers have realized that this task too has to be faced together with other preparatory training (de la Cruz and la Veck, 1973).

In line with current thinking it is felt that sex education is a legitimate and necessary subject of educational work with the subnormal (Kratten and Thorne, 1957; Goodman et al., 1971). Extreme difficulties are however caused by the fact that this aspect cannot be tackled without coming to terms with the many issues relating to marriage and parenthood of mentally subnormal people (Bass, 1963, 1964). It involves questions such as sterilization and use of contraceptives and teachers', parents' and doctors' management of controversial issues (Bass, 1967; Meyen and Retish, 1971; Goodman et al., 1971). There is little literature available which discusses the actual educational programme for subnormals relating to this aspect, but some of the published work on therapy touches on it (Oliver *et al.*, 1973). There are only few discussions of experiences with less rigidly controlled segregation policies (Birkelund and Jacobsen, 1960). Harris and Kinney (1947), in describing a comprehensive treatment programme in an institution, emphasize co-education as providing the residents with opportunities for casual social relationships which they consider particularly important during adolescence. There is no formal tabulation of success and failure, but the authors conclude that one of the factors which seems to have played a direct part in reducing the incidence of maladjustment in the institution was due to 'providing a co-educational programme which approximates as nearly as possible with that of the community'. Smith (1957) describes an employment project in an institution where for the last ten years patients were permitted 'working in couples – a boy with his best girl'. No major problems arose and 'tone and discipline have . . . always been excellent, and it was achieved with little effort and fuss'.

A proportion of female patients are admitted to the institution because their mental subnormality had been associated with promiscuity and illegitimate off-spring. The mental defective, however, whether male or female, does not appear to be more libidinous than the normal contemporary despite the great number of women admitted to hospital for so-called immorality. Apart from a few 'over-sexed' girls (Burt, 1944, estimated that there were no more than 7 per cent of this type in the sample) most of the immorality of the young girls can be traced to the subnormal's impulsiveness, lack of judgment, great suggestibility, and lack of control. Their inability to resist temptation on one side and their desire for sexual gratification, affection and a home, make them a particularly difficult problem. They are even more resentful than the men of the sexual frustration imposed upon them (Milner, 1949), and training seems to make little inroad in this sphere. Much of the trouble, however, is due to adolescent instability, and if assistance is given during that period, time itself may effect stabilization. This must not be interpreted as suggesting that one should wait until the childbearing age has been passed and the 'safe time' has arrived. The reaction of many mildly subnormal women who see their years slip by with the maternal, home-making and sex instincts unsatisfied and without a possibility of sublimation, is severe. Even the risk of venereal disease, or pregnancies, seems scarcely large enough to justify their continued segregation. There is no evidence to suggest that patients on parole or licence produce considerably more illegitimate children than the general population of the same age, and in fact reports indicate a very low rate; e.g. 14 illegitimate children borne to 1,439 mentally deficient girls during 14 years under supervision (quoted by Wallin, 1956); 25 pregnancies during 20 years for 1,174 women sent on full licence in Birmingham (Middleton, 1956). Withdrawals from 'leave' are often due to association with the opposite sex which is against the conditions of this period on trial. However, it must not be forgotten that much of this so-called sexual misdemeanour, while not exactly ethical or moral, is condoned by society in the case of the ordinary man and woman, and is a biologically inescapable necessity.

In the Emma Hjorths Hjem in Norway 'several of our patients of all ages have during many years kept "firm company" with their sweethearts. The couples have kept together.' The authors of this report also state that 'the patients themselves arrange their leisure time, and have mixed freely "outdoors" for several years. Ample opportunities for free intercourse between the sexes are present and, in fact, to the same extent as if they were living outside the institution . . .' Nevertheless they came to the conclusion that this permissive and tolerant institutional arrangement has not led to a worsening of the situation but resulted in well adjusted, happy and more content patients (Birkelund and Jacobsen, 1960).

(b) MOTIVATION

Probably most teachers of the mentally handicapped would agree that the dominant problem is to make him *want* to learn, and to make him persist in his effort when he faces difficulties. Earl (1961) considered this 'weakness of drive' to be the fundamental characteristic of the mentally handicapped and regards it as far more important than the cognitive weaknesses which themselves might be affected by the mentally handicapped's unconcern for success.

Various systems and approaches have been tried out in educational work. On the lowest levels of ability, particularly in conditioning experiments, simple rewards in the form of candy and chocolates were found adequate, but for the more capable trainees, monetary rewards and incentive schemes have been introduced (Clark, 1960).

Within the educational system various forms of the sophisticated 'token-economy' (Ayllon and Azrin, 1968) have been applied in various contexts. In this system tokens are used as tangible reinforcers of approved behaviour, and can be exchanged for a wide range of goods, activities, privileges, hobbies, etc.

(c) ACTIVITY TRAINING (INCLUDING INDUSTRIAL TRAINING)

The term 'activity training' has been chosen to refer not merely to the adult activities known variously as occupational (OT) and industrial training but also to those aspects which help to occupy pleasurably (leisure activities) and to activate and stimulate people to take an interest in their surroundings. In recent years there has been much insistence on the introduction of various highly complex and spectacular work training schemes for mentally handicapped adults of varying levels of ability (Stahlecker, 1967) because it was felt that work efficiently executed was the one area where many subnormals could achieve a reasonable degree of success, and with it give satisfaction to themselves, employers, relations and training personnel. Indeed, the success of scientifically devised training methods (see Chapter 13), even in cases of very profoundly handicapped people (Williams, 1967), has encouraged a rapid development of work centres and realistic contacts with industry which often adversely affects the time and effort which should be devoted to further education.

In practical terms it is necessary to define carefully the distinction between 'training' which is to lead to a higher level of competence and 'occupation' which is to maintain a level of competence. In the first case the activities are chosen and directed with a view *to prepare* for more demanding situations, whilst in the second instance activities are *provided* for what is, in effect, a pleasurable way of spending time, with the special purpose of stopping mental and physical deterioration. This is a generalization which helps to some extent to evaluate the significant various activities towards a particular aim and to decide how much time should be devoted to certain activities within a programme of further education.

It is important that the training and 'employment' aspects should be clearly differentiated in any vocational scheme for the adult mentally defective. Training represents a systematic effort to raise the efficiency level of the 'worker' to a reasonable extent, corresponding to his abilities. The major aim will be to achieve a level of competence which would enable the subnormal to take his place – as a worker – alongside people with average intelligence in ordinary work conditions. If, however, it is not possible for him to function in 'normal' work situations – either because he requires supervision on account of his personality make-up, or because his work efficiency is not up to 'normal' demands – he should be prepared for work in a sheltered and less demanding workshop. In either case work training which *prepares* for employment in some form will have to share time and teaching effort with other training schemes which aim at developing other aspects of functioning, such as social competence and use of leisure. It must be clearly accepted as part of the operational philosophy that training in work attitudes and habits, in work skills and manipulation, demands much individual effort on the teacher's part. The attention to the needs of the trainee will affect adversely and very considerably the assembly line, the factory atmosphere which has been carefully created to introduce the trainee to normal working conditions. It has therefore been suggested (Gunzburg 1963b; Morley, 1973) that the full production assembly line, with its aim of maintaining a satisfactory and financially rewarding level of output, is properly the province of the 'sheltered workshop' to which trainees will be admitted for employment after they have been through a stage of training and cannot be placed in the open community.

Training is thus a time-limited stage of highly concentrated attention to the individual person, followed by 'employment' when attention invariably centres on production and not so much on the worker (Whelan, 1973).

Morley (1973) points out that 'employment training' would be a better term because it refers to many possible facets of employment rather than concentrating on industrial skills only. He points out that mentally handicapped persons can be grouped into:

(i) those who will obviously benefit from such training;
(ii) those who may possibly benefit in the foreseeable future;
(iii) those who appear unlikely to benefit but should not be overlooked;
(iv) those who are clearly unlikely even to benefit.

Using this grouping as a guide he suggests that employment training 'will range from 80 per cent of the syllabus time with Group I to none at all with Group IV'.

In practical terms this means that provisions should be arranged to cater for the different needs of the different groups, rather than providing the same scheme for these groups regardless of their future. Morley goes on to describe a three-tier scheme at Croydon consisting of an adult training centre, an advanced adult training centre and a sheltered workshop.

> Each centre is open-ended. Any trainee able to benefit can progress upwards so that there is a constant movement between the three Units, and, as far as the sheltered workshop is concerned, between that Unit and open employ-ment. In the adult training centre the programme is based on a much broader syllabus, in which industrial training plays an important, but relatively minor role. At the advanced centre, industrial training has the majority role, whilst at the sheltered workshop the emphasis is entirely on work. (Morley, 1973; see also Morley and Appell, 1974.)

(i) *Training activities in work habits and attitudes*

The practical work executed within the framework of an employment scheme will obviously depend on local conditions and the labour market. Industrial areas offer great advantages and it has often been found possible to enlist the cooperation of manufacturers who supply materials and tools for carrying out industrial processes. Among these are found: assembly of switchboxes, filing and trimming, cleaning of rubber mouldings, drilling of holes into metal discs, soldering of wireless terminals, folding of cardboard boxes, making of paper bags, cutting of rubber hoses, painting and cleaning of plastic discs, etc. (Clarke and Clarke, 1954; Gunzburg, 1963b). The great advantage of such skilled and semi-skilled work is its realistic nature and that it can provide the basis for industrial habit training. The repetitiveness of the job enables the worker to develop gradually increasing skill and speed and with that a certain pride in his accomplishments. Most of these above-mentioned tasks are within the capabilities of the mentally subnormal; they can be scaled, and appropriate daily or weekly targets for output can be set; they offer opportunities for impressing the trainee with the need for maintaining satisfactory quality and quantity, with the necessity for punctuality, and with the paramount demand of persisting with the job, despite its dullness.

The success of schemes of this type obviously depends on suitable motivation. Clearly defined incentives should be employed, both short-term and long-term. These include: payment by results leading to an increasing personal savings account and spending money; adequate pocket money; the encouragement to buy clothes and other personal possessions (under guidance where necessary); and above all – for institutionalized people – the opportunity for 'promotion' to outside employment. In order for such incentives to be effective, they must be clearly and repeatedly explained to the trainees, who must never be left in doubt as to their present position and future prospects (Tizard and O'Connor, 1952; Clarke and Clarke, 1954; Gunzburg, 1957; Smith, 1957; Clark, 1960).

Training should involve a gradual change from simpler to more complex work which at first should be broken down into its constituents. The more varied the tasks learned the better. In this connection the attitude of the supervisor is crucial; subnormal people tend to be very conservative, disliking and fearing change, and it is all too easy to let them settle into one task and leave them to it. Only by planned changes of work can this tendency be overcome. The safest rule would be that whenever a patient has learned a task to perfection he should be given a new one to master. In this way he will become used to change which is essential to life 'outside'.

Flexibility is required from the supervisory staff. *Laissez-faire* supervision is not often found in industrial life and is just as unsupportive for our patient as the non-directive passive therapist attitude discussed in the next chapter. Strict supervision – not harsh supervision – where criticism and blame, but no praise for work well done, are given, is bearable by many patients except the anxious and neurotic ones. The compromise between those two extremes, the friendly supervision, where praise and encouragement are given, appears to succeed like the strict supervision, even though some tough-minded patients might take advantage of the situation. This has been demonstrated in a research under controlled conditions (Tizard, 1953) where it also became clear that individual patients showed considerable differences in their response to different types of supervision.

Morley (1973) enumerated some of the basic elements which are essential in employment training. They should include:

Continuous assessments on graded and varied work processes to determine levels of abilities;
Observation over a period of time of speed and accuracy of performances, judgment and reliability, physical and mental limitations;
Training for as long as is necessary in processes in which aptitude is shown and which will have significance in future employment opportunities, together with relevant aspects of social and educational competence in the workshop situation.

The placement of women as domestic helpers in private residences and institutions, and of men as handymen in the kitchens and gardens of hotels, restaurants, and boarding-houses, has been undertaken by many hospitals for the mentally subnormal over a long period of time, often with successful results.

The advantages of such a procedure are:

1. that during periods of full industrial employment mildly subnormal patients are frequently acceptable to private employers;
2. that such jobs often offer residential accommodation, providing the patient with an opportunity of becoming entirely self-supporting relatively rapidly;
3. that for some patients the intimate, supportive atmosphere of a good home or domestic departments of hotels provides the most suitable environment for their adjustment.

The disadvantages appear to be:

1. The risks of exploitation are much greater than in industry where usually standard rates of pay, hours of work, and conditions of service obtain. This danger applies, of course, more to private establishments than to hospitals.
2. The work involved may demand a considerable degree of versatility, initiative, and a variety of skills, and will tend to be of a non-repetitive nature.
3. Not infrequently patients brought up in institutions or large subcultural families feel insecure, lonely, and out of their depth in the new cultural milieu of a middle-class home. The problem of interpersonal relationships may present great difficulties, particularly where the patient is unstable.
4. The opportunities for economic and trade advancement tend to be poor.

For those patients who have a clear preference or aptitude for domestic work, the problem of vocational inadequacy may be dealt with by providing within the training scheme opportunities for learning and daily practising of non-industrial vocational skills, which might be required in the home, in canteen work or in shops.

For a genuine assessment of the rate of success emerging from training schemes, a long-term follow-up such as that of Charles (1953) or Wildenskov (1957) is needed, and no industrial training project for the mildly subnormal has been running sufficiently long for such a final evaluation to have been made. Success rates themselves are affected by a number of factors:

1. the type of person rehabilitated;
2. the quality of training;
3. the type of job;
4. the quality of supervision while first in the community, both by the hospital and by the employers;
5. the economic circumstances at the time.

O'Connor and Tizard (1956) analysed the success and failure of patients placed, on the one hand, in a large factory and, on the other, in non-industrial forms of employment. The follow-up was short, being a maximum of two years, but it was shown that only 18 per cent failed in the factory while 44 per cent failed in other employment, a figure almost exactly corroborated in an unpublished study at The Manor Hospital. With longer periods of follow-up, failure rates obviously will tend to increase, and Clarke and Clarke (1954) estimate that over about three years between one-quarter and one-third fail in their first job in industry. What emerges quite clearly from longer periods of study, however, is that the vast majority, even under traditional methods of training and placement, succeed perhaps in their second, third, or even fourth job.

Stanley and Gunzburg (1957) believe that character defects are the major category under which failures can be subsumed, but indicate that most of these are remediable. In evaluating success and failure of the handicapped, it is profitable not only to compare the effects of different types of training and placement but also to study failure of normal young men and women in similar jobs. Thus O'Connor and Tizard (1956) showed that the failure rates of defective boys employed on a building site were less than those of normal day-labourers. Moreover, it is sometimes not appreciated that many normal young men and women change jobs quite frequently for various reasons, including those which would be termed 'failure' in mental deficiency practice. Sometimes more puritanical standards of conduct are demanded of the mentally deficient than society asks of normal people, and this demand is imposed on persons presumably less able to exercise normal emotional control.

Gunzburg (1957), commenting on factors affecting success on leave in general, states that (1) the tested intellectual level can be quite low before setting a definite limit to employability outside the hospital (some of the young men in his study having Wechsler IQs below 40); and (2) the repetition of delinquency – even of a sexual nature – is so infrequent that pre-admission delinquency does not suggest a poor social prognosis. The latter point is supported by the work of Tong and MacKay (1959) who found that an early history of heterosexual misbehaviour and violence was associated with a good prognosis. Low intelligence by itself is not necessarily an obstacle to living and working in the community. Saenger (1957) found that 27 per cent of his sample of severely subnormal people living in the community were employed for remuneration. Craft (1962a) showed that 75 per cent of an imbecile group were employed, compared with 77 per cent of a group with IQs above 50.

Morley (1973) reports that in the sheltered workshop at Croydon all forty-five subnormal people are *employed* – 'men over 21 years receiving a basic wage of £14 per week and the women £10·29 plus free midday meals, reimbursement of fares to and from work, two weeks' paid annual holiday and full trade union representation'.

One of the latest English studies, discussing the results of a comprehensive training scheme of mentally handicapped adults which comprised industrial and social aspects, is that by Baranyay (1971). In her follow-up of 67 trainees who had gone through the training programme, she found 11 young men and girls (16 per cent) had proceeded to open employment. Their intelligence scores ranged from 34 to 47 (Stanford–Binet) with a mean IQ of 42. Their mental ages ranged from 4 years 2 months to 7 years 2 months. Social ages as measured on the Vineland Social Maturity Scale were available on entry and on discharge for 10 of the group. The mean increase in social competence was 3·5 years, though the length of training had ranged only from 1 year to 2 years seven months.

Baranyay states that 'all in this group had intelligence scores on entry below 50; all had a social age value of 11 years or higher at the end of training. The trainee with the lowest intelligence score, a mongol with IQ 34, achieved an increase in social age of 3·6 years, rising to 11·3 on discharge as against 7·7 on entry'. The longest period of employment at the time of this study was 5 years, and the shortest 6 months. The members of this group (which included 3 mongols) were employed as canteen assistants (2), kitchen porter (1), hotel workers (2), workers in light industry (3), garage worker (1), assistant in nursery group (1), pantry maid (1). Ten of the 11 were living at home and negotiating their own journeys to and from work.

(ii) *Occupational activities*

The enthusiasm with which 'normal' industrial activities have been introduced into the workshops for the severely mentally handicapped and have taken the place of the old fashioned basket, mat and rug-making suggests that there has been much doubt about the usefulness of these traditional activities from the patients' point of view. However, recently some further doubts have arisen regarding the over-emphasis on the production side which leaves little time for other activities. Links with industry result in firm commitments regarding delivery time and output, which create a useful atmosphere of industriousness and exercise pressure on trainees in preparation for the demands of a less protective setting. This appears to be conducive to training for life even though these conditions may mislead staff to regard their set-up as a factory rather than as a training environment. The 100 per cent work situation is justified in the 'sheltered workshop' where demands are made and met which would satisfy ordinary employers, even though these workers require these particular sheltered work conditions. Criticism becomes more persistent if the same approach is imposed on the severely subnormal person who has little prospect of working in normal conditions and for whom industrial employment provides neither particular satisfaction nor stimulation. Nevertheless, a sheltered work environment is created for him where he is encouraged to carry out industrial tasks, which have been adjusted to his limited capacity (Williams, 1967). To some extent one might consider this programme as a 'watered down' industrial training scheme, in the same way as a 'watered down' education is derived for the severely subnormal child from an educational programme designed for the more capable child. Again, the question will have to be asked whether an imitation of an industrial training programme, which in the majority of cases will not lead to employment either in or outside the protective shelter, is in the best interest of the mentally handicapped adult. It may well be thought that working a full day at a monotonous stereotyped job could in due course result in deterioration of attitudes, interests, motivation and personality. If the purpose of adult education and training is to encourage a fuller development of a potential which will help the mentally handicapped person to participate more fully in activities and to be more capable of relative independence, the available time and energy could well be devoted to activities which stimulate, activate and encourage interest in active participation.

Cortazzi (1969) describes a training programme for profoundly retarded patients with MA 2 to 5 and IQs for the most part below 25. They had been in closed wards for periods of up to twenty years for repeated attacks on staff or patients, frequent tearing of clothes, smashing of windows and furniture, continued running away or total inability to adapt to life in an open ward, to understand instructions or to follow a simple routine.

The aims of the training were defined as

1. Developing contact and positive communication
2. Arousing interest
3. Learning control
4. Increasing attention
5. Teaching skills at infant school level
6. Gradually by stages to full-time Occupational Therapy as practised at the hospital – i.e. half-day technical work, half-day education, recreational and social training, plus evening activities . . .

Such points as developing initiative, taking turns, exercising a choice must, it was felt, be encouraged right from the start, and at every possible opportunity, since they were so noticeably absent from the protective routine of the ward.

The author made the point that it was important to make 'a strong appeal to the emotions, and music, rhythm, colour, movement and touch must be all involved in the early stages'. Adopting this as the underlying philosophy for making these extremely disturbed severely handicapped people more accessible to the more conventional, Cortazzi reports that these patients were 'resocialised to the point where they not only enjoy being members of a group and begin to learn (as opposed to just being occupied) but they also *want* to learn'.

Unfortunately Cortazzi's work is exceptional because there is little note yet taken that it is essential to devise programmes which cater for the many personal needs of the severely handicapped, and not only for his occupation.

If such a programme is successful, these severely mentally handicapped people may well contribute to some extent to the sheltered workshop production line at a later stage, provided this achievement is not regarded as the desirable and final end result of training. Considering the extreme limitations of this group of people an enriched environment will be required for maintaining the level achieved rather than the concentration of effort on a narrow front as in the sheltered environment (Cortazzi, 1974).

(iii) *Leisure activities*

Attention has focused in recent years on the need to train and educate even in this area, which might be regarded by many as requiring no special organization (Carlson and Ginglend, 1968). With the increasing conviction that a good proportion of people who are at present housed in institutions, where life is arranged for them, should as soon as possible be given opportunities to live in the open community (Leck *et al.*, 1967; McKeown and Teruel, 1970; Browne *et al.*, 1971), there has also been an increasing awareness of the possible danger points. Among these, the aimless drifting after working hours of the unoccupied mentally handicapped presents a very real risk. Many of his delinquent acts originate in these periods when he is neither able to evolve a spontaneous leisure-time interest, nor participates in the social activities of his contemporaries (Edgerton, 1967). Indeed, as has been pointed out, 'the maturing retardate has special need for organized recreation because all too often he is among the socially deprived' (Carlson and Ginglend, 1968).

Many of the city-dwelling youths spend most of their free time in the 'pictures' and are unable to develop more active interests. It may be possible to widen the range of interests if patients are encouraged to develop hobbies while still in hospital. Fitzpatrick (1956) reports that patients on 'parole' have outside interests which they pursue in the company of their normal contemporaries. Many belong to a speedway club, others join local football clubs. 'The more solitary may prefer to explore the countryside on bicycles or join fishing clubs and take part in their competitions. Recently, a band of healthy young men volunteered their services to the local flower show committee; others, more conscious of the power of money, take on spare-time jobs in the weekend.'

Far too little time has been spent guiding the subnormal patient into organizations and clubs which would give him support, interest, and occupation during those hours when he is left to his own devices. He should be taught and trained in hobbies, skills, and games to overcome his distrust in his own abilities when facing competition in sport and games with normal people, but also to establish a further bridge to normal, busy, ordered life (Baranyay, 1971).

Discussion and conclusions

There is a consensus of opinion that further education should be carried out for the mentally subnormal after the conventional educational period has come to an end. The adolescent mentally subnormal is very often more likely to benefit by education and instruction at that stage than when he was younger, and in any case he still needs to learn essentials which he was unable to acquire during his schooldays. Opinions, however, differ widely as to the extent to which he should still be taught and as to the contents of a further education syllabus.

There are many who feel that the subnormal himself will benefit most by increased self-respect when he sees himself accepted as a worker who receives financial remuneration, and there are others who would regard this as a shortsighted policy because it does not take into account his needs as a social being. Those who advocate that 'training for work' is the paramount task of the adolescent and adult stage will be content to carry out 'further education' in evening classes or a few weekly sessions during worktime. To some extent this would conform to the practices of industrial 'normal' life for which the subnormal is to be prepared if at all possible. Advocates of the 'further education' approach feel that a work-dominated training stage, whilst desirable as such, is usually entered on far too early and that provisions must be made for a transitional stage where full-time education with adult orientation takes precedence over work training.

It is also felt that education at that stage (and in childhood) must be far more comprehensive than could be achieved in a few formal sessions. This applies to all subnormals whether living at home, in institutions, community homes, etc. What is, in effect, aimed at is 'Education in Living' and this can only have a chance to be effective by making systematic use of the many learning opportunities which are offered by normal life. Further education for the subnormal comprises therefore not only those 'subjects' which are conventionally and automatically included in an educational syllabus, but also those skills of living which will assist him in coping more competently with everyday situations, and the acquisition of which must not be left to chance and informal learning.

In addition, further education will have to assist in developing aspects in the subnormal's personality which have been scarcely regarded so far as a proper educational concern: developing initiative, stimulating curiosity, encouraging interest, learning to choose, making decisions. Many if not all of present-day arrangements for the subnormal are based on traditional care ideas where everything is done for somebody utterly handicapped, but little confidence is placed in his latent ability to do something for himself. Though it is only realistic not to expect that education and training will result in normal efficiency, over-protective and unexpectant attitudes are responsible for not realizing adequately the subnormal's potential for functioning on a higher level than he has been given credit for.

The vocational and social training is for many subnormals the only therapeutic help required – they are not in need of special psychotherapy nor do they care for educational help. It attempts to instil those skills which have remained underdeveloped for lack of encouragement, stimulation, lack of application, absence of opportunity, and many other reasons; it should never primarily be an attempt only to occupy, but always a systematic effort to make them acquire modes of behaviour acceptable to society.

The Senior Training Centres organized in the community are, in some ways, better placed than the institution to carry out vocational and social training. The Training Centres must, however, appreciate that teaching and training of 'social skills' are often the main needs even though carried out in the more adult atmosphere of the workshop. Unless this task is accepted and the Senior Training Centre manages to provide an 'educative environment' (Scott Report, 1962) the differences between Training Centre and Sheltered Workshop will become indistinct; similarly, the difference between community provisions and the hospital's occupational therapy and maintenance workshops will be merely one of day versus full-time attendance for the purpose of being occupied.

The vocational and social training provides the broadest, most comprehensive, and most realistic area of rehabilitation efforts. We have at present, however – as with so many other areas of mental deficiency – no reliable evidence which would 'prove' the efficacy of particular approaches. This state of affairs is scarcely good enough – traditional beliefs, emotional thinking, and narrow experience ranges affect too much the validity of our conclusions. Much of the evidence gathered from past reports and researches is outdated and invalid – not only have methods changed and with them the attitudes of the mentally handicapped, but so have the economics of society and the attitudes and views which have made the defective more tolerated than ever before.

It cannot, therefore, be too strongly emphasized that even in the field of vocational and social training, which has the longest history in mental deficiency work, we must not rely too much on the findings of the past, but must reconsider the problem against the background of a changing world.

References

ABERCROMBIE, M. L. J. (1964) *Perceptual and Visuo-motor Disorders in Cerebral Palsy*. London: Heinemann.

ADLER, S. (1964) *The Non-verbal Child*. Springfield, Ill.: Charles C. Thomas.

AINSWORTH, S. A. (1959) *An Exploratory Study of Educational, Social and Emotional Factors in the Education of Mentally Retarded Children in Georgia Public Schools*. Athens: US Office of Educ., Coop. Res. Program., Univ. of Georgia.

AXLINE, V. M. (1947) Non-directive therapy for poor readers. *J. consult. Psychol.*, **11**, 61–9.

AYLLON, T. and AZRIN, T. (1968) *The Token Economy System, a Motivational System for Therapy and Rehabilitation*. New York: Appleton-Century-Crofts.

BADT, M. I. (1958) Levels of abstraction in vocabulary definitions of mentally retarded schoolchildren. *Amer. J. ment. Defic.*, **63**, 241–6.

BALLA, D. A., BUTTERFIELD, E. C. and ZIGLER, E. (1974) Effects of institutionalization on retarded children *Amer. J. ment. Defic.* 78, 530–49.

BALTHAZAR, E. E. (1972) *Balthazar Scales of Adaptive Behavior. Sect. I:*

The scales of functional independence. Palo Alto, Calif.: Consulting Psychologists' Press.

BALTHAZAR, E. E. (1973) *Balthazar Scales of Adaptive Behavior. Sect. II: Scales of social adaptation.* Palo Alto, Calif.: Consulting Psychologists' Press.

BALTHAZAR, E. E. and ENGLISH G. E. (1969) A system for the social classification of the more severely retarded. *Amer. J. ment. Defic.,* **74,** 361–8.

BANK-MIKKELSEN, N. E. (1969) A metropolitan area in Denmark: Copenhagen. In KUGEL, R. B. and WOLFENSBERGER, W. P. (eds.) *Changing Patterns in Residential Services for the Mentally Retarded.* Washington, DC: President's Committee on Mental Retardation.

BARANYAY, E. P. (1971) *The Mentally Handicapped Adolescent.* Oxford: Pergamon.

BARCLAY, A., GOULET, L. R. and SHARP, A. R. (1964) Short-term changes in intellectual and social maturity of young non-institutionalised retardates. In ØSTER, J. (ed.) *Proc. Copenhagen Congr. Internat. Assoc. Scient. Stud. Ment. Defic.,* 679–83. Copenhagen: Statens Åndssvageforsorg.

BARHAM, J. (1971) Nature study activities with severely subnormal children. *Forward Trends,* **15,** 29–32.

BARRETT, B. H. (1971) Behavioral differences among an institution's backward residents. *Ment. Retard.,* **9,** 4–9.

BARTON, R. (1961) The institutional mind and the subnormal mind. *J. ment. Subn.,* **VII,** 37–44.

BASS, M. S. (1963) Marriage, parenthood and prevention of pregnancy. *Amer. J. ment. Defic.,* **68,** 318–31.

BASS, M. S. (1964) Marriage for the mentally deficient. *Ment. Retard.,* **2,** 198–202.

BASS, M. S. (1967) Attitudes of parents of retarded children toward voluntary sterilization. *Eugen. Quart.,* **14,** 45–53.

BATEMAN, B. (1965) *The Illinois Test of Psycholinguistic Abilities in Current Research: Summaries of Studies.* Urbana: Univ. of Illinois Press.

BAYES, K. and FRANCKLIN, S. (1971) *Designing for the Handicapped.* London: George Godwin.

BEIER, E. G., STARKWEATHER, J. A. and LAMBERT, M. J. (1969) Vocabulary usage of mentally retarded children. *Amer. J. ment. Defic.,* **73,** 927–34.

BELL, P. (1970) *Basic Teaching for Slow Learners.* London: Muller.

BENDER, L. (1938) A visual-motor Gestalt test and its clinical uses. *Amer. Orthopsychiat. Assoc. Res. Monogr.,* 3. New York.

BENSBERG, G. J., COLWELL, C. N. and CASSEL, R. H. (1965) Teaching the profoundly retarded self-help activities by behavior shaping techniques. *Amer. J. ment. Defic.,* **69,** 674–9.

BENSBERG, G. J., COLWELL, C. N., ELLIS, N. R., ROOS, P. and

WATSON, L. S. (1969) *Report on Symposium on Environmental Modifications for the Profoundly Retarded.* Albany, NY: New York State Dept of Mental Hygiene.

BENTON, A. L. (1955) *Benton Visual Retention Test* (rev. edn). New York: Psychol. Corporation.

BEREITER, C. and ENGELMANN, S. (1966) *Teaching Disadvantaged Children in the Pre-School.* Englewood Cliffs, NJ: Prentice-Hall.

BIJOU, S. W. (1965) Application of operant principles to the teaching of reading, writing and arithmetic to retarded children. In *New Frontiers in Special Education.* Washington, DC: Council for Exceptional Children.

BILOVSKY, D. and SHARE, J. (1965) The ITPA and Down's syndrome: an exploratory study. *Amer. J. ment. Defic.,* **70,** 78–82.

BIRCH, H. G. (1964) *Brain Damage in Children.* New York: Williams & Wilkins.

BIRCH, H. G., BELMONT, L., BELMONT, I. and TAFT, L. T. (1967) Brain damage and intelligence in educable mentally subnormal children. *J. nerv. ment. Dis.,* **144,** 246–57.

BIRKELUND, L. and JACOBSEN, J. R. (1960) Normal relationships between institutionalized subnormals. *J. ment. Subn.,* **VI,** 13–18.

BLACKMAN, L. S. and CAPOBIANCO, R. J. (1965) An evaluation of programmed instruction with the MR utilizing teaching machines. *Amer. J. ment. Defic.,* **70,** 262–9.

BLAND, G. A. (1968) *Education in Hospital Schools for the Mentally Handicapped.* London: College of Special Education.

BLAND, G. A. (1974) Encouraging communicative skills in the institutionalized adolescent mentally handicapped. In GUNZBURG, H. C. (ed.) *Experiments in the Rehabilitation of the Mentally Handicapped.* London: Butterworths.

BLATT, B. (1958) The physical personality and academic status of children who are mentally retarded attending special classes as compared with children who are mentally retarded attending regular classes. *Amer. J. ment. Defic.,* **62,** 810–18.

BLATT, B. and KAPLAN, F. (1966) *Christmas in Purgatory.* Boston: Allyn & Bacon.

BLOUNT, W. R. (1968) Language and the more severely retarded: a review. *Amer. J. ment. Defic.,* **73,** 21–9.

BOBATH, K. (1966) *The Motor Deficit in Patients with Cerebral Palsy.* Clin. Developm. Med. No. 23. London: Spastics Soc. and Heinemann.

BODMAN, F. (1946) Social maturity test. *J. ment. Sci.,* **92,** 532–41.

BRIMER, M. A. and DUNN, L. M. (1966) *English Picture Vocabulary Test.* London: National Foundation for Educational Research.

British Psychological Society (1966) *Children in Hospitals for the Subnormal: A Survey of Admissions and Educational Facilities.* London: British Psychological Society.

BROOK, J. R. (1966) Spontaneous spoken vocabulary of a group of severely mentally subnormal children. *Brit. J. dis. Comm.*, **1**, 131–5.

BROWN, R. I. (1966) Problems of attention in the education and training of the subnormal. In GUNZBURG, H. C. (ed.) *The Application of Research to the Education and Training of the Severely Subnormal Child*, 74–9. J. ment. Subn. Monogr.

BROWN, R. I. (1967) A remedial reading program for the adolescent illiterate. *J. spec. Educ.*, **1**, 409–17.

BROWN, R. I. and BOOKBINDER, G. E. (1966) Programmed reading for spastics. *Spec. Educ.*, **55**, 26–9.

BROWN, R. I. and BOOKBINDER, G. E. (1968) *The Clifton Audio-Visual Reading Programme.* Harlow: ESA.

BROWN, R. I. and DYER, L. (1963) Social arithmetic training for the subnormal: a comparison of two methods. *J. ment. Subn.*, **IX**, 8–12.

BROWNE, R. A., GUNZBURG, H. C., JOHNSTON HANNAH, L. G. W., MACCOLL, K., OLIVER, B. and THOMAS, A. (1971) The needs of patients in subnormality hospitals if discharged to community care. *Brit. J. ment. Subn.*, **XVII**, 1–18.

BRYANT, P. E. (1967) Selective attention and learning in severely subnormals. In RICHARDS, B. W. (ed.) *Proc. 1st Congr. Internat. Assoc. Scient. Stud. Ment. Defic.*, 264–9. Reigate: M. Jackson.

BURLAND, R. (1969) The development of the verbal regulation of behaviour in cerebrally palsied (multiply handicapped) children. *J. ment. Subn.*, **XV**, 85–9.

BURNS, M. E. and SIMON, G. B. (1968) Biochemical factors in subnormality. In O'GORMAN, G. (ed.) *Modern Trends in Mental Health and Subnormality.* London: Butterworths.

BURNS, P. C. (1961) Arithmetic fundamentals for the educable mentally retarded. *Amer. J. ment. Defic.* **66**, 57–62.,

BURT, C. (1922) *Mental and Scholastic Tests* (2nd edn, 1924). London: P. S. King.

BURT, C. (1944) *The Young Delinquent.* London: Univ. of London Press.

BUTTERFIELD, E. C. (1968) The role of environmental factors in the treatment of institutionalized mental retardates. In BAUMEISTER, A. A. (ed.) *Mental Retardation: Appraisal, Education and Rehabilitation.* London: Univ. of London Press.

BUTTERFIELD, E. C. and ZIGLER, E. (1965) The influence of differing institutional climates on the effectiveness of social reinforcement in the mentally retarded. *Amer. J. ment. Defic.*, **70**, 48–56.

CAIN, L. F. and LEVINE, S. (1963) *Effects of Community and Institutional School Programmes on Trainable Mentally Retarded Children.* Washington, DC: Council for Exceptional Children.

CAIN, L. F., LEVINE, S. and ELZEY, F. F. (1963) *Cain–Levine Social Competency Scale.* Palo Alto, Calif.: Consulting Psychologists' Press.

CARLSON, B. W. and GINGLEND, D. R. (1968) *Recreation for Retarded Teenagers and Young Adults*. New York: Abingdon Press.

CARR, D. L., BROWN, L. F. and RICE, J. A. (1967) The PPVT in the assessment of language deficits. *Amer. J. ment. Defic.*, **71**, 937-9.

CARTER, J. A. (1966) *The Effect of a Group Language Stimulation Program upon Negro Culturally Disadvantaged First Grade Children*. Doctoral dissertation, Univ. of Texas.

CASSIDY, V. M. and STANTON, J. E. (1959) *An Investigation of Factors involved in the Educational Placement of Mentally Retarded Children*. Columbus: US Office of Educ., Coop. Res. Program., Ohio State Univ.

CATTELL, P. (1947) *The Measurement of Intelligence of Infants and Young Children*. New York: Psychol. Corporation.

CHALL, J. S. (1967) *Learning to Read: The Great Debate, I.* New York: McGraw-Hill.

CHARLES, D. C. (1953) Ability and accomplishment of persons earlier judged mentally deficient. *Genet. Psychol. Monogr.*, **47**, 3-71.

CLARK, D. F. (1960) Visual feedback in the social learning of the subnormal. *J. ment. Subn.*, **IV**, 30-9.

CLARKE, A. D. B. and CLARKE, A. M. (1954) Cognitive changes in the feebleminded. *Brit. J. Psychol.*, **45**, 173-9.

CLARKE, A. D. B., CLARKE, A. M. and REIMAN, S. (1958) Cognitive and social changes in the feeble-minded – three further studies. *Brit. J. Psychol.*, **49**, 144-57.

COLWELL, C. N. and CASSEL, R. H. (1955) Teaching the profoundly retarded self-help activities by behavior shaping techniques. *Amer. J. ment. Defic.*, **69**, 674-9.

CORTAZZI, D. (1969) The bottom of the barrel. *J. ment. Subn.*, **XV**, 3-10.

CORTAZZI, D. (1974) 'You don't want him'. In GUNZBURG, H. C. (ed.) *Experiments in the Rehabilitation of the Mentally Handicapped*. London: Butterworths.

COTTON, E. and PARNWELL, M. (1973) Conductive education. In GUNZBURG, H. C. (ed.) *Advances in the Care of the Mentally Handicapped*. London: Baillière Tindall.

CRAFT, M. J. (1962) The rehabilitation of the imbecile: a follow-up report. *J. ment. Subn.*, **8**, 26-7.

CRAIB, M. F. and WOODWARD, M. (1958) A survey of 44 children admitted to the Fountain Group Hospital under the Mental Deficiency Act and subsequently accepted as educable. *J. ment. Sci.*, **104**, 115-22.

CRUICKSHANK, W. M. (1946) Arithmetic vocabulary of mentally retarded boys. *Except. Child.*, **13**, 65-9.

CRUICKSHANK, W. M., BENTZEN, F. A., RATZEBERG, F. E. and TANNHOUSER, M. T. (1961) *A Teaching Method for Brain-injured Hyperactive Children*. Syracuse, NY: Syracuse Univ. Press.

DANIELS, J. C. and DIACK, H. (1958) *The Standard Reading Tests*. London: Chatto & Windus.

DANIELS, J. C. and DIACK, H. (1960) *Progress in Reading in the Infant School*. Nottingham: Univ. of Nottingham Inst. of Education.

DAWE, A. (1959) Progress in curriculum and method with mentally handicapped children. *Amer. J. ment. Defic.*, **64**, 19–23.

DAWE, H. G. (1942) A study of the effect of an educational program upon language development and related mental functions in young children. *J. exp. Educ.*, **11**, 200–9.

DE LA CRUZ, F. F. and LA VECK, G. D. (1973) *Human Sexuality and the Mentally Retarded*. New York: Brunner-Mazel.

Department of Health and Social Security (1971) *Buildings for Mentally Handicapped People*. London: HMSO.

DE VRIES-KRUYT, T. (1971) *Small Ship – Great Sea (The Life Story of a Mongoloid Boy)*. London: Collins.

DOLL, E. A. (1953) *The Measurement of Social Competence: A Manual for the Vineland Social Maturity Scale*. Washington, DC: Educational Test Bureau.

DOLL, E. A. (1966) *P-A-R (Preschool Attainment Record) Manual*. Minneapolis: Amer. Guidance Service Inc.

DUNCAN, J. (1942) *The Education of the Ordinary Child*. London: Nelson.

DUNN, L. M. (1959) *Peabody Picture Vocabulary Test*. Minneapolis: Amer. Guidance Service Inc.

DUNN, L. M. (1968) Special education for the mildly retarded – is much of it justifiable? *Except. Child.*, **35**, 5–22.

DUNN, L. M. and MUELLER, M. W. (1966) *The Effectiveness of the Peabody Language Development Kits and the Initial Teaching Alphabet with Disadvantaged Children in the Primary Grades after One Year*. Nashville: Inst. Ment. Retard. Intellect. Developmt. Sci. Monogr.

DUNN, L. M. and SMITH, J. O. (1964) *The Peabody Language Development Kit*. Minneapolis: Amer. Guidance Service Inc.

DUNN, L. M., POCHANART, P. and PFOST, P. (1967) *The Effectiveness of the Peabody Language Development Kits and the Initial Teaching Alphabet with Disadvantaged Children in the Primary Grades after Two Years*. Nashville: Inst. Ment. Retard. Intellect. Developmt. Sci. Monogr.

DYBWAD, G. (1967) Changing patterns of residential care for the mentally retarded. In RICHARDS, B. (ed.) *Proc. 1st Congr. Internat. Assoc. Scient. Stud. Ment. Defic.* Reigate: Michael Jackson.

DYBWAD, G. (1970) Architecture's role in revitalizing the field of mental retardation. *J. ment. Subn.*, **XVI**, 45–8.

EARL, C. J. C. (1961) *Subnormal Personalities: Their Clinical Investigation and Assessment*. London: Baillière, Tindall & Cox.

EDGERTON, R. B. (1967) *The Cloak of Competence*. Berkeley: Univ. of California Press.

EDMONSON, B., JUNG, J. E. and LELAND, H. (1965) Social perceptual (non-verbal communication) training of retarded adolescents. *Ment. Retard.*, **3**, 7–9.

EDMONSON, B., LELAND, H., JUNG, J. E. and LEACH, E. M. (1967) Increasing social cue interpretations (visual decoding) by retarded adolescents through training. *Amer. J. ment. Defic.*, **71**, 1017–24.

EISENBERG, L. and KANNER, L. (1956) Early infantile autism, 1943–1955. *Amer. J. Orthopsychiat.*, **26**, 556–66.

ELLIOT, R. and MACKAY, D. N. (1971) Social competence of subnormal and normal children living under different types of residential care. *Brit. J. ment. Subn.*, **XVII**, 48–53.

ELLIS, N. R., BARNETT, C. D. and PRYER, M. W. (1960) Operant behaviour in mental defectives. *J. exp. Anal. Behav.*, **3**, 63–9.

EVANS, D. and SAMPSON, M. (1968) The language of mongols. *Brit. J. dis. Comm.*, **3**, 171–81.

EWERHARDT, P. (1938) Reading difficulties in subnormal children. *Proc. Amer. Assoc. ment. Defic.*, **43**, 188–93.

FELDMAN, I. S. (1953) Psychological differences among moron and border-line mental defectives as a function of etiology. *Amer. J. ment. Defic.*, **57**, 484–94.

FINLEY, C. J. (1962) Arithmetic achievement in mentally retarded children. *Amer. J. ment. Defic.*, **67**, 281–6.

FITZPATRICK, F. K. (1956) Training outside the walls. *Amer. J. ment. Defic.*, **60**, 827–37.

FRANCEY, R. E. (1966) Psychological test changes in mentally retarded children during training. In JORDAN, T. E. (ed.) *Perspectives in Mental Retardation*. Carbondale and Edwardsville: Southern Illinois Univ. Press.

FROSTIG, M. and HORNE, D. (1964) *The Frostig Program for the Development of Visual Perception*. Chicago: Follett, in collaboration with Curriculum Materials Laboratory.

FROSTIG, M., LEFEVER, D. W. and WHITTLESEY, J. R. B. (1961) A developmental test of visual perception for evaluating normal and neurologically handicapped children. *Percept. mot. Skills*, **12**, 383–94.

GALLAGHER, J. J. (1960) *The Tutoring of Brain-Injured Mentally Retarded Children*. Springfield, Ill.: Charles C. Thomas.

GALLAGHER, J. J. (1962) Changes in verbal and non-verbal ability of brain-injured mentally retarded children following removal of special stimulation. *Amer. J. ment. Defic.*, **66**, 774–81.

GANN, E. (1945) *Reading Difficulty and Personality Organization*. New York: King's Crown Press.

GARDNER, J. M. (1969) Behavior modification research in mental retardation. Search for an adequate paradigm. *Amer. J. ment. Defic.*, **73**, 844–51.

GARDNER, J. M. and WATSON, L. S. (1969) Behavior modification of the mentally retarded: an annotated bibliography. *Ment. Retard. Abstrs.*, 6, 181–93.

GARDNER, L. (1969) Planning for planned dependence. *Spec. Educ.*, 58, 27–30.

GARDNER, W. I. and NISONGER, H. W. (1962) A manual on program development in mental retardation. *Amer. J. ment. Defic. Suppl.*, 66(1).

GATES, A. I. (1935) *Improvement of Reading.* New York: Macmillan.

GESELL, A. (1954) *The First Five Years of Life.* London: Methuen.

GIRARDEAU, F. L. (1962) The effect of secondary reinforcement on the operant behavior of mental defectives. *Amer. J. ment. Defic.*, 67, 441–9.

GIRARDEAU, F. L. and SPRADLIN, J. E. (1964) Token rewards in a cottage program. *Ment. Retard.*, 2, 345–51.

GOFFMAN, E. (1961) *Asylums: Essays on the Social Situation of Mental Patients and other Inmates.* Garden City, NY: Doubleday.

GOLDSTEIN, H., MOSS, J. and JORDAN, L. (1964) *The Efficacy of Special Class Training on the Development of Mentally Retarded Children.* US Office of Education, Cooperative Research Program, Project No. 619. Urbana: Univ. of Illinois Inst. for Research on Exceptional Children.

GOODMAN, L., BUDNER, S. and LESH, B. (1971) The parents' role in sex education for the retarded. *Ment. Retard.*, 9, 43–5.

GORTON, C. E. and HOLLIS, J. H. (1965) Redesigning a cottage unit for better programming and research for the severely retarded. *Ment. Retard.*, 3, 16–21.

GOULET, L. R. and BARCLAY, A. (1962) The Vineland Social Maturity Scale: utility in assessment of Binet MA. *Amer. J. ment. Defic.*, 67, 916–21.

GRIFFITHS, R. (1954) *The Abilities of Babies.* London: Univ. of London Press.

GRUNEWALD, K. (1971) A test ward for the mentally retarded. *Brit. J. ment. Subn.*, XVII, 66–71.

GULLIFORD, R. (1971) *Special Educational Needs.* London: Routledge & Kegan Paul.

GUNZBURG, A. L. (1967) Architecture for social rehabilitation. *J. ment. Subn.*, XIII, 84–7.

GUNZBURG, A. L. (1974) The physical environment as a supportive factor in rehabilitation. In GUNZBURG, H. C. (ed.) *Experiments in the Rehabilitation of the Mentally Handicapped.* London: Butterworths.

GUNZBURG, H. C. (1948) The subnormal boy and his reading interests. *Libr. Quart.*, 18, 264–74.

GUNZBURG, H. C. (1957) Therapy and social training for the feebleminded youth. *Brit. J. med. Psychol.*, 30, 42–8.

GUNZBURG, H. C. (1960) *Social Rehabilitation of the Subnormal.* London: Baillière, Tindall & Cox.

GUNZBURG, H. C. (1963a) *Junior Training Centres: An Outline of the Principles and Practices of Social Education and Training of the Mentally Subnormal Child.* London: National Association for Mental Health.

GUNZBURG, H. C. (1963b) *Senior Training Centres: An Outline of the Principles and Practices of Social Education and Training for Older Mentally Subnormal People.* London: National Association for Mental Health.

GUNZBURG, H. C. (1964a) The reliability of a test of psycholinguistic abilities (ITPA) in a population of young male subnormals. *J. ment. Subn.,* **X,** 101–12.

GUNZBURG, H. C. (1964b) Social competence of the imbecile child. In ØSTER, J. (ed.) *Proc. Copenhagen Congr. Internat. Assoc. Scient. Stud. Ment. Defic.* Copenhagen: Statens Åndssvageforsorg.

GUNZBURG, H. C. (1968) *Social Competence and Mental Handicap.* London: Baillière, Tindall & Cassell.

GUNZBURG, H. C. (1969) *Progress Evaluation Index (PEI).* London: National Society for Mentally Handicapped Children.

GUNZBURG, H. C. (1970) The hospital as a normalizing training environment. *J. ment. Subn.,* **XVI,** 71–83.

GUNZBURG, H. C. (1973) 39 steps leading towards normalized living practices in living units for the mentally handicapped. *Brit. J. ment. Subn.,* **XIX,** 91–9.

GUNZBURG, H. C. (1974a) The monitoring of rehabilitation programmes. In GUNZBURG, H. C. (ed.) *Experiments in the Rehabilitation of the Mentally Handicapped.* London: Butterworths.

GUNZBURG, H. C. (1974b) *The P-A-C-Manual* (3rd edn). London: National Society for Mentally Handicapped Children.

GUNZBURG, H. C. and GUNZBURG, A. L. (1973) *Mental Handicap and Physical Environment.* London: Baillière Tindall.

HAMILTON, J. and ALLEN, P. (1967) Ward programming for severely retarded institutionalized retardates. *Ment. Retard.,* **5,** 22–4.

HARRIS, L. A. and KINNEY, C. (1947) A program for reducing maladjustments in an institution for the mentally deficient. *Amer. J. ment. Defic.,* **52,** 78–84.

HARRISON, S. (1959) Integration of developmental language activities with an educational program for mentally retarded children. *Amer. J. ment. Defic.,* **63,** 967–70.

HEADRICK, N. W. (1963) Operant conditioning in mental deficiency. *Amer. J. ment. Defic.,* **67,** 924–9.

HEBER, R. (1968) The role of environmental variations in etiology of cultural-familial mental retardation. In RICHARDS, B. (ed.) *Proc. 1st Congr. Internat. Assoc. Scient. Stud. Ment. Defic.* Reigate: Michael Jackson.

HEBER, R. (1971) An experiment in prevention of cultural-familial mental retardation. In PRIMROSE, D. A. (ed.) *Proc. 2nd Congr. Internat. Assoc.*

Scient. Stud. Ment. Defic. Warsaw: Ars Polona; Amsterdam: Swets & Zeitlinger.

HEBER, R. and DEVER, R. (1970) Research on education and habilitation of the mentally retarded. In HAYWOOD, H. C. (ed.) *Social-Cultural Aspects of Mental Retardation.* New York: Appleton-Century-Crofts.

HERMELIN, B. and O'CONNOR, N. (1960) Reading ability of severely subnormal children. *J. ment. Defic. Res.,* 4, 144–7.

HINDLEY, C. H. (1960) The Griffiths Scale of Infant Development scores and predictions from 3 to 18 months. *J. Child Psychol. Psychiat.,* 1, 99–112.

HOLLIS, J. H. and GORTON, C. E. (1967) Training severely and profoundly developmentally retarded children. *Ment. Retard.,* 5, 20–4.

HORNE, B. M. and JUSTISS, W. A. (1967) Clinical indicators of brain damage in mentally retarded children. *J. clin. Psychol.,* 23, 464–5.

HUDSON, M. (1955) Some theoretical aspects to curriculum building for the severely retarded child. *Amer. J. ment. Defic.,* 60, 270–7.

HUNDZIAK, M., MAURER, R. and WATSON, L. S. (1965) Operant conditioning in toilet training for severely mentally retarded boys. *Amer. J. ment. Defic.,* 70, 120–4.

HUNGERFORD, R. H. (1948) *Enrichment through Difference: Occupational Education.* New York.

HUNT, N. (1967) *The World of Nigel Hunt (The Diary of a Mongoloid Youth).* New York: Garrett Publications.

ILLINGWORTH, R. S. (1961) The predictive value of developmental tests in the first year with special reference to the diagnosis of mental subnormality. *J. Child Psychol. Psychiat.,* 2, 210–15.

ILLINGWORTH, R. S. (1966) *The Development of the Infant and Young Child.* Edinburgh and London: Livingstone.

ILLINGWORTH, R. S. and BIRCH, L. B. (1959) The diagnosis of mental retardation in infancy. *Arch. dis. Child,* 34, 269–73.

INGRAM, C. P. (1953) *Education of the Slow-Learning Child.* New York: The Ronald Press.

IRWIN, B. (1959) Oral language for slow-learning children. *Amer. J. ment. Defic.,* 64, 32–40.

JASTAK, J. (1949) A rigorous criterion of feeblemindedness. *J. abn. soc. Psychol.,* 44, 367–78.

JASTAK, J. (1952) Psychological tests, intelligence and feeblemindedness. *J. clin. Psychol.,* 8, 107–12.

JEFFREE, D. M. (1971) A language teaching programme for a mongol child. *Forward Trends,* 15, 33–8.

JEFFREE, D. M. and CASHDAN, A. (1971) Severely subnormal children and their parents: an experiment in language improvement. *Brit. J. clin. Psychol.,* 41, 184–93.

JOHNSON, G. O. (1958) The education of mentally handicapped children.

In CRUICKSHANK, W. M. and JOHNSON, G. O. (eds.) *Education of Exceptional Children and Youth*. Englewood Cliffs, NJ: Prentice-Hall.

KEATING, L. E. (1962) A pilot experiment in remedial reading at the Hospital School. *Brit. J. educ. Psychol.*, **32**, 62–5.

KEITH, K. D. and LANGE, B. M. (1974) Maintenance of behavior change in an institution-wide training program. *Ment. Retard.*, **12**, 34–7.

KELLMER PRINGLE, M. L. (1951) Social maturity and social competence. *Educ. Res.*, **3**, part 1, 113–28; part 2, 183–95.

KELLMER PRINGLE, M. L. (1960) Social learning and its measurement. *Educ. Res.*, **11**, 194–206.

KELLMER PRINGLE, M. L. (1964) *The Emotional and Social Adjustment of Blind Children*. Occasional Publ. No. 10. London: National Foundation for Educational Research.

KELLMER PRINGLE, M. L. (1966) *Social Learning and its Measurement*. London: Longmans.

KERN, W. H. and PFAEFFLE, H. (1962) A comparison of social adjustment of mentally retarded children in various educational settings. *Amer. J. ment. Defic.*, **67**, 407–13.

KIERNAN, C. C. (1974) Application of behaviour modification in the ward situation. In GUNZBURG, H. C. (ed.) *Experiments in the Rehabilitation of the Mentally Handicapped*. London: Butterworths.

KING, R. and RAYNES, N. (1968) An operational measure of inmate management in residential institutions. *Soc. Sci. Med.*, **2**, 41–53.

KIRK, S. A. (1934) The effects of remedial reading on the education progress and personality adjustment of high-grade mentally deficient problem children: ten case studies. *J. juv. Res.*, **18**, 140–62.

KIRK, S. A. (1940) *Teaching Reading to Slow Learning Children*. Boston: Houghton Mifflin.

KIRK, S. A. (1958) *Early Education of the Mentally Retarded*. Urbana: Univ. of Illinois Press.

KIRK, S. A. (1962) *Educating Exceptional Children*. Boston: Houghton Mifflin.

KIRK, S. A. (1964) Research in education. In STEVENS, H. A. and HEBER, R. (eds.) *Mental Retardation: A Review of Research*. Chicago and London: Univ. of Chicago Press.

KIRK, S. A. and BATEMAN, B. (1962) Diagnosis and remediation of learning disabilities. *J. except. Child.*, **29**, 73–8.

KIRK, S. A. and JOHNSON, G. O. (1951) *Educating the Retarded Child*. Boston: Houghton Mifflin.

KIRK, S. A. and MCCARTHY, J. T. (1961) The Illinois Test of Psycholinguistic Abilities: an approach to differential diagnosis. *Amer. J. ment. Defic.*, **66**, 399–412.

KIRK, S. A., KARNES, M. B. and KIRK, W. D. (1955) *You and Your Retarded Child*. New York: Macmillan.

KIRK, S. A., MCCARTHY, J. J. and KIRK, W. D. (1968) *Examiners' Manual, Illinois Test of Psycholinguistic Abilities* (rev. edn). Urbana: Univ. of Illinois Press.

KLABER, M. M. (1969) The retarded and institutions for the retarded – a preliminary research report. In SARASON, S. B. and DORIS, J. (eds.) *Psychological Problems in Mental Deficiency* (4th edn). New York: Harper & Row.

KLABER, M. M., BUTTERFIELD, E. C. and GOULD, L. J. (1969) Responsiveness to social reinforcement among institutionalized retarded children. *Amer. J. ment. Defic.*, **73**, 890–5.

KOLBURNE, L. L. (1965) *Effective Education for the Mentally Retarded Child.* New York: Vantage Press.

KRATTEN, F. E. and THORNE, G. D. (1957) Sex education for retarded children. *Amer. J. ment. Defic.*, **62**, 44–8.

KUSHLICK, A. (1966) A community service for the mentally subnormal. *Soc. Psychiat.*, **1**, 73–82.

LABON, D. (1967) But does i.t.a. help slow learners? *Spec. Educ.*, **56**, 17–20.

LAWRENCE, W. and KARTYE, J. (1971) Extinction of social competency skills in severely and profoundly retarded females. *Amer. J. ment. Defic.*, **75**, 630–4.

LECK, I., GORDON, W. L. and MCKEOWN, T. (1967) Medical and social needs of patients in hospitals for the mentally subnormal. *Brit. J. prev. soc. Med.*, **21**, 115–21.

LELAND, H., NIHIRA, K., FOSTER, R. and SHELLHAAS, M. (1967) The demonstration and measurement of adaptive behaviour. In RICHARDS, B. (ed.) *Proc. 1st Congr. Internat. Assoc. Scient. Stud. Ment. Defic.* Reigate: Michael Jackson.

LENNEBERG, E. H., NICHOLS, I. A. and ROSENBERGER, E. F. (1968) Primitive stages of language development in mongolism. *Proc. Assoc. Res. nerv. ment. Dis.*, 119–37.

LINDE, T. (1962) Techniques for establishing motivation through operant conditioning. *Amer. J. ment. Defic.*, **67**, 437–40.

LOCKING, J. R. (1966) An arithmetic programme for the subnormal pupil. In GUNZBURG, H. C. (ed.) *The Application of Research to the Education and Training of the Severely Subnormal Child.* J. ment. Subn. Monogr.

LORENZO, E. G. C. (1967) Investigation in spontaneous development and development in a group of subjects studied from birth. In RICHARDS, B. (ed.) *Proc. 1st Congr. Internat. Assoc. Scient. Stud. Ment. Defic.* Reigate: Michael Jackson.

LORENZO, E. G. C. (1970) The importance of early stimulation. In PRIMROSE, D. A. (ed.) *Proc. 2nd Congr. Internat. Assoc. Scient. Stud. Ment. Defic.* Warsaw: Ars Polona; Amsterdam: Swets & Zeitlinger.

LOTTER, V. (1966) Epidemiology of autistic conditions in young children. *Soc. Psychiat.*, **1**, 124–37.

LUNZER, E. A. (1966) *The Manchester Scales of Social Adaptation.* London: National Foundation for Educational Research.

LURIA, A. R. (1963) *The Mentally Retarded Child.* New York: Pergamon Press.

LYLE, J. G. (1959) The effect of an institution environment upon the verbal development of imbecile children. Part I: Verbal intelligence. *J. ment. Defic. Res.,* **3,** 122–8.

LYLE, J. G. (1960) The effect of an institution environment upon the verbal development of imbecile children. Parts II and III. *J. ment. Defic. Res.,* **4,** 1–23.

MACANDREW, C. and EDGERTON, R. B. (1964) The everyday life of the institutionalized 'idiot'. *Human Org.,* **23,** 312–8.

MCCARTHY, J. J. (1964) Research on the linguistic problems of the mentally retarded. *Ment. Retard. Abstrs.,* **1,** 3–27.

MCCARTHY, J. J. and KIRK, S. A. (1961) *Illinois Test of Psycholinguistic Abilities: Experimental Edition.* Urbana: Univ. of Illinois Press.

MCCARTHY, J. J. and SCHEERENBERGER, R. G. (1966) A decade of research on the education of the mentally retarded. *Ment. Retard. Abstrs.,* **3,** 481–501.

MCCOULL, G. (1971) *Newcastle upon Tyne Regional Aetiological Survey (Mental Retardation).* Regional Hosp. Bd. Unpubl. Rep.

MACKAY, D. N. (1974) The alleged effects of hospital care on the mentally subnormal. In GUNZBURG, H. C. (ed.) *Experiments in the Rehabilitation of the Mentally Handicapped.* London: Butterworths.

MCKEOWN, T. and TERUEL, J. R. (1970) An assessment of the feasibility of discharge of patients in hospitals for the subnormal. *Brit. J. prev. soc. Med.,* **24,** 116–19.

MACKIE, R., DUNN, L. M. and CAIN, L. F. (1960) *Professional Preparation for Teachers of Exceptional Children: An Overview.* Washington, DC: Government Printing Office.

MARSHALL, A. (1967) *The Abilities and Attainments of Children Leaving Junior Training Centres.* London: National Association for Mental Health.

MATTHEWS, C. G. (1964) The social competence of the subnormal school leaver. *J. ment. Subn.,* **10,** 83–8.

MECHAM, M. J. (1958) *Verbal Language Development Scale.* Minneapolis: Amer. Guidance Service Inc.

MECHAM, M. J. (1963) Developmental schedules of oral-aural language as an aid to the teacher of the mentally retarded. *Ment. Retard.,* 359–69.

MECHAM, M. J., BERKO, M. J., GIDEN, F. and PALMER, M. F. (1966) *Communication Training in Childhood Brain Damage.* Springfield, Ill.: Charles C. Thomas.

MEIN, R. (1968) Changes in intelligence test scores in cerebral palsied patients under treatment. In RICHARDS, B. W. (ed.) *Proc. 1st Congr. Internat. Assoc. Scient. Stud. Ment. Defic.* Reigate: Michael Jackson.

MEIN, R. and O'CONNOR, N. (1960) A study of the oral vocabularies of severely subnormal patients. *J. ment. Defic. Res.*, **4**, 130–43.

MEYEN, E. L. and RETISH, O. M. (1971) Sex education for the mentally retarded: influencing teachers' attitudes. *Ment. Retard.*, **9**, 46–9.

MIDDLETON, T. H. (1956) The mental defective on licence: a survey of 20 years in Birmingham. *J. Midland ment. Defic. Soc.*, **2**, 41–9.

MILLER, A. (1967) Symbol accentuation: outgrowth of theory and experiment. In RICHARDS, B. (ed.) *Proc. 1st Congr. Internat. Assoc. Scient. Stud. Ment. Defic.* Reigate: Michael Jackson.

MILNER, K. O. (1949) Delinquent types of mentally defective persons. *J. ment. Sci.*, **95**, 842–59.

MINGE, R. and BALL, T. S. (1967) Teaching of self-help skills to profoundly retarded residents. *Amer. J. ment. Defic.*, **71**, 864–8.

MITCHELL, A. C. (1955) A study of the social competence of a group of institutionalized retarded children. *Amer. J. ment. Defic.*, **60**, 354–61.

MITCHELL, A. C. and SMERIGLIO, V. (1970) Growth in social competence in institutionalized mentally retarded children. *Amer. J. ment. Defic.*, **74**, 666–73.

MITTLER, P. (1968) *Aspects of Autism.* London: British Psychological Society.

MITTLER, P., GILLIES, S. and JUKES, E. (1966) Prognosis in psychotic children: report of a follow-up study. *J. ment. Defic. Res.*, **10**, 73–83.

MORLEY, K. G. (1973) Industrial training – problems and implications. In CLARKE, A. D. B. and CLARKE, A. M. (eds.) *Mental Retardation and Behavioural Research.* London: Churchill Livingstone.

MORLEY, K. G. and APPELL, J. (1974) An appraisal of the social progress of 59 mentally handicapped persons in community centres. In GUNZBURG, H. C. (ed.) *Experiments in the Rehabilitation of the Mentally Subnormal.* London: Butterworths.

MORRIS, P. (1969) *'Put Away': A Sociological Study of Institutions for the Mentally Retarded.* London: Routledge & Kegan Paul.

MUELLER, M. W. and SMITH, J. O. (1964) The stability of language age modifications over time. *Amer. J. ment. Defic.*, **68**, 537–9.

MULLEN, F. and ITKIN, W. (1961) *Achievement and Adjustment of Educable Mentally Handicapped Children in Special Classes and in Regular Grades.* Chicago: Board of Education.

MUNDY, L. (1957) Environmental influence on intellectual function as measured by intelligence tests. *Brit. J. med. Psychol.*, **13**, 194–201.

NAWAS, M. M. and BRAUN, S. H. (1970) An overview of behaviour modification with the severely and profoundly retarded. *Ment. Retard.*, **8**, 4–11.

NEALE, M. D. (1966a) *The Neale Analysis of Reading Ability.* London: Macmillan.

NEALE, M. D. (1966b) Perceptual development of severely retarded children through motor experience. In GUNZBURG, H. C. (ed.) *The Application of Research to the Education and Training of the Severely Subnormal Child.* J. ment. Subn. Monogr.

NEALE, M. D. and CAMPBELL, W. J. (1963) *Education for the Intellectually Limited Child and Adolescent.* Sydney: Ian Novak.

NICHOLLS, R. H. (1963) Programming Piaget in practice. *Teaching Arithmetic,* 1(3).

NICKELL, V. (1951) *Educating the Mentally Handicapped in the Secondary School.* Illinois Secondary School Curriculum Program, Bull. No. 12. Springfield: Dept of Public Instruct.

NIHIRA, K., FOSTER, R., SHELLHAAS, M. and LELAND, H. (1969) *Adaptive Behavior Scales.* Washington, DC: American Association on Mental Deficiency.

NIRJE, B. (1969) The normalization principle and its human management implications. In KUGEL, R. B. and WOLFENSBERGER, W. P. (eds.) *Changing Patterns in Residential Services for the Mentally Retarded.* Washington, DC: President's Committee on Mental Retardation.

NIRJE, B. (1970) The normalization principle – implications and comments. *J. ment. Subn.,* XVI, 62–70.

NORRIS, D. (1968) *Some Observations on the School Life of Severely Retarded Children.* J. ment. Subn. Monogr.

O'CONNOR, N. and HERMELIN, B. (1961) Like and cross-modality recognition in subnormal children. *Quart. J. exp. Psychol.,* 13, 48–52.

O'CONNOR, N. and HERMELIN, B. (1963) *Speech and Thought in Severe Subnormality.* London: Pergamon.

O'CONNOR, N. and TIZARD, J. (1956) *The Social Problems of Mental Deficiency.* London: Pergamon.

O'GORMAN, G. (1970) *The Nature of Childhood Autism.* London: Butterworths.

O'HARA, J. (1968) The role of the nurse in subnormality: a reappraisal. *J. ment. Subn.,* XIV, 19–24.

OLIVER, B., SIMON, G. B. and CLARK, B. (1973) Group discussions with adolescent female patients in a mental subnormality hospital. In GUNZBURG, H. C. (ed.) *Advances in the Care of the Mentally Handicapped.* London: Baillière Tindall.

OLSON, J. L. (1961) Deaf and sensory aphasic children. *Except. Child.,* 27, 422–4.

OLSON, J. L., HAHN, H. R. and HERMANN, A. L. (1965) Psycholinguistic curriculum. *Ment. Retard.,* 3, 14–19.

ORLANDO, R. and BIJOU, S. W. (1960) Single and multiple schedules of reinforcement in developmentally retarded children. *J. exp. Anal. Behav.,* 3, 339–48.

OSGOOD, C. E. (1957) *Contemporary Approaches to Cognition, a Behavioristic Analysis.* Cambridge, Mass.: Harvard Univ. Press.

PAPANIA, N. A. (1954) Qualitative analysis of vocabulary responses of institutionalized mentally retarded children. *J. clin. Psychol.*, **10**, 361–5.

PECK, J. R. and SEXTON, L. C. (1960) *A Comparative Investigation of the Learning and Social Adjustment of Trainable Children in Public School Facilities, Segregated Community Centers and State Residential Centers.* Austin: Univ. of Texas.

PITT, D. (1968) The multiply-handicapped retarded child. In RICHARDS, B. (ed.) *Proc. 1st Congr. Internat. Assoc. Scient. Stud. Ment. Defic.*, 751–3. Reigate: Michael Jackson.

POPE, L. and HAKLAY, A. (1970) Reading disability. In WORTIS, J. (ed.) *Mental Retardation.* New York: Grune & Stratton.

President's Panel on Mental Retardation (1962) *A Proposed Program for National Action to Combat Mental Retardation.* Washington, DC: Government Printing Office.

QUAY, L. C. (1963) Academic skills. In ELLIS, N. R. (ed.) *Handbook of Mental Deficiency.* New York: McGraw-Hill.

RAYNES, N. and KING, R. (1968) The measurement of child management in residential institutions for the retarded. In RICHARDS, B. (ed.) *Proc. 1st Congr. Internat. Assoc. Scient. Stud. Ment. Defic.* Reigate: Michael Jackson.

REED, M. (1970) Deaf and partially hearing children. In MITTLER, P. (ed.) *The Psychological Assessment of Mental and Physical Handicaps.* London: Methuen.

RENFREW, C. and MURPHY, K. (1964) *The Child Who Does Not Talk.* London: Heinemann.

REYNELL, J. (1969) *Reynell Developmental Language Scales.* London: National Foundation of Educational Research.

RICHARDS, H. E. and STONE, D. R. (1970) The learning and transference of the Piagetian concept of conservation. *Ment. Retard.*, **8**, 34–7.

RICHARDSON, S. O. (1967) Language training for mentally retarded children. In SCHIEFELBUSCH, R. L. *et al.* (eds.) *Language and Mental Retardation.* New York: Holt, Rinehart & Winston.

ROOS, P. (1970) Normalization, de-humanization and conditioning – conflict or harmony. *Ment. Retard.*, **8**, 12–14.

ROOS, P. and OLIVER, M. (1969) Evaluation of operant conditioning with institutionalized retarded children. *Amer. J. ment. Defic.*, **74**, 325–30.

ROSENBERG, S. (1970) Problems of language development in the retarded. In HAYWOOD, H. C. (ed.) *Social-Cultural Aspects of Mental Retardation.* New York: Appleton-Century-Crofts.

ROSENZWEIG, L. (1959) How far have we come? *Amer. J. ment. Defic.*, **64**, 12–18.

ROSS, D. (1970) Incidental learning of number concepts in small group games. *Amer. J. ment. Defic.*, **74**, 718–25.

ROSWELL-HARRIS, D. (1958) *Some Aspects of Cognitive and Personality Test*

Changes in a Group of One Hundred Feebleminded Young Men. Unpubl. MA thesis, Univ. of Reading.

RUDOLF, G. de M. (1949) Retesting of the IQ and the social age. *J. ment. Sci.*, **95**, 696–702.

RYCHLAK, J. R. and WADE, I. (1963) American usage of the terms 'Educable' vs 'Trainable' mental retardates. *J. ment. Subn.*, **IX**, 70–5.

SAENGER, G. (1957) *The Adjustment of Severely Retarded Adults in the Community.* Albany: New York State Interdepartmental Health Resources Board.

SAMPSON, O. C. (1962) Speech development and improvement in the severely subnormal child. *J. ment. Subn.*, **VIII**, 70–7.

SAMPSON, O. C. (1964) The conversational style of a group of severely subnormal children. *J. ment. Subn.*, **X**, 89–100.

SAMPSON, O. C. (1966) Helping the severely subnormal child to develop language. In GUNZBURG, H. C. (ed.) *The Application of Research to the Education and Training of the Severely Subnormal.* J. ment. Subn. Monogr.

SANGREN, P. V. (1927) *The Measurement of Achievement in Silent Reading.* Kalamazoo: West State Teachers' College.

SARASON, S. B. and DORIS, J. (1969) *Psychological Problems in Mental Deficiency* (4th edn). New York: Harper & Row.

SCANLAN, J. B., LEBERFELD, D. T. and FREIBRUN, R. (1963) Language training in the treatment of the autistic child functioning on a retarded level. *Ment. Retard.*, **1**, 305–10.

SCHIEFELBUSCH, R. L., COPELAND, R. H. and SMITH, J. D. (1967) *Language and Mental Retardation.* London: Holt, Rinehart & Winston.

SCHIPHORST, B. (1968) Social education of the subnormal. *J. spec. Educ.*, **57**, 26–9.

SCHLANGER, B. B. (1954) Environmental influences on the verbal output of mentally retarded children. *J. speech hear. Dis.*, **19**, 339–43.

SCHMIDT, B. G. (1946) Changes in personal, social and intellectual behaviour of children originally classified as feebleminded. *Psychol. Monogr.*, **60**, 1–144.

Scott Report, The (1962) *The Training of Staff of Training Centres for the Mentally Subnormal.* London: HMSO.

SHAW, H. J., MATTHEWS, C. G. and KLOVE, H. (1966) The equivalence of WISC and PPVT IQs. *Amer. J. ment. Defic.*, **70**, 601–6.

SHERIDAN, M. (1960) *The Developmental Progress of Infants and Young Children.* London: HMSO.

SIEVERS, D. J. (1959) A study to compare the performance of brain-injured and non-brain-injured mentally retarded children on the differential language facility test. *Amer. J. ment. Defic.*, **63**, 839–47.

SIEVERS, D. J. and ESSA, S. H. (1961) Language development in institutionalized and community mentally retarded children. *Amer. J. ment. Defic.*, **66**, 413–20.

SIEVERS, D. J. and ROSENBERG, C. M. (1960) The differential language facility test and electroencephalograms of brain-injured mentally retarded children. *Amer. J. ment. Defic.*, **65**, 46–50.

SILVERSTEIN, A. B., AUGER, R. and KRUDIS, B. R. (1964) The meaning of indefinite number terms for mentally retarded children. *Amer. J. ment. Defic.*, **69**, 419–24.

SKEELS, H. M. (1966) Adult status of children with contrasting early life experiences. *Monogr. Soc. Res. Child Developm.*, **31**, (105).

SKEELS, H. M. and DYE, H. B. (1939) A study of the effects of differential stimulation on retarded children. *Proc. Amer. Assoc. ment. Defic.*, **44**, 114–36.

SKEELS, H. M. and HARMS, I. (1948) Children with inferior social histories, their mental development in adoptive homes. *J. Genet. Psychol.*, **72**, 283–94.

SKINNER, B. F. (1965) The technology of teaching. *Proc. Roy. Soc.*, **162**, 427–43.

SKODAK, M. (1968) Adult status of individuals who experienced early intervention. In RICHARDS, B. (ed.) *Proc. 1st Congr. Internat. Assoc. Scient. Stud. Ment. Defic.* Reigate: Michael Jackson.

SKODAK, M. and SKEELS, H. M. (1949) A final follow-up study of one hundred adopted children. *J. genet. Psychol.*, **75**, 85–125.

SMITH, H. W. (1957) A sheltered employment project in an institution for mental defectives. *Amer. J. ment. Defic.*, **61**, 665–71.

SMITH, J. O. (1962) Group language development for educable mental retardates. *Except. Child.*, **29**, 95–101.

SMITH, M. (1966) Right backward pupils and i.t.a. *Spec. Educ.*, **55**, 19–22.

SPRADLIN, J. E. (1963a) Language and communication in mental defectives. In ELLIS, N. R. (ed.) *Handbook of Mental Deficiency.* New York: McGraw-Hill.

SPRADLIN, J. E. (1963b) Assessment of speech and language of retarded children: the Parsons Language Sample. *J. speech hear. Dis. Monogr. Suppl.*, **10**, 8–31.

SPRADLIN, J. E. (1968) Environmental factors and the language development of retarded children. In ROSENBERG, S. (ed.) *Developments in Applied Psycholinguistic Research.* New York: Macmillan.

STAHLECKER, L. V. (1967) *Occupational Information for the Mentally Retarded.* Springfield, Ill.: Charles C. Thomas.

STANLEY, R. J. and GUNZBURG, H. C. (1957) A survey of residential licences from a mental deficiency hospital. *Internat. J. soc. Psychiat.*, **2**, 207–13.

STANTON, J. R. and CASSIDY, V. N. (1964) Effectiveness of special classes for educable mentally retarded. *Ment. Retard.*, **2**, 8–13.

STERNLICHT, M. and SIEGEL, L. (1968) Institutional residence and intellectual functioning. *J. ment. Defic. Res.*, **12**, 119–27.

STEVENS, G. D. (1958) An analysis of the objectives for the education of children with retarded mental development. *Amer. J. ment. Defic.*, **63**, 225–35.

STEVENS, M. (1968) *Observing Children who are Severely Subnormal.* London: Edward Arnold.

STEVENS, M. (1971) *The Educational Needs of Severely Subnormal Children.* London: Edward Arnold.

STOLUROW, L. M. (1963) Programmed instruction for the mentally retarded. *Rev. educ. Res.*, **33**, 126–36.

STOTT, D. H. (1962a) Abnormal mothering as a cause of mental subnormality. I, A critique of some classic studies of maternal deprivation in the light of possible congenital factors. *J. Child Psychol. Psychiat.*, **3**, 79–91.

STOTT, D. H. (1962b) Abnormal mothering as a cause of mental subnormality. II, Case studies and conclusions. *J. Child Psychol. Psychiat.*, **3**, 133–48.

STRAUSS, A. A. and KEPHART, N. C. (1955) *Psychopathology and Education of the Brain-Injured Child.* New York: Grune & Stratton.

STRAUSS, A. A. and LEHTINEN, L. E. (1967) *Psychopathology and Education of the Brain-injured Child.* New York: Grune & Stratton.

TANSLEY, A. E. and GULLIFORD, R. (1960) *The Education of Slow Learning Children.* London: Routledge & Kegan Paul.

THOMPSON, G. E. (1962) What arithmetic shall we teach our educationally subnormal children? *Spec. Educ.*, **LI**(3).

THORMALEN, P. W. (1965) *A Study of On-The-Ward Training of Trainable Mentally Retarded Children in a State Institution.* California Mental Health Research Monogr. No. 4. State of California, Dept. of Mental Hygiene.

THRESHER, J. M. (1962) A problem for educators: arithmetical concept formation in the mentally retarded child. *Amer. J. ment. Defic.*, **66**, 766–73.

THURSTONE, T. G. (1960) *An Evaluation of Educating Mentally Handicapped Children in Special Classes and in Regular Classes.* Grambling, La.: Grambling College.

TIZARD, J. (1950) The abilities of adolescent and adult high-grade male defectives. *J. ment. Sci.*, **96**, 889–907.

TIZARD, J. (1953) The effects of different types of supervision on the behavior of mental defectives in a sheltered workshop. *Amer. J. ment. Defic.*, **58**, 143–61.

TIZARD, J. (1962) The residential care of mentally handicapped children. In RICHARDS, B. W. (ed.) *Proc. Lond. Conf. Scient. Stud. Ment. Defic.*, 659–66. Dagenham: May & Baker.

TIZARD, J. (1964) *Community Services for the Mentally Handicapped.* London: Oxford Univ. Press.

TIZARD, J. (1968) *The Role of Social Institutions in the Causation, Prevention and Alleviation of Mental Retardation.* Peabody NIMH Conference on Socio-cultural Aspects of Mental Retardation.

TIZARD, J. (1970) The role of social institutions in the causation, prevention and alleviation of mental retardation. In HAYWOOD, H. C. (ed.) *Social-Cultural Aspects of Mental Retardation.* New York: Appleton-Century-Crofts.

TIZARD, J. and GRAD, J. C. (1961) *The Mentally Handicapped and their Families*. London: Oxford Univ. Press.

TIZARD, J. and O'CONNOR, N. (1952) The occupational adaptation of high-grade mental defectives. *Lancet*, ii, 620–3.

TONG, J. E. and MACKAY, G. W. (1959) A statistical follow-up of mental defectives of dangerous or violent propensities. *Brit. J. Delinq.*, 9, 276–84.

TREFFRY, D., MARTIN, G., SAMELS, J. and WATSON, C. (1970) Operant conditioning of grooming behaviour of severely retarded girls. *Ment. Retard.*, 8, 29–33.

TUBBS, V. K. (1966) Types of linguistic disability in psychotic children. *J. ment. Defic. Res.*, 10, 230–40.

VAIL, D. J. (1967) *Dehumanization and the Institutional Career*. Springfield, Ill.: Charles C. Thomas.

WALLIN, J. E. W. (1955) *Education of Mentally Handicapped Children*. New York: Harper & Row.

WALLIN, J. E. W. (1956) *Mental Deficiency*. Brandon, Vt: J. clin. Psychol.

WALTON, D. and BEGG, T. L. (1957) Cognitive changes in low-grade defectives. *Amer. J. ment. Defic.*, 62, 96–102.

WARNER, W. L., HAVIGHURST, R. J. and LOEB, M. B. (1946) *Who Shall Be Educated?* London: Routledge & Kegan Paul.

WATSON, L. S. (1968) Application of behaviour-shaping devices to training severely and profoundly mentally retarded children in an institutional setting. *Ment. Retard.*, 6, 21–3.

WATTS, A. F. (1944) *The Language and Mental Development of Children*. London: Harrap.

WEBB, C. E. and KINDE, S. (1967) Speech, language and hearing of the mentally retarded. In BAUMEISTER, A. A. (ed.) *Mental Retardation*. London: Univ. of London Press.

WEINBERG, B. and ZLATIN, M. (1970) Speaking fundamental frequency characteristics of five and six year old children with mongolism. *J. speech hear. Res.*, 13, 418–25.

WHALEN, C. K. and HENKER, B. A. (1969) Creating therapeutic pyramids using mentally retarded patients. *Amer. J. ment. Defic.*, 74, 331–7.

WHALEN, C. K. and HENKER, B. A. (1971) Pyramid therapy in a hospital for the retarded: methods, program evaluation and long-term effects. *Amer. J. ment. Defic.*, 75, 414–34.

WHELAN, E. (1973) Developing work skills: a systematic approach. In MITTLER, P. (ed.) *Assessment for Learning in the Mentally Handicapped*. Edinburgh: Churchill Livingstone; Baltimore, Md: Williams & Wilkins.

WHELAN, R. J. and HARING, N. (1966) Modification and maintenance of behaviour through systematic application of consequences. *Except. Child.*, 32, 281–9.

WHITCOMB, M. A. (1945) A comparison of social and intellectual levels of 100 high-grade adult mental defectives. *Amer. J. ment. Defic.*, 50, 257–62.

WHITE, W. D. and WOLFENSBERGER, W. P. (1969) The evolution of dehumanization in our institutions. *Ment. Retard.*, **VII**, 5–9.

WILDENSKOV, H. O. T. (1957) A symposium: the social adjustment of the mentally deficient – family care in Denmark – III. *Amer. J. ment. Defic.*, **62**, 304–9.

WILLIAMS, C. E. (1966) A blind idiot who became a normal blind adolescent. *Developm. med. Child. neurol.*, **8**, 166–9.

WILLIAMS, H. M. and WALLIN, J. E. W. (1959) *Education of the Severely Retarded Child.* Washington, DC: Government Printing Office.

WILLIAMS, P. (1967) Industrial training and remunerative employment of the profoundly retarded. *J. ment. Subn.*, **XIII**, 14–23.

WISEMAN, D. E. (1965) A classroom procedure for identifying and remediating language problems. *Ment. Retard.*, **3**, 20–4.

WOLFSENBERGER, W. P. (1972) *The Principle of Normalization in Human Services.* Toronto: Leonard Crainford.

WOLFSENBERGER, W. P., MEIN, R. and O'CONNOR, N. (1963) A study of the oral vocabularies of severely subnormal patients: III core vocabulary, verbosity and repetitiousness. *J. ment. Defic. Res.*, **7**, 38–45.

WOODWARD, M. (1959) The behaviour of idiots interpreted by Piaget's theory of sensori-motor development. *Brit. J. educ. Psychol.*, **XXIX**, 60–71.

WOODWARD, M. (1961) Concepts of number in the mentally subnormal studied by Piaget's method. *J. Child. Psychol. Psychiat.*, **2**, 249–59.

WOODWARD, M. (1962a) The application of Piaget's theory to the training of the subnormal. *J. ment. Subn.*, **VIII**, 17–25.

WOODWARD, M. (1962b) Concepts of space in the mentally subnormal studied by Piaget's method. *Brit. J. soc. clin. Psychol.*, **1**, 25–37.

WOODWARD, M. (1963a) Early experiences and behaviour disorders in severely subnormal children. *Brit. J. soc. clin. Psychol.*, **2**, 174–84.

WOODWARD, M. (1963b) The application of Piaget's theory to research in mental deficiency. In ELLIS, N. R. (ed.) *Handbook of Mental Deficiency.* New York: McGraw-Hill.

WOODWARD, M. (1970) The assessment of cognitive processes: Piaget's approach. In MITTLER, P. (ed.) *The Psychological Assessment of Mental and Physical Handicaps.* London: Methuen.

WOODWARD, M. and STERN, D. J. (1963) Developmental patterns of severely subnormal children. *Brit. J. educ. Psychol.*, **33**, 10–21.

YOUNGHUSBAND, E., BIRCHALL, D., DAVIE, R. and KELLMER PRINGLE, M. L. (1970) *Living with Handicap.* London: National Bureau for Cooperation in Child Care.

ZARFAS, D. E. (1970) Moving toward the normalcy principle in a large government-operated facility for the mentally retarded. *J. ment. Subn.*, **XVI**, 84–92.

22

H. C. Gunzburg

Psychotherapy

Introduction

It could be successfully argued that all activities with the mentally retarded which aim at improving his functioning are of a psychotherapeutic nature, if they do not directly depend on medication or deal mainly with physical aspects, such as in physiotherapy. It is indeed difficult not to call psychotherapy the conscious establishment of a relationship and the consistent application of knowledge of human nature for the purpose of attaining better adjustment to people and a better functioning within a person. It seems irrelevant whether psychotherapeutic work is carried out via special media, such as art and movement (recreational therapy), or weaving and woodwork (occupational therapy), or whether it is done by other people than trained psychotherapists, such as social workers (social casework), and clergymen (pastoral counselling), or even whether psychotherapy is effected indirectly by manipulating the human and physical milieu (environmental therapy). A great range of adjustment techniques could claim legitimately to provide psychotherapy and indeed this variety of approaches is required in overcoming the many difficulties presented by the different handicaps of the mentally subnormal. Excellent discussions of the whole range of various techniques are given by various authors (e.g. Beier, 1964; Robinson and Robinson, 1965; Bialer, 1967).

However, for the purpose of the following discussion the term psychotherapy with the mentally retarded will be defined somewhat narrowly and traditionally to refer to one specific type of approach, without denying that it requires the full support of other kinds of psychotherapy to be fully effective. Indeed, it is one of the most marked shortcomings of many 'psychotherapy' accounts, discussed in the following pages, that they have been carried out in isolation and that only a few therapists were aware of the need to consolidate and enhance the effectiveness of their work by utilizing other forms of support (Thorne, 1948; Maisner, 1950; May and May, 1959; Gunzburg, 1970).

This chapter will, therefore, emphasize particularly psychotherapeutic efforts with the mentally handicapped which are characterized

(a) by the systematic, regular and planned application of psychological techniques by a trained person;

(b) by a consistent effort to establish interpersonal relationships for the purpose of ameliorating personal and social problems;

(c) by an attempt to assess and measure objectively the effectiveness of the psychotherapeutic procedures.

Practically all published literature on this subject relates to the mentally subnormal in institutions. This is primarily due to the fact that the specialist in subnormality tends to be based in institutions and that it is the problem case who will be institutionalized, whilst the adjusted and amenable will be accommodated in the community as long as possible. However, the concentration of subnormal persons in institutions produces in its turn new problems due to institutionalization: the psychotherapists have to deal with many problems which are caused by the institutional residence and which are not those instrumental in necessitating admission to the institution in the first instance (Barton, 1961; Goffman, 1961).

The specific aspects which colour and determine psychotherapeutic approaches with the institutionalized person will be discussed under separate headings. Accessibility to psychotherapy, which employs mainly or even exclusively verbal contact, requires an intelligent grasp of the situation, but perhaps also some realization on the patient's part of the problem that needs to be solved. Another important aspect is the need to identify the particular problems which are responsible for the underfunctioning and underachieving which are so characteristic for the majority of institutionalized mental defectives. If the 'hospital' for the mentally defective is to fulfil a role which cannot effectively be carried out in the community, then intensive psychotherapy by specialized staff working in a therapeutic environment will be a primary task. This applies not only to the unstable, immature 'psychopathic' personality (Craft, 1965), but also extends to the less attention-drawing, inadequate mentally handicapped, whose potential is unfulfilled because of emotional difficulties which have not become overt. Indeed, it is important to remember that subnormality is not simply a problem of a cognitive deficit, but that one deals with a person (Earl, 1961), who more often than not is unable to protest against unfairness, even by such primitive means as aggression and running away. Masland, Sarason and Gladwin (1958) put this very clearly when they stated:

> To what extent a condition of subnormality predisposes the individual to an exacerbation of neurotic symptoms, or to what extent the subnormality is an effect of these conflicts, is impossible to say. What we feel could be said is that for any individual whose functioning is considered subnormal, we can assume the presence of longstanding neurotic conflicts, which, so to speak, have added insult and injury to whatever handicaps he may originally have had.

Similarly, Neham (1951) comments that 'the evidence resulting from the use of projective techniques with mental defectives points out that mental deficiency may be symptomatic of personality disorder rather than of intellectual inferiority'. It must, however, be pointed out that these ideas derive usually from the records obtained from mildly and borderline defectives and that the authors do not apply this thinking to the whole range of subnormality.

Malfunctioning personalities

The tendency to view all the difficulties experienced by the mentally handicapped as a direct consequence of his mental disability has made his personal problems appear less important. Indeed, it has been argued that 'a person of low intelligence is less likely to have mental conflict than a person of higher intelligence' (Morgan, 1950). Yet, Feldman (1946) reports the case of a young man with low intelligence (IQ 41 and 39) who 'revealed a surprising depth of feeling regarding his failures and inadequacies. He recounted his simple achievements in work and at home before entering service and asked several times, 'Why can't I do things like everybody else?" and "Why am I different?" '

Jolles (1947) found such severe emotional maladjustment in a group of thirty-four mentally deficient children that he concluded that,

> mental deficiency of the familial and undifferentiated types is, in many instances, a symptom of personality disorder, and it is unlikely that in such cases it represents a failure of the intellect to develop normally. It is quite probable that many mental defectives may be treated successfully by psychotherapeutic techniques.

Similar views have been voiced by other research workers (Ackerman and Menninger, 1936; Hackbusch and Klopfer, 1946; Sloan, 1947).

Little reliance can be placed on the findings of surveys relating to the incidence of neurosis and psychosis among the mentally handicapped. This is as much due to the different criteria employed by the psychiatrists as to the repercussions that different institutional regimes have on the functioning of the residents. Craft (1959) estimated that 7 per cent of his sample of 324 patients suffered from mental illnesses and 33 per cent showed personality disorders. O'Connor (1951), using psychometric criteria rather than clinical diagnosis, judged 12 per cent neurotic and 44 per cent as emotionally unstable in a sample of 104 consecutive admissions. A recent survey of 317 patients in an institution (Browne *et al.*, 1971) put 23 per cent of the sample into a category characterized by displaying psychotic features 'of some kind', and Williams (1971) found in a survey that 442 subnormals out of 752 patients exhibited psychiatric disorders. Though it is often thought that these conditions occur predominantly in the mildly and borderline retarded, it has been shown that the less able institutionalized mentally defective has similar symptoms (e.g. Menolascino, 1967, found psychiatric disturbances in 37 per cent of a sample of 95 institutionalized mongols).

There is little doubt that much of the subnormal's inadequate functioning can be ascribed to emotional disturbances which make it difficult, sometimes impossible, for him to make adequate use of his meagre mental capital.

Earl (1961) suggests that the question should never be, 'Is this person mentally defective' but 'Has this personality proved inadequate? If so, to what extent is the inadequacy organismal in origin, and to what extent environmental? What areas or aspects of personality are mainly involved? What is the most suitable treatment?'

Areas of malfunctioning and psychotherapy

In a discussion of group therapy, Slavson suggested that its real value for dull patients is the 'discharge of emotions through anger, rage, disgust and quarrelling' because their inability to express themselves verbally requires acting out of their feelings (Slavson, 1950). Therapists in institutions, whilst keeping in mind the cathartic effect of group experience, tend to express their aims more positively. Some want, for example, to 'create a ward atmosphere in which patients could make as adequate a social adjustment within the hospital as allowed by the intelligence . . . also desired was the reduction in the minds of patients of the importance of an extra-mural placement' (Stubblebine and Roadruck, 1956). This use of psychotherapy as a sedative is in some contrast to therapy aimed at better adjustment to an environment of a non-institutional character. In this latter case patients receive therapy to make them more capable of dealing with problems outside the institution, to correct and improve social and personality defects and to re-establish better interpersonal relations (Ringelheim and Polatsek, 1955; Astrachan, 1955).

Abel (1953) suggests a programme of gradual steps

> because the goal of treatment should be modest and simpler than the goal one usually, but not necessarily, anticipates in working with more intelligent individuals . . . If we set out at first with the purpose of changing total attitudes and many aspects of behaviour, we are likely to be defeated, but this does not mean that as one goal is achieved another one cannot be set and further work done.

Wilcox and Guthrie (1957) describe four stages in therapy to develop increased frustration tolerance and to make the defectives more socially competent: (1) to reduce the suspiciousness felt towards outsiders; (2) to release aggressions; (3) to encourage feelings of self-confidence and self-work; (4) to develop feelings of responsibility for their actions.

The general aim expressed by practically all therapists consists of alleviating 'emotional and behavioural abnormalities that are inexplicable on the basis of mental deficiency alone' (Fisher and Wolfson, 1953). Yet it appears desirable that a statement of aims should be specific and provide guidance for therapeutic work.

Such a programme was published in 1947 by Frederick C. Thorne, then Medical Director of a mental deficiency hospital. He pointed out that

psychotherapy with defectives involved: (a) accepting the mental defective as being a worthy individual in spite of his defects, (b) permitting expression and clarification of emotional reactions, (c) patiently teaching him methods for resisting frustration and achieving emotional control, (d) outlining standards for acceptable conduct within the ability of each child, (e) building up self-confidence and respect by providing experience of success and (f) training the child to seek help intelligently through counselling when faced with insurmountable problems. (Thorne, 1948)

The same author also pointed out (1950) that

the constitutionally inadequate are characteristically dependent upon others because of inability to compete well and become involved in circular reactions of frustration, secondary unhealthy personality reactions, social reflection and dependency. Lacking the personality resources to solve major problems alone, it may require active directive methods of counselling to supplement what the mental defective can do for himself.

Suitability of mentally handicapped people for psychotherapy

To a large extent psychotherapeutic work depends on verbal communication between the therapist and his patient. The mentally handicapped person's limitation in understanding and expressing himself have, therefore, frequently discouraged psychotherapists (Wiest, 1955).

Classical psychotherapy, for example, has not been frequently used in mental subnormality except in a few early cases (Clark, 1931; Chidester, 1934; Ackerman and Menninger, 1936; Chidester and Menninger, 1936; Stogdill, 1938). Indeed, the master himself, Sigmund Freud, had given directives relating to this field in an address to the College of Physicians in Vienna in 1904, when he stated: 'Those patients who do not possess a reasonable degree of education and a reliable character should be refused. The qualification which is the determining factor of fitness for psycho-analytic treatment is – whether the patient is educable'. Nevertheless, adaptations of the technique were developed and Ackerman and Menninger (1936) used psychoanalysis 'when a thorough study indicates a strong suspicion that early psychodynamic distortions have contributed in degree to the inhibition of intellectual development.' Chidester and Menninger (1936) admitted 'how extraordinary it is to get such information and fantasies from retarded children', and Mundy (1957a) found that 'analytical interpretation of a simple, but deep going kind . . . was understood more often than might have been expected at the apparent mental level in some cases.' Nevertheless, most therapists would probably agree with De Martino (1957) that 'in general it seems highly unlikely that much therapeutic progress could be achieved with retardates who have IQs below a borderline classification using only orthodox client centred procedures.'

The difficulties assumed to face the therapist when dealing with subnormal patients have been summarized by Sarason (1949). Such persons, he states, have been considered unable to delay or control emotional expression, to seek or to accept socially appropriate substitute activities in the face of frustrations and restrictions; to view objectively the behaviour of others; to adjust or to want to adjust to the needs of others; to realize the sources and consequences of their behaviour; to verbalize the interpersonal nature of their problems; to seek help or to understand the purpose of the individual offering it. It must, however, be pointed out that many of these opinions derive from prior concepts of mental deficiency.

Low intelligence test results alone are not indicative of a patient's inability to respond to therapeutic approaches. The test scores may have been lowered by emotional problems and, in any case, do not express the patient's ability for establishing some kind of a relationship with the therapist (Williams and Belinson, 1953). Slavson (1950) included dull patients in his group therapy and, though they participated only occasionally in group discussions, they proved to be capable of keeping up with the general trend of the talks and seemed to derive considerable benefit from them. It was found that in order to formulate and verbalize the problems and to have some understanding of interpretation 'the intelligence level need not be very high' (Slavson, 1950). Glassman (1943) and Cooley (1945), comparing the treatment results of dull children with those of bright children, came to the conclusion that therapy with those of lower mentality was at least as favourable, if not better, as with bright children. Shapiro (1962) points out that:

the hypothesis on which treatment is based is that the therapeutic effect is due not to the intellectual appreciation of the theoretical constructs, but to the working through the previous phases of negatively affected development within the therapeutic relationship. This is possible at any level of intelligence within the feebleminded range. Psychoanalysis of children as young as 4 or 5 years is regularly and successfully carried out, and the feebleminded has a mental age well above this.

Mundy (1957a), working with imbecile children, comments that a sound transference situation can easily be established and that therapy leads to a marked development of verbal ability. It can well be argued that withholding psychotherapy on grounds of lack of intelligence may deprive a person of just that treatment which might be successful in restoring effective mental functioning.

Findings such as those of Healy and Bronner (1936), who recorded failure of psychotherapy in 66 per cent of children with IQ 70–79, but only in 10 per cent of children with IQ above 110, suggest only that the usual type of psychotherapeutic treatment is unsuitable for the mental defective patient, but not that the patient is unsuitable for psychotherapeutic treatment.[1]

Who in particular requires this treatment?

Even though the selection of patients is primarily dependent on the aims, method and magnitude of the planned investigation or therapeutic situation, local conditions have obviously to be taken into account.

The most common principle of selection of patients for treatment appears to be in terms of behaviour. Patients are chosen who are 'creating problems in their classrooms' (Cotzin, 1948) who 'show overt anxiety as their principal symptom' (Ringelheim and Polatsek, 1955), or are either 'aggressive, uncooperative, hyperactive and attention demanding' or in whom the tendencies of submissiveness, withdrawal and fantasy indulgence are prominent (Fisher and Wolfson, 1953). A slightly different idea seems to underlie Stubblebine and Roadruck's (1956) approach; they used psychotherapy as a preventative measure because 'adolescent males with their high energy levels and pubertal troubles seemed to need an improved treatment programme'. Thorne, looking not only at the behavioural aspect, but also at the patient's accessibility to treatment, selected from his 'most unstable and maladjusted mental defectives' those who had sufficient personality resources to assume some responsibility for self-regulation and 'who were integrated enough to enter into a therapeutic relationship long enough for reasonably adequate counselling to be performed' (Thorne, 1948).

With a few exceptions (Mehlman, 1953; O'Connor and Yonge, 1955) most groups lack homogeneity in important variables like age and intelligence levels. In both these aspects the range is usually very wide though the groups are comparatively small (Astrachan, 1955; Vail, 1955; Stubblebine and Roadruck, 1956; Stubblebine, 1957). At times patients are included whose diagnosis suggests clinical abnormality. Few therapists attempt to deal with mixed groups, and sex is the only variable held constant by most investigators, except those using sociodrama methods (Sarbin, 1946; Lavalli and Levine, 1954; Pilkey *et al.*, 1961). While the pioneering character of these first tentative steps in psychotherapy made it permissible to cast the net often indiscriminately wide, it is well to keep in mind the heterogeneous composition of the groups, the different selection principles and the varying aims of therapeutic endeavours when comparing the results reported in the literature.

It is inadvisable to make general statements regarding subnormals suitable for therapy of one or the other kind. Low intelligence scores, extreme resistance

---

[1] A closer study of these unpromising cases in the lower IQ range reveals such a complexity of other factors is involved in the poor response to psychotherapy that it seems hardly permissible to single out the low intelligence by itself. The 33 per cent favourable adjustments in Healy and Bronner's study received all the sympathetic support of a good and understanding environment in addition to psychotherapy – but that factor was missing in the other cases.

and shallow personality may well be the result of maladjustment, and it will require careful appraisal in the individual case before treatment is withheld on these grounds. Generally speaking, however, therapeutic assistance of varying degree and form should be made available to all defectives who have enough 'insight' to be concerned about their failure to adjust. Limits will be imposed by the existence of organic factors, of sensory defects, of particular low intelligence on one side and time and competence of the therapist on the other side.

A fact only too often overlooked and leading to rash and unjustified conclusions is the need for flexibility in therapeutic techniques. In the same way as responses of patients may vary with different therapists and with different projective tests, inappropriate therapeutic media may also fail to obtain full rapport. The techniques so far discussed require verbalizing and listening. Schaefer–Simmern (1944, 1948) demonstrated the therapeutic value of artistic activity in the mentally deficient. A silent, morose 16-year-old boy of borderline intelligence became accessible to therapy only after four months of frequent 'drawing sessions'. The same paper refers also to another report showing 'how only through finger painting a deficient child was able at first to communicate his problems' (Abel, 1953). A concerted approach through therapy in occupation, music, speech and remedial reading for the treatment of a retarded and hyperactive child has been described by Knight *et al.* (1957). Other examples have been reported by Lowenfeld (1941).

Epileptic defectives, who are particularly vulnerable to physical hazards, present a special problem in the institution and are in many ways excluded from the activities and privileges and from the usual stages in the rehabilitation process. Their comparative isolation and the seeming 'unfairness' of their situation produces a characteristic antisocial disgruntled attitude. Stubblebine (1957), giving psychotherapy to six epileptics of the non-working institution population, describes them as '. . . disliked by their fellows . . . chronically sullen, irritable, temperamental and having . . . an extremely narrow range of social activities'. Though this author thinks that 'insight in the dynamic sense does not seem possible in the brain-damaged patient' the results of therapy indicated that some of the patients 'seemed to profit from the greater than average time spent with them in a group setting while searching for some measure of mutual understanding'.

Mundy (1957a) reports changes in intelligence scores and social adjustment in a group of imbecile children, aged 5–12 years. Among them were deaf mutes, post-meningitis cases and children with aphasia, many of whom showed social improvement. She observed also that cases with cerebral palsy or epilepsy do not profit considerably from therapy.

Various psychotherapeutic approaches

There are now so many useful accounts of the wide variety of psychotherapeutic work that only a few aspects can be singled out for discussion in this section.

The majority of published reports deal with therapeutic methods applied to groups – play therapy (Maisner, 1950; Mundy, 1957a; Stacey and De Martino, 1957; Leland *et al.*, 1959; Leland and Smith, 1962), discussion groups – and less often with individual counselling. Group therapy has found much favour with the therapists because it is economical of time and energy and concentrates on the weak personal relationships of the defective. Discussion of problems in a group setting makes the individual patient aware that his case is one of many and helps to break down tendencies of isolation and withdrawal. Working through problems in a group setting makes it possible to reorientate the patient towards his immediate environment, to give opportunities for becoming aware of the other people's viewpoints and of *feeling* instead of only *knowing* the implications of social approval and disapproval.

Group sessions provide an opportunity to relieve situational anxiety caused by misunderstood or only half-understood happenings. Questions freely answered by the therapist provide an opportunity for disseminating information, counteracting disturbing rumours and for utilizing institutional incidents for concrete demonstrations of community demands and regulations. They make it possible to clarify misunderstandings on the spot, to dispel doubts, to reassure the insecure and to suggest solutions to the hesitant (Ringelheim and Polatsek, 1955; Stubblebine and Roadruck, 1956; Wilcox and Guthrie, 1957; Kaldeck, 1958; Morris *et al.*, 1959).

Though true insight is perhaps rather exceptional among these patients, it seems quite possible that in this way an understanding may dawn on them of their limitations and position in society. In group therapy 'the concrete samples of behaviour or personality difficulties given by themselves and seen by them in others may be the source of insight. Such an artificially structured situation may approach, for defectives, the discussion in groups for people with normal intellect' (Cotzin, 1948). The problems and conflicts of the mentally deficient are of a very concrete, realistic nature; they relate to the present, to the immediate past and the immediate future, and the assistance of the therapist must, therefore, be given on the same realistic plane on which the problems are experienced (Burton, 1954). Counselling, whether used in a group setting or individually, tackles the conflicts when they arise and usually in a very direct fashion. The immediate problems encountered most frequently are the patient's position as a known mentally subnormal person, his future, his personal relationships. Here the counsellor will reassure and encourage, persuade and explain in an effort to overcome feelings of personal inferiority, of rejection, of anxiety and of insecurity (Feldman, 1946; Sarason, 1949; Gunzburg, 1956, 1957; Woody, 1966).

Oliver *et al.* (1965) describe the contents of group discussions with adolescent mentally defective women. Commonly arising topics discussed were ambition relating to employment, their own background, financial matters, problems of sex and marriage and relations with parents and others. An attempt was made to establish a more realistic attitude to life and to deal with the antisocial and inadequate responses which are a characteristic of this group.

Evaluation of psychotherapeutic approaches

Evaluating success or failure of formal psychotherapy has proved delicate, difficult and perhaps impossible in the case of neurotic patients of normal intellect where a wealth of evidence is available. When it comes to the handful of studies relating to mental subnormality, the position is even more unsatisfactory. Most experiments have been undertaken in a pioneering clinical spirit with more thought for the patient than for objective criteria for evaluating results.

Not only the group compositions, the intelligence levels, ages and the clinical categories differ considerably from one experiment to the other; methods are different and often inadequately described; such important factors as local conditions, hospital regulations and 'general atmosphere' vary also to a large extent. Criteria for improvement or non-improvement, even when supported at times by hospital records, are not only subjective but may also differ with different investigators. The length and frequency of psychotherapy sessions vary a good deal and there is nearly always a complete lack of follow-up studies to indicate whether the results of therapy are of a permanent nature. Published investigations tend to report 'successes' rather than 'failures', and few investigators seem to have had either the same experience or the same courage as Vail, who declared 'that those patients who attended the group the least number of times have shown the greatest progress' (1955). In a study which employed a comparison group for evaluating the results of a programme of '48 half-hour therapy' sessions, Albini and Dinitz (1965) came to the regretful conclusion that 'faith in the efficacy of short term psychotherapy may have to be tempered'. They found that out of six measures utilized in their investigation only the 'reported number of negative classroom behaviours and teacher ratings of the subjects' habits and attitudes toward learning' revealed any trend toward, but not any significant improvement in, the behaviour of the disturbed subjects. Similarly, Subotnik and Callahan (1959) came to the conclusion that nothing in the results of their individual therapy programme of '16 forty-five minute therapy contacts in a playroom' suggested that measurable improvements could be achieved in institutionalized, educable retarded boys. Gorlow *et al.* (1963) assessed the effects of twelve weeks of thrice-weekly hour therapy sessions on the institutional behaviour and self attitudes of young female residents in an institution. As far as their assessment measures and comparisons with a control group indicated, there were no differences.

Discouraging as these investigators' conclusions are, one has to remember the somewhat naïve assumption by many experimenters that the crude assessment instruments of doubtful reliability which have to be used would reflect changes after the comparatively short psychotherapy efforts, thereby oversimplifying the situation which requires psychotherapeutic action. There is a marked absence of recognition of the following facts: the emotional disturbance in a mentally handicapped is usually of long standing; he has little innate ability to assist the therapist in his work; it needs much experience of the 'subnormal personality' to get at his 'wavelength' and have adequate rapport; the subnormal is a 'slow learner' and much more time must be spent on therapeutic work than research-minded investigators are prepared to give; the available assessment instruments to register any changes which might occur are generally not sensitive enough and usually quite irrelevant to the issues; and any success which might be achieved in short personal contacts will be neutralized by adverse experiences in non-supportive environments.

On the other hand, the methodological shortcomings of studies with negative results can also be observed in studies reporting successes. Halo effects, the unreliability of rater's observations, the absence of control groups and the marked lack of follow-up studies combine to produce a picture of less persuasiveness than the proponents of psychotherapy would favour.

Besides the reports on systematic investigations of group methods there are a few case studies which confirm the findings of most group therapists. Four years of psycho-analytic treatment for a mentally deficient boy resulted in the disappearance of his extreme selfishness, his inability to establish relationships and his isolation. There was a marked improvement in his attitude and relations with other children – 'he began to see himself in relation to his environment and made definite efforts to be like others and to accept reality' (Chidester and Menninger, 1936).

Sarason reports that at the end of ten months of counselling, Lottie's 'periods of sullenness and depression had noticeably decreased, she was more spontaneous, she did not avoid new people and situations with as much apprehension, her efficiency at work had improved and she did not feel as personally isolated as previously'. Stephen 'by facing rather than avoiding certain problems . . . was able to resolve conflicts which had previously reinforced unhealthy attitudes towards self and others. He was not plagued as much by feelings of guilt and worthlessness, he achieved a more realistic conception of his physical adequacy' (Sarason, 1949).

Two months of counselling treatment of a mentally retarded soldier resulted in evident improvement. His tension had disappeared and he spoke no longer of his feelings of inferiority, stating 'that he considered himself "one of the fellows" again' (Feldman, 1946).

Two out of nineteen children in a community-based mental retardation clinic made such significant gains in behaviour and intelligence that they could no longer be considered retarded (Chess, 1962). Axline (1949, 1950) found that about one-third of her children in a non-directive play therapy programme showed impressive gain in measured intelligence.

From a scientific point of view the results of these investigations cannot, of course, convince. In view of the lack of control groups it is not known, for example, whether these changes would not have been brought about in the same way by traditional methods, or by time itself. More impressive is the changed attitude of the staff because 'perhaps the most difficult thing is to convince employees that they largely make their own problems through failure to use psychological methods of studying and handling the children under their care'. Their observation indicated that the patients were happier, that the 'total abolition of corporal punishment and repressive methods . . . [and] minimal use of punishment has been associated with improved behaviour', that the patients 'became extremely critical of offenders' and 'to a large extent . . . discipline themselves', and there was a 'lessened incidence of reactive emotional disturbance', and that there was a 'greater loyalty and co-operativeness' (Thorne, 1948). Similarly, Stubblebine and Roadruck (1956) quoted the opinions of people having known the patients before treatment and who 'commented on their increased maturation, self-reliance and improved behaviour and social abilities'.

Only a few experiments published so far make use of control groups and objective criteria for the assessment of patients under treatment (Mehlman, 1953; Yonge and O'Connor, 1954; O'Connor and Yonge, 1955; Mundy, 1957a; Wilcox and Guthrie, 1957). Mehlman's carefully designed investigation reports statistically significant increases in adjustment measured by ratings, but no significant changes in intelligence scores. His main observation was 'that the mentally retarded child, despite his intellectual limitations, can grow in therapy because therapeutic progress does not depend on intellectual ability'. O'Connor reported significant changes in the attitude of the group under therapy accompanied by changes in behaviour and performances in a workshop situation. In particular there was an increase in 'zest' coupled with an increase in 'fanciful ambitions', but even more in 'feasible aspirations'. There was a definite change in attitude to 'authority figures' from negative to positive and the 'progressive release of hostility to be expected in a permissive group atmosphere showed in negative attitudes to group members as well as in increase of the "criticism of others" '. The end of the six months of psychotherapy saw also a nearly complete disappearance of initially fairly frequent masochistic, sadistic and other morbid ideas.

A large-scale study of the effect of psychotherapy on mentally defective delinquent males was carried out by Craft (1965) at the Balderton Unit for psychopathic mental defectives. The results of the investigation dealt in the end with 44 admissions (though 100 boys provide the bulk of the evidence) 'on probation with a condition of residence' whose IQ was over 59. They were all considered 'as having such mental disorder as to necessitate treatment in a hospital psychopathic unit rather than elsewhere'. They were placed on a strictly alternate basis in a group psychotherapy ward and authoritarian villa respectively.

The psychotherapy ward was administered to some extent by a ward council, which consisted of the 'patients' and staff members. Each 'student' on admission joined the small 'deep psychotherapy group' most concerned with his problems, respectively consisting of sex deviants, older and more mature offenders, or the young and unstable. These groups, meeting two or three times weekly to discuss their problems, were supervised by a psychiatrist. 'Boys were helped to interpret their own motives and behaviour and there was enough time to carry out depth psychotherapy.' The psychiatrist devoted approximately fifteen hours per week to the thirty-bedded villa.

In the authoritarian villa 'noise and disarray were not tolerated, peace and quiet being enforced by putting offenders to bed, by fines, deprivation of privileges, or isolation in a single room. These disciplinary methods reinforced the hierarchical system of control by doctors and nurses who adopted an enlightened, sympathetic but authoritarian basis.' 'Little more than superficial psychotherapy was possible' (approximately five hours per week in a fifty-bedded unit). On both wards 'staff were taught that the main treatment function with psychopathic adolescents was to develop a good relationship, using this on the one ward to discuss motivation and changes in attitude, and on the authoritarian ward to direct energy into constructive rather than destructive activity'.

Various evaluation techniques were used in the analysis of the progress of these groups, each member of which stayed at least three months in the hospital. These included personality tests (MMPI, Stott's Social Adjustment Guides, Porteus Maze) the results of which were inconclusive, and a follow-up during the second year after discharge. Taken as a whole, comments the author, the results 'suggest that the authoritarian ward provided the more effective treatment of the psychopathic delinquent'. He further states, 'if the present results of this study do not show the authoritarian ward to be more effective on all the evaluatory scales, they certainly do not support the hypothesis that greater personal attention from adults – "psychotherapy" in a wide sense – is any more effective than a minimum of attention'. And with some regret perhaps Craft concludes that 'this project has indicated that treatment with psychotherapy designed to change personality orientation seems no better on short term evaluation than standard hospital training', and finds it 'surprising that at this stage the cheaper method of treatment appears to be better'.

It may well be possible that the treatment was not intensive or good enough to effect significant results of the kind expected. Craft (1965) quotes results of earlier surveys suggesting that successful treatment took 'an average 6·4 years', but it would certainly be difficult to decide how much of the success is due to 'psychotherapy' itself and how much to a process of conforming gradually to the directives of authority.

To some extent Craft's poor results of 'non-directive' therapy and his conclusion that 'work training alone in a friendly but disciplined residential setting is probably better than work training with group psychotherapy in a relatively permissive residential setting' supports the opinion of many workers that the adult mental defective requires guidance and advice as much in a therapeutic setting as in other situations. Though there is no evidence available comparing directly the long-term results of directive versus non-directive therapy with mental defectives, Craft's careful and honest analysis of his three years of psychiatric work goes a long way towards finding an effective way of helping the mentally handicapped. In the same way as Tizard's investigation (1953) showed that the *laissez-faire* supervision in workshops was unsupportive and unproductive in industrial terms compared with the friendly supervision with praise and encouragement, non-directive approaches may be less helpful with the majority of the disturbed mentally handicapped. Craft's investigation indicated not that psychotherapy was not as successful as 'standard hospital training', but merely that this particular approach of non-directive psychotherapy is most likely unsuitable for the mentally handicapped.

Some information relating to IQ changes is contained in a few studies (Axline, 1948, 1949), and one of the most striking features is the variability of the IQs reported. Sarason's cases, Lottie and Stephen show IQs ranging from 45 to 74 and 63 to 76 (Sarason, 1949), an imbecile soldier testing 41 and 39 before treatment showed on retest an IQ 59, which appeared 'to be considerably lower than the Rorschach indication, which suggested dull normal intelligence' (Feldman, 1946). A boy under Freudian treatment showed a change in IQ from 62 to 90 (Chidester and Menninger, 1936).

Kriegman and Hilgard (1944) considered that psychotherapy may increase intelligence scores in some cases and they thought that they achieved best results with the anxious, guilty child.

A large pilot study by Tarjan and Benson (1953) mentions that several patients undergoing psychotherapy 'showed a distinct rise in measurable intelligence'. In some cases this increase amounted to as much as 20 IQ points.

Mundy (1957b) comparing the Stanford–Binet IQs of 15 young children before and after psychotherapy with the IQ of 10 untreated children found a highly significant increase of 7 IQ points in the first group. In a second comparison she used 8 children as their 'own controls' and found that there was a highly significant increment of 22 IQ points during the therapy period, but only 2 IQ points change in the pre-therapy period of comparable length. The IQ changes of these very young children were paralleled by very pronounced improvement in social adjustment.

Obviously much will depend on the selection of tests used and of patients treated, and not every intelligence test may be sensitive to the particular changes brought about by treatment. Thus while Ringelheim and Polatsek (1955) report little observable changes in personality, dynamics or mental level (without indicating what tests were employed), O'Connor and Yonge (1955) arrived at quite different results. Using three groups, two of which served as controls, all matched on sex, age and IQ, they observed that pre- and post-treatment scores of the experimental group showed a significant change at the 5 per cent level on the Wechsler Verbal Scale but not on Raven's Progressive Matrices. The control groups did not change. The gain in IQ had a mean of 9 points and was equivalent to one standard deviation with this group. The improvement was mostly due to an increase in the comprehension subtest of the Wechsler Scale, significant at the 2 per cent level.

The final judgment as to whether psychotherapy directly contributes to an increase in intellectual efficiency measurable by intelligence tests will have to be postponed until more carefully designed studies are available. Most of the work so far available is no more than suggestive, and those IQ changes reported could just as well be attributed to maturation, changes in environment, spontaneous stabilization, inadequate testing and to familiarity with the test situation on a second occasion (Kriegman and Hilgard, 1944), as well as to selective factors favouring the more promising patients being chosen for therapy.

Conclusions

In summary one might well be cautious and merely state that the published evidence suggests that apparently changes take place in attitude, behaviour and outlook of mentally deficient patients who receive some special attention. The changes seem to be most marked in patients showing behaviour disorders, even if of a degree permitting the label 'psychopathy'. The psychotherapeutic approach seems to have no, or little, effect in schizophrenics, or even simple schizoid cases (Astrachan, 1955; Stubblebine and Roadruck, 1956). Viewing the vagueness of the methodology of the actual therapeutic methods one might well wonder whether the form of approach is of considerable importance since all activities and all relationships are potentially psychotherapeutic if handled with this intention. Much of the success of psychotherapy with the mentally subnormal may be due to the presence of 'someone to think both with him and for him' (Hartwell, 1940).

Perusing the literature, one gains the impression that a good deal of the work reported has been carried out by complete novices who embarked on the venture of psychotherapy with little or no knowledge of methods or patients. Whilst this is unavoidable in a first generation of therapists in mental subnormality, it may perhaps also account for the difficulties met, and for the sceptical reception of these attempts.

One or two further considerations are indicated before engaging in an indiscriminate experimentation in therapy. Many of the therapeutic investigations appeared to be of fairly short duration. In some cases a practical result was placement of patients in more congenial employment, but in most cases the end of the therapy sessions coincided with the end of any special endeavours to help. The ensuing disappointments, when 'warm' therapeutic sessions which have aroused hope end abruptly and the everyday institution life comes into full force again without any apparent changes, throws some doubt on the value of such isolated experimentation for the patient. It seems that far from being helpful, the lack of concrete results and the disappearance of personal interest may well strengthen the anti- and asocial attitudes of the patients who have once again been 'let down'.

There seems to be little justification for initiating therapy of that type merely in order to learn or to prove that it has value, unless it can be reinforced and followed up by concrete achievements. The therapist must, therefore, have some definite administrative power and some weight in the decisions concerning the future life of his patients (Thorne, 1948; Gunzburg, 1956, 1957).

Psychotherapy may be undertaken with either individuals or groups; it may be directive or non-directive; it may seek to explore and modify the fundamental personality structure, or it may be concerned with relatively superficial problems, frequently acknowledged by the patient, though probably not fully understood by him. This latter approach, often called counselling, attempts to modify behaviour patterns which have resulted in social maladjustment. It appears to be a method which is admirably suited to the needs of people who require only guidance and assistance in sorting out problems which, despite their distressing nature, are fairly near to the surface and are easily accessible to the therapist. Counselling is most frequently directed towards the solution of specific, limited problems of adaptation as they occur from day to day and aims at finding practical *ad hoc* solutions without attempting to change the basic personality organization. Faced with the emergence of deep-seated conflicts under the assistance of the therapist, few defectives would have either the ability, or insight, to deal with them.

Psychotherapy with children, attempting to reopen disturbed communications between the child and the environment, is often less concerned with working out and solving problems than with providing the warmth and affection of which the child has been starved. This applies to young and older children, who often come from severely disturbed home backgrounds and have become confused in their emotional relationships. They are withdrawn and isolated and deeply worried about their own disloyalties towards the parents and their parents' disloyalty towards them. Therapy with these children takes place on an entirely emotional plane, the therapist providing a father and mother substitute with warm, close bodily contact offering shelter, acceptance and love. Not infrequently hugging and cuddling – so essential for the development of a mentally healthy child – has to be provided by the therapist in a late stage and in unfavourable conditions and he has to be fully aware of the responsibilities he shoulders in creating a transference situation. Social adjustment will follow once the security of the relationship is comprehended emotionally.

Both approaches, deep psychotherapy and counselling, represent considered attempts by a trained therapist to modify and improve *by word and deed* the conditions which will enable a person to live and work with others and to adjust to their reasonable demands. These forms of treatment, particularly counselling for adults, are given increasingly more weight in modern mental deficiency practice with the mounting realization that the factors of character and temperament are frequently more decisive in the rehabilitation of the feeble-minded than the intellectual aspects (Zisfein and Rosen, 1973).

Group and individual therapy sessions break the ground and encourage the adoption of a new outlook by persuasion and explanation, but therapy can only initiate and not carry the whole burden of readjustment. The proof of the veracity of the therapist's assertions is given through the patient's reception of his immediate environment, when with great doubts he makes his first hesitant attempts at reorientation. The final therapy is administered by the environment, the institution in the first place and the community after that.

References

ABEL, T. M. (1953) Resistances and difficulties in psychotherapy of mental retardates. *J. clin. Psychol.*, **9**, 107–9.

ACKERMAN, N. W. and MENNINGER, C. E. (1936) Treatment techniques for mental retardation in a school for personality disorders in children. *Amer. J. Orthopsychiat.*, **6**, 294–313.

ALBINI, J. L. and DINITZ, S. (1965) Psychotherapy with disturbed and defective children: an evaluation of changes in behaviour and attitudes. *Amer. J. ment. Defic.*, **69**, 560–7.

ASTRACHAN, M. (1955) Group psychotherapy with mentally retarded female adolescents and adults. *Amer. J. ment. Defic.*, **60**, 152–6.

AXLINE, V. M. (1947) Non-directive therapy for poor readers. *J. consult. Psychol.*, **11**, 61–9.

AXLINE, V. M. (1948) Some observations on play therapy. *J. consult. Psychol.*, **12**, 209–16.

AXLINE, V. M. (1949) Mental Deficiency – symptom or disease. *J. consult. Psychiat.*, **13**, 313–27.

AXLINE, V. M. (1950) Play therapy experiences as described by child participants. *J. consult. Psychiat.*, **14**, 53–63.

BARTON, R. (1961) The institutional mind and the subnormal mind. *J. ment. Subn.*, **VII**, 37–44.

BEIER, D. (1964) Behavioral disturbance. In STEVENS, H. A. and HEBER, R. F. (eds.) *Mental Retardation – A Review of Research*. Chicago: Univ. of Chicago Press.

BIALER, I. (1967) Psychotherapy and other adjustment techniques with the mentally retarded. In BAUMEISTER, A. A. (ed.) *Mental Retardation*. London: Univ. of London Press.

BROWNE, R. A., GUNZBURG, H. C., JOHNSTON-HANNAH, L. G. W., MACCOLL, K., OLIVER, B. and THOMAS, A. (1971) The needs of patients in subnormality hospitals if discharged to community care. *Brit. J. ment. Subn.*, **XVII**, 7–24.

BURTON, A. (1954) Psychotherapy with the mentally retarded. *Amer. J. ment. Defic.*, **58**, 486–9.

CHESS, S. (1962) Psychiatric treatment of the mentally retarded child with behavior problems. *Amer. J. Orthopsychiat.*, **32**, 863–9.

CHIDESTER, L. (1934) Therapeutic results with mentally retarded children. *Amer. J. Orthopsychiat.*, **4**, 464–72.

CHIDESTER, L. and MENNINGER, K. A. (1936) The application of psychoanalytic methods to the study of mental retardation. *Amer. J. Orthopsychiat.*, **6**, 616–25.

CLARK, L. P. (1931) Child analysis: a motion picture dramatization. *Proc. and Addr. Amer. Assoc. Stud. Feebleminded.*, **36**, 111–15.

COOLEY, J. M. (1945) The relative amenability of dull and bright children to child guidance. *Smith Coll. Stud. soc. Wk.*, **16**, 26–43.

COTZIN, M. (1948) Group psychotherapy with mentally defective problem boys. *Amer. J. ment. Defic.*, **53**, 268–83.

CRAFT, M. (1959) Mental disorder in the defective. A psychiatric survey among in-patients. *Amer. J. ment. Defic.*, **63**, 829–34.

CRAFT, M. (1965) *Ten Studies into Psychopathic Personality*. Bristol: John Wright & Sons.

DE MARTINO, M. F. (1957) Some observations concerning psychotherapeutic techniques with the mentally retarded. In STACEY, C. L. and DE MARTINO, M. F. (eds.) *Counseling and Psychotherapy with the Mentally Retarded*. Glencoe, Ill.: The Free Press.

EARL, C. J. C. (1961) *Subnormal Personalities; Their Clinical Investigation and Assessment*. London: Baillière, Tindall & Cox.

FELDMAN, F. (1946) Psychoneuroses in the mentally retarded. *Amer. J. ment. Defic.*, **51**, 247–54.

FELDMAN, I. S. (1953) Psychological differences among moron and borderline mental defectives as a function of aetiology. *Amer. J. ment. Defic.*, **57**, 484–94.

FISHER, L. A. and WOLFSON, I. N. (1953) Group therapy of mental defectives. *Amer. J. ment. Defic.*, **57**, 463–76.

GLASSMAN, L. A. (1943) Is dull normal intelligence a contraindication for psychotherapy? *Smith Coll. Stud. soc. Wk.*, **13**, 275–98.

GOFFMAN, E. (1961) *Asylums*. Harmondsworth: Penguin.

GORLOW, L., BUTLER, A., EINIG, K. G. and SMITH, J. A. (1963) An appraisal of self attitudes and behaviour following group psychotherapy with retarded young adults. *Amer. J. ment. Defic.*, **67**, 893–8.

GUNZBURG, H. C. (1956) The role of the psychologist in the Mental Deficiency Hospital. *Internat. J. soc. Psychiat.*, **I**, 31–6.

GUNZBURG, H. C. (1957) Therapy and social training for the feebleminded youth. *Brit. J. med. Psychol.*, **30**, 42–8.

GUNZBURG, H. C. (1970) The hospital as a normalizing training environment. *J. ment. Subn.*, **XVI**, 71–83.

HACKBUSCH, F. and KLOPFER, B. (1946) The contribution of projective techniques to the understanding and treatment of children psychometrically diagnosed as feebleminded. *Amer. J. ment. Defic.*, **51**, 15–34.

HARTWELL, S. W. (1940) *Fifty-five 'Bad Boys'*. New York: Knopf.

HEALY, W. and BRONNER, A. F. (1936) *New Light on Delinquency and its Treatment*. New Haven, Conn.: Yale Univ. Press.

JOLLES, I. (1947) The diagnostic implications of Rorschach's Test in Case studies of mental defectives. *Genet. Psychol. Monogr.*, **36.**

KALDECK, R. (1958) Group psychotherapy with mentally defective adolescents and adults. *Internat. J. Group Psychother.* **8,** 185–93

KNIGHT, D., LUDWIG, A. J., STRAZZULLA, M. and POPE, L. (1957) The role of varied therapies in the rehabilitation of the retarded child. *Amer. J. ment. Defic.*, **61,** 508–15.

KRIEGMAN, G. and HILGARD, J. R. (1944) Intelligence level and psychotherapy with problem children. *Amer. J. Orthopsychiat.*, **14,** 251–65.

LAVALLI, A. and LEVINE, M. (1954) Social and guidance needs of mentally handicapped adolescents as revealed through sociodramas. *Amer. J. ment. Defic.*, **58,** 554–62.

LELAND, H. and SMITH, D. (1962) Unstructured material in playtherapy for emotionally disturbed brain damaged mentally retarded children. *Amer. J. ment. Defic.*, **66,** 621–8.

LELAND, H., WALKER, J. and TABODA, A. N. (1959) Group play therapy with a group of post-nursery male retardates. *Amer. J. ment. Defic.*, **63,** 848–51.

LOWENFELD, V. (1941) Self adjustment through creative activity. *Amer. J. ment. Defic.*, **45,** 366–73.

MAISNER, E. A. (1950) Contributions of playtherapy techniques to total rehabilitative design in an institution for high-grade mentally deficient and borderline children. *Amer. J. ment. Defic.*, **55,** 235–50.

MASLAND, R. L., SARASON, S. B. and GLADWIN, T. (1958) *Mental Subnormality.* New York: Basic Books.

MAY, J. M. and MAY, M. A. (1959) The treatment and education of the atypical autistic child in a residential school situation. *Amer. J. ment. Defic.*, **64,** 435–43.

MEHLMAN, B. (1953) Group playtherapy with mentally retarded children. *J. abn. soc. Psychol.*, **48,** 53–60.

MENOLASCINO, F. J. (1967) Psychiatric findings in a sample of institutionalized mongoloids. *J. ment. Subn.*, **XIII,** 67–74.

MORGAN, J. J. B. (1950) *The Psychology of the Unadjusted School Child.* New York: Macmillan.

MORRIS, C. C., NELLIS, B. and STROMBERG, C. E. (1959) The development of an inter-disciplinary psychotherapeutic program in an institution for the mentally retarded. *Amer. J. ment. Defic.*, **63,** 605–10.

MUNDY, L. (1957a) Therapy with physically and mentally handicapped children in a mental deficiency hospital. *J. clin. Psychol.*, **13,** 3–9.

MUNDY, L. (1957b) Environmental influence on intellectual function as measured by intelligence tests. *Brit. J. med. Psychol.*, **30,** 194–201.

NEHAM, S. (1951) Psychotherapy in relation to mental deficiency. *Amer. J. ment. Defic.*, **55,** 557–72.

O'CONNOR, N. (1951) Neuroticism and emotional instability in high-grade male defectives. *J. Neurosurg. Psychiat.*, **14**, 226–30.

O'CONNOR, N. and YONGE, K. A. (1955) Methods of evaluating the group psychotherapy of unstable defective delinquents. *J. genet. Psychol.*, **87**, 89–101.

OLIVER, B. E., SIMON, G. B. and CLARK, B. (1965) Group discussions with adolescent female patients in a mental subnormality hospital. *J. ment. Subn.*, **XI**, 53–7.

PILKEY, L., GOLDMAN, M. and KLEINMAN, B. (1961) Psychodrama and empathic ability in the mentally retarded. *Amer. J. ment. Defic.*, **65**, 595–605.

RINGELHEIM, D. and POLATSEK, I. (1955) Group therapy with a male defective group. *Amer. J. ment. Defic.*, **60**, 157–62.

ROBINSON, H. B. and ROBINSON, N. M. (1965) *The Mentally Retarded child*. New York: McGraw-Hill.

SARASON, S. B. (1949) *Psychological Problems in Mental Deficiency* (2nd edn., 1953). New York: Harper & Row.

SARBIN, T. R. (1946) Spontaneity training of the feebleminded. In MORENO, J. L. (ed.) *Group Psychotherapy*. New York: Beacon House.

SCHAEFER-SIMMERN, H. (1948) *The Unfolding of Artistic Activity*. Berkeley: Univ. of California Press.

SCHAEFER-SIMMERN, H. and SARASON, S. B. (1944) Therapeutic implications of artistic activity. *Amer. J. ment. Defic.*, **49**, 185–96.

SHAPIRO, A. (1962) Problems of psychotherapy. *Proc. Lond. Conf. Scient. Stud. Ment. Defic.*, *1960*, **I**, 263–70. Dagenham: May & Baker.

SLAVSON, S. R. (1950) *Analytic Group Psychotherapy, with Children, Adolescents and Adults*. New York: Columbia Univ. Press.

SLOAN, W. (1947) Mental deficiency as a symptom of personality disturbance. *Amer. J. ment. Defic.*, **52**, 31–6.

STACEY, C. L. and DE MARTINO, M. F. (1957) *Counseling and Psychotherapy with the Mentally Retarded*. Glencoe, Ill.: The Free Press.

STOGDILL, R. M. (1938) Some behavior adjustment techniques in use with mentally retarded children. *J. except. Child.*, **5**, 25–30.

STUBBLEBINE, J. M. (1957) Group psychotherapy with some epileptic mentally deficient adults. *Amer. J. ment. Defic.*, **61**, 725–30.

STUBBLEBINE, J. M. and ROADRUCK, R. D. (1956) Treatment program for mentally deficient adolescents. *Amer. J. ment. Defic.*, **60**, 552–6.

SUBOTNIK, L. and CALLAHAN, R. J. (1959) A pilot study in short term play therapy with institutionalized educable mentally retarded boys. *Amer. J. ment. Defic.*, **63**, 730–5.

TARJAN, G. and BENSON, F. (1953) Report on the pilot study at Pacific Colony. *Amer. J. ment. Defic.*, **57**, 453–62.

THORNE, F. C. (1948) Counselling and psychotherapy with mental defectives. *Amer. J. ment. Defic.*, **52**, 263–71.

THORNE, F. C. (1950) *Principles of Personality Counselling: An Eclectic Viewpoint.* Brandon, Vt: J. clin. Psychol.

TIZARD, J. (1953) The effects of different types of supervision on the behavior of mental defectives in a sheltered workshop. *Amer. J. ment. Defic.,* **58,** 143–61.

VAIL, D. J. (1955) An unsuccessful experiment in group therapy. *Amer. J. ment. Defic.,* **60,** 144–51.

WIEST, G. (1955) Psychotherapy with the mentally retarded. *Amer. J. ment. Defic.,* **59,** 640–4.

WILCOX, G. T. and GUTHRIE, G. M. (1957) Changes in adjustment of institutionalized female defectives following group psychotherapy. *J. clin. Psychol.,* **13,** 9–13.

WILLIAMS, C. E. (1968) Psychiatric problems of blind children. In O'GORMAN, G. (ed.) *Modern Trends in Mental Health and Subnormality.* London: Butterworth.

WILLIAMS, C. E. (1971) A study of the patients in a group of mental subnormality hospitals. *Brit. J. ment. Subn.,* **XVII,** 29–41.

WILLIAMS, J. R. and BELINSON, L. (1953) Neurosis in a mental defective. *Amer. J. ment. Defic.,* **57,** 601–12.

WOODY, R. H. (1966) Counselling the mentally subnormal: an American model. *J. ment. Subn.,* **XII,** 73–9.

YONGE, K. A. and O'CONNOR, N. (1954) Measurable effects of group psychotherapy with defective delinquents. *J. ment. Sci.,* **100,** 944–52.

ZISFEIN, L. and ROSEN, M. (1973) Personal adjustment training: a group counseling program for institutionalized mentally retarded persons. *Ment. Retard.,* **11,** 16–20.

23

C. C. Kiernan

Behaviour modification

Introduction

The aims of this chapter will be to present a description of the behaviour modification approach to analysis of the behaviour of the mentally handicapped and to discuss representative programmes within this context. It will not attempt an overall critical review of the application of these methods, since the volume of available data is far too extensive. In addition, several reviews have appeared recently which have accomplished this task (e.g. Bandura, 1969; J. M. Gardner, 1971; W. I. Gardner, 1971; Sherman and Baer, 1969). Rather the chapter will aim to develop the approach and to indicate some of its implications.

The application of operant techniques to the behaviour of mentally handicapped individuals began over thirty years ago (Fuller, 1949). Since then its extent has increased at a rapid rate in North America, although in Great Britain and Continental Europe it is lagging several years behind.

The conceptual roots of this application lie firmly in the work of Skinner (1938, 1953). Early use of the term 'behaviour modification' did not tie it specifically to the operant tradition. R. I. Watson (1962) related it to situations which were studies of learning, with a particular intent – 'the clinical goal of treatment'. Among Watson's situations were structured interviews, experimental neuroses and doctor-patient relationships. Krasner and Ullman (1966) focus it further in terms of an elimination of hypothetical constructs, a consequent emphasis on behavioural explanations and an emphasis on social reinforcement. The social learning approach was further developed by Bandura (1969) and by Patterson (1969).

An alternative phrase used in describing the application of operant principles is the 'experimental analysis of behaviour'. The experimental analysis referred to is operant analysis (cf. Bijou and Baer, 1961, 1965, 1967; Keller and Schoenfeld, 1950). This has tended to be used far more precisely but the approach it designates has also been identified by the term behaviour 'modification' (cf. W. I. Gardner, 1971).

One terminological problem is that not all attempts to modify behaviour would be classed under 'behaviour modification' and not all attempts to analyse behaviour experimentally would be classified under the rubric 'experimental analysis of behaviour'.

A further problem is that much work in the applied field does not involve the extensive experimental manipulation of variables which characterizes infra-human experimental analysis of behaviour. The term 'applied behaviour analysis' is preferred by some workers anxious to emphasize the applied orientation as opposed to more analytic studies.

The phrases 'behaviour therapy' or 'behavioural psychotherapy' are rejected by most workers in this field, since they relate to a range of techniques not covered by operant analyses. Furthermore it would be overextending the word 'therapy' to include under it the bulk of work with the mentally handicapped.

The term 'behaviour modification' will be used in this chapter. This usage is a matter of convenience rather than conviction. It reflects an emphasis on the social learning aspects of the application of operant techniques. Much more importantly it reflects an emphasis on the need to re-interpret phenomena described outside the operant tradition in operant contexts. Moreover, it will be interpreted to designate areas of educational, child care and clinical interest rather than restricting it to clinical situations.

The specific argument presented in this chapter will be that operant analysis and operant principles offer a valuable model in the context of which the behaviour of the mentally handicapped may be interpreted and modified. In particular it will be suggested that the model can integrate and systematize diverse approaches to behaviour, including psychological, sociological, bio-logical, education and ecological studies. Many of these disciplines have involved studies which are broadly descriptive in nature and translation of their findings into operant terms serves both to give a unification of theoretical language and to suggest new approaches to the behavioural phenomena involved (Michael, 1970).

It will be evident that this definition of the scope of behaviour modification is broader than other uses quoted. The emphasis on social learning is coupled with an emphasis on environmental modification as a means of effecting change in behaviour through change in the impact of variables isolated as critical within the operant framework.

The first part of this chapter will present a description of the behaviour modification approach with an attempt to show how it develops out of basic principles. Later sections will concern broader factors related to the environment and the curriculum.

The basic approach

The radical behaviourist position represented by behaviour modification has been discussed and analysed fully both in its general application to human behaviour and development (e.g. Bijou and Baer, 1961; Skinner, 1953) and with particular reference to disturbed behaviour or the behaviour of the mentally handicapped (e.g. Bijou, 1966; Spradlin and Giradeau, 1966; Whaley and Malott, 1968; W. I. Gardner, 1971). No attempt will be made here to describe or defend the approach in full. The aim of this section will be to characterize the main outline of the theory and then to examine its chief propositions as they relate to the behaviour of the mentally handicapped.

The fundamental assumptions are that the control and explanation of behaviour are best accomplished in terms of environmental variables which affect behaviour and that therefore this explanation does not require recourse to hypothetical constructs or intervening variables. The heuristic virtues of this approach were outlined by Skinner (1950) in terms of emphasizing the study of behaviour rather than theoretical constructs. In terms of the analysis of human behaviour this emphasis has led to attention being focused on the day-to-day behaviour of the individual, on 'retarded behaviour' rather than on 'retarded mentality' as an abstract entity (Bijou, 1966).

The behaviour of the mentally handicapped is seen within the theory as a function of a number of factors. These include current environmental factors and the history of the individual. Biological variables affecting stimulus reception or response potential are also seen as critical. However behaviour is not 'caused by' biological defects. The defects set the occasion for a failure to learn or for anomalous learning. Similarly environmental factors related to the occurrence of behaviour do not 'cause it'. The attitude of hospital staff does not affect the individual. It is the restriction on the behaviour of the inmate brought about through the behaviour of the staff which is critical (cf. King *et al.*, 1971). Attitudes are critical only in that they correlate with behaviour – behaviour is prime.

In short, biological, sociological and other factors affect the probability of a large number of events. Subnormal behaviour is seen as a failure of learning. Aetiology and history are critical only to the extent that they may affect the formation of stimulus-response relationships. A full analysis of the current behaviour and the factors maintaining it may reveal procedures which will overcome apparent limiting biological factors or lead to a reformulation of arguments relating to the influence of other variables.

RESPONSES AND STIMULI

The basic assumption of behaviour modification is that all responses can be classified in terms of a respondent-operant distinction. Respondents are responses which are elicited by preceding stimulation in a 'reflexive' or 'involuntary' manner. Salivation, pupillary dilation, and patellar responses are all examples of this class. Respondents are seen as being controlled, not by consequences, but rather by antecedent events.

Operants are defined as behaviours which are 'best understood as functionally related to their consequences in the environment' (Bijou and Baer, 1961). These are behaviours which are 'goal-directed', 'purposeful', or 'instrumental' in attaining goals. Antecedent stimulation may set the occasion for operant but the stimulus which controls emission of the operant is the consequent or reinforcing stimulus.

Since the original major statement of the theory (Skinner, 1938) data have accumulated which indicate that responses which would normally be termed respondents may be brought under control of their consequences, i.e. behave as operants. The work of Miller and his associates (DiCara and Miller, 1968; Miller and Banuazizi, 1968; Miller and DiCara, 1967; Trowill, 1967) and others (e.g. Brener and Hothersall, 1967) has demonstrated that responses such as heart rate, vasoconstriction, and intestinal responses may be brought under control of their consequences.

These studies have carefully excluded the possibility that operant components are mediating the observed changes. Thus it is unlikely that heart rate changes are mediated by the subject being conditioned to change skeletal activity in order indirectly to promote the heart rate change (cf. Katkin and Murray, 1968).

These studies do not require any fundamental revision in the operant-respondent distinction. The distinction was always drawn empirically, and in fact it is even arguable that Skinner anticipated the data on operant conditioning of so-called autonomic functions (Skinner, 1938, pp. 112–15). What these studies have stimulated is a further definition of the variables concerned with the operant-respondent distinction (e.g. Catania, 1971). This work is likely to lead in the future to exciting developments but for the moment the critical point is that the operant-respondent distinction can still be meaningfully drawn.

Applications of the theory in the mentally handicapped have tended to deal almost exclusively with operants. In fact, the study of respondents in general have been de-emphasized by the behaviour modification approach. Almost all work of note with the mentally handicapped within this tradition is concerned with operant behaviour.

Stimuli are conceptualized in a variety of ways within the theory. The stimulus may be seen in terms of its physical properties, or in terms of the function it subserves. A stimulus may be measurable physically but may have no function in relation to behaviour. Respondents are elicited by certain classes of stimuli. In relation to operants, the stimulus may serve either a reinforcing or discriminative function. Its reinforcing properties concern its effect on behaviour where it follows a consequence of a response. Consequent stimuli may function to increase the probability of a response, to decrease it or may not affect it.

Consequent events, reinforcing events, may follow a response each time it is emitted. In this case the contingency is termed continuous. However, a contingency may be set up on any one of a wide variety of schedules of reinforcement on an intermittent basis.

The discriminative function of a stimulus refers to the extent to which it will set the occasion for an operant. Thus a green light at a traffic junction and the instruction 'do it if you like' can both function as discriminative stimuli for operants. Discriminative stimuli may be either positive 'go' stimuli or negative 'no-go' stimuli, at any degree of complexity.

A special class of discriminative stimuli, 'setting events', is distinguished by several writers (Kantor, 1958; Bijou and Baer, 1961). A setting event is defined as a stimulus-response interaction which affects a whole set of succeeding events. Physical injury, drugs, deprivation of social contact and some verbal formulations are all seen as such to the extent that they affect a substantial number of subsequent behaviours. Although setting events can be analysed into component stimulus events, it is considered sometimes more convenient and efficient to use the setting concept (Bijou and Baer, 1961). We have already seen that the theory conceptualizes the biological occurrences relating to handicapping conditions in this way.

CONSEQUENCES

The experimental variable most frequently manipulated in behaviour modification is the consequence of the response. As already indicated, operants are seen as being controlled by their consequences. Consequences may be either accelerating, decelerating or neutral, i.e. they may result in the increase or decrease in probability of a response – or they may not affect it. The relationship between a response and its consequences is specified in terms of contingencies, or schedules of reinforcement. Specification of a contingency or schedule of reinforcement indicates when consequences are to be delivered for responses. Lindsley (1970) has pointed out that Skinnerians were at one time the world experts on contingencies. This arose from the fact that responses (pecking or lever pressing) and consequences (grain or rat pellets) were held constant and only contingencies allowed to vary in their studies. Interest in the applied area has broadened the scope of the approach to include greater concern with different types of response and consequence, and also a concern with programmes involving many stimuli, responses, contingencies and consequences. To the extent that behaviour modification is currently involved with shaping new responses, contingencies are often simplified to continuous reinforcement. Certainly the elaborate study of 'schedules' is not evident in the applied field, almost to the point of suggesting that this parameter may not be as important in practice as the initial emphasis of experimental analysis of behaviour would suggest.

The events used as consequences are classified as positive or negative reinforcers. A positive reinforcer is one which, when made to follow a response, leads to an increase in the frequency of that response. A negative reinforcer is defined as an event which results in a decrease in frequency of the response it follows. Thus events are defined by the effects they produce when they are presented as consequences of responding rather than in terms of their apparent 'reward' or 'punishment' value. This serves to emphasize the individualized nature of the approach to behaviour. What is a positive reinforcer for one individual may be negative to another (cf. Bucher and Lovaas, 1968).

The terms positive and negative reinforcer must be understood relativistically in another sense. Premack (1959, 1965) has propounded an influential principle which defines reinforcers in terms of their ability to sustain responding. What Premack has emphasized is that an activity may serve either to reinforce behaviour or be reinforced depending on the alternatives open to the organism at any particular time. Therefore a child may play cooperatively (Event A) if rewarded by adult attention (Event B), when adult attention and cooperative play represent the range of possible events (B reinforces A). The same child may however perform an academic task (Event C) in order to be allowed to play cooperatively if the academic task is less preferred than cooperative play (Event B now reinforces Event C). Therefore the same event, cooperative playing, may be either reinforced or reinforcing depending on the consequences available in the setting (Homme *et al.*, 1963; Spradlin, 1964).

Accelerating consequences may be of two types. Increase in frequency of a response may result from presenting a positive reinforcer or withdrawing a negative. These training procedures are normally termed 'reward training' and 'aversion relief', 'avoidance' or 'escape training'. Decelerating consequences may also be of two types. Decrease in response probability may result from presentation of a negative reinforcer (punishment training) or withdrawal of a positive reinforcer. This latter procedure is usually termed 'time-out' from positive reinforcement and involves the withdrawal of the individual from a situation in which he can attain positive reinforcement, or in which he is being positively reinforced continuously. A variant on time-out, in which the reinforcer is withdrawn completely, is the normal extinction procedure.

The laws governing consequation have been investigated at the human level with mentally handicapped and normal individuals. These studies show a general agreement for basic principles with the more extensive infra-human literature.

The theory argues that the most effective consequence for rapid acquisition of a response will be one which is presented immediately following the response, will be one which is large rather than small, or more intense rather than less intense, and presented on a continuous one-to-one contingency (cf. Hetherington *et al.*, 1964; Schoelkopf and Orlando, 1965, 1966; Ross *et al.*, 1965; Candland and Manning, 1966; Hom *et al.*, 1966; Hom, 1967; Hetherington and Ross, 1967; Piper, 1971).

These empirical laws are seen as holding for both positive and negative reinforcers, i.e. the most effective punishing consequence will be one which follows the to-be-decelerated response immediately, is intense and is presented on a continuous reinforcement schedule (Church, 1963).

Generally speaking, those accelerating consequences which serve to produce maximum rate of acquisition produce maximum rate of loss of response when withdrawn. Thus acquisition of a response is most rapid when each occurrence of the response is rewarded (a continuous reinforcement or *crf* contingency). If responses are rewarded only intermittently during acquisition, the rate of acquisition will be lowered (for example interval or ratio schedules). However, when the consequence is eliminated, decline in rate of responding will be *fastest* following *crf* and delayed under intermittent reinforcement. The same considerations apply with other parameters, for example delay of reinforcement, and to a large extent this generalization holds with decelerative as well as accelerative consequences. Thus recovery of a punished response will be fastest following punishment training on *crf* and slower when punishment has been intermittently presented (Orlando and Bijou, 1960; Bijou and Orlando, 1961; Orlando, 1965; Spradlin *et al.*, 1965).

At their simplest level of statement, these laws would not raise controversy. In complex situations, and especially where 'cognitive' aspects are assumed to be powerful, the laws may require extensive qualification. However, in many of the applications to the behaviour of the mentally handicapped they can be seen to be operating effectively.

METHODOLOGY OF BEHAVIOUR MODIFICATION

Several aspects of the methodology of behaviour modification require special comment. This has been traditionally individual-based (Skinner, 1938). The type of law which has been of interest has concerned the effect of contingencies and consequences on the behaviour of the individual. This led to a rejection of the concepts of Fisherian statistics and the development of an approach which failed to make contact with experimental design in the rest of psychology (Sidman, 1960; Skinner, 1966).

The technique of experimentation developed under the general rubric of applied behaviour analysis has mainly derived from earlier established ones. The basic form of demonstration of the effects of a variable involves a baseline phase in which existent behaviour is assessed, usually over several successive periods and an experimental phase in which the experimental variable is applied and its effects assessed by the extent and pattern of change from the former to the latter phase.

This design suffers several faults, prime among which is the possibility that events other than those manipulated may be changing at the same time as the shift from baseline to experimental operation. Two basic techniques have been developed to deal with this situation (Baer *et al.*, 1968). The *reversal* technique involves the withdrawal of the experimental variable either once or on several successive reversals during the experiment. If the variable is critical, behavioural measures should follow the direction of experimental manipulations. This technique makes the assumption that behaviour is 'reversible', i.e. that baselines can be recovered (Sidman, 1960).

For example Twardosz and Sajwaj (1972) modified hyperactive behaviour in a 4-year-old boy described as retarded. Percentage of time spent sitting during a free play period was recorded over 7 baseline sessions. The child scored zero in each of these sessions. In phase one of the study the child was rewarded for sitting at the table with attention, praise and tokens exchangeable for sweets and trinkets. During the first 8 experimental days the rate of sitting rose to a median of 62·5 per cent of the 30-minute free play period.

During this training phase the teacher's approach to the child shifted from an initial strategy, where she seated the child, to the situation at the end of the 8-day period where the child had to touch the table or chair before being verbally requested to sit and play at the table.

During the reversal phase, attention, praise and tokens were withdrawn and sitting declined virtually to zero. Reintroduction of reward led to recovery of the sitting behaviour.

There are several reasons why reversal procedures may not always be feasible. In particular there may be ethical reasons why a behaviour cannot be reversed, for example, if head-banging has been eliminated by an experimental operation. In addition, new responses may be socially valued. Consequently once they are produced by the subject they may become dependent on the operation of variables in the natural environment. Production of speech or response to requests represent examples of behaviours which would allow the individual to be 'trapped' by the natural environment (cf. Baer and Wolf, 1967; Baer *et al.*, 1968). In the study described above, Twardosz and Sajwaj found that an increase in the amount of sitting was correlated with a decrease in posturing from 81·5 to 18 per cent and an increase in the use of toys and proximity to other children. In this study, reward for sitting was also reward for play and reward for proximity.

A second technique, the *multiple baseline* technique, avoids several of the problems resulting from reversal. This involves the establishment of concurrent baselines for several behaviours which the individual may exhibit. The experimenter then applies the experimental variable to one of these, while continuing to record all. He may note changes in this behaviour with little or no alteration in others. Rather than now removing the experimental variable, he applies it to a second response and observes its effects. If change occurs also in this response, as a function of the experimental variable, there will be evidence of its effectiveness. Clearly the technique can be extended to cover a number of responses. It is advantageous in not involving withdrawal of an experimental variable but it nonetheless allows precise conclusions to be drawn about the effectiveness of these.

Barton, Guess, Garcia and Baer (1970) provide an example of the use of this methodology. Barton and her colleagues worked with a group of severely handicapped hospitalized males. They recorded mealtime behaviours for the group, and isolated several unacceptable behaviours including stealing, inappropriate eating with the fingers, pushing food off the plate, spilling food, and eating spilled food or eating food by mouth directly off the table. These responses were grouped under several headings and then successively eliminated by removing food for 15 seconds on emission of the inappropriate response or, exceptionally, by removing the meal completely (no loss of weight was recorded).

All responses were recorded throughout the 120-meal duration of the study. In general, the results showed that as the contingency was applied to each response that response decreased in frequency without a substantial effect on other responses. However, with a decrease in the use of fingers, there was an increase in the messy use of the spoon. In addition, the authors comment on an apparent cumulative effect of the consequence. As the study progressed, it appeared to become more potent.

The central focus of the reversal and multiple baseline techniques is replication of effects. Replication is on an intra-subject basis with either multiple reversals or with the multiple baseline procedure. Inter-subject replication is achieved by manipulating the same experimental variables with several subjects. Sidman (1960) argued that the number of replications required in order for an effect to be accepted depended on several factors – the main one being the novelty of the effect demonstrated. Thus a demonstration that a subject would avoid an unpleasant event would require only minimal replication. If an *increase* in the possibility of response followed the experience of an unpleasant event this surprising result would require several replications before it would be accepted as a phenomenon and would then need further analysis. Sidman's concern is for the development of a model which would allow experimental results to be evaluated in relation to the extent to which they 'fit' with established phenomena rather than against chance as in the Fisherian model. The concern that the psychological or behavioural significance of data should not be confused with statistical significance is reflected powerfully outside the applied behaviour analysis field (e.g. Bolles, 1962; Lykken, 1968). The need for the adoption of a statistical model which more closely reflects the requirements of behavioural experimentation appears also in the increasing interest in Bayesian statistics (e.g. McGee, 1971).

The methodology of behaviour modification has a basic core of procedures which owe their origin to the Skinnerian tradition. These techniques all involve intra-subject comparisons. This emphasis on single subject designs is almost certainly one reason why behaviour modification has advanced quickly in the research on mental handicap. It represents a rigorous way of dealing with the single subject which is closed to more conventional methodologies.

Workers in applied behaviour analysis are more willing than their colleagues in infra-human research to allow of the desirability of other methodological traditions for the answer to questions concerning the relative value of different educational programmes or services. Inter-group comparisons, in addition to intra-group comparisons, appear desirable if these problems are to receive adequate answer (Baker and Ward, 1971; Kiernan *et al.*, 1971). There is a convergence of methodologies as the requirements of certain problems become clearer in experimental terms (Campbell and Stanley, 1963).

The techniques of behaviour modification experimentation have been developed in the natural environment and have demonstrated the feasibility, if not the ease, of this type of experimentation. In addition, experimentation in the natural environment allows the practitioner to demonstrate that particular experimental variables are not only effective in changing behaviour in the laboratory but also in the 'real life' setting. Put another way, experimentation in the natural environment can demonstrate the effectiveness or power of manipulated variables as they affect behaviour. Thus attention may be focused on potent variables and on variables which actually affect behaviour. This feature is likely to lead to an increased contact between research and practice and increased relevance of research to practice. In this, behaviour modification embraces a theme emphasized by other traditions within psychology over a considerable period of history (Barker and Wright, 1955; Willems and Raush, 1969), but in this case the critical feature is manipulation of variables, which allows decisions on the effectiveness of variables in changing behaviour in the natural environment to be made.

Mention should be made of the 'probe' procedure used in behaviour modification methodology to assess the effects of transfer or generalization of learning. The technique involves the use of a 'test' set of trials which is related in content to the training set, but on which the individual is never trained. Thus in an imitation training study the probe set may involve responses similar to those being trained which are presented for imitation at regular intervals, for instance after each segment of training in which a different type of response has been trained (Garcia *et al.*, 1971).

The probe procedure can be easily adapted for use in the classroom and other 'natural' settings. Here the effects of training are difficult to log on a trial-by-trial basis and the probe procedure offers a method of assessing progress in a standardized way within this type of teaching setting. This approach is characteristic of the use of precision teaching in behaviour modification. (cf. Tharp and Wetzel, 1969; Council for Exceptional Children, 1971).

THE LEARNING SITUATION

Procedures used in behaviour modification are potentially unrestricted in scope. Its central focus is changing behaviour, and any technique which is shown to be effective in this goal may be adopted (Krasner and Ullman, 1966). However, in general, workers in this area proceed on the assumption that the techniques are re-analysed in operant terms before use. The strength of the approach derives from the fact that basic principles can be used to analyse and, potentially, to improve the precision and effectiveness of practices of teaching.

(a) *Establishing responses and response sequences*

At the basis of the most commonly used procedures in behaviour modification is the concept of teaching through successive approximation to target behaviours. In turn the notion of behavioural analysis underlies the use of successive approximation. Successive approximation involves the analysis of behaviour into small steps and the reinforcement of progressively closer approximations to the final behaviour required, the target response, on successive trials.

There are two critical features of this strategy. Firstly, a very clear idea of the target behaviour must be worked out and objectively expressed. Once this task is completed it is possible to break down the steps necessary for achievement of the target response. Here again objective statement allows the teacher to identify appropriate and inappropriate approximations to the target behaviour. The second critical feature of the approach is that, given small enough step sizes, the level of success can be kept to 100 per cent. This question of rate of change of programme requirement is one of the major problems with shaping.

Within the behaviour modification framework these considerations lead in two directions. First, there has been an adoption of techniques used by workers in parallel traditions. These include an extension of educational technology with a particular emphasis on the statement of behavioural objectives, task analysis and systems analysis (Budde and Menolascino, 1971; Davies, 1971). The second direction leads to what may best be called 'art'. Procedures involving interaction between individuals are likely to require changes within the framework of any teaching session which allow for the shift in influence of different variables as a function of previous interactions. Therefore, although basic principles may be clearly stated, the application of these procedures may require moment by moment analysis of the situation concerned and response to this momentary state. Skill in successive approximation will then constitute a sensitivity to the optimal rate of change in requirements for appropriate performance. This aspect may be termed an 'art' since it represents a responsiveness to unique situations, but it must be emphasized that this 'art' is built on principles which can be explicitly stated and taught (Bricker, 1970).

(b) *Forward and backward chaining*

Some behaviours may be seen as single responses; for example, pressing a key on a typewriter or making the sound '*a*'. However, most responses are organized into sequences or chains with a definite temporal ordering. Turning on a water tap involves several responses, including identifying the position of the tap, extending the hand, gripping the tap and then turning it in a specified direction. Single responses within chains can usually be broken down into differently specified response sequences, possibly described in terms of sets of muscular movements.

The level of molarity of description of response sequences used in any programme will depend on the initial pattern of responses, i.e. the capabilities of the subject and the target behaviour aimed at. Whatever the level of specification, the sequence of training of components of the response chain presents a problem.

The behaviour modification approach suggests that behaviour chains should be established by beginning with the response which immediately precedes reinforcement. Once this is established, the second to last response is trained, and so on. Therefore, in putting on a jumper, the last response in the sequence may be pulling the jumper down to the waist, the second last pulling it over the head, etc. The first response trained would therefore be pulling the garment down, the second pulling it over the head. This strategy is termed *backward chaining*. The alternative strategy, *forward chaining*, would involve teaching the individual to pick up the jumper as a first step, then to position it for putting on, etc.

The suggested superiority of backward chaining stems from the fact that this strategy involves the trainee in first learning a rewarded response, then learning another response which leads directly to the already learned response, then a third also leading to learned responses and reward, and so on. In this way the trainee is always working into an already learned behaviour which continues to be rewarded. The learned behaviour is likely also to have conditioned reinforcing properties thus providing immediate reward.

In the forward chaining setting, the individual learns a response which continues to be rewarded only so long as it is the end of the chain. When another response is added, the initial response ceases to be rewarded unless the to-be-learned step follows readily. The effect of this procedure is likely to depend on the probability of the second unlearned step occurring, given the first. If the probability is high, either by the nature of the response or because step two is prompted, forward chaining may be effective. If the probability is low, extinction of the first response in the chain, with the possibility of emotional reactions to the learning situation, may substantially interfere with acquisition. Clearly this type of chaining is at best more 'risky' than backward chaining (but see Mahoney *et al.*, 1971, later).

In the management of learning situations a mixture of forward and backward chaining may be used. W. I. Gardner (1971) describes a situation in which a group of severely handicapped adults were taught a work task involving placing a leather washer on a 4-inch long nail, putting 18 completed units into a box, closing the box and putting it in a basket on the edge of the work bench. These tasks were trained using backward chaining, i.e. the first response trained was stacking closed boxes in the basket. The other responses in the sequence were then added. However, at the beginning of the study the trainees would not sit down at the work table. Therefore, initially they were rewarded for approaching and sitting at the table. This set of responses was rewarded as a separate chain until the work task was acquired at which stage the separate reward for sitting was progressively phased out.

A similar situation occurs in any setting where some responses are pre-requisite for correct performance. For example, in training correct imitation of a model Kiernan and Saunders (1972) found it necessary to teach initially uncooperative severely handicapped children to sit on a chair as a first pre-requisite, secondly to attend to the model on cue, and then to imitate appropriately. This use of forward chaining was necessary because the likelihood of appropriate modelling occurring without both types of pretraining was considered extremely low. The first components were pretrained in order to increase the probability of occurrence of correct responding in the situation of interest.

(c) *Establishing stimulus control*

We have already seen that stimuli can serve several functions within the behaviour modification framework. Stimuli may be discriminative for operants or may reinforce them. A response is considered to be under stimulus control when the probability of the response is high following presentation of the S^D or positive discriminative stimulus and low following the negative discriminative stimulus or S^Δ.

The concept of stimulus control is a very broad one. It encompasses those of generalization and discrimination and may relate to responses as simple as turning the eyes to a sound or light or as complex as delivering a lecture. The stimulus concept here is also broad, ranging from the onset of a simple light, through instructions which may be simple or highly complex, to complicated and subtle situational cues. The use of the term 'stimulus control' stems from the need to distinguish empirical functions of stimuli from process usages of terms like discrimination and generalization (Terrace, 1966).

The strategy for building stimulus control involves the positive reinforcement of appropriate responses in the presence of the S^D and either non-reinforcement or negative reinforcement of responses in S^Δ.

Simple examples of the establishment of stimulus control come from the use of operant techniques in sensory testing. Macht (1971) evaluated visual acuity in a group of 5 non-verbal severely handicapped children and 2 normal adults. The procedure consisted of 4 phases.

In Phase 1 the subject was taught to press a lever with a consumable reinforcer. During this phase the S^D, an illuminated E, was displayed all the time in front of the subject in the darkened test room. Phase 2 was initiated when there was a pause in responding. At this the illuminated display was darkened for 2 to 3 seconds building up to 10 seconds by the end of Phase 2. If lever-pressing occurred during this time the examiner said 'no', gave the subject a slight slap on the responding hand and did not deliver positive reinforcement. Criterial behaviour in this phase was defined as depressing the lever in the presence of E with the lights on, and not pressing the lever at other times.

During Phases 1 and 2 the S^Δ, a reversed E, was covered by a black card. During Phase 3 a reversed E was presented; initially completely covered by a card and then, in 11 steps the reversed E was gradually revealed. Criterion behaviour at the end of Phase 3 involved response in the presence of the correct E and non-response to the reverse E. In Phase 4 Macht assessed acuity by gradually increasing the distance between the subject and the display until responding broke down and it was necessary to move the subject closer in order to re-establish responding.

Macht's procedure is similar to several others developed to assess visual or auditory acuity (Bricker and Bricker, 1969; Spradlin *et al.*, 1969). For example Stolz and Wolf (1969) describe a complex study in which a 16-year-old retarded boy diagnosed as organically blind and treated by those around him as such was taught fine-grain discriminations in a two-choice setting, was taught to make and maintain eye contact on request, and was taught complex self-help skills depending on vision. The Stoltz and Wolf study represents an extensive development of stimulus control in dealing with a single case. Several approaches to establishing control were used, including instructing the subject's responses. It is worth emphasizing that workers in the behaviour modification tradition use verbal instruction and guidance where appropriate, often in conjunction with other procedures. Hence, in this case, the boy's plate was removed for 10 seconds for certain types of inappropriate eating behaviour. When this happened the boy was told the reason.

It is sometimes suggested that behaviour modification techniques are too elaborate for the problems they face. For example it is suggested that, rather than have a complex prompt and fade programme, it would be simpler and more direct to instruct the subject verbally. Clearly, however, verbal instructions are a form of prompt, and in any case the individual has to learn to follow instructions and can be taught to do so using behaviour modification techniques (Whitman *et al.*, 1971).

In practice a behaviour modification programme would include a pre-test phase during which the potentiality of the individual for following such prompts would be investigated.

A further important point concerns stimulus control. Although a stimulus, like the delivery of a consumable, or an event like cuddling a child and smiling, may function primarily as a reinforcement, it will also have discriminative aspects. Spradlin, Girardeau and Hom (1966) present evidence which shows that, after acquisition and extinction of a response, the delivery of free reinforcement leads to the recommencement of responding. In this laboratory study, the response was lever pressing. However, the authors point out that there are possible implications for other responses and settings. If a reinforcer, for example adult attention, has been contingent on undesirable behaviour, then giving attention may lead to recurrence of this behaviour.

This 'priming' function of reinforcement is illustrated in an unpublished study by Kiernan and Burgess (1971). They rewarded upright walking in a severely handicapped blind child. Initially social reinforcement was used but abandoned when it was found to cue the child to circle round on one spot whilst smiling and laughing. Observation outside the experimental setting showed that this behaviour was frequently reinforced by the child being picked up and swung round or cuddled. Use of an alternative reinforcer, the opportunity to ring and throw a hand-bell, produced appropriate walking when the child's name was called from a distance.

In this case the social reinforcer apparently performed a discriminative function for circling and laughing. Similar findings are reported by Stolz and Wolf (1969), by Ayllon and Azrin (1968) with psychiatric patients, and by Bernal (1969) with emotionally disturbed children. Patterson and Reid (1970) provide an interesting theoretical discussion of dyadic interaction in behaviour modification terms. Stolz and Wolf (1969) showed that the appropriate, i.e. non-blind, behaviour of their subject was dependent on the behaviour of those around him. As soon as he was reinforced for single behaviours related to blindness, other behaviours in this class recurred. This setting function of reinforcement is also demonstrated with a blind individual by Brady and Lind (1961) and Grosz and Zimmerman (1965).

Studies by Redd and Birnbrauer (1969) and Redd (1969) demonstrate that normal adults take on discriminative functions for handicapped children which are related to the reinforcement history of the child with the adult. Redd and Birnbrauer used a procedure in which two subjects were positively reinforced for play by an adult who came into the playroom for two 5-minute periods out of a 39-minute session. A second adult dispensed rewards on a non-contingent basis over two separate 5-minute periods. Amount of attention and amount of reward was controlled between adults, the systematically manipulated variable being whether the adult required appropriate play from the children before reward was dispensed. Redd and Birnbrauer showed that the play behaviour of the children did not change when the 'non-contingent' adult came into the room, in fact the children ignored him. When the 'contingent' adult entered the room the children began to play appropriately. In other words the play behaviour of the children was under discriminative stimulus control of the contingent adult, but not of the non-contingent adult despite his free dispensing of reward.

This result indicates the necessity for contingent reinforcement in changing behaviour. It also contrasts with the studies quoted above (Spradlin *et al.*, 1966; Kiernan and Burgess, 1971) in that here the reinforcer did not control behaviour. The behaviour was under control of the adult as a discriminative stimulus probably because the adult was a more reliable predictor of response requirements than the reinforcer.

An extension and replication of this study by Redd (1969) showed the same general effects. In addition however Redd investigated the effects of a 'mixed' régime, i.e. discriminative stimulus properties of an adult who sometimes rewarded contingently and sometimes non-contingently. Redd showed that non-contingent delivery of reward by this adult produced no change in behaviour until he withheld reward. At this point the children began playing in the manner required for reinforcement. In this instance we see a demonstration of the discriminative or setting properties of the adult with appropriate behaviour being cued by the *absence* of reward at the end of the non-contingent session (cf. Spradlin *et al.*, 1966).

This discussion does not exhaust the complexities of considerations raised by the stimulus control concept. It is hoped that the discussion illustrates the shortcomings of a simplistic approach. One aspect which will be given more attention later is the consideration of generalization from one setting or teacher to another. What has been said already should serve to illustrate some of the problems with this operation.

(d) *Teaching techniques*

The breakdown of behaviour into steps, the successive approximation of the reinforced response, using a chaining procedure and under particular stimulus control, represents one dimension of the behaviour modification approach. The teaching technique used within this framework represents a further dimension. As with other features of behaviour modification these methods are not novel. They are traditional procedures which are informed by the operant theory.

(i) *Shaping*. Response shaping refers to the procedure whereby a subject is rewarded for successive approximations to the target behaviour with each trial or block of trials requiring a more developed response. Characteristically a backward chaining procedure is used when there is a particular topography of response to be produced. Alternatively, the frequency of a response may be modified through differential reinforcement.

Examples of simple shaping where responses are chained are rare in the literature. The reason is that it is often more economical to use prompts and physical guidance rather than waiting for successive variants of a response to occur. Exceptions are speech sound production where the initial production of some speech sounds may be difficult to prompt completely. Even here, however, the individual may be taught to imitate such responses as opening and shutting the mouth, placing the tongue, blowing out matches, or playing the kazoo, and the child's lips, tongue and mouth may be physically guided (Sloane *et al.*, 1968).

Shaping in terms of increasing the frequency of a response is a more common procedure. In this case the response topography is not deliberately modified. Examples vary from increase in the frequency of lever pressing or panel pushing to responses as complex as social interaction (Orlando, 1965, lever pressing; Hopkins, 1968, smiling; Whitman *et al.*, 1970, social interaction).

Positive reinforcement for non-responding or negative reinforcement for responding as shaping techniques for eliminating behaviour are also fairly commonly used. For example, Paul and Miller (1971) used a procedure in which negative behaviours, including self-destruction, tantrums, spitting and throwing objects including faeces, were reduced by negative reinforcement (time-out) and positive behaviours increased through reinforcement with a consumable reward.

The critical feature of shaping as a training procedure is that the teacher does not intervene in terms of physical guidance, provision of prompts or other props. Other aspects of the procedure, i.e. the use of a graded series of tasks and principles of chaining are shared with other procedures.

(ii) *Prompt and fade.* Two types of procedure are often included under this head. Physical guidance may be given to the handicapped individual, or a verbal or visual prompt may be used. In both cases the individual's behaviour is reinforced when appropriate, regardless of prompting. In both cases rapid withdrawal of the prompt is desirable.

The procedures represent examples of development of stimulus control. In the case of training using physical guidance, the control is transferred from manual or other cues provided by the trainer to the self-generated, propriocep-tive or visual cues guiding particular responses. Prompt and fade procedures involving verbal or visual cueing with a gradual fading or modification of the cue by the trainer may not involve a change in the form of response, only of its timing.

Zeiler and Jervey (1968) describe a typical prompt and fade procedure involving guidance. They worked with a 15-year-old severely handicapped institutionalized girl. The child did not feed herself with a spoon; at first her hand was placed on the spoon with an overhard grip. The spoon was loaded with food and brought to her mouth with the teacher moving both spoon and hand and also putting the spoon in the child's mouth for the first few spoonfuls. On subsequent trials, the teacher released the spoon just in front of her lips, the child continuing the movement of the spoon to her mouth without help. In a second session the spoon was released progressively further from the child's mouth until by the end of the session she was moving it from her plate. Other steps were accomplished in subsequent sessions. It will be noted that this procedure involved backward chaining and successive approximation.

Physical guidance and verbal or visual prompting are typically used together in single programmes. Thus a dressing programme may involve a first step of physical guidance and verbal prompting, as skill in putting on individual garments is established. Once individual garments can be put on, the control of initiation of, for example, putting on shoes may be transferred from verbal cues to the sight of feet with socks on and shoes near.

In complex uses of prompt and fade procedures careful task analysis, a graded series of tasks and the principle of backward chaining are typically used (cf. Zeiler and Jervey, 1968).

Prompt and fade procedures are probably the most commonly used methods in behaviour modification studies. This is especially so where new responses are to be established. Here physical guidance is very common. Experience with this suggests the desirability of rapid elimination of prompts, especially of prompts provided at the end of the response sequence. If these are not eliminated rapidly they can become discriminative stimuli for pausing on the part of the trainee until prompted (Kiernan and Saunders, 1972).

A good example of the use of verbal prompting and physical guidance is provided by Whitman, Zakaras and Chardos (1971). They trained two severely handicapped children to follow sets of instructions ranging from 'sit down' to 'put the pencil in the box' or 'put your hands under the table'. Each response was initially physically guided completely but rewarded none the less. Guidance was withdrawn on a backward chaining principle until the children were initiating the responses given only the verbal instruction. The study showed the dependence of correct responding on positive reinforcement and also demonstrated a generalization of instruction – following a set of instructions which were not rewarded. This latter finding suggested that the children concerned were being brought under general stimulus control rather than simply learning a specific set of responses to instructions.

(iii) *Imitation or modelling.* These terms tend to be used fairly interchangeably in behaviour modification literature. They refer to a procedure whereby the to-be-learned response is modelled, usually by a normal adult. Typically the handicapped individual is cued to attend – 'Timmy, look – do this' – the behaviour modelled and then the individual allowed time to imitate before re-presentation of the same or a different model.[1]

Imitation training has been used widely with the mentally handicapped from the time of Séguin and Itard (Ball, 1970). Recently it has received increased attention, partly because of its advantages over shaping as a means of training. Clearly, if a response can be demonstrated and then imitated by the handicapped individual, rate of acquisition can be enhanced very substantially. This strength has led to the development of techniques for training the generalized tendency to imitate, a topic to which we will return later in this chapter.

Modelling or imitation can be seen as a form of prompt and fade procedure. The essential difference lies in the fact that the individual is required to reproduce, not simply to follow, the prompt. However, as in the prompt and fade procedure the prompt may be eliminated in the course of training.

Paloutzian, Hasazi, Streifel and Edgar (1971) provide an example of extensive use of imitation training. The social interaction of twenty children in one ward of an institution was recorded. Ten of these were then randomly assigned to a training group and taught individually to imitate a set of behaviours modelled by an adult. These ranged from folding hands to moving a chair or tugging an ear lobe. During this stage physical prompts were used and all appropriate responses rewarded, regardless of whether they had been physically guided. The next phase of the experiment involved modelling social interaction with other children from the ward. Children were trained in pairs, the exact composition of each pair was changed frequently to promote generalization. The social interaction responses were modelled and physically prompted as necessary. These included walking up to another subject and gently stroking his face, pushing another child in a swing, pulling a peer in a wagon and passing a bean bag. Paloutzian and his colleagues showed a generalization from the off-ward

[1] In fact Bandura's research would suggest that the model ought to be rewarded for his performance in order to demonstrate that reward occurs. Bandura (1965), using normal children, showed that performance was significantly influenced by this factor. The practice has not been followed in behaviour modification work and it is possible that its influence is overridden by reinforcement of the individual trained.

training situation to social interaction on the ward as a result of this training. No change from pre-test to post-test was shown by control subjects. After completion of the study, generalization was assisted by having the ward staff deliver positive social reinforcement, contingent on positive responses in the ward setting. In addition the fact that the children apparently enjoyed the new activities probably significantly assisted the maintenance of the new responses.

Imitation or modelling procedures have been used widely in behaviour modification studies, especially in the area of language understanding and acquisition (cf. Peterson, 1968; Bricker and Bricker, 1970; Buddenhagen, 1971; W. A. Bricker, 1972; D. D. Bricker, 1972). As such they represent potentially powerful procedures for promoting change in the behaviour of the handicapped which unite the strengths of other procedures (Bandura, 1969). However one point about behaviour modification uses of modelling is the relative divorce from general psychological work on imitation (Flanders, 1968). It is to be hoped that valuable features of this research may be explored within a behaviour modification context in the future.

(iv) *Other procedures*. The techniques of training listed above represent the main strategies used in behaviour modification. In the case of the elimination of avoidance behaviour, desensitization through counterconditioning based on the principles of successive approximation, chaining and stimulus control would be one typical strategy (Bandura, 1969; Sherman and Baer, 1969; Kanfer and Phillips, 1970). In this author's experience such studies are rare with the mentally handicapped.

Punishment training and escape training procedures follow the basic principles outlined above. In the case of punishment training, most studies report that shaping procedures are used (e.g. Hamilton *et al.*, 1967). In the very rare documented instances of escape training, shaping was again utilized (Bucher and Lovaas, 1968). In the case of escape training, prompting of the escape response would be likely to speed acquisition.

Implications of behaviour modification

So far, this discussion has been restricted to the presentation and explanation of the basic approach taken by behaviour modification to the behaviour of the handicapped. This has far-reaching implications which will now be considered.

It will be argued that if behaviour modification is accepted as a basic approach, the strategy for modifying the behaviour of the mentally handicapped requires several steps or stages. These are: the initial setting of goals and the assessment of behaviour in relation to these goals both before and after modification; change in the physical layout of the teaching environment in order to maximize the initial probability of responding; change in the structure of interaction between the mentally handicapped individual and the teacher such that the latter provides appropriate discriminative stimuli and immediate appropriate reinforcement for behaviour; and a modification of the social and material environment in which the individual lives in order to maximize the probability of transfer or generalization from the teaching to the living environment.

These stages may be summarized as involving a need to specify goals, a need to modify the teaching environment to allow learning to occur with maximum ease, a need to reinforce appropriately and a need to modify the living environment as necessary, to ensure transfer of new behaviour.

Finally, the approach raises questions concerning the curriculum for the mentally handicapped. It is important to emphasize at this stage that the method does not and cannot dictate the goals of education. Behaviour modification is not a content area – it consists only of a set of procedures to modify behaviour and does not state which behaviours should be modified. The goals of education must be derived from other sources (MacMillan and Forness, 1970). But the approach has important implications for the route by which goals may be achieved.

Assessment may perform a critical role within an administrative framework. For example, a child may be assigned to one type of educational setting or another primarily on the basis of IQ and related assessments. On the other hand, assessment may provide guidance at any degree of specificity within a particular educational framework, right down to the dictation of particular remedial procedures (Clarke and Clarke, 1973).

Within the behaviour modification framework assessment plays a specific role in describing the current state of behaviour. This assessment is normally termed functional analysis since it analyses the effects of variables which are functional in the control of behaviour in any specified setting. It will be readily appreciated that more usual types of assessment do not have this goal, nor can they achieve it since they do not normally involve any systematic evaluation of functional stimuli (Kiernan, 1973a).

There are three steps followed in functional analysis (W. I. Gardner, 1971; Kiernan, 1973a). These are, firstly, the description of behaviour; secondly, the analysis of discriminative stimuli supporting behaviour; and thirdly, the analysis of reinforcing or consequating stimuli (Bijou *et al.*, 1968; W. I. Gardner, 1971; Kiernan, 1973a).

Descriptions of behaviour are in terms of its topography, frequency and any other relevant characteristics. Behaviour is specified at the same level of description which is to be used in modification. Bijou, Peterson and Ault (1968), in describing this approach, emphasize the need to specify the environmental setting in effective terms, to specify the behaviour which is being observed and to define objectively relevant stimuli and responses. These workers distinguish between specific and general observational codes. The former relate to particular problems or sets of problems, e.g. occurrence of spontaneous speech, occurrence of temper tantrums. The latter relate to more general events, for instance, vocalizations or physical contacts. Much behaviour modification with the mentally handicapped requires the development of specific codes for problem behaviours. However, general codes may be used in the training or teaching setting.

For example, a study by Hall and Broden (1967) demonstrated successful modification of rates of play behaviour in brain-injured children through social reinforcement. Up to 5 informal pre-data observation sessions were employed with each child. Then observers and teachers established criteria for the occurrence of the behaviour of interest. Once these criteria were established, and inter-observer reliability was checked, a formal recording sheet was adopted. In this case, a code was evolved which allowed a continuous record of play behaviour of the child, and verbalizations and proximity of the adult, during each 10-second interval of each session.

The initial description of behaviour is likely to generate hypotheses concerning discriminative or setting stimuli. These functional stimuli may be either precise, closely defined stimulus classes or very general setting stimuli. The extent to which a stimulus functions either as discriminative, setting or reinforcing can only be established by manipulating it in the applied setting (Bijou *et al.*, 1968; Kiernan, 1973a). This represents the critical difference between a purely observational form of assessment and one concerned with functional analysis. Manipulation of stimuli in the applied setting in order to investigate their functional properties represents the paradigm of experimental analysis. However, precise analysis of the discriminative and reinforcing functions of stimuli is rare in published literature. This consideration applies particularly to discriminative functions. Most workers appear to rely on a clear specification of the behaviour to be modified, a clear baseline record of this behaviour and the manipulation of potent reinforcing stimuli to change behaviour. The attempt may be made to override any effects of existing discriminative stimuli by eliminating some sources during training and supplying new ones which are then associated with known reinforcers. Generalization back to the natural environment is then ideally graded and carefully controlled.

Rate of reinforcement may be manipulated without a very precise analysis of the nature of the reinforcing event. Thus attention may be made contingent on correct performance when level of relevant attending behaviour on the part of adults has been low (Hall, 1970) or the response of adults may be considered to be maintaining aberrant behaviour, for instance vomiting (Wolf *et al.*, 1970). The experimental procedure in these cases involved paying attention to appropriate behaviour, and withdrawing all reinforcement for inappropriate behaviour. However, no attempt was made in these studies to break down the discriminative stimuli controlling behaviour. In the Wolf study, operant vomiting apparently occurred only in the classroom setting. Although it is possible that particular discriminative stimuli were setting the occasion for vomiting, the intervention strategy involved an increase in the amount of positive reinforcement given during non-vomiting periods and a withdrawal of the usual event of return to dormitory following a vomiting episode without analysis of particular discriminative stimuli.

This approach can be justified in several ways. Firstly, the reinforcers supporting behaviour may be maintaining behaviour on an intermittent schedule and therefore may be relatively difficult to identify (Kiernan, 1973a). Secondly, stimulus control may be loose and based on the individual responding to a highly idiosyncratic discriminative stimulus class (Kiernan and Burgess, 1971).

In fact, it seems most likely that effects such as those described earlier in the section on stimulus control will characterize many real life settings. To try to unravel the effects of a complex reinforcement history may or may not be a useful enterprise. As already noted, most workers appear to adopt a strategy of using settings and reinforcers designed to override preceding history.

Further analysis of discriminative and reinforcing stimuli may be necessary if the attempt at modification fails. Clearly this will be expected and will not appear in the literature unless successful modification eventually occurs, because of the tendency to publish only accounts of successful modification (Gelfand and Hartmann, 1968; J. M. Gardner, 1971).

However, attention needs to be paid to discriminative stimuli in studies of pre-academic or academic performance. For example, the series of studies by Sidman and Stoddard (1967) in circle-ellipse discrimination, the subsequent researches by Sidman and Touchette (e.g. Touchette, 1968, 1969, 1971) and the work of Bijou (1968) on the development of left-right concepts, all show the necessity for sensitive analysis of the discriminative stimuli controlling the individual's behaviour.

Conclusion

The implications of behaviour modification for assessment are that techniques are required which allow a continuity of recording between baseline and experimental procedures. An analysis of the extent to which stimuli in the situation function as discriminative or reinforcing is necessary in order to formulate hypotheses concerning control of behaviour. It has been argued, however, that detailed analysis is not usual provided change occurs. This is likely if potent reinforcers are used as consequences for new behaviour in modified settings with a gradual transfer to the normal living environment or a modification of that setting.

Implications for the establishment of learning situations

In this section, problems arising in the practical implementation of behaviour modification in a natural setting will be considered. These include the selection of reinforcers, and of techniques of training and type of consequence, the reorganization of the learning and living environment and the modification of the behaviour of normal adults in the life-space of the handicapped individual.

First the various types of reinforcer used with the mentally handicapped will be described.

TYPES OF REINFORCERS

An exhaustive listing of possible reinforcers would be impossible. However, certain classifications are perhaps helpful. One class is directly available in the teaching setting. Such reinforcers may be consumable, including the individual's normal diet of food or drink, or extra items like sweets, savouries, ice cream, or drinks of juice. Manipulable reinforcers include toys or trinkets which the individual may be allowed to retain and items which may be available only during training. Sensory reinforcers, flashing lights, vibration, music or other noises are fairly frequently used. Clearly some of these, specifically trinkets, may be stored and removed from the experimental setting. In this case storing may be either enforced by the teacher or may be optional (Bijou and Sturges, 1959).

Rather than supplying consumable, manipulable or sensory reinforcers directly in the experimental setting, whether they are stored or not, the reinforcer can be supplied following training, in exchange for tokens or points gained during teaching. In this case, consumables and other reinforcers function as back-up reinforcers to the generalized conditioned reinforcers, tokens or points. When these latter are exchanged the individual can be given a choice of reinforcers with individuals functioning at an appropriate level. Events like trips out to the cinema or other 'treats' may be traded in exchange for tokens or points.

Positive social rewards can be classed in several ways (Bersoff, 1971). On the positive side, social rewards in the form of attention may be either distal (a smile) or proximal (a cuddle). They may or may not involve verbalization.

Negative reinforcers are equally variable. Non-social sensory reinforcers include the occasional use of brief electric shock, and the more frequent use of withdrawal of the individual from settings where he is experiencing positive consumable, manipulable or sensory reinforcers. In distinction to the positive case, negative reinforcers cannot be 'stored up', except in the situation where tokens or points are used. Here tokens or points may be removed immediately following behaviour and thereby negatively affect availability of back-up reinforcers. This operation, however, corresponds to a simple reduction in amount of positive reinforcement available. Threats of future punishment of a more active kind are, fortunately, not used in behaviour modification programmes.

Negative social reinforcers may again be either distal or proximal and again may or may not involve verbalization. By far the most common form of negative social reinforcement is withdrawal of attention. It may also be the most effective. Simple negative social reinforcement, saying 'no' or, less frequently, slapping, is reported in some studies, often in conjunction with positive reinforcement for desirable behaviour. Other types of negative social reinforcement include the use of holding and 'restitution'. Holding is a technique which has been successfully used in the elimination of problem behaviours like toy throwing and hitting with pre-school retarded children. It consists in holding the child still by the arms until the child ceases to resist being held (Bricker, personal communication). Restitution is described by Azrin and Foxx (1972). This involves the offending individual in 'making good' the situation created by aberrant behaviour. Thus an individual who throws objects would be required to pick them up, to tidy other items in his environment and possibly to calm individuals upset by the throwing. This procedure is clearly more complex as a negatively reinforcing event than are others quoted. Azrin and Foxx claim that this procedure is effective with long-standing problems and it has more positive aspects than most negative reinforcers.

This description of reinforcers is not meant to be either exhaustive or to suggest that all mentally handicapped individuals will respond to all reinforcers. As with other facets of behaviour modification, the question of applicability in the individual case is an empirical one. Reinforcers may be highly idiosyncratic. Recently we came across a child who was rewarded by being allowed to feed the adult with sweets; she herself would not eat them. Considerable ingenuity is required in identifying such reinforcers.

SELECTION OF REINFORCERS

The appropriate selection of a reinforcing event is critical for the success of behaviour modification. It may be suggested that, in general, the problems of the mentally handicapped relate to the fact that their behaviour is not apparently controlled by conventional reinforcers including social, food and drink. Nurses, teachers and parents often point out that it is difficult to find what is a reward or punishment for their charges. Since the success of a behaviour modification programme is dependent on appropriate reinforcer selection, these constraints could be very serious. This is a substantial problem but it is often possible to identify reinforcers which may however be idiosyncratic and clumsy to use.

There are several ways in which reinforcers may be identified. Firstly, adults familiar with the child may be asked to describe events which appear rewarding or punishing and which can be then systematically explored in learning situations. A direct questioning approach may be used with some mentally handicapped individuals (cf. Addison and Homme, 1966; Clements and McKee, 1968) but clearly this would not apply with the severely handicapped. Indirect preference techniques may be used. For example, severely handicapped hospitalized children were presented with five potential rewards, all edibles which they were known to like to some extent. The children were allowed free choice and the order in which the items were selected and the latency of selection were recorded. Repeated testing over a ten-day period showed a very high stability of choices (Riddick and Kiernan, 1972). A review of scaling techniques by Siegel (1968) serves to emphasize the complexity of scaling problems presented by reinforcer selection. What is clear from his review is that if there is an interest in modification of a particular behaviour, it may well be best to select the reinforcer by a technique which examines reinforcement in a setting close to the training setting. In particular, it would appear that the relation between the technique used to establish preference and the type of measure used in training, i.e. rate, error, etc., needs careful consideration. In the study mentioned above there appears to be a close relation between free choice preference and control of rate of performance in simple tasks (Riddick and Kiernan, 1972).

The approach taken by Premack (1959, 1965) to reinforcer selection involves observing the proportion of time spent engaged in different activities, when free choice is allowed in the natural or experimental environment. Premack argues that the longer the duration of time spent in an activity the higher its reward value.

This approach indicates a second technique for selecting reinforcing activities. However, the settings in which handicapped individuals live are often such as to provide very few possible activities in which they can engage. It seems likely that one way round the difficulty of identifying reinforcers in these settings would be to provide an 'enriched' environment which could be 'sampled' by the handicapped individual on a cafeteria basis. The preference hierarchy then observed could be used to identify rewarding behaviours. It seems clear, however, that some individuals may fail to interact with this type of environment and in this case active interventionist tactics may be essential. This may involve a period during which the individual is positively encouraged to touch, taste, feel or see a set of potential reinforcers.

The vagueness of specification of procedures at this level stems from the fact that little is known about the ways in which basic reinforcers develop. This is the phenomenon that Murphy (1947) referred to as canalization, but despite its early description little relevant work appears to be available in the general developmental literature.

A central point so far as the operant approach is concerned is that there may be a need with some individuals to build up rewarding events *before* behaviour modification can be attempted.

THE IDEAL REINFORCER

There are several defining features of the ideal reinforcer which can be deduced from the basic laws of learning taken in relation to the general aims of behaviour modification.

It should be possible to deliver the reinforcer *immediately* following the defined response. Therefore the fact that sweets or other consumables cannot be easily delivered direct into the mouth means that they are not ideal. Similarly, it is often difficult to arrange the environment in such a way that rewarding activities, like playing with a toy, follow immediately on the desired response. The best type of reinforcement from the immediacy viewpoint is a sensory event. Therefore visual displays, sounds, or vibration which can be produced immediately may be ideal (Bailey and Meyerson, 1969; Greene and Hoats,

1969). Conditioned reinforcers, especially verbal social reinforcers, are also excellent in this respect.

A second important defining feature of the ideal reinforcer is that it should be *easy* to deliver and withdraw. In terms of ease of delivery the main problems relate to the bahaviour of the modifier rather than that of the handicapped individual. One can suggest as a 'law' that the less effortful the operation of reinforcement for the behaviour modifier, the more likely he or she is to persist in modification. Once again verbal social reinforcers or tokens, as opposed to edible reinforcers, appear to have an advantage. It 'costs' little in terms of energy expenditure to praise an individual or to hand out a token whereas much effort and organization may be involved in the preparation and delivery of edible or manipulable reinforcers.

A third characteristic of the ideal reinforcer is that it should not interfere with, or interrupt, appropriate behaviour but should still provide an ongoing reinforcement control. Once again the drawbacks of contingently delivered edibles are clear. The use of social reinforcement, or other sensory reinforcement, may also be a problem under certain settings (for example, where the individual is 'distracted' by it), but in general, the use of tokens, points which are given or removed, social and sensory reinforcement are likely to interfere less with ongoing behaviour.

The fourth characteristic of the ideal reinforcer is that it should not be subject to rapid satiation effects. However, little research on satiation has been undertaken within the operant framework. Some types of reinforcer are clearly subject to satiation effects. Prime among these are food and drinks. The evidence provided by Gewirtz (1967) suggests that children may satiate for social reinforcement. Satiation effects within sessions may be minimized if the reinforcers delivered are conditioned ones which are backed up outside the training sessions. Social interaction and tokens or points all fall into this category.

The fifth characteristic appears rather trivial at first sight, but is of substantial importance. Some reinforcers take time to consume, for example sweets or other edibles. Time spent in this way can obviously be cut down by using small quantities and reinforcing frequently. However, their use can be cumbersome. The opportunity to play with toys can produce greater problems. The child usually has to be required to give up the toy after, say, 30 to 60 seconds if the teaching session is not to be infinitely extended. This is likely to be negatively reinforcing for the child or adult concerned. Clearly the optimal reinforcer is one which, when presented, disappears quickly and painlessly, or which is retained by the trainee without on-the-spot 'consumption'. Thus again verbal social reinforcement proves ideal; cuddling or other types of physical contact may present problems of termination if the handicapped individual does not wish to be released. Tokens, points, or edibles which are cumulated during the session and exchanged at the end also satisfy this requirement.

A final critical characteristic of the ideal reinforcer is that it is transituational. In other words, the ideal reinforcer would be usable in a wide variety of settings and by a wide variety of administering individuals. This characteristic is of central importance. If the generalization of trained behaviour is to occur in a variety of non-training situations, there is a serious danger of the handicapped individual learning to discriminate between the settings, and to produce the trained behaviour only in those where reinforcement of a particular type is provided. Thus, if material reinforcers are used consistently in a training situation, transfer to settings where material rewards are not provided is not likely to be complete and may not occur at all.

For example, Kiernan and Saunders (1972) showed that generalization of learned imitation of models, who had not trained the handicapped child, was minimal until the child was reinforced in generalization tests by them. When a prompted response was reinforced, full imitation of a probe set occurred. This evidence suggests that the child was discriminating clearly between settings in which he was reinforced and settings in which this did not occur. This is another example of complex stimulus control (see earlier discussion of stimulus control).

It would seem centrally important to build up reinforcers which can be used transituationally. Clearly social reinforcers meet this criterion most completely. If the individual becomes appropriately responsive to social reinforcement, he has become integrated into the natural reinforcing setting provided by the society (Baer and Wolf, 1967). Time spent in establishing social reinforcers may pay off in terms of more rapid and extensive generalization of responses. This will only occur, however, if the form and scheduling of social reinforcement as well as the frequency of back-up reinforcement is sufficiently similar to the training setting. It is always possible that the reinforcement scheduling provided by the natural environment may not be adequate to support the behaviour of the handicapped individual. Furthermore, handicapped individuals may be less able to provide self-reinforcement than the normal individual and therefore be at a continual disadvantage in a normal setting (cf. Bandura, 1969).

The alternative form of conditioned reinforcement, tokens or points, has strengths and weaknesses similar to social reinforcement. Points or tokens are in addition 'storable' and do suggest the possibility of generalization to the use of normal currency. Again, however, the degree to which generalization to the natural environment can occur will depend on the extent to which the programme teaches the handicapped individual to work within the contingencies provided by the natural environment and the degree to which the individual's behaviour can be maintained by the contingencies provided in this environment.

MULTIPLE REINFORCEMENT

One practical solution to the difficulties of providing adequate reinforcement is to use several reinforcers concurrently (Logan *et al.*, 1971). This may be done either by using a variety of them on each trial, for example a social reward, immediately delivered, followed by a material reward, offered after 2 or 3 seconds, and another social reward, a cuddle, delivered after 5 to 8 seconds, or by giving a different selection on each trial.

The overall effect of this technique should be to provide both a more powerful overall reinforcement and also a situation in which weak social reinforcers may become more powerful through conditioning effects. Once again the precise nature of these effects needs exploration under controlled conditions in order to investigate the interaction of different positive reinforcers and the additivity of effects.

Intermittent presentation of reinforcers will clearly delay satiation to any single reinforcer. This could be capitalized on by using several different reinforcers at different times during the session. Thus multiple reinforcers would be used but in a successive rather than a simultaneous manner.

In all cases it is likely that the effects of multiple reinforcers offset the defects of less than optimal individual ones in the training setting, but in all cases there is still substantial room for applied research which would investigate interaction effects.

McReynolds (1970) suggests a further dimension. She demonstrated that verbal responses which were not modified early in training by social reinforcers were modified when ice cream was used as reward. These responses could then be maintained by social reinforcement. McReynolds suggests that initial acquisition may require more 'effort' on the part of the subject and hence stronger reinforcers than maintenance of the response once acquired. The author points out that typically speech therapists avoid material reinforcers and indeed the study she describes was on a 4-year-old brain-damaged child who had been 'found unsuitable for speech training'.

MECHANICAL AIDS

A word should be added concerning the use of mechanical aids to deliver reinforcement. These may be of various types, ranging from a switch to turn on a light, or a button to press to produce a sound, up to a complex and expensive reinforcement dispenser. There is a mystique surrounding the use of mechanical aids; such aids are only of use to the extent that they mediate the immediate delivery of reinforcement. To this end they can be of immense value. However, it is clear that they tend to lack generality, they are not likely to be available in a variety of settings, and must therefore serve primarily to provide a means whereby conditioned reinforcement, especially social reinforcement, can be either established or backed up.

CONDITIONED REINFORCEMENT

A good deal has been said in the previous section about the value of conditioned reinforcers, especially tokens or points, and some types of social reinforcement. These are termed generalized conditioned reinforcers since they signify the availability of a wide range of back-up reinforcers (Kelleher and Gollub, 1962).

Ayllon and Azrin (1968) argue that tokens have advantages over other forms of generalized conditioned reinforcers mainly on the grounds that they are tangible and therefore storable, portable, usable in a wide range of contexts and can be durable. In this respect they provide a tangible means of bridging time gaps in a way not possible when social reinforcers only are used.

Kazdin and Bootzin (1972) add that tokens provide a visible record of improvement and facilitate social reinforcement from staff members, as well as self-reinforcement. In effect, they instate all of the values which bank managers urge on their clients.

Despite the obvious parallel with normal money, and the possibility of phasing out tokens and phasing in money as currency, the token system retains a certain artificiality in the ways noted previously. Conditioned social reinforcers are clearly the type more usually dispensed in a face-to-face setting, especially for children. Since part of the problem posed by mental handicap involves adequate integration into natural communities, where social reinforcement is the currency, a direct approach to the establishment of social reinforcers may be more appropriate. Token systems may be more useful where a variety of individuals, no one of whom may have consistent contact with the mentally handicapped individual, have dealings with him. Thus ward-based programmes, with constantly changing staff, may need to run on a token basis in order to overcome problems inherent in each staff member having to develop relationships with each 'patient'. The desirability of this situation represents a separate question. If large, poorly staffed wards exist, it would be inhumane to reject even unsatisfactory part-solutions to their problems.

The establishment of generalized conditioned reinforcers occurs, according to the theory, through a consistent pairing of the initially neutral event with an established reinforcer, the neutral event always preceding the latter. This generalization holds for the establishment of both positive and negative conditioned reinforcers. For example, Locke (1969) showed that the reinforcing value of 'good' was enhanced when it was paired with delivery of a valued token. He also found that precise pairing was not essential for increase in reward value, but that the occurrence of 'good' and the delivery of the valued token in the same setting was essential. Bucher and Lovaas (1968) report that pairing the word 'no' with electroshock for inappropriate behaviour produces behaviour suppression in retarded autistic children. They also report the use of a 'relief' procedure for building positive responsiveness. Here the child could avoid shock for inappropriate behaviour by turning to the adult. Clear indication of the acquisition of reward value was shown by means of a pre- and post-test.

Work at the infra-human level would suggest that the conditioned reinforcer should be uniquely discriminative for established reinforcement (Egger and Miller, 1962). In other words, saying 'good' and following this by pulling out a packet of sweets to give the child one will not necessarily lead to the word good becoming a conditioned reinforcer. Other cues in the situation – reaching to the pocket, the sight of a paper bag etc. – may be much more reliable predictors of reward than the word good. This is especially likely to happen if the child has difficulty in understanding speech. In the establishment of generalized reinforcers the pairing of the reinforcer with a large variety of established reinforcers, each one of which has a different cue pattern preceding delivery, should isolate the conditioned reinforcer as a non-redundant cue (Skinner, 1953).

Once the reinforcer has become established, an intermittent pairing of the reinforcer with back-up reinforcers becomes essential if it is to retain its ability to maintain behaviour (D. W. Zimmerman, 1959; J. Zimmerman, 1963; Findley and Brady, 1965).

Conclusion

Some general conclusions emerge from this discussion. First, it is clear that social reinforcement, and in particular verbal or other distal social reinforcement, meets all the criteria for the ideal reinforcer. This suggests that, in terms of the establishment of an educational programme, first priority should be given to the development of social reinforcers or to their strengthening if they are already partially established. The use of multiple reinforcement procedures is one technique which can be adopted for the establishment of social reinforcers, while maintaining behaviour during training. At first the emphasis in the multiple reinforcement procedure can be placed on known material rewards.

One area which has as yet received very little attention concerns the comparative effectiveness of different reinforcers in the same setting. Part of the reason for this neglect lies in the fact that the value of reinforcers is likely to vary from individual to individual and time to time. However, some work in this direction has already been undertaken within the behaviour modification framework (Burchard and Barrera, 1972). There are interesting possibilities in linking behaviour modification work with studies on social reinforcement in experimental contexts. Of especial potential value is the research of Zigler and his colleagues, indicating a greater responsiveness to social reinforcement of moderately handicapped institutionalized individuals (cf. Zigler, 1968).

SELECTION OF BASIC PROCEDURES AND TECHNIQUES

In general one training procedure, *reward training*, and one training technique, *prompt and fade*, emerge as favoured in teaching in applied work with the mentally handicapped. This holds whether the prime interest is in acquisition of new responses or in the elimination of undesirable behaviour. The precise value of the procedures will obviously also depend on the skill in their application and on the suitability of the technique for the particular handicapped individual. Clearly, if an individual is not able to imitate, the modelling procedure is not going to be effective, and if physical contact is highly aversive, prompt procedures will be rendered less efficient.

(i) *Reward training and other procedures*

There are many reasons why reward training has been favoured over other training techniques. These range from ethical issues to empirical factors. Happily the evidence would suggest that empirical and ethical considerations both indicate the same conclusions. In other words, both suggest the desirability of using reward training as the central procedure.

At the broad level of logic and theory, procedures can be compared on whether they aim primarily at the strengthening or elimination of responses, and the question can be asked as to whether there is a case for eliminating a response rather than trying to shape it into a different form. The behaviour of many severely handicapped individuals tends to involve few response classes, and to try to eliminate any of these seems relatively unacceptable. Thus, on very general grounds, it would seem desirable to build up behaviour rather than trying to eliminate it.

Still at a general level, if any procedure is to be maximally effective it will involve high values of reinforcers. The most rapid acquisition will occur when the rewards are of high value, and conversely the most effective punishment training procedure will involve high levels of punishment (Church, 1963). The same considerations hold for escape training and time-out. Clearly there are substantial ethical problems involved here as well as practical issues of trainer behaviour. Some professionals, having once used punishment, refuse to use it as a procedure again. The dangers of such methods in the hands of non-professionals are obvious.

At the theoretical level, there are contrasts between reward training and escape training as procedures for building up new responses. Reward training will normally involve reinforcement contingent on *completion* of the desired response or response sequence. Therefore the procedure emphasizes the desirability of completing the response as fast as is compatible with correct responding. In escape training, reinforcement follows *initiation* of the response, i.e. the aversive stimulation ceases when the trainee begins to respond – other-wise desired behaviour is punished. Aversive stimulation may begin again when the individual pauses, thus punishing pausing, or reward may follow complete correct performance, but a pure escape training procedure will by its very nature reinforce the initiation rather than the completion of a desired response. This could clearly lead to the situation in which the speed of responding under escape contingencies is very slow and in which performance may be poor. Typically responses based on 'nagging' as a training procedure have these qualities. This would suggest that the only type of response which is suitable for escape training is one which is very brief, for example the response of turning to the adult in order to escape shock used by Bucher and Lovaas (1968).

A related practical issue, concerned with temporal order, is that techniques for eliminating behaviour (punishment training and time-out from reward) should be most effective if they are used at the beginning of the response sequence to be eliminated. Punishment of throwing behaviour will be most effective if it is applied at the beginning of the relevant response sequence than at the end (cf. Skinner, 1953). Similarly time-out for stealing food will be more effective if it follows the beginning of the response sequence leading to stealing than at the end.

These requirements lead to problems concerned with identification of the relevant response sequences. For example, the initial components of the to-be-punished sequence may be common to other desirable sequences. It is likely that the physical arrangement for detection and punishment will be difficult to guarantee and that the individual may be intermittently reinforced, with consequent slowing down of elimination through punishment training. The individual may, alternatively, learn strategies for avoiding punishment. Very fast responding may be acquired if such responding allows the individual to complete the response before punishment or the response may become discriminated. Thus if hitting another person and causing them to cry is reinforcing, a punishment procedure may result in the handicapped person learning to hit only when the punishing adult is not present, or alternatively in learning to hit very quickly, so that the likely reinforcing events of hitting and seeing the other person cry occur despite the punishment. In this case, escalation of punishment or a change in its form are the only solutions.

The considerations so far outlined suggest the general desirability of the use of reward training, largely in terms of an avoidance of the use of negative reinforcement in the punishment or escape training context. This suggests that reward training and time-out from reward would be optimal procedures for building up and eliminating behaviour, respectively.

At this stage it is necessary to introduce a further factor, response competition. This may be said to occur where new responses, which are incompatible with existing behaviours, are rewarded in the presence of particular sets of discriminative or setting stimuli. So throwing toys is replaced by fine manipulation of these toys. It will be argued that response competition lies at the base of the effective use of time-out and punishment training. This concept is also seen as having substantial implications for the arrangement of the teaching and living environment.

(ii) *Development of competing responses – time-out*

The critical feature of a time-out procedure is that there should be a period in which positive reinforcement is not available to the subject following an undesirable response. At this simple level of operation its value has been in doubt in the infra-human literature for some time (Leitenberg, 1961). Studies with mentally handicapped subjects also suggest that unless the environment or activity from which the individual is withdrawn is heavily rewarding, time-out does not lead to elimination of undesirable behaviour.

Time-out has been used most effectively in the feeding situation to control a variety of aberrant behaviours. Several studies report effective control through removal of food for a specified duration of time (Bensberg and Slominski, 1965;

Whitney and Barnard, 1966; Hamilton and Allen, 1967; Zeiler and Jervey, 1968; Stolz and Wolf, 1969; Barton *et al.*, 1970), or by removing the individual from the table at which he is being fed (Barton *et al.*, 1970; Berkowitz *et al.*, 1971). O'Brien, Bugle and Azrin (1972) report a technique in which inappropriate responses were interrupted, and in all cases satisfactory elimination of these was reported. In the feeding situation, appropriate behaviour is positively reinforced with food (if food is not positively reinforcing it is not likely that inappropriate feeding will be the problem shown). Therefore the basis of modification lies in the fact that responses, which may have an initial low level of emission, are strengthened as other responses are punished. The alternative response topographies will be incompatible in this setting. In other situations, the reinforcement for 'other behaviour' may require independent manipulation. Birnbrauer, Wolf, Kidder and Tague (1965) report a study of the interaction of a token system and time-out from a classroom setting. When tokens for good behaviour were withdrawn, two subjects 'competed' to be put into a time-out room separate from the classroom. Birnbrauer suggests that 'removing a child from a classroom is effective to the extent that it is, in fact, time-out from positive reinforcement'.

The bulk of studies have followed this precept and actively built up competing responses which may or may not be topographically incompatible. In some cases, as in the Birnbrauer study just quoted, this may involve an increase in the overall amount of reward delivered. In others the primary shift may be to transfer positive reinforcement from unacceptable to acceptable behaviours, although this is typically not reported. For example, Bostow and Bailey (1969) used time-out in the form of being removed from a chair, placed on the floor and ignored, as a consequence for loud and abusive verbal behaviour on the part of a non-ambulatory hospitalized woman. She remained on the floor for a minimum of 2 minutes, after which a 15-second interval of silence was required before she was put back on to her chair. In addition, she was not allowed to have things she liked until she had been quiet in her chair for a 10-minute period. If the loud and abusive behaviour did not occur she was given a treat, favoured object or attention at least once every 30 minutes. The base rate of positive reinforcement was not reported by Bostow and Bailey, and it is therefore not possible to say whether absolute rate of positive reinforcement was affected. However, they do report consistent improvement with no additional strain on staff resources which suggests that the rate of positive reinforcement necessary to maintain the new behaviour was not substantially discrepant from base rate.

On the other hand, a study by Husted, Hall and Agin (1971) showed reduction in aggressive and self-destructive behaviour during training sessions involving positive reinforcement for acceptable behaviours. The authors found, however, that they could not successfully generalize this behaviour to non-training periods because of a need for high levels of reward. They conclude that time-out programmes are not economical in terms of staff time.

This study raises a critical question. It seems reasonable to suggest that there are environments which are lacking in sources of suitable reinforcement to support appropriate behaviours. The 'back-wards' of institutions possibly represent the clearest examples. In these, the mentally handicapped individual may resort to inappropriate behaviours if these are positively reinforced by custodians or peers (cf. Bostow and Bailey, 1969). Buehler, Patterson and Furniss (1966) gathered data which indicate that delinquent responses are rewarded in a correctional institution. If regular sources of positive social or other types of reinforcement are absent, the result may be that socially unobtrusive behaviour (e.g. sitting still or mild self-stimulation) may occur. Alternatively, socially obstructive or self-injurious behaviour may result, e.g. shouting, eye-gouging, head-banging, or aggression towards other inmates. If the responses have developed in an environment barren of extrinsic positive reinforcers, 'time-out' in the sense of removal from the environment for unacceptable behaviour is not likely to be effective. These environments are typically settings in which only certain types of behaviour lead to reward. These behaviours are either independent of the environment – eye-gouging – or completed rapidly – hitting. Removal will clearly not affect the first type. In the second case the individual is moved from his initial situation as a function of his tapping his only source of reward. Since the maintenance and time-out environments are likely to be very similar, time-out may serve only to increase the likelihood of the response on return from time-out. Clearly the only solution in this case is to introduce new forms of positive reinforcement for new behaviours in the living environment. In general, where there are clear sources of positive reinforcement for other behaviour, time-out is effective. This holds whether it takes place in an instructional context (e.g. McReynolds, 1969) or in a more general setting where presence of other members of a group functions as the reinforcer (Peterson and Peterson, 1968; Tyler and Brown, 1967; Pendergrass, 1972).

(iii) *Development of competing responses – punishment training*

Many of the comments made concerning time-out from positive reinforcement can be applied to punishment training. In both cases infra-human research suggests quite clearly that, unless other acceptable responses in the training situation are positively reinforced, punishment training will result in temporary elimination of the punished response (Azrin and Holz, 1966). Lasting elimination only occurs if other competing responses are positively reinforced. The infra-human research also suggests that punishment must be used at high levels from the beginning of training to be maximally effective. Miller (1960) and others have shown that gradually increasing intensity of punishment serves only to habituate the organism to the punishment. This poses clear ethical problems requiring the person administering punishment to be very sure of its value before using it.

Punishment training has been employed mainly in an attempt to eliminate behaviour which is considered to be endangering the health of the individual or others in his environment. Several studies have used electric shock in attempts to eliminate head-banging, ruminating or vomiting (e.g. Insalaco and Hamilton, 1966; Luckey *et al.*, 1968; White and Taylor, 1967). Others have used a variety of punishments including physical restraint (Hamilton *et al.*, 1967) and hair pulling (Banks and Locke, 1966) for self-abusive, destructive or aggressive behaviours. In many of these studies incompatible behaviours have been positively reinforced often on a systematic basis (Mazik and MacNamara, 1967).

One advantage of punishment training over other procedures for the elimination of inappropriate behaviour is that it can be very rapid in its effects. Lovaas quotes several instances in which behaviour which had persisted over long periods of time was eliminated within a very few trials. In one study, Lovaas and Simmons (1969) allowed self-destructive behaviour to extinguish, up to 9,000 self-destructive responses (hitting self) occurring before the criterion was reached. This effect did not generalize to other settings as shown by recordings taken in those settings. A total of twelve 1-second electroshocks over fourteen sessions eliminated hitting completely in that setting. No 'substitute' self-destructive behaviour was observed.

On the other hand, the fact that punishment can eliminate behaviour rapidly can be a disadvantage also. Given time pressure on therapists, there may be a tendency to use punishment because it can produce a rapid change in behaviour, heavily reinforcing to custodians and therapists alike. If, in addition, other approaches require the expenditure of funds, there may be a general pressure to use punishment as a 'coping' procedure. Other disadvantages of punishment were heralded by Skinner (1953) and others. In particular, Skinner suggested that the use of punishment would lead to the individual administering punishment becoming a negative conditioned reinforcer. This danger appears to have been overstressed. The evidence tends not to support the prediction (e.g. Risley, 1968; Whaley and Tough, 1970), and indeed Martin (1963) quotes evidence which suggests that use of positive and negative reinforcers by the same individual may enhance the effects of positive reinforcement (Solomon, 1964). Research on variables affecting identification could clearly be relevant in considering this aspect of the use of punishment.

One finding has emerged fairly clearly in several studies. Punishment effects are likely to be specific to the individual and setting in which training is done (Birnbrauer, 1968; Risley, 1968; Lovaas and Simmons, 1969). This is a parallel result to that seen in reward training but is a more acute problem with punishment since it is less acceptable to recommend it in several contexts. A study by Corte, Wolf and Locke (1971) demonstrated that generalization from one adult to another took place only as several observers independently punished self-injurious behaviour. They also found that setting effects were specific. After behaviour had been suppressed in one setting, it was necessary to punish in a separate setting, in order to attain generalization. They point out the need for a 'planned programme of treating the behaviour under as many different conditions as necessary to produce a generalized effect'.

A related problem is the durability of punishment effects. There are few ethical problems raised by re-programming a natural environment to produce positive reinforcement, but clear difficulties if punishment is to be programmed. Few authors report follow-up. Corte *et al.* (1971) report that one of their four subjects showed a recurrence of self-injurious behaviour within two months.

It would be dangerous to draw any firm conclusions on the advisability or otherwise of punishment training. Where self-destructive behaviour is involved the approach may be most justified but success cannot be guaranteed. Unsuccessful uses of punishment are not likely to be published. On the other hand, there are circumstances where punishment training appears indicated but where other approaches may be equally effective.

As already noted, several studies have used electric shock to eliminate ruminating and/or vomiting behaviour in severely handicapped individuals (White and Taylor, 1967; Luckey *et al.*, 1968). The same type of behaviour has been dealt with successfully by the withdrawal of social reinforcement (Smeets, 1970; Wolf *et al.*, 1970). Similarly, Vukelich and Hake (1971) report a study in which dangerous aggressive behaviour in a severely handicapped institutionalized woman was reduced by a systematic programme involving time-out for aggressive behaviour and initial massive positive social reinforcement for non-aggressive behaviour.

It is clearly foolhardy to attempt a comparison of studies, but one feature which emerges clearly in the latter is that a great increase in attention was necessary especially at first in order to compete out aggressive behaviour. The authors then phased out extra attention but found that when the woman was unrestrained all day and received no extra attention aggressive behaviour recurred. Extra attention at the rate of 6 minutes every 30 minutes phasing down to 6 minutes per hour was programmed during the final phase and successfully controlled her aggression. The authors conclude that 'for severely retarded residents, positive reinforcers are frequently scarce and they may have to be increased by the staff to increase the likelihood of success of treatment programmes . . . that are based on positive reinforcement'. This conclusion is reminiscent of that drawn by Husted, Hall and Agin (1971). Both papers suggest the need for change in the amount of reward given in the environment before procedures can be expected to work. It seems reasonable to suggest that the use of punishment may be avoided if sufficient time can be spent in actively programming for the handicapped individual. However, if this cannot be done, or if the nature of the behaviour is such that it is necessary to eliminate it rapidly, punishment training may be a more humane alternative to restraint or what Baer (1970) has referred to as the 'half-living death of 24-hour-per-day stupor'.

(iv) *Physical organization*

The behaviour modification approach has several implications for environmental organization. It is necessary, first of all, to distinguish between the optimal training environment and the optimal maintenance or living environment.

The optimal training environment, from a behaviour modification viewpoint, can be constructed from a consideration of basic principles; it is one in which the probability of the to-be-trained response is as high as possible in the first instance. This ideal may be reached by eliminating stimuli which would lead to responses which would interfere with the to-be-trained response. Similarly, the environment should be one in which the response made by the individual can be identified precisely as soon as it occurs and reinforced immediately. These considerations suggest a small, simple environment which can be adapted to various needs for modifying different types of response.

The ideal maintenance environment is one which can be geared closely to two factors; firstly, the need to encourage transfer or generalization from the training environment; secondly, the discussion of competing responses in the previous section indicates a further factor. It may be suggested that, without an adequate maintenance environment, the effectiveness of time-out, punishment and especially differential positive reinforcement procedures is likely to be low. We have already suggested that the behaviours usually attacked by these procedures may be a direct function of maintenance environments in which rate of positive reinforcement is chronically low. These environments may be behaviourally toxic or pathogenic in that the only behaviours which lead to positive reinforcement may be either socially obtrusive and unacceptable, self-destructive, or simply result in the individual learning not to respond by sitting and rocking mildly, playing with a piece of material, or many other 'dead' behaviours. If these behaviours are a function of poor environments then the environments must be changed before the behavioural techniques can be expected to operate (cf. Gewirtz, 1968). The approach from behaviour modification would suggest the need for several classes of provision in the ideal maintenance environment. Firstly, the material environment of the living area must provide sources of positive reinforcement from suitable recreational, educational or work settings. This is not simply a 'rich stimulating environment' involving substantial sensory bombardment, but an environment with which the individual actively interacts by producing reinforced overt responses. Martin (1972) describes an environment in which additional cues for behaviour and other supports related to the specific training situation were included.

Secondly, the broader living environment, the community within which the living environment is set, should be capable of complementing the direct living environment to the extent of providing a variety of educational and reinforcing settings. Kiernan (1973b) has discussed this point in relation to a hospital setting and has suggested that if hospitals are to match general communities in the extent of provision of support facilities, the financial expenditure would be very great. Finally, if the individual is to be seen as part of a community of non-handicapped individuals, adequate provision must be made for social interaction resulting in social learning. Newly learned social behaviour should mesh in with, and be trapped by, the reinforcement contingencies provided by the maintenance environment (Baer and Wolf, 1967).

The realization of these ideal environments in the hospital, hostel, school or home setting may require considerable physical and social reorganization. In general it would seem that the more closely the maintenance environment approximates the natural community, the better the chances of habilitation. In fact, in many ways it would appear that segregation from the community is justifiable only if the period of segregation is one in which intensive training related to adjustment is undertaken.

SOCIAL ORGANIZATION

In order to implement behaviour modification programmes it may be necessary radically to reorganize the social setting in which the individual is living.

(i) *Numbers of staff*

It follows from the last section that some programmes require heavy staffing if they are to be implemented. This problem may be acute where all staff have to be hired and paid. One solution adopted by many programmes is to use parents and other members of the individual's family as teachers.

(ii) *Training of change-agents*

There is general agreement amongst behaviour modifiers on two points. Firstly, that training is necessary if effective programmes are to be run (Martin, 1972; Kazdin and Bootzin, 1972). Secondly, it is generally considered that parents, teachers, nurses and other 'untrained therapists' can be taught to be effective behaviour modifiers (Risley and Baer, 1972).

One of the most impressive series of studies is reported by Whalen and Henker (1969, 1971a, b). They taught mentally handicapped adolescents to use behaviour modification techniques with younger children in a hospital setting. The programme was monitored and evaluated. Gains for both trainees and trainers were demonstrated. Many training programmes appear to rely on lectures, reading and examination. There are several training manuals which are designed to assist at this level (e.g. Bensberg, 1965; Larsen and Bricker, 1968; Patterson and Guillon, 1968; Gardner, 1969; Homme *et al.*, 1969; Meacham and Weisen, 1970; Mink, 1970; Hall, 1971; Becker *et al.*, 1971; Kiernan and Riddick, 1972). Lectures, reading and discussion probably affect staff attitudes but may or may not affect behaviour.

Martin (1971) found that staff who were taught to observe behaviour and record it, in addition to being taught basic concepts through examined lectures, discussions and reading, did not in general apply the procedures at all. A second group which, in addition to the experience of Group 1, observed demonstrations and modified one individual's behaviour did rather better. Just under 50 per cent attempted some further work. With a third group the ward was rearranged and cue lights, rules for procedure, etc. were set up in addition to the basic care programme. This group was also required to train a handicapped individual both on and off ward. All of the thirty-one staff in this group subsequently used operant conditioning in the ward setting.

Two points in Martin's account may be emphasized: firstly, the need to have the trainees actually train behaviour with a handicapped individual or at least role play training (cf. J. M. Gardner, 1972); secondly, Martin's stress on the reorganization of the physical and organizational structure of the maintenance environment is echoed elsewhere.

We have already commented on the physical aspects of reorganization. From the viewpoint of job definition other points arise.

The general questions which must be asked are how, and from what sources, the behaviour of the nurse, parent, or other custodian is reinforced. Several possible sources have been suggested. When behaviour changes rapidly, progress of the individual may act as reward or the individual may be rewarded for any efforts he may make, regardless of their value, either by social or financial means. Panyan, Boozer and Morris (1970) argue that, if the individual's progress is slow, additional special reinforcers may be required. Panyan and her colleagues show that, following training, there was a decrease in frequency with which sessions were run in wards. Using a multiple baseline design, Panyan provided feedback to the wards of number of sessions completed beginning at four different dates following the end of training. The results indicate that the effect of feedback from the unit level was to bring about progressive increases in percent sessions completed, from around 25 per cent up to an asymptote of around 95 per cent. Other authors have used more direct forms of reinforcement including trading stamps and videotape records and time off from work (Bricker *et al.*, 1968; Watson *et al.*, 1971; Martin, 1972).

The approach adopted by Panyan, Boozer and Morris involves a redefinition of the job of ward personnel from a custodial to a training role. To this extent, feedback represents a measure for the staff of their effectiveness. In addition the programme described by Panyan and also that described by Watson, Gardner and Sanders (1971) involve staff in making decisions about which behaviours are to be trained and how this is to be done. In other words, autonomy is given to the individual who is to implement the programme. Work in organizational psychology and in the sociology of institutions suggests that this granting of important decision-making functions may be a powerful reinforcer when coupled with feedback on the appropriateness of these decisions (Davies, 1971; King *et al.*, 1971).

The same general considerations apply to parents both in terms of training and motivation. Reported research suggests that effective intervention results when parents are trained in practical application of techniques with feedback on specific programmes. Many factors such as socio-economic status of the parent, crowding in the home and poor physical support may influence effective participation. These variables clearly need investigation but some authors report that as many as 85 per cent of parents participate effectively in training programmes (Terdal and Buell, 1969; Mira, 1970; Fredericks *et al.*, 1971). The development of parent training programmes, especially for parents of pre-school children, represents a potentially important development. It could lead to a situation in which behaviour problems and educational difficulties within adequate pre-school provision could be avoided for many children (Bricker and Bricker, 1972). This type of advance is clearly not necessarily related to the behaviour modification approach. However, the desirability of modifying the behaviour of custodians and the recognition that behaviour change is unlikely to result from half-hour sessions once per week are conclusions which follow from a behavioural model.

Implications for the curriculum

We have already seen that the behaviour modification does not prescribe the goals of education. Behaviour modification represents a set of techniques which can be used to change behaviour, but the direction of modification of behaviour is not dictated. However, several points require discussion concerning the way in which goals may be attained, the feasibility of different types of goals and the types and form of programmes within the behaviour modification framework.

ROUTES OF ACHIEVEMENT OF GOALS

Two points follow from the behaviour modification approach. Firstly, as has already been suggested, if the overall goal is a specified change in behaviour, and if the modifier does not wish to use punishment training, there is an apparent need to use reward training procedures. This, in turn, may require a substantial shift in the provision of material and/or staff in the teaching and maintenance environment.

A second point which follows from an overall learning approach to mental handicap or child development is that it is assumed that such concepts as 'readiness' for particular activities are analysable into component skills and competences each of which may be taught (Gagné, 1968). Consequently, education of the mental handicapped is an active teaching process regardless of the initial abilities of the child. Further, education can and should be started at the earliest possible age. As already noted, the feasibility of this aspect of the approach is currently being investigated at several centres in the United States (Bricker and Bricker, 1972; Eastern Nebraska Community Office of Retardation, 1972).

SPECIFICATION OF GOALS

The behaviour modification approach is predicated on the need to specify the goals of any programme. There are two reasons why these need to be discussed thoroughly. Behaviour modification represents a powerful and, to an extent, prestigious set of techniques. In this context there are considerable dangers inherent in their use; they can be misapplied and employed to achieve goals which are unacceptable. Or, alternatively, practices which are substantially misconceived within the behaviour modification framework may be used in the name of behaviour modification. Any procedures which may legitimatize deprivation of food or drink or administration of punishment clearly require thorough discussion. At a less dramatic, but no less tragic, level the handing out of 'Smarties' and raisins in totally inappropriate ways may do little direct harm, but almost certainly does little good. Furthermore, if behaviour modification techniques are judged in light of such practices, incalculable damage may be done through the failure to allow their development in other areas. What seems essential is that there should be thorough discussion of goals and techniques. In North America these issues have already received considerable public airing resulting in sets of working rules being devised (e.g. Lucero *et al.*, 1968). The main critical considerations are that each individual must be provided with a programme which involves as little use of deprivation or other aversive procedure as is possible, and that where the living environment of the individual can be seen as possibly at fault, this environment is modified (cf. Ulrich *et al.*, 1970, Section 12). Secondly, it has already been indicated that these procedures assume the value of an active structured approach to the education of the mentally handicapped, with active participation by parents, teachers, nurses or other custodians. In addition, these individuals require clear feedback on the success of their efforts in terms of clearly specified goals.

The question then becomes one of who should set the goals. Several possibilities offer themselves. The prime change-agents, the custodians, parents, nurses or teachers, could set goals. The need to motivate change-agents and the fact that these individuals have to deal with the handicapped on a day-to-day basis, and also probably know the individuals concerned better than anyone else, gives them a clear right to participate in goal setting. However, clear problems arise if the prime custodians are to be prime goal-setters. These individuals may not be in a position to judge the relationship between their own short-term needs and the long-term needs of the handicapped individual. For instance, it may appear essential for the disruptive behaviour of a handicapped child to be eliminated within a home, school or hospital environment. But another child who simply sits in a corner and plays with his fingers all day may not be seen as requiring such a high priority of modification. Under situations of environmental stress, or if custodians are poorly trained, the quiet child may be seen as 'no trouble' and allowed to remain undisturbed. The general philosophy of 'readiness' has unfortunately provided legitimatization to this approach. Part of the deteriorative effect of the institutional environment may be the result of this type of factor (Francis, 1970).

Alternative sources of goals are offered by the 'normalization' principle and by work in child development and general psychology. These sources offer two types of alternative: on the one hand, specified goals derived from an analysis of the needs of society, and on the other, suggested sequences of goals through which competency may be developed (Kiernan, 1973a).

The behaviour modification approach would suggest that, if these goals are to be achieved, it is necessary to specify them clearly, to train in specific environments and then to mediate generalization into the final target environment.

One of the most impressive examples of this approach within the relevant literature is the Mimosa C programme run in Parsons, Kansas (Lent *et al.*, 1967). Lent and his colleagues built up a token programme for twenty-seven moderately handicapped adolescent girls (IQ 25–55), in which the target behaviours were designed to allow the girls to integrate in the local community. Aspects of personal appearance, dress, hair styles, gait etc. were analysed, in addition to basic social interactive and adaptive skills including sewing, ironing, leisure time activities, town orientation, cooking, housecleaning and general education. Transfer of new skills into the general community environment was mediated through members of the project staff, who modified behaviour *in situ*. The authors point out that 'on-the-job supervision allowed for gradual, rather than abrupt, shifts of control of the child's behaviour from cottage contingencies to those provided in the community environment'.

Given the goal of adapting the individual to a normal environment it is critical that generalization into the natural community is demonstrated. After reviewing token economy studies, Kazdin and Bootzin (1972) conclude that unfortunately such demonstrations of generalization are rare and although there are several procedures for augmenting generalization and resistance to extinction they have not been used extensively to date.

The use of research findings in child development and general psychology as sources of guidance for programmes in behaviour modification is a relatively recent trend (Kiernan, 1973a). Its basis is to use information derived from studies of normal development or of normal individuals as compared with the handicapped to provide guidance for modification of behaviour. It would seem essential to make use of such information in planning behaviour modification programmes. The limitations on this approach will be explored in the last section of this chapter.

TYPES OF PROGRAMME

The range of programmes which can be implemented using behaviour modification procedures is virtually unlimited. Studies have been reported which have shown modification of basic mobility in profoundly handicapped individuals (Fuller, 1949) on training of self-help skills such as eating, dressing, washing, toileting (J. M. Gardner, 1971; Groves and Carroccio, 1971; Martin *et al.*, 1971; Williams, 1972, for review). Numerous investigations have been reported on the elimination of problem behaviours ranging from self-mutilative actions to the use of foul language (J. M. Gardner, 1970; W. I. Gardner, 1971).

Finally, there are studies showing modification of pre-academic, academic and work behaviours, language and communication, all of which show successful modification of behaviour (W. I. Gardner, 1971; Schiefelbusch, 1972).

Many of these researches can be said to involve 'habit training' in the sense of modification of relatively specific response classes such as washing or responding to instructions. It is often argued that behaviour modification is only suitable for habit-training and that 'rule-learning' cannot be accomplished using these techniques. Secondly, it is often assumed that the behaviour trained in behaviour modification studies lacks flexibility and spontaneity.

Two types of study demonstrate clearly that such techniques can be applied to 'rule-learning'. There are now several studies of generalized imitation which involve mentally handicapped individuals. Baer, Peterson and Sherman (1967) showed that if mentally handicapped children were taught, through prompt and fade procedures with reward, to imitate a number of responses, the children would generalize the tendency to imitate to responses which were not rewarded. The children had not been observed to imitate before training. Baer showed that imitation of non-rewarded responses persisted while other imitated responses were being reinforced, but declined when reinforcement was withdrawn. This, and subsequent experiments, demonstrate that the individual can learn the 'rule' that if he imitates the model he will attain reinforcement (Gewirtz and Stingle, 1968; Sherman, 1971). The inference that a 'rule' has been learned is drawn from the fact that diverse responses which are not reinforced are imitated. This approach follows the basic paradigm of learning set training, i.e. that diverse examples, each illustrating the same 'rule', are taught to the individual. This view of imitation training is not new (cf. Ball, 1970), but current research suggests that the individual learns statements of the rule which are limited by the training set. Thus Garcia, Baer and Firestone (1971) divided training responses into small motor, large motor, and short vocal responses. Training each set separately, Garcia and his colleagues showed that generalization of imitation was limited to the topographical type receiving training or which had previously received training. This study and others suggest that verbal and motor imitation can be seen as separate response classes. The ability to teach rule-following through behaviour modification techniques has contributed substantially to the development of operant language training. Procedures developed for language training involve a progression from generalized motor imitation to head and mouth imitations with a heavier and heavier speech related component and finally to simple vocal imitations. Imitation training is used to establish simple chaining and blending to produce words, at which point control is transferred from the vocal model to named objects. Baer, Guess and Sherman (1972) and others report that at this stage the individual may acquire new labels in a single trial (cf. Bricker and Bricker, 1966; Lovaas, 1967; Risley and Wolf, 1967). Any tendency to maintain imitative behaviour in an inappropriate way is eliminated in these studies by appropriately discriminating settings in which imitation is to occur, i.e. 'do this . . . . . .', and by differential reinforcement of appropriate behaviour (Johnston, 1968; Risley and Wolf, 1967).

Several studies in the language area have demonstrated grammatical 'rule' acquisition. Guess, Sailor, Rutherford and Baer (1968) and Guess (1969) demonstrate the establishment of a generative use of plurals in institutionalized children. Sailor (1971) demonstrated the acquisition of productive plural allomorphs (-s and -z) in two institutionalized handicapped children. The trained allomorph was shown to be generalized to probe items in a manner indicating 'rule' acquisition. Schumaker and Sherman (1970) taught institutionalized children to produce past and present forms of verbs in response to questions like 'Now the man is painting. Yesterday he . . . . . . ' or 'Yesterday the man painted. Now he is . . . . . . '

These studies are clearly only initial demonstrations but they serve to illustrate that surface grammar can be acquired through behaviour modification techniques (Baer *et al.*, 1972).

A second group of studies relates to the question of 'inflexibility' and 'stereotyping' of trained responses. In theory behaviour modification techniques can be used to train any type of behaviour which can be specified, including behaviour which is highly variable. This would be accomplished by selectively reinforcing new responses, or responses which were in general investigative in nature. Goetz and Baer (1971) describe a study in which normal 4-year-old children were reinforced for producing novel constructions with blocks. Juvonen (1972) selectively reinforced 'constructive play' in two severely handicapped pre-school children. Constructive play was defined as involving combining objects together, separating parts, etc. A decline in throwing, banging and other non-rewarded response classes was observed. Both studies showed an increase in 'flexible' and 'spontaneous' behaviours. Morales (1972) taught two severely handicapped children to make simple exploratory responses, for example pushing and shaking objects. Transfer of these newly acquired behaviours to novel objects under conditions of non-reinforcement was demonstrated. This study suggests that the child can acquire responses which may be useful to him in exploring and analysing his environment.

The studies reviewed in this section have been described in order to try to establish two points. First, that behaviour modification techniques can be used to teach 'rules', and second, that the techniques can be employed to teach behaviours which may be termed novel, creative or exploratory. There is no reason why other divergent behaviours, such as decision taking or creative art work, should not be taught using these techniques. Provided criteria can be established for reinforcement, even if the target is specified in an open way, 'a response which the individual has not produced before', the methods can be applied.

At an advanced level the regulation of behaviour by the individual himself through self-reinforcement is an area which is being actively investigated at the present time (Bandura, 1969; Kanfer, 1970). This line of research is clearly exciting in terms of future application with the less handicapped, or as an advanced stage of a curriculum. It also leads to the situation where the individual is offered means of control over his own 'inner' behaviour. Homme (1966) has argued that 'coverants' such as thinking or imagining are amenable to the same general control as operants. This point has been taken up in terms of clinical application by Goldiamond (1965), Cautela (1966), Kanfer and Phillips (1966), and Davison (1968).

FORM OF PROGRAMMES

We turn finally to the question of the implications of behaviour modification for the way in which programmes are set up in practice. Two main issues must be covered, the way in which a complex programme is conceptualized, and the way in which the programmes can be put into practice. There are several reasons why overall planning of a programme is required especially within a behaviour modification context. First, any programme based on an analysis of task requirements (Gagné, 1968; Davies, 1971) will have built into it the logical necessity to establish some competencies before others can be built up. At the fundamental level the individual must be able to walk or crawl independently before he can climb stairs. Similar considerations relate to programmes based on developmental or other theoretical assumptions. These sequences or curriculum components can be highly complex and therefore require some means of overall statement which will allow sequence of steps in training to be delineated.

The second main reason why overall planning is required within the behaviour modification framework is because of the emphasis on goal setting. Within the overall structure of a programme, subprogrammes will represent subgoals. These subgoals are critical in relation to the overall aim of the programme but also serve several other functions which require specific statement. They serve to provide a focus for feedback to the individuals implementing the programme, a factor which we have already argued can be of substantial importance. Secondly, the explicit statement of goals and subgoals is that the behaviour modification approach sees the whole environment as critical, i.e. parents, teachers and nurses are all vital to its success. If these individuals are to be effectively integrated into a scheme, that scheme must be explicitly stated and in a way which is comprehensible to those involved.

The explicit statement of goals requires that the goal-set has been at least seriously considered, i.e. that there is an agreed set of aims for the individual. We have already suggested that the parents, teachers or nurses involved in immediate contact with the individual should play a critical part in deciding on the goals set, but that inputs from a consideration of general long-term adaptation to the normal environment and from child development and psychology are necessary. In this case child development may be taken as an inter-disciplinary area involving both physical and psychological development. Thus inputs from physiotherapy, speech therapy and education as well as psychological and sociological work need to be considered.

The need for an overall assessment procedure to establish the capabilities and progress of the individual is clear. This assessment is also necessary in order to establish priorities of teaching.

The type of assessment required by behaviour modification at this level of analysis is more molar than that involved in functional analysis. What is necessary at this level is an analysis which states the subgoals and major goals of a teaching scheme. An increasing number of workers are using systems analysis, flow chart analysis and parallel schemes to describe this structural aspect of the curriculum and to allow placement of the individual within the system (Davies, 1971). One such analysis is the Lattice Systems Approach (Budde and Menolascino, 1971). The lattice approach involves the breakdown into a logical sequence of a complex problem. For example, Budde and Menolascino (1971) describe an application of it in a vocational rehabilitation setting with severely and moderately handicapped individuals. A simplified version of their Programme Lattice is reproduced in Fig. 17.

The lattice is a summary of a complex training programme involving several subprogrammes. It is read from the left and upwards to indicate progression through training. Base-line cells represent teaching programmes. Cells above the base-line represent developmental modules – signifying completion of base-line programmes. Thus Cell 8B (Social Skills Development Complete) has three base-line cells representing interdependent components (A3, Critical Social Skills Training; A5, Job Related Social Skills Training; A8 Placement Related Social Skills Training). Each of the three base-line cells represents a training programme. Each base-line training programme within this type of system can be broken down into other lattices which can specify particular programme components.

From the assessment viewpoint it is clear that this type of arrangement requires specification of criterion behaviour for each component, and that the individual should not 'graduate' from the programme until all requirements are met. Thus assessment serves to place an individual at the appropriate point on the training lattice and to allow clear decisions on final achievements to be made.

One very ambitious development of the Lattice Systems Approach is the Client Progress System developed by the Nebraska State Office of Mental Retardation in conjunction with the Eastern Nebraska Community Office of Retardation (Falls, 1972). This system of assessment involves forty-five Developmental Ladders covering areas from Attending to Budgeting and including cognitive, social and work skills. Each consists of up to eight or so steps, all defined objectively in terms of acquisition criteria. The system represents a training and assessment scheme for use by attendants, teachers, foster parents and others involved in the care and education of the handicapped. As would be

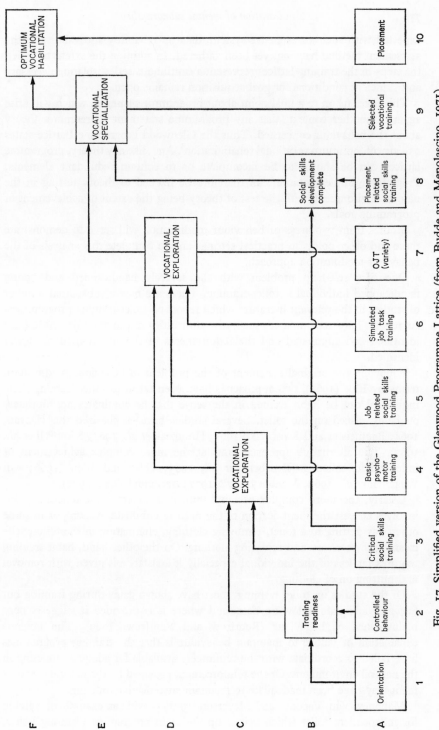

Fig. 17 Simplified version of the Glenwood Programme Lattice (from Budde and Menolascino, 1971).

expected with such an extensive system, data on reliability and validity of the assessment method have not yet been gathered. In addition the extent to which the steps in the training lattices represent a continuous series isolating necessary and sufficient conditions for goal acquisition remains open.

This takes us on to a final point about programme planning, which will arise again in another context, that any programme statement represents a theory about the behaviour concerned. Thus the Glenwood Programme Lattice states a theory of 'optimum vocational rehabilitation'. And, like any theory, programme lattices can be shown to be incomplete or to contain redundant elements. Programme implementation can therefore be likened to theory testing in the natural environment, with the test of theory being the extent of achievement of programme goals.

Studies from two areas of behaviour modification will serve to demonstrate these and other points in practical settings and to complete this analysis of the behaviour modification approach.

One core self-help problem with the severely handicapped and young handicapped individual is toilet-training. There are now a substantial number of studies in the relevant literature which report on toilet-training programmes. As reports have accumulated, successive difficulties in programming have been identified and eliminated and the requirements of the situation more clearly identified.

Following the original statement of the problem in behaviour modification terms by Ellis (1963), two approaches have been taken to toilet training. The individual can be habit trained in the sense that he eliminates appropriately on being placed on the toilet. Several studies have emphasized this (Dayan, 1964; Baumeister and Klosowski, 1965; Hundziak *et al.*, 1965; Kimbrell *et al.*, 1967). The alternative approach aims at the more complex achievement of independent toileting (Bensberg *et al.*, 1965; Giles and Wolf, 1966; van Wagenen *et al.*, 1969; Mahoney *et al.*, 1971; Azrin and Foxx, 1971).

Clearly, the more complex accomplishment is independent toileting. This involves at least the identification of the need to eliminate, walking or in some other way getting to a toilet, removing clothing, eliminating in the toilet, self-cleaning if necessary and replacing clothing. On the other hand, habit training requires far less of the individual especially if assistance is given with removal and putting on of clothing.

Of the studies on toilet training, most have shown gains during training but few give adequate follow-up data, and where it is provided it suggests poor maintenance of behaviour (Rentfrow and Rentfrow, 1969). The obvious explanation of failure to maintain behaviour is that the training programmes have failed to coordinate with the reinforcers available for adequate toileting in the natural environment. Or the reinforcement provided by the natural environment may have been inadequate to maintain any effective toileting.

Mahoney, Van Wagenen and Meyerson (1971) provide an example of training for independent toilet which brings up the main programme planning issues.

They trained a group of 3 young normal children (18–20 months old) and a group of 5 handicapped children (4–9 years old). The procedure involved a pre-test and 6 training phases. During the pre-test phase the children were observed daily for $3\frac{1}{2}$ hours over a 5-day period in order to assess base-line behaviour. During the first major stage of training the child was taught prerequisite toileting behaviour. An auditory signal generator was worn by the child which could be activated either by the subject urinating or by the experimenter. In Phase I when it was turned on the experimenter approached the child and invited and prompted him to go to the potty. Compliance, at first under prompt and subsequently independently, was rewarded with food and social praise. In Phase II the child was taught in addition to lower his pants, again with initial physical prompting. In Phase III the child was taught to sit on the toilet seat or take the proper male stance when facing it. Reinforcement in Phase III was given for sitting or standing appropriately for 30 seconds having approached the toilet and adjusted clothing appropriately.

During these phases no attempt was made to effect actual elimination. The aim had been to teach prerequisite skills. In the second three phases, attention was switched to elimination. In Phase 4 subjects were given 10 ounces of extra liquid during training sessions in order to increase the probability of urination. Clearly the low operant level of elimination makes for problems of programming if the response is to be reinforced. Giving extra liquid is reported as effective in increasing operant levels (Giles and Wolf, 1966; Azrin and Foxx, 1971). During Phase 4 the experimenter generated the auditory signal. If the subject urinated during the 30 seconds at the toilet he was reinforced. Otherwise his pants were pulled up and he was allowed to return to play. If elimination occurred during play the auditory signal sounded. If the child then walked to the toilet and re-started urination he was rewarded. If not he was not rewarded. Wet pants were removed without comment at this stage.

Once the child had urinated successfully in the toilet on one occasion the strategy changed. Now if the child eliminated inappropriately the experimenter said, 'No! Go potty'. Again reward followed urination in the toilet.

The various features of the Mahoney–van Wagenen approach are common to other programmes. Aside from increasing the frequency of response the immediate identification of urination is seen as essential if reinforcers are to be appropriately administered (Mowrer and Mowrer, 1938; van Wagenen and Murdock, 1966; Watson, 1966; Azrin *et al.*, 1971; Azrin and Foxx, 1971). Typically these authors have devised 'trainer pants' worn by the subject during training or have constructed specially wired toilets to detect elimination immediately it occurs appropriately. The other function of these cues is to provide conditioned reinforcers to which internal cues may be conditioned as discriminative stimuli. This immediate detection is likely to be critical. Toileting has in fact got a 'natural' reinforcement sequence built in provided the individual is taught to sit on the toilet. It would be normal under these circumstances to allow the individual off only when he had performed, and it is also likely that the custodian would also initiate social interaction at this stage which would not be present whilst the individual was seated. This sequence was observed as a standard pattern in wards in an institution. It represents a setting in which reward should operate for correct toileting – if the fact that the individual has eliminated is detected. Unfortunately, elimination is characteristically not detected under block treatment unless special cues are developed. In un-modified block treatment appropriate toilet behaviour does not develop.

A third common feature is the joint emphasis on reward for appropriate and punishment for inappropriate behaviour. Azrin and Foxx argue that 'normal toileting is not simply a matter of learning to respond to bladder and bowel pressures by relaxing the sphincter but rather is a complex operant and social learning process that has been hindered (in the institutionalized handicapped individual) by a reduced learning capacity and by institutionalization' (1971, p. 89). They argue that the negative aspects of unsuccessful toileting are critical in control of behaviour. In their study the institutionalized severely handicapped men who served as subjects experienced elaborate consequences for incorrect elimination during training. These included verbal reprimands, an hour of time-out from a heightened level of positive reinforcement, and cleanliness training including being given a tepid shower, changing all his clothes, carrying soiled clothes to the sink, washing them out and hanging them to dry. He also had to clean up all traces of soiling.

The fifth phase of the Mahoney–van Wagenen procedure involved teaching the child to pull up pants. Mahoney and his colleagues hold that the optimal sequence for toilet training is a forward chaining procedure. It will be noted that at each potential problem phase success is assisted by physical prompting thereby minimizing extinction problems. Other authors teach dressing skills as part of the toilet training programme (cf. Giles and Wolf, 1966; Azrin and Foxx, 1971).

The final phase of the Mahoney programme involved the removal of the auditory signal. Mahoney and his colleagues report that by this stage of the study they had learned to identify for each subject specific overt responses which often preceded the act of elimination, for example tugging at pants, or a sudden increase in activity. During this phase the experimenter initiated the auditory signal when the subject showed these signs. The final training component followed when the subject had correctly eliminated three times following the auditory signal. At this time the device was removed. Reinforce-ment was then given for the complete sequence of behaviour without signals or prompts.

In other studies this final transition to independent toileting may begin earlier in training. Azrin and Foxx faded physical prompts for sitting on the toilet from early in training. In their study subjects were on the toilet for much longer periods of time at first (up to 20 minutes of every 30 if appropriate elimination did not occur). Thus isolation of pre-urination behaviour was not as critical. Azrin and Foxx argue that the anticipation of positive reinforcement and the avoidance of disapproval were the basis for toilet approach in their study.

Following basic training, Mahoney and his colleagues ran three days of post-test and then instructed the parents in aspects of the procedures to be continued at home. Follow-up over a period of six months was completed with only two subjects. They showed a low level of inappropriate responses.

Azrin and Foxx instituted a post-training ward maintenance procedure which involved encouragement of proper toileting and social disapproval and cleanliness training for 'accidents'. This procedure was introduced by assigning one

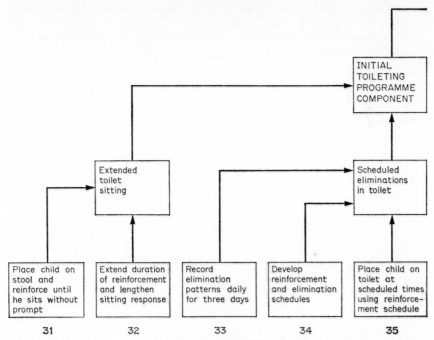

Fig. 18 Isolated component of a Behaviour Modification Training Process Lattice (from Budde, 1971).

attendant on each shift the responsibility of overseeing the trainees and recording behaviour. After one month regular checks were reduced in frequency. This type of modification to the maintenance environment is similar to that discussed by Panyan, Boozer and Morris (1970).

In both the studies discussed, good acquisition of independent toileting was reported. Azrin and Foxx report good maintenance of independent toileting.

Several general points may be made which arise out of this detailed presentation of a programme. Firstly, the environment was modified in order to allow rapid detection and reinforcement of appropriate and inappropriate behaviour. In the Azrin and Foxx study the subjects spent the four days of the training phase actually in the toilet area. Secondly, since the programming was intensive,

Report Symbol 7020/13   TOILET TRAINING   ACCIDENTS

TIME   U   BM

| | | | | | | | | | | | | AM |
| | | | | | | | | | | | | PM |

MON. AM TRAINER_____ PM TRAINER_____

TIME

| | | | | | | | | | | | | AM |
| | | | | | | | | | | | | PM |

TUES. AM TRAINER_____ PM TRAINER_____

TIME

| | | | | | | | | | | | | AM |
| | | | | | | | | | | | | PM |

WED. AM TRAINER_____ PM TRAINER_____

TIME

| | | | | | | | | | | | | AM |
| | | | | | | | | | | | | PM |

THU. AM TRAINER_____ PM TRAINER_____

TIME

| | | | | | | | | | | | | AM |
| | | | | | | | | | | | | PM |

FRI. AM TRAINER_____ PM TRAINER_____

TIME

| | | | | | | | | | | | | AM |
| | | | | | | | | | | | | PM |

SAT. AM TRAINER_____ PM TRAINER_____

TIME

| | | | | | | | | | | | | AM |
| | | | | | | | | | | | | PM |

SUN. AM TRAINER_____ PM TRAINER_____

Mark a 'U' for urination or 'BM' for bowel movement in the appropriate box.
Mark a '−' if no elimination occurs. ·Place slash marks (///) in accident column.

PROCEDURE: 1. Children should be placed on the toilet every 2 hours
           2. Assign the children to specific stools so that they are toileted in the same
              place every day
           3. Each child should remain on the commode until he urinates and/or
              defecates, or for 15 minutes
           4. The Nurse should be with the children every moment they are on the
              stool and be in a position to see when elimination occurs
           5. The moment a child begins to eliminate, he should be reinforced immediately
           6. When the child has had no accidents for 2 weeks, his training is
              considered successful and a new child should be begun

CRITERION FOR GRADUATION: Three or less accidents per week for 2 weeks. Begin a new
                          child in training at this point

WEEK OF_____   CHILDS NAME_____

Fig. 19 Programming sheet used by ward attendants in a large institution in the
United States.

staff, in this case research staff, were assigned specially to training. In these studies ward staff and parents did not participate. In other institutional, pre-school and home settings, parents, teachers or nurses can and do record programmes of the type described (Watson *et al.*, 1971; Boozer, 1972, personal communication; Galloway, 1972, personal communication).

With this type of programme it becomes critical for some form of programme planning of the type offered by the Lattice Systems method to be used in order to establish sequencing. This may be done either through a Lattice Systems Approach or by less formal means. Fig. 18 shows a component of the toilet training programme developed by Budde (1971) which specifies on the base-line several component programmes. Fig. 19 is a programming sheet used by ward attendants in a large institution in the United States (Boozer, 1972, personal communication).

The final point concerning the toilet training programmes is that they clearly differ on some points, in particular on the emphasis on negative reinforcement. These and similar disagreements represent differences in theoretical approach which it is to be hoped will be empirically resolved.

Rather different points concerning programme planning emerge from the consideration of language training. Here there is a greater possibility of deriving programme sequences and structures from linguistic theory or from work on the development of language in normal children.

Normative work on the development of language and other behaviours offers a dubious direct source of programmes. Language scales and other scales of development are normally derived with the explicit aim of isolating behaviours which show differences between different age groups. The implication of this is that, if a behaviour occurs in a particular sequence with other behaviours, but at an unpredictable time, it will not be selected. Thus Behaviour A may characterize the 20-month-old child, Behaviour C the 30-month-old. Behaviour B may occur at any time between 20 and 30 months. In this case it will be a poor item for a developmental test based on age. However B may not be able to occur before A and may be a necessary precondition for C. Thus at a teaching level it may be critical. Scale items are not normally selected in line with any theory of development and scales are not constructed with a view to giving an indication of critical stages of development.

Developmental scales would not be expected to be able to specify all necessary and sufficient steps to the achievement of goals. They therefore represent poor bases for the construction of programme systems (Kiernan, 1973a).

This suggests that either linguisitic or developmental theories, for example Piagetian theory, plus logical analyses of task requirements may offer a better basis for programme construction (Gagné, 1968). This approach also offers a rigorous method of theory testing not usually open to developmental theories. If the theory states all the necessary and sufficient steps towards an achievement, and if these component steps are trained, then the achievement should emerge, given the correctness of the theory.

The unification of linguistic theory and behaviour modification appears in the work of Bricker and Baer (Baer *et al.*, 1972; Lynch and Bricker, 1972). It leads in Bricker's case to the establishment of a complex language training programme (Bricker and Bricker, 1970; Bricker, 1972). The training lattice of this programme is reproduced in Fig. 14 (see p. 569). In this lattice cells below the ridge line all specify programme steps. This programme is highly complex involving a large number of subprogrammes. Each of these can be seen as involving teaching in formal and informal settings or an extensive breakdown into further subprogrammes relevant to the training situation. For example, Fulton (1972) described the development of sets of audiological procedures which include standard puretone audiometry, speech audiometry, 'general' auditory tests and Bekesy audiometry, which would fit into one of the cells of the programme.

In terms of implementation of component programmes in school or home settings, the type of schemes arising from the Lattice Systems Approach may involve a mixture of formal and informal teaching. Thus a motor imitation component may involve the following steps.[1] Firstly, the establishment of reinforcement control in which it is ensured that the subject responds reliably to presentation of reward. Secondly, the subject is assessed for the extent to which he 'attends' in the sense of looking at the teacher when called. This level appears critical for performance in imitation. If the individual does not orient appropriately on around 60 per cent of trials it is desirable to bring behaviour up to this level otherwise test and training is very slow. At this stage motor imitation, with reinforcement for correct responding, is assessed. The test set involves a variety of types of motor responses, i.e. self-oriented, object oriented, gross and fine motor imitation (Kiernan and Saunders, 1972). If the individual does not reach a preset criterion or if performance suggests deficiencies in certain areas of imitation a training programme is introduced. This programme involves either a full twenty minute session once per day with recording of all performances during the training, or a less formal training session with a probe test at the end of each session. In this case the responses to probe may be the only behaviour recorded. In our own case the full sessions are used with nurses. The former approach may be beyond the resources of many parents, teachers or nurses. However, Hall has shown that parents can set up and record not simply single sessions but also full experiments using reversal designs (Hall *et al.*, 1972). The second procedure, involving only recording of responses to probes, tends to be favoured by proponents of precision teaching (Galloway, 1972, personal communication). This method has the obvious virtue of placing less strain on the individual running the teaching session.

Whatever approach is used, this type of individualized teaching can be generalized for all bar research purposes to non-training settings. Thus if motor

---

[1] These steps are similar to those at present being used in a motor imitation programme for young handicapped children by the author. A debt in the development of this programme is owed to Diane and Bill Bricker whose work suggested many of the steps.

imitation is being trained, reinforcement of appropriate behaviour in the home or classroom would be encouraged. Characteristically this type of casual reinforcement is not recorded.

The training set for individual sessions is devised to cover relevant dimensions of imitation. The individuals running sessions are normally involved in devising such sets. In addition, generalization sets may be introduced to assess degree of acquisition of generalized imitation.

Following achievement of agreed criterion behaviour in training sets reassessment on the original test set yields a further measure of acquisition of generalized imitation. Progression to the next component in training follows successful acquisition.

Programmes of the type described exist in several centres. What characterizes them is their emphasis on accurate assessment of training needs and then a mixture of formal training and informal training before reassessment.

This type of programme planning clearly differs from that involved in the toilet training programmes. The latter may be classed as total programmes in the sense that they require full-time attention of at least one individual whilst in operation.

Such programmes require more communication between individuals involved in teaching and hence will be more difficult to arrange than individual programmes. In terms of staff economies it may not be possible to run more than one total programme on toilet training or behaviour problems at any one time in a ward, classroom or home. Individual teaching session programmes may be run in addition to a general programme. In this respect specific timetabling of individual sessions appears essential (Kiernan, 1973b). Notices giving instructions to individuals running training, cue lights signifying particular times for events, also assist in programme integration (G. L. Martin, 1972).

Conclusions

The functions of a theory are to allow a systematization of existing data, to make testable predictions, and to provide a more general heuristic framework which stimulates ideas and allows general integration of thinking within an area. This chapter has aimed at presenting the behaviour modification approach in such a way that its potential value in relation to these criteria could be appreciated. No serious attempt has been made to 'evaluate' behaviour modification. The concentration here has been on developing the basic model and indicating what this author feels are its implications for our dealings with the mentally handicapped.

There are several reasons for adopting this approach. Partly it is conditioned by the large amount of published research.[1] More, it is conditioned by the fact that research and practice are several years ahead of publication. There appears,

[1] See Gardner and Watson, 1969, for a bibliography to that date: *Mental Retardation Abstracts* include behaviour modification research.

therefore, to be a case for selection of studies which exemplify particular important points and indicate apparent trends. Research and practice in this area is progressing beyond basic demonstrations and it is to these areas of development that attention has been directed.

The main emphases in the current position appear to be as follows. As Lindsley (1970) has pointed out there is now a greater emphasis on programmes of education or remediation rather than on individual one-off training (cf. Gelfand and Hartmann, 1968; Gardner, 1969a; Sherman and Baer, 1969). The phase of basic demonstration of effectiveness of reinforcement in changing behaviour in individual cases appears to have passed. As the editor of an international journal has put it, 'many studies have demonstrated that the law of effect has not yet been repealed'. Within this framework three elements dominate: the need to specify clear target behaviours, the need to modify the social and material environment in order to allow the modification and maintenance of behaviour, and finally the emphasis on consequation by whatever reinforcers are effective, be they social or material.

The emphasis on programmes has extended the thinking of workers in the behaviour modification area beyond the specific interaction of the reinforcement event to broader variables which precondition availability of reinforcement. Thus attention in studies within institutions has shifted to institutional reorganization at both the social and material level. The result of this has been to blur edges between different approaches and also to break down the isolation characteristic of operant workers (Krantz, 1971). Baker and Ward (1971), reporting a study in which a behaviour modification programme was implemented on a living unit in an institution, conclude that

in the last analysis . . . it is not meaningful conceptually to separate the milieu from reinforcement therapy. The availability of reinforcers in the environment, both tangible (as toys or TV) and social (as closer contact with attendants and volunteers) is essential to a total reinforcement therapy program. The reinforcement model becomes helpful in designing the physical milieu so as to provide opportunities and meaningful rewards for learning, along with formal contingencies introduced within that milieu. (1971, p. 133)

Similar blurring appears necessary across disciplines. Michael (1970) has pointed out that behaviour modification can offer a common set of procedures covering several areas including medical and vocational rehabilitation. One can extend the list to include methods used by parents, teachers, nurses, speech therapists, occupational therapists, physiotherapists, music therapists, art therapists, and so forth. These workers have diverse goals but they are all directly concerned with behaviour change. While it has been emphasized that the goals of education are not necessarily the business of behaviour modification, the routes to achievement of these goals could be a matter of concern. Michael (1970) suggests a role of 'primary authority in the arrangement of the environment so as to produce, maintain, or eliminate behaviour' (1970, p. 54). The essence of the argument is that behaviour is a unitary phenomenom which may not be happily split along professional lines which have arisen in the West largely through historical chance.

The broadening of the scope of practice of behaviour modification makes it necessary to ensure that the pure research on which it is based is well founded. In addition studies on the effectiveness of programmes are essential.

Common basic criticisms have been expressed by J. M. Gardner (1968, 1969a, 1971), Gelfand and Hartmann (1968) and Sherman and Baer (1969). No attempt will be made to detail these but it is essential to state the main problems outlined and to comment on issues raised. Gardner (1969) has pointed out that many independent variables are inadequately specified in behaviour modification research, and in a surprisingly large number of cases potentially important variables such as age, diagnostic category, physical condition and test scores are omitted. He and other authors have also drawn attention to the large number of single case studies published (Gelfand and Hartmann, 1968). It has already been noted that the danger here is that only successful cases will be reported. The fact that the 'worst' subjects in institutions were selected especially in earlier studies does not circumvent this difficulty. Even when a sample of subjects are used there is still the likelihood that the samples involved will be biased (Bricker, 1970). Gardner also criticizes the failure to specify relevant experimenter variables including attitude and training in behaviour modification. On the dependent variable side, again the failure to specify the precise effects of a programme and also its more generalized effects is emphasized.

These criticisms reflect problems which are in some ways a function of the behaviour modification approach itself and in others are general problems. For example, the specification of general behaviour before and after modification requires efficient assessment procedures. Some workers have used existing cognitive tests and have shown that these can detect change as a result of behaviour modification programmes. Thus, Sachs (1971) showed WISC score changes resulting from the operation of a token economy. However, these tests are likely to be too gross and insensitive as methods of assessing behaviour change. Gardner's criticisms relate in part to the failure to provide the type of assessment described above in context of programme planning, i.e. a system which allows an extensive specification of progress towards target behaviours. J. M. Gardner (1971) describes a check list system which provides such a frame (Gardner and Hoffman, 1969). Kiernan, Donoghue and Hawks (1971) describe the use of a checklist system devised by Williams and Kushlick (1970).

An interesting further development at a research level which relates to Gardner's main thesis is the appearance of studies in which several dependent variables are assessed simultaneously, usually in an attempt to detect the 'side-effects' of behaviour modification. These investigations have produced some interesting results, all bar one study show positive effects – and in the study showing adverse effects, in addition to positive side-effects, the adverse results were brought under control with an extension of the procedure (Buell *et al.*,

1968; Risley, 1968; Sajwaj *et al.*, 1972). This type of study is too rare in the behaviour modification literature.

The problem of single case studies is partly a function of the methodology of operant research, coupled with problems concerned with the time required to complete researches of this type. Although the numbers of subjects run in most studies is remarkably low, most reports of programme research involve larger numbers of subjects and, in these, negative findings can be and are reported. For example, many of the studies reported by Kazdin and Bootzin (1972) on token economies include discussion of programme failures. Clearly these data are critically important in improvement of programmes if other relevant data are also available which will allow hypotheses related to failure to be formulated. Non-representativeness of samples raises other issues, prime among which is, representative of what ? At one level, studies based on epidemiologically representative samples of the population are necessary, and again it is to be hoped that these will be reported from centres in which programmes are being developed. At another level, it would appear that behavioural techniques have been shown to apply to at least some individuals with all degrees of handicap from the most severe.

Another criticism made by Gardner and others is that behaviour modification research fails to report relevant situational variables. This criticism is especially important if the extension of the behaviour modification model to situational variables is to be taken seriously (Baker and Ward, 1971). In addition, as already noted, many studies specify discriminative stimuli generally, if at all. Again, part of the problem facing the behaviour modifier is the availability of relevant measuring instruments. Kiernan, Donoghue and Hawks (1971) used a combination of direct observation, questionnaires on basic ward data, such as number of ambulant children, plus the Child Management Schedule devised by King, Raynes and Tizard (1971), a questionnaire which gives data on management procedures shown relevant to development. There appears to be a clear need for studies which examine the effects of ecological factors on behaviour in relation to the behaviour modification approach.

A critical problem mentioned by all reviewers is the lack of studies showing adequate follow-up, and this raises particular issues for behaviour modification. The approach asserts that behaviour is responsive to environmental change, and therefore environmental changes are used to modify behaviour. However, it also follows that if the contingencies which support new behaviour are removed or reversed the behaviour may well follow. It has been argued throughout this chapter that generalization to non-training conditions must take into account the contingencies in that environment. Successful maintenance of behaviour will then reflect at least two factors: the extent to which training has been geared to the non-training environment and the extent to which the latter has been adapted to accommodate the new behaviour. To expect the techniques to produce lasting change without allowing for this consideration is to test the theory beyond its boundary conditions. The studies by Azrin and Foxx (1971) and Vukelich and Hake (1971) reported earlier exemplify this approach. In both cases maintenance of behaviour was programmed by modifying the environmental setting to ensure sources of check and reinforcement.

Similar considerations apply to the use of conventional control groups. Within the behaviour modification approach the concept of no-treatment control is meaningless. Similarly, alternative approaches to behaviour modification programmes would be expected to be analysable in terms of procedural or content variables. These could be studied in terms of behaviour modification techniques and content, a strategy which may reveal important new content or procedures. But there is no one behaviour modification approach; each programme may be well or poorly carried out, have good or poor content (Kuypers *et al.*, 1968), and therefore the comparison of any particular package with another is a false one. What does seem both valuable and essential is the comparison of different procedures, for example modelling as opposed to verbal prompting in the teaching of particular content, or the comparison of different programme content with procedures held at a common level of efficiency in the achievement of set goals.

The behaviour modification approach provides a challenging and hopeful trend in work with the mentally handicapped. Its main strengths appear to lie in the fact that it is applicable to very young and very severely handicapped individuals to whom little has been offered by other methods. In fact the emphasis on external control of behaviour in the behaviour modification approach as it is currently developed may make it particularly applicable to these individuals. It offers exciting prospects in the active testing of theory in practice. Its emphasis on dealing with the whole social and physical environment and of integrating diverse approaches and disciplines is clearly challenging and promises substantial benefits.

References

ADDISON, R. M. and HOMME, L. E. (1966) The reinforcing event (RE) menu. *National Society for Programmed Instruction Journal*, 5, 8–9.

AYLLON, T. and AZRIN, N. (1968) *The Token Economy.* New York: Appleton-Century-Crofts.

AZRIN, N. H. and FOXX, R. M. (1971) A rapid method of toilet training the institutionalized retarded. *J. appl. Behav. Anal.*, 4, 89–99.

AZRIN, N. H. and HOLZ, W. C. (1966) Punishment. In HONIG, W. K. (ed.) *Operant Behavior: Areas of Research and Application.* New York: Appleton-Century-Crofts.

AZRIN, N. H., BUGLE, C. and O'BRIEN, F. (1971) Behavioral engineering: two apparatuses for toilet training retarded children. *J. appl. Behav. Anal.*, 4, 249–53.

BAER, D. M. (1970) A case for selective reinforcement of punishment. In NEURINGER, C. and MICHAEL, J. L. (eds.) *Behavior Modification in Clinical Psychology.* New York: Appleton-Century-Crofts.

BAER, D. M. and WOLF, M. M. (1967) The entry into natural communities of reinforcement. In ULRICH, R., STACHNIK, T. and MABRY, J. (eds.) *Control of Human Behavior. Vol. Two: From Cure to Prevention.* Glenview, Ill.: Scott, Foresman.

BAER, D. M., GUESS, D. and SHERMAN, J. A. (1972) Adventures in simplistic grammar. In SCHIEFELBUSCH, R. L. (ed.) *Language of the Mentally Retarded.* Baltimore, Md.; Univ. Park Press.

BAER, D. M., PETERSON, R. F. and SHERMAN, J. A. (1967) The development of imitation by reinforcing behavioral similarity to a model. *J. exp. Anal. Behav.*, **10**, 405–16.

BAER, D. M., WOLF, M. M. and RISLEY, T. R. (1958) Some current dimensions of applied behavior analysis. *J. appl. Behav. Anal.*, **1**, 91–7.

BAILEY, J. and MEYERSON, L. (1969) Vibration as a reinforcer with a profoundly retarded child. *J. appl. Behav. Anal.*, **2**, 135–7.

BAKER, B. L. and WARD, M. H. (1971) Reinforcement therapy for behavior problems in severely retarded children. *Amer. J. Orthopsychiat.*, **41**, 124–35.

BALL, T. S. (1970) Training generalized imitation: variations on a historical theme. *Amer. J. ment. Defic.*, **75**, 135–41.

BANDURA, A. (1965) Influence of model's reinforcement contingencies on the acquisition of imitative responses. *J. Pers. soc. Psychol.*, **1**, 589–95.

BANDURA, A. (1969) *Principles of Behaviour Modification.* New York: Holt, Rinehart & Winston.

BANKS, M. and LOCKE, B. (1966) *Self-injurious Stereotypes and Mild Punishment with Retarded Subjects.* Working Paper No. 123. Parsons State Hospital and Training Centre.

BARKER, R. G. and WRIGHT, H. F. (1955) *Midwest and its Children.* New York: Harper & Row.

BARTON, E. S., GUESS, D., GARCIA, E. and BAER, D. M. (1970) Improvements of retardates' mealtime behaviours by timeout procedures using multiple baseline techniques. *J. appl. Behav. Anal.*, **3**, 77–84.

BAUMEISTER, A. and KLOSOWSKI, R. (1965) An attempt to group toilet train severely retarded patients. *Ment. Retard.*, **3**, 24–6.

BECKER, W. C., ENGELMANN, S. and THOMAS, D. R. (1971) *Teaching: A Basic Course in Applied Psychology.* Chicago: Science Research Associates.

BENSBERG, G. J. (1965) *Teaching the Mentally Retarded.* Atlanta, Ga: Southern Regional Education Board.

BENSBERG, G. J. and SLOMINSKI, A. (1965) Helping the retarded learn self-care. In BENSBERG, G. J. (ed.) *Teaching the Mentally Retarded.* Atlanta, Ga: Southern Regional Educational Board.

BENSBERG, G. J., COLWELL, C. N. and CASSEL, R. H. (1965) Teaching the profoundly retarded self-help skill activities by behavior-shaping techniques. *Amer. J. of ment. Defic.*, **69**, 674–9.

BERKOWITZ, S., SHERRY, P. J. and DAVIS, B. A. (1971) Teaching self-feeding skills to profound retardates using reinforcement and fading procedures. *Behav. Therapy*, **2**, 62–7.

BERNAL, M. (1969) Behavioural feedback in the modification of rat behaviours. *J. nerv. ment. Dis.*, **148**, 375–85.

BIJOU, S. W. (1966) A functional analysis of retarded development. In ELLIS, N. R. (ed.) *International Review of Research in Mental Retardation*, Vol. 1. New York: Academic Press.

BIJOU, S. W. (1968) Studies in the experimental development of left-right concepts in retarded children using fading techniques. In ELLIS, N. R. (ed.) *International Review of Research in Mental Retardation*, Vol. 3. New York: Academic Press.

BIJOU, S. W. and BAER, D. M. (1961) *Child Development 1: A systematic and Empirical Theory*. New York: Appleton-Century-Crofts.

BIJOU, S. W. and BAER, D. M. (1965) *Child Development II. Universal Stages of Infancy*. New York: Appleton-Century-Crofts.

BIJOU, S. W. and BAER, D. M. (1967) *Child Development: Readings in Experimental Analysis.* New York: Appleton-Century-Crofts.

BIJOU, S. W. and ORLANDO, R. (1961) Rapid development of multiple-schedule performances with retarded children. *J. exp. Anal. Behav.*, **4**, 7–16.

BIJOU, S. W. and STURGES, P. T. (1959) Positive reinforcers for experimental studies with children consumables and manipulables. *Child Developm.*, **30**, 151–70.

BIJOU, S. W., PETERSON, R. F. and AULT, M. H. (1968) A method to integrate descriptive and experimental field studies at the level of data and empirical concepts. *J. appl. Behav. Anal.* **1**, 175–91.

BIRNBRAUER, J. S. (1968) Generalization of punishment effects – a case study. *J. appl. Behav. Anal.*, **1**, 201–11.

BIRNBRAUER, J. S., WOLF, M. M., KIDDER, J. D. and TAGUE, C. E. (1965) Classroom behaviour of retarded pupils with token reinforcement. In SLOANE, H. N. and MACAULAY, B. D. (eds.) *Operant Procedures in Remedial Speech and Language Training*. Boston: Houghton Mifflin.

BOE, E. E. and CHURCH, R. M. (1968) *Punishment: Issues and Experiments*. New York: Appleton-Century-Crofts.

BOLLES, R. C. (1962) The difference between statistical hypotheses and scientific hypotheses. *Psychol. Rep.*, **11**, 639–45.

BOSTOW, D. E. and BAILEY, J. B. (1969) Modification of severe disruptive and aggressive behaviour using brief time-out and reinforcement procedures. *J. appl. Behav. Anal.*, **2**, 31–7.

BRADY, J. P. and LIND, D. L. (1961) Experimental analysis of hysterical blindness. *Arch. Gen. Psychiat.*, **4**, 331–9.

BRENER, J. and HOTHERSALL, D. (1967) Heart rate control under conditions of augmented sensory feedback. *Psychophysiol.*, **4**, 1–6.

BRICKER, D. D. (1972) Imitative sign training as a facilitator of word-object association with low-functioning children. *Amer. J. ment. Defic.*, **76**, 509–16.

BRICKER, D. D. and BRICKER, W. A. (1972) *Toddler Research and Intervention Project. Report Year One.* Nashville, Tenn.· IMRID, Peabody College.

BRICKER, W. A. (1970) Identifying and modifying behavioral deficits. *Amer. J. ment. Defic.*, **75**, 16–21.

BRICKER, W. A. (1972) A systematic approach to language training. In SCHIEFELBUSCH, R. L. (ed.) *The Language of the Mentally Retarded.* Baltimore, Md.: Univ. Park Press.

BRICKER, W. A. and BRICKER, D. D. (1966) The use of programmed language training as a means for differential diagnosis and educational remediation among severely retarded children. In *Peabody Papers in Human Development.* Nashville, Tenn.: Peabody College.

BRICKER, W. A. and BRICKER, D. D. (1969) Four operant procedures for establishing auditory stimulus control with low functioning children. *Amer. J. ment. Defic.*, **73**, 981–7.

BRICKER, W. A. and BRICKER, D. D. (1970) A program of language training for the severely language handicapped child. *Except. Child.*, 101–11.

BRICKER, W. A., MORGAN, D. and GRABOWSKI, J. (1968) Token reinforcement of attendants who work with low-functioning children. *Abstracts of Peabody Studies in Mental Retardation 1965–8*, **4**.

BUCHER, B. and LOVAAS, O. I. (1968) Use of aversive stimulation in behaviour modification. In JONES, M. R. (ed.) *Miami Symposium on the Prediction of Behaviour, 1967: Aversive Stimulation.* Coral Gables, Fla.: Univ. of Miami Press.

BUDDE, J. F. (1971) *The Lattice Systems Approach: A Developmental Tool for Behavioural Research and Program Models.* Working Paper No. 250. Parsons, Kans.: Parsons Research Centre.

BUDDE, J. F. and MENOLASCINO, F. J. (1971) Systems technology and retardation: applications to vocational habilitation. *Ment. Retard.*, **9**, 11–16.

BUDDENHAGEN, R. G. (1971) *Establishing Vocal Verbalization in Mute Mongoloid Children.* Champaign, Ill.: Research Press Company.

BUEHLER, R. E., PATTERSON, G. R. and FURNISS, J. M. (1966) The reinforcement of behaviour in institutional settings. *Behav. Res. Therapy*, **4**, 157–67.

BUELL, J., STODDARD, P., HARRIS, F. R. and BAER, D. M. (1968) Collateral social development accompanying reinforcement of outdoor play in a preschool child. *J. appl. Behav. Anal.*, **1**, 167–73.

BURCHARD, J. D. and BARRERA, F. (1972) An analysis of timeout and response cast in a programmed environment. *J. appl. Behav. Anal.*, **5**, 271–82.

CAMPBELL, D. T. and STANLEY, J. C. (1963) Experimental and quasi-experimental designs for research. In GAGE, N. L. (ed.) *Handbook of Research on Teaching*. New York: Rand, McNally.

CANDLAND, D. K. and MANNING, S. A. (1966) Elementary learning patterns in mental retardates. *Training School Bull.*, **63**, 57–99.

CATANIA, A. C. (1971) Elicitation, reinforcement and stimulus control. In GLASER, R. (ed.) *The Nature of Reinforcement*. New York: Academic Press.

CAUTELA, J. H. (1966) Treatment of compulsive behaviour by covert sensitization. *Psychol. Rec.*, **16**, 33–41.

CHURCH, R. M. (1963) The varied effects of punishment on behaviour. *Psychol. Rev.*, **70**, 369–402.

CLARKE, A. M. and CLARKE, A. D. B. (1973) What are the problems? An evaluation of recent research relating to theory and practice. In CLARKE, A. D. B. and CLARKE, A. M. (eds.) *Mental Retardation and Behavioural Research*. London: Churchill Livingstone.

CLEMENTS, C. B. and MCKEE, J. M. (1968) Programmed instruction for institutionalized offenders: contingency management and performance contacts. *Psychol. Rep.*, **22**, 957–64.

CORTE, H. E., WOLF, M. M. and LOCKE, B. J. (1971) A comparison of procedures for eliminating self-injurious behaviour of retarded adolescents. *J. appl. Behav. Anal.*, **4**, 201–13.

Council for Exceptional Children (1971) *Teaching Exceptional Children* (Special Issue on Precision Teaching). Arlington, Va.

DAVIES, I. K. (1971) *The Management of Learning*. London: McGraw-Hill.

DAVISON, G. C. (1968) The elimination of a sadistic fantasy by a client-controlled counterconditioning technique: a case study. *J. abn. Psychol.*, **73**, 84–90.

DAYAN, M. (1964) Toilet training retarded children in a state residential institution. *Ment. Retard.*, **2**, 116–17.

DICARA, L. V. and MILLER, N. E. (1968) Changes in heart rate instrumentally learned by curarized rats as avoidance responses. *J. comp. physiol. Psychol.*, **65**, 8–12.

Eastern Nebraska Community Office of Retardation (1972) *General Information Papers*.

EGGER, M. D. and MILLER, N. E. (1962) Secondary reinforcement in rats as a function of information value and reliability of a stimulus. *J. exp. Psychol.*, **64**, 97–104.

ELLIS, N. R. (1963) Toilet training the severely defective patient: An S-R reinforcement analysis. *Amer. J. ment. Defic.*, **68**, 98–103.

FALLS, C. W. (1972) *Client Progress System*. Lincoln: Nebraska State Office of Mental Retardation.

FINDLEY, J. D. and BRADY, J. V. (1965) Facilitation of large ratio perform-ance by use of conditioned reinforcement. *J. exp. Anal. Behav.*, **8**, 125–9.

FLANDERS, J. P. (1968) A review of research on imitative behaviour. *Psychol. Bull.*, **69**, 316–37.

FOXX, R. M. and AZRIN, N. H. (1972) Restitution: a method of eliminating aggressive-disruptive behavior of retarded and brain damaged patients. *Behav. Res. Ther.*, **10**, 15–27.

FRANCIS, S. H. (1970) Behaviour of low-grade institutionalized mongoloids: changes with age. *Amer. J. ment. Defic.*, **75**, 92–101.

FREDERICKS, H. D. B., BALDWIN,V. L., MCDONALD, J. J., HOFFMAN, R. and HARTER, J. (1971) Parents educate their trainable children. *Ment. Retard.*, **9**, 24–6.

FULLER, P. R. (1949) Operant conditioning of a vegetative human organism. *Amer. J. Psychol.*, **62**, 587–90.

FULTON, R. T. (1972) A program of developmental research in audiological procedures. In SCHIEFELBUSCH, R. L. (ed.) *Language of the Mentally Retarded*. Baltimore, Md.: Univ. Park Press.

GAGNÉ, R. M. (1968) Contributions of learning to human development. *Psychol. Rev.*, **75**, 177–93.

GARCIA, E., BAER, D. M. and FIRESTONE, I. (1971) The development of generalized imitation with topographically determined boundaries. *J. appl. Behav. Anal.*, **4**, 101–12.

GARDNER, J. M. (1968) The behaviour modification model. *Ment. Retard.*, **6**, 54–5.

GARDNER, J. M. (1969a) Behaviour modification research in mental retarda-tion: Search for an adequate paradigm. *Amer. J. ment. Defic.*, **73**, 844–51.

GARDNER, J. M. (1969b) *The Training Proficiency Scale: Manual.* Columbus, Ohio: Columbus State Institute.

GARDNER, J. M. (1971) Behaviour modification in mental retardation: a review of research and analysis of trends. In RUBIN, R. D., FENSTERHEIM, H., LAZARUS, A. A. and FRANKS, C. M. (eds.) *Advances in Behaviour Therapy*. New York: Academic Press.

GARDNER, J. M. (1972) Teaching behaviour modification skills to nonprofessionals. *J. appl. Behav. Anal.*, **5**, 517–21.

GARDNER, J. M. and HOFFMAN, D. (1969) *The Resident Comprehensive Behaviour Check List: Manual.* Columbus, Ohio: Columbus State Institute.

GARDNER, J. M. and WATSON, L. S. (1969) Behaviour modification of the mentally retarded: An annotated bibliography. *Ment. Retard. Abstrs.*, **6**, 181–93.

GARDNER, W. I. (1969) Use of punishment procedures with the severely retarded. *Amer. J. ment. Defic.*, **74**, 86–103.

GARDNER, W. I. (1971) *Behavior Modification in Mental Retardation.* Chicago: Aldine, Atherton.

GELFAND, D. M. and HARTMANN, D. P. (1968) Behavior therapy with children: a review and evaluation of research methodology. *Psychol. Bull.*, **69**, 204–15.

GEWIRTZ, J. L. (1967) Deprivation and satiation of social stimuli as determinants of their reinforcing efficacy. In HILL, J. P. (ed.) *Minnesota Symposia on Child Psychology*, Vol. 1. Minneapolis: Univ. of Minnesota Press.

GEWIRTZ, J. L. (1968) On designing the functional environment of the child to facilitate behavioural development. In DITTMAN, L. L. (ed.) *Early Child Care: The New Perspectives*. New York: Atherton.

GEWIRTZ, J. L. and STINGLE, K. G. (1968) Learning of generalized imitation as the basis for identification. *Psychol. Rev.*, **75**, 374–97.

GILES, D. K. and WOLF, M. M. (1966) Toilet training institutionalized, severe retardates: an application of behavior modification techniques. *Amer. J. ment. Defic.*, **70**, 766–80.

GOETZ, E. N. and BAER, D. M. (1971) Descriptive social reinforcement of 'creative' block building by young children. In RAMP, E. A. and HOPKINS, B. L. (eds.) *A New Direction for Education: Behavior Analysis*. Laurence; Univ. of Kansas.

GOLDIAMOND, I. (1965) Self-control procedures in personal behavioural problems. *Psychol. Rep.*, **17**, 851–68.

GREENE, R. J. and HOATS, D. L. (1969) Reinforcing capabilities of television distortion. *J. appl. Behav. Anal.*, **2**, 139–41.

GROSZ, H. J. and ZIMMERMAN, J. (1965) Experimental analysis of hysterical blindness: a follow-up report and new experimental data. *Arch. gen. Psychiat.*, **13**, 255–60.

GROVES, I. D. and CARROCCIO, D. F. (1971) A self-feeding programme for the severely and profoundly retarded. *Ment. Retard.*, **9**, 10–12.

GUESS, D. (1969) A functional analysis of receptive language and productive speech: acquisition of the plural morpheme. *J. appl. Behav. Anal.*, **2**, 55–64.

GUESS, D., SAILOR, W., RUTHERFORD, G. and BAER, D. M. (1968) An experimental analysis of linguistic development: The productive use of the plural morpheme. *J. appl. Behav. Anal.*, **1**, 297–306.

HALL, R. V. (1970) Reinforcement procedures and the increase of functional speech by a brain-injured child. In GIRARDEAU, F. L. and SPRADLIN, J. E. (eds.) *A Functional Approach to Speech and Language*. ASHA Monogr. No. 14. Washington, DC: American Speech and Hearing Association.

HALL, R. V. (1971) *Behaviour Management Series. Part 1: The Measurement of Behaviour. Part II: Basic Principles. Part III: Applications in School and Home*. Kansas City, Miss.: H. & H. Enterprises.

HALL, R. V. and BRODEN, M. (1967) Behaviour changes in brain-injured children through social reinforcement. *J. exp. Child Psychol.*, **5**, 463–79.

HALL, R. V., AXELROD, S., TYLER, L., GRIEF, E., JONES, F. C. and
ROBERTSON, R. (1972) Modification of behaviour problems in the home
with a parent as observer and experimenter. *J. appl. Behav. Anal.*, 5,
53–64.

HAMILTON, J. and ALLEN, P. (1967) Ward programming for severely
retarded institutionalized retardates. *Ment. Retard.*, 5, 22–4.

HAMILTON, J., STEPHENS, L. and ALLEN, P. (1967) Controlling
aggressive and destructive behavior in severely retarded
institutionalized residents. *Amer. J. ment. Defic.*, 71, 852–6.

HETHERINGTON, E. M. and ROSS, L. E. (1967) Discrimination learning
by normal and retarded children under delay of reward and interpolated
task conditions. *Child Developm.*, 38, 639–47.

HETHERINGTON, E. M., ROSS, L. E. and PICK, H. L. (1964) Delay of
reward and learning in mentally retarded and normal children. *Child
Developm.*, 35, 653–9.

HOM, G. L. (1967) Effects of amount of reinforcement on the concurrent
performance of retardates. *Psychol. Rep.*, 20, 887–92.

HOM, G. L., CORTE, E., SPRADLIN, J. E. and MICHAEL, J. (1966)
Effects of amount of reinforcement on the performance of mildly retarded
adolescent girls. *Psychol. Rep.*, 19, 1191–4.

HOMME, L. E. (1966) Perspectives in psychology – XXIV. Control of
coverants, the operants of the mind. *Psychol. Rec.*, 15, 501–11.

HOMME, L. E., CGANYI, A., GONZALES, M. and RECHS, J. (1969)
How to Use Contingency Contacting in the Classroom. Champaign, Ill.:
Research Press.

HOMME, L. E., de BACA, P., DEVINE, J. V., STEINHORST, R. and
RICKERT, E. J. (1963) Use of the Premack Principle in controlling the
behaviour of nursery school children. *J. exp. Anal. Behav.*, 6, 544.

HOPKINS, B. (1968) Effects of candy and social reinforcement, instructions,
and reinforcement schedule learning in the modification and maintenance
of smiling. *J. appl. Behav. Anal.*, 1, 121–30.

HUNDZIAK, M., MAURER, R. A., and WATSON, L. S. (1965) Operant
conditioning in toilet training severely mentally retarded boys. *Amer. J.
ment. Defic.*, 70, 120–4.

HUSTED, J. R., HALL, P. and AGIN, B. (1971) The effectiveness of
time-out in reducing maladaptive behavior of autistic and retarded
children. *J. Psychol.*, 79, 189–96.

INSALACO, C. and HAMILTON, J. (1966) *Modification of Self-Abusive
Behaviour with the Use of Punishment and Reward in a Free Operant
Situation.* Paper read at the Southeastern Meeting of the American
Association on Mental Deficiency, Atlanta.

JOHNSTON, M. (1968) Echolalia and automatism in speech. In
SLOANE, H. N. and MACAULAY, B. D. (eds.) *Operant Procedures in
Remedial Speech and Language Training.* Boston: Houghton Mifflin.

JUVONEN, L. (1972) *Development of Play Behaviour in Two Severely Retarded Preschool Children*. Unpubl. Master's thesis, Univ. of London Institute of Education.

KANFER, F. H. (1970) Self regulation: research, issues, and speculations. In NEURINGER, C. and MICHAEL, J. L. (eds.) *Behaviour Modification in Clinical Psychology*. New York: Appleton-Century-Crofts.

KANFER, F. H. and PHILLIPS, J. S. (1966) Behaviour therapy: a panacea for all ills or a passing fancy? *Arch. Gen. Psychiat.*, **15**, 114–28.

KANFER, F. H. and PHILLIPS, J. S. (1970) *Learning Foundations of Behavior Therapy*. New York: Wiley.

KANTOR, J. R. (1958) *Interbehavioral Psychology*. Bloomington, Ind.; Principia Press.

KATKIN, E. S. and MURRAY, E. N. (1968) Instrumental conditioning of autonomically mediated behaviour. *Psychol. Bull.*, **70**, 52–68.

KAZDIN, A. E. and BOOTZIN, R. R. (1972) The token economy: an evaluative review. *J. appl. Behav. Anal.*, **5**, 343–72.

KELLEHER, R. T. and GALLUB, L. R. (1962) A review of positive conditioned reinforcement. *J. exp. Anal. Behav.*, **5**, 543–97.

KELLER, F. S. and SCHOENFELD, W. N. (1950) *Principles of Psychology*. New York: Appleton-Century-Crofts.

KIERNAN, C. C. (1973a) Functional analysis. In MITTLER, P. (ed.) *Assessment for Learning in the Mentally Handicapped*. London: Churchill Livingstone; Baltimore, Md: Williams & Wilkins.

KIERNAN, C. C. (1973b) Application of behaviour modification in the ward situation. In GUNZBURG, H. C. *Experiments in Rehabilitation of the Mentally Handicapped* (in press).

KIERNAN, C. C. and BURGESS, I. S. (1971) *Shaping Walking in a Profoundly Retarded Blind Child*. Unpubl. manuscript.

KIERNAN, C. C. and RIDDICK, B. (1972) *A Draft Programme for Training in Operant Techniques*. London: Univ. of London Institute of Education.

KIERNAN, C. C. and SAUNDERS, C. (1972) Generalized imitation: experiments with profoundly retarded children. *Second European Conference on Behaviour Modification, Wexford, Ireland*.

KIERNAN, C. C., DONOGHUE, E. C. and HAWKS, G. D. (1971) *A Ward Wide Programme for Profoundly Subnormal Children*. Paper to the 3rd Conference of the Behavioural Engineering Association, Wexford.

KIMBRELL, D. L., LUCKEY, R. E., BARBUTO, P. F. P. and LOVE, J. G. (1967) Operation dry pants: an intensive habit-training program for severely and profoundly retarded. *Ment. Retard.*, **5**, 32–6.

KING, R. D., RAYNES, N. V. and TIZARD, J. (1971) *Patterns of Residential Care*. London: Routledge & Kegan Paul.

KRANTZ, D. L. (1971) The separate worlds of operant and non-operant research. *J. appl. Behav. Anal.*, **4**, 61–70.

KRASNER, L. and ULLMAN, L. P. (1966) *Research in Behaviour Modification.* New York: Holt, Rinehart & Winston.

KUYPERS, D. S., BECKER, W. C. and O'LEARY, K. D. (1968) How to make a token system fail. *Except. Child.* 35, 101–8.

LARSEN, L. A. and BRICKER, W. A. (1968) *A Manual for Parents and Teachers of Severely and Moderately Retarded Children.* IMRID Papers V, No. 22. Nashville, Tenn.: IMRID.

LEITENBERG, H. (1961) Is time-out from positive reinforcement an aversive event? *Psychol. Bull.,* 64, 428–41.

LENT, J. R., LeBLANC, J. and SPRADLIN, J. E. (1967) Designing a rehabilitative culture for moderately retarded, adolescent girls. In ULRICH, R., STACHNIK, T. and MABRY, J. (eds.) *Control of Human Behaviour. Volume Two. From Cure to Prevention.* Glenview, Ill.: Scott, Foresman.

LINDSLEY, O. R. (1970) Procedures in common described by a common language. In NEURINGER, C. and MICHAEL, J. L. (eds.) *Behaviour Modification in Clinical Psychology.* New York: Appleton-Century-Crofts.

LOCKE, B. J. (1969) Verbal conditioning with retarded subjects: establishment and reinstatement of effective reinforcing consequences. *Amer. J. ment. Defic.,* 73, 621–6.

LOGAN, D. L., KINSINGER, J., SHELTON, G. and BROWN, J. M. (1971) The use of multiple reinforcers in a rehabilitation setting. *Ment. Retard.,* 9, 3–6.

LOVAAS, O. I. (1967) A behaviour therapy approach to the treatment of childhood schizophrenia. In HILL, J. (ed.) *Minnesota Symposium on Child Psychology.* Minneapolis: Univ. of Minnesota Press.

LOVAAS, O. I. and SIMMONS, J. Q. (1969) Manipulation of self-destructive behavior in three retarded children. *J. appl. Behav. Anal.,* 1, 143–57.

LUCERO, R. J., VIAL, D. J. and SCHERBER, J. (1968) Regulating operant-conditioning programs. *Hospital and Community Psychiatry,* 53–4.

LUCKEY, R., WATSON, C. and MUSICK, J. (1968) Aversive conditioning as a means of inhibiting vomiting and rumination. *Amer. J. ment. Defic.,* 73, 139–42.

LYKKEN, D. T. (1968) Statistical significance in psychological research. *Psychol. Bull.,* 70, 151–9.

LYNCH, J. and BRICKER, W. A. (1972) Linguistic theory and operant procedures: toward an integrated approach to language training for the mentally retarded. *Ment. Retard.,* 10, 12–17.

MCGEE, V. E. (1971) *Principles of Statistics: Traditional and Bayesian.* New York: Appleton-Century-Crofts.

MACHT, J. (1971) Operant measurement of subjective visual acuity in non-verbal children. *J. appl. Behav. Anal.,* 4, 23–36.

MACMILLAN, D. L. and FORNESS, S. R. (1970) Behaviour modification: limitations and liabilities. *Except. Child.*, 291–7.

MCREYNOLDS, L. V. (1969) Application of time-out from positive reinforcement for increasing the efficiency of speech training. *J. appl. Behav. Anal.*, **2**, 199–205.

MCREYNOLDS, L. V. (1970) Reinforcement procedures for establishing and maintaining echoic speech by a non-verbal child. In GIRARDEAU, F. L. and SPRADLIN, J. E. (eds.) *A Functional Approach to Speech and Language*. ASHA Monogr., No. 14. Washington, DC: American Speech and Hearing Association.

MAHONEY, K., VAN WAGENEN, R. K. and MEYERSON, L. (1971) Toilet training of normal and retarded children. *J. appl. Behav. Anal.*, **4**, 173–81.

MARTIN, B. (1963) Reward and punishment associated with the same goal response: a factor in the learning of motives. *Psychol. Bull.*, **60**, 441–51.

MARTIN, G. L. (1972) Teaching operant technology to psychiatric nurses, aides and attendants· In CLARK, F. W., EVANS, D. R. and HAMERLYNCK, L. A. (eds.) *Implementing Behavioural Programs for Schools and Clinics*. Champaign, Ill.: Research Press.

MARTIN, G. L., KEHOE, B., BIRD, E., JENSEN, V. and DARBYSHIRE, M. (1971) Operant conditioning in dressing behaviour of severely retarded girls. *Ment. Retard*, **9**, 27–31.

MARTIN, J. A. (1971) The control of imitative and non-imitative behaviours in severely retarded children through 'generalized-instruction following'. *J. exp. Child Psychol.*, **11**, 390–400.

MAZIK, K. and MACNAMARA, R. (1967) Operant conditioning at the training school. *Training School Bull.*, **63**, 153–8.

MEACHAM, M. and WEISEN, A. (1970) *Changing Classroom Behaviour: A Manual for Precision Teaching*. Scranton, Penn.: International Textbook Co.

MICHAEL, J. L. (1970) Rehabilitation. In NEURINGER, C. and MICHAEL, J. L. (eds.) *Behaviour Modification in Clinical Psychology*. New York.: Appleton-Century-Crofts.

MILLER, N. E. (1960) Learning resistance to pain and fear: effects of overlearning, exposure, and rewarded exposure in context *J. comp. physiol. Psychol.*, **60**, 137–45.

MILLER, N. E. and BANUAZIZI, A. (1968) Instrumental learning by curarized rats of a specific visceral response, intestinal and cardiac. *J. comp. physiol. Psychol.* **65**, 1–7.

MILLER, N. E. and DICARA, L. (1967) Instrumental learning of heart rate changes in curarized rats: shaping, and specificity to discriminative stimulus. *J. comp. physiol. Psychol.* **63**, 12–19.

MINK, O. (1970) *The Behaviour Change Process*. Chicago: Harper & Row.

MIRA, M. (1970) Results of a behavior modification training program for parents and teachers. *Behav. Res. Therapy*, **8**, 309–11.

MORALES, I. (1972) *Application of Operant Techniques to Some Aspects of Exploratory Behaviour in Two Severely Retarded Children*. Unpubl. Master's thesis, Univ. of London Institute of Education.

MOWRER, O. H. and MOWRER, W. M. (1938) Enuresis: a method for its study and treatment. *Amer. J. Orthopsychiat.*, **8**, 436–59.

MURPHY, G. (1947) *Personality: a Biosocial Approach to Origins and Structure*. New York: Harper & Row.

O'BRIEN, F., BUGLE, C. and AZRIN, N. H. (1972) Training and maintaining a retarded child's proper eating. *J. appl. Behav. Anal.*, **5**, 67–72.

ORLANDO, R. (1965) Shaping multiple schedule performances in retardates: Establishment of baselines by systematic and special procedures. *J. exp. Child Psychol.*, **2**, 135–53.

ORLANDO, R. and BIJOU, S. W. (1960) Single and multiple schedules of reinforcement in developmentally retarded children. *J. exp. Anal. Behav.*, **3**, 339–48.

PALOUTZIAN, R. F., HASAZI, J., STREIFEL, J. and EDGAR, C. L. (1971). Promotion of positive social interaction in severely retarded young children. *Amer. J. ment. Defic.*, **75**, 519–24.

PANYAN, M., BOOZER, H. and MORRIS, N. (1970) Feedback to attendants as a reinforcer for applying operant techniques. *J. appl. Behav. Anal.*, **3**, 1–4.

PATTERSON, G. R. (1969) Behavioral techniques based on social learning: An additional base for developing behavior modification technologies. In FRANKS, C. M. (ed.) *Behavior Therapy: Appraisal and Status*. New York: McGraw-Hill.

PATTERSON, G. R. and GUILLON, M. (1968) *Living with Children: New Methods for Parents and Teachers*. Champaign, Ill.: Research Press.

PATTERSON, G. R. and REID, J. B. (1970) Reciprocity and coercion: two facets of social systems. In NEURINGER, C. and MICHAEL, J. L. (eds.). *Behavior Modification in Clinical Psychology*. New York: Appleton-Century-Crofts.

PAUL, H. A. and MILLER, J. R. (1971) Reduction of extreme deviant behaviours in a severely retarded girl. *Training School Bull.*, **67**, 193–7.

PENDERGRASS, V. E. (1972) Timeout from positive reinforcement following persistent, high rate behaviour in retardates. *J. appl. Behav. Anal.*, **5**, 85–91.

PETERSON, R. (1968) Imitation: A basic behavioural mechanism. In SLOANE, H. N. and MACAULAY, B. D. (eds.) *Operant Procedures in Remedial Speech and Language Training*. Boston: Houghton Mifflin.

PETERSON, R. F. and PETERSON, L. R. (1968) The use of positive reinforcement in the control of self-destructive behavior in a retarded boy. *J. exp. Child Psychol.*, **6**, 351–60.

PIPER, T. J. (1971) Effects of delay of reinforcement on retarded children's learning. *Except Child.*, 139–45.

PREMACK, D. (1959) Toward empirical behavior laws: 1. Positive reinforcement. *Psychol. Rev.*, **66**, 219–33.

PREMACK, D. (1965) Reinforcement theory. In LEVINE, D. (ed.) *Nebraska Symposium on Motivation.* Lincoln: Univ. of Nebraska Press.

REDD, W. H. (1969) Effects of mixed reinforcement contingencies on adults' control of children's behaviour. *J. appl. Behav. Anal.*, **2**, 249–54.

REDD, W. H. and BIRNBRAUER, J. S. (1969) Adults as discriminative stimuli for different reinforcement contingencies with retarded children. *J. exp. Child Psychol.*, **7**, 440–7.

RENTFROW, R. K. and RENTFROW, D. K. (1969) Studies related to toilet training of the mentally retarded. *Amer. J. occup. Therapy*, **23**, 425–30.

RIDDICK, B. and KIERNAN, C. C. (1972) *Stability of Preferences for Rewards in Profoundly Retarded Children.* Unpubl. manuscript.

RISLEY, T. R. (1968) The effects and side effects of punishing the autistic behaviors of a deviant child. *J. appl. Behav. Anal.,* **1**, 21–34.

RISLEY, T. R. and BAER, D. M. (1972) Operant behaviour modification: the deliberate development of child behaviour. In CALDWELL, B. and RICCIUTI, D. *Review of Child Development Research. Vol III: Social Influence and Social Action.* New York: Russell-Sage.

RISLEY, T. R. and WOLF, M. M. (1967) Establishing functional speech in echolalic children. *Behav. Res. Therapy,* **5**, 73–88.

ROSS, L. E., HETHERINGTON, M. and WRAY, N. P. (1965) Delay of reward and the learning of a size problem by normal and retarded children. *Child Developm.* **36**, 509–17.

SACHS, D. A. (1971) WISC changes as an evaluative procedure within a token economy. *Amer. J. ment. Defic.*, **76**, 230–4.

SAILOR, W. (1971) Reinforcement and generalization of productive plural allomorphs in two retarded children. *J. appl. Behav. Anal.*, **4**, 305–10.

SAJWAJ, T., TWARDOSZ, S. and BURKE, M. (1972) Side effects of extinction procedures in a remedial preschool. *J. appl. Behav. Anal.*, **5**, 163–75.

SCHIEFELBUSCH, R. L. (1972) *Language of the Mentally Retarded.* Baltimore, Md.: Univ. Park Press.

SCHOELKOPF, A. M. and ORLANDO, R. (1965) Delayed versus immediate reinforcement in simultaneous discrimination problems with mentally retarded children. *Psychol. Rec.*, **15**, 15–23.

SCHOELKOPF, A. M. and ORLANDO, R. (1966) Reinforcement delay gradients of retardates with a concurrent discrimination task procedure. *Psychol. Rec.*, **16**, 113–28.

SCHUMAKER, J. and SHERMAN, J. A. (1970) Training generative verb usage by imitation and reinforcement procedures. *J. Appl. Behav. Anal.*, **3**, 273–87.

SHERMAN, J. A. (1971) Imitation and language development. In REESE, H. W. (ed.) *Advances in Child Development and Behavior.* New York: Academic Press.

SHERMAN, J. A. and BAER, D. M. (1969) Appraisal of operant therapy techniques with children and adults. In FRANKS, C. M. *Behavior Therapy: Appraisal and Status.* New York: McGraw-Hill.

SIDMAN, M. (1960) *Tactics of Scientific Research: Evaluating Experimental Data in Psychology.* New York: Basic Books.

SIDMAN, M. and STODDARD, L. T. (1967) Programmed perception and learning for retarded children. In ELLIS, N. R. (ed.) *International Review of Research in Mental Retardation,* Vol. 2. New York: Academic Press.

SIEGEL, P. S. (1968) Incentive motivation in the mental retardate. In ELLIS, N. R. (ed.) *International Review of Research in Mental Retardation,* Vol. 3. New York: Academic Press.

SKINNER, B. F. (1938) *The Behavior of Organisms.* New York: Appleton-Century-Crofts.

SKINNER, B. F. (1950) Are theories of learning necessary? *Psychol. Rev.,* **57,** 193–216.

SKINNER, B. F. (1953) *Science and Human Behavior.* New York: Macmillan.

SKINNER, B. F. (1966) Operant behavior. In HONIG, W. K. (ed.) *Operant Behavior: Areas of Research and Application.* New York: Appleton-Century-Crofts.

SKINNER, B. F. (1969) *Contingencies of Reinforcement.* New York: Appleton-Century-Crofts.

SLOANE, H. N., JOHNSTON, M. K. and HARRIS, F. R. (1968) Remedial procedures for teaching verbal behaviour to speech deficient or defective young children. In SLOANE, H. N. and MACAULAY, B. D. (eds.) *Operant Procedures in Remedial Speech and Language Training.* Boston: Houghton Mifflin.

SMEETS, P. M. (1970) Withdrawal of social reinforcers as a means of controlling rumination and regurgitation in a profoundly retarded person. *Amer. Inst. ment. Stud.,* **67,** 44–51.

SOLOMON, R. L. (1964) Punishment. *Amer. Psychol.,* **19,** 237–53.

SPRADLIN, J. E. (1964) *The Premack Hypothesis and Self-feeding by Profoundly Retarded Children: A Case Report.* Working Paper No. 79. Parson, Kans.: Parsons Research Centre.

SPRADLIN, J. E. and GIRARDEAU, F. L. (1966) The behavior of moderately and severely retarded persons. In ELLIS, N. R. *International Review of Research in Mental Retardation,* Vol. 1. New York: Academic Press.

SPRADLIN, J. E., GIRARDEAU, E. L. and CORTE, E. (1965) Fixed ratio and fixed interval behavior of severely and profoundly retarded subjects. *J. exp. Child Psychol.,* **2,** 340–53.

SPRADLIN, J. E., GIRARDEAU, F. L. and HOM, G. L. (1966) Stimulus properties of reinforcement during extinction of a free operant response. *J. exp. Child Psychol.*, **4**, 369–80.

SPRADLIN, J. E., LOCKE, B. J. and FULTON, R. T. (1969) In FULTON, R. T. and LLOYD, L. L. (eds.) *Audiometry for the Retarded: With Implications for the Difficult-to-Test.* Baltimore, Md.: Williams & Wilkins.

STOLZ, S. B. and WOLF, M. M. (1969) Visually discriminated behavior in a 'blind' adolescent retardate. *J. appl. Behav. Anal.*, **2**, 65–77.

TERDAL, L. and BUELL, J. (1969) Parent education in managing retarded children with behavior deficits and inappropriate behaviours. *Ment. Retard.*, **7**, 10–13.

TERRACE, H. S. (1966) Stimulus control. In HONIG, W. K. (ed.) *Operant Behavior: Areas of Research and Application.* New York: Appleton-Century-Crofts.

THARP, R. G. and WETZEL, R. J. (1969) *Behavior Modification in the Natural Environment.* New York: Academic Press.

TOUCHETTE, P. E. (1968) The effects of graduated stimulus change on the acquisition of a simple discrimination in severely retarded boys. *J. exp. Anal. Behav.*, **11**, 39–48.

TOUCHETTE, P. E. (1969) Tilted lines as complex stimuli. *J. exp. Anal. Behav.*, **12**, 211–14.

TOUCHETTE, P. E. (1971) Transfer of stimulus control: measuring the moment of transfer. *J. exp. Anal. Behav.*, **15**, 347–54.

TROWILL, J. A. (1967) Instrumental conditioning of the heart rate in the curarized rat. *J. comp. physiol. Psychol.*, **63**, 7–11.

TWARDOSZ, S. and SAJWAJ, T. (1972) Multiple effects of a procedure to increase sitting in a hyperactive, retarded boy. *J. appl. Behav. Anal.*, **5**, 73–8.

TYLER, V. O. and BROWN, G. D. (1967) The use of swift, brief isolation as a group control device. *Behav. Res. Therapy*, **5**, 1–9.

ULRICH, R., STACHNIK, T. and MABRY, J. (1970) *Control of Human Behavior. Volume Two: From Cure to Prevention.* Glenview, Ill.; Scott, Foresman.

VAN WAGENEN, R. K. and MURDOCK, E. E. (1966) A transistorized signal-package for toilet training of infants. *J. exp. Child Psychol.*, **3**, 312–14.

VAN WAGENEN, R. K., MEYERSON, L., KERR, N. J. and MAHONEY, K. (1969) Field trials of a new procedure for toilet training. *J. exp. Child Psychol.*, **8**, 147–59.

VUKELICH, R. and HAKE, D. F. (1971) Reduction of dangerously aggressive behavior in a severely retarded resident through a combination of positive reinforcement procedures. *J. Appl. Behav. Anal.*, **4**, 215–25.

WATSON, L. S. (1966) Application of behavior shaping devices to training severely and profoundly mentally retarded children in an institutional setting. *Ment. Retard.*, **6**, 21–3.

WATSON, L. S., GARDNER, J. M. and SANDERS, C. (1971) Shaping and maintaining behavior modification skills in staff members in an M.R. Institution: Columbus State Institute Behavior Modification Program. *Ment. Retard.*, **9**, 39–42.

WATSON, R. I. (1962) The experimental tradition and clinical psychology. In BACHRACH, A. J. (ed.) *Experimental Foundations of Clinical Psychology*. New York: Basic Books.

WHALEN, C. K. and HENKER, B. A. (1969) Creating therapeutic pyramids using mentally retarded patients. *Amer. J. ment. Defic.*, **74**, 331–7.

WHALEN, C. K. and HENKER, B. A. (1971a) Pyramid Therapy in a hospital for the retarded: methods, program evaluation, and long-term effects. *Amer. J. ment. Defic.*, **75**, 414–34.

WHALEN, C. K. and HENKER, B. A. (1971b) Play therapy conducted by mentally retarded patients. *Psychotherapy: Theory, Research and Practice*, **8**, 236–45.

WHALEY, D. L. and MALOTT, R. W. (1968) *Elementary Principles of Behavior*. Ann Arbor, Mich; Edwards Brothers.

WHALEY, D. L. and TOUGH, J. (1970) Treatment of a self-injuring mongoloid with shock-induced suppression and avoidance. In ULRICH, R, STACHNIK, T. and MABRY, J. (eds.) *Control of Human Behavior. Vol. Two: from Cure to Prevention*. Glenview, Ill.; Scott, Foresman.

WHITE, J. C. and TAYLOR, D. J. (1967) Noxious conditioning as a treatment for rumination. *Ment. Retard.*, **5**, 30–3.

WHITMAN, T. L., MERCURIO, J. R. and CAPONIGRI, V. (1970) Development of social responses in two severely retarded children. *J. appl. Behav. Anal.*, **3**, 133–8.

WHITMAN, T. L., ZAKARAS, M. and CHARDOS, S. (1971) Effects of reinforcement and guidance procedures on instruction–following behavior of severely retarded children. *J. appl. Behav. Anal.*, **4**, 283–90.

WHITNEY, L. R. and BARNARD, K. E. (1966) Implications of operant learning theory for nursing care of the retarded child. *Ment. Retard.*, **4**, 26–9.

WILLEMS, E. P. and RAUSH, H. L. (1969) *Naturalistic Viewpoints in Psychological Research*. New York: Holt, Rinehart & Winston.

WILLIAMS, P. (1973) Psychological assessment of the mentally handicapped: social skills. In MITTLER, P. (ed.) *Assessment for Learning in the Mentally Handicapped*. London: Churchill Livingstone; Baltimore, Md: Williams & Wilkins.

WILLIAMS, P. and KUSHLICK, A. (1970) *Interview Schedule for the Social Assessment of Mentally Handicapped Children*. Wessex Regional Hospital Board.

WOLF, M. M., BIRNBRAUER, J. S., LAWLER, J. and WILLIAMS, T. (1970) The operant extinction, reinstatement and re-extinction of vomiting behavior in a retarded child. In URICH, R., STACHNIK, T. and MABRY, J. (eds.) *Control of Human Behaviour. Vol. Two: From Cure to Prevention.* Glenview, Ill.: Scott, Foresman.

ZEILER, M. D. and JERVEY, S. S. (1968) Development of behaviour self-feeding. *J. consult. clin. Psychol.*, **32**, 164–8.

ZIGLER, E. (1968) Research on personality structure in the retardate. In ELLIS, N. R. (ed.) *International Review of Research in Mental Retardation*, Vol. I. New York: Academic Press.

ZIMMERMAN, D. W. (1959) Sustained performance in rats based on secondary reinforcement. *J. comp. physiol. Psychol.*, **52**, 353–8.

ZIMMERMAN, J. (1963) Technique for sustaining behavior with conditioned reinforcement. *Science*, **142**, 682–4.

PART FIVE

Services for the mentally subnormal and their parents

24

J. Carr

The effect of the severely subnormal
on their families

Introduction

Over the last decade a wealth of data has accumulated showing that severely subnormal children brought up in their own homes are more forward in their development than are those brought up in institutions (Tizard, 1960; Lyle, 1960; Centerwall and Centerwall, 1960; Stedman and Eichorn, 1964; Shipe and Shotwell, 1965; Bayley et al., 1966; Carr, 1970). Partly as a result of these findings there has been increased pressure on parents to keep their mentally handicapped child at home, and the question arises as to the effect this has on the child's family, and in particular on the parents and siblings. (The effect on the more extended family members, such as grandparents, uncles or aunts, has been scarcely considered.)

Wolfensberger (1967) in a chapter that is highly recommended, both for its exhaustive coverage of the field and for its readability, points out that to read the literature of twenty years ago is to be hardly aware that parents existed: 'very little mention was made of parents, of their feelings and sensibilities, or of the impact of the diagnosis on them'. This was followed in the mid-1940s–1950s by 'a trickle of armchair papers' discussing parent dynamics ('Sampson [1947] was one of the first professionals who, in effect, proposed that it was time to be nice to parents') and later by 'almost a flood of such papers' (Wolfensberger, 1967). More recently, studies have become more research- and experiment-oriented; workers have compared the effects on the families of, for example, a retarded child in an institution or one brought up at home, of children with different types of handicap, or of a handicapped or a normal child. Kelman (1964) discusses the limitations of many such studies. Many suffer from population bias in that the populations on which they are based are either users of services or members of parent-sponsored organizations. Being 'self-selected', they may consist of parents who have been particularly affected by the impact of a handicapped child. He discusses the assumptions on which a number of studies appear to rest – that family behaviour is governed by the nature of the child's impairment, and thus that differences in family behaviour can be accounted for by differences in the impairment of the children – which Kelman rightly regards as unrealistic and of dubious validity. Another limitation common to many studies is that of a limited time perspective: 'Clinical contacts are office-bound, sporadic and short-term . . . virtually absent from the existing literature are longitudinal prospective family studies.' However, both Wolfensberger and Kelman emphasize that to recognize the shortcomings of these studies is not to say that they have no value, but that it is essential to recognize their biases if their contribution to our knowledge of the situation for parents of retarded children is to be adequately assessed.

Socio-economic factors

In contrast with the families of the mildly retarded, who have been found predominantly in working-class populations (Stein and Susser, 1960; Saenger, 1962; Rutter *et al.*, 1970), families of the severely subnormal are 'evenly distributed among all the social strata in society' (Kushlick, 1966). Penrose (1938) found that while high-grade and low-grade retarded subjects were equally represented among families of clerical workers downwards, there were twice as many low-grade as there were high-grade subjects coming from the professional classes (see Chapter 3). It has been noted anecdotally (Giannini and Goodman, 1963) that the socio-economic level of families of mongols appeared to be higher than those of the community as a whole. This was also found in a recent population study of one year's intake of mongol births in Surrey (Carr, 1975); 62 per cent of the families were in social classes I and II (Registrar General [1960] Classification of Occupations) compared with 34 per cent for Surrey as a whole. Since the numbers of Surrey babies in this study was very small (twenty-nine) the proportions of mongol and non-mongol severely subnormal children recorded in the Camberwell Register[1] were also examined. Children were included in the figures for Table 24 who were under the age of 15 and whose home addresses were in the former London Borough of Camberwell at some time during the period 31 December 1967 to 30 June 1971. This table also includes social class figures for the population of Camberwell (1961 census).

The table shows that the families of both groups of children were evenly distributed in comparison with the population from which they were drawn, with the possible exception of an excess of social class V non-mongols. So this study does not lend support to the suggestion that mongols occur more often in middle-class families; Giannini and Goodman's own explanation for their observation, that the mongol child, 'the most stigmatised of the retarded, physically and socially, represents an assault to middle class strivings and

[1] This is a cumulative register of patients, both adults and children, who have home addresses in Camberwell and who contact psychiatric or mental retardation services. Children were also traced through the 'at risk' register which has operated in the area since 1965, and through examination of the registers of other possible sources (such as Local Authority and private homes, all subnormality hospitals that had taken LCC patients, etc.) (Wing, 1971).

aspirations and culturally determined goals', and that middle-class families are more likely to seek for and demand services and thus come to the notice of those providing services, seems the more likely. This explanation does not account for the finding in the Surrey study, which is probably due to chance and small numbers.

Tizard and Grad (1961) found that families with a severely subnormal child at home were significantly worse off where housing and income were concerned than were families with such a child in an institution. Twice as many of those with a child at home were judged to be overcrowded (40 per cent, compared with 20 per cent of those with a child in an institution) and to be poor (25 per

TABLE 24. *Distribution according to social class: families of mongol and non-mongol severely subnormal children on the Camberwell Register (Wing, 1971) and for the population of Camberwell (1961 census)*

Social class	Mongols		Non-mongols		Population of Camberwell
	Numbers	%	Numbers	%	%
I and II	4	9	12	8	10
III NM	6 ⎫		22 ⎫		
	⎬24	53	⎬82	52	59·7
III M	18 ⎭		60 ⎭		
IV	10	22	29	18	17·3
V	7	16	34	22	13
	45*	100	157*	100	100

* Note: There were in addition 9 families of mongols and 16 of non-mongols where the social class rating was not known.

cent compared with 13 per cent of those with a child in an institution). However, in each case the differences between the two groups disappeared if the variables were recalculated for the institution group as if the retarded child were at home. The differences seem to be due entirely to the fact that the families with a child in an institution were one member short, so that available resources such as living space and income could be spread more generously among the remaining members of the family. Although Tizard and Grad suggest that expenses in the families of the handicapped were heavier on such things as special foods, medicines or replacement clothing than they would be in families of the general population, it seems possible that a similar effect could be observed in families of normal children, and that living standards in these would also rise if one member left the family group.

Standards of housing were compared for a group of thirty-nine families of mongol children and for a matched group of normal children (Carr, 1975). Ratings were made on a 4-point scale, from 'very comfortable' to 'poor', on spaciousness, furnishings, equipment and so forth. The standards for the families of mongols were rated slightly higher than were those for the control group – 26 per cent of homes of mongols and 14 per cent of homes of controls were rated as very comfortable; 39 per cent of homes of mongols and 48 per cent of homes of controls were rated as low-average or poor. The differences are not significant, but at least in this group, the families of mongols do not appear to have been worse off for housing than were families of normal children, at any rate while the children were young (up to 4 years old).

Home or institution care

Many studies, particularly those from America, have focused on the families' decision on whether or not the child should be sent to an institution. Indeed, in the earlier American literature the question was often not so much 'whether' as 'when'. One early study, for example, bore the unequivocal title, 'When should the seriously retarded infant be institutionalised?' (Jolly, 1953). Others of the same period discussed the need for the caseworker to help parents to overcome their reluctance to place the child and, once he was in the institution, to leave him there (Wardell, 1947; Walker, 1949). 'Acceptance' of the child seemed to imply acceptance of his condition and hence of the need for institutional placement (Stone, 1948). Caseworkers were urged to encourage parents to take this step by pointing out the advantages to the child; they should emphasize the training, education and specialized medical care that he would receive in the institution, while the parents should be helped to view the parting as if he were going away to boarding school or Scout Camp (Wardell, 1947). If the advisor could 'emphasise the positive features of institutional life parents will come to . . . see the logic of separation' (Jolly, 1953). The aim of this article was to discourage the very early institutionalization of retarded infants, especially likely in the case of mongols; but institutionalization was seen as eventually inevitable. The author urged that parents should take their baby home; but this was in order that they might gradually become more detached from him and 'realise that the child needs the special facilities of an institution'. The article ends with a case report of a child institutionalized at the age of 12 by his family, who then regretted it, and Jolly comments: 'Somewhere along the way this family's advisors had failed in their responsibility . . . the best time for separation had passed by.'

Running through these papers is an over-valuation of institutions for the mentally retarded, and an over-optimistic view of what they were able or likely to achieve for their residents. Disenchantment with institutions may have followed more realistic appraisal of their régimes and methods.

More recently, the institution has been seen less as the invariable choice for parents, and attention has turned to the factors which make institutionalization of a child more or less likely. Graliker, Koch and Henderson (1965) studied the families of a group of 32 children who had been placed in an institution, and of 37 who had been recommended for institutional care but whose parents had not accepted the recommendation. There were no differences between the groups on social class, religion, educational level and age of the parents. The institution group had an average of 3·6 siblings each, as against 3·2 in the home group. First-born children were found to be more likely, last-born children least likely to be institutionalized, the difference between these being significant at the ·05 level; children who were more retarded were more likely to be institutionalized. Mongols were more numerous in the home group (54·1 per cent), and less numerous in the institution group (31·3 per cent), while the reverse was true for children with congenital cerebral defects (29·7 per cent and 43·7 per cent respectively).

Families of mongol children under 9 years old were investigated by Stone (1967). In 50 families the child was on the waiting list for a place in an institution: 20 families were eager for the child to go in ('Placers'), while 30 families wished to defer placement ('Postponers'). Fifty-three had not applied for placement ('Non-applicants'). Forty-six of these 103 families refused to participate in the study; it is not clear how many fell into each of the three groups, though the proportions of applicants and non-applicants were said to be not significantly different. 'Placers' came from families that were rated poorest in socio-economic status, in family relationships and overall family adaptation. 'Postponers' had the most favourable social situation. Older children (over 5) were more likely to be placed, especially if they were boys. Parents who participated in parent groups were likely to be well informed about mongolism and mental retardation, while well-informed parents were likely to be more unwilling to institutionalize the child. It is difficult to reconcile the author's statement that social status was not associated with placement willingness (and hence with level of information and participation in parent groups) in view of earlier statements that 'Placers' were of the lowest and 'Postponers' of the highest socio-economic level, but no figures are presented which would enable firm conclusions on this point.

One of the earliest of these studies formed part of the major work of Tizard and Grad (1961). One hundred and fifty families with a defective child or adult living at home, and one hundred with a defective in hospital were interviewed. The institution cases included many more who were extremely retarded on the Vineland Scale, and fewer who were more advanced: 62 per cent of the institution sample had social ages below 3 years, compared with only 25 per cent of the home sample; only 17 per cent of the institution sample had a social age of 6 years or more, compared with 54 per cent of the home sample. The authors point out that as the institution sample was tested after admittance to the institution, the greater degree of retardation in this sample could have been due in part to the effect of institutionalization. Nevertheless this finding, that the more retarded subjects are more likely to be institutionalized, is consistent with findings from other studies (Saenger, 1962; Graliker *et al.*, 1965). Tizard and Grad showed also that many more subnormals with numerous problems (of degree of retardation, health, temperament, management, and special disabilities such as cerebral palsy or sensory defects) were institutionalized. This was true whether the problems were rated as major ones or major and minor ones combined – chi squares were significant in each case at the ·001 level. For example, 64 per cent of the home sample, but only 32 per cent of the institution sample presented no major problem apart from mental defect: only 12 per cent of the home sample compared with 33 per cent of the institution sample presented three to four major problems. Mongols seemed less likely than other defectives to be institutionalized: 40 per cent of the home group were mongols, compared with 21 per cent of the institution group. Tizard and Grad note that very few of the mongols were idiots, the majority being 'middle grade imbeciles'; very few had serious problems of health, and only 3 per cent had fits compared with 26 per cent of the non-mongol population. So the mongols as a group presented fewer difficulties in management, and this may have been important in enabling the parents to keep them at home. Another factor, however, may have been the services available to the parents. Of those with a child in an institution, 29 per cent said that more adequate provision of services would have enabled them to keep the child at home.

Saenger (1962) investigated representative samples of admissions to state schools for the retarded in New York City and of retarded people who had never before been institutionalized; 1,050 families were interviewed. Degree of retardation was found to be highly related to institutionalization: 'All idiots (in New York City) are committed within a short period after diagnosis', compared with 1 out of every 9 imbeciles and 1 out of every 90–100 morons. There was no difference between the samples in incidence of mongolism or special sense defects, but cases with severe motor defect, epilepsy and cerebral palsy were slightly more likely to be institutionalized. Among high-grade subjects institutionalization was highest – 4 out of 5 cases – where the parents were inadequate and the child had run into trouble with the community, mainly through sexual offences and offences against property and persons. This finding agrees with that of Hobbs (1964) that the factor which best discriminated between the two groups, one of institutionalized and one of non-institutionalized adolescents and young adults, was antisocial and immoral behaviour. On the other hand, Saenger found that difficulties at home without accompanying trouble in the community led to institutionalization mainly among low-grade subnormals from middle-class homes. When home and institution samples were matched for degree of retardation, family income and ethnic background, family adequacy and adjustment of the retarded (all of which had been shown to be associated with institutionalization), low-grade cases remaining at home had received a significantly higher level of services, such as speech and occupational therapy, compared with the institution sample. Saenger, like Tizard and Grad, concluded that increasing the services for the retarded and making special efforts to reach those who needed the services might do much to stem the flow into institutions.

Summing up, it seems that the children most likely to be institutionalized were the more retarded, the more handicapped, children from larger families, those whose families had had little help from services, boys rather than girls, and non-mongols rather than mongols. It may be that these findings are already out of date – the studies quoted are between seven and fifteen years old – and that the need for institutional care will change as more services become available and the attitudes of the general public towards the retarded become more tolerant.

How the parents were told

Initial counselling is generally regarded, by parents as well as professionals, as of crucial importance. Raech (1966), himself the father of a retarded child, says:

> Of particular importance, in my view, is the *initial* counselling experience. Usually this is given by a medical person untrained for the task. Yet, this interview is likely to be the source of the parents' greatest single emotional trauma in what is commonly a life-long struggle. Since this is true, it is important that the experience be handled as skilfully as possible. . . . I submit that, in many cases, being told that one's child is retarded may well be the most severe shock that one may experience in a normal lifetime full of trying experiences.

Perhaps the three major aspects of this initial interview are its timing, what is told, and how it is told. Since many forms of retardation do not become apparent at any particular period of the child's life, the timing of the interview and the parents' reactions to this are best studied in relation to mongols, whose handicap is discoverable at birth. Table 25 summarizes the findings from five studies as to when the mothers were told and how many were satisfied with the time of telling.

Table 25 shows that consistently over the studies a higher proportion of mothers told early were satisfied, compared with those who were told later. In two studies (Drillien and Wilkinson, 1964; Carr, 1970) 2 and 5 per cent, respectively, of mothers who had been told very early, before ten days, felt they should have been told earlier still – 'when I asked'. A majority of mothers, 60 to 90 per cent in several studies, said emphatically that they would prefer to know as soon as possible (Tizard and Grad, 1961; Drillien and Wilkinson, 1964; Valaes and Marouli-Agathonos, 1969; Carr, 1970), although a small minority (between 1 and 7 per cent in the same studies) would have liked to have been informed later than they were.

Table 25 shows, too, that there has been a tendency over the years for the mothers to be told earlier, from 55 per cent told by one year in Tizard and Grad's study to almost 100 per cent by that time in Carr's and in Berg's study of later-born children. Since the majority of mothers want to be informed early, perhaps this development gives grounds for cautious optimism.

If parents want to be told of their child's condition early, they want also to hear the truth, as Raech (1966) explains. 'The truth must be expressed. No purpose can possibly be served by concealing the truth and indeed a great deal of damage may be done in not stating the facts clearly yet gently.' Nearly half the mothers in two studies (Drillien and Wilkinson, 1964; Carr, 1970) suspected before being told that there was something wrong with the child, and other studies, too, have noted the bitterness that mothers experience when they feel that they have been fobbed off with reassurances, or that information that they urgently asked for was withheld, or that they were told lies (Tizard and Grad, 1961; Hutton, 1966). 'The fact that it was hidden did us more harm than the

TABLE 25. *The times at which mothers were told their children were mongols, and whether they were satisfied with the time of telling in five studies*

Authors	Date of study	N	Mongols born between:	Time of telling:		Satisfied – told by:	
				By 1 month %	By 1 year %	1 month %	1 year %
Tizard and Grad	1961	80	1915–55	—	55		
Drillien and Wilkinson	1964	71	1950–6	25	72	78	31
Berg et al.	1969	(1) 44	1929–48	16	68⎫	84	33
		(2) 51	1949–68	61	98⎭		
Hutton	1966	44	<1950–≤62	66			
Carr	1970	46	1963–4	60	96	68	33

fact of her condition', and 'They should have told me when I kept asking' were typical comments (Carr, 1970). Many professionals accept that parents must be told the truth (Kanner, 1962; Wolfensberger, 1967). Since no examples have been found of professionals who advocate actually deceiving parents, this, where it has happened, has probably been due to the idea that early information is somehow harmful. Cowie (1967) suggests that the doctor's own anxiety 'may subconsciously make him defer telling the parents, contenting himself with the rationalisation that the delay is to their advantage, for the time is not ripe'. However, Cowie's own recommendation of giving the news to parents in 'divided doses' over a period of six to seven days might well result in parents feeling equally dissatisfied. There are many parents who would not be content to wait for seven days after hearing that the doctor was worried about the child's future development to learn the reason for his concern; many, as we have seen, would want the truth at once.

After the first shock of hearing that their child is retarded, most parents want detailed information and advice on the possible prognosis, the expectations they can have of the child, how to handle him. Many doctors feel that this ·information cannot be absorbed at the first interview and that the parents should be offered the chance to return later for further discussion (Evans, 1962; Smithells, 1963). Drillien and Wilkinson found that such a service resulted in a higher proportion of mothers who were satisfied with the way they were told.

Much has been made of the question of who should tell the parents, especially in relation to the view that parents will feel resentful towards the doctor who tells them (Cowie, 1966). These fears seem unfounded: half the parents in Carr's (1970) study said they would be glad to see the teller again to discuss the baby, and of the rest, most felt little need of discussion, and only four (9 per cent) seemed antagonistic towards the person who told them. Of far greater importance than who does the telling is how it is done. All the studies quoted agree that the informant should take trouble and, if need be, time over the telling, be sympathetic towards the parents, and answer their questions fully. Resentment arises when the teller seems unfeeling (worse still, facetious – cf. Tizard and Grad) or informs the parents briefly or abruptly – what Raech calls the 'get-it-over-with' school. Questions need to be answered fully, but some writers (Tizard and Grad, 1961; Hewett, 1970) go further and recognize that in many cases the parents are not able to formulate the questions that they want to ask and that it may be necessary for the doctor to offer a little more information than that for which he is asked. Where prognosis is concerned, doctors are often warned against over-optimism and raising false hopes, but in some cases it seems they go too far in the opposite direction and are unnecessarily discouraging (Tizard and Grad, 1961; Dembo, 1964; Raech, 1966; Berg *et al.*, 1969). Parents may be given the impression that their child will never walk, talk, feed himself or become toilet-trained. To engender such feelings of hopelessness is probably at least as unkind as it is to overestimate the child's future potential. From the many comments of parents to this effect (Zwerling, 1954; Raech, 1966) the following one was made to the writer: 'We thought she would always be a vegetable, we had no idea she would be able to do all the things she has done. I think he [the teller] might have stressed the positive side a bit more.'

Family adjustment

In spite of all the difficulties, the embarrassment and humiliations, the inconveniences and problems of management, most families manage to adjust to having a mentally retarded child, and 'the great majority of parents wish to keep their mentally subnormal children at home' (Tizard and Grad, 1961). Schipper (1959), in a study of forty-three families with a mongol child, felt that in nearly three-quarters the family's way of life was not adversely affected, while in about half of the rest the mongol baby was 'the last straw' to a family already suffering from financial or social problems. Caldwell and Guze (1960) found most mothers to be adjusting well to the situation. In contrast Holt

(1958a) suggests that families suffer under a great many difficulties; it seems that of the 201 families of mildly and severely subnormal children that he studied, at least 31 per cent presented severe problems, but his figures are presented in such a way that it is not possible to analyse them in greater detail.

The effect of the retarded child on the relationship between the parents has received some attention, especially in comparing families with the child at home or in an institution. Tizard and Grad (1961) rated the relationships in the families on a four-point scale, from 'good' to 'very disturbed'. They found a higher proportion of families with the child at home to have good relationships compared with the institution sample (62 per cent as against 42 per cent) and fewer to be very disturbed (3 per cent as against 13 per cent), though this difference between the groups disappeared if the ratings were collapsed from four to two, 'satisfactory' and 'disturbed'. They concluded that it was not possible to show that keeping a retarded child at home had an adverse effect on family life but that, on the contrary, the better-adjusted families seemed better able to cope with the problems of an abnormal child. Farber (1959), in a study of 240 families, 175 with a retarded child at home and 65 with one in an institution, has explored the effect on 'marital integration' of the child's sex, age and degree of dependence. A retarded boy living at home affected 'marital integration', especially in lower-class families, more than did a retarded girl; this effect increased as the boy grew older and tended to disappear if he were institutionalized. Degree of dependence of the child did not affect 'marital integration'. These results were not confirmed by Fowle (1968) who found no differences in 'marital integration' between the families of twenty male and fifteen female retardates living at home and a similar group whose child was in an institution. Fowle did not assess the effect of the sex of the retarded child, but as there were more boys than girls in her group her findings might have been expected to support those of Farber. Farber's concept of marital integration depends on measures of similarity between the spouses on rankings of domestic values ('a place in the community', 'moral and religious unity' etc.) and on personality traits ('sense of humour', 'likes belonging to organizations'). Farber states that the score has been found to have a positive relationship with such factors as high stress on social-emotional aspects of family life, and high degree of identification of the wife with at least one of her children; and in families with a severely retarded child at home, with both parents reporting that they were happy in their marriage. Such validation seems to the present writer inadequate, especially in view of the doubtful *a priori* value of the premise that success or happiness in marriage depends on the partners' thinking and behaving alike on most subjects. (More recent sociological writing suggests that complementarity in couples is as important as similarity, e.g. Winch, 1967.) Wolfensberger (1967), too, has criticized Farber's studies on the grounds that the sample studied was population-biased, often split down into very small, unequal numbers, based in some cases on inadequate measurements, and lacked a control group.

Many writers have taken as self-evident the fact that parents of retarded children feel guilty, reject their children, and/or over-protect them. Wardell (1947), in a discussion of the way in which parents approach institutionalization, writes: 'Parents rarely discuss institutional placement for their child without also expressing a feeling of guilt for having produced such a child. . . . [They] are at one time over-protecting and then rejecting of the child.' Again, Walker (1949):

> Probably every woman bearing a defective child develops some sense of guilt . . . [which may] be very openly expressed by such statements as the child is 'her cross to bear' . . . [or] projected towards the institution in a spirit of fault-finding solicitation for the patient's welfare, or shown by an overt attempt to make up to the child by frequent visitations [*sic*].

It becomes difficult to imagine how any woman who did not feel guilty could demonstrate the fact.

Holt (1958a) considers that, in the 201 mothers whom he visited, 'the emotions of guilt and shame were very noticeable in most parents'. Two mothers showed 'very open guilt reactions, regarding the child's condition as a punishment for past transgressions', but in others it was shown as over-anxiety and over-devotion to the retarded child. No figures are given. Others (Hutchison, 1966; Illingworth, 1966) also speak of 'pathological attachment' of the mother as a source of damage to the family, but Wright (1960) believes that in some cases over-protection may be the result of real love and concern for the child, and advises parents to do whatever they feel will benefit their child, as no matter what they do they will be criticized. Bearing in mind the views expressed in some of the papers previously discussed this seems realistic advice.

Other writers again feel that 'the general tendency to characterise parents of handicapped children as guilt-ridden, anxiety-laden, over-protective and reject-ing beings is unfortunate. While it is true that such cases exist, the majority of parents are unduly stigmatised by this generalisation' (Barsch, 1968). Saenger (1962) found that with the exception of a few cases of severe rejection, the proportion of devoted and affectionate parents was equal amongst those with the child at home or in an institution. Roith (1963) sent questionnnaires to 120 mothers of retarded patients in Monyhull Hospital, and received a 60 per cent response rate; 94 per cent of these said that they did not feel guilty or that they had somehow brought the child's condition about. Roith points to the frequent use of the words guilt, shame and hostility in articles, and feels that their usage in relation to parents of handicapped children is copied from one textbook to another, and comments, 'No matter what the parents did they were construed as guilty'.

Wolfensberger (1967) takes a novel approach to the role of guilt. He suggests, first, that guilt may not be inappropriate, as for instance when retardation actually results from abortion attempts (he quotes, and the present writer knows of, no evidence that this often or indeed ever happens); and second, that guilt may be beneficial:

Perhaps a bit of guilt may go a long way in motivating a parent to provide the extra attention, effort, and even love a retarded child may need. Perhaps it may prevent premature institutional placement, thus serving the welfare of the child, society and perhaps even the family, and instead of being alleviated, some parents may need to be helped to a realistic and manageable dose of it.

Although this begs the question of whether guilt has a distorting effect on the person's actions and emotions, and so might undermine their value to the object of them, there is no denying that this is a refreshing view of the place of guilt in parents of the retarded. On the whole, however, the reported studies of the subject are unsatisfactory. On the one hand there are a number of intuitive, subjective reports which infer from a wide variety of parental behaviour, or even from armchair reasoning, the guilt parents must feel. On the other there are a few studies where parents have been asked point blank whether they feel guilty and have said they did not. Neither approach is adequate; what is needed is a standardized and validated research tool which could measure objectively the guilt felt by these parents. Until such an assessment method becomes available perhaps we should be less hasty in ascribing guilt to the parents or in invoking it to explain their behaviour.

Social isolation, too, is often thought to be part of the penalty parents must suffer for having a handicapped child. Tizard and Grad found a significant difference in this respect between those with a child in an institution and at home; 26 per cent and 45 per cent respectively were judged to have limited social contacts. Carr (1975) found that although mothers of mongols went out significantly less than did mothers of normal children, this was to some extent due to the difference in age between the two groups of mothers, and an equal proportion in each group (about two-thirds) felt they went out as much as they wanted to. No differences were found regarding holidays; 92 per cent of families of mongols and 85 per cent of controls had had at least one holiday during the four years of the child's lifetime. Only 21 per cent of the mothers said that having a handicapped child had made them lonely; the majority disagreed, some strenuously, while nearly a quarter felt that they had made friends through the child. Hewett (1970) also found only 21 per cent of lonely mothers, and that a similar proportion of parents of normal and cerebral palsied children – 30 to 40 per cent – seldom went out together. (This throws new light on Holt's finding that 41 per cent of parents of handicapped children never went out together, and 17 per cent never had a holiday, which seemed significant until compared with figures for parents of normal children.) Compared with the mongols in Carr's study, significantly fewer cerebral palsied children – 71 per cent – had been taken away for a holiday, which is the more striking since two-thirds of these children were up to five years older than the mongols, giving their families that much more opportunity for taking a holiday. While differences in social class and, perhaps, in level of income between the two groups of families of mongols and cerebral palsied children may have been partly responsible, it seems likely that the difference in handicap would account for most of the difference in holiday-taking. The majority of the mongols could reasonably be treated as ordinary children of half their age, but about one-third of the cerebral palsied children were severely physically handicapped, half of these being mentally handicapped as well. The problems posed by taking one of these children on holiday might make it hardly worth attempting.

In general, then, these and other studies (Schipper, 1959; Barsch, 1968) found that most families are not isolated on account of the child. Tizard and Grad, however, found families with the child at home significantly more isolated than were those where he was institutionalized. Since the subjects in this study were older (two-fifths were over 16, compared with none in the other studies quoted) this problem may become more difficult as the children grow older; alternatively the situation for the family may have improved over the years. Comparison of the two older studies – Tizard and Grad, and Holt – with the more recent ones of Hewett and Carr suggests that families nowadays feel that handicapped children are more accepted and understood by the general public than they were; 74 per cent of Holt's families found their neighbours objectionable or reserved, compared with 45 per cent of families of mongols and 18 per cent of cerebral palsied children who received little support from friends and neighbours. Tizard and Grad say: 'There were few families who did not comment on the sense of humiliation they felt, or had felt on occasion in the past, when strangers stared at their child, or made comments.'

Although similar comments were occasionally encountered in the studies of Hewett and Carr, they were relatively rare, and over 70 per cent of the mothers in both, said they welcomed the interest of strangers when they took the child out. As Hewett says, 'Genuine, sensible and non-advisory approaches are likely to be welcome. Tactless comment and gratuitous advice are not.' Although some mothers disliked 'noseyness' and 'remarks', most mothers were glad of a friendly interested attitude from strangers. It seems that there has been some real and welcome progress in public attitudes to handicapped children which may do much to help their parents.

Genetic counselling and family limitation

Much has been written about the need for genetic counselling for parents of handicapped children (Illingworth, 1966; Hutchison, 1966) but, as in other areas, awareness of need outstrips the provision made for it. Only one-third of the mothers in Tizard and Grad's study had had medical advice about the risks to further children; 45 per cent of the mothers in Hewett's and in Carr's studies had discussed with a doctor the question of future children. In spite of the paucity of genetic advice it has seemed to some writers (Holt, 1958b;

Tips *et al.*, 1963) that parents have tended to limit their families after the birth of a retarded child, though these findings have not always been confirmed (Sigler *et al.*, 1967; Fraser and Latour, 1968). In Holt's study nearly two-thirds of the mothers did not want more children, either because they feared further children might be similarly affected, or because of the strain of caring for the retarded child. He estimates that further pregnancies in the group that did not want more children was reduced by 21 per cent when compared with the group that wanted more children, and concludes that this reduction may be attributed to the presence of the retarded child in the family. He also showed that two factors, age of the mother and number of children in the family, were significantly associated with the mother's wish to have or not to have more children; mothers aged 30 years and less when the retarded child was born, and those for whom the retarded child was the first-born, were more likely to be willing to face a further pregnancy. However, these two factors, of age and parity of the mother, appear not to have been taken into account in calculating the incidence of pregnancies in those families wanting more children, or its reduction in those families not wanting more children, so the estimation of reduction may be somewhat exaggerated. Nevertheless his finding that 60 per cent of younger mothers whose retarded child was the first-born did not want more children is striking. Barsch (1968) found age of mother (over or under 30) to be a significant factor in family limitation, but did not consider the effect of the number of children in the family. Fraser and Latour (1968) comparing the reproductive history of mothers, aunts and aunts-in-law of mongol children (N=45) and of children with cleft lip and palate (N=62) and with hay fever (N=104) found a decline in birth-rate which began well before the birth of the index child and which was similar for the three groups. Age of the mother (of mongols) was taken into account in this study, but not the number of children in the family. The authors conclude that the decline in the birth-rate following the birth of an affected child is largely due to the normal decline in fertility with advancing age, and that there is little reason to think that relatives of affected children will be discouraged from having babies.

Similar results were obtained by Sigler *et al.* (1967) who studied 216 mothers of mongols and 216 mothers of normal children, matched for sex, race, place of birth and age of mother. No differences were found between the groups on the number of pregnancies either before or after the birth of the index child.

Significant differences were found between the mothers in Carr's and Hewett's studies; 79 per cent of mothers of mongols and 51 per cent of mothers of cerebral palsied children had not changed their minds about having more children, while 13 per cent and 34 per cent respectively felt discouraged from having the further children they had wanted. These differences are probably due to the high proportion of mothers of mongols (61 per cent) who did not, before the birth, want further children and felt the same after the birth. This in turn may well be due to the different average age of the mothers in the two studies (33 per cent of mothers of mongols but 80 per cent of the mothers of cerebral palsied children were under 40 at the time of the interview). The size of the families in the two groups was similar.

It seems clear that some parents may be put off by the birth of a handicapped child from adding to their families, but that this effect may not be as serious as has been suggested. Further studies might clarify the situation if they took into account the three important factors – age of the mother, the size of her family at the handicapped child's birth, and whether or not she had hoped to have more children following that pregnancy – and if comparable control groups were used.

Parent counselling

The literature on parent counselling is vast, and will be touched on here only briefly. (For a fuller and excellent review, the reader is referred to Wolfensberger, 1967, especially pp. 356–69). Although at one time the diagnostic session contained all the counselling that parents were likely to get, increasingly it has come to be realized that parents cannot absorb in one interview all that they need to know. Many writers (Schumacher, 1945; Yates and Lederer, 1961; Richards, 1964; Wolfensberger, 1967; Pinkerton, 1970) have stressed the need for repeated interviews with the parents, to allow them to assimilate information, express their feelings and adjust as far as possible to the situation. These recommendations seem to have gained general acceptance but the evidence on whether repeated interviews are helpful to the parents is slight. Caldwell *et al.* (1961) found that the more contact parents had had with a clinic, the higher was their expressed satisfaction, while Drillien and Wilkinson (1964) stated that mothers were more satisfied with the way they had been told if 'they were encouraged to return to the family doctor or paediatrician with any further queries or problems' (though no figures are given). It seems likely that doctors regard outpatient follow-up appointments as serving the purpose of repeated interviews, but in many cases these are not adequate. Well over half the mothers in Hewett's (1970) and Carr's (1975) studies found their hospital visits very unhelpful, complaining of a long wait for a short interview, lack of discussion or advice, and a perfunctory attitude on the part of the doctor. Unless these visits are carefully designed to allow for adequate discussion and exchange of information they are likely to be seen by the parents as no more than a tiresome waste of time.

Much of the literature on counselling is concerned with the need for ways of dealing with the parents' own psychodynamic problems. 'The parents are often viewed as being problem-ridden, anxious and maladjusted' (Wolfensberger, 1967); Wolfensberger also remarks on 'a certain prevalent psychiatric orientation that views parents as "patients" and that sees the source of their problems as residing within them'. A parent of a retarded child (personal communication) quotes the recent White Paper (Department of Health and Social Security, 1971, paragraph 140); this discusses the parents' need for help with emotional problems, which may, the paper suggests, lead to rejection or over-protection of the child and the neglect of the other children. He comments that:

> My reaction to this paragraph is that it is impertinent in the extreme. It gives the impression that the parents can do nothing right, but that if they are lucky they might get some professional worker to help them cope with the worst emotional problems that they have got themselves into.

Similar feelings of frustration and irritation have probably been felt by other parents who, asking for information or practical advice, have received psychotherapy instead (cf. Yates and Lederer, 1961; Cummings and Stock, 1962). Undoubtedly in many cases parents do want the chance to talk and to express their feelings, and they should be given the opportunity to do so, but this should not be all that they get. To quote Wolfensberger again: 'The parents, as is apparent over and over, want counsel on child management and facts about retardation. The professionals often want to give them therapy.'

The participation of parents in their child's training and education

One of the most dispiriting things that parents can be told is that nothing they do will make any difference to their child. 'The consultant said, "She's a mongol." We said, "What can we do ?" and he said, "Nothing, there's nothing you can do" ' (Carr, 1975). Compare this with the views of the parent quoted earlier:

> Our own experience was that our attitudes changed in one evening when it was suggested to us, 'These children can learn, why don't you start by trying to teach Adrian shapes ?' . . . We, like many parents, found a special joy in the achievements of our handicapped child and the knowledge of our contribution to these achievements.

These remarks are typical of those made by other parents who have been helped to help their own children.

That parents, who have the most prolonged contacts with the child and the strongest motivation for helping him, *should* be involved in their children's education seems obvious. Training Centres,[1] for example, might have been expected to be eager to bring in the parents both as helpers in the Centre and to enable them to carry on at home the methods and programmes used by the teachers. However, books for teachers of the mentally retarded mention parents only as those to whom the child goes at the end of the day, or disparagingly – 'the home life may be destructive rather than conducive to growth' (Baumgartner, 1965); or as money-raisers (Weber, 1962); or, more honourably, as being encouraged to train the child appropriately in self-help skills and to attend parents' meetings, but with little suggestion that they would receive any help

[1] Now ESN schools.

in doing so, except in speech training where they should use 'any special methods suggested by the Centre' (McDowall, 1964). In view of this it is perhaps not surprising that in Carr's (1975) study only a quarter of the mothers felt that they had learnt anything from the 'schools' that they could put into practice at home to help their children.

Some programmes of teaching parents to deal with their retarded children have been reported. These may be divided into two groups, those in which the parents are taught how to stimulate and teach their children, and those in which parents are taught how to deal with behaviour problems (although often there is a good deal of overlap). Many of the stimulation programmes are concerned primarily with mongols, presumably because the children can be identified early in life. One of the first of these (de Coriat *et al.*, 1967) describes a programme of instruction given to the mothers of mongol infants. The mothers were seen every 2–4 weeks by a teacher, physician or psychologist who gave each a verbal and written set of instructions for daily activities to be carried out with the child – exercises, verbal contact, development of hand–eye coordination, locomotion, language, self-feeding etc. Gesell Tests were administered every 3–6 months to both the 'educated' group and a control group, those 'left alone to spontaneous evolution'. The programme appears to have been applicable to the child's first year, but test results are given for 10 semesters (5 years). Results are given for a maximum of 80 'educated' children, declining to 9 at 5 years, compared with a maximum of 182 'infants of spontaneous evolution', declining to 15. Median IQs and standard deviations are reported. The IQs of the 'educated' group are consistently higher, roughly 17 points above those of the 'spontaneous evolution' group. The authors say the difference is significant, without giving any details. They comment that 'Even more noticeable is the positive attitude adopted by the parents towards their children'. In this programme, a sophisticated range of physical stimulation contrasts with the rather simple and non-specific psychological stimulation suggested, so that the apparently good results from the whole programme are the more remarkable. However, no details are given as to the social class composition of the groups, nor sex distribution, nor how the children were allocated to one or other of the groups, so it is not possible to be sure that the two groups of children were comparable in the first place.

Brinkworth (1973) reports on a comparison between 5 experimental and 12 control mongol babies. The parents of the experimental group had advice and demonstrations for up to 4 hours weekly, and had a worksheet to follow. Tests were given at 6 months for the experimental group and at ages varying between 7 and 13 months for the controls, and again 6 months later. At the first test there was a significant difference between the mean DQs (experimental group = 101·8, sd = 18·45; controls = 75·0, sd = 17·21) but not at the second test (experimental group = 81·07, sd = 4·9; controls = 75·0, sd = 17·21). The study suffers from serious drawbacks, in that, first, it seems that the testing was done by the author, who was also solely responsible for the remedial programme; and secondly, it seems that although the experimental group were 'no longer under direct surveillance' after 6 months, at this point at least some of the control group appear to have been involved in the remedial programme, so that the distinctions between the groups are blurred. So there is no conclusive evidence yet as to whether or not the author's methods made any significant difference to the developmental progress of the children, though there is no reason to doubt his statements that the parents were active and interested in teaching their children and felt that the children benefited. Nor should the inconclusiveness of the results of Brinkworth's study be allowed to detract from his pioneering efforts in giving help to parents of retarded children.

An important project in progress is that of Ludlow (personal communication). Approximately fifty mongols living in East Kent, referred from 1964 onwards, constitute the experimental group: the infants are assessed on the Griffiths Scale in their own homes, and the parents offered a monthly counselling service consisting of a review of progress, discussion of problems and advice to the mother for further activities. When the child is 1–1½ years, the mother is invited to bring him to a Special Care Clinic two or three times a week for playgroup activities under the supervision of a qualified nurse or teacher. Mothers are taught how best to stimulate their children, and are able to share their problems and experiences with other mothers. Counselling classes for the mothers are held at three-monthly intervals where relevant problems are discussed in a group.

Assessments are carried out at 6 months and 1 year, and then annually until 5 years. Results are to be compared with similar test results from a control group, matched for age and social class; these are mongol babies living in West Kent where counselling and Special Care Clinics are not available, and East Kent mongols whose parents opted out of the scheme. This study, when completed, should enable an accurate assessment to be made of the value to the children in developmental terms of the help given to their parents.

The Parents' Workshop (Cunningham and Jeffree, 1971) came into being after a series of lectures to parents organized by the NSMHC had proved to be too general to be of practical help; 41 parents contacted through the Society enrolled for an 8-week course, consisting of lectures, discussions, and, importantly, tutor-groups, with one tutor to 10 parents. By means of developmental charts (derived from infant scales such as Griffiths, Bayley etc.) the parents assessed their own child's present level of functioning, and were then helped to find ways to stimulate him to the next appropriate stage of activity. This teaching of parents how to teach, and also how to manage behavioural problems in their own children, was largely carried out in the tutor groups. Although it is emphasized that this was not a research project, it was carefully (albeit impressionistically) evaluated through records and tape-recordings of tutors' notes and questions asked by parents, and by evaluation sheets filled in by parents at the end of the course. Attendance was very high, averaging 86 per cent of parents per session. The responses to the evaluation sheets showed that in general the parents felt the course to have been useful; that at least 50 per cent had successfully applied the teaching model to a wide variety of tasks; that 'success' did not appear to correlate with the parents' educational background; and that most parents did not feel they had spent more time with their children as a result of the course. On the negative side, the course was felt to have been least helpful to the parents of very severely retarded children.

In the Toddler Project (Bricker and Bricker, 1971) 10 handicapped children (7 of them mongols) were enrolled in special stimulation classes, and their parents were asked to weekly parents' meetings. When the parents indicated that they would like to be more involved they were invited to bring their children half an hour before the regular time for the classes and were given intensive training in the training of their children, by operant techniques. The children were assessed on the Bayley Scales, and over a period of 10 months the average gain in mental ages for 9 children retested twice was 7·3 months. While, as the authors point out, these gains cannot, in the absence of a control group, be described as significant, they are undoubtedly impressive: in Carr's (1975) study the average gain of children of roughly comparable age over a period of 12 months was about 4 months. This study has also been criticized on the grounds that the families of the children in the project were self-selected and may therefore have been those who would have been likely to be higher grade, and likely to make better progress anyway. However, when the results from the highest 10 children in Carr's study were examined, it was found that their average gain in MA over the same (10-month) period was 5 months: so there is little evidence that the Brickers' results are due entirely to an artifact of selection.

Finally Barnard (1968) reports on an individual programme to teach the parents of a retarded 18-month-old how to teach him to feed himself. Operant methods were used, with careful base-line observations, breaking down of the skill into small steps, shaping, prompting and fading. The study is of particular interest in that, after the original interdisciplinary evaluation, all the observations and parent training were done by a nurse.

Of the programmes aimed at helping parents deal with their children's behaviour, one of the earliest, that described by Weingold and Hormuth (1953), seems to have been primarily aimed at providing group discussion of the feelings of mothers having difficulties with their mongol children. However, management problems were also discussed, and the authors report that there was a 'remarkable change' in the parents and improved adjustment and behaviour in the children, as reported by the parents.

In Terdal and Buell's (1969) project, parents of retarded children were trained to observe their child's and their own behaviour accurately, and taught methods of eliminating undesirable behaviours and building up appropriate behaviours. The children first went through an intensive diagnostic screening and were observed by staff both in the clinic and, where necessary, at home. These observations, together with the parents' own description of their difficulties, formed the basis of the individual treatment plan for the family.

The authors emphasize the role of the parents' attention in governing their child's behaviour, and the fact that in some cases their attention may actually be aversive to the child; in this extraordinarily difficult and discouraging situation the authors suggest using potent extrinsic reinforcers paired with verbal or gestural responses that may later become reinforcers. In the more common situation, where parental attention is reinforcing to the child, the authors discuss the frequently-encountered necessity to teach parents how to respond to a child who is being good: 'The patterns of response which involve "leaving him alone when he's not getting into trouble" are so strong that it has taken several sessions to teach the mother to respond to the child as he is behaving appropriately.' Treatment sessions were carried out first in the clinic, sometimes with a therapist modelling a behaviour while the mother observed what was going on and discussed it with another therapist, and then as the mother gained in confidence the sessions were transferred to the home. No details are given of results, but the programme of help for parents is usefully described with many relevant examples.

Other descriptions of similar programmes for parents of individual mentally handicapped children with behaviour problems are to be found in Hawkins *et al.* (1966), Schell and Adams (1968), Johnson and Brown (1969). Holland (1970), at one further remove, counsels those who would counsel parents, presenting a twenty-one step interview guide which would be useful to the beginner and perhaps also to those more experienced in behaviour modification techniques. A programme designed especially for parents of autistic children, but equally applicable to parents of retarded children with behaviour problems, is described by Schopler and Reichler (1970).

Parental attitudes and child-rearing practices

Studies of parental attitudes, using the PARI (Parental Attitudes Research Instrument) (Schaefer and Bell, 1958) suggest that mothers are colder and more rejecting towards mentally retarded than towards normal or emotionally disturbed children (Ricci, 1970), and that mothers of mongols, cerebral palsied and blind children are more punitive and authoritarian towards them than are mothers of children who are deaf or suffer from organic defects (Cook, 1963). This last study also found degree of handicap to be important: mothers of mildly handicapped children tended to be rejecting; of the more severely handicapped, over-protecting. How far this would be true of the mentally retarded, as a separate group, is not clear: Ricci found rejection highest in mothers of the mentally retarded and least in mothers of normals, and quotes a study by Hurley which found an inverse relationship between IQ and rejection. Pitfield and Oppenheim (1964), using an attitude scale developed by Oppenheim, found parents of mongols to be more detached and somewhat stricter than were parents of either normal or psychotic children; while Fredericks (1957), using a variety of attitude scales, found mothers of retarded children more repressive and domineering than mothers of normal and orthopaedically handicapped children. Barsch (1968) found results almost identical with Cook's in that mothers of mongols and cerebral palsied children were more authoritarian and punitive, and of the blind more authoritarian, than were mothers of deaf and organically handicapped children; and that mothers of mildly handicapped children were rejecting and those of severely handicapped children over-protective.

The study of child-rearing practices, as opposed to attitudes, has received little attention where the severely subnormal are concerned. Barsch (1968) found that practices of mothers of children with various handicaps were essentially the same as those employed with normal sibs. He contrasts this unvarying approach with the ingenuity shown by therapists and teachers in devising special apparatus and methods for handicapped children. He concludes that the lack of ingenuity shown by the parents is due to the lack of useful advice available for them: 'Since no parent is ever prepared to be the parent of a handicapped child, and since available resources to coach them in a different approach are rare, it is not surprising that they adopt a single child-rearing approach, and apply it to all their children' (p. 344). Carr (1975) also felt that the mothers' frequently expressed belief that a mongol child should be brought up the same as a normal child, while it sometimes reflected the mother's determination not to let the child be set apart from the rest of the world, often seemed to result from the lack of any alternative; with no advice as to special methods that might help a handicapped child there was little else to do but bring him up the only way she knew.

In Carr's study, however, some differences were found in the child-rearing practices of mothers of mongol and of normal children. In their answers to questions on their attitude to the child's sucking, crying, toilet training, or naughtiness, the mothers of mongols were found to be less punitive and more permissive than were the mothers of matched normal children. This was not related to the sex of the child, age of the mother, size of family or presence in the family of other young children, although there was a significant tendency for middle-class mothers in both groups to be less punitive and more permissive than were working-class mothers. The difference was greatest at 15 months, while by 4 years old the gap between the two groups had narrowed a good deal, especially in how the mothers handled tempers, how much they smacked and how much they believed in smacking. It is suggested that this tougher attitude on the part of the parents may have been brought about partly by increased tiresomeness of the children (by 4 they were having as many tempers and were judged naughtier than the controls), and partly by the fact that by 4 they did not seem as fragile as they had at 15 months; they had a firmer grasp on life and need not be treated so tenderly. Although the differences between the two groups as to the mothers' handling were not significant at 4 years old, yet they were in every case in the direction of gentler treatment for the mongols. The progress towards equal treatment had begun but was not complete. It seems possible that, when these children are older, the tendencies will be reversed, and the mongol children will then be treated less permissively than the control children. It seems likely that the differences between the attitudes of mothers in Carr's study, and those of Pitfield and Oppenheim, Cook, Ricci and Barsch, is due to differences in the children's age – in these latter studies the mean age of the children was never less than 5, compared with a maximum age of 4 in Carr's study. It may be that the mentally handicapped child is treated more gently when he is young and more strictly when he is older than is his normal counterpart.

The effect on the siblings

Many parents are worried in case the presence of a severely retarded child will have a harmful effect on their other children. They worry that the normal children will be disturbed by the retarded child's behaviour, and ashamed of him so that they may be unwilling to bring their friends home, or that the retarded child will take so much of the parents' time that the normal children will be neglected.

Perhaps the most serious effect recorded was that noticed by Holt (1958a) who found that 12 per cent of the siblings in his study had suffered physical attacks by the retarded child. The majority of the children who suffered in this way were younger than the retarded child. Compared with this the disadvantages found in other studies were minor. Siblings were found to be affected[1] by a young, very dependant child living at home; normal sisters, especially the eldest, were more likely to be affected than normal brothers (Farber, 1959; Fowle, 1968). Wolfensberger has criticized this work on the grounds that the data on the normal children's adjustment was derived from the mother's observations and not from assessment of the children themselves. It would be more accurate to say, in fact, not that the siblings, but that the mother's view of the siblings, was affected by the factors described. This in itself might be important, but is different from the interpretations given by the authors.

The conclusion that normal siblings are adversely affected by a retarded child is challenged by Graliker *et al.* (1962) who interviewed 21 teenage siblings, 6 boys and 15 girls, of 16 retarded children. All but 2 of the retarded children were living at home, ages ranged from 10 months to $5\frac{1}{2}$ years, all but 3 were severely retarded. No social class data are given. The siblings were pleasant, nice-looking, church-going individuals prepared to do chores at home; on ratings on a 5-point scale on relationships with their parents 14 scored the maximum of 5 and the rest 4; all but 1 said their home life was happy, all but 1 had no hesitation about their friends meeting the retarded child. The teenagers appeared not to feel burdened with responsibility for the retarded

---

[1] In 'role tension': this was measured by the sum of ratings on a 5-point scale by the mother on a series of unpleasant personality traits – stubborn, self-centred etc. A high degree of 'role tension' is indicated by a high level of unfavourable ratings by the mother.

child, and accepted that the parents' ways of handling the child and their plans for his future were the right ones. While this group seems to have been noticeably well adjusted and conforming, the findings from this study are closely similar to those of Caldwell and Guze (1960). Schipper (1959) felt that three-quarters of the siblings of mongols in her study were happily adjusted and that, of those who were disturbed, in only about half the cases (in 6 out of a total of 43 families) did the retarded child appear to be the cause of the maladjustment. In another study (Barsch, 1968) the majority of parents of different types of handicapped children thought the child was well accepted by his siblings, of whom only a minority (12 per cent) were thought to show predominately negative attitudes. In a larger sample than those discussed above, Tizard and Grad (1961) found that, contrary to expectation, significantly fewer of the siblings of the severely retarded living at home had mental health problems than those of the severely retarded in institutions, the proportions being 12 per cent (home) and 26 per cent (institution). There was no difference between the two groups as to problems of physical health. Tizard and Grad comment: 'This interesting difference does not support the view that keeping a defective in the family upsets the other children; but it does suggest that parents who have more than one difficult child to cope with are more likely to seek institutional care for a mental defective.'

Many of the studies of the effect on the siblings of a retarded child have suffered from methodological drawbacks, in particular those of small selected samples. Nevertheless what emerges from the studies (apart from Holt's) is a consistent lack of support for the still widely-held view that normal children will suffer from the presence of a retarded child in the home (cf. a recent article in *The Times* in which a 'wise physician' advised a mother to institutionalize her mongol daughter because 'you must always think first of your normal children'.) The other main finding is that the siblings will usually reflect the attitudes of their parents; as Wolfensberger says: 'If problems exist [in relation to the sibs] they may be of the parents' making, and planning may be more effective if directed at them instead of being rationalised around the siblings' benefit.'

Problems of everyday life

Most studies have examined the effect of a retarded child on their families principally in terms of the effect on the feelings and attitudes of the family. A few have attempted to investigate also the day-to-day problems involved in caring for a retarded child (Barsch, 1968; Hewett, 1970). The findings from one such study, hitherto unpublished (Carr, 1975) will be briefly discussed. Thirty-nine mothers of mongol children and 42 mothers of normal children matched with the mongols for age, sex and social class were interviewed when their children were 15 months and again at 4 years old. The mongols were the survivors of a population sample (all mongol babies born in Surrey and the former boroughs of Camberwell and Lewisham in the year 1 December 1963–30 November 1964) so the investigation did not suffer from selection bias. Since, however, numbers are so small, and since the group studied included certain features which would probably not be found in most other groups of parents of handicapped children, the findings cannot be applied uncritically to families of retarded children in general. Nevertheless, they may be of some interest.

In some respects the problems involved in caring for young mongol children were no more than those involved in caring for young normal children. The mongols were if anything less trouble over sleeping – they needed less help to go to sleep, slept rather longer, woke less at night and stayed awake for a shorter time (although none of these differences were individually significant). At 15 months they cried less; more mongols were said to cry rarely and none (compared with 10 per cent of the normal children) to cry often, and fewer kept up the crying for a long time (again none of these individual differences were significant). At 15 months significantly fewer of the mongols were said to have temper tantrums – 44 per cent, compared with 15 per cent of the normal children, never had tantrums, and no mongols, compared with 21 per cent of the normals, had tantrums frequently. At 4 years old this significant difference had disappeared, although the tendency was still for the mongols to have fewer tantrums. The reasons for tantrums differed between the 2 groups at 15 months; significantly more control children were said to have tantrums when they were prevented from doing or having something they wanted (86 per cent, compared with 59 per cent of mongols), more mongols had tantrums when they were made to do things they did not want to do (36 per cent, compared with 6 per cent of the controls). By 4 years old this difference too had disappeared. Mischief was less of a problem for the mothers of mongols at 15 months, in that they were less destructive (partly because they were much less mobile at this age than were the normal children). Of those who were said to be naughty (and over half the mothers of mongols and a third of the mothers of controls said flatly that their children were not naughty, using such phrases as 'they can't be naughty at this age') the most frequent complaints of the mongols were of attacks on the mother and others – pulling hair, biting, scratching and grabbing at glasses, followed by misbehaviour at meals – blowing, upsetting or throwing food. These two categories accounted for two-thirds of all the mongol naughtinesses but only a quarter of that of the controls, who were more likely to be thought of as naughty because of disobedience or exploratory inquisitiveness. Finally, 90 per cent of each group were said at 4 years old to be happy children, and only one in each group was said to be a miserable child. Over half the mothers in each group found the child very easy to manage, while 5 mothers of mongols and 6 of controls found them so difficult as to constitute a problem. All the mongols whose mothers found them a problem had low-medium mental ages, between 17 and 22 months; none of the very low-grade (and rather passive) children, with mental ages going down to 9 months, nor of the brighter more biddable children, whose mental ages ranged up to 36 months, were found very difficult to deal with.

Other areas in which the families of mongols did not appear to be worse off than the families of normal children were 'school' attendance for the child, holidays for the family, and the mother's health. Over half the children in each group went to 'school' of some sort, mostly part-time in playgroups, normal nursery schools and day nurseries; many more of the mongols (those attending Junior Training Centres) went to 'school' full-time – 46 per cent compared with 2 per cent of the controls. Ninety-two per cent of the families of mongols and 85 per cent of the families of controls had had at least one holiday during the child's lifetime, and more than two-thirds of these had been away more than once. The large majority of these holidays had been a success; 1 mongol and 3 control children had spoilt the holiday for the family. Over half the mothers in each group said that their own health was good; 1 mother in each group said it was poor. Just over two-thirds in each group had had no medical attention; 10 per cent of mothers of mongols and 15 per cent of mothers of controls had been to their doctors for tranquillizers, 12 per cent in each group had had tonics or other medicines, and 1 mother in each group had been seen by a psychiatrist.

These then were the areas in which there was little difference in the problems faced by the families of mongols or of normal children. There were other areas, however, particularly in matters of independence, in which the mongols were more of a problem. Feeding was more difficult, and especially so when the children were babies. Breast-feeding was less often attempted and given up sooner; more mongol babies never demanded a feed – 33 per cent, compared with 2 per cent of controls; they were more likely to be still on the bottle when they were 15 months old – half of them, compared with a quarter of the controls; and nearly two-thirds of them, but only 14 per cent of the controls, were at 15 months still given most of their nourishment by bottle. More mothers of mongols – 21 per cent, compared with 5 per cent of mothers of controls – spoke of the early feeding situation as 'very difficult', and although this difference is not significant, there was no doubt that the mothers had a real and probably justified fear that the mongols, sleepy undemanding babies who sucked feebly, might not take enough food to stay alive. By 15 months the mongols were less skilful at feeding themselves; a third or less could feed themselves with fingers, a cup or a spoon, compared with 95–57 per cent of controls. These differences were still evident at 4, when nearly all the controls but only two-thirds to three-quarters of the mongols could feed themselves, drink without help and eat ordinary food.

Dressing was another problem. Nearly half the mongols, but only 12 per cent of the controls, gave very little help or had to be entirely dressed by their mothers.

Little difference was found between the two groups at 15 months on toilet training, mainly because neither felt that, at this stage, it mattered greatly;

about a third of the mothers in each, had not begun to pot their child by 15 months. In fact, significantly more mongols were using the pot successfully at that time (41 per cent, compared with 19 per cent of controls), though, as more normal children had given up using the pot when they had previously done so, this difference may be due to less rebelliousness among the mongols. By 4 years old, however, the mongols were much slower where toilet training was concerned. Significantly fewer of them were clean and dry by day (38 per cent) and by day and by night (18 per cent) compared with 88 per cent and 71 per cent respectively of the controls. Nearly a third but no controls were still in nappies during the day, and two-thirds of the mongols but only 7 per cent of the controls at night. Only 10 per cent of the mongols could manage the toilet by themselves, compared with 63 per cent of the controls; 80 per cent of the mongols, but only 10 per cent of the controls, always used a potty rather than the lavatory.

An independence score, derived from scores on walking, eating, drinking, dressing and toilet training was calculated for each child; the lower his score, the more independent he was. Significantly more controls than mongols had lower (better) independence scores; 68 per cent, but only 5 per cent of the mongols, scored between 0 and 5; 98 per cent of controls and 38 per cent of mongols scored between 0 and 7.

For the mongols a linear correlation between their independence scores and MA at 4 years old on the Bayley Mental Scale was carried out; $r = -\cdot732$ (significant at less than the 1 per cent level). So the children with higher mental ages were more likely to be the more independent – a predictable finding. Inspection of the individual scores showed that: some of the brightest children scored badly on independence (3 children with MAs over 24 months had independence scores between 12 and 22); the moderately bright children had independence scores over most of the range, between 4 and 21; but all the very dull children, with MAs below 15 months, scored badly on independence, their scores ranging from 16–29. This suggests that other factors (such as the mother's interest and effort) may affect the independence of the medium- and high-grade children, but that they are not effective for the most retarded mongols.

Until now we have noted how much more independent the control children were, and how far the mongols lagged behind them. It is useful to look more closely at the achievement of the mongols, to see what they could do despite their handicaps. By the age of 4 nearly all could walk alone. More than two-thirds could feed themselves, eat ordinary food, and drink without help. Well over half (59 per cent) rarely dirtied their pants, and over a third (38 per cent) were virtually clean and dry during the day; nearly half (46 per cent) could manage toileting with little or no help. On an independence scale nearly 40 per cent scored within the normal range for their age. So between a half and a third of the mongols needed little more looking after in feeding, dressing, and toileting than do normal children of this age. In view of the severity of their handicap, this seems a considerable achievement.

Besides having greater problems of independence the mongols also showed more ill-health than the controls, but not as much more as had been expected. Significantly more had had frequent colds (51 per cent compared with 27 per cent of controls), and rather more were apt to get constipated (38 per cent of mongols, 17 per cent of controls). The mongols had had more, but not significantly more, coughs, bronchitis, diarrhoea and temperatures, while the groups were equal for other minor complaints – ear-ache, tummy-ache, catarrh and allergies. Of the infectious diseases – measles, mumps, chickenpox, German measles and pneumonia – more mongols had had at least one badly (50 per cent of mongols, 22 per cent of controls) while more controls had had only one disease mildly or none at all (73 per cent of controls, 41 per cent of mongols). In particular, measles and pneumonia had affected the mongols more seriously; thus more mongols had had measles badly (9/18 mongols, 2/13 controls); 9 mongols had had pneumonia (and 2 more had died of it between 15 months and 4 years) but no controls. The mongols had caught rather more infectious diseases; 39 mongols had had a total of 43 diseases, 42 controls a total of 32. Since the 2 groups of children had been judged to have had roughly equal contacts with other children, with slightly more mongols judged to have had very restricted social contacts (21 per cent mongols, 10 per cent controls) it seems that the mongols did pick up illnesses more easily, and tended to have them more severely.

However, there were no significant differences in the mothers' ratings of their children's health; about half in each group rated them as of average health, while the majority of the rest rated them as particularly strong. Only 5 mothers of mongols and 1 of a control rated them as delicate. Many mothers of mongols had been warned that their children might be delicate, and it seems possible that the fact that the child was in many cases sturdier than they had expected him to be led them to overrate his standard of health.

So the mothers of mongols did experience, in some areas, more problems than did the mothers of controls. Of these, only the feeding was felt to have been a serious problem, by 40 per cent of the mothers, while to a third the most severe problem was her feeling of distress at the child's condition, of disappointment and worry, 'knowing that he is what he is'. Other problems were felt to be minor ones, and this finding was unexpected, especially as a pilot study of 11 mothers of similar-aged mongols, not in the main study, had suggested that by 4 years old a good many difficulties would emerge. The mothers in the main study probably cannot be regarded as typical, simply because they had been involved in the study. Most mothers had been visited three to four times by the psychiatrist (Dr Valerie Cowie) and seven times by the psychologist in the four years; although these visits were not designed to be supportive, a warm relationship was soon established between the psychologist and (most of) the mothers. They discussed problems, sometimes asked for advice, and occasionally were given help, as for instance with holidays, contact with other mothers or the NSMHC. The mothers felt the visits to be helpful and spoke compassionately of other mothers who, to their surprise, had not received equal support. It seems possible that this played a part in enabling the mother to adjust to, and so to minimize, her problems. If so, then these mothers are not typical of mothers of mongol children, let alone of retarded children; a similar study of those might reveal more, and more serious, problems of child-rearing. Nevertheless, perhaps the study shows that, given this degree of support and interest, the lives of other mothers of retarded children might be made easier, and more enabled to live at home, to their own benefit and that of the community.

Conclusions

With the increasing emphasis in recent years on the benefits of home care for the retarded has come an increasing concern with the effect that this may have on their families. In general, most families want to keep their retarded child at home, and most adjust to doing so. The situation is more difficult for them where the child is more severely retarded and presents more problems of behaviour and management, and where the families are larger and already beset by a multiplicity of other problems. That most parents manage to cope should be a cause for admiration of them rather than of the existing services and facilities, in which there are still numerous shortcomings. There are welcome signs that those responsible for conveying the news that a child is retarded are doing so earlier and more compassionately, but too many parents still complain of delay, deception and carelessness. Medical supervision of the child is valued by the parents, but might be more useful if, instead of relatively frequent, brief and superficial interviews, fewer appointments, planned to allow time for questions and discussion on both health and management, were offered. In particular the crying need, where advisory services are concerned, is for special-ized help, as soon as the diagnosis becomes apparent, on all aspects of handling of the child – feeding, toilet training, speech training, discipline, and so on – and on how the parents themselves can stimulate and train their child. The parents need to learn as early as possible about the facilities, national and local, available to help them; schools, special care units, sheltered workshops, holiday homes, hostels, trustee schemes, and perhaps above all about the various parent associations. While it is a truism that these facilities need to be greatly expanded if they are to serve adequately all who need them, even those that are available are of little help to people who have no idea they exist.

At present parents in this country are unlikely to get any or much of this help and information unless they are participating in a special research or other project. More could be helped in the first place by a series of books and pamphlets setting out clearly the information they need, supplied where necessary and supplemented by visits by health visitors or social workers from the Social Services Departments. These would need to have 'an encyclopaedic knowledge of all the services and the special financial and other assistance available' (Corbett and Wing, 1972). They should ideally also have some knowledge of child development and of behaviour modification techniques, so that they could advise on the most appropriate training methods and on management problems. It is unlikely that all health visitors and social workers could have these skills, but perhaps a number in each area could undergo specialized training in order to work particularly with these families. Such specialization may be essential if families are to get the benefits they need and deserve. To the parents the world looks a very different place when they find they are not alone, and that they will have help in their task of bringing up their retarded child.

References

BARNARD, K. (1968) Teaching the retarded child is a family affair. *Amer. J. Nursing*, **68**, 305–11.

BARSCH, R. H. (1968) *The Parent of the Handicapped Child*. Springfield, Ill.: Charles C. Thomas.

BAUMGARTNER, B. B. (1965) *Guiding the Retarded Child: An Approach to a Total Educational Program*. New York: John Day.

BAYLEY, N., RHODES, L. and GOOCH, B. (1966) A comparison of the development of institutionalized and home-reared mongoloids. *California ment. Hlth. Res. Digest*, **4**, 104–5.

BERG, J. M., GILDERDALE, S. and WAY, J. (1969) On telling parents of a diagnosis of mongolism. *Brit. J. Psychiat.*, **115**, 1195–6.

BRICKER, D. and BRICKER, W. (1971) Toddler research and intervention project: report – year 1. *IMRD Behav. Sci. Monog.*, No. 20. Nashville, Tenn.: George Peabody College.

BRINKWORTH, R. (1973) The unfinished child. Effects of early home training on the mongol infant. In CLARKE, A. D. B. and CLARKE, A. M. (eds.) *Mental Retardation and Behavioural Research*. London: Churchill-Livingstone; Baltimore, Md.: Williams & Wilkins.

CALDWELL, B. M. and GUZE, S. (1960) A study of the adjustment of parents and siblings of institutionalised and non-institutionalised retarded children. *Amer. J. ment. Defic.*, **66**, 845–61.

CALDWELL, B. M., MANLEY, E. J. and SEELYE, B. J. (1961) Factors associated with parental reaction to a clinic for retarded children. *Amer. J. ment. Defic.*, **65**, 590–4.

CARR, J. (1970) Mongolism: telling the parents. *Developm. med. Child Neurol.*, **12**, 213–21.

CARR, J. (1975) *A Comparative Study of the Development of Mongol and Normal Children from 0–4 years*. Unpubl. Ph.D. thesis, Univ. of London.

CENTERWALL, S. A. and CENTERWALL, W. H. (1960) A study of children with mongolism reared in the home compared to those reared away from home. *Pediatrics*, **25**, 678–85.

COLLINS, J. and BRINKWORTH, R. (1969) *Improving Mongol Babies.* London: National Society for Mentally Handicapped Children.

COOK, J. J. (1963) Dimensional analysis of child-rearing attitudes of parents of handicapped children. *Amer. J. ment. Defic.*, **68**, 354–61.

CORBETT, J. and WING, L. (1972) A plan for a comprehensive service for the mentally retarded. In WING, J. K. and HAILEY, A. M. (eds.) *Evaluating a Community Psychiatric Service.* London: Oxford Univ. Press.

COWIE, V. (1966) Genetic counselling. *Proc. Roy. Soc. Med.*, **59**, 15–16.

COWIE, V. (1967) Parental counselling and spina bifida. *Developm. med. Child Neurol.*, **9**, 110–12.

CUMMINGS, S. T. and STOCK, D. (1962) Brief group therapy of mothers of retarded children outside the speciality clinic setting. *Amer. J. ment. Defic.*, **66**, 739–48.

CUNNINGHAM, C. C. and JEFFREE, D. M. (1971) *Working with Parents: Developing a Workshop Course for Parents of Young Mentally Handicapped Children.* Manchester: National Society for Mentally Handicapped Children, NW Region.

DE CORIAT, L. F., THESLENCO, L. and WAKSMAN, J. (1967) The effects of psychomotor stimulation on the IQ of young children with Trisomy 21. In RICHARDS B. (ed.) *Proc. 1st Congr. Internat. Assoc. Scient. Stud. Ment. Defic.* Reigate: Michael Jackson.

DEMBO, T. (1964) Sensitivity of one person to another. In NOLAND, R. (ed.) *Counseling Parents of the Mentally Retarded.* Springfield, Ill.: Charles C. Thomas.

Department of Health and Social Security (1971) *Better Services for the Mentally Handicapped.* Cmnd 4383. London: HMSO.

DRILLIEN, C. M. and WILKINSON, E. M. (1964) Mongolism: when should parents be told. *Brit. med. J.*, **2**, 1306–7.

EVANS, K. A. (1962) Mentally handicapped children. *Lancet*, **i**, 974.

FARBER, B. (1959) *Effects of a Severely Mentally Retarded Child on Family Integration.* Monogr. Soc. Res. Child Developm. No. 71, **24**.

FINNIE, N. (1968) *Handling the Young Cerebral Palsied Child at Home.* London: Baillière, Tindall & Cox.

FOWLE, C. M. (1968) The effect of the severely mentally retarded child on his family. *Amer. J. ment. Defic.*, **73**, 468–73.

FRASER, F. C. and LATOUR, A. (1968) Birth rates in families following birth of a child with Mongolism. *Amer. J. ment. Defic.*, **72**, 883–6.

FREDERICKS, M. U. (1957) *A Comparative Study of Expressed Parent Attitudes: Mothers of Mentally Retarded and Orthopaedically Handicapped vs. Mothers of Non-handicapped Children.* Unpubl. doctoral dissertation, Univ. of Oregon. Quoted by Wolfensberger, 1967.

GIANNINI, M. J. and GOODMAN, L. (1963) Counseling families during the crisis reaction to mongolism. *Amer. J. ment. Defic.*, **67**, 740–7.

GRALIKER, B. V., FISHLER, K. and KOCH, R. (1962) Teenage reaction to a mentally retarded sibling. *Amer. J. ment. Defic.*, **66**, 838–43.

GRALIKER, B. V., KOCH, R. and HENDERSON, R. A. (1965) A study of factors influencing placement of retarded children in a state residential institution. *Amer. J. ment. Defic.*, **69**, 553–9.

HAWKINS, R. P., PETERSON, R. F., SCHWEID, E. and BIJOU, S. W. (1966) Behaviour therapy in the home: amelioration of problem parent-child relations with the parent in a therapeutic role. *J. exp. Child Psychol.*, **4**, 99–107.

HEWETT, S. (1970) *The Family and the Handicapped Child*. London: Allen & Unwin.

HOBBS, M. T. (1964) A comparison of institutionalised and non-institutionalised mentally retarded. *Amer. J. ment. Defic.*, **69**, 206–10.

HOLLAND, C. J. (1970) An interview guide for behavioural counselling with parents. *Behav. Therapy*, **1**, 70–9.

HOLT, K. S. (1958b) The influence of a retarded child upon family limitation. *Pediatrics*, **22**, 744–55.

HOLT, K. S. (1958b) The influence of a retarded child upon family limitation. *J. ment. Defic. Res.*, **2**, 28–36.

HUTCHISON, A. (1966) Stress on families of the mentally handicapped. In *Stress on Families of the Mentally Handicapped*. Third Internat. Congr., Internat. League of Societies for the Mentally Handicapped.

HUTTON, LADY V. (1966) Breaking the news. In *Stress on Families of the Mentally Handicapped*. Third Internat. Congr., Internat. League of Societies for the Mentally Handicapped.

ILLINGWORTH, R. S. (1966) Counselling. In *Stress on Families of the Mentally Handicapped*. Third Internat. Congr., Internat. League of Societies for the Mentally Handicapped.

JOHNSON, S. M. and BROWN, R. A. (1969) Producing behaviour change in parents of disturbed children. *J. Child Psychol. Psychiat.*, **10**, 107–21.

JOLLY, D. H. (1953) When should the seriously retarded infant be institutionalised? *Amer. J. ment. Defic.*, **57**, 632–6.

KANNER, L. (1962) Parent counseling. In ROTHSTEIN, J. (ed.) *Reading and Resources*. New York: Holt, Rinehart & Winston. Quoted by Wolfensberger, 1967.

KELMAN, H. R. (1964) The effect of a brain-damaged child on the family. In BIRCH, H. G. (ed.) *Brain Damage in Children; the Biological and Social Aspects*. Baltimore, Md: Williams & Wilkins.

KUSHLICK, A. (1966) Subnormality – the size of the problem. In *Mental Handicap*. Basle, Switzerland: Geigy.

LYLE, J. G. (1960) The effect of an institution environment upon the verbal development of imbecile children. III: The Brooklands residential family unit. *J. ment. Defic. Res.*, **4**, 14–23.

MCDOWALL, E. B. (1964) *Teaching the Severely Subnormal*. London: Edward Arnold.

PENROSE, L. S. (1938) A clinical and genetic study of 1,280 cases of mental defect. *Spec. Rep. Ser. Med. Res. Coun.*, No. 229. London: HMSO.

PINKERTON, P. (1970) Parental acceptance of the handicapped child. *Developm. med. Child Neurol.*, **12**, 207–12.

PITFIELD, M. and OPPENHEIM, A. N. (1964) Child rearing attitudes of mothers of psychotic children. *J. Child Psychol. Psychiat.*, **5**, 51–7.

RAECH, H. (1966) A parent discusses initial counselling. *Ment. Retard.*, **2**, 25–6.

RICCI, C. S. (1970) Analysis of child-rearing attitudes of mothers of retarded, emotionally disturbed and normal children. *Amer. J. ment. Defic.*, **74**, 756–61.

RICHARDS, B. W. (1964) Mental subnormality in the general hospital. *J. ment. Subn.*, **10**, 19–22.

ROITH, A. I. (1963) The myth of parental attitudes. *J. ment. Subn.*, **9**, 51–4.

RUTTER, M., TIZARD, J. and WHITMORE, K. (1970) *Education, Health and Behaviour*. London: Longmans.

SAENGER, G. (1962) Social factors in the institutionalisation of retarded individuals. In RICHARDS, B. W. (ed.) *Proc. Lond. Conf. Scient. Stud. Ment. Defic.*, 1960. Dagenham: May & Baker.

SAMPSON, A. H. (1947) Developing and maintaining good relations with parents of mentally deficient children. *Amer. J. ment. Defic.*, **52**, 187–94. Quoted by Wolfensberger, 1967.

SCHAEFER, E. S. and BELL, R. Q. (1958) Development of a parental attitude research instrument. *Child Developm.*, **29**, 339–61.

SCHELL, R. E. and ADAMS, W. P. (1968) Training parents of a young child with profound behaviour deficits to be teacher-therapists. *J. spec. Educ.*, **2**, 439–53.

SCHIPPER, M. T. (1959) The child with mongolism in the home. *Pediatrics*, **24**, 132–44.

SCHOPLER, E. and REICHLER, R. J. (1970) *Developmental Therapy by Parents with Their Own Autistic Child*. Paper read at a Colloquium on Infantile Autism, Ciba Foundation, London.

SCHUMACHER, H. C. (1945) Contribution of the child guidance clinic to the problem of mental deficiency. *Amer. J. ment. Defic.*, **50**, 277–83.

SHIPE, D. and SHOTWELL, A. (1965) Effect of out-of-home care on mongoloid children: a continuation study. *Amer. J. ment. Defic.*, **69**, 649–52.

SIGLER, A. T., COHEN, B. H., LILIENFELD, A. M., WESTLAKE, J. E. and HETZNECKER, W. H. (1967) Reproductive and marital experience of parents of children with Down's syndrome (mongolism). *J. Pediat.*, **70**, 608–14.

SMITHELLS, R. W. (1963) *The Early Diagnosis of Congenital Abnormalities*. London: Cassell.

STEDMAN, D. J. and EICHORN, D. H. (1964) A comparison of the growth and development of institutionalised and home-reared mongoloids during infancy and early childhood. *Amer. J. ment. Defic.*, **69**, 381–401.

STEIN, Z. and SUSSER, M. (1960) Families of dull children. *J. ment. Sci.*, **106**, 1296–319.

STONE, M. M. (1948) Parental attitudes to retardation. *Amer. J. ment. Defic.*, **53**, 363–72.

STONE, N. D. (1967) Family factors in willingness to place the mongoloid child. *Amer. J. ment. Defic.*, **72**, 16–20.

TERDAL, L. and BUELL, J. (1969) Parent education in managing retarded children with behaviour deficits and inappropriate behaviours. *Ment. Retard.*, **7**, 10–13.

TIPS, R. L., SMITH, G. S., PERKINS, A. L., BERGMAN, E. and MEYER, D. L. (1963) Genetic counseling problems associated with Trisomy 21, Down's disorder. *Amer. J. ment. Defic.*, **68**, 334–9.

TIZARD, J. (1960) The residential care of mentally handicapped children. In RICHARDS, B. W. (ed.) *Proc. Lond. Conf. Scient. Stud. Ment. Defic.* Dagenham: May & Baker.

TIZARD, J. and GRAD, J. C. (1961) *The Mentally Handicapped and their Families.* London: Oxford Univ. Press.

VALAES, T. and MAROULI-AGATHONOS, H. (1969) The child with Down's syndrome. Parental reactions to the announcement of the diagnosis. *Iatriki*, **15**, 378–84.

WALKER, G. H. (1949) Some considerations of parental reactions to institutionalisation of defective children. *Amer. J. ment. Defic.*, **54**, 108–14.

WARDELL, W. (1947) Casework with parents of mentally deficient children. *Amer. J. ment. Defic.*, **52**, 91–7.

WEBER, E. W. (1962) *Educable and Trainable Mentally Retarded Children.* Springfield, Ill.: Charles C. Thomas.

WEINGOLD, J. T. and HORMUTH, R. P. (1953) Group guidance of parents of mentally retarded children. *J. clin. Psychol.*, **9**, 118–24.

WINCH, R. F. (1967) Another look at the theory of complementary needs in mate selection. *J. Marriage & the Family*, **29**, 756–62.

WING, L. (1971) Severely retarded children in a London area: prevalence and provision of services. *Psychol. Med.*, **1**, 405–15.

WOLFENSBERGER, W. (1967) Counselling parents of the retarded. In BAUMEISTER, A. (ed.) *Mental Retardation.* London: Univ. of London Press.

WRIGHT, B. A. (1960) *Physical Disability – A Psychological Approach.* New York: Harper & Row. Quoted by TRETAKOFF, M. (1969) Counselling parents of handicapped children: a review. *Ment. Retard.*, **7**, 31–4.

YATES, M. L. and LEDERER, R. (1961) Small, short-term group meetings with parents of children with mongolism. *Amer. J. ment. Defic.*, **65**, 467–72.

ZWERLING, I. (1954) Initial counseling of parents with mentally retarded children. *J. Pediat.*, **44**, 469–79.

25

J. Tizard

Services and the evaluation
of services

During the last twenty-five years or so, major changes have taken place in attitudes towards the mentally retarded and in administrative policy concerned with their well-being. Throughout the latter part of the nineteenth century and the first half of the present one, mental deficiency services, in virtually all countries which provided them, were governed by legislation which defined mental deficiency in terms of social incompetence 'existing from birth or from an early age' (WHO, 1955). Social incapacity of the sort that led magistrates to 'certify' individuals as mentally deficient was thought to be largely genetic in origin: a direct and inevitable consequence of low intelligence, and one that was largely unmodifiable. The outlook was pessimistic and the concept of mental defect was itself simple minded.[1] This bleak attitude towards the mentally retarded persisted in spite of the fact that the evidence in favour of it was not very strong and despite a good deal of contradictory evidence. Thus Burt (1921) and others pointed out the distinction between low intelligence (a psychological concept) and mental retardation (an administrative one); longitudinal studies gave only weak support to the view that the IQ was constant; cross section studies of relations between IQ and other personal and behavioural characteristics (apart from academic performance at school) resulted in only low correlations; longitudinal studies of the adjustment of persons who at one time or another were classified as mentally retarded indicated that mental handicap was not 'incurable'. Moreover, critics commented that legislation designed ostensibly to protect the liberty of the subject, in practice took away his liberty (a mentally handicapped person could not for example enter a mental deficiency institution as a voluntary inmate, but only on committal by magistrate's order, and once committed he could not in most cases leave of his own free will, nor could his parents have him home again except with the law's consent). Still other critics, in Europe and in the United States, repeatedly attacked the inadequacy and poor quality of the services provided for the retarded. (See also Chapter 2.)

[1] Kugel and Wolfensberger (1969) have written an authoritative account of American experience; a sociological and historical survey of British practice, and of the philosophy upon which it was based, has yet to be undertaken. There is a rich store of primary source material upon which to draw.

Criticisms of the traditional wisdom regarding mental handicap, and of the services provided for them, mounted in many countries after the second world war, and, during the 1950s and 1960s, a rethinking of the basis for services took place (WHO, 1954). In Britain the change was marked by the *Report of the Royal Commission on the Law relating to Mental Illness and Mental Deficiency* (1957), by a new Mental Health Act (1959) and by a recent White Paper, *Better Services for the Mentally Handicapped* (1972). In Denmark, an Act of 1959 laid down a new legal basis for the treatment, teaching and care of the mentally retarded, and ushered in a newly structured national service (Bank-Mikkelsen, 1964, gives a useful historical summary of the development of services in Denmark and an account of the new service). Similar events have occurred in Sweden (Nirje, 1969) and in some other European countries. In the United States in the following year the President's Panel on Mental Retardation, established by President Kennedy in 1961, proposed a 'programme of national action to combat mental retardation'; this, and the subsequent activities of the President's Committee have been highly influential in affecting developments in that country.

All over the world, then, changes were taking place which, in their effects, were as important as those which occurred in the 1840s following the work of Guggenbühl. Séguin's words, applied to that time, are equally applicable to the present one: 'at certain times and eras, the whole race of Man, as regards the discovery of truth, seems to arrive at once at a certain point' (Kanner, 1964).

A good deal of solemn stuff has been written about the principles which underlie the provision of services for the mentally retarded. The matter can, however, be summarized in Bank-Mikkelsen's (1964) rather informal remarks to the International Copenhagen Congress on the Scientific Study of Mental Retardation. We must, he said, regard the mentally retarded person as a fellow human being, one with a handicap and perhaps with more than one handicap – which, however, do not make the mentally retarded individual any more odd than people are in general. Because he is first of all a fellow being, he must as a matter of equality have full rights as a fellow citizen. There is therefore no occasion for a 'special ideology' in the treatment of the mentally retarded. 'If this has been understood the rest is rather easy, because it is only a question of the best treatment of the mentally retarded from a humane and professional viewpoint.' If this is not understood, 'there is a risk of ending simply in sentimental pity, in theories of over-protection, in group discrimination or in something worse. . . . The aim is to give the mentally retarded a normal existence, that is to say to assist with treatment of any kind and ensure living quarters and work in the ordinary community for as many as possible.'

The central importance of epidemiology

To plan services which are adequate to meet needs it is necessary to know the numbers of persons who will make use of them. As Kushlick and Blunden (Chapter 3) have pointed out, a number of recent surveys have shown that in industrialized countries prevalence rates for *severe* mental handicap (IQ under 50) can be fairly accurately estimated. The 'peak' prevalence rate among children and young persons is 3·6 to 3·7/1,000. Hence in a population of 100,000, of both sexes and all ages, having a crude birth rate of 18/1,000, in which therefore there are 1,800 births a year, only 6–8 are likely to be children with severe mental handicap. Many of them will have additional handicaps (see Chapter 3).

No precise figures for the expected numbers of *mildly* handicapped children can be given: the term is an administrative one which lacks clear social and biological definition and in this respect resembles terms such as 'poverty' or 'social deprivation'. There is no doubt that many people are 'poor': but poverty in the United States or in the United Kingdom has a different meaning from poverty in, for example, India. It may be mentioned, however, that many educational systems have found that, in practice, between 1 and 2 per cent of schoolchildren are too backward to be educated in ordinary classes without special help, and for these children some kind of special educational provision, either in the ordinary class or in a special class or school, is needed. To the extent that special provision within the education system is not made for the numbers of children who are officially recognized to need it, there are unmet needs. Whether the educational needs of mildly retarded children are best met in the normal school system or through special classes is a matter of controversy. Kirk (1964) gives a reasoned statement of a case for education in special classes; Dunn (1968) has argued cogently against such provision. The matter is not further discussed here.

One estimate of the numbers of retardates, adults and children for whom further services would have to be provided in a population of 100,000 persons, is given in Table 26.

The numbers are considerably higher than those reported in most surveys, and are to some extent conjectural. The rates were based partly on data obtained in an earlier survey carried out in London (Goodman and Tizard, 1962), and partly on estimates of what the administrative needs would be in a population of 100,000 which made *adequate* provision for all its mentally retarded. In this sense, they constitute an *administrative* prevalence rate, that is, a rate based on 'the numbers for whom services would be required in a community which made provision for all who needed them' (Tizard, 1964, p. 17). Though they may well be too high to be used as a basis for planning at the present time, the writer believes that numbers of this order will have to be dealt with within the next ten or twenty years. More detailed analyses of the numbers, and handicaps, of retardates actually known to the authorities at the present time in southern England have been prepared by Kushlick and Blunden (Chapter 3).

According to the estimate on which Table 26 is based, in a population of 100,000 the diagnostic and treatment services dealing with problems of mental retardation would have to cope with about 90 severely subnormal children, of whom up to 30 might require residential care outside their own homes. About half of those in institutions would be profoundly retarded, or children with gross physical problems who required basic nursing. The figure of 90 does not include 'educable' retarded children (IQ over 50) who would remain in the education system proper and if necessary go to boarding schools, foster care or children's homes which took other children 'deprived of normal home life'.

There would be a further 375 retardates, aged 15 or over, of whom about half (180) would be employable. It is estimated that about 75 of these would be in residential units or in lodgings, while 105 would be at home and would require only occasional supervision and help. Whether these two groups should be regarded as mentally retarded at all is questionable. Their needs can best be considered within a more general social context of providing welfare services

TABLE 26. *An estimate of the numbers of mentally subnormal persons requiring services of various sorts in a city of 100,000 total population.*

Age group	Employable		Ambulant and trainable		Cot and chair and bedfast		Total		
	I	C	I	C	I	C	I	C	T
0–14	—	—	15	45	15	15	30	60	90
15	30	70	15	15	5	10	50	95	145
25	20	20	20	10	5	5	45	35	80
35	15	10	20	5	5	—	40	15	55
45	10	5	25	5	5	—	40	10	50
55	—	—	15	—	10	—	25	—	25
65	—	—	10	—	10	—	20	—	20
Total	75	105	120	80	55	30	250	215	465

I = In institutions. C = At home.

for those who require them. Special difficulties which arise out of the high-grade retardate's *mental* limitations are likely to be few, and on the whole easily dealt with. The psychiatric and other medical problems of the high-grade retarded could, and indeed should, be dealt with by a general community mental health service, since mentally retarded persons do not present *special* psychiatric problems not encountered among other sections of the population.

Of the remaining 195 severely retarded persons aged 15 or over included in Table 26, 140 would be ambulant and trainable, while 55 would be profoundly retarded, or housebound or bedfast. Nearly three-quarters would require residential care (145 out of 195) but their needs would differ considerably according to age and degree of handicap. About half of them are likely to have major physical and mental handicaps, but perhaps only 40 would have disabilities severe enough to warrant the classification of idiocy or profound mental retardation.

The figures given in Table 26 assume rates of residential provision which are higher than those reported in any area known to the writer. They were drawn up about ten years ago (Tizard, 1964) at a time when it was known that existing services were inadequate to meet expressed need, and when the implications of the increase in mean life span of severely retarded persons were beginning to become apparent. The estimates of numbers of residential places, particularly for younger retardates, may today be somewhat too high, since subsequent experience has shown that if really adequate services are provided for retardates living at home and for their families, the demand for residential care is greatly reduced. This point is currently being made in Britain by *Campaign for the Mentally Handicapped*, a pressure group campaigning on the basis of current knowledge for better services for the mentally retarded; and comprehensive service patterns such as that operated by the Salford (England) Local Authority (Susser, 1968) and by the Eastern Nebraska Community Office of Retardation (Lensink, personal communication) in the United States, have amply demonstrated that as day services improve the pressure on residential services sharply declines.

What is important about Table 26, however, is not so much the figures presented as the method of approach, which is epidemiological. In order to plan comprehensive services we must investigate needs. A first step (logically though not necessarily temporally) is to make estimates of the numbers of persons who have different types of handicap of differing degrees of severity. We can then consider how best to meet their needs.

The organization of services

The organization of *day* services has to be based on the needs of populations residing within easy travelling distance of the facilities they require. In cities and large towns distances are short but travelling time is slow; in more rural areas, the opposite. It is suggested that the *maximum* acceptable area for planning of day services should be one in which any member is within an hour's journey of any centre which he will need to attend frequently. The median travelling time should therefore be very much less than this. For planning purposes, the size of an effective region naturally depends on the density of the population, the administrative boundaries of local government units, and the adequacy of communications. It is obvious that quite different administrative arrangements will be required in the northern half of Sweden, or for the Highlands and Islands of Britain, for example, from those required for Stockholm, Edinburgh or London. In the proposals that follow, a base-line population of 100,000 has been used. For urbanized countries such as Britain, and much of Europe, North America and Australia, in which the majority of the population live in, or near, large aggregates of people, an urban model may be used to give guidelines. Modifications would be required for rural areas and for particular circumstances.

The planning of *residential* services is not closely tied by the constraints that affect the planning of day services. In practice, most residential services have traditionally served much larger catchment areas – populations as large as 1 or even 2 million have been served by a single institution. There is growing dissatisfaction with this system, and over Northern Europe and North America increasing efforts are being made to provide residential services in areas which are coterminous with those for planning day services. The arguments in favour of this policy have been presented elsewhere (Tizard, 1964, 1970).

The following section sketches out one possible model for services which would provide, in a geographically defined population of 100,000 persons, for the needs of all retarded persons and their families without requiring to have recourse to hospital and other facilities outside the catchment area save in quite exceptional instances and for quite specific purposes.

DIAGNOSTIC, COUNSELLING AND EDUCATIONAL SERVICES FOR CHILDREN

The essential elements of the services are that they should be available to all children at risk and their parents – an estimated 1 to 3 per cent – and that the emphasis should be on the full range of diagnostic services coupled with remedial treatment. The remedial aspect should include parent counselling and material support for parents, including constant attendance allowances, free nappy services etc. Remedial services including general education, speech therapy and physical therapy should be available from birth if necessary and should work both through neighbourhood pre-school facilities and through parent training in conjunction with the school where possible. The emphasis of this service must be on massive effective early intervention coupled with accurate diagnosis.

The same basic pattern of diagnostic services linking closely with extensive remedial services should continue at school age. Close collaboration with schools is essential. Psychologists should have special responsibilities for schools and should spend much of their time working with teachers on programmes for individual children.

Schools

A special school with fifty to sixty places would probably prove adequate for trainable (IQ less than 50) children of school age. To this centre would go both the children living in their own homes and those in residential care.

For children whose handicaps were too severe to enable them to profit from the programme provided by the day school, some kind of day hospital or 'special care' unit should be provided. This could usefully be attached to the special school; but it would require special staffing.

Residential places for children

If thirty places are needed, about half would be for the profoundly retarded or for children with severe physical handicaps or behaviour problems, and half for 'trainable' children, capable of attending the special school. The severely handicapped group might be placed in a long stay annexe attached to a children's ward or hospital, while the less severely handicapped imbecile group would be in a special residential home. Alternatively, a single unit, or two units each containing about fifteen children, or four or five smaller units, might be established, each unit having both severely and profoundly retarded children in it. Yet another form of residential provision is foster care. Efforts to get foster homes for severely or profoundly retarded children have not met with great success in the past, possibly because the social workers making the enquiries have themselves been half-hearted about them. More experience is needed in this area.

ADULTS

The services required for adults include vocational guidance and placement for educationally backward school-leavers and others, and where necessary, supervision of those who require it; training courses, sheltered workshops with recreational and other facilities for the more handicapped who cannot easily participate in normal group activities, hostel provision for high-grade defectives who are going out to work and for others who work in sheltered workshops or not at all; homes for old people. With adults, as with children, efforts should be made to find foster homes and family placements.

Sheltered workshops

It is not possible to make more than the most tentative estimate of the number of places required in sheltered workshops for the retarded (140 places have been allowed for in Table 26.) But in spite of uncertainty as to numbers, a great deal is known about how to organize such centres effectively. Both in the United Kingdom and in the Netherlands, as also in other countries, highly successful workshops in which the trainees do simple industrial work have been established. This kind of work appears to be particularly suitable for the subnormal (because they can do it, and do it well), and there is no reason why there should not be, in a sheltered workshop, people with other types of disability also. The numbers of places required would depend on the scope of the service they provide (whether 'high-grade' and 'low-grade' trainees are taken on and whether, for example, some are schizophrenics or adults disabled by epilepsy) and on the prevailing level of employment and the possibility of finding work for marginally employable workers.

The emphasis placed here on work should not be misunderstood. For many centuries the ability to work has been the milestone marking the boundary between childhood and adult life. Handicapped adults who can work, even if only in a limited way, are more likely to be accepted as adults and treated accordingly than are adults who are totally dependent upon others for their subsistence. The handicapped themselves know this – and it is for this reason, and not simply on economic grounds, that the organization of work is stressed here. The dangers to be avoided are, first, that the retardates will be exploited, or made to work in sweatshops; secondly that, out of a laudable desire to maintain efficient workshops, authorities will pay little attention to the social and cultural needs of the retarded who work in them. An adequate programme for young people and handicapped adults must provide for education and make possible a satisfying social life in an environment which is interesting, and which is part of the environment of a wider community.

Residential services for adults

In our supposed population of 100,000, perhaps 15–20 educationally retarded youths would leave school each year. London experience suggests that about 10 would need some kind of special supervision, but that only 2 would require residential care. Hence 2 hostels, with between 10 and 20 places, or an equivalent number of foster homes, would suffice for the needs of adolescents and young adults. English experience suggests that it is desirable to have separate hostels for high-grade retardates who are working out, and for lower grade, dependent retardates. These hostels, it is suggested, should contain both young men and young women. Their function should be to prepare school leavers and young adults for independent living in ordinary lodgings or in their own homes. At the same time they could serve as social centres, to which other young people, living at home, could come.

Long-stay homes for adults

The greatest need for residential accommodation is for long-stay homes for adults who are mentally retarded. In the future these are likely to comprise three-fifths of the total for whom residential care is required. However, very few adult retardates will be severely handicapped, physically or behaviourally. It is suggested that the needs of these people could best be met in small family type units which were separate from but reasonably close to the main sheltered workshops in which many of them would be employed during the day. These hostels should also serve a wider community function, as clubs and meeting places for other retardates who lived at home. There is much room for experiment and innovation here.

PARENTS AND COMMUNITY

The problems that face parents and relatives of the mentally handicapped have already been referred to – but they require special mention since they are seldom dealt with adequately, despite a great deal of knowledge of how to do so.

Few parents to whom a handicapped child is born have any prior knowledge about problems of handicap. Nor are they psychologically prepared for the shock and grief which the birth of a handicapped child brings. They therefore require both to be told about the baby's condition and its implications, and to be helped to come to terms with it. As the baby develops the parents are likely to encounter problems not commonly met by other mothers, so the need for counselling, for practical advice and for practical help continues. These needs persist, though the nature of the problems changes throughout the lifetime of the retarded person.

There has been a good deal of study made of social and family problems associated with mental handicap. For a 'general approach to parents of deformed or ill babies' see Davies *et al.* (1972) who write authoritatively of medical care of newborn babies; Bricker has described the contribution which psychologists can make to parent education and to the development of handicapped children of pre-school age; Carr (Chapter 24) gives a detailed account of family and upbringing problems of young children with Down's syndrome, and Hewett (1970) of children with cerebral palsy; the social casework approach to the mentally handicapped of all ages is comprehensively treated in Adams (1971, 1972). Fuller treatments of the problems of organizing community-based *services* for the mentally handicapped are to be found in Tizard and Grad (1961), WHO (1954, 1968), Tizard (1964, 1970), Kushlick (1968), Susser (1968), *Better Services for the Mentally Handicapped* (HMSO, 1971), *Campaign for the Mentally Handicapped* (1972), among other sources. Changing patterns in residential services are comprehensively reviewed by Kugel and Wolfensberger (1969).

Evaluation of services

Today it is fashionable to talk about the evaluation of different types of service for handicapped persons. The subject is complex and is one which presents unusually rich opportunities for research. In mental retardation most studies have been made of the efficacy of various kinds of education in special classes or in ordinary classes (see Chapters 1, 19 and 20 of this book) or of projects under the Head-Start Programme (see Chapter 7). Very much less work has been done on the evaluation of other services for mentally handicapped persons and their families.

A model for research on *residential* services has been prepared and is being investigated by Kushlick; the studies which he and his colleagues are carrying out are among the very few large-scale inquiries which both explore the needs of whole communities (i.e. are epidemiologically based) and also attempt to control and investigate the quality as well as the form of the provisions being studied. A brief description of this programme illustrates the types of problems involved and the methods available to deal with them. (See also Chapter 3.)

Kushlick's starting point was a practical problem facing the Wessex Regional Hospital Board, the Hospital Authority responsible under the National Health Service for providing hospital services (including mental subnormality hospital services) for 2 million total population living in the Wessex region of southern England. The Authority knew that it had a shortage of residential places for mentally retarded persons of the region, but it was uncertain as to the amount of provision it was likely to need in the future, and it was doubtful about the wisdom of adding to the size of existing hospitals. It was in this setting that Kushlick carried out his survey of the prevalence of mental retardation over the whole region.

It emerged from the survey that in every 100,000 of the total population about 25 residential places for severely and profoundly retarded children were required. About 30 per cent of these children were non-ambulant, and 20 per cent were ambulant but had a severe behaviour disorder. The remaining 50 per cent were ambulant and without severe behaviour problems, though two-fifths of them were incontinent.

Instead of building an additional 600-bed hospital to provide for unmet needs, the Board agreed to try experimentally a different pattern of service in parts of the region. There were a number of alternatives to choose from. Two were selected: the traditional all-age hospital, and 20-bed comprehensive units taking *all* severely and profoundly handicapped children in particular areas who required residential care. A number of demographically comparable areas were paired, and children in one half placed in small homes, whereas children in the other half went into, or remained in, the existing hospitals. Extensive data about the children and their families were collected. Progress is being monitored.

So far we have a classical quasi-experimental situation, with several replications, of the traditional sort. A novel feature is, however, now being introduced by Kushlick. He observed, as others have done, that treatment in the hospitals left a good deal to be desired as compared with treatment given to the children in the new residential homes which were established. He is, therefore, persuading the hospital authorities to implement the same operational policy as has been drawn up for the new hostels. (For example, changes in staff ratios, the movement of children whose homes are in the same part of the region into the same ward, the issue of personal clothing to children, and so on.) Thus, the two environments – for the children – are being made as similar as possible, though organizationally of course they remain very different. The interest of the research team is to see whether the environments remain, or can remain, alike – and more important what the effects of the different types of *services* are upon the families, the communities, the staff of the units, and the Regional Hospital Board. What are the administrative problems, what are the costs, what realistically are the benefits and drawbacks of different types of provision when the cards are not all stacked in favour of one type rather than another?

Studies of this sort are extremely difficult to carry out. First, they require an active partnership – which is not easy to establish and maintain – between research workers and bodies responsible for providing services. In this situation the research worker is likely to wish to influence policy, or to suggest alternative ways of doing things, but he cannot as a research worker direct policy. Moreover, if his task is to evaluate the effectiveness of different policies he must remain uncommitted in support of any one of them.

Secondly, field trials of the efficacy of different patterns of service are only possible if the objectives of the service can be specified. In practice this is rarely done: if aims are stated at all, it is usually only in terms of unexceptionable generality. To evaluate success in attaining objectives however it is necessary both to state just what these objectives are, and to devise ways of measuring how far they have been attained – within a specified period of time.

Thirdly, in the design of experimental trials, like has to be compared with like. The subjects (or children or patients or clients) who are studied have to be similar, and the quality of treatment they are offered has also to be, in a specifiable manner, similar. In practice it is often not possible to allocate subjects living in the same geographical area randomly to different treatments; the only practicable procedure is to compare total communities which are in specifiable ways matched and which are then allocated, if possible on a chance basis, one or other form of treatment. In this kind of study it is the community rather than the individual patient that constitutes the element requiring to be replicated.

To specify the quality of treatment is much more difficult than to match communities. There is, however, little point in comparing treatments which differ greatly in quality – for example poorly staffed, grossly overcrowded institutions of one type with generously staffed, well housed institutions of another – if one's interest is to explore differences in the type of institution rather than in, for example, the staff-patient ratios. Kushlick has attempted to get round this problem by working out, with the staff concerned in running the mental subnormality institutions he is studying, an operational policy to which they all subscribe. Moreover the Wessex Regional Hospital Board is attempting to equate staffing ratios and staff workloads in the different types of establishment being studied.

A fourth difficulty in the specification of criteria of effectiveness stems from the fact that there is no *single* objective. In the Wessex studies, for example, use has been made of four types of criteria: the effects on patients, the effects on parents and on the general community, the cost of running different types of service, and problems of management. It may well be that types of care which appear best when viewed from one angle appear worst when viewed from another. If this is so it will pose problems for those responsible for policy decisions: and such problems are substantive not statistical.

Other practical problems in the design of experimental field trials arise from the difficulty in achieving adequate numbers of replications, and from the time scale over which evaluation is possible. In practice it is rarely if ever possible to achieve enough replications for adequate statistical tests to be made of even simple hypotheses. Because in evaluating services the hypotheses are far from simple, and because idiosyncratic features associated with particular establishments account for much of the variance between establishments, conclusions about the relative efficacy of different types of institution have inevitably to be drawn on the basis of inadequate data. Quantitative findings must therefore be supported by assertions based on more or less adequate case studies, or on purely theoretical grounds. Most of those who have carried out evaluative studies have attempted to obfuscate this issue. Often it is difficult for the reader to distinguish between what is asserted and what is statistically validated – and sometimes even the researchers themselves appear to slide from one level of reporting to another without being clearly aware that they have done so. When this happens the results are inevitably suspect.

A factor which makes adequate objective data gathering impossible on a routine replicable scale, is that for many outcome variables (e.g. those associated with the well-being of those for whose benefit the services are ostensibly provided) there are no criteria of quality. This deficiency tends to lead tender-minded researchers to make assertions as though they were based on facts, and tough-minded critics to deny that differences exist because they cannot be measured.

Another type of problem relates to the time scale over which evaluation occurs. For example, critics of current proposals to set up mental subnormality hostels to replace some or all of the large hospitals have argued that they may be all right in the short run, but that over a longer time span they will prove difficult to staff and impossible to run. Equally, however, it can be argued, on the basis of history, that large institutions may be temporarily reformed from time to time but that such places tend inexorably to revert to their ideal type, namely that of the total institution. This view is an explicit part of Goffman's thesis (1961) and Kugel and Wolfensberger (1969) have provided powerful documentary support for it as far as American mental subnormality institutions are concerned. Either or both of these views may be correct; the point is that the time scale argument is one which it is difficult to cope with experimentally. This would not matter very much were it not for the fact that, for planning purposes, it is long-term rather than short-term outcomes which are of crucial importance, because of the long lead-in time between planning and the execution of plans. For this reason policies which permit action to be taken quickly and which do not tie up large amounts of capital resources over long periods of time have much to commend them. This is a fact which should be – though it rarely is – taken into account by planners.

Despite all these limitations, social experiment to help decide issues of urgent practical importance is at least feasible in principle. Moreover studies which have this aim can also explore factors which influence the manner in which institutions differ one from another. In doing so they direct attention to questions of institutional functioning which are of great importance and interest.

Measuring the quality of care

It has been mentioned that for many aspects of care no criteria of quality exist. This has led many investigators to concentrate on matters for which tests or scales already exist (e.g. to measure IQ or educational attainments, or sight vocabulary), irrespective of the relevance of such measures to the problems they are studying. The exploration of other indicators of institutional quality has been remarkably unadventurous, and often very indirect (e.g. through attitude questionnaires to staff rather than direct observations of staff behaviour, and so on). There is however good reason to believe that simple and direct observation of behaviour, and straightforward questions rather than oblique open-ended ones, can go a long way towards exploring differences between types of institutional care. An example taken from the work of our own research group may illustrate the fruitfulness of direct studies of the quality of care.

Our inquiries (King *et al.*, 1971) began with a practical issue which was as follows: institutions differ in patterns of child management. These differences are usually attributed to staff shortages, to staff attitudes, or to the large size of residential institutions. Confident opinions are expressed as to why standards of care differ, but the explanations are often mutually contradictory, and no very clear empirically based description of the ways in which institutions differ had in fact been given. We believed that child management practices were strongly influenced by the manner in which institutions were organized, and we thought that differences in child management practices were therefore likely to be attributable to differences in the organizational structure of institutions which determined staff roles and how they were performed. These differences in child management practices were, in their turn, thought likely to have an influence on the behaviour of children brought up in different regimens. We set out, therefore, to explore a number of hypotheses to account for differences in institutional functioning.

In a series of inquiries lasting over 5 years more than 100 different residential units were examined. In a major study 8 hostels, 5 wards in mental subnormality hospitals, and 3 voluntary homes were investigated. An objective and highly reliable scale of child management practices was devised which enabled us to score patterns of staff behaviour in a quantitative manner which permitted comparisons to be made between one institution and another. Time sampling observations of staff behaviour were carried out, and staff were interviewed using structured interview schedules of predetermined reliability.

There were striking differences in child management practices as scored on the child management scale, with no overlap in scale scores between any of the hostel units and any of the hospital wards. Hospital wards all had high scale scores indicative of institutionally oriented child management practices, whereas hostels had low scores indicative of child-oriented practices. The evidence suggested that differences in child care practices were not due to differences in the handicaps of the children.

Child care practices differed with the size of the institution and the size of the child care units in which the children lived, but differences in unit size did not seem able to account for the differences in child management practices. Nor could differing child care practices be ascribed to differences in assigned staff ratios, though in child-oriented units more staff were available at peak periods.

The organizational structure of child-oriented units was indeed very different, and it was this which appeared to be the principal determinant of differences in patterns of child care. In child-oriented units the person in charge had very much greater responsibility to make decisions about matters which affected all aspects of the unit's functioning. Perhaps because they were accorded greater autonomy, senior staff in these establishments tended to share their responsibilities with their junior colleagues: role differentiation was reduced (e.g. senior staff were more often engaged in child care than were their counterparts in institution-oriented units, who spent far more time on administration and even domestic work, and far less time in child care). Staff stability was also much greater in child-oriented units – partly because staff were not moved from one unit to another to meet crises in units which were short staffed, partly because students in training were not moved about in order to 'gain experience'. Role performances also differed. In child-oriented units staff were more likely to involve the children in their activities. They spoke to them more often, and were more 'accepting' of them, and less often 'rejecting'. Junior staff tended to behave in ways similar to those in which the head of the unit acted.

Though the social organization of the institution appeared to be largely responsible for the differences in staff behaviour, the nature of staff training also seemed important. Trained nurses were in general less child-oriented than were staff with child care training. They were more authoritarian and when the person in charge was a nurse the unit tended to be characterized by sharp role differentiation.

Mentally handicapped children in units which were child-care oriented were significantly more advanced in feeding and dressing skills, and in speech, than were those in institution-oriented units. Though no very adequate study was made of other personality characteristics of the children, fewer of those in child-oriented institutions appeared to be psychiatrically disturbed (Tizard, 1972).

The point about these studies is that they show that there were marked differences between different types of institution: but the factors usually thought to be responsible for differences in the quality of care turned out not to be the significant ones. Thus, by looking directly at particular characteristics of child-care practices which appeared to have beneficial or detrimental effects upon children in residential care at the same time as we examined characteristics of organizational structure in contrasting institutions, we were able to throw light on relationships between organizational structure and organizational function. And in doing this we were also able to examine the effects of specific aspects of child-care practices upon the development of children. It should be added that in a later series of studies carried out by Barbara Tizard (Tizard and Joseph, 1970; Tizard and Tizard, 1971; Tizard et al., 1972) in residential nurseries for normal children deprived of normal home life, strong associations were found between *specific* aspects of the institutional regimen and *specific* aspects of the children's development.

Conclusion

Because mental handicap, at least in its severe form, is an easily identifiable condition, and because services for the mentally retarded have been established for a long period of time, the subject of mental retardation lends itself to social as well as clinical study. Services for the mentally retarded are at present changing and expanding: there is thus opportunity to introduce changes on a planned basis and to explore their consequences. A number of *models* of different types of service have been proposed, some of them well established, others which have been tried out only experimentally in demonstration projects, and still others which have yet to be implemented. Today there is an interest in the evaluation of different types of service, such evaluation forming one of the bases for future policy. Problems of service evaluation are indeed complex. However experience in how to proceed with such studies is rapidly accumulating, and the evaluation of services offers one of the most fruitful avenues for social research.

References

ADAMS, M. (1971) *Mental Retardation and its Social Dimensions*. New York and London: Columbia Univ. Press.

ADAMS, M. and LOVEJOY, H. (1972) *The Mentally Subnormal: The Social Casework Approach*. London: Heinemann.

BANK-MIKKELSEN, N. E. (1964) The ideological and legal basis of the Danish National Service, of the treatment, teaching, training etc. of the mentally retarded, as well as a description of the structure of the National Service. In ØSTER, J. (ed.) *Proceedings of the International Copenhagen Conference on the Scientific Study of Mental Retardation*. Copenhagen: Statens Åndssvageforsorg.

BURT, C. (1921) *Mental and Scholastic Tests*. L.C.C. Rep. No. 2052. London.

Campaign for the Mentally Handicapped (1972) *Even Better Services for the Mentally Retarded*. London: Campaign for the Mentally Handicapped, Central Action Group.

CARR, J. (1971) A comparative study of the development of mongol and normal children from 0–4 years. Unpubl. Ph.D. thesis, Univ. of London.

DAVIES, P. A., ROBINSON, R. J., SCOPES, J. W., TIZARD, J. P. M. and WIGGLESWORTH, J. S. (1972) *Medical Care of Newborn Babies*. London: Heinemann and Washington: Lippincott, for Spastics International Medical Publications.

DUNN, L. M. (1968) Special education for the mildly retarded: is much of it justified? *Except. Child.*, **35**, 5–22.

GOFFMAN, E. (1961) *Asylums: Essays on the Social Situation of Mental Patients and Other Inmates*. New York: Doubleday.

GOODMAN, H. and TIZARD, J. (1962) Prevalence of imbecility and idiocy among children. *Brit. med. J.*, **1**, 216–19.

HEWETT, S. (1970) *The Family and the Handicapped Child*. London: Allen & Unwin.

HMSO (1957) *Royal Commission on the Law Relating to Mental Illness and Mental Deficiency*. Cmnd 169. London.

HMSO (1971) *Better Services for the Mentally Handicapped.* Government White Paper. London.

KANNER, L. (1964) *A History of the Care and Study of the Mentally Retarded.* Springfield, Ill.: Charles C. Thomas.

KING, R. D., RAYNES, N. V. and TIZARD, J. (1971) *Patterns of Residential Care: Sociological Studies in Institutions for Handicapped Children.* London: Routledge & Kegan Paul.

KIRK, S. A. (1958) *Early Education of the Mentally Retarded.* Urbana: Univ. of Illinois Press.

KIRK, S. A. (1964) Research in education. In STEVENS, H. and HEBER, R. (eds.) *Mental Retardation.* Chicago and London: Univ. of Chicago Press.

KUGEL, R. B. and WOLFENSBERGER, W. (1969) *Changing Patterns in Residential Services for the Mentally Retarded.* Washington, D.C.: President's Committee on Mental Retardation.

KUSHLICK, A. (1968) The Wessex Plan for evaluating the effectiveness of residential care for the severely subnormal. In RICHARDS, B. (ed.). *Proc. 1st Congr. Internat. Assoc. Scient. Stud. Ment. Defic., Montpellier, September 1967.* Reigate: Michael Jackson.

NIRJE, B. (1969) The normalization principle and its human management implications. In KUGEL, R. B. and WOLFENSBERGER, W. (eds.) *Changing Patterns in Residential Services for the Mentally Retarded.* Washington, D.C.: President's Committee on Mental Retardation.

SUSSER, M. (1968) *Community Psychiatry.* New York: Random House.

TIZARD, B. and JOSEPH, A. (1970) Today's foundlings: A survey of young children admitted to care of Voluntary Societies in England. *New Society,* **16,** (410), 585.

TIZARD, B., COOPERMAN, O., JOSEPH, A. and TIZARD, J. (1972) Environmental effects on language development: a study of young children in long-stay residential nurseries. *Child Developm.,* **43,** 337–58.

TIZARD, J. (1964) *Community Services for the Mentally Handicapped.* London: Oxford Univ. Press.

TIZARD, J. (1970) The role of social institutions in the causation, prevention and alleviation of mental retardation. In HAYWOOD, H. C. (ed.) *Social-Cultural Aspects of Mental Retardation: Proceedings of the Peabody–NIMH Conference.* New York: Appleton-Century-Crofts.

TIZARD, J. (1972) Research into services for the mentally handicapped: science and policy issues. *Brit. J. ment. Subn.,* **XVIII,** Part 1 (34), 1–12.

TIZARD, J. and GRAD, J. C. (1961) *The Mentally Handicapped and Their Families.* Maudsley Monogr. No. 7. London: Oxford Univ. Press.

TIZARD, J. and TIZARD, B. (1971) The social development of two-year-old children in residential nurseries. In SCHAFFER, H. R. (ed.) *The Origins of Human Social Relations.* London: Academic Press.

World Health Organization (1954) *The Mentally Subnormal Child.* WHO Tech. Rep. Ser., No. 75. Geneva.

World Health Organization (1955) Hospitalisation of mental patients. *Int. Dig. Hlth. Leg.*, **6,** 1–100.

World Health Organization (1968) *International Classification of Disease, 8th Revision.* Geneva.

Name Index

Subject Index

McCrary–Hunter hypothesis, 286
malaria, maternal, 102
malnutrition, 6, 229, 231
maple syrup urine disease, 89
Maroteaux-Lamy's syndrome, 90
measles, 105
memory, 283
  in autism, 362
  LTM, 287, 332
  STM, 283, 332
meningitis, 94, 105
Mental Deficiency Act (1913), 16, 209
Mental Deficiency Act (1927), 20
Mental Health Act (1959), 21, 32, 209
mercury, 102, 118
microcephaly, 91, 122, 655
mild mental subnormality, 4
  diagnosis of, 234
  differences from severe subnormality,
    223
  longitudinal study of, 234
  prevalence, 36, 62, 64
  prognosis, 36
  social rehabilitation, 657
Milwaukee study, 186, 231
Minamata disease, 118
minimal brain damage, 127
  and social class, 58, 127
Ministry of Education, 37, 56, 63, 78
Ministry of Health, 59, 78
moderate subnormality, 4
mongolism, *see* Down's syndrome
Morquio's syndrome, 90
mortality rate, 38
mosaicism, 14, 47
motivation to learn, 677
motor disorder, categories, 483
motor skill, tests of, 456
  Lincoln Oseretzky, 456
  Rail Walking Test, 456
mucopolysaccharide metabolism, 90
  mucopolysaccharidosis, 132
multi-disciplinary needs, 633
multiply handicapped children, 632

nephrogenic diabetes insipidus, 92
neurofibromatosis, 86
'neuropathic diathesis', 130
neuropsychology of subnormality, 331
normalization, 650, 769

obsessional behaviour, 352
obstetric complications, 6, 103
occupational training, 677; *see also*
  activity training
oculocerebrorenal syndrome, 92
Onondaga County Survey, 71, 78
'open' class words, 574

operant conditioning, 730
  in severe subnormality, 655
  see also behaviour modification

parents
  behaviour modification training
    programmes, 768
  counselling, 132, 813, 845
  education of, 188
  emotional reactions, 508, 817
  genetic counselling, 6, 69, 87, 820
  Parental Attitudes Research Instrument,
    826
  workshop for, 553
partial deletion of No. 18 chromosome,
  97
Patau's syndrome, 96
pathological factors, 82–107
pathological/subcultural dichotomy, 27
pauperism, 17
perceptual-motor tests, 435
  Bender Gestalt Test, 435
  Benton Visual Retention Test, 437
  Graham–Kendall Memory for Designs
    Test, 437
perceptual processes, studies of, 265
personality disorders, 710
personality factors affecting adjustment,
  237
personality tests, 453
  Eysenck/Withers Personality
    Inventory, 454
  Rorschach Test, 453
  Thematic Apperception Test of the
    Symonds Picture Story Test, 453
phenylketonuria, 8, 88, 123
Piaget's theory of intellectual
  development, 157
'pivots', 575
prematurity, 55, 103, 131, 229
pre-school programmes, 184, 186–201,
  231, 232
President's Committee on Mental
  Retardation, 3, 11, 201, 204, 648,
  701
prevalence, 9, 22, 31–72, 226–34, 482
prevention, 5–7; *see also* aetiology
primary mental abilities, 153
profound subnormality, 4, 654
prognosis, 18, 32, 224, 232
  for ESN school-leavers, 40
  for the mildly subnormal, 22, 38
  relevance of test data, 393, 443
  see also assessment
psycholinguistics, 531, 567, 574
psychometric assessment, 371
psychoneurosis, 47, 709
psychopathy, 50